The American Pageant

D. C. Heath and Company
Lexington, Massachusetts   Toronto

8th Edition

The American Pageant

A History of the Republic

Thomas A. Bailey

David M. Kennedy

Stanford University

Acquisitions Editor: Linda Halvorson
Developmental Editor: Sylvia Mallory
Production Editor: Rosemary Rodensky
Designer: Cia Boynton
Production Coordinator: Michael O'Dea
Photo Researcher: Martha Shethar
Text Permissions Editor: Margaret Roll

COVER: *Armistice Celebration Parade, Fifth Avenue, 1919,* by Hayley Lever, Sotheby's, New York.

Published simultaneously in Canada.

Printed in the United States of America.

International Standard Book Number: 0-669-10810-3

Library of Congress Catalog Card Number: 86-80501

5 6 7 8 9

THOMAS A. BAILEY, a native Californian, taught American history for nearly forty years at Stanford University, his alma mater. Always a popular teacher, he also served as a visiting professor at Harvard, Cornell, Johns Hopkins, and other institutions. Long regarded as among the nation's leading diplomatic historians, he was honored by his colleagues in 1968 by election to the presidency of the Organization of American Historians. Though he was the author, co-author, or editor of some twenty books in the field of American history, he was most proud of *The American Pageant*, through which, he liked to say, he had taught American history to some two million students.

DAVID M. KENNEDY, a native of Seattle, received his undergraduate education at Stanford University. He earned his Ph.D. at Yale University in American Studies, combining the fields of history, literature, and economics. His first book, *Birth Control in America: The Career of Margaret Sanger* (1970), was honored with both the Bancroft Prize and the John Gilmary Shea Prize. His study of World War I, *Over Here: The First World War and American Society* (1980), was a Pulitzer Prize nominee. Kennedy is the 1988–1989 holder of the Harmsworth Professorship of American History at Oxford University. A member of the Stanford History Department since 1967, Kennedy has twice been recognized by the graduating class for the effectiveness of his teaching. He has also chaired the university's program in international relations and served as Associate Dean of the School of Humanities and Sciences. His most recent book is *Power and Responsibility: Case Studies in American Leadership* (1986). He is currently working on a volume covering the Great Depression and World War II in *The Oxford History of the United States.*

Preface

Revising *The American Pageant* for this eighth edition posed the vexing problem of how to make a good thing better. The *Pageant* has long enjoyed a deserved reputation as one of the most accessible, popular, and effective textbooks in the field of American history. Thomas A. Bailey gave to the book a distinctive personality that mirrored the vast learning and the sparkling classroom style that he had cultivated during his nearly four decades of teaching at Stanford University. He stamped every page of the text with the charm of his inventive prose, his passion for clarity, his disdain for clutter, and his mastery of the narrative form.

Clearly, these outstanding attributes of the book had to be preserved, even strengthened. But like the United States itself, sometimes described as the only nation that was born perfect and yet aspired to progress, the *Pageant* presented possibilities for improvement in certain areas. Specifically, I have tried to preserve the book's basic personality while incorporating the rich new scholarship in social, economic, cultural, and intellectual history that has appeared in the last generation. I have been guided in this effort by two principles: first, the desire to bring to light the "inner" histories of people—including women, the poor, blacks, Hispanics, and certain religious communities—who until recently were only imperfectly visible to historians; second, the belief that the main drama and the urgent interest of American history reside in the public arena where these and other groups contend and cooperate with one another. In that sometimes noisy forum, Americans have shaped the civic culture in which they all necessarily live. Thus this eighth edition of *The American Pageant*, like earlier editions, gives special emphasis to the great public issues—such as constitution making, slavery and civil war, the rights of minorities, economic regulation, and foreign policy—that have dominated national life. It also gives considerable attention to tracing the evolution of major public institutions like the agencies of government and political parties. Public affairs, in short, form the spine of the *Pageant*'s account of American history.

This edition includes much new material on the history of the family from colonial times to the twentieth century; on the influence of religion in American life; on the role of ideas in the making of the Revolution, the Constitution, and the two-party system, and in the struggle for women's rights; on the effects of urbanization and suburbanization; and on the causes and consequences of immigration, old and new.

In addition, readers will find expanded discussion of pre-Columbian history and Native Americans; an entirely new chapter on colonial life in the seventeenth century; an extensively revised account of Jacksonian America, stressing the novelty of mass-based political parties and the emergence of the two-party system; new treatment of the rise of a market economy and its implications for women and families in antebellum America; an updated account of the character of slavery and the nature of abolitionism; a completely revised explanation of Reconstruction; and a virtually all-new chapter on the rise of the city in post-Civil War America. The coverage of twentieth-century American history has likewise been revised and now includes a fresh discussion, in a single chapter, of the domestic and diplomatic dimensions of World War I; new material on the home front during World War II, and on the war's shaping influence on postwar society; an updated account of the origins of the Cold War; a substantial reworking of the entire post-1945 portion of the text, including a new chapter on Ronald Reagan and the conservative resurgence; and a thoroughly revised concluding chapter on the character of American society since World War II. I have also woven into the text narrative new biographies of more than a dozen figures, such as Charles Grandison Finney, Jane Addams, and Eleanor Roosevelt, and have expanded the biographical material on many others, including Brigham Young and Martin Luther King, Jr.

Other improvements include the expansion of most "Varying Viewpoints" essays to reflect recent scholarship and to stimulate classroom discussion; updated end-of-chapter bibliographies, with an added subsection recommending primary-source documents for further study; many new boxed quotations; a much-expanded appendix featuring tables and graphics with extensive information on American social and economic history; and, not least, an attractive new text design with full-color maps and illustrations—many of them new—and the generous use of color throughout.

A new text supplement, the *Instructor's Resource Guide,* is also available with this edition. It features summaries of chapter themes, chapter outlines, suggestions and resources for lectures, character sketches of key historical figures, ideas for classroom debates, and discussion questions. The student *Guidebook* and instructor's *Quizbook* have both been completely rewritten and expanded to incorporate a wealth of useful new material. In addition, *The American Spirit,* a companion collection of primary-source documents, has been thoroughly revised to reflect the changes in the *Pageant.*

While undertaking these improvements, I have tried to preserve all the elements that have made the *Pageant* distinctive, especially a strong chronological narrative and a writing style that emphasizes clarity, concreteness, and a measure of wit. I believe that Thomas A. Bailey would have been proud of this new edition of *The American Pageant.* No scholar ever loved his subject with more gusto and devotion than Thomas A. Bailey loved American history. He originally wrote the *Pageant* so that others could share in the sheer delight and rich satisfaction that he took from his scholarship. In keeping with that tradition, I hope that the readers of this book will enjoy learning from it and come to savor, as Thomas A. Bailey so exuberantly did, the pleasures and rewards of historical study.

DAVID M. KENNEDY
Stanford University

Acknowledgments

Many people contributed to this revision. Foremost among them are the countless students and teachers who have written unsolicited letters of comment or inquiry. I have learned from each of them. I want also to thank the hundreds of current *Pageant* users who generously responded to an extensive mail survey. Too numerous to name here, they provided me with the best possible advice on how to make the book most suitable for classroom use. Several colleagues also gave me the benefit of their expertise in particular areas, including:

Professor Geoffrey Blodgett, Oberlin College
Professor Stuart Bruchey, Columbia University
Professor Michael Holt, University of Virginia
Professor Regina Markell Morantz-Sanchez, University of Kansas
Professor Nell Irvin Painter, University of North Carolina
Professor Mel Piehl, Valparaiso University
Professor Jack N. Rakove, Stanford University

My warm thanks to each of them.

Contents

CHAPTER **1** *New World Beginnings*   **1**

Europe in the sixteenth century ⋆ The search for a water route to the East ⋆ Columbus and the early explorers ⋆ Native Americans and the ecological consequences of the European discovery ⋆ Spanish America and rivalry with England ⋆ England on the eve of colonization ⋆ The planting of Virginia and Maryland ⋆ Settling the Carolinas and Georgia

CHAPTER **2** *Completing the Thirteen Colonies*   **21**

The Puritan faith ⋆ Plymouth Colony ⋆ The Puritan commonwealth of Massachusetts Bay Colony ⋆ Rhode Island and Connecticut ⋆ The Dominion of New England, 1686–1689 ⋆ New Netherland becomes New York ⋆ Pennsylvania, the Quaker colony ⋆ New Jersey and Delaware

CHAPTER **3** *American Life in the Seventeenth Century*   **39**

Life and labor in the Chesapeake tobacco region ⋆ Indentured servants and Bacon's Rebellion in Virginia, 1676 ⋆ The spread of slavery ⋆ Afro-American culture ⋆ Families in New England ⋆ Declining Puritan piety ⋆ The Salem witchcraft trials, 1692 ⋆ Daily life in the colonies

CHAPTER **4** *Colonial Society on the Eve of Revolution*   **54**

Immigration and population growth ⋆ Colonial social structure ⋆ Earning a living ⋆ The Atlantic economy ⋆ The role of religion ⋆ The "Great Awakening" of the 1730s ⋆ Education and culture ⋆ Political patterns

CHAPTER **5** *The Duel for North America*   74

New France ⋆ Fur-traders and Indians ⋆ Anglo-French colonial
rivalries ⋆ Europe, America, and the first "world wars" ⋆ The
French and Indian War, 1754–1763 ⋆ The ousting of France from
North America, 1763 ⋆ The question of colonial union

CHAPTER **6** *The Road to Revolution*   89

The merits and menace of mercantilism ⋆ The Stamp Act crisis,
1765 ⋆ The Townshend Acts, 1767 ⋆ The Boston Tea Party,
1773 ⋆ The "Intolerable Acts" and the Continental Congress, 1774 ⋆
Lexington, Concord, and the gathering clouds of war, 1775

CHAPTER **7** *America Secedes from the Empire*   108

Early skirmishes, 1775 ⋆ The Declaration of Independence, 1776 ⋆
The Loyalists ⋆ The role of the militia ⋆ The fighting fronts ⋆
The French alliance, 1778 ⋆ Yorktown, 1781 ⋆ The Peace of
Paris, 1783

CHAPTER **8** *The Confederation and the Constitution*   127

Changing political sentiments ⋆ The new state constitutions ⋆
Economic troubles ⋆ The Articles of Confederation, 1781–1788 ⋆
The Northwest Ordinance, 1787 ⋆ Shays's Rebellion, 1786 ⋆
The Constitutional Convention, 1787 ⋆ Ratifying the Constitution,
1787–1790

CHAPTER **9** *Launching the New Ship of State*   149

Problems of the young Republic ⋆ The Bill of Rights, 1791 ⋆
The first presidency, 1789–1793 ⋆ Hamilton's economic policies ⋆
The Whiskey Rebellion, 1794 ⋆ The emergence of political parties

CHAPTER **10** *Federalists and Foreign Friction*   163

Foreign policy conflicts ⋆ Jay's Treaty, 1794 ⋆ President Adams
keeps the peace ⋆ The Alien and Sedition Acts, 1798 ⋆ The
Virginia and Kentucky Resolutions, 1798–1799 ⋆ Jefferson defeats
the Federalists, 1800

CHAPTER **11**   *The Triumph of Jeffersonian Democracy*   **179**

The Jefferson presidency   ☆   John Marshall and the Supreme
Court   ☆   Barbary pirates   ☆   The Louisiana Purchase, 1803   ☆
The Anglo-French War   ☆   The Embargo, 1807–1809

CHAPTER **12**   *James Madison*
and the Second War for Independence   **197**

Napoleon manipulates Madison   ☆   War Hawks and the West   ☆
Invasion of Canada, 1812   ☆   The war at sea   ☆   Triumph at New
Orleans, 1815   ☆   Treaty of Ghent, 1814   ☆   The Hartford
Convention, 1814–1815   ☆   A new national identity

CHAPTER **13**   *The Postwar Upsurge of Nationalism,*
1815–1824   **212**

The tariff of 1816   ☆   James Monroe and the Era of Good Feelings   ☆
The Panic of 1819   ☆   The Missouri Compromise, 1820   ☆   The
Supreme Court under John Marshall   ☆   Canada and Florida   ☆   The
Monroe Doctrine, 1823

CHAPTER **14**   *The Rise of Jacksonian Democracy*   **231**

Politics for the common man   ☆   Sources of the "new democracy"   ☆
The "corrupt bargain" of 1824   ☆   President John Quincy Adams,
1825–1829   ☆   The "Tariff of Abominations," 1828   ☆   The triumph
of Andrew Jackson, 1828   ☆   The Jacksonian philosophy   ☆   The
spoils system   ☆   The Maysville Road veto, 1830   ☆   The
Webster-Hayne debate, 1830

CHAPTER **15**   *Jacksonian Democracy at Flood Tide*   **250**

The South Carolina nullification crisis, 1832   ☆   Jackson's war on the
Bank of the United States   ☆   The removal of the Indians from the
Southeast   ☆   Revolution in Texas, 1835–1836   ☆   The emergence of
the Whig party, 1836   ☆   Martin Van Buren in the White House,
1837–1841   ☆   The depression of 1837   ☆   The Independent
Treasury   ☆   William Henry Harrison's "log cabin" campaign,
1840   ☆   The establishment of the two-party system

CHAPTER **16**   *Manifest Destiny in the Forties*   **270**

"Tyler Too" becomes president, 1841   *   Fixing the Maine boundary,
1842   *   The annexation of Texas, 1845   *   Oregon and
California   *   James K. Polk, the "dark horse" of 1844   *   War with
Mexico, 1846–1848

CHAPTER **17**   *Shaping the National Economy,*
1790–1860   **289**

The coming of the factory system   *   Capitalists and workers   *
The ripening of commercial agriculture   *   The transportation
revolution   *   The market economy and the family   *   The
emergence of a continental economy   *   America and the Atlantic
economy   *   Clipper ships and the Pony Express

CHAPTER **18**   *Creating an American Character,*
1790-1860   **311**

Pioneer democracy   *   European immigration   *   The Germans and
the Irish   *   Religious revivals   *   The Mormons   *   Educational
advances   *   The changing American family

CHAPTER **19**   *The Ferment of Reform and Culture,*
1790–1860   **333**

Religion and reform   *   Temperance   *   Women's roles and
women's rights   *   Utopian experiments   *   Art and architecture   *
A national literature

CHAPTER **20**   *The South and the Slavery Controversy*   **349**

The economy of the Cotton Kingdom   *   Poor whites and free
blacks   *   The plantation system   *   The human face of the
"peculiar institution"   *   The abolitionist crusade   *   The white
Southern response   *   Abolition and the Northern conscience

CHAPTER **21** *Renewing the Sectional Struggle,*
1848–1854 **369**

The bitter fruits of victory in the Mexican War ★ "Popular
sovereignty" ★ Zachary Taylor, Millard Fillmore, and California
statehood ★ The Compromise of 1850 ★ The inflammatory
Fugitive Slave Law ★ President Pierce and expansion, 1853–1857 ★
Senator Douglas and the Kansas-Nebraska Act, 1854

CHAPTER **22** *Drifting toward Disunion, 1854–1861* **391**

Uncle Tom's Cabin and the spread of abolitionist sentiment in the
North ★ The contest for Kansas ★ The election of James
Buchanan, 1856 ★ The *Dred Scott* case, 1857 ★ The Panic of
1857 ★ The Lincoln-Douglas debates, 1858 ★ John Brown's raid
on Harpers Ferry, 1859 ★ Lincoln and Republican victory, 1860 ★
Secession

CHAPTER **23** *The War for Southern Independence* **414**

The attack on Fort Sumter, April 1861 ★ The crucial border
states ★ The threat of European intervention ★ Southern and
Northern assets ★ The Emancipation Proclamation, 1863 ★ Grant
in the West ★ Sherman in Georgia ★ Hammering the Army of
Virginia ★ Appomattox, 1865

CHAPTER **24** *Behind the Lines: North and South* **440**

Friction with France and England ★ Men in uniform ★ Financing
the Blue and the Gray ★ The economic impact of the war ★
Lincoln and civil liberties ★ Wartime politics ★ The assassination
of Lincoln, 1865

CHAPTER **25** *The Ordeal of Reconstruction* **457**

The defeated South ★ The freed slaves ★ President Andrew
Johnson's Reconstruction policies ★ Moderate and radical
Republicans ★ Congressional Reconstruction policies ★ Johnson
clashes with Congress ★ Military Reconstruction, 1867–1877 ★
"Black Reconstruction" and the Ku Klux Klan ★ The impeachment of
Andrew Johnson ★ The legacy of Reconstruction

CHAPTER **26** *Politics in the Gilded Age, 1869–1889*   **480**

Ulysses S. Grant, soldier-president   ★   Corruption and reform in the
post-Civil War era   ★   The depression of the 1870s   ★   Political
parties and partisans   ★   The Compromise of 1877 and the end of
Reconstruction   ★   Civil service reform   ★   Grover Cleveland and the
tariff

CHAPTER **27** *Industry Comes of Age, 1865–1900*   **504**

The railroad boom   ★   Speculators and financiers   ★   Early efforts at
government regulation   ★   Lords of industry   ★   The New South   ★
The laboring class   ★   The rise of trade unions

CHAPTER **28** *America Moves to the City, 1865–1900*   **529**

The rise of the city   ★   Skyscrapers, tenements, and suburbs   ★
The "new immigration"   ★   Settlement houses and social workers   ★
Nativists and immigration restriction   ★   Churches in the city   ★
Black leaders: Booker T. Washington and W. E .B. Du Bois   ★   Literary
achievements   ★   The urban family   ★   The "New Woman" and the
new morality

CHAPTER **29** *The Great West and the Agricultural
Revolution, 1865–1890*   **556**

The conquest of the Indians   ★   The mining and cattle frontiers   ★
Free lands and fraud   ★   The industrialization of agriculture   ★
The Populist protest

CHAPTER **30** *The Revolt of the Debtor, 1889–1900*   **578**

President Harrison and the "Billion-Dollar Congress"   ★   Cleveland
regains the White House, 1892   ★   The Panic of 1893   ★   The
Pullman strike, 1894   ★   The Wilson-Gorman Tariff, 1894   ★   Bryan
versus McKinley, 1896

CHAPTER **31** *The Path of Empire*   **595**

The sources of American expansionism   ★   Cleveland and the
Venezuelan boundary dispute, 1895–1896   ★   The explosion of the
Maine, February 15, 1898   ★   The Spanish-American War, 1898   ★
The liberation of Cuba   ★   Acquiring Hawaii (1898) and the
Philippines (1899)

CHAPTER **32** *America on the World Stage, 1899–1909* **615**

Crushing the Filipino insurrection ★ The Open Door Notes, 1899 ★ TR becomes president, 1901 ★ The Panama Canal ★ The "Roosevelt Corollary" to the Monroe Doctrine, 1905 ★ Roosevelt and the Far East

CHAPTER **33** *Progressivism and the Republican Roosevelt* **631**

The muckrakers ★ The politics of progressivism ★ Roosevelt, labor, and the trusts ★ Consumer protection ★ Conservation ★ Roosevelt's legacy ★ The troubled presidency of William Howard Taft ★ Taft's "Dollar Diplomacy" ★ Roosevelt breaks with Taft

CHAPTER **34** *Wilsonian Progressivism at Home and Abroad* **653**

The election of 1912: The New Freedom versus the New Nationalism ★ Wilson, the tariff, the banks, and the trusts ★ Wilson's diplomacy in Mexico ★ War in Europe and American neutrality ★ The reelection of Wilson, 1916

CHAPTER **35** *The War to End War, 1917–1918* **673**

German submarines push America into war, 1917 ★ Wilsonian idealism and the Fourteen Points ★ Mobilizing minds and machines ★ Propaganda and civil liberties ★ The American Expeditionary Force fights in France ★ Wilsonian peacemaking at Paris ★ The Senate rejects the Versailles Treaty

CHAPTER **36** *American Life in the "Roaring Twenties"* **697**

The "Red Scare," 1919–1920 ★ Immigration restriction, 1921–1924 ★ Prohibition and gangsterism ★ The emergence of a mass-consumption economy ★ The automobile age ★ Radio and the movies ★ Music and literature in the "delirious decade" ★ The economic boom

CHAPTER **37** *The Politics of Boom and Bust,*
1920–1932   **720**

The Republicans return to power, 1921   ⋆   Disarmament and
isolation   ⋆   The Harding scandals   ⋆   Calvin Coolidge's foreign
policies   ⋆   The international debt snarl   ⋆   Herbert Hoover, cautious
progressive   ⋆   The Great Crash, 1929   ⋆   Hoover and the Great
Depression

CHAPTER **38** *The Great Depression and the New Deal*   **745**

The "Hundred Days," 1933   ⋆   The National Recovery Administration,
1933–1935   ⋆   The Agricultural Adjustment Administration,
1933–1936   ⋆   The Social Security Act, 1935   ⋆   Gains for organized
labor   ⋆   The election of 1936 and the "Roosevelt coalition"   ⋆   The
Supreme Court fight, 1937

CHAPTER **39** *Franklin D. Roosevelt and the Shadow*
of War   **772**

Roosevelt's early foreign policies   ⋆   The Neutrality Acts,
1935–1939   ⋆   The destroyer-bases deal with Britain, 1940   ⋆   The
Lend-Lease Act, 1941   ⋆   The Atlantic Charter, 1941   ⋆   Pearl
Harbor, December 7, 1941

CHAPTER **40** *America in World War II*   **792**

The internment of Japanese-Americans   ⋆   The war ends the New
Deal   ⋆   Mobilizing the economy   ⋆   Women, blacks, and minorities
in wartime   ⋆   The economic and social impact of war   ⋆   Turning
the Japanese tide in the Pacific   ⋆   Campaigns in North Africa (1942)
and Italy (1943)   ⋆   "D-Day" in Normandy (France), June 6, 1944   ⋆
Germany surrenders, May 1945   ⋆   The atomic bombing of Hiroshima
and Nagasaki, August 1945

CHAPTER **41** *Harry S Truman and the Cold War*   **819**

Truman takes command, 1945   ⋆   The Yalta Conference (February
1945) and its legacy   ⋆   Origins of the Cold War   ⋆   The
International Monetary Fund, the World Bank, and the United
Nations   ⋆   The containment doctrine   ⋆   The Truman Doctrine, the
Marshall Plan, and NATO   ⋆   The Truman administration at home   ⋆
The outbreak of the Korean War, 1950   ⋆   The election of Dwight D.
Eisenhower, 1952

CHAPTER **42** *The Eisenhower Era, 1953–1960*   **842**

Eisenhower's leadership style ★ The menace of McCarthyism ★
Desegregating the South ★ John Foster Dulles and the "New Look" in
foreign policy ★ Eisenhower's reelection, 1956 ★ John F. Kennedy
defeats Richard Nixon, 1960

CHAPTER **43** *The Stormy Sixties*   **859**

The Kennedy spirit ★ The abortive Bay of Pigs invasion (1961) and
the missile crisis (1962) in Cuba ★ Kennedy assassinated, November
22, 1963 ★ Lyndon Baines Johnson and the "Great Society" ★ The
civil rights movement and the black revolution ★ The Vietnam
disaster ★ The election of Richard Nixon, 1968

CHAPTER **44** *The Stalemated Seventies*   **882**

Nixon and the Vietnam War ★ New policies toward Russia and
China ★ Nixon and the Supreme Court ★ Nixon trounces
McGovern, 1972 ★ The Watergate trauma ★ Israelis, Arabs, and
oil ★ Nixon resigns, August 9, 1974 ★ The Ford interlude ★
The election of Jimmy Carter, 1976 ★ Carter's diplomatic successes
in Panama and the Middle East ★ The energy crisis and inflation ★
The Iranian hostage humiliation

CHAPTER **45** *Ronald Reagan and the Conservative
Resurgence*   **906**

The "new right" and Reagan's election, 1980 ★ Budget battles and
tax cuts ★ Problems in Central America ★ Middle Eastern
woes ★ Terrorist traumas ★ The Strategic Defense Initiative
("Star Wars") ★ Abortion, school prayer, and affirmative action ★
Assessing the "Reagan Revolution"

CHAPTER **46** *The American People since World War II*   **921**

Postwar prosperity ★ The sagging economy in the 1970s ★ The
emergence of a "postindustrial" economy ★ The rise of the
"Sunbelt" ★ The postwar population boom ★ Demographic
trends ★ The newest immigrants ★ Minorities on the march ★
The feminist revolution ★ The modern American family ★
Culture and "counterculture" ★ The American prospect

APPENDIX   *Declaration of Independence*   **i**

Constitution of the United States of America   **v**

An American Profile: The U.S. and Its People   **xxiii**

Growth of U.S. Population and Area   ⋆   Characteristics of the U.S.
Population   ⋆   Changing Lifestyles in the Twentieth Century   ⋆
Characteristics of the U.S. Labor Force   ⋆   Leading Economic Sectors
(Various Years)   ⋆   Per Capita Disposable Personal Income in Constant
(1982) Dollars, 1929–1985   ⋆   U.S. Foreign Trade Since 1900   ⋆
Tariff Levies on Dutiable Imports, 1821–1985   ⋆   Gross National
Product in Current and Constant (1972) Dollars, 1900–1985   ⋆
Presidential Elections   ⋆   Presidents and Vice-Presidents   ⋆   Admission
of States   ⋆   Estimates of Total Costs and Number of Battle Deaths of
Major U.S. Wars

INDEX   **xxxv**

Maps

Territorial Growth of the United States
  Inside front cover
The United States Today
  Inside back cover
The World Known to Europe, 1492 **2**
Trade Routes with the East **3**
North American Indian Tribes at the Time of
  European Colonization **5**
Principal Voyages of Discovery **9**
Principal Spanish Explorations and Conquests **9**
Main Sources of English Colonists **11**
Early Maryland and Virginia **16**
Early Carolina and Georgia Settlements **18**
New England Settlements about 1650 **22**
The Great Puritan Migration **24**
Massachusetts Bay, the Hub of New England **27**
Andros's Dominion of New England **29**
Early Settlements in the Middle Colonies **31**
Main Sources of African Slaves c. 1500–1900 **43**
Immigrant Groups in 1775 **55**
The Colonial Economy **59**
Colonial Trade Patterns, c. 1770 **61**
Early French Settlements **75**
France's American Empire at Greatest Extent,
  1700 **76**
Fur-Trading Posts **77**
British Territory after Two Wars, 1713 **80**
Scenes of the French Wars **81**
The Ohio Country, 1753–1754 **81**
Events of 1775–1760 **84**
North America before 1754 **85**
North America after 1763 **85**
Settled Areas at End of French and Indian War,
  1763 **87**
Quebec before and after 1774 **101**
Revolution in the North, 1775–1776 **111**
New York and New Jersey, 1776–1777 **116**
New York, Pennsylvania Theater, 1777–1778 **117**
War in the South, 1780–1781 **120**
George Rogers Clark's Campaign, 1778–1779 **122**
Western Lands, 1783 **133**
Western Lands, 1802 **133**
Surveying the Old Northwest **134**

Main Centers of Spanish and British Influence after
  1783 **135**
The Struggle over Ratification **143**
American Posts Held by British after 1783 **166**
Presidential Election of 1800 **176**
Four Barbary States of North Africa **184**
Louisiana Purchase, 1803 **186**
Exploring the Louisiana Purchase **187**
The Three U.S. Thrusts of 1812 **202**
Campaigns of 1813 **202**
The Southwest, 1814–1815 **204**
Presidential Election of 1812 **207**
The Missouri Compromise and Slavery,
  1820–1821 **220**
U.S.–British Boundary Settlement, 1818 **224**
Acquiring the Floridas, 1810–1819 **224**
The West and Northwest, 1819–1824 **226**
Presidential Election of 1828 **241**
Southern Tribes before Transplanting **257**
The Texas Revolution, 1835–1836 **260**
Maine Boundary Settlement, 1842 **274**
The Oregon Controversy **277**
Texas, 1845–1846 **282**
Major Campaigns of Mexican War **284**
Cumberland (National) Road and Main
  Connections **298**
Erie Canal and Main Branches **300**
Principal Canals in 1840 **301**
Railroads in Operation in 1850 **303**
Railroads in Operation in 1860 **303**
Industry and Agriculture, 1860 **305**
Main Routes West before the Civil War **308**
Westward Movement of Center of Population,
  1790–1980 **312**
The Mormon Trek, 1846–1847 **323**
Southern Cotton Production, 1820 **352**
Southern Cotton Production, 1860 **353**
Distribution of Slaves, 1820 **354**
Distribution of Slaves, 1860 **355**
Early Emancipation in the North **361**
California Gold Rush Country **372**
Texas and the Compromise of 1850 **374**
Slavery after the Compromise of 1850 **378**

The Legal Status of Slavery from the Revolution to the Civil War **380**

Central America, c. 1850, Showing British Possessions and Proposed Canal Routes **382**

Gadsden Purchase, 1853 **385**

Kansas and Nebraska, 1854 **388**

Bleeding Kansas, 1854–1860 **393**

Presidential Election of 1856 **398**

Presidential Election of 1860 [Electoral] **407**

Presidential Election of 1860 [Popular] **407**

Southern Opposition to Secession, 1860–1861 **409**

Proposed Crittenden Compromise, 1860 **410**

Seceding States **417**

Main Thrusts, 1861–1865 **425**

Peninsular Campaign, 1862 **429**

Emancipation in the South **431**

The Mississippi River and Tennessee, 1862–1863 **433**

Sherman's March, 1864–1865 **434**

Lee's Chief Battles, December 1862–July 1863 **435**

Grant's Virginia Campaign, 1864–1865 **436**

Presidential Election of 1864 **453**

Military Reconstruction, 1867 **469**

Alaska and the Lower Forty-Eight States **476**

Hayes-Tilden Disputed Election of 1876 **489**

Presidential Election of 1884 **498**

Federal Land Grants to Railroads **505**

Early Pacific Railway Lines **508**

American Industry in 1900 **520**

Woman Suffrage before the Nineteenth Amendment **549**

Indian Wars, 1860–1890 **560**

Cattle Trails **564**

Average Annual Precipitation **567**

American Agriculture in 1900 **571**

Presidential Election of 1892 **582**

Presidential Election of 1896 **591**

The Venezuela–British Guiana Boundary Dispute **597**

The Pacific **599**

Dewey's Route in the Philippines, 1898 **604**

The Cuban Campaign, 1898 **608**

Big Stick in the Caribbean **623**

Far East, 1904–1905 **627**

Presidential Election of 1912 **656**

The United States in the Caribbean **661**

The United States and Mexico, 1914–1917 **663**

British Military Area and German Submarine War Zone **667**

Presidential Election of 1916 **670**

Major U.S. Operations in France, 1918 **683**

Presidential Election of 1920 **694**

Presidential Election of 1924 **729**

Presidential Election of 1928 **734**

The Extent of Erosion, 1934 **757**

TVA Area **759**

Destroyer-Bases Deal **783**

Presidential Election of 1940 **785**

Main Flow of Lend-Lease Aid **786**

Internal Migration in the United States during World War II **798**

Corregidor-Bataan **802**

United States Thrusts in the Pacific, 1942–1945 **804**

Allied Thrusts in North Africa and Italy, 1942–1945 **806**

Final Allied Thrusts in Europe, 1944–1945 **809**

Battle of the Bulge **811**

Postwar Partition of Germany **824**

United States Foreign Aid, Military and Economic, 1945–1954 **827**

The Shifting Front in Korea **837**

Presidential Election of 1952 **838**

The Far East, 1955–1956 **848**

Presidential Election of 1956 **850**

Presidential Election of 1960 **856**

Vietnam and Southeast Asia **863**

Presidential Election of 1964 **868**

Presidential Election of 1968 **879**

Presidential Election of 1972 **888**

Presidential Election of 1980 **908**

The Middle East **913**

Central America and the Caribbean **914**

Population Increase in the Sunbelt States, 1950–1982 **929**

Charts and Tables

4,000 B.C. Recorded History Begins—World War II Ends **1**

Columbus's Discovery—World War II Ends **2**

The Tudor Rulers of England **13**

The Thirteen Original Colonies **17**

The Stuart Dynasty in England **29**

Estimated Population Elements, 1790 **56**

The Colonial Social Pyramid, 1775 **57**

Estimated Religious Census, 1775 **63**

Established (Tax-Supported) Churches in the Colonies, 1775 **64**

Colonial Colleges **67**

Later English Monarchs **79**

The Nine World Wars **79**

Britain against the World **119**

Evolution of Federal Union **140**

Strengthening the Central Government **142**

Ratification of the Constitution **144**

Evolution of the Cabinet **151**

Hamilton's Financial Structure Supported by Revenues **154**

War Vote in House of Representatives, 1812 **199**

House Vote on Tariff of 1816 **214**

Election of 1824 **235**

House Vote on Tariff of 1828 **237**

House Vote on Tariff of 1832 **251**

House Vote on Compromise Tariff of 1833 **252**

House Vote on Tariff of 1846 **279**

Population Increase, Including Slaves and Indians, 1790–1860 **315**

Irish and German Immigration by Decade **316**

Slaveowning Families, 1850 **353**

Compromise of 1850 **377**

Election of 1860 **408**

Manufacturing by Sections, 1860 **420**

Immigration to U.S., 1860–1866 **421**

Enlistees North and South **444**

Union Party, 1864 **451**

Principal Reconstruction Proposals and Plans **466**

Southern Reconstruction by State **470**

Lynching: Aftermath of Reconstruction **474**

Composition of the Electoral Commission, 1877 **489**

Growth of Classified Civil Service **495**

Cotton Manufacturing Moves South **521**

The Shift to the City **531**

Annual Immigration, 1860–1984 **532**

Old and New Immigration **537**

Educational Levels, 1870–1985 **542**

Marriages and Divorces, 1890–1980 **549**

Homesteads from the Public Lands **569**

The Presidential Vote, 1912 **655**

Organization of Holding Companies **659**

Principal Foreign Elements in the United States **666**

U.S. Exports to Belligerents, 1914–1916 **667**

Approximate Comparative Losses in World War I **685**

Interlocking Treaty Structure **695**

Annual Immigration and the Quota Laws **700**

The Cost of a Model T Ford, 1908–1924 **708**

Limits Imposed by Washington Conference **724**

Aspects of the Financial Merry-Go-Round, 1921–1933 **731**

Index of Common Stock Prices **735**

Selected Stock Prices, Sept.–Nov. 1929 **735**

Principal New Deal Acts during Hundred Days Congress, 1933 **749**

Bank Failures and the Banking Act of 1933 **751**

Farm Foreclosures and Defaults, 1929–1945 **752**

Later Major New Deal Measures, 1933–1939 **753**

The Rise of Organized Labor, 1900–1982 **763**

Unemployment, 1929–1942 **768**

Federal Budget Surpluses or Deficits, 1930–1985 **800**

National Debt, 1930–1985 **800**

Merchant Tonnage Sunk by German U-Boats **805**

National Defense Budget, 1940–1985 **923**

Median Money Incomes of Families, 1950–1983 **925**

Government Expenditures for Public Welfare, 1940–1980 **925**

U.S. Population below the Poverty Line,
    1959–1983   **927**
The History of the Consumer Price Index,
    1967–1985   **928**
Comparative Tax Burdens   **929**
Occupational Distribution of Working Women,
    1900–1985   **937**

Percentage of Working Married Women with
    Children, (Husband Present), 1948–1984   **938**
Women in the Labor Force, 1900–1980   **938**
The Federal Budget Dollar and How It Is Spent by
    Major Category   **947**

Sail, sail thy best, ship of Democracy,
Of value is thy freight, 'tis not the Present only,
The Past is also stored in thee,
Thou holdest not the venture of thyself alone, not of
    the Western continent alone,
Earth's résumé entire floats on thy keel, O ship, is
    steadied by thy spars,
With thee Time voyages in trust, the antecedent
    nations sink or swim with thee,
With all their ancient struggles, martyrs, heroes, epics,
    wars, thou bear'st the other continents,
Theirs, theirs as much as thine, the destination-port
    triumphant. . . .

Walt Whitman
Thou Mother with Thy Equal Brood, 1872

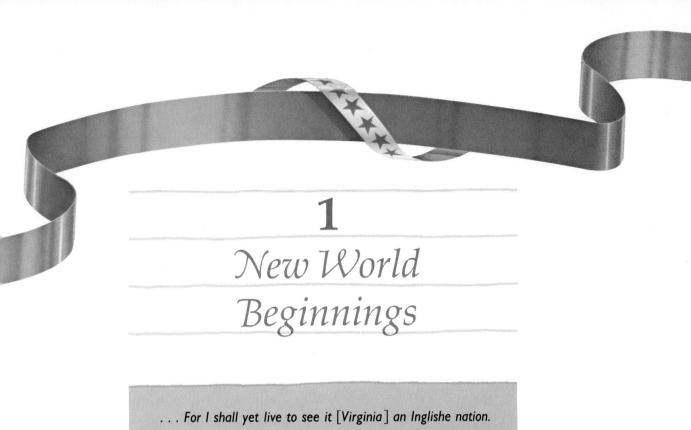

1
New World Beginnings

> *. . . For I shall yet live to see it [Virginia] an Inglishe nation.*
>
> Sir Walter Raleigh, 1602

Planetary Perspectives

Several billion years ago that whirling speck of dust known as the earth, fifth in size among the planets, came into being.

About six thousand years ago—only the day before yesterday geologically—recorded history of the Western world began. Certain peoples of the Middle East, developing a primitive culture, gradually emerged from the haze of the past.

Nearly five hundred years ago—only yesterday—European explorers stumbled on the American continents. This epochal achievement, one of the most dramatic in the chronicles of humankind, opened breathtaking new vistas and forever altered the future of both the Old World and the New.

The two new American continents eventually brought forth a score of sovereign republics. By far the most influential of this brood—the United States—was born a pygmy and grew to be a giant. It was destined to leave a deep imprint upon the rest of the world as a result of its refreshingly liberal ideals, its revolutionary democratic experiment, and its boundless opportunities for the common folk of foreign lands. The enormous output of its robust economy ultimately made it a decisive weight in the world balance of power. Its achievements in science, technology, and the arts shaped people's lives in every corner of the planet.

The American Republic, which is still relatively young when compared with the Old World, was from the outset richly favored. It started from scratch on a vast and virgin continent, which was so sparsely peopled by Indians that they could be eliminated or shouldered aside. This unique opportunity for a great social and political experiment may never come again, for no other huge, fertile, and relatively unin-habited areas are left in the temperate zones of this increasingly crowded planet.

Despite its marvelous development, the United States will one day reach its peak, like Greece and Rome. Its glory will eventually fade, as did theirs. But whatever uncertainties the future may hold, the past at least is secure and will richly repay examination.

Indirect Discoverers of the New World

The American continents were slow to yield their virginity. The all-conquering Romans, a half century after the birth of Christ, expanded their empire northwestward as far as Britain. But for nearly fifteen hundred years thereafter, the New World lay unknown and unsuspected to Europeans, awaiting its discoverers. Blond-bearded Norse seafarers from Scandinavia chanced upon the northeastern shoulder of North America about A.D. 1000. They landed at a place abounding in wild grapes, which they named Vinland. But their settlements were soon abandoned, and the discovery was forgotten, except in Scandinavian saga and song.

America was to be mainly a child of Europe, not of a specific country, such as England. One must seek in the Old World that momentous chain of events which led to a drive toward the Far East—and a completely accidental discovery of the New World.

Christian Crusaders must take high rank among the indirect discoverers of America. Tens of thousands of these European warriors, clad in shining armor, invaded Palestine from the eleventh to the fourteenth century. They were avowedly attempting to wrest the Holy Land from the polluting hand of the Moslem "infidel." Foiled in their repeated assaults, these Christian soldiers did manage to come into closer contact with the exotic delights of Asia—delights already introduced to Europe on a limited scale. European "barbarians" learned more fully the value of spices for spoiled and monotonous food; of silk for rough skins; of drugs for aching flesh; of perfumes for unbathed bodies; and of colorful draperies for gloomy castles.

But the luxuries of the Far East were prohibitively expensive in Europe. They had to be transported enormous distances from the Spice Islands (Indonesia), China, and India, in creaking ships and on swaying camel back, to the ports of the eastern Mediterranean. Moslem middlemen exacted a heavy toll en route. By the time the strange-smelling goods reached the Italian merchants at Venice and Genoa, they

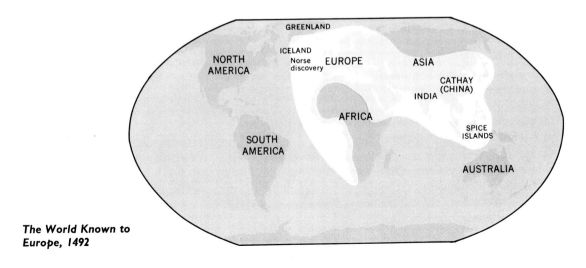

The World Known to Europe, 1492

were so costly that purchasers and profits alike were narrowly limited. Consumers and distributors of Western Europe were naturally eager to find a less costly route to the riches of Eastern Asia—one that would also break the monopoly of the Italian cities.

European appetites were further whetted when footloose Marco Polo, an Italian adventurer, returned to Europe in 1295, after a stay of nearly twenty years in China. Several years later, while a war prisoner, he dictated a classic account of his travels. He, too, must be regarded as an indirect discoverer of the New World, for his book, with its descriptions of rose-tinted pearls and golden pagodas, stimulated European desires for a cheaper route to the treasures of the Indies.

An urge to find a shortcut waterway to Eastern Asia was strong, but success awaited new horizons and new technology. Fortunately the Renaissance, which dawned in the fourteenth century, shot hopeful rays of light through the mists of the Middle Ages. An atmosphere of rebirth nurtured a healthy spirit of optimism, self-reliance, and venturesomeness. Better maps reduced superstitious fears of the unknown. The mariner's compass, possibly borrowed from the Arabs, eliminated some of the uncertainties of navigation. Printing presses, introduced about 1450, facilitated the spread of scientific knowledge.

Columbus Comes upon a New World

The spirit of the Renaissance also stimulated the ambition of several European monarchs. As these kings gradually subordinated the nobles, the modern national state emerged in Western Europe from the feudalism of the Middle Ages. This new type of government alone had the unity, power, and resources to shoulder the formidable tasks of discovery, conquest, and colonization.

The first nations to unite were the first to flourish as colonial empire builders—Portugal, Spain, England, France, and the Netherlands. Those countries that did not achieve unity until the nineteenth century, notably Germany and Italy, were left with crumbs dropped by the early feasters.

Little Portugal took the lead in discovering what came to be the coveted water route to the Indies. A courageous band of Portuguese navigators, edging cautiously down the pistol-handle coast of Africa, pushed southeasterly in the general direction of Asia. In 1488, four years

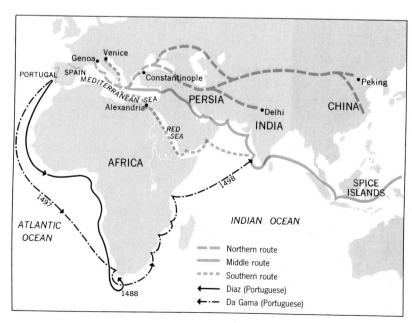

Trade Routes with the East
Goods on the early routes were passed through so many hands along the way that their ultimate source remained mysterious to Europeans.

before Columbus chanced upon America, Bartholomeu Diaz rounded the southernmost tip of the Dark Continent. Complete success crowned Portuguese efforts in 1498 when Vasco da Gama finally reached India (hence the name "Indies," given to all the mysterious lands of the Orient). He coaxed few jewels and spices from the natives, but later voyagers reaped lush profits from this treasure trove.

Portuguese empire builders ultimately established flourishing trading stations in India, Africa, China, and the East Indies. Immense wealth flowed to European coffers from these ventures. In turn, the ballooning prices of Asian products collapsed, and the monopolistic grip of the Italian commercial cities was broken.

The kingdom of Spain became united—an event pregnant with destiny—late in the fifteenth century. This new unity resulted primarily from the marriage of two sovereigns, Ferdinand and Isabella, and from the brutal expulsion of the "infidel" Moslem Moors. Glorying in their new strength, the Spaniards were eager to outstrip their Portuguese rivals in the race for the fabled Indies.

Christopher Columbus, a skilled Italian seaman, now stepped upon the stage of history. A man of vision, energy, resourcefulness, and courage, he finally managed, after heartbreaking delays, to gain the ear of the Spanish rulers. Like all of his informed contemporaries, he was convinced that the world was round. Then why not find the way to East Asia by sailing directly westward into the darkness of the Atlantic, instead of eastward for unnecessary miles around Africa?

The Spanish monarchs at last decided to gamble on the persistent mariner. They helped outfit him with three tiny but seaworthy ships, manned by a motley crew. Daringly, he spread the sails of his cockleshell craft. Winds were friendly and progress was rapid, but the superstitious sailors, fearful of sailing over the edge of the world, grew increasingly mutinous. Nearly six long weeks passed and failure loomed ahead when, on October 12, 1492, land was sighted—an island in the Bahamas. A new world thus swam within the vision of Europeans.

Columbus's sensational achievement has obscured the fact that he was one of the most successful failures of history. Seeking a new water route to the fabled Indies of the East, he had in fact bumped into an enormous land barrier blocking the ocean pathway. For decades thereafter explorers strove to get through it—or around it. The truth gradually dawned that sprawling new continents had been discovered. Yet Columbus stubbornly maintained until his death in 1506 that he had skirted the rim of the "Indies." So certain was he that he called the near-naked natives "Indians," a gross geographical misnomer that somehow stuck.

The Earliest Americans

Ironically, the remote ancestors of these native Americans were the true discoverers of America. Some twenty thousand years earlier, they had begun to venture from Asia across the land bridge that then connected Siberia and Alaska.

Aztec History   *This drawing recounts the founding of the Aztec capital of Tenochtitlan, now the site of Mexico City. The bottom panel shows the conquest of neighboring cities. (Library of Congress; Loubat,* Codex Mendoza.*)*

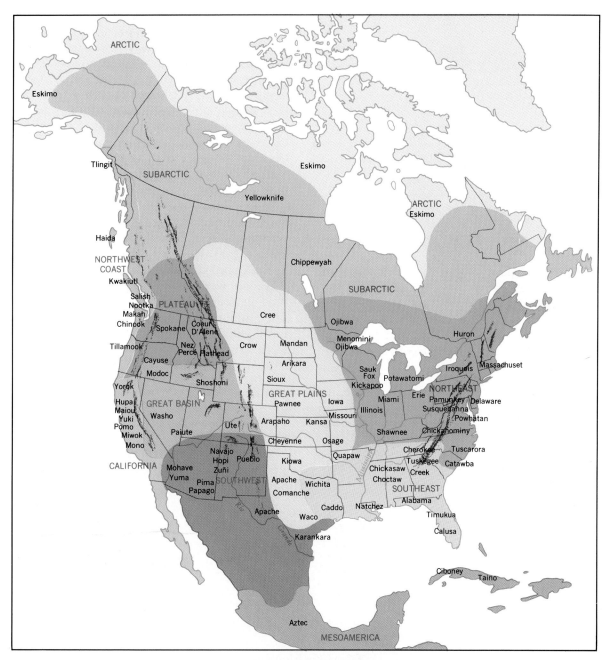

North American Indian Tribes at the Time of European Colonization *This map illustrates the great diversity of the Indian population—and suggests the inappropriateness of identifying all the Native American peoples with the single label* Indian. *The more than two hundred tribes were deeply divided by geography, language, and life-style.*

Roaming slowly southward through the silent vastness of the untracked wilderness, they eventually reached the far tip of South America. They continued to trek across the Asian-American isthmus for thousands of years, until rising seas submerged it and left this far-flung part of the family of man marooned for millennia on the now-isolated American continents.

Time did not stand still for these aboriginal Americans. Over the centuries they split into

Incan Art　*This golden figurine, wrapped in Peruvian cloth, illustrates both the wealth and the refinement of Incan society. (Lee Boltin, private collection.)*

hundreds of tribes, with different languages, religions, and cultures. Some of them evolved stunning civilizations. Incas in Peru, Aztecs in Mexico, and Mayans in Central America developed advanced agricultural techniques, based primarily on the cultivation of corn. Numbering their population in the millions, these sophisticated societies erected bustling, elaborately carved stone cities, rivaling in size those of Columbus's Europe. They carried on commerce, studied mathematics, and made strikingly accurate astronomical observations.

Indian life in North America was cruder, though some groups reached high levels of development. The Mound Builders of the lower Mississippi Valley built large permanent settlements around rectangular plazas. They used iron tools, wore woven fabrics, and buried their dead in collective graves covered by mounds. Their influence radiated as far as the Great Lakes area until—around the time of Columbus's discovery—powerful enemies virtually destroyed their culture. The Pueblos in the Rio

Taos Indian Pueblo　This sprawling adobe apartment house in present-day New Mexico looks today much as it did when Spanish explorers penetrated the upper Rio Grande Valley in the sixteenth century. Among the Spanish contributions to Pueblo Indian culture were the dome-shaped baking ovens, whose design, in turn, had entered Spain from Africa. (Shostal Associates, New York.)

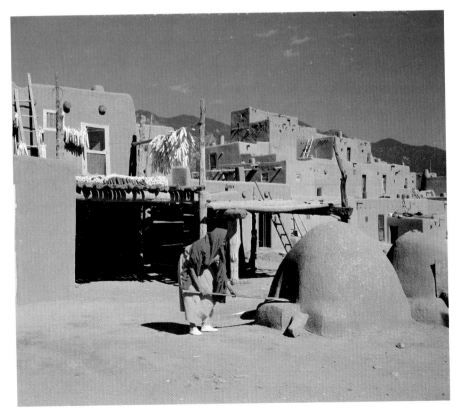

Grande Valley constructed elaborate irrigation systems and were dwelling in villages of multi-storied, terraced buildings when the Spanish made contact with them in the late sixteenth century. (*Pueblo* means "village" in Spanish.) The Creeks in the Southeast practiced a democratic style of government that led Europeans later to include them among the "civilized tribes." The Iroquois in the Northeast, inspired by their legendary leader Hiawatha, developed the political skills to sustain a robust military confederacy, which menaced Indian and European neighbors alike for more than a century.

These exceptions aside, most native peoples lived in small, scattered, and impermanent settlements. Tribes would gather into dense encampments along a riverbank at spawning time and then disperse in small bands of two or three families for the winter's hunting. In more settled agricultural tribes, women tended the crops while men hunted, fished, gathered fuel, and cleared fields for planting—often by setting massive forest fires. Deliberate torching of thousands of acres of woods also created better hunting habitats, especially for deer. This Indian burning accounted for the open, parklike character of the eastern woodlands that so amazed early European explorers.

But for the most part the land did not heavily feel the hand of the Indians upon it—partly because the Indians were so few in number. Perhaps ten million Native Americans dwelled in all of the present-day United States at the time of Columbus's arrival. They were so thinly spread across the land that vast areas were virtually uninhabited, with whispering, primeval forests and sparkling, virgin waters.

When Worlds Collide

Two ecosystems—the fragile, naturally evolved networks of relations among organisms in a stable environment—commingled and clashed when Columbus waded ashore. The flora and fauna of the Old and New Worlds had been separated from one another for thousands of years. European explorers marveled at the strange sights that greeted them—buffalo, iguanas, and "snakes with castanets" (rattlesnakes). Native

Benjamin Franklin later commented on the attractiveness of Indian life to Europeans: "When an Indian child has been brought up among us, taught our language and habituated to our customs, yet if he goes to see his relations and make one Indian ramble with them, there is no persuading him ever to return. [But] when white persons of either sex have been taken prisoners by the Indians, and lived awhile among them, though ransomed by their friends, and treated with all imaginable tenderness to prevail with them to stay among the English, yet in a short time they become disgusted with our manner of life, and the care and pains that are necessary to support it, and take the first good opportunity of escaping again into the woods, from whence there is no reclaiming them." (Letter to Peter Collinson, May 9, 1753.)

New World plants like tobacco, corn (maize), beans, tomatoes, and especially the lowly potato revolutionized the international economy and fed the rapid population growth of Europe. These were among the most important Indian gifts to the Europeans.

In exchange, the Europeans introduced cattle, swine, and horses to the New World. Indian tribes like the Blackfoot, the Sioux, and the Apaches swiftly adopted the horse, transforming their culture. They became less sedentary and more nomadic, roaming on horseback over the grassy Great Plains in pursuit of the buffalo.

Unwittingly, the Europeans also brought other organisms in the dirt on their boots and the dust on their clothes, as well as in their bodies—such as the seeds of Kentucky bluegrass, dandelions, and daisies and the germs that caused smallpox, yellow fever, and malaria. Old World diseases devastated the Native Americans. During their millennia of isolation in the Americas, the Indians had rooted out most of the Old World's killer maladies. But generations of freedom from those illnesses had also wiped out necessary antibodies. Devoid of any natural resistance to European sicknesses, Indians died in droves. In the century after Columbus's landfall, nearly 90 percent of the Native American

A Carolina Indian Woman and Child   *A painting by John White, who was a member of the Raleigh expedition of 1585. Note that the Indian girl carries a European doll, illustrating the mingling of cultures that had already begun. (The Granger Collection.)*

population perished. By 1592, a combination of disease, enslavement, and armed Spanish aggression had reduced the civilization of the Arawaks in Hispaniola from about 5 million people to 250. Enraged and vengeful, Indians kneaded infected blood into their masters' bread, to little effect. Perhaps it was poetic justice that the Indians took a kind of revenge by infecting the early explorers with syphilis, injecting that noxious disease for the first time into Europe.

The Spanish Conquistadores

Gradually Europeans realized that the American continents held rich prizes of their own—especially the glittering gold of the advanced Indian civilizations in the southern continent.

Spain secured its claim to Columbus's discoveries in the Treaty of Tordesillas (1494), dividing with Portugal the "heathen lands" of the New World. The lion's share went to Spain, but Portugal received compensating territory in Africa and Asia, and also title to lands that would one day be Brazil.

Spain now became the dominant exploring and colonizing power in the 1500s. Love of God joined with the lure of gold in spurring the Spaniards on, as zealous priests sought to convert the pagan natives to Catholic Christianity. On Spain's long roster of heroic deeds two spectacular exploits must be headlined. Vasco Nuñez Balboa, hailed as the discoverer of the Pacific Ocean, waded into the foaming waves off Panama in 1513 and claimed for his king all the lands washed by that sea! Ferdinand Magellan started from Spain in 1519 with five tiny ships. After discovering the storm-lashed strait off South America that bears his name, he was slain by the natives in the Philippines, but his one remaining vessel creakily completed the first circumnavigation of the globe in 1522.

Exploratory beginnings were launched by other adventuresome Spaniards in what was destined to be the United States. In 1513 Juan Ponce de León discovered Florida, which he thought an island. Debauched by high living, he was seeking the mythical fountain of youth. He found instead death—from an Indian arrow. Francisco Coronado, in quest of golden cities that turned out to be adobe pueblos, wandered in 1540–1542 with a clanking cavalcade through Arizona and New Mexico as far east as Kansas. His expedition discovered en route two impressive natural wonders: the Grand Canyon of the Colorado and enormous herds of buffalo (bison). A half-century later, Spanish settlers began to trickle into the Rio Grande Valley. They treated the Indians cruelly—severing one foot of each survivor of a battle in 1599—and were temporarily driven out of the region by an Indian uprising in 1680.

Hernando de Soto, with six hundred armor-plated men, undertook a fantastic gold-seeking expedition during 1539–1542. Floundering through marshes and pine barrens, from Florida westward, he discovered and crossed the majestic Mississippi north of the Arkansas River. After brutally misusing the Indians with

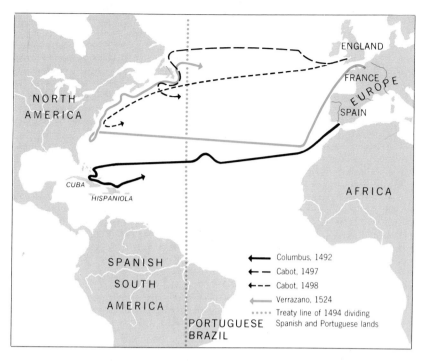

Principal Voyages of Discovery
Spain, Portugal, France, and England reaped the greatest advantages from the New World, but much of the earliest exploration was done by Italians, notably Christopher Columbus of Genoa. John Cabot, another native of Genoa (his original name was Giovanni Caboto), sailed for England's King Henry VII. Giovanni da Verrazano was a Florentine employed by France.

iron collars and fierce dogs, he at length died of fever and wounds. His remains were secretly buried at night in the Mississippi, lest the Indians abuse the dead body of their abuser.

Hernando Cortés, with seven hundred men and eighteen horses (which awed the horseless natives), tore open the coffers of the Mexican Aztecs in 1519–1521. Francisco Pizarro, an ironfisted conqueror, crushed the Peruvian Incas in 1532 and added another incredible hoard of gold and silver to the loot from Mexico. The Spanish invaders not only robbed the Indians but subsequently enslaved them and put them to work digging up precious metals. By 1600,

Principal Spanish Explorations and Conquests *Note that Coronado traversed northern Texas and Oklahoma. In present-day eastern Kansas he found, instead of the great golden city he sought, a drab encampment, probably of Wichita Indians.*

Spain was swimming in New World silver, mostly from the fabulously rich mines at Potosí in present-day Bolivia.

The Spanish conquerors (*conquistadores*), curiously enough, were indirect founders of the United States. Their phenomenal success excited the envy of the English and helped spur some of the early attempts at colonization. Moreover, the dumping of the enormous Indian treasure chests upon Europe inflated the currency and drove prices upward. The pinch further distressed underpaid English toilers, many of whom in turn were later driven to the New World. There, ironically, they challenged Spanish supremacy.

These plunderings by the Spaniards unfortunately obscured their substantial colonial achievements and helped give birth to the "black legend." This false concept meant that the conquerors merely tortured and butchered the Indians ("killing for Christ"), stole their gold, infected them with smallpox, and left little but misery behind. The Spanish invader did kill thousands of natives and exploit the rest, but he intermarried with them as well, creating a distinctive South American culture of *mestizos*—

people of mixed Indian and European heritage. He erected a colossal empire, sprawling from California and the Floridas to Tierra del Fuego. He transplanted and engrafted his culture, laws, religion, and language and laid the foundations for a score of Spanish-speaking nations.

The bare statistics of Spain's colonial empire are alone impressive. By 1574, thirty-three years before the first primitive English shelters in Virginia, there were about two hundred Spanish cities and towns in North and South America. A total of 160,000 Spanish inhabitants, mostly men, had subjugated some 5 million Indians—all in the name of the gentle Jesus. Majestic cathedrals dotted the land, printing presses were turning out books, and literary prizes were being awarded. Two distinguished universities were chartered in 1551, one at Mexico City and the other at Lima, Peru. Both of them antedated Harvard, the first college established in the English colonies, by eighty-five years.

It is clear that the Spaniards, who had more than a century's head start over the English, were genuine empire builders in the New World. As compared with their Anglo-Saxon ri-

North Carolina Indians Sitting at Meate   *Painted by John White, a member of Sir Walter Raleigh's second expedition, 1585. Indians such as these may have absorbed the more than one hundred "lost colonists" from Raleigh's ill-starred venture on Roanoke Island. In one nearby county of present-day North Carolina, blue-eyed and fair-haired characteristics have persisted among the Indians, along with Elizabethan words and the family names of forty-one Roanoke colonists. (Library of Congress.)*

vals, their colonial establishment was larger and richer, and it lasted more than a quarter of a century longer.

England's Imperial Stirrings

Feeble indeed were the efforts of England in the 1500s to compete with the sprawling Spanish Empire. As Spain's ally in the first half of the century, England took little interest in establishing its own overseas colonies. But after the Protestant Queen Elilzabeth mounted the English throne in 1558, rivalry with Catholic Spain intensified.

Hardy English freebooters swarmed out upon the shipping lanes. They sought to promote the twin goals of Protestantism and plunder by seizing Spanish treasure ships and raiding Spanish settlements, even though England and Spain were technically at peace. The most famous of these semipiratical "sea dogs" was the courtly Francis Drake. He plundered his way around the planet, returning in 1580 with his ship heavily ballasted with Spanish booty. The venture netted profits of about 4,600 percent to his financial backers, among whom, in secret, was Queen Elizabeth. Defying Spanish protest, she brazenly knighted Drake on the deck of his barnacled ship.

The bleak coast of Newfoundland was the scene of the first English attempt at colonization, which collapsed when its promoter, Sir Humphrey Gilbert, lost his life at sea in 1583. Gilbert's ill-starred dream inspired his gallant half brother Sir Walter Raleigh to try again in warmer climes. Raleigh organized a group of settlers who landed in 1585 on North Carolina's Roanoke Island, off the coast of Virginia—a vaguely defined region named by the "Virgin Queen" Elizabeth in honor of herself. With Raleigh busy at home, the hapless Roanoke colony mysteriously vanished, swallowed up by the wilderness.

These pathetic English failures at colonization contrasted embarrassingly with the glories of the Spanish Empire, whose profits were enriching Spain beyond its most ambitious dreams of avarice. Philip II of Spain, self-anointed foe of the Protestant Reformation, used part of his imperial gains to amass an "Invincible Armada" of

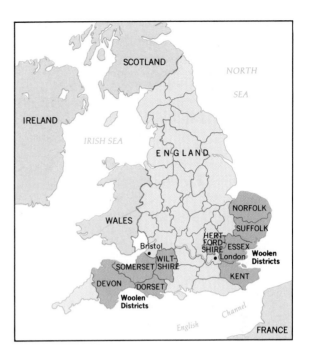

Main Sources of the Puritan "Great Migration" to New England, 1620–1650

Sir Walter Raleigh (c. 1552–1618) Here he is shown *"drinking tobacco,"* as smoking was first called. He is credited with introducing both tobacco and the potato into England. A dashing courtier, he launched important colonizing failures in the New World. After seducing (and marrying) one of Queen Elizabeth's maids of honor, he fell out of favor and was ultimately beheaded for treason.

Elizabeth I (1533–1603) *Although accused of being vain, fickle, prejudiced, and miserly, she proved to be an unusually successful ruler. She never married (the "Virgin Queen"), although various royal matches were projected. (National Portrait Gallery, London.)*

ships for an invasion of England. The showdown came in 1588, when the lumbering Spanish flotilla, 130 strong, hove into the English Channel. The English sea dogs fought back. Using craft that were swifter, more maneuverable, and more ably manned, they inflicted heavy damage on the cumbersome, overladen Spanish ships. Then a devastating storm arose (the "Protestant wind"), scattering the crippled Spanish fleet.

The defeat of the Spanish Armada was a red-letter day in American history. It dampened the fighting spirit of Spain and helped to ensure England's naval dominance in the North Atlantic. It started her well on her way to becoming mistress of the seas—a fact of enormous importance to the American people.

A wondrous flowering of the English national spirit also bloomed in the wake of the Spanish Armada's defeat. A golden age of literature dawned in this exhilarating atmosphere, with Shakespeare, at its forefront, making occasional poetical references to England's American colonies. The English were seized with restlessness, with thirst for adventure, and with curiosity about the unknown. Everywhere there blossomed a new spirit of self-confidence, of vibrant patriotism, and of boundless faith in the future of the English nation. When England and Spain finally signed a treaty of peace in 1604, the English people were poised to plunge headlong into the planting of their own colonial empire in the New World.

England on the Eve of Empire

England's scepter'd isle, as Shakespeare called it, throbbed with social and economic change as the seventeenth century opened. Her population was mushrooming, from some 3 million people in 1550 to about 4 million in 1600. In the evergreen English countryside, landlords were "enclosing" croplands for sheep grazing, forcing many small farmers ("yeomen") into precarious tenancy or off the land altogether. It was no accident that the woolen districts of eastern and western England—where Puritanism had taken strong root—supplied many of the earliest immigrants to America. When economic depression hit the woolen trade in the late 1500s, thousands of footloose yeomen took to the roads. They drifted about England, chronically unemployed, often ending up as beggars and paupers in cities like Bristol and London.

This remarkably mobile population alarmed many contemporaries. They concluded that England was burdened with a "surplus population," though twentieth-century London holds twice as many people as did all of England in 1600.

At the same time, laws of primogeniture decreed that only eldest sons were eligible to inherit landed estates. The landholders' ambitious younger sons—like Gilbert, Raleigh, and Drake —were forced to seek their fortunes elsewhere. Bad luck plagued their early, lone-wolf enterprises. But by the early 1600s the joint-stock company—forerunner of the modern corporation—was perfected. It enabled a considerable number of investors, called "adventurers," to pool their capital.

Peace with a chastened Spain provided the opportunity for English colonization. Population growth provided the workers. Unemployment, as well as a thirst for adventure, for markets, and for religious freedom, provided the motives. Joint-stock companies provided the financial means. The stage was now set for a historic effort to establish an English beachhead in the still uncharted American wilderness.

England Plants the Jamestown Seedling

In 1606, two years after peace with Spain, the hand of destiny beckoned toward Virginia. A joint-stock company, known as the Virginia Company of London, received a charter from King James I of England for a settlement in the New World. The main attraction was the promise of gold, combined with a strong desire to convert the Indians to Christianity and to find a passage through America to the Indies. Like most joint-stock companies of the day, the Virginia Company was intended to endure for only a few years, after which its stockholders hoped to liquidate it for a profit. This arrangement put severe pressure on the luckless

King James I had scant enthusiasm for the Virginia experiment, partly because of his hatred of tobacco smoking, which had been introduced into the Old World by the Spanish discoverers. In 1604 he published the pamphlet A Counterblast to Tobacco: *"A custom loathsome to the eye, hateful to the nose, harmful to the brain, dangerous to the lungs, and in the black stinking fume thereof, nearest resembling the horrible Stygian smoke of the pit [Hades] that is bottomless."*

colonists, who were threatened with abandonment in the wilderness if they did not quickly strike it rich on the company's behalf. Few of the investors thought in terms of long-term colonization. Apparently no one even faintly suspected that the seeds of a mighty nation were being planted.

The charter of the Virginia Company is a significant document in American history. It guaranteed to the overseas settlers the same rights of Englishmen that they would have enjoyed if they had stayed at home. This precious boon was gradually extended to the other English colonies and became a foundation stone of American liberties.

Unluckily, the site selected in 1607 for the tiny colony was Jamestown, on the wooded and malarial banks of the James River, named in honor of King James I. Although it was mosquito-infested and unhealthful, the spot was easy to defend.

The Tudor Rulers of England *

NAME, REIGN	RELATION TO AMERICA
Henry VII, 1485–1509	Cabot voyages, 1497, 1498
Henry VIII, 1509–1547	English Reformation begun
Edward VI, 1547–1553	Strong Protestant tendencies
"Bloody" Mary, 1553–1558	Catholic reaction
Elizabeth, 1558–1603	Break with Rome final; Drake; Spanish Armada defeated

* See p. 29 for continuation of table.

The early years at Jamestown proved to be a nightmare for all concerned—except the buzzards. Forty would-be colonists perished during the initial voyage in 1606–1607. Another expedition in 1609 lost its leaders and many of its precious supplies in a shipwreck in Bermuda. Of the 400 settlers who managed to make it to Virginia, only 60 survived the "starving time" winter of 1609–1610. Ironically, the woods rustled with game and the rivers flopped with fish, but the greenhorn settlers wasted valuable time grubbing for nonexistent gold when they should have been gathering provisions. Diseased and despairing, the colonists dragged themselves aboard homeward-bound ships in the spring of 1610—only to be met at the mouth of the James River by a relief party, which ordered them back to Jamestown.

Disease continued to reap a gruesome harvest among the Virginians, and Indian raids added to the death toll. One Indian uprising in 1622 left 347 settlers dead. By 1625, Virginia contained only some 1200 hard-bitten survivors of the nearly 8000 adventurers who had tried to start life anew in the ill-fated colony.

Virginia was saved from collapse at the start largely by the leadership and resourcefulness of an intrepid young adventurer, Captain John Smith. Taking over in 1608, he whipped the gold-hungry colonists into line with the rule, "He who will not work shall not eat." The brown-skinned Indian maiden Pocahontas may not have saved his life, as he dramatically related, by suddenly interposing her head between his and the war clubs of his Indian captors, but there can be little doubt that she contributed to the salvation of the colony by helping to preserve peace and provide foodstuffs. At times of scarcity the settlers were forced to eat "dogges, Catts, Ratts, and Myce." One hungry man killed, salted, and ate his wife, for which misbehavior he was executed.

Virginia: Child of Tobacco

John Rolfe, who married Pocahontas in 1614 and became father of the tobacco industry, was also an economic savior of the Virginia colony. By 1616 he perfected methods of raising and curing the pungent weed, eliminating much of the bitter tang. Tobacco-rush days began, as crops were planted even in the streets of Jamestown and between the numerous graves. So heavy was the concentration on the yellow leaf that some foodstuffs had to be imported.

Virginia's prosperity was finally built on tobacco smoke. This "bewitching weed" played a vital role in putting the colony on firm foundations and in setting an example for other successful colonizing experiments. But tobacco—King Nicotine—was something of a tyrant. It was ruinous to the soil when greedily planted in successive years, and it enchained the prosperity of Virginia to the fluctuating price of a single crop. Tobacco also promoted the broad-acred plantation system and with it a brisk demand for fresh labor.

In 1619, the year before the Plymouth Pilgrims landed in New England, what was described as a Dutch warship appeared off Jamestown and sold some twenty black Africans. (The scanty record does not reveal whether they were purchased as lifelong slaves or as servants committed to limited years of servitude.) Yet black slaves were too costly for most of the hard-pinched white colonists to acquire, and for

Pocahontas (c. 1595–1617) Taken to England by her husband, she was received as a princess. She died when preparing to return, and her infant son ultimately reached Virginia, where hundreds of his descendants have lived, including the second Mrs. Woodrow Wilson. (National Portrait Gallery, Smithsonian Institution, Washington, D.C.)

decades they were imported only in driblets. Virginia counted but three hundred blacks in 1650, although by the end of the century blacks made up approximately 14 percent of the colony's population.

Representative self-government was also born in primitive Virginia, in the same cradle with slavery and in the same year—1619. The London Company authorized the settlers to summon an assembly, known as the House of Burgesses. A momentous precedent was thus feebly established, for this assemblage was the first of many miniature parliaments to mushroom from the soil of America.

As time passed, James I grew increasingly hostile to Virginia. He detested tobacco and he distrusted the representative House of Burgesses, which he branded a "seminary of sedition." In 1624 he revoked the charter of the bankrupt and beleaguered Virginia Company, thus making Virginia a royal colony directly under his control.

Maryland: Catholic Haven

Maryland—the second plantation colony but the fourth English colony to be planted—was founded in 1634 by Lord Baltimore, of a prominent English Catholic family. He embarked upon the venture partly to reap financial profits and partly to create a refuge for his co-religionists. Protestant England was still persecuting Roman Catholics; among numerous discriminations, a couple seeking wedlock could not be legally married by a Catholic priest.

Absentee proprietor Lord Baltimore hoped that the 200 settlers who founded Maryland at St. Mary's, on Chesapeake Bay, would be the vanguard of a vast new feudal domain. Huge estates were to be awarded to his largely Catholic relatives, and gracious manor houses, modeled on those of England's aristocracy, were intended to sprout from the fertile forests. As in Virginia, colonists proved willing to come only if offered the opportunity to acquire land of their own. Soon they were dispersed around the Chesapeake region on modest farms, and the haughty land barons, mostly Catholic, were surrounded by resentful backcountry planters, mostly Protestant. Resentment flared into open

Advertisement of a Voyage to America, 1609

rebellion near the end of the century, and the Baltimore family for a time lost its proprietary rights.

Despite these tensions, Maryland prospered. Like Virginia, it blossomed forth in acres of tobacco. Like Virginia, it depended for labor in its early years mainly on white indentured ser-

> *The wife of a Virginia governor wrote to her sister in England in 1623 of her voyage: "For our Shippe was so pestered with people and goods that we were so full of infection that after a while we saw little but throwing folkes over board: It pleased god to send me my helth till I came to shoare and 3 dayes after I fell sick but I thank god I am well recovered. Few else are left alive that came in that Shippe. . . ."*

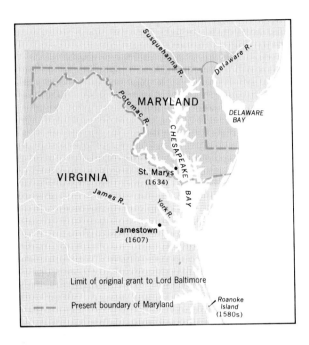

Early Maryland and Virginia

Colonizing the Carolinas

Civil wars convulsed England in the 1640s. King Charles I had dismissed Parliament in 1629, and when he eventually recalled it in 1640, the members were mutinous. Finding their great champion in the Puritan-soldier Oliver Cromwell, they ultimately beheaded Charles in 1649, and Cromwell ruled England for nearly a decade. Finally, Charles II, son of the decapitated king, was restored to the throne in 1660.

Colonization had been interrupted during this period of bloody unrest. Now, in the so-called Restoration period, empire building resumed with even greater intensity—and royal involvement. The Carolinas, named in honor of the restored king, were formally created in 1670, after Charles II granted to eight of his court favorites—Lords Proprietors—an expanse of wilderness ribboning across the continent to the Pacific. These aristocratic founders hoped to grow foodstuffs to provision the sugar plantations in Barbados and to export non-English products like wine, silk, and olive oil.

South Carolina prospered by developing close economic ties with the flourishing British West Indies. In a broad sense, the mainland colony was but the most northwesterly of those islands.

vants—penniless persons who bound themselves to work for a number of years to pay their passage. In both colonies it was only in the later years of the seventeenth century that black slaves began to be imported in large numbers.

Lord Baltimore, a canny soul, permitted unusual freedom of worship at the outset. He hoped that he would thus purchase toleration for his own fellow worshipers. But the heavy tide of Protestants threatened to submerge the Catholics and place severe restrictions on them, as in England. Faced with disaster, the Catholics of Maryland threw their support behind the famed Act of Toleration, which was passed in 1649 by the local representative assembly.

Maryland's new religious statute guaranteed toleration to all Christians. But it decreed the death penalty for those, like Jews and atheists, who denied the divinity of Jesus. The law thus sanctioned less toleration than had previously existed in the settlement, but it did extend a temporary cloak of protection to the uneasy Catholic minority. One result was that when the colonial era ended, Maryland probably sheltered more Roman Catholics than any other English-speaking colony in the New World.

Cecelius Calvert (Lord Baltimore), c. 1605–1675
Inheriting the land grant from his father, he served as the first proprietor of Maryland, named after the English queen. He never saw his colony but governed through deputies. The present Anne Arundel county, embracing Annapolis and Baltimore, was named after his wife. (Enoch Pratt Free Library. Photograph from the Maryland Historical Society.)

Indian slaves were among the colony's earliest exports. Manacled captives from the colony's interior were sent to work in the West Indian cane fields and sugar mills. Others were dispatched to New England. One Rhode Island town in 1730 counted over two hundred Indian slaves from Carolina in its midst.

After much experimentation, rice emerged as the principal export crop in South Carolina. Rice was then an exotic food in England; no rice seeds were sent out from London in the first supply ships to South Carolina. But rice was grown in Africa, and the Carolinians were soon paying premium prices for west African slaves experienced in rice cultivation. The Africans' agricultural skill and their relative immunity to malaria (thanks to a genetic trait that also made them and their descendants susceptible to sickle-cell anemia) made them ideal laborers on the hot and swampy rice plantations. By 1710 they constituted a majority of Carolinians.

Moss-festooned Charles Town—also named for the king—rapidly became the busiest seaport in the South. Many high-spirited sons of English landed families, deprived of an inheritance, came to the Charleston area and gave it a rich aristocratic flavor. The village became a colorfully diverse community, to which French Protestant refugees and others were attracted by religious toleration.

Nearby, in Florida, the Catholic Spaniards bitterly resented the intrusion of these Protestant English heretics. South Carolina's frontier

The Thirteen Original Colonies

NAME	FOUNDED BY	YEAR	CHARTER	MADE ROYAL	1775 STATUS
1. Virginia	London Co.	1607	1606 1609 1612	1624	Royal (under the Crown)
Plymouth	Separatists	1620	None		(Merged with Mass., 1691)
Maine	F. Gorges	1623	1639		(Bought by Mass., 1677)
2. New Hampshire	John Mason and others	1623	1679	1679	Royal (absorbed by Mass., 1641–1679)
3. Massachusetts	Puritans	c. 1628	1629	1691	Royal
4. Maryland	Lord Baltimore	1634	1632	——	Proprietary (controlled by proprietor)
5. Connecticut	Mass. emigrants	1635	1662	——	Self-governing (under local control)
6. Rhode Island	R. Williams	1636	1644 1663	——	Self-governing
New Haven	Mass. emigrants	1638	None		(Merged with Conn., 1662)
7. N. Carolina	Virginians	1653	1663	1729	Royal (separated informally from S.C., 1691)
8. New York	Dutch	c. 1613			
	Duke of York	1664	1664	1685	Royal
9. New Jersey	Berkeley and Carteret	1664	None	1702	Royal
10. S. Carolina	Eight nobles	1670	1663	1729	Royal (separated formally from N.C., 1712)
11. Pennsylvania	William Penn	1681	1681	——	Proprietary
12. Delaware	Swedes	1638	None	——	Proprietary (merged with Penn., 1682; same governor, but separate assembly, granted 1703)
13. Georgia	Oglethorpe and others	1733	1732	1752	Royal

was often aflame. Spanish-incited Indians brandished their tomahawks, and armor-clad warriors of Spain frequently unsheathed their swords during the successive Anglo-Spanish wars. But by 1700 South Carolina was too strong to be wiped out.

The wild northern expanse of the huge Carolina grant bordered on Virginia. From the older colony there drifted down a motley group of poverty-stricken outcasts and religious dissenters. Many of them had been repelled by the rarefied atmosphere of Virginia, dominated as it was by big-plantation aristocrats belonging to the Church of England. North Carolinians, as a result, have been called "the quintessence of Virginia's discontent." The newcomers, who frequently were "squatters" without legal right to the soil, raised their tobacco and other crops on small farms, with little need for slaves.

Distinctive traits developed rapidly in North Carolina. The poor but sturdy inhabitants, regarded as riffraff by their snobbish neighbors, earned a reputation for being irreligious and hospitable to pirates. Isolated from neighbors by raw wilderness and stormy Cape Hatteras, "graveyard of the Atlantic," the North Carolinians developed a strong spirit of resistance to authority. Their location between aristocratic Virginia and aristocratic South Carolina caused the area to be dubbed "a vale of humility between

two mountains of conceit." Following much friction with governors, North Carolina was officially separated from South Carolina in 1712, and subsequently each segment became a royal colony.

North Carolina shares with tiny Rhode Island several distinctions. These two outposts were the most democratic, the most independent-minded, and the least aristocratic of the original thirteen English colonies.

Late-Coming Georgia: The Buffer Colony

Pine-forested Georgia, with the harbor of Savannah nourishing its chief settlement, was formally founded in 1733. It proved to be the last of the thirteen colonies to be planted—fifty-two years after Pennsylvania. Chronologically it belongs elsewhere, but geographically it may be grouped with its southern neighbors.

Georgia was valued by the English crown chiefly as a buffer. It would serve to protect the more valuable Carolinas from inroads by vengeful Spaniards from Florida and by the hostile French from Louisiana. Georgia in truth suffered much buffeting, especially when wars broke out between Spain and England in the European cockpit. As a vital link in imperial defense, the exposed colony received monetary subsidies from the British government at the outset—the only one of the "original thirteen" to enjoy this boon in its founding stage.

Named in honor of George II of England, Georgia was launched by a high-minded group of philanthropists. Aside from producing silk and wine, and strengthening the empire, they were determined to create a haven for wretched souls imprisoned for debt. The ablest of the founders was the dynamic soldier-statesman James Oglethorpe, who became keenly interested in prison reform after one of his friends had died in a debtor's jail. As an able military leader, Oglethorpe repelled savage Spanish attacks. As an imperialist and a philanthropist, he saved "the Charity Colony" by his energetic leadership and by mortgaging heavily his own personal fortunes.

Early Carolina and Georgia Settlements

The hamlet of Savannah, like Charleston, was a melting-pot community. German Lutherans and kilted Scots Highlanders, among others, added color to the pattern. All Christian worshipers except Catholics enjoyed religious toleration. Many Bible-toting missionaries arrived to work among debtors and Indians. Prominent among them was young John Wesley, who later returned to England and founded the Methodist church.

Georgia grew with painful slowness and at the end of the colonial era was perhaps the least populous of the colonies. Prosperity through a large-plantation economy was thwarted by an unhealthful climate, by early restrictions on black slavery, and by demoralizing Spanish attacks.

The Plantation Colonies

Certain distinctive features were shared by England's southern mainland colonies: Maryland, Virginia, North Carolina, South Carolina, and Georgia.

Broad-acred, these outposts of empire were all in some degree dominated by a plantation economy. Profitable staple crops were the rule, notably tobacco and rice, though to a lesser extent in small-farm North Carolina. Slavery was found in all the plantation colonies, though only after 1750 in reform-minded Georgia. Immense acreage in the hands of a favored few fostered a strong aristocratic atmosphere, except in North Carolina and to some extent in debtor-tinged Georgia. The wide scattering of plantations and farms, often along stately rivers, made the establishment of churches and schools both difficult and expensive. In 1671 the governor of Virginia thanked God that no free schools or printing presses existed in his colony.

All the plantation colonies permitted some religious toleration. The tax-supported Church of England became the dominant faith, though weakest of all in nonconformist North Carolina.

All the plantation colonies were in some degree expansionary. "Soil butchery" by excessive growing of tobacco drove settlers westward, and the long, lazy rivers invited penetration of the continent.

Varying Viewpoints

The history of discovery and the earliest colonization raises perhaps the single most fundamental question about all American history. Should it be understood as the extension of European civilization into the New World or as the gradual development of a uniquely "American" culture? An older school of thought tended to emphasize the Europeanization of America. Historians of that persuasion thus paid close attention to the situation in Europe, particularly in England and Spain, in the fifteenth and sixteenth centuries. They also focused on the various means by which the values and institutions of the mother continent were exported to the new lands in the western sea. Some European writers have varied this general question by asking what transforming effect the discovery of America had on Europe itself. But both of these approaches are Eurocentric. More recently, historians have concentrated on the distinctive aspects of America, especially the interactions among the various races in the Western Hemisphere. This approach stresses the adaptations of native, African, and European cultures to the challenges of life in a strange new environment and emphasizes the creation of a uniquely *American* society and culture.

Select Readings

Primary Source Documents

Richard Hakluyt, *Divers Voyages Touching the Discovery of America and the Islands Adjacent,** edited by J. W. Jones (1850), supplied the rationale for the establishment of English colonies in North America. John Smith, "Generall Historie of Virginia," in *Travels and Works of Captain John Smith,** edited by Edward Arber (1910), is the account of the amazing, vain man who steered Jamestown through its first few years.

Secondary Sources

The international economic background to colonization is sketched in Ralph Davis, *The Rise of the Atlantic Economies* (1973). More theoretical is Immanuel Wallerstein, *The Modern World-System: Capitalist Agriculture and the Origins of the European World in the Sixteenth Century* (1974). The immediate English backdrop is colorfully presented in Peter Laslett, *The World We Have Lost* (1965), and in Carl Bridenbaugh, *Vexed and Troubled Englishmen, 1590–1642* (1968). Samuel E. Morison has written several masterful accounts of the discoveries; among the best are *Admiral of the Ocean Sea* (2 vols., 1942; condensed as *Christopher Columbus, Mariner,* 1956), *The European Discovery of America: The Northern Voyages,* A.D. *500–1600* (1971), and *The European Discovery of America: The Southern Voyages,* A.D. *1492-1616* (1974). A modern classic is Wallace Notestein, *The English People on the Eve of Colonization, 1603–1630* (1954). The ablest summation of the Spanish experience is Charles Gibson, *Spain in America* (1966); James Lang, *Conquest and Commerce: Spain and England in the Americas* (1975), is

a comparative chronicle of colonial rivalries. A fascinating brief synthesis of early European contact with the Americas is J. H. Elliott, *The Old World and the New, 1492–1650* (1970). A marvelously illustrated volume, portraying the impact of America on the European imagination, is Hugh Honour, *The New Golden Land* (1975). Contact between Indian and European cultures is handled in Wilcomb E. Washburn, *The Indian in America* (1975), and in Francis Jennings, *The Invasion of America* (1975). Nathan Wachtel presents the Indians' view of the Spanish conquest in *The Vision of the Vanquished* (1977). See also Karen Ordahl Kupperman, *Settling with the Indians: The Meeting of English and Indian Cultures in America, 1580–1640* (1980). The impact of Indian-white relations on the environment is the subject of William Cronon's intriguing *Changes in the Land* (1983) and Calvin Martin's provocative *Keepers of the Game* (1978). Alfred Crosby discusses *The Columbian Exchange: The Biological Consequences of 1492* (1972). The Chesapeake region has recently received much fresh attention, especially in Aubrey C. Land et al., *Law, Society, and Politics in Early Maryland* (1977); Thad W. Tate and David L. Ammerman, eds., *The Chesapeake in the Seventeenth Century* (1979); and Paul G. E. Clemens, *The Atlantic Economy and Colonial Maryland's Eastern Shore* (1980). The role of slavery in early colonial society gets perceptive treatment in Edmund S. Morgan, *American Slavery, American Freedom* (1975). See also Winthrop Jordan's monumental *White over Black* (1968) and Peter Wood's account of South Carolina, *Black Majority* (1974). Gary Nash analyzes relations among all three races in *Red, White, and Black: The Peoples of Early America* (1974).

---

*An asterisk indicates that the document, or an excerpt from it, can be found in Thomas A. Bailey and David M. Kennedy, eds., *The American Spirit: United States History as Seen by Contemporaries, 6th ed.* (Lexington, Mass.: D. C. Heath and Company, 1987).

2

Completing the Thirteen Colonies

*God hath sifted a Nation that he might send
Choice Grain into this Wilderness.*

William Stoughton
[of Massachusetts Bay], 1699

The Protestant Reformation Produces Puritanism

Little did the German monk Martin Luther know, when he nailed his protests against Catholic doctrines to the door of Wittenberg's cathedral in 1517, that he was shaping the destiny of a yet unheralded nation. Denouncing the authority of priests and popes, Luther declared that the Bible alone was the source of God's word. He ignited a fire of religious reform (the "Protestant Reformation") that licked its way across Europe for more than a century, dividing peoples, toppling sovereigns, and kindling the spiritual fervor of millions of men and women—some of whom helped to found America.

The reforming flame burned especially brightly in the bosom of John Calvin of Geneva. This somber and severe religious radical elaborated Luther's ideas in ways that profoundly affected the thought and character of generations of Americans yet unborn. Calvinism became the dominant theological credo not only of the New England Puritans but of other American settlers as well, including Scotch Presbyterians, French Huguenots, and communicants of the Dutch Reformed church.

Calvin spelled out his basic doctrine in a learned Latin tome of 1536, *Institutes of the Christian Religion*. God, he argued, was all-powerful and all-good. Humans, because of the corrupting effect of original sin, were weak and wicked. God was also all-knowing—and he knew who was going to heaven and who to hell. Since the first moment of creation, some souls —the *elect*—had been destined for eternal bliss and others for eternal torment. Good works could not save those whom *predestination* had marked for the infernal fires.

But neither could the elect count on their predetermined salvation and lead lives of wild, immoral abandon. For one thing, no one could be certain of his or her status in the heavenly ledger. Gnawing doubts about their eternal fate plagued Calvinists. They constantly sought, in themselves and others, signs of *conversion*, or the receipt of God's free gift of saving grace. Conversion was thought to be an intense, identifiable personal experience in which God revealed to the elect their heavenly destiny. Thereafter they were expected to lead "sanctified" lives, demonstrating by their holy behavior that they were among the "visible saints."

These doctrines swept into England just as King Henry VIII was breaking his ties with the Roman Catholic church in the 1530s, making himself the head of the Church of England. Henry would have been content to retain Roman rituals and creeds, but his action powerfully stimulated some English religious reformers to undertake a total purification of English Christianity. Many of these *Puritans*, as it happened, came from the commercially depressed woolen districts. Calvinism, with its message of stark but reassuring order in the divine plan, fed on this social unrest and provided spiritual comfort to the economically afflicted. As time

went on, Puritans grew increasingly unhappy over the snail-like progress of the Protestant Reformation in England. They burned with pious zeal to see the Church of England wholly de-Catholicized.

All Puritans agreed that only "visible saints" should be admitted to church membership. But the Church of England was open to all comers, which meant that the "saints" had to share pew and communion rail with the damned. Gagging on this unholy fraternizing, a group of extreme Puritans, known as Separatists, vowed to break away entirely from the Church of England.

King James I, a shrewd Scotsman, was head of both the state and the church in England. He quickly perceived that if his subjects could defy him as their spiritual leader, they might one day defy him as their political leader, as in fact they later defied his son, Charles I. He therefore threatened to harass the more bothersome Separatists out of the land.

The Pilgrims End Their Pilgrimage at Plymouth

The most famous congregation of Separatists, fleeing royal wrath, departed for Holland in 1608. During the ensuing twelve years of toil and poverty, they were increasingly distressed by the "Dutchification" of their children. They longed to find a haven where they could live and die as English men and women—and as purified Protestants. America was the logical refuge, despite the early ordeals of Jamestown, and despite tales of cannibals roasting steaks from their white victims before open fires.

A group of the Separatists in Holland, after negotiating with the Virginia Company, at length secured rights to settle under its jurisdiction. But their crowded *Mayflower*, sixty-five days at sea, missed its destination and arrived off the rocky coast of New England in 1620, with a total of 102 persons. One had died en route—an unusually short casualty list—and one had been born and appropriately named Oceanus. Fewer than half of the entire party were Separatists. Prominent among the nonbelongers was a peppery and stocky soldier of fortune, Captain Myles Standish, dubbed by one of

New England Settlements about 1650

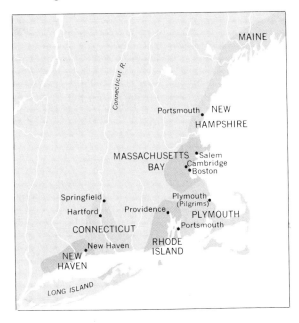

his critics "Captain Shrimp." He later rendered indispensable service as an Indian fighter and negotiator.

The Pilgrims did not make their initial landing at Plymouth Rock, as commonly supposed, but undertook a number of preliminary surveys. They finally chose for their site the shore of inhospitable Plymouth Bay. This area was outside the domain of the Virginia Company, and consequently the settlers became squatters. They were without legal right to the land and without specific authority to establish a government.

Before disembarking, the Pilgrim leaders drew up and signed the brief Mayflower Compact. Though setting an invaluable precedent for later written constitutions, this document was not a constitution at all. It was a simple agreement to form a body politic and to submit to the will of the majority under the regulations agreed upon. The compact was signed by forty-one adult males, eleven of them with the exalted rank of "mister," though not by the servants and two seamen. The pact was a promising step toward genuine self-government, for soon the adult male settlers were assembling to make their own laws in open-discussion town meetings—a great laboratory of liberty.

The Pilgrims' first winter of 1620–1621 took a grisly toll. Only 44 out of the 102 survived. At one time only 7 were well enough to lay the dead in their frosty graves. Yet when the *Mayflower* sailed back to England in the spring, not a single one of the courageous band of Separatists left. As one of them wrote, "It is not with us as with other men, whom small things can discourage."

God made his children prosperous so the Pilgrims believed. The next autumn, that of 1621, brought bountiful harvests and with them the first Thanksgiving Day in New England. In time the frail colony found sound economic legs in fur, fish, and lumber. The beaver and the Bible were the early mainstays: the one for the sustenance of the body, the other for the sustenance of the soul. Plymouth proved that the English could maintain themselves in this uninviting region.

The Pilgrims were extremely fortunate in their leaders. Prominent among them was the cultured William Bradford, a self-taught scholar

William Bradford wrote in Of Plymouth Plantation, "Thus out of small beginnings greater things have been produced by His hand that made all things of nothing, and gives being to all things that are; and, as one small candle may light a thousand, so the light here kindled hath shone unto many, yea in some sort to our whole nation."

who read Hebrew, Greek, Latin, French, and Dutch. He was chosen governor thirty times in the annual elections. Among his major worries was his fear that independent, non-Puritan settlers "on their particular" might corrupt his godly experiment in the wilderness. Bustling fishing villages and other settlements did sprout to the north of Plymouth, on the storm-lashed shores of Massachusetts Bay, where many people were as much interested in cod as God.

Quiet and quaint, the little colony of Plymouth was never important economically or numerically. It claimed only seven thousand souls by 1691, when, still charterless, it merged with its giant neighbor, the Massachusetts Bay Colony. But the tiny settlement of Pilgrims was big both morally and spiritually.

The Bay Colony Bible Commonwealth

The Separatist Pilgrims were dedicated extremists—the purest Puritans. More moderate Puritans sought to reform the Church of England by boring from within. Though resented by bishops and monarchs, they slowly gathered support, especially in Parliament. But when Charles I dismissed Parliament in 1629 and sanctioned the anti-Puritan persecutions of the reactionary Archbishop William Laud, many Puritans saw catastrophe in the making.

In 1629, an energetic group of non-Separatist Puritans, fearing for their faith and for England's future, secured a royal charter to form the Massachusetts Bay Company. They proposed to plant a sizable settlement in the infertile Massachusetts area, with Boston soon becoming its hub. Stealing a march on both king

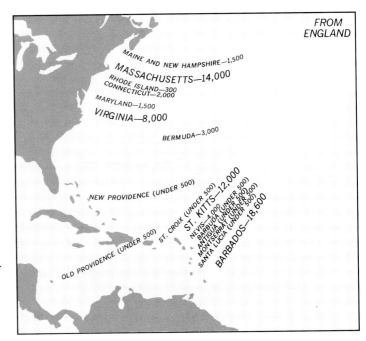

FROM ENGLAND

MAINE AND NEW HAMPSHIRE—1,500
MASSACHUSETTS—14,000
RHODE ISLAND—300
CONNECTICUT—2,000
MARYLAND—1,500
VIRGINIA—8,000
BERMUDA—3,000
NEW PROVIDENCE (UNDER 500)
ST. KITTS—12,000
NEVIS—4,000 (UNDER 500)
BARBUDA (UNDER 500)
ANTIGUA (UNDER 500)
MONTSERRAT (UNDER 500)
SANTA LUCIA (UNDER 500)
ST. CROIX (UNDER 500)
BARBADOS—18,600
OLD PROVIDENCE (UNDER 500)

The Great Puritan Migration   *Much of the early history of the United States was written by New Englanders, who were not disposed to emphasize the larger exodus of Puritans to the southerly islands. When the mainland colonials declared independence in 1776, they hoped that these island outposts would join them, but the existence of the British navy had a chilling effect.*

and church, the newcomers brought their charter with them. For many years they used it as a kind of constitution, out of easy reach of royal authority. They steadfastly denied that they wanted to separate from the Church of England, only from its impurities. But back in England the highly orthodox Archbishop Laud snorted that the Bay Colony Puritans were "swine which rooted in God's vineyard."

The Massachusetts Bay enterprise was singularly blessed. The well-equipped expedition of 1630, with eleven vessels carrying nearly a thousand immigrants, started the colony off on a larger scale than any of the other English settlements. Continuing turmoil in England tossed up additional enriching waves of Puritans on the shores of Massachusetts in the following decade. During the "Great Migration" of the 1630s, about seventy-five thousand refugees left mother England. But not all of them were Puritans, and only about fifteen thousand came to Massachusetts. Many were attracted to the warm and fertile West Indies, especially the sugar-rich island of Barbados. More Puritans came to this Caribbean islet, rather surprisingly, than to all of Massachusetts.

Many fairly prosperous, educated persons immigrated to the Bay Colony, including Governor John Winthrop, a well-to-do pillar of English so-ciety. A successful attorney and manor lord in England, Winthrop eagerly accepted the offer to become governor of the Massachusetts Bay Colony, believing that he had a *calling* from God to lead the new religious experiment. He served as governor or deputy governor for nineteen years. The resources and skills of talented settlers like Winthrop helped Massachusetts to prosper, as fur trading, fishing, and shipbuilding blossomed into important industries, especially fish and ships. Massachusetts Bay Colony rapidly shot to the fore as both the biggest and the most influential of the New England outposts.

Massachusetts also benefited from a shared sense of purpose among most of the first settlers. "We shall be as a city upon a hill," a beacon to humanity, declared Governor Winthrop. The Puritan bay colonists believed that they had a *covenant* with God, an agreement to build a holy society that would be a model for humankind.

Building the Bay Colony

These common convictions deeply shaped the infant colony's life. Soon after arrival, the franchise was extended to all "freemen"—adult males who belonged to the Puritan congregations, which in time came to be called collectively the Congregational church. Unchurched men remained voteless in provincial elections, as did women. On this basis, about two-fifths of adult males enjoyed the franchise in provincial affairs, a far larger proportion than in contemporary England. Town governments, which conducted much important business, were even more inclusive. There all male property holders, and in some cases other residents as well, enjoyed the priceless boon of publicly discussing local issues, often with much heat, and of voting on them by a majority-rule show of hands.

Yet the provincial government, liberal by the standards of the time, was not a democracy. The able Governor Winthrop feared and distrusted the "commons" as the "meaner sort" and thought that democracy was the "meanest and worst" of all forms of government. "If the people be governors," asked one Puritan clergyman, "who shall be governed?" True, the freemen annually elected the governor and his assistants, as well as a representative assembly called the General Court. But only Puritans—the "visible saints" who alone were eligible for church membership—could be freemen. And according to the doctrine of the covenant, the whole purpose of government was to enforce God's laws—which applied to believers and unbelievers alike. Moreover, unbelievers as well as believers paid taxes for the government-supported church.

Religious leaders thus wielded enormous influence in the Massachusetts "Bible Commonwealth." They powerfully influenced admission to church membership, by conducting public interrogations of persons claiming to have experienced conversion. Prominent among the early clergy was fiery John Cotton. Educated at England's Cambridge University, a Puritan citadel, he emigrated to Massachusetts to avoid persecution for his criticism of the Church of England. In the Bay Colony he devoted his considerable learning to defending the government's duty to enforce religious rules. Profoundly pious, he sometimes preached and prayed up to six hours in a single day.

But the power of the preachers was not absolute. A congregation had the right to hire and fire its minister and to set his salary. Clergymen were also barred from holding formal political office. Puritans in England had suffered too much at the hands of a "political" Anglican clergy to permit in the New World another unholy union of religious and governmental power. In a limited way, the bay colonists thus endorsed the idea of the separation of church and state.

The Puritans were a worldly lot, despite—or even because of—their spiritual intensity. Like John Winthrop, they believed in the doctrine of a "calling" to do God's work on this earth. They shared in what was later called the "Protestant ethic," involving serious commitment to work and to engagement in the world of affairs. Legend to the contrary, they also enjoyed simple pleasures: they ate plentifully, drank heartily, sang songs occasionally, and made love discreetly. Like other peoples of their time, in both America and Europe, they passed laws aimed at making sure these pleasures stayed simple by repressing certain human instincts. In New Haven, for example, a young married couple was fined twenty shillings for the crime of kissing in public, and in later years Connecticut came to be dubbed "the Blue Law State."

Yet life was serious business, and hellfire was real—a hell where sinners shriveled and shrieked for divine mercy. An immensely popular poem in New England, selling one copy for every twenty persons, was clergyman Michael Wigglesworth's "Day of Doom" (1662). Especially horrifying were his descriptions of the fate of the damned:

> They cry, they roar for anguish sore,
>   and gnaw their tongues for horrour.
> But get away without delay,
>   Christ pitties not your cry:
> Depart to Hell, there may you yell,
>   and roar Eternally.

Trouble in the Bible Commonwealth

The Bay Colony enjoyed a high degree of social harmony, stemming from common beliefs, in its early years. But even in this tightly knit community, dissension soon appeared. Quakers, who flouted the authority of the Puritan clergy, were persecuted with fines, floggings, and banishment. In one extreme case, four Quakers who defied expulsion, one of them a woman, were hanged on the Boston Common.

Anne Hutchinson, Dissenter *Mistress Hutchinson (1591–1643) held unorthodox views that challenged the authority of the clergy and the very integrity of the Puritan experiment in Massachusetts Bay Colony. (Mike Mazzaschi/ Stock, Boston.)*

A sharp challenge to Puritan orthodoxy came from Mistress Anne Hutchinson. She was an unusually intelligent, strong-willed, and talkative woman, ultimately the mother of fourteen children. Swift and sharp in theological argument, she carried to logical extremes the Puritan doctrine of predestination. She claimed that a holy life was no sure sign of salvation and that the truly saved need not bother to obey the law of either God or man. This assertion, known as *antinomianism* (from the Greek, "against the law"), was high heresy.

Brought to trial in 1638, the quick-witted Hutchinson bamboozled her clerical inquisitors for days, until she eventually boasted that she had come by her beliefs through a direct revelation from God. This was even higher heresy. The Puritan magistrates had little choice but to banish her, lest she pollute the entire Puritan experiment. She set out on foot for Rhode Island, though pregnant. She finally moved to New York, where she and all but one of her household were killed by Indians. Back in the Bay Colony, the pious John Winthrop sadly saw "God's hand" in her fate.

More threatening to the Puritan leaders was a personable and popular Salem minister, Roger Williams. Williams was a young man with radical ideas and an unrestrained tongue. An extreme Separatist, he hounded his fellow clergymen to make a clean break with the corrupt Church of England. He also challenged the legality of the Bay Colony's charter, which he condemned for expropriating the land from the Indians without fair compensation. As if all this were not enough, he went on to deny the authority of civil government to regulate religious behavior—a seditious blow at the Puritan idea of government's very purpose.

Their patience exhausted by 1635, the Bay Colony authorities found Williams guilty of disseminating "newe & dangerous opinions" and ordered him banished. He was permitted to remain several months longer because of illness, but he kept up his criticisms. The outraged magistrates, fearing that he might organize a rival colony of malcontents, then planned to exile him to Engand.

The Rhode Island "Sewer"

Aided by friendly Indians, Roger Williams fled to the Rhode Island area in 1636, in the midst of a bitter winter. At Providence, the courageous and far-visioned Williams built a Baptist church, probably the first in America. He established complete freedom of religion, even for Jews and Catholics. In this respect he was not only far ahead of his age but ahead of any of the other English settlements in the New World. He demanded no oaths regarding one's religious beliefs, no compulsory attendance at worship, no taxes to support a state church. He even sheltered the abused Quakers, although disagreeing sharply with their views.

Those outcasts who clustered about Roger Williams enjoyed additional blessings. They exercised simple manhood suffrage from the start, though this boon was later modified by a property qualification. Opposed to special privilege of any sort, the doughty Rhode Islanders managed to achieve remarkable freedom of opportunity.

Other scattered settlements soon dotted Rhode Island. They consisted largely of malcontents and exiles, some of whom could not bear the stifling theological atmosphere of the Bay Colony. Many of these restless souls in "Rogues' Island," including Anne Hutchinson, had little in common with Roger Williams—except banishment. The Puritan clergy back in Boston sneered at Rhode Island as "that sewer" in which the "Lord's debris" had collected and rotted.

Planted by dissenters and exiles, Rhode Island became strongly individualistic and stubbornly independent. With good reason "Little Rhody" was later known as "the traditional home of the otherwise minded." Begun as a squatter colony in 1636 without legal standing, it finally established rights to the soil when it secured a charter from Parliament in 1644. A huge bronze statue of the "Independent Man" appropriately stands today on the dome of the state house in Providence.

New England Spreads Out

The smiling valley of the Connecticut River, one of the few highly fertile expanses of any size in all New England, had meanwhile attracted a sprinkling of Dutch and English settlers. Hartford was founded in 1635. The next year witnessed a spectacular beginning of the centuries-long westward movement across the continent. An energetic group of Boston Puritans, led by the Reverend Thomas Hooker, swarmed as a body into the Hartford area, with Mrs. Hooker riding a horse litter.

Three years later, in 1639, the settlers of the new Connecticut River colony drafted in open meeting a trailblazing document known as the Fundamental Orders. It was in effect a modern constitution, which established a regime democratically controlled by the "substantial" citizens. Essential features of the Fundamental

Massachusetts Bay, the Hub of New England *All earlier colonies grew into it; all later colonies grew out of it.*

Orders were later borrowed by Connecticut for her colonial charter and ultimately for her state constitution.

Another flourishing Connecticut settlement began to spring up at New Haven in 1638. It was a prosperous community, founded by Puritans who contrived to set up an even closer church-government alliance than in Massachusetts. Although only squatters without a charter, the colonists dreamed of making New Haven a flourishing seaport. But they fell into disfavor with Charles II, as a result of having sheltered two of the judges who had condemned his father, Charles I, to death. In 1662, to the acute distress of the New Havenites, the crown granted a charter to Connecticut that merged New Haven with the more democratic settlements in the Connecticut Valley.

Far to the north, enterprising fishermen and fur traders had been active on the coast of Maine for a dozen or so years before the founding of Plymouth. After disheartening attempts at colonization in 1623 by Sir Ferdinando Gorges, this land of lakes and forests was absorbed by Massachusetts Bay after a formal purchase in 1677 from the Gorges heirs. It remained a part of Massachusetts for nearly a century and a half and then became a separate state.

Granite-ribbed New Hampshire also sprang from the fishing and trading activities along its narrow coast. It was absorbed in 1641 by the *(New Hampshire)* grasping Bay Colony, under a strained interpretation of the Massachusetts charter. The king, annoyed by this display of greed, arbitrarily separated New Hampshire from Massachusetts in 1679 and made it a royal colony.

Seeds of Colonial Unity and Independence

A path-breaking experiment in union was launched in 1643, when four colonies banded together to form the New England Confederation. Old England was then deeply involved in civil wars, and hence the colonials were thrown upon their own resources. The primary purpose of the confederation was defense against foes or potential foes, notably the Indians, the French, and the Dutch. Purely intercolonial problems,

Philip, King of Mount Hope   *Philip was not only shot and killed but, as a "traitor" to the king, beheaded, drawn, and quartered. His head was exhibited at Plymouth for many years. (An engraving by Paul Revere, Courtesy of The American Antiquarian Society.)*

such as runaway servants and criminals who had fled from one colony to another, also came within the jurisdiction of the confederation. Each member, regardless of size, wielded two votes—an arrangement highly displeasing to the most populous one, Massachusetts Bay.

The confederation was essentially an exclusive Puritan club. It consisted of the two Massachusetts colonies (the Bay Colony and bantam-sized Plymouth) and the two Connecticut colonies (New Haven and the scattered valley settlements). The Puritan leaders blackballed Rhode Island, as well as the Maine outposts. These places, it was charged, harbored too many heretical or otherwise undesirable characters. Shockingly, one of the Maine towns had made a tailor its mayor and had even sheltered an excommunicated minister of the gospel.

Weak though it was, the confederation was the first notable milestone on the long and rocky road toward colonial unity. The delegates took tottering but urgently needed steps toward acting together on matters of intercolonial importance. Rank-and-file colonists, for their part, received valuable experience in delegating their votes to properly chosen representatives.

The New England Confederation functioned usefully during the bloody war in 1675–1676 with the Indian chieftain King Philip, whose followers struck back at encroachments by whites on their lands. Several hundred settlers were killed and dozens of towns were burned, but the whites finally emerged victorious. If the confederation had been continued and strengthened, it almost certainly would have spared the colonials much grief in their subsequent conflicts with the French and Indians.

Back home in England, the king had paid little attention to the American colonies during the early years of their planting. They were allowed, in effect, to become semiautonomous commonwealths. This era of benign neglect was prolonged when the crown, struggling to retain its power, became enmeshed during the 1640s in civil wars with the parliamentarians.

But when Charles II was restored to the English throne in 1660, the royalists and their Church of England allies were once more firmly in the saddle. Puritan hopes of eventually purifying the old English church withered. Worse,

The Stuart Dynasty in England*

NAME, REIGN	RELATION TO AMERICA
James I, 1603–1625	Va., Plymouth founded; Separatists persecuted
Charles I, 1625–1649	Civil wars, 1642–1649; Cavalier tradition; Mass., Md. founded
(Interregnum, 1649–1660)	Commonwealth; Protectorate (the Cromwells)
Charles II, 1660–1685	The Restoration; Carolinas, Penn., N.Y. founded; Conn. chartered
James II, 1685–1688	Catholic trend; Glorious Revolution, 1688
William & Mary, 1689–1702	King William's War, 1689–1697
(Mary died 1694)	

*See p. 13 for predecessors; p. 79 for successors.

Charles II was determined to take an active, aggressive hand in the management of the colonies. His plans ran headlong against the habits that decades of relative independence had bred in the colonists.

Deepening colonial defiance was nowhere more glaringly revealed than in Massachusetts. One of the king's agents in Boston was mortified to find that royal orders had no more effect than old issues of the London *Gazette*. Punishment was soon forthcoming. As a slap at Massachusetts, Charles II gave rival Connecticut in 1662 a sea-to-sea charter grant, which legalized the squatter settlements. The very next year the outcasts in Rhode Island received a new charter, which gave kingly sanction to the most religiously tolerant government yet devised in America. A final and crushing blow fell on the stiff-necked Bay Colony in 1684, when her precious charter was revoked by the London authorities.

Andros Promotes the First American Revolution

Massachusetts suffered further humiliation in 1686, when the Dominion of New England was created by royal authority. Unlike the homegrown New England Confederation, it was imposed from London. Embracing at first all New England, it was expanded two years later to include New York and East and West Jersey. The Dominion also aimed at bolstering colonial defense in the event of war with the Indians, and hence from the imperial viewpoint of London was a statesmanlike move.

More importantly, the Dominion of New England was designed to promote urgently needed efficiency in the administration of the English Navigation Laws. Those laws reflected the intensifying colonial rivalries of the seventeenth century. They sought to stitch England's overseas possessions more tightly to the motherland, by throttling American trade with countries not ruled by the English crown. Like colonial peoples everywhere, the Americans chafed at such confinements, and smuggling became an increasingly common and honorable occupation.

At the head of the new dominion stood autocratic Sir Edmund Andros, an able English military man, conscientious but tactless. Establishing headquarters in Puritanical Boston, he

Andros's Dominion of New England

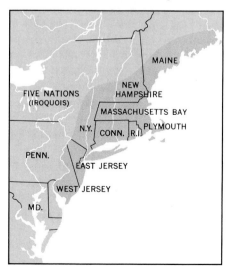

generated much hostility by his open affiliation with the despised Church of England. The colonials were also outraged by his noisy and Sabbath-profaning soldiers, who were accused of teaching the people "to drink, blaspheme, curse, and damn."

Andros was prompt to use the mailed fist. He ruthlessly curbed the cherished town meetings; laid heavy restrictions on the courts, the press, and the schools; and revoked all land titles. Dispensing with the popular assemblies, he taxed the people without the consent of their duly elected representatives. He also strove to enforce the unpopular Navigation Laws and suppress smuggling. Liberty-loving colonials, accustomed to unusual privileges during long decades of neglect, were goaded to the verge of revolt.

The people of old England, likewise resisting oppression, stole a march on the people of New England. In 1688–1689 they engineered the memorable Glorious (or Bloodless) Revolution. Dethroning the despotic and unpopular Catholic James II, they enthroned the Protestant rulers of the Netherlands, the Dutch-born William III and his English wife, Mary, daughter of James II.

When the news of the Glorious Revolution reached America, the ramshackle Dominion of New England collapsed like a house of cards. A Boston mob, catching the fever, rose against the existing regime. Sir Edmund Andros attempted to flee in woman's clothing but was betrayed by boots protruding beneath his dress. He was then shipped off to England.

Massachusetts, though rid of the despotic Andros, did not gain as much from the upheaval as she had hoped. In 1691 she was arbitrarily made a royal colony, with a new charter and a new royal governor. The permanent loss of the ancient charter was a staggering blow to the proud Puritans, who never fully recovered. Worst of all, the privilege of voting, once a monopoly of church members, was now to be enjoyed by all qualified male property holders.

England's Glorious Revolution had a far-flung impact, for unrest erupted from New England to the Carolinas. The upheaval resulted in a permanent abandonment of many of the objectionable features of the Andros system,

as well as a temporary breakdown of the new imperial policy of enforcing the Navigation Laws.

Yet residues remained of Charles II's effort to assert tighter administrative control over his empire. More British officials—judges, clerks, customs officials—were now staffing the courts and strolling the wharves of British America. Many were incompetent, corrupt hacks who knew little and cared less about American affairs. Appointed by influential patrons in far-off England, they blocked by their presence the rise of local leaders to positions of political power. Aggrieved Americans viewed them with mounting contempt and resentment as the eighteenth century wore on.

Old Netherlanders at New Netherland

Late in the sixteenth century, the oppressed people of the Netherlands unfurled the standard of rebellion against Catholic Spain. After bloody and protracted fighting, they finally succeeded, with the aid of Protestant England, in winning their independence.

The seventeenth century—the era of Rembrandt and other famous artists—was a golden age in Dutch history. This vigorous little lowland nation finally emerged as a major commercial and naval power and then ungratefully challenged the supremacy of her former benefactor, England. Three great Anglo-Dutch naval wars were fought in the seventeenth century, with as many as a hundred ships on each side. The sturdy Dutch dealt blows about as heavy as they received.

Holland also became a leading colonial power, with by far her greatest activity in the East Indies. There she maintained an enormous and profitable empire for over three hundred years. The Dutch East India Company was virtually a state within a state and at one time supported an army of 10,000 men and a fleet of 190 ships, 40 of them men-of-war.

Seeking greater riches, this enterprising company employed an English explorer, Henry Hudson. Disregarding orders to sail northeast, he ventured into Delaware Bay and New York

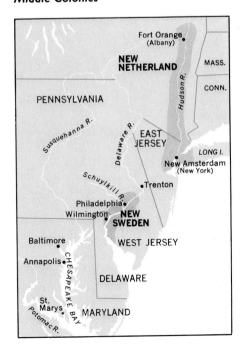

New Netherland Like many early mapmakers, the Dutch cartographer who drew this map was sometimes fanciful in his geography, especially regarding the unexplored backcountry. More reliable is the inset view of New Amsterdam in 1673. (The Granger Collection.)

Bay in 1609 and then ascended the Hudson River, hoping that at last he had chanced upon the coveted shortcut through the continent. But, as the event proved, he merely filed a Dutch claim to a magnificently wooded and watered area.

Much less powerful than the mighty Dutch East India Company was the Dutch West India Company, which maintained profitable enterprises in the Caribbean. At times it was less interested in trading than in raiding and at one fell swoop in 1628 captured a fleet of Spanish treasure ships laden with loot worth $15 million. The company also established outposts in Africa and a flourishing sugar industry in Brazil, which for several decades was its principal center of activity in the New World.

New Netherland, in the beautiful Hudson River area, was planted in 1623–1624 on a permanent basis. Established by the Dutch West India Company for its quick-profit fur trade, it was never more than a secondary interest of the founders. The company's most brilliant stroke

Early Settlements in the Middle Colonies

New Amsterdam, c. 1653   *The site of latter-day New York, this colonial village was still in Dutch hands in 1653, as illustrated by the Dutch-style windmill. (Museum of the City of New York.)*

was to buy Manhattan Island from the Indians (who did not actually "own" it) for trinkets worth about $24—22,000 acres of what is now perhaps the most valuable real estate in the world for one-tenth of a cent an acre.

New Amsterdam—later New York City—was a company town. It was run by and for the Dutch company, in the interests of the stockholders. The investors had no enthusiasm for religious toleration, free speech, or democratic practices; and the governors appointed by the company as directors-general were usually harsh and despotic. In response to repeated protests by the colonists, a semirepresentative body was at length reluctantly granted. Religious dissenters who opposed the official Dutch Reformed church were looked upon with suspicion, and for a while Quakers were savagely abused.

This picturesque Dutch colony took on a strongly aristocratic tinge and retained it for generations. Vast feudal estates fronting the Hudson River, known as patroonships, were granted to promoters who would settle fifty persons on them. One of the largest in the Albany areas was slightly larger than the later state of Rhode Island.

Colorful little New Amsterdam attracted a cosmopolitan population, as is common in seaport towns. A French Jesuit missionary, visiting in the 1640s, noted that eighteen different languages were being spoken in the streets.

The later babel of immigrant tongues was thus foreshadowed.

Friction with English and Swedish Neighbors

Vexation of various sorts beset the Dutch company-colony from the beginning. The directors-general were largely incompetent, though Washington Irving's later characterization of one of them as "a beer barrel on skids" is unfair. Company shareholders demanded their dividends, even at the expense of the colony's welfare. The Indians, infuriated by Dutch cruelties, retaliated with horrible massacres. As a defense measure, the hard-pressed settlers on Manhattan Island erected a stout wall, from which Wall Street derived its name.

New England was hostile to the growth of its Dutch neighbor, and the people of Connecticut finally ejected intruding Hollanders from their verdant valley. Three of the four member colonies of the New England Confederation were eager to wipe out New Netherland with military force. But Massachusetts, which would have had to provide most of the troops, vetoed the proposed foray.

The Swedes in turn trespassed on Dutch preserves, from 1638 to 1655, by planting the anemic colony of New Sweden on the Delaware River. This was the golden age of Sweden, during and following the Thirty Years' War of 1618–1648, in which its brilliant King Gustavus Adolphus had carried the torch for Protestantism. This outburst of energy in Sweden caused it to enter the costly colonial game in America, though on something of a shoestring.

Resenting the Swedish intrusion on the Delaware, the Dutch dispatched a small military expedition in 1655. It was led by the ablest of the directors-general, the energetic and hotheaded Peter Stuyvesant, who was dubbed "Father Wooden Leg" by the Indians. The main fort fell after a bloodless siege, whereupon Swedish rule came to an abrupt end. The colonists were absorbed by New Netherland.

New Sweden was never important. It faded away, leaving behind in later Delaware a sprinkling of Swedish place names and Swedish log cabins (the first in America), as well as an admixture of Swedish blood.

Dutch Residues in New York

The days of the Dutch on the Hudson were numbered, for the English regarded them as intruders. In 1664, after the imperially ambitious Charles II had granted the area to his brother, the Duke of York, a strong English squadron appeared off the decrepit defenses of New Amsterdam. A fuming Peter Stuyvesant, short of all munitions except courage, was forced to surrender without firing a shot. New Amsterdam was thereupon renamed New York, in honor of the Duke of York. England won a splendid harbor, strategically located in the middle of the mainland colonies, and a stately Hudson River penetrating the interior. The English banner now waved triumphantly, with the removal of this foreign wedge, over a solid stretch of territory from Maine to the Carolinas.

As the neglected stepchild of a trading company, New Netherland was destined from the beginning to be English. Lacking vitality, and representing only a secondary commercial interest of the Dutch, it lay under the shadow of the vigorous English colonies to the north. In addition, it was honeycombed with New England immigrants. Numbering about one-half of New Netherland's ten thousand souls in 1664,

Peter Stuyvesant (1602–1682) *Despotic in government and intolerant in religion, he lived in a constant state of friction with the prominent men of New Netherland. When protests arose, he replied that he derived his power from God and the company, not the people. He opposed popular suffrage on the grounds that "the thief" would vote "for the thief" and "the rogue for the rogue."*

they might in time have seized control from within.

The conquered Dutch province tenaciously retained many of the illiberal features of earlier days. An autocratic spirit survived, and the aristocratic element gained strength when certain corrupt English governors granted immense acreage to their favorites. Influential landowning families—such as the Livingstons and the De Lanceys—wielded disproportionate power in the affairs of colonial New York. These monopolistic land policies, combined with the lordly atmosphere, discouraged many European immigrants from coming. The physical growth of New York was correspondingly retarded.

The short-lived Dutch colony contributed little of major significance, whether to democracy, government, education, toleration, or literature. A possible exception would be the Knicker-bocker themes that Washington Irving developed in the nineteenth century with such charm. The Dutch peppered place names over the land, including Harlem (Haarlem), Brooklyn (Breuckelen), and Hell Gate (Hellegat). They likewise left their imprint on the gambrel-roofed architecture. As for social customs and folkways, no other foreign group of comparable size has made so colorful a contribution. Note-worthy were Easter eggs, Santa Claus, waffles, sauerkraut, bowling, sleighing, skating, and kolf (golf)—a dangerous game played with heavy clubs and forbidden in settled areas.

Penn's Holy Experiment in Pennsylvania

A remarkable group of dissenters, commonly known as Quakers, arose in England during the mid-1600s. Their name derived from the report that they "quaked" when under deep religious emotion. Officially they were known as the Religious Society of Friends.

Quakers were especially offensive to the authorities, both religious and civil. They refused to support the established Church of England with taxes. They built simple meetinghouses, without a paid clergy, and "spoke up" themselves in meetings when moved. Believing that they were all children in the sight of God, they kept their broad-brimmed hats on in the presence of their "betters" and addressed others with simple "thees" and "thous," rather than with conventional titles. They would take no

Quakers Abused in England *New England persecutions were similarly harsh.*

oaths, because Jesus had said, "Swear not at all." This peculiarity often embroiled them with government officials, for "test oaths" were still required to establish the fact that a person was not a Roman Catholic.

The Quakers, beyond a doubt, were a people of deep conviction. They abhorred strife and warfare and refused military service. As advocates of passive resistance, they would turn the other cheek and rebuild their meetinghouse on the site where their enemies had torn it down. Their courage and devotion to principle finally triumphed. Though at times they seemed stubborn and unreasonable, they were a simple, devoted, democratic people, contending in their own high-minded way for religious and civic freedom.

William Penn, a well-born and athletic young Englishman, was attracted to the Quaker faith in 1660, when only sixteen years old. His father, disapproving, administered a sound flogging. After various adventures in the army (the best portrait of the peaceful Quaker has him in armor), the youth firmly embraced the despised faith and suffered much persecution. The courts branded him a "saucy" and "impertinent" fellow. Several hundred of his less fortunate coreligionists died of cruel treatment, and thousands more were fined, flogged, or cast into "nasty stinking prisons."

Penn's thoughts naturally turned to the New World, where a sprinkling of Quakers had already fled, notably to Rhode Island, North Carolina, and New Jersey. Eager to establish an asylum for his people, he also hoped to experiment with liberal ideas in government and at the same time make a profit. Finally, in 1681, he managed to secure from the king an immense grant of fertile land, in consideration of a monetary debt owed to his deceased father by the crown. The king called the area Pennsylvania ("Penn's Woodland") in honor of the sire. But the modest son, fearing that critics would accuse him of naming it after himself, sought unsuccessfully to change the name.

Pennsylvania was by far the best advertised of all the colonies. Its founder—the "first American advertising man"—sent out paid agents and distributed countless pamphlets printed in English, Dutch, French, and German. Unlike the

William Penn Signs a Treaty with the Indians *The peace-loving Quaker founder of Pennsylvania made a serious effort to live in harmony with the Indians, but the westward thrust of white settlement eventually caused friction, as in other colonies. (The Thomas Gilcrease Institute of American History and Art, Tulsa, Oklahoma.)*

lures of many another American real estate promoter, then and later, Penn's inducements were generally truthful. He especially welcomed forward-looking spirits and substantial citizens, including industrious carpenters, masons, shoemakers, and other manual workers. His liberal land policy, which encouraged substantial holdings of land, was instrumental in attracting a heavy inflow of immigrants.

Quaker Pennsylvania and Its Neighbors

Penn formally launched his colony in 1681. His task was simplified by the presence of several thousand "squatters"—Dutch, Swedes, English, Welsh—who were already scattered along the banks of the Delaware River. Philadelphia, meaning "brotherly love" in Greek, was more carefully planned than most colonial cities and consequently enjoyed wide and attractive streets. Penn farsightedly bought land from the Indians, including Chief Tammany, later patron

saint of New York's political Tammany Hall. His treatment of the native peoples was so fair that the Quaker "broad brims" went among them unarmed and even employed them as baby tenders.

Penn's new proprietary regime was unusually liberal and included a representative assembly elected by the landowners. There was no tax-supported state church. Freedom of worship was guaranteed to all residents, although Penn, under pressure from London, was forced to deny Catholics and Jews the privilege of voting or holding office. The death penalty was imposed only for treason and murder, as compared with some two hundred capital crimes in England.

Among other noteworthy features, no provision was made by the peaceloving Quakers of Pennsylvania for a military defense. No restrictions were placed on immigration, and naturalization was made easy. The humane Quakers early developed a strong dislike of black slavery, and in the genial glow of Pennsylvania some progress was made toward social reform.

With its many liberal features, Pennsylvania attracted a rich mix of ethnic groups. They included numerous religious misfits who were repelled by the harsh practices of neighboring colonies. This Quaker haven boasted a surprisingly modern atmosphere in an unmodern age and to an unusual degree afforded economic opportunity, civil liberty, and religious freedom. Even so, there were some "blue laws" aimed at "ungodly revelers," stage plays, playing cards, dice, May games, and excessive hilarity.

Under such generally happy auspices, Penn's brainchild grew lustily. The Quakers were shrewd businesspeople, and in a short time the settlers were exporting grain and other foodstuffs. Within two years Philadelphia claimed three hundred houses and twenty-five hundred people. Within nineteen years—by 1700—the colony was surpassed in population and wealth only by long-established Virginia and Massachusetts.

William Penn, who altogether spent about four years in Pennsylvania, was never fully appreciated by his colonists. His governors, some of them incompetent and tactless, quarreled bitterly with the people, who were constantly demanding greater political control. Penn himself became too friendly with James II, the deposed Catholic king. Thrice arrested for treason, thrust for a time into a debtors' prison, and racked by apoplectic seizures, he died full of sorrows. His enduring monument was not only a noble experiment in government but also a new commonwealth. Based on civil and religious liberty, and dedicated to freedom of conscience and worship, it held aloft a hopeful torch in a world of semidarkness.

Small Quaker settlements flourished next door to Pennsylvania. New Jersey was started in 1664, when two noble proprietors received the

area from the Duke of York. A substantial number of New Englanders, including many whose weary soil had petered out, flocked to the new colony. One of the proprietors sold West New Jersey in 1674 to a group of Quakers, who here set up a sanctuary even before Pennsylvania was launched. East New Jersey was also acquired in later years by the Quakers, whose wings were clipped in 1702 when the crown combined the two Jerseys in a royal colony.

Swedish-tinged Delaware consisted of only three counties—two at high tide, the witticism goes—and was named after Lord de la Warr. Harboring some Quakers, and closely associated with Penn's flourishing colony, Delaware was granted its own assembly in 1703. But until the American Revolution it remained under the governor of Pennsylvania.

The Middle Way in the Middle Colonies

The middle colonies—New York, New Jersey, Delaware, and Pennsylvania—enjoyed certain features in common.

In general, the soil was fertile and the expanse of land was broad, unlike rock-bestrewn New England. Pennsylvania, New York, and New Jersey came to be known as the "bread colonies," by virtue of their heavy exports of grain.

Rivers also played a vital role. Broad, languid streams—notably the Susquehanna, the Delaware, and the Hudson—tapped the fur trade of the interior and beckoned adventuresome spirits into the backcountry. The rivers had few cascading waterfalls, unlike New England's, and hence presented little inducement to manufacturing with water-wheel power.

A surprising amount of industry nonetheless flourished in the middle colonies. Virginal forests abounded for lumbering and shipbuilding. The presence of deep river estuaries and landlocked harbors stimulated both commerce and the growth of seaports, such as New York and Philadelphia. Even Albany, more than a hundred miles up the Hudson, was a port of some consequence in colonial days.

In a Boston lecture (1869), Ralph Waldo Emerson declared, "the sect of the Quakers in their best representatives appear to me to have come nearer to the sublime history and genius of Christ than any other of the sects."

The middle colonies were in many respects midway between New England and the southern plantation group. Except in aristocratic New York, the landholdings were generally intermediate in size—smaller than in the big-acreage South but larger than in small-farm New England. Local government lay somewhere between the personalized town meeting of New England and the diffused county government of the South. There were fewer industries in the middle colonies than in New England, more than in the South.

Yet the middle colonies, which in some ways were the most American part of America, could claim certain distinctions in their own right. Generally speaking, the population was more ethnically mixed than that of other settlements. The people were blessed with an unusual degree of religious toleration and democratic control. Earnest and devout Quakers, in particular, made a contribution to human freedom out of all proportion to their numbers. Desirable land was more easily acquired in the middle colonies than in New England or in the tidewater South. One result was that a considerable amount of economic and social democracy prevailed, though less so in aristocratic New York.

Modern-minded Benjamin Franklin, entering Philadelphia as a seventeen-year-old youth with a roll of bread under each arm, found a congenial home in the urbane atmosphere of the city. It is true that he was born a Yankee in Puritanical Boston, but, as one Pennsylvanian later boasted, "He came to life at seventeen, in Philadelphia."

By the mid–eighteenth century, the thirteen colonies as a group revealed striking similarities, even though they had developed wide differences. They were all basically English. They all exercised certain priceless Anglo-Saxon freedoms. They all possessed some measure of self-government, though by no means complete democracy. They all enjoyed some degree of religious toleration and educational opportunity. They all afforded unusual advantages for economic and social self-development. Finally—and perhaps most significantly—they were all separated from home authority by a billowing ocean moat three thousand miles (4,800 kilometers) wide.

Varying Viewpoints

For many years, historians of the first century of colonial life in British North America focused on the efforts of the colonists to stake out a social order free of the constraints of the mother country. The struggle of the Massachusetts Bay Puritans to escape the regimentation of English society and to seize the religious freedom and economic equality proffered by the American wilderness formed the centerpiece of this interpretation, which was conspicuous in the work of Perry Miller, among others. Similarly, the founding of Quaker settlements in New Jersey and Pennsylvania, and the attempt of Dutch New Yorkers to maintain their cultural heritage, revealed the discord between the colonies and the mother country.

Recent studies, including those by Gary Nash and Patricia Bonomi, have shifted the drama of early American history from the transatlantic to the domestic stage. This perspective emphasizes the contests for economic and political supremacy within the colonies, such as the efforts of the Massachusetts Bay elite to ward off the challenges of religious "heretics" and an increasingly restless lower class. Nowhere was such internal conflict so prevalent as in the ethnically diverse middle colonies, where factional conflict became the distinguishing feature of public life. Some historians even find, in the turbulent middle colonies, the seeds of the later competitive American political system.

Select Readings

Primary Source Documents

John Winthrop, "A Modell of Christian Charity" (1630), in *The American Primer,* edited by Daniel Boorstin, outlines the goals of the Puritan errand into the wilderness. Winthrop's "Speech on Liberty"* (1645), in his *History of New England* (1853), established the colony's fundamental political principles. William Bradford, *Of Plymouth Plantation,* * edited by Samuel E. Morison (1952), is a rich contemporary account.

Secondary Sources

New England has received more scholarly attention than any other colonial region. An incisive short account is Edmund S. Morgan's *The Puritan Dilemma: The Story of John Winthrop* (1958). A brilliant and complex intellectual history is Perry Miller's *The New England Mind* (2 vols., 1939, 1953), a work that has long been a landmark for other scholars. Sacvan Bercovitch traces the heritage of the New England temperament in *The Puritan Origins of the American Self* (1975). See also his *The American Jeremiad* (1978). Edmund S. Morgan describes the crisis that beset the original Puritans when their children displayed a lesser degree of religiosity in *Visible Saints* (1963). Economic questions receive critical attention from Bernard Bailyn in *The New England Merchants in the Seventeenth Century* (1955). Sidney Ahlstrom's *Religious History of the American People* (1972) is comprehensive. John T. Ellis pays special attention to religious issues in *Catholics in Colonial America* (1965), as does Edmund S. Morgan in *Roger Williams: The Church and State* (1967). Areas outside New England are dealt with in Gary Nash, *Quakers and Politics: Pennsylvania, 1681–1726* (1971); Patricia Bonomi, *A Factious People: Politics and Society in Colonial New York* (1971); and Frederick Tolles, *Meetinghouse and Countinghouse* (1948). Timothy H. Breen, *Puritans and Adventurers* (1980), draws contrasts between Virginia and New England.

3

American Life in the Seventeenth Century

Being thus passed the vast ocean, and a sea of troubles before in their preparation . . . , they had now no friends to wellcome them, nor inns to entertaine or refresh their weatherbeaten bodys, no houses or much less towns to repaire too, to seeke for succore.

William Bradford, Of Plymouth Plantation

The Unhealthy Chesapeake

Life in the American wilderness was nasty, brutish, and short for the earliest Chesapeake settlers. Malaria, dysentery, and typhoid took a cruel toll, cutting ten years off the life expectancy of newcomers from England. Half the people born in early Virginia and Maryland did not survive to celebrate their twentieth birthdays. Few of the remaining half lived to see their fiftieth—or even their fortieth, if they were women.

The disease-ravaged settlements of the Chesapeake grew only slowly in the seventeenth century, mostly through fresh immigration from the mother country. The great majority of immigrants were single men in their late teens and early twenties, and most perished soon after arrival. Surviving males competed for the affections of the extremely scarce women, whom they outnumbered nearly six to one in 1650 and still outnumbered by three to two at the end of the century. Eligible women did not remain single for long.

Families were both few and fragile in this ferocious environment. Most men could not find mates. Most marriages were destroyed by the death of a partner within seven years. Scarcely any children reached adulthood under the care of two loving parents, and almost no one knew a grandparent. Weak family ties were reflected in the many pregnancies among unmarried young girls. In one Maryland county, more than a third of all brides were already pregnant when they spoke their marriage vows.

Yet despite these hardships, the Chesapeake colonies struggled on. The native-born inhabitants eventually acquired immunity to the killer diseases that had ravaged the original immigrants. The presence of more women allowed more families to form, and by the end of the seventeenth century the white population of the Chesapeake was growing on the basis of its own birthrate. As the eighteenth century opened, Virginia, with some fifty-nine thousand souls, was the most populous colony. Maryland, with about thirty thousand, was the third largest (after Massachusetts).

The Tobacco Economy

Though unhealthy for human life, the Chesapeake was immensely hospitable to tobacco cultivation. Profit-hungry settlers often planted tobacco before they planted corn. (Cornfields were also feared as staging areas for Indian ambushes.) Seeking fresh fields to plant to tobacco, these new immigrants plunged ever farther up the river valleys, provoking Indian attacks.

Leaf-laden ships annually hauled some 1.5 million pounds (680,000 kilograms) of tobacco out of Chesapeake Bay by the 1630s and almost 40 million pounds (18 million kilograms) a year by the end of the century. This enormous production depressed prices, but colonial Chesapeake tobacco growers responded to falling prices in the familiar way of farmers: by planting still more acres to tobacco and bringing still more product to market.

More tobacco meant more labor, but where was it to come from? Families formed too slowly to provide it by natural population increase. Indians died too quickly on contact with whites to be a reliable labor force. African slaves cost too much money. But England still had a "surplus" of displaced yeoman farmers, desperate for employment. Many of them, as "indentured servants," voluntarily mortgaged the sweat of their bodies for several years to Chesapeake masters. In exchange they received transatlantic passage and eventual "freedom dues," including a few barrels of corn, a suit of clothes—and perhaps a small parcel of land.

Both Virginia and Maryland employed the "headright" system to encourage the importation of servant workers. Under its terms, whoever paid the passage of a laborer received the right to acquire fifty acres of land. Masters—not the servants themselves—thus reaped the benefits of landownership from the headright system. Some masters, men who already had at least some modest financial means, soon parlayed their investments in servants into huge fortunes in real estate. They became the great

A Tobacco Plantation As the white managers look on, slave workers load tobacco in barrels for shipment on the waiting vessels in the background. (The Granger Collection.)

merchant-planters, lords of vast riverfront estates that came to dominate the agriculture and commerce of the southern colonies. Hungry for both labor and land, Chesapeake planters brought some 100,000 indentured servants to the region by 1700. These "white slaves" represented more than three-quarters of all European immigrants to Virginia and Maryland in the seventeenth century.

Indentured servants led a hard but hopeful life in the early days of the Chesapeake settlements, as they looked forward to becoming free and acquiring land of their own after completing their term of servitude. But as prime land became scarcer, masters became increasingly resistant to including land grants in "freedom dues." The servants' lot grew harsher as the seventeenth century wore on. Misbehaving servants, such as a housemaid who became pregnant or a laborer who killed a hog, might be punished with an extended term of service. Even after formal freedom was granted, penniless freed workers often had little choice but to hire themselves out for pitifully low wages to their former masters.

Frustrated Freedmen and Bacon's Rebellion

An accumulating mass of footloose, impoverished freemen was drifting discontentedly about the Chesapeake region by the late seventeenth century. Mostly single young men, they were frustrated by their broken hopes of acquiring land, as well as by their gnawing failure to find single women.

The swelling numbers of these wretched bachelors rattled the established planters. The Virginia assembly in 1670 disenfranchised most of the landless knockabouts, accusing them of "having little interest in the country" and causing "tumults at the election to the disturbance of his majesty's peace." Virginia's Governor Berkeley lamented his lot as ruler of this rabble: "How miserable that man is that governs a people where six parts of seven at least are poor, endebted, discontented, and armed."

Berkeley's misery soon increased. About a thousand Virginians broke out of control in

Early Tobacco Advertising *Crude woodcut labels like this were used to identify various "brands" of tobacco. (The Granger Collection.)*

1676, under the leadership of a twenty-nine-year-old planter, Nathaniel Bacon. Many of the rebels were frontiersmen who had been forced into the untamed backcountry in search of virgin land. They fiercely resented Berkeley's friendly policies toward the Indians, whose thriving fur trade the governor monopolized. When Berkeley refused to retaliate for a series of savage Indian attacks on frontier settlements, Bacon and his followers took matters into their own hands. They fell murderously upon the Indians, friendly and hostile alike, chased Berkeley from Jamestown, and put the torch to the capital. Chaos swept the raw colony, as frustrated freemen and resentful servants—described as "a rabble of the basest sort of people"—went on a rampage of plundering and pilfering.

As this civil war in Virginia ground on, Bacon suddenly died of disease, like so many of his fellow colonials. Berkeley thereupon crushed the uprising with brutal cruelty, hanging more than

The "Middle Passage"   *Human cargo in the hold of a slave ship. (The Mariners Museum.)*

twenty rebels. Back in England Charles II complained, "That old fool has put to death more people in that naked country than I did here for the murder of my father."

The distant English king could scarcely imagine the depths of passion and fear that Bacon's Rebellion excited in Virginia. Bacon had ignited the smoldering unhappiness of landless former servants, and he had pitted the hardscrabble backcountry frontiersmen against the haughty gentry of the tidewater plantations. The rebellion was now suppressed, but these tensions remained. Lordly planters, surrounded by a still-seething sea of malcontents, anxiously looked about for less-troublesome laborers to toil in the restless tobacco kingdom. Their eyes soon lit on Africa.

Colonial Slavery

Perhaps 10 million Africans were carried in chains to the New World in the three centuries or so following Columbus's discovery. Only about 400,000 of them ended up in North America, the great majority arriving after 1700. Most of the early human cargoes were hauled to Spanish and Portuguese South America or to the sugar-rich West Indies.

Africans had been brought to Jamestown as early as 1619, but as late as 1670 they numbered only about 2,000 in Virginia (out of a total population of some 35,000 persons) and about 7 percent of the 50,000 people in the southern plantation colonies as a whole. Hard-pinched white colonists, struggling to stay alive and to hack crude clearings out of the forests, could not afford to pay high prices for slaves who might die soon after arrival. White servants might die, too, but they were far less costly.

Drastic change came in the 1680s. Rising wages in England shrank the pool of penniless folk willing to gamble on a new life or an early death as indentured servants in America. At the same time, the large planters were growing increasingly fearful of the multitudes of potentially mutinous former servants in their midst. By the mid-1680s, for the first time, black slaves outnumbered white servants among the plantation colonies' new arrivals. In 1698 the Royal African Company lost its crown-granted monopoly on carrying slaves to the colonies. Enterprising Americans, especially Rhode Islanders, rushed to cash in on the lucrative slave trade, and the supply of slaves increased steeply. More than ten thousand Africans were pushed ashore in America in the decade after 1700, and tens of thousands more in the next half-century. Blacks accounted for nearly half the population of Virginia by 1750. In South Carolina they outnumbered whites two to one.

Most of the slaves who reached North America came from the west coast of Africa, including the area stretching from present-day Senegal to Angola. They were originally captured by African coastal tribes, who traded them in crude markets on the shimmering tropical beaches to itinerant European—and American—flesh merchants. Usually branded and bound, the captives were herded aboard sweltering ships for

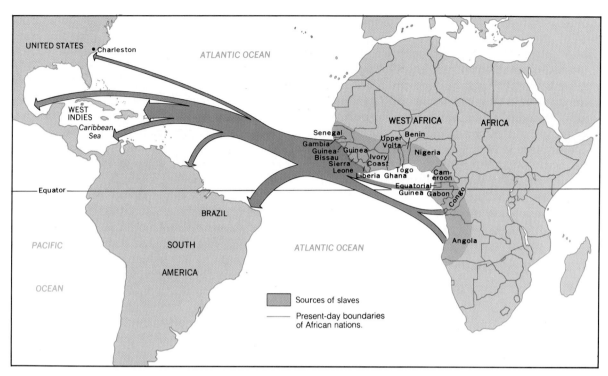

Main Sources of African Slaves, c. 1500 to c. 1800 *The three centuries of the "African Diaspora" scattered blacks all over the New World, with about 400,000 coming to the English colonies.*

the gruesome "middle passage," on which death rates ran as high as 20 percent. Terrified survivors were eventually shoved onto auction blocks in New World ports like Newport, Rhode Island, or Charleston, South Carolina, where a giant slave market flourished for more than a century.

A few of the earliest African immigrants gained their freedom, and some even became slaveowners themselves. But as the number of

Charleston, South Carolina *Nearly a century old when this painting was done about 1773, Charleston was the largest city in the mostly rural southern colonies. (Museum of Early Southern Decorative Arts.)*

Africans in their midst increased dramatically toward the end of the seventeenth century, white colonists reacted remorselessly to this supposed racial threat. Laws began to appear on the books that formally decreed the iron conditions of black slavery. These earliest "slave codes" made blacks and their children the property for life of their white masters and in some colonies made it a crime even to teach a slave to read or write. Not even conversion to Christianity could qualify a slave for freedom. Thus did the God-fearing whites put the fear of God into their hapless black laborers.

Africans in America

In the deepest South, slave life was especially harsh. The climate was hostile to health, and the labor was life-draining. The widely scattered South Carolina rice and indigo plantations were lonely hells on earth where gangs of mostly male Africans toiled and perished. Only fresh imports could sustain the slave population under these cruel conditions.

Blacks in the tobacco-growing Chesapeake region had a somewhat easier lot. Tobacco was a less physically demanding crop than those of the deeper South. Tobacco plantations were larger and closer to one another than rice plantations. The size and proximity of these plantations permitted the slaves more frequent contact with friends and relatives. By about 1720 the proportion of females in the Chesapeake slave population had begun to rise, making family life possible. The captive black population of the Chesapeake area soon began to grow not only through new imports but also through its own fertility—making it one of the few slave societies in history to perpetuate itself by its own natural reproduction.

Native-born Afro-Americans contributed to the growth of a stable and distinctive slave culture, a mixture of African and American elements of speech, religion, and folkways. On the sea islands off South Carolina's coast, blacks evolved a unique language, *Gullah* (probably a corruption of *Angola*, the African region from which many of them had come). It blended English with several African languages, including Yoruba, Ibo, and Hausa. Through it many African words have passed into American speech—such as *goober* (peanut), *gumbo* (okra), and *voodoo* (witchcraft). The ringshout, a West African religious dance performed by shuffling in a circle while answering a

An Indigo Plantation
Indigo, used to make blue dye for textiles, was a major product of the southernmost colonies. As shown here, black slaves furnished most of the labor on indigo plantations. (The New York Public Library.)

George Mason (1725–1792) *(left)   Later a leading figure in the Revolution and at the Constitutional Convention, Mason was a Virginia planter-aristocrat who built a magnificent estate, Gunston Hall, in the 1750s.*   **The "Chinese Room" at Gunston Hall** *(right)   Shown here with the table set for a dinner party, this elegant interior reflects the opulent lifestyle of the southern planter aristocracy. (Board of Regents of Gunston Hall, The National Society of the Colonial Dames of America.)*

preacher's shouts, was brought to colonial America by slaves and eventually contributed to the development of jazz. The banjo and the bongo drum were other African contributions to American culture.

Slaves also helped powerfully to build the country with their labor. A few became skilled artisans—carpenters, bricklayers, and tanners. But chiefly they performed the sweaty toil of clearing swamps, grubbing out trees, and other menial tasks. Condemned to life under the lash, slaves naturally pined for freedom. A slave revolt erupted in New York City in 1712 that cost the lives of a dozen whites and caused the execution of twenty-one blacks, some of them burned at the stake over a slow fire. More than fifty resentful South Carolina blacks exploded in revolt in 1739 and tried to march to Spanish Florida, only to be stopped by the local militia. But in the end the slaves in the South proved to be a more reliable labor force than the white indentured servants they gradually replaced. No slave rebellion in American history matched the scale of Bacon's Rebellion.

Southern Society

As slavery spread, the gaps in the South's social structure widened. The rough equality of poverty and disease of the early days was giving way to a defined hierarchy of wealth and status in the early eighteenth century. At the top of the social ladder perched a small but powerful covey of great planters. Owning gangs of slaves and vast domains of land, they ruled the region's economy and virtually monopolized political power. A clutch of extended clans—such as the Fitzhughs, the Lees, and the Washingtons—possessed among them horizonless tracts of Virginia real estate, and together they dominated the House of Burgesses. Just before the Revolutionary War, 70 percent of the leaders of the Virginia legislature came from families established in Virginia before 1690—the famed "first families of Virginia," or "FFVs."

Yet, legend to the contrary, these great seventeenth-century merchant planters were not silk-swathed cavaliers gallantly imitating the ways of English country gentlemen. They did eventually build stately riverfront manors, occasionally rode to the hounds, and some of them even cultivated the arts and accumulated distinguished libraries. But for the most part they were a hardworking, businesslike lot, laboring long hours over the problems of plantation management. Few problems were more vexatious than the unruly, often surly servants. One Virginia governor had such difficulty keeping his servants sober that he struck a deal allowing them to get drunk the next day if they would only lay off the liquor long enough to look after his guests at a celebration of the queen's birthday in 1711.

Beneath the planters—far beneath them in wealth, prestige, and political power—were the small farmers, the largest social group. They tilled their modest plots and might own one or two slaves, but they lived a ragged, hand-to-mouth existence. Still lower on the social scale were the landless whites, most of them luckless former indentured servants. Beneath them were those persons still serving out the term of their

indenture. Their numbers gradually diminished as black slaves increasingly replaced white indentured servants toward the end of the seventeenth century. The oppressed black slaves, of course, remained enchained in society's basement.

Few cities sprouted in the colonial South, and consequently an urban professional class, including lawyers and financiers, was slow to emerge. Southern life revolved around the great plantations, distantly isolated from one another. Waterways provided the principal means of transportation. Roads were so wretched that in bad weather funeral parties could not reach church burial grounds—an obstacle that accounts for the development of family burial plots in the South, a practice unlike anything in old England or New England.

The New England Family

Nature smiled more benignly on pioneer New Englanders than on their disease-plagued fellow colonists to the south. Clean water and cool temperatures retarded the spread of killer microbes. In stark contrast to the fate of Chesapeake immigrants, settlers in seventeenth-century New England *added* ten years to their life spans by migrating from the Old World. One settler claimed that "a sip of New England's air is better than a whole draft of old England's ale." The first generations of Puritan colonists enjoyed, on the average, about seventy years on this earth—not very different from the life expectancy of present-day Americans.

In further contrast with the Chesapeake, New Englanders tended to migrate not as single individuals but as families, and the family remained at the center of New England life. Almost from the outset, New England's population grew from natural reproductive increase. The people were remarkably fertile, even if the soil was not.

Early marriage encouraged the booming birthrate. Women typically wed by their early twenties and produced babies about every two years thereafter until menopause. Ceaseless childbearing drained the vitality of many pioneer women, as the weather-eroded colonial

Mrs. Elizabeth Freake and Baby Mary *This portrait of a Boston mother and child in about 1674 suggests the strong family ties that characterized early New England society. (Worcester Art Museum.)*

Early Advertising *Appeal in England for American colonists.*

from the earliest days of her marriage until the day of her death, and child raising became virtually her full-time occupation.

The longevity of the New Englanders contributed to family stability. Children grew up in nurturing environments where they received love and guidance not only from their parents but from their grandparents as well. This novel intergenerational continuity has inspired the observation that New England "invented" grandparents. Family stability was reflected in low premarital pregnancy rates (again in contrast with the Chesapeake) and in the generally strong, tranquil social structure characteristic of colonial New England.

Life in the New England Towns

Sturdy New Englanders evolved a tightly knit society, the basis of which was small villages and farms. This development was natural in a people anchored by geography and hemmed in by the Indians, the French, and the Dutch. Puritanism likewise made for unity of purpose—and for concern about the moral health of the whole community. It was no accident that the nineteenth-century crusade for abolishing black

tombstones eloquently reveal. A number of the largest families were borne by several mothers, though claims about the frequency of death in childbirth have probably been exaggerated. But the dread of death in the birthing bed haunted many women, and it was small wonder that they came to fear pregnancy. A married woman could expect to experience up to ten pregnancies and rear as many as eight surviving children. Massachusetts governor William Phips was one of twenty-seven children, all by the same mother. A New England woman might well have dependent children in her household

Graveyard Art *These New England colonists evidently died in the prime of life. Carving likenesses on grave markers was a common way of commemorating the dead. (American Antiquarian Society.)*

A Colonial Kitchen *Simple but well-provisioned, this restored kitchen from a Massachusetts house of 1684 illustrates the tidy, unpretentious prosperity of colonial New England. (Essex Institute.)*

slavery—with Massachusetts agitators at the forefront—sprang in some degree from the New England conscience, with its Puritan roots.

In the Chesapeake region the expansion of settlement was somewhat random and was usually undertaken by lone-wolf planters on their own initiative, but New England society grew in a more orderly fashion. New towns were legally chartered by the colonial authorities, and the distribution of land was entrusted to the steady hands of sober-minded town fathers, or "proprietors." After receiving a grant of land from the colonial legislature, the proprietors

moved themselves and their families to the designated place and laid out their town. It usually consisted of a meetinghouse, which served as both the place of worship and the town hall, surrounded by houses. Also marked out was a village green, where the militia could drill. Each family received several parcels of land, including a woodlot for fuel, a tract suitable for growing crops, and another for pasturing animals.

Towns of more than fifty families were required to provide elementary education, and a majority of the adults knew how to read and write. As early as 1636, just eight years after the colony's founding, the Massachusetts Puritans established Harvard College, today the oldest corporation in America, to train local boys for the ministry. Only in 1693, eighty-six years after the founding of Jamestown, did the Virginians establish their first college, William and Mary.

Puritans ran their own churches, and democracy in Congregational church government led logically to democracy in political government. The town meeting, in which the freemen met together and each man voted, exhibited democracy in its purest form. New England villagers from the outset gathered regularly in their meetinghouses to elect their officials, appoint schoolmasters, and discuss such mundane matters as road repairs. The town meeting, observed Thomas Jefferson, was "the best school of political liberty the world ever saw."

Puritan Textbooks *A page from the* New England Primer; *and the hornbook for children, so called because the printing was protected by transparent horn.*

The Half-Way Covenant and the Salem Witch Trials

Yet worries plagued the God-fearing pioneers of these tidy New England settlements. The pressure of a growing population was gradually dispersing the Puritans onto outlying farms, far from the control of church and neighbors. And while the core of Puritan belief still burned brightly, the passage of time was dampening the first generation's flaming religious zeal. About the middle of the seventeenth century a new form of sermon began to be heard from Puritan pulpits—the "jeremiad." Taking their cue from the doom-saying Old Testament prophet Jeremiah, earnest preachers scolded parishioners for their waning piety. Especially alarming was the apparent decline in conversions—testimonials by individuals that they had received God's grace and therefore deserved to be admitted to the church as members of the elect. Troubled ministers in 1662 announced a new formula for church membership, the "Half-Way Covenant." It offered partial membership rights to persons not yet converted.

The "Half-Way Covenant" dramatized the difficulty of maintaining at fever pitch the religious devotion of the founding generation. Jeremiads continued to thunder from the pulpits, but as time went on, the doors of the Puritan churches swung fully open to all comers, whether converted or not. This widening of church membership gradually erased the distinction between the "elect" and other members of society. In effect, strict religious purity was somewhat sacrificed to the cause of wider religious participation. Interestingly, from about this time onward women made up a larger proportion of Puritan congregations.

Women also played a prominent role in one of New England's most frightening religious episodes. A group of adolescent girls in Salem, Massachusetts, claimed to have been bewitched by certain older women. A hysterical "witch-hunt" ensued, leading to the legal lynching in 1692 of twenty persons, nineteen of whom were hanged and one of whom was pressed to death. Two dogs were also hanged. Larger-scale witchcraft persecutions were then common in Europe, and several outbreaks had already

The Wonders of the Invisible World:

Being an Account of the

TRYALS

OF

Several Witches,

Lately Excuted in

NEW-ENGLAND:

And of several remarkable Curiosities therein Occurring.

Together with,

I. Observations upon the Nature, the Number, and the Operations of the Devils.

II. A short Narrative of a late outrage committed by a knot of Witches in Swede-Land, very much resembling, and so far explaining, that under which New-England has laboured.

III. Some Councels directing a due Improvement of the Terrible things lately done by the unusual and amazing Range of Evil-Spirits in New-England.

IV. A brief Discourse upon those Temptations which are the more ordinary Devices of Satan.

By COTTON MATHER.

Published by the Special Command of his EXCELLENCY the Govenour of the Province of the Massachusetts-Bay in New-England.

Printed first, at Boston in New-England; and Reprinted at London, for John Dunton, at the Raven in the Pudtry. 1693.

Salem Witchcraft Hysteria *In this notorious tract of 1693, the Puritan minister Cotton Mather defended the death-sentence verdicts of several trials for witchcraft. (The Granger Collection.)*

flared forth in the colonies. But the reign of horror in Salem grew not only from the superstitions of the age but also from the unsettled social and religious conditions of the rapidly evolving Massachusetts village. The Salem witchcraft delusion marked an all-time high in American experience of popular passions run wild and seriously weakened the prestige of the Puritan clergy, some of whom had supported it.

The New England Way of Life

Oddly enough, the story of New England was largely written by rocks. The heavily glaciated soil was strewn with countless stones, many of

The Saugus Iron Works   *Built in 1646, this primitive Massachusetts iron works flourished for only a few years. Now restored, it stands as mute testimony to New England's painful struggle, beginning even in the seventeenth century, for economic self-sufficiency. (Saugus Iron Works NHS.)*

which were forced to the surface after a winter freeze. In a sense the Puritans did not possess the soil; it possessed them by shaping their character. Scratching a living from the protesting earth was an early American success story. Back-bending toil put a premium on industry and penny-pinching frugality, for which New Englanders became famous. Traditionally sharp Yankee traders, some of them palming off wooden nutmegs, made their mark. Connecticut came in time to be called good-humoredly "the Nutmeg State." Cynics exaggerated when they said that the three stages of progress in New England were "to get on, to get honor, to get honest."

The grudging land also left colonial New England less ethnically mixed than its southern neighbors. European immigrants were not attracted in great numbers to a site where the soil was so stony—and the religion so sulfurous.

Climate likewise molded New England, where the summers were often uncomfortably hot and the winters cruelly cold. Many early immigrants complained of the region's extremes of weather. Yet the soil and climate of New England eventually encouraged a diversified agriculture and industry. Staple products like tobacco did not flourish, as in the South. Black slavery, although attempted, could not exist profitably on small farms, especially where the

surest crop was stones. No broad, fertile hinterland, comparable to that of the South, beckoned people inland. The mountins ran fairly close to the shore, and the rivers were generally short and rapid.

Repelled by the rocks, the hardy New Englanders turned instinctively to their fine natural harbors. Hacking timber from their dense forests, they became experts in shipbuilding and commerce. They also ceaselessly exploited the self-perpetuating codfish lode off the coast of Newfoundland—the fishy "gold mines of New England," which have yielded more wealth than all the treasure chests of the Aztecs. During colonial days the wayfarer seldom got far from the sound of the ax and hammer, or the swift rush of the ship down the ways to the sea, or the smell of rotting fish. As a reminder of the importance of fishing, a handsome replica of the "sacred cod" is proudly displayed to this day in the Massachusetts State House in Boston.

The Sacred Cod   *As displayed in the Boston State House. (George M. Cushing.)*

The combination of Calvinism, soil, and climate in New England made for energy, purposefulness, sternness, stubbornness, self-reliance, and resourcefulness. Righteous New Englanders prided themselves on being God's chosen people. They long boasted that Boston was "the hub of the universe"—at least spiritually. A famous jingle of later days ran:

> I come from the city of Boston
> The home of the bean and the cod
> Where the Cabots speak only to Lowells
> And the Lowells speak only to God.

New England's impact on the rest of the nation has been incalculable. Countless thousands of New Englanders, ousted by their sterile soil, were destined to pull up stakes and re-create New England towns from Ohio to Oregon and all the way to Hawaii. A people courageous, conscientious, and willing to sacrifice for their beliefs, they made the idealism represented by Plymouth Rock a national symbol. As flinty as their stones, as stiff as their cuffs and collars, they cross-fertilized innumerable other communities with their ideals and democratic practices. The New England conscience inspired many later reformers and added something indispensable to the fiber and backbone of the American people.

The Early Settlers' Days and Ways

The cycles of the seasons and the sun set the schedules of all the earliest American colonists, men as well as women, blacks as well as whites. The overwhelming majority of colonists were farmers. They planted in the spring, tended their crops in the summer, harvested in the fall, and prepared in the winter to begin the cycle anew. They usually rose at dawn and went to bed at dusk. Chores might be performed after nightfall only if they were "worth the candle," a phrase that has persisted in American speech.

Women, slave or free, on southern plantations or northern farms, wove, cooked, cleaned, and cared for children. Men cleared land; fenced, planted, and cropped it; cut firewood; and butchered livestock as needed. Children helped with all these tasks, while picking up such schooling as they could.

Life and Death in Colonial America *This embroidery suggests the stoic resolve of a colonial mother, with one child in a coffin and another in its cradle. (The Connecticut Historical Society.)*

Life was humble but comfortable by contemporary standards. Compared to most seventeenth-century Europeans, Americans lived in affluent abundance. Land was relatively cheap, though somewhat less available in the planter-dominated South than elsewhere. In the northern and middle colonies, an acre of virgin soil cost about what American carpenters could earn in one day as wages, which were roughly three times those of their European counterparts.

"Dukes don't emigrate," the saying goes, for if people enjoy wealth and security, they are not likely to risk exposing their lives in the wilderness. Similarly, the very poorest members of a society may not possess even the modest means needed to pull up stakes and seek a fresh start in life. Accordingly, most white migrants to early colonial America came neither from the aristocracy nor from the dregs of European society.

Crude frontier life did not in any case permit the flagrant display of class distinctions, and seventeenth-century society in all the colonies had a certain simple sameness to it, especially in the more egalitarian New England and middle colonies. Yet many settlers, who considered themselves to be of the "better sort," tried to recreate on a modified scale the social structure they had known in the Old World. To some extent, they succeeded, though yeasty democratic forces frustrated their full triumph. Resentment against upper-class pretensions helped to spark outbursts like Bacon's Rebellion of 1676 in Virginia and the uprising of Maryland's Protestants toward the end of the seventeenth century. In New York, animosity between lordly landholders and aspiring merchants fueled Leisler's Rebellion, an ill-starred and bloody little insurgency that rocked New York City from 1689 to 1691.

For their part, would-be American blue bloods resented the pretensions of the "meaner sort" and passed laws to try to keep them in their place. Massachusetts in 1651 prohibited poorer folk from "wearing gold or silver lace," and in eighteenth-century Virginia a tailor was fined and jailed for arranging to race his horse—"a sport only for gentlemen." But these efforts to reproduce the finely stratified societies of Europe proved feeble in the early American wilderness, where equality and democracy found fertile soil—at least for white people.

Varying Viewpoints

The simultaneous evolution of a rigid racial caste system and democratic political traditions in the British colonies has long perplexed students of early America. For many generations historians, most of them of Yankee stock, resolved the apparent paradox by locating the seeds of democracy in New England. The aggressive independence of the people, best expressed by the boisterous town meetings, spawned the American obsession with freedom. On the other hand, this view holds, the slave societies of the South were hierarchical, aristocratic communities under the sway of a few powerful planters.

Recent studies have questioned this interpretation. First, they point out the many undemocratic features of colonial New England. Second, they note that Washington, Jefferson, and Madison—the architects of American government and its commitment to liberty—all hailed from slaveholding Virginia. In fact, nowhere were republican principles stronger than in Virginia. This realization has sparked new speculation about the relationship between American slavery and American freedom. Some scholars, notably Edmund S. Morgan, see the willingness of wealthy planters to concede the equality and freedom of all white males as a device to ensure racial solidarity and mute class conflict. In this view, the concurrent emergence of slavery and democracy poses no paradox. Racism muffled animosity between rich and poor and fostered the devotion to equality (for whites) that became the hallmark of American democracy.

Select Readings

Primary Source Documents

Adolph B. Benson, ed., *The America of 1750*; *Petar Kalm's Travels in North America* (1937), records the observations of a visiting Swedish naturalist with a keen eye for the behavior of human fauna. The first slave laws of Virginia are collected in Warren M. Billings, ed., *The Old Dominion in the Seventeenth Century** (1975), as are firsthand accounts of Bacon's Rebellion. See also George L. Burr, ed., *Narratives of the Witchcraft Cases, 1648–1706* (1914).*

Secondary Sources

A general survey is Clarence Ver Steeg, *The Formative Years* (1964). On life and labor in the Chesapeake, consult Thad W. Tate and David L. Ammerman, eds., *The Chesapeake in the Seventeenth Century* (1979); Wesley F. Craven, *The Southern Colonies in the Seventeenth Century* (1949); and Edmund S. Morgan, *American Slavery, American Freedom* (1975), which concentrates on race and class relations. Further probing economic conflicts and their role in the introduction of slavery is Timothy H. Breen and Stephen Innes, *Myne Owne Ground: Race and Freedom on Virginia's Eastern Shore, 1640–1676* (1980). Gloria Main chronicles *The Tobacco Colony: Life in Early Maryland, 1650–1719* (1982). Daniel Blake Smith looks *Inside the Great House: Planter Family Life in Eighteenth Century Chesapeake Society* (1980). Winthrop Jordan's magnificent *White over Black: American Attitudes toward the Negro, 1550–1812* (1968) discusses the evolution of racial attitudes. Life in New England's towns and homes is scrutinized in Edmund S. Morgan, *Puritan Family* (1944); Bernard Bailyn, *Education in the Forming of American Society* (1960); Sumner C. Powell, *Puritan Village* (1963); Darrett Rutman, *Winthrop's Boston* (1965); John Demos, *A Little Commonwealth: Family Life in Plymouth Colony* (1970); Philip Greven, *Four Generations: Population, Land, and Family in Colonial Andover, Massachusetts* (1970); Kenneth Lockridge, *New England Town: Dedham* (1970); Roger Thompson, *Women in Stuart England and America* (1974); Lyle Koehler, *A Search for Power: The "Weaker Sex" in Seventeenth-Century New England* (1980); Laurel T. Ulrich, *Good Wives: Image and Reality in the Lives of Women in Northern New England, 1650–1750* (1982); Stephen Innes, *Labor in a New Land: Economy and Society in Seventeenth Century Springfield* (1983); and Philip Greven, *The Protestant Temperament* (1977), which analyzes child-rearing practices. Robert Pope examines *The Half-Way Covenant: Church Membership in Puritan New England* (1969). Witchcraft is the subject of Paul Boyer and Stephen Nissenbaum's *Salem Possessed* (1974) and John Demos's massive *Entertaining Satan* (1982).

4

Colonial Society on the Eve of Revolution

Driven from every other corner of the earth, freedom of thought and the right of private judgment in matters of conscience direct their course to this happy country as their last asylum.

Samuel Adams, 1776

Conquest by the Cradle

The common term *thirteen original colonies* is misleading. There were thirty-two colonies under British rule in North America by 1775, including Canada, the Floridas, and the various islands of the Caribbean. But only thirteen of them unfurled the standard of revolt. A few of the nonrebels, such as Canada and Jamaica, were larger, wealthier, or more populous than some of the thirteen. And even among the revolting thirteen, dramatic differences in economic organization, social structure, and ways of life were evident.

All the eventually rebellious colonies did have one outstanding feature in common: their population was growing by leaps and bounds. In 1700 they contained fewer than 300,000 souls, about 20,000 of whom were black. By 1775, 2.5 million persons inhabited the thirteen colonies, of whom about half a million were black. White immigrants made up nearly 400,000 of the increased number, and black "forced immigrants" accounted for almost as many again. But most of the spurt stemmed from the remarkable natural fertility of all Americans, white and black. To the amazement and dismay of Europeans, the colonists were doubling their numbers every twenty-five years. Unfriendly Dr. Samuel Johnson, back in England, growled that the Americans were multiplying like their own rattlesnakes. They were also a youthful people, whose average age in 1775 was about sixteen.

This population boom had political consequences. In 1700 there were twenty English settlers for each American colonist. By 1775 the English advantage in numbers had fallen to three to one—setting the stage for a momentous shift in the balance of power between colonies and the mother country.

The bulk of the population was cooped up east of the Alleghenies, although by 1775 a vanguard of pioneers had trickled into the stump-studded clearings of Tennessee and Kentucky. The most populous colonies in 1775 were Virginia, Massachusetts, Pennsylvania, North Carolina, and Maryland—in that order. There were only four communities that might properly be called cities: Philadelphia, including suburbs, was first with about 34,000, while New York, Boston, and Charleston were strung out behind. About 90 percent of the people lived in rural areas.

A Mingling of the Races

Colonial America was a melting pot and had been from the outset. The population, although basically English in stock and language, was picturesquely mottled with numerous foreign groups.

Heavy-accented Germans constituted about 6 percent of the total population, or 150,000, by 1775. Fleeing religious persecution, economic oppression, and the ravages of war, they had flocked to America in the early 1700s and had settled chiefly in Pennsylvania. They belonged to several different Protestant sects—primarily Lutheran—and thus further enhanced the religious diversity of the colony. Known popularly but erroneously as the Pennsylvania Dutch (a corruption of the German word *Deutsch*), they totaled about one-third of the colony's population. In Philadelphia the street signs were painted in both German and English.

A young Frenchman named Crèvecoeur wrote about 1770 of the diverse population: "They are a mixture of English, Scotch, Irish, French, Dutch, Germans, and Swedes. From this promiscuous breed, that race now called Americans have arisen. . . . I could point out to you a family whose grandfather was an Englishman, whose wife was Dutch, whose son married a French woman, and whose present four sons have now four wives of different nations."

Immigrant Groups in 1775 *America was already a nation of diverse nationalities in the colonial period. This map shows the great variety of immigrant groups, especially in Pennsylvania and New York. It also illustrates the tendency of later arrivals, particularly the Scotch-Irish, to push into the backcountry.*

These German newcomers moved into the backcountry of Pennsylvania, where their splendid stone barns gave—and still give—mute evidence of industry and prosperity. Not having been brought up as Englishmen, they had no deep-rooted loyalty to the British crown, and they clung tenaciously to their German language and customs.

The Scotch-Irish, who in 1775 numbered about 175,000, or 7 percent of the population, were an important non-English group, although English-speaking. They were not Irish at all, but turbulent Scots Lowlanders. Over a period of many decades, they had first been transplanted to Northern Ireland, where they had not prospered. The Irish Catholics already there, hating Scotch Presbyterianism, resented the intruders and still do. The economic life of the Scotch-Irish was severely hampered, especially when the English government placed burdensome restrictions on their production of linens and woolens.

Early in the 1700s tens of thousands of embittered Scotch-Irish finally pulled up stakes and came to America, chiefly to tolerant and deep-soiled Pennsylvania. Finding the best acres already taken by Germans and Quakers, they pushed out onto the frontier. There many of them illegally but defiantly squatted on the unoccupied lands and quarreled with both Indian and white owners. When the westward-flowing Scotch-Irish tide lapped up against the Allegheny barrier, it was deflected southward into the backcountry of Maryland, down Virginia's Shenandoah Valley, and into the western Carolinas. Already experienced colonizers and agitators in Ireland, the Scotch-Irish proved to be superb frontiersmen, though their readiness to visit violence on the Indians repeatedly inflamed the western districts. By the mid–eighteenth century, a chain of Scotch-Irish settlements lay scattered along the "great wagon road," which hugged the eastern Appalachian foothills from Pennsylvania to Georgia.

It was said, somewhat unfairly, that the Scotch-Irish kept the Sabbath—and all else they could lay their hands on. Pugnacious, lawless, and individualistic, they brought with them the Scottish secrets of whiskey distilling and dotted the Appalachian hills and hollows with their stills. They cherished no love for the British government that had uprooted them—or for any other government, it seemed. They led the armed march of the Paxton Boys on Philadelphia in 1764, protesting the Quaker oligarchy's lenient policy toward the Indians, and a few years later spearheaded the Regulator movement in North Carolina, a small but nasty insurrection against eastern domination of the colony's affairs. Many of them—including the youthful Andrew Jackson—eventually joined the embattled American revolutionists. All told, about a dozen future presidents were of Scotch-Irish descent.

Approximately 5 percent of the multicolored colonial population consisted of other European groups. These embraced French Huguenots, Welsh, Dutch, Swedes, Jews, Irish, Swiss, and Scots Highlanders—as distinguished from the Scotch-Irish. Except for the Scots Highlanders, such hodgepodge elements felt little loyalty to the British crown. By far the largest single non-English group was African, accounting for nearly 20 percent of the colonial population in 1775 and heavily concentrated in the South.

The population of the thirteen colonies, though mainly Anglo-Saxon, was perhaps the most mixed to be found anywhere in the world. The South, holding about 90 percent of the slaves, already displayed its historic black-and-white racial composition. New England, mostly staked out by the original Puritan migrants, showed the least ethnic diversity. The middle colonies, especially Pennsylvania, received the bulk of later white immigrants and boasted an

Estimated Population Elements, 1790 *
(Based on Family Names)

ETHNIC GROUPS	NUMBER	PERCENTAGE
English and Welsh	2,605,699	66.3%
Scotch (including		
Scotch-Irish)	221,562	5.6
German	176,407	4.5
Dutch	78,959	2.0
Irish	61,534	1.6
French	17,619	0.4
All other whites	10,664	0.3
African	757,181	19.3
GRAND TOTAL	3,929,625	

*Rossiter, *A Century of Population Growth* (1909). Later estimates by Barker and Hansen (1931) are not used here because they are confused by the inclusion of Spanish and French elements *later* a part of the United States.

A Pennsylvania Advertisement for Slaves in the 1760s Note that the slaves are said to have had smallpox and to be able to speak English. (Rare Book Division, The New York Public Library, Astor, Lenox and Tilden Foundations.)

astonishing variety of peoples. Outside of New England, about one-half the population was non-English in 1775. Of the fifty-six signers of the Declaration of Independence in 1776, eighteen were non-English, and eight had not been born in the colonies.

The Structure of Colonial Society

In contrast with contemporary Europe, eighteenth-century America was a shining land of equality and opportunity—with the notorious exception of slavery. No titled nobility dominated society from on high, and no pauperized underclass threatened it from below. Most white Americans, and even some free blacks, were small farmers. Clad in buckskin breeches, they owned modest holdings and tilled them with their own hands and horses. The cities contained a small class of skilled artisans, with their well-greased leather aprons, as well as a few shopkeepers and tradespeople, and a handful of unskilled casual laborers. The most remarkable feature of the social ladder was the rags-to-riches ease with which an ambitious colonial, even a former indentured servant, might rise from a lower rung to a higher one, quite unlike in old England.

Yet in contrast with seventeenth-century America, colonial society on the eve of the Revolution was beginning to show signs of stratification and barriers to mobility that raised worries about the "Europeanization" of America. The gods of war contributed to these developments. The armed conflicts of the 1690s and early 1700s had enriched a number of merchant princes in the New England and middle colonies. They laid the foundations of their fortunes with profits made as military suppliers. Roosting regally atop the social ladder, these elites now feathered their nests more finely. They sported imported clothing and dined at tables laid with English china and gleaming silverware. Prominent persons came to be seated in churches and schools according to their social rank. (Future President John Adams was placed fourteenth in a class of twenty-four at Harvard, where ability also affected one's standing.)

The plague of war also created a class of widows and orphans, who became dependent for their survival on charity. Both Philadelphia and New York built almshouses in the 1730s to care for the destitute. Yet the numbers of poor people remained tiny compared to the numbers in England, where about a third of the population lived in impoverished squalor.

In the New England countryside the descendants of the original settlers faced more limited prospects than had their pioneering forebears. As the supply of unclaimed soil dwindled and families grew, existing landholdings were subdivided and the average size of farms shrank drastically. Younger sons were increasingly

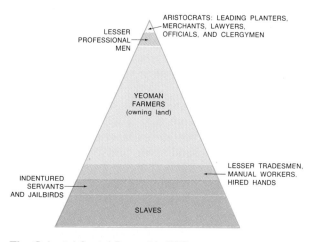

The Colonial Social Pyramid, 1775
(an approximation)

Slave-Catcher Advertisement   *Runaway slaves were so numerous in colonial days that newspapers kept on hand stock woodcuts like those here reproduced. One Virginia owner offered five pounds reward for the return of Toby, a fourteen-year-old mulatto boy "with a scar on the right side of his throat" and with "an old brown jacket, tow shirt and check trousers, which are supposed to be worn out by this time."*

forced to hire out as wage laborers—or eventually, to seek virgin tracts of land beyond the Appalachians.

In the South the power of the great planters continued to be bolstered by their disproportionate ownership of slaves. The riches created by the growing slave population in the eighteenth century were not distributed evenly among the whites. Wealth was concentrated in the hands of the largest slaveowners, widening the gap between the prosperous gentry and the "poor whites," who were increasingly forced to become tenant farmers.

In all the colonies the ranks of the lower classes were further swelled by the continuing stream of indentured servants, many of whom ultimately achieved prosperity and prestige. Two became signers of the Declaration of Independence.

Far less fortunate than the voluntary indentured servants were the paupers and convicts involuntarily shipped to America. Altogether, about fifty thousand "jayle birds" were dumped on the colonies by the London authorities. This riffraff crowd—including robbers, rapists, and murderers—was generally sullen and undesirable, and not bubbling over with goodwill for the king's government. But many convicts were the unfortunate victims of circumstances and of a viciously unfair English penal code that included about two hundred capital crimes. Some

of the deportees, in fact, came to be highly respectable citizens.

Least fortunate of all, of course, were the black slaves. They enjoyed no equality with whites and dared not even dream of ascending the ladder of opportunity. Oppressed and degraded, the slaves were America's closest approximation to Europe's volatile lower classes, and fears of black rebellion plagued the white colonists. Some colonial legislatures, notably South Carolina's in 1760, sensed the dangers present in a heavy concentration of resentful slaves and attempted to restrict or halt their importation. But the British authorities vetoed all such efforts. Many colonials looked upon this veto as a callous disregard of their welfare, although it was done primarily in the interests of imperial policy and of the British and New England slave trade. Thomas Jefferson, himself a slaveholder, assailed such vetoes in an early draft of the Declaration of Independence, but his proposed clause was finally dropped, largely out of regard for southern sensibilities.

Clerics, Physicians, and Jurists

Most honored of the professions was the Christian ministry. In 1775 the clergy wielded less influence than in the early days of Massachusetts, when piety had burned more warmly. But they still occupied a position of high prestige.

Most physicians, on the other hand, were poorly trained and not highly esteemed. Not until 1765 was the first medical school established, although European centers attracted some students. Aspiring young doctors served

On doctors and medicine Benjamin Franklin's Poor Richard's Almanack offered some homely advice:

"God heals and the doctor takes the fee."

"He's the best physician that knows the worthlessness of most meicines."

"Don't go to the doctor with every distemper, nor to the lawyer with every quarrel, nor to the pot for every thirst."

for a while as apprentices to older practitioners and were then turned loose on their "victims." Bleeding was a favorite and frequently fatal remedy; when the physician was not available, a barber was often summoned.

Plagues were a constant nightmare. Especially dreaded was smallpox, which afflicted one out of five persons, including the heavily pock-marked George Washington. A crude form of inoculation was introduced in 1721, despite the objections of many physicians and some of the clergy, who opposed tampering with the will of God. Powdered dried toad was a favorite prescription for smallpox. Diphtheria was also a deadly killer, especially of young people. One epidemic in the 1730s took the lives of thousands. This grim reminder of their mortality may have helped to prepare many colonists in their hearts and minds for the religious revival that was soon to sweep them up.

At first the law profession was not favorably regarded. In this pioneering society, which required much honest manual labor, the parties to a dispute often presented their own cases in court. Lawyers were commonly regarded as noisy windbags or troublemaking rogues; an early Connecticut law classed them with drunkards and brothel keepers. When future President John Adams was a young law student, the father of the woman whom he eventually married frowned upon him as a suitor.

By about 1750, seaboard society had passed the pioneering stage, and trained attorneys were generally recognized as useful. Able to defend colonial rights against the crown on legal grounds, lawyers like the eloquent James Otis and the flaming Patrick Henry took the lead in the agitation that led to revolt. Other lawyer-orators played hardly less important roles in forging new constitutions and in serving in representative bodies.

Workaday America

Agriculture was the leading industry, involving about 90 percent of the people. Tobacco continued to be the staple crop in Maryland and Virginia. The fertile middle ("bread") colonies produced large quantities of grain, and by 1759 New York alone was exporting eighty thousand

The Colonial Economy *By the eighteenth century, the various colonial regions had distinct economic identities. The northern colonies grew grain and raised cattle, harvested timber and fish, and built ships. The Chesapeake colonies and North Carolina were still heavily dependent on tobacco, while the southernmost colonies grew mostly rice and indigo. Cotton, so important to the southern economy in the nineteenth century, had not yet emerged as a major crop.*

barrels of flour a year. Seemingly the farmer had only to tickle the soil with a hoe and it would laugh with a harvest. Overall, Americans probably enjoyed a higher standard of living than the masses of any country in history up to that time.

Fishing (including whaling), though ranking far below agriculture, was rewarding. Pursued in all the colonies, this harvesting of the sea was a major industry in New England, which exported smelly shiploads of dried cod to the Catholic countries of Europe. The fishing fleet also stimulated shipbuilding and served as a nursery for the seamen who manned the navy and merchant marine.

A bustling commerce, both coastwise and overseas, enriched all the colonies, especially the New England group, New York, and Pennsylvania. Commercial ventures and land speculation, in the absence of later get-rich-quick schemes, were the surest avenues to speedy wealth. Yankee seamen were famous in many climes not only as skilled mariners but as tightfisted traders. They provisioned the Caribbean sugar islands with food and forest products. They hauled Spanish and Portuguese gold, wine, and oranges to London, to be exchanged for industrial goods, which were then sold for a juicy profit in America.

The so-called triangular trade was infamously profitable, though small in relation to total colonial commerce. A skipper, for example, would leave a New England port with a cargo of rum and sail to the Gold Coast of Africa. Bartering the fiery liquor with African chiefs for captured African slaves, he would proceed to the West Indies with his screaming and suffocating cargo sardined below deck. There he would exchange the survivors for molasses, which he would then carry to New England, where it would be distilled into rum. He would then repeat the trip, making a handsome profit on each leg of the triangle.

Manufacturing in the colonies was of only secondary importance, although there was a surprising variety of small enterprises. As a rule, workers could get ahead faster in soil-rich America by tilling the land. Huge quantities of "kill devil" rum were distilled in Rhode Island and Massachusetts; and even some of the "elect of the Lord" developed an overfondness for it. Handsome beaver hats were manufactured in quantity, despite British restrictions. Smoking iron forges, including Pennsylvania's Valley

Sea Captains Carousing in Surinam, 1757–1758 *This playful portrayal of Yankee sea captains in Dutch Guiana is a reminder of the distant trade connections established by American shippers in the colonial era. The lively ale-house merriment also confirms that not all seamen were sober-sided Puritans. (The Saint Louis Art Museum.)*

Colonial Trade Patterns, c. 1770 *Future President John Adams noted about this time that "the commerce of the West Indies is a part of the American system of commerce. They can neither do without us, nor we without them. The Creator has placed us upon the globe in such a situation that we have occasion for each other."*

Forge, likewise dotted the land and in fact were more numerous in 1775, though generally smaller, than those of England. In addition, household manufacturing, including spinning and weaving by womenfolk, added up to an impressive output. As in all pioneering countries, strong-backed laborers and skilled craftspeople were scarce and highly prized. In early Virginia a carpenter who had committed a murder was freed because his woodworking skills were needed.

Lumbering was perhaps the most important single manufacturing activity. Countless cartloads of virgin timber were consumed by shipbuilders, at first chiefly in New England and then elsewhere in the colonies. By 1770 about four hundred vessels of assorted sizes were splashing down the ways each year, and about one-third of the British merchant marine was American-built.

Colonial naval stores—such as tar, pitch, rosin, and turpentine—were highly valued, for Britannia was anxious to gain and retain a mastery of the seas. London offered generous bounties to stimulate production of these items; otherwise Britain would have had to turn to the uncertain and possibly hostile Baltic areas. Towering trees, ideal as masts for His Majesty's navy, were marked with the king's broad arrow for future use. The luckless colonial who was

caught cutting down this reserved timber was subject to a fine. Even though there were countless unreserved trees and the ones marked were being saved for the common defense, this shackle on free enterprise engendered considerable bitterness.

Americans held an important flank of a thriving, many-sided Atlantic economy by the dawn of the eighteenth century. Yet strains appeared

Early Lumbering *An eighteenth-century sawmill in colonial New York. (The William L. Clements Library.)*

in this complex network as early as the 1730s. Fast-breeding Americans demanded more and more English products—yet the slow-growing English population early reached the saturation point for absorbing imports from America. How, then, could the colonists sell the goods to make the money to buy what they wanted in the mother country? The answer was obvious: by seeking foreign (non-English) markets.

By the eve of the Revolution the bulk of Chesapeake tobacco was filling pipes in France and other Continental countries, though it passed through the hands of British re-exporters, who took a slice of the profits. More important was the trade with the West Indies, especially the French islands. West Indian purchases of North American timber and foodstuffs provided the crucial cash for the colonists to continue to make their own purchases in England. In 1733, bowing to pressure from influential British West Indian planters, Parliament passed the Molasses Act, aimed at squelching North American trade with the *French* West Indies. If successful, this scheme would have struck a crippling blow to American international trade and to the colonists' standard of living. American merchants responded by bribing and smuggling their way around the law. Thus was foreshadowed the impending imperial crisis, when headstrong Americans would revolt rather than submit to the dictates of a far-off Parliament, apparently bent on destroying their very livelihood.

Horsepower and Sailpower

All sprawling and sparsely populated pioneer communities are cursed with oppressive problems of transportation. America, with a scarcity of both money and workers, was no exception.

Not until the 1700s were there roads connecting even the major cities, and these dirt thoroughfares were treacherously poor. A wayfarer could have rumbled along more rapidly over the Roman highways in the days of Julius Caesar, nearly two thousand years earlier. It actually took twenty-nine days for the news of the Declaration of Independence—the story of the year—to reach Charleston from Philadelphia.

Roads were often clouds of dust in the summer and quagmires of mud in the winter. Stagecoach travelers braved such additional dangers as tree-strewn roads, rickety bridges, carriage overturns, and runaway horses. A wayfarer venturesome enough to journey from Philadelphia to New York, for example, would not think it amiss to make a will and assemble the family for prayers before departing.

Where man-made roads were wretched, heavy reliance was placed on God-grooved waterways. Population tended to cluster along the banks of navigable rivers. There was also much coastwise traffic, and although it was slow and undependable, it was relatively cheap and pleasant.

Taverns sprang up along the main routes of travel, as well as in the cities. Their attractions customarily included such items as bowling alleys, pool tables, bars, and gambling equipment. Before a cheerful, roaring log fire all social classes would mingle, including the village loafers and drunks. The tavern was yet another cradle of democracy.

Gossips also gathered at the taverns, which were clearinghouses of information, misinformation, and rumor—frequently stimulated by alcoholic refreshment and impassioned political talk. A successful politician, like the wire-pulling Samuel Adams, was often a man who had a large alehouse acquaintance in places like Boston's Green Dragon Tavern. Taverns were important in crystallizing public opinion and proved to be hotbeds of agitation as the Revolutionary movement gathered momentum.

An intercolonial postal system was established by the mid-1700s, although private couriers remained. Some mail was handled on credit. Service was slow and infrequent, and secrecy was problematical. Mail carriers, serving long routes, would sometimes pass the time by reading the letters entrusted to their care.

Dominant Denominations

Two "established," or tax-supported, churches were conspicuous in 1775: the Anglican and the Congregational. A considerable segment of the population, surprisingly enough, did not

The Green Dragon Tavern, Boston *Alehouses like this provided not only food, drink, and shelter, but also raucous arenas for the exchange of political ideas. (American Antiquarian Society.)*

worship in any church. And in those colonies where there was an "established" religion, only a minority of the people belonged to it.

The Church of England, whose members were commonly called Anglicans, became the official faith in Georgia, North and South Carolina, Virginia, Maryland, and a part of New York. Established also in England, it served in America as a major prop of kingly authority. British officials naturally made vigorous efforts to impose it on additional colonies, but they ran into a stone wall of opposition.

In America the Anglican church fell distressingly short of its promise. Secure and self-satisfied, like the parent establishment in England, it clung to a faith that was less fierce and more worldly than the religion of Puritanical New England. Sermons were shorter; hell was less scorching; and amusements, like Virginia fox hunting, were less frowned upon. So dismal was the reputation of the Anglican clergy in seventeenth-century Virginia that the College of William and Mary was founded in 1693 to train a better class of clerics.

The influential Congregational church, which had grown out of the Puritan church, was formally established in all the New England colonies, except independent-minded Rhode Island. At first Massachusetts taxed all residents to support Congregationalism but later relented and exempted members of other well-known denominations. Presbyterianism, though closely associated with Congregationalism, was never made official in any colonies.

Ministers of the gospel, turning from the Bible to this sinful world, increasingly grappled with burning political issues. As the early rumblings of revolution against the British crown

Estimated Religious Census, 1775

NAME	NUMBER	CHIEF LOCALE
Congregationalists	575,000	New England
Anglicans	500,000	N.Y., South
Presbyterians	410,000	Frontier
German churches (incl. Lutheran)	200,000	Pa.
Dutch Reformed	75,000	N.Y., N.J.
Quakers	40,000	Pa., N.J., Del.
Baptists	25,000	R.I., Pa., N.J., Del.
Roman Catholics	25,000	Md., Pa.
Methodists	5,000	Scattered
Jews	2,000	N.Y., R.I.
EST. TOTAL MEMBERSHIP	1,857,000	
EST. TOTAL POPULATION	2,493,000	
PERCENTAGE CHURCH MEMBERS	74%	

could be heard, sedition flowed freely from pulpits. Presbyterianism, Congregationalism, and rebellion were triplets. Many of the leading Anglican clergymen, aware of what side their tax-provided bread was buttered on, naturally supported their king.

Anglicans in the New World were seriously handicapped by not having a resident bishop, whose presence would be convenient for the ordination of young ministers. American students of Anglican theology had to travel to England to be ordained. On the eve of the Revolution there was serious talk of creating an American bishopric, but the scheme was violently opposed by many non-Anglicans, who feared a tightening of the royal reins. This controversy poured holy oil on the smoldering fires of rebellion.

Religious toleration had indeed made enormous strides in America, at least when compared with halting steps abroad. Roman Catholics were still generally discriminated against, as in England, even in office holding. But there were fewer Catholics in America, and hence the antipapist laws were less severe and

Franklin's Poor Richard's Almanack contained such thoughts on religion as:

"A good example is the best sermon."

"Many have quarreled about religion that never practiced it."

"Serving God is doing good to man, but praying is thought an easier service, and therefore more generally chosen."

"How many observe Christ's birthday; how few his precepts! O! 'tis easier to keep holidays than commandments."

less strictly enforced. In general, people could worship—or not worship—as they pleased.

The Great Awakening

In all the colonial churches, religion was less fervid in the early eighteenth century than it had been a century earlier, when the colonies were first planted. The Puritan churches in particular sagged under the weight of two burdens: their elaborate theological doctrines and their compromising efforts to liberalize membership requirements. Churchgoers increasingly complained about the "dead dogs" who droned out tedious, overerudite sermons from Puritan pulpits. Some ministers, on the other hand, worried that many of their parishioners had gone soft and that their souls were no longer kindled by the hellfire of orthodox Calvinism. Liberal ideas began to challenge the old-time religion, and some worshipers now proclaimed that human beings were not necessarily predestined to damnation but might save themselves by good works. A few churches grudgingly conceded that spiritual conversion was not necessary for church membership. Together, these twin trends toward clerical intellectualism and lay liberalism were sapping the spiritual vitality from many denominations.

The stage was thus set for a rousing religious revival. Known as the Great Awakening, it exploded in the 1730s and 1740s and swept through the colonies like a fire through prairie grass. The Awakening was first ignited in

Established (Tax-Supported) Churches in the Colonies, 1775 *

COLONIES	CHURCHES	YEAR DISESTABLISHED
Mass. (incl. Me.)	Congregational	1833
Connecticut		1818
New Hampshire		1819
New York	Anglican (in N.Y. City and three neighboring counties)	1777
Maryland	Anglican	1777
Virginia		1786
North Carolina		1776
South Carolina		1778
Georgia		1777
Rhode Island	None	
New Jersey		
Delaware		
Pennsylvania		

*Note the persistence of the Congregational establishment in New England.

Northampton, Massachusetts, by a tall, delicate, and intellectual pastor, Jonathan Edwards. Perhaps the deepest theological mind ever nurtured in America, Edwards proclaimed with burning righteousness the folly of believing in salvation through good works and affirmed the need for complete dependence on God's grace. Warming to his subject, he painted in lurid detail the landscape of hell and the eternal torments of the damned. "Sinners in the Hands of an Angry God" was the title of one of his most famous sermons. He believed that hell was "paved with the skulls of unbaptized children."

Edwards' preaching style was learned and closely reasoned, but his stark doctrines sparked a warmly sympathetic reaction among his parishioners in 1734. Four years later, the itinerant English parson George Whitefield loosed a different style of evangelical preaching on America and touched off a conflagration of religious ardor that revolutionized the spiritual life of the colonies. A former alehouse attendant, Whitefield was an orator of rare gifts. His magnificent voice boomed sonorously over thousands of enthralled listeners in an open field. One of England's greatest actors of the day commented enviously that Whitefield could make audiences weep merely by pronouncing the word *Mesopotamia* and that he would "give a hundred guineas if I could only say 'O!' like Mr. Whitefield."

Triumphally touring the colonies, Whitefield trumpeted his message of human helplessness and divine omnipotence. His eloquence reduced Jonathan Edwards to tears and even caused the skeptical and thrifty Benjamin Franklin to empty his pockets into the collection plate. During these roaring revival meetings, countless

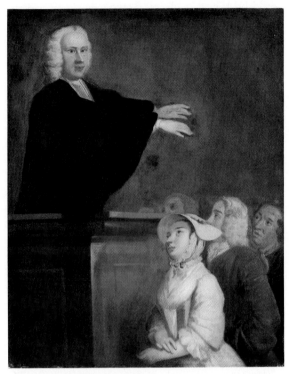

George Whitefield Preaching *Americans of both sexes and all races and sections were spellbound by Whitefield's emotive oratory. (National Portrait Gallery, London.)*

Jonathan Edwards preached hellfire, notably in one famous sermon: "The God that holds you over the pit of hell, much as one holds a spider or some loathsome insect over the fire, abhors you, and is dreadfully provoked. His wrath toward you burns like fire; he looks upon you as worthy of nothing else but to be cast into the fire."

sinners professed conversion, while hundreds of the "saved" groaned, shrieked, or rolled in the snow from religious excitation. Whitefield soon inspired American imitators. Taking up his electrifying new style of preaching, they heaped abuse on sinners and shook enormous audiences with emotional appeals. One preacher cackled hideously in the face of hapless wrongdoers. Another, naked to the waist, leaped frantically about in the light of flickering torches.

Orthodox clergymen, known as "old lights," were deeply skeptical of the emotionalism and the theatrical antics of the revivalists. "New light" ministers, on the other hand, defended the Awakening for its role in revitalizing American religion. Congregationalists and Presbyterians split over this issue, and many of the believers in religious conversion went over to the Baptists and other sects more prepared to make room for emotion in religion. The Awakening left many lasting effects. Its emphasis on direct, emotive spirituality seriously undermined the older clergy whose authority had derived from their education and erudition. The schisms it set off in many denominations greatly increased the numbers and the competitiveness of American churches. It encouraged a fresh wave of missionary work among the Indians and even among black slaves, many of whom also attended the mass open-air revivals. It led to the founding of such "new light" centers of higher learning, as Dartmouth, Brown, Rutgers, and Princeton. Perhaps most significant, the Great Awakening was the first spontaneous mass movement of the American people. It tended to break down sectional boundaries as well as denominational lines and contributed to the growing sense that Americans had of themselves as a single people, united by a common history and shared experiences.

Schools and Colleges

A time-honored English ideal regarded education as a boon reserved for the aristocratic few, not for the unwashed many. Education should be for leadership, not citizenship, and primarily for the male sex. Only slowly and painfully did the colonials break the chains of these ancient restrictions.

Puritan New England, largely for religious reasons, was more zealously interested in education than any other section. Dominated by the Congregational church, it stressed the need for Bible reading by the individual worshiper. The primary goal of the clergy was to make good Christians rather than good citizens. A more

> *John Adams, the future second president, once wrote to his wife: "The education of our children is never out of my mind. Train them to virtue. Habituate them to industry, activity, and spirit. . . . For God's sake make your children hardy, active, and industrious; for strength, activity, and industry will be their only resource and dependence."*

secular approach was evident late in the eighteenth century, when some children were warned:

> He who ne'er learns his A.B.C.
> Forever will a blockhead be.
> But he who learns his letters fair
> Shall have a coach to take the air.

Education, principally for boys, flourished almost from the outset in New England. This densely populated region boasted an impressive number of graduates from the English universities, especially Cambridge, the intellectual center of England's Puritanism. New Englanders, at a relatively early date, established primary and secondary schools, which varied widely in the quality of instruction and in the length of time that their doors remained open each year. Back-straining farm labor drained much of the youth's time and energy.

Fairly adequate primary and secondary schools were also hammering knowledge into the heads of reluctant "scholars" in the middle colonies and in the South. Some of these institutions were tax-supported; others were privately operated. The South, with its white and black population diffused over wide areas, was severely handicapped in attempting to establish an effective school system. Wealthy families leaned heavily on private tutors.

The general atmosphere in the colonial schools and colleges continued grim and gloomy. Most of the emphasis was placed on religion and on the classical languages, Latin and Greek. The stress was not on experiment and reason, but on doctrine and dogma. The age was one of orthodoxy, and independence of thinking was discouraged. Discipline was quite severe, with many a mettlesome lad being sadistically "birched" with a switch cut from a birch tree. Sometimes punishment was inflicted by indentured-servant teachers, who could themselves be whipped for their failures as workers and who therefore were not inclined to spare the rod.

College education was regarded—at least at first in New England—as more important than instruction in the ABCs. Churches would wither if a new crop of ministers was not trained to lead the spiritual flocks. Many well-to-do families, especially in the South, sent their boys abroad to English institutions.

For purposes of convenience and economy, nine local colleges were planted during the colonial era. Student bodies were small, numbering about 200 boys at the most; and at one time a few lads as young as eleven were admitted to Harvard. Instruction was poor by present-day standards. The curriculum was still heavily loaded with theology and the "dead" languages, although by 1750 there was a distinct trend toward "live" languages and other modern subjects. A significant contribution was made by Benjamin Franklin, who had a large hand in launching what became the University of Pennsylvania, the first American college free from denominational control.

Culture in the Backwoods

The dawn-to-dusk toil of pioneer life left little vitality or aptitude for artistic effort. Americans were too busy chopping down trees to sit around painting landscapes, especially when a hostile Indian might burst from a nearby bush. There was no strong esthetic tradition; many of the clergy, in fact, regarded art as an invention of the Devil.

As the colonists gradually acquired some wealth and leisure, their surplus energy went

Harvard College, c. 1770   *Engraving by Paul Revere, Boston silversmith of "midnight ride" fame. (Harvard University.)*

into religious and political leadership, not art. The materialistic atmosphere was not favorable to artistic endeavor. One famous painter, John Trumbull of Connecticut (1756–1843), was discouraged in his youth by his father with the chilling remark, "Connecticut is not Athens." Charles W. Peale (1741–1827), best known for his portraits of George Washington, ran a museum, stuffed birds, and practiced dentistry. Gifted Benjamin West (1738–1820) and precocious John S. Copley (1738–1815) succeeded in their ambition to become famous painters, but they had to go to England to complete their training. Only there could they find subjects who had the leisure to sit for their portraits and the money to pay handsomely for them. Copley

Colonial Colleges

NAME	ORIGINAL NAME (IF DIFFERENT)	LOCATION	OPENED OR FOUNDED	DENOMINATION
1. Harvard		Cambridge, Mass.	1636	Congregational
2. William and Mary		Williamsburg, Va.	1693	Anglican
3. Yale		New Haven, Conn.	1701	Congregational
4. Princeton	College of New Jersey	Princeton, N.J.	1746	Presbyterian
5. Pennsylvania	The Academy	Philadelphia, Pa.	1751	Nonsectarian
6. Columbia	King's College	New York, N.Y.	1754	Anglican
7. Brown	Rhode Island College	Providence, R.I.	1764	Baptist
8. Rutgers	Queen's College	New Brunswick, N.J.	1766	Dutch Reformed
9. Dartmouth (begun as an Indian missionary school)		Hanover, N.H.	1769	Congregational

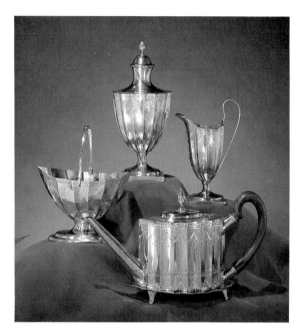

Tea Set, by Paul Revere *The famed horseman of the Revolution was a silversmith by trade. These finely wrought pieces illustrate not only the high degree of his skill, but also the growing prosperity and refined tastes of his clients in late eighteenth-century Boston. (The Metropolitan Museum of Art, Bequest of A.T. Clearwater, 1933.)*

was regarded as a Loyalist during the Revolutionary War, while West, a close friend of George III and official court painter, was buried in London's St. Paul's Cathedral.

Architecture was largely imported from the Old World and modified to meet the peculiar climatic and religious conditions of the New World. Even the lowly log cabin was apparently borrowed from Sweden. The red-bricked Georgian style, so common in the pre-Revolutionary decades, was introduced about 1720 and is best exemplified by the beauty of now-restored Williamsburg, Virginia.

Colonial literature, like art, was generally undistinguished, and for much the same reasons. One noteworthy exception was the precocious poet Phillis Wheatley (c. 1753–1784), a slave girl brought to Boston at age eight and never formally educated. Taken to England when twenty years of age, she published a book of verse and subsequently wrote other polished poems that revealed the influence of Alexander Pope. Her verse compares favorably with the

best of the poetry-poor colonial period, but the remarkable fact is that, considering her grave handicaps, she could write any poetry at all.

Many-sided Benjamin Franklin, often called "the first civilized American," also shone as a literary light. Although his autobiography is now a classic, he was best known to his contemporaries for *Poor Richard's Almanack,* which he edited from 1732 to 1758. This famous publication, containing many pithy sayings culled from the thinkers of the ages, emphasized such homespun virtues as thrift, industry, morality, and common sense. Examples are: "What maintains one vice would bring up two children"; "Plough deep while sluggards sleep"; "Honesty is the best policy"; and "Fish and visitors stink in three days." *Poor Richard's* was well known in Europe and was more widely read in America than anything else except the Bible. As a teacher of both old and young, Franklin had an incalculable influence in shaping the American character.

Science, rising above the shackles of superstition, was making some progress, though lagging behind the Old World. A few botanists, mathematicians, and astronomers had won some repute, but Benjamin Franklin was perhaps the only first-rank scientist produced in the American colonies. His spectacular but dangerous experiments with electricity, including the kite-flying episode, won him numerous honors in Europe. But his mind had a practical turn, and among his numerous inventions were bifocal spectacles and the highly efficient Franklin stove. His lightning rod, not surprisingly, was condemned by the less-liberal clergy as "presuming on God" by attempting to control the "artillery of the heavens."

Pioneer Presses

Stump-grubbing Americans were too poor to buy quantities of books and too busy to read them. One South Carolina merchant in 1744 advertised the arrival of a shipment of "printed books, Pictures, Maps, and Pickles." A few private libraries of fair size could be found, especially among the clergy. The Byrd family of Virginia enjoyed perhaps the largest collection in the colonies, consisting of about four thousand volumes. Bustling Benjamin Franklin established in Philadelphia the first privately supported circulating library in America; and by 1776 there were about fifty public libraries and collections supported by subscription.

Hand-operated printing presses were active in running off pamphlets, leaflets, and journals. On the eve of the Revolution there were about forty colonial newspapers, chiefly weeklies that consisted of a single large sheet folded once. Columns ran heavily to dull essays, frequently signed with such pseudonyms as *Cicero, Philosophicus*, and *Pro Bono Publico* (for the public good). The "news" often lagged many weeks behind the event, especially in the case of overseas happenings, in which the colonials were deeply interested. Newspapers proved to be a powerful agency for airing colonial grievances and building up opposition to British control.

A celebrated legal case, in 1734–1735, involved John Peter Zenger, a newspaper printer. Significantly, the case arose in New York, reflecting the tumultuous give-and-take of politics in the middle colonies, where so many different ethnic groups jostled against one another. Zenger's newspaper had assailed the corrupt royal governor. Charged with seditious libel, the accused was haled into court, where he was defended by a distinguished Philadelphia lawyer, Andrew Hamilton, then nearly eighty. Zenger argued that he had printed the truth, while the bewigged royal chief justice ruled that the mere fact of printing, irrespective of the truth, was enough to convict. Yet the jury, swayed by the eloquence of Hamilton, defied the red-robed judges and daringly returned a verdict of "not guilty." Cheers burst from the spectators.

The Zenger decision was epochal. It pointed the way to the kind of freedom of expression required by the diverse society that was colonial New York and that all America was to become. Though contrary to existing law and not accepted by other royal judges, in time it helped set a precedent against judicial tyranny in libel suits. Newspaper editors had something of a burden lifted from their backs, even though complete freedom of the press was unknown during the pre-Revolutionary era.

Andrew Hamilton concluded his eloquent plea in the Zenger case with these words: "The question before the court and you, gentlemen of the jury, is not of small nor private concern. It is not the cause of a poor printer, nor of New York alone, which you are now trying. No! It may, in its consequence, affect every freeman that lives under a British government on the main[land] of America. It is the best cause. It is the cause of liberty."

The Great Game of Politics

American colonials may have been backward in natural or physical science, but they were making noteworthy contributions to political science.

The thirteen colonial governments presented a varied structure. By 1775, eight of the colonies had royal governors, who were appointed by the king. Three were under proprietors who themselves chose the governors—Maryland, Pennsylvania, and Delaware. And two—Connecticut and Rhode Island—elected their own governors under self-governing charters.

Practically every colony utilized a two-house legislative body. The upper house, or council, was normally appointed by the crown in the royal colonies and by the proprietor in the proprietary colonies. It was chosen by the voters in the self-governing colonies. The lower house, as the popular branch, was elected by the people—or rather by those persons who owned enough property to qualify as voters. In several of the colonies, the backcountry elements were seriously underrepresented, and they hated the ruling colonial clique perhaps more than they did kingly authority. Legislatures, in which the people enjoyed direct representation, voted such taxes as they chose for the necessary expenses of colonial government. Self-taxation through representation was a precious privilege that Americans had come to cherish above most others.

Governors appointed by the king were generally able men, sometimes outstanding figures,

> *Junius, the pseudonym for a critic (or critics) of the British government from 1768 to 1772, published a pointed barb in criticizing one new appointee: "It was not Virginia that wanted a governor but a court favorite that wanted a salary."*

and their households were an important outcropping of Europe's cultural frontier. But the appointees were sometimes incompetent or corrupt and included broken-down politicians badly in need of jobs. The worst of the group was impoverished Lord Cornbury, first cousin of Queen Anne, who was made governor of New York and New Jersey in 1702. He proved to be a drunkard, a spendthrift, a grafter, an embezzler, a religious bigot, and a vain fool, especially when he appeared in public dressed like a woman. Even the best of the king's appointees had trouble with the colonial legislatures, basically because the royal governor embodied a bothersome transatlantic authority some 3,000 miles (4,800 kilometers) away.

But the colonial assemblies were by no means defenseless. Some of them employed the trick of withholding the governor's salary unless he yielded to their wishes. He was normally in need of money—otherwise he would not have come to this godforsaken country—so the power of the purse usually forced him to terms. But one governor of North Carolina died with his salary eleven years in arrears.

The London government, in leaving the colonial governor to the tender mercies of the legislature, was guilty of poor administration. In the interests of simple efficiency the British authorities should have arranged to pay him from independent sources. As events turned out, control over the purse by the colonial legislatures led to prolonged bickering, which proved to be one of the persistent irritants that generated a spirit of revolt.*

---

*Parliament finally arranged for separate payment of the governors through the Townshend taxes of 1767, but by then the colonials were in such an ugly mood over taxation that this innovation only added fresh fuel to the flames.

Administration at the local level was also varied. County government remained the rule in the plantation South; town-meeting government predominated in New England; and a modification of the two developed in the middle colonies. In the town meeting, with its open discussion and open voting, direct democracy functioned at its best. In this unrivaled cradle of self-government, Americans learned to cherish their privileges and exercise their duties as citizens of the New World commonwealths.

Yet the ballot was by no means a birthright. Religious or property qualifications for voting, with even stiffer qualifications for office holding, existed in all the colonies in 1775. The privileged upper classes, fearful of democratic excesses, were unwilling to grant the ballot to every "biped of the forest." Perhaps half of the adult white males were thus disfranchised. But because of the ease of acquiring land and thus satisfying property requirements, the right to vote was not beyond the reach of most industrious and enterprising colonials. Yet somewhat surprisingly, eligible voters often did not exercise this precious privilege. They frequently acquiesced in the leadership of their "betters," who ran colonial affairs—though always reserving the right to vote misbehaving rascals out of office.

By 1775 America was not yet a true democracy—socially, economically, or politically. But it was far more democratic than England and Europe. Colonial institutions were giving freer rein to the democratic ideals of tolerance, educational advantages, equality of economic opportunity, freedom of speech, freedom of the press, freedom of assembly, and representative government. And these democratic seeds, planted in rich soil, were to bring forth a lush harvest in later years.

Colonial Folkways

Everyday life in the colonies may now seem glamorous, especially as reflected in antique shops. But judged by modern standards, it was drab and tedious. For the mass of the people, the labor was heavy and constant—from daybreak to backbreak.

Food was plentiful, though the diet could be coarse and monotonous. Americans probably ate more bountifully, especially of meat, than any people in the Old World. Lazy or sickly was the person whose stomach was empty.

Basic comforts now taken for granted were lacking. Churches were not heated at all, except for charcoal foot-warmers which the womenfolk carried. During the frigid New England winters, the preaching of hellfire may not have seemed altogether unattractive. Drafty homes were poorly heated, chiefly by inefficient fireplaces. There was no running water in the houses, no plumbing, and probably not a single bathtub in all colonial America. Flickering lights were inadequate, for illumination was provided by candles and whale-oil lamps. Garbage disposal was primitive. Long-snouted hogs customarily ranged the streets to consume refuse, while buzzards, protected by law, flapped greedily over tidbits of waste.

Amusement was eagerly pursued where time and custom permitted. The militia assembled periodically for "musters," which consisted of several days of drilling, liberally interspersed with merrymaking and eyeing the girls. On the frontier, pleasure was often combined with work at house-raisings, quilting bees, husking bees, and apple parings. Funerals and weddings everywhere afforded opportunities for social gatherings, which customarily involved the swilling of much strong liquor.

Winter sports were common in the North, while in the South card playing, horse racing, cockfighting, and fox hunting were favorite pastimes. George Washington, not surprisingly, was a superb rider. In the non-Puritanical South, dancing was the rage—jigs, square dances, the Virginia reel—and the agile Washington could swing his fair partner with the best of them.

Other diversions beckoned. Lotteries were universally approved, even by the clergy, and were used to raise money for churches and colleges, including Harvard. Stage plays became popular in the South but were disapproved in the Quaker and Puritan colonies and in some places were even forbidden by law. Many of the New England clergy regarded playacting as time-consuming and immoral; they preferred

Heated Public Gathering *The spirit of the New England town meeting. (Library of Congress.)*

religious lectures, from which their flocks derived much spiritual satisfaction.

Holidays were everywhere celebrated, but Christmas was frowned upon in New England as an offensive reminder of "Popery." "Yuletide is fooltide" was a common Puritan sneer. Thanksgiving Day came to be a truly American festival, for it combined thanks to God with an opportunity for jollification, gorging, and guzzling.

England's American colonists in 1775 were a remarkable people: restless, energetic, ambitious, resourceful, ingenious, and independent-minded. With every passing year they were less willing to bow their necks to the yoke of overseas authority. They were like a fast-growing and vigorous youngster who is coming of age and who expects to be treated as an adult and not as a lackey. With a boundless continent before them, with impressive pioneer achievements behind them, and with an astonishing fertility within them, they had caught a vision of their destiny and were preparing to grasp it. Woe unto him who should try to thwart them!

Varying Viewpoints

Many historians, notably Richard Bushman, see pre-Revolutionary America as an expanding, opening society. In this view, colonial society was losing the religious discipline and social hierarchy of the founding generations, as Americans poured out onto the frontier or sailed the commercial seaways in search of fortune and adventure. These scholars portray the Great Awakening as further evidence of the erosion of social constraints. They argue that unbridled religious enthusiasm, directed by itinerant preachers, displayed the kind of questing for personal autonomy that eventually led to demands for national independence.

The opposing view, shown by Gary Nash and Kenneth Lockridge, emphasizes declining opportunities in colonial society. Pressure on land and the continued dominance of church and parental authority gave rise to a landless class, forced to till tenant plots in the countryside or find manual labor in the cities. The simmering discontent of this growing lower class, according to this interpretation, exploded first in the Great Awakening and later in the American Revolution.

Select Readings

Primary Source Documents

Noting the ethnic diversity of colonial American society, Michel Guillaume Jean de Crèvecoeur's *Letters from an American Farmer* (1904)* and Benjamin Franklin's "Observations on the Increase of Mankind,"* in Jared Sparks, ed., *The Works of Benjamin Franklin* (1840), respectively celebrate and express unease at that diversity. Franklin's entertaining *Autobiography** (1868) is an indispensable guide to the values and preoccupations of his time. It includes an account of George Whitefield's visit to Philadelphia during the Great Awakening.

Secondary Sources

Social history is painted with broad strokes in James Henretta, *The Evolution of American Society, 1700–1815* (1973), and Daniel Boorstin, *The Americans: The Colonial Experience* (1958). Richard Hofstadter takes a suggestive snapshot view in *America at 1750* (1971). Population trends are detailed in Evarts B. Greene and Virginia D. Harrington, *American Population before the Federal Census of 1790* (1932), and in Robert V. Wells, *The Population of the British* *Colonies in America before 1776* (1975). Black "immigrants" are studied in Philip D. Curtin, *The African Slave Trade: A Census* (1969); indentured servants, in Abbot E. Smith, *Colonists in Bondage* (1947); and colonial immigration in general, in the early portions of Maldwyn Jones, *American Immigration* (1960). Jackson T. Main astutely analyzes *The Social Structure of Revolutionary America, 1763–1788* (1965). Access to the ballot is scrutinized in Chilton Williamson, *American Suffrage: From Property to Democracy, 1760–1860* (1961). Large-scale economic patterns are traced in Edwin J. Perkins, *The Economy of Colonial America* (1980), and in Alice H. Jones, *The Wealth of a Nation to Be: The American Colonies on the Eve of the Revolution* (1980). The toiling classes are probed in Gerald W. Mullin, *Flight and Rebellion: Slave Resistance in Eighteenth-Century Virginia* (1972); Gary B. Nash, *The Urban Crucible: Social Change, Political Consciousness and the Origins of the American Revolution* (1979); and Rhys Isaac, *The Transformation of Virginia, 1740–1790* (1982). The latter two volumes link social conflict to the Great Awakening, as does Richard L. Bushman, *From Puritan to Yankee: Character and Social Order in Connecticut, 1690–1765*

(1967). Religious revivalism is chronicled in Edwin S. Gaustad, *The Great Awakening in New England* (1957). Cultural history is imaginatively presented in Howard M. Jones, *O Strange New World: American Culture in the Formative Years* (1964). Comprehensive is Henry May, *The Enlightenment in America* (1976). The sometimes heroic dedication to education is portrayed by Lawrence Cremin, *American Education: The Colonial Experience, 1607–1783* (1970); and the general social implications of the early educational system are studied in James Axtell, *School upon a Hill* (1974). Colonial politics are interpreted in a most suggestive way in Bernard Bailyn, *The Origins of American Politics* (1965). More fine-grained local studies are Charles S. Sydnor, *Gentlemen Freeholders* (1952); Patricia Bonomi, *A Factious People: Politics and Society in Colonial New York* (1971); James T. Lemon, *The Best Poor Man's Country* (1972), which deals with Pennsylvania; and Daniel Blake Smith, *Inside the Great House: Planter Family Life in Eighteenth-Century Chesapeake Society* (1980).

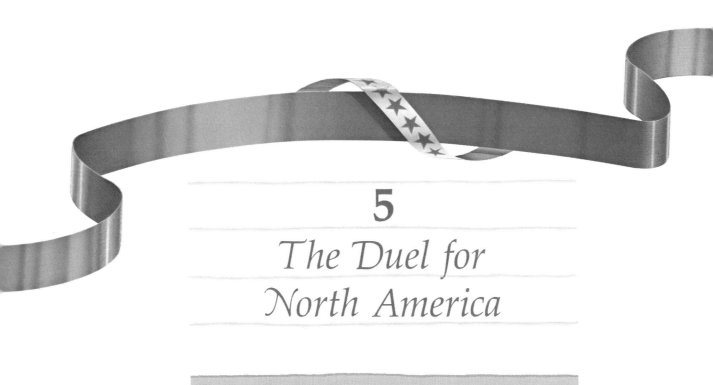

5

The Duel for North America

A torch lighted in the forests of America set all Europe in conflagration.

Voltaire, c. 1756

France Finds a Foothold in Canada

France was another latecomer in the scramble for New World real estate, like England and Holland, and for basically the same reasons. It was convulsed during the 1500s by foreign wars and domestic strife, including the frightful clashes between the Roman Catholics and the Protestant Huguenots. On St. Bartholomew's Day, 1572, over ten thousand Huguenots—men, women, and children—were butchered in cold blood.

A new era dawned in 1598 when the Edict of Nantes, issued by the crown, granted limited toleration to the French Protestants. Religious wars ceased, and in the 1600s France blossomed into the mightiest and most feared nation in Europe. Leadership of a high order was provided by a series of brilliant ministers and by the vainglorious King Louis XIV. *Le Grand Monarque* reigned majestically, beginning as a five-year-old boy, for an incredible seventy-two years (1643–1715). Though involved with a glittering court and numerous mistresses, he was deeply interested in overseas colonies and bestirred himself to promote their welfare.

Success finally crowned the exertions of France in the New World. In 1608, the year after Jamestown, the permanent beginnings of a vast empire were established at Quebec, a rocky sentinel commanding the St. Lawrence River. The leading figure was Samuel de Champlain, an intrepid soldier and explorer whose energy and leadership fairly earned for him the title "Father of New France."

Champlain entered into friendly relations—a fateful friendship—with the nearby Huron Indian tribes. Yielding to their entreaties, he joined them in battle against their feathered foes, the federated Iroquois tribes of the upper

Early French Settlements *By the 1980s French-speakers made up nearly 30 percent of the total Canadian population of about 24 million, and a strong separatist movement had developed among them in Quebec—just one legacy of the colonial-era duel for North America.*

New York area. Two shots from the "lightning sticks" of the whites routed the terrified Indians, who left behind three dead and one wounded. France, to its sorrow, thus earned the lasting enmity of the Iroquois tribes. They thereafter hampered French penetration of the Ohio Valley, ravaged French settlements, and served as allies of the British in the prolonged struggle for supremacy on the continent.

The government of New France (Canada) finally fell under the direct control of the king, after various commercial companies had faltered or failed. This royal regime was almost completely autocratic. There were no popularly elected assemblies, as in the English colonies; there was no trial by jury—merely the decision of the magistrate.

Population in Catholic New France grew with painful slowness: as late as 1750 there were only sixty thousand or so whites. Landowning French peasants, unlike the dispossessed English tenant farmers who embarked for the British colonies, had little economic motive to move. Protestant Huguenots, who might have had a religious motive to migrate, were denied a refuge in this raw colony. The French

Champlain Fights the Iroquois, 1609 *This illustration commemorates the battle on Lake Champlain. Champlain's explorations extended French claims as far inland as Wisconsin. He was fittingly buried in Quebec. (By permission of the Houghton Library, Harvard University.)*

government, in any case, favored its Caribbean island colonies, rich in sugar and rum, over the snow-cloaked wilderness of Canada.

New France Fans Out

New France did contain one valuable resource: the beaver. European fashion-setters valued beaver-pelt hats for their warmth and opulent appearance. To adorn the heads of Europeans, French fur-trappers ranged over the woods and waterways of North America in pursuit of beaver. These colorful *coureurs de bois* (runners of the woods) were also runners of risks—two-fisted drinkers, free spenders, free livers and lovers. They littered the land with scores of place names, including Baton Rouge (red stick), Terre Haute (high land), Des Moines (some monks), and Grand Teton (big breast).

Singing, paddle-swinging French *voyageurs* also recruited Indians into the fur business. The Indian fur flotilla arriving in Montreal in 1693 numbered four hundred canoes. But the fur trade had some disastrous drawbacks. Indians were decimated by the white man's diseases

France's American Empire at Greatest Extent, 1700

Chief of the Taensa Indians Receiving LaSalle, March, 1682   *Driven by the dream of a vast North American empire for France, LaSalle spent years exploring the Great Lakes region and the valleys of the Illinois and Mississippi Rivers. This scene of his encounter with an Indian chieftain is imaginatively recreated by the nineteenth-century artist George Catlin. (A Detail. The National Gallery of Art, Washington, D.C., The Paul Mellon Collection.)*

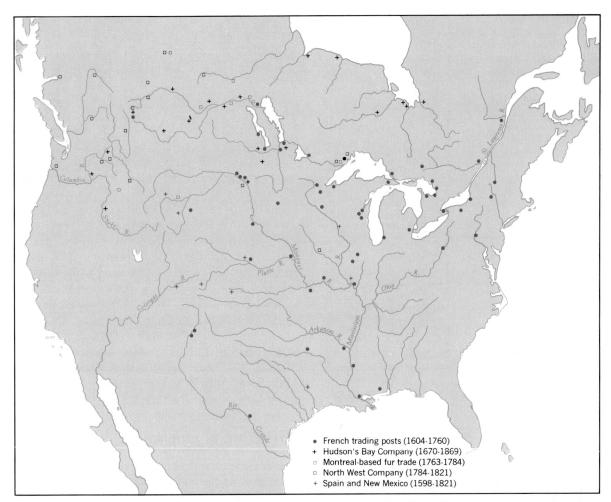

● French trading posts (1604-1760)
+ Hudson's Bay Company (1670-1869)
□ Montreal-based fur trade (1763-1784)
□ North West Company (1784-1821)
+ Spain and New Mexico (1598-1821)

Fur-Trading Posts   *To serve the needs of European fashion, fur-traders pursued the beaver for more than two centuries over the entire continent of North America. They brought many Indians for the first time into contact with white culture.*

and debauched by his alcohol—"firewater"—often adulterated with pepper. Slaughtering beaver by the boatload violated many Indians' religious beliefs and sadly demonstrated the shattering effect that contact with Europeans wreaked on traditional Indian ways of life.

Pursuing the sharp-toothed beaver ever deeper into the heart of the continent, the French trappers and their Indian partners hiked, rode, snowshoed, sailed, and paddled amazing distances. They trekked in a huge arc across the Great Lakes, into present-day Saskatchewan and Manitoba, along the valleys of the Platte, the Arkansas, and the Missouri, west to the Rockies, and south to the border of Texas. In the process, they extinguished the beaver population in many areas, inflicting incalculable ecological damage.

French Catholic missionaries, notably the Jesuits, labored zealously to save the Indians for Christ and from the fur-trappers. Some of the Jesuit missionaries, their efforts scorned, suffered unspeakable tortures at the hands of the Indians. But though they made few permanent converts, the Jesuits played a vital role as explorers and geographers.

Other explorers sought neither souls nor beaver, but empire. To thwart English settlers pushing into the Ohio Valley, Antoine Cadillac founded Detroit, "the City of Straits," in 1701. To check Spanish penetration into the region of the Gulf of Mexico, haughty and ambitious

New Orleans, About 1720 This early French map shows the modest beginnings of the strategic river-port, gateway to the Mississippi (here called the "St. Louis River"). (The Granger Collection.)

Plan de la Nouvelle Orleans Capitale de la Louisiane [1]

Robert de La Salle floated down the mighty Mississippi in 1682 to the point where it mingles with the gulf. He named the great interior basin "Louisiana," in honor of his sovereign, Louis XIV. Dreaming of empire, he returned to the gulf three years later with a colonizing expedition of four ships. But he failed to find the Mississippi delta, landed in Spanish Texas, and in 1687 was murdered by his mutinous men.

Undismayed, French officials persisted in their efforts to block Spain on the Gulf of Mexico. They planted several fortified posts in what is now Mississippi and Louisiana, the most important of which was New Orleans (1718). Commanding the mouth of the Mississippi River, this strategic semitropical outpost also tapped the fur trade of the huge interior valley. The fertile Illinois country—where the French established forts and trading posts at Kaskaskia, Cahokia, and Vincennes—became the garden of France's North American empire. Surprising amounts of grain were floated down the Mississippi for transshipment to the West Indies and to Europe.

The Clash of Empires

As the seventeenth century neared its sunset, a titanic struggle was shaping up for mastery of the North American continent. It involved three civilizations: English, French, and Spanish. From 1688 to 1763, four bitter wars convulsed Europe. All four of these conflicts were world wars. They amounted to a death struggle for domination in Europe as well as in the New World and were fought on the waters and on the soil of two hemispheres. Counting these first four clashes, there have been nine world wars since 1688. The American people, whether as British subjects or as American citizens, were unable to stay out of a single one of them. Isolation from the broils of Europe was all too often a hope rather than a reality.

The first two wars, known in America as King William's War and Queen Anne's War, pitted British colonials against the French *coureurs de bois* and their Indian allies. Both France and England at this stage did not consider America worth the commitment of regular

Later English Monarchs*

NAME, REIGN	RELATION TO AMERICA
William III, 1689–1702	War of Spanish Succession begun
Anne, 1702–1714	Queen Anne's War, 1702–1713
George I, 1714–1727	Navigation Laws laxly enforced ("salutary neglect")
George II, 1727–1760	Ga. founded; King George's War; French and Indian War
George III, 1760–1820	American Revolution, 1775–1783

* See pp. 13, 29 for earlier ones.

troops, so a kind of primitive guerrilla warfare prevailed. French-inspired Indians ravaged with torch and tomahawk the British colonial frontiers, visiting especially horrible violence on the villages of Schenectady, New York, and Deerfield, Massachusetts. Spain, eventually allied with France, probed from its Florida base at outlying South Carolina settlements. For their part, the English colonials failed miserably in attempts to capture Quebec and Montreal but did temporarily seize the stronghold of Port Royal in Acadia.

Peace terms, signed at Utrecht in 1713, revealed how badly France and its Spanish ally had been beaten. England was rewarded with French-populated Acadia (renamed Nova Scotia, or New Scotland) and the wintry wastes of Newfoundland and Hudson Bay. These immense tracts applied the pincers to the St. Lawrence settlements of France, foreshadowing their ultimate doom. A generation of peace ensued, during which Britain provided its American colonies with decades of "salutary neglect"—fertile soil for the roots of independence.

By the treaty of 1713 the British had won limited trading rights in Spanish America, but these later involved much friction over smuggling. Ill feeling flared up when the English Captain Jenkins, encountering Spanish revenue authorities, had one ear sliced off by a sword. The Spanish commander reportedly sneered, "Carry this home to the King, your master, whom, if he were present, I would serve in like fashion." The victim, with a tale of woe on his tongue and a shriveled ear in his hand, aroused furious resentment when he returned home to England.

The War of Jenkins' Ear, curiously but aptly named, broke out in 1739 between the English and the Spaniards. It was confined to the Caribbean Sea and to the much-buffeted buffer colony of Georgia, where philanthropist-soldier James Oglethorpe fought his Spanish foe to a standstill.

The Nine World Wars

DATES	IN EUROPE	IN AMERICA
1688–1697	War of the League of Augsburg	King William's War, 1689–1697
1701–1713	War of Spanish Succession	Queen Anne's War, 1702–1713
1740–1748	War of Austrian Succession	King George's War, 1744–1748
1756–1763	Seven Years' War	French and Indian War, 1754–1763
1778–1783	War of the American Revolution	American Revolution, 1775–1783
1793–1802	Wars of the French Revolution	Undeclared French War, 1798–1800
1803–1815	Napoleonic Wars	War of 1812, 1812–1814
1914–1918	World War I	World War I, 1917–1918
1939–1945	World War II	World War II, 1941–1945

British Territory after Two Wars, 1713

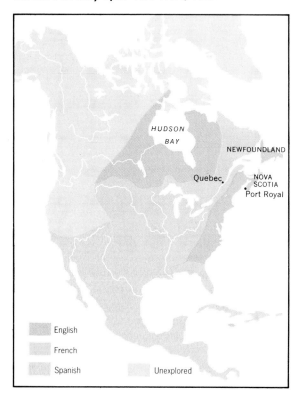

HUDSON BAY

NEWFOUNDLAND

Quebec

NOVA SCOTIA
Port Royal

English

French

Spanish

Unexplored

This small-scale scuffle with Spain in America soon merged with the large-scale War of Austrian Succession in Europe. Once again, France allied itself with Spain. Once again, a rustic force of New Englanders invaded New France. With help from a British fleet and with much good luck, the raw and sometimes drunken recruits captured a reputedly impregnable French fortress, Louisbourg, on Cape Breton Island, commanding the approaches to the St. Lawrence River.

When the peace treaty of 1748 handed Louisbourg back to their French foe, the victorious New Englanders were outraged. The glory of their arms—never terribly lustrous in any event—seemed tarnished by the wiles of Old World diplomats. Worse, Louisbourg was still a cocked pistol pointed at the heart of the American continent. France, powerful and unappeased, still clung to its vast holdings in North America.

New Englanders Capture Louisburg, 1745 *When the final peace settlement returned this fortress to France, the American colonials felt betrayed by their British masters. (Yale University Art Gallery, The Mabel Brady Garvan Collection.)*

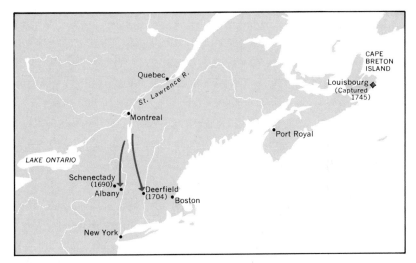

Scenes of the French Wars *The arrows indicate French-Indian attacks. The primitive settlement of Schenectady was burned to the ground in the raid of 1690. At Deerfield the attackers killed fifty inhabitants, took over one hundred prisoners, and sent the rest of the village's three hundred residents fleeing for their lives into the wintry February wilderness.*

George Washington Inaugurates War with France

As the drama unfolded in the New World, the Ohio Valley became the chief bone of contention between the French and British. The Ohio country was the critical area into which the westward-pushing English would inevitably penetrate. It was the key to the continent that the French had to retain, particularly if they were going to link their Canadian holdings with those of the lower Mississippi Valley. By the mid-1700s the English colonials, painfully aware of these basic truths, were no longer so reluctant to bear the burdens of empire. Alarmed by French land-grabbing and cutthroat fur-trade competition in the Ohio Valley, they were determined to fight for their economic security and for the supremacy of their way of life in North America.

Rivalry for the lush lands of the upper Ohio Valley brought tensions to the snapping point. In 1749 a group of English colonial speculators, chiefly influential Virginians, including the Washington family, had secured rights to some 500,000 acres in this region. In the same disputed wilderness the French were in the process of erecting a chain of forts commanding the strategic Ohio River. Especially formidable was Fort Duquesne at the strategic point where the Monongahela and Allegheny rivers join to form the Ohio—the later site of Pittsburgh.

In 1754 the governor of Virginia ushered George Washington, a twenty-one-year-old surveyor and fellow Virginian, onto the stage of history. Washington was sent to the Ohio country as a lieutenant colonel in command of about 150 Virginia militiamen. Encountering a small detachment of French troops in the forest about forty miles from Fort Duquesne, the Virginians opened fire—the first shots of the globe-girdling new war. The French leader was killed, and his men retreated. An exultant Washington wrote: "I heard the bullets whistle, and believe me, there is something charming in the sound." It soon lost its charm.

The French promptly returned with reinforcements, which surrounded Washington in

The Ohio Country, 1753–1754

back of his hastily constructed breastworks, Fort Necessity. After a ten-hour siege he was forced to surrender his entire command in July 1754—ironically the Fourth of July. But he was permitted to march his men away with the full honors of war.

With the shooting already started and in danger of spreading, the British authorities in Nova Scotia took vigorous action. Understandably fearing a stab in the back from the French Acadians, whom England had acquired in 1713, the British brutally uprooted some four thousand of them in 1755. These unhappy French deportees were scattered as far south as Louisiana, where the descendants of the French-speaking Acadians are now called "Cajuns" and number nearly a million.

Global War and Colonial Disunity

The first three Anglo-French colonial wars had all started in Europe, but the tables were now reversed. A fourth struggle, known as the French and Indian War, began in America. Touched off by George Washington in the wilds of the Ohio Valley in 1754, it rocked along on an undeclared basis for two years and then widened into the most far-flung conflict the world had yet seen—the Seven Years' War. It was fought not only in America but in Europe, in the West Indies, in the Philippines, in Africa,

and on the ocean. The Seven Years' War was a seven-seas war.

In Europe the principal adversaries were England and Prussia on one side, arrayed against France, Spain, Austria, and Russia on the other. The bloodiest theater was in Germany, where Frederick the Great deservedly won the title of "Great" by repelling French, Austrian, and Russian armies, often with the opposing forces outnumbering him three to one. The London government, unable to send him effective troop reinforcements, liberally subsidized him with gold. Luckily for the English colonials, the French wasted so much strength in this European bloodbath that they were unable to throw an adequate force into the New World. "America was conquered in Germany," declared Britain's great statesman William Pitt.

In previous colonial clashes, the Americans had revealed an astonishing lack of unity. Colonists who were nearest the shooting had responded much more generously with volunteers and money than those enjoying the safety of remoteness. Even the Indians had laughed at the inability of the colonials to pull together. Now, with musketballs already whining in the Ohio country, the crisis demanded concerted action.

In 1754 the British government summoned an intercolonial congress to Albany, New York, near the Iroquois Indian country. Travel-weary delegates from only seven of the thirteen colonies showed up. The immediate purpose was to keep the scalping knives of the Iroquois tribes loyal to the British in the spreading war. The chiefs were harangued at length and then presented with thirty wagonloads of gifts, including guns.

The longer-range purpose at Albany was to achieve greater colonial unity and thus bolster the common defense against France. A month before the congress assembled, ingenious Benjamin Franklin published in his *Pennsylvania Gazette* the most famous cartoon of the colonial era. Showing the separate colonies as parts of a disjointed snake, it broadcast the slogan, "Join, or Die."

Franklin himself, a wise and witty counselor, was the leading spirit of the Albany congress. His outstanding contribution was a well-devised

Famous Cartoon by Benjamin Franklin *Delaware and Georgia were omitted.*

scheme for colonial home rule. It was unanimously adopted by the Albany delegates but was spurned by the individual colonies and by the London regime. To the colonials, it did not seem to give enough independence; to the British officials, it seemed to give too much. The disappointing result confirmed one of Franklin's sage observations: all people agreed on the need for union, but their "weak noddles" were "perfectly distracted" when they attempted to agree on details.

Braddock's Blundering and Its Aftermath

The opening clashes of the French and Indian War went badly for the English colonials. Haughty and bullheaded General Braddock, a sixty-year-old officer experienced in European warfare, was sent to Virginia with a strong detachment of British regulars. After gathering scanty supplies from the reluctant colonists, he set out in 1755 with some two thousand men to capture Fort Duquesne. A considerable part of his force consisted of ill-disciplined colonial militiamen ("buckskins"), whose behind-the-tree methods of fighting Indians won "Bulldog" Braddock's professional contempt.

Braddock's expedition, dragging heavy artillery, moved slowly. Axmen laboriously hacked a path through the dense forest, thus opening a road that was later to be an important artery to the West. A few miles from Fort Duquesne, Braddock encountered a much smaller French and Indian army. At first the enemy force was repulsed, but it quickly melted into the thickets and poured a murderous fire into the ranks of the redcoats. George Washington, an energetic and fearless aide to Braddock, had two horses shot from under him and four bullet holes in his coat, and Braddock himself was mortally wounded. The entire force was routed after appalling losses.

Inflamed by this easy victory, the Indians took to a wider warpath. The whole frontier from Pennsylvania to North Carolina, left virtually naked by Braddock's bloody defeat, felt their fury. Scalping forays occurred within eighty miles of Philadelphia, and in desperation

the local authorities offered bounties for Indian scalps: $50 for a woman's and $130 for a brave's. George Washington, with only three hundred men, did heroic work in helping to defend the scorched frontier.

The British launched a full-scale invasion of Canada in 1756, now that the undeclared war in America had at last merged into a world conflict. But they unwisely tried to attack a number of exposed wilderness posts simultaneously, instead of throwing all their strength at Quebec and Montreal. If these strongholds had fallen, all the outposts to the west would have withered on the vine for lack of riverborne supplies. But the British ignored such sound strategy, and defeat after defeat tarnished their arms, both in America and in Europe.

Pitt's Palms of Victory

In the hour of crisis Britain brought forth, as it repeatedly has, a superlative leader—William Pitt. A tall and imposing figure, whose flashing eyes were set in a hawklike face, he

William Pitt (1708–1778) *He opposed the king's stubborn policies against the colonies but never favored complete independence. Fort Duquesne, falling to Britain in the French and Indian War, was renamed Pittsburgh in his honor.*

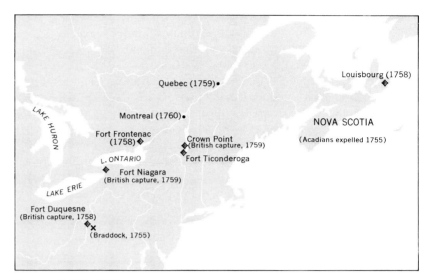

Events of 1755–1760

was popularly known as the "Great Commoner." Pitt drew much of his strength from the common people, who admired him so greatly that on occasion they kissed his horses. A splendid orator endowed with a majestic voice, he believed passionately in his cause, in his country, and in himself.

In 1757 Pitt became a foremost leader in the London government. Throwing himself headlong into his task, he soon earned the title "Organizer of Victory." He wisely decided to soft-pedal assaults on the French West Indies, which had been bleeding away much British strength, and to concentrate on the vitals of Canada—the Quebec-Montreal area. He also picked young and energetic leaders, thus bypassing incompetent and cautious old generals.

Pitt first dispatched a powerful expedition in 1758 against Louisbourg. The frowning fortress, though it had been greatly strengthened, fell after a blistering siege. Wild rejoicing swept England, for this was the first significant British victory of the entire war.

Quebec was next on Pitt's list. For this crucial expedition he chose the thirty-two-year-old James Wolfe, who had been an officer since the age of fourteen. Though slight and sickly, Wolfe combined a mixture of dash with painstaking attention to detail. The British attackers were making scant progress when Wolfe, in a daring

move, sent a detachment up a poorly guarded part of the rocky eminence protecting Quebec. This vanguard scaled the cliff, pulling itself upward by the bushes and showing the way for the others. In the morning the two armies faced each other on the Plains of Abraham on the outskirts of Quebec, the British under Wolfe and the French under the Marquis de Montcalm. Both commanders fell fatally wounded, but the French were defeated and the city surrendered.

The battle of Quebec ranks as one of the most significant engagements in British and American history. When Montreal fell in 1760, the French flag waved in Canada for the last time. By the peace settlement at Paris (1763), French power was thrown completely off the continent of North America, leaving behind a fertile French population that is to this day a strong minority in Canada. This bitter pill was sweetened somewhat when the French were allowed to retain several small but valuable sugar islands in the West Indies, and two never-to-be-fortified islets in the Gulf of St. Lawrence for fishing stations. A final blow came when the French, to compensate their luckless Spanish ally for its losses, ceded to Spain all trans-Mississippi Louisiana, plus the outlet of New Orleans. Spain, for its part, turned Florida over to England in return for Cuba, where Havana had fallen to British arms.

North America before 1754

North America after 1763 (after French losses)

Great Britain thus emerged as the dominant power in North America, while taking its place as the leading naval power of the world.

Mother-and-Daughter Friction

England's colonials, baptized by fire, emerged with increased confidence in their military strength. They had borne the brunt of battle at first; they had fought bravely beside the crack British regulars; and they had gained valuable experience, officers and men alike. In the closing days of the conflict some twenty thousand American recruits were under arms.

The French and Indian War, while bolstering colonial self-esteem, simultaneously shattered the myth of British invincibility. On Braddock's bloody field the "buckskin" militia had seen the demoralized regulars huddling helplessly together or fleeing their unseen enemy.

Ominously, friction had developed during the war between arrogant English officers and the raw colonial "boors." Displaying the contempt of the professional soldier for amateurs, the British refused to recognize any American militia commission above the rank of captain—a demotion humiliating to "Colonel" George Washington.

They also showed the usual condescension of snobs from the civilized Old Country toward the "scum" who had confessed failure by fleeing to the "outhouses of civilization." General Wolfe referred to the colonial militia, with exaggeration, as "in general the dirtiest, most contemptible, cowardly dogs that you can conceive." Energetic and hardworking American settlers, on the other hand, sensed that they were the cutting edge of British civilization. They believed that they deserved credit rather than contempt for risking their lives to erect a New World empire.

British officials were further distressed by the reluctance of the colonials to support the common cause wholeheartedly. American shippers, using fraudulent papers, developed a golden traffic with the enemy ports of the Spanish and French West Indies. This treasonable trade in foodstuffs actually kept some of the hostile islands from starving at the very time when the British navy was trying to subdue them. In the last year of the war the British authorities, forced to resort to drastic measures, forbade the export of all supplies from New England and the middle colonies.

Other colonials, self-centered and regarding the war as remote, refused to provide troops and

Anti-Quaker Cartoon *Noncombatant Pennsylvania Quakers traded with the French, and in this cartoon (c. 1760) Franklin points out that the Quaker (with fox's head) will flourish, regardless of who wins. (The Historical Society of Pennsylvania.)*

money for the conflict. They demanded the rights and privileges of Englishmen, without the duties and responsibilities of Englishmen. Not until Pitt had offered to reimburse the colonies for a substantial part of their expenditures—some £900,000—did they move with some enthusiasm. If the Americans had to be bribed to defend themselves against a relentless and savage foe, would they ever unite to strike the mother country?

The curse of intercolonial disunity, present from early days, had continued throughout the recent hostilities. It had been caused mainly by enormous distances; by geographical barriers like rivers; by conflicting religions, from Catholic to Quaker; by varied nationalities, from German to Irish; by differing types of colonial governments; by many boundary disputes; and by the resentment of the crude backcountry settlers against the aristocratic bigwigs.

Yet unity received some encouragement during the French and Indian War. When soldiers and statesmen from widely separated colonies met around common campfires and council tables, they were often agreeably surprised by what they found. Despite deep-seated jealousy and suspicion, they discovered that they were all fellow Americans who generally spoke the same language and shared common ideals. Bar-

riers of disunity began to melt, although a long and rugged road lay ahead before a nation could emerge.

Americans: A People of Destiny

The removal of the French menace in Canada profoundly affected American attitudes. While the French hawk had been hovering in the North and West, the colonial chicks had been forced to cling close to the wings of the mother hen. Now that the hawk was killed, they could range far afield with a new spirit of independence.

The French, humiliated by the British and saddened by the fate of Canada, consoled themselves with one wishful thought. Perhaps the loss of their American empire would one day result in Britain's loss of its American empire. In a sense the history of the United States began with the fall of Quebec and Montreal; the infant republic was cradled on the Plains of Abraham.

The Spanish and Indian menaces, in like manner, were removed by the recent war. Spain was eliminated from Florida, although now entrenched in Louisiana and New Orleans. And the Indian allies of France were left in the lurch. A violent postwar flare-up against the whites occurred in the Ohio Valley and Great Lakes region in 1763, with the vengeful chieftain Pontiac as the principal leader. Catching the British napping, the Indians wiped out a number of their posts. But the whites swiftly

The Reverend Andrew Burnaby, an observant Church of England clergyman who visited the colonies in the closing months of the French and Indian War, scoffed at any possibility of unification (1760): ". . . for fire and water are not more heterogeneous than the different colonies in North America. Nothing can exceed the jealousy and emulation which they possess in regard to each other. . . . In short . . . were they left to themselves there would soon be a civil war from one end of the continent to the other, while the Indians and Negroes would . . . impatiently watch the opportunity of exterminating them all together."

Settled Areas at End of French and Indian War, 1763 *This map, showing the colonies thirteen years before the Declaration of Independence, helps to explain why the British would be unable to conquer their offspring. The colonials were spreading rapidly into the backcountry, where the powerful British navy could not flush them out. During the Revolutionary War, the British at one time or another captured the leading colonial cities—Boston, New York, Philadelphia, and Charleston; but the more remote interior remained a sanctuary for rebels.*

and cruelly retaliated. The British commander ordered blankets infected with smallpox to be distributed among the Indians. Such tactics crushed the uprising and pacified the frontier, temporarily.

Land-hungry American colonials were now free to burst over the dam of the Appalachian Mountains, and flood out over the grassy western lands. A tiny rivulet of pioneers like Daniel Boone had already trickled into Tennessee and Kentucky; other courageous settlers were preparing for the long trek over the mountains.

Then, out of a clear sky, the London government issued its Proclamation of 1763. It flatly prohibited settlement in the area beyond the Appalachian Mountains, pending further adjustments. The truth is that this hastily drawn document was not designed to oppress the colonials at all, but to work out the Indian problem fairly and prevent another bloody eruption like Pontiac's uprising.

But countless Americans, especially land speculators, were dismayed and angered. Was not the land beyond the mountains their birthright? Had they not, in addition, bought it with their blood in the recent war? In complete defiance of the paper proclamation, they clogged the westward trails. In 1765 an estimated one thousand wagons rolled through the town of Salisbury, North Carolina, on their way "up west." This wholesale flouting of royal authority boded ill for the longevity of British rule in America.

The French and Indian War also caused the colonials to develop a new vision of their ultimate destiny. With the path cleared for the conquest of a continent, with their birthrate high and their energy boundless, they sensed that they were a potent people on the march. And they were in no mood to be restrained.

Lordly Britons, whose suddenly swollen empire had tended to produce swollen heads, were in no mood for back talk. Puffed up over their recent victories, they were already annoyed with their unruly colonials. The stage was set for a violent family quarrel.

Varying Viewpoints

The duel for North America was but one episode in the epochal story of the worldwide expansion of European commerce and culture after 1500. Dominated by the "imperial school," a group of historians who see transatlantic economic stresses as leading to revolution, scholarly inquiry has revolved around four principal questions: How did New World developments fit into the overall pattern of rivalries among the great European powers? What were the relative strengths and weaknesses of the British and French imperial systems that spelled the final triumph of the British and the defeat of the French? How well or poorly did the British Empire function? Finally, were the Americans well or badly treated in the British imperial system? In short, how economically justifiable was the eventual American Revolution?

Social historians have recently looked at the colonial rivalries in a different light. They view the social and economic dislocations wrought by war as a stimulus to class conflict and revolutionary ferment. Some scholars have also asked whether the Revolution would have occurred at all without the British victory over the French in North America. If a powerful, Catholic, hostile France had retained its foothold in Canada, the British colonials might have thought twice about challenging their mother country.

Select Readings

Primary Source Documents

"The Albany Plan of the Union" was the first great statement of colonial unity; "The Proclamation of 1763" forbade settlement west of the Appalachians. Both are collected in Henry Steele Commager, *Documents of American History.*

Secondary Sources

The workings of the British mercantile system are detailed in Charles M. Andrews' vast *Colonial Period of American History* (4 vols., 1935–1938) and in Lawrence H. Gipson's still more ambitious *British Empire before the American Revolution* (15 vols., 1936–1970). Recent efforts to analyze the colonial empire are James Henretta, *"Salutary Neglect": Colonial Administration under the Duke of Newcastle* (1972), and Michael Kammen's especially interesting *Empire and Interest* (1970). The French colonial effort is described in George M. Wrong, *The Rise and Fall of New France* (2 vols., 1928). Calvin Martin, *Keepers of the Game* (1978), offers a provocative interpretation of the fur trade and its impact on Indian societies. See also Shepard Krech III, ed., *Indians, Animals and the Fur Trade: A Critique of Keepers of the Game* (1981). The Anglo-French struggle is recounted in Howard H. Peckham, *The Colonial Wars, 1689–1762* (1964). Alan Rogers, *Empire and Liberty: American Resistance to the British Authority 1755–1763* (1974), investigates American participation in the Seven Years' War. Classic accounts are Francis Parkman's several volumes, including *Count Frontenac and New France under Louis XIV* (1877), *Montcalm and Wolfe* (2 vols., 1884), and *A Half-Century of Conflict* (1892). Parkman's tomes are condensed, without serious loss of flavor, in *The Battle for North America*, edited by John Tebbel (1948), and *The Parkman Reader*, edited by Samuel E. Morison (1955). An impressive biography is Douglas S. Freeman, *Young Washington* (2 vols., 1948), a subject treated in less detail in James T. Flexner, *George Washington: The Forge of Experience* (1965). See also Bernhard Knollenberg's revealing *George Washington: The Virginia Period* (1965).

6

The Road to Revolution

> The Revolution was effected before the war commenced. The Revolution was in the minds and hearts of the people.
>
> *John Adams, 1818*

The Deep Roots of Revolution

In a broad sense, the American Revolution was not the same thing as the American War of Independence. The war itself lasted only eight years. But the Revolution lasted over a century and a half and began when the first permanent English settlers set foot on the new continent. Insurrection of thought usually precedes insurrection of deed. Over the years such a ferment had occurred in the thinking of the colonists that the Revolution was partially completed in their minds before the musketballs began to fly. America was a revolutionary force from the day of its discovery.

England's colonies were settled largely by emigrants who were discontented or rebellious in spirit—by people who had failed to adjust themselves to their harsh lot in the Old World. Most of them had not been able to get along, whether socially, politically, economically, or religiously. Some of them were tired of taking off their hats and standing bareheaded in the presence of their "betters." Others wanted a larger share in government, or a richer portion of this world's goods, or an opportunity to worship God in their own peculiar way.

The nightmare of crossing the Atlantic normally lasted about six to eight weeks, often much longer. Ships were frequently turned into "floating coffins" by food shortages or epidemics of disease; in one extreme case 350 of 400 passengers and crew perished. Cannibalism was not unknown, and starving voyagers fought over the bodies of vermin. As a sailor's song ran:

> We ate the mice, we ate the rats,
> And through the hold we ran like cats.

Such a perilous crossing left many emotional scars. Survivors who staggered ashore on the promised land were, as a rule, isolated spiritually from the faraway Old World. They were more than ever aware that the long arm of the London government, enfeebled by 3,000 miles

(4,800 kilometers) of ocean, could not reach them nearly so effectively as at home. Distance weakens authority; great distance weakens authority greatly.

America's lonely wilderness likewise stimulated ideas of independence. Back in England some villagers had lived near graveyards that contained the bones of their ancestors for a thousand years past. Born into such conservative surroundings, the poor peasants did not question the social rut in which they found themselves. But in the New World they were not held down by the scowl of their overlords.

In America all was strange, crude, different. Dense forests and the rugged pioneering conditions changed patterns of living and consequently habits of thought. Those wretched settlers perished who could not adapt themselves to their raw surroundings, and hundreds of the early Virginia colonists paid the supreme penalty. Before long, Americans were eating Indian corn, wearing Indian moccasins and buckskin, and in extreme instances on the frontier uttering the war whoop as they scalped their fallen Indian foe. Hacking a home out of the wildwood with an ax developed strength, self-confidence, individualism, and a spirit of independence.

As the Americans matured, they acquired privileges of self-government enjoyed by no other colonial peoples. They set up thirteen parliaments of their own and aped the parliamentary methods of the mother country. Ultimately they came to regard their own legislative bodies as more or less on a footing with the great mother of parliaments in London. One governor of Rhode Island would wear no wig unless it had been made in England and was exactly like that worn by the speaker of the British House of Commons.

> Adam Smith, the Scottish "Father of Modern Economics," frontally attacked mercantilism in 1776: "To prohibit a great people, however, from making all that they can of every part of their own produce, or from employing their stock and industry in the way that they judge most advantageous to themselves, is a manifest violation of the most sacred rights of mankind."

The Mercantile Theory

Britain's empire was acquired in a "fit of absent-mindedness," as the old saying goes, and there is much truth in it. Not one of the original thirteen colonies, except Georgia, was formally planted by the British government. The actual founding was done haphazardly by trading companies, religious groups, land speculators, and others. Ignoring the high-minded and far-visioned aspirations of pioneering Puritans, Quakers, and other colonizers, authorities in London did not even dream that a new nation was being born.

Machinery in Britain for controlling the colonies was relatively simple. As it had evolved by 1696, the principal agency was the Board of Trade, joined in an advisory capacity by certain other prominent officials. With the passage of time, interest in the board flagged, and membership on it became something of a joke. Yet the recommendations of the board regarding the colonies were often made into law, either by act of Parliament or in regulations adopted by the Privy Council (the king's advisers).

The theory that shaped and justified English exploitation of the American colonies was mercantilism. According to this doctrine the colonies existed for the benefit of the mother country; they should add to its wealth, prosperity, and self-sufficiency. Otherwise, why go to all the trouble and expense of governing and protecting them? The settlers were regarded more or less as tenants. They were expected to produce tobacco and other products needed in England and not to bother their heads with dangerous experiments in agriculture or self-government.

Specifically, how were the American colonies to benefit the mother country? First of all, they were to ensure Britain's naval supremacy by furnishing ships, ships' stores, sailors, and trade. In addition, they were to provide a profitable consumers' market for the English manufacturers at home. Finally, they were to keep gold and silver money within the empire by growing products, such as sugar, that otherwise would have to be bought from foreigners. The ideal of "buy British" would thus be promoted in a manner that foreshadowed later protective tariffs.

Mercantilist Trammels on Trade

Parliament passed numerous measures to enforce the mercantile system. Most famous were the Navigation Laws. The first of these, enacted in 1650, was aimed at rival Dutch shippers who were elbowing their way into the American carrying trade. The Navigation Laws worked to restrict commerce to and from the colonies to English vessels. Such regulation not only kept money within the empire but bolstered the British—and colonial—merchant marine, which in turn was an indispensable auxiliary to the Royal Navy.

An alert Parliament from time to time enacted additional laws that were favorable to the motherland. European goods consigned to America had to be landed first in England, where customs duties could be collected and where the British middleman would get his cut of the profit. Still other curbs required certain "enumerated" products, notably tobacco, to be shipped to England and not to a foreign market, though prices in Europe might be higher.

In the interests of the empire, settlers were even restricted in what they might produce at home. They were forbidden to manufacture for export certain products, such as woolen cloth and beaver hats, because the colonies were supposed to complement and not compete with English industry.

Americans also felt the pinch in the area of currency. No banks existed in the colonies, and the money problem on the eve of the Revolution was acute. Industrious colonials were now busily buying more goods from England than they were selling to her, so the difference had to be made up in hard cash. Every year gold and silver money, much of it in quaint Spanish coins from the West Indies, was drained out of the colonies. The colonials simply did not have enough left for the convenience of everyday purchases. Barter became necessary, and even butter, nails, pitch, and feathers were used for purposes of exchange.

Currency problems came to a boil when dire need finally forced many of the colonies to issue paper money, which unfortunately depreciated. British merchants and creditors, understandably worried, squawked so loudly that Parliament was compelled to act. It restrained the

> As the Boston Gazette declared in 1765, "A colonist cannot make a button, a horseshoe, nor a hobnail, but some snooty ironmonger or respectable buttonmaker of Britain shall bawl and squall that his honor's worship is most egregiously maltreated, injured, cheated, and robbed by the rascally American republicans."

colonial legislatures from printing paper currency and from passing lax bankruptcy laws—practices that might result in defrauding British merchants. The Americans, who felt that their welfare was again being sacrificed, reacted angrily. Another burning grievance was thus heaped upon the pile of combustibles already smoldering.

London officialdom naturally kept a watchful eye on the legislation passed by the colonial assemblies. If such laws conflicted with British regulations or policy, they might be summarily declared null and void by the Privy Council.

The Female Combatants Britain is symbolized as a lady of fashion, and her rebellious daughter as an Indian princess. (Courtesy of The Print Collection, Lewis Walpole Library, Yale University.)

This "royal veto" was in fact used rather sparingly—469 times in connection with 8,563 laws. But the colonists nevertheless fiercely resented it. They felt aggrieved when, in the interests of the mother country, they were forbidden to make reforms that they deemed desirable, such as curbing the degrading trade in African slaves.

The Merits of Mercantilism

Red-blooded Americans have long regarded the British mercantile system as thoroughly selfish and deliberately oppressive, if not downright malicious. The truth is that until 1763 the Navigation Laws imposed no intolerable burden, partly because they were laxly enforced. Ingenious colonial merchants early learned to disregard or evade restrictions that they found vexatious. In fact, some of the early American fortunes were amassed by wholesale smuggling. Wealthy and vain John Hancock of Massachusetts came to be known as the "King of Smugglers," though his illicit activity was greatly exaggerated.

Americans, in addition, were fortunate enough to reap direct benefits from the mercantile system. London paid liberal bounties or price supports to those colonials who produced ships' parts and ships' stores, even though English competitors complained heatedly. When independence came, the bounties dried up and many of these American producers were forced to the wall.

Virginia tobacco planters, in particular, enjoyed valuable privileges. While forbidden to ship their pungent yellow leaf to any place other than England, the planters were guaranteed a monopoly of the British market. Tobacco growing was also outlawed in England and Ireland, although the plant had already been raised in England with some success.

American colonials additionally fared well in other fields. They enjoyed the undiluted rights of Englishmen, as well as unusual opportunities for self-government. They were not compelled to tax themselves to support a professional army and navy for protection against the French, Dutch, Spaniards, Indians, and pirates. Although the colonists went to some little expense in "training" militias, they enjoyed the shield of a strong army of British redcoats and the mightiest navy in the world—without a penny of cost. After independence, the American people would themselves be required to pay the costs of maintaining a tiny army and navy, both of which afforded inadequate protection.

In manufacturing and trade the New World settlers did not fare badly. They were denied the privilege of fabricating specified articles for export, notably fur hats, but this regulation worked no serious hardships, because it was laxly enforced and because other pursuits were usually more profitable. Americans were forced to deal with the British middleman, but they would have done so anyhow, owing to a common language, standard pounds and shillings,

Paul Revere, c. 1768 *This painting by John Singleton Copley of the famed silversmith-horseman challenged convention—but reflected the new democratic spirit of the age—by portraying an artisan in working clothes. Note how Copley has depicted the serene confidence of the master craftsman and Revere's quiet pride in his work. (Museum of Fine Arts, Boston. Gift of Joseph W., William B., and Edward H. R. Revere.)*

liberal credit arrangements, and familiar business methods.

"Prosperity trickles down" is a common saying; and it is true that the Americans enjoyed a generous share of Britain's profits under the time-honored mercantile system. The average American was probably better off economically than the average English person at home. If the colonies existed for the benefit of the mother country, it was hardly less true that the mother country existed for the benefit of the colonies. The well-meaning officials in London were working for the welfare of the empire as a whole, and they gave overall unity to its policies. A wise owner does not disembowel or starve the goose that lays the golden eggs. Mistakes were made by the British authorities, but they were not, until revolt had erupted, the mistakes of malice.

Mercantilism had sufficient merit to be widely adopted and long perpetuated. All other colonial nations of that age, including Spain and France, embraced mercantilistic principles completely and enforced them ironhandedly. Mercantilism has endured to the present century, even in the United States. Interested groups of Americans seek to ensure prosperity for manufacturers and wage earners by protective tariffs and to bolster the national defense by subsidies to shipbuilders. American navigation laws—shades of the seventeenth century!—are still designed to prevent foreign shippers from encroaching on coastwise trade, even that between Hawaii and the mainland.

The Menace of Mercantilism

Even when painted in its rosiest colors, the mercantile system burdened the colonials with annoying liabilities. Economic initiative was stifled because Americans were not at complete liberty to buy, sell, ship, or manufacture under conditions that they found most profitable. The southern colonies, as "pets," were generally favored over the northern ones, chiefly because they grew non-English products like tobacco, sugar, and rice. Revolution was one seed that sprouted vigorously from the stony soil of New England, for the proud descendants of the Puri-

English statesman Edmund Burke warned in 1775: "Young man, there is America—which at this day serves for little more than to amuse you with stories of savage men and uncouth manners; yet shall, before you taste of death, show itself equal to the whole of that commerce which now attracts the envy of the world."

tans greatly resented being treated like unwanted relatives.

One-crop Virginians, despite London's preference for the southern colonies, also nursed rankling grievances. Forced to sell their tobacco in England, they were at the mercy of British merchants, who often gouged them. Many of the fashionable Virginia planters were plunged into debt by the falling price of tobacco and were forced to buy their necessities in England by mortgaging future crops. Some debts, becoming hereditary, were bequeathed from one generation to the next.

Impoverished Virginia thus joined restless Massachusetts in agitating for revolt against England. Unfriendly critics sneered that the Virginians' cry, "Liberty or Death," might better have been "Liberty or Debt." While this charge was unfair in many cases, countless Virginians welcomed the opportunity to end their economic bondage to the mother country.

Finally—and of supreme importance—mercantilism was debasing to the Americans. The colonies, many of them felt, were being used or milked, as cows are milked. They were to be kept in a state of perpetual economic adolescence and never allowed to come of age. As Benjamin Franklin wrote in 1775:

> We have an old mother that peevish is
> grown;
> She snubs us like children that scarce walk
> alone;
> She forgets we're grown up and have sense
> of our own.

Revolution broke out, as Theodore Roosevelt later remarked, because England failed to recognize an emerging nation when it saw one.

The Stamp Tax Uproar

The costly Seven Years' War, which ended in 1763, marked a new relationship between Britain and her transatlantic colonies. A revolution in British colonial policy precipitated the American Revolution.

Victory-flushed Britain emerged from the conflict possessing one of the biggest empires in the world—and also, less happily, the biggest debt. It amounted to £140 million, about half of which had been incurred in defending the American colonies. British officials wisely had no intention of asking the colonials to help pay off this crushing burden. But London felt that the Americans should be asked to defray one-third the cost of maintaining a garrison of some ten thousand redcoats, presumably for the colonies' own protection.

Prime Minister George Grenville, an honest and able financier not noted for tact, moved vigorously. Dedicated to efficiency, he aroused the resentment of the colonials in 1763 by ordering the British navy to enforce the Navigation Laws. He also secured from Parliament the so-called Sugar Act of 1764, the first law ever passed by that body for raising revenue in the colonies for the crown. Among various provisions, it increased the duty on foreign sugar imported from the West Indies. After bitter protests from the colonials, the duties were lowered substantially, and the agitation died down. But resentment was kept burning by the Quartering Act of 1765. It required certain colonies to provide food and quarters for British troops.

Then in the same year, 1765, Grenville imposed the most ominous measure of all: a stamp tax, to raise revenues to support the new military force. The Stamp Act required the use of stamped paper or the affixing of stamps, certifying payment of tax. Involved were about fifty trade items and certain types of commercial and legal documents, including playing cards, pamphlets, newspapers, diplomas, bills of lading, and marriage licenses.

Grenville regarded all these measures as reasonable and just. He was simply asking the Americans to pay their fair share for colonial defense, through taxes that were already familiar in England. In fact, Englishmen for two generations had endured a stamp tax far heavier than that passed for the colonies.

Yet the Americans were angrily aroused at what they regarded as Grenville's fiscal aggression. The new laws pinched their pocketbooks and, even more ominously, menaced the local liberties they had come to assume as a matter of right. Thus, some colonial assemblies defiantly refused to comply with the Quartering Act or voted only a fraction of the supplies that it called for.

Worse still, Grenville's noxious legislation seemed to jeopardize the basic rights of the colonists as Englishmen. Both the Sugar Act and the Stamp Act provided for trying offenders in the hated admiralty courts, where juries were not allowed. The burden of proof was on the defendants, who were assumed to be guilty unless they could prove themselves innocent. Trial by jury and the doctrine of "innocent until proved guilty" were ancient privileges that the English people everywhere, including the American colonials, held most dear.

And why was a British army needed at all in the colonies, now that the French were expelled from the continent and Pontiac's warriors crushed? Could its real purpose be to whip rebellious colonials themselves into line? Many Americans began to sniff the strong scent of a conspiracy to strip them of their historic liberties. They lashed back violently, and the Stamp Act became a target that drew their most ferocious fire.

Angry throats raised the cry, "No taxation without representation." There was some irony in the slogan, because the seaports and tidewater towns that were most wrathful against the Stamp Act had long denied full representation

A Royal Stamp *The motto in French is translated "Shame to him who evil thinks."*

A Parody of the "Fatal Stamp"

The famous circular letter from the Massachusetts House of Representatives (1768) stated: ". . . considering the utter impracticability of their ever being fully and equally represented in Parliament, and the great expense that must unavoidably attend even a partial representation there, this House think that a taxation of their constituents, even without their consent, grievous as it is, would be preferable to any representation that could be admitted for them there."

to their own backcountry pioneers. But now the agitated colonials took the high ground of principle. They vividly recollected the theories of popular government developed during England's own Puritan revolution a century earlier. American firebrands hurled these doctrines back at their English masters, who were stunned at the keenness of the colonials' historical memory.

The Americans made a distinction between "legislation" and "taxation." They conceded the right of Parliament to legislate about matters that affected the entire empire, including the regulation of trade. But they steadfastly denied the right of Parliament, in which no Americans were seated, to impose taxes on Americans. Only their own elected colonial legislatures, the Americans insisted, could legally tax them. Taxes levied by the distant English Parliament amounted to robbery, a piratical assault on the sacred rights of property.

Grenville dismissed these American protests as hairsplitting absurdities. The power of Parliament was supreme and undivided, he asserted, and in any case the Americans *were* represented in Parliament. Elaborating the theory of

"virtual representation," Grenville claimed that every member of Parliament represented all British subjects, even those Americans in Boston or Charleston who had never voted for a member of the London Parliament.

The Americans scoffed at the notion of virtual representation. And at bottom, they did not really want direct representation in Parliament, which might have seemed like a sensible compromise. If they had obtained it, any gouty member of the House of Commons could have proposed an oppressive tax bill for the colonies, and the American representatives, few in numbers, would have stood bereft of a principle with which to resist.

Thus the principle of no taxation without representation was supremely important, and the colonials clung to it with tenacious consistency. When the English replied that the sovereign power of government could not be divided between "legislative" authority in London and "taxing" authority in the colonies, they forced the Americans to deny the authority of Parliament altogether and to begin to consider their own political independence. This chain of logic eventually led to revolutionary consequences.

Nicholas Cresswell, a Tory, observed in 1774: "The New Englanders by their canting, whining, insinuating tricks have persuaded the rest of the Colonies that the Government is going to make absolute slaves of them."

Parliament Forced to Repeal the Stamp Act

Colonial outcries against the hated stamp tax took various forms. The most conspicuous assemblage was the Stamp Act Congress of 1765, which brought together in New York City

Boycott Handbill

WILLIAM JACKSON,

an IMPORTER; at the

BRAZEN HEAD,

North Side of the TOWN-HOUSE,

and Opposite the Town-Pump, in

Corn-hill, BOSTON.

It is defired that the Sons and Daughters of LIBERTY, would not buy any one thing of him, for in fo doing they will bring Difgrace upon themfelves, and their Pofterity, for ever and ever, AMEN.

twenty-seven distinguished delegates from nine colonies. After dignified debate, the members drew up a statement of their rights and grievances and besought the king and Parliament to repeal the odious legislation.

The Stamp Act Congress, which was largely ignored in England, made little splash at the time in America. But it did do something to break down sectional suspicions, for it brought together around the same table leaders from the different and rival colonies. It was one more halting but significant step toward intercolonial unity.

More effective than the congress was the widespread adoption of nonimportation agreements against British goods. Woolen garments of homespun became fashionable, and the eating of lamb chops was discouraged so that the wool-bearing sheep would be allowed to mature. Nonimportation agreements were in fact a promising stride toward union; they spontaneously united the American people for the first time in common action.

Violence also attended colonial protests. Groups of ardent spirits, known as Sons of Liberty and Daughters of Liberty, took the law into their own hands. Crying "Liberty, Property, and No Stamps," they enforced the nonimportation agreements against violators, often with a generous coat of tar and feathers. Houses of unpop-

ular officials were ransacked, their money was stolen, and stamp agents were hanged on liberty poles, albeit in effigy.

Shaken by violence, the machinery for collecting the tax broke down. On that dismal day in 1765 when the new act was to go into effect, the stamp agents had all been forced to resign, and there was no one to sell the stamps. While flags flapped at half-mast, the law was openly and flagrantly defied—or rather, nullified.

England was hard hit. America then bought about one-quarter of all British exports, and about one-half of British shipping was devoted to the American trade. Merchants, manufacturers, and shippers suffered from the colonial nonimportation agreements, and hundreds of laborers were thrown out of work. Loud demands converged on Parliament for repeal of the Stamp Act. But many of the members could not understand why 7.5 million Britons had to pay heavy taxes to protect the colonies, while some 2 million colonials refused to pay for only one-third of the cost of their own defense.

After a stormy debate, and as a matter of expediency and not of right, Parliament in 1766 reluctantly repealed the Stamp Act. At the same time, and by an overwhelming vote, it saved face by passing the Declaratory Act. This futile measure proclaimed that Parliament had the right "to bind" the colonies "in all cases whatsoever." A bare assertion of this right was but a feeble victory for parental authority, for the unruly colonials had proved that the London government could be forced to yield to boycotts and mob action.

America forthwith burst into an uproar of rejoicing. Grateful residents of New York erected a leaden statue to King George III—a tribute that was later melted into thousands of bullets to be fired at his own troops.

The Townshend Tea Tax and the Boston "Massacre"

Control of the British ministry was now seized by the gifted but erratic "Champagne Charley" Townshend, a man who could deliver brilliant speeches in Parliament while drunk. Rashly promising to pluck feathers from the colonial

Hanging John Huske in Effigy *A Paul Revere engraving showing the fate in America of an alleged supporter of the Stamp Act. (American Antiquarian Society.)*

royal governors into line by controlling the purse, regarded Townshend's tax as another attempt to enchain them. Their worst fears took on greater reality when the London government, after passing the Townshend taxes, suspended the legislature of New York for failure to comply with the Quartering Act in 1767.

Nonimportation agreements, previously potent, were quickly revived against the Townshend Acts. But they proved less effective than those devised against the Stamp Act. The colonials, again enjoying prosperity, took the new tax less seriously than might have been expected, largely because it was light and indirect. They found, moreover, that they could secure smuggled tea at a cheap price, and consequently smugglers increased their activities, especially in Massachusetts.

British officials, faced with a breakdown of law and order, landed two regiments of troops in Boston in 1768. Many of the soldiers, as might be expected, were drunken and profane characters. Liberty-loving colonials, resenting

goose with a minimum of squawking, he persuaded Parliament in 1767 to pass the Townshend Acts. The most important of these new regulations was a light import duty on glass, white lead, paper, and tea. Townshend, seizing on a dubious distinction between internal and external taxes, made this tax, unlike the Stamp Act, an indirect customs duty payable at American ports. But to the colonials, this was a distinction without a difference. For them, the real difficulty remained taxes—in any form—without representation.

Flushed with their recent victory over the stamp tax, the colonists were in a rebellious mood. The impost on tea was especially irksome, for an estimated 1 million persons drank the refreshing brew twice a day, and even tipplers used it when alcohol was not available.

The new Townshend revenues, worse yet, would be used to pay the salaries of the royal governors and judges in America. From the standpoint of efficient administration by London, this was a reform long overdue. But the ultrasuspicious Americans, who had beaten the

Redcoats Landing in Boston

The Boston Massacre, 1770 *This widely reprinted engraving by Paul Revere was both art and propaganda. (Library of Congress.)*

the presence of the red-coated "ruffians," taunted the "bloody backs" unmercifully.

A clash was inevitable. On the evening of March 5, 1770, a crowd of some sixty townspeople set upon a squad of about ten "bloody backs," one of whom was hit by a club and another of whom was knocked down. Acting apparently without orders but under extreme provocation, the troops opened fire and killed or wounded eleven "innocent" citizens. One of the first to die was Crispus Attucks, described by contemporaries as a powerfully built runaway "mulatto" and as a leader of the mob. Both sides were in some degree to blame, and in the subsequent trial only two of the soldiers could be found guilty of manslaughter. They were released after being branded on the hand.

The so-called Boston Massacre further inflamed the colonials against the British, especially after the conviction spread that the Americans had been wholly unoffending. Paul Revere, the artist-horseman, wrote:

> Unhappy Boston! see thy sons deplore
> Thy hallowed walks besmear'd with guiltless
>   gore.

Massacre Day was observed in Boston as a patriotic holiday until 1776, when the more glorious Fourth of July eclipsed it.

The Seditious Committees of Correspondence

By 1770 King George III, then only thirty-two years old, was strenuously attempting to restore the declining power of the British monarchy. He was a good man in his private morals, but he proved to be a bad ruler. Earnest, industrious, stubborn, lustful for power, and later plagued with periodic fits of supposed madness, he surrounded himself with cooperative "yes men," notably his corpulent prime minister, Lord North.

The ill-timed Townshend Acts had failed to produce revenue, though producing near-rebellion. Net proceeds from the tax in one year were £295, and during that time the annual military costs to Britain in the colonies had mounted to £170,000. Nonimportation agreements, though feebly enforced, were pinching British manufacturers. The government of Lord North, bowing to various pressures, finally persuaded Parliament to repeal the Townshend revenue duties. But the three-pence tax on tea was retained to keep alive the principle of parliamentary taxation.

Flames of discontent in America continued to be fanned by numerous incidents, including the redoubled efforts of the British officials to enforce the Navigation Laws. Resistance was further whipped up by a master propagandist and engineer of rebellion, Samuel Adams of Boston, a cousin of John Adams. Unimpressive in appearance (his hands trembled), he lived and breathed only for politics. His friends had to buy him a presentable suit of clothes when he left Massachusetts on intercolonial business. Zealous, tenacious, and courageous, he was ultrasensitive to infractions of colonial rights. Cherishing a deep faith in the common people, he appealed effectively to what was called his "trained mob." Skillful also as a pamphleteer, he soon became known as the "Penman of the Revolution."

Samuel Adams' signal contribution was to organize in Massachusetts the local committees of correspondence. After he had formed the first one in Boston during 1772, some eighty towns in the colony speedily set up similar organizations. Their chief function was to spread propaganda and information by interchanging letters and thus keep alive opposition to British policy. One critic referred to the committees as "the foulest, subtlest, and most venomous serpent ever issued from the egg of sedition." No more effective device for stimulating resistance could have been contrived, and modern communist revolutionists have adopted some of its underground techniques in establishing "cells."

Intercolonial committees of correspondence were the next logical step. Virginia led the way in 1773 by creating such a body as a standing committee of the House of Burgesses. Within a short period of time every colony had established a central committee through which it could exchange ideas and information with other colonies. These intercolonial groups, which were supremely significant in stimulating and disseminating sentiment in favor of united action, evolved directly into the first American congresses.

Tea Parties at Boston and Elsewhere

Thus far—that is, by 1773—nothing had happened to make rebellion inevitable. Nonimportation was weakening. Increasing numbers of colonials were reluctantly paying the tea tax, because the legal tea was now cheaper than the smuggled tea and cheaper than tea in England. Even John Adams on one occasion hoped that the tea he was drinking was smuggled Dutch tea, but he could not be sure and did not want to know.

A new ogre entered the picture in 1773. The powerful British East India Company, overburdened with 17 million pounds of unsold tea, was facing bankruptcy. If it collapsed, the London government would lose heavily in tax revenue. The ministry therefore decided to assist the company by awarding it a complete monopoly of the American tea business. The terms thus granted would enable the giant corporation to sell the coveted leaves more cheaply than ever before, even with the three-pence tax added. But to many American consumers, principle was more important than price.

If British officials insisted on the letter of the law, violence would be inevitable, for the new tea monopoly had many features that were hateful to the colonials. Above all, it seemed like a shabby attempt to trick the Americans, with the bait of cheaper tea, into acceptance of the detested tax. Fatefully, the British colonial authorities decided to enforce the law literally, and once more the colonials rose in their wrath. Not a single one of the several thousand chests of tea shipped by the company reached the hands of the consignees. At Annapolis, the Marylanders burned both the cargo and the vessel, while proclaiming "Liberty and Independence or death in pursuit of it." At Boston, which was host to the most famous tea party of all, a band of white townsfolk, disguised as Indians, boarded the three tea ships on December 16, 1773. They smashed open 342 chests and dumped the "cursed weed" into the harbor, while a silent crowd watched approvingly from the wharves as salty tea was brewed for the fish.

Reactions varied. Extremists in America rejoiced; conservatives shuddered. This wanton destruction of private property was going too

Public Punishment *Boston customs official, John Malcolm, paraded after being tarred and feathered, January 25, 1774. (Detail from an English cartoon. Harvard College Library.)*

far. The British at home were outraged; even friends of America hung their heads. Punishment and coercion were the only possible responses of the London authorities, as long as the mercantilist philosophy prevailed and the colonials refused to accept responsibility. The granting of some kind of home rule to the Americans might have prevented rebellion, but not many Britons of that age were blessed with such vision. Edmund Burke, a friend of America in Parliament, stoically declared, "To tax and to please, no more than to love and be wise, is not given to men."

> *Josiah Quincy, a prominent Boston patriot and orator, lashed out against the Boston Port Act: "Blandishments will not fascinate us, nor will threats of a 'halter' [noose] intimidate. For, under God, we are determined that wheresoever, whensoever, or howsoever we shall be called to make our exit, we will die free men." He died at sea the next year while on a diplomatic mission to England.*

Parliament Passes the "Intolerable Acts"

An outraged Parliament responded speedily to the Boston Tea Party with measures that brewed a revolution. By huge majorities in 1774 it passed a series of "Repressive Acts," which were designed to chastise Boston in particular, Massachusetts in general. They were branded in America as "the massacre of American Liberty."

Most drastic of all was the Boston Port Act. It closed the tea-stained harbor until damages were paid and order could be assured. By other "Intolerable Acts"—as they were called in America—many of the chartered rights of colonial Massachusetts were swept away. Restrictions were likewise placed on the precious town meetings. Contrary to previous practice, enforcing officials who killed colonials in the line of duty could now be sent to England for trial. There, suspicious Americans assumed, they would be likely to get off scot-free.

By a fateful coincidence, the "Intolerable Acts" were accompanied in 1774 by the Quebec Act. Passed at the same time, it was erroneously regarded in English-speaking America as one of the "repressive" measures. Actually, the Quebec Act was a good law in bad company. For many years the British government had debated how it should administer the sixty thousand or so conquered French subjects in Canada, and it had finally framed this farsighted and statesmanlike measure. The French were guaranteed their Catholic religion. They were also permitted to retain many of their old customs and institutions, which did not include a representative assembly or trial by jury in civil cases. In addition, the old boundaries of the Province of Quebec were now extended southward all the way to the Ohio River.

The Quebec Act, from the viewpoint of the French Canadians, was a shrewd and conciliatory measure. If England had only shown as much foresight in dealing with its English-speaking colonies, it might not have lost them.

But from the viewpoint of the American colonials as a whole, the Quebec Act was especially noxious. All the other "repressive" laws slapped directly at Massachusetts, but this one had a much wider range. It seemed to set a dangerous precedent in America against jury trials and popular assemblies. It alarmed land speculators, who were distressed to see the huge trans-Allegheny area snatched from their grasp. It aroused the host of anti-Catholics, who were shocked by the extension of Roman Catholic jurisdiction southward into a huge region that had once been earmarked for Protestantism—a region about as large as the thirteen original colonies. One angry Protestant cried that there ought to be a "jubilee in hell" over this enormous gain for "popery."

The Continental Congress and Bloodshed

American dissenters, outraged by the Quebec Act, responded sympathetically to the plight of Massachusetts. It had put itself in the wrong by the wanton destruction of the tea cargoes; now the mother country had put itself in the wrong by brutal punishment that did not seem to fit the crime. Flags were flown at half-mast throughout the colonies on the day that the Boston Port Act went into effect, and sister colonies rallied to send food to the stricken city. Rice was shipped even from faraway South Carolina.

Quebec before and after 1774 *Young Alexander Hamilton voiced the fears of many colonists when he warned that the Quebec Act of 1774 would introduce "priestly tyranny" into Canada, making that country another Spain or Portugal. "Does not your blood run cold," he asked, "to think that an English Parliament should pass an act for the establishment of arbitrary power and Popery in such a country?"*

Samuel Adams (1722–1803) *A second cousin of John Adams, he contributed a potent pen and tongue to the American Revolution as a political agitator and organizer of rebellion. He was the leading spirit in hosting the Boston Tea Party. A failure in the brewing business, he was sent by Massachusetts to the First Continental Congress of 1774. He signed the Declaration of Independence and served in Congress until 1781. (Museum of Fine Arts, Boston.)*

Most memorable of the responses to the "Intolerable Acts" was the summoning of a Continental Congress in 1774. It was to meet in Philadelphia to consider ways of redressing colonial grievances. Twelve of the thirteen colonies, with Georgia alone missing, sent fifty-five distinguished men, among them Samuel Adams, John Adams, George Washington, and Patrick Henry. Intercolonial frictions were partially melted away by social activity after working hours; in fifty-four days George Washington dined at his own lodgings only nine times.

The First Continental Congress deliberated for seven weeks, September 5 to October 26, 1774. It was not a legislative but a consultative body; it was a convention rather than a congress. John Adams played a stellar role. Eloquently swaying his colleagues to a revolution-

ary course, he helped defeat by the narrowest of margins a proposal by the moderates for a species of American home rule under British direction. After prolonged argument, the Congress drew up several dignified papers. These included a ringing Declaration of Rights, as well as solemn appeals to other British American colonies, to the king, and to the British people.

The most significant action of the Congress was the creation of The Association. Unlike previous nonimportation agreements, this one called for a *complete* boycott of British goods: nonimportation, nonexportation, and nonconsumption. A document known as The Association, by providing for concerted action, was the closest approach to a written constitution that the colonies as a unit had yet devised. But still there was no genuine drive toward independence—merely an effort to bring about a repeal of the offensive legislation and a return to the happy days before parliamentary taxation. If

Abigail Adams *The wife of Revolutionary leader and future president John Adams, she was a prominent Patriot in her own right. She was also among the first Americans to see, however faintly, the implications of Revolutionary ideas for changing the status of women. (New York State Historical Association, Cooperstown, New York.)*

colonial grievances were redressed, well and good; if not, the Congress was to meet again in May 1775.

But the deadly drift toward war continued. The petitions of the Continental Congress were rejected, after considerable debate, by strong majorities in Parliament. In America chickens squawked and tar kettles bubbled as violators of The Association were tarred and feathered. Muskets were being collected, men were openly drilling, and a clash seemed imminent.

In April 1775, the British commander in Boston sent a detachment of troops to nearby Lexington and Concord. They were to seize stores of colonial gunpowder and also to bag the "rebel" ringleaders, Samuel Adams and John Hancock. At Lexington, the colonial "Minute Men" refused to disperse rapidly enough, and shots were fired that killed eight Americans and wounded several more. The affair was more the "Lexington Massacre" than a battle. The redcoats pushed on to Concord, whence they were forced to retreat by the homespun Americans, whom Emerson immortalized:

> By the rude bridge that arched the flood,
> Their flag to April's breeze unfurled,
> Here once the embattled farmers stood,
> And fired the shot heard round the world.*

The bewildered British, fighting off murderous fire from militiamen crouched behind thick stone walls, finally regained the sanctuary of Boston. Licking their wounds, they could count about three hundred casualties, including some seventy killed. England now had a war on her hands.

Imperial Strength and Weakness

Aroused Americans had brashly rebelled against a mighty empire. The population odds were about three to one against the rebels—some 7.5 million Britons to 2.5 million colonials. The odds in monetary wealth and naval power were overwhelmingly in favor of the mother country.

Black people were only a partial asset to the American cause, for they could hardly be ex-

---

*Ralph Waldo Emerson, "Concord Hymn."

Privately (1776) General Washington expressed his distrust of militia: "To place any dependence upon militia is assuredly resting on a broken staff. . . . The sudden change in their manner of living . . . brings on sickness in many, impatience in all, and such an unconquerable desire of returning to their respective homes that it not only produces shameful and scandalous desertions among themselves, but infuses the like spirit in others. . . . If I was called upon to declare upon oath whether the militia have been most serviceable or hurtful upon the whole, I should subscribe to the latter."

pected to fight for a society that had enslaved them. Still, about five thousand saw military service, whether as freemen or as slaves promised freedom, and in a number of engagements fought bravely. Even larger numbers, often guaranteed freedom with no strings attached, fled to enemy lines and left the country when the British departed.

Britain then boasted a professional army of some fifty thousand men, as compared with the numerous but wretchedly trained American militia. George III, in addition, had the money with which to hire foreign soldiers, and some thirty thousand Germans—so-called Hessians—were ultimately employed. The British enrolled about fifty thousand American Loyalists and enlisted the services of many Indians, who though unreliable fair-weather fighters, ravaged long stretches of the frontier. One British officer boasted that the war would offer no problems that could not be solved by an "experienced sheep herder."

Yet the mother country was weaker than she seemed at first glance. Oppressed Ireland was a latent volcano, and British troops had to be detached to watch it. France, bitter from its recent defeat, was awaiting an opportunity to stab Britain in the back. The London government was confused and inept. There was no William Pitt, "Organizer of Victory," only the stubborn George III and his pliant Lord North.

Many earnest and God-fearing Britons had no desire whatever to kill their American cousins. William Pitt withdrew a son from the army rather than see him thrust his sword into fellow Anglo-Saxons struggling for liberty. The English Whig factions, opposed to Lord North's Tory factions, openly cheered American victories—at least at the outset. Aside from trying to embarrass the Tories politically, many Whigs believed that the battle for English freedom was being fought in America. If George III triumphed, his rule at home might become tyrannical. This outspoken sympathy in England, though plainly that of a minority, greatly encouraged the Americans. If they continued their resistance long enough, the Whigs might come into power and deal generously with them.

Britain's army in America had to operate under endless difficulties. The generals were second-rate; the soldiers, though on the whole capable, were brutally treated. There was one extreme case of eight hundred lashes on the bare back for striking an officer. Provisions were often scarce, rancid, and wormy. On one occasion a supply of biscuits, captured some fifteen years earlier from the French, was softened by dropping cannonballs on them.

Other handicaps loomed. The redcoats had to conquer the Americans; a draw would be a victory for the colonials. Britain was operating some 3,000 miles (4,800 kilometers) from her home base, and distance added greatly to the delays and uncertainties arising from storms and other mishaps. Military orders were issued in London that, when received months later, would not fit the changing situation.

America's geographical expanse was enormous: roughly 1,000 by 600 miles (1,600 by 970 kilometers). The united colonies had no urban nerve center, like France's Paris. British armies captured every city of any size, yet like a boxer punching a feather pillow, they made little more than a dent in the entire country. The Americans wisely traded space for time. Benjamin Franklin calculated that during the prolonged campaign in which the redcoats captured Bunker Hill and killed some 150 Yankees, about 60,000 American babies were born.

General Lafayette (1757–1834)   He gave to America not only military services but some $200,000 of his private funds. He returned to France after the American Revolution to play a conspicuous but disappointing role in the French Revolution. (The Granger Collection.)

American Pluses and Minuses

The revolutionists were blessed with outstanding leadership. George Washington was a giant among men; Benjamin Franklin was a master among diplomats. Open foreign aid, theoretically possible from the start, eventually came from France. Numerous European officers, many of them unemployed and impoverished, volunteered their swords for pay. In a class by himself was a wealthy young French nobleman, the Marquis de Lafayette. Fleeing from boredom, loving glory and ultimately liberty, at age nineteen the "French gamecock" was made a major general in the colonial army. His commission was largely a recognition of his family influence and political connections, but the services of this teenage general in securing further aid from France were invaluable.

Other conditions aided the Americans. They were fighting defensively, with the odds, all things considered, favoring the defender. In agriculture, the colonies were mainly self-sustaining, like a kind of Robinson Crusoe's island. Colonial "buckskins," moreover, were a tough, self-reliant people. As marksmen, they far outshone the British, who often pointed rather than aimed their muskets. A competent American rifleman could hit a man's head at 200 yards (183 meters).

In addition, the Americans enjoyed the moral advantage that came from belief in a just cause. The historical odds were not impossible. Other peoples had triumphed in the face of greater obstacles: the Greeks against Persians, the Swiss against Austrians, the Dutch against Spaniards.

Yet the American rebels were badly organized for war. From the earliest days they had been almost fatally lacking in unity, and the new nation lurched forward uncertainly like an uncoordinated centipede. Even the Continental Congress, which directed the conflict, was hardly more than a debating society, and it grew feebler as the struggle dragged on. "Their Congress now is quite disjoint'd," jibed an English satirist, "Since Gibbits (gallows) [are] for them appointed." Disorganized colonials fought almost the entire war before adopting a written constitution—the Articles of Confederation—in 1781.

Jealousy everywhere raised its hideous head. Individual states, proudly regarding themselves as sovereign, resented the attempts of Congress to exercise its weak powers. Sectional jealousy boiled up over the appointment of military leaders; some distrustful New Englanders almost preferred British officers to Americans from other sections.

Economic difficulties were well-nigh insuperable. Metallic money had already been heavily drained away. A cautious Continental Congress, unwilling to raise anew the explosive issue of taxation, was forced to print "Continental" paper money in great amounts. As this currency poured from the presses, it depreciated until the expression became current, "not worth a Continental." One barber contemptuously papered his shop with the almost worthless dollars. The confusion worsened when the individual states were compelled to issue depreciated paper money of their own.

Inflation of the currency inevitably skyrocketed prices. Families of the soldiers at the fighting front were hard hit, and hundreds of anxious husbands and fathers deserted. Debtors easily acquired handfuls of the semiworthless money and gleefully paid their debts "without mercy"—sometimes with the bayonets of the authorities to back them up.

A Thin Line of Heroes

Basic military supplies in the colonies were dangerously scanty, especially firearms and powder. Benjamin Franklin seriously proposed going back to the bow and arrow. Even where food was accumulated, wagons were often not available to haul it. At Valley Forge, in the winter of 1777–1778, the shivering American soldiers were without bread for three successive days. In one southern campaign some men fainted for lack of food.

Manufactured goods were generally in short supply in agricultural America, and clothing and shoes were appallingly scarce. The path of the patriot fighting men was often marked by bloody snow. At frigid Valley Forge, during one anxious period, twenty-eight hundred men were barefooted or nearly naked. Woolens were desperately needed against the wintry blasts; and in general the only real uniform of the colonial army was uniform raggedness. During a grand parade at Valley Forge, some of the officers appeared wrapped in woolen bed covers. One Rhode Island unit was known as the "Ragged, Lousy, Naked Regiment."

American militiamen were numerous but also highly unreliable. Able-bodied American males—perhaps several hundred thousand of them—had received rudimentary training, and many of these recruits served for short terms in the rebel armies. But poorly trained plowboys, though better shots, could not stand up in the open field against professional British troops advancing with bare bayonets. Many of these undisciplined warriors would, in the words of Washington, "fly from their own shadows."

> *General Washington's disgust is reflected in a diary entry for 1776: "Chimney corner patriots abound; venality, corruption, prostitution of office for selfish ends, abuse of trust, perversion of funds from a national to a private use, and speculations upon the necessities of the times pervade all interests."*

A few thousand regulars—perhaps seven thousand or eight thousand at war's end—were finally whipped into shape by stern drillmasters. Notable among these officers was an organizational genius, the salty German Baron von Steuben. He spoke no English when he reached America, but he soon taught his men that bayonets were not for broiling beefsteaks over open fires. As they gained experience, these soldiers of the Continental line could hold their own in open battle against crack British troops.

Morale in the Revolutionary army was badly undermined by American profiteers. These grasping gentry, putting profits before patriotism, sold to the British because the invader could pay in gold. Speculators forced prices sky-high; and some Bostonians made profits of 50 percent to 200 percent on army clothing while the American army was freezing at Valley Forge. Washington never had as many as twenty thousand effective troops in one place at one time, despite bounties of land and other inducements. Yet if the rebels had thrown themselves into the struggle with Revolutionary zeal, they could easily have raised many times that number.

The brutal truth is that only a select minority of the American colonials attached themselves to the cause of independence with a spirit of selfless devotion. These were the dedicated souls who bore the burden of battle and the risks of defeat; these were the freedom-loving patriots who deserved the gratitude and esteem of generations yet unborn. Seldom have so few done so much for so many.

Varying Viewpoints

Historians once assumed that the Revolution was just another chapter in the unfolding story of human liberty—a kind of divinely ordained progress toward perfection in human affairs. This approach is often called the Whig view of history. Around the beginning of this century, the concept was sharply challenged by the so-called progressive historians, who argued that not God but a sharp struggle among different social groups brought about change. "Progressives" thus saw the Revolution as stemming from class conflict and ending in a truly transformed social order. As Carl Becker put it, the Revolution was not only about home rule but about "who should rule at home." Since World War II, scholars have questioned this interpretation. They have uncovered evidence that the British imperial system really was not unduly burdensome to the colonists and, more important, that colonial society was *already* fairly democratic before 1776 (at least as regards white people).

Two questions naturally arise: What really caused the divorce of mother country and colonists, and precisely how "revolutionary" was the Revolution? Interestingly, recent scholarship, especially the work of Bernard Bailyn, has tended to emphasize not economic or political friction but ideological and even psychological factors. The root causes of the Revolution may well have been the need to resist what the colonists feared to be the conspiracy of a corrupt British government to deprive them of their liberties. Opposition to this "ministerial plot" forced Americans to reformulate their fundamental political principles and led eventually to revolution.

Select Readings

Primary Source Documents

Adam Smith's *An Inquiry into the Nature and Causes of the Wealth of Nations** (1776) is a penetrating analysis of British mercantilism. Patrick Henry's "Speech before the Virginia House of Burgesses against the Stamp Act"* (1765) was an influential statement of colonial opposition to British policy, as was John Dickinson's response to the Townshend Acts, *Letters from a Farmer in Pennsylvania* (1768). For contemporary accounts of the beginning of hostilities, see Peter Force, ed., *American Archives,* Fourth Series, Vol. 2 (1839).*

Secondary Sources

Edmund S. Morgan, *The Birth of the Republic, 1763–1789* (1959), is among the best brief accounts of the Revolutionary era. It stresses the happy coincidence of the revolutionaries' principles and their interests. Lawrence Gipson, *The Coming of the Revolution, 1763–1775* (1954), summarizes his 15-volume masterwork (cited in Chapter 5). Merrill Jensen, *The Founding of a Nation* (1968), is a more recent effort at a general synthesis, as is Robert Middlekauff's *The Glorious Cause: The American Revolution, 1763–1789* (1982). Robert R. Palmer, *The Age of the Democratic Revolution: A Political History of Europe and America, 1760–1800* (2 vols., 1959, 1964), masterfully places American events in the larger context of Western history. Three enlightening collections of essays are Jack P. Greene, ed., *The Reinterpretation of the American Revolution, 1763–1789* (1968); Stephen Kurtz and James Hutson, eds., *Essays on the American Revolution* (1973); and Alfred F. Young, ed., *The American Revolution* (1976), which generally represents a "new left" revisionist view. An interesting effort to blend British and American perspectives is Ian R. Christie and Benjamin W. Labaree, *Empire or Independence, 1760–1776* (1976). The sources of American dissatisfaction with the British imperial system can be traced in Carl Ubbelohde, *The American Colonies in the British Empire, 1607–1763* (1968), and Thomas C. Barrow, *Trade and Empire: The British Customs Service in Colonial America* (1967). Oliver M. Dickerson, *The Naviga-*tion Acts and the American Revolution* (1951), concludes that the navigation system did not put undue burdens on the colonies. Bernhard Knollenberg examines the effects of the British tightening of the imperial system in the 1760s in *Origin of the American Revolution, 1759–1766* (1960), as does Michael Kammen in *Empire and Interest* (1970). John Shy imaginatively explores an important aspect of the imperial system's effect on America in *Toward Lexington: The Role of the British Army in the Coming of the American Revolution* (1965). A perceptive short account of the American reaction to British initiatives is Edmund S. Morgan and Helen M. Morgan, *The Stamp Act Crisis* (1953). Benjamin W. Labaree discusses another instance of American reaction in *The Boston Tea Party* (1964). P. Maier focuses on the crucial role of the "mob" in *From Resistance to Revolution: Colonial Radicals and the Development of American Opposition to Britain, 1765–1776* (1972). The British side is told in Peter D. G. Thomas, *British Politics and the Stamp Act Crisis* (1975). Clinton Rossiter, *Seedtime of the Republic* (1953), stresses the importance of ideas in pushing the Revolution forward, as does Bernard Bailyn's seminal *Ideological Origins of the American Revolution* (1967), which also emphasizes the colonists' fears of a conspiracy against their liberties. Helpful biographies of key Revolutionary figures include John C. Miller, *Sam Adams* (1936); Robert D. Meade, *Patrick Henry* (1957); Merrill D. Peterson, *Thomas Jefferson and the New Nation* (1970); Dumas Malone, *Jefferson and His Time* (5 vols., 1948–1974); and Pauline Maier, *The Old Revolutionaries: Political Lives in the Age of Samuel Adams* (1980). Imaginative cultural history is found in Robert A. Gross, *The Minutemen and Their World* (1976). Edward A. Countryman emphasizes class conflict in *A People in Revolution: The American Revolution and Political Society in New York, 1760–1790* (1981). Two recent books take a psychological approach to the problem of the Revolutionary generation's assault on established authority: Kenneth S. Lynn, *A Divided People* (1977), and Jay Fliegelman, *Prodigals and Pilgrims: The American Revolution against Patriarchal Authority, 1750–1800* (1982).

7

America Secedes from the Empire

> These are the times that try men's souls. The summer soldier and the sunshine patriot will, in this crisis, shrink from the service of their country; but he that stands it now, deserves the love and thanks of man and woman.
>
> Thomas Paine, December 1776

Congress Drafts George Washington

Bloodshed at Lexington and Concord, in April of 1775, was a clarion call to arms. About twenty thousand musket-bearing "Minute Men" swarmed around Boston, there to coop up the outnumbered British.

The Second Continental Congress met in Philadelphia the next month, on May 10, 1775; and this time the full slate of thirteen colonies was represented. The conservative element in Congress was still strong, despite the shooting in Massachusetts. There was no real sentiment for independence—merely a desire to continue fighting in the hope that king and Parliament would consent to a redress of grievances. Congress hopefully drafted new appeals to the British people and king—appeals that were spurned. Anticipating a possible rebuff, the del-

egates also adopted measures to raise money and to create an army and navy.

Perhaps the most important single action of the Congress was to select George Washington, one of its members already in officer's uniform, to head the hastily improvised army besieging Boston. This choice was made with considerable misgivings. The tall, powerfully built, dignified, blue-eyed Virginia planter, then forty-three, had never risen above the rank of a colonel in the militia. His largest command had numbered only twelve hundred men, and that had been some twenty years earlier. Falling short of true military genius, Washington was actually destined to lose more pitched battles than he won.

But the distinguished Virginian was gifted with outstanding powers of leadership and immense strength of character. He radiated pa-

The Battle of Lexington and Concord, 1775 *Amos Doolittle, a Connecticut militiaman, portrayed the redcoats' costly retreat to Boston in this contemporary engraving. (Albany Institute of History and Art.)*

tience, courage, self-discipline, and a sense of justice. He was a great moral force rather than a great military mind—a symbol and a rallying point. People instinctively trusted him; they sensed that when he put himself at the head of a cause, he was prepared, if necessary, to go down with the ship. He insisted on serving without pay, though he kept a careful expense account amounting to more than $100,000. Later he sternly reprimanded his steward at Mount Vernon for providing the enemy, under duress, with supplies. He would have preferred instead to see the enemy put the torch to his mansion.

The Continental Congress, though dimly perceiving Washington's qualities of leadership, chose more wisely than it knew. His selection, in truth, was largely political. Americans in other sections, already jealous, were beginning to distrust the large New England army being collected around Boston. Prudence suggested a commander from Virginia, the largest and most populous of the colonies. As a man of wealth, both by inheritance and by marriage, Washington could not be accused of being a fortune seeker. As an aristocrat, he could be counted on to check the excesses of the masses.

Martha Washington (1732–1802) *Destined to be the first First Lady, she was the daughter of a prominent Virginia planter. Her first husband died, leaving her a wealthy young widow with two children. Two years later she married George Washington. Known as "Lady Washington" for her charm and aristocratic graciousness, she brought considerable status to the Patriot cause. She bore Washington no children. It was said that fate had ordained that he was to be only the Father of his Country.*

Bunker Hill and Hessian Hirelings

The clash of arms continued on a strangely contradictory basis. On the one hand, the Americans were emphatically affirming their loyalty to the king and earnestly voicing their desire to patch up existing difficulties. On the other hand, they were raising armies and shooting down His Majesty's soldiers. This curious war of inconsistency was fought for fourteen long months—from April 1775 to July 1776—before the fateful plunge into independence was taken.

Gradually the tempo of warfare increased. In May 1775 a tiny American force, under Ethan Allen and Benedict Arnold, surprised and captured the British garrisons at Ticonderoga and Crown Point, on the scenic lakes of upper New York. A priceless store of powder and artillery for the siege of Boston was thus secured. In June 1775 the colonials seized a hill, now known as Bunker Hill (actually Breed's Hill), from which they menaced the enemy in Boston. The British, instead of cutting off the retreat of their foes by flanking them, blundered bloodily when they launched a frontal attack with three thousand men. Sharpshooting Americans, numbering fifteen hundred and strongly entrenched, mowed down the advancing foe with frightful slaughter. But the colonials' scanty store of powder finally gave out, and they were forced to abandon the hill in disorder. With two more such victories, remarked the French foreign minister, the British would have no army left in America.

Following Bunker Hill, the king slammed the door on all hope of reconciliation. In August 1775 he formally proclaimed the colonies in rebellion, with all that this implied in the way of future hangings. The next month he further widened the chasm when he completed arrangements for hiring thousands of German troops (so-called Hessians) to help crush his rebellious subjects. Six German princes involved in the transaction needed the money (one reputedly had seventy-four children); George III needed the men.

News of the Hessian deal shocked the colonials. The quarrel, they felt, was within the family. Why bring in outside mercenaries, especially fiercely mustached foreigners, who had an exaggerated reputation for butchery and bestiality?

Hessian hirelings proved to be good soldiers in a mechanical sense, but many of them were more interested in booty than in duty. For good reason they were dubbed "Hessian flies." Seduced by American promises of land, hundreds of them finally deserted and remained in the United States to become respected citizens.

The Abortive Conquest of Canada

The unsheathed sword continued to take its toll. In October 1775, on the eve of a cruel winter, the British burned Falmouth (Portland), Maine. In that same autumn the rebels daringly undertook a two-pronged invasion of Canada. American leaders believed, erroneously, that the conquered French were explosively restive under the British yoke. A successful assault on Canada would add a fourteenth colony, while depriving Britain of a valuable base for striking at the colonies in revolt. But this large-scale attack, involving some two thousand American troops, contradicted the claim of the colonials that they were merely fighting defensively for a redress of grievances. Invasion northward was undisguised offensive warfare.

This bold stroke for Canada narrowly missed success. One invading column under the Irish-born General Richard Montgomery, formerly of the British army, pushed up the Lake Champlain route and captured Montreal. He was joined at Quebec by the bedraggled army of General Benedict Arnold, whose men had been reduced to eating dogs and shoe leather during their grueling march through the Maine woods. An assault on Quebec, launched on the last day of 1775, was beaten off. The able Montgomery was killed; the dashing Arnold was wounded in one leg. Scattered remnants under his command retreated up the St. Lawrence River, reversing the way Montgomery had come. French-Canadian leaders, who had been generously treated by the British in the Quebec Act of 1774, showed no real desire to welcome the plundering anti-Catholic invaders.

Bitter fighting continued in the colonies, though the Americans still disclaimed all desire

Revolution in the North, 1775–1776
Benedict Arnold's troops were described as "pretty young men" when they sailed from Massachusetts. They were considerably less pretty on their arrival in Quebec, after eight weeks of struggling through wet and frigid forests, often without food. "No one can imagine," one of them wrote, "the sweetness of a roasted shot-pouch [ammunition bag] to the famished appetite."

for independence. In January 1776, the British set fire to the Virginia town of Norfolk. In March they were finally forced to evacuate Boston, taking with them the leading friends of the king. (Evacuation Day is still celebrated annually in Boston.) In the South the rebellious colonials won two victories in 1776—one in February against some fifteen hundred Loyalists at Moore's Creek Bridge, in North Carolina, and the other in June against an invading British fleet at Charleston harbor.

Thomas Paine Preaches Common Sense

Why did Americans continue to deny any intention of independence? Loyalty to the empire was deeply ingrained; colonial unity was poor; and open rebellion was dangerous, especially against a formidable Britain. Irish rebels of that day were customarily hanged, drawn, and quartered. American rebels might have fared no better. As late as January 1776—five months before independence was declared—the king's health was being toasted by the officers of Washington's mess near Boston. "God save the king" had not yet been replaced by "God save the Congress."

Gradually the Americans were shocked into an awareness of their inconsistency. Their eyes were opened by harsh British acts like the burning of Falmouth and Norfolk, and especially by the hiring of the Hessians. Early in 1776 came the publication of *Common Sense,* one of the most potent pamphlets ever written. Its author was the radical Thomas Paine, once an impoverished corset-maker's apprentice, who had come over from England a year earlier. His tract became a whirlwind best-seller and within a few months reached the astonishing total of 120,000 copies.

Paine flatly branded the shilly-shallying of the colonials as contrary to "common sense." Why not throw off the cloak of inconsistency? Nowhere in the physical universe did the smaller heavenly body control the larger one. Then why should the tiny island of England control the vast continent of America? As for the king, whom the Americans professed to revere, he was nothing but "the Royal Brute of Great Britain." America had a sacred mission—a

> *Paine rose to heights of eloquence in* Common Sense: *"O! ye that love mankind! Ye that dare oppose not only the tyranny but the tyrant, stand forth! Every spot of the Old World is overrun with oppression. Freedom hath been hunted round the globe. Asia and Africa have long expelled her. Europe regards her as a stranger and England hath given her warning to depart. O! receive the fugitive and prepare in time an asylum for mankind."*

moral obligation to the world—to set herself up as an independent, democratic republic, untainted by association with corrupt and monarchical Britain.

Paine's passionate protest was simple and somewhat shallow, but it was direct and persuasive. It was both high-class journalism and high-class propaganda. Thousands of American waverers, their eyes jolted open, were prodded into going the whole way. They not only perceived the folly of their position, but—perhaps most important—they realized that they could not hope for open aid from France as long as they swore allegiance to the king. The French crown was interested in the destruction of the British Empire, not in its reconstruction under a plan of reconciliation.

Jefferson's "Explanation" of Independence

Members of the Philadelphia Congress, instructed by their respective colonies, gradually edged toward a clean break. On June 7, 1776, fiery Richard Henry Lee of Virginia moved that "These United Colonies are, and of right ought to be, free and independent states. . . ." After considerable debate, the motion was adopted nearly a month later, on July 2, 1776.

The passing of Lee's resolution was the formal "declaration" of independence by the American colonies, and technically this was all that was needed to cut the British tie. John Adams wrote confidently that ever thereafter July 2 would be celebrated annually with fireworks.

But something more was required. An epochal rupture of this kind called for some formal explanation to "a candid world." An inspirational appeal was also needed to enlist other English colonies in the Americas, to invite assistance from foreign nations, and to rally resistance at home.

Shortly after Lee made his memorable motion on June 7, Congress appointed a committee to prepare an appropriate statement. The task of drafting it fell to Thomas Jefferson, a tall, freckled, sandy-haired Virginia lawyer of thirty-three. Despite his youth, he was already recognized as a brilliant writer, and he measured up splendidly to his opportunity. After some debate and amendment, the Declaration of Independence was formally approved by the Congress on July 4, 1776. It might better have been called "the Explanation of Independence" or, as one contemporary described it, "Mr. Jefferson's advertisement of Mr. Lee's resolution."

Jefferson's pronouncement, couched in a lofty style, was magnificent. He gave his appeal universality by invoking the "natural rights" of humankind—not just British rights. He argued persuasively that because the king had flouted these rights, the colonials were justified in cutting their connection. He then set forth a long list of the presumably tyrannous misdeeds of George III. The overdrawn bill of indictment included imposing taxes without consent, dispensing with trial by jury, abolishing valued laws, establishing a military dictatorship, maintaining standing armies in peacetime, cutting off trade, burning towns, hiring mercenaries, and inciting savage Indians.*

Jefferson's withering blast was admittedly one-sided. But he was in effect the prosecuting attorney, and he took certain liberties with historical truth. He was not writing history; he was making it through what has been called "the world's greatest editorial." He owned many slaves, and his affirmation that "all men are created equal" was to haunt him and his fellow citizens for generations.

The formal declaration of independence cleared the air as a thundershower does on a

---

*For an annotated text of the Declaration of Independence, see the Appendix.

George III (1738–1820) *America's last king, he was a good man, unlike some of his scandal-tainted brothers and sons, but a bad king. Doggedly determined to regain arbitrary power for the crown, he antagonized and then lost the thirteen American colonies. During much of his sixty-year reign, he seemed to be insane, but recently medical science has found that he was suffering from a rare metabolic and hereditary disease called porphyria. (Reproduced by courtesy of the Trustees of the British Museum.)*

muggy day. Foreign aid could be solicited with greater hope of success. Those patriots who defied the king were now rebels, not loving subjects shooting their way into reconciliation. They must all hang together, Franklin is said to have grimly remarked, or they would all hang separately. Or, in the eloquent language of the great declaration, "We mutually pledge to each other our lives, our fortunes and our sacred honor."

Jefferson's defiant Declaration of Independence had a universal impact unmatched by any other American document. This "shout heard round the world" has been a source of inspiration to countless revolutionary movements against arbitrary authority. Lafayette hung a copy on a wall in his home, leaving beside it room for a future French Declaration of the Rights of Man—a declaration that was officially born thirteen years later.

Patriots and Loyalists

The War of Independence, strictly speaking, was a war within a war. Colonials loyal to the king (Loyalists) fought the American rebels (Patriots), while the rebels also fought the British redcoats. Loyalists were derisively called "Tories," after the dominant political factions in England, while Patriots were called "Whigs," after the opposition factions in England. A popular definition of a Tory among the Patriots betrayed bitterness: "A Tory is a thing whose head is in England, and its body in America, and its neck ought to be stretched."

Like many revolutions, the American Revolution was a minority movement. Many colonists were apathetic or neutral, including those Byrds of Virginia who sat on the fence. The opposing forces contended not only against each other but also for the allegiance and support of the civilian population. In this struggle for the hearts and minds of the people, the British proved fatally inept, and the Patriot militias played a crucial role. The British military proved able to control only those areas where it could maintain a massive military presence. Elsewhere, as soon as the redcoats had marched on, the rebel militiamen appeared and took up the task of "political education"—sometimes by coercive means. Often lacking bayonets but always loaded with political zeal, the ragtag militia units proved remarkably effective agents of Revolutionary ideas. They convinced many colonists, even those indifferent to indepen-

The American signers had reason to fear for their necks. In 1802, twenty-six years later, George III approved this death sentence for seven Irish rebels: ". . . you are to be hanged by the neck, but not until you are dead; for while you are still living your bodies are to be taken down, your bowels torn out and burned before your faces, your heads then cut off, and your bodies divided each into four quarters, and your heads and quarters to be then at the King's disposal; and may the Almighty God have mercy on your souls."

New York Patriots Pull down the Statue of King George III *Erected after the repeal of the Stamp Act in 1766, this statue was melted down by the revolutionaries into bullets to be used against the king's troops. (Dr. Gilbert Darlington Collection.)*

dence, that the British army was an unreliable friend and that they had better throw in their lot with the Patriot cause. They also mercilessly harassed small British detachments and occupation forces. One British officer ruefully observed that "the Americans would be less dangerous if they had a regular army."

Loyalists, numbering perhaps 20 percent of the American people, remained true to their king. Families often split over the issue of independence: Benjamin Franklin supported the Patriot side, while his handsome illegitimate son, William Franklin (the last royal governor of New Jersey), upheld the Loyalist cause.

The Loyalists were tragic figures. For generations the English in the New World had been taught fidelity to their king. Loyalty is ordinarily regarded as a major virtue—loyalty to one's family, one's friends, one's country. If the king had triumphed, as he seemed likely to do, the Loyalists would have been acclaimed patriots, and defeated rebels like Washington would have been disgraced, severely punished, and probably forgotten.

Conservative Americans generally remained loyal—the people of education and wealth, of culture and caution. These moderate souls were satisfied with their lot and believed that any violent change would only be for the worse. They feared that the "dirty rabble," inflamed by violence, might break out of control. "If I must be devoured," moaned one aristocrat, "let me be devoured by the jaws of a lion, and not gnawed to death by rats and vermin." Loyalists were also more numerous among the older generation. Young people make revolutions, and from the outset energetic, purposeful, and militant young people surged forward—figures like the sleeplessly scheming Samuel Adams and the impassioned Patrick Henry. His flaming outcry before the Virginia Assembly—"Give me liberty or give me death!"—still quickens patriotic pulses.

Loyalists also included the king's officers and other beneficiaries of the crown—people who knew which side their daily bread came from. The same was generally true of the Anglican clergy and a large portion of their flocks, all of whom had long been taught obedience to the king.

Usually the Loyalists were most numerous where the Anglican church was strongest. A notable exception was Virginia, where the debt-burdened Anglican aristocrats flocked into the rebel camp. The king's followers were well entrenched in aristocratic New York City and Charleston, and also in Quaker Pennsylvania and New Jersey, where General Washington felt that he was fighting in "the enemy's country." While his men were starving at Valley Forge, nearby Pennsylvania farmers were selling their produce to the British for the king's gold.

Loyalists were least numerous in New England, where self-government was especially strong and mercantilism was especially weak. Rebels were the most numerous where Presbyterianism and Congregationalism flourished, notably in New England. Invading British armies vented their contempt and anger by using Yankee churches for pigsties.

The Loyalist Exodus

Before the Declaration of Independence in 1776, persecution of the Loyalists was relatively mild. Yet they were subjected to some brutality, including tarring and feathering and riding astride fence rails.

After the Declaration of Independence, which sharply separated Loyalists from Patriots, harsher methods prevailed. The rebels naturally desired a united front. Putting loyalty to the colonies first, they regarded their opponents, not themselves, as traitors. Loyalists were roughly handled; hundreds were imprisoned; and a few noncombatants were hanged. But there was no wholesale reign of terror comparable to that which later bloodied both France and Russia. For one thing, the colonials reflected Anglo-Saxon regard for order; for another, the leading Loyalists were prudent enough to flee to the British lines.

About eighty thousand loyal supporters of George III were driven out or fled, but several hundred thousand or so of the mild Loyalists were permitted to stay. The estates of many of the fugitives were confiscated and sold—a relatively painless way of helping to finance the war. Confiscation often worked great hardship, as, for example, when two aristocratic old ladies

Tory Suspended, While Goose Is Plucked for Coat of Feathers *(The Bettmann Archive, Inc.)*

were forced to live in their former chicken house.

Some fifty thousand Loyalist volunteers at one time or another bore arms for the British. They also helped the king's cause by serving as spies, by inciting the Indians, and by keeping Patriot soldiers at home to protect their families. Ardent Loyalists had their hearts in their cause, and a major blunder of the haughty British was not to make full use of them in the fighting.

General Washington at Bay

With Boston evacuated in March 1776, the British concentrated on New York as a base of operations. Here was a splendid seaport, centrally located, where the king could count on cooperation from the numerous Loyalists. An awe-inspiring British fleet appeared off New York in July 1776. It consisted of some five hundred ships and thirty five thousand men— the largest armed force to be seen in America until the Civil War. General Washington, dangerously outnumbered, could muster only eighteen thousand ill-trained troops with which to meet the crack army of the invader.

Disaster befell the Americans in the summer and fall of 1776. Outgeneraled and outmaneuvered, they were routed at the Battle of Long Island, where panic seized the raw recruits. By the narrowest of margins, and thanks to a favoring wind and fog, Washington escaped to Manhattan Island. Retreating northward, he crossed the Hudson River to New Jersey and finally reached the Delaware River with the British close at his heels. Tauntingly, enemy buglers sounded the fox-hunting call, so familiar to Virginians of Washington's day. The Patriot cause was at low ebb when the rebel remnants fled across the river, after collecting all available boats to forestall pursuit.

The wonder is that Washington's adversary, General William Howe, did not speedily crush the demoralized American forces. But he was no military genius, and he well remembered the horrible slaughter at Bunker Hill, where he had commanded. The country was rough, supplies were slow in coming, and as a professional soldier Howe did not relish the rigors of winter

campaigning. He evidently found more agreeable the bedtime company of his mistress, the wife of one of his subordinates—a scandal with which American satirists had a good deal of ribald fun.

Washington, who was now almost counted out, stealthily recrossed the ice-clogged Delaware River. At Trenton, on December 26, 1776, he surprised and captured a thousand Hessians who were sleeping off the effects of their Christmas celebration. A week later, leaving his campfires burning as a ruse, he slipped away and inflicted a sharp defeat on a smaller British detachment at Princeton. This brilliant New Jersey campaign, crowned by these two lifesaving victories, revealed "Old Fox" Washington at his military best.

Burgoyne's Blundering Invasion

London officials adopted an intricate scheme for capturing the vital Hudson River Valley in 1777. If successful, the British would sever New England from the rest of the states and paralyze the American cause. The main invading force, under an actor-playwright-soldier, General ("Gentleman Johnny") Burgoyne, would push down the Lake Champlain route from Canada. General Howe's troops in New York, if needed, could advance up the Hudson River to meet Burgoyne near Albany. A third and much smaller British force, commanded by Colonel St. Leger, would come in from the west by way of Lake Ontario and the Mohawk Valley.

British planners did not reckon with General Benedict Arnold. After his repulse at Quebec in 1775, he had retreated slowly along the St. Lawrence River back to the Lake Champlain area, by heroic efforts keeping an army in the field. The British had pursued his tattered force to Lake Champlain in 1776. But they could not move farther south until they had won control of the lake, which, in the absence of roads, was indispensable for carrying their supplies.

Tireless, Arnold assembled a small fleet, and the British had to stop to construct a larger one. His tiny flotilla was finally destroyed after desperate fighting, but winter was descending and the British were forced to retire to Canada. General Burgoyne had to start anew from this base

New York and New Jersey, 1776–1777

the following year. If Arnold had not contributed his daring and skill, the British invaders of 1776 almost certainly would have penetrated as far south as Fort Ticonderoga. If Burgoyne had started from this springboard in 1777, instead of Canada, he almost certainly would have succeeded in his venture. (At last the apparently futile American invasion of Canada in 1775 was beginning to pay rich dividends.)

General Burgoyne began his fateful invasion with seven thousand regular troops. He was encumbered by a heavy baggage train and a considerable number of women, many of whom were wives of his officers. Progress was painfully slow, for sweaty axmen had to chop a path through the forest, while American militiamen began to gather like hornets on Burgoyne's flanks.

General Howe, meanwhile, was causing astonished eyebrows to rise. At a time when it seemed obvious that he should be starting up the Hudson River from New York to join his slowly advancing colleague, he deliberately embarked with the main British army for an attack on Philadelphia, the rebel capital. As scholars now know, he wanted to force a general engagement with Washington's army, destroy it, and leave the path wide open for Burgoyne's thrust. Howe apparently assumed that he had ample time to assist Burgoyne directly, should he be needed.

General Washington, keeping a wary eye on the British in New York, hastily transferred his army to the vicinity of Philadelphia. There, late in 1777, he was defeated in two pitched battles, at Brandywine Creek and Germantown. Pleasure-loving General Howe then settled down comfortably in the lively capital, leaving Burgoyne to flounder through the wilds of upper New York. Benjamin Franklin, recently sent to Paris as an envoy, truthfully jested that Howe had not captured Philadelphia but that Philadelphia had captured Howe. Washington finally retired to winter quarters at Valley Forge, a strong, hilly position some twenty miles northwest of Philadelphia, and there his frostbitten and hungry men were short of about everything except misery. This rabble was nevertheless whipped into a professional army by the recently arrived Prussian drillmaster, the profane but patient Baron von Steuben.

Burgoyne meanwhile had begun to bog down north of Albany, while a host of American militiamen, scenting the kill, swarmed about him. In a series of sharp engagements, in which General Arnold was again shot in the leg wounded at Quebec, the British army was trapped. Meanwhile the Americans had driven back St. Leger's force at Oriskany. Unable to advance or retreat, Burgoyne was forced to surrender his entire command at Saratoga, on October 17, 1777, to the American General Gates.

Saratoga ranks high among the decisive battles of both American and world history. The victory immensely revived the faltering colonial cause. Even more important, it made possible the urgently needed foreign aid from France which in turn helped ensure American independence.

Strange French Bedfellows

France, thirsting for revenge, was eager to inflame the quarrel that had broken out in America. The New World colonies were by far Britain's most valuable overseas possessions. If they could be wrested from Britain, it presumably would cease to be a front-rank power.

France might then regain its former position and prestige, the loss of which in the recent Seven Years' War rankled deeply.

America's cause rapidly became something of a fad in France. The bored aristocracy, which had developed some interest in the writings of liberal French thinkers like Rousseau, was rather intrigued by the ideal of American liberty. Hardheaded French officials, on the other hand, were not prompted by a love for America but by a realistic concern for the interests of France. Any marriage with the United States would be strictly one of convenience.

After the shooting at Lexington, in April 1775, the French agents undertook to blow on the embers. They secretly provided the Americans with lifesaving amounts of powder and other munitions, chiefly through a sham company rigged up for that purpose. About 90 percent of all the gunpowder used by the Americans in the first two and a half years of the war came from French arsenals.

Secrecy enshrouded all these French schemes. Open aid to the American rebels might provoke England into a declaration of war; and France, still weakened by its recent defeat, was not ready to fight. It feared that the American rebellion might fade out, for the colonies were proclaiming their desire to patch up differences. But the Declaration of Independence in 1776 showed that the Americans really meant business; and the smashing victory at Saratoga seemed to indicate that they had an excellent chance of winning their freedom.

After the humiliation at Saratoga in 1777, the British Parliament belatedly passed a measure that in effect offered the Americans home rule within the empire. This was essentially all that the colonials had ever asked for—except independence. If the French were going to break up the British Empire, they would have to bestir themselves. Wily and bespectacled old Benjamin Franklin, whose simple fur cap and witty sayings had captivated the French public, played skillfully on France's fears of reconciliation.

The French king, Louis XVI, was reluctant to intervene. Although somewhat stupid, he was alert enough to see grave dangers in aiding the

Americans openly and incurring war with Britain. But his ministers at length won him over. They argued that hostilities were inevitable, sooner or later, to undo the victor's peace of 1763. If England should regain its colonies, it might join with them to seize the sugar-rich French West Indies and thus secure compensation for the cost of the recent rebellion. The French had better fight while they could have an American ally, rather than wait and fight both Britain and its reunited colonials.

So France, in 1778, offered the Americans a treaty of alliance. Their treaty promised everything that Britain was offering—plus independence. Both allies bound themselves to wage war until the United States had won its freedom and until both agreed to terms with the common foe.

This was the first entangling military alliance in the experience of the Republic and one that later caused prolonged trouble. The American people, with ingrained isolationist tendencies, accepted the French entanglement with distaste. They were painfully aware that it involved a hereditary foe that was also a Roman Catholic power. But when one's house is on fire, one does not inquire too closely into the background of those who carry the water buckets.

After concluding the alliance, France sent a minister to America, to the delight of one Patriot journalist: "Who would have thought that the American colonies, imperfectly known in Europe a few years ago and claimed by every pettifogging lawyer in the House of Commons, every cobbler in the beer-houses of London, as a part of their property, should to-day receive an ambassador from the most powerful monarchy in Europe."

The Colonial War Becomes a World War

England and France thus came to blows in 1778, and the shot fired at Lexington rapidly widened into a global conflagration. Spain entered the fray against Britain in 1779, as did Holland. Combined Spanish and French fleets outnumbered those of England, and on two occasions the British Isles seemed to be at the mercy of hostile warships.

The weak maritime neutrals of Europe, who had suffered from Britain's dominance over the seas, now began to demand more respect for

Britain against the World

BRITAIN AND ALLIES		ENEMY OR UNFRIENDLY POWERS	
Great Britain Some Loyalists and Indians 30,000 hired Hessians (*Total population on Britain's side: c. 8 million*)	Belligerents (*Total population: c. 39.5 million*)	United States, 1775–1783 France, 1778–1783 Spain, 1779–1783 Holland, 1779–1783	
		Ireland (restive)	
	Members of the Armed Neutrality (with dates of joining)	Russia, 1780 Denmark-Norway, 1780 Sweden, 1780 Holy Roman Empire, 1781 Prussia, 1782 Portugal, 1782 Two Sicilies, 1783 (after peace signed)	

their rights. In 1780 the imperious Catherine the Great of Russia took the lead in organizing the Armed Neutrality, which she later sneeringly called the "Armed Nullity." It lined up almost all the remaining European neutrals in an attitude of passive hostility toward England. The war was now being fought not only in Europe and North America, but also in South America, the Caribbean, and Asia.

To say that America, with some French aid, defeated England is like saying, "Daddy and I killed the bear." To the mother country, struggling for her very life, the scuffle in the New World became secondary. The Americans deserve credit for having kept the war going until 1778, with secret French aid. But they did not achieve their independence until the conflict erupted into a multipower world war that was too big for Britain to handle. From 1778 to 1783, France provided the rebels with large sums of money, immense amounts of equipment, about one-half of America's regular armed forces, and practically all of the new nation's naval strength.

France's entrance into the conflict forced the British to change their basic strategy in America. Hitherto they could count on blockading the colonial coast and commanding the seas.

War in the South, 1780–1781

Now the French had powerful fleets in American waters, chiefly to protect their own valuable West Indian islands, but in a position to jeopardize Britain's blockade and lines of supply. The British therefore decided to evacuate Philadelphia and concentrate their strength in New York City.

In June 1778 the withdrawing redcoats were attacked by General Washington at Monmouth, New Jersey, on a blisteringly hot day. Scores of men collapsed or died from sunstroke. But the battle was indecisive, and the British escaped to New York, although about one-third of their Hessians deserted. Henceforth, except for the Yorktown interlude of 1781, Washington remained in the New York area hemming in the British.

Blow and Counterblow

In the summer of 1780 a powerful French army of six thousand regular troops, commanded by the Comte de Rochambeau, arrived in Newport, Rhode Island. The Americans were somewhat suspicious of their former enemies; in fact, several ugly flare-ups, involving minor bloodshed, had already occurred between the new allies. But French gold and goodwill melted restraints. Dancing parties were arranged with the prim Puritan maidens; and one French officer related, doubtless with exaggeration, "The simple innocence of the Garden of Eden prevailed." No real military advantage came immediately from this French reinforcement, although preparations were made for a Franco-American attack on New York.

Improving American morale was staggered later in 1780, when General Benedict Arnold turned traitor. A leader of undoubted dash and brilliance, he was ambitious, greedy, unscrupulous, and suffering from a well-grounded but petulant feeling that his valuable services were not fully appreciated. He plotted with the British to sell out the key stronghold of West Point, which commanded the Hudson River, for £6,300 and an officer's commission. By the sheerest accident the plot was detected in the nick of time, and Arnold fled to the British. "Whom can we trust now?" cried General Washington in anguish.

The British meanwhile had devised a plan to roll up the colonies, beginning with the South, where the Loyalists were numerous. The colony of Georgia was ruthlessly overrun in 1778–1779; Charleston, South Carolina, fell in 1780. The surrender of the city to the British involved the capture of five thousand men and four hundred cannon and was a heavier loss to the Americans, in relation to existing strength, than that of Burgoyne was to the British.

Warfare now intensified in the Carolinas, where Patriots bitterly fought their Loyalist neighbors. It was not uncommon for prisoners on both sides to be butchered in cold blood after they had thrown down their arms. A turn of the tide came later in 1780 and early in 1781, when American riflemen wiped out a British detachment at King's Mountain and then defeated a smaller force at Cowpens. In the Carolina campaign of 1781, General Nathanael Greene, a Quaker-reared tactician, distinguished himself by his strategy of delay. Standing and then retreating, he exhausted his foe, General Cornwallis, in vain pursuit. By losing battles but winning campaigns, the "Fighting Quaker" finally succeeded in clearing most of Georgia and South Carolina of British troops.

Joseph Brant, Mohawk Chief *Siding with the British, Brant led Indian frontier raids so savage that he was dubbed "monster Brant." When he later met King George III, he declined to kiss the king's hand, but asked instead to kiss the hand of the queen. (New York State Historical Association, Cooperstown, New York.)*

The Land Frontier and the Sea Frontier

The West was ablaze during much of the war. Indian allies of George III, hoping to protect their land, were busy with torch and tomahawk; they were egged on by British agents branded as "hair buyers" because they allegedly paid bounties for American scalps. Fateful 1777 was known as "the bloody year" on the frontier. Yet the human tide of westward-moving pioneers did not halt its flow. Eloquent testimony is provided by place names in Kentucky, such as Lexington (named after the battle) and Louisville (named after America's new ally, Louis XVI).

In the wild Illinois country the British were vulnerable to attack, for they held scattered posts which they had captured from the French. An audacious frontiersman, George Rogers Clark, conceived the idea of seizing these forts by surprise. With the blessing of Virginia and £1,200 in depreciated currency, he floated down the Ohio River with about 175 men and captured in quick succession the forts Kaskaskia, Cahokia, and Vincennes. These daring forays no doubt helped quiet the Indians. But Clark's admirers have also assumed, without positive proof, that his occupation of the southwest corner of the great area north of the Ohio River forced the British to cede the whole region to the United States at the peace table in Paris.

America's infant navy had meanwhile been laying the foundations of a brilliant tradition. The naval establishment consisted of only a handful of nondescript ships, commanded by daring officers, the most famous of whom was a hard-fighting young Scotsman, John Paul Jones. As events turned out, this tiny naval

George Rogers Clark's Campaign, 1778–1779

force never made a real dent in Britain's thunderous fleets. Its chief contribution was in destroying British merchant shipping and thus carrying the war into the waters around the British Isles. An English song of the time, critical of the Royal Navy, began:

> The tradesmen stand still, and the merchant
>   bemoans
> The losses he meets with from such as Paul
>   Jones.

More numerous and damaging than ships of the regular American navy were swift privateers. These craft were privately owned armed ships—legalized pirates in a sense—specifically authorized by Congress to prey on enemy shipping. Altogether over a thousand American privateers, responding to the call of patriotism and profit, sallied forth with about seventy thousand men ("sailors of fortune"). They captured some six hundred British prizes, while British warships captured about as many American merchantmen and privateers.

Privateering was not an unalloyed asset. It had the unfortunate effect of diverting manpower from the main war effort and involving Americans, including Benedict Arnold, in speculation and graft. But the privateers brought in urgently needed gold, harassed the enemy, and raised American morale by providing victories at a time when victories were few. British shipping was so badly riddled by privateers and by the regular American navy that insurance rates skyrocketed. Merchant ships were compelled to

sail in convoy, and British shippers and manufacturers brought increasing pressure on Parliament to end the war on honorable terms.

Yorktown and the Final Curtain

One of the darkest periods of the war was 1780–1781, before the last decisive victory. Inflation of the currency was continuing at full gallop. Not only was the government virtually bankrupt but Congress had been forced to repudiate its financial obligations, in part, on a forty-to-one basis. Despair was prevalent; disunion was increasing among the states; and mutiny over back pay was spreading in the army.

Meanwhile the British General Cornwallis was blundering into a trap. After futile operations in Virginia, he had fallen back to Chesapeake Bay at Yorkton, there to await seaborne supplies and reinforcements. He assumed that Britain would continue to control the sea. But these few fateful weeks just happened to be one of the brief periods during the war in America when British naval superiority slipped away.

The French were now prepared to cooperate energetically in a brilliant stroke. Admiral de Grasse, operating with a powerful fleet in the West Indies, advised the Americans that he was free to join with them in an assault on Cornwallis at Yorktown. Quick to seize this opportunity, General Washington made a swift march of more than 300 miles (483 kilometers) to the Chesapeake from the New York area. Accompanied by Rochambeau's French army, he beset the British by land, while De Grasse blockaded them by sea after beating off the British fleet. Completely cornered, Cornwallis surrendered his entire force of seven thousand men, on October 19, 1781, as his band appropriately played "The World Turn'd Upside Down." The triumph was no less French than American: the French provided essentially all the seapower and about half of the regular troops in the besieging army of some sixteen thousand men.

Stunned by news of the disaster, Prime Minister Lord North cried, "Oh God! It's all over! It's all over!" But it was not. George III stubbornly planned to continue the struggle, for

Lord George Germain, secretary of state for the colonies and a chief architect of war plans, swelled with confidence after Yorktown: "So very contemptible is the Rebel Force now in all Parts, and so vast is Our Superiority everywhere, that no resistance on their [Americans'] Part is to be apprehended, that can materially obstruct the Progress of the King's Army in the Speedy Suppression of the Rebellion."

England was far from being crushed. She still had fifty-four thousand troops in North America, including thirty-two thousand in the United States. Washington returned with his army to New York, there to continue keeping a vigilant eye on the British force of ten thousand men.

Fighting actually continued for more than a year after Yorktown, with Patriot-Loyalist warfare in the South especially savage. "No quarter for Tories" was the common battle cry. One of Washington's most valuable contributions was to keep the languishing cause alive, the army in the field, and the states together during these critical months. Otherwise a satisfactory peace treaty might never have been signed.

Peace at Paris

After Yorktown, the war-weary British were increasingly ready to come to terms. They had suffered heavy reverses in India and in the West Indies. The island of Minorca in the Mediterranean had fallen; the Rock of Gibraltar was tottering. Lord North's ministry collapsed in March 1782, temporarily ending the personal rule of George III. A Whig ministry, rather favorable to the Americans, replaced the Tory regime of Lord North.

Three American peace negotiators had meanwhile gathered at Paris: the aging but astute Benjamin Franklin; the flinty John Adams, vigilant for New England interests; and the impulsive John Jay of New York, deeply suspicious of Old World intrigue. The three envoys had explicit instructions from Congress to make no separate peace and to consult with their French

allies at all stages of the negotiations. But the American representatives chafed under this directive. They well knew that it had been written by a subservient Congress, with the French Foreign Office indirectly guiding the pen.

France was in a painful position. It had induced Spain to enter the war on its side, in part by promising to deliver British-held Gibraltar. Yet the towering rock was defying frantic joint assaults by French and Spanish troops. Spain also coveted the immense trans-Allegheny area, on which restless American pioneers were already settling.

Benjamin Franklin (1706–1790) He left school at age ten, and became a wealthy businessman, a journalist, an inventor, a scientist, a legislator, and preeminently a statesman-diplomatist. He was sent to France in 1776 as the American envoy at age seventy, and he remained there until 1785, negotiating the alliance with the French and helping to negotiate the treaty of peace. His fame had preceded him, and when he discarded his wig for the fur cap of a simple "American agriculturist," he took French society by storm. The ladies, with whom he was a great favorite, honored him by adopting the high coiffure à la Franklin in imitation of his cap. (C. W. Peale, Historical Society of Pennsylvania.)

Blundering George III, a poor loser, wrote this of America: "Knavery seems to be so much the striking feature of its inhabitants that it may not in the end be an evil that they become aliens to this Kingdom."

France, ever eager to smash Britain's empire, desired an independent United States, but one feebly independent. It therefore schemed to keep the new republic cooped up east of the Allegheny Mountains. A weak America—like a horse gentle enough to plow but not vigorous enough to kick—would be easier to manage in promoting French interests and policy. France was paying a heavy price in men and treasure to win America's independence, and it wanted to get its money's worth.

But John Jay was unwilling to play France's game. Suspiciously alert, he perceived that the French could not satisfy the conflicting ambitions of both Americans and Spaniards. He saw signs—or thought he did—that indicated that the Paris Foreign Office was about to betray America's trans-Allegheny interests to satisfy those of Spain. He therefore secretly made separate overtures to London, contrary to his instructions from Congress. The hard-pressed British, eager to entice one of their enemies from the alliance, speedily came to terms with the Americans. A preliminary treaty of peace was signed in 1782; the final peace, the next year.

By the Treaty of Paris of 1783, the British formally recognized the independence of the United States. In addition, they granted generous boundaries, stretching majestically to the Mississippi on the west, to the Great Lakes on the north, and to Spanish Florida on the south. (Spain had recently captured Florida from Britain.) The Yankees, though now divorced from the Empire, were to retain a share in the priceless fisheries of Newfoundland. The Canadians, of course, were profoundly displeased.

The Americans, on their part, had to yield important concessions. Loyalists were not to be

The Reconciliation between Britannia and Her Daughter America *America (represented by an Indian) is invited to buss (kiss) her mother. (Detail from an English cartoon. New York Public Library.)*

further persecuted, and Congress was to *recommend* to the state legislatures that confiscated Loyalist property be restored. As for the debts long owed to British creditors, the American states were bound to put no lawful obstacles in the way of their collection. Unhappily for future harmony, the assurances regarding both debts and Loyalists were not carried out in the manner hoped for by London.

A New Nation Legitimized

Britain's terms were liberal almost beyond belief. The enormous trans-Allegheny area was thrown in as a virtual gift, for George Rogers Clark had captured only a small segment of it. Why the generosity? Had the United States beaten the mother country to her knees?

The key to the riddle may be found in the Old World. At the time the peace terms were drafted, England was trying to seduce America from its French alliance, so it made the terms as alluring as possible. The shaky Whig ministry, hanging on by its fingernails for only a few months, was more friendly to the Americans than were the Tories. It was determined, by a policy of liberality, to salve recent wounds, reopen old trade channels, and prevent future wars over the coveted trans-Allegheny region. This far-visioned policy was regrettably not followed by the successors of the Whigs.

In spirit, the Americans made a separate peace—contrary to the French alliance. In fact, they did not. The Paris Foreign Office formally approved the terms of peace, though disturbed by the lone-wolf course of its American ally. France was immensely relieved by the prospect of bringing the costly conflict to an end and of freeing itself from its embarrassing promises to the Spanish crown.

America alone gained from the world-girdling war. The British, though soon to stage a comeback, were battered and beaten. The French gained sweet revenge but plunged headlong down the slippery slope to bankruptcy and revolution. In truth, Dame Fortune smiled benignly on the Americans. Snatching their independence from the furnace of world conflict, they began their national career with a splendid territorial birthright and a priceless heritage of freedom. Seldom, if ever, have any people been so favored.

Varying Viewpoints

As the first colonial struggle for "national liberation," the Revolutionary War has long captured the attention of military historians. Early accounts concentrated on the engagements between British regulars and the Continental army, and the war's place in the context of European rivalries. The French alliance, the dramatic battles at Saratoga and Yorktown, and the terrible winter at Valley Forge receive the greatest emphasis in these studies.

During the last thirty years, the proliferation of guerrilla conflicts in the Third World has prompted scholars to emphasize another distinctive feature of the War for American Independence—the "triangularity" of the Revolutionary struggle. Focusing on the efforts of the patriot militia to disrupt British supply lines and win the loyalty of the general public, recent accounts, most notably those of John Shy and Charles Royster, portray the conflict less as a battle between two armies than as a contest between the British and the militia for control of the civilian population. By forcing the apathetic majority to associate actively with the Patriot cause, the militia won this war for the hearts and minds of the people and made it unlikely that the British could have recovered the loyalty of the colonists, even had they achieved a military victory.

Select Readings

Primary Source Documents

Thomas Paine's fiery *Common Sense** (1776) is the manifesto of the Revolution. "The Declaration of Independence"* (1776) is one of the foundations of American political theory. See also the "Treaty of Peace with Great Britain" (1783), in Henry Steele Commager, *Documents of American History.*

Secondary Sources

The war is sketched in John R. Alden, *A History of the American Revolution* (1969), and in Don Higgenbotham's excellent military history, *The War of American Independence: Military Attitudes, Policies and Practice, 1763–1789* (1971). On the implications of the Revolutionary conflict, see John Shy, *A People Numerous and Armed: Reflections on the Military Struggle for American Independence* (1976), and Charles Royster, *A Revolutionary People at War: The Continental Army and the American Character* (1980). The conflict is considered in its European setting in Piers Mackesy, *The War for America, 1775–1783* (1964). Carl Becker's classic *The Declaration of Independence* (1922) is masterful; on the same subject, see also Garry Wills, *Inventing America: Jefferson's Declaration of Independence* (1980). Propaganda is analyzed in Carl Berger, *Broadsides and Bayonets* (1961). The role of the Loyalists is treated in William H. Nelson, *The American Tory* (1961); Robert M. Calhoon, *The Loyalists in Revolutionary America* (1973); Mary Beth Norton, *The British-Americans: The Loyalist Exiles in England* (1972); and Bernard Bailyn's unusually sensitive biography of the governor of colonial Massachusetts, *The Ordeal of Thomas Hutchinson* (1974). A general treatment of an often neglected subject is Benjamin Quarles, *The Negro in the American Revolution* (1961). See also Duncan J. MacLeod, *Slavery, Race and the American Revolution* (1974), and David B. Davis, *The Problem of Slavery in the Age of Revolu-*

tion, 1770–1823 (1975), an able, gracefully written book. International implications are developed in Samuel F. Bemis, *The Diplomacy of the American Revolution* (1935); James H. Hutson, *John Adams and the Diplomacy of the American Revolution* (1980); and Richard B. Morris, *The Peacemakers: The Great Powers and American Independence* (1965). Attention to the social history of the Revolution has been largely inspired by John F. Jameson's seminal *The American Revolution Considered as a Social Movement* (1926). Jackson T. Main, *The Social Structure of Revolutionary America* (1969), takes the exploration further along the same lines, with conclusions somewhat at variance with Jameson's. Local studies of this issue include Edward A. Countryman, *A People in Revolution: The American Revolution and Political Society in New York, 1760–1790* (1981); Gary Nash, *The Urban Crucible: Social Change, Political Consciousness and the Origins of the American Revolution* (1979); and Ronald Hoffman, *A Spirit of Dissension: Economics, Politics, and the Revolution in Maryland* (1973). Interesting biographies are Samuel E. Morison's swashbuckling *John Paul Jones* (1959); Eric Foner, *Tom Paine and Revolutionary America* (1976); James T. Flexner, *George Washington in the American Revolution, 1775–1783* (1968); and Charles Royster, *Light Horse Harry Lee and the Legacy of the American Revolution* (1981). British troubles are laid bare in Gerald S. Brown, *The American Secretary: The Colonial Policy of Lord George Germain, 1775–1778* (1963), and in William B. Willcox, *Portrait of a General: Sir Henry Clinton in the War of Independence* (1964). Women are the subject of Linda K. Kerber, *Women of the Republic: Intellect and Ideology in Revolutionary America* (1980), and Mary Beth Norton, *Liberty's Daughters: The Revolutionary Experience of American Women* (1980). Michael Kammen brilliantly evokes the ways that the Revolution has been enshrined in the national memory in *A Season of Youth: The American Revolution and the Historical Imagination* (1978).

8

The Confederation and the Constitution

> *This example of changing the constitution by assembling the wise men of the state, instead of assembling armies, will be worth as much to the world as the former examples we have given it.*
>
> *Thomas Jefferson*

A Revolution of Sentiments

The American Revolution was not a revolution in the sense of a radical or total change. It did not suddenly and violently overturn the entire political and social framework, as later occurred in the French and Russian revolutions. What happened was accelerated evolution rather than outright revolution. During the conflict itself people went on working and praying, marrying and playing. Most of them were not seriously disturbed by the actual fighting, and many of the more isolated communities scarcely knew that a war was on.

Yet some striking changes were ushered in, affecting social customs, political institutions, and ideas about society and government. The exodus of some eighty thousand substantial Loyalists robbed the new ship of state of conservative ballast. This weakening of the aristocratic upper crust, with all its culture and elegance, paved the way for new, Patriot elites to emerge. It also cleared the field for the "leveling" ideas of unbridled democracy to sweep across the land.

Equality was everywhere the watchword. When a group of Continental Army officers in 1783 formed an exclusive military order, the Society of the Cincinnati, they were roundly denounced for their aristocratic pretensions. Most states reduced (but usually did not eliminate altogether) property-holding requirements for voting. Social democracy was further stimulated by the growth of trade organizations for artisans and laborers. Citizens in several states, flushed with republican fervor, also sawed off the remaining shackles of medieval inheritance laws, such as primogeniture, which awarded all of a father's property to the eldest son.

A protracted fight for separation of church and state resulted in notable gains. Although the well-entrenched Congregational church continued to be legally established in some New England states, the Anglican church, tainted by association with the British crown, was humbled. De-Anglicized, it re-formed as the Protestant Episcopal church and was everywhere disestablished. The struggle for divorce between religion and government proved to be bitterest in Virginia. It was prolonged to 1786, when free-thinking Thomas Jefferson and his co-reformers, including the lowly Baptists, won a complete victory with the passage of the Virginia Statute for Religious Freedom. (See table of established churches, p. 64.)

The egalitarian sentiments unleashed by the war likewise challenged the institution of slavery. Philadelphia Quakers in 1775 founded the world's first antislavery society. Hostilities hampered the noxious trade in "black ivory," and the

> The impact of the American Revolution was worldwide. About 1783 a British ship stopped at some islands off the East African coast, where the natives were revolting against their Arab masters. When asked why they were fighting they replied: "America is free. Could not we be?"

Continental Congress in 1774 called for the complete abolition of the slave trade, a summons to which most of the states responded positively. Several northern states went further and either abolished slavery outright or provided for the gradual emancipation of blacks.

These laws codified the Declaration's ringing concept that "all men are created equal," though laws against interracial marriage sprang up at the same time. Even in slave-burdened Virginia, a few idealistic masters freed their human chattels. In this still sadly incomplete revolution of sentiments, symbolized and inspired by the Declaration of Independence, were to be found the first frail sprouts of the later abolitionist movement.

But why in this dawning democratic age did abolition not go further and cleanly blot the evil of slavery from the fresh face of the new nation? The sorry truth is that the fledgling idealism of the Founding Fathers was sacrificed to political expediency. A fight over the slavery issue would have fractured the fragile national unity that was so desperately needed. Nearly a century later, the same issue did wreck the Union—temporarily.

Likewise incomplete was the extension of the doctrine of equality to women. Some women did serve (disguised as men) in the military, and New Jersey's new constitution in 1776 even temporarily enabled women to vote. But though Abigail Adams teased her husband John in 1776 that "the ladies" were determined "to foment a rebellion" of their own if they were not given political rights, most of the women in the Revolutionary era were still doing traditional women's work.

Charleston Slave Advertisement
(State Gazette of South Carolina, 1787.)

Constitution Making in the States

The Continental Congress in 1776 called upon the colonies to draft new constitutions. In effect, the Congress was asking the colonies to summon themselves into being as new states, whose sovereignty, according to the theory of republicanism, would rest on the authority of the people. For a period of time the manufacturing of governments was more pressing than the manufacturing of gunpowder. In Connecticut and Rhode Island the yellowing colonial charters were kept essentially intact but were retouched a bit to reflect the new vigor of republican thinking. Elsewhere, constitution writers worked tirelessly to capture the democratic spirit of the age on black-inked parchment.

Massachusetts contributed one especially noteworthy innovation when it called a special convention to draft its constitution and then submitted the final draft directly to the people for ratification. Once adopted in 1780, the Massachusetts constitution could be changed only by another specially called constitutional convention. This procedure was later imitated in the drafting and ratification of the federal Constitution.

The newly penned state constitutions enjoyed many features in common. Their similarity, as it turned out, made easier the drafting of a workable federal charter when the time was ripe. As *written* documents, the state constitutions were intended to represent a *fundamental* law, superior to the transient whims of ordinary legislation. Most of these documents included bills of rights, specifically guaranteeing long-prized liberties against later legislative encroachment. Most of them required the annual election of legislators, who were thus forced to stay in touch with the mood of the people. All of them deliberately created weak executive and judicial branches, at least by present-day standards. A generation of quarreling with His Majesty's officials had implanted a deep distrust of despotic governors and arbitrary judges.

In all the new state governments, the legislatures, as presumably the most democratic branch of government, were given sweeping powers. But as Thomas Jefferson warned, "173 despots [in a legislature] would surely be as oppressive as one." Many Americans soon came to agree with him.

The democratic character of the new state legislatures was vividly reflected by the presence of many members from the recently enfranchised poorer western districts. Their influence was powerfully felt in their several successful movements to relocate state capitals from the haughty eastern seaports into the less pretentious interior. In the Revolutionary era, the capitals of New Hampshire, New York, Virginia, North Carolina, South Carolina, and Georgia were all moved westward. These geographical shifts portended political shifts with which many more conservative Americans grew increasingly uncomfortable.

Economic Crosscurrents

Economic changes begotten by the war were likewise noteworthy, but not overwhelming. States seized control of former crown lands, and although rich speculators had their day, many of the large Loyalist holdings were confiscated and eventually cut up into small farms. Roger Morris's huge estate in New York, for example, was sliced into 250 parcels—thus accelerating the spread of economic democracy. The frightful excesses of the French Revolution were avoided, partly because cheap land was easily available. People do not chop off heads so readily when they can chop down trees. It is highly significant that in the United States, economic democracy, broadly speaking, preceded political democracy.

A sharp stimulus was given to manufacturing by the prewar nonimportation agreements and later by the war itself. Goods that had formerly been imported from England were mostly cut off, and the ingenious Yankees were forced to make their own. Ten years after the Revolution the busy Brandywine Creek, south of Philadelphia, was turning the waterwheels of numerous mills along an eight-mile (thirteen-kilometer) stretch. Yet America remained overwhelmingly a nation of soil-tillers.

Thomas Jefferson, then minister to France, was not overjoyed by the prospect of much manufacturing. As he wrote (1784): "While we have land to labor then, let us never wish to see our citizens occupied at a work-bench, or twirling a distaff. . . . For the general operations of manufacture, let our workshops remain in Europe. . . . The mobs of great cities add just so much to the support of pure government, as sores do to the strength of the human body."

Economically speaking independence had drawbacks. Much of the coveted commerce of the mother country was still reserved for the loyal parts of the empire; and now that the Americans were aliens, they were forced to find new customers. Fisheries were disrupted, and bounties for ships' stores had abruptly ended. In some respects, the hated British Navigation Laws were more disagreeable after independence than before.

New commercial outlets, fortunately, compensated partially for the loss of old ones. Americans could now trade freely with foreign nations, subject to local restrictions—a boon they had not enjoyed in the old days of mercantilism. Enterprising Yankee shippers ventured boldly—and profitably—into the Baltic and China seas. In 1784 the *Empress of China*, carrying a valuable weed (ginseng) that was highly prized by Chinese herb doctors as a cure for impotence, led the way into the East Asian markets.

Yet the general economic picture was far from being rosy. War had spawned demoralizing extravagance, speculation, and profiteering, with profits as indecently high as 300 percent. Runaway inflation had been ruinous to many citizens, and Congress had failed in its feeble attempts to curb economic laws by fixing prices. Probably the average citizen was worse off financially at the end of the shooting than before.

The whole economic and social atmosphere was unhealthy. A newly rich class of profiteers was noisily conspicuous, while many once-wealthy people were left destitute. The controversy leading to the war had bred a keen distaste for taxes; and the wholesale seizure of Loyalist estates had encouraged disrespect for private property and for the majesty of the law generally. John Adams had been shocked when gleefully told by a horse-jockey neighbor that the courts of justice were all closed—a plight that proved to be only temporary.

A Shaky Start toward Union

What would the Americans do with the independence they had so dearly won? London had dumped the responsibility of creating and operating a new central government squarely into their laps.

Prospects for erecting a lasting regime were far from bright. It is always difficult to set up a new government, doubly difficult to set up a new type of government. The picture was further confused in America by leaders preaching "natural rights" and looking suspiciously at all persons clothed with authority. America was more a name than a nation, and unity ran little deeper than the color on the map.

Disruptive forces stalked the land. The departure of the conservative Tory element left the political system inclined toward experimentation and innovation. Patriots had fought the war with a high degree of disunity, but they had at least enjoyed the unifying cement of a common cause. Now even that was gone. It would have been almost a miracle if any government fashioned in all this confusion had long endured.

Hard times, the bane of all regimes, set in shortly after the war and hit bottom in 1786. As if other troubles were not enough, British manufacturers, with dammed-up surpluses, began flooding the American market with cut-rate goods. War-baby American industries, in particular, suffered industrial colic from such ruthless competition. One Philadelphia newspaper in 1783 urged the use of ill-fitting homespun cloth:

> Of foreign gewgaws let's be free,
> And wear the webs of liberty.

Independence Hall   *Originally built in the 1730s as a meeting place for the Pennsylvania colonial assembly, this building witnessed much history: Here Washington was given command of the Continental Army, the Declaration of Independence was signed, and the Constitution hammered out. The building began to be called "Independence Hall" only in the 1820s. (Historical Society of Pennsylvania.)*

Yet hopeful signs could be discerned. The thirteen sovereign states were basically alike in governmental structure and functioned under similar constitutions. Americans enjoyed a rich political inheritance, derived partly from England and partly from their own homegrown devices for self-government. Finally, they were blessed with political leaders of a high order in men like George Washington, James Madison, John Adams, Thomas Jefferson, and Alexander Hamilton.

Creating a Confederation

The Second Continental Congress of Revolutionary days was little more than a conference of ambassadors from the thirteen states. It was totally without constitutional authority and in general did only what it dared to do, though it asserted some control over military affairs and foreign policy. In nearly all respects the states were sovereign, for they coined money, raised armies and navies, and erected tariff barriers. The legislature of Virginia even ratified separately the treaty of alliance of 1778 with France.

Shortly before declaring independence in 1776, the Congress appointed a committee to draft a written constitution for the new nation. The finished product was the Articles of Confederation. Adopted by Congress in 1777, it was translated into French after the battle of Saratoga so as to convince France that America had a genuine government in the making. In due course this new constitution was sent out to the states for their approval. But final action was delayed for four years, until 1781, less than eight months before the victory at Yorktown.

The chief apple of discord was western lands. Six of the jealous states, including Pennsylvania and Maryland, had no holdings beyond the Allegheny Mountains. Seven, notably New York and Virginia, were favored with enormous acreage, in most cases on the basis of earlier sea-to-sea charter grants. The six landless states argued that their more fortunate sisters would not have retained possession of this splendid prize if all the other states had not fought for it also. A major complaint was that the land-blessed states could sell their trans-Allegheny tracts and thus pay off pensions and other debts incurred in the common cause. States without such holdings would have to tax themselves heavily to defray these obligations. Why not turn the whole western area over to the central government?

Unanimous approval of the Articles of Confederation by the thirteen states was required, and landless Maryland stubbornly held out until March 1, 1781. It at length gave in when New York surrendered its western claims and Virginia seemed about to do so. To sweeten the pill, Congress pledged itself to dispose of these vast areas for the "common benefit." It further agreed to carve from the new public domain not colonies but a number of "republican" states, which in time would be admitted to the Union on terms of complete equality with all the others. This extraordinary commitment faithfully reflected the anticolonial spirit of the Revolution, and the pledge was later fully redeemed in the famed Northwest Ordinance of 1787.

Fertile public lands thus transferred to the central government proved to be an invaluable bond of union. The states that had thrown their heritage into the common pot had to remain in the Union if they were to reap their share of the advantages from the land sales. An army of westward-moving pioneers purchased their farms from the federal government, directly or indirectly, and they learned to look to the national capital, rather than to the state capitals—with a consequent weakening of local influence. Finally, a uniform national land policy was made possible.

The Articles of Confederation: America's First Constitution

The Articles of Confederation—some have said "Articles of Confusion"—provided for a loose confederation or "firm league of friendship." Thirteen independent states were thus linked together for joint action in dealing with common problems, such as foreign affairs. A clumsy Congress was to be the chief agency of government. There was no executive branch—George III had left a bad taste—and the vital judicial arm was left almost exclusively to the states, which remained sovereign.

Congress, though dominant, was closely hobbled. Each state had a single vote, so that some 68,000 Rhode Islanders had the same voice as more than ten times that many Virginians. All bills dealing with specified subjects of importance required at least a two-thirds vote; any amendment of the Articles themselves required a unanimous vote. Unanimity was almost impossible, and this meant that the amending process, perhaps fortunately, was unworkable. If it had been workable, the Republic might have struggled along with a patched-up Articles of Confederation rather than adopting an effective new Constitution.

The shackled Congress was weak—and was purposely designed to be weak. Suspicious states, having just won control over taxation and commerce from Britain, had no desire to yield their newly acquired privileges to an American parliament—even one of their own making.

Two handicaps of the Congress were crippling. It had no power to regulate commerce, and this weakness left the states free to establish conflictingly different laws regarding tariffs

> Jefferson was never a friend of strong government (except when himself president), and he viewed with suspicion the substitute that was proposed for the Articles of Confederation: "Indeed, I think all the good of this new Constitution might have been couched in three or four new articles, to be added to the good, old, and venerable fabric."

and navigation. Nor could the Congress enforce its tax-collection program. It established a tax quota for each of the states and then asked them please to contribute their share on a voluntary basis. The central authority—a "government by supplication"—was lucky if in any year it received one-fourth of its requests.

The feeble national government in Philadelphia could advise and recommend and request. But in dealing with the independent states, it could not command or coerce or enforce. It could not act directly upon the individual citizens of a sovereign state; it could not even protect itself against gross indignities. In 1783 a dangerous threat came from a group of mutinous Pennsylvania soldiers who demanded back pay. After Congress had appealed in vain to the state for protection, the members were forced to move in disgrace to Princeton College in New Jersey. The new Congress, with all its paper powers, was even less effective than the old Continental Congress, with no constitutional powers at all.

Yet the Articles of Confederation, weak though they were, proved to be a landmark in government. They were for those days a model of what a loose *con*federation ought to be. Thomas Jefferson enthusiastically hailed the new structure as the best one "existing or that ever did exist." To compare it with the European governments, he thought, was like comparing "heaven and hell." But although the Confederation was praiseworthy as confederations went, the troubled times demanded not a loose *con*federation but a tightly knit federation. This involved the yielding by the states of their sovereignty to a completely new federal government, which in turn would leave them free to control their local affairs.

In spite of their defects, the Articles of Confederation were a significant stepping-stone toward the present Constitution. They clearly outlined the general powers that were to be exercised by the central government, such as making treaties and establishing a postal service. As the first written constitution of the Republic, the Articles kept alive the flickering ideal of union and held the states together—until such time as they were ripe for the establishment of a strong constitution by peaceful,

Western Lands, 1783

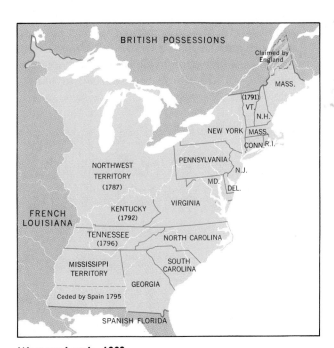

Western Lands, 1802

evolutionary methods. The anemic Articles represented what the states regarded as an alarming surrender of their power. Without this intermediary jump, they probably would never have consented to the breathtaking leap from the old boycott Association of 1774 to the Constitution of the United States.

Landmarks in Land Laws

Handcuffed though the Congress of the Confederation was, it succeeded in passing supremely farsighted pieces of legislation. These related to an immense part of the public domain recently acquired from the states and commonly known as the Old Northwest. This area of land lay northwest of the Ohio River, east of the Mississippi River, and south of the Great Lakes.

The first of these red-letter laws was the Land Ordinance of 1785. It provided that the acreage of the Old Northwest should be sold and that the proceeds should be used to help pay off the national debt. The vast area was to be surveyed before sale and settlement, thus forestalling endless confusion and lawsuits. It was to be divided into townships six miles square, each of which in turn was to be split into thirty-six sections of one square mile each. The sixteenth section of each township was set aside to be sold for the benefit of the public schools—a priceless gift to education in the Northwest. The orderly settlement of the Northwest Territory, where the land was methodically surveyed and titles duly recorded, contrasted sharply with the chaos south of the Ohio River, where uncertain ownership and fraud were rampant.

Even more noteworthy was the Northwest Ordinance of 1787, which related to governing of the Old Northwest. This law came to grips with the problem of how a nation should deal with its colonial peoples—the same problem that had bedeviled the king and Parliament in London. The solution provided by the Northwest Ordinance was a judicious compromise: temporary tutelage, then permanent equality. First, there would be two evolutionary territorial stages, during which the area would be subordinate to the federal government. Then, when a territory could boast sixty thousand inhabitants, it might be admitted by Congress as a state, with all the privileges of the thirteen charter members. (This is precisely what the Continental Congress had promised the states when they surrendered their lands in 1781.) The ordinance also forbade slavery in the Old Northwest—a pathbreaking gain for freedom.

Surveying the Old Northwest   *Sections of a township under Ordinance of 1785.*

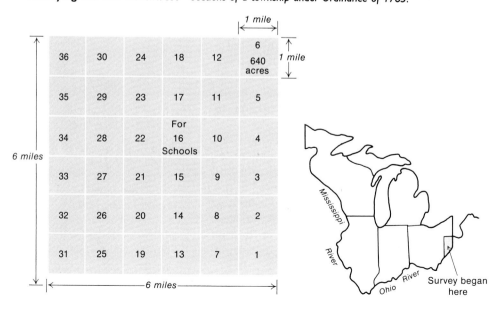

The wisdom of Congress in handling this explosive problem deserves warm praise. If it had attempted to chain the new territories in permanent subordination, a second American Revolution almost certainly would have erupted in later years, fought this time by the West against the East. Congress thus neatly solved the seemingly insoluble problem of empire. The scheme worked so well that its basic principles were ultimately carried over from the Old Northwest to other frontier areas.

The World's Ugly Duckling

Foreign relations, especially with London, continued troubled during these anxious years of the Confederation. The mother country resented the stab in the back from her rebellious offspring, and for eight years she refused to send a minister to America's "backwoods" capital. She suggested, with barbed irony, that if she sent one, she would have to send thirteen.

Britain flatly declined to make a commercial treaty or to repeal its ancient Navigation Laws. Lord Sheffield, whose ungenerous views prevailed, argued persuasively in a widely sold pamphlet that England would win back America's trade anyhow. Commerce, he insisted, would naturally follow old channels. So why go to the Americans hat in hand? The British also officially shut off their profitable West Indian trade from the United States, though the Yankees, with their time-tested skill in smuggling, illegally shared some of it nonetheless.

Scheming British agents were also active along the far-flung northern frontier. They intrigued with the disgruntled Allen brothers of Vermont and sought to annex that troubled area to Britain. Along the northern border the redcoats continued to hold a chain of trading posts on United States soil, and there they maintained their profitable fur trade with the Indians. One plausible excuse for remaining was the failure of the American states to carry out the treaty of peace in regard to debts and Loyalists. But probably the main purpose of Britain in hanging on was to curry favor with the Indians and keep their tomahawks lined up on the side of the king as a barrier against future American attacks on Canada.

Main Centers of Spanish and British Influence after 1783 *This map shows graphically that the United States in 1783 achieved complete independence in name only, particularly in the area west of the Appalachian Mountains. Not until twenty years had passed did the new Republic, with the purchase of Louisiana from France in 1803, eliminate foreign influence from the area east of the Mississippi River.*

All these grievances against England were maddening to patriotic Americans. Some citizens demanded, with more heat than wisdom, that the United States force the British into line by imposing restrictions on their imports to America. But Congress could not control commerce, and the states refused to adopt a uniform tariff policy. Some "easy states" deliberately lowered their tariffs in order to attract an unfair share of trade.

Spain, though recently an enemy of England, was openly unfriendly to the new Republic. It controlled the mouth of the all-important Mississippi, down which the pioneers of Tennessee and Kentucky were forced to float their produce and in 1784 closed the river to American commerce. The West was thus threatened with strangulation. Spain likewise claimed a large area north of the Gulf of Mexico, including Florida, granted to the United States by the

British in 1783. At Natchez, on disputed soil, it held an important fort. It also intrigued with the neighboring Indians, grievously antagonized by the rapacious land policies of Georgia and North Carolina, to hem the Americans in east of the Alleghenies. Spain and England together, radiating their influence out among warlike Indian tribes, prevented America from exercising effective control over about half of its total territory.

Even America's French ally, now that it had humbled Britain, cooled off. It demanded the repayment of money loaned during the war; it restricted trade with its bustling West Indies and other ports.

Pirates of the North African states, including the arrogant Dey of Algiers, were ravaging America's Mediterranean commerce and enslaving Yankee sailors. The British purchased protection for their own subjects, and as colonials the Americans had enjoyed this shield. But as an independent nation the United States was too weak to fight and too poor to bribe. A few Yankee shippers engaged in the Mediterranean trade with forged British protection papers, but not all were so bold or so lucky.

John Jay, secretary for foreign affairs, derived some hollow satisfaction from these insults. He hoped they would at least humiliate the American people into framing a new government at home that would be strong enough to command respect abroad.

The Horrid Specter of Anarchy

Economic storm clouds continued to hang low in the mid-1780s. The requisition system of raising money was breaking down; some of the states refused to pay anything, while complaining bitterly about the tyranny of "King Congress." Interest on the public debt was piling up at home, while the nation's credit was evaporating abroad.

Individual states were getting out of hand. Several of them were having quarrels over boundaries, which generated numerous minor pitched battles. Some of the states were levying duties on goods from their neighbors; New York, for example, taxed firewood from Con-

necticut and cabbages from New Jersey. A number of the states were again starting to grind out depreciated paper currency, and a few of them had passed laws sanctioning the semi-worthless "rag money." As a contemporary rhymester put it:

> Bankrupts their creditors with rage pursue;
> No stop, no mercy from the debtor crew.

An alarming uprising, known as Shays's Rebellion, flared up in western Massachusetts in 1786. Impoverished backcountry farmers, many of them Revolutionary War veterans, were losing their farms through mortgage foreclosures and tax delinquencies. Led by Captain Daniel Shays, a veteran of the Revolution, these desperate debtors demanded cheap paper money, lighter taxes, and a suspension of mortgage foreclosures. Hundreds of angry agitators, again seizing their muskets, attempted to enforce their demands.

Massachusetts authorities responded with drastic action. Supported partly by contributions from wealthy citizens, they raised a small army under General Lincoln. Several skirmishes occurred—at Springfield three Shaysites were killed, and one was wounded—and the movement collapsed. Daniel Shays, who believed that he was fighting anew against tyranny, was condemned to death but was later pardoned.

Shays's followers were crushed—but the nightmarish memory lingered on. The outbursts of these and other distressed debtors struck fear in the hearts of the propertied class, who began to suspect that the Revolution had created a Frankenstein's monster of "mobocracy." "Good God!" burst out George Washington, who felt that only a Tory or a Briton could have predicted such disorders. There was obviously a crying need for a stronger central government. A few panicky citizens even talked of importing a European monarch to carry on where George III had failed.

How critical were conditions under the Confederation? Conservatives, anxious to safeguard their wealth and position, naturally exaggerated the seriousness of the nation's plight. They were eager to persuade their fellow citizens to scrap the Articles of Confederation, under which the states were sovereign, in favor of a muscular central government, in which the federal authority would be sovereign. But the poorer states' rights people, who favored at most a simple amending of the Articles, pooh-poohed the talk of anarchy. Many of them were debtors who feared that a powerful federal government would force them to pay their creditors.

Yet friends and critics of the Confederation generally agreed that it needed strengthening. Popular toasts were "Cement to the Union" and "A hoop to the barrel." The chief differences arose over how this goal should be attained and how a maximum amount of states' rights could be reconciled with a strong central government. America probably could have muddled through somehow with amended Articles of Confederation. But the adoption of a completely new constitution certainly spared the Republic much costly indecision, uncertainty, and turmoil.

The nationwide picture was actually brightening before the Constitution was drafted. Nearly half the states had not issued semiworthless paper currency; and some of the monetary black sheep showed signs of returning to the sound-money fold. Congressional control of commerce was in sight, specifically by means of an amendment to the Articles of Confederation. Prosperity was beginning to emerge from the fog of depression. By 1789 overseas shipping had largely regained its place in the commercial world. If conditions had been as grim in 1787 as painted by foes of the Articles of Confederation, the move for a new constitution would hardly have encountered such heated opposition.

A Convention of "Demi-Gods"

Control of commerce, more than any other problem, touched off the chain reaction that led to a constitutional convention. Interstate squabbling over this issue had become so alarming by 1786 that Virginia, taking the lead, issued a call for a convention at Annapolis, Maryland. Nine states appointed delegates, but only five were finally represented. With so feeble a showing, nothing could be done about the ticklish question of commerce. A classic-featured New Yorker, thirty-one-year-old Alexander Hamilton,

> Regarding popular disorders, Jefferson wrote privately in 1787: "A little rebellion, now and then, is a good thing, and as necessary in the political world as storms in the physical. . . . It is a medicine necessary for the sound health of government."

brilliantly saved the convention from complete failure by engineering the adoption of his report. It called upon Congress to summon a convention to meet in Philadelphia the next year, not to deal with commerce alone but to bolster the entire fabric of the Articles of Confederation.

Congress, though slowly dying in New York City, was reluctant to take a step that might be the signing of its own death warrant. But after six of the states had seized the bit in their teeth and appointed delegates anyhow, Congress belatedly issued the call for a convention "*for the sole and express purpose of revising*" the Articles of Confederation.

Every state chose representatives, except independent-minded Rhode Island (still "Rogues' Island"), a stronghold of paper-moneyites. These leaders were all appointed by the state legislatures, whose members had been elected by voters who could qualify as property holders. This double distillation inevitably brought together a select group of propertied men.

A quorum of the fifty-five emissaries from twelve states finally convened at Philadelphia on May 25, 1787, in the imposing red-brick statehouse. The smallness of the assemblage facilitated intimate acquaintance and hence compromise. Sessions were held in complete secrecy, with armed sentinels posted at the doors. Delegates knew that they would generate heated differences, and they did not want to advertise their own dissensions or put crippling arguments into the mouths of the opposition.

The caliber of the participants was extraordinarily high—"demi-gods," Jefferson called them. The crisis was such as to induce the ablest men to drop their personal pursuits and come to the aid of their country. Most of the

Alexander Hamilton clearly revealed his class-interest views of an aristocratic government in his Philadelphia speech (1787): *"All communities divide themselves into the few and the many. The first are the rich and wellborn, the other the mass of the people . . . The people are turbulent and changing; they seldom judge or determine right. Give therefore to the first class a distinct, permanent share in the government. They will check the unsteadiness of the second, and as they cannot receive any advantage by change, they therefore will ever maintain good government."*

members were lawyers, and most of them fortunately were old hands at constitution making in their own states.

George Washington, towering austere and aloof among the "demi-gods," was unanimously elected chairman. His enormous prestige, as "the Sword of the Revolution," served to quiet overheated tempers. Benjamin Franklin, then eighty-one, added the urbanity of an elder statesman, though he was inclined to be indiscreetly talkative in his declining years. James Madison, then thirty-six and a profound student of government, made contributions so notable that he has been dubbed "the Father of the

Alexander Hamilton (1755–1804) *He was one of the youngest and most brilliant of the Founding Fathers, who might have become president but for his ultraconservatism, an adulterous scandal, and a duelist's bullet. (Copyright Yale University Art Gallery.)*

Constitution." Alexander Hamilton, then only thirty-two, was present as an advocate of a super-powerful central government. His five-hour speech in behalf of his plan, though the most eloquent of the convention, left only one delegate convinced—himself.

Most of the flaming Revolutionary leaders of 1776 were absent. Thomas Jefferson, John Adams, and Thomas Paine were in Europe; Samuel Adams and John Hancock were not elected by Massachusetts. Patrick Henry, ardent champion of states' rights, was chosen as a delegate from Virginia but declined to serve, declaring that he "smelled a rat." It was perhaps well that these architects of revolution were absent. The time had come to yield the stage to leaders interested in fashioning solid political systems.

Patriots in Philadelphia

The fifty-five delegates were a conservative, well-to-do body: lawyers, merchants, shippers, land speculators, and moneylenders. Not a single spokesperson was present from the poorer debtor groups. They were young (the average age was about forty-two) but experienced statesmen. Above all, they were nationalists, more interested in preserving and strengthening the young Republic than in further stirring the roiling cauldron of popular democracy.

The delegates hoped to crystallize the last evaporating pools of revolutionary idealism into a stable political structure that would endure. They strongly desired a firm, dignified, and respected government. They believed in republicanism but sought to protect the American democratic experiment from its weaknesses abroad and excesses at home. In a broad sense the piratical Dey of Algiers, who drove the delegates to their work, was a Founding Father. They aimed to clothe the central authority with genuine power, especially in controlling tariffs, so that the United States could wrest satisfactory commercial treaties from foreign nations. The shortsighted hostility of the British mercantilists spurred the constitution framers to their task, and in this sense the illiberal Lord Sheffield was a Founding Father.

Other motives were present in the stately Philadelphia hall. Delegates were determined to preserve the union, forestall anarchy, and ensure security of life and property against dangerous uprisings by the "mobocracy." Above all, they sought to curb the unrestrained democracy rampant in the various states. "We have, probably, had too good an opinion of human nature in forming our confederation," George Washington concluded. The specter of the recent outburst in Massachusetts was especially alarming, and in this sense Daniel Shays was a Founding Father. Grinding necessity extorted the Constitution from a reluctant nation. Fear occupied the fifty-sixth chair.

Hammering Out a Bundle of Compromises

Some of the travel-stained delegates, when they first reached Philadelphia, decided upon a daring step. They would completely *scrap* the old Articles of Confederation, despite explicit instructions from Congress to *revise*. Technically, these bolder spirits were determined to overthrow the existing government of the United States by peaceful means. The sovereign states were in danger of losing their sovereignty.

A scheme proposed by populous Virginia, and known as "the large-state plan," was first pushed forward as the framework of the Constitution. Its essence was that representation in both houses of a bicameral Congress should be based on population—an arrangement that would naturally give the larger states an advantage.

> Jefferson, despite his high regard for the leaders at the Philadelphia convention, still was not unduly concerned about Shaysite rebellions. He wrote (November 1787): "What country before ever existed a century and a half without a rebellion?. . . The tree of liberty must be refreshed from time to time with the blood of patriots and tyrants. It is its natural manure."

Gouverneur Morris (1752–1816) *A delegate from Pennsylvania to the Constitutional Convention of 1787, he spoke more frequently than any other member and served as principal draftsman of that superbly written document. A wealthy and rock-ribbed conservative, he had joined the Revolutionary movement with reluctance and to the end feared the "riotous mob." (The New-York Historical Society.)*

Tiny New Jersey, suspicious of Virginia, countered with "the small-state plan." This provided for equal representation in a unicameral Congress by states, regardless of size and population, as under the existing Articles of Confederation. The weaker states feared that under the Virginia scheme the stronger states would band together and lord it over the rest. Angry debate, heightened by a stifling heat wave, led to deadlock. The danger loomed that the convention would break up in complete failure. Even skeptical old Benjamin Franklin seriously proposed that the daily sessions be opened with prayer by a local clergyman.

After bitter and prolonged debate, the "Great Compromise" of the convention was hammered out and agreed upon. A cooling of tempers came coincidentally with a cooling of the temperature. The larger states were conceded representation by population in the House of Representatives (Art. I, Sec. II, para. 3; see Appendix at the end of this book), and their smaller sisters were appeased by equal representation in the Senate (see Art. I, Sec. III, para. 1). Each state, no matter how poor or small, would have two senators. The big states, which would have to bear the major burden of taxation, obviously yielded more. As a sop to them, the delegates agreed that every tax bill or revenue measure must originate in the House, where population counted the more heavily (see Art. I, Sec. VII, para. 1). This critical compromise broke the log jam, and from then on success seemed within reach.

In a significant reversal of the arrangement most state constitutions had embodied, the framers provided for a strong, independent executive in the presidency. The president was to be military commander in chief and to have wide powers of appointment to domestic offices—including judgeships. The president was also to have veto power over legislation.

The Constitution as drafted was a bundle of compromises; they stand out in every section. A vital compromise was the method of electing the president indirectly by the Electoral College, rather than by direct means (see Art. II, Sec. I, para. 2). One Virginia delegate insisted that to leave the choice to the people was like asking a blind person to choose colors.

Sectional jealousy also intruded. Should the voteless slave of the southern states count as a person in apportioning direct taxes and also representation in the House of Representatives? The South, not wishing to be deprived of influence, answered "yes." The North replied "no," arguing that the North might as logically have additional representation based on its horses. As a compromise between total representation and none at all, it was decided that a slave might count as three-fifths of a person. Hence the memorable, if somewhat illogical, "three-fifths compromise" (see Art. I, Sec. II, para. 3), an idea seriously discussed four years earlier.

Most of the states wanted to shut off the African slave trade. But South Carolina and Georgia, requiring slave labor in their rice paddies and malarial swamps, raised vehement protests. By way of compromise the convention stipulated that the slave trade might continue until the end of 1807, at which time Congress could turn off the spigot (see Art. I, Sec. IX, para 1). It did so as soon as the prescribed interval had elapsed. Meanwhile all the new state constitutions except Georgia's forbade overseas slave trade.

Safeguards for Conservatism

Heated clashes among the delegates have been overplayed. The area of agreement was actually large; otherwise the convention would have speedily disbanded. Economically, the members generally saw eye to eye; they demanded sound money and the protection of private property. Politically, they were in basic agreement; they favored a stronger government, with three branches and with checks and balances among them—what critics called a "triple-headed monster." Finally, the convention was virtually unanimous in believing that manhood-suffrage democracy—government by "democratick babblers"—was something to be feared and fought.

Daniel Shays, the prime bogeyman, still frightened the conservative-minded delegates. They deliberately erected safeguards against the excesses of the "mob," and they made these barriers as strong as they dared. The awesome

Evolution of Federal Union

YEARS	ATTEMPTS AT UNION	PARTICIPANTS
1643–1684	New England Confederation	4 colonies
1686–1689	Dominion of New England	7 colonies
1754	Albany Congress	7 colonies
1765	Stamp Act Congress	9 colonies
1772–1776	Committees of Correspondence	13 colonies
1774	First Continental Congress (adopts The Association)	12 colonies
1775–1781	Second Continental Congress	13 colonies
1781–1789	Articles of Confederation	13 states
1789–1790	Federal Constitution	13 states

federal judges were to be appointed for life. The powerful president was to be elected *indirectly* by the Electoral College; the lordly senators were to be chosen *indirectly* by state legislatures (see Art. I, Sec. III, para. 1). Only in the case of one-half of one of the three great branches—the House of Representatives—were qualified (propertied) citizens permitted to choose their officials by *direct* vote (see Art. I, Sec. II, para. 1).

Yet the new charter also contained democratic elements. Above all, it stood foursquare on the great principle that the only legitimate government was one based on the consent of the governed. "We the people," the preamble began, in a ringing affirmation of the doctrine of popular sovereignty.

At the end of seventeen muggy weeks—May 25 to September 17, 1787—only forty-two of the original fifty-five members remained to sign the Constitution. Three of the forty-two, refusing to do so, returned to their states to resist ratification. The remainder, adjourning to the City Tavern, appropriately celebrated the occasion. They little suspected that one day an Eighteenth Amendment would be added forbidding the manufacture and sale of alcoholic beverages.

No members of the convention were completely happy about the result. They were too near their work—and too weary. Whatever their personal desires, they finally had to compromise and adopt what was acceptable to the entire body, and what presumably would be acceptable to the entire country.

The Clash of Federalists and Anti-Federalists

The Framing Fathers early foresaw that nationwide acceptance of the Constitution would not be easy to obtain. A formidable barrier was unanimous ratification by all thirteen states, as required for amendment by the still-existent Articles of Confederation. But since absent Rhode Island was certain to veto the Constitution, the delegates boldly adopted a different scheme. They stipulated that when *two-thirds* of the

One of the Philadelphia delegates recorded in his journal a brief episode involving Benjamin Franklin, who was asked by a lady when the convention ended, "Well, Doctor, what have we got, a republic or a monarchy?" He answered, "A republic, if you can keep it."

states—that is, nine—had registered their approval through specially elected conventions, the Constitution would become the supreme law of the land in those states ratifying (see Art. VII).

This was extraordinary, even revolutionary. It was in effect an appeal over the heads of the Congress that had called the convention, and over the heads of the legislatures that had chosen its members, to the people—or those of the people who could vote. In this way the framers could claim greater popular sanction for their handiwork. Congress reluctantly submitted the document to the states on this basis, without recommendation of any kind.

People were somewhat shocked, so well had the secrets of the convention been kept. The public had expected the old Articles of Confederation to be patched up; now it was handed a frightening document in which, many thought, the precious jewel of state sovereignty was swallowed up. One of the hottest debates of American history forthwith erupted. The anti-federalists, who opposed the stronger federal government, were arrayed against the federalists, who naturally favored it.

A motley crowd gathered in the anti-federalist camp. It consisted primarily, though not exclusively, of the states' rights devotees, the backcountry dwellers, the one-horse farmers, the work-soiled artisans, the ill-educated and illiterate—in general, the poorer classes. They were joined by paper-moneyites and debtors, many of whom feared that a potent central government would force them to pay off their debts—and at full value. Large numbers of anti-federalists suspected that something sinister was being put over on them by the aristocrats.

Silver-buckled federalists were more respectable; they generally embraced the cultured and properted groups. Most of them lived in the settled areas along the seaboard, not in the raw backcountry. They were in outlook rather closely akin to the conservative Loyalist group of Revolutionary days. In fact, many of the remaining former Loyalists gave vigorous support to the Constitution; without them it might have failed of ratification.

Anti-federalists, their worst fears aroused, voiced vehement objections to the "gilded trap" known as the Constitution. They cried with much truth that it had been drawn up by the aristocratic elements and hence was antidemocratic. They likewise charged that the sovereignty of the states was being swallowed up and that the freedoms of the individual were jeopardized by the absence of a bill of rights. They decried the dropping of annual elections for congressional representatives, the setting up of a federal stronghold ten miles square (later the District of Columbia), the creation of a standing army, the omission of any reference to God, and the highly questionable procedure of ratifying with only two-thirds of the states. A Philadelphia newspaper added that Benjamin Franklin was "a fool from age" and George Washington "a fool from nature."

The Great Debate in the States

Special elections, some apathetic but others hotly contested, were held in the various states for members of the ratifying conventions. The candidates—federalist or anti-federalist—were elected on the basis of their pledges for or against the Constitution.

The newly forged document was quickly accepted by four small states, for they had come off much better than they could have expected. Pennsylvania, number two on the list of ratifiers, was the first large state to act, but not until high-handed irregularities had been employed by the federalist legislature in calling a convention. These included the forcible seating of two anti-federalist members, their clothes torn and their faces red with rage, in order to complete a quorum.

Massachusetts, the second most populous state, provided an acid test. If the Constitution had failed there, the entire movement might easily have bogged down. The Boston ratifying convention at first contained an anti-federalist majority. It included weather-beaten Shaysites and the suspicious Samuel Adams, that aging "Engineer of Revolution" who now distrusted

Strengthening the Central Government

UNDER ARTICLES OF CONFEDERATION	UNDER FEDERAL CONSTITUTION
A loose confederation of states	A firm union of people
1 vote in Congress for each state	2 votes in Senate for each state; representation by population in House (see Art. I, Secs. II, III)
$\frac{2}{3}$ vote (9 states) in Congress for all important measures	Simple majority vote in Congress, subject to presidential veto (see Art. I, Sec. VII, para. 2)
Laws executed by committees of Congress	Laws executed by powerful president (see Art. II, Secs. II, III)
No congressional power over commerce	Congress to regulate both foreign and interstate commerce (see Art. I, Sec. VIII, para. 3)
No congressional power to levy taxes	Extensive power in Congress to levy taxes (see Art. I, Sec. VIII, para. 1)
No federal courts	Federal courts, capped by Supreme Court (see Art. III)
Unanimity of states for amendment	Amendment less difficult (see Art. V)
No authority to act directly upon individuals and no power to coerce states	Ample power to enforce laws by coercion of individuals and to some extent of states

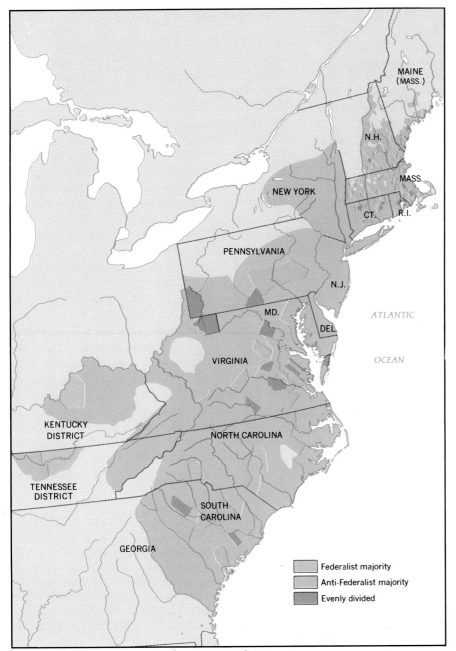

The Struggle over Ratification This mottled map shows that federalist support tended to cluster around the coastal areas, which had enjoyed profitable commerce with the outside world, including the export of grain and tobacco. Impoverished frontiersmen, suspicious of a powerful new central government under the Constitution, were generally anti-federalists.

Federalist majority

Anti-Federalist majority

Evenly divided

change. The assembly buzzed with dismaying talk of summoning another constitutional convention, as though the nation had not already shot its bolt. Clearly the choice was not between this Constitution and a better one, but between this Constitution and the creaking Articles of Confederation. The absence of a bill of rights alarmed the anti-federalists. But the federalists gave solemn assurances that the first Congress would add such a safeguard by amendment, and ratification was then secured in Massachusetts by the rather narrow margin of 187 to 168.

> Richard Henry Lee, a prominent anti-federalist, attacked the proposed constitution in 1788: "'Tis really astonishing that the same people, who have just emerged from a long and cruel war in defense of liberty, should now agree to fix an elective despotism upon themselves and their posterity."

Three more states fell into line. The last of these was New Hampshire, whose convention at first had contained a strong anti-federalist majority. The federalists cleverly engineered a prompt adjournment and then won over enough waverers to secure ratification. Nine states—all but Virginia, New York, North Carolina, and Rhode Island—had now taken shelter under the "new federal roof," and the document was officially adopted on June 21, 1788. Francis Hopkinson exulted in his song "The New Roof":

> Huzza! my brave boys, our work is complete;
> The world shall admire Columbia's fair seat.

But such rejoicing was premature so long as the four dissenters, conspicuously New York and Virginia, remained outside the fold.

The Four Laggard States

Proud Virginia, the biggest and most populous state, provided fierce anti-federalist opposition. There the college-bred federalist orators, for once, encountered worthy antagonists, including the fiery Patrick Henry. He professed to see in the fearsome parchment the death warrant of liberty. George Washington, James Madison, and John Marshall, on the federalist side, lent influential support. With New Hampshire about to ratify, the new Union was going to be formed anyhow, and Virginia could not very well continue comfortably as an independent state. After a close and exciting debate in the state convention, ratification carried, 89 to 79.

New York, which also experienced an uphill struggle, was the only state that permitted a manhood-suffrage vote for the members of the ratifying convention. The result was a heavy anti-federalist majority. Alexander Hamilton at heart favored a much stronger central government than that under debate, but he contributed his sparkling personality and persuasive eloquence to whipping up support. He also joined John Jay and James Madison in penning a masterly series of articles for the New York newspapers. Though designed as propaganda, these essays remain the most penetrating com-

Ratification of the Constitution

STATE	DATE	VOTE IN CONVENTION	RANK IN POPULATION	1790 POPULATION
1. Delaware	Dec. 7, 1787	Unanimous	13	59,096
2. Pennsylvania	Dec. 12, 1787	46 to 23	3	433,611
3. New Jersey	Dec. 18, 1787	Unanimous	9	184,139
4. Georgia	Jan. 2, 1788	Unanimous	11	82,548
5. Connecticut	Jan. 9, 1788	128 to 40	8	237,655
6. Massachusetts (incl. Maine)	Feb. 7, 1788	187 to 168	2	475,199
7. Maryland	Apr. 28, 1788	63 to 11	6	319,728
8. South Carolina	May 23, 1788	149 to 73	7	249,073
9. New Hampshire	June 21, 1788	57 to 46	10	141,899
10. Virginia	June 26, 1788	89 to 79	1	747,610
11. New York	July 26, 1788	30 to 27	5	340,241
12. North Carolina	Nov. 21, 1789	195 to 77	4	395,005
13. Rhode Island	May 29, 1790	34 to 32	12	69,112

A Triumphant Cartoon It appeared in the Massachusetts Centinel on August 2, 1788. Note the two laggards, especially the sorry condition of Rhode Island.

mentary ever written on the Constitution and are still widely sold in book form as *The Federalist*. Probably the most famous of these is Madison's "*Federalist No. 10*," which brilliantly refuted the conventional wisdom of the day that it was impossible to extend a republican form of government over a large territory.

New York finally yielded. Realizing that the state could not prosper apart from the Union, the convention ratified the document by the close count of 30 to 27. At the same time, it approved thirty-two proposed amendments and—vain hope—issued a call for yet another convention to modify the Constitution.

Last-ditch dissent developed in only two states. A hostile convention met in North Carolina, then adjourned without taking a vote. Rhode Island did not even summon a ratifying convention. The two most ruggedly individualist centers of the colonial era—homes of the "otherwise minded"—thus ran true to form. They were to change their course, albeit unwillingly, only after the new government had been in operation for some months.

The battle for ratification, despite much apathy, was close and extremely bitter in some localities. No lives were lost, but riotous disturbances broke out in New York, and Pennsylvania, involving bruises and bloodshed. There was much behind-the-scenes pressure on delegates who had solemnly promised their constituents

to vote against the Constitution. The last four states ratified, not because they wanted to but because they had to. They could not safely exist apart from the Union.

A Conservative Triumph

The minority had triumphed—doubly. A militant minority of American radicals had engineered the military Revolution that cast off the unwritten British constitution. A militant minority of conservatives—now embracing many of the earlier radicals—had engineered the peaceful revolution that overthrew the inadequate constitution known as the Articles of Confederation. Eleven states, in effect, had se-

> Referring to the belief that self-government is better than good government, Fisher Ames of Massachusetts, a Federalist member of the new Congress, is quoted as having said: "A monarchy is like a merchantman [merchant ship]. You get on board and ride the wind and tide in safety and elation but, by and by, you strike a reef and go down. But democracy is like a raft. You never sink, but, damn it, your feet are always in the water."

Hamiltonian Frigate   *A victory parade in New York City honoring Hamilton and the ratification of the Constitution. At the key New York ratifying convention at Poughkeepsie, Hamilton, by sheer eloquence and cogent argument, turned a two-thirds majority against the Constitution into a majority of three in favor of it. (The Granger Collection.)*

ceded from the Confederation, leaving two out in the cold.

A majority had not spoken. Only about one-fourth of the adult white males in the country, chiefly the propertied people, had voted for delegates to the ratifying conventions. Careful estimates indicate that if the new Constitution had been submitted to a manhood-suffrage vote, as in New York, it would have encountered much more opposition, probably defeat.

Conservatism was victorious. Safeguards had been erected against mob-rule excesses, and the democratic gains of the Revolution were conserved in the face of possible anarchy. Radicals like Patrick Henry, who had overthrown British rule, had in turn been overthrown by American conservatives. The result was a kind of peaceful counterrevolution. It restored the

economic and political stability of colonial years and set the drifting ship of state on a more promising course.

Yet if the architects of the Constitution were conservative, it is worth emphasizing that what they conserved was the principle of popular, democratic government, made forever sacred in the fires of the Revolution. By an ingenious system of checks and balances, the Constitution reconciled the potentially conflicting principles of liberty and order. It represented a marvelous achievement; one that preserved the ideals of the Revolution while setting limits to them. One of the distinctive—and enduring—paradoxes of American history was thus revealed: in the United States, conservatives and radicals alike have championed the heritage of democratic revolutionism.

Varying Viewpoints

Charles Beard's book, *An Economic Interpretation of the Constitution of the United States* (1913), has long defined the area around which debate on the constitutional period has revolved. Beard described the Constitution as the "reactionary" phase of the Revolutionary era—a shrewd maneuver by conservative property owners to curtail the democratic excesses let loose in 1776. Most modern scholars, if they accept Beard's argument at all, accept it only with severe qualifications. The most recent discussions of the Constitution have been cast in terms of reflections on the ancient riddle of republicanism: Does republican self-government rest on the virtue of the people or on the formal political institutions that control human behavior? Seen in this light, the framers of the Constitution appear more "radical" than their opponents.

The anti-federalists who opposed the Constitution, in this view, so feared human weakness for corruption that they shuddered at the prospect of putting powerful political weapons in the hands of a central government. They saw small governments susceptible to local control as the only safeguard against tyranny. The federalists who made the Constitution, on the other hand, believed that a strong, balanced national government would rein in selfish human instincts and channel them toward the pursuit of the common good. Alarmed by the excesses of the state governments, the federalists developed the novel idea of an "extensive republic," a polity that would achieve stability by virtue of its great size and diversity. This conception, scholars such as Gordon S. Wood have concluded, challenged the conventional wisdom that a republic could only survive if it extended over a small area with a homogeneous population. In this sense, the Constitution represented a bold experiment—the fulfillment, rather than the repudiation, of the most advanced ideas of the Revolutionary era.

This appraisal of the making of the Constitution builds on Bernard Bailyn's interpretation of the "ideological origins" of the Revolution. Scholars following Bailyn's approach see disputes over the principles of republicanism—not economic and social conflict—as the force driving the evolution of American institutions. The federalists and their opponents, in this view, debated the proper application to American society of republican theory—a body of ideas Americans borrowed from the eighteenth-century English "country party" opposition to the power and alleged corruption of the court. "Country" politicians had emphasized the importance of public virtue, the preservation of an independent citizenry, and the election of government officials who would unselfishly serve the common good. All of these ideas seemed to apply with peculiar force in the rustic, egalitarian setting of democratic America. Indeed, many recent historians have cast the entire history of the pre–Civil War era in terms of a protracted debate over the extent to which American society conformed to republican ideals.

Select Readings

Primary Source Documents

A comparison of the text of the Articles of Confederation (1781), in Henry Steele Commager, *Documents of American History*, with the Constitution* makes an intriguing study. See also Madison, Hamilton, and Jay's explanations of the Constitution in *The Federalist Papers*, especially "Federalist No. 10."*

Secondary Sources

John Fiske, in *The Critical Period of American History* (1888), portrayed America under the Articles of Confederation as a crisis-ridden country. His view has been sharply qualified by Merrill Jensen in *The New Nation* (1950). Jack N. Rakove's *The Beginnings of National Politics* (1979) offers a history of the Continental Congress that substantially revises Jensen's work. Especially learned is Gordon S. Wood's massive and brilliant study of the entire period, *The Creation of the American Republic, 1776–1787* (1969). An influential transatlantic perspective on the roots of American republicanism is J. G. A. Pocock, *The Machiavellian Moment: Florentine Political Thought and the Atlantic Republican Tradition* (1975). On the state constitutions, see Jackson T. Main, *The Sovereign States, 1775–1783* (1973), and Willi P. Adams, *The First American Constitutions* (1980). On the Constitutional Convention, see Clinton Rossiter, *1787: The Grand Convention* (1966). Robert A. Rutland's *The Ordeal of the Constitution* (1966) describes the ratification struggle. Charles A. Beard shocked conservatives with *An Economic Interpretation of the Constitution of the United States* (1913). It is seriously weakened by two blistering attacks: Robert E. Brown, *Charles Beard and the Constitution* (1956), and Forrest McDonald, *We the People: The Economic Origins of the Constitution* (1958). See also the latter author's *E Pluribus Unum: The Formation of the American Republic, 1776–1790* (1965). Jackson T. Main, *The Anti-Federalists* (1961), partially rehabilitates Beard. Staughton Lynd explores another aspect of the topic in *Class Conflict, Slavery, and the United States Constitution* (1967). Sectionalism is discussed in William N. Chambers, *Political Parties in a New Nation* (1963). Finance is treated fully in Curtis P. Nettles, *The Emergence of a National Economy, 1775–1815* (1962). David Szatmary is perceptive on *Shays's Rebellion* (1980). Relevant biographical studies of merit are John C. Miller, *Alexander Hamilton: Portrait in Paradox* (1959); and Irving Brant, *James Madison* (6 vols., 1941–1961).

9

Launching the
New Ship of State

> I shall only say that I hold with Montesquieu, that a government must be fitted to a nation, as much as a coat to the individual; and, consequently, that what may be good at Philadelphia may be bad at Paris, and ridiculous at Petersburg [Russia].
>
> Alexander Hamilton, 1799

A New Ship on an Uncertain Sea

When the Constitution was launched in 1789, the Republic was continuing to grow at an amazing rate. Population was still doubling about every twenty-five years, and the first official census of 1790 recorded almost 4 million souls. Cities had blossomed proportionately: Philadelphia numbered 42,000; New York, 33,000; Boston, 18,000; Charleston, 16,000; and Baltimore, 13,000.

America's population was still about 90 percent rural, despite the flourishing cities; all but 5 percent of the people lived east of the mountains. The trans-Allegheny overflow was concentrated chiefly in Kentucky, Tennessee, and Ohio, all of which were welcomed as states within fourteen years. (Vermont had preceded them, becoming the fourteenth state in 1791.) Foreign travelers everywhere looked down their noses at the roughness and crudity resulting from ax-and-rifle pioneering life. Yet, critical though they might be, they were impressed by evidences of energy, self-confidence, and material well-being.

The new ship of state, despite these promising signs of fair weather, did not spread its sails to the most favorable breezes. Within twelve troubled years the American people had risen up and thrown overboard their first two constitutions: the British constitution and the Articles of Confederation. A decade of constitution smashing and law breaking was not the best training for government making. Americans

> The French statesman Turgot had high expectations for a united America: "This people is the hope of the human race. . . . The Americans should be an example of political, religious, commercial and industrial liberty. . . . But to obtain these ends for us, America . . . must not become . . . a mass of divided powers, contending for territory and trade."

had come to regard a central authority, replacing that of George III, as a necessary evil—something to be distrusted, watched, and curbed.

People of the western waters—in the stump-studded clearings of Kentucky, Tennessee, and Ohio—were restive and dubiously loyal. The mouth of the Mississippi, their life-giving outlet, lay in the hands of unfriendly Spaniards. Smooth-tongued Spanish and British agents, jingling gold, moved freely among the settlers and held out seductive promises of independence.

Finances of the infant government were likewise precarious. The revenue had declined to a trickle, while the public debt, with interest heavily in arrears, was mountainous. Worthless paper money, both state and national, was as plentiful as metallic money was scarce.

The Americans, moreover, were brashly trying to erect a Republic on an immense scale, something that no other people had attempted and that traditional political theory held to be impossible. The eyes of a skeptical world were on the upstart United States, and the bejeweled monarchs of Europe in particular feared that the new republic would provide a dangerous example for their long-oppressed subjects.

Washington's Pro-Federalist Regime

General Washington, the esteemed war hero, was unanimously drafted as president by the Electoral College in 1789—the only presidential nominee ever to be honored by unanimity. He would not run for the office; he would not run from the office. His presence was imposing: 6 feet 2 inches, 175 pounds (1.88 meters, 79.5

kilograms), broad and sloping shoulders, strongly pointed chin, and pockmarks (from smallpox) on nose and cheeks. Much preferring the quiet of Mount Vernon to the turmoil of politics, he was perhaps the only president who did not in some way angle for this exalted office. But his name and fame, which had spread throughout two hemispheres, made him an "indispensable man." Balanced rather than brilliant, he commanded his followers by strength of character rather than by the arts of the politician.

Washington's long journey from Mount Vernon to New York City, the temporary capital, was a triumphal procession. He was greeted by roaring cannon, pealing bells, flower-carpeted roads, and singing and shouting citizens. With appropriate ceremony, he solemnly and somewhat nervously took the oath of office on April 30, 1789, on a crowded balcony overlooking Wall Street, which some have regarded as a bad omen. A cold but able New Englander, John Adams, was sworn in as vice-president—an office that Benjamin Franklin thought should have carried the title "His Superfluous Excellency."

The Constitution does not mention a cabinet; it merely provides that the president "may require" written opinions of the heads of the exec-

Washington Being Sworn In at Federal Hall, New York *Being the first president under the Constitution, Washington could neither cite precedents nor blame a predecessor. (Stokes Collection, New York Public Library.)*

President-Elect Washington Honored in New Jersey
Before leaving home he wrote, "My movements to the chair of government will be accompanied by feelings not unlike those of a culprit who is going to the place of his execution." (Lithograph, Library of Congress.)

utive-branch departments (see Art. II, Sec. II, para. 1). But this system proved so cumbersome, and involved so much homework, that cabinet meetings gradually evolved in the Washington administration. The president thus secured an invaluable body of special advisers.

Along with numerous other features not specifically authorized, the cabinet has become an integral part of the "unwritten Constitution."

At first there were only three full-fledged department heads under the president: Secretary of State Thomas Jefferson, Secretary of the

Evolution of the Cabinet

POSITION	DATE ESTABLISHED	COMMENTS
Secretary of state	1789	
Secretary of treasury	1789	
Secretary of war	1789	Loses cabinet status, 1947
Attorney general	1789	Not head of Justice Dept. until 1870
Secretary of navy	1798	Loses cabinet status, 1947
Postmaster general	1829	Loses cabinet status, 1970
Secretary of interior	1849	
Secretary of agriculture	1889	
Secretary of commerce and labor	1903	Office divided in 1913
Secretary of commerce	1913	
Secretary of labor	1913	
Secretary of defense	1947	Subordinate to this secretary, without cabinet rank, are secretaries of army, navy, and air force.
Secretary of health, education, and welfare	1953	Office divided in 1979
Secretary of housing and urban development	1965	
Secretary of transportation	1966	
Secretary of energy	1977	
Secretary of health and human services	1979	
Secretary of education	1979	

Treasury Alexander Hamilton, and Secretary of War Henry Knox. The last-named was a 300-pound (136-kilogram) Revolutionary general to whom were entrusted both the infant army and the newborn navy.

The shining star in this government galaxy was smooth-faced Alexander Hamilton, just thirty-four years old. He was once called the "bastard brat of a Scotch peddler," though the sneer was unfair. His parents could not legally marry because of a technicality connected with his mother's divorce from her first husband. Hamilton's genius was unquestioned, but doubts about his character and his loyalty to the democratic experiment always swirled about his head. He was said to have shocked Jefferson by exclaiming, "Your people, sir, are a Great Beast!"

Critics claimed that Hamilton loved his country more than he loved his countrymen. Born on a tiny island in the British West Indies, he never developed that passionate loyalty to his home state that dominated so many Americans. Hamilton regarded himself as a kind of prime minister in Washington's cabinet and on occa-

sion thrust his hands into the affairs of other departments, including that of his arch-rival, Thomas Jefferson.

The Bill of Rights

Drawing up a bill of rights headed the list of tasks facing the new government. Many anti-federalists had sharply criticized the Constitution drafted at Philadelphia for its failure to provide guarantees of individual rights such as freedom of religion and trial by jury. Many states had ratified the federal Constitution on the understanding that it would soon be amended to include such guarantees.

Amendments to the Constitution could be proposed in either of two ways—by a new constitutional convention requested by two-thirds of the states or by a two-thirds vote of both houses of Congress. Fearing that a new convention might unravel the narrow federalist victory in the ratification struggle, James Madison determined to draft the amendments himself. He then submitted them to Congress, where his scholarly and political skills were quickly making him the leading figure.

Adopted by the necessary number of states in 1791, the first ten amendments to the Constitution, popularly known as the Bill of Rights, safeguarded some of the most precious of American principles. Among these are protections for freedom of religion, speech, and the press; the right to bear arms and to be tried by a jury; and the right to assemble and petition the government for redress of grievances. The Bill of Rights also prohibited cruel and unusual punishments, and arbitrary government seizure of private property.

To guard against the danger that enumerating such rights might lead to the conclusion that they were the only ones protected, Madison inserted the crucial Ninth Amendment. It declared that specifying certain rights "shall not be construed to deny or disparage others retained by the people." In a gesture of reassurance to the states' righters, he included the equally significant Tenth Amendment, which reserved all rights not explicitly delegated or prohibited by the federal Constitution "to the

Confidence in the Constitution *This late eighteenth-century printer's cut caught the spirit of optimism and hope that prevailed in the infant Republic. (The Granger Collection.)*

States respectively, or to the people." By preserving a strong central government while specifying protections for minority and individual liberties, Madison's amendments partially swung the federalist pendulum back in an antifederalist direction. (See Amendments I–X, in the Appendix.)

The first Congress also nailed other newly sawed governmental planks into place. It created effective federal courts under the Judiciary Act of 1789. The act organized the Supreme Court, with a chief justice and five associates, as well as federal district and circuit courts, and established the office of attorney general. New Yorker John Jay, Madison's collaborator on *The Federalist Papers* and one of the young Republic's most seasoned diplomats, became the first chief justice of the United States.

Hamilton Revives the Corpse of Public Credit

Financial vexations, which had crippled the Articles of Confederation, were also pressing. Alexander Hamilton, a financial wizard, sprang to the rescue. His plan was to shape the fiscal policies of the administration in such a way as to favor the wealthier groups. They, in turn, would gratefully lend the government monetary and moral support. The new federal regime would flourish, the propertied classes would grow fat, and prosperity would trickle down to the masses.

The youthful financier's first objective was to bolster the national credit. Without public confidence in the government, Hamilton could not secure the funds with which to float his risky schemes. He therefore boldly urged Congress to "fund" the entire national debt at par and to assume completely the debts incurred by the states during the recent war.

"Funding at par" meant that the federal government would pay off its debts at face value, plus accumulated interest—a then-enormous total of more than $54 million. So many people believed the infant Treasury incapable of meeting those obligations that government bonds had depreciated to ten or fifteen cents on the dollar. Yet speculators held fistfuls of them, and

> One of the most eloquent tributes to Hamilton came from Daniel Webster in the Senate (1831): "He smote the rock of the national resources, and abundant streams of revenue gushed forth. He touched the dead corpse of public credit, and it sprung upon its feet."

when Congress passed Hamilton's measure in 1790, they grabbed for more. Some of them galloped into rural areas ahead of the news, buying for a song the depreciated paper holdings of farmers, war veterans, and widows.

Hamilton was bitterly reproached for not having sought out the original holders of these securities. But such a course would have been impossible to carry out with complete fairness. Besides, Congress, with some speculators in its ranks, flatly rejected such a proposal.

Some cynics have dubbed the first congressmen "Funding Fathers," with reference to their pocket-lining practices. Yet many of these legislators were convinced that the success of the new government depended on their approval of Hamilton's schemes. They could hardly have been expected to vote "nay" just because principle and personal profit happened to coincide.

Assuming the State Debts

Hamilton was willing, even eager, to have the new government shoulder additional obligations. While pushing the funding scheme, he urged Congress to assume the debts of the states, totaling some $21.5 million.

The secretary made a convincing case for "assumption." The state debts could be regarded as a proper national obligation, for they had been incurred in the war for independence. But foremost in Hamilton's thinking was the belief that assumption would chain the states more tightly to the "federal chariot." Thus, the secretary's maneuver would shift the attachment of wealthy creditors from the states to the federal government. The support of the rich for the national administration was a crucial link in

Hamilton's political strategy of strengthening the central government.

States that were burdened by heavy debts, like Massachusetts, were delighted by Hamilton's proposal. States that had small debts, or had taken energetic steps to pay them off, were less happy. They saw no good reason why they should be taxed by the central government to pull their less thrifty sisters out of a fiscal hole. The fight against assumption was vigorously led by Virginia and took on the semblance of another North-South sectional struggle. In some of the states there was even irresponsible talk of leaving the Union.

The stage was set for some old-fashioned horse trading. Virginia did not want the state debts assumed, but it did want the forthcoming federal district*—now the District of Columbia—to be located on the Potomac River. It would thus gain in commerce and prestige. Hamilton persuaded a reluctant Jefferson, who had recently come home from France, to line up enough votes in Congress for assumption. In return, Virginia would have the federal district on the Potomac. The bargain was carried through in 1790, though Jefferson later claimed that he had been outwitted. It proved to be one of the earliest instances of congressional log-rolling.[†]

Customs Duties and Excise Taxes

The new ship of state thus set sail dangerously overloaded. The national debt had swelled to $75 million owing to Hamilton's insistence on honoring the outstanding federal and state obligations alike. Anyone less determined to establish such a healthy public credit could have sidestepped $13 million in back interest and could have avoided the state debts entirely.

But Hamilton, "Father of the National Debt," was not greatly worried. His objectives were as much political as economic. He believed that,

---

*Authorized by the Constitution, Art. I, Sec. VIII, para. 17.
[†]On the frontier, heavy logs in clearings were rolled into place by enlisting the assistance of neighbors. Mutual aid in legislative bodies to pass laws for special interests came to be called logrolling—"an aye for an aye."

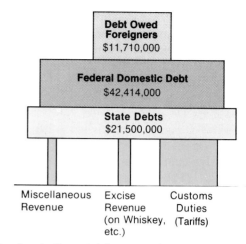

Hamilton's Financial Structure Supported by Revenues

within limits, a national debt was a "national blessing"—a kind of cement of union. The more creditors to whom the government owed money, the more people there would be with a personal stake in the success of his ambitious enterprise. His unique contribution was to make a debt—ordinarily a liability—an asset for vitalizing the financial system as well as the government itself.

Where was the money to come from to pay interest on this huge debt and run the government? Hamilton's first answer was customs duties, derived from a tariff. Tariff revenues, in turn, depended on a vigorous foreign trade, another crucial link in Hamilton's overall economic strategy for the new Republic.

The first tariff law, imposing a low tariff of about 8 percent on the value of dutiable imports, was speedily passed by the first Congress in 1789, even before Hamilton was sworn in. Revenue was by far the main goal, but the measure was also designed to erect a low protective wall around infant industries, which bawled noisily for more shelter than they received. Hamilton had the vision to see that the industrial revolution would soon reach America, and he argued strongly in favor of more protection for the well-to-do manufacturing groups—another vital element in his economic program. But Congress was still dominated by the agricultural and commercial interests, and it voted only two slight increases in the tariff during Washington's presidency.

Hamilton, with characteristic vigor, sought additional internal revenue and in 1791 secured from Congress an excise tax on a few domestic items, notably whiskey. The new levy of seven cents a gallon was borne chiefly by the distillers who lived in the backcountry, where the wretched roads forced the farmer to reduce bulky bushels of grain to horseback proportions. Whiskey flowed so freely on the frontier that it was used for money; a gallon of the fiery liquid passed for one shilling—or about twenty-five cents.

But Hamilton was not unduly bothered by the cries of outrage from the backwoods. The federal regime had to be bolstered, no matter how unpopular his measures. Besides, the excise would accustom the people, especially the reluctant states' rights advocates, to a direct tax by the federal government. In any case, the secretary had little sympathy for the western distillers, many of whom from the outset had opposed the powerful new Constitution and Hamilton's centralizing schemes.

Hamilton Battles Jefferson for a Bank

As the capstone of his financial system, Hamilton proposed a Bank of the United States. An enthusiastic admirer of most things English, he took as his model the Bank of England. Specifically, he proposed a powerful private institution, of which the government would be the major stockholder and in which the federal Treasury would deposit its surplus monies. The central government not only would have a convenient strongbox, but federal funds would stimulate business by remaining in circulation. The bank would also print urgently needed paper money and thus provide a sound and stable national currency, badly needed since the days when the Continental dollar was "not worth a Continental."

Ardent champions of states' rights, spearheaded by Secretary of State Jefferson, cried out against a giant bank. They predicted that their cherished state banks could not survive competition from this monopolistic monster. More alarming, the states' righters feared that their precious liberties would be jeopardized by a grasping banking colossus that, in fact, came to enjoy a virtual monopoly of the government's surplus funds.

Jefferson, whose written opinion Washington requested, argued vigorously against the bank. There was, he insisted, no specific authorization in the Constitution for such a financial octopus. He was convinced that all powers not specifically granted to the central government were reserved to the states, as provided in the about-to-be-ratified Bill of Rights (see Art. X). He therefore concluded that the states, not Congress, had the power to charter banks. Believing that the Constitution should be interpreted "literally" or "strictly," Jefferson and his states' rights disciples zealously embraced the theory of "strict construction."

Hamilton, also at Washington's request, prepared a brilliantly reasoned reply to Jefferson's arguments. He boldly invoked that clause of the Constitution which stipulates that Congress may pass any laws "necessary and proper" to carry out the powers vested in the various governmental agencies (see Art. I, Sec. VIII, para. 18). The government was explicitly empowered to collect taxes and regulate trade. In carrying out these basic functions, Hamilton argued, a national bank would be not only "proper" but "necessary." By inference or implication—that is, by virtue of "implied powers"—Congress would be fully justified in establishing the Bank of the United States. In short, Hamilton contended for a "loose" or "broad" interpretation of the Constitution. He and his federalist followers thus evolved the theory of "loose construction" by invoking the "elastic clause" of the Constitution—a precedent for enormous federal powers.

Hamilton's financial views prevailed. His eloquent and realistic arguments were accepted by Washington, who reluctantly signed the bank measure into law. This explosive issue had been debated with much heat in Congress, where the old North-South cleavage again appeared ominously. The most enthusiastic support for the bank naturally came from the commercial and financial centers of the North, while the strongest opposition arose from the agricultural South.

The First Bank of the United States *The first Bank of the United States, established in Philadelphia, lasted from 1789 to 1811; the second, from 1816 to 1836. (Library of Congress.)*

The Bank of the United States, as created by Congress in 1791, was chartered for twenty years. Located in Philadelphia, it was to have a capital of $10 million, one-fifth of it owned by the federal government. Stock was thrown open to public sale. To the agreeable surprise of Hamilton, a milling crowd oversubscribed in less than two hours, pushing aside many would-be purchasers.

Mutinous Moonshiners in Pennsylvania

The Whiskey Rebellion, which flared up in southwestern Pennsylvania in 1794, sharply challenged the new national government. Hamilton's excise bore harshly on these home-spun pioneer folk. They regarded it not as a tax on a luxury but as a burden on an economic ne-

cessity and a medium of exchange. Even preachers of the gospel were paid in "Old Monongahela rye." Defiant distillers finally erected whiskey poles, similar to the liberty poles of anti–stamp tax days in 1765, and raised the cry "Liberty and No Excise." Boldly tarring and feathering revenue officers, they brought collections to a halt.

President Washington, once a revolutionist, was alarmed by what he called these "self-created societies." With the warm encouragement of Hamilton, he summoned the militia of several states. Anxious moments followed the call for there was much doubt as to whether men in other states would muster to crush a rebellion in a sister state. Despite some opposition, an army of about thirteen thousand rallied to the colors, and two widely separated columns marched briskly forth in a gorgeous, leaf-tinted Indian summer, until knee-deep mud slowed their progress. Washington accompanied the troops a part of the way; Hamilton, all the way.

The federal force was overpoweringly strong—larger in fact than Washington's army during much of the Revolutionary War. When the troops reached the hills of western Pennsylvania, they found no insurrection. The "Whiskey Boys" were overawed, dispersed, or captured. Washington, with an eye to healing old sores, pardoned the two small-fry convicted culprits. Hamilton, disgusted by this turn of affairs, wanted to punish the real ringleaders. Ironically, crushing the rebels cost more than three years' net revenue from the excise.

The Whiskey Rebellion was small—some three rebels were killed—but its consequences were large. George Washington's government, now substantially strengthened, commanded a new respect. Yet the numerous foes of the federalists condemned the administration for its brutal display of force—for having used a sledge hammer to crush a gnat. The ranks of the Jeffersonians were consequently enlarged. Backcountry settlers, taught a harsh lesson, now saw the wisdom of forsaking the tar kettle for the ballot box—and voting for Jefferson.

The Hamiltonian Balance Sheet

Almost overnight Hamilton's fiscal feats had established the public credit. The Treasury was now able to secure needed funds in the Netherlands on terms more favorable than those being extended to any other borrowing nation.

The dynamic secretary, under the leadership of Washington, also strengthened the government politically while bolstering it financially. His major schemes—funding, assumption, the excise, the bank—all encroached sharply upon states' rights. This trend, facilitated by "loose construction," was destined to continue its controversial course to the Civil War and beyond.

States' rights people naturally condemned Hamilton in harsh terms. The Constitution had been ratified by a painfully narrow margin; and if the voters had foreseen how the states were going to be overshadowed by the federal colossus, they almost certainly would have voted it

down. Hamilton in general believed that what the Constitution did not forbid it permitted; Jefferson in general believed that what it did not permit it forbade.

Though a skillful planner, Hamilton was at heart a gambler—a taker of calculated risks. He was playing for enormous stakes, and the outcome might be either a resounding success or a crashing failure. The huge debt, which he had so confidently urged Congress to assume, could be paid off only if ample receipts flowed into the customshouses. Disaster would befall the nation if foreign trade languished or if it were choked off by war with America's best customer, Great Britain.

Luck was with Hamilton. Returning prosperity preceded the Constitution and floated it over the financial reefs. A full-blown foreign war was avoided for more than two decades, and by that time the experimental stage had passed. Even so, the race between mounting expenditures and increasing revenues was nip and tuck for about ten years.

Government by the Wellborn

Hamilton navigated skillfully on the sea of economic policy, but politically he encountered increasingly heavy weather. Out of the resentment against Hamilton's revenue-raising and centralizing policies an organized opposition began to emerge.

National political parties, in the modern sense, were unknown to America when George Washington took the inaugural oath. There had been Whigs and Tories, federalists and anti-federalists, but these groups were factions rather than parties. They had sprung into existence over hotly contested special issues; they had faded away when their cause had triumphed or had become hopelessly lost.

The Founding Fathers at the Philadelphia Constitutional Convention had not envisioned the existence of political parties. Organized opposition to the government seemed tainted with disloyalty, an affront to the spirit of national unity that the glorious cause of the Revolution had inspired. This notion of a formal party apparatus was a novelty. Jefferson and Madison first organized their opposition to the Hamilton program only in Congress and did not anticipate creating a permanent, popular party. But as their antagonism to Hamilton endured, and as the amazingly noisy and widely read newspapers of the day spread their political message, and Hamilton's, among the people, primitive semblances of political parties began to emerge. American political parties date their birth from these bitter clashes between Hamilton and Jefferson, chiefly over fiscal policy and foreign affairs. By 1792–1793 two well-defined groupings had crystallized: the Hamiltonian Federalists and the Jeffersonian Republicans. The two-party system has existed in the United States since that time and has provided indispensable machinery for self-government. The party of the "outs" has traditionally played the invaluable role of both critic and brake—"the loyal opposition."

As might be expected, federalists of the pre-Constitution period (1787–1789) became Federalists in the Washington era. By 1793 they were welded into an effective group, largely through the magnetic leadership and organizational genius of Alexander Hamilton.

Federalists openly advocated rule by the "best people." They believed in a government by the upper classes, with secondary attention to the masses. "Those who own the country," remarked Federalist John Jay, "ought to govern it." With their intellectual arrogance and Tory tastes, the Hamiltonians deplored democratic tendencies and distrusted the common people. They regarded democracy as the mother of all mischiefs and feared the "swayability" of the crowd. Let the rich rule, insisted many Federalist leaders, for they had the leisure with which to study the problems of governing. They also enjoyed all the advantages of intelligence, education, and culture. The untutored masses would only throw monkey wrenches into the machinery; democracy was too important to be left to the people.

Hamiltonians likewise advocated a potent central government. It would maintain law and order, crush democratic excesses (like Shays's Rebellion), and protect the lives and estates of the wealthy. The foreign-born Hamilton, in pursuit of these goals, would subordinate the sovereignty-loving states.

Hamiltonian Federalists also believed that the national government should foster business, not interfere with it. This attitude was only natural in a group dominated by merchants, manufacturers, and shippers. The great majority of Federalists lived in the urban areas of the seaboard, where commerce and manufacturing flourished. If a gunner could have fired a cannonball 50 miles (80.5 kilometers) inland, it would have hit few Hamiltonians.

The Federalists, in addition, were at bottom pro-British. Though Americans first of all, they felt that the nation's foreign policy should be slanted toward friendship with England, above any other outside power. Foreign trade, especially with England, was a key element in Hamilton's entire fiscal machinery. Many Hamiltonians were mild Loyalists, leftovers from Revolutionary days. Basically conservative in their outlook, they welcomed the Federalist bias for the mother country, to which they retained much sentimental attachment.

Jeffersonian Republican Leaflet *It treats Federalists as Tories as late as 1807.*

The finifhing
STROKE.
Every Shot's a Vote,
and every Vote
KILLS A TORY!
DO YOUR DUTY, REPUBLICANS
Let your exertions this day
Put down the Kings
AND TYRANTS OF BRITAIN.
LAST DAY.
April, 1807.

Jeffersonian Idealism and Idealists

Leading the anti-Federalist forces was Thomas Jefferson. Lanky and relaxed in appearance, lacking personal aggressiveness, weak-voiced, and unable to deliver a rabble-rousing speech, he became a master political organizer through his ability to lead people rather than drive them. His strongest appeal was to the middle class and to the underprivileged—the "dirt" farmers, the laborers, the artisans, and the small shopkeepers.

Liberal-thinking Jefferson, with his aristocratic head set on a farmer's frame, was a bundle of inconsistencies. By one set of tests he should have been a Federalist, for he was a Virginia aristocrat and slaveowner who lived in an imposing hilltop mansion at Monticello. A so-called traitor to his upper class, Jefferson cherished uncommon sympathy for the common people, especially the down-trodden, the oppressed, and the persecuted. As he wrote in 1800, "I have sworn upon the altar of God eternal hostility against every form of tyranny over the mind of man."

Jeffersonian Republicans—or Democratic-Republicans, as they were called—demanded a weak central regime. They believed that the best government was the one that governed least. The bulk of the power, Jefferson argued, should be retained by the states. There the people, in intimate contact with local affairs, could keep a more vigilant eye on their public servants. Otherwise, a dictatorship might develop. Central authority—a kind of necessary evil—was to be kept at a minimum through a strict interpretation of the Constitution. The national debt, which Jefferson regarded as a curse illegitimately bequeathed to later generations, was to be paid off.

Thomas Jefferson   *Among America's greatest statesmen, he wrote his own epitaph: "Here was buried Thomas Jefferson, Author of the Declaration of Independence, of the Statute of Virginia for Religious Freedom, and Father of the University of Virginia." (Alan P. Kirby Collection of Historical Paintings, LaFayette College.)*

> Jefferson, who became one of the ablest political organizers in American history, was distrustful of the evils spawned by parties. He wrote in 1789, "If I could not go to Heaven but with a party I would not go there at all."

Jeffersonians, themselves primarily agrarians, insisted that there should be no special privileges for special classes, particularly manufacturers. Agriculture, to Jefferson, was the favored branch of the economy. He regarded farming as essentially ennobling; it kept people away from wicked cities, out in the sunshine and close to the sod—and God. Most of his followers naturally came from the agricultural South and Southwest.

Above all, Jefferson advocated the rule of the people. But he did not propose thrusting the ballot into the hands of *every* adult white male.

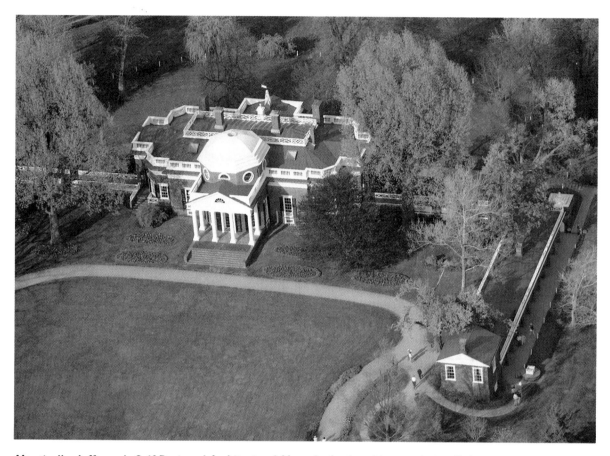

Monticello, Jefferson's Self-Designed Architectural Marvel   *A talented inventor, he installed a number of gadgets, including a device for pulling up chilled bottles of wine from the cellar to the dining table. (Robert Llewellyn.)*

He favored government *for* the people, but not by *all* the people—only by those men who were literate enough to inform themselves and wear the mantle of American citizenship worthily. Universal education would have to precede universal suffrage. The ignorant, he argued, were incapable of self-government. But he had profound faith in the reasonableness and teachableness of the masses and in their collective wisdom when taught. His enduring appeal was to America's better self.

The open-minded Jefferson championed free speech, because without free speech the misdeeds of tyranny could not be exposed. He even went so far as to say that as between "a government without newspapers" and "newspapers without a government," he would choose the latter. Yet no other American leader, except perhaps Abraham Lincoln, ever suffered more foul abuse from editorial pens; Jefferson might well have prayed for freedom *from* the Federalist press.

Jeffersonian Republicans, unlike the Federalist "British boot-lickers," were basically pro-French. They earnestly believed that it was to America's advantage to support the liberal ideals of the French Revolution, rather than applaud the reaction of the English Tories. So it was that foreign policy and domestic politics became perilously intermingled, as the fledgling American Republic was caught up in the bloody international conflicts of the French Revolutionary era.

*Evolution of Major Parties**

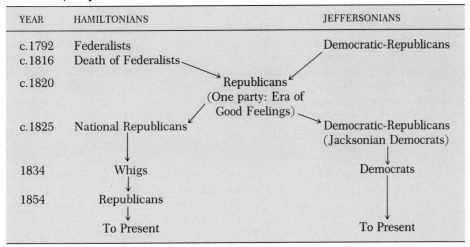

YEAR	HAMILTONIANS	JEFFERSONIANS
c.1792	Federalists	Democratic-Republicans
c.1816	Death of Federalists	
c.1820		Republicans (One party: Era of Good Feelings)
c.1825	National Republicans	Democratic-Republicans (Jacksonian Democrats)
1834	Whigs	Democrats
1854	Republicans	
	To Present	To Present

*See Appendix (Presidential Elections) for third parties.

Varying Viewpoints

The Federalist era witnessed some of the sharpest political conflicts in American history. The first students of the period framed these disputes as a contest between two opposing philosophies—the Jeffersonian demand for small government and strict construction of the Constitution, versus the loose constructionism and belief in active government of Hamilton and his allies.

This view was challenged in the early years of the twentieth century by historians who emphasized the economic rivalries at the root of political debates. They saw the Hamiltonian-Jeffersonian dispute as a smoke screen for battles between creditors and debtors, commercial interests and agrarian interests, northern merchants and southern planters.

Recently, the pendulum has swung back in the other direction, and ideological issues have regained prominence in the historical literature. The new interpretations, advanced by scholars like Lance Banning and Drew McCoy, see the turmoil of the Federalist era as a continuation of the debate over the proper conduct of a republican government that gave rise to the Revolution and the Constitution.

Select Readings

Primary Source Documents

"The Report on Manufactures" (in Daniel Boorstin, ed., *American Primer*), the last of Alexander Hamilton's messages to Congress, presented the case for the development of American industry. Thomas Jefferson expounded his views in *Notes on the State of Virginia* (1784). For further study of the Hamiltonian-Jeffersonian debate, see Henry Cabot Lodge, ed., *The Works of Alexander Hamilton** (1904), and Paul L. Ford, ed., *The Writings of Thomas Jefferson** (1985).

Secondary Sources

Perceptive introductions are provided by Marcus Cunliffe's succinct *The Nation Takes Shape, 1789–1837* (1959) and John C. Miller's more detailed *The Federalist Era, 1789–1801* (1960). On administration, consult Leonard D. White, *The Federalists* (1948); on finance, the book by Curtis P. Nettles cited in the previous chapter. On party politics, see William N. Chambers, *Political Parties in the New Nation* (1963), and Richard Hofstadter's thoughtful *The Idea of a Party System* (1969). Among the new interpretations of that subject, stressing the ideology of republicanism, are Drew McCoy, *The Elusive Republic: Political Economy in Jeffersonian America* (1980), and Lance Banning, *The Jeffersonian Persuasion* (1978). For a trenchant analysis of Jeffersonianism, see Joyce Appleby, *Capitalism and a New Social Order: The Republican Vision* (1984). Also illuminating is Gerald Stourzh, *Alexander Hamilton and the Idea of Republican Government* (1970). A comprehensive biography is James T. Flexner, *George Washington and the New Nation, 1783–1793* (1969). Consult also Forrest McDonald, *The Presidency of George Washington* (1974). Of special interest is Richard H. Kohn, *Eagle and Sword: The Federalists and the Creation of the Military Establishment in America, 1783–1802* (1975).

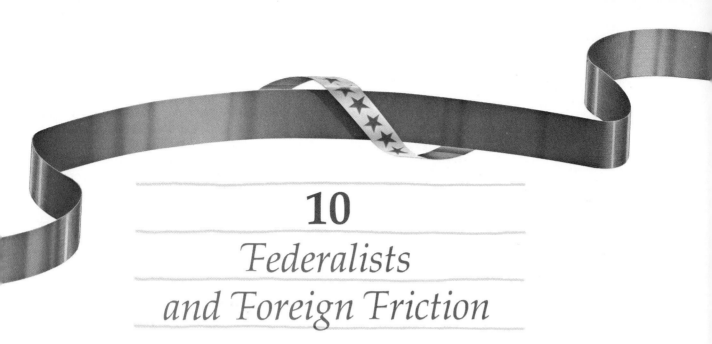

10
Federalists and Foreign Friction

And ne'er shall the sons of Columbia be slaves, While the earth bears a plant, or the sea rolls its waves.

Popular Song by Robert Treat Paine
"Adams and Liberty," 1798

The Impact of the French Revolution

When Washington's first administration ended, early in 1793, domestic controversies had already formed two political camps—Hamiltonian Federalists and Jeffersonian Republicans. As his second term began, issues of foreign policy brought differences to a fever pitch.

Only a few weeks after Washington's inauguration in 1789, the curtain had risen on the first act of the French Revolution. Twenty-six years were to pass before the seething continent of Europe settled back into a peace of exhaustion. Few non-American events have left a deeper scar on American political and social life. In a sense, the French Revolution was misnamed: it was a *world* revolution that touched all civilized peoples.

In its early stages the upheaval was surprisingly peaceful, involving as it did a successful attempt to impose constitutional shackles on Louis XVI. The American people, loving liberty and deploring despotism, were pleased. They were flattered to think that the outburst in France was but the second chapter of their own glorious Revolution, as to some extent it was. Only a few ultraconservative Federalists—fearing change, reform, and "leveling" principles—were from the outset dubious or outspokenly hostile to the "despicable mobocracy." The more ardent Jeffersonians were overjoyed.

The French Revolution entered upon a more ominous phase in 1792, when France declared war on hostile Austria. Powerful ideals and powerful armies alike were on the march. Late in that year the electrifying news reached America that French citizen armies had hurled back the invading foreigners and that France had proclaimed itself a republic. American enthusiasm found expression in singing "The Marseillaise"

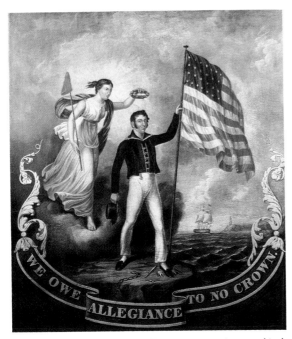

Democracy Triumphant   *This patriotic, anti-monarchical banner was displayed in Fourth of July parades in Philadelphia in the early nineteenth century. (Collection of Davenport West, Jr.)*

and other rousing French Revolutionary songs and in renaming thoroughfares. King Street in New York, for example, became Liberty Street, while in Boston Royal Exchange Alley became Equality Lane.

But centuries of pent-up poison could not be purged without baleful results. The guillotine was set up, the king was beheaded in 1793, Christianity was abolished, and the head-rolling Reign of Terror was begun. Back in America, God-fearing Federalist aristocrats nervously fingered their tender white necks and eyed the Jeffersonian masses apprehensively. Lukewarm Federalist approval of the early Revolution turned, almost overnight, to heated opposition to "blood-drinking cannibals."

Sober-minded Jeffersonians regretted the bloodshed. But they felt, with Jefferson, that one could not expect to be carried from "despotism to liberty in a feather bed" and that a few thousand aristocratic heads were a cheap price to pay for human freedom. When the news came of Louis XVI's beheading, the Pittsburgh *Gazette* brutally rejoiced, "Louis Capet has lost his caput."

Such gloating was shortsighted, for dire peril loomed ahead. The earlier battles of the French Revolution had not hurt America directly, but now Britain was sucked into the titanic conflict. The conflagration speedily spread to the New World, where it vitally affected the expanding young American Republic. Thus was repeated the familiar story of every major European war, beginning with 1689, that involved a death struggle for control of the Atlantic Ocean. (See table on p. 79.)

Washington's Neutrality Proclamation

Ominously, the Franco-American alliance of 1778 was still on the books. By its own terms it was to last "forever." It bound the United States to help the French defend their West Indies against future foes; and the booming British fleets were certain to attack these strategic islands.

Many Jeffersonian Republicans favored honoring the alliance, though dubious about defending the French island outposts at the risk of war. Aflame with the liberal ideals of the French Revolution, red-blooded Jeffersonians were eager to enter the conflict against Britain, the recent foe, at the side of France, the recent friend. America owed France its freedom, they argued, and now was the time to pay the debt of gratitude.

But President Washington, levelheaded as usual, was not swayed by the clamor of the crowd. Backed by Hamilton, he perceived that

> *William Cobbett wrote of the frenzied reaction in America to the death of Louis XVI: "Never was the memory of any man so cruelly insulted as that of this mild and humane monarch. He was guillotined in effigy, in the capital of the Union [Philadelphia], twenty or thirty times every day, during one whole winter and part of the summer. Men, women and children flocked to the tragical exhibition, and not a single paragraph appeared in the papers to shame them from it."*

The Contrast *Adaptation of an English cartoon. C. C. Coffin, Building a Nation, 1882. (Boston Public Library.)*

war had to be avoided at all costs. The nation in 1793 was militarily weak, economically wobbly, and politically disunited. But solid foundations were being laid, and American cradles were continuing to rock a bumper crop of babies. Washington sagaciously reasoned that if America could avoid the broils of Europe for a generation or so, it would then be populous enough and strong enough to assert its maritime rights with vigor and success. Otherwise, it might invite disaster. This strategy of delay—of playing for time while the birthrate fought America's battles—was a cardinal policy of the Founding Fathers. Hamilton and Jefferson, often poles apart on other issues, were in agreement here.

Accordingly, Washington boldly issued his Neutrality Proclamation in 1793, shortly after the outbreak of war between Britain and France. This epochal document not only proclaimed the government's official neutrality in the widening conflict but sternly warned American citizens to be impartial toward both armed camps. It was America's first formal declaration of aloofness from Old World quarrels and as such proved to be a major prop of the spreading isolationist tradition.

The pro-French Jeffersonians were enraged by the Neutrality Proclamation, especially by Washington's method of announcing it unilaterally, without consulting Congress. The pro-British Federalists were heartened. A few days earlier an impetuous, thirty-year-old representative of the French Republic, Citizen Genêt, had landed at Charleston, South Carolina. With unrestrained zeal, he undertook to fit out priva-

teers and otherwise take advantage of the existing Franco-American alliance. The giddy-headed envoy—all sail and no anchor—was soon swept away by his enthusiastic reception by the Jeffersonian Republicans. He foolishly came to believe that the Neutrality Proclamation did not reflect the true wishes of the American people, and he consequently embarked upon unneutral activity not authorized by the French alliance. Even Madison and Jefferson were soon disillusioned by his conduct. After he had threatened to appeal over the head of "Old Washington" to the sovereign voters, the president demanded Genêt's withdrawal and the Frenchman was replaced by a less impulsive spokesperson.

Washington's Neutrality Proclamation clearly illustrates the truism that self-interest is the basic cement of alliances. In 1778, both France and America stood to gain; in 1793, only France. Technically, the Americans did not flout their obligation, because France never officially called upon them to honor it. Its homeland, and especially its blockaded West Indian islands, were urgently in need of Yankee

A contemporary later wrote, "Can it ever be forgotten what a racket was made with the citizen Genêt? The most enthusiastic homage was too cold to welcome his arrival; and his being the first minister of the infant [French] republic . . . was dwelt upon. . . . What hugging and tugging! What addressing and caressing!"

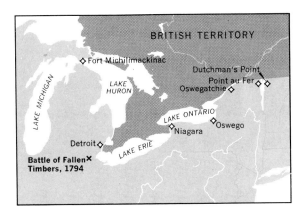

American Posts Held by British after 1783

foodstuffs. If the Americans had entered the war, the British fleets would have blockaded their coasts and cut off those desperately needed supplies. America was much more useful to France as a prosperous provider than as a prostrate partner.

Embroilments with Britain

President Washington's far-visioned policy of neutrality was sorely tried by the British. For ten long years they had been retaining the chain of northern frontier posts on United States soil, all in defiance of the peace treaty of 1783. There they openly sold firearms and firewater to the Indians, who continued to attack palefaced pioneers invading their lands. When General "Mad Anthony" Wayne crushed the northwest Indians at the Battle of Fallen Timbers on August 20, 1794, the fleeing foe left on the field British-made arms, as well as the corpses of a few British-Canadians. In the Treaty of Greenville in 1795, the Indians, finally abandoned by their red-coated friends, ceded their claims to a vast virgin tract in the Ohio country.

On the sea frontier, the British were eager to starve out the French West Indies and naturally expected the United States to defend them under the Franco-American alliance. Hard-boiled commanders of the Royal Navy, acting under instructions from London in 1793, struck savagely. They seized about three hundred American merchant ships in the West Indies, im-

pressed scores of seamen into service on English vessels, and threw hundreds of others into foul dungeons.

These outrages were intolerable. A mighty outcry arose, chiefly from Jeffersonians, that America should once again fight George III in defense of its liberties. At the very least, it should cut off all supplies to its oppressor through a nationwide embargo.

But the Federalists stoutly resisted all demands for drastic action. War with Britain would be a lethal blow at the heart of the Hamiltonian financial system. About 90 percent of the revenue supporting the nation's still-shaky financial structure flowed from customs duties, and some 75 percent of all customs duties came from British imports. An armed clash with England would dry up this life-giving revenue.

John Jay Negotiates a Treaty

President Washington, in a last desperate gamble to avert war, decided to send Chief Justice John Jay to London in 1794. The Jeffersonians were acutely unhappy over the choice, partly because they feared that so notorious a Federalist and Britain-lover would sell out his country. Arriving in London, Jay gave the Jeffersonians further cause for alarm when, at the presentation ceremony, he routinely kissed the queen's hand.

Unhappily, Jay entered the negotiations with weak cards, which were further weakened by Hamilton. The latter, fearful of war with England, secretly supplied the British with the details of America's bargaining strategy. Not surprisingly, Jay won few concessions. The British did promise to evacuate the chain of posts on

Evidently satirizing Jay's obeisance to the British queen, one American journal wrote "Hear the voice of truth, hear and believe! John Jay, ah! the arch traitor—seize him, drown him, hang him, burn him, flay him alive! Men of America, he betrayed you with a kiss!"

United States soil—a concession that inspired little confidence, since it had been made before in Paris (to the same John Jay!) in 1783. In addition, Britain consented to pay damages for the recent seizures of American ships. But the British stopped short of pledging anything about *future* maritime seizures and impressments or about Indian butcheries. And they forced Jay to give ground by binding the United States to pay the debts still owed to British merchants on pre-Revolutionary accounts.

When the Jeffersonians learned of Jay's concessions, their rage was fearful to behold. The treaty seemed like an abject surrender to Britain, as well as a betrayal of the Jeffersonian South. Southern planters would have to pay the major share of the pre-Revolutionary debts, while rich Federalist shippers were collecting damages for recent British seizures. Jeffersonian mobs hanged, burned, and guillotined in effigy that "damn'd archtraitor, Sir John Jay." His unpopular pact, more than any other issue, vitalized the newborn Democratic-Republican party of Thomas Jefferson.

President Washington was now confronted with an agonizing decision. He realized that the treaty was highly disappointing, but he also perceived, as did Hamilton, that the choice was either this treaty or none. If it was none, war would almost certainly ensue. And war might well be ruinous, given America's financially overstrained condition. So Washington, in one of the most courageous acts of a courageous life, threw his immense prestige behind the pact.

The president's course was both condemned and condoned. "Damn George Washington," reportedly cried John Randolph of Virginia in a public toast. Other violent Jeffersonians guillotined the president in effigy. But the Senate, after a stormy debate, approved the treaty by the narrowest of margins. War with Great Britain was thus averted for seventeen years.

A memorable pact with Spain was one of the aftermaths of Jay's Treaty, which in some ways was more important for its by-products than for its provisions. Spain feared that the Anglo-American pact foreshadowed an Anglo-American alliance—to its detriment. It therefore made haste to conclude with the United States the Pinckney Treaty of 1795. Unlike Jay's Treaty, it conceded virtually everything the Americans demanded. At long last Spain granted free navigation of the Mississippi; it yielded the large area north of Florida that had been in dispute for over a decade. (See map on p. 135.) America's totally unexpected diplomatic successes in this quarter were again a direct result of Spain's European distresses.

George Washington's Farewell

A weary Washington had hoped to retire in 1793, at the end of his first term. But his friends and advisers, including the arch-rivals Jefferson and Hamilton, begged him to stay. This was no time to turn from a leader of international eminence to one of sectional stature, like the disagreeably stiff New Englander, John Adams. Washington was unanimously reelected, simply because the nation could not do without him. Many people could still sing "God save great Washington," to the tune of "God Save the King."

But two full terms were enough. Washington was not only exhausted physically, but he was weary of verbal abuse. Having lost his nonpartisan standing when he became a Federalist, he was being assailed by political foes as an "American Caesar" and as the "Stepfather of His Country." Although he had no serious constitutional scruples against a third election, his decision to retire contributed powerfully to establishing the two-term tradition.*

Washington's Farewell Address was not delivered orally but was published in the newspapers of 1796. The bulk of the document, legend to the contrary, was not concerned with foreign affairs. About two-thirds of it was devoted to domestic problems, including a sage warning against partisan bitterness. Its admonition about alliances has been most misunderstood. Washington did not say that the nation should never make any alliances of any kind under any circumstances. As a military man, he favored

---

*Not broken until 1940 by Franklin D. Roosevelt and made a part of the Constitution in 1951 by the Twenty-second Amendment.

> *Thomas Paine, then in France and resenting George Washington's anti-French policies, addressed the president in an open letter (1796) that reveals his bitterness: "And as to you, sir, treacherous in private friendship (for so you have been to me, and that in the day of danger) and a hypocrite in public life, the world will be puzzled to decide, whether you are an apostate or an imposter; whether you have abandoned good principles, or whether you ever had any."*

"temporary alliances" for "extraordinary emergencies." But he strongly advised the avoidance of "permanent alliances," like the still-vexatious French Treaty of 1778.

Washington added still other words of paternal wisdom. With the pro-British Federalists and the pro-French Jeffersonians clearly in mind, he urged that the Republic avoid tying its political fortunes to the tail of a foreign kite. Subservience to overseas nations would cause America to become "in some degree a slave." With the plottings of Genêt and other French agents fresh in memory, Washington urged that the nation banish foreign intrigue from both domestic and diplomatic affairs.

The Farewell Address was not received with unanimous acclaim. Jeffersonians, on fire to help the French ally, assailed Washington's impartial words as though they were a declaration of war on France. The truth is that the president, in urging no "permanent" foreign entanglements, was giving admirable advice to a weak and divided nation in the year 1796. But what is sound counsel for a growing youth may not apply later to a muscular giant.

Washington's contributions as president were enormous, even though the sparkling Hamilton at times seemed to outshine him. The central government, its fiscal feet now under it, was solidly established. The West was expanding. The merchant marine was plowing the seas. Above all, Washington had kept the nation out of both overseas entanglements and foreign wars. The experimental stage had passed, and the presidential chair could now be turned over to a less impressive figure. But republics are

notoriously ungrateful. When Washington left office in 1797, he was showered with the brickbats of partisan abuse, quite in contrast with the bouquets that had greeted his coming. Though the vast majority of his countrymen honored his name, the more venomous Jeffersonians hailed his departure as ending tyranny and graft. "This day," cried journalist Benjamin Franklin Bache, a grandson of "Old Ben," "ought to be a jubilee in the United States."

"Bonny Johnny" Adams Becomes President

Who should succeed the exalted "Father of His Country"? Alexander Hamilton was the best-known member of the Federalist party, now that Washington had bowed out. But his financial policies, some of which had fattened the speculators, had made him so unpopular that he could not hope to be elected president. The Federalists were forced to turn to the experienced but ungracious John Adams, a rugged chip off old Plymouth Rock. The Democratic-Republicans naturally rallied behind their master organizer and leader, Thomas Jefferson.

Political passions ran feverishly high in the presidential canvass of 1796. The presence of Washington had hitherto imposed some restraints; now the lid was off. Cultured Federalists like Fisher Ames referred to the Jeffersonians as "fire-eating salamanders, poison-sucking toads." Federalists and Democratic-Republicans even drank their liquor in separate taverns. The issues of the campaign, as it turned out, focused heavily on personalities. But the Jeffersonians again assailed the too-forceful crushing of the Whiskey Rebellion and, above all, the negotiation of Jay's hated treaty.

> *Jefferson wrote privately of John Adams in 1787: "He is vain, irritable, and a bad calculator of the force and probable effect of the motives which govern men. This is all the ill which can possibly be said of him. He is as disinterested as the Being who made him."*

John Adams, with most of his support in New England, squeezed through by the narrow margin of 71 votes to 68 in the Electoral College. The resulting taunt, "President by three votes," was galling to his pride, which was highly developed. Jefferson, as runner-up, became vice-president.*

One of the ablest statesmen of his day, Adams at sixty-two was a stuffy figure. Sharp-featured, bald, short (5 feet 7 inches; 1.7 meters), and thickset ("His Rotundity"), he impressed observers as a man of stern principles who did his duty with stubborn devotion. Though learned and upright, he was a tactless and prickly intellectual aristocrat, with no appeal to the masses and with no desire to cultivate any. Many citizens regarded him with "respectful irritation."

The crusty New Englander suffered from other handicaps. He had stepped into Washington's shoes, which no successor could hope to fill. In addition, Adams was hated by Hamilton, who had resigned from the Treasury in 1795 and who now headed the war faction of the Federalist party. The famed financier even secretly plotted with certain members of the cabinet against the president, who had a conspiracy rather than a cabinet on his hands. Most ominous of all, Adams inherited a violent quarrel with France—a quarrel that foreshadowed blazing gunpowder.

Unofficial Fighting with France

The French were infuriated by Jay's Treaty. They condemned it as the initial step toward an alliance with England, their relentless foe. They further assailed the pact as a flagrant violation of the Franco-American Treaty of 1778. French warships, in retaliation, began to seize defenseless American merchant vessels, altogether about three hundred by mid-1797. Adding insult to outrage, the Paris regime haughtily re-

John Adams Second president of the United States, Adams reflected the optimistic, forward-looking values of the eighteenth-century Enlightenment in his views on education: "I must study politics and war, that my sons may have liberty to study mathematics and philosophy. My sons ought to study mathematics and philosophy, geography, natural history and naval architecture, in order to give their children a right to study painting, poetry, music, architecture, statuary, tapestry and porcelain." (Harvard University Portrait Collection.)

fused to receive America's newly appointed envoy and even threatened him with arrest.

President Adams kept his head, temporarily, even though the nation was mightily aroused. True to Washington's policy of steering clear of war at all costs, he tried again to reach an agreement with the French and appointed a diplomatic commission of three men, including John Marshall, the future chief justice.

Adams' envoys, reaching Paris in 1797, hoped to meet Talleyrand, the crafty French foreign minister. They were secretly approached by three go-betweens, later referred to

*The possibility of such an inharmonious two-party combination in the future was removed by the Twelfth Amendment to the Constitution in 1804. (See text in the Appendix.)

The XYZ Affair   *When President Adams's envoys to Paris were asked to pay a huge bribe as the price of doing diplomatic business, humiliated Americans rose up in wrath against France. Here an innocent young America is being plundered by Frenchmen as John Bull looks on in amusement. (The Lilly Library, Indiana University, Bloomington.)*

as X, Y, and Z in the published dispatches. The French spokesmen, among other concessions, demanded an unneutral loan of 32 million florins, plus what amounted to a bribe of $250,000 for the privilege of merely talking with Talleyrand.

These terms were intolerable. The American trio knew that bribes were standard diplomatic devices in Europe, but they gagged at paying a quarter of a million dollars for mere talk, without any assurances of a settlement. Negotiations quickly broke down, and John Marshall, on reaching New York in 1798, was hailed as a conquering hero for his steadfastness.

War hysteria swept the United States, catching up President Adams. The slogan of the hour

Preparation for War to Defend Commerce
The building of the frigate Philadelphia. In 1803 this frigate ran onto the rocks near Tripoli harbor, and about three hundred officers and men were imprisoned by the Tripolitans. The ship was refloated for service against the Americans, but Stephen Decatur led a party of men that set her afire. (Prints Division, the New York Public Library, Astor, Lenox and Tilden Foundations.)

became "Millions for defense, but not one cent for tribute." The song of the hour was "Hail Columbia," which was sung lustily in theaters and taverns:

> Immortal patriots, rise once more!
> Defend your rights, defend your shore.

The Federalists were delighted at this unexpected turn of affairs, while all except the most rabid Jeffersonians hung their heads over the misbehavior of their fine-feathered French friends.

War preparations in America were pushed feverishly, despite considerable Jeffersonian opposition in Congress. The Navy Department was created; the three-ship navy was expanded; the Marine Corps was established. A new army of ten thousand men was authorized (but never fully raised), to be headed by the redoubtable but aging General Washington. He reluctantly heeded the call of duty but stipulated that the active command be entrusted to the younger Alexander Hamilton, who became a major general. A frustrated military genius, Hamilton was intoxicated by dreams of conquest. He would lead a victorious American army, supported by the British navy, against the possessions of France's Spanish ally—specifically the Floridas, Louisiana, Mexico, and perhaps points south.

Bloodshed was confined to the sea, and principally to the West Indies. In two and one-half years of undeclared hostilities (1798–1800), American privateers and men-of-war of the new navy captured over eighty armed vessels flying the French colors, though several hundred Yankee merchantmen were lost to the enemy. Evidently only a slight push would plunge both nations into a full-dress war.

Adams Puts Patriotism above Party

Embattled France, its hands full in Europe, wanted no war. An outwitted Talleyrand realized that to fight the United States would merely add one more foe to his enemies. The British, who were lending the Americans cannon and other war supplies, were actually driven closer to their wayward cousins than

> Adams' firmness was revealed in his message to Congress (June 1798): "I will never send another minister to France without assurances that he will be received, respected, and honored as the representative of a great, free, powerful, and independent nation."

they were to be again for many years. Talleyrand therefore let it be known, through roundabout channels, that if the Americans would send a new minister, he would be received with proper respect.

This French furor brought to Adams a degree of personal acclaim that he had never known before—and was never to know again. The song "Adams and Liberty" was hardly less popular than "Hail Columbia." He doubtless perceived that a full-fledged war, crowned by the conquest of the Floridas and Louisiana, would bring new plaudits to the Federalist party—and perhaps a second term to himself. But the heady wine of popularity did not sway his final judgment. He realized full well, like other Founding Fathers, that war must be avoided while the country was relatively weak.

Adams unexpectedly exploded a bombshell when, early in 1799, he submitted to the Senate the name of a new minister to France. Hamilton and his war-hawk faction were enraged. But public opinion—Jeffersonian and reasonable Federalist alike—was favorable to one last try for peace.

America's envoys (now three) found the political skies brightening when they reached Paris early in 1800. The ambitious "Little Corporal," the Corsican Bonaparte, had recently seized dictatorial power. He was eager to free his hands of the American squabble so that he might continue to redraw the map of Europe and perhaps create a New World empire in Louisiana. The distresses and ambitions of the Old World were again working to America's advantage.

After much haggling, a memorable treaty known as the Convention of 1800 was signed in Paris. France agreed to grant a divorce from the twenty-two-year-old marriage of (in)conven-

In 1815 Adams wrote privately: "I will defend my missions to France, as long as I have an eye to direct my hand, or a finger to hold my pen. They were the most disinterested and meritorious actions of my life. I reflect upon them with . . . satisfaction."

ience, but as a kind of alimony the United States itself agreed to pay the damage claims of American shippers. So ended the nation's only peacetime military alliance for a century and a half. Its troubled history does much to explain the traditional antipathy of the American people to foreign entanglements.

Adams, flinty to the end, deserves immense credit for his belated push for peace, even though moved in part by jealousy of Hamilton. He not only avoided the hazards of war, but unwittingly smoothed the path for the peaceful purchase of Louisiana three years later. He should indeed rank high among the forgotten purchasers of this vast domain. If America had drifted into a full-blown war with France in 1800, Napoleon would not have sold her Louisiana on any terms in 1803.

President Adams, the bubble of his popularity pricked by peace, was aware of his signal contribution to the nation. He later suggested as the epitaph for his tombstone (not used): "Here lies John Adams, who took upon himself the responsibility of peace with France in the year 1800."

The Federalist Witch Hunt

Exulting Federalists had meanwhile capitalized on the anti-French frenzy to drive through Congress in 1798 a sheaf of laws designed to reduce or gag their Jeffersonian foes.

The first of these oppressive laws was aimed at supposedly pro-Jeffersonian "aliens." Most European immigrants, lacking wealth, were scorned by the aristocratic Federalist party. But they were welcomed as voters by the less prosperous and more democratic Jeffersonians. The Federalist Congress, hoping to discourage the

"dregs" of Europe, erected a disheartening barrier. They raised the residence requirements for aliens who desired to become citizens from a tolerable five years to an intolerable fourteen. This drastic new law violated the traditional American policy of open-door hospitality and speedy assimilation.

Two additional Alien Laws struck heavily at undesirable immigrants. The president was empowered to deport dangerous foreigners in time of peace and to deport or imprison them in time of hostilities. Though defensible as a war measure—and an officially declared war with France seemed imminent—this was an arbitrary grant of power contrary to American tradition and to the spirit of the Constitution.

But the Alien Laws were not so senseless as they may seem. Hundreds of foreign firebrands, fleeing the wrath of the homeland authorities, were pouring into America from France, England, and Ireland. Most of these outcasts joined the ranks of the Jeffersonians, where they naturally clamored for an anti-British policy. A few of them were French spies who should have been expelled; many were what President Adams called "foreign liars."

The stringent Alien Laws were never enforced. But they frightened out of the country certain foreign agitators, including a reported two shiploads of French citizens. In addition, an undetermined number of other foreigners were discouraged from sailing to the now not-so-promising promised land.

The "lockjaw" Sedition Act, the last of the harsh Federalist measures, was a direct slap at two priceless freedoms guaranteed in the Constitution by the Bill of Rights—freedom of speech and freedom of the press (First Amendment). This law provided that anyone who impeded the policies of the government or falsely defamed its officials, including the president, would be liable to a heavy fine and imprisonment. Severe though the measure was, the Federalists believed that it was justified. The verbal violence of the day was unrestrained, and foul-penned editors, some of them exiled aliens, assailed Adams' anti-French policy in vicious terms.

Many outspoken Jeffersonian editors were indicted under the Sedition Act, and ten were brought to trial. All of them were convicted, of-

Congressional Pugilists
Satirical representation of Matthew Lyon's fight in Congress with the Federalist Representative Roger Griswold. (The Bettmann Archive.)

ten by packed juries swayed by prejudiced Federalist judges. A few of the victims were harmless partisans, who should have been spared the notoriety of martyrdom. Among them was Congressman Matthew Lyon (the "Spitting Lion"), who had earlier gained fame by spitting in the face of a Federalist. He was sentenced to four months in jail for writing of President Adams' "unbounded thirst for ridiculous pomp, foolish adulation, and selfish avarice." Another culprit was lucky to get off with a fine of $100 after he

> James Callender published in 1800 a pamphlet that assailed the president in this language: "The reign of Mr. Adams has, hitherto, been one continued tempest of malignant passions. As president, he has never opened his lips, or lifted his pen, without threatening and scolding. The grand object of his administration has been to exasperate the rage of contending parties, to calumniate and destroy every man who differs from his opinions. . . . Every person holding an office must either quit it, or think and vote exactly with Mr. Adams." For such blasts Callender was prosecuted under the Sedition Act, fined $250, and sentenced to prison for nine months.

had expressed the wish that the wad of a cannon fired in honor of Adams had landed in the seat of the president's breeches.

The Sedition Act, at least in spirit, was in direct conflict with the Constitution. But the Supreme Court, dominated by Federalists, was of no mind to declare this Federalist law unconstitutional. (The law expired, in March 1801, to much rejoicing from Jeffersonians.) This attempt by the Federalists to crush free speech and silence the opposition party, high-handed as it was, undoubtedly made many converts for the Jeffersonians.

Yet the Alien and Sedition Laws, despite pained outcries from the Jeffersonians, commanded widespread popular support. Anti-French hysteria played directly into the hands of witch-hunting conservatives. In the congressional elections of 1798–1799, the Federalists, riding a wave of popularity, scored the most sweeping victory of their entire history.

The Virginia (Madison) and Kentucky (Jefferson) Resolutions

Resentful Jeffersonians naturally refused to take the Alien and Sedition Laws lying down. Jefferson himself feared that if the Federalists managed to choke free speech and free press, they would then wipe out other precious constitutional guarantees. His own political party might even be stamped out of existence. If this had happened, the country might have drifted into a dangerous one-party dictatorship.

As vice-president under Adams, Jefferson was in an awkward position to protest openly against the Alien and Sedition Laws. Fearing prosecution for sedition, he secretly penned a series of resolutions, which the Kentucky legislature approved in 1798 and 1799. His friend and fellow Virginian James Madison drafted a similar but less extreme statement, which was adopted by the legislature of Virginia in 1798.

Both Jefferson and Madison stressed the compact theory—a theory popular among English political philosophers in the seventeenth and eighteenth centuries. As applied to America by the Jeffersonians, this concept meant that the thirteen sovereign states, in creating the federal government, had entered into a "compact," or contract, regarding its jurisdiction. The national government was consequently the agent or creation of the states. Since water can rise no higher than its source, the individual states were the final judges of whether their agent had broken the "compact" by overstepping the authority originally granted. Invoking this logic, Jefferson's Kentucky resolutions concluded that the federal regime had exceeded its constitutional powers and that with regard to the Alien and Sedition Acts "nullification" was the "rightful remedy."

If Federalists bent the bow too far in passing the Alien and Sedition Acts, Jefferson bent the bow too far in his reply. If the Federalist indiscretion had made many Jeffersonian voters, Jefferson's indiscretion made many Federalist voters. No other state legislatures, despite Jefferson's hopes, fell into line. Some of them flatly refused to endorse the Virginia and Kentucky resolutions. Others, chiefly in Federalist states, added ringing condemnations. Many Federalists argued that the people, not the states, had made the original compact, and that it was up to the Supreme Court—not the states—to nullify unconstitutional legislation passed by Congress. This practice, though not specifically authorized by the Constitution, was finally adopted by the Supreme Court in 1803.

The Virginia and Kentucky resolutions were a brilliant formulation of the extreme states'-rights view regarding the Union. They were later used by southerners to support nullification—and ultimately secession. Yet neither Jefferson nor Madison, as Founding Fathers of the Union, had any intention of breaking it up: they were groping for ways to preserve it. Their resolutions were basically campaign documents designed to crystallize opposition to the Federalist party and to unseat it in the upcoming presidential election of 1800. The only real nullification that Jefferson had in view was the nullification of Federalist abuses.

Federalist and Republican Mudslingers

In the heated presidential contest of 1800, Adams and Jefferson were again the standard-bearers of their respective parties. The Federalists labored under heavy handicaps. Their Alien and Sedition Acts had aroused a host of enemies, although most of these critics were dyed-in-the-wool Jeffersonians anyhow. The Hamiltonian wing of the Federalist party, robbed of its glorious war with France, split openly with President Adams. Hamilton, a victim of arrogance, was so indiscreet as to attack the president in a privately printed pamphlet. Jeffersonians soon got hold of the pamphlet and gleefully published it.

The most damaging blow to the Federalists was the refusal of Adams to give them a rousing fight with France. Their feverish war preparations had swelled the public debt and had required disagreeable new taxes, including a stamp tax. After all these unpopular measures, the war scare had petered out, and the country was left with an all-dressed-up-but-no-place-to-go feeling. The military preparations now seemed not only unnecessary but extravagant, as seamen for the "new navy" were called "John Adams' Jackasses." Adams himself was known as "the Father of the American Navy."

Thrown on the defensive, the Federalists concentrated their fire on Jefferson himself, who became the victim of one of the earliest "whispering campaigns." He was accused of having robbed a widow and her children of a

The Providential Detection (Federalist Propaganda) *The American eagle snatches the Constitution from Jefferson, who is about to burn it (together with the works of Voltaire, Paine, and others) on the altar to French Revolutionary despotism. (Massachusetts Historical Society.)*

trust fund and of having fathered numerous mulatto children by his own slave women. As a liberal in religion, he had earlier incurred the wrath of the orthodox clergy, largely through his successful struggle to separate church and state in Virginia. From the New England stronghold of Federalism and Congregationalism, the preachers thundered against his atheism, although he did believe in God. Old ladies

> The Reverend Timothy Dwight, president of Yale College, predicted that in the event of Jefferson's election "the Bible would be cast into a bonfire, our holy worship changed into a dance of [French] Jacobin phrensy, our wives and daughters dishonored, and our sons converted into the disciples of Voltaire and the dragoons of Marat."

of Federalist families, fearing Jefferson's election, even buried their Bibles or hung them in wells.

The Jeffersonian "Revolution of 1800"

Jefferson won by a majority of 73 electoral votes to 65. But the colorless and presumably unpopular Adams polled more electoral strength than he had gained four years earlier—except for New York. The Empire State fell into the Jeffersonian basket, and with it the election, largely because Aaron Burr, a master wire-puller, turned New York to Jefferson by the narrowest of margins. The Virginian polled the bulk of his strength in the South and West, particularly in those states where manhood suffrage had been adopted.

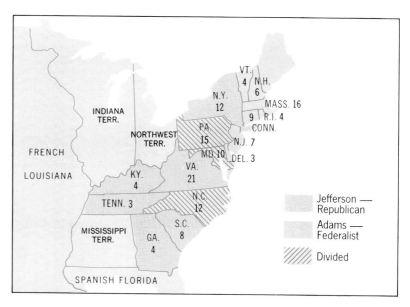

Presidential Election of 1800 (with electoral vote by state) *New York was the key state in this election, and Aaron Burr helped swing it away from the Federalists with tactics that anticipated the political "machines" of a later day. Federalists complained that Burr "travels every night from one meeting of Republicans to another, haranguing... them to the most zealous exertions. [He] can stoop so low as to visit every low tavern that may happen to be crowded with his dear fellow citizens." But Burr proved that the price was worth it. "We have beat you," Burr told kid-gloved Federalists after the election, "by superior Management."*

Jeffersonians rejoiced wildly over the end of the "Federalist Reign of Terror." Some of them, with alcoholic enthusiasm, bawled the song "Jefferson and Liberty":

> Lord! how the Federalists will stare
> At Jefferson, in Adams' chair!

But Jeffersonian joy was dampened by an unexpected deadlock. Through a technicality Jefferson, the presidential candidate, and Burr, his vice-presidential running mate, received the same number of electoral votes for the presidency. Under the Constitution the tie could be broken only by the House of Representatives (see Art. II, Sec. I, para. 2). This body was controlled for several more months by the lame-duck Federalists, who had been swept into office during the French war scare and who were eager to elect Burr.*

Voting in the House moved slowly to a climax. As ballots were taken in wearisome succession, representatives snored in their seats; a

---

*A "lame duck" has been humorously defined as a politician whose political goose has been cooked at the recent elections. The possibility of another such tie was removed by the Twelfth Amendment in 1804 (for text, see the Appendix). Before then, each elector had two votes, with the second-place finisher becoming vice-president.

sick member lay in an adjoining room. Historians used to think that Hamilton, bargaining secretly with Jefferson, played a decisive role. But the evidence indicates that the deadlock was broken when a few Federalists, despairing of electing Burr and hoping for moderation from Jefferson, refrained from voting. The election then went to the rightful candidate.

Jefferson later claimed that the election of 1800 was a "revolution" comparable to that of 1776. But it was no revolution in the sense of a massive popular upheaval or an upending of the political system. In truth, Jefferson had narrowly squeaked through to victory. A switch of some 250 votes in New York would have thrown the election to Adams. What *was* revolutionary was the peaceful and orderly transfer of power on the basis of an election whose results all parties accepted. This was a remarkable—indeed, even "revolutionary"—achievement for a raw young nation, especially after all the partisan bitterness that had agitated the country during Adams' presidency. It was particularly remarkable in that age; comparable developments would not take place in Britain for another generation. Americans could take justifiable pride in the vigor of their experiment in democracy.

The Federalist Finale

John Adams, as fate would have it, was the last Federalist president of the United States. His party sank slowly into the mire of political oblivion and ultimately disappeared completely in the days of Andrew Jackson.

Whatever their shortcomings, the Federalists were a party of the elite. They boasted a much higher concentration of brains, talent, and ability than any other major American political party, past or present. Their political and financial leaders had built enduring foundations for the new government. Their diplomats, with a strong helping hand from Europe's distresses, had signed advantageous treaties with England, Spain, and France. Their leaders had kept the peace during a crucial period when peace had to be kept.

After all the turmoil of the American Revolution, a conservative party served a needed function in preserving democratic gains and fending off anarchy. The Federalists provided a welcome breathing spell, a chance for the nation to get its bearings. They served, in the words of historian Henry Adams, great-grandson of John Adams, as the "half-way house between the European past and the American future."

But by 1800 the Federalists, blessed with more talent than wisdom, were out of place. The bustling new Republic knew instinctively where it was going. It was eager to take the high road over the mountains that would one day lead to the fulfillment of America's democratic experiment. The Federalists lost out because they were content to mark time and failed to get in step with the westward march of progress. They were unable or unwilling to unbend and appeal to the common people. They could not adapt—so they died, like the dinosaur. Distinguished though their past service had been, it was no substitute for a capacity to grapple democratically with future problems. The victorious Jeffersonians were prepared to keep the Federalist edifice while ousting the Federalist architects.

Varying Viewpoints

Historians have rightly regarded the Federalist era as the seedtime of the nation's foreign policy. As debate continues over America's role abroad, so does argument still swirl about the diplomacy of the Federalists. Was George Washington the father of unreasoning "isolationism," or did he set forth a realistic policy for the infant nation to follow? Could Washington reasonably expect that "in extending our commercial relations" with foreign nations, the United States could "have with them as little political connection as possible"? Was that policy equally applicable when the infant nation had matured? What was the historical basis of Washington's ideas? Some scholars regard his policies as opportune rationalizations of the country's weak position. Others, especially Felix Gilbert, see them as high expressions of all the best Enlightenment thought about an ideal international order. This question—concerning the degree to which American foreign policy reflects self-interest or idealism—has continued to be argued from Washington's day to the present.

Select Readings

Primary Source Documents

Important salvos in the battle between national power and state sovereignty, and between Federalists and Jeffersonians, were the Virginia and Kentucky resolutions* (1798) and the reply of Rhode Island* (1799). Washington's Farewell Address* (1796) established the foundation for American attitudes about party politics and foreign policy. See also Benjamin Franklin Bache's stinging editorial on Washington's retirement, Philadelphia *Aurora** (1797).

Secondary Sources

See the titles by Marcus Cunliffe and John C. Miller cited in the preceding chapter. On the rise of parties, consult Noble E. Cunningham, *The Jeffersonian Republicans* (1958). On aspects of foreign policy, see Alexander De Conde, *Entangling Alliance* (1958), and his *Quasi-War: The Politics and Diplomacy of the Undeclared War with France, 1797–1801* (1966); Gilbert Lycan, *Alexander Hamilton and American Foreign Policy* (1970); Jerald Combs, *The Jay Treaty* (1970); Lawrence S. Kaplan, *Colonies into Nation: American Diplomacy, 1763–1801* (1972); Louis M. Sears, *George Washington and the French Revolution* (1960); Paul A. Varg, *Foreign Policies of the Founding Fathers* (1963); Felix Gilbert, *To the Farewell Address* (1961); and Julian Boyd, *Number 7* (1964), on Hamilton's devious dealings with the British. For the view from across the Atlantic, see Charles R. Ritcheson, *Aftermath of Revolution: British Policy toward the United States, 1783–1795* (1969). On Adams, consult Page Smith, *John Adams* (2) vols., (1962), and Stephen G. Kurtz, *The Presidency of John Adams* (1957). John C. Miller, *Crisis in Freedom* (1951), and James M. Smith, *Freedom's Fetters* (1956), treat the Alien and Sedition Laws, as does Leonard Levy, *Legacy of Suppression* (1960).

11

The Triumph of Jeffersonian Democracy

Timid men . . . prefer the calm of despotism to the boisterous sea of liberty.

Thomas Jefferson, 1796

Responsibility Breeds Moderation

"Long Tom" Jefferson was inaugurated president on March 4, 1801, in the swampy village of Washington, the crude new national capital. Tall (6 feet 2.5 inches; 1.89 meters), with large hands and feet, reddish hair ("The Red Fox"), and prominent cheekbones and chin, he was an arresting figure. Believing that the customary pomp did not befit his democratic ideals, he spurned a horse-drawn coach and simply walked over to the Capitol from his boardinghouse.

The inaugural address, beautifully phrased, was a classic statement of democratic principles. Seeking to allay Federalist fears of a bull-in-the-china-closet overturn, Jefferson blandly stated, "We are all Republicans, we are all Federalists." As for foreign affairs, he pledged "honest friendship with all nations, entangling alliances with none."

With its rustic setting, Washington lent itself admirably to the simplicity and frugality of the Jeffersonian Republicans. In this respect, it contrasted sharply with the elegant atmosphere of Federalist Philadelphia, the former temporary capital. Extending democratic principles to etiquette, Jefferson established the rule of pell-mell at official dinners—that is, seating without regard to rank. The resplendent British minister, who had enjoyed precedence among the pro-British Federalists, was insulted.

Jefferson's toleration was reflected in his inaugural address. "If there be any among us who would wish to dissolve this Union or to change its republican form, let them stand undisturbed as monuments of the safety with which error of opinion may be tolerated where reason is left free to combat it."

Washington and Jefferson Contrasted   *Note the emphasis on Jefferson's fondness for freethinkers like Paine and Voltaire. Jefferson liked the democratic way of thinking and the aristocratic way of living. His personal wine bill at the White House ran to over $10,000. (New-York Historical Society.)*

As a widower, Jefferson was shockingly unconventional. Having no wife to police his apparel, he would receive callers in sloppy attire—once in a dressing gown and heelless slippers. He started the precedent, unbroken for 112 years, of sending messages to Congress to be read by a clerk. Personal appearances, in the Federalist manner, suggested too strongly a monarchical speech from the throne. Besides, Jefferson was painfully conscious of his weak voice and unimpressive platform presence.

As if plagued by an evil spirit, Jefferson was forced to reverse many of the political principles he had so vigorously championed. There were in fact two Thomas Jeffersons. One was the private citizen, who had philosophized in his study. The other was the public official, who made the disturbing discovery that bookish theories worked out differently in the noisy arena of practical politics. The open-minded Virginian was therefore consistently inconsistent; it is easy to quote one Jefferson to refute the other.

The triumph of Jefferson's Democratic-Republicans and the eviction of the Federalists marked the first party overturn in American history. The vanquished naturally feared that the victors would grab all the spoils of office for themselves. But Jefferson, in line with his conciliatory inaugural address, showed unexpected moderation. To the dismay of his office-seeking friends, the new president dismissed few public servants for political reasons. Patronage-hungry Jeffersonians watched the Federalist appointees grow old in office and grumbled that "few die, none resign."

Jefferson quickly proved an able politician. He was especially effective in the informal atmosphere of a dinner party. There he wooed congressional representatives while personally pouring imported wines and serving the tasty dishes of his French cook.

In part, Jefferson had to rely on his personal charm because his party was so weak-jointed. Denied the power to dispense patronage, the Democratic-Republicans could not build a loyal political following. Opposition to the Federalists was the chief glue holding them together, and as the Federalists faded, so did Democratic-Republican unity. The era of well-developed, well-disciplined political parties still lay in the future.

Jeffersonian Restraint Helps to Further a "Revolution"

At the outset, Jefferson was determined to undo the Federalist abuses begotten by the anti-French hysteria. The hated Alien and Sedition

Laws had already expired. The incoming president speedily pardoned the "martyrs" serving sentences under the Sedition Law, and the government returned many fines. Shortly after the Congress met, the Jeffersonians enacted the new naturalization law of 1802. The law reduced the unreasonable requirement of fourteen years of residence to the former and more reasonable requirement of five years.

Jefferson actually kicked away only one substantial prop of the Hamiltonian system. He hated the excise tax, which bred bureaucrats and bore heavily on his farmer following, and he early persuaded Congress to repeal it. His devotion to principle thus cost the federal government about a million dollars a year in urgently needed revenue.

Swiss-born and French-accented Albert Gallatin, "Watchdog of the Treasury," proved to be as able a secretary of the treasury as Hamilton. Gallatin agreed with Jefferson that a national debt was a bane rather than a blessing and by strict economy succeeded in reducing it substantially while balancing the budget.

Except for excising the excise tax, the Jeffersonians left the Hamiltonian framework essentially intact. They did not tamper with the Federalist programs for funding the national debt at par and assuming the Revolutionary War debts of the states. They launched no attack on the Bank of the United States, and they did not repeal the mildly protective Federalist tariff. In later years they embraced Federalism to such a degree as to recharter a bigger bank and to boost the protective tariff to higher levels.

Paradoxically, Jefferson's moderation thus further cemented the gains of the "Revolution of 1800." That revolution had consisted above all in the peaceful replacement of one govern-

ing party by another. By shrewdly absorbing the major Federalist programs, Jefferson showed that a change of regime need not be disastrous for the defeated group. His restraint pointed the way toward the two-party system that was later to become a characteristic feature of American politics.

The "Dead Clutch" of the Judiciary

The "deathbed" Judiciary Act of 1801 was one of the last important laws passed by the expiring Federalist Congress. It created sixteen new federal judgeships and other judicial offices. President Adams remained at his desk until nine o'clock in the evening of his last day in office, allegedly signing the commissions of the Federalist "midnight judges." (Actually only three commissions were signed on his last day.)

This Federalist-sponsored Judiciary Act, though a long-overdue reform, aroused bitter resentment. "Packing" these lifetime posts with anti-Jeffersonian partisans was, in Republican eyes, a brazen attempt by the defeated party to entrench itself in one of the three powerful branches of government. Jeffersonians condemned the "midnight judges" in violent language. To them, the trickery of the Federalists was open defiance of the people's will, as recently expressed at the polls.

The newly elected Republican Congress bestirred itself to repeal the Judiciary Act of 1801 in the year after its passage. Jeffersonians thus swept sixteen benches from under the recently appointed "midnight judges." Frustrated Federalists, in turn, were acidly critical of this "assault" on the judicial arm.

Jeffersonians likewise had their knives sharpened for the scalp of Chief Justice John Marshall, whom Adams had appointed to the Supreme Court (as a fourth choice) in the dying days of his term. The lanky Marshall, with his rasping voice and steel-trap mind, was a cousin of Thomas Jefferson. As a Virginia Federalist, he was cordially disliked by the states' rights Jeffersonians. He served for about thirty days under a Federalist administration and thirty-four years under the administrations of the Jeffersonian Republicans and their successors.

President John F. Kennedy later greeted a large group of Nobel Prize winners as "the most extraordinary collection of talent, of human knowledge, that has ever been gathered together at the White House, with the possible exception of when Thomas Jefferson dined alone."

The Federalist party died out, but Marshall went on handing down Federalist decisions serenely for many more years. He probably did more than Hamilton to engraft the Hamiltonian concept of a powerful central government upon the American political and economic system.

One of the "midnight judges" of 1801 presented John Marshall with a historic opportunity. He was obscure William Marbury, whom President Adams had named a justice of the peace for the District of Columbia. When Marbury learned that his commission was being held up by the new secretary of state, James Madison, he sued for its delivery. Chief Justice Marshall knew that his Jeffersonian rivals, entrenched in the executive branch, would hardly spring forward to enforce a writ to deliver the commission to his fellow Federalist Marbury. He therefore dismissed Marbury's suit, avoiding a direct political showdown. But the wily Marshall snatched a victory from the jaws of this judicial defeat. In explaining his ruling, Marshall said that the part of the Judiciary Act of 1789 on which Marbury tried to base his appeal was unconstitutional. The act had attempted to assign to the Supreme Court powers that the Constitution had not foreseen.

In this self-denying opinion, Marshall greatly magnified the authority of the Court—and slapped at the Jeffersonians. Until the case of *Marbury* v. *Madison* (1803), controversy had clouded the question of who had the final authority to determine the meaning of the Constitution. Jefferson in the Kentucky resolutions (1798) had tried to assign that right to the individual states. But now his cousin on the Court had cleverly promoted the contrary principle of "judicial review"—that the black-robed tribunal of the Supreme Court alone had the last word on the question of constitutionality. In this epochal case, Marshall inserted the keystone into the arch that supports the tremendous power of the Supreme Court in American life.*

Jefferson Threatens the Supremacy of the Supreme Court

Marshall's decision regarding Marbury spurred the Jeffersonians in their desire to lay rough hands on the Supreme Court through impeachment. Certain Federalist judges had become highly offensive, especially in Sedition Law cases, by delivering harangues from the bench against the Republican "mobocracy." Jefferson favored free speech, but not this kind of free speech. Accordingly, he urged action against an arrogant Supreme Court justice, Samuel Chase, who was so unpopular that Republicans named vicious dogs after him.

Early in 1804 impeachment charges against Chase were voted by the House of Representatives, which then passed the question of guilt or innocence on to the Senate. The indictment by the House was based on "high crimes and misdemeanors," as specified in the Constitution.[†]

In his decision in Marbury v. Madison, *Chief Justice Marshall vigorously asserted his view that the Constitution embodied a "higher" law than ordinary legislation, and that the Court must interpret the Constitution:*

"The Constitution is either a superior paramount law, unchangeable by ordinary means, or it is on a level with ordinary legislative acts, and, like other acts, is alterable when the legislature shall please to alter it.

"If the former part of the alternative be true, then a legislative act contrary to the constitution is not law; if the latter part be true, then written constitutions are absurd attempts, on the part of the people, to limit a power in its own nature illimitable . . .

"It is emphatically the province and duty of the judicial department to say what the law is . . .

"If, then, the courts are to regard the Constitution, and the Constitution is superior to any ordinary act of the legislature, the Constitution, and not such ordinary act, must govern the case to which they are both applicable."

---

*The next invalidation of a federal law by the Supreme Court came fifty-four years later, with the explosive Dred Scott decision (see p. 399).
†For impeachment, see Art. I, Sec. II, para. 5; Art. I, Sec. III, paras. 6, 7; Art. II, Sec. IV, in the Appendix.

Mad Tom in a Rage *A Federalist cartoon shows "Mad Tom" Jefferson, assisted by brandy and the Devil, trying to pull down the federal edifice erected by Washington and Adams. (Houghton Library, Harvard.)*

Yet the evidence was plain that the intemperate judge had not been guilty of "high crimes" but of bad manners, injudicious statements, and unrestrained partisanship. The Senate, after a determined prosecution, failed to muster enough votes to convict and remove Chase. The precedent thus established was fortunate. From that day to this, no really serious attempt has been made to reshape the Supreme Court by the impeachment weapon.

John Marshall viewed the attack on Chase with deep misgivings. He suspected, not unreasonably, that if it succeeded, he would be next—and then his other Federalist colleagues. These fears were now laid to rest. Jefferson's ill-advised attempt at "judge breaking" was a reassuring victory for the independence of the judi-

ciary and for the separation of powers among the three branches of the federal government.

The Pacifist Jefferson Turns Warrior

As a passionate champion of freedom, Jefferson distrusted large standing armies as a standing invitation to dictatorship. Navies, though also suspect, were less to be feared: they could not march inland and "endanger liberties." Pinning his faith to the frail reed of an ill-trained militia, Jefferson reduced the military establishment to a mere police force of 2,500 officers and men. The Republicans, primarily agrarians, saw little point in protecting a few Federalist shippers with a costly navy that all the taxpayers would have to support. Pledged to rigid economy, Jefferson gladly reduced the navy to a peacetime footing, in accordance with legislation already passed by the outgoing Federalist Congress.

But harsh realities forced a penny-pinching Jefferson to change his tune on navies and war. Pirates of the North African states had long made a national industry of blackmailing and plundering merchant ships that ventured into the Mediterranean. Preceding Federalist administrations, in fact, had been forced to buy protection. At the time of the French crisis of 1798, when Americans were shouting, "Millions for defense, but not one cent for tribute," twenty-six barrels of blackmail dollars were being shipped to piratical Algiers.

At this price, war seemed cheaper than peace, and the showdown came in 1801. The Pasha of Tripoli, dissatisfied with his share of protection money, informally declared war on the United States by cutting down the flagstaff of the American consulate. A challenge was thus thrown squarely into the face of Jefferson—the noninterventionist, the pacifist, the critic of a big-ship navy, and the political foe of Federalist shippers. He reluctantly rose to the occasion by dispatching the infant navy to the "shores of Tripoli," as related in the song of the U.S. Marine Corps. After four years of intermittent fighting, marked by hair-raising exploits, Jefferson succeeded in extorting a treaty

Four Barbary States of North Africa

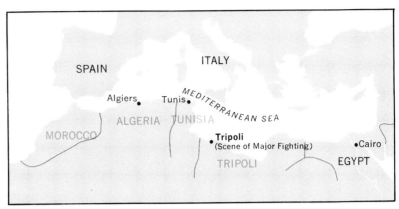

of peace from Tripoli in 1805. It was secured at the bargain price of only $60,000—a sum representing ransom payments for captured Americans.

With the pattern thus set, the punishment of other North African corsairs continued, off and on, until after the War of 1812. The navy reaped a rich harvest of experience, while strengthening its budding tradition. Foreign nations in general, and the Barbary cutthroats in particular, developed a wholesome respect for the United States—a nation willing and able to defend its rights with blazing guns.

Small gunboats, which the navy had used with some success in the Tripolitan War, fascinated Jefferson. Pledged to tax reduction, he advocated a large number of tiny coastal craft—"Jeffs" or the "mosquito fleet," as they were contemptuously called. He believed that these frail vessels would prove valuable in guarding American shores, although not in defending Federalist merchantmen on the high seas.

About two hundred tiny gunboats were constructed, democratically in small shipyards where votes could be made for Jefferson. Often mounting only one unwieldy gun, they were sometimes more of a menace to the crew than to the prospective enemy. During a hurricane and tidal wave at Savannah, Georgia, one of them was deposited eight miles (12.9 kilometers) inland in a cornfield, to the derisive glee of the Federalists. They drank toasts to American gunboats as the best in the world—on land. Jefferson's pinchpenny economizing backfired badly when the War of 1812 broke out and the whole swarm of gunboats proved virtually stingless. The money could have been much more wisely invested in a few frigates of the *Constitution* class.

The Louisiana Godsend

A secret pact, fraught with peril for America, was signed in 1800. Napoleon Bonaparte induced the King of Spain to cede to France, for attractive considerations, the immense trans-Mississippi region of Louisiana, which included the New Orleans area.

Rumors of the transfer were partially confirmed in 1802, when the Spaniards at New Orleans withdrew the right of deposit guaranteed America by the treaty of 1795. Deposit privileges were vital to frontier farmers who floated their produce down the Mississippi to its mouth, there to await oceangoing vessels. A roar of anger rolled up the mighty river and into its tributary valleys. American pioneers talked wildly of descending upon New Orleans, rifles in hand. Had they done so, the nation probably

---

Explaining the western outburst over the closing of the river, James Madison wrote to Pinckney: "The Mississippi is to them every thing. It is the Hudson, the Delaware, the Potomac, and all the navigable rivers of the Atlantic States, formed into one stream."

would have been involved in war with both Spain and France.

Thomas Jefferson, both pacifistic and anti-entanglement, was again on the griddle. Louisiana in the senile grip of Spain posed no real threat; America could seize the territory when the time was ripe. But Louisiana in the iron fist of Napoleon, the preeminent military genius of his age, foreshadowed a dark and blood-drenched future. The United States would probably have to fight to dislodge him; and because it alone was not strong enough to defeat his armies, it would have to seek allies, contrary to the deepening anti-alliance policy.

Hoping to quiet the clamor of the West, Jefferson moved decisively. Early in 1803 he sent James Monroe to Paris to join forces with the regular minister there, Robert R. Livingston. The two envoys were instructed to buy New Orleans and as much land to the east as they could get for a maximum of $10 million. If these proposals should fail and the situation should become critical, negotiations were to be opened with England for an alliance.

Nothing could better illustrate Jefferson's concern. Though a passionate hater of war and an enemy of entangling alliances, he was proposing to make an alliance with his old foe, England, against his old friend, France, with the object of waging a defensive war.

Napoleon now suddenly decided to sell all Louisiana and abandon his dream of a New World empire. He had failed in his efforts to reconquer the sugar-rich island of Santo Domingo, for which Louisiana was to serve as a granary. Infuriated ex-slaves, ably led by a gifted black, Toussaint L'Ouverture, had put up a stubborn resistance that was ultimately broken. Then the island's second line of defense—mosquitoes carrying yellow fever—had swept away thousands of crack French troops. Santo Domingo could not be reconquered, except perhaps at a staggering cost; hence, there was no need for the granary. "Damn sugar, damn coffee, damn colonies!" burst out Napoleon.

Bonaparte was about to end the twenty-month lull in his deadly conflict with Britain. Because the British controlled the seas, he feared that he might be forced to make them a

Toussaint L'Ouverture (c. 1774–1803) *A self-educated ex-slave and military genius, L'Ouverture was finally betrayed by the French, who imprisoned him in a chilly dungeon in France, where he coughed his life away. By indirection he did much to set up the sale of Louisiana to the United States. (Library of Congress.)*

gift of Louisiana. Rather than drive America into the arms of England by attempting to hold the area, he decided to sell the huge wilderness to the Americans and pocket the money for his schemes nearer home. He hoped that the United States, strengthened by Louisiana, would one day grow up to be a military and naval power that would thwart the ambitions of the lordly British in the New World. The distresses of France in Europe were again paving the way for America's diplomatic successes.

Events now moved dizzily. The American Minister Livingston, pending the arrival of Monroe, was busily negotiating in Paris for a window on the Gulf of Mexico at New Orleans. Suddenly, out of a clear sky, the French foreign minister asked him how much he would give for all Louisiana. Scarcely able to believe his ears (he was partially deaf anyhow), Livingston nervously entered upon the negotiations. After about a week of haggling, while the fate of America trembled in the balance, treaties were

Louisiana Purchase, 1803 *Seeking to avert friction with France by purchasing all of Louisiana, Jefferson bought trouble because of the vagueness of the boundaries. Among the disputants were Spain in the Floridas, Spain and Mexico in the Southwest, and Great Britain in Canada.*

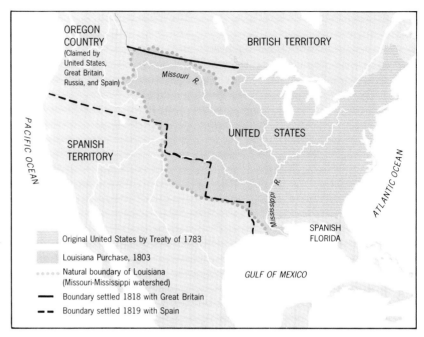

signed, under the date April 30, 1803, ceding Louisiana to the United States for about $15 million.

Out-Federalizing the Federalists in Louisiana

When the news of the bargain reached America, Jefferson was startled. He had authorized his envoys to offer not more than $10 million for New Orleans, and as much to the *east* in the Floridas as they could get. Instead, they had signed three treaties that pledged $15 million for New Orleans, plus a vast wilderness entirely to the *west*—an area that would more than double the United States. They had bought a wilderness to get a city.

Once again the two Jeffersons wrestled with each other in private: the theorist and former strict constructionist versus the realist and public official. Where in his beloved Constitution was the president authorized to negotiate treaties incorporating a huge new expanse into the union—an expanse containing some fifty thousand red, white, and black inhabitants? There was no such clause.

Conscience-stricken, Jefferson secretly proposed that a constitutional amendment be passed. But his friends pointed out in alarm that in the interval Napoleon, for whom thought was action, might suddenly change his mind. So Jefferson shamefacedly submitted the treaties to the Senate, while privately admitting that the purchase was unconstitutional.

The senators were less finicky than Jefferson. Reflecting enthusiastic public support, they registered their prompt approval of the transaction. Land-hungry Americans were not disposed to split constitutional hairs when confronted with perhaps the most magnificent real

> In accepting the Louisiana Purchase, Jefferson thus compromised with conscience in a private letter: "It is the case of a guardian, investing the money of his ward in purchasing an important adjacent territory; and saying to him when of age, I did this for your good; I pretend to no right to bind you: you may disavow me, and I must get out of the scrape as I can: I thought it my duty to risk myself for you."

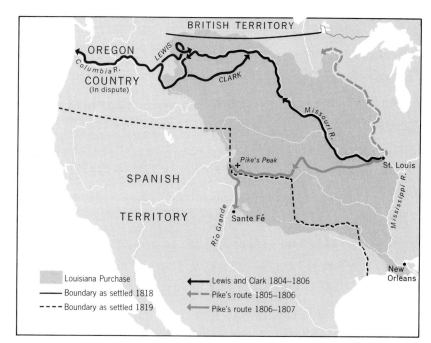

estate bargain in history—828,000 square miles (2,144,520 square kilometers) at about three cents an acre.

If Louisiana made Jefferson a loose constructionist, it made many Federalists strict constructionists. (Hamilton, to his credit, was a partial exception.) Federalists argued vehemently that there was no constitutional warrant for the transfer. (Shades of the Federalists who had chartered the Bank of the United States!) Louisiana, so they claimed, was a worthless desert that would cost too much at a time when the Jeffersonians were pledged to rigid economy: $15 million in one pile of silver dollars would reach three miles into the air. (Shades of the Federalists who had cheerfully assumed Hamilton's debt of $75 million!)

What really worried the Federalists was that the signing of the Louisiana treaties was the signing of their own political death warrant. New states would be carved from the immense area—states that would outvote the thirteen charter members, including Federalist New England. The Jeffersonian agrarians would then become unassailable. At Williams College in Massachusetts, a debating group voted fifteen to one that the purchase of Louisiana was undesirable. A few Federalist extremists even threatened to secede from the Union.

The purchase of Louisiana—the most glorious achievement of Jefferson as president—was a triumph for which neither he nor anyone else could claim much direct credit. Napoleon, for reasons purely selfish, dumped this rich prize into the laps of Livingston, Monroe, and Jefferson. Louisiana was so desirable that Jefferson found it less embarrassing to reverse himself on strict construction than to lose the magnificent windfall.

Louisiana in the Long View

Jefferson's bargain with France was epochal. By scooping up Louisiana, America secured at one bloodless stroke the western half of the richest river valley in the world and further laid the foundations of a future major power. The ideal of a great agrarian democracy, as envisioned by Jefferson, would have elbowroom in the vast "Valley of Democracy." At the same time, the transfer established a precedent that was to be followed repeatedly: the acquisition of foreign territory and peoples by purchase.

The extent of the huge new area was more fully unveiled by a series of explorations under the direction of Jefferson. He was keenly interested in the natural treasures of his purchase, including an enormous (and nonexistent) mountain of salt. The expedition of Meriwether Lewis and William Clark ascended the "Great Muddy" Missouri River and struggled through the Rockies to the mouth of the Columbia River. This hazardous venture into the uncharted western wilderness, from 1804 to 1806, bolstered America's claim to Oregon, while further opening the West to Indian trade and exploration. Zebulon M. Pike, in 1805–1806, explored the Louisiana territory near the headwaters of the Mississippi River and in 1806–1807 ventured into Colorado and New Mexico, sighting the peak that bears his name.

> The French minister who negotiated the Louisiana Purchase treaties recalled that Minister Livingston had remarked at the signing: "We have lived long, but this is the noblest work of our whole lives . . . From this day the United States take their place among the powers of the first rank. . . . The instruments which we have just signed will cause no tears to be shed: they prepare ages of happiness for innumerable generations of human creatures."

Jefferson's reluctant purchase of Louisiana proved to be a landmark in American foreign policy. Overnight he avoided a possible rupture with France and the consequent entangling alliance with England. The nation was thus able

Flathead Indians, c. 1805 (left) *William Clark served as the artist and cartographer of the Lewis and Clark Expedition. Here he has sketched the Flathead Indians of present-day Montana, showing the skull-molding practice from which they got their name.* **Cock of the Plains** (right) *A drawing from nature by William Clark. (Missouri Historical Society.)*

to continue the noninterventionist policies of the Founding Fathers, though it later quarreled with Spain and Britain over the vague boundaries of Louisiana, north, south, and west. Not needing the navy of the mother country, the United States drifted away from her and eventually fought her in 1812. But by that time, the Republic was bigger and stronger, and had Louisiana securely in its possession.

The Louisiana godsend likewise boosted national unity. Once-proud Federalists, now mere sectionalists, sank ever lower in public esteem as they were reduced to whining impotence. A few of their more extreme members attempted to plot with scheming Aaron Burr for the secession of New England and New York. But the intrigue failed, largely owing to the vigilance of Alexander Hamilton, who subsequently provoked Burr to a duel. The pistol that killed Hamilton in 1804 blew the brightest brain out of the Federalist party—and destroyed its one remaining hope of effective leadership.

A once-restive West, which now toasted the "immortal Jefferson," was more securely riveted to the Union by the purchase. People of the western waters were grateful to the federal government for having safeguarded their interests, particularly in securing the mouth of the Mississippi. A new spirit of unity surged through the West.

Aaron Burr, turning his disunionist plottings to the trans-Mississippi West, was arrested in 1806 for treason. Tried the next year at Richmond, Virginia, he was freed after the presiding judge, Chief Justice Marshall, had infuriated the Jeffersonians by what seemed to be bias in favor of the accused. The government's case collapsed when two witnesses to the same overt act of treason could not be found, as required by the Constitution (See Art. III, Sec. III). Burr's schemes are still somewhat shrouded in mystery, but he apparently planned to separate the western part of the United States from the eastern and unite it with to-be-conquered Spanish territory west of the Louisiana Purchase. The very fact that so dashing a figure as Burr could muster only threescore followers was quite significant. It indicated, among other things, that the West was developing a deeper sense of loyalty to the Washington government.

Meriwether Lewis   *He is portrayed here as he looked on his return from the great expedition. (Charles Saint-Mémin, New-York Historical Society.)*

America: A Nutcrackered Neutral

Jefferson was triumphantly reelected in 1804, with 162 electoral votes to only 14 for his Federalist opponent. His success was not so much due to Republicanizing the Federalists, as he fondly supposed, as to Federalizing the Republicans. The iron hand of reality gradually forced him, quite unintentionally, to kill off the opposition party by stealing many of its principles and embracing them as his own. He caught the Federalists in bathing, it was said, and made off with their clothes.

But the laurels of Jefferson's first administration soon withered under the blasts of the new

England (John Bull) Eats French Warships   *Contemporary English caricature.*

storm that broke in Europe. After unloading Louisiana in 1803, Napoleon deliberately provoked a renewal of his war with Britain—a conflict that crashed to an awesome close eleven long years later.

For two years a maritime United States—the number one neutral carrier since 1793—enjoyed juicy commercial pickings. But a setback came in 1805. At the Battle of Trafalgar, one-eyed Lord Nelson achieved immortality by smashing the combined French and Spanish fleets off the coast of Spain, thereby ensuring Britain's supremacy on the seas. At the Battle of Austerlitz in Austria—the Battle of the Three Emperors—Napoleon crushed the combined Austrian and Russian armies, thereby ensuring his mastery of the land. Like the tiger and the shark, France and Britain were supreme in their chosen elements. England ruled the waves and waived the rules.

Unable to hurt each other directly, the two antagonists were forced to strike indirect blows. The London government, beginning in 1806, issued a series of Orders in Council. These edicts closed the ports under French continental control to foreign shipping, including American, unless the vessels first stopped at a British port. There they would pay the necessary fees and, if acceptable, secure clearance papers. Napoleon struck back savagely in a series of decrees. In effect, they ordered the seizure of all merchant

Intercourse or Impartial Dealings   *A cartoon by "Peter Pencil" (1809) shows Jefferson being victimized by both England (left) and France (right). (Houghton Library, Harvard.)*

ships, including American, that entered British ports.

Yankee skippers, like their predestined Calvinist ancestors, were seemingly damned if they did, damned if they did not. Even so, their trade prospered, because the greater the risk, the greater the profit. If only one vessel in three sailed over the reefs of French decrees and past the shoals of British Orders in Council, the owner could make a comfortable gain.

British Man-Stealing

Even more galling to American pride than the seizure of wooden ships was the seizure of flesh-and-blood American seamen. Impressment—the forcible enlistment of sailors—was a crude form of conscription which the British, among others, had employed for over four centuries. Clubs and stretchers (for men knocked unconscious) were standard equipment of press-gangs from His Majesty's man-hungry ships.

The London authorities themselves set limits to this ugly practice. They claimed the right to impress only British subjects on their own soil, in their own harbors, or on merchant ships on the high seas. But many fair-skinned Americans looked like Englishmen and the benefit of the doubt was seldom given to an experienced seaman in those shorthanded days. The result was that some six thousand bona fide United States citizens, according to the best estimates, were impressed by the "piratical man-stealers" of England from 1808 to 1811 alone. A number of these luckless souls died or were killed in the service, leaving their kinfolk and friends bereaved and embittered.

On their side, the British had countercomplaints. America's navy and merchant marine openly encouraged the enlistment of deserters from the "floating hells" of the British navy, where discipline was taught to the tune of the cat-o'-nine-tails. An expanding American merchant marine, also short of sailors, paid seductively high wages—"dollars for shillings." British deserters, conniving with ingenious Americans, would often secure fraudulent naturalization papers. (One resourceful female con-

niver had an oversized cradle in her shop so she could swear she had known the sailor "from the cradle.") His Majesty's press-gangs laughed aside such documents, whether genuine or not, holding to the principle "Once an Englishman, always an Englishman." But the Americans, who had recently decided *en masse* to be English no longer, claimed that individuals had the right to choose their own country.

Britain had its back to the wall, and its desperate plight colored its views. If the Yankee "dollar grubbers" had not encouraged so much desertion, the British impressers might have been willing to make fewer mistakes in acquiring sailors. But England would not abandon its brutal practice of sailor-snatching at the behest of an upstart United States. Britons were making war; Americans were making money. The British feared that they would lose the war if they gave up their hoary method of conscription—and they would fight before they did.

Britain's determination was spectacularly highlighted in 1807. A royal frigate overhauled a United States frigate, the *Chesapeake,* about ten miles off the coast of Virginia. The British captain bluntly demanded the surrender of four alleged deserters. London had never claimed the right to seize sailors from a foreign warship, and the American commander, though totally unprepared to fight, refused the request. The British warship thereupon fired three devastating broadsides at close range, killing three Americans and wounding eighteen. Four deserters were dragged away, and the bloody hulk called the *Chesapeake* limped back to port.

An infuriated America—Federalists and Republicans alike—now joined in an outburst of

Regarding the Chesapeake *affair, the Washington* Federalist *reported: "We have never, on any occasion, witnessed the spirit of the people excited to so great a degree of indignation, or such a thirst for revenge, as on hearing of the late unexampled outrage on the* Chesapeake. *All parties, ranks, and professions were unanimous in their detestation of the dastardly deed, and all cried aloud for vengeance."*

national wrath. Nothing like it had been seen since the French XYZ insults of 1797. Jefferson, the peace lover, could easily have had war if he had wanted it. As the event proved, if America were going to fight at all, it should have fought when the country was united.

Britain was clearly in the wrong, as the London Foreign Office admitted. But Jefferson unwisely attempted to use the *Chesapeake* outrage as a lever to force the British to renounce impressment altogether. This they flatly refused to do. The affair rankled for five years; and when reparation was finally made, it came too late to salve old wounds.

Jefferson's Backfiring Embargo

National honor would not permit a slavish submission to British and French mistreatment. Yet a large-scale foreign war was contrary to the settled policy of the new Republic—and in addition it would be futile. The navy was weak, thanks largely to Jefferson's antinavalism; and the army was even weaker. A disastrous defeat would not improve America's plight.

The warring nations in Europe were heavily dependent upon the United States for raw materials and foodstuffs. In his eager search for an alternative to war, Jefferson seized upon this essential fact. He reasoned that if America voluntarily cut off its exports, the offending powers would be forced to come, hat in hand, and agree to respect its rights.

Responding to the presidential lash, Congress hastily passed the Embargo Act late in 1807. This rigorous law forbade the export of all goods from the United States, whether in American or in foreign ships. It was a compromise between submission and shooting.

Jefferson, the onetime strict constructionist, had once more flip-flopped into the camp of the loose constructionists. In the interests of the Federalist shippers, whom he disliked, he was rereading the Constitution with strange bifocals. To him, it now meant that Congress, under its authority to "regulate" commerce, could go so far as to stop foreign trade altogether. Regulation thus became strangulation.

Federalist New England could well have prayed for relief from its newly found Virginia friend, "Mad Tom" Jefferson. Forests of dead masts gradually filled once-flourishing harbors; docks that had once rumbled were deserted (except for illegal trade); and soup kitchens cared for some of the hungry unemployed. Jeffersonian Republicans probably hurt the commerce of New England, which they avowedly were trying to protect, far more than Old England and France together were doing.

Farmers of the South and West, the strongholds of Jefferson, suffered no less disastrously than New England. They were alarmed by the mounting piles of exportable cotton, grain, and tobacco. Tart-tongued John Randolph of Virginia remarked that enacting the embargo was like cutting off one's toes to cure one's corns. Jefferson in truth seemed to be waging war on his fellow citizens, rather than on the offending belligerents.

The American people, from the days of the colonial Navigation Acts, have never submitted meekly to unpopular legislation. Though basically law-abiding, they habitually flout laws that are opposed by large numbers of the population. An enormous illicit trade mushroomed in 1808, especially along the Canadian border, where bands of armed Americans on loaded rafts overawed or overpowered federal agents. Irate citizens cynically transposed the letters of "Embargo" to read "O Grab Me," "Go Bar 'Em," and "Mobrage," while heartily denouncing the "Dambargo."

Jefferson nonetheless induced Congress to pass iron-toothed enforcing legislation. It was so

> *A Federalist circular in Massachusetts against the embargo cried out: "Let every man who holds the name of America dear to him, stretch forth his hands and put this accursed thing, this Embargo from him. Be resolute, act like sons of liberty, of God, and your country; nerve your arm with vengeance against the Despot [Jefferson] who would wrest the inestimable germ of your independence from you—and you shall be Conquerors!!!"*

The Embargo (Ograbme) *As a snapping turtle, it halts overseas shipments. (Prints Division, New York Public Library, Astor, Lenox and Tilden Foundations.)*

inquisitorial and tyrannical as to cause some Americans to think more kindly of George III, whom Jefferson had berated in the Declaration of Independence. One indignant New Hampshire poet burst out in song:

> Our ships all in motion,
> Once whiten'd the ocean;
>   They sail'd and return'd with a Cargo;
> Now doom'd to decay
>   They are fallen a prey,
> To Jefferson, worms, and EMBARGO

New England seethed with talk of secession; and Jefferson later admitted that he felt the foundations of government tremble under his feet.

An alarmed Congress, bowing to the storm of public anger, finally repealed the embargo, on March 1, 1809, three days before Jefferson's retirement. A half-loaf substitute was provided by the Non-Intercourse Act. This measure formally reopened trade with all the nations of the world, except the two most important, England and France. Though thus watered down, economic coercion continued to be the policy of the Jeffersonians from 1809 to 1812, when the nation finally plunged into war.

The Wooden-Gun Embargo: A Successful Failure

Why did the embargo, Jefferson's most daring act of statesmanship, collapse after fifteen dismal months? First of all, he underestimated the bulldog determination of the British, as others have, and overestimated their dependence on America's trade. Bumper grain crops blessed the British Isles during these years, and the revolutionary Latin American republics unexpectedly threw open their ports for compensating commerce.

The hated embargo was not continued long enough or tightly enough to achieve the desired results. But leaders must know the temper of their people, and Jefferson should have foreseen that such a self-crucifying weapon could not possibly command public support. The Americans, notoriously people of action, did not take kindly to the passive type of heroism. They much preferred commercial activity, with all its risks, to enforced inactivity, with no chance of profit.

A crestfallen Jefferson himself admitted that the embargo was three times more costly than war. The irony is that with only a fraction of its cost to the country, he could have built a fairly

Crowningshield's Wharf, Salem, Massachusetts *Like many another New England port, Salem saw its economy throttled by Jefferson's embargo policy. (Peabody Museum of Salem.)*

strong navy. Such a fighting force would have won more respect for American rights on the high seas and might well have prevented the War of 1812.

The embargo further embroiled relations with both Britain and France. It embittered the British, partly because it hit them more forcibly than it did Napoleon. The French despot naturally applauded the embargo, for it was an indirect American blockade of his foe. He cynically helped enforce it by seizing scores of Yankee merchant ships in his ports; by the terms of the Embargo Act, he argued, these vessels should have been tied up at home. His "cooperation" merely rubbed salt into old sores.

A stoppage of exports hurt Federalist shipping but temporarily revived the Federalist party. Gaining new converts, its leaders hurled their nullification of the embargo into the teeth of the "Virginia lordlings" in Washington. In 1804, the discredited Federalists had polled only 14 electoral votes out of 176; in 1808, the embargo year, the figure rose to 47 out of 175.

Curiously enough, New England plucked a new prosperity from the ugly jaws of the embargo. With shipping tied up and imported goods scarce, the resourceful Yankees reopened old factories and erected new ones. The real foundations of modern America's industrial might were laid behind the protective wall of the embargo, followed by nonintercourse and the War of 1812. Jefferson, the avowed critic of factories, may have unwittingly done more

for American manufacturing than Alexander Hamilton, the outspoken friend of factories.

Jefferson's embargo, followed in modified form by nonintercourse, undeniably pinched England. Many British importers and manufacturers suffered severe losses, especially those dependent on American cotton. As thousands of factory workers were thrown out of jobs, agitation mounted for a repeal of the restrictions that had brought on the embargo. A petition to Parliament in 1812, from the city of Birmingham alone, bore twenty thousand names on a sheet of parchment 150 feet long. So strong was public pressure that two days before Congress declared war in June 1812, the British foreign secretary announced that the offensive Orders in Council would be immediately suspended. The supreme irony is that Jefferson's policy of economic coercion did win in the end, but America was not patient enough to reap the reward of its sacrifices.

The Living Jefferson

Thomas Jefferson retained much of his popularity, even though it was severely tarnished by the embargo. One public toast ran: "May he receive from his fellow citizens the reward of his merit, a halter, [hangman's noose]." But his grip on his party was such that he could easily have won a third nomination and election. The international crisis was still acute; and although Jefferson was sixty-five years old, he was mentally alert and physically vigorous. He lived eighteen more years, glad to have escaped what he called the "splendid misery" of the presidential penitentiary.

Jefferson, rather than Washington, was the real father of the two-term tradition. Unlike the first president, who had no serious constitutional qualms, he feared that more than two terms might open the door to dictatorship. Yet Jefferson strongly favored the nomination and election of a kindred spirit, his friend and fellow Virginian, the quiet, intellectual, and unassuming James Madison.

Though bitterly assailed, Jefferson left office with the consolation that he had remained true to the guiding star of the other Founding Fathers. He had kept the country out of a serious foreign war. Despite numerous reversals of policy under the whiplash of practicality, he never lost his faith in democracy and in the common people. He brought a renovation rather than a revolution; the real revolution that did occur was in his own thinking. If the Federalists were the stepping-stone between monarchical Europe and republican America, then the

> *Early in 1805 Jefferson privately foresaw the two-term Twenty-Second Amendment (1951): "General Washington set the example of voluntary retirement after eight years. I shall follow it, and a few more precedents will oppose the obstacle of habit to anyone after a while who shall endeavor to extend his term. Perhaps it may beget a disposition to establish it by an amendment of the Constitution."*

Jeffersonians were the stepping-stone between aristocratic Federalism and democratic Jacksonianism.

Thomas Jefferson and John Adams died on the same day—appropriately the Fourth of July, 1826. The last words of Adams, then ninety-one, were: "Thomas Jefferson still survives." He was wrong, for three hours earlier Jefferson had breathed his last. But Thomas Jefferson still survives in the democratic ideals and liberal principles of the great nation that he risked his all to found and that he served so long and faithfully.

Varying Viewpoints

The Jeffersonian era has long presented observers with a series of paradoxes, none greater than the question of how the man who proclaimed, "We are all Republicans, we are all Federalists," came to preside over one of the most bitterly partisan periods in American history.

Some scholars play down the importance of party conflict in this era. Stressing the early parties' lack of concern for organizing the electorate, these accounts note that the Jeffersonians and the Federalists distrusted parties; saw them only as temporary, necessary evils; and looked forward to their elimination. Thus, historians like James S. Young argue that the Jeffersonian era possessed no true party system.

Others, among them Noble E. Cunningham, see the organizations of the early national period as the prototypes of the modern American party system. Conceding that the Federalists and Jeffersonians never became mass-based organizations like the later Jacksonian parties, this interpretation emphasizes the innovations of the period. The Jeffersonians created a partisan press, maintained control of Congress by dominating committee chairmanships, and pioneered campaign tactics like stump speaking and door-to-door canvassing. Most important, the experiences of the Federalists and Jeffersonians, in the two decades after the ratification of the Constitution, led both groups to accept, grudgingly, the idea that party competition was inevitable and potentially beneficial in a republican society. This realization paved the way for the evolution of a full-blown two-party system in the 1830s.

Select Readings

Primary Source Documents

Jefferson's "First Inaugural Address" (1801), in Henry Steele Commager, *Documents of American History*, echoed the themes of Washington's Farewell and set the tone for his presidency. Reuben G. Thwaites, ed., *Original Journals of the Lewis and Clark Expedition* * (1904), chronicles the explorers' adventures. For the political flavor of the age, see the debate over the Embargo Act* (1807); For Constitutional history, read the decision of John Marshall in *Marbury* v. *Madison* * (1803).

Secondary Sources

A monument of American historical writing is Henry Adams, *History of the United States during the Administrations of Jefferson and Madison* (9 vols., 1889–1891), available in a one-volume abridgement edited by Ernest Samuels. Especially fascinating are Adams' epilogue and prologue on the United States in 1800 and 1817. A brief introduction is given in Marshall Smelser, *The Democratic Republic, 1801–1815* (1968). Problems with the judiciary can be traced in Albert J. Beveridge's still-respected *Life of John Marshall* (4 vols., 1919). A more recent and succinct analysis is Richard E. Ellis, *The Jeffersonian Crisis: Courts and Politics in the New Republic* (1971). Politics are treated in a broad, imaginative context in James S. Young, *The Washington Community, 1800– 1829* (1966), and more traditionally in Noble E. Cunningham's rebuttal, *The Process of Government under Jefferson* (1979). See also the Joyce Appleby, Lance Banning, and Drew McCoy volumes cited in Chapter 9. The development of political parties is dissected in William N. Chambers, *Political Parties in a New Nation* (1963), and in Noble E. Cunningham, *The Jeffersonian Republicans: The Formation of Party Organization, 1789–1801* (1958). See also Richard Buel, Jr., *Securing the Revolution* (1972), and Robert E. Shalhope, *John Taylor of Carolina* (1980). The standard scholarly biography is Merrill D. Peterson, *Thomas Jefferson and the New Nation* (1970). Peterson has also scrutinized *The Jefferson Image in the American Mind* (1960). Leonard D. White brings administrative history to life in *The Jeffersonians* (rev. ed., 1959). Forrest McDonald is highly critical of his subject in *The Presidency of Thomas Jefferson* (1976). Leonard Levy debunks Jefferson's liberalism in *Jefferson and Civil Liberties* (1963), while Bernard W. Sheehan examines another important aspect of policy in *Seeds of Extinction: Jeffersonian Philanthropy and the American Indian* (1973). See also Reginald Horsman, *Expansion and American Indian Policy, 1783–1812* (1967). A first-class study of the negotiator of the Louisiana Purchase is George Dangerfield, *Chancellor Robert R. Livingston of New York* (1960). An expansionist thesis is fully developed in Alexander De Conde, *This Affair of Louisiana* (1976). The embargo is treated in Burton Spivak, *Jefferson's English Crisis: Commerce, Embargo and the Republican Revolution* (1979). Daniel Boorstin vividly evokes the intellectual climate of the age in *The Lost World of Thomas Jefferson* (1948). John C. Miller, *The Wolf by the Ears: Thomas Jefferson and Slavery* (1977), probes the third president's attitudes on an important question. Irving Brant looks at *James Madison, Secretary of State* (1953), and F. E. Ewing examines Jefferson's powerful treasury secretary in *America's Forgotten Statesman: Albert Gallatin* (1959).

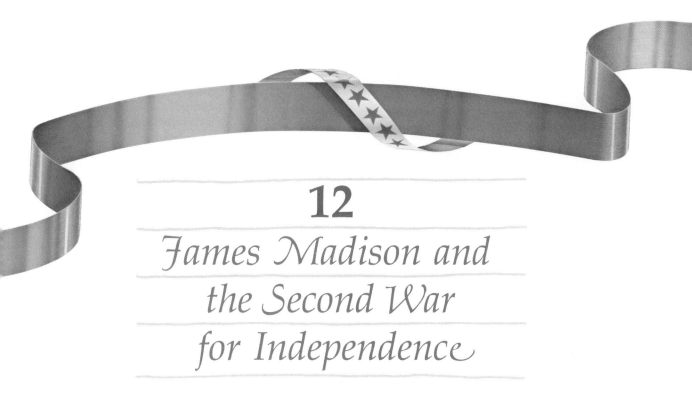

12

James Madison and the Second War for Independence

Madison: Dupe of Napoleon

Scholarly James Madison took the presidential oath on March 4, 1809, as the awesome conflict in Europe was roaring to its climax. Small of stature (5 feet 4 inches; 1.62 meters), light of weight (about 100 pounds; 45 kilograms), bald of head, and weak of voice, he fell tragically short of providing vigorous executive leadership. Crippled also by factions within his cabinet, he was unable to dominate his party, as Jefferson had once done.

The Non-Intercourse Act of 1809—the limited substitute for the embargo aimed solely at Britain and France—would expire in about a year. Congress, desperately attempting to uphold American rights, adopted in 1810 a bar-

gaining measure known as Macon's Bill No. 2. While permitting American trade with all the world, it dangled an attractive lure. If either England or France repealed its commercial restrictions, America would restore nonimportation against the nonrepealing nation. In short, the United States would bribe the belligerents into respecting its rights.

This opportunity was made to order for Napoleon, a past master of deceit. He was eager to have nonimportation clamped down once more on the British, because it would serve as a partial blockade, which he would not have to raise a finger to enforce. He was hopeful that such a boycott would embroil the Americans in war with Britain, for then they would be serving as his indirect allies to weaken his arch-enemy.

President James Madison (1751–1836) *Though an eminent constitutionalist, legislator, and diplomatist, he was not a strong Chief Executive. Foolishly, he was the only President ever to go directly to the fighting front, but he quickly rode away as the British advanced on Washington in 1814. (White House Historical Association.)*

Accordingly, he blandly announced, in August 1810, that his objectionable decrees had been repealed.

Responsible Americans, rising above self-delusion, should have examined the hollow-sounding French announcement with extreme caution. Napoleon, prince of liars, had no intention whatever of repealing his damaging de-

> "The injuries received from France," insisted the editor of Niles' Weekly Register (June 27, 1812), "do not lessen the enormity of those heaped upon us by England. . . . In this 'straight betwixt two' we had an unquestionable right to select our enemy. We have given the preference to Great Britain . . . on account of her more flagrant wrongs."

crees. But Madison, frantically seeking to wrest a recognition of American rights from England, accepted French bad faith as good faith. He formally announced, in November 1810, that France had complied with the terms of Macon's Bill No. 2 and that nonimportation would consequently be reestablished against Britain.

Madison's decision was fateful. Britons were angered by America's apparent willingness to be the dupe and partner of Napoleon. Once Madison had aligned his nation against England commercially, he found himself gravitating toward France politically—and edging toward the whirlpool of war.

War Whoops Arouse the War Hawks

The complexion of the Twelfth Congress, which met late in 1811, differed markedly from that of its predecessor. Recent elections had swept away many of the older "submission men" and replaced them with young hotheads, chiefly from the South and West. The youthful newcomers—"the boys," John Randolph sneeringly called them—were on fire for a new war with the old enemy. Not having had a conflict in their own generation, these war hawks were weary of hearing how their fathers had "whipped" the British single-handedly. They won control of the House of Representatives and elevated to the speakership the tall (6 feet 2 inches; 1.88 meters), eloquent, and magnetic Henry Clay of Kentucky, the gallant "Harry of the West," then only thirty-four years old.

Western war hawks, first of all, were eager to wipe out the renewed Indian resistance against the white settlers streaming steadily into the western wilderness. As this white flood spread through the green forests, more and more Indians were pushed farther and farther toward the setting sun. Two remarkable Shawnee twin brothers, Tecumseh and the Prophet, knew that if this onrushing tide were ever to be stopped, that time had come. They began to weld together a far-flung confederacy of all the tribes east of the Mississippi. Their braves forswore firewater in order to be fit for the last-ditch battle with the "paleface" intruders. To make matters worse, the sturdy pioneers and their war

War Vote in House of Representatives, 1812,
Showing Western and Southwestern War Sentiment

STATES	REGIONS	FOR WAR	AGAINST WAR
N.H.	} Frontier New England	3	2
Vt.		3	1
Mass.	Maritime and Federalist New England; Mass. (includes frontier Maine)	6	8
R.I.		0	2
Conn.		0	7
N.Y.	Commercial and Federalist middle states	3	11
N.J.		2	4
Del.		0	1
Pa.	} Jeffersonian middle states	16	2
Md.		6	3
Va.	Jeffersonian southern states	14	5
N.C.		6	3
S.C.		8	0
Ga.		3	0
Ohio	The trans-Allegheny West—nest of the war hawks	1	0
Ky.		5	0
Tenn.		3	0
		79	49

hawk representatives in Congress widely believed that the Indians' firearms and scalping knives were being furnished by British "hair buyers" in Canada.

Only a few days after the war hawk Congress convened in Washington, news of stirring events on the frontier further inflamed anti-Indian and anti-British feeling. General William H. Harrison, advancing with one thousand men upon the Indian headquarters, repelled a surprise attack at Tippecanoe, in present Indiana, on November 7, 1811. He then put the torch to the settlement.

Harrison's onslaught broke the back of the Indian rebellion. It also made the blood course faster in the veins of the impetuous war hawks. People like Representative Felix Grundy of Tennessee, three of whose brothers had been murdered, cried that there was only one way to remove the menace of the Indians: wipe out their Canadian base. Canada was a lush prize—so near, so desirable, and apparently so defenseless. "On to Canada, on to Canada" was the war hawks' ominous chant. Southern expansionists, less vocal, cast a covetous eye on Florida, then weakly held by Britain's ally Spain.

Henry Clay (1777–1852) *A glamorous, eloquent, and ambitious member of the House and Senate for many years, Clay was thrice an unsuccessful candidate for the highest office in the land. "Sir," he declared in the Senate in 1850, "I would rather be right than be President." Right or wrong, he never made the grade but his devotion to the Union was inspirational. (Library of Congress.)*

Tecumseh (1768?–1813) A Shawnee Indian born in the Ohio country, he was probably the most gifted organizer and leader of his people in U.S. history. A noted warrior, he fought the tribal custom of torturing prisoners and opposed the practice of permitting any one tribe to sell land that, he believed, belonged to all Indians. (Field Museum of Natural History, Chicago.)

Militant war hawks, with scattered but essential support from other sections, finally engineered a declaration of war in June 1812. The vote in the House was 79 to 49, in the Senate 19 to 13. The close tally betrayed a dangerous degree of national disunity. Representatives from the pro-British maritime and commercial centers, as well as from the middle Atlantic states, almost solidly opposed hostilities. Thus, the West and Southwest, mostly landlocked, presented the sea-fronting East with a war for a free sea that the East vehemently resented.

Mr. Madison's War

But why fight Britain rather than France, which had committed nearly as many maritime offenses? The traditional Republican attachment to France partly explains the choice of foe, as does the visibility of British impressments and the British arming of the Indians, who were smashing into pioneer cabins on the frontier.

The choice prize of Canada also beckoned from the north. Americans fondly (but wrongly) believed that taking Canada would be absurdly simple, a "frontiersman's frolic." If this northern mirage had not been so inviting, the administration would have waited a few more months and thereby learned of London's intention to repeal the Orders in Council. In fact, the announcement of the intention to repeal was made two days *before* Congress voted for war. Had there been an Atlantic cable, the war hawks probably could not have forced a declaration of hostilities through the Senate.

Seafaring New England damned the war for a free sea. The news of the declaration of war was greeted with muffled bells, flags at half-mast, and public fasting.

Why the opposition? To New Englanders, impressment was an old and exaggerated wrong. New England shippers and manufacturers were still raking in money, and profits dull patriotism. Pro-British New England Federalists also sympathized with the mother country and resented the Virginia dynasty's sympathy with Napoleon, whom they regarded as the "Corsican butcher" and "the anti-Christ of the age."

The war hawks wanted "Free Trade and Sailors' Rights," as well as free land. It may seem strange that settlers beyond the mountains, many of whom had never seen a body of salt water larger than a salt lick, should want to fight for maritime rights. But the proud, nationalistic westerners were outraged by the manhandling of American sailors and by the British Orders in Council that dammed up their agricultural products from shipment to Europe. Westerners also joined many of their fellow citizens in believing that only a vigorous assertion of American rights could demonstrate the viability of American nationhood—and of democracy as a form of government. If America could not fight to protect itself, its experiment in republicanism would be discredited in the eyes of a scoffing world.

*I left with you a precious Casket of choicest Blessings Supported by three Pillars —
Desist my Sons from pulling at them Should you remove one you destroy the whole*

The Present State of Our Country
Partisan disunity over the War of 1812 threatens the nation's very existence. The prowar Jeffersonian at the left is attacking the pillar of federalism; the antiwar Federalist at the right is trying to pull down Democracy. The spirit of Washington warns that the country's welfare depends upon all three pillars, including Republicanism. (A cartoon by William Charles, New York Public Library.)

Federalists also condemned the War of 1812 because they opposed the acquisition of Canada, which would merely add more agrarian states from the wild Northwest. This, in turn, would increase the voting strength of the Jeffersonian Republicans. New England Federalists were determined, wrote one versifier:

> To rule the nation if they could,
> But see it damned if others should.

The bitterness of New Englanders against "Mr. Madison's War" led them to treason or near-treason. In a sense America fought two enemies simultaneously: old England and New England. New England gold holders probably lent more dollars to the British than to the federal treasury. New England farmers sent huge quantities of supplies and foodstuffs to Canada, enabling British armies to invade New York. New England governors stubbornly refused to permit their militia to serve outside their own states.

Fight over Canada on Land and Lakes

The War of 1812, largely because of widespread disunity, ranks as one of America's worst-fought wars. There was no burning national anger, as there had been in 1807, following the *Chesapeake* outrage. War hawks in Congress were no more than a zealous minority. President Madison, while supporting their aims, knew that there was serious disunity. The supreme lesson of this conflict was the folly of leading a divided and apathetic people into war.

The Republic was dangerously unprepared, despite warnings going back nineteen years to the outbreak of the European war in 1793. The nation was still suffering from its own embargo and nonintercourse, which it had partially enforced for the better part of four years. Congress had shortsightedly permitted the Bank of the United States to expire in 1811, at a time when a powerful financial institution was needed. It was knifed largely by the jealousies of the competing state banks.

The regular army was scandalously inadequate, for it was ill-trained, ill-disciplined, and widely scattered. It had to be supplemented by the even more poorly trained militia, who were sometimes distinguished by speed of foot in leaving the battlefield. Some of the ranking generals were semisenile heirlooms from the Revolutionary War, rusting on their laurels and lacking in vigor and vision.

The offensive strategy in Canada was poorly conceived. Had the Americans captured Montreal, the center of population and transportation, everything to the west would have died, just as the leaves of a tree wither when the

The Three U.S. Thrusts of 1812   *The thin red line delineates the Canadian border.*

Campaigns of 1813   *The thin red line denotes the Canadian boundary.*

trunk is girdled. But instead of laying ax to the trunk, the Americans frittered away their strength in the three-pronged invasion of 1812. The trio of invading forces that set out from Detroit, Niagara, and Lake Champlain were all beaten back shortly after they had crossed the Canadian border.

By contrast, the British and Canadians displayed energy from the outset. Early in the war they captured the American fort of Michilimackinac, which commanded the upper Great Lakes and the Indian-inhabited area to the south and west. Their brilliant defensive operations were led by the inspired British general Isaac Brock and assisted (in the American camp) by "General Mud" and "General Confusion."

When several American land invasions of Canada were again hurled back in 1813, Americans looked for success on water. Control of the Great Lakes was vital, and an energetic American naval officer, Oliver Hazard Perry, managed to build a fleet of green-timbered ships on the shores of Lake Erie, manned by even greener seamen. When he captured a British fleet in a furious engagement on Lake Erie, he reported to his superior, "We have met the enemy and they are ours." Perry's victory and his slogan infused new life into the drooping American

cause. Forced to withdraw from Detroit and Fort Malden, the retreating redcoats were overtaken by General Harrison's army and beaten at the Battle of the Thames in October 1813. The gifted Indian leader Tecumseh, now a brigadier general in the British army, lost his life in the battle.

Despite these successes, the Americans by late 1814, far from invading Canada, were grimly defending their own soil against the invading British. In Europe, the diversionary power of Napoleon was destroyed in mid-1814, and the dangerous despot was marooned on the Mediterranean isle of Elba. The United States, which had so brashly provoked war behind the protective skirts of Napoleon, was now left to face the music alone. As thousands of redcoated veterans began to pour into Canada, Europe's distresses, for once, failed the Americans.

Assembling some ten thousand crack troops, the British prepared in 1814 for a crushing blow into New York, along the familiar lake-river route. In the absence of roads, the invader was forced to bring supplies over the Lake Champlain waterway. A weaker American fleet, commanded by the thirty-year-old Thomas Macdonough, challenged the British. The ensuing battle was desperately fought near Plattsburg, on September 11, 1814, on floating slaughterhouses. The American flagship at one point was in grave trouble. But Macdonough, unexpectedly turning his ship about with cables, confronted the enemy with a fresh broadside and snatched victory from the fangs of defeat.

The results of this heroic naval battle were momentous. The invading British army was forced to retreat. Macdonough thus saved at least upper New York from conquest, New England from further disaffection, and the Union from possible dissolution. He also profoundly affected the concurrent negotiations of the Anglo-American peace treaty in Europe.

Washington Burned and New Orleans Defended

A second formidable British force, numbering about four thousand, landed in the Chesapeake Bay area in August 1814. Advancing rapidly on Washington, it easily dispersed some six thousand panicky militia at Bladensburg ("the Bladensburg races"). The invaders then entered the capital and set fire to most of the public buildings, including the Capitol and the White House ("the Yankee Palace"). President Madison and his aides, chased into the surrounding hills like frightened rabbits, witnessed from afar the billowing smoke. The British fleet next appeared before Baltimore, a nest for privateers, but was beaten off by the doughty defenders at Fort McHenry, despite "bombs bursting in air." At the same time, the American land defenders, though driven back at first, caused the attacking army to withdraw. The memory of the Chesapeake campaign was further kept alive when Francis Scott Key, a detained American anxiously watching the bombardment at Baltimore from a British ship, was inspired to write the words of "The Star-Spangled Banner." Set to the tune of a saucy old English tavern refrain, the song quickly attained popularity.

A third British blow of 1814, aimed at New Orleans, menaced the entire Mississippi Valley. Gaunt and hawk-faced Andrew Jackson, fresh from crushing the southwest Indians at the Battle of Horseshoe Bend in what is now Alabama, was placed in command. His hodgepodge force consisted of seven thousand sailors, regulars, pirates, and Frenchmen, as well as militiamen

The Burning of Washington   *America's military fortunes hit rock bottom on August 24, 1814, when British forces, having routed a ragtag American army on the outskirts of the capital, put the torch to Washington, D.C. (Courtesy of the New-York Historical Society, New York City.)*

The Southwest, 1814–1815

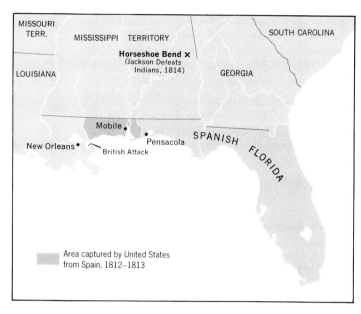

MISSOURI TERR.
MISSISSIPPI TERRITORY
SOUTH CAROLINA
Horseshoe Bend ✕ (Jackson Defeats Indians, 1814)
LOUISIANA
GEORGIA
Mobile
Pensacola
New Orleans
British Attack
SPANISH FLORIDA

Area captured by United States from Spain, 1812–1813

from Louisiana, Kentucky, and Tennessee. Among the defenders were two Louisiana regiments of free black volunteers, numbering about four hundred men. The Americans threw up their entrenchment, and in the words of a popular song:

> Behind it stood our little force—
> None wished it to be greater;
> For ev'ry man was half a horse,
> And half an alligator.

The overconfident British, numbering some eight thousand battle-seasoned veterans, blundered badly. They made the mistake of launching a frontal assault, on January 8, 1815, on the entrenched American riflemen and cannoneers. The attackers suffered the most devastating defeat of the entire war, losing over two thousand, killed and wounded, in half an hour, as compared with some seventy for the Americans. This slaughter was as useless as it was horrible, for the treaty of peace had been signed at Ghent, in Europe, two weeks earlier. But Jackson became more than ever the hero of the West.

The "glorious news" from New Orleans reached Washington early in February 1815, and about two weeks later came the tidings of the treaty of peace. Naive citizens promptly concluded that the British, beaten to their knees by Jackson, had hastened to make terms.

Ship Duels and Privateer Prizes

Man for man and ship for ship the American navy did much better than the army. But the results of its heroism have been exaggerated.

Britain's navy in 1812 boasted more than 800 men of war. Of these oaken craft, 219 were ships of the line of the 74-gun class, and 296 were frigates of roughly the 44-gun class. America, by contrast, had only 16 ships in its entire navy, the largest of which were a few 44-gun frigates, unable to stand up to British ships of the line. There could obviously be no saltwater fleet engagements in the slam-bang Trafalgar tradition; the only fleet battles were fought on the interior lakes.

American frigates and smaller sloops did clash with the enemy in a series of spectacular duels. In the frigate class, the Americans won four out of five of the single-ship contests; and in the sloop class, eight out of nine. American craft on the whole were more skillfully handled, had better gunners, and were manned by non-press-gang crews who were burning to avenge numerous indignities. The American frigates

**Constitution and Guerrière,
1812** *The Guerrière was heavily outweighed and outgunned, yet its British captain eagerly—and foolishly—sought combat. His ship was totally destroyed. Historian Henry Adams later concluded that this duel "raised the United States in one half hour to the rank of a first-class Power in the world." (U.S. Naval Academy Museum.)*

were specially designed superfrigates, notably the *Constitution* ("Old Ironsides"). They had thicker sides, heavier firepower, and larger crews, of which one sailor in six was a free black.

The British were deeply humiliated by their naval defeats, all the more so because they had sneered at America's "few fir-built frigates, manned by a handful of bastards and outlaws." In a few months they lost more warships to the Yankees than the French and Spaniards together had captured in years of fighting.

Swift and annoying American privateers—the "militia of the sea"—numbered about 500. They were in fact much more damaging than the regular navy and had an important bearing on the coming of peace. Built to fly from stronger ships, rather than fight them, these speedy craft captured or destroyed some 1,350 British merchantmen, even pursuing them into the English Channel and the Irish Sea. Assisted by fast-sailing sloops of the navy, Yankee privateers were so destructive that Lloyd's of London refused to insure unconvoyed British merchantmen crossing the Irish Sea. (At the same time, British warships and privateers were capturing hundreds of American merchant ships.)

Yet the American privateers were not an unmixed blessing. They lost scores of their own craft and diverted valuable manpower from the navy and army. But they brought urgently needed wealth into the country, boosted sagging morale, and slowed up British operations in Canada and elsewhere by capturing arms and supplies. More than that, the privateers brought the war home to British manufacturers, merchants, and shippers, who in turn exerted strong pressure on Parliament to end this costly conflict.

Its wrath aroused, the Royal Navy finally retaliated by throwing a ruinous naval blockade along America's coast and by landing raiding parties almost at will. American economic life,

Smarting from wounded pride on the sea, the London Times *urged chastisement for Americans: "The people—naturally vain, boastful, and insolent—have been filled with an absolute contempt of our maritime power, and a furious eagerness to beat down our maritime pretensions. Those passions, which have been inflamed by success, could only have been cooled by what in vulgar and emphatic language has been termed 'a sound flogging.'"* (Dec. 30, 1814)

A Wasp on a Frolic *U.S. sloops-of-war* Wasp *and Hornet* sting *John Bull's pride. The* Wasp *captured the* Frolic. *Contemporary American cartoon.*

including fishing, was crippled. Customs revenues were choked off, and near the end of the war the bankrupt Treasury was unable to meet its maturing obligations.

The Treaty of Ghent

Czar Alexander I of Russia, hard-pressed by Napoleon's army and not wanting his British ally to fritter away its strength in America, proposed mediation between the clashing Anglo-Saxon cousins in 1812. The czar's feeler eventually set in motion the machinery that brought five American peacemakers to the quaint Belgian city of Ghent in 1814. The bickering group was headed by early-rising, puritanical John Quincy Adams, son of John Adams, who deplored the late-hour card playing of his high-living colleague Henry Clay.

Confident after their military successes, Britain's envoys made sweeping demands for a

neutralized Indian buffer state in the Great Lakes region, control of the Great Lakes, and a substantial part of conquered Maine. The Americans flatly rejected these terms, and the talks appeared stalemated. But news of British reverses in upper New York and at Baltimore, and increasing war-weariness in Britain, made London more willing to compromise. Preoccupied with the Congress of Vienna and still-dangerous France, the British lion resigned itself to licking its wounds. Revenge against its upstart American offspring would be sweet—but expensive. Once again European distress brought American diplomatic success, for the War of 1812 was "won" by the United States, so far as it was won at all, in Europe.

The Treaty of Ghent, signed on Christmas Eve in 1814, was essentially an armistice. Both sides simply agreed to stop fighting and to restore conquered territory. No mention was made of those grievances for which America had ostensibly fought: the Indian menace, search and seizure, Orders in Council, impressment, and confiscations. These maritime omissions have often been cited as further evidence of the insincerity of the war hawks. Rather, they are proof that the Americans did not defeat the British decisively. With neither side able to impose its will, the treaty negotiations—like the war itself—ended as a virtual draw.

The news from Ghent triggered an outburst of rejoicing in the United States. Many Americans had rather expected to lose some territory, so dark was the military outlook early in 1815. But when the treaty arrived, the public mood rocketed from gloom to glory. The popularity of the pact was so overwhelming that it was unanimously approved by the Senate. A slogan of the hour became "Not One Inch of Territory Ceded or Lost"—a watchword that contrasted strangely with "On to Canada" at the outset of the war.

Federalist Grievances and the Hartford Convention

Defiant New England remained a problem. It was by far the most prosperous section during the conflict, owing largely to illicit trade with the enemy in Canada and to the absence of a

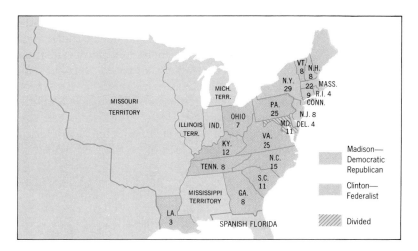

Presidential Election of 1812 (with electoral vote by state) *The Federalists showed impressive strength in the North and their presidential candidate, DeWitt Clinton, the future "father of the Erie Canal," almost won. If the 25 electoral votes of Pennsylvania had gone to the New Yorker, he would have won, 114 to 103.*

British blockade until 1814. But the embittered opposition of the Federalists to the war continued unabated. Late in 1812, when the first wartime presidential election was held, unhappy Federalists combined with disaffected Republicans and almost unseated President Madison. If the state of Pennsylvania alone had been transferred to their electoral column, they would have won.

As the war dragged on, New England extremists became more vocal. A small minority of them proposed secession from the Union, or at least a separate peace with England. Ugly rumors were afloat about "Blue Light" Federalists—treacherous New Englanders who supposedly flashed lanterns on the shore so that blockading British cruisers would be alerted to the attempted escape of American ships.

The most spectacular manifestation of Federalist discontent was the ill-omened Hartford Convention. Late in 1814, when the capture of New Orleans seemed imminent, Massachusetts issued a call for a convention at Hartford, Connecticut. The states of Massachusetts, Connecticut, and Rhode Island dispatched full delegations, while New Hampshire and Vermont sent partial representation. This group of prominent men, twenty-six in all, met in complete secrecy for about three weeks—December 15, 1814, to January 5, 1815—to discuss their grievances and to seek redress for their wrongs.

In truth, the Hartford Convention was less radical than alarmists supposed. Its immediate goal was to secure financial assistance from Washington, because the shores of New England were then being menaced by British blockading squadrons. A minority of the delegates gave vent to much wild talk of secession, but they were outvoted by the moderate Federalists. The report and resolutions adopted by the convention, in fact, resemble a modern political platform.

The Hartfordites, resenting the war-bent policies of the administration, were eager to restore New England to her stellar role on the national stage. They recommended amendments to the Constitution aimed at hobbling Congress and restoring Federalist influence by a kind of minority veto. These proposals would require a two-thirds vote before an embargo could be imposed, before new western states could be admitted, and before war could be declared—except in case of invasion.

The War of 1812 won a new respect for America among many Britons. Michael Scott, a young lieutenant in the British navy, wrote: "I don't like Americans; I never did, and never shall like them. . . . I have no wish to eat with them, drink with them, deal with, or consort with them in any way; but let me tell the whole truth, nor fight with them, were it not for the laurels to be acquired, by overcoming an enemy so brave, determined, and alert, and in every way so worthy of one's steel, as they have always proved."

"Three Wise Men of Gotham Went to Sea in a Bowl—" *This satirical anti-Federalist cartoon shows three Massachusetts men sailing precariously for Washington in a large chamber pot bearing Hartfordite demands. They are quieting their fears of sinking by exchanging off-color remarks. (Massachusetts Historical Society.)*

Three special envoys from Massachusetts, bearing demands of the Hartford Convention for financial support to promote defense, journeyed to the burned-out capital of Washington. The trio arrived just in time to be overwhelmed by the glorious news from New Orleans, followed by that from Ghent. Pursued by the sneers and jeers of the press, they slunk away into obscurity and disgrace.

The Hartford resolutions, as it turned out, were the death song of the Federalist party. In 1816, the next year, the Federalists nominated their last presidential candidate. He was lopsidedly defeated by James Monroe, yet another Virginian.

Unhappily, the stench of treason has clung to the Hartford Convention. The taint was not justified by its formal resolutions. Yet if the war had not ended when it did, the convention might well have paved the way for treasonable courses.

Federalist doctrines of disunity, which long survived the party, blazed a fateful trail. Until 1815, there was far more talk of nullification and secession in New England than in any other section, including the South. The outright flouting of the Jeffersonian embargo and the later crippling of the war effort were the two most damaging acts of nullification in America prior to the events leading to the Civil War.

The Second War for American Independence

The War of 1812 was a small war, involving about 6,000 Americans killed or wounded. It was but a footnote to the mighty European conflagration. In 1812, when Napoleon invaded Russia with about 500,000 men, Madison tried to invade Canada with about 5,000 men. But if the American conflict was globally unimportant, its results were highly important to the United States.

Americans wrested no formal recognition of their rights on the high seas, but informally they did. No longer did British aristocrats jeer at the "striped bunting" over "American cockboats." The Republic had shown that it would resent, sword in hand, what it regarded as grievous wrongs. Other nations developed a new respect for American fighting men. Naval officers like Perry and Macdonough were the most effective type of negotiators; the hot breath of their broadsides spoke the most eloquent diplomatic language. America's diplomats abroad were henceforth treated with less scorn. In a diplomatic sense, if not in a military sense, the conflict could be called the Second War for American Independence.

A new nation, moreover, was welded in the fiery furnace of armed conflict. Sectionalism, now identified with discredited New England Federalists, was given a black eye. The painful events of the war glaringly revealed, as perhaps nothing else could have done, the folly of sectional disunity. In a sense, the most conspicuous casualty of the war was the Federalist party.

The nation thrilled to the victories of its warriors. A brilliant naval tradition, already well launched, was strengthened by the exploits of the gallant seamen. The ineptitude of insubordinate or fleeing militia was forgotten. The battle-singed regular army, which in the closing months of the war had fought bravely and well, had won its spurs. War heroes emerged, such as Andrew Jackson and William Henry Harrison, both of whom were to become president.

Hostile Indians in the South had been crushed by Jackson at Horseshoe Bend (1814) and those in the North by Harrison at the Battle of the Thames (1813). Left in the lurch by their British friends at Ghent, the Indians were forced to make such terms as they could. They reluctantly consented, in a series of treaties, to relinquish vast areas of forested land north of the Ohio River.

Manufacturing increased behind the fiery wooden wall of the British blockade. In an economic sense, as well as in a diplomatic sense, the War of 1812 may be regarded as the Second War for American Independence. The industries that were thus stimulated by the fighting rendered America less dependent on the workshops of Europe.

International Legacies

Regrettably, the war revived and intensified bitterness toward the mother country. The uglier incidents of the conflict, notably the burning of Washington, added fuel to a century of Britain hating and Britain baiting. Mutual suspicion and hate were perhaps the most enduring heritages of this frustrating little war. Few Americans could have guessed in 1815 that it was to be the nation's last armed conflict with England.

Canadian patriotism and nationalism, no less than American patriotism and nationalism, received a powerful stimulus from the clash. The outnumbered Canadians, fighting bravely in defense of their homeland against the Yankee invaders, won their full share of the laurels. Their stirring song "The Maple Leaf" ringingly recalls these battles, including Chippewa and Lundy's Lane, which Americans regard as their victories.

Many Canadians felt betrayed by the treaty of Ghent. They were especially aggrieved by the failure to secure an Indian buffer state or even mastery of the Great Lakes. Canadians fully expected the frustrated Yankees to come again, and for a time the Americans and British engaged in a naval armaments race on the Great Lakes. But in 1817 the Rush-Bagot agreement between Britain and the United States severely limited naval armament on the lakes. Better relations brought the last border fortifications down in the 1870s, with the happy result that

The U.S. Frigate Constitution *It was the pride of the scant American fleet.*

the United States and Canada came to share the longest unfortified boundary in the world—5,527 miles (8,899 kilometers) long.

After Napoleon's final defeat at Waterloo in 1815, Europe slumped into a peace of exhaustion. Deposed monarchs returned to battered thrones, as the mother continent took the rutted road back to conservatism, illiberalism, and reaction.

But the American people were largely unaffected by these European developments. Freed from the humiliating side blows of the belligerents, they no longer had to scan the Atlantic horizon for approaching sails—sails that might bring news of impending calamities. Americans thrilled to a new sense of nationality. They were like subject peoples attaining their majority and for the first time shaking off the shackles of colonialism. Turning their backs on the Old World, they faced resolutely toward the untamed West. Unlike monarchy-cursed Europe, Americans were ready to take the high road toward democracy, liberalism, and freedom. The steady tramp, tramp, tramp of the westward-moving pioneers came to be the giant drumbeat of a new destiny.

Varying Viewpoints

The causes and consequences of the War of 1812 have long sparked spirited debate. Was war the result of western war-hawk expansionism or of British provocations on the high seas? Most recent historians emphasize the naval issue. The young nation's pride and independence, they argue, could not tolerate John Bull's repeated affronts. The Jeffersonian Republicans accepted the need for war because they believed that the future of their party, and indeed of the entire American experiment in republican government, rested on the infant nation's ability to prove that it could meet external challenges.

Perhaps more interestingly, scholars also have seen the first vague outlines of an American identity emerging from the smoke of the War of 1812. Henry Adams' magisterial *History* made this theme a central motif; Adams found evidence of a distinctive American character even in the tactics and techniques of Yankee seamen. The war does appear to have dissolved many localisms and to have begun the forging of a genuine national consciousness—thus paving the way for an upsurge of expansionism and nationalism in the so-called Era of Good Feelings.

Select Readings

Primary Source Documents

See James Madison's "War Message"* (1812), in James D. Richardson, ed., *Messages and Papers of the Presidents* (1896), Vol. I, pp. 500–504; and the protest of thirty-four Federalist congressmen, *Annals of Congress* * 12 Cong., I sess., II cols. 2219–2221 (1812). Timothy Dwight offers a participant's view of the opposition to the war in *The History of the Hartford Convention* * (1833).

Secondary Sources

An important recent work that sets the War of 1812 in a broad context of early American history is J. C. A. Stagg, *Mr. Madison's War: Politics, Diplomacy and Warfare in the Early American Republic* (1983). On the causes of the war, Julius W. Pratt, *Expansionists of 1812* (1925), stresses western pressures; Bradford Perkins, *Prologue to War: England and the United States, 1805–1812* (1961), and Reginald Horsman, *The Causes of the War of 1812* (1962), discuss free seas; Roger H. Brown, *The Republic in Peril: 1812* (1964), emphasizes the need for saving the republican form of government. The relevant volumes of Henry Adams' nine-volume *History of the United States* (1889–1891) still contain magnificent reading, both on the war and on the peace. Federalist reaction to Republican foreign policy is vividly etched in David H. Fisher, *The Revolution of American Conservatism* (1965), and James M. Banner, *To the Hartford Convention: The Federalists and the Origins of Party Politics in Massachu-* setts (1970). Consult also James H. Broussard, *The Southern Federalists, 1800–1816* (1979). Irving Brant continues his strong pro-Madison bias in the relevant volumes of his six-volume work, *James Madison: Commander in Chief, 1812–1836* (1961). See also Ralph Ketcham, *James Madison: A Biography* (1971). Other useful biographical studies are Bernard Mayo, *Henry Clay: Spokesman of the New West* (1937); Glyndon G. Van Deusen, *The Life of Henry Clay* (1937); and Marquis James's spirited *Andrew Jackson: The Border Captain* (1933).

13

The Postwar Upsurge of Nationalism, 1815–1824

The American continents . . . are henceforth not to be considered as subjects for future colonization by any European powers.

James Monroe, December 2, 1823

Nascent Nationalism

The most impressive by-product of the War of 1812 was a heightened nationalism—the spirit of nation-consciousness or national oneness. America may not have fought the war as one nation, but it emerged one nation. So exhilarating was the postwar era that President Madison, despite his blunders, enjoyed the unusual distinction of being more popular when he left the White House in 1817 than when he entered it in 1809.

A weak nationalism had existed since Revolutionary days, but the vibrant new nationalism was composed of many additional ingredients. It sprang partly from pride in recent victories, partly from the setback to Federalist sectionalism and states' rightism, partly from a lessening of economic and political dependence on Europe, and partly from an exulting confidence in the future. Swelling numbers of citizens—although probably not yet a majority—were coming to regard themselves as first of all Americans and secondarily as citizens of their respective states.

The changed mood even manifested itself in the birth of a distinctively national literature. Washington Irving and James Fenimore Cooper attained international recognition in the 1820s, significantly as the nation's first writers of importance to use American scenes and themes. School textbooks, often British in an earlier era, were now being written by Americans for Americans. In the world of magazines, the highly intellectual *North American Review* saw the light of day in 1815—the year of the triumph at New Orleans. Even American painters increasingly celebrated the glories of American landscapes on their canvases.

A fresh nationalistic spirit could be recognized in many other areas. A more handsome national capital began to rise from the ashes of Washington—a capital fit to symbolize America's prospective greatness. The army was expanded to ten thousand men. The navy further covered itself with glory in 1815 when it administered a thorough beating to the piratical plunderers of North Africa. These gratifying victories, inspired by the spirit of nationalism, further inflamed nationalism. Stephen Decatur, naval hero of the War of 1812 and the North African expeditions, pungently captured the nationalist mood in a famous toast made on his return from these Mediterranean triumphs: "Our

country! In her intercourse with foreign nations may she always be in the right; but our country, right or wrong!"

A rising tide of nation-consciousness also touched finance. The War of 1812 had demonstrated the folly of permitting the Bank of the United States to expire in 1811, on the very eve of hostilities. Weak state banks, responding to the vacuum, had seemingly sprung up beside every village tavern. The country was flooded with depreciated bank notes that, incidentally, had hampered the war effort.

A revived Bank of the United States, in response to these obvious needs, was voted by Congress in 1816. It was modeled on the first one but had a total capital of $35 million—three and one-half times that of the original. Jeffersonian Republicans, taught a bitter lesson during the war, supported the revived institution. In fact, they cleverly but inconsistently borrowed the same arguments for a bank that Hamilton had used against Jefferson back in 1791. The

Washington, D.C., 1824　*This view of the Capitol building, much smaller than it is today, reveals the rustic conditions of the early days in the nation's capital. (Metropolitan Museum of Art, Purchase, 1942, Joseph Pulitzer Bequest.)*

Federalist minority in Congress, opposing the Republican measures with its dying gasps, no less inconsistently denounced the Federalist-spawned bank as being unconstitutional. The "moneyed monster," as it was branded by its enemies, further broadened nationalism as it thrust its numerous branches out across state boundaries.

"The American System"

Nationalism likewise manifested itself in manufacturing. Patriotic Americans took pride in the factories that had recently mushroomed forth, largely as a result of the self-imposed embargoes and the war.

When hostilities ended in 1815, British competitors undertook to recover lost ground. They began to dump the contents of their bulging warehouses on the United States, often cutting their prices below cost in an effort to strangle the American war-baby factories in the cradle. The infant industries bawled lustily for protection. To many red-blooded Americans it seemed as though the British, having failed on the battlefield to crush Yankee fighters, were now seeking to crush Yankee factories.

A nationalist Congress, out-Federalizing the old Federalists, responded by passing the pathbreaking Tariff of 1816. The legislators were impressed with the desirability of saving the new industries for the national defense, while at the same time promoting the general welfare. The Tariff of 1816, significantly, was the first in American history with aims that were primarily protective. Its rates—roughly 20 to 25 percent on the value of dutiable imports—were not high

House Vote on Tariff of 1816*

REGIONS	FOR	AGAINST
New England	17	10
Middle states	44	10
West (Ohio)	4	0
South and Southwest	23	34
TOTAL	88	54

* Even in South Carolina, Calhoun's state, the vote in favor of the bill was 4 to 3.

enough to provide completely adequate safeguards, but the law was a bold beginning. A strongly protective trend was started that stimulated the appetites of the protected for more protection.

The battle in Congress over the Tariff of 1816 reflected North-South sectional crosscurrents. Thirty-four-year-old Representative John C. Calhoun of South Carolina—slender, handsome, black-haired, intense, and intellectual—played a stellar role in the debates. A recent war hawk and an ardent nationalist, he supported the tariff bill with all his eloquence and vigor. In 1816 there was some likelihood that the destiny of his native South lay in manufacturing, as well as in the intensive cultivation of cotton. But within a few years Calhoun became a relentless foe of a highly protective tariff. He sadly concluded that it was being used to enrich a few Yankee manufacturers, rather than to build up the economic self-sufficiency and well-being of the entire nation.

Calhoun encountered a worthy adversary in Daniel Webster of New Hampshire, also thirty-four. Stocky, bushy-browed, and dark-haired, "Black Dan" Webster eloquently opposed the highly protective duties of the Tariff of 1816. He took this stand even though he was later to be a zealous nationalist and an ardent champion of high protection. The explanation is simple. Manufacturing in New England had not yet pushed shipping into a back seat, and the shippers of Webster's New Hampshire district feared that a tariff would interfere with their carrying trade. New England, though favoring some protection, was not yet completely willing to exchange the mainsail for the loom—but that day was slowly dawning.

Nationalism was further highlighted by a grandiose plan of Henry Clay for developing a profitable home market. Still radiating the nationalism of war hawk days, he threw himself behind an elaborate scheme known by 1824 as the American System. This system began with the protective tariff, behind which eastern manufacturing would flourish. Revenues gushing from the tariff would provide funds for roads and canals, especially in the fast-developing Ohio Valley. Through these new arteries of transportation would flow foodstuffs and raw

Protariff Woodcut Showing Foreign Goods on Shelves *Many Americans feared foreign goods more than foreign armies.*

materials from the South and West to the North and East. In exchange, a stream of manufactured goods would flow in the return direction.

Persistent and eloquent demands by Henry Clay and others for internal improvements struck a responsive chord with the public. The recent attempts to invade Canada had all failed partly because of oath-provoking roads—or no roads at all. People who have dug wagons out of hub-deep mud do not quickly forget their blisters and backaches. An outcry for better transportation, rising most noisily in the road-poor West, was one of the most striking aspects of the nationalism inspired by the War of 1812.

But attempts to secure federal funding for roads and canals stumbled on Republican constitutional scruples. Congress passed Calhoun's Bonus Bill in 1817, which would have parceled out $1.5 million to the states for internal improvements. But President Madison sternly vetoed this handout measure as unconstitutional. Madison's successor, James Monroe, generally followed the same line of negative reasoning. The individual states were thus forced to venture ahead with construction programs of their own, including the Erie Canal, triumphantly completed by New York in 1825. Jeffersonian Republicans, who had gulped down Hamiltonian loose constructionism on other important problems, choked on the idea of direct federal support of intrastate internal improvements.

The enfeebled Federalists, now turncoat strict constructionists, could grudgingly applaud the vetoes of the Jeffersonian Republican presidents. New England, in particular, strongly opposed federally constructed roads and canals, because such outlets would further drain away population and create competing states beyond the mountains.

The So-Called Era of Good Feelings

James Monroe—6 feet (1.83 meters) tall, somewhat stooped, courtly, and mild-mannered—was nominated for the presidency in 1816 by the Republicans. They thus undertook to continue the so-called Virginia dynasty of Washington, Jefferson, and Madison. The fading Federalists ran a candidate for the last time in their checkered history, and he was crushed by 183 electoral votes to 34.

The death of the once-proud Federalist party was due to various diseases, shortcomings, and misfortunes. A list would include its disgraceful war record, its inability to choke down the new nationalistic program, and the theft of its tenets by the Jeffersonians. Many Federalists followed their stolen principles into the opposition camp; others gradually crawled away to the political graveyard. The irony is that the original Hamiltonians, while the party of the "ins," had been conspicuously nationalistic; now, as the party of the "outs," they scorned the nationalism of the Republicans.

In James Monroe, the man and the times auspiciously met. As the last president to wear an old-style cocked hat, he straddled two generations: the bygone age of the Founding Fathers and the emergent age of nationalism. Never brilliant, and perhaps not great, the serene Virginian with gray-blue eyes was in intellect and personal force the least distinguished of the first eight presidents. But the times called for sober administration, not heroics. And Monroe was an experienced, levelheaded executive, with an ear-to-the-ground talent for interpreting popular rumblings.

President James Monroe (1758–1831) *Monroe fought in the Revolution (suffering a wound), served as minister to France, became copurchaser of Louisiana, and rose to the presidency in 1817. An excellent administrator, he presided over the Era of Good Feelings. His inaugural address declared: "National honor is national property of the highest value." His name is imperishably attached to the Monroe Doctrine and Monrovia, the capital city of Liberia in Africa. He had strongly backed the colonization there of ex-slaves. His wife and two daughters had expensive tastes, and like plantation owner Jefferson, he died deeply in debt. (The Metropolitan Museum of Art, Bequest of Seth Low, 1929.)*

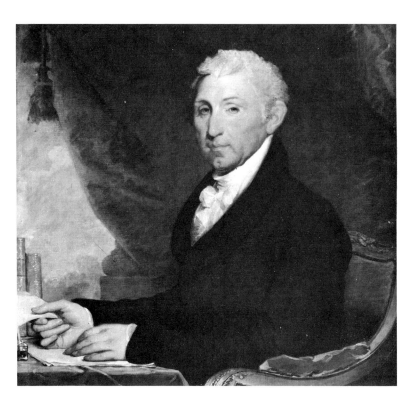

Emerging nationalism was further cemented by a goodwill tour that Monroe undertook early in 1817, ostensibly to inspect military defenses. He pushed northward deep into New England, and then westward to Detroit, viewing en route the Niagara Falls. Even in Federalist New England, "the enemy's country," he received a heartwarming welcome; a Boston newspaper was so far carried away as to announce that an "Era of Good Feelings" had been ushered in.

Boston's **Columbian Centinel** *was not the only newspaper to regard President Monroe's early months as the Era of Good Feelings. The* **Washington** *National* **Intelligencer** *observed in July 1817: "Never before, perhaps, since the institution of civil government, did the same harmony, the same absence of party spirit, the same national feeling, pervade a community. The result is too consoling to dispute too nicely about the cause."*

This happy phrase since then has been commonly used to describe the administrations of Monroe.

The Era of Good Feelings, unfortunately, was something of a misnomer. Considerable tranquillity and prosperity did in fact smile upon the early years of Monroe, but the period was a troubled one. The acute issues of the tariff, the bank, internal improvements, and the sale of public lands were being hotly contested. Sectionalism was crystallizing, and the conflict over slavery was beginning to raise its hideous head.

A vanquished Federalist party was breathing its dying gasps, leaving the field to the triumphant Republicans and one-party rule. But where there is only one party, or where one of the parties enjoys a lopsided majority, the tendency is for factions to develop and fight among themselves. By the early 1820s there was an Era of Inflamed Feelings. Political giants—men like Clay, Calhoun, Jackson, and John Quincy Adams—were elbowing for power and championing the clashing economic interests of their respective sections.

The Panic of 1819 and the Curse of Hard Times

Much of the goodness went out of the good feelings in 1819, when a paralyzing economic panic descended. It brought deflation, depression, bankruptcies, bank failures, unemployment, soup kitchens, and overcrowded pesthouses known as debtors' prisons.

This was the first of the national financial panics since President Washington took office. It was to be followed by a succession of others every twenty or so years, in what seemed an inevitable cycle. Many factors contributed to the catastrophe of 1819, but looming large was overspeculation in frontier lands. The Bank of the United States, through its western branches, had become deeply involved in this popular type of outdoor gambling.

Financial paralysis from the panic, which lasted in some degree for several years, gave a rude setback to the nationalistic ardor. Various parts of the country tended to drift back toward the old sectionalism, as they concentrated on bailing themselves out. The West was especially hard hit. When the pinch came, the Bank of the United States forced the speculative ("wildcat") western banks to the wall and foreclosed mortgages on countless farms. All this was technically legal but politically unwise. In the eyes of the western debtor, the bank soon became a kind of financial devil.

A more welcome child of the panic was fresh legislation for the public domain. The plight of the western farmer, combined with the evils of land speculation, laid bare the defects of the Land Act of 1800, as amended in 1804. By its terms, the pioneer could buy a minimum of 160 acres at $2 an acre over a period of four years, with a down payment of $80. When hard times came, whole communities would default on their installments. An improved Land Act of 1820 lightened the burden somewhat, for it permitted the buyer to secure 80 virgin acres at a minimum of $1.25 an acre in cash—for a total cost of $100. There was less acreage but less outlay.

The panic of 1819 also created backwashes in the political and social world. It hit especially hard the poorer classes—the one-suspender men—and hence helped cultivate the seedbed of Jacksonian democracy. It also directed attention to the inhumanity of imprisoning debtors. In extreme cases, often overplayed, mothers were torn from their infants for owing a few dollars. Mounting agitation against imprisonment for debt bore fruit in remedial legislation in an increasing number of states.

Growing Pains of the West

Beyond doubt the West, out of which had swooped the war hawks of 1812, was by far the most nationalistic of the sections. Being new, it had no long-established states' rights tradition. Moreover, it had early learned to lean on the national government, from which it had secured most of its land, directly or indirectly. It was a mixing bowl within the huge American melting pot, for people from all the sections rubbed elbows on the frontier.

Marvelous indeed had been the onward march of the West; nine frontier states had joined the original thirteen between 1791 and 1819. With an eye to preserving the North-South sectional balance, most of these commonwealths had been admitted alternately, free or slave. (See Admission of States in the Appendix.)

Why this explosive expansion? Fundamentally, there was the generations-old westward movement, which had been going on since early colonial days. In addition, the siren call of cheap lands—"the Ohio fever"—had a special appeal to European immigrants. Quaintly garbed newcomers from abroad were beginning to shuffle down the gangplanks in impressive numbers, especially after the war of embargoes and bullets. Land exhaustion in the older tobacco states, where the soil was "mined" rather than cultivated, likewise drove people westward. Glib-tongued speculators, accepting small down payments, made easier the purchase of new holdings.

The western boom was stimulated by additional developments. Acute distress during the embargo years turned many saddened faces toward the setting sun. The crushing of the Indians in the Northwest and South, by Generals

A Frontier Log Cabin, 1826 Pioneers in the fast-filling West were at first too busy (and too poor) to build elegant residences. (The Granger Collection.)

Harrison and Jackson, soothed the frontier and opened up vast virgin tracts of land. The building of highways improved the land routes to the Ohio Valley. A noteworthy route was the Cumberland Road, begun in 1811, which ran ultimately from western Maryland to Illinois. The employment of the first steamboat on western waters, also in 1811, heralded a new era of upstream navigation.

But the West, despite the inflow of settlers, was still weak in population and influence. Not potent enough politically to make its voice heard, it was forced to ally itself with sister sections. Thus strengthened, it demanded cheap acreage and partially achieved its goal in the Land Act of 1820. It demanded cheap transportation and slowly got it, despite the constitutional qualms of the presidents and the hostility of easterners. Finally, the West demanded cheap money, issued by its own "wildcat" banks, and fought the powerful Bank of the United States to attain its goal.

Wagons West This busy scene on the Frederick Road, leading westward from Baltimore, was typical as pioneers flooded into the newly secured West in the early 1800s. (Maryland Historical Society.)

Slavery and the Sectional Balance

Sectional tensions were nakedly revealed in 1819, when the territory of Missouri knocked on the doors of Congress for admission as a slave state. This fertile and well-watered area contained sufficient population to warrant statehood. But the House of Representatives threw a monkey wrench into the plans of the Missourians by passing the incendiary Tallmadge amendment. It stipulated that no more slaves should be brought into Missouri and also provided for the gradual emancipation of children born to slave parents already there. A mounting roar of anger burst from slaveholding southerners. They were joined by many depression-cursed pioneers who favored unhampered expansion of the West and by many northerners, especially diehard Federalists, who were eager to play politics.

Southerners saw in the Tallmadge amendment, which was defeated in the Senate, an ominous threat to the sectional balance. When the Constitution was adopted in 1788, the North and South were running neck and neck in wealth and population. But with every passing decade the North was becoming wealthier and also more thickly settled—an advantage reflected in an increasing northern majority in the House of Representatives. Yet in the Senate, with eleven states free and eleven slave, the southerners had maintained equality. They were therefore in a good position to thwart any northern effort to interfere with the expansion of slavery, and they did not want to lose this veto.

The future of the slave system caused southerners profound concern. Missouri was the first state entirely west of the Mississippi River to be carved out of the Louisiana Purchase, and the Missouri emancipation amendment might set a damaging precedent for all the rest of the area. Even more disquieting was another possibility. If Congress could abolish the "peculiar institution" in Missouri, might it not attempt to do likewise in the older states of the South? The wounds of the Constitutional Convention of 1787 were once more ripped open.

Burning moral questions also protruded, even though the main issue was political and

Contemporary Antislavery Propaganda   *This also appeared as "Am I Not a Woman and a Sister?"*

economic balance. A small but growing group of antislavery agitators in the North seized the occasion to raise an outcry against the evils of slavery. They were determined that the plague of human bondage should not spread further into the virgin territories.

The Uneasy Missouri Compromise

Deadlock in Washington was at length broken in 1820 by the time-honored American solution of compromise—actually a bundle of three compromises. Courtly Henry Clay of Kentucky, gifted conciliator, played a leading role. Congress, despite abolitionist pleas, agreed to admit Missouri as a slave state. But at the same time, free-soil Maine, which until then had been a part of Massachusetts, was admitted as a separate state. The balance between North and South was thus kept at twelve states each and remained there for fifteen years. Although Missouri was permitted to retain slaves, all future bondage was prohibited in the remainder of the

While the debate over Missouri was raging, Jefferson wrote to a correspondent: "I thank you for your information on the progress and prospects of the Missouri question. It is the most portentous one which ever yet threatened our Union. In the gloomiest moment of the revolutionary war I never had any apprehensions equal to what I feel from this source." He also wrote that the "question, like a firebell in the night, awakened and filled me with terror." With slavery, the aging ex-president declared, "we have the wolf by the ears, and we can neither hold him nor safely let him go."

Louisiana Purchase north of the line of 36° 30'—the southern boundary of Missouri.

This horse-trading adjustment was politically evenhanded, though denounced by extremists on each side as a "dirty bargain." Both North and South yielded something; both gained something. The South won the prize of Missouri as an unrestricted slave state. The North won the concession that Congress could forbid slavery in the remaining territories. More gratifying to many northerners was the fact that the immense area north of 36° 30', except Missouri, was forever closed to the blight of slavery. Yet the restriction on future slavery in the territories was not unduly offensive to the slaveowners, partly because the northern prairie land did not seem adapted to slave labor. Even so, a majority of southern congressmen voted against the compromise.

Neither North nor South was acutely displeased, although neither was completely happy. Fortunately, the Missouri Compromise lasted thirty-four years—a vital formative period in the life of the young Republic—and during that time it preserved the shaky compact of the states. Yet the embittered dispute over slavery heralded the future breakup of the Union. Ever after, the morality of the South's "peculiar institution" was an issue that could not be swept under the rug. The Missouri Compromise only ducked the question—it did not resolve it. Sooner or later, Thomas Jefferson predicted, it will "burst on us as a tornado."

The Missouri dispute proved to be another serious setback to nationalism and a tremendous stimulus to sectionalism—in the North, South, and West. From this time forward the embattled South began to develop a nationalism of its own—a kind of sectional nationalism. Needing sectional reinforcements, it cast flirtatious eyes upon the adolescent West, which in turn was seeking allies.

The Missouri Compromise and Slavery, 1820–1821 In the 1780s Thomas Jefferson had written of slavery in America: "Indeed I tremble for my country when I reflect that God is just; that his justice cannot sleep forever; that . . . the Almighty has no attribute which can take side with us in such a contest." Now, at the time of the Missouri Compromise, Jefferson feared that his worst forebodings were coming to pass. "I considered it at once," he said of the Missouri question, "as the knell of the Union."

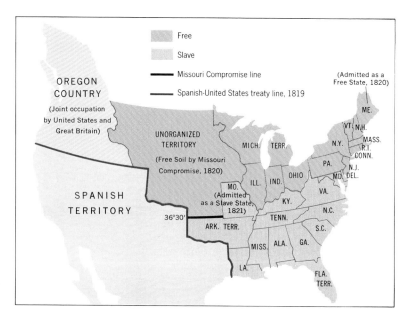

Hotheads in both the North and South, numbering only a tiny minority, clamored for secession or a shooting showdown in 1820. But fortunately for the Union, hostilities were postponed. With every passing decade the North was becoming stronger in population, wealth, industry, and transportation—all of which added up to military strength.

Admittedly, the Missouri solution was a compromise—a partial surrender on both sides. Subsequent generations have tended to sneer at Henry Clay and the other architects of the settlement as weak—as "appeasers." Yet the fact should not be overlooked that compromise and statesmanship are often Siamese twins. In a free and peaceful association of once-sovereign states, no group of them could lord it over the others—that is, if they were all going to live together under the same roof. Without compromise there could have been no Constitution in 1787. Compromise made the Union in 1789; compromise saved the Union until 1860. When compromise broke down, the Union broke up.

The Missouri Compromise and the concurrent panic of 1819 should have dimmed the political star of President Monroe. Certainly both unhappy events had a dampening effect on the Era of Good Feelings. But smooth-spoken James Monroe was so popular, and the Federalist opposition so weak, that in the presidential election of 1820 he received every electoral vote except one. Unanimity was an honor reserved for George Washington. Monroe, as it turned out, was the only president in American history to be reelected after a term in which a major financial panic began.

John Marshall and Judicial Nationalism

Upsurging nationalism of the post-Ghent years, despite setbacks, was further reflected and strengthened by the Supreme Court.

The august tribunal was dominated by the tall, thin, and aggressive Chief Justice John Marshall, a "deathbed" Federalist appointee of John Adams' expiring administration. He had served at Valley Forge during the Revolution and while suffering from cold and hunger had

John Marshall (1755–1835) *Born in a log cabin on the Virginia frontier, he attended law lectures for just a few weeks at the college of William and Mary—his only formal education. (National Portrait Gallery, Smithsonian Institution, Washington, D.C.)*

been painfully impressed with the drawbacks of feeble central authority. Before Marshall mounted the supreme bench in 1801, the judiciary had been the weakest and most timid of the three arms of the federal government. But he boldly asserted the doctrine of judicial review of congressional legislation in the case of *Marbury* v. *Madison* (1803).* And long before the end of his thirty-four years of service, he had made the judiciary, in some respects, the strongest branch of the national government.

Marshall, whose formal legal schooling had lasted only six weeks, was a judicial statesman rather than a strictly impartial judge. He examined a case through the colored lenses of his Federalist philosophy and then undertook to find legal precedents to support his Hamiltonian preconceptions. Sure of his ground, he

*See p. 182.

wrote some of his most important decisions even before the lawyers had concluded their arguments.

In the vain hope of offsetting Marshall's Federalism, President Jefferson and his successors appointed Republicans to the Supreme Court. But by this time many Republicans had come to accept the Federalist ideal of a strong central government, and the masterful Marshall found it easy to lead his colleagues the rest of the way. The Jeffersonians raged, while Jefferson himself privately condemned the "twistifications" of his cousin, "the crafty chief judge." But Marshall pushed ahead inflexibly on his Federalist course, though bending slightly in his final years before the rising popular demands for a more democratic control of government.

For over three decades, the ghost of Alexander Hamilton spoke through the lanky, black-robed judge. As a shaper of the Constitution in the direction of a more potent central government, Marshall ranks as the foremost of the Molding Fathers. As a wealthy businessman and land speculator, he instinctively shared Hamilton's preference for the propertied class. As a Virginia aristocrat, he deplored democratic excesses and opposed manhood suffrage and the rule of the unwashed masses.

The Supreme Court Curbs States' Rights

One group of Marshall's decisions—perhaps the most famous—resulted in bolstering the power of the federal government at the expense of the states. A notable case in this category was *McCulloch* v. *Maryland* (1819). The suit involved an attempt by the state of Maryland to destroy a branch of the Bank of the United States by imposing a tax on its notes. John Marshall, speaking for the Court, declared the bank constitutional by invoking the Hamiltonian doctrine of implied powers (see p. 155). At the same time, he strengthened federal authority and slapped at state infringements when he denied the right of Maryland to tax the bank. With ringing emphasis, he affirmed "that the power to tax involves the power to destroy" and "that a power to create implies a power to preserve."

Marshall's ruling in this case gave the doctrine of "loose construction" its most famous formulation. The Constitution, he said, derived from the consent of the people and thus permitted the government to act for their benefit. He further argued that the Constitution was "intended to endure for ages to come and, consequently, to be adapted to the various crises of human affairs." Finally, he declared: "Let the end be legitimate, let it be within the scope of the Constitution, and all means which are appropriate, which are plainly adapted to that end, which are not prohibited, but consist with the letter and spirit of the Constitution, are constitutional."

Two years later (1821) the case of *Cohens* v. *Virginia* gave Marshall one of his greatest opportunities. The Cohens, found guilty by the Virginia courts of illegally selling lottery tickets, appealed to the highest tribunal. Virginia won, in that the conviction of the Cohens was upheld. But it lost, in that Marshall resoundingly asserted the right of the Supreme Court to review the decisions of the state supreme courts in all questions involving powers of the federal government. The states' rights people were aghast.

Hardly less significant in Marshall's career was the celebrated "steamboat case," *Gibbons* v. *Ogden* (1824). The suit grew out of an attempt by the state of New York to grant to a private concern a monopoly of waterborne commerce between New York and New Jersey. Marshall sternly reminded the upstart state that the Constitution conferred on Congress alone the control of interstate commerce (see Art. I, Sec. VIII, para. 3). He thus struck another blow at states' rights, while upholding the sovereign powers of the federal government. Interstate streams were thus cleared of this judicial snag, while the departed spirit of Hamilton may have applauded.

Judicial Dikes against Democratic Excesses

Another sheaf of Marshall's decisions bolstered judicial barriers against democratic or demagogic attacks on property rights.

The notorious case of *Fletcher* v. *Peck* (1810) arose when a Georgia legislature, swayed by bribery, granted 35 million acres in the Yazoo River country (Mississippi) to private speculators. The next legislature, yielding to an angry public outcry, canceled the crooked transaction. But the Supreme Court, with Marshall presiding, decreed that the legislative grant was a contract (even though fraudulently secured) and that the Constitution forbids state laws "impairing" contracts (Art. I, Sec. X, para. 1). The decision is perhaps most noteworthy as further protecting property rights against popular pressures. It is also one of the earliest clear assertions of the right of the Supreme Court to invalidate state laws conflicting with the federal Constitution.

A similar principle was upheld in the case of *Dartmouth College* v. *Woodward* (1819), perhaps the best remembered of Marshall's decisions. The college had been granted a charter by King George III in 1769, but the democratic New Hampshire state legislature had seen fit to change it. Dartmouth appealed the case, employing as counsel its most distinguished alumnus, Daniel Webster ('01). The "Godlike Daniel" reportedly pulled out all the stops of his tear-inducing eloquence when he declaimed, "It is, sir, as I have said, a small college. And yet there are those who love it."

Marshall needed no dramatics in the Dartmouth case. He put the states firmly in their place when he ruled that the original charter must stand. It was a contract—and the Constitution protected contracts against state encroachments. The Dartmouth decision had the fortunate effect of safeguarding business enterprise from domination by the states. But it had the unfortunate effect of creating a precedent that enabled chartered corporations, in later years, to escape the handcuffs of needed public control.

If John Marshall was a Molding Father of the Constitution, Daniel Webster was an Expounding Father. Time and again he left his seat in the Senate, stepped downstairs, and there expounded his Federalistic and nationalistic philosophy before the supreme bench. The eminent chief justice, so Webster reported, approvingly drank in the familiar arguments as a

> When Supreme Court Chief Justice John Marshall died, a New York newspaper rejoiced that "the chief place in the supreme tribunal of the Union will no longer be filled by a man whose political doctrines led him always . . . to strengthen government at the expense of the people."

baby sucks in its mother's milk. The two men dovetailed with each other. Webster's classic speeches in the Senate, challenging states' rights and nullification, were largely repetitions of the arguments that he had earlier presented before a sympathetic Supreme Court.

Marshall's decisions are felt even today. In this sense his nationalism was the most tenaciously enduring of the era. He buttressed the federal Union and helped to create a stable, nationally uniform environment for business. At

Daniel Webster (1782–1852) *Premier orator and statesman, he served many years in both Houses of Congress and also as secretary of state. Often regarded as presidential timber, he was somewhat handicapped by an overfondness for good food and drink and was frequently in financial difficulties. His devotion to the Union was inflexible. "One country, one constitution, and one destiny," he declaimed in 1837. (The Metropolitan Museum of Art, Gift of I. N. Phelps Stokes, Edward S. Hawes, Alice Mary Hawes, Marion Augusta Hawes, 1937.)*

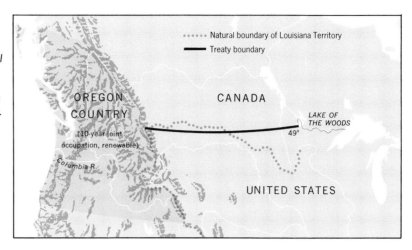

U.S.-British Boundary Settlement, 1818 *Note that the United States gained considerable territory by securing a treaty boundary rather than the natural boundary of the Missouri River watershed. The line of 49° was extended westward to the Pacific Ocean under the Treaty of 1846 with Britain (see p. 280).*

the same time, Marshall checked the excesses of popularly elected state legislatures. In an age when white manhood suffrage was flowering and America was veering toward stronger popular control, Marshall almost single-handedly shaped the Constitution along conservative, centralizing lines that ran somewhat counter to the dominant spirit of the new century. Through him the conservative Hamiltonians triumphed from the tomb.

Sharing Oregon and Acquiring Florida

The yeasty nationalism of the years after the War of 1812 was likewise reflected in the shaping of foreign policy. To this end, the nationalistic President Monroe teamed with his nationalistic secretary of state, John Quincy Adams, the cold and scholarly son of the frosty and bookish ex-president. The younger Adams, a statesman of the first rank, happily rose above the ingrown Federalist sectionalism of his native New England and proved to be one of the great secretaries of state.

To its credit, the Monroe administration negotiated the much-underrated Treaty of 1818 with England. It permitted Americans to share the coveted Newfoundland fisheries with their Canadian cousins. This multisided agreement also fixed the vague northern limits of Louisiana along the forty-ninth parallel from the Lake of the Woods to the Rocky Mountains. The

treaty further provided for a ten-year joint occupation of the untamed Oregon country, without a surrender of the rights or claims of either America or Britain.

To the south lay semitropical Spanish Florida, which many Americans believed geography and providence had destined to become part of the United States. Americans already claimed West Florida, where uninvited American settlers had torn down the hated Spanish flag in 1810. Congress ratified this grab in 1812, and during the War of 1812 against Spain's ally, Britain, a small American army seized the Mobile region. But the bulk of Florida remained, tauntingly, under Spanish rule.

Acquiring the Floridas, 1810–1819

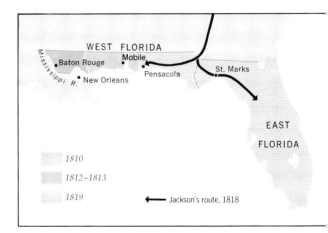

When an epidemic of revolutions broke out in South America, Spain was forced to denude Florida of troops to fight the rebels. A chaotic situation rapidly developed in the swampy peninsula. Bands of Indians, runaway slaves, and white outcasts poured across the border into American territory, burning and scalping, and then fled to safety behind the surveyor's line.

General Andrew Jackson, idol of the West and scourge of the Indians, reappeared in 1817. The Monroe administration formally commissioned him to punish the Indians, and, if necessary, to pursue them into Florida. But he was to respect all posts under the Spanish flag.

Early in 1818 Jackson swept across the Florida border with all the fury of an avenging angel. He hanged two Indian chiefs without ceremony and, after hasty military trials, executed two British subjects for assisting the Indians. He also seized the two most important Spanish posts in the area, St. Marks and then Pensacola, where he deposed the Spanish governor, who was lucky enough to escape Jackson's jerking noose.

Jackson had clearly exceeded his instructions from Washington. Alarmed, President Monroe consulted his cabinet. Its members were for disavowing or disciplining the overzealous Jackson—all except the lone wolf John Quincy Adams, who refused to howl with the pack. An ardent patriot and nationalist, the flinty New Englander finally won the others over to his point of view. Far from apologizing, he took the offensive and emphatically informed Spain that she had violated the Spanish-American Treaty of 1795 by not suppressing the outlaws of Florida. He then insisted that the alternatives were

Warrior Andrew Jackson, 1814 *A self-taught and popularly elected major general of the militia, Andrew Jackson became a major general of the U.S. Army in 1814. He was noted for his stern discipline, iron will ("Old Hickory"), and good luck. (National Gallery of Art, Washington, Andrew W. Mellon Collection.)*

for the Spaniards to control the area (a task that they admitted was impossible) or cede it to the United States (a course that was galling to their pride).

Distressed in Latin America and at home, and believing that they were going to lose Spanish Florida in any case, the Spanish decided to dispose of the alligator-infested area while they could still get something for it. In the mislabeled Florida Purchase Treaty of 1819, Spain ceded Florida, as well as shadowy Spanish claims to Oregon, in exchange for America's abandonment of equally shadowy claims to Texas, soon to become part of independent Mexico. The hitherto vague western boundary of Louisiana was made to run zigzag along the Rockies to the forty-second parallel and then to turn due west to the Pacific, dividing Oregon from Spanish holdings.

The successful invasion of Spain, so Secretary of State Adams recorded in his diary, caused panic in official Washington: "I find him [President Monroe] . . . alarmed, far beyond anything that I could have conceived possible, with the fear that the Holy Alliance [of European powers] are about to restore immediately all South America to Spain."

The Menace of Monarchy in America

After the Napoleonic nightmare, the rethroned autocrats of Europe banded together in a kind of monarchical protective association. Determined to restore the good old days, they undertook to stamp out the democratic tendencies that had sprouted from soil richly manured by the ideals of the French Revolution. The world must be made safe *from* democracy.

The crowned despots acted promptly. With complete ruthlessness, they smothered the embers of rebellion in Italy (1821) and in Spain (1823). According to the European rumor factory, they were also gazing across the Atlantic. Russia, Austria, Prussia, and France, acting in partnership, would presumably send powerful fleets and armies to the revolted colonies of Spanish America and there restore the autocratic Spanish king to his ancestral domains.

Many Americans were alarmed. Sympathetic to democratic revolutions everywhere, they had cheered when the Latin American republics rose from the ruins of monarchy. Americans feared that if the European powers intervened in the New World, the cause of republicanism would suffer irreparable harm. The physical security of the United States—the mother lode of democracy—would be endangered by the proximity of powerful and unfriendly forces.

The southward push of the Russian bear, from the chill region now known as Alaska, had already publicized the menace of monarchy to North America. In 1821 the czar of Russia issued a decree extending Russian jurisdiction over 100 miles (161 kilometers) of the open sea down to the line of 51°, an area that embraced most of the coast of present-day British Columbia. The energetic Russians had already established trading posts almost as far south as the entrance to San Francisco Bay, and the fear prevailed in the United States that they were planning to cut the Republic off from California, its prospective window on the Pacific.

Great Britain, still Mistress of the Seas, was now beginning to play a lone-hand role on the complicated international stage. In particular, it recoiled from joining hands with the continental European powers in crushing the newly won liberties of the Spanish-Americans. These

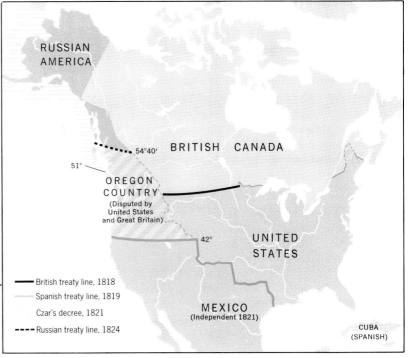

The West and Northwest, 1819–1824   *The British Hudson's Bay Company moved to secure its claim to the Oregon country in 1824, when it sent a heavily armed expedition led by Peter Skene Ogden into the Snake River country. In May 1825, Ogden's party descended the Bear River "and found it discharged into a large Lake of 100 miles in length"—the first documented sighting by white explorers of Great Salt Lake.*

British treaty line, 1818
Spanish treaty line, 1819
Czar's decree, 1821
Russian treaty line, 1824

revolutionists had thrown open their monopoly-bound ports to outside trade, and British shippers, as well as Americans, had found the profits sweet.

Accordingly, in August 1823, George Canning, the haughty British foreign secretary, approached the American minister in London with a startling proposition. Would not the United States join with Britain in a joint declaration, specifically warning the European despots to keep their harsh hands off the Latin American republics? The American minister, lacking instructions, referred this fateful scheme to his superiors in Washington.

Mr. Monroe and His Doctrine

Reactions in America to the Canning proposal varied. The intimate advisers of President Monroe, including the aged Jefferson and Madison, recommended that the Republic lock arms with the hitherto distrusted mother country. The one notable exception was again the lone-wolf nationalist, Secretary Adams, who was hard-headed enough to beware of Britons bearing gifts. Why should the lordly British, with the mightiest navy afloat, need America as an ally—an America that had neither naval nor military strength? Such a union, argued Adams, was undignified—like a tiny American "cockboat" sailing "in the wake of the British man-of-war."

Adams, ever alert, thought that he detected the joker in the Canning proposal. The British feared that the aggressive Yankees would one day seize Spanish territory in the Americas—perhaps Cuba—which would jeopardize England's possessions in the Caribbean. If Canning could seduce the United States into joining with him in support of the territorial integrity of the New World, America's own hands would be morally tied.

A self-denying alliance with Britain would not only hamper American expansion, concluded Adams, but it was unnecessary. He suspected—correctly—that the European powers had not agreed upon any definite plans for invading the Americas. In any event, the British navy would not permit hostile fleets to come, because the South American markets had to be kept open at all costs for English merchants. It was presumably safe for Uncle Sam, behind the protective wooden petticoats of the British navy, to blow a defiant, nationalistic blast at all Europe. The distresses of the Old World again set the stage for another American diplomatic coup.

The Monroe Doctrine was born late in 1823, when the nationalistic Adams won the nationalistic Monroe over to his way of thinking. The president, in his regular annual message to Congress of December 2, 1823, incorporated a stern warning to the European powers. Its two basic features were (1) noncolonization and (2) nonintervention.

Monroe first directed his verbal blast primarily at the lumbering Russian bear in the Northwest. With emphatic tones he proclaimed, in effect, that the era of colonization in the Americas had ended and that henceforth there would be a permanently closed season. What the great powers had they might keep, but neither they nor any other Old World powers could seize or otherwise acquire more. This lofty declaration was later resented by those nations, notably Germany and Italy, that were not unified and hence unable to take out colonial hunting licenses until late in the century.

At the same time, Monroe sounded a trumpet blast against foreign intervention. He was clearly concerned with regions to the south, where fears were felt for the newly fledged Spanish-American republics. Monroe bluntly warned the crowned heads of Europe to keep their hated monarchical systems out of this hemisphere. For its part, the United States would not intervene in the war that the Greeks were then fighting against the Turks for their independence.

Monroe's Dictum Abroad

Monroe's ringing declaration quickened the patriotic pulse of nationalistic young America. The American people were thrilled, even though they had no effective army or navy, to shake their collective fists at all the European despots and loudly warn them to stay away. While gratifying national pride and striking a blow for democratic rule, Monroe was also striking a blow for the "Almighty Dollar," as represented by the freshly opened Latin American markets.

Reactions in England were mixed. The British press, likewise savoring the juicy Latin American markets, was generally favorable to Monroe's forceful warning. But Canning was irked, for he perceived that the Monroe Doctrine was aimed at possible land-grabbing by Britain, as well as by Europe. "Hands off" applied to all outside powers, including proud Britain.

The ermined monarchs of Europe were angered. Having resented the incendiary American experiment from the beginning, they were now deeply offended by Monroe's high-flown pronouncement—all the more so because of the gulf between America's loud pretensions and her weak military strength. But though offended by the upstart Yankees, the European powers found their hands tied, and their frustration increased their annoyance. Even if they had worked out plans for invading the Americas, they would have been helpless before the booming broadsides of the British navy.

Monroe's solemn warning, when issued, made little splash in the newly hatched republics to the south. Anyone could see that Uncle Sam was only secondarily concerned about his neighbors, because he was primarily concerned about defending himself against future invasion. Only a relatively few upper-class Latin Americans knew of the message, and they generally recognized that the British navy—not the paper pronouncement of James Monroe—stood between them and a hostile Europe.

In truth, Monroe's message did not have much contemporary significance. Americans applauded it and then forgot it as they turned back to such activities as felling trees and fighting Indians. Not until 1845 did President Polk revive it, and not until midcentury did it become an important national dogma.

The new doctrine was not even necessary, in a narrow sense, when given to the world. Secretary Adams, in firm diplomatic notes, had already warned Russia against trespassing on the northwest coast. Even before Monroe's stiff message, the czar had decided to retreat. This he formally did in the Russo-American Treaty of 1824, which fixed his southernmost limits at the line of 54° 40′—the present southern tip of the Alaska panhandle.

Monroe's Doctrine Appraised

The Monroe Doctrine might more accurately have been called the Self-Defense Doctrine. President Monroe was concerned basically with the security of his own country—not of Latin America. The United States has never willingly permitted a powerful foreign nation to secure a foothold near its stragetic Caribbean vitals. Yet in the absence of the British navy or other allies, the strength of the Monroe Doctrine has never been greater than America's power to eject the trespasser. The doctrine, as often noted, was just as big as the nation's armed forces—and no bigger. But attaching Monroe's name to the Self-Defense Doctrine has given it the prestige that comes from a distinguished personage.

Monroe and Adams must share about equally the credit for the authorship of the so-called Monroe Doctrine. But its basic principles, in one form or another, had been set forth earlier by Washington, Jefferson, Hamilton, and others. Monroe and Adams merely collected and codified existing ideas, giving them a new emphasis and slant.

The Monroe Doctrine has had a long career of ups and downs. It was never law—domestic or international. It was not, technically speaking, a pledge or an agreement. It was merely a simple, personalized statement of the policy of President Monroe. What one president says, another may unsay. And Monroe's successors have ignored, revived, distorted, or expanded the original version, chiefly by adding interpre-

Prince Metternich, the Austrian chancellor, wrote bitterly of the "dangerous" new manifesto with its "unprovoked attacks . . . indecent declarations . . . evil doctrines and pernicious examples."

tations. Like ivy on a tree, it has grown with America's growth.

But the Monroe Doctrine in 1823 was largely an expression of the post-1812 nationalism energizing the United States. Although directed at a specific menace in 1823, and hence a kind of period piece, the doctrine proved to be the most famous of all the long-lived offspring of that na-

tionalism. While giving vent to a spirit of patriotism, it simultaneously deepened the illusion of isolationism. Many Americans falsely concluded, then and later, that the Republic was in fact isolated from European dangers simply because it wanted to be and because, in a nationalistic outburst, Monroe had publicly warned the Old World powers to stay away.

Varying Viewpoints

The Era of Good Feelings, at first, generated little ill feeling among historians. They generally agreed in seeing the period in terms not of conflict but of consolidation. There were then few irreconcilable controversies, but rather a remarkable consensus on laying the new nation's institutional base. In effect, the era set up a political program for the future; defined the power of the Supreme Court and its relation to the other branches of government; stabilized national bound-

aries; and established basic elements of foreign policy in the Monroe Doctrine.

Recently, historians have uncovered the smoldering tensions seething under the calm surface of the period. One-party rule masked deep divisions over economic and sectional issues that would soon erupt into bitter struggles over the tariff, expansion, and especially, slavery. The tenuous Missouri Compromise revealed the fragility of the era's buoyant nationalism.

Select Readings

Primary Source Documents

Charles F. Adams, ed., *Memoirs of John Quincy Adams* * (1875), offers a behind-the-scenes portrait of the creation of the Monroe Doctrine. See also the text of Monroe's public statement in James D. Richardson, ed., *Messages and Papers of the Presidents* * (1896), vol. II, pp. 207 ff. John Marshall's decision in *McCulloch* v. *Maryland* *, 4 Wheaton 316 (1819), is a leading statement of the era's surging nationalism. "The Missouri Compromise" (1819–1820), in Henry Steele Commager, *Documents of American History*, reveals the dangerous sectional animosities underlying such national pride.

Secondary Sources

An excellent introduction is George Dangerfield, *The Awakening of American Nationalism, 1815–1828* (1965), which supplements his *Era of Good Feelings*

(1952). See also Robert H. Wiebe's ambitious *Opening of American Society: From the Adoption of the Constitution to the Eve of Disunion* (1984). Perry Miller, *The Life of the Mind in America* (1965), contains suggestive insights on legal thought and the role of the legal profession in the Marshall era. This and other topics are astutely placed in context by Lawrence Friedman in *A History of American Law* (1973). R. Kent Newmyer, *The Supreme Court under Marshall and Taney* (1968), briefly charts constitutional development. More comprehensive is Alfred H. Kelly, Winfred A. Harbison and Herman Belz, *The American Constitution: Its Origin and Development* (6th ed., 1983). George R. Taylor's classic *Transportation Revolution* (1955) remains a valuable source on that subject. Glover Moore, *The Missouri Controversy, 1819–1821* (1953), and Charles S. Sydnor, *The Development of Southern Sectionalism,*

1819–1848 (1948), place the Missouri Compromise in a broader context. On the Monroe Doctrine, the best single volume is Dexter Perkins, *A History of the Monroe Doctrine* (1955). More recently, Ernest R. May has somewhat unconvincingly tied the doctrine to domestic politics, especially the impending election of 1824, in *The Making of the Monroe Doctrine* (1975). Related to the doctrine is John A. Logan, Jr., *No Transfer: An American Security Princi-* ple (1961). See also Harry Ammon, *James Monroe: The Quest for National Identity* (1971). On Calhoun consult Margaret L. Coit, *John C. Calhoun* (1950); Gerald M. Capers, *John C. Calhoun, Opportunist* (1960); and Richard N. Current, *John C. Calhoun* (1963). See also Samuel F. Bemis, *John Quincy Adams and the Foundations of American Foreign Policy* (1949).

14

The Rise of
Jacksonian Democracy

In the full enjoyment of the gifts of Heaven and the fruits of superior industry, economy, and virtue, every man is equally entitled to protection by law; but when the laws undertake to add to those natural and just advantages artificial distinctions . . . and exclusive privileges . . . the humble members of society—the farmer, mechanics, and laborers . . . have a right to complain of the injustice of their government.

Andrew Jackson, 1832

Politics for the People

Democracy was something of a taint in the days of the lordly Federalists. Martha Washington, the first First Lady, was shocked after a presidential reception to find a greasy smear on the wallpaper—left there, she was sure, by an uninvited "filthy democrat."

But by the 1820s, if not before, aristocracy was becoming a taint, and democracy was becoming respectable. Politicians were now forced to unbend and curry favor with the voting masses. Lucky indeed was the aspiring office seeker who could boast of birth in a log cabin. In 1840 Daniel Webster publicly apologized for not being able to claim so humble a birthplace,

though quickly adding that his brothers could. Fatally handicapped was the candidate who appeared to be too clean, too well dressed, too grammatical, too high-browishly intellectual. In the West, especially, the belief was spreading that a man was well qualified for high office if he was a superior militia commander or a victorious Indian fighter, like Andrew Jackson, or even an outstanding hunter, like Davy Crockett. The semiliterate Crockett was elected to Congress mainly on the basis of his prowess with a rifle. He once killed 105 bears in a season, and his Tennessee constituents began to talk of running him for the presidency. Yet coloful characters like Crockett were exceptions. Most high political offices continued to be filled by

David ("Davy") Crockett (1786–1836) *A semiliterate Tennesseean, he failed at farming but won distinction as a rifleman, soldier, scout, humorist, and three-time congressman. Rejected in politics, he left Tennessee to fight for Texas against the Mexicans and fell, bullet-riddled, in the final assault on the Alamo.*

"leading citizens." But now these wealthy and prominent men had to forsake all social pretensions and cultivate the common touch if they hoped to win elections.

Jeffersonian democracy had proclaimed that the people should be governed as little as possible; Jacksonian democracy now added that whatever governing was to be done should be done directly by the people. The common man was at last moving to the center of the national political stage: the sturdy American who donned plain trousers rather than silver-buckled knee breeches, who besported a plain haircut and a coonskin cap rather than a powdered wig, and who wore no man's collar, often not even one of his own. Instead of the old divine right of kings, America was now witnessing the divine right of the people.

The New Democracy, so called, was based on universal white manhood suffrage rather than the old property qualifications. The frontier state of Vermont, admitted to the Union in 1791, was the first to place the ballot in the hands of all adult white males. This trend continued, notably in the West, where land was so easily obtained as to render almost meaningless the old property qualifications. Property tests for officeholding were also widely abolished, and even judges were now being popularly elected. The South trailed other regions in giving up property requirements, but it, too, eventually extended suffrage and the right to hold office to all white men.

Snobbish bigwigs, unhappy over the change, sneered at "coonskin congressmen" and at the newly enfranchised "bipeds of the forest." To them, the tyranny of King Numbers was no less offensive than that of King George. But they protested in vain. The masses marched unswervingly toward a fuller measure of control over the Republic's political affairs. If they made mistakes, they made them themselves and were not the victims of aristocratic domination. If at times they stumbled, they stumbled forward. The New Democracy had arrived to stay.

Nourishing the New Democracy

What caused this lush flowering of political democracy? In part it was simply the logical outgrowth of the egalitarian ideas that had taken root in colonial days and been lavishly fertilized during the Revolutionary era. More immediately, the panic of 1819 and the Missouri Compromise of 1820 rank high on the list of the New Democracy's nutrients.

The economic downturn was blamed by many workers and farmers on banking irregularities and speculation. In particular, the panic nurtured burning resentment at the government-granted privileges of the banks. Farmers unable to pay their debts usually lost their farms; overextended bankers unable to fulfill their obligation to redeem their paper bank notes in coin simply suspended payment and escaped any further threat to their property. Holders of bank notes were left with worthless paper and might next find their own property under foreclosure, as the bank called in its debts. These kinds of practices reeked of favoritism and seemed to mock the democratic principles of equality and fair play. The desire to purge the land of this sort of "corruption" and restore the republican ideals of Jefferson's day invigorated the interest of many Americans in politics—especially the followers of Andrew Jackson. They sought control of government in order to tear the banks from its protective embrace, to substitute hard money for bank notes, and even to abolish the banks altogether. Opposed to the Jacksonians were those persons who favored the current banking system and, more generally, who believed that the federal government had a legitimate role to play in promoting economic growth.

The Missouri Compromise likewise awakened many Americans, especially white southerners, to the importance of politics. The spectacle of organized northern resistance to admission of Missouri as a slave state aroused fears in the white South about further federal aggressions against states' rights—especially the right to perpetuate slavery. Controlling the federal government in order to prevent that result thus became a prime goal of white southerners, stimulating heightened involvement in politics.

Economic distress and the slavery issue together raised the political stakes in the 1820s, ushering in a whole new chapter in the history of American politics. The deference, apathy, and virtually nonexistent party organizations of the Era of Good Feelings gave way to the boisterous democracy, frenzied vitality, and strong political parties of the Jacksonian era. Voter turnout rose dramatically; only about one-quarter of eligible voters cast a ballot in the presidential election of 1824, but that proportion doubled in 1828, and in the election of 1840 it reached 78 percent. A new style of politicking emerged, as candidates made increasing use of banners, badges, parades, barbecues, free drinks, and baby kissing in an effort to "get out the vote." The old suspicion of political parties as illegitimate disrupters of society's natural harmony was replaced by an acceptance of the sometimes wild contentiousness of political life. Vigorous political conflict even came to be celebrated as necessary for the health of democracy.

Everywhere the people flexed their political muscles. To an increasing degree, members of

The New Politics *Politicians in the Jacksonian era had to take their message to the common man, as shown in this painting by George Caleb Bingham. (Nelson-Atkins Museum of Art, Kansas City, Missouri, Nelson Fund.)*

An Election Day Scene in the Age of Jackson *Though politics was serious business in the Jacksonian era, it also provided the occasion for much socializing and merriment. This election-day crowd in Philadelphia appears in an especially festive mood. (Historical Society of Pennsylvania.)*

the Electoral College were being chosen directly by the people, rather than by state legislatures. Presidential nominations by a congressional caucus, meeting secretly, took on a bad odor. This procedure was now condemned as furtive, elitist, and subversive of democracy. The delicate checks and balances among the three federal branches were thought to be weakened when the president was indirectly indebted to Congress for his exalted office.

New and more democratic methods of nominating presidential candidates were devised. In 1824 the voters, crying "The People Must Be Heard" and "Down with King Caucus," turned against the candidate (Crawford) who had been selected by the congressional clique. For a brief period nominations were made by some of the state legislatures. But these did not seem democratic either, and in 1831 the first of the circuslike national nominating conventions was held (by the short-lived but significant Anti-Masonic party). Here the people appeared to exercise greater control, though their will was often thwarted by paunchy bosses in smoke-filled rooms.

The Adams-Clay "Corrupt" Bargaining

The woods were full of presidential timber in 1824. Four candidates towered above the others: Andrew Jackson of Tennessee, the tall, silver-maned, and hollow-cheeked "Old Hero" of New Orleans; Henry Clay of Kentucky, the gamy and gallant "Harry of the West"; William H. Crawford of Georgia, a giant of a man, able though ailing; and John Quincy Adams of Massachusetts, highly intelligent, experienced, and aloof.

All four rivals professed to be "Republicans." Well-organized parties had not yet emerged, as illustrated by the fact that John C. Calhoun appeared as the vice-presidential candidate on both the Adams and the Jackson tickets.

The results of the noisy campaign were interesting but confusing. Jackson, the war hero, clearly had the strongest personal appeal, especially in the West. Foreshadowing the themes that would later shape the historical identity of his presidency, his campaign appealed for the salvation of republicanism from the forces of corruption and privilege in government, especially as embodied in "King Caucus." He polled almost as many popular votes as his next two rivals combined, but he failed to win a majority of the electoral vote. In such a deadlock the House of Representatives, as directed by the Twelfth Amendment (see the Appendix), must choose among the top three candidates. Clay was thus eliminated, yet he still presided over the very chamber that had to pick the winner. Since he enjoyed all the influence of a popular Speaker of the House, he was in a position to throw the election to the candidate of his choice.

Clay reached his fateful decision by a process of elimination. Crawford, recently felled by a paralytic stroke, was out of the picture. Clay hated the "military chieftain" Jackson, his archrival for the allegiance of the West. Jackson, in turn, bitterly resented Clay's public denunciation of his Florida foray in 1818. The only candidate left was the puritanical Adams, with whom Clay—a free-living gambler and duelist—had never established cordial personal relations. But the two men had much in common politically: both were fervid nationalists and advocates of the American System. Shortly before the final balloting in the House, Clay met privately with Adams and assured him of his support.

Decision day came early in 1825. The House of Representatives met amid tense excitement, with sick members being carried in on stretchers. On the first ballot, thanks largely to Clay's behind-the-scenes influence, Adams was elected president. A few days later, the victor announced that Henry Clay would be the new secretary of state.

The secretaryship of state was then the prize plum, even more so than today. Three of the four preceding secretaries had reached the

> Suspicions of a "corrupt bargain" have been strengthened by entries in Adams' diary. On January 1, 1825, after a public dinner, we find: "He [Clay] told me [in a whisper] that he should be glad to have with me soon some confidential conversation upon public affairs. I said I should be happy to have it whenever it might suit his convenience." The diary entry for January 9 reads in part: "Mr. Clay came at six, and spent the evening with me in a long conversation explanatory of the past and prospective of the future." Exactly a month later, with Clay's backing, Adams was elected.

presidency, and the high cabinet office was regarded as an almost certain runway to the White House. By allegedly dangling the secretaryship as a bribe before Clay, Adams, the second choice of the people, apparently defeated the first choice of the people, Andrew Jackson.

Masses of angered Jacksonians, most of them common folk, raised a roar of protest against the "corrupt bargain." The clamor continued for nearly four years. Jackson condemned Clay as the "Judas of the West," and John Randolph of Virginia publicly assailed the alliance between "the Puritan [Adams] and the black-leg [Clay]," who, he added "shines and stinks like rotten mackerel by moonlight." Clay, outraged, challenged Randolph to a duel, the bloodless outcome of which proved nothing, except perhaps shaky nerves and poor marksmanship.

No positive evidence has yet been unearthed to prove that Adams and Clay entered into a formal bargain, corrupt or otherwise. But appearances were so damning as to render denials unconvincing. Even if a bargain had been struck,

Election of 1824

CANDIDATES	ELECTORAL VOTE	POPULAR VOTE	POPULAR PERCENTAGE
Jackson	99	153,544	42.16%
Adams	84	108,740	31.89
Crawford	41	46,618	12.95
Clay	37	47,136	12.99

it was not necessarily corrupt, for "deals" of a similar nature are the stock-in-trade of politicians. But this "bargain" differed from others in its apparent flouting of the popular will by both Adams and Clay. Both men erred, the one by offering the post in circumstances sure to arouse suspicion, the other by accepting it. The best that can be said of them is that neither avoided the appearance of evil.

A Yankee Misfit in the White House

John Quincy Adams was a chip off the old family glacier. Short (5 feet 7 inches; 1.7 meters), thickset, and billiard-bald, he was even more frigidly austere than his presidential father, John Adams. Shunning people, he often went for early morning swims, sometimes stark naked, in the then-pure Potomac River. Essentially a closeted thinker rather than a politician, he was irritable, sarcastic, and tactless. Yet few individuals have ever come to the presidency

President John Quincy Adams (1767–1848) *Adams wrote in his diary, in June 1819, nearly six years before becoming president, "I am a man of reserved, cold, austere, and forbidding manners: my political adversaries say, a gloomy misanthropist, and my personal enemies an unsocial savage."*

with a more brilliant record in statecraft, especially in foreign affairs. He ranks as one of the most successful secretaries of state, yet one of the least successful presidents.

A man of puritanical honor, Adams entered upon his four-year "sentence" in the White House smarting under charges of "bargain," "corruption," and "usurpation." Fewer than one-third of the voters had voted for him. As the first "minority president," he would have found it difficult to win popular support even under the most favorable conditions. Possessing almost none of the arts of the politician, he had achieved high office by commanding respect rather than by courting popularity. In an earlier era, an aloof John Adams could win the votes of propertied men by sheer ability. But with the raw New Democracy in the driver's seat, his cold-fish son could hardly hope for success at the polls.

Political spoilsmen annoyed Adams. Whether through high-mindedness or ineptitude, he resolutely declined to oust efficient officeholders in order to create vacancies for political supporters. During his entire administration he removed only twelve public servants from the federal payroll. Such stubbornness caused countless Adams followers to throw up their hands in despair. If the president would not reward party workers with political plums, why should they labor to keep him in office?

Adams' nationalistic views involved him in further woes. The old Jeffersonian Republican party was breaking into fragments, most of which tended to coalesce around a common hatred of the Adams-Clay partnership. The flinty president refused to recognize that the popular tide was turning away from the post-Ghent nationalism toward states' rights and sectionalism. Confirmed nationalist that he was, Adams urged upon Congress in his first annual message the construction of roads and canals. He renewed George Washington's proposal for a national university and went so far as to advocate federal support for an astronomical observatory, similar to Europe's more than 130 "lighthouses of the skies."

The public reaction to some of these proposals was prompt and unfavorable. To many workaday Americans grubbing out stumps, astronomical observatories seemed like a scandalous waste of public funds. The South in particular bristled up. If the federal government should take on such heavy financial burdens, it would have to continue the hated tariff duties. If it could meddle in local concerns like education and roads, it might even try to lay its hand on the "peculiar institution" of black slavery.

Adams' land policy likewise antagonized the westerners. They clamored for wide-open expansion and were angered by the president's well-meaning attempts to curb feverish speculation in the public domain. The fate of the Cherokee Indians, who were about to be evicted from their holdings in Georgia, generated additional bitterness. Ruggedly honest Adams attempted to deal fairly with the friendless Indians, further offending the West in general and the state of Georgia in particular. The governor, who threatened a resort to arms, successfully resisted the efforts of the Washington government to interpose federal authority on behalf of the Indians. Another fateful chapter was thus written in the nullification of the national will.

The Tricky "Tariff of Abominations"

The touchy tariff issue became one of Adams' biggest headaches. Congress had increased the general tariff in 1824, from about 23 percent on dutiable goods to about 37 percent. But wool manufacturers, dissatisfied with their share of protection, bleated for still-higher barriers.

Rabid Jacksonites, seeking to unhorse Adams, seized this opportunity to play politics with the Tariff of 1828. They rigged up a bill that was seemingly more concerned with manufacturing a president than with protecting manufacturers. A part of their scheme was to push the duties as high as about 45 percent on the value of certain manufactured items. At the same time, they would impose a heavy tariff on certain raw materials, notably wool. These materials were so urgently needed for manufacturing, especially in New England, that even this industrial section would presumably vote against the entire measure. Adams, whose stronghold was New England, would thus be given another political black eye, and Jackson

would receive a boost, especially in the middle states. There many voters were politically uncertain but protection-prone.

But the New Englanders spoiled this clever little game. Though disliking the proposed duties, they were anxious to continue the principle of protection. As a consequence, enough of them choked down the dishonest Tariff of 1828, as amended, to force its passage. Daniel Webster, who had earlier fought the mild Tariff of 1816, and John C. Calhoun, who had sponsored it, had by this time completely reversed their positions. They and others now clearly saw that the future of New England lay in the factory, rather than on the waves, while the destiny of the South lay in the cotton fields.

Southerners, as heavy consumers of manufactured goods, were shocked by what they regarded as the outrageous rates of the Tariff of 1828. Hotheads promptly branded it the "Black Tariff" or the "Tariff of Abominations." Several southern states adopted formal protests; in South Carolina flags were lowered to half-mast. "Let the *New* England beware how she imitates the *Old,*" cried one eloquent Carolinian who remembered 1776.

Why did the South, especially South Carolina, react so angrily against the tariff? Underlying the southern outcry were growing anxieties about possible federal interference with the institution of slavery. The congressional debate on the Missouri Compromise had kindled those anxieties, and they were further fed by an ominous slave rebellion in Charleston in 1822, led by a free black, Denmark Vesey. The South Carolinians, still closely tied to the British West

House Vote on Tariff of 1828 ("Tariff of Abominations")*

REGIONS	FOR	AGAINST
New England	16	23
Middle states	57	11
West (Ohio, Ind., Ill., Mo.)	17	1
South (incl. La.)	3	50
Southwest (Tenn., Ky.)	12	9
TOTAL	105	94

*Compare 1816 tariff, p. 214.

Indies, also knew full well how their slaveowning West Indian cousins were feeling the mounting pressure of British abolitionism on the London government. Abolitionism in America might similarly use the power of the government in Washington to suppress slavery in the South. If so, now was the time, and the tariff was the issue, for taking a strong stand on principle against all federal encroachments on states' rights.

Nearer the surface was the real economic distress of the Old South—the seaboard area first settled. It was now the least flourishing of all the sections. The bustling Northeast was experiencing a boom in manufacturing; the developing West was prospering from rising property values and a multiplying population; and the energetic Southwest was expanding into virgin cotton lands. Overcropped acres of the Old South were petering out, and the price of cotton was falling sharply. John Randolph of Virginia grimly quipped that masters would soon cease to advertise for their fugitive slaves, and slaves would advertise for their fugitive masters. So the Old South was seeking a scapegoat, and the tariff proved to be a convenient and plausible one.

The Tariff Yoke in the South

Southerners believed, not illogically, that the "Yankee tariff" discriminated against them. They sold their cotton and other farm produce in a world market completely unprotected by tariffs and were forced to buy their manufactured goods in an American market heavily protected by tariffs.

The plight of the South may be illustrated by a hypothetical case. Suppose that in 1828 an English manufacturer sold shoes in South Carolina at $1.25 a pair, whereas a Massachusetts shoemaker, paying higher wages, would have to charge $1.50 for a pair of equal quality. South Carolinians would naturally buy the British footwear. But if a tariff of $0.50 a pair were levied on foreign shoes at the Charleston customshouse, the British shoes would cost $1.75 a pair. The Massachusetts shoemaker could now safely raise the price to anything less than $1.75—say, $1.74—and still undercut the British competitor by selling the cheapest shoes in South Carolina. South Carolinians would thus be forced to pay higher prices, while the profits of the Yankee manufacturer were commensurately fattened. This artificial inflation of prices

Tariff Inequalities, North and South   *The protective tariff under which the North grows fat and prosperous brings economic hardship to the South. (United States Weekly Telegram, 1832.)*

has always been among the most objectionable features of high tariffs.

The South also objected to other consequences of towering tariffs. Higher prices generally lead to a reduced volume of purchases. And if Americans bought fewer English textiles, the British would in turn buy less southern cotton with which to make the textiles. Southerners thus would suffer both as consumers and as producers, as importers and as exporters. Little wonder that southern leaders regarded the protective tariff as a foe of their economic development. On the other hand, many failed to appreciate that in the long run a prosperous manufacturing economy in the Northeast could itself contribute to their prosperity by consuming their cotton and other farm products.

South Carolinians took the lead in protesting against the "Tariff of Abominations." Their legislature went so far as to publish in 1828, though without formal endorsement, a pamphlet known as "The South Carolina Exposition." It had been secretly written by John C. Calhoun, one of the few topflight political theorists ever produced by America. (As vice-president, he was forced to conceal his authorship.) "The Exposition" boldly denounced the recent tariff as unjust and unconstitutional. Going a stride beyond the Kentucky and Virginia resolutions of 1798, it bluntly and explicitly proposed that the states should nullify the tariff—that is, they should declare it null and void within their borders.

Calhoun found himself caught in an awkward straddle. Still a Unionist and a nationalist, he was also a southern sectionalist. He therefore desperately sought a formula that would protect the minority in the South from the "tyranny of the majority" in the North and West. Seizing upon nullification, he undertook by this explosive device to preserve the Union and prevent secession. Calhoun's aim was not to destroy the Union but to salvage it by quieting the fears of those forces that might one day destroy it.

Calhoun's "Exposition," at least immediately, was a false alarm. No other state joined South Carolina in her heated antitariff protest. But the disruptive theory of nullification was further publicized, while the even more dangerous doc-

John C. Calhoun (1782–1850) *Calhoun was a South Carolinian, educated at Yale. Beginning as a strong nationalist and Unionist, he reversed himself and became the ablest of the sectionalists and disunionists in defense of the South and slavery. As a foremost nullifier, he died trying to reconcile strong states' rights with a strong Union. In his last years he advocated a Siamese-twin presidency, probably unworkable, with one president for the North and one for the South. His former plantation home is now the site of Clemson University. (National Archives.)*

trine of secession was foreshadowed. South Carolina was not then prepared to force the controversy to a showdown. The election of Carolina-born Andrew Jackson to the presidency had occurred two weeks earlier, and the "Old Hero"—a fellow cotton planter and slaveowner—was expected to sympathize with the plight of the South.

Going "Whole Hog" for Jackson in 1828

The presidential campaign for Andrew Jackson had started early. It began on February 9, 1825, the day of John Quincy Adams' controversial election by the House, and continued noisily for nearly four years.

Even before the election of 1828, the temporarily united Republicans of the Era of Good Feelings had split into two camps. One was the National Republicans, with the ultranationalistic Adams as their standard-bearer. The other was the Democratic-Republicans, with the fiery Jackson heading their ticket. Rallying cries of the Jackson zealots were "Bargain and Corruption," "Huzza for Jackson," and "All Hail Old Hickory." Jacksonites planted hickory poles for their hickory-tough hero; "Adamites" adopted the oak as the symbol of their oakenly independent candidate.

"Shall the people rule?" was the chief issue of 1828, at least to Jacksonians. They argued that the will of the voters had been thwarted in 1825 by the backstairs "bargain" of Adams and Clay. The only way to right the wrong was to seat Jackson, who would then bring about "reform" by sweeping out the "dishonest" Adams gang. "Jackson and Reform" was a widely mouthed

> One anti-Jackson newspaper declared, "General Jackson's mother was a Common Prostitute, brought to this country by the British soldiers! She afterwards married a MULATTO MAN with whom she had several children, of which number GENERAL JACKSON is one."

slogan, while hickory brooms were brandished as tokens of a forthcoming "clean sweep." Seldom has the public mind been so successfully poisoned against an honest and high-minded president.

Mudslinging reached a disgraceful level, partly as a result of the taste of the new mass electorate for bare-knuckle politics. Adams would not stoop to gutter tactics, but many of his backers were less squeamish. They described Jackson's mother as a prostitute; they printed black-bordered handbills, shaped like coffins, recounting his numerous duels and brawls and trumpeting his hanging of six mutinous militiamen. The "Old Hero" was also branded an adulterer. He had married an estimable woman, Rachel Robards, confident that her divorce had been granted. To the consternation of both, they discovered two years later that it had not been, and they made haste to correct the marital miscue.

Rachel Jackson was crushed by the vicious charges of bigamy and adultery. She lived to see her husband win the presidency, but she died—supposedly of a broken heart—before she could become First Lady. Jackson, devotedly attached to his wife, was convinced that his enemies had killed her. He never forgave them.

Jackson men also hit below the belt. President Adams had purchased, with his own money and for his own use, a billiard table and a set of chessmen. In the mouths of rabid Jacksonites, these items became "gaming tables" and "gambling furniture" for the "presidential palace." Criticism was also unfairly directed at the large sums that Adams had received over the years in federal salaries, well earned though they had been. He was even accused of having procured a servant girl for the lust of a Russian nobleman while minister to Russia—in short, of having served as a pimp.

Mrs. Andrew Jackson   *A devoted wife who did not live to become First Lady, she had unwittingly, and hence innocently, involved herself and her husband in scandal. (National Archives.)*

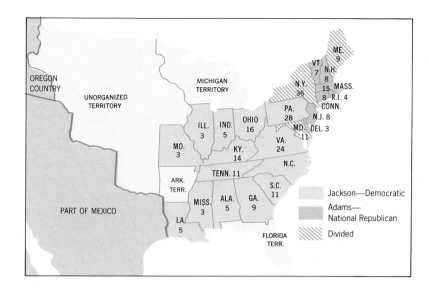

Presidential Election of 1828 (with electoral vote by state) Note that Jackson swept the South and West, while Adams retained the old Federalist stronghold of the Northeast. Yet Jackson's inroads in the Northeast were decisive. He won twenty of New York's electoral votes, and all twenty-eight of Pennsylvania's. If those votes had gone the other way, Adams would have been victorious—by a margin of one vote.

The Jacksonian "Revolution of 1828"

General Jackson, victorious on the battlefields, was no less victorious at the ballot boxes. The popular tally was 647,286 votes for him to 508,064 for Adams, with an electoral count of 178 to 83. Support for Jackson came mainly from the West and South, and to a considerable extent from the sweat-stained laborers of the eastern seaboard. Generally speaking, the common people—though by no means all of them—voted for the Hero of New Orleans. Adams won the backing of his own New England, as well as the propertied "better elements" of the Northeast.

The election of 1828 has often been called the "Revolution of 1828." Actually, as in 1800, there was no upheaval or landslide that swept out the incumbent. Adams, in fact, polled a respectable 44 percent of the popular vote. A considerable part of Jackson's support, moreover, was lined up by machine politicians, especially in New York and Pennsylvania, and not entirely among the leather-aproned artisans and other manual workers.

But the concept of a *political* revolution in 1828 is not completely farfetched. The increased turnout of voters proved that the common people, especially in the universal-white-manhood-suffrage states, now had the vote and the will to use it for their ends. A discontented West, with its numerous rustics and debtors, generally voted for Jackson. The results show that the political center of gravity was continuing to shift away from the conservative seaboard East toward the emerging states across the mountains.

So in a broader sense the election was a "revolution," more than in 1800. It was a peaceful revolution, achieved by ballots instead of bullets, by counting heads instead of crushing them. "Shall the people rule?" cried the Jacksonians. The answering roar seemed to say, "The people shall rule!" In the struggle between the poorer masses and the entrenched classes, the homespun folk scored a resounding triumph. Rejecting the candidate who lacked the common touch, they rejoiced as they had been delivered from some impending danger.

America hitherto had been ruled by an elite of brains and wealth, whether aristocratic Federalist shippers or aristocratic Jeffersonian planters. Jackson's victory accelerated the transfer of national power from the counting-house to the farmhouse, from the East to the West, and from the snobs to the mobs. If Jefferson had been the hero of the gentleman farmer, Jackson was the hero of the dirt farmer. The plowholders were now ready to take over the government—their government.

Adams, though president-reject, was still destined for an enviable public career. Ever high-minded, he did not deem it beneath his dignity as an ex-president to accept election to the House of Representatives from Massachusetts. ("No person can be degraded by serving the people," he declared.) There he served with conspicuous success for seventeen fruitful years. Affectionately known as "Old Man Eloquent," he fought stalwartly for free government, free speech, free soil, and free people. A rough and savage debater, he finally was stricken on the floor of the House in 1848, at age eighty. His funeral was the greatest pageant of its kind that Washington had yet seen. Ironically, the popularity that had escaped him in life came to him in death.

The Advent of "Old Hickory" Jackson

Andrew Jackson cut a striking figure—tall (6 feet 1 inch; 1.86 meters), gaunt, and with bushy iron-gray hair brushed high above a prominent forehead, craggy eyebrows, and blue eyes. His irritability and emaciated condition (140 pounds; 64 kilograms) probably had resulted in part from long-term bouts with dysentery, malaria, tuberculosis, and lead poisoning from two bullets that he carried in his body from near-fatal duels. His autobiography was largely written in his lined face.

To a considerable degree, Jackson personified the new West. He reflected its individualism, its jack-of-all-trades versatility, its opportunism, its energy, its directness, and its prejudices. He was a genuine folk hero—an uncommon common man. The backwoods preacher who cried that Jesus was "just another Andrew Jackson" reflected a sentiment that did not seem out of place to some.

Jackson's upbringing was not of the best. Born in the Carolinas and early orphaned, "Mischievous Andy" grew up without parental restraints. As a youth, he displayed much more interest in brawling and cockfighting than in his scanty opportunities for reading and spelling. Although he ultimately learned to express himself in writing with vigor and clarity, his grammar was always rough-hewn, and his spelling was often original, like that of many contemporaries. He sometimes misspelled a word two different ways in the same letter.

The youthful Carolinian had the foresight to emigrate "up West" to Tennessee, where a fighting man was more highly regarded than a writing man. There—through native intelligence, force of personality, and powers of leadership—he became a judge and a member of Congress. His passions were so terrible that on occasion he would choke into silence when he tried to speak. He won his greatest fame as a commander of militia troops, who dubbed him "Old Hickory" in honor of his toughness. Afflicted with a violent temper, he early became involved in numerous duels, stabbings, and other bloody frays. But, rough and forthright as democracy itself, he made things move.

The first president from the West, and the first without a college education, except Washington, Jackson was unique. His university was adversity. He had risen from the masses, but he was not one of them, except insofar as he shared many of their prejudices. Essentially a frontier aristocrat, he owned many slaves, cultivated broad acres, and lived in one of the finest mansions in America—the Hermitage, near Nashville, Tennessee. More westerner than easterner, more country gentleman than common clay, more courtly than crude, he was hard to fit into a neat category:

> He's none of your old New England stock,
> Or your gentry-proud Virginians,
> But a regular Western fighting-cock
> With Tennessee opinions.*

As befitted an authentic man of the people and hero of the one-suspender man, Jackson's political ideas had a stark simplicity. Like the anti-federalists of an earlier day, he was suspicious of the federal government as a bastion of privilege, an institution dangerously remote from popular scrutiny. He was therefore determined to reduce it "to that simple machine

---

*"Andrew Jackson," from *A Book of Americans*, by Rosemary & Stephen Vincent Benét. Copyright, 1933, by Rosemary & Stephen Vincent Benét. Copyright renewed ©, 1961, by Rosemary Carr Benét. Reprinted by permission of Brandt & Brandt Literary Agency, Inc.

which the Constitution created," which meant, among other things, hostility to the active federal economic role envisioned in Henry Clay's American System. Conversely, he and especially his followers were generally friendly toward the frothy democracy bubbling up in the states and looked with some favor on economic activism on the part of state governments. Yet Jackson was destined to disappoint some of his states' rights supporters in the South by his insistence on the sacredness of the Union and the ultimate supremacy of federal power over that of the states.

While president, Jackson proved to be a storm center. As a former military man, he demanded prompt and loyal support from his subordinates. If one was not for him, one was against him. Cherishing strong ideas as to his constitutional prerogatives, he ignored the Supreme Court on several conspicuous occasions. He likewise defied or dominated Congress as few presidents have done. His six predecessors had wielded the veto ten times; during his two terms he employed it twelve times, sometimes on grounds of personal distaste rather than constitutional principle. Jackson's modest use of the veto ax was perfectly legitimate, but his numerous enemies condemned him as "King Andrew the First."

Jackson's inauguration symbolized the newly won ascendancy of the masses. "Hickoryites" poured into Washington from far places, sleeping on hotel floors or in hallways. They were curious to see their hero take office and perhaps to pick up a well-paying office for themselves. Nobodies mingled with notables as the White House, for the first time, was thrown open to the multitude. A milling crowd of clerks, shopkeepers, hobnailed artisans, and grimy laborers

"*King Andrew the First*" Jackson is here assailed as a tyrant who tramples underfoot the Constitution, the courts, and domestic welfare. (Houghton Library, Harvard.)

surged in, wrecking the china and furniture, and threatening the "people's champion" with cracked ribs. Jackson was hastily spirited through a side door, and the White House miraculously emptied itself when the word was passed that huge bowls of well-spiked punch had been placed on the lawns. Such was "the inaugural brawl."

To conservatives, this orgy seemed like the end of the world. "King Mob" reigned triumphant as Jacksonian vulgarity replaced Jeffersonian simplicity. Old ladies of both sexes shuddered, drew their blinds, and recalled the opening scenes of the French Revolution.

Jackson Nationalizes the Spoils System

Under Jackson the spoils system—that is, rewarding political supporters with public office—was introduced into the federal government on

> In 1824, Jefferson said of Jackson: "When I was President of the Senate he was a Senator; and he could never speak on account of the rashness of his feelings. I have seen him attempt it repeatedly, and as often choke with rage. His passions are no doubt cooler now . . . but he is a dangerous man."

a large numerical scale. On a percentage basis, Jefferson, with reluctance and discrimination, had already made about as large a beginning. Jackson, with more ruthlessness, extended it to more people, while complaining about those "clamoring for a public tit from which to suck the treasury."

The basic idea was as old as politics. Its name came later from Senator Marcy's classic remark in 1832, "To the victor belong the spoils of the enemy." The system had already secured a firm hold in New York and Pennsylvania, where well-greased machines were operating. Professional politicians, by ladling out the "gravy" of office, had been able to make politics a full-time business, rather than a sideline. The emphasis was more on spoils than on responsibilities.

A housecleaning of some sort in Washington was clearly needed. No party overturn had occurred since the defeat of the Federalists in 1800, and even that had not produced wholesale evictions. During the ensuing twenty-eight years, festering evils had developed in the civil service. The old colonial-system ideal of holding office during good behavior had bred some incompetence and corruption, as well as considerable indifference and insolence ("uncivil servants"). A few officeholders, their commissions signed by President Washington, were lingering on into their eighties, drawing breath and salary but doing little else.

Jackson fully shared the view of the New Democracy that "every man is as good as his neighbor"—perhaps "equally better." As this was believed to be so, and as the routine of office was also thought to be simple enough for any upstanding American to learn quickly, why encourage the development of an aristocratic, bureaucratic, officeholding class? Experience, of course, had some value. But alertness and new blood had more—at least in the eyes of Jacksonians.

The New Democracy also trumpeted the ideal of "rotation in office"—or "a turn about is fair play." Since experience was discounted, and since officeholding provided valuable training for citizenship, let as many citizens as possible feed at the public trough for at least a short time. This was a polite way of saying "Throw the rascals out and put our rascals in."

More Victors Than Spoils

Elected as a reformer, Jackson believed that the swiftest road to reform was to sweep out the Adams-Clay gang and bring in his own trusted henchmen. Furiously aroused against his foes, he agreed that the old Adams "barnacles" must "be scraped clean from the Ship of State."

The spoilsmen now had their inning. Office seekers hounded Jackson at every turn and even invaded his privacy: for every appointee there were seemingly ten disappointees. In view of such pressures, one may marvel that he removed so few incumbents rather than so many. During his eight years, only about one-fifth of the old civil servants were dismissed, leaving more than nine thousand out of the original eleven thousand. The "clean sweeps" were to come in later administrations.

Even so, a demoralizing practice was begun on a national scale. Insecurity replaced security and discouraged many able citizens from entering the public service. Terrible hardships were worked on poor men with large families. One discharged employee cut his throat from ear to ear; another went raving mad. Fitness, merit, and the ideal of public service were subordinated, while offices were prostituted to political ends. The questions were not "What can he do for the country?" but "What has he done for the party?" or "Is he loyal to Jackson?"

Scandal inevitably accompanied the new system. Men were appointed to high office who

One elderly postmaster, a Revolutionary War veteran, while personally appealing to Jackson not to evict him from office, removed his coat to display his war wounds. Jackson later exclaimed: "By the eternal! I will not remove the old man. Do you know that he carries a pound of British lead in his body?"

had openly bought their posts by campaign contributions. Illiterates, incompetents, and plain crooks were given positions of public trust; they lusted for the spoils of office rather than the toils of office. Samuel Swartwout, despite ample warnings of his untrustworthiness, was awarded the high-salaried post of collector of the customs of the port of New York. Nearly nine years later he "Swartwouted out" for England, leaving his accounts more than a million dollars short—the first person to steal a million from the Washington government.

Finally, the spoils system built up a potent, personalized political machine. Its delicate gears were lubricated by gifts from expectant party members and by percentage levies on the salaries of officeholders—a kind of political job insurance. The system at length secured such a tenacious hold that more than half a century passed before its grip could be even partially loosened.

Cabinet Crises and Nationalistic Setbacks

Jackson's cabinet was mediocre; its members were used primarily as executive clerks. The only person of conspicuous ability was the smooth-tongued and keen-witted secretary of state, Dutch-descended Martin Van Buren of New York, who shone as a gifted conciliator and wire-puller. A balding, sharp-featured little man, he was affectionately addressed by Jackson as "Matty." But he was known to his enemies as the "Little Magician."

The official cabinet of six was privately supplemented by an extraofficial cabinet of about thirteen every-shifting members. It grew out of Jackson's informal meetings with his advisers, some of whom were newspaper people who kept him in touch with the fickle winds of public opinion. The enemies of the president branded these shirt-sleeved cronies "the Kitchen Cabinet." Subsequent generations have retained the picture of an uncouth clique gathering in the kitchen and spitting tobacco juice in the general direction of grimy spittoons. Actually, the group did not gather in the kitchen;

it never met officially; its overall influence has been grossly exaggerated; and it was not unconstitutional. Presidents are free to consult with such unofficial advisers as they desire.

The regular cabinet was wrecked in 1831, as a result of the "Eaton malaria." Secretary of War Eaton had married the daughter of Washington boardinghouse keeper, pretty Peggy O'Neal, whom the tongue of scandal had perhaps unfairly linked with the male boarders. She was consequently snubbed by the ladies of Jackson's official family, conspicuously by the blue-blooded wife of Vice-President Calhoun. The president, whose own spouse had been victimized by scandalmongers, was chivalrously aroused in behalf of Mrs. Eaton's chastity. With a zeal worthy of a better cause, he tried to force the social acceptance of the black-haired beauty. But the all-conquering general finally had to acknowledge defeat in the "Petticoat War" at the hands of the female phalanx.

The Eaton scandal played directly into the hands of Secretary Van Buren. As a fancy-free widower, he further curried favor with Jackson by paying marked attention to Mrs. Eaton, whose physical charms helped to lighten this

Peggy Eaton (1796–1879) *Though scandal raised her to notoriety, she retained Jackson's favor. After her husband left the cabinet, the president appointed him minister to Spain. For four years she basked in a brilliant Madrid society that had no prejudice against a woman with a past. (Library of Congress.)*

self-imposed task. Jackson turned increasingly against Calhoun, and finally broke with him completely. Followers of the South Carolinian were purged from the cabinet in 1831. Calhoun himself, resigning the vice-presidency the next year, entered the Senate as a champion of South Carolina.

It would be absurd to say that Peggy Eaton caused the Civil War. But up to this time Calhoun had publicly been a strong nationalist, despite his secret espousal of nullification in "The South Carolina Exposition" of 1828. As vice-president, he thought himself in line for the presidency after Jackson had served one term. The open break with the incumbent, though foreshadowed earlier, blighted his hopes. He gradually abandoned his weakening nationalism and became an inflexible defender of southern sectionalism. Seeking extreme medicines for protecting the states and preserving the Union, the "Great Nullifier" contributed to the almost fatal illness of the Union.

Jackson himself, consistent with his Jeffersonian principles, dealt nationalism a body blow by his hostility to localized roads and canals. It is true that he signed a number of measures that appropriated federal funds for ambitious internal improvements. But his states' rights principles rebelled against spending money from the pinched Washington Treasury for roads built entirely within individual states and unrelated to an interstate network. He headlined his antagonism in 1830, when he vigorously vetoed a bill for improving the Maysville Road, which lay completely within Henry Clay's Kentucky (but which was connected with an interstate artery). This setback slapped at the internal improvements aspect of the American System, so ardently championed by Clay, the "corrupt bargainer" whom Jackson never forgave. "Old Hickory's" veto was also a signal victory for eastern and southern states' rightism in its struggle with Jackson's own West.

The Webster-Hayne Forensic Duel

Sectional jealousies found a spectacular outlet in the Senate during 1829–1830. Hidebound New England, resenting the marvelous expansion of the West, was determined to call a halt. The lavish distribution of western acreage was draining off eastern population while further upsetting political balance. Late in 1829, therefore, a New England senator introduced a resolution designed to curb the sale of public lands.

Sectional passions flared forth angrily in the Senate, as the western senators sprang furiously to the defense of their interests. The South, seeking sectional allies in its controversies with the Northeast, promptly sided with the West. Its most persuasive spokesman was Robert Y. Hayne, of South Carolina, one of the silver-tongued orators of his generation.

Hayne's oratorical effort in the Senate was impressive. He roundly condemned the obvious disloyalty of New England during the War of 1812, as well as her selfish inconsistency on the protective tariff. Airing in detail the grievances of the South, he reserved his heavy fire for the "Tariff of Abominations" (1828). He then acclaimed Calhoun's dangerous doctrine of nullification as the only means of safeguarding the minority interests of his section. Hayne, like Calhoun, did not advocate a breakup of the Union; rather, he was seeking to protect southern rights within the Union and under the Constitution. But his arguments were carefully stored up by nullifiers and secessionists for future use.

The "Godlike Daniel" Webster, spokesman for New England, now took the floor. Matchless orator and leader of the American bar, he awed audiences by his majestic presence, including craglike brows, flashing eyes, a sonorous voice, a noble head, and a well-chested frame. His life up to this point, including his frequent appear-

> *In 1839 Daniel Webster visited England, where his distinguished bearing and intellectual power made a great impression. The Reverend Sydney Smith, a merciless critic of America, reportedly remarked, "Daniel Webster struck me much like a steam-engine in trousers." He was also a "living lie, because no man on earth could be so great as he looked."*

> *Webster challenged Hayne in these words:*
> "The proposition that, in case of a supposed violation of the Constitution by Congress, the states have a constitutional right to interfere and annul the law of Congress is the proposition of the gentleman. I do not admit it. If the gentleman had intended no more than to assert the right of revolution for justifiable cause, he would have said only what all agree to. But I cannot conceive that there can be a middle course, between submission to the laws, when regularly pronounced constitutional, on the one hand, and open resistance, which is revolution or rebellion, on the other" *(January 26, 1830).* Webster and Hayne thus clashed over the same question that had vexed Jefferson in the Kentucky resolutions and Marshall in Marbury v. Madison. Where did final authority to interpret the Constitution lie?

Websterian Cement for the Union

Webster did not overpower Hayne with his thunderous oratory; Hayne did not defeat Webster with his seductive eloquence. There were no official judges. The polished southerner was sounder on historical and economic grounds; the impassioned New Englander was sounder on constitutional practicalities and common sense—on things as they were rather than as they had been. Each section was satisfied with its champion.

The impact of Webster's reply was spectacular. About forty thousand copies were printed in three months, and arguments for the Union were seared into the minds of countless northerners. Among them was young Abraham Lincoln, just turning twenty-one and moving from Indiana to the Illinois frontier. Webster's inspirational peroration was printed in the school

ances before Chief Justice Marshall, had been a preparation for this nine-day running debate with Hayne in January of 1830.

After defending New England with vigor, if not complete candor, Webster, the ex-Federalist, passed on to the larger issue of Union. Insisting that the *people* and not the *states* had framed the Constitution (here he was on shaky historical ground*), he decried the insidious doctrine of nullification. Either the Supreme Court would judge the constitutionality of laws, or the Republic would be torn by revolution. If each of the twenty-four states were free to go its separate way in obeying or rejecting federal statutes, there would be no union but only a "rope of sand." Webster's concluding outburst, which brought tears to listeners' eyes, was a magnificent tribute to the Union, ending with those imperishable words: "Liberty and Union, now and forever, one and inseparable."

---

*The original preamble of the Constitution of 1787 had read: "We the people of the states of"—and then they were listed by name. But when it was objected that all the states might not ratify, the formula "We the people of the United States" was adopted. (For the text of the preamble, see the Appendix.)

A Jackson Campaign Poster, 1832 *Note the emphasis on democracy and union. (Tennessee State Library and Archives.)*

"The man who has filled the measure of his Country's Glory."
JEFFERSON.

Jackson,

DEMOCRACY,

And our Country.

"The Union must be Preserved."

readers and was memorized by tens of thousands of impressionable lads—the Boys in Blue who in 1861–1865 were willing to lay down their lives for the Union.

Webster, beyond a doubt, had a large hand in winning the Civil War. He probably did more than any other person to arouse the oncoming generation of northerners to fight for the ideal of Union. His admirers have claimed that the nation was saved hardly less by the thunder of Webster's replies to Hayne than by the thunder of General Grant's replies to the cannonading of General Lee.

Hot-tempered "Old Hickory" had meanwhile been keeping strangely silent on southern grievances. States' rights leaders, at a Jefferson Day banquet in 1830, schemed to smoke him out. Their strategy was to devise a series of toasts in honor of Jefferson, onetime foe of centralization, that would lean toward states' rights and nullification. The plotters assumed that the "Old Hero"—a fellow southerner—would be swept along by the tenor of the toasts and speak up in favor of states' rights.

Jackson, forewarned and inwardly fuming, had carefully prepared his response. At the proper moment he rose to his full height, fixed his eyes on Calhoun, and with dramatic intensity proclaimed:

"Our Union: It must be preserved!"

The southerners were dumbfounded, and Calhoun haltingly replied, in part:

"The union, next to our liberty, most dear!"

Some seventy other anticlimactic toasts followed this exchange, but in effect the party was over.

Jackson's military ire was aroused. As commander in chief, he would stand for no back talk from the states or particularly from the hated Calhoun. But, as fate decreed, the showdown with defiant South Carolina was postponed for over two years.

Varying Viewpoints

Aristocratic nineteenth-century historians damned Jackson as a backwoods barbarian. They criticized Jacksonianism as democracy run riot—an irresponsible, backcountry outburst that overturned the electoral system and raised hob with the national financial structure. Early twentieth-century "progressive" historians followed the lead of Frederick Jackson Turner in his famous 1893 essay "The Significance of the Frontier in American History." They saw the frontier as the fount of democratic virtue, and they hailed Jackson as a popular hero sprung from the forests of the West. But with the publication of Arthur M. Schlesinger, Jr.'s *The Age of Jackson* in 1945, the focus of the debate on Jacksonianism shifted. Contending that the urban working people of the Northeast formed the backbone of Jackson's support, Schlesinger argued that its identification with a social class, rather than a geographic section, was the most important characteristic of Jacksonianism. In the last twenty years, historical discussion has again shifted, from considerations of class to an emphasis on ethnic and religious conflict. This "ethnocultural school," following Lee Bensen's pioneering study of New York, sees disputes between ethnic groups, especially over local issues, as the basis for political alignments in the Jacksonian era.

Select Readings

Primary Source Documents

Davy Crockett's *Exploits and Adventures in Texas** (1836) is a lively description of the democratic political order of Jacksonian America. C.W. Janson, *The Stranger in America, 1793–1806** (1807), exposes the seamier aspects of American egalitarianism. On the Tariff of Abominations and its implications, see the "Webster-Hayne Debate"* (1830). Webster's reply to Hayne is one of the greatest specimens of American political oratory.

Secondary Sources

A still-living classic treatise on the Jacksonian period is Alexis de Tocqueville, *Democracy in America* (1835, 1840). General introductions are Glyndon G. Van Deusen, *The Jacksonian Era* (1959), and Edward Pessen, *Jacksonian America: Society, Personality and Politics* (rev. ed., 1978). The latter volume sharply disputes Tocqueville's findings. Marvin Meyers, *The Jackson Persuasion* (1957), and John William Ward, *Andrew Jackson: Symbol for an Age* (1955), examine the broader cultural significance of Old Hickory and his supporters. Arthur M. Schlesinger, Jr., in his seminal *The Age of Jackson* (1945), stresses the support of eastern labor for Jackson, a view that has come under attack in Lee Bensen, *The Concept of Jacksonian Democracy: New York as a Test Case* (1961). On the evolution of mass-based political parties, see Richard P. McCormick, *The Second American Party System* (1966), and two books by Ronald P. Formisano, *The Birth of Mass Political Parties: Michigan, 1827–1861* (1971) and *The Transformation of Political Culture: Massachusetts Parties, 1790s–1840s* (1983). Three works that consider Jacksonian politics in the South are William J. Cooper, *The South and the Politics of Slavery, 1828–1856* (1978); J. Mills Thornton III, *Politics and Power in a Slave Society: Alabama, 1800–1860* (1978); and Harry L. Watson, *Jacksonian Politics and Community Conflict: The Emergence of the Second American Party System in Cumberland County, North Carolina* (1981), which discusses the opponents of Jackson. Samuel Flagg Bemis, *John Quincy Adams and the Union* (1956), is the second volume of a distinguished biography, as is Robert V. Remini, *Andrew Jackson and the Course of American Freedom, 1822–1832* (1981). See also Sydney Nathans, *Daniel Webster and Jacksonian Democracy* (1973). The standard work on the subject is Frank W. Taussig, *The Tariff History of the United States* (1931).

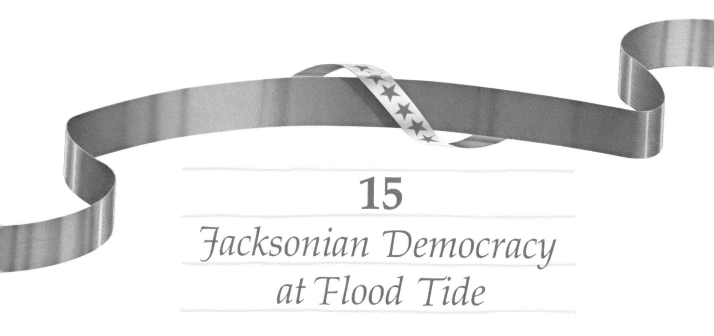

15

Jacksonian Democracy at Flood Tide

The vain threats of resistance by those who [in South Carolina] have raised the standard of rebellion shew their madness and folly. . . . In forty days, I can have within the limits of So. Carolina fifty thousand men. . . . The Union will be preserved.

Andrew Jackson, 1832

"Nullies" in South Carolina

The "abominable" Tariff of 1828 continued to rankle with hot-blooded South Carolinians. They persisted in seeing it not only as economically punitive in the short run, but as a possible entering wedge for later federal interference with slavery in the southern states. In protest, some South Carolinians took to wearing ill-fitting garments of homespun, untaxed by the hated Yankee tariff, while their slaves sported discarded broadcloth. The nullifiers—"nullies," they were called—tried strenuously to muster the necessary two-thirds vote for nullification in the South Carolina legislature. But they were blocked by a determined minority of Unionists, scorned as "submission men."

Back in Washington, Congress touched off the fuse by passing the new Tariff of 1832, which fell far short of meeting all southern demands. The measure did pare away the worst of the "abominations" of 1828, and it did lower the imposts to about the level of the moderate Tariff of 1824—roughly 35 percent, or a reduction of 10 percent. Yet the new law was frankly protective, and to many southerners it had a disquieting air of permanence.

South Carolina was now nerved for drastic action. Nullifiers and Unionists clashed head-on in the state election of 1832. "Nullies," defiantly wearing palmetto ribbons on their hats, emerged with more than a two-thirds majority. The state legislature then called for a special convention. Several weeks later the delegates, meeting in Columbia, solemnly declared the existing federal tariff to be null and void within South Carolina. The hotheaded assemblage also called upon the state legislature to undertake any necessary military preparations. As a final act of defiance, the convention threatened to take South Carolina out of the Union if the Washington regime attempted to collect the customs duties by force.

President-General Jackson, his military instincts rasped, reacted violently. Hating Calhoun and pledged to uphold the Union, he privately threatened to hang the nullifiers. But fortunately for compromise, he was much less pugnacious in public. He dispatched modest naval and military reinforcements to the Palmetto State, while quietly preparing a sizable army. He also issued a ringing proclamation against nullification, to which the governor of South Carolina, ex-Senator Hayne, responded with a counterproclamation. If civil war were to be avoided, one side would have to surrender, or both would have to compromise.

Conciliatory Henry Clay of Kentucky, now in the Senate, stepped forward. An unforgiving foe of Jackson, he had no desire to see his old enemy win new laurels by crushing the Carolinians and returning with the scalp of Calhoun dangling from his belt. The gallant Kentuckian therefore threw his influence behind a compromise bill that would gradually reduce the Tariff of 1832 by about 10 percent over a period of eight years. By 1842 the rates would be at approximately the mildly protective level of

Calhoun Criticized *This contemporary cartoon shows Calhoun reaching for power over the dead bodies of the Constitution and the Union. Jackson, at the far right, threatens to hang the nullifiers. (The New York Public Library, Astor, Lenox and Tilden Foundations.)*

1816—that is, 20 percent to 25 percent on the value of dutiable goods.*

The compromise Tariff of 1833 finally squeezed through Congress. Debate was bitter, with most of the opposition naturally coming from protectionist New England and the middle states. Calhoun and the South favored the compromise, so it was evident that Jackson would

---

*For the history of tariff rates, see the Appendix, page xxviii.

House Vote on Tariff of 1832*

REGIONS	FOR	AGAINST	EXPLANATIONS
New England	17	17	Divided on moderate tariff
Middle states	52	18	Pa., N.Y., protectionist strongholds
West (Ohio, Ind., Ill., Mo.)	18	0	Undeveloped West for tariff to support improvements
South (incl. La.)	27	27	Note division on moderate tariff
Southwest (Tenn., Ky.)	18	3	West favorable to tariff
TOTAL	132	65	

*The vote was badly divided because the bill was really a compromise between extreme protection and free trade. Compare vote on 1828 tariff, p. 237.

House Vote on Compromise Tariff of 1833

REGIONS	FOR	AGAINST	EXPLANATIONS
New England	10	28 ⎫	Opposition in manufacturing centers to
Middle states	24	47 ⎭	lowered tariff
West	10	8	Divided on moderate tariff
South and Southwest	75	2	Strong southern support for compromise
TOTAL	119	85	

not have to use firearms and rope. But at the same time, and partly as a face-saving device, Congress passed the Force Bill, known among Carolinians as the "Bloody Bill." It authorized the president to use the army and navy, if necessary, to collect federal tariff duties.

Militant South Carolinians welcomed this opportunity to extricate themselves without loss of face from a dangerously tight corner. To the consternation of the Calhounites, no other southern states had sprung to their support, though Georgia and Virginia toyed with the idea. Moreover, an appreciable Unionist minority within South Carolina was gathering guns, organizing militia, and nailing the Stars and Stripes to flagpoles. Faced with civil war within and invasion from without, the Columbia convention met again and repealed the ordinance of nullification. As a final but futile gesture of fist-shaking, it nullified the unnecessary Force Act and adjourned.

A Victory for Both Union and Nullification

Neither Jackson nor the "nullies" won a clear-cut triumph. Admirers of "Old Hickory" insisted that he had avoided an armed clash, induced the South Carolinians to repeal their ordinance of nullification, and preserved the Union. On the other hand, the danger of disunion seems to have been exaggerated.

South Carolina actually emerged with colors flying. Although confronted with overwhelming odds, it had forced a reduction of the tariff to as reasonable a level as it could have expected. It had not only saved face but it had surrendered

no principle. Unrepentant and defiant, it felt that it had won; and the people of Charleston—the "Cradle of Secession"—gave a gala "victory ball" for the volunteer troops. But ominously the South Carolinians gradually abandoned nullification in favor of the more extreme remedy of secession.

Later generations, gazing back through the smoke of the Civil War, have condemned the "appeasement" of South Carolina in 1833 as sheer folly. Unbloody and unbowed, it could have been voted the state most likely to secede. (In 1860 it was the first to go.) If Jackson had only strangled the serpent of secession in the cradle, so the argument runs, there might have been no costly Civil War. During the crisis of 1832 medals were struck off in honor of Calhoun bearing the words, "First President of the Southern Confederacy."

Yet force was the risky solution. The flare-up in South Carolina was no mere Whiskey Rebellion, and the nation was not yet ready to drink the cup of blood. Violence tends to beget violence. Armed invasion might have aroused other southern states and touched off a civil war, at a time when the Unionists were even worse prepared for fighting than in 1861. Force is a confession that statesmanship has failed. Reasonable compromise was in the American tradition, and in 1833 any other course seemed unwise.

The Bank as a Political Football

President Jackson did not hate all banks and all businesses, but he distrusted monopolistic banking and overbig business, as did his followers. A man of violent dislikes, he came to share the prejudices of his own West against the "moneyed monster" known as the Bank of the United States (BUS). He might have tolerated a renewal of its charter in 1836, with adequate safeguards. But hated Henry Clay aroused his ire by throwing himself behind a premature move in the Senate to recharter the bank in 1832—four years early. "Gallant Harry" was the leading candidate of the National Republicans for the presidency, and with fateful blindness he looked upon the bank issue as a surefire winner.

Clay's scheme was to ram a recharter bill through Congress and then send it on to the White House. If Jackson signed it, he would alienate his worshipful western followers. If he vetoed it, as seemed certain, he would presumably lose the presidency in the forthcoming election by alienating the wealthy and influential groups in the East. Clay seems not to have fully realized that the "best people" were now only a minority and that they generally feared Jackson anyhow. The president growled privately, "The Bank . . . is trying to kill me, but I will kill it."

The recharter bill slid through Congress on greased skids, as planned, but was killed by a scorching veto from Jackson. The "Old Hero" assailed the plutocratic and monopolistic bank as unconstitutional. Of course, the Supreme Court had earlier declared it constitutional in the case of *McCulloch* v. *Maryland* (1819), but Jackson acted as though he regarded the executive branch as superior to the judicial branch.

He had taken an oath to uphold the Constitution as he understood it, not as his foe John Marshall understood it.

Jackson's veto message went on to condemn the bank as not only antiwestern but anti-American. A substantial minority of its stockholders were foreigners, chiefly Britons, for whom Americans still harbored a war-born hate. Thus, at one bold stroke, Jackson succeeded in mobilizing the prejudices of the West against the East. He was setting the log cabin against the business office, the apprehensive debtor against the steely-eyed creditor. More than that, the president was arousing the "native" American against the foreigner, the states' righter against the centralizer.

The gods continued to misguide Henry Clay. Delighted with the financial fallacies of Jackson's message, but blind to its political appeal, he arranged to have thousands of copies printed as a campaign document. The president's sweeping accusations may indeed have seemed demagogic to the moneyed people of the country, but they made good sense to the common people. The bank issue was now thrown into the noisy arena of the Clay-Jackson presidential canvass of 1832.

Brickbats and Bouquets for the Bank

What of Jackson's vigorous charges? The bank was undeniably antiwestern in its strong hostility to the wobbly "wildcat banks" that provided financial fuel—often volatile paper—for western expansion. It had foreclosed on many western farms and had thus drained "tribute" into eastern coffers. For that era, it was a mammoth superbank—a "monster monopoly"—and hence out of touch with the sweaty New Democracy. It was undeniably plutocratic, run by an elite moneyed aristocracy, headed by the able but high-handed Nicholas Biddle (dubbed "Czar Nicholas I"). The bank was also in some degree autocratic and tyrannical, especially when it turned the screws on the weak "rag money" banks.

The charge that the bank was a "hydra of corruption" contained much truth. Biddle cleverly lent funds where they would make

> *Banker Biddle wrote to Henry Clay (August 1, 1832) expressing his satisfaction: "I have always deplored making the Bank a party question, but since the President will have it so, he must pay the penalty of his own rashness. As to the veto message, I am delighted with it. It has all the fury of a chained panther biting the bars of his cage. It is really a manifesto of anarchy . . . and my hope is that it will contribute to relieve the country of the domination of these miserable [Jackson] people."*

Nicholas Biddle (1786–1844)   *A precociously brilliant linguist, writer, magazine editor, diplomat, legislator, and financier, he entered the University of Pennsylvania at age ten and completed the requirements for graduation at age thirteen. Drawn into high finance, he mastered the business and became president of the Bank of the United States. (Historical Society of Pennsylvania.)*

influential friends. In 1831 alone, a total of fifty-nine members of Congress borrowed sums from "Biddle's Bank" totaling about a third of a million dollars. Even a dog does not ordinarily bite the hand that feeds it. During one period Daniel Webster was a director of the bank, its chief paid counsel, its debtor in the sum of thousands of dollars, and a member of the United States Senate, where he eloquently battled for his employer's interests. Judicious loans by Biddle to newspaper editors likewise ensured a "good press" and led to the sneer, "Emperor Nick of the Bribery Bank." Whomever he could not corrupt, it was believed, he crushed.

Yet the bank had much to commend it. An eminently sound organization, it was the only national financial institution of its kind in American history. It imposed some restraint on fly-by-night-banks—banks that often consisted of little more than a few chairs and a suitcase full of printed notes. It reduced bank failures and, at a time when the country was flooded with depreciated paper money, issued sound bank notes ("Old Nick's Money"). It promoted economic expansion by making credit and sound currency reasonably abundant. It was a safe depository for the funds of the Washington government, which it also served by transferring and disbursing money. Admittedly it had a monopoly of surplus federal funds, but that monopoly had been specifically authorized by the people's representatives in Congress.

The bank, in short, was a highly important and useful institution that had fallen into the hands of a wealthy clique. Its officers not only were arrogant but were also not fully aware of their responsibilities to society in the management of what amounted to a public trust.

"Old Hickory" Crushes Clay in 1832

Clay, as a National Republican, and Jackson, as a Democrat, were the chief gladiators in the presidential contest of 1832. The gaunt old general, who had earlier favored one term for a president and rotation in office, was easily persuaded by his cronies not to rotate himself out of office. Presidential power is a heady brew—and habit-forming.

The ensuing campaign was colorful and noisy. The "Old Hero's" adherents again raised the hickory pole and bellowed, "Jackson Forever: Go the Whole Hog." Admirers of Clay shouted, "Freedom and Clay," while his foes harped on his dueling, gambling, cockfighting, and fast living.

Novel features made the campaign of 1832 especially memorable. For the first time, a third party entered the field—the newborn Anti-Masonic party, which opposed the fearsome secrecy of the Masonic order. Energized by the mysterious disappearance and probable murder in 1826 of a New Yorker who was threatening to expose the secret rituals of the Masons, the Anti-Masonic party quickly became a potent political force in New York and spread its influence throughout the middle Atlantic and New England states. The Anti-Masons appealed to long-standing American suspicions of secret societies, which they condemned as citadels of privilege and monopoly—a note that harmonized with the democratic chorus of the Jacksonians. But since Jackson himself was a Mason, and publicly gloried in his membership, the Anti-Masonic party was also an anti-Jackson party. Moreover, the Anti-Masons attracted support from many evangelical Protestant groups seeking to use political power to effect moral and religious reforms, such as prohibiting mail deliveries on Sundays and otherwise keeping the Sabbath holy. This moral busybodiness was anathema to the Jacksonians, who were generally opposed to all government meddling in social and economic life.

A further novelty of the presidential contest in 1832 was the calling of national nominating conventions (three of them) to name candidates. The Anti-Masons and a group of National Republicans added still another innovation when they adopted formal platforms, publicizing their positions on the issues.

Henry Clay and his overconfident National Republicans enjoyed impressive advantages. Ample funds flowed into their campaign chest, including $50,000 in "life insurance" from the BUS. Most of the newspaper editors, some of them "bought" with Biddle's bank loans, dipped their pens in acid when they wrote of Jackson.

Oratorical big guns, including the incomparable Webster, were lined up on the side of Clay, as was true of the middle- and upper-income groups.

Yet Jackson won easily over the sparkling Kentuckian. The popular count stood at 687,502 to 530,189; the electoral count, 219 to 49. The Anti-Masons carried only Vermont. A Jacksonian wave swept over the West and South, washed into Pennsylvania and New York, and even broke into rock-ribbed New England.

Henry Clay, long bitten by the presidential bug, was crushed. Himself magnetically appealing, he had enlisted on his side the big money, the brilliant oratory, the "solid" citizenry, and the sound financial reasoning. But the peppery president, the idol of the masses, won because he had the votes. The poor always outnumber the rich—and in 1832, as in 1824 and 1828, the poor voted for "Old Andy" Jackson.

Badgering Biddle's Bank

A vindictive Jackson was not one to let the financial octopus die in peace. He was convinced that he now had a "mandate" from the voters, and he had good reason to fear that the slippery Biddle might try to manipulate the

"Race Over Uncle Sam's Course" Clay, with his American System, is supposed to gain the White House as Jackson, with his veto club and Van Buren as running mate, falls on the bank issue in 1832. A falsely optimistic Whig cartoon. (Boston Public Library.)

bank (as he did) so as to force its recharter. Jackson therefore decided to weaken the bank by "removing" federal deposits from its vaults. He proposed depositing no more funds with Biddle and gradually shrinking existing deposits by using them to defray the day-to-day expenses of the government. By slowly siphoning off the government's funds, he would bleed the bank dry and ensure its demise when its charter expired in four years.

"Removing" the deposits involved nasty complications. Jackson, his dander up, was forced to reshuffle his cabinet before he could find a secretary of the treasury who would bend to his iron will. Surplus federal funds henceforth were placed in several dozen state institutions—the so-called pet banks or Jackson's pets. These new depositories were selected partly because of their pro-Jackson sympathies, but in general they were not nearly so weak as pictured by the president's enemies.

Biddle, for his part, was compelled to retrench after losing the federal deposits. But he called in loans with unnecessary severity and evidently for the purpose of forcing a reconsideration of the charter by Congress. A number of the wobblier banks were driven to the wall by "Biddle's Panic," and the vengeful conduct of the dying "monster" seemed to justify the earlier accusations of its foes.

The teetering financial structure of the country received an additional shock in 1836, the year the bank breathed its last. "Wildcat" currency had become so unreliable, especially in the West, that Jackson authorized the Treasury to issue a Specie Circular—a decree that required all public lands to be purchased with "hard," or metallic, money. This drastic step was overdue, but coming at that time it gave the speculative bubble another sharp prick. Hard money brought hard feelings and hard times for the West.

Yet inflationary pressure continued. By 1835 the national debt was finally liquidated for the first time, but additional funds still poured into the federal Treasury. This revenue flowed principally from the customshouses, which were benefiting from the high tariff duties and the heavy imports resulting from flush times. In 1836 a scheme passed Congress for distributing the surplus above $5 million to the states. When this transfer began, early in 1837, the risky speculative spiral was given another boost. Later that year the panic broke, and the bothersome problem of the surplus became the even more bothersome problem of a deficit.

Transplanting the Tribes

Wondrous indeed was the continued expansion of the American population. The unflagging fertility of the people, reinforced by immigration, brought the total figure to nearly 13 million by 1830—or more than three times that of 1790.* Most of the states east of the Mississippi had been admitted, leaving islands of Indians marooned on lands coveted by their white neighbors.

President Jackson, the veteran Indian fighter known as "Big Knife," was convinced of the folly of continuing to regard the tribes as separate nations within the individual states. When Georgia attempted to exercise control over the Cherokees, and the Supreme Court thrice upheld the rights of the Indians, Jackson viewed continued defiance by the state with unaccustomed composure. A state might flout federal

---

"The times are dreadfully hard," wrote a New York diarist, Philip Hone on December 30, 1833. "The . . . act of tyranny which the President exercised in removing the deposits has produced a state of alarm and panic unprecedented in our city. . . . The truth is, we are smarting under the lash which the vindictive ruler of our destinies [Jackson] has inflicted upon us as a penalty for the sin which Nicholas Biddle committed in opposing his election. My share of the punishment amounts to $20,000, which I have lost by the fall of stocks in the last sixty days."

---

*For population figures since 1790, see the Appendix.

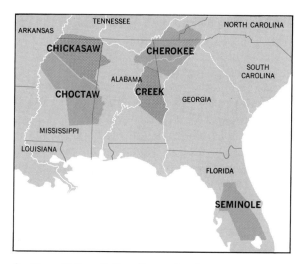

Southern Tribes Before Transplanting

jured race"? Jackson proposed a bodily removal of the remaining eastern tribes—chiefly Cherokee, Creek, Choctaw, and Chickasaw—beyond the Mississippi. Individual Indians might remain if they adopted white society's ways. Emigration should be voluntary, since it would be "cruel and unjust to compel the aborigines to abandon the graves of their fathers."

Jackson's policy was high-sounding, but it led to the more or less forcible uprooting of more than 100,000 Indians in the 1830s. Many died on the "Trail of Tears" to the newly established Indian Territory (present Oklahoma), where they were to be "permanently" free of white encroachments. The Bureau of Indian Affairs was established in 1836 to administer relations with America's original inhabitants. But as the land-hungry "palefaces" pushed west faster than anticipated, the government's guarantees went up in smoke. The "permanent" frontier lasted about fifteen years.

Suspicious of white intentions from the start, braves from Illinois and Wisconsin, ably led by Black Hawk, resisted eviction. They were bloodily crushed in 1832 by regular troops, including Lieutenant Jefferson Davis of Mississippi, and by volunteers, including Captain Abraham Lincoln of Illinois.

In Florida the Seminole Indians, joined by runaway black slaves, retreated to the swampy

law if whites thereby profited at the Indians' expense. In a callous sneer at the Indians' defender, Jackson reportedly snapped, "John Marshall has made his decision; now let him enforce it."

Yet Jackson also harbored protective feelings toward the Indians. Their present condition, he told Congress in 1829, "contrasted with what they once were, makes a most powerful appeal to our sympathies." Could not something be done, he implored, to preserve "this much in-

Black Hawk War, c. 1832
Resisting Indians in the Illinois country are dispatched by the white men's "fire sticks." (Rare Book Division, New York Public Library, Astor, Lenox and Tilden Foundations.)

Proud in Defeat *Chief Black Hawk and his son are here depicted in captivity. After their surrender in the Black Hawk War in 1832, they were put on public display throughout the United States. (Thomas Gilcrease Institute, Tulsa, Oklahoma.)*

granting a huge tract of land to Stephen Austin, with the understanding that he would bring in three hundred American families. Immigrants were to be of the established Roman Catholic faith and in addition were to become properly Mexicanized.

These two restrictions were largely ignored. Hardy Texan pioneers remained Americans at heart, resenting the trammels imposed by a "foreign" government. They were especially annoyed by the presence of Mexican soldiers, many of whom were ragged ex-convicts.

Virile and prolific, Texas-Americans numbered about thirty thousand by 1835. Most of them were law-abiding, God-fearing people, but some of them had left the "states" only one or two jumps ahead of the sheriff. "G. T. T." (Gone to Texas) became current descriptive slang. Among the adventurers were Davy Crockett, the fabulous rifleman, and James Bowie, the

Everglades. For seven years (1835–1842) they waged a bitter guerrilla war that took the lives of some fifteen hundred soldiers and proved to be the costliest Indian conflict in American experience. The spirit of the Seminoles was at last broken in 1837, when the American field commander treacherously seized their half-breed leader, Osceola, under a flag of truce. Some fled deeper into the Everglades, where their descendants now live, but about four-fifths of them were moved to present Oklahoma, where about three thousand of the tribe survive.

The Lone Star of Texas Flickers

Americans, greedy for land, continued to covet the vast expanse of Texas, which the United States had abandoned to Spain when acquiring Florida in 1819. The Spanish authorities were desirous of populating this virtually unpeopled area, but before they could carry through their contemplated plans, the Mexicans won their independence. A new regime in Mexico City thereupon concluded arrangements in 1823 for

Samuel ("Sam") Houston (1793–1863) *After a promising career in Tennessee as a soldier, lawyer, congressman, and governor, Houston became the chief leader and hero of the Texas rebels. Elected to the U.S. Senate and the governorship of Texas, he was forced into retirement when his love for the Union caused him to spurn the Confederacy in the Civil War.*

The Alamo *An abandoned mission at San Antonio, the Alamo occupies a glorious spot in Texas history. Known as "The Cradle of Texas Liberty," the Alamo was constructed as a Franciscan chapel in the days of Spanish colonization in the eighteenth century. It had been abandoned for some time prior to its famous use as a fort in 1836. Destroyed in the Mexican attack, the Alamo was purchased by the state of Texas in 1883 and subsequently restored. (D. W. C. Baker, A Brief History of Texas, New York: A. S. Barnes, 1873.)*

presumed inventor of the murderous knife that bears his name. It was widely known in the Southwest as the "genuwine Arkansas toothpick." A distinguished latecomer and leader was an ex-governor of Tennessee, Sam Houston. His life had been temporarily shattered in 1829 when his bride of a few weeks left him and he took up transient residence with the Arkansas Indians, who dubbed him "Big Drink." He subsequently took the pledge of temperance.

The pioneer individualists who came to Texas were not easy to push around. Friction rapidly increased between Mexicans and Texans over such issues as slavery, immigration, and local rights. Slavery was a particularly touchy issue. Mexico emancipated its slaves in 1830 and prohibited their further importation into Texas, as well as further settlement by troublesome Americans. The Texans refused to honor this decree. They kept their slaves in bondage, and new American settlers kept bringing more slaves into Texas. When Stephen Austin went to Mexico City in 1833 to negotiate these differences with the Mexican government, dictator Santa Anna clapped him in jail for eight months. The explosion finally came in

1835, when Santa Anna wiped out all local rights and started to raise an army to suppress the upstart Texans.

Early in 1836 the Texans declared their independence and unfurled their Lone Star flag—with Sam Houston as commander in chief. Santa Anna, at the head of about six thousand men, swept ferociously into Texas. Trapping a band of nearly two hundred pugnacious Texans at the Alamo in San Antonio, he wiped them out to a man after a thirteen-day siege. Their commander, Colonel W. B. Travis, had heroically declared, "I shall never surrender nor retreat. . . . Victory or Death." The victims included Jim Bowie, who was shot as he lay sick and crippled on his cot, and Davy Crockett, whose body was found riddled with bullets and surrounded by enemy corpses. But the Mexican losses were extremely heavy. A short time later a band of about four hundred surrounded and defeated American volunteers, having thrown down their arms at Goliad, were butchered as "pirates." All these operations further delayed the Mexican advance.

Texan war cries—"Remember the Alamo!" "Remember Goliad!" and "Death to Santa

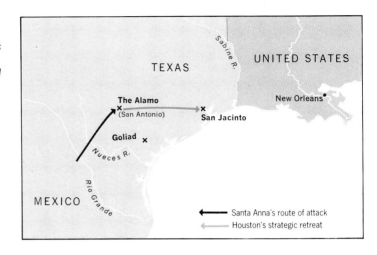

The Texas Revolution, 1835–1836 *General Houston's strategy was to retreat and use defense in depth. His line of supply from the United States was shortened as Santa Anna's lengthened. The Mexicans were forced to bring up supplies by land because the Texas navy controlled the sea. This force consisted of only four small ships, but it was big enough to do the job.*

Anna!"—swept up into the United States. Scores of vengeful Americans seized their rifles and rushed to the aid of relatives, friends, and compatriots. But despite their efforts, the Lone Star was in grave danger of being dimmed forever as General Sam Houston's small army continued its thirty-seven-day eastward retreat.

But Houston proved equal to the occasion. A commanding figure of a man and a natural leader of the Texans, he lured the pursuers onward to San Jacinto, near the site of the city that now bears his name. The invaders numbered about thirteen hundred men; the Texans, about nine hundred. Suddenly, on April 21, 1836, Houston turned. Taking full advantage of the Mexican siesta hour, he wiped out the invading force and captured Santa Anna, who was found cowering in the tall grass near the battlefield. Confronted with thirsty bowie knives, the quaking dictator was speedily induced to sign two treaties. By their terms he agreed to withdraw Mexican troops and to recognize the Rio Grande as the extreme southwestern boundary of Texas. When released, he repudiated the whole agreement as illegal and as extorted under duress.

Texas: An International Derelict

Mexico no doubt had a genuine grievance against the United States. The Texans, though courageous, could hardly have won their independence without unneutral help in men and supplies from their American cousins. The Washington government, as the Mexicans bitterly complained, had a solemn obligation under international law to enforce its leaky neutrality statutes. But American public opinion, overwhelmingly favorable to the Texans, openly nullified the existing legislation. The federal authorities were powerless to act.

Jackson's heart was torn by the Texas issue. He disliked the Mexican overlords and admired the heroism of Sam Houston, his old comrade-in-arms against the Indians. But Jackson was in no haste to recognize Texas formally as an independent republic. To do so would touch off the whole explosive issue of slavery, at a time when he was trying to engineer the election of his handpicked successor, Martin Van Buren. But after Van Buren had come safely under the wire, Jackson extended the right hand of recognition, on the day before he left office in 1837.

Texas had every reason to expect a union with the United States, for what nation in its right mind would refuse so princely a dowry? The radiant Texan bride, officially petitioning for annexation in 1837, presented herself for marriage. But the expectant groom, Uncle Sam, was jerked back by the black hand of the slavery issue. Antislavery crusaders in the North were opposing annexation with increasing vehemence; they contended that the whole scheme was merely a conspiracy cooked up by the southern "slavocracy" to bring new slave pens into the Union.

At first glance, a "slavery plot" charge seemed plausible. Most of the early settlers in Texas, as well as American volunteers during the revolution, had come from the states of the South and Southwest. But scholars have concluded that the settlement of Texas was merely the normal and inexorable march of the westward movement. Most of the immigrants came from the South and Southwest simply because these states were closer. The explanation was proximity rather than conspiracy. Yet the fact remained that many Texans were slaveholders, and admitting Texas to the Union inescapably meant enlarging American slavery.

The jilted Texas bride was left in a dangerous predicament. Fearing the return of the "villain," Santa Anna, she understandably went so far as to flirt openly with Britain and France for support. An ugly situation, involving balance-of-power politics, began to develop below the underbelly of the United States. It could not be allowed to go on indefinitely.

The Birth of the Whigs and the Election of 1836

New political parties were gelling as the 1830s lengthened. As early as 1828, the Democratic-Republicans of Andrew Jackson had unashamedly adopted the once-tainted name of "Democrats." Jackson's opponents, fuming at his ironfisted exercise of presidential power, condemned him as "King Andrew I" and began to coalesce as the *Whigs*—a name deliberately chosen to recollect eighteenth-century British and Revolutionary American opposition to the monarchy.

The Whig party contained so many diverse elements that it was mocked at first as "an organized incompatibility." Hatred of Jackson and his "executive usurpation" was its only apparent cement in its formative days. The Whigs first emerged as an identifiable group in the Senate, where Clay and Calhoun joined forces in 1834 to pass a motion censuring Jackson for his single-handed removal of federal deposits from the Bank of the United States. Thereafter, the Whigs rapidly evolved into a potent national political force by attracting other groups alienated by Jackson: supporters of Clay's American System; southern states' righters offended by Jackson's stand on nullification; the larger northern industrialists and merchants; and eventually, many of the evangelical Protestants associated with the Anti-Masonic party.

As the presidential election of 1836 neared, the still-ramshackle organization of the Whigs showed in their inability to nominate a single presidential candidate. Their long-shot strategy was instead to run several prominent "favorite sons," who would so scatter the vote that no candidate would win a majority. The deadlock would then have to be broken by the House of Representatives, where the Whigs might have a chance. With Henry Clay rudely elbowed aside, the leading "favorite son" was heavy-jawed General William Henry Harrison of Ohio, hero of the Battle of Tippecanoe.

Martin Van Buren of New York, a smooth-as-silk politician, was Jackson's choice for "appointment" as his successor. The hollow-cheeked Jackson, now nearing seventy, was too old and ailing to consider a third term. But he was not loath to try to serve a third term through Van Buren, something of a "yes man." Leaving nothing to chance, the general carefully rigged the nominating convention and rammed his favorite down the throats of the delegates. Van Buren was supported by the Jacksonites without wild enthusiasm, even though he had promised "to tread generally" in the military-booted footsteps of his predecessor.

The finespun schemes of the Whigs availed nothing. Van Buren, the dapper "Little Van," squirmed into office by the close popular vote of 765,483 to 739,795, but by the comfortable margin of 170 votes to 73 in the Electoral College. Jackson could now step down.

In retrospect, the Jackson years were yeasty ones. It is true that they were marred by noise and bluster, as well as by bull-in-the-china-closet financial policies. Yet the rough-hewn general—through forthrightness, energy, and strength of character—left a lasting imprint on the presidency. He demonstrated anew the value of strong executive leadership; he led the common people into national politics; he united

Martin Van Buren (1782–1862) *He has been generally underrated as a President because of his skill as a politician. It was said of him that he rowed toward his objectives "with muffled oars." Yet he eventually took a strong stand against the expansion of slavery by his hopeless run for the presidency as the candidate of the Free Soil Party in 1848. (Library of Congress.)*

them into the powerful and long-lived Democratic party; and he proved that they could be trusted with the vote. Reasserting the prestige of the presidency, he amazed weak-kneed politicians by showing that the courageous course often wins the most votes.

The other side of the ledger is less satisfying. Jackson cannot escape blame for his encouragement of the spoils system and of unsound finance, with its heartbreaking legacy of a century of thousands of bank failures. No one can deny that the BUS was a powerful and ultimately a corrupting monopoly, which needed to have its wings clipped. But chopping off its

head instead of its wings was of dubious benefit to the entire nation.

Big Woes for the "Little Magician"

Martin Van Buren, eighth president, was the first to be born under the American flag. Bland of face, bald of head, slender of figure, the adroit little New Yorker has been described as "a first-class second-rate man." An accomplished wire-puller and spoilsman—"the wizard of Albany"—he was also a statesman of wide experience in both legislative and administrative life. In intelligence, education, and training, he was above the average of the presidents since Jackson. The myth of his complete mediocrity sprouted from a series of misfortunes over which he had no control.

From the outset, the new politician-president labored under severe handicaps. As a machine-made candidate, he incurred the resentment of many Democrats—those who objected to having a "bastard politician" smuggled into office beneath the tails of the old general's military coat. Jackson, the master showman, had been the dynamic type of executive whose administration had resounded with furious quarrels and cracked heads. Easygoing Martin Van Buren seemed to rattle about in the military boots of his testy predecessor. The people felt let down. Inheriting Andrew Jackson's mantle without his popularity, the polished New Yorker also inherited the ex-president's numerous and vengeful enemies.

Van Buren's four years overflowed with toil and trouble. A rebellion in Canada in 1837 stirred up ugly incidents along the northern frontier and threatened to trigger war with Britain. The president's attempt to play a neutral game led to the cry "Woe to Martin Van Buren!" The antislavery agitators in the North were in full cry and among other grievances were condemning the prospective annexation of Texas.

Worst of all, Van Buren inherited the making of a searing depression from Jackson. Much of his energy had to be devoted to the purely negative task of battling the panic, and there were not enough rabbits in the "Little Magician's" tall silk hat. Hard times ordinarily blight the reputation of a president—and Van Buren was no exception.

Depression Doldrums and the Independent Treasury

The panic of 1837 was a symptom of the financial sickness of the times. Its basic cause was evidently overspeculation, prompted by a mania of get-rich-quickism. Gamblers in western lands were doing a "land-office business" on borrowed capital, much of it in the shaky currency of "wildcat banks." The speculative craze spread to canals, roads, railroads, and slaves.

But speculation alone did not cause the crash. Jacksonian finance, including the Bank War and the Specie Circular, gave an additional jolt to an already teetering structure. Failures of wheat crops, ravaged by the Hessian fly, deepened the distress. Grain prices were forced so high that mobs in New York City, three weeks before Van Buren took the oath, stormed warehouses and broke open flour barrels. The panic really began before Jackson left, but its full fury burst about Van Buren's bewildered head.

Financial stringency abroad likewise left its imprint on America. Late in 1836, while Jackson was still president, the failure of two prominent British banks created tremors, and these in turn caused English investors to call in foreign loans. The resulting pinch in the United States, combined with other setbacks, heralded the beginning of the panic. Europe's economic distresses have often been America's distresses, for every major American financial panic has been affected by conditions overseas.

Hardship was acute and widespread. American banks collapsed by the hundreds, including some "pet banks," which carried down with them several millions in government funds. Commodity prices drooped, sales of public lands fell off, and customs revenues dried to a rivulet. Factories closed their doors; unemployed workers darkened the streets.

Increasingly, the Whigs were coming forward with proposals for active government

> Philip Hone, a New York businessman, described in his diary (May 10, 1837) a phase of the financial crisis: "The savings-bank also sustained a most grievous run yesterday. They paid 375 depositors $81,000. The press was awful; the hour for closing the bank is six o'clock, but they did not get through the paying of those who were in at that time till nine o'clock. I was there with the other trustees and witnessed the madness of the people—women nearly pressed to death, and the stoutest men could scarcely sustain themselves; but they held on as with a death's grip upon the evidences of their claims, and, exhausted as they were with the pressure, they had strength to cry 'Pay! Pay!'"

remedies for the economy's ills. They called for the expansion of bank credit, higher tariffs, and subsidies for internal improvements. But Van Buren, shackled by the Jacksonian philosophy of keeping the government's paws off the economy, scorned all such ideas.

The beleaguered Van Buren tried to apply vintage Jacksonian medicine to the ailing economy through his controversial "Divorce Bill." Convinced that some of the financial fever was fed by the injection of federal funds into private banks, he championed the principle of "divorcing" the government from banking altogether. By establishing a so-called independent treasury, the government could lock its surplus money in vaults in several of the larger cities. Government funds would thus be safe, but they would also be denied to the banking system as reserves, thereby shriveling available credit resources. Van Buren's desire for political purity triumphed over enlightened economics.

Van Buren's "divorce" scheme was never highly popular. It was supported only lukewarmly by his fellow Democrats, many of whom longed for the risky but lush days of the "pet banks." The new policy was condemned by the Whigs, primarily because it would dampen their hopes for a revived Bank of the United States. After a prolonged struggle, the Independent Treasury Bill passed Congress in 1840. Repealed the next year by the victorious Whigs, the scheme was reenacted by the triumphant Democrats in 1846 and then continued until merged with the Federal Reserve System in the next century.

"Tippecanoe" Versus "Little Van"

Martin Van Buren, though panic-tainted, was renominated by the Democrats in 1840, albeit without terrific enthusiasm. The party had no

President William Henry Harrison (1773–1841)
Harrison can claim several distinctions. At sixty-eight, he was the oldest man to be sworn in until Ronald Reagan's inauguration 140 years later; he delivered the longest inaugural address (two hours); dying of pneumonia, he served the shortest term (thirty-one days); he obviously accomplished the least of any president; and he was responsible for the most progeny: 10 children, 48 grandchildren, 106 great-grandchildren. One of his grandchildren, Benjamin Harrison, became the twenty-third president. (National Portrait Gallery, Smithsonian Institution, Washington, D.C.)

acceptable alternative to what the Whigs called "Martin Van Ruin."

The Whigs, hungering for the spoils of office, scented victory in the breeze. Pangs of the panic were still being felt; and voters blindly blamed their woes on the party in power. The Whigs turned again not to their ablest statesman—Clay or Webster—but to their presumably ablest vote-getter: General Harrison, a coarse-featured military chieftain, with a long, thin face and medium build (5 feet 8 inches; 1.72 meters).

The aging hero, nearly sixty-eight when the campaign ended, was a small-bore candidate. Despite an inflated reputation, he had been only moderately successful in civilian and military life, notably at the Battles of Tippecanoe (1811) and the Thames (1813). "Old Tippecanoe" was then living quietly in a sixteen-room mansion, located on a three-thousand-acre farm near North Bend, Ohio. His views on current issues were only vaguely known. He was nominated primarily because he was issueless and enemyless—and a most unfortunate precedent was thus set. John Tyler of Virginia, an afterthought, was selected as his vice-presidential running mate.

The Whigs benefited from the economic distresses of Van Buren's term, and they were generally perceived as advocates of positive governmental steps to revive the economy. But officially, the Whigs played the political game with the cards close to their vests. They published no platform, because they feared making bothersome commitments and were unwilling to reveal the deep divisions within their own patchwork party. They hoped to sweep their hero into office with a frothy huzza-for-Harrison campaign.

A dull-witted Democratic editor played directly into Whig hands. Stupidly insulting the West, he sneered at Harrison as an impoverished old farmer who would be content with a pension, a log cabin, and a barrel of hard cider—the poor westerner's champagne. Whigs gleefully took up the challenge and, stressing the hard cider and log cabin theme, turned the campaign into a huge political revival meeting. Harrisonites portrayed their hero as the poor

The Hard Cider Campaign, 1840 *An almanac cover promoting Harrison's candidacy. (The Granger Collection.)*

"Farmer of North Bend," who had been called from his plow and his log cabin to drive corrupt Jackson spoilsmen from the "presidential palace."

A nonexistent candidate rapidly began to take shape in the hands of Whig mythmakers. The real Harrison was not lowborn, but from one of the FFVs (first families of Virginia). He was not poverty-stricken; he did not live in a one-room log cabin; he did not swill down gallons of hard cider (he evidently preferred whiskey); and he did not plow his fields with his own "huge paws."

Whig propagandists made merry with little "Matty" Van Buren, the "Flying Dutchman." Although reared in poverty, he was denounced as a supercilious aristocrat, who wore corsets and ate French food with golden teaspoons from golden plates. Jackson's rough-timbered Democratic party, deeply rooted in the West, was thus saddled with a simpering dandy from the aristocratic East. The aristocratic Whig party of Webster and Biddle, no less inconsistently, had come up with a backwoods nominee from the Democratic West—a reasonably good facsimile of wrinkled old General Jackson. As a jeering Whig campaign song proclaimed:

> Old Tip, he wears a homespun shirt,
>   He has no ruffled shirt, wirt, wirt.
> But Matt, he has the golden plate,
>   And he's a little squirt, wirt, wirt.

The Log Cabins and Hard Cider of 1840

Eager Democrats, who had hurrahed Jackson into the White House, now discovered to their chagrin that this was a game two could play. Acres of Whig audiences and miles of Whig marchers shouted such slogans as: "Harrison, Two Dollars a Day and Roast Beef" and "With Tip and Tyler We'll Bust Van's Biler." Log cabins were dished up in every conceivable form. Bawling Whigs, stimulated by fortified cider, rolled huge inflated balls from village to village and state to state—balls that represented the snowballing majority for "Tip and Ty." As they pushed, they sang:

> Tippecanoe, and Tyler too.
> And with them we'll beat little Van, Van, Van,
> Oh! Van is a used-up man.

Claptrap was king, as the electoral debauch reached an all-time intellectual low. There was little sober discussion of solid issues. Democrats inquired earnestly about the bank, internal improvements, and the tariff. The replies were "log cabin," "hard cider," and "Harrison is a poor man." Van Burenites, protesting futilely, were drowned in a tidal wave of apple juice as America experienced its first mass-turnout election.

Harrison won by the surprisingly close margin of 1,274,624 popular votes to 1,127,781, but

A Hard Road to Hoe! *Jackson urges Van Buren toward the White House over a road littered with log cabins and hard cider. Van Buren, handicapped also by his unpopular subtreasury policy, would evidently prefer the smoother road back to his Kinderhook home. A campaign cartoon of 1840. (Library of Congress.)*

by the overwhelming electoral count of 234 to 60. The hard-ciderites had seemingly received a mandate to go to Washington, tear down the White House, and erect a log cabin.

Basically, the vote was a protest against hard times—a thunderous shout of "Out with the old and in with the new." But the blatant bunkum and silly slogans set an unfortunate example for future campaigns. Democracy calls for hard thinking, not hard cider; for dignity, not delirium. Yet an able, well-organized, and well-entrenched political party, committed to solid principles, was hooted out of office by an inane hoopla campaign.

The Democrats were baffled. They complained with much bitterness and no little truth that they had been shouted down, sung down, lied down, and drunk down. Yet, though outsloganed, they had kept their ranks intact. Even in defeat they were a stronger party than the Whigs. Though temporarily overdosed with hard cider, the Democrats would be heard from again.

The Two-Party System Emerges

The Jeffersonians of an earlier day had been so successful in absorbing the programs of their Federalist opponents that a full-blown two-party system had never truly emerged in the subsequent Era of Good Feelings. The idea had prevailed that parties of any sort smacked of conspiracy and "faction" and were injurious to the health of the body politic in a virtuous republic.

But the American political world changed dramatically in the era of the New Democracy. One of Andrew Jackson's most lasting legacies was the impetus he gave to the formation of a vigorous and durable two-party system, which had fully come of age by 1840.

Both parties, the Democrats as well as the Whigs, grew out of the rich soil of Jeffersonian republicanism, and each laid claim to different aspects of the republican inheritance. Jacksonians glorified the liberty of the individual and were fiercely on guard against the inroads of "privilege" into government. Whigs trumpeted the natural harmony of society and the value of community, and were willing to use government to realize their objectives. Whigs also berated those leaders—and they considered Jackson to be one—whose appeals to self-interest fostered conflict among individuals, classes, or sections.

Democrats clung to states' rights and federal restraint in social and economic affairs as their basic doctrines. Whigs, on the other hand, tended to favor a renewed national bank; protective tariffs; internal improvements; public schools; and increasingly, moral reforms such as the prohibition of liquor and eventually the abolition of slavery.

The two parties were thus separated by real differences of philosophy and policy. But they also had much in common. Both were mass-

Andrew Jackson advised a supporter in 1835 on how to tell the difference between Democrats and "Whigs, nullies, and blue-light federalists." In doing so, he neatly summarized the Jacksonian philosophy: "The people ought to inquire [of political candidates]—are you opposed to a national bank; are you in favor of a strict construction of the Federal and State Constitutions; are you in favor of rotation in office; do you subscribe to the republican rule that the people are the sovereign power, the officers their agents, and that upon all national or general subjects, as well as local, they have a right to instruct their agents and respresentatives, and they are bound to obey or resign; in short, are they true Republicans agreeable to the true Jeffersonian creed?"

Politics for the Common Man   Artist George Caleb Bingham here gently satirizes the drinking and wheeler-dealing that sometimes marred the electoral process in the boisterous age of Jacksonian politics. (Boatman's National Bank of St. Louis.)

based, "catchall" parties that tried deliberately to mobilize as many voters as possible for their cause. Though it is true that Democrats tended to be more humble folk and Whigs more prosperous, both parties nevertheless commanded the loyalties of all kinds of Americans, from all social classes and in all sections. The social diversity of the two parties had important implications. It fostered horse-trading compromises *within* each party that prevented either from assuming extreme or radical positions. By the same token, the geographical diversity of the two parties retarded the emergence of purely sectional political parties—temporarily suppressing, through compromise, the ultimately uncompromisable issue of slavery. When the two-party system began to creak in the 1850s, the Union was mortally imperiled.

Varying Viewpoints

As the debate over Jacksonianism shifted from a concern with geography to a consideration of social class, and later to an analysis of religion and ethnicity, historical evaluations of the rival parties have also changed. Patrician historians of the nineteenth century made the Whigs the champions of enlightened civilization against the excesses of the Jacksonian rabble. The progressive historians of the early years of this century reversed those assessments. They praised the Jacksonians as the representatives of freedom and equality and damned the Whigs as self-serving, aristocratic snobs. That view held sway until recent times, when historians began exploring the operation of the party system on a local level and the variations in party positions from state to state. Studies such as those by Ronald Formisano and Michael Holt stress the two parties' connections with various religious and immigrant groups and have encouraged a more balanced assessment of the merits of both parties.

Select Readings

Primary Source Documents

An incisive commentary on Jacksonian politics is novelist James Fenimore Cooper's *The American Democrat** (1838). On the Bank War, see Andrew Jackson's "Veto Message" (July 10, 1832), in James D. Richardson, ed., *Messages and Papers of the Presidents* (1896), vol. II, pp. 576 ff,* and Daniel Webster's "Speech on Jackson's Veto of the U.S. Bank Bill" (1832), in Richard Hofstadter, ed., *Great Issues in American History.*

Secondary Sources

Glyndon G. Van Deusen, *The Jacksonian Era, 1828–1848* (1959), is an excellent introduction. More thorough is the concluding volume of Robert V. Remini's biography, *Andrew Jackson and the Course of American Democracy, 1833–1845* (1984). Incisive analysis can be found in Richard Hofstadter's essay on Jackson in *The American Political Tradition* (1948). A superior monograph is William W. Freehling, *Prelude to Civil War: The Nullification Controversy in South Carolina* (1966). Jacksonians are charged with ignorance and hypocrisy in Bray Hammond, *Banks and Politics in America from the Revolution to the Civil War* (1957), and Thomas P. Govan defends *Nicholas Biddle: Nationalist and Public Banker* (1959). John McFaul looks at the broader picture in *The Politics of Jacksonian Finance* (1972). Robert V. Remini focuses on political questions in *Andrew Jackson and the Bank War* (1967). Jackson's

Indian policies are scrutinized in Ronald N. Satz, *American Indian Policy in the Jacksonian Era* (1975), and Michael P. Rogin's heavily psychoanalytic *Fathers and Children: Andrew Jackson and the Subjugation of the American Indians* (1975). Important political transformations are handled in the Ronald P. Formisano and Richard P. McCormick volumes cited in Chapter 14. See also the opening chapters of Michael F. Holt's *The Political Crisis of the 1850s* (1978). Daniel W. Howe provides a stimulating analysis of Jackson's opponents in *The Political Culture of the American Whigs* (1980). Peter Temin interprets *The Jacksonian Economy* (1969). The color of the frothy presidential campaign of 1840 comes through in Robert G. Gunderson, *The Log-Cabin Campaign* (1957).

16

Manifest Destiny
in the Forties

Our manifest destiny [is] to overspread the continent allotted by Providence for the free development of our yearly multiplying millions.

John L. O'Sullivan, 1845*

The Accession of "Tyler Too"

A horde of hard-ciderites descended upon Washington early in 1841, clamoring for the spoils of office. Newly elected President Harrison, bewildered by the uproar, was almost hounded to death by Whig spoilsmen.

The real leaders of the Whig party regarded "Old Tippecanoe" as little more than an impressive figurehead. Daniel Webster, as secretary of state, and Henry Clay, the uncrowned king of the Whigs and their ablest spokesman in the Senate, would grasp the helm. The aging general was finally forced to rebuke the overzealous Clay and pointedly remind him that William

---

*Earliest known use of the term *Manifest Destiny*, sometimes called "manifest desire."

Henry Harrison was president of the United States.

Unluckily for Clay and Webster, their schemes soon hit a fatal snag. Before the new term had fairly started, Harrison came down with pneumonia. Wearied by official functions and plagued by office seekers, the enfeebled old warrior died after only four weeks in the White House—the shortest administration by far in American history, following by far the longest inaugural address.

The "Tyler too" part of the Whig ticket, hitherto only a rhyme, now claimed the spotlight. What manner of man did the nation now find in the presidential chair? Six feet (1.83 meters) tall, slender, blue-eyed, and fair-haired, with classical features and a high forehead, Tyler was a Virginia gentleman of the old school—gracious and kindly, yet stubbornly attached to principle. He had earlier resigned from the United States Senate, quite unnecessarily, rather than accept distasteful instructions from the Virginia legislature. Still a lone wolf, he had forsaken the Jacksonian Democratic fold for that of the Whigs, largely because he could not stomach the dictatorial tactics of Jackson.

Tyler's enemies accused him of being a Democrat in Whig clothing, but this charge was only partially true. The Whig party, like the Democratic party, was something of a catchall, and the accidental president belonged to the minority wing, which embraced a number of Jeffersonian states' righters. Tyler had in fact been put on the ticket partly to attract the vote of this influential group, many of whom were southern gentry.

Yet Tyler, high-minded as he was, should never have consented to run on the ticket. Though the dominant Clay-Webster group had published no platform, every alert politician knew what the unpublished platform contained. And on virtually every major issue the obstinate Virginian was at odds with the majority of his Whig party, which was probank, pro–protective tariff, and pro–internal improvements. "Tyler too" rhymed with "Tippecanoe," but there the harmony ended. As events turned out, President Harrison, the Whig, served for only four weeks, while Tyler, the ex-Democrat who was still largely a Democrat at heart, served for 204 weeks.

President John Tyler (1790–1862) *The first "accidental president," he was faithful to his states' rights convictions until death. A member of the Virginia secession convention in 1861, he served in the provisional congress of the Confederacy and was elected to a seat in the Confederate house of representatives. Invading Northern troops vengefully despoiled his beautiful Virginia estate, Sherwood Forest. (Chicago Historical Society.)*

John Tyler: A President without a Party

After their hard-won, hard-cider victory, the Whigs brought their not-so-secret platform out of Clay's waistcoat pocket. To the surprise of no one, it outlined a strongly nationalistic program.

Financial reform came first. The Whig Congress hastened to pass a law ending the independent treasury system, and President Tyler, disarmingly agreeable, signed it. Clay next drove through Congress a bill for a "Fiscal Bank," which would establish a new Bank of the United States.

Tyler's hostility to a centralized bank was notorious, and Clay—the "Great Compromiser"

—would have done well to conciliate him. But the Kentuckian, robbed repeatedly of the presidency by lesser men, was in an imperious mood and riding for a fall. When the bank bill reached the presidential desk, Tyler flatly vetoed it on both practical and constitutional grounds. A drunken mob gathered late at night near the White House and shouted insultingly, "Huzza for Clay!" "A Bank! A Bank!" "Down with the Veto!"

The stunned Whig leaders tried once again. Striving to meet Tyler's objections to a "Fiscal Bank," they passed another bill providing for a

"Fiscal Corporation." But the president, still unbending, vetoed the offensive substitute. Democrats were jubilant: they had been saved from another financial "monster" only by the pneumonia that had felled Harrison.

Whig extremists, boiling with indignation, condemned Tyler as "His Accidency" and as an "Executive Ass." Widely burned in effigy, he received numerous letters threatening him with death. A wave of influenza then sweeping the country was called the "Tyler grippe." To the delight of Democrats, the stiff-necked Virginian was formally expelled from his party by a caucus of Whig congressmen, and a serious attempt to impeach him was made in the House of Representatives. His entire cabinet resigned in a body, except Secretary of State Webster, who was then in the midst of delicate negotiations with England.

The proposed Whig tariff also felt the prick of the president's well-inked pen. Surprisingly enough, Tyler did sign a law passed in 1841 for bringing additional revenue to the depression-drained Treasury. But he looked with a frosty eye on the major tariff scheme of the Whigs. It provided, among other features, for a distribution among the states of revenue from the sale of public lands in the West. Tyler could see no point in squandering federal money when the federal Treasury was not overflowing, and he again wielded an emphatic veto.

Chastened Clayites redrafted their tariff bill. They chopped out the offensive dollar-distribution scheme and pushed down the rates to about the moderately protective level of 1832, roughly 32 percent on dutiable goods. Tyler had no fondness for a protective tariff, but realizing the need for additional revenue, he reluctantly signed the law of 1842. In subsequent months, the pressure for higher customs duties slackened as the country gradually edged its way out of the depression. The Whig slogan, "Harrison, Two Dollars a Day and Roast Beef," was rewritten by unhappy Democrats to read, "Ten Cents a Day and Bean Soup."

A War of Words with England

Hatred of England during the nineteenth century came to a head periodically and had to be lanced by treaty settlement or by war. The poison had festered ominously by 1842.

"Life In An American Hotel" *An English caricature of American rudeness and readiness with the pistol. (Punch, 1856.)*

Anti-British passions were compounded of many ingredients. At bottom lay the bitter, red-coated memories of the two Anglo-American wars. In addition, the genteel pro-British Federalists had died out, eventually yielding to the boisterous Jacksonian Democrats. British travelers, sniffing with aristocratic noses at the crude scene, wrote acidly of American tobacco spitting, slave auctioneering, lynching, eye gouging, and other unsavory features of the rustic civilization. Travel books penned by these critics, whose views were avidly read on both sides of the Atlantic, stirred up angry outbursts in America.

But the literary fireworks did not end here. British magazines added fuel to the flames when, enlarging on the travel books, they launched sneering attacks on Yankee shortcomings. American journals struck back with "you're another" arguments, thus touching off the "Third War with England." Fortunately, this British-American war was fought with paper broadsides, and only ink was spilled. British authors, including Charles Dickens, entered the fray with gall-dipped pens, for they were being denied rich royalties by the absence of an American copyright law.*

Sprawling America, with expensive canals to dig and railroads to build, was a borrowing nation in the nineteenth century. Imperial Britain, with its overflowing coffers, was a lending nation. The tightfisted creditor is never popular with the debtor, and the phrase "bloated British bondholder" rolled bitterly from many an American tongue. When the panic of 1837 broke, and several states defaulted on their bonds or repudiated them openly, honest Englishmen assailed Yankee trickery. One of them offered a new stanza for an old song:

> Yankee Doodle borrows cash,
> Yankee Doodle spends it,
>   And then he snaps his fingers at
> The jolly flat [simpleton] who lends it.

Troubles of a more dangerous sort came closer to home in 1837, when a short-lived insurrection erupted in Canada. It was supported by such a small minority of Canadians that it never had a real chance of success. Yet hundreds of hot-blooded Americans, hoping to strike a blow for freedom against the hereditary enemy, furnished military supplies or volunteered for armed service. The Washington regime tried arduously, though futilely, to uphold its weak neutrality regulations. But again, as in the case of Texas, it simply could not enforce unpopular laws in the face of popular opposition.

A provocative incident on the Canadian frontier brought passions to boil in 1837. An American steamer, the *Caroline*, was engaged in carrying supplies to the insurgents across the swift Niagara River. It was finally attacked on the New York shore by a determined British force, which set the vessel on fire. Lurid American illustrators showed the flaming ship, laden with shrieking souls, plunging over the Niagara Falls. The craft evidently sank short of the falls, and only one American was killed.

This unlawful invasion of American soil—a counterviolation of neutrality—had alarming aftermaths. The Washington officials lodged vigorous but ineffective protests. Three years later, in 1840, the incident was dramatically revived in the state of New York. A Canadian named McLeod, after allegedly boasting in a tavern of his part in the *Caroline* raid, was arrested and indicted for murder. The London Foreign Office, which regarded the *Caroline* raiders as members of an armed force and not as criminals, made clear that his execution would mean war. Fortunately, McLeod was freed after establishing an alibi. It must have been airtight, for it was good enough to convince a New York jury. The tension forthwith eased, but it snapped taut again in 1841, when British officials in the Bahamas offered asylum to 130 Virginia slaves who had rebelled and captured the American ship *Creole*.

Manipulating the Maine Maps

An explosive controversy of the early 1840s involved the Maine boundary dispute. The St. Lawrence River is icebound several months of

---

*Not until 1891 did Congress extend copyright privileges to foreign authors.

the year, as the British, remembering the War of 1812, well knew. They were determined, as a defensive precaution against the Yankees, to build a road westward from the seaport of Halifax to Quebec. But the proposed route ran through disputed territory—claimed also by Maine under the misleading peace treaty of 1783. Tough-knuckled lumberjacks from both Maine and Canada entered the disputed no-man's-land of the tall-timbered Aroostook River Valley. Ugly fights flared up and both sides summoned the local militia. The small-scale lumberjack clash, which was dubbed the "Aroostook War," threatened to widen into a full-dress shooting war.

As the crisis deepened in 1842, the London Foreign Office took an unusual step. It sent to Washington a nonprofessional diplomat, the conciliatory financier Lord Ashburton, who had married a wealthy American woman. He speedily established cordial relations with Secretary Webster, who had recently been lionized during a visit to England.

The two statesmen, their nerves frayed by protracted negotiations in the heat of a Washington summer, finally agreed to compromise on the Maine boundary. On the basis of a rough, split-the-difference arrangement, the Americans were to retain some 7,000 square miles (18,130 square kilometers) of the 12,000 square miles (31,080 square kilometers) of wilderness in dispute. The British got less land

> The London Morning Chronicle greeted the Webster-Ashburton treaty thusly: "See the feeling with which the treaty has been received in America; mark the enthusiasm it has excited. What does this mean? Why, either that the Americans have gained a great diplomatic victory over us, or that they have escaped a great danger, as they have felt it, in having to maintain their claim by war."

but won the desired Halifax-Quebec route. During the negotiations the *Caroline* affair, dragged out since 1837, was patched up by an exchange of diplomatic notes.

The surrender of 5,000 square miles (12,950 square kilometers) of allegedly American soil to the British proved highly unpopular, especially among loyal Maine citizens. One irate United States senator branded the treaty a "solemn bamboozlement." But Webster had obtained an ancient map which indicated, ironically, that the British were entitled to the entire area in dispute. When he secretly displayed his find in Washington, the treaty quickly slipped through the Senate on greased skids.

British imperialists likewise condemned Lord Ashburton for his "capitulation." But their opposition also evaporated when the London officials turned up with another yellowing map: it proved that the *Americans* were entitled to the entire area in contention. Thus each party to the negotiation secretly held the other's trump card in the historic "Battle of the Maps."

Historians have since proved that the United States had a valid claim to the entire territory. This fact was not known at the time, perhaps fortunately, for the British were in no mood to give up the Halifax route. The yielding of 5,000 square miles (12,950 square kilometers) of pine-forested land, at least in 1842, seemed like a cheap price to pay for avoiding a senseless war.

An overlooked bonus was won in the same treaty when the British, in adjusting the boundary to the west, surrendered 6,500 square miles (16,835 square kilometers). The area was later found to contain the priceless Mesabi iron ore of Minnesota.

Maine Boundary Settlement, 1842

The Lone Star of Texas Shines Alone

The jilted Texas bride, during the uncertain eight years since 1836, had led a precarious existence. Mexico, refusing to recognize her independence, regarded the Lone Star Republic as a province in revolt, to be reconquered in the future. Mexican officials loudly threatened war if the American eagle should gather the fledgling republic under its protective wings.

The Texans were forced to maintain a costly military establishment. Vastly outnumbered by their Mexican foe, they could not tell when he would strike again. Mexico actually did make two halfhearted raids which, though ineffectual, foreshadowed more fearsome efforts. Confronted with such perils, Texas was driven to open negotiations with England and France, in the hope of securing the defensive shield of a protectorate. In 1839 and 1840, the Texans concluded treaties with France, Holland, and Belgium.

Britain was intensely interested in an independent Texas. Such a republic would check the southward surge of the American colossus, whose bulging biceps posed a constant threat to nearby British possessions in the New World. A puppet Texas, dancing to strings pulled by Britain, could be turned upon the Yankees. Subsequent clashes would create a smoke-screen diversion, behind which foreign powers could move into the Americas and challenge the insolent Monroe Doctrine. French schemers were likewise attracted by the hoary game of divide and conquer. These actions would result, they hoped, in the fragmentation and militarization of America.

Dangers threatened from other foreign quarters. British abolitionists were busily intriguing for a foothold in Texas. If successful in freeing the few blacks there, they presumably would inflame the nearby slaves of the South. In addition, British merchants regarded Texas as a potentially important free-trade area—an offset to the tariff-walled United States. British manufacturers likewise perceived that those vast Texan plains constituted one of the great cotton-producing areas of the future. An independent Texas would relieve British looms of their fatal dependence on American fiber—a supply that might be cut off in time of crisis by embargo or war.

The Belated Texas Nuptials

Partly because of the fears aroused by British schemers, Texas became a leading issue in the presidential campaign of 1844. The foes of expansion assailed annexation, while southern hotheads cried, "Texas or Disunion." The proexpansion Democrats under James K. Polk finally triumphed over the Whigs under Henry Clay, the hardy perennial candidate. Lame-duck President Tyler thereupon interpreted the narrow Democratic victory, with dubious accuracy, as a "mandate" to acquire Texas.

Eager to crown his troubled administration with this splendid prize, Tyler deserves much of the credit for shepherding Texas into the fold. Many "conscience Whigs" feared that Texas in the Union would be red meat to nourish the lusty "slave power." Aware of their opposition, Tyler despaired of securing the needed two-thirds vote for a treaty in the Senate. He therefore arranged for annexation by a joint resolution. This solution required only a simple majority in both houses of Congress. After a spirited debate, the resolution passed early in 1845, and Texas was formally invited to become the twenty-eighth star on the American flag. After some coyness, the waiting bride unpacked her mildewing wedding dress and was formally embraced as a full-fledged state.

Mexico angrily charged that the Americans had despoiled it of Texas. This was to some extent true in 1836, but hardly true in 1845, for the area was no longer Mexico's to be despoiled of. As the years stretched out, realistic observers could see that the Mexicans would not be able to reconquer their lost province. Yet Mexico left the Texans dangling by denying their right to dispose of themselves as they chose.

By 1845, the Lone Star Republic had become a danger spot, inviting foreign intrigue that menaced the American people. Its continued existence as an independent nation threatened to involve the United States in a series of ruinous wars, both in America and in Europe. Americans were in a "lick all creation" mood when they sang "Uncle Sam's Song to Miss Texas":

> If Mexy back'd by secret foes,
>   Still talks of getting you, gal;
> Why we can lick 'em all you know
>   And then annex 'em too, gal.

What other power would have spurned the imperial domain of Texas? The bride was so near, so rich, so fair, so willing. Whatever the peculiar circumstances of the Texas revolution, the United States can hardly be accused of unseemly haste in achieving annexation. Nine long years were surely a decent wait between the beginning of the courtship and the consummation of the marriage.

Oregon Fever Populates Oregon

The so-called Oregon Country was an enormous wilderness. It sprawled magnificently west of the Rockies to the Pacific Ocean, and north of California to the line of 54° 40′—the present southern tip of the Alaska panhandle. All or substantial parts of this immense area were claimed at one time or another by four nations: Spain, Russia, Britain, and the United States.

Two claimants dropped out of the scramble. Spain, though the first to raise its banner in Oregon, bartered away its claims to the United States in the so-called Florida Treaty of 1819. The Russian bear retreated to the line of 54° 40′ by the treaties of 1824 and 1825 with America and Britain. These two remaining rivals now had the field to themselves.

British claims to Oregon were strong—at least to that portion north of the Columbia River. They were based squarely on prior discovery and exploration, on treaty rights, and on actual occupation. The most important colonizing agency was the far-flung Hudson's Bay Company, which was trading profitably with the Indians of the Pacific Northwest for their furs.

Americans, for their part, could also point pridefully to exploration and occupation. Cap-

Oregon Fever   *Thousands of pioneers like these pulling away from St. Louis said farewell to civilization as they left the Mississippi River and headed across the untracked plains to Oregon in the 1840s. (St. Louis Art Museum, Eliza McMillan Purchase Fund.)*

The Oregon Controversy

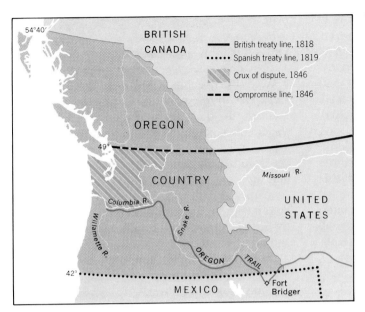

tain Robert Gray in 1792 had stumbled upon the majestic Columbia River, which he named after his ship; and the famed Lewis and Clark expedition of 1804–1806 had ranged overland through the Oregon Country to the Pacific. This shaky American toehold was ultimately strengthened by the presence of missionaries and other settlers, a sprinkling of whom reached the grassy Willamette River Valley, south of the Columbia, in the 1830s. These men and women of God, in saving the soul of the Indian, were instrumental in saving the soil of Oregon for the United States. They stimulated interest in a faraway domain that countless Americans had earlier assumed would not be settled for centuries.

> In winning Oregon the Americans had great faith in their procreative powers. "Our people are spreading out," boasted one congressman in 1846, "with the aid of the American multiplication table. Go to the West and see a young man with his mate of eighteen; after the lapse of thirty years, visit him again, and instead of two, you will find twenty-two. That is what I call the American multiplication table."

Scattered American and British pioneers in Oregon continued to live peacefully side by side. At the time of negotiating the Treaty of 1818, the United States had sought to divide the vast domain at the forty-ninth parallel. But the British, who regarded the Columbia River as the St. Lawrence of the West, were unwilling to yield this vital artery. A scheme for peaceful "joint occupation" was thereupon adopted, pending future settlement.

The handful of Americans in the Willamette Valley was suddenly multiplied in the early 1840s, when "Oregon fever" seized hundreds of restless pioneers. In increasing numbers their creaking covered wagons jolted over the 2,000-mile (3,200-kilometer) Oregon Trail as the human rivulet widened into a stream.* By 1846 there were about five thousand American settlers south of the Columbia River, some of them tough "border ruffians," expert with bowie knife and "revolving pistol."

The British, in the face of this rising torrent of humanity, could muster only seven hundred

---

*The average rate of progress in covered wagons was 1 to 2 miles an hour. This amounted to about 100 miles (161 kilometers) a week, or about five months for the entire journey. Thousands of humans, in addition to horses and oxen, died en route. One estimate is seventeen deaths a mile for men, women, and children.

or so subjects north of the Columbia. Losing out lopsidedly in the population race, they were beginning to see the wisdom of arriving at a peaceful settlement before being engulfed by their neighbors.

A curious fact is that only a relatively small segment of the Oregon Country was in actual controversy by 1845. The area in dispute consisted of the rough triangle between the Columbia River on the south and the 49th parallel on the north. Britain had repeatedly offered the line of the Columbia; America had repeatedly offered the forty-ninth parallel. The whole fateful issue was now tossed into the presidential election of 1844, where it was largely overshadowed by the question of annexing Texas.

A Mandate (?) for Manifest Destiny

The two major parties nominated their presidential standard-bearers in May 1844. Ambitious but often frustrated Henry Clay, easily the most popular man in the country, was enthusiastically chosen by the Whigs at Baltimore. The Democrats, meeting later in the same city, seemed hopelessly deadlocked. Finally the expansionists, dominated by the pro-Texas southerners, trotted out and nominated James K. Polk of Tennessee, the nation's first "dark horse" or "surprise" presidential candidate.

Polk may have been a dark horse, but he was hardly an unknown or decrepit nag. Speaker of the House of Representatives for four years and governor of Tennessee for two terms, he was a determined, industrious, ruthless, and intelligent public servant. Sponsored by Andrew Jackson, his friend and neighbor, he was rather implausibly built up by Democrats as yet another "Young Hickory." Whigs attempted to jeer him into oblivion with the taunt, "Who is James K. Polk?" They soon found out.

The campaign of 1844 was in part an expression of the mighty emotional upsurge known as Manifest Destiny. Countless citizens in the 1840s and 1850s, feeling a sense of mission, believed that Almighty God had "manifestly" destined the American people for a hemispheric career. They would irresistibly spread their uplifting and ennobling democratic institutions over at least the entire continent, and possibly over South America as well. Land greed and ideals were thus conveniently conjoined.

Expansionist Democrats were strongly swayed by the intoxicating spell of Manifest Destiny. They came out flat-footedly in their platform for the "Reannexation of Texas"* and the "Reoccupation of Oregon," all the way to 54° 40′. Out-bellowing the Whig log-cabinites in the game of slogans, they shouted "All of Oregon or None." They also condemned Clay as a "corrupt bargainer," a dissolute character, and a slaveowner. (Their own candidate, Polk, also owned slaves—a classic case of the pot calling the kettle black.)

The Whigs, as noisemakers, took no back seat. They countered with such slogans as "Hooray for Clay" and "Polk, Slavery, and Texas, or Clay, Union, and Liberty." They also spread the lie that a gang of Tennessee slaves had been seen on their way to a southern market with the initials J.K.P. (James K. Polk) branded on them.

On the crucial issue of Texas, the acrobatic Clay tried to ride two horses at once. The "Great Compromiser" appears to have compromised away the presidency when he wrote a series of confusing letters. They seemed to say that while he personally favored annexing slaveholding Texas (an appeal to the South), he also favored postponement (an appeal to the North). He might have lost more ground if he had not "straddled," but he certainly alienated the more ardent antislaveryites.

In the stretch drive, "Dark Horse" Polk nipped Henry Clay at the wire, 170 to 105 votes in the Electoral College and 1,338,464 to 1,300,097 in the popular column. Clay would have won if he had not lost New York State by a scant 5,000 votes. There the tiny antislavery Liberty party absorbed nearly 16,000 votes, many of which would otherwise have gone to the unlucky Kentuckian. Ironically, the anti-Texas Liberty party, by helping to ensure the

---

*The United States had given up its claims to Texas in the so-called Florida Purchase Treaty with Spain in 1819 (see p. 225). The slogan "Fifty-four forty or fight" was evidently not coined until two years later, in 1846.

election of pro-Texas Polk, hastened the annexation of Texas.

Land-hungry Democrats, flushed with victory, proclaimed that they had received a mandate from the voters to take Texas. But a presidential election is seldom, if ever, a clear-cut mandate on anything. The only way to secure a true reflection of the voters' will is to hold a special election on a given issue. The picture that emerged in 1844 is not one of mandate but of muddle. What else could there have been when the results were so close, the personalities so colorful, and the issues so numerous—including Oregon, Texas, the tariff, slavery, the bank, and internal improvements? Yet this unclear "mandate" was interpreted by President Tyler as a clear mandate to annex Texas—and he signed the joint resolution three days before leaving the White House.

Polk the Purposeful

"Young Hickory" Polk, unlike "Old Hickory" Jackson, was not an impressive figure. Of middle height (5 feet 8 inches; 1.72 meters), lean, white-haired (worn long), gray-eyed, and stern-faced, he took life seriously and drove himself mercilessly into a premature grave. His burdens were increased by an unwillingness to delegate authority. Methodical and hardworking but not brilliant, he was shrewd, narrow, conscientious, and persistent. "What he went for he fetched," wrote a contemporary. Purposeful in the highest degree, he developed a positive four-point program and with remarkable success achieved it completely in less than four years.

One of Polk's goals was a lowered tariff. His secretary of the treasury, wispy Robert J. Walker, devised a tariff-for-revenue bill that reduced the average rates of the Tariff of 1842 from about 32 percent to 25 percent. With the strong support of low-tariff southerners, Walker lobbied the measure through Congress, though not without loud complaints from the Clayites, especially in New England and the middle states, that American manufacturing would be ruined. But these prophets of doom missed the mark. The Walker Tariff of 1846 proved to be an excellent revenue producer, largely because

James K. Polk (1795–1849) *Distinguished for both determination and deviousness, Polk added more territory to the United States (by questionable means) than any other president. In tenaciously pursuing his goals, he broke himself down with overwork and died 103 days after his single term ended. His childless wife (and secretary) had banned all drinking and dancing in the White House. (National Archives.)*

it was followed by boom times and heavy imports.

A second objective of Polk was the restoration of the independent treasury, unceremoniously dropped by the Whigs in 1841. Probank Whigs in Congress raised a storm of opposition, but victory at last rewarded the president's efforts in 1846.

The third and fourth points on Polk's "must list" were the acquisition of California and the settlement of the Oregon dispute.

House Vote on Tariff of 1846*

REGIONS	FOR	AGAINST
New England	9	19
Middle states	18	44
West and Northwest	29	10
South and Southwest	58	20
TOTAL	114	93

*Compare vote on 1832 tariff, p. 251.

President Polk's Flimsy House of Cards *He appears to be hatching troublesome eggs relating to vexatious issues. (Yankee Doodle.)*

and that the turbulent American hordes might one day seize the Oregon Country. Why fight a hazardous war over this wilderness on behalf of an unpopular monopoly, the Hudson's Bay Company, which had already "furred out" much of the area anyhow?

Early in 1846 the British, hat in hand, came around and themselves proposed the line of 49°. President Polk, irked by the previous rebuff, threw the decision squarely into the lap of the Senate. The senators speedily accepted the offer and approved the subsequent treaty, despite a few diehard shouts of "fifty-four forty forever!" and "Every foot or not an inch!" The fact that the United States was then a month deep in a war with Mexico doubtless influenced the Senate's final vote.

Satisfaction with the Oregon settlement among Americans was not unanimous. The northwestern states, hotbed of Manifest Destiny and "fifty-four fortyism," joined the antislavery forces in condemning what they regarded as a base betrayal by the South. Why *all* of Texas and not *all* of Oregon? Because, sneered the expansionist Senator Benton of Missouri, "Great Britain is powerful and Mexico is weak."

So Polk, despite all the campaign bluster, got neither "fifty-four forty" nor a fight. But he did get something that in the long run was better: a reasonable compromise without shedding a drop of blood.

"Reoccupation" of the "whole" of Oregon had been promised northern Democrats in the campaign of 1844. But southern Democrats, once they had annexed Texas, rapidly cooled off. Polk, himself a southerner, had no intention of insisting on the 54° 40′ pledge of his own platform. But feeling bound by the three offers of his predecessors to London, he again proposed the compromise line of 49°. The British minister in Washington, on his own initiative, brusquely spurned this olive branch.

The next move on the Oregon chessboard was up to Britain. Fortunately for peace, the ministry began to experience a change of heart. British antiexpansionists ("Little Englanders") were now persuaded that the Columbia River after all was not the St. Lawrence of the West

Ridiculous Exhibition *"Yankee noodle" putting his head into the British lion's mouth. British view of American bluster on the Oregon issue. (Punch, 1846.)*

Misunderstandings with Mexico

Faraway California was another worry of Polk's. He and other disciples of Manifest Destiny had long coveted its verdant valleys, and especially the spacious bay of San Francisco. This splendid harbor was widely regarded as America's future gateway to the Pacific Ocean.

The population of California in 1845 was curiously mixed. It consisted of some seven thousand sun-blessed Spanish-Mexicans, plus more than ten times as many dispirited Indians. There were fewer than a thousand foreigners, mostly Americans, some of whom had "left their consciences" behind them as they rounded Cape Horn. Given time, these transplanted Yankees might yet bring California into the Union by "playing the Texas game."

Polk was eager to buy California from Mexico, but relations with Mexico City were dangerously embittered. Among other friction points, the United States had claims against the Mexicans for some $3 million in damages to American citizens and their property. The revolution-riddled regime in Mexico had formally agreed to assume most of this debt but had been forced to default on its payments.

A more serious bone of contention was Texas. The Mexican government, after threatening war if the United States should acquire the Lone Star Republic, had recalled its minister from Washington following annexation. Diplomatic relations were completely severed.

Deadlock with Mexico over Texas was further tightened by a question of boundaries. During the long era of Spanish-Mexican occupation, the southwestern boundary of Texas had been the Nueces River. But the expansive Texans, on rather farfetched grounds, were claiming the more southerly Rio Grande instead. Polk, for his part, felt a strong moral obligation to defend Texas in her claim, once she was annexed.

The Mexicans were far less concerned about this boundary quibble than the United States. In their eyes all of Texas was still theirs, although temporarily in revolt, and a dispute over the two rivers seemed pointless. Yet Polk was careful to keep American troops out of virtually all of the explosive no-man's-land between the Nueces and the Rio Grande, as long as there was any real prospect of peaceful adjustment.

The golden prize of California continued to cause Polk much anxiety. Disquieting rumors (now known to have been ill-founded) were circulating that the British lion was about to buy or seize California—a grab that Americans could not tolerate under the Monroe Doctrine. In a last desperate throw of the dice, Polk dispatched John Slidell to Mexico City as minister late in 1845. The new envoy, among other alternatives, was instructed to offer a maximum of $25 million for California and territory to the east. But the proud Mexican people would not even permit Slidell to present his "insulting" proposition.

American Blood on American (?) Soil

A frustrated Polk was now prepared to force a showdown. On January 13, 1846, he ordered four thousand men, under General Zachary Taylor, to march from the Nueces River to the Rio Grande, provocatively near Mexican forces. Polk's presidential diary reveals that he expected at any moment to hear of a clash. When none occurred after an anxious wait, he informed his cabinet on May 9, 1846, that he proposed to ask Congress to declare war on the basis of (1) unpaid claims and (2) Slidell's rejection. These, at best, were rather flimsy pretexts. Two cabinet members spoke up and said that they would feel better satisfied if Mexican troops should fire first.

That very evening, as fate would have it, news of bloodshed arrived. On April 25, 1846, Mexican troops had crossed the Rio Grande and attacked General Taylor's command, with a loss of sixteen Americans killed or wounded.

Polk, further aroused, sent a vigorous war message to Congress. He declared that despite "all our efforts" to avoid a clash, hostilities had been forced upon the country by the shedding of "American blood on the American soil." A patriotic Congress overwhelmingly voted for war, and enthusiastic volunteers cried, "Ho for the Halls of the Montezumas!" and "Mexico or Death!" Inflamed by the war fever, even antislavery Whig centers joined with the rest of the

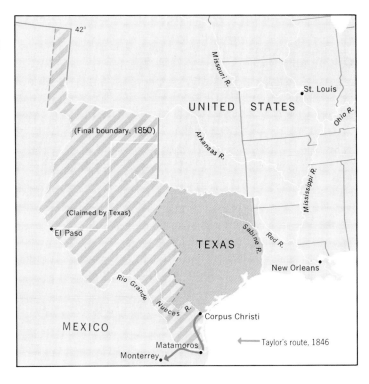

Texas, 1845–1846 *Texas President Mirabeau Buonaparte Lamar, flushed with imperial dreams, tried to secure the Texas claim to the large striped area on this map by leading a military expedition in 1841 against the Mexicans at Santa Fe. But the weak and outgunned "army" of the Lone Star Republic, made up mostly of American drifters and adventurers, was speedily smashed. The Texans drew in their horns thereafter and with renewed vigor sought annexation to the United States, rather than further expansion to the west of their precariously independent nation.*

nation, though they later condemned "Jimmy Polk's war." As James Russell Lowell of Massachusetts lamented,

> Massachusetts, God forgive her,
> She's akneelin' with the rest.

In his message to Congress Polk was making history—not writing it. If he had been a historian, he would have explained that American blood had been shed on soil that the Mexicans had good reason to regard as their own. A gangling, rough-featured Whig congressman from Illinois, one Abraham Lincoln, introduced certain resolutions that requested information as to the precise "spot" on American soil where American blood had been shed. He pushed his "spot" resolutions with such persistence that he came to be known as the "spotty Lincoln," who could die of "spotted fever." The more extreme antislavery agitators of the North, many of them Whigs, branded the president a liar—"Polk the Mendacious."

Did Polk provoke war? California was an imperative point in his program, and Mexico would not sell it at any price. The only way to get it was to use force or wait for an internal American revolt. Yet delay seemed dangerous, for the claws of the British lion might snatch the ripening California fruit from the talons of the American eagle. Grievances against Mexico were annoying yet tolerable; in later years America endured even worse ones. But in 1846 patience had ceased to be a virtue, as far as Polk was concerned. So he pushed the quarrel to a bloody showdown.

Both sides, in fact, were spoiling for a fight. Hotheaded Americans, especially southwestern expansionists, were eager to teach the Mexi-

> *Less than a year before he became president, Lincoln wrote that "the act of sending an armed force among the Mexicans was unnecessary, inasmuch as Mexico was in no way molesting or menacing the United States or the people thereof; and that it was unconstitutional, because the power of levying war is vested in Congress, and not in the President" (June 1, 1860).*

cans a lesson. The Mexicans, in turn, were burning to humiliate the "Bullies of the North." Possessing a considerable standing army, heavily overstaffed with generals, they boasted of invading the United States, freeing the black slaves, and lassoing whole regiments of Americans. They were hoping that the quarrel with Britain over Oregon would blossom into a full-dress war, as it came near doing, and further pin down the hated *yanquis*. A conquest of Mexico's vast and arid expanses seemed fantastic, especially in view of the bungling American invasion of Canada in 1812.

Both sides were fired by moral indignation. The Mexican people could fight with the flaming sword of righteousness, for had not the "insolent" Yankee picked a fight by polluting their soil? Many earnest Americans, on the other hand, sincerely believed that Mexico was the aggressor.

The Mastering of Mexico

Polk wanted California—not war. But when war came, he hoped to fight it on a limited scale and then pull out when he had won the prize. The dethroned Mexican dictator Santa Anna, then exiled with his teenage bride in Cuba, let it be known that if the American blockading squadron would permit him to slip into Mexico, he would sell out his country. This discreditable intrigue was finally carried through. But the double-crossing Santa Anna, self-styled "Napoleon of the West," rallied the Mexicans to a desperate defense of their soil.

American operations in the Southwest and in California were completely successful. In 1846 General Stephen W. Kearny led a detachment of seventeen hundred troops over the famous Santa Fe trail from Fort Leavenworth to Santa Fe. This sunbaked outpost, with its drowsy

War News from Mexico   *The new-fangled telegraph kept the nation closely informed of events in far-off Mexico. (National Academy of Design.)*

Major Campaigns of the Mexican War *The conflict was far more popular in the West than in the longer-settled parts of the country. The Mississippi Valley and Texas supplied nearly 50,000 volunteers to the army, while the original thirteen states furnished only 13,000. One lasting literary legacy of the war was Henry David Thoreau's famed essay "On the Duty of Civil Disobedience" (1849), written to justify his refusal to pay taxes in protest against the war.*

plazas, was easily captured. But before Kearny could reach California, the fertile province was won. When war broke out, Captain John C. Frémont, the dashing explorer, just "happened" to be there with several dozen well-armed men. In helping to overthrow Mexican rule in 1846, he collaborated with American naval officers and with the local Americans, who had hoisted the banner of the short-lived California Bear Flag Republic.

General Zachary Taylor meanwhile had been spearheading the main thrust. Known as "Old Rough and Ready" because of his iron constitution and incredibly unsoldierly appearance—he sometimes wore a Mexican straw hat—he fought his way across the Rio Grande into Mexico. After several gratifying victories, he reached Buena Vista. There, on February 22–23, 1847, his weakened force of five thousand men was attacked by some twenty thousand march-weary troops under Santa Anna. The Mexicans were finally repulsed with extreme difficulty, and overnight Zachary Taylor became the "Hero of Buena Vista." One Kentuckian was heard to say that "Old Zack" would be elected

president in 1848 by "spontaneous combustion."

Sound American strategy now called for a crushing blow at the enemy's vitals—Mexico City. General Taylor, though a good leader of modest-sized forces, could not win decisively in the semideserts of northern Mexico. The command of the main expedition, which pushed inland from the coastal city of Vera Cruz early in 1847, was entrusted to General Winfield Scott. A handsome giant of a man, Scott had emerged as a hero from the War of 1812 and had later earned the nickname of "Old Fuss and Feathers" because of his resplendent uniforms and strict discipline. He was severely handicapped in the Mexican campaign by inadequate numbers of troops, by expiring enlistments, by a more numerous enemy, by mountainous terrain, by disease, and by political backbiting at home. Yet he succeeded in battling his way up to Mexico City by September 1847 in one of the most brilliant campaigns in American military annals. He proved to be the most distinguished general produced by his country between 1783 and 1861.

Fighting Mexico for Peace

Polk was anxious to end the shooting as soon as he could secure his territorial goals. Accordingly, he sent along with Scott's invading army the chief clerk of the State Department, Nicholas P. Trist, who among other weaknesses was afflicted with an overfluid pen. Trist and Scott arranged for an armistice with Santa Anna, at a cost of $10,000. The wily dictator pocketed the bribe and then used the time to bolster his defenses.

Negotiating a treaty with a sword in one hand and a pen in the other was ticklish business. Polk, disgusted with his blundering envoy, abruptly recalled Trist. The wordy diplomat then dashed off a sixty-five-page letter explaining why he was not coming home. The president was furious. But Trist, grasping a fleeting opportunity to negotiate, signed the Treaty of Guadalupe Hidalgo on February 2, 1848, and forwarded it to Washington.

The terms of the treaty were breathtaking. They confirmed the American title to Texas and yielded the enormous area stretching westward to Oregon and the ocean and embracing coveted California. This total expanse, including Texas, was about one-half of Mexico. The United States agreed to pay $15 million for the land and to assume the claims of its citizens against Mexico in the amount of $3,250,000.

Polk submitted the treaty to the Senate. Although Trist had proved highly annoying, he had generally followed his original instructions. And speed was imperative. The antislavery Whigs in Congress—dubbed "Mexican Whigs" or "Conscience Whigs"—were condemning this "damnable war" with increasing heat. Having secured control of the House in 1847, they were even threatening to vote down supplies for the armies in the field. If they had done so, Scott probably would have been forced to retreat, and the fruits of victory might have been tossed away.

Another peril impended. A swelling group of expansionists, intoxicated by Manifest Destiny, was clamoring for all of Mexico. If America had seized it, the nation would have been saddled with an expensive and vexatious policing problem. Farseeing southerners like Calhoun,

Early in 1848 the New York *Evening* Post demanded: "Now we ask, whether any man can coolly contemplate the idea of recalling our troops from the [Mexican] territory we at present occupy . . . and . . . resign this beautiful country to the custody of the ignorant cowards and profligate ruffians who have ruled it for the last twenty-five years? Why, humanity cries out against it. Civilization and Christianity protest against this reflux of the tide of barbarism and anarchy." Such was one phase of Manifest Destiny.

alarmed by the mounting anger of antislavery agitators, realized that the South would do well not to be too greedy. The treaty was finally approved by the Senate, 38 to 14. Oddly enough, it was condemned both by those opponents who wanted all of Mexico and by opponents who wanted none of it.

Victors rarely pay an indemnity, especially after a costly conflict has been "forced" on them. Yet Polk, who had planned to offer $25 million before the war, arranged to pay $18,250,000 after winning the war. Cynics have charged that the Americans were pricked by guilty consciences; apologists have pointed proudly to the "Anglo-Saxon spirit of fair play." A decisive factor was the need for haste, while there was still a responsible Mexican government to carry out the treaty and before political foes in the United States, notably the antislavery zealots, sabotaged Polk's expansionist program.

Profit and Loss in Mexico

As wars go, the Mexican War was a small one. It cost some thirteen thousand American lives, most of them taken by disease. But the fruits of the fighting were enormous.

America's total expanse, already vast, was increased by about one-third (counting Texas)—an addition even greater than that of the Louisiana Purchase. A sharp stimulus was given to the spirit of Manifest Destiny, for as the proverb has it, the appetite comes with eating.

As fate ordained, the Mexican War was the blood-splattered schoolroom of the Civil War. The campaigns provided priceless field experience for most of the officers destined to become leading generals in the forthcoming conflict, including Captain Robert E. Lee and Lieutenant U. S. Grant. The Military Academy at West Point, founded in 1802, fully justified its existence through the well-trained officers. Useful also was the navy, which did valuable work in throwing a crippling blockade around Mexican ports. The Marine Corps, in existence since 1798, won new laurels, and to this day sings in its stirring hymn about the Halls of Montezuma.

The army waged war without defeat and without a major blunder, despite formidable obstacles and a half-dozen or so achingly long marches. Chagrined British critics, as well as other foreign skeptics, reluctantly revised upward their estimate of Yankee military prowess. Opposing armies, moreover, emerged with increased respect for each other. The Mexicans, though poorly led, fought heroically. At Chapultepec, near Mexico City, the teenage lads of the military academy there (*los niños*) perished to a boy.

Long-memoried Mexicans have never forgotten that their northern enemy tore away about half of their country. The argument that they were lucky not to lose all of it, and that they had been paid something for their land, did not lessen their bitterness. The war also marked an ugly turning point in the relations between the United States and Latin America as a whole. Hitherto, Uncle Sam had been regarded with some complacency, even friendliness. Henceforth, he was increasingly feared as the "Colossus of the North." Suspicious neighbors to the south condemned him as a greedy and untrustworthy bully, who might next despoil them of their soil.

Most ominous of all, the war rearoused the snarling dog of the slavery issue, and the beast did not stop yelping until drowned in the blood of the Civil War. Abolitionists assailed the Mexican conflict as one provoked by the southern "slavocracy" for its own evil purposes. As James Russell Lowell had Hosea Biglow drawl in his Yankee dialect:

> They jest want this Californy
>   So's to lug new slave-states in
> To abuse ye, an' to scorn ye,
>   An' to plunder ye like sin.

In line with Lowell's charge, the bulk of the American volunteers were admittedly from the South and Southwest. But, as in the case of

A Cartoon from Yankee Doodle, 1847 *This satiric drawing was symbolic of the "lick all creation" spirit of the times.*

PLUCKED:

THE MEXICAN EAGLE BEFORE THE WAR!   THE MEXICAN EAGLE AFTER THE WAR!

the Texan revolution, the basic explanation was proximity rather than conspiracy.

Quarreling over slavery extension also erupted on the floors of Congress. In 1846, shortly after the shooting started, Polk requested an apropriation of $2 million with which to buy a peace. Representative David Wilmot of Pennsylvania, fearful of the southern "slavocracy," introduced a fateful amendment. It stipulated that slavery should never exist in any of the territory to be wrested from Mexico.

The disruptive Wilmot amendment twice passed the House, but not the Senate. Southern members, unwilling to be robbed of prospective slave states, fought the restriction tooth and nail. Antislavery men in Congress and out, bat-tled no less bitterly for the exclusion of slaves. The "Wilmot Proviso," eventually endorsed by the legislatures of all but one of the free states, soon came to symbolize the burning issue of slavery in the territories.

In a broad sense, the opening shots of the Mexican War were the opening shots of the Civil War. President Polk left the nation the splendid physical heritage of California and the Southwest, but also the ugly moral heritage of an embittered slavery dispute. Mexicans could later take some satisfaction in knowing that the territory wrenched from them had proved to be a frightful apple of discord that could well be called Santa Anna's revenge.

Varying Viewpoints

Historians have long probed for the real meaning behind the pulse-stirring phrase *Manifest Destiny*. Some have emphasized the idealistic impulses behind continental expansion. Others have stressed the supposed "superiority" of Anglo-Saxon culture over Indian and Spanish civilizations. Still other writers have seen American expansion as simply another chapter in the familiar story of territorial conquest. In recent years, many historians, no doubt influenced by the general reappraisal of America's relations with the rest of the world, have stressed the "imperialistic" forces behind America's territorial growth. These writers identify economic considerations—the quest for markets, the desire for cheap land, the demands for the expansion of slavery—as the motivations for conquest. Scholars have also begun to show more interest in, and sympathy for, the people displaced or absorbed in America's sweep to the western sea. They condemn the racial doctrines that had earlier been used to justify expansionism.

Select Readings

Primary Source Documents

The colorful reminiscences of the pioneers are collected in Dale Morgan, ed., *Overland in 1846: Diaries and Letters of the California-Oregon Trail** (1963). The outbreak and conduct of the Mexican War come alive in the fascinating *Diary of James K. Polk*, edited by Milo Milton Quaife (1910).

Secondary Sources

A brief introduction is Ray A. Billington, *The Far Western Frontier, 1830–1860* (1956); more compre-hensive is his *Westward Expansion* (rev. ed. 1974). Still useful is Albert K. Weinberg, *Manifest Destiny* (1935), though it should be supplemented by two works of Frederick Merk, *Manifest Destiny and Mission in American History* (1963) and *Monroe Doctrine and Expansionism, 1843–1849* (1966). Paul Horgan, *Great River* (1954), is a magnificent history of the Southwest and the Rio Grande. *The Texas Revolution* is the subject of William C. Binkley's 1952 study. It should be supplemented by Frederick W. Merk, *Slavery and the Annexation of Texas* (1972). For the Pacific region, see Francis Parkman's classic

The California and Oregon Trail (1849) and Norman A. Graebner's general account, *Empire on the Pacific* (1955). On the conflict with Mexico, see K. Jack Bauer, *The Mexican-American War, 1846–1848* (1974). The other side's perspective is given in Gene M. Brack, *Mexico Views Manifest Destiny, 1821–1846* (1976). John H. Schroeder analyzes an important aspect of the conflict in *Mr. Polk's War: American Opposition and Dissent, 1846–1848* (1973). David M. Pletcher gives an overall view in *The Diplomacy of the Annexation of Texas, Oregon, and the Mexican War* (1973). See also Bernard DeVoto's popular *Year of Decision, 1846* (1943). William H. Goetzmann brings to life *Army Exploration in the American West, 1803–1863* (1959). Unusually colorful social history of the westward movement is provided in John Mack Faragher, *Women and Men on the Overland Trail* (1979), and John D. Unruh, Jr., *The Plains Across: The Overland Emigrants and the Trans-Mississippi West, 1840–1860* (1979). Julie Roy Jeffrey focuses on *Frontier Women* (1979), while William R. Brock summarizes the politics of the 1840s in *Parties and Political Conscience: American Dilemmas, 1840–1850* (1979).

17
Shaping the National Economy, 1790–1860

> *The progress of invention is really a threat [to monarchy].*
> *Whenever I see a railroad I look for a republic.*
>
> *Ralph Waldo Emerson, 1866*

The March of Mechanization

A gifted group of British inventors, beginning about 1750, perfected a series of machines for the mass production of textiles. This enslavement of steam multiplied the power of human muscles some ten thousandfold and ushered in the modern factory system.

The so-called industrial revolution has been misnamed. It was not a revolution in the sense of an overnight change or upheaval. The machines developed in England were gradually improved over several decades, and the people there were scarcely aware that a significant shift was taking place. Nor was the industrial revolution solely industrial. It was accompanied by a no less spectacular transformation in the methods of transportation and communication.

The factory system gradually spread from England—"the world's workshop"—to other lands. It took a generation or so to reach western Europe, and then the United States. Why was the youthful American Republic, destined to be an industrial giant, so slow to embrace the machine?

For one thing, virgin soil in America was cheap. Land-starved descendants of land-starved peasants were not going to coop themselves up in smelly factories when they might till their own acres in God's fresh air and sunlight. Labor was therefore generally scarce, and enough nimble hands to operate the machines were hard to find. Money for capital investment, moreover, was not plentiful in pioneering America. Raw materials lay undeveloped, undiscovered, or unsuspected. The Republic was one day to become the world's leading coal producer, but much of the coal burned in colonial times was imported all the way from England.

Just as labor was scarce, so were consumers. The young country at first lacked a domestic market large enough to make factory-scale manufacturing profitable.

Long-established British factories, which provided cutthroat competition, posed another problem. Their superiority was attested by the fact that a few unscrupulous Yankee manufacturers, out to make a dishonest dollar, learned to stamp their own products with faked English trademarks.

The British also enjoyed a monopoly of the textile machinery, whose secrets they were anxious to hide from foreign competitors. Parliament enacted laws, in harmony with the mercantilistic system, forbidding the export of the machines or the emigration of mechanics able to reproduce them.

Despite all these drawbacks, a surprising amount of small-scale manufacturing existed when the Republic was launched. As early as 1791, Alexander Hamilton reported that the wheels of seventeen different kinds of enterprises were humming. Yet the future industrial colossus was still snoring. Not until well past the middle of the next century did the value of the output of the factories exceed that of the farms.

Whitney Ends the Fiber Famine

Samuel Slater has been acclaimed the "Father of the Factory System" in America, and seldom can the paternity of a movement more properly be ascribed to one person. A skilled British mechanic of twenty-one, he was attracted by bounties being offered to English workers familiar with the textile machines. After memorizing the plans for the machinery, he escaped in disguise to America, where he won the backing of Moses Brown, a Quaker capitalist in Rhode Island. Laboriously reconstructing the essential apparatus with the aid of a blacksmith and a carpenter, he put into operation in 1791 the first efficient American machinery for spinning cotton thread.

The ravenous mechanism was now ready, but where was the cotton fiber? Handpicking 1 pound (0.45 kilogram) of lint from 3 pounds (1.36 kilograms) of seed was a full day's work for one slave, and this process was so expensive that cotton cloth was relatively rare. In 1785 eight bales of American cotton were seized for fraudulent entry at Liverpool, England. The incredulous officials charged that so much cotton could not have been produced in America.

Another mechanical genius, Massachusetts-born Eli Whitney, now made his mark. After graduating from Yale College, he journeyed to Georgia to serve as a private tutor while preparing for the law. There he was told that the poverty of the South would be relieved if someone could only invent a workable device for separating the seed from the short-staple cotton fiber. Within ten days, in 1793, he constructed a crude machine that was fifty times more effective than the handpicking process. The cotton gin (short for e*ngine*) was so simple that rivals infringed on his patent, and he was to net only relatively small profits from this particular brainchild.

Few machines have ever wrought so wondrous a change. The gin affected not only the history of America but that of the world. Almost overnight the raising of cotton became highly profitable, and the South was tied hand and foot to the throne of King Cotton. Human bondage had been dying out, but the insatiable demand for cotton reriveted the chains on the limbs of the luckless southern blacks.

South and North both prospered. Slave-driving planters cleared more acres for cotton, pushing the Cotton Kingdom westward off the depleted tidewater plains, over the Piedmont, and onto the black loam bottomlands of Alabama and Mississippi. Humming gins poured out avalanches of snowy fiber for the spindles of the Yankee machines, though for decades to come the mills of old England bought the lion's share of southern cotton. The American phase of the industrial revolution, which first blossomed in cotton textiles, was well on its way. Yet many decades were to pass before the old-fashioned spinning wheel was driven into the attic, and from there into the antique shops.

Winter Scene in Brooklyn c. 1817–1820, by Francis Guy (1760–1820) *Life in the cities of the early Republic was devoid of many of the amenities that made urban living attractive to later generations of Americans. This painting of Brooklyn, near the site of the later Brooklyn Bridge, shows that city-dwellers, like their country counterparts, still had to split their own firewood, draw their own water, and brave the icy elements as they went about their daily business. (The Brooklyn Museum, Gift of the Brooklyn Institute for Arts and Sciences.)*

Early textile factories merely spun the fiber into cotton thread. The actual weaving into cloth was done laboriously by hand in the home or by contract weavers. Not until 1814, at Waltham, Massachusetts, was the first dual-purpose plant established: it spun the fiber and wove the finished cloth under the same roof. Water power and steam power were gradually supplanting mother-and-daughter power.

Factories at first flourished most actively in New England, though branching out into the more populous areas of New York, New Jersey, and Pennsylvania. The South, increasingly wedded to the production of cotton, could boast of comparatively little manufacturing. Its capital was bound up in slaves; its local consumers for the most part were desperately poor.

New England was singularly favored as an industrial center for several reasons. Its narrow belt of stony soil discouraged farming and hence made manufacturing more attractive than elsewhere. A relatively dense population provided labor; shipping brought in capital; and snug seaports made easy the import of raw materials and the export of the finished products. Finally, the rapid rivers—notably the Merrimack in Massachusetts—provided abundant water power to turn the cogs of the machines.

One observer in 1836 published a newspaper account of conditions in some of the New England factories: "The operatives work thirteen hours a day in the summer time, and from daylight to dark in the winter. At half past four in the morning the factory bell rings, and at five the girls must be in the mills. . . . So fatigued . . . are numbers of girls that they go to bed soon after receiving their evening meal, and endeavor by a comparatively long sleep to resuscitate their weakened frames for the toil of the coming day."

By 1860, more than 400 million pounds (182,000 metric tons) of southern cotton poured annually into the gaping maws of over a thousand mills, mostly in New England.

Marvels in Manufacturing

America's factories spread slowly until about 1807, when there began the fateful sequence of the embargo, nonintercourse, and the War of 1812. Stern necessity dictated the manufacture of substitutes for normal imports, while the stoppage of European commerce was temporarily ruinous to Yankee shipping. Both capital and labor were driven from the waves onto the factory floor, as New England, in the striking phrase of John Randolph, exchanged the trident for the distaff. Generous bounties were offered by local authorities for homegrown goods; "Buy American" and "Wear American" became popular slogans; and patriotism prompted the wearing of baggy homespun garments. President Madison donned some at his inauguration, where he was said to have been a walking argument for the better processing of native wool.

But the manufacturing boomlet broke abruptly with the peace of Ghent in 1815. British competitors unloaded their dammed-up surpluses at ruinously low prices, and American newspapers were so full of British advertisements for goods on credit that little space was left for news. In one Rhode Island district, all 150 mills were forced to close their doors, ex-

cept the original Slater plant. Responding to pained outcries, Congress provided some relief when it passed the mildly protective Tariff of 1816.

As the factory system flourished, it embraced numerous other industries in addition to textiles. Prominent among them was the manufacturing of firearms, and here the wizardly Eli Whitney again appeared with an epochal contribution. Frustrated in his earlier efforts to monopolize the cotton gin, he turned to the mass production of muskets for the United States Army. Up to this time each part of a firearm had been hand-tooled, and if the trigger of one broke, the trigger of another might or might not fit. About 1798 Whitney seized upon the idea of having machines make each part, so that all the triggers, for example, would be as much alike as the successive imprints of a copperplate engraving. Journeying to Washington, he reportedly dismantled ten of his new muskets in the presence of skeptical officials, scrambled the parts together, and then quickly reassembled ten different muskets.

The principle of interchangeable parts was widely adopted by 1850, and it ultimately became the basis of modern mass-production, assembly-line methods. It gave to the North the vast industrial plant that ensured military preponderance over the South. The Yankee Eli Whitney, by perfecting the cotton gin, gave slavery a renewed lease on life and perhaps made inevitable the Civil War. The same Whitney, by popularizing the principle of interchangeable parts, caused factories to flourish in the North and contributed heavily to the winning of that war by the Union.

Industrialization in the North received another strong boost about 1850, with the perfection of the sewing machine for making clothing, both in the home and in the factory. Here emerged the figure of Elias Howe, who suffered such extreme poverty that when his wife died, he had to wear borrowed "Sunday" clothes to her funeral. He finally succeeded commercially where others had failed; and the royalties from his invention, patented in 1846, rapidly mounted to $4,000 a week. Even more successful in improving and promoting the machine was the versatile inventor Isaac Singer, whose name is still a household word. A new stitching device was also adapted before the Civil War for the mass production of boots and shoes.

The sewing machine was of incalculable significance. It was the foundation of the ready-made clothing industry, which took root about the time of the Civil War. It drove many a seamstress from the shelter of the private home to the factory, where, like a human robot, she tended the clattering mechanisms.

Momentous inventions seem to unchain the human imagination and stimulate other inventions. American ingenuity before the Civil War is best revealed by the number of patents registered in Washington. The decade ending in 1800 saw only 306; the decade ending in 1860 saw the amazing total of 28,000. America was truly the land of the fertile-minded and the home of the ingenious. Yet in 1838 the clerk of the Patent Office had resigned in despair, complaining that all worthwhile inventions had been discovered.

Elias Howe's First Sewing Machine *The young Republic often lacked the money to match the genius of its inventors, and Howe had to travel to England to secure the financial backing necessary to turn his revolutionary invention to practical use. (National Museum of History and Technology, Smithsonian Institution, Washington, D.C.)*

Building the Business World

All these advances spurred changes in the form and legal status of business organizations. To take proper advantage of the new machine gadgetry, people needed to command great concentrations of capital and to find means to organize efficiently their far-flung affairs. Capital began to accumulate more rapidly as the principle of limited liability gained acceptance—permitting individual investors, in cases of legal claims or bankruptcy, to risk no more than their own

"The patent system," said Abraham Lincoln in a lecture in 1859, ". . . secured to the inventor for a limited time exclusive use of his invention, and thereby added the fuel of interest to the fire of genius in the discovery and production of new and useful things." Ten years earlier Lincoln had received patent No. 6469 for a scheme to buoy steamboats over shoals. It was never practically applied, but he remains the only president ever to have secured a patent.

share of the corporation's stock. Fifteen Boston families formed one of the earliest and most powerful joint-capital ventures, the Boston Associates. They came to dominate not only the textile industry but also the railroad, insurance, and banking business in all of Massachusetts.

The state of New York gave a powerful boost to budding capitalism in 1848, when it passed a General Incorporation Law. Businesspeople no longer needed to apply for charters from the legislature; they could simply create a corporation if they complied with the terms of the law. "Free incorporation" statutes reflected the Jacksonian climate and were widely adopted in other states. They poured economic adrenaline into the veins of enterprising capitalists.

Other inventions tightened the sinews of an increasingly complex business world. Prominent among them was the telegraph, developed by patriarch-bearded Samuel F. B. Morse, whose name is immortalized by the Morse code. A distinguished portrait painter, he was compelled by poverty to forsake his brush for the telegraph key. After prolonged disappointments and hunger, he finally secured from Congress, to the accompaniment of the usual jeers, an appropriation of $30,000 to support his experiment with "talking wires."

In 1844 Morse strung a wire 40 miles (64 kilometers) from Washington to Baltimore and clicked out the historic message, "What hath God wrought?" The government might have controlled the telegraph, as it did the post office, but declined on the ground that the new device would not pay. Yet the invention brought fame and fortune to Morse, as he put distantly separated men of affairs in almost instant communication with one another.

Northern "Wage Slaves"

One ugly offspring of the factory system was an increasingly acute labor problem. Hitherto manufacturing had been done in the home, or in the small shop, where the master craftsman and his apprentice, rubbing elbows at the same bench, could maintain an intimate and friendly relationship. The industrial revolution submerged this personal association in the impersonal ownership of stuffy factories in "spindle cities." Around these, like tumors, the slumlike hovels of the "wage slaves" tended to cluster.

Clearly the early factory system did not shower its benefits evenly on all. While many owners waxed fat, workingpeople often wasted away at their workbenches. Hours were long, wages were low, and meals were skimpy and hastily gulped. Workers were forced to toil in unsanitary buildings that were poorly ventilated, lighted, and heated. They were forbidden by law to form labor unions to raise wages, for such cooperative activity was regarded as a criminal conspiracy. Not surprisingly, only twenty-four recorded strikes occurred before 1835.

The Master Craftsman *Dignity and pride of workmanship are evident in this tidy wheelwright's shop. Small-scale, intimate workplaces like this were eventually overshadowed by the mass-production, impersonal factory system as in the illustration on p. 297. (Collection of E. F. Fisher.)*

Textile Workers of Lawrence (Massachusetts)   *Engraving by Winslow Homer, a famous painter. Born in Boston in 1836, Homer first became famous as a magazine illustrator. His drawings of battlefield scenes for Harper's Weekly during the Civil War made the conflict come to life for thousands of home-bound readers. He abandoned illustration in 1876 and gained even greater renown as a painter in oils and watercolors, especially with his depictions of marine scenes and life among blacks. (Harper's Weekly, 1868.)*

Women and children were also sucked into the clanging mechanism of factory production. They typically toiled six days a week, earning a pittance for dreary stints of twelve or thirteen hours—"from dark to dark." The Boston Associates pridefully pointed to their textile mill at Lowell, Massachusetts, as a showplace factory. The workers were virtually all New England farm girls, carefully supervised on and off the job by watchful matrons. Escorted regularly to church from their company boardinghouses, forbidden to form unions, they were as disciplined and docile a labor force as any employer could wish. To the surprise of visitors, including Charles Dickens, they published their own newspaper. But the "Song of the Manchester Factory Girl" was no doubt overdrawn:

> She tends her loom, she watches the spindle,
>   And cheerfully talketh away;
> Mid the din of wheels, how her bright eyes
>   kindle!
>   And her bosom is ever gay.

Few observers harbored such happy illusions about child workers. In 1820, half the nation's industrial toilers were children under ten years of age. Victims of factory labor, many children were mentally blighted, emotionally starved, physically stunted, and even brutally whipped in special "whipping rooms." In Samuel Slater's mill of 1791, the first machine tenders were seven boys and two girls, all of whom were under twelve years of age.

Triumphs for American Toilers

The lot of the wage worker improved markedly in the 1820s and 1830s. In the full flush of Jacksonian democracy, many of the states granted the laboring man the vote. Brandishing the ballot, he first strove to lighten his burden through workingmen's parties. Aside from such goals as the ten-hour day, higher wages, and tolerable working conditions, he demanded public education for his children and an end to the inhuman practice of imprisonment for debt.

Employers, abhorring the rise of the "rabble" in politics, fought the ten-hour day to the last ditch. They argued that reduced hours would lessen production, increase costs, and demoralize the workers. Laborers would have so much leisure time that the Devil would lead them into mischief. A red-letter gain was at length registered for labor in 1840, when President Van Buren established the ten-hour day for federal employees on public works. In ensuing years a number of states gradually fell into line by reducing the hours of workingpeople.

Day laborers at last learned that their strongest weapon was to lay down their tools, even at the risk of prosecution under the law. Dozens of strikes erupted in the 1830s and 1840s, most of them for higher wages, some for the ten-hour day, and a few for such unusual goals as the right to smoke on the job. The workers usually lost more strikes than they won, for the employer could resort to such tactics as the importing of strikebreakers—often derisively called "scabs" or "rats," and often fresh off the boat from the Old World. Labor long raised its voice against the unrestricted inpouring of wage-depressing and union-busting immigrant workers.

Labor's early and painful efforts at organization had netted some 300,000 trade unionists by 1830. But such encouraging gains were dashed on the rocks of hard times following the severe depression of 1837. As unemployment spread, union membership shriveled. Yet toilers won a hope-giving legal victory in 1842. The supreme court of Massachusetts ruled in the case of *Commonwealth* v. *Hunt* that labor unions were not illegal conspiracies, provided that their methods were "honorable and peaceful." This enlightened decision did not legalize the strike overnight throughout the country, but it was a significant signpost of the times. Trade unions still had a rocky row to hoe, stretching ahead for about a century, before they could meet management on relatively even terms.

Western Farmers Reap a Revolution in the Fields

As smoke-belching factories altered the eastern skyline, flourishing farms were changing the face of the West. The trans-Allegheny region—especially the Ohio-Indiana-Illinois tier—was fast becoming the nation's breadbasket. Before long, it would become a granary to the world.

Pioneer farmers first hacked a clearing out of the forest and then planted their painfully furrowed fields to corn. The yellow grain was amazingly versatile. It could be fed to hogs ("corn on the hoof") or distilled into liquor ("corn in the bottle"). Both these products could be more easily transported than the bulky grain itself, and they became the early western farmer's staple market items. So many hogs were butchered, traded, or shipped at Cincinnati that the city was known as the "Porkopolis" of the West.

Most western produce was at first floated down the Ohio-Mississippi river system, to feed the lusty appetite of the booming Cotton Kingdom. But western farmers were as hungry for profits as southern slaves and planters were for food. These soil-tillers, spurred on by the easy availability of seemingly boundless acres, sought ways to bring more and more land into cultivation.

Ingenious inventors came to their aid. One of the first obstacles that frustrated the farmers was the thickly matted soil of the West, which snagged and snapped fragile wooden plows. John Deere of Illinois in 1837 finally produced a steel plow that broke the virgin soil. Sharp and

> *Violence broke out along the New York waterfront in 1836 when laborers striking for higher wages attacked "scabs." "The Mayor," Philip Hone's diary records, "who acts with vigour and firmness, ordered out the troops, who are now on duty with loaded arms. . . . These measures have restored order for the present, but I fear the elements of disorder are at work; the bands of Irish and other foreigners, instigated by the mischievous councils of the trades-union and other combinations of discontented men, are acquiring strength and importance which will ere long be difficult to quell."*

McCormick Reaper Works, 1850s *Contrast this scene of "Mass Production" with the workplace depicted in "The Master Craftsman" on p. 294. (McCormick Collection, State Historical Society of Wisconsin.)*

effective, it was also light enough to be pulled by horses, rather than oxen.

In the 1830s Virginia-born Cyrus McCormick contributed the most wondrous contraption of all: a mechanical mower-reaper. The clattering cogs of McCormick's horse-drawn machine were to the western farmers what the cotton gin was to the southern planters. Seated on his red-chariot reaper, a single husbandman could do the work of five men with sickles and scythes.

No other American invention cut so wide a swath. It made ambitious capitalists out of humble plowmen, who now scrambled for more acres on which to plant more fields of billowing wheat. Subsistence farming gave way to production for the market, as large-scale ("extensive"), specialized, cash-crop agriculture came to dominate the trans-Allegheny West. With it followed mounting indebtedness, as farmers bought more land and more machinery to work it. Soon hustling farmer-businesspeople were annually harvesting a larger crop than the South—which was becoming self-sufficient in food production—could devour. They began to dream of markets elsewhere—in the mushrooming factory towns of the East, or across the faraway Atlantic. But they were still largely landlocked. Commerce moved north and south

Harvesting Grain by Hand and by McCormick Reaper (Above, *Prints Division, New York Public Library;* below, *from a company advertisement.*)

on the river systems. Before it could begin to move east-west in bulk, a transportation revolution would have to occur.

Highways and Byways

In 1789, when the Constitution was launched, primitive methods of travel were still in use. Waterborne commerce, whether along the coast or on the rivers, was slow, uncertain, and often dangerous. Stagecoaches and wagons lurched over bone-shaking roads. Passengers would be routed out to lay nearby fence rails across muddy stretches, and occasionally horses would drown in muddy pits while wagons sank slowly out of sight.

Cheap and efficient carriers were imperative if raw materials were to be transported to the factories and if the finished product were to be delivered to the consumer. On December 3, 1803, a firm in Providence, Rhode Island, sent a shipment of yarn to a point 60 miles (97 kilometers) away, notifying the purchaser that the consignment could be expected to arrive in "the course of the winter."

A promising change for the better came in the 1790s, when a private company completed the Lancaster turnpike in Pennsylvania. It was a broad, hard-surfaced highway that thrust 62 miles (100 kilometers) westward, from Philadelphia to Lancaster. As drivers approached the toll gate, they were confronted with a barrier of sharp pikes, which were turned aside when they paid their toll. Hence, the term *turnpike*.

The Lancaster Pike proved to be a highly successful venture, returning as high as 15 percent annual dividends to its stockholders. It attracted a rich trade to Philadelphia and touched off a turnpike-building boom that lasted about twenty years. It also stimulated western development. The turnpikes beckoned to the canvas-covered Conestoga wagons, whose creakings heralded an advance that would know no real retreat.

Western road building, always expensive, encountered many obstacles. Looming large among them were the noisy states' righters, who opposed federal aid to local projects. Eastern states also protested against being bled of their populations by the westward-reaching arteries.

Westerners scored a notable triumph in 1811 when the federal government began to construct the elongated National Road, or Cumberland Road. This highway ultimately stretched from Cumberland, in western Maryland, to Vandalia, in Illinois, a distance of 591 miles (952 kilometers). The War of 1812 interrupted construction, and states' rights shackles on internal improvements hampered federal grants. But the thoroughfare was belatedly brought to its destination, in 1852, by a combination of aid from the states and the federal government.

The famed Cumberland Road, with numerous branches, was a marvelous stimulant to American prosperity. As the vital highway to the West, it made freight carrying cheaper and faster. It hastened the flow of European immigrants over the mountains; it swelled popula-

Cumberland (National) Road and Main Connections

tion centers; it enhanced land values. It also wrote a colorful chapter in the history of transportation. Brightly painted stagecoaches, named after prominent statesmen and pulled by four to six foam-flecked horses, careened down the dusty highroad at breakneck speed, often better than 20 miles (32 kilometers) an hour. The age of rapid land transportation was dawning.

Fulton Reverses the Rivers

The steamboat craze, which overlapped the turnpike craze, was touched off by an ambitious painter-engineer named Robert Fulton. Several other entrepreneurs had earlier built steamboats, but these craft had all proved unprofitable, largely because of weak engines and even weaker financing.

Fulton, shrewder and luckier than the others, won financial backing from a wealthy New Yorker. He installed a powerful steam engine in a vessel that posterity came to know as the *Clermont* but that a dubious public dubbed "Fulton's Folly." On a historic day in 1807, the quaint little ship, belching sparks from its single smokestack, churned steadily from New York City up the Hudson River toward Albany. It made the run of 150 miles (242 kilometers) in 32 hours.

The success of the steamboat was sensational. People could now in large degree defy wind, wave, tide, and downstream current. Within a few years Fulton had changed all of America's navigable streams into two-way arteries, thereby doubling their carrying capacity. Hitherto keelboats had been pushed up the Mississippi, with quivering poles and raucous profanity, at less than one mile an hour—a process that was prohibitively costly. Now the steamboats could churn rapidly against the current, ultimately attaining speeds in excess of 10 miles (16 kilometers) an hour. The mighty Mississippi had now met her master.

By 1820 there were some sixty steamboats on the Mississippi and its tributaries; by 1860, about one thousand, some of them luxurious river palaces. Keen rivalry among the swift and gaudy steamers led to memorable races. Excited passengers would urge the captain to pile on wood at the risk of bursting the boilers, which all too often exploded with tragic results for the floating firetraps.

Chugging steamboats played a vital role in the opening of the West and South, both of which were richly endowed with navigable rivers. Like bunches of grapes on a vine, population clustered along the banks of the broad-flowing streams. Cotton growers and other farmers made haste to take up the now-profitable virgin soil. Not only could they float their produce out to market but, hardly less important, they could ship in at low cost their shoes, hardware, and other manufactured necessities.

"Clinton's Big Ditch" in New York

A canal-cutting craze paralleled the boom in turnpikes and steamboats. A few canals had been built around falls and elsewhere in colonial days, but ambitious projects lay in the future. Resourceful New Yorkers, cut off from federal aid by states' righters, themselves dug the Erie Canal, linking the Great Lakes with the Hudson River. They were blessed with the driving leadership of Governor DeWitt Clinton, whose grandiose project was scoffingly called "Clinton's Big Ditch" or "the Governor's Gutter."

Begun in 1817, the canal eventually ribboned 363 miles (585 kilometers). On its completion in 1825, a garland-bedecked canal boat glided from Buffalo, on Lake Erie, to the Hudson River and on to New York harbor. There, with colorful ceremony, Governor Clinton emptied a cask of water from the lake to symbolize "the marriage of the waters."

The water from Clinton's cask baptized an Empire State. Mule-drawn passengers and bulky freight could now be handled with cheapness and dispatch, at the dizzy speed of 5 miles (8 kilometers) an hour. The cost of shipping a ton of grain from Buffalo to New York City fell from $100 to $5, and the time of transit from about twenty days to six.

Ever-widening economic ripples followed the completion of the Erie Canal. The value of land along the route skyrocketed, and new cities—such as Rochester and Syracuse—blossomed.

Erie Canal and Main Branches *The Erie Canal system, and others like it, tapped the fabulous agricultural potential of the Midwest, while canal construction and maintenance provided employment for displaced eastern farmers squeezed off the land by competition from their more productive midwestern cousins. The transportation revolution thus simultaneously expanded the nation's acreage under cultivation and speeded the shift of the work force from agricultural to manufacturing and "service" occupations. In 1820 more than three-quarters of American workers labored on farms; by 1850 only a little more than half of them were so employed.*

Industry in the state boomed. The new profitability of farming in the Old Northwest —notably in Ohio, Michigan, Indiana, Illinois— attracted thousands of European immigrants to the unaxed and untaxed lands now available. Flotillas of steamships soon plied the Great Lakes, connecting with canal barges at Buffalo. Interior waterside villages like Cleveland, Detroit, and Chicago exploded into mighty cities.

Other profound economic and political changes followed the completion of the canal. The price of potatoes in New York City was cut in half, and many dispirited New England farmers, no longer able to face this ruinous competition, abandoned their rocky holdings and went elsewhere. Some became mill hands, thus speeding the industrialization of America. Others, finding it easy to go west over the Erie Canal, took up new farmlands south of the Great Lakes, where they were joined by countless thousands of New Yorkers and other northerners. Still others shifted to fruit, vegetable, and dairy farming. These transformations in the Northeast showed how long-established local market structures could be swamped by the emerging behemoth of a continental economy.

A Set of Locks on the Erie Canal *An engineering marvel, it had to raise boats 571 feet (174 meters) from the Hudson to Lake Erie. Thousands of laborers died of afflictions ranging from malaria to snakebite—conspicuously Irish immigrant laborers, some of whom worked for $37\frac{1}{2}$ cents an hour plus whiskey. (Courtesy of the New-York Historical Society, New York City.)*

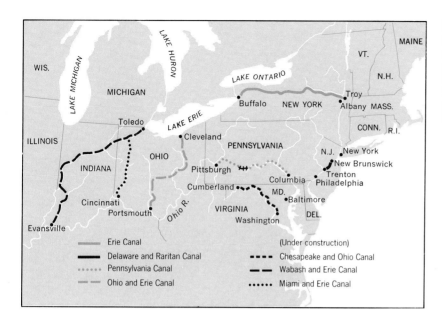

Principal Canals in 1840 *Note that the canals mainly facilitated east-west traffic, especially along the great Lake Erie artery. No comparable network of canals existed in the South—a disparity that helps to explain Northern superiority in the Civil War that came two decades later.*

The astonishing success of the Erie Canal stimulated competition, especially from the urban rivals of New York City. Ingenious Philadelphians, defying both geography and gravity, constructed a temporarily profitable canal over the Allegheny Mountains. At a unique portage, a special railroad lifted barges to an elevation of nearly 2,300 feet (700 meters), from which they were lowered on the other side.

A web of canals was likewise dug in the Old Northwest to connect with the Great Lakes and the Mississippi River. On one of the Ohio waterways, the youthful James A. Garfield, later to become president, drove balky mules down the towpath.

When the Iron Horse Was a Colt

The railroad proved to be the most significant contribution to a solution of the great American problem of distance. It was fast, reliable, cheaper than canals to construct, and not frozen over in winter. Able to go almost anywhere, even through the Allegheny barrier, it defied terrain and weather.

Early experiments with railroads involved the use of various kinds of power, including wind, dogs, horses, and finally steam. The first important line was begun by the Baltimore and Ohio Company, significantly on Independence Day, 1828. At the colorful dedication ceremony, the first stone was laid at Baltimore by Charles Carroll, then aged ninety, the only surviving signer of the Declaration of Independence. But the steam locomotive for railroads—truly a declaration of independence from primitive transportation—was not, as commonly supposed, a Yankee invention. It had already been used to a limited extent in England.

American locomotives, though soon to make the grade, encountered initial setbacks. A famous nine-mile race was staged in 1830 between a horse-drawn car and the "Tom Thumb," the crack locomotive of the Baltimore and Ohio. The noisy iron horse was winning when it broke down. The gray quadruped then clattered on to victory, amid wild cheers from the foes of mechanical progress. But dumb animals rapidly lost out, as numerous railroads began to radiate from the main cities like spokes from the hub of a wheel. By 1860, only thirty-two years after the Baltimore and Ohio ceremony, the United States boasted 30,000 miles (48,000 kilometers) of railroad track, three-fourths of it running through the rapidly industrializing North.

The Stourbridge Lion   *On August 8, 1829, at Honesdale, Pennsylvania, this smoke-belching beast made the first successful trip in America by a steam locomotive. (The Bettmann Archive.)*

Pioneer Railroad Promoters

Inevitably the hoarse screech of the locomotive sounded the doom of various vested interests. They railed against progress and in defense of their pocketbooks, as victims of change so often do. Turnpike investors and tavern keepers did not relish the loss of business, and farmers feared for their hay-and-horse market. The canal backers were especially violent. Mass meetings were held along the Erie Canal, and in 1833 the legislature of New York, anxious to protect its canal investment, prohibited the railroads from carrying freight—at least temporarily.

Objections to the Iron Monster did not end there. It was branded as undemocratic, for no ordinary citizen could own one. It was sacrilegious, for God had given humans and animals legs. Finally, it was a public menace. Sparks set fire to haystacks and houses, and supposedly frightened chickens into not laying eggs. Good old four-legged Dobbin was preferred. He sent out no sparks, carried his own fuel, made little noise, and would not explode.

Early railway coaches were torture chambers on wheels, and no place for weaklings or cowards. Live cinders burned holes in clothes—one woman found thirteen in her gown. The brakes were so feeble that the engineer might miss the station twice, both coming and backing up. The rails were flimsy iron strips fastened on wood; and appalling accidents turned the wooden "miniature hells" into flaming funeral pyres.

Railroad pioneers ran into additional obstacles. Arrivals and departures were conjectural; timetables were little better than ill-kept promissory notes. Further complications were caused by the variance in gauge (or space between the rails). When passengers came to a different line, they would often have to change cars, after wiping cinders from their eyes. In

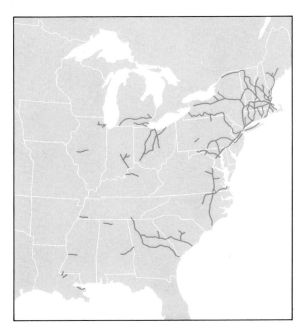

Railroads in Operation in 1850

Railroads in Operation in 1860   Note concentration in North.

1840 there were seven transfers between Philadelphia and Charleston. Violence flared up in Erie, Pennsylvania, in 1853, when the hotel and trucking workers rebelled. Fearing that the trains would go through without stopping, they unsuccessfully attempted to prevent standardization of the gauge.

But needed railway improvements were gradually installed. Gauges became standardized, safety devices were adopted, solid iron rails were laid, and the Pullman sleeping "palace" was introduced in 1859. America at long last was being bound together with ribs of iron—later steel.

The Transport Web Binds the Union

More than anything else, the desire of the East to tap the West stimulated the "transportation revolution." Until about 1830, the produce of the western region drained southward to the cotton belt or to the heaped-up wharves of New Orleans. The steamboat vastly aided the reverse flow of finished goods up the watery western ar-

teries and helped bind West and South together. But the truly revolutionary changes in commerce and communication came in the three decades before the Civil War, as canals and railroad tracks radiated out from the East, across the Alleghenies and into the blossoming heartland. The ditchdiggers and tie-layers were attempting nothing less than a conquest of nature itself. They would offset the "natural" flow of trade on the interior rivers by laying down an impressive grid of "internal improvements."

The builders succeeded beyond their wildest dreams. The Mississippi was increasingly robbed of its traffic, as goods moved eastward on chugging trains, puffing lake boats, and mule-tugged canal barges. Governor Clinton had in effect picked up the mighty Father of Waters and flung it over the Alleghenies, forcing it to empty into the sea at New York City. By the 1840s the city of Buffalo handled more western produce than New Orleans. Between 1836 and 1860, grain shipments through Buffalo increased a staggering sixtyfold. New York City became the seaboard queen of the nation, a gigantic port through which a vast hinterland

The Levee at New Orleans   *With the expansion of cotton-growing into the new states of the trans-Appalachian Southwest, and the coming of the steamboat, the entire Cotton Kingdom paid economic tribute to New Orleans, Queen City of the South. (The Granger Collection.)*

poured its wealth and to which it daily paid economic tribute.

By the eve of the Civil War, a truly continental economy had emerged. The principle of division of labor, which spelled productivity and profits in the factory, applied on a national scale as well. Each region now specialized in a particular type of economic activity. The South raised cotton for export to New England and old England; the West grew grain and livestock to feed factory workers in the East and in Europe; the East made machines and textiles for the other two regions.

The economic pattern thus woven had fateful political and military implications. Many southerners regarded the Mississippi as a silver chain that naturally linked together the upper valley states and the Cotton Kingdom. They were convinced, as secession approached, that some or all of these states would have to secede with them or be strangled. But they overlooked the man-made links that now bound the upper Mississippi Valley to the East in intimate commercial union. Southern rebels would have to fight not only Northern armies, but the tight bonds of an interdependent continental economy. Economically, the two northerly sections were Siamese twins.

The emergence of a specialized, continental-scale economy also had far-reaching social effects. As more and more Americans—mill hands as well as farmers, women as well as men—linked their economic fate to the burgeoning market economy, the self-sufficient households of colonial days were transformed. Most families had once raised all their own food, spun their own wool, and bartered with their neighbors for the few necessities they could not make themselves. In growing numbers, they now scattered to work for wages in the mills, or they planted just a few crops for sale at market and used the money to buy goods made by strangers in far-off factories. As store-bought fabrics, candles, and soap replaced

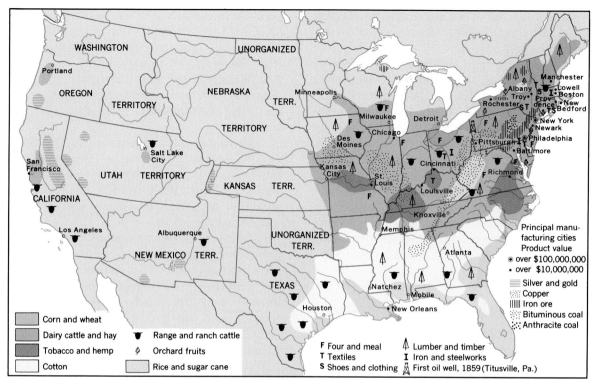

Industry and Agriculture, 1860   *Still a nation of farmers on the eve of the Civil War, Americans had nevertheless made an impressive start on their own industrial revolution, especially in the Northeast.*

homemade products, a quiet revolution occurred in the household division of labor and status. Traditional women's work was rendered superfluous and devalued. The home itself, once a center of economic production in which all family members cooperated, grew into a place of refuge from the world of work, a refuge that became increasingly the special and separate sphere of women.

Wealth and Poverty

Revolutionary advances in manufacturing and transportation brought increased prosperity to all Americans, but they also widened the gulf between the rich and the poor. Millionaires had been rare in the early days of the Republic, but by the eve of the Civil War several specimens of colossal financial success were strutting across

the national stage. Spectacular was the case of fur trader and real estate speculator John Jacob Astor, who left an estate of $30 million on his death in 1848.

Cities bred the greatest extremes of economic inequality. Unskilled workers, then as always, fared worst. Many of them came to make up a floating mass of "drifters," buffeted from town to town by the shifting prospects for menial jobs. These wandering workers accounted at various times for up to half the population of the brawling industrial centers. Though their numbers were large, they left little behind them but the homely fruits of their transient labor. Largely unstoried and unsung, they are among the forgotten men and women of American history.

Many myths about "social mobility" grew up over the buried memories of these luckless day laborers. Mobility did exist in industrializing

America—but not in the proportions that legend often portrays. Rags-to-riches success stories were relatively few.

Yet America, with its dynamic society and wide-open spaces, undoubtedly provided more "opportunity" than did the contemporary countries of the Old World—which is why millions of immigrants packed their bags and headed for New World shores. Moreover, a rising tide lifts all boats, and the improvement in overall standards of living was real. Wages for unskilled workers in a labor-hungry America rose about 1 percent a year from 1820 to 1860. This general prosperity helped defuse the potential class conflict that might otherwise have exploded—and that did explode in many European countries.

Commerce and Cables

A new pattern of American foreign trade also emerged in the antebellum years, though businesspeople concentrated on developing the wondrously rewarding domestic market. (Foreign commerce seldom added up to more than 7 percent of the national product.) Abroad as at home, cotton was king and regularly accounted for more than half the value of all American exports. After the repeal of the British exclusionary Corn Laws in 1846, the wheat gathered by McCormick's reapers began to play an increasingly important role in trade with Great Britain. Americans generally exported agricultural products and imported manufactured goods—and they generally imported more than they exported.

Most American foreign trade involved Great Britain. As time went on, a bustling Anglo-American transatlantic economy took shape. In 1818 New York's Black Ball Line inaugurated a regularly scheduled passenger and shipping service to England.

In 1858 Cyrus Field, a wealthy New York paper manufacturer, finally succeeded in stretching a cable between Newfoundland and Ireland. As "the greatest wire-puller of modern times," he had tried and failed in four previous attempts, amid much ridicule, to lay the cable through the 2 miles (3.2 kilometers) deep North Atlantic waters. When he achieved his goal, wild rejoicing rocked the nation. New York City reveled in a two-day cable carnival, and Queen Victoria exchanged congratulatory messages with President Buchanan. After three weeks and several hundred cablegrams, the cable went dead and remained useless for eight years.

A Clipper Ship   (The Peabody Museum of Salem, Massachusetts, photo by Mark Sexton.)

Fur Traders Descending the Missouri, 1844 *Missourian George Caleb Bingham captured in this painting a moment of calm in the usually strenuous life of the rough-and-tumble fur traders. The fragile dugout canoe on the ominously placid water, the tethered animal in the bow, and the recently shot duck (contrasted with the flock on the wing in the distant sky) evoke the pioneer's relentless battle with nature. (The Metropolitan Museum of Art, Morris K. Jesup Fund, 1933.)*

Heroes became villains overnight, and skeptics falsely accused the promoter of having sent faked messages so as to sell his stock at a high figure. But Field did not despair. In 1866, after the Civil War and another aborted try, he laid a heavier cable with gratifying success. The derided dreamer again became an honored hero.

Clipper Captains and Pony Riders

The United States merchant marine encountered rough sailing during much of the early nineteenth century. American vessels had been repeatedly laid up by the embargo, the War of 1812, and the panics of 1819 and 1837. The American naval designers made few contributions to maritime progress. A pioneer American steamer, the *Savannah*, had crept across the Atlantic in 1819, but it used sail most of the time

and was pursued for a day by a British captain who thought it afire.

In the 1840s and 1850s a golden age dawned for American shipping. Yankee naval yards, notably Donald McKay's at Boston, began to send down the ways sleek new craft called clipper ships. Long, narrow, and majestic, they glided across the sea under towering masts and clouds of canvas. In a fair breeze they could outrun any steamer.

> Stately as churches, swift as gulls,
> They trod the oceans, then—
> No man had seen such ships before
> And none will see again*

───────────

*"Clipper Ships and Captains," from *A Book of Americans*, by Rosemary & Stephen Vincent Benét. Copyright, 1933, by Rosemary & Stephen Vincent Benét. Copyright renewed ©, 1961, by Rosemary Carr Benét. Reprinted by permission of Brandt & Brandt Literary Agency, Inc.

Main Routes West before the Civil War   *Mark Twain described his stagecoach trip to California in the 1860s:*

We began to get into country, now, threaded here and there with little streams. These had high, steep banks on each side, and every time we flew down one bank and scrambled up the other, our party inside got mixed somewhat. First we would all be down in a pile at the forward end of the stage, . . . and in a second we would shoot to the other end, and stand on our heads. And . . . as the dust rose from the tumult, we would all sneeze in chorus, and the majority of us would grumble, and probably say some hasty thing, like: "Take your elbow out of my ribs!—can't you quit crowding?"

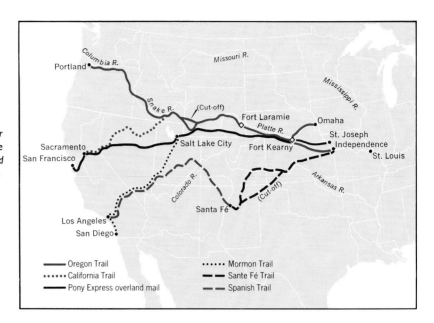

The stately clippers sacrificed cargo space for speed, and their captains made killings by hauling high-value cargoes in record times. They wrested much of the tea-carrying trade between the Far East and England from their slower-moving British competitors, and they sped thousands of impatient adventurers to the gold fields of California and Australia.

But the hour of glory for the clipper was relatively brief. On the eve of the Civil War the British had clearly won the world race for maritime ascendancy with their iron tramp steamers ("teakettles"). Though slower and less romantic than the clipper, these vessels were steadier, more capacious, more reliable, and hence more profitable.

> *As late as 1877 stagecoach passengers were advised in print: "Never shoot on the road as the noise might frighten the horses. . . . Don't point out where murders have been committed, especially if there are women passengers. . . . Expect annoyances, discomfort, and some hardships."*

No story of rapid American communication would be complete without including the Far West. By 1858 horse-drawn overland stages, immortalized by Mark Twain's *Roughing It*, were a familiar sight. Their dusty tracks stretched into California from the right bank of the muddy Missouri River.

Even more dramatic was the Pony Express, established in 1860 to carry mail speedily the 2,000 lonely miles (3,220 kilometers) from St. Joseph, Missouri, to Sacramento, California. Daring, lightweight riders, leaping onto wiry ponies saddled at stations approximately 10 miles (16 kilometers) apart, could make the trip in an amazing ten days. These unarmed horsemen galloped on, summer or winter, day or night, through dust or snow, past red Indians and white bandits. The speeding postmen missed only one trip, though the whole enterprise lost money heavily and folded after only eighteen legend-leaving months.

Just as the clippers had succumbed to steam, so were the express riders unhorsed by Morse's clacking keys, which began tapping messages to California in 1861. The swift ships and the fleet ponies ushered out a dying technology of wind and muscle. In the future, machines would be in the saddle.

Varying Viewpoints

Economic history was once simply a tale of industrious inventors and inventive industrialists. But economics has become a sophisticated science, and so has the story of the material past. Historians now seek to know just why economic growth occurred. Many scholars emphasize the plentiful resources of the United States. These resources, especially the abundance of arable land, led to high agricultural productivity and stimulated advances in transportation and communication that raised land values. The availability of land, this view holds, in turn limited the industrial labor supply, driving up wages and inducing manufacturers to adopt laborsaving machinery. Thus, the natural plenty of the continent set off a chain reaction that unleashed explosive economic growth.

Other historians stress the contribution of human resources to America's economic progress. They focus on the large population of natives and immigrants to till the soil and fill the factories, the exploitation of slaves, legal and political innovations like the tariff and the general incorporation laws, and the technical genius of the American people, which by 1860 had become the envy of the entire Atlantic world.

Historians are also increasingly interested in the question: Which people benefited most from economic growth? This is known as the "welfare" question, as distinct from the fact of growth alone. Recently, labor historians, such as Sean Wilentz, have described the emergence of an increasingly self-conscious working class in antebellum America. These studies reveal the efforts of urban workers to protect themselves against the dislocations of industrialization and to secure a fair share of the benefits of economic development.

Select Readings

Primary Source Documents

Seth Luther, *An Address to the Working-Men of New-England** (1833), is the eloquent appeal of an uneducated working-class labor reformer. On the transportation revolution, see John H. B. Latrobe's *Western Waters** (1871) and Mark Twain's classic *Life on the Mississippi* (1883). Lemuel Shaw's decision of 1842 in *Commonwealth* v. *Hunt*, 4 Metc. III (in Henry Steele Commager, *Documents of American History*) is regarded as the "Magna Charta of American labor organization."

Secondary Sources

Solid introductions are George R. Taylor, *The Transportation Revolution, 1815–1860* (1951); Clarence H. Danhoff, *Change in Agriculture: The Northern United States, 1820–1870* (1969)*;* and Douglas C. North, *Economic Growth in the United States, 1790–1860* (1961). See also North's *Growth and Welfare in the American Past* (rev. ed., 1974). The events of the period are placed in a larger context of economic history in Stuart Bruchey, *The Roots of American Economic Growth, 1607–1861* (1965), and in Walt W. Rostow, *The Stages of Economic Growth* (rev. ed., 1971). Thomas C. Cochrane, *Frontiers of Change: Early Industrialism in America* (1981), sees industrialization as culturally inspired change. Two fascinating case studies of the coming of industrialism are Alan Dawley, *Class and Community: The Industrial Revolution in Lynn* (1977), and Anthony F. C. Wallace, *Rockdale: The Growth of an American Village in the Early Industrial Revolution* (1978). The laboring classes are chronicled in Joseph Rayback, *History of American Labor* (1966). Consult also Herbert Gutman's path-breaking *Work, Culture, and Society in Industrializing America* (1976) and Sean Wilentz's insightful *Chants Democratic: New York City and the Rise of the American Working Class, 1788–1850* (1984). The experiences of women workers are the focus of Thomas Dublin, *Women at Work: The Transformation of Work and Community in Lowell, Massachusetts, 1826–1860* (1979). On the introduction of technology, see the provocative anthology edited by S. B. Saul, *Technological Change:*

The U.S. and Britain in the Nineteenth Century (1970). Ideological aspects of this process are described in John F. Kassen, *Civilizing the Machine: Technology and Republican Values in America, 1776–1900* (1976). The canal era is comprehensively described in Carter Goodrich, *Government Promotion of American Canals and Railroads, 1800–1890* (1960). See also H. N. Schreiber, *The Ohio Canal Era* (1968). On railroads, consult Robert Fogel, *Railroads and American Economic Growth* (1964), which presents the startling thesis that the iron horse in fact did little to promote growth. For a different view, see Albert Fishlow, *American Railroads and the Transformation of the Ante-Bellum Economy* (1965). The clipper ships are lovingly described in Carl C. Cutler, *Greyhounds of the Sea* (1930), and Samuel E. Morison, *By Land and By Sea* (1953). An excellent introduction to the romance of the tall ships is Richard H. Dana Jr.'s personal narrative, *Two Years before the Mast* (1840).

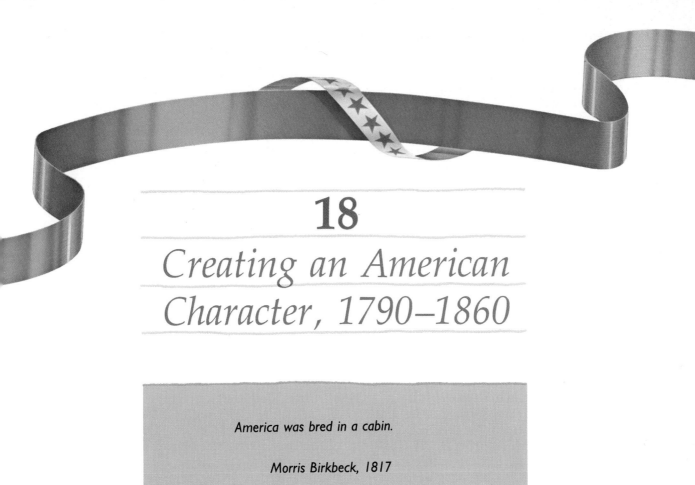

18

Creating an American Character, 1790–1860

America was bred in a cabin.

Morris Birkbeck, 1817

American Children of Environment

"In the United States," wrote twentieth-century novelist Gertrude Stein, "there is more space where nobody is than where anybody is. This is what makes America what it is." Even today, as a highly industrialized and technologically sophisticated people, Americans have not fully shaken off the effects of their centuries-long battle with the wilderness.

The West, with its raw frontier, was the most typically American part of America. George Washington, a product of tidewater Virginia, was outwardly an English aristocrat, who lived most of his life under the British flag; Andrew Jackson, a product of frontier Tennessee, was clearly an American. As Ralph Waldo Emerson wrote in 1844, "Europe stretches to the Alleghenies; America lies beyond."

The "go-aheaditive" Americans sprang from a restless breed of people. Thanks to an invigorating climate and the challenge of tremendous tasks, they were nervous and energetic. Born hustlers—always "a-doin'"—they were footloose and frequently on the move. One "tall tale" of the frontier described chickens that voluntarily crossed their legs every spring, waiting to be tied for the annual move west. Even in repose, Americans were often whittling, sewing, chewing, jiggling, or rocking. The rocking chair—"the chair that travels but stays at home"—was a typically American device. At the dinner table, the rule seemed to be "gobble, gulp, and go." Americans had no time for four o'clock tea, as

Westward Movement of Center of Population, 1790–1980 *Note the remarkable equilibrium of the north-south pull from 1790 onward and the strong spurt west and south after 1940. The 1980 census revealed that the nation's center of population had at last moved west of the Mississippi River.*

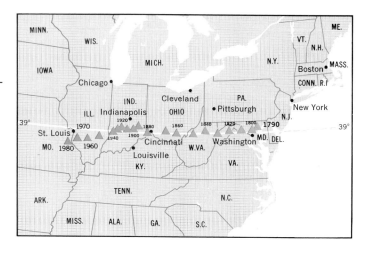

the English did. There was too much cream to be skimmed off the continent—furs, timber, wildlife—with a consequent wasting of soil and natural resources in some areas. All this restlessness came partly from youth; as late as 1850 the majority of Americans were under thirty.

The West attracted these nervous particles of human energy like a magnet. By 1840 the "demographic center" of the American population map had crossed the Alleghenies. On the eve of the Civil War, it had marched beyond the Ohio River. Legend portrays an army of muscular axmen triumphantly carving civilization out of the western woods. But in reality life was downright grim for most pioneer families. Poorly fed, ill-clad, housed in hastily erected shanties, they were perpetual victims of disease, depression, and premature death. Above all, there was the awful loneliness, especially for women, who sometimes cracked under the strain. They were often cut off from human contact, especially neighbors, for whole days or even weeks, while confined to the cramped orbit of a dark cabin erected in a crude and secluded clearing. Breakdowns and even madness were all too frequently the "opportunities" that the frontier offered to pioneer women.

Rugged Pioneers

A mad scramble for riches led not only to waste but to superficiality. Wooden bridges were flung across streams, until time permitted the hurry-up American to build stone spans. The breathless pursuit of treasure inevitably led to accusations of money-chasing and crass materialism. John Stuart Mill, the noted English writer, remarked in the 1840s that in America the life of one sex was "devoted to dollar hunting, and of the other to the breeding of dollar hunters." Dollar grabbing was undeniably important, but the thrill of the chase was hardly less so. Wealth was everywhere recognized as the badge of success and the symbol of power.

The rough-and-tough American—especially the westerner—was often crude, ruthless, brutal. Tobacco chewing and indelicate spitting— "the salivary propensity"—became a national scandal in the decades before the Civil War. One visiting Briton suggested that the spittoon, not the eagle, should be America's national emblem; and a group of Japanese visitors in 1860 noted that the white man had brown saliva. Frontier wrestling, often of the no-holds-barred type, sanctioned such niceties as the biting off of noses or the gouging out of eyes. "Look out, or I'll measure the length of your eyestrings [eye muscles]" was an expressive frontier warning. Nor was brutality directed solely at fellow whites. The Indians stood in the way of expansion, and when they fought back, they were brushed aside or killed off, like the wild animals.

Americans were ingenious, inventive, adaptable, self-sufficient—jacks-of-all-trades. They had to be, especially on the frontier, where there was no place for specialists. "Root, hog, or die"—the western saying directed at hogs left to root up their own food—might well have been the national motto.

Average Americans were strenuous, courageous, aggressive—overendowed with the "lick all creation" spirit. They had unshakable faith in their military prowess, untrained though they might be. They were tough and tenacious. Learning to laugh at adversity, they fought the elements, the wild animals ("varmints"), their Canadian and Mexican neighbors, and above all, the Indians. The Englishman Rudyard Kipling later wrote in grudging admiration of the American pioneer:

> He greets the embarrassed Gods, nor fears
> To shake the iron hand of Fate
> Or match with Destiny for beers.

Gamblers All

Marooned by geography, Americans were self-centered, provincial, and isolationist, whether in their hometowns or in the world community. First and foremost they were individualists. The men depended on their own trusty axes and especially their rifles, which, in the western phrase, made them all "equally tall." Their political and social beliefs might not bear a radical stamp, for many observers noted the remarkable conformity of American opinion. But they were convinced that their way in the world was for them alone to make. Emerson's popular lecture-essay "Self-Reliance" struck a deeply responsive chord. Popular literature of the period abounded in portraits of heroically unique, even isolated, figures like Cooper's Natty Bumppo

"The Spitter"   *The famed English author, Charles Dickens, laid out his clothes one night on an American canal boat. The next morning he found them liberally bedewed with tobacco juice, the result of "a perfect storm and tempest of spitting." (Vanity Fair.)*

and Melville's Captain Ahab—just as Jacksonian politics aimed to emancipate the lone-wolf, enterprising businessperson. Vast space and fabulous economic abundance fostered this fond self-image and gave it a certain reality. Yet even in this heyday of "rugged individualism," there were exceptions. Pioneers, in tasks clearly beyond their own individual resources, would call upon their neighbors for logrolling and barn raising, and upon their federal government for help in building internal improvements.

Americans in general were confident, buoyant, optimistic—born boosters, tellers of "tall tales," admirers of the giant lumberjack, the fabled Paul Bunyan. Pessimism was a kind of treason; "knockers" were not wanted. The ancestors of the Americans, as well as the immigrants themselves, had to be courageously optimistic to undertake the stormy Atlantic crossing. "The cowards never started; the weak died on the way," ran the saying.

Those who reached the New World were all gamblers. They gambled their lives against disease and Indians, and their crops and fortunes

> A British magazine thus satirized American boastfulness in 1870: "If an Arkansaw man cannot boast of the education of a Boston man, at any rate he can chew more tobacco and spit more, farther and straighter than any other man. If the Mississippi steamers are not so magnificent as some on the Hudson River, they sail faster and blow up oftener and shoot men higher than any other steamers in the country."

against the elements. The American people are distilled not only from a select group of brave men and women but also from a long line of risk-takers. Even those who failed had at least one satisfaction: someone had to take the first steps if the Republic were to achieve its ultimate destiny. "It's better to be a has-been," one heard, "than a never-was."

Americans were boastful—a trait growing out of their easy optimism. The game of poker ("brag"), with its premium on successful bluffing, attained great popularity in the West, especially with Henry Clay. Americans were painfully aware of their nation's many physical and cultural shortcomings, and while smarting under the sneers of monocled foreigners, they would brag loudly and defensively about the splendid cities that would one day spring from their malarial swamps. Significantly, they boasted of the future, while Europeans boasted of their past. They also learned to worship bigness, partly because America excelled in size. Above all, they had unbounded faith in the future, in progress, in the "American dream."

The Torch of Democracy

The American people were essentially democratic—except, conspicuously, for the blight of slavery. In their social democracy, especially beyond the mountains, they set little store by caste, tradition, or family trees. The first question was not "Who are you?" but "What can you do?" On the frontier, where all people were "equally better," a common expression was "I'm as good as you be." Or as a Hungarian immigrant later remarked, "The President is Mister and I am Mister too." The very first sentence of Alexis de Tocqueville's great treatise on *Democracy in America* (1835) proclaimed: "Nothing struck me more forcibly than the general equality of conditions among the people." One rousing song sung at religious camp meetings ran:

> Come hungry, come thirsty, come ragged, come bare,
> Come filthy, come lousy, come just as you are.

Political democracy was one of the nation's proudest boasts. White manhood suffrage came

to be the rule. The people realized that the world was skeptically watching their vast experiment in political democracy, and this awareness contributed further to self-conscious boastfulness. Emerson once observed that the American eagle was something of a peacock.

Americans, moreover, were lovers of freedom. Not to be pushed about, they had forcibly overthrown George III and set up a republic. They cherished states' rights and localism, largely because these ideals enabled them to keep a more watchful eye on their public servants. They hailed freedom abroad, as well as in America. Responding to the flattery of imitation, they applauded democratic revolutions whenever they occurred and often assisted them with money and volunteers. They cheered as thrones crashed, and they openly pitied people who did not have the "gumption" to rise up and break their autocratic chains. Mark Twain caught the spirit of antimonarchical America when he had his character Huck Finn remark, "Sometimes I wish we could hear of a country that's out of kings."

Americans were intensely patriotic and nationalistic—America lovers, who annually cheered flag-flapping Fourth of July oratory. Instead of inheriting the land, they had subdued it themselves, battling both the elements and the Indians. And one especially cherishes the possessions one has had to fight for.

The March of the Millions

An amazing multiplication of people continued decade after decade, without serious slackening. By midcentury the population was still doubling approximately every twenty-five years, as in fertile colonial days.

By 1860 the original thirteen states had more than doubled in number: thirty-three stars graced the American flag. The United States was the fourth most populous nation in the western world, exceeded by only three European countries—Russia, France, and Austria.

Urban growth continued explosively. In 1790 there had been only two cities that could boast 20,000 or more souls: Philadelphia and New York. By 1860 there were forty-three; and about

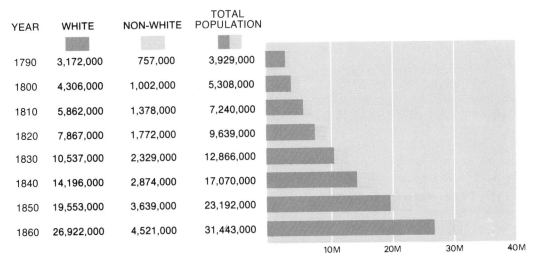

YEAR	WHITE	NON-WHITE	TOTAL POPULATION
1790	3,172,000	757,000	3,929,000
1800	4,306,000	1,002,000	5,308,000
1810	5,862,000	1,378,000	7,240,000
1820	7,867,000	1,772,000	9,639,000
1830	10,537,000	2,329,000	12,866,000
1840	14,196,000	2,874,000	17,070,000
1850	19,553,000	3,639,000	23,192,000
1860	26,922,000	4,521,000	31,443,000

Population Increase, Including Slaves and Indians, 1790–1860

three hundred other places claimed over 5,000 inhabitants apiece. New York was the metropolis; New Orleans, the "Queen of the South"; and Chicago, the swaggering lord of the Midwest, destined to be "hog butcher for the world."

Such overrapid urbanization unfortunately brought undesirable by-products. It intensified the problems of smelly slums, feeble street lighting, inadequate policing, impure water, foul sewage, ravenous rats, and improper garbage disposal. Hogs poked their scavenging

Cincinnati in 1843 *Famous as a processor of hogs, this "Queen City of the West" was a town of 2,540 people in 1800 and 161,044 in 1860, 45 percent of them foreign-born. Though tied to the South by downriver commerce on the Ohio and Mississippi rivers, it remained loyal to the North during the Civil War. (Cincinnati Public Library.)*

Irish and German Immigration by Decade

YEARS	IRISH	GERMAN	ALL OTHERS	GRAND TOTAL
1820–1830	Unknown	Unknown	Unknown	151,824
1831–1840	207,381	152,454	239,290	599,125
1841–1850	780,719	434,626	497,906	1,713,251
1851–1860	914,119	951,667	732,428	2,598,214
1861–1870	435,778	787,468	1,091,578	2,314,824
1871–1880	436,871	718,182	1,657,138	2,812,191
1881–1890	655,482	1,452,970	3,138,161	5,246,613
1891–1900	388,416	505,152	2,793,996	3,687,564

snouts about many city streets as late as the 1840s. Boston in 1823 pioneered with a sewage system; and New York in 1842 abandoned wells and cisterns for a piped-in water supply. The city thus unknowingly eliminated the breeding places of many disease-carrying mosquitoes.

A continuing high birthrate accounted for most of the increase in population, but by the 1840s the tides of immigration were adding hundreds of thousands more. Before this decade, immigrants had been flowing in at a rate of about 60,000 a year, but suddenly the influx was tripled in the 1840s and then quadrupled in the 1850s. During these two feverish decades, over a million and a half Irish, and nearly as many Germans, swarmed down the gangplanks. Why did they come?

The immigrants came partly because Europe seemed to be running out of room. The population of the Old World more than doubled in the nineteenth century, and Europe began to generate a great seething pool of apparently "surplus" people. They were displaced and footloose in their homelands before they felt the tug of the American magnet. Indeed, at least as many people moved about *within* Europe as crossed the Atlantic. America benefited from these people-churning changes but did not set them all in motion. Nor was the United States the sole beneficiary of the process: of the nearly 60 million persons who abandoned Europe in the century after 1840, about 25 million went somewhere other than the United States.

Yet America still beckoned most strongly to the struggling masses of Europe, and the ma-

jority of migrants headed for the "land of freedom and opportunity." There was freedom from aristocratic caste and state church; there was abundant opportunity to secure broad acres and better one's condition. Much-read letters sent home by immigrants—"America letters"—often described in glowing terms the richer life: low taxes, no compulsory military service, and "three meat meals a day." The introduction of transoceanic steamships also meant that the immigrants could come speedily, in a matter of ten or twelve days instead of ten or twelve weeks. They were still jammed into unsanitary quarters, thus suffering an appalling death rate, but the nightmare was more endurable because it was shorter.

The Emerald Isle Moves West

Ireland, already groaning under the heavy hand of British overlords, was prostrated in the mid-1840s. A terrible rot attacked the potato crop, on which the people had become dangerously dependent, and about one-fourth of them were swept away by disease and hunger. Starved bodies were found dead by the roadsides with grass in their mouths. All told, about 2 million perished.

Tens of thousands of destitute souls, fleeing the Land of Famine for the Land of Plenty, flocked to America in the "Black Forties." Ireland's great export has been population; and the Irish take their place beside the Jews as a dispersed people.

These uprooted newcomers—too poor to move west and buy the necessary land, livestock, and equipment—swarmed into the larger seaboard cities. Noteworthy were Boston and particularly New York, which rapidly became the largest Irish city in the world. Before many decades had passed, more people of Hibernian blood lived in America than on the "ould sod" of Erin's Isle.

The luckless Irish received no red-carpet treatment. Forced to live in squalor, they worsened already vile slum conditions. They were scorned by the older American stock, especially "proper" Protestant Bostonians, who regarded the scruffy Catholic newcomers as a social menace. Barely literate "Biddies" (Bridgets) took jobs as kitchen maids. Broad-shouldered "Paddies" (Patricks) were pushed into pick-and-shovel drudgery on canals and railroads, where thousands left their bones as victims of disease and accidental explosions. It was said that an Irishman lay buried under every railroad tie. As wage-depressing competitors for jobs, the Irish were hated by native workers. "No Irish Need Apply" was a sign commonly posted at factory gates and was often abbreviated to NINA. The Irish, for similar reasons, fiercely resented the blacks, with whom they shared society's basement. Race riots between black and Irish dockworkers flared up in several port cities, and the Irish were always cool to the abolitionist cause.

The friendless "Famine Irish" were forced to fend for themselves. The Ancient Order of Hibernians, a semisecret society founded in Ireland to fight rapacious landlords, served in America as a benevolent society, aiding the downtrodden. It also helped to spawn the "Molly Maguires," a shadowy Irish miners' union that rocked the Pennsylvania coal districts in the 1860s and 1870s.

The Irish tended to remain in low-skill occupations but gradually improved their lot, usually

Ragged Irish Immigrants Arriving in America Bewildered Irish newcomers were often whisked to "boardinghouses"—filthy hovels above a "grog shop" where whiskey flowed and a saucer of free tobacco sat on the bar. The hard-drinking Irish scandalized old-stock Americans, but Boston's Orestes Brownson predicted in 1852: "Out from these . . . dirty streets will come forth some of the noblest sons of our country, whom she will delight to own and honor." (The Granger Collection.)

by acquiring modest amounts of property. The education of children was cut short as families struggled to save money to purchase a home. But for humble Irish peasants, cruelly cast out of their homeland, property ownership counted as a grand "success."

Politics quickly attracted these gregarious Gaelic newcomers. A poet urged them in 1852:

> Fellow exiles! claim your station
>   In the councils of the nation;
> Be not aliens in the soil
>   Which exacts your sweat and toil

They soon began to gain control of powerful city machines, notably New York's Tammany Hall, and reaped the patronage rewards. Before long, beguilingly brogued Irishmen dominated police departments in many big cities, where they now drove the "Paddy wagons" that had once carted their brawling forebears to jail.

American politicians made haste to cultivate the Irish vote, especially in the politically potent state of New York. Irish hatred of the British lost nothing in the transatlantic transplanting. As the Irish-Americans increased in number—nearly 2 million arrived between 1830 and 1860—officials in Washington glimpsed political gold in those Hibernian hills. Politicians often found it politically profitable to fire verbal volleys at London—a process vulgarly known as "twisting the British lion's tail."

The German Forty-Eighters

The influx of refugees from Germany between 1830 and 1860 was hardly less spectacular than that from Ireland. During these troubled years, over a million and a half thrifty Germans stepped onto American soil. The bulk of them were uprooted farmers, displaced by crop failures and by other hardships. But a strong sprinkling were liberal political refugees. Saddened by the collapse of the democratic revolutions of 1848, they had decided to leave the autocratic fatherland and flee to America—the one brightest hope of democracy.

The liberal German "Forty-Eighters," who came to America for free government, are not to be confused with the "Forty-Niners," who came

to California for free gold. The future history of Germany—and indeed of the world—might well have been less war-torn if these rare spirits had remained at home as a seedbed for genuine democracy. But Germany's loss was America's gain. Zealous German liberals like the lanky and public-spirited Carl Schurz, a relentless foe of slavery and public corruption, contributed richly to the elevation of American political life.

Many of the Germanic newcomers, unlike the Irish, possessed a modest amount of this world's goods. Most of them pushed out to the lush lands of the Middle West, notably Wisconsin, where they settled and established model farms. Like the Irish, they formed an influential body of voters whom American politicians shamelessly wooed. But the Germans were less potent politically because their strength was more widely scattered.

The hand of Germans in shaping American life was widely felt in still other ways. They had fled from the militarism and wars of Europe and consequently came to be a bulwark of isolationist sentiment in the upper Mississippi Valley. Better educated on the whole than the stump-grubbing Americans, they warmly supported public schools, including their *Kindergarten* (children's garden). They likewise did much to stimulate art and music. As outspoken champions of freedom, they became relentless enemies of slavery during the fevered years before the Civil War.

Yet the Germans—often dubbed "damned Dutchmen"—were occasionally regarded with suspicion by their old-stock American neighbors. Seeking to preserve their language and culture, they sometimes settled in compact "colonies" and kept aloof from the surrounding community. Accustomed to the "Continental Sunday" and uncurbed by Puritan tradition, they made merry on the Sabbath and drank huge quantities of an amber beverage called *Bier* (beer), which dates its real popularity in America to their coming.* Their Old World drinking habits, like those of the Irish newcomers, gave a severe setback to the movement for greater temperance in the use of alcohol.

---

*Frederick Pabst and Joseph Schlitz were among the German immigrant brewers who "made Milwaukee famous."

Flare-Ups of Antiforeignism

The invasion by this so-called immigrant "rabble" in the 1840s and 1850s inflamed the hates of American "nativists." They feared that these foreign hordes would outbreed, outvote, and overwhelm the old "native" stock. Not only did the newcomers take jobs from "native" Americans, but the bulk of the displaced Irish were Roman Catholics, as were a substantial minority of the Germans. The Church of Rome was still widely regarded by many old-line Americans as a "foreign" church; convents were commonly referred to as "Popish brothels."

Roman Catholics were now on the move. Seeking to protect their children from Protestant indoctrination in the public schools, they began in the 1840s to construct an entirely separate Catholic educational system—an enormously expensive undertaking for a poor immigrant community, but one that revealed the strength of its religious commitment. They had formed a negligible minority during colonial days, and their numbers had increased gradually. But with the enormous influx of the Irish and Germans in the 1840s and 1850s, the Catholics became a powerful religious group. In 1840 they had ranked fifth, behind the Baptists, Methodists, Presbyterians, and Congregational-

Strong antiforeignism was reflected in the platform of the American (Know-Nothing) party in 1856: "Americans must rule America; and to this end, native-born citizens should be selected for all state, federal, or municipal offices of government employment, in preference to naturalized citizens."

ists. By 1850, with some 1.8 million communicants, they had bounded into first place—a position they have never lost.

"Native" Americans were alarmed by these mounting figures. They professed to believe that in due time the "alien riffraff" would "establish" the Catholic church at the expense of Protestantism and would introduce "Popish idols." The noisier American "nativists" rallied for political action. In 1849 they formed the Order of the Star-Spangled Banner, which soon developed into the formidable American, or "Know-Nothing," party—a name derived from its secretiveness. "Nativists" agitated for rigid restrictions on immigration and naturalization and for laws authorizing the deportation of alien paupers. They also promoted a lurid literature of exposure, much of it pure fiction. The authors,

Crooked Voting   *A bitter "nativist" cartoon charging Irish and German immigrants with "stealing" elections. (New York Public Library.)*

sometimes posing as escaped nuns, described sin as they imagined it behind brick convent walls, including the secret burial of babies. One of these books—Maria Monk's *Awful Disclosures* (1836)—sold over 300,000 copies.

Even uglier was occasional mass violence. As early as 1834 a Catholic convent near Boston was burned by a howling mob, and in ensuing years there were a few scattered attacks on Catholic schools and churches. The most frightful flare-up occurred during 1844 in Philadelphia, where the Irish Catholics fought back against the threats of the "nativists." The City of Brotherly Love did not quiet down until two Catholic churches had been burned and some thirteen citizens had been killed and fifty wounded in several days of fighting. These outbursts of intolerance, though infrequent and generally localized in the larger cities, remain an unfortunate blot on the record of America's treatment of minority groups.

Reviving Religion

Church attendance was still a regular ritual for about three-fourths of the 23 million Americans in 1850. Alexis de Tocqueville declared that there was "no country in the world where the Christian religion retains a greater influence over the souls of men than in America." Yet the religion of these years was not the old-time religion of colonial days. The austere Calvinist rigor had long been seeping out of the American churches. The rationalist ideas of the French Revolutionary era had done much to soften the older orthodoxy. Thomas Paine's widely circulated book *The Age of Reason* (1794) had shockingly declared that all churches were "set up to terrify and enslave mankind, and monopolize power and profit." American anticlericalism was seldom that virulent, but many of the Founding Fathers, including Jefferson and Franklin, embraced the liberal doctrines of Deism that Paine promoted. Deists relied on reason rather than revelation, on science rather than the Bible. They rejected the concept of original sin and denied Christ's divinity. Yet Deists believed in a Supreme Being who had created a knowable universe and endowed human beings with a capacity for moral behavior.

Deism helped to inspire an important spin-off from the severe Puritanism of the past—the Unitarian faith, which began to gather momentum in New England at the end of the eighteenth century. Unitarians held that God existed in only *one* person (hence *uni*tarian), and not in the orthodox Trinity. Although denying the divinity of Jesus, Unitarians stressed the essential goodness of human nature rather than its vileness; they proclaimed their belief in free will and the possibility of salvation through good works; they pictured God not as a stern Creator but as a loving Father. Embraced by many leading thinkers (including Ralph Waldo Emerson), the Unitarian movement appealed mostly to intellectuals whose rationalism and optimism contrasted sharply with the hellfire doctrines of Calvinism, especially predestination and human depravity.

A boiling reaction against the growing liberalism in religion set in about 1800. A fresh wave of roaring revivals, beginning on the southern frontier but soon rolling even into the cities of the Northeast, sent a Second Great Awakening surging across the land. Sweeping up even more people than the First Great Awakening almost a century earlier, the Second Awakening was one of the most momentous episodes in the history of American religion. This tidal wave of spiritual fervor left in its wake countless converted souls, shattered and reorganized churches, and new sects. It also encouraged an effervescent evangelicism that bubbled up into innumerable areas of American life—including prison reform, the temperance cause, the women's movement, and the crusade to abolish slavery.

The Second Awakening was spread to the masses on the frontier by huge "camp meetings," where as many as twenty-five thousand persons would gather for an encampment of several days to drink the hellfire gospel as served up by an itinerant preacher. Thousands of spiritually starved souls "got religion" at these gatherings and in their ecstasy engaged in orgies of rolling, dancing, barking, and jerking. Many of the "saved" soon backslid into their for-

A Camp Meeting at Sing Sing, New York   Note the preacher with uplifted hands under the canopy at the left. A British visitor wrote in 1839 of a revival meeting: "In front of the pulpit there was a space railed off and strewn with straw, which I was told was the anxious seat, and on which sat those who were touched by their consciences." (Library of Congress.)

mer sinful ways, but the revivals massively stimulated church membership and a variety of humanitarian reforms. Easterners were moved to engage in missionary work in the Indian backwoods, in Hawaii, and in faraway Asia.

Methodists and Baptists reaped the biggest harvest of souls from the fields fertilized by revivalism. Both sects stressed personal conversion (contrary to predestination), a relatively democratic control of church affairs, and a rousing emotionalism. As a frontier jingle ran:

> The devil hates the Methodist
> Because they sing and shout the best.

Powerful Peter Cartwright (1785–1872) was the best known of the Methodist "circuit riders," or traveling frontier preachers. This ill-educated but sinewy servant of the Lord ranged for a half-century from Tennessee to Illinois, calling upon sinners to repent. With bellowing voice and flailing arms, he converted thousands of souls to the Lord. Not only did he lash the Devil with his tongue, but with his fists he knocked out rowdies who tried to break up his meetings. His Christianity was definitely muscular.

Bell-voiced Charles Grandison Finney was the greatest of the revival preachers. Trained as a lawyer, Finney abandoned the bar to become an evangelist after a deeply moving conversion experience as a young man. Tall and athletically built, Finney held huge crowds spellbound with the power of his oratory and the pungency of his message. He led massive revivals in Rochester and New York City in 1830 and 1831. Finney preached a version of the old-time religion, but he was also an innovator. He devised the "anxious bench," where repentant sinners could sit in full view of the congregation, and he encouraged women to pray aloud in public. Holding out the promise of a perfect Christian kingdom on earth, Finney denounced both alcohol and slavery. He eventually served

The Circuit Preacher   *(From the drawing by A. R. Waud in* Harper's Weekly, *October 12, 1867.)*

as president of Oberlin College in Ohio, which he helped to make a hotbed of revivalist activity and abolitionism.

Denominational Diversity

Revivals also furthered the fragmentation of religious faiths. Western New York, where many descendants of New England Puritans had settled, was so blistered by sermonizers preaching "hellfire and damnation" that it came to be known as the "Burned-Over District."

Millerites, or Adventists, who mustered several hundred thousand adherents, rose from the superheated soil of the Burned-Over region in the 1830s. Named after the eloquent and commanding William Miller, they interpreted the Bible to mean that Christ would return to earth on October 22, 1844. Donning their go-to-meeting clothes, they gathered in prayerful assemblies to greet their Redeemer. The failure of Jesus to descend on schedule dampened but did not destroy the movement.

Like the First Great Awakening, the Second Great Awakening tended to widen the lines between classes and regions. The more prosperous and conservative denominations in the East were little touched by revivalism, while Episcopalians, Presbyterians, Congregationalists, and Unitarians continued to rise mostly from the wealthier, better-educated levels of society. Methodists, Baptists, and the members of the other new sects spawned by the swelling evangelistic fervor tended to come from less prosperous, less "learned" communities in the rural South and West.

Religious diversity further reflected social cleavages when the churches faced up to the slavery issue. By 1844–1845 both the southern Baptists and the southern Methodists had split with their northern brethren over human bondage. The Methodists came to grief over the case of a slaveowning bishop in Georgia, whose second wife added several household slaves to his estate. In 1857 the Presbyterians, North and South, parted company. The secession of the southern churches foreshadowed the secession of the southern states. First the churches split, then the political parties split, and then the Union split.

A Desert Zion in Utah

The smoldering spiritual embers of the Burned-Over District kindled one especially ardent flame in 1830. In that year Joseph Smith—a tall, powerfully built visionary, proud of his prowess at wrestling—reported that he had received some golden plates from an angel. When deciphered, they constituted the Book of Mormon, and the Church of Jesus Christ of Latter-Day Saints (Mormons) was launched. It was a native American product, a new religion, destined to spread its influence worldwide.

After establishing a religious oligarchy, Smith ran into serious opposition from his non-Mormon neighbors, first in Ohio, and then in Missouri and Illinois. His cooperative sect rasped rank-and-file Americans, who were individualistic and dedicated to free enterprise. The Mormons aroused further antagonism by voting as a unit and by openly but understandably drilling their militia for defensive purposes. Accusations of polygamy likewise arose and increased in intensity, for Joseph Smith was reputed to have several wives.

The Mormon Trail *Utah-bound Mormons with handcarts. (The Church of Jesus Christ of Latter-Day Saints.)*

Continuing hostility finally drove the Mormons to desperate measures. In 1844 Joseph Smith and his brother were murdered and mangled by a mob in Carthage, Illinois, and the movement seemed near collapse. The falling torch was seized by a remarkable Mormon Moses named Brigham Young. Stern and austere in contrast to Smith's charm and affability, the barrel-chested Brigham Young had received only eleven days of formal schooling. But he quickly proved to be an aggressive leader, an eloquent preacher, and a gifted administrator. Determined to escape further persecution, Young in 1846–1847 led his oppressed and despoiled Latter-Day Saints over vast rolling plains to Utah as they sang "Come, Come, Ye Saints."

Overcoming pioneer hardships, the Mormons soon made the desert bloom like a new Eden by means of ingenious and cooperative methods of irrigation. The crops of 1848, threatened by hordes of crickets, were saved when flocks of gulls appeared, as if by a miracle, to gulp down the invaders. (A monument to the sea gulls stands in Salt Lake City today.)

Semiarid Utah grew remarkably. By the end of 1848 some five thousand settlers had arrived, and other large bands were to follow them.

The Mormon Trek, 1846–1847 *Accompanied by livestock, the first pioneer band, led by Brigham Young, set out for Utah in 1846. The party consisted of 146 young men and women driving seventy-three wagons.*

Polygamy was an issue of such consequence that it was bracketed with slavery in the Republican national platform of 1856: "It is both the right and the imperative duty of Congress to prohibit in the Territories those twin relics of barbarism—Polygamy and Slavery."

dusty ditch. Fortunately, the quarrel was finally adjusted without serious bloodshed. The Mormons later ran afoul of the antipolygamy laws passed by Congress in 1862 and 1882, and their unique marital customs delayed statehood for Utah until 1896.

Daily Diversions

Many dedicated Mormons in the 1850s actually made the 1,300-mile (2,090-kilometer) trek across the plains pulling two-wheeled carts.

Under the rigidly disciplined management of Brigham Young, the community became a prosperous frontier theocracy and a cooperative commonwealth. Young married as many as twenty-seven women—some of them wives in name only—and begot fifty-six children. The population was further swelled by thousands of immigrants from Europe, where the Mormons had established a flourishing missionary movement.

A crisis developed when the Washington government was unable to control the hierarchy of Brigham Young, who had been made territorial governor in 1850. A federal army marched in 1857 against the Mormons, who harassed its lines of supply and rallied to die in their last

As the log-clearing phase passed, the masses were left with more leisure to enjoy the good things of life. The simple amusements of colonial days were continued, such as country dances, and the people still derived much satisfaction from religious and political meetings, which were primly attended in "Sunday best" clothes. But a wider range of diversions gradually beckoned.

The stage took on greater respectability as the nineteenth century unfolded, even in Boston, where the Puritans had frowned upon the theater as "the Devil's chapel." Resourceful promoters attempted to quiet prejudices by stressing the moral value of their productions: one of Shakespeare's famous plays was advertised as: "Hamlet: Filial Piety." Classical English dramas continued their popularity, while in the 1850s *Uncle Tom's Cabin* and *Ten Nights*

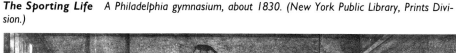

The Sporting Life   *A Philadelphia gymnasium, about 1830. (New York Public Library, Prints Division.)*

in a Barroom were also playing to packed houses.

Early in the century many of the leading actors were visitors from England, but eventually local stars began to flash across the American stage. Handsome and arrogant Edwin Forrest (1806–1872) was the first topflight American performer, and his rivalry with a visiting English artist stirred up his New York devotees and inflamed them to riot in 1849. This frightful affair ended with twenty-two persons killed and thirty-six wounded.

Other headliners had their day. English-born Junius Brutus Booth (1796–1852), a marvelously gifted though alcoholic tragedian, often broke engagements and even upbraided audiences. Two of his sons trod the boards as tragedians: Edwin T. Booth (1833–1893), who gained fame as an actor; John Wilkes Booth (1838—1865), who gained infamy as the assassin of Lincoln. The most talented American actress of the century was contralto-voiced Charlotte Cushman (1816–1876), who proved to be a smash hit in male and female roles, including both Romeo and Juliet.

Sports continued to relieve the monotony of everyday drudgery. Horse racing still attracted an enthusiastic and open-pursed following. Embryonic baseball had attained so much popularity by 1845 that a uniform set of rules was adopted. Flashy and flammable showboats were churning the main rivers, bringing their variety shows to a gaping public. The traveling circus was drawing appreciative crowds, although the huge three-ring spectacles were not introduced until after the Civil War.

The most famous showman of the era was Phineas T. Barnum (1810–1891), a shrewd and cynical Connecticut Yankee, "the Prince of Humbug." He got his start during the 1830s and 1840s in New York City, where he displayed bearded ladies and other freaks. Realizing that the American public loved to be "humbugged," he operated on the golden assumption that a "sucker" was born every minute. One of his prize hoaxes was the wizened black "nurse" of George Washington, alleged to be 161 years old. (An autopsy indicated that she was about 80.)

Other activities were less amusing. Light-fingered gamblers were ever present to fleece the greedy and unwary, especially on the palatial river steamers. Dueling died hard in the honor-conscious South, its last stronghold. Crimes of violence still persisted in alarming numbers, partly as a result of the brutalizing influence of the frontier. Rough western justice—often hempen injustice—still manifested itself to an alarming degree in lynching bees, popularly known as "necktie parties."

For the upper crust, fashionable "watering places" were established at Saratoga Springs (New York) and also at Newport (Rhode Island). These resorts were frequented by the gaudily dressed elite, including many cotton-rich southerners. Growing numbers of wealthier Americans were also making the "grand tour" of Europe.

Culturally, by 1860 America had traveled a long and uphill road since crude pioneering days. But a high degree of polish and sophistication, at least by European standards, lay in the lap of the future.

Free Schools for a Free People

Tax-supported primary schools were scarce in the early years of the Republic. They had the odor of pauperism about them, since they existed chiefly to educate the children of the

> Lincoln wrote of his education (1859): "There were some schools so-called [in Indiana], but no qualification was ever required of a teacher beyond 'readin', writin' and cipherin'' to the rule of three. . . . There was absolutely nothing to excite ambition for education. Of course, when I came of age I did not know much. Still, somehow, I could read, write and cipher to the rule of three, but that was all. I have not been to school since. The little advance I now have upon this store of education, I have picked up from time to time under the pressure of necessity. I was raised to work, which I continued till I was twenty-two."

The Country School   *Stark and simple by latter-day standards, the one-room schoolhouse never-theless contributed richly to the development of the young Republic. From a painting by Winslow Homer. (St. Louis Art Museum, Museum Purchase.)*

poor—the so-called ragged schools. Advocates of "free" public education met stiff opposition. A middlewestern legislator cried that he wanted only this simple epitaph when he died: "Here lies an enemy of public education."

Well-to-do, conservative Americans gradually saw the light. If they did not pay to educate "other folkses brats," the brats might grow up into a dangerous, ignorant rabble—armed with the vote. Taxation for education was an insurance premium that the wealthy paid for stability and democracy.

Tax-supported public education, though miserably lagging in the slavery-cursed South, triumphed between 1825 and 1850. Grimy-handed laborers wielded increased influence and demanded instruction for their children. Most important was the gaining of manhood suffrage for whites in Jackson's day. A free vote cried aloud for free education. A civilized nation that was both ignorant and free, declared Thomas Jefferson, "never was and never will be."

The famed little red schoolhouse—with one room, one stove, one teacher, and often eight grades—became the shrine of American democracy. Regrettably, it was an imperfect shrine. Early free schools stayed open only a few months of the year. Schoolmasters were too often ill trained, ill tempered, and ill paid. They frequently put more stress on "lickin'" (with a hickory stick) than on "larnin'." These knights of the blackboard often "boarded around" in the community, and some knew scarcely more than their older pupils. They usually taught only the "three Rs"—"readin', 'ritin', and 'rithmetic." To many rugged Americans, suspicious of "book larnin'," this was enough.

Reform was urgently needed. Into the breach stepped Horace Mann (1796–1859), a brilliant and idealistic graduate of Brown University. As secretary of the Massachusetts Board of Education, he campaigned effectively for more and better schoolhouses, longer school terms, higher pay for teachers, and an expanded curriculum. His influence radiated out to other states, and impressive improvements were chalked up. Yet education remained an expensive luxury for many communities. As late as 1860 the nation counted only about a hundred public secondary schools—and nearly a million white adult illiterates. Black slaves in the South were legally forbidden to receive instruction in reading or writing, and even free blacks, in the North as well as the South, were usually excluded from the schools.

Educational advances were aided by improved textbooks, notably those of Noah Webster (1758–1843), a Yale-educated Connecticut Yankee who was known as the "Schoolmaster of the Republic." His "reading lessons," used by millions of children in the nineteenth century, were partly designed to promote patriotism. He devoted twenty years to his famous dictionary, published in 1828, which helped to standardize the American language.

Equally influential was Ohioan William H. McGuffey (1800–1873), a teacher-preacher of rare power. His grade-school readers, first published in the 1830s, sold 122 million copies in the following decades. *McGuffey's Reader*s hammered home lasting lessons in morality, patriotism, and idealism. One copy-exercise ran:

> Beautiful hands are they that do
>   Deeds that are noble good and true;
> Beautiful feet are they that go
>   Swiftly to lighten another's woe.

Higher Goals for Higher Learning

Higher education was likewise stirring. The religious zeal of the Second Great Awakening, beginning about 1800, led to the planting of many small, denominational, liberal arts colleges, chiefly in the South and West. Too often they were educationally anemic, established more to satisfy local pride than genuinely to advance the cause of learning. Like their more venerable, ivy-draped brethren, the new colleges offered a narrow, tradition-bound curriculum of Latin, Greek, mathematics, and moral philosophy. On new and old campuses alike there was little intellectual vitality and much boredom.

The first state-supported universities sprang up in the South, beginning with North Carolina

in 1795. Federal land grants nourished the growth of state institutions of higher learning. Conspicuous among the early group was the University of Virginia, founded in 1819. It was largely the brainchild of Thomas Jefferson, who designed its beautiful architecture and who at times watched its construction through a telescope from his hilltop home. He dedicated the university to freedom from religious or political shackles, and modern languages and the sciences received unusual emphasis.

Women's higher education was frowned upon in the early decades of the nineteenth century. A woman's place was in the home, and training in needlecraft seemed more important than training in algebra. In an era when the clinging-vine bride was the ideal, coeducation was regarded as frivolous. Prejudices also prevailed that too much learning injured the feminine brain, undermined health, and rendered a young lady unfit for marriage. The teachers of Susan B. Anthony, the future feminist, refused to instruct her in long division.

Women's schools at the secondary level began to attain some respectability in the 1820s, thanks in part to the dedicated work of Emma Willard (1787–1870). In 1821 she established the Troy (New York) Female Seminary. Oberlin College, in Ohio, jolted traditionalists in 1837 when it opened its doors to women as well as men. (Oberlin had already created shock waves by admitting black students.) In the same year, Mary Lyon established an outstanding women's school, Mount Holyoke Seminary (later College), in South Hadley, Massachusetts. Mossback critics scoffed that "they'll be educatin' cows next."

Adults who craved more learning satisfied their thirst for knowledge at private subscription libraries or, increasingly, at tax-supported libraries. House-to-house peddlers also did a

---

Horace Mann deplored indolence when he said, "Lost, yesterday, somewhere between sunrise and sunset, two golden hours, each set with sixty diamond minutes. No reward is offered, for they are gone forever."

Mary Lyon (1797–1849) *An intrepid pioneer in the field of higher education for women, Mary Lyon was a gifted teacher who achieved an important breakthrough when, in the face of much antagonism, she managed to raise enough money to launch her "Female Seminary," now Mount Holyoke College. The year after it opened in 1837, she had to turn away some four hundred applicants. She served as principal for twelve years.*

lush business in feeding the public appetite for culture. Traveling lecturers helped to carry learning to the masses through the lyceum lecture associations, which numbered about three thousand by 1835. The lyceums provided platforms for speakers in such areas as science, literature, and moral philosophy. Talented talkers like Ralph Waldo Emerson journeyed thousands of miles on the lyceum circuits, casting their pearls of civilization before appreciative audiences.

Magazines flourished in the pre–Civil War years, but most of them withered after a short life. The *North American Review*, founded in 1815, was the long-lived leader of the intellectu-

als. *Godey's Lady's Book*, founded in 1830, survived until 1898 and attained the enormous circulation (for those days) of 150,000. It was devoured devotedly by countless millions of women.

The Changing American Family

The rustling pages of publications like *Godey's Lady's Book*, perused in parlors all over America, quietly heralded a subtle, slow-moving, but eventually sweeping revolution in American society. Women were growing more conscious of themselves as individuals and as one another's "sisters" in a world where male and female sexual roles were becoming more sharply divided. Prompted in part by the wide circulation of women's magazines like *Godey's*, this dawning self-consciousness was beginning to change women's lives—and to transform society's most fundamental institution, the family.

It was still a man's world, in America and Europe, when the nineteenth century opened. A wife was supposed to immerse herself in her home and subordinate herself to her lord and master. Like black slaves, she could not vote; like black slaves, she could be legally beaten by her overlord "with a reasonable instrument." When she married, she could not retain title of her property; it passed to her husband.

Yet American women, though legally regarded as perpetual minors, fared better than their European cousins, partly because of their scarcity in frontier communities. A western woman could warn her spouse to be respectful, for "if you don't there's plenty will." Few American husbands were brutes; and women always had quiet ways of protecting themselves, regardless of law.

Despite these relative advantages, women were still "the submerged sex" in America in the early part of the century. But as the decades unfolded, women increasingly emerged to breathe the air of freedom and self-determination. In contrast to colonial times, many women avoided marriage altogether—about 10 percent of adult women remained "spinsters" at the time of the Civil War.

Opportunities for women to be economically self-supporting were still scarce and consisted mainly of low-paying factory jobs, nursing, and especially teaching. The dedicated Catharine Beecher, unmarried daughter of a famous preacher and sister of Harriet Beecher Stowe, tirelessly urged women to enter the teaching profession. She eventually succeeded beyond her dreams, as men left teaching for other lines of work and schoolteaching became a thoroughly "feminized" occupation. Other work "opportunities" for women beckoned in domestic service. Perhaps one white family in ten employed servants at midcentury, most of whom were poor white, immigrant, or black women. About 10 percent of white women were working

Godey's Lady's Book   *The most popular women's magazine of the era. (Schlesinger Library, Radcliffe College; photo by Barry Donahue.)*

for pay outside their own homes in 1850, and estimates are that about 20 percent of all women had been employed at some time prior to marriage.

The vast majority of working women were single. Upon marriage, they left their paying jobs and took up their new work (without wages) as wives and mothers. In the home they were enshrined in a "cult of domesticity," a widespread cultural creed that glorified the traditional functions of the homemaker. From their pedestal, married women commanded immense moral power, and they increasingly made decisions that altered the character of the family itself.

Families are like air—they surround most people completely and so constantly that they have tended to be invisible, historically speaking. But though they long went unrecorded, some important changes were overtaking the life of the nineteenth-century home—the traditional "women's sphere." Love, not parental "arrangement," more and more frequently determined the choice of a spouse—yet parents often retained the power of veto. Families thus became more closely knit and affectionate, providing the emotional refuge that made the threatening impersonality of big-city industrialism tolerable to many people.

Most striking, families grew smaller. The average household had nearly six members at the end of the eighteenth century but fewer than five members a century later. The "fertility rate," or number of births among women aged 14 to 45, dropped sharply among white women in the years after the Revolution and, in the course of the nineteenth century as a whole, fell by half. Birth control was still a taboo topic for polite conversation, and contraceptive technology was primitive, but clearly some form of family limitation was being practiced quietly and effectively in countless families, rural and urban alike. Women undoubtedly played a large part—perhaps the leading part—in decisions to have fewer children. This newly assertive role for women has been called "domestic feminism," because it signified the growing power and independence of women, even while they remained trapped in the "cult of domesticity."

Smaller families, in turn, meant child-centered families, since where children are fewer, parents can lavish more care on them individually. European visitors to the United States in the nineteenth century often complained about the unruly behavior of American "brats." But though American parents may have increasingly spared the rod, they did not spoil their children. Lessons were enforced by punishments other than the hickory stick. When the daughter of novelist Harriet Beecher Stowe neglected to do her homework, her mother sent her from the dinner table and gave her "only bread and water in her own apartment." What Europeans saw as permissiveness was in reality the consequence of an emerging new idea of child rearing, in which the child's will was not to be simply broken, but shaped. In the little republic of the family, as in the Republic at large, good citizens were raised not to be meekly obedient to authority, but to be independent individuals who could make their own decisions on the basis of internalized moral standards. Thus, the outlines of the "modern" family were clear by midcentury: it was small, affectionate, child-centered, and provided a special arena for the talents of women. Feminists of a later day might decry the stifling atmosphere of the Victorian home, but to many women of the time it seemed a big step upward from the conditions of grinding toil—often alongside men in the fields—in which their mothers had lived.

Journalistic Giants

The newspaper—"the university of the public"—was further popularized by free, compulsory education and a consequent increase of literacy. Before 1830 a daily journal cost about six cents, a sum that the dollar-a-day manual laborer could ill afford to pay. The New York *Sun*, seeking the economies of mass production, reduced its price in 1833 to one cent. It thus inaugurated the era of the "penny dreadful"—dreadful because it featured murders, scandals, and other human-interest stories in the manner of the modern tabloid.

A leader in the new "gutter journalism" was erratic James Gordon Bennett, who in 1835 founded the New York *Herald*. His office desk consisted of two flour barrels with a plank laid across them; and he was editor, reporter, proofreader, folder, and cashier. He aggressively expanded the definition of "news," printing facts about all kinds of topics. Bennett also believed that the function of newspapers was not only to instruct people but also to startle them, and he and other editors lowered the public taste while lowering the price of their sheets. In any event, more Americans were now reading than ever before.

The influence of journalism was vastly increased by the march of mechanization. Telegraphy instantly updated the news, and "scoops" became the newspaper reporter's driving demon. Quick contact with events only hours old whetted the public's appetite for more newsprint, and publishers sought to multiply the output of their clanking presses. In 1846 Richard Hoe came to their aid with a cylindrical press that could spew forth eight thousand papers in an hour.

The decades just before the Civil War marked the dawn of the golden age of personal journalism. Newspaper publishing had not yet become a big business, and editors like Horace Greeley of the New York *Tribune* owned and published their own newspapers. His weekly edition enjoyed a wide circulation outside New York State, and since the idealistic Greeley was a merciless foe of slavery, his word was law among a host of followers. "Wait until the *Weekly Tribune* arrives," remarked a New York farmer when asked his opinion, "and then I can tell you what I think about it."

Passions ran incredibly high during this era of personalized, hit-below-the-belt journalism. The writing-fighting editors were frequently caned, stabbed, or shot by those whom they verbally abused. "You lie, you villain," wrote Greeley of a rival editor, "you sinfully, wickedly, basely lie."

Despite this violence and vulgarity, America was making praiseworthy progress in lifting the mental horizons of the masses. More people than ever were now able to inform themselves on current issues; and with increased knowledge went an increased ability to make democracy work.

Varying Viewpoints

Ever since its publication in 1835, Alexis de Tocqueville's *Democracy in America* has defined the terms for discussion of the American character. Most accounts of the era between the Revolution and the Civil War have ratified Tocqueville's claims that individualism and equality formed the distinguishing values of antebellum American life.

Nearly twenty-five years ago, the historian David M. Potter raised a challenge to Tocqueville. How would our conception of the American character change, Potter asked, if we remembered that half of all Americans were women? How did the ideal of equality apply to women? Does a focus on women cause us to revise the belief that individualism and suspicion of the "community" were hallmarks of the national character? In the last ten years, historians such as Nancy Cott have offered answers to Potter's question. Women's concern for their families and for a larger network of human associations, these scholars argue, nurtured strong traditions of community ties and reform activity in antebellum America.

Select Readings

Primary Source Documents

Joseph Smith, *The Pearl of Great Price* * (1829), contains an account of the Mormon leader's religious visions, which capture the religious ferment of the age. William H. McGuffey, *Fifth Eclectic Reader* * (1879), was the most popular school text of the age. Catharine Beecher and Harriet Beecher Stowe, *The American Woman's Home* * (1869), discusses the role of women. Stowe's classic *Uncle Tom's Cabin* (1852) offers an emotional appeal against slavery and a fascinating portrait of slavery, religion, and family life in antebellum America.

Secondary Sources

Satisfying detail may be found in Russell B. Nye, *The Cultural Life of the New Nation, 1776–1830* (1960), and the same author's *Society and Culture in America, 1830–1860* (1974). Alexis de Tocqueville's classic account of life in the young Republic is brilliantly analyzed by James R. Schlieffer in *The Making of Tocqueville's "Democracy in America"* (1980). Richard A. Easterlin analyzes *Population, Labor Force, and Long Swings in Economic Growth: The American Experience* (1968). Maldwyn Jones, *American Immigration*, is a standard work. Sydney E. Ahlstrom, *Religious History of the American People* (1972), is sweeping. William W. Sweet, *Religion in the Development of American Culture, 1765–1840* (1952), concentrates on the early national period. On revivalism, see William G. McLoughlin, *Modern Revivalism: Charles Grandison Finney to Billy Graham* (1959), and Whitney Cross's absorbing *The Burned-Over District* (1950). McLoughlin's *Revivals, Awakenings and Reform: An Essay on Religion and Social Change in America, 1607–1977* (1978) is highly original, as is Paul Johnson, *A Shopkeeper's Millennium: Society and Revivals in Rochester, New York, 1815–1837* (1978). On education, see Lawrence A. Cremin, *American Education: The National Experience, 1789–1860* (1980); David Nasaw, *Schooled to Order: A Social History of Public Schooling in the United States* (1979); and Carl F. Kaestle and Maris A. Vinovskis, *Education and Social Change in Nineteenth-Century Massachusetts* (1980). An alternative interpretation of the rise of public education can be found in Michael Katz, *The Irony of Early School Reform* (1968), and Samuel Bowles and Herbert Gintis, *Schooling in Capitalist America* (1976). Recent work of note on women and the family includes Joseph F. Kett, *Rites of Passage: Adolescence in America, 1790 to the Present* (1977); Lewis Perry, *Childhood, Marriage, and Reform: Henry Clarke Wright, 1797–1870* (1980); Carl N. Degler, *At Odds: Women and the Family in America from the Revolution to the Present* (1980); Mary P. Ryan, *Cradle of the Middle*

Class: The Family in Oneida County, New York (1981); and Nancy Cott's particularly sensitive *The Bonds of Womanhood: "Woman's Sphere" in New England, 1780–1835* (1977). See also Kathryn Kish Sklar, *Catharine Beecher: A Study in Domesticity* (1973). Suzanne Lebsock, *The Free Women of Petersburg* (1984), discusses these issues in a southern context. On life in the slave societies of the South, see the detailed listings in Chapter 20. Special topics are treated in Lewis O. Saum, *The Popular Mood of Pre–Civil War America* (1980); Morton J. Horowitz, *The Transformation of American Law, 1780–1860* (1977); James W. Hurst, *Law and Social Order in the United States* (1977); and James H. Kettner, *The Development of American Citizenship, 1608–1870* (1978).

19

The Ferment of Reform and Culture, 1790–1860

> We [Americans] will walk on our own feet; we will work with our own hands; we will speak our own minds.
>
> Ralph Waldo Emerson,
> "The American Scholar," 1837

An Age of Reform

As the young Republic grew, reform campaigns of all types flourished in sometimes bewildering abundance. There was not "a reading man" who was without some scheme for a new utopia in his "waistcoat pocket," claimed Ralph Waldo Emerson. Reformers promoted rights for women as well as miracle medicines, communal living, polygamy, celibacy, rule by prophets, and guidance by spirits. Societies were formed against alcohol, tobacco, profanity, and the transit of mail on the Sabbath. Fad diets proved popular, including the whole-wheat bread and crackers regimen of Sylvester Graham. Eventually overshadowing all other reforms was the crusade against slavery.

Many reformers were simply crackbrained cranks. But most were intelligent, inspired idealists, usually touched by the fire of evangelical religion then licking through the pews and pulpits of American churches. The optimistic promises of the Second Great Awakening inspirited countless souls to do battle against earthly evils. These modern idealists dreamed anew the old Puritan vision of a perfected society: free from cruelty, war, intoxicating drink, discrimination, and—ultimately—slavery. Women were particularly prominent in these reform crusades, especially in their own struggle for suffrage. For many middle-class women, the reform campaigns provided a unique opportunity to escape the confines of home and enter the arena of public affairs.

In part, the practical, activist Christianity of these reformers resulted from their desire to reaffirm traditional values as they plunged ever further into a world disrupted and transformed by the turbulent forces of a market economy. Mainly middle-class descendants of pioneer farmers, they were often blissfully unaware that they were witnessing the dawn of the industrial era, which posed unprecedented problems and called for novel ideas. They either ignored the factory workers, for example, or blamed their problems on bad habits. With naive single-mindedness, reformers sometimes applied conventional virtue to refurbishing an older order—while events hurtled them headlong into the new.

Imprisonment for debt continued to be a nightmare, though its extent has been exaggerated. As late as 1830 hundreds of penniless persons were languishing in filthy holes, some-times for owing less than one dollar. The poorer working classes were especially hard hit by this merciless practice. But as the embattled laborer won the ballot and asserted himself, state legislatures gradually abolished debtors' prisons.

Criminal codes in the states were likewise being softened, in accord with more enlightened European practices. The number of capital offenses was being reduced, and brutal punishments, such as whipping and branding, were being slowing eliminated. A refreshing idea was taking hold that prisons should reform as well as punish—hence "reformatories," "houses of correction," and "penitentiaries" (for penance).

Sufferers from so-called insanity were still being treated with incredible cruelty. The medieval concept had been that the mentally deranged were cursed with unclean spirits; the nineteenth-century idea was that they were willfully perverse and depraved—to be treated only as beasts. Many crazed persons were chained in jails or poorhouses with sane people.

Into this dismal picture stepped a quiet New England teacher-author, Dorothea Dix (1802–1887). A frail spinster afflicted with persistent lung trouble, she possessed infinite compassion and willpower. Never raising her voice to a screech, she traveled some 60,000 miles (97,000 kilometers) in eight years and assembled her damning reports on insanity from firsthand observations. Her classic petition of 1843 to the Massachusetts legislature, describing cells so foul that visitors were driven back by the stench, turned legislative stomachs and hearts. Her persistent prodding resulted in improved conditions and in a gain for the concept that the demented were not willfully perverse but mentally ill.

Agitation for peace also gained some momentum in the pre–Civil War years. In 1828 the American Peace Society was formed, with a ringing declaration of war on war. A leading spirit was William Ladd, who orated when his legs were so badly ulcerated that he had to sit on a stool. His ideas were finally to bear some fruit in the international organizations for collective security of the twentieth century. The American peace crusade, linked with the European crusade, was making promising progress by midcentury, when it was set back by

Dorothea Dix (1802–1887) *A tireless reformer, she worked mightily to improve the treatment of the mentally ill. At the outbreak of the Civil War she was appointed superintendent of women nurses for the Union forces. (National Portrait Gallery, Smithsonian Institution, Washington, D.C.)*

the bloodshed of the Crimean War in Europe and the Civil War in America.

Demon Rum—The "Old Deluder"

The ever-present drink problem attracted dedicated reformers. Custom, combined with a hard and monotonous life, led to the excessive drinking of hard liquor, even among women, clergymen, and members of Congress. Weddings and funerals all too often became disgraceful brawls, and occasionally a drunken mourner would fall into the open grave with the corpse. Heavy drinking decreased the efficiency of labor, while the introduction of poorly safeguarded machinery increased the danger of accidents occuring at work. Drunkenness also fouled the sanctity of the family, threatening the spiritual welfare—and physical safety—of women and children.

After earlier and feebler efforts, the American Temperance Society was formed at Boston in 1826. Within a few years about a thousand local groups sprang into existence. They implored drinkers to sign the temperance pledge and organized children's clubs, known as the "Cold Water Army." Temperance crusaders also made effective use of pictures, pamphlets, and lurid lecturers, some of whom were reformed drunkards. A popular temperance song ran:

> We've done with our days of carousing,
> Our nights, too, of frolicsome glee;
> For now with our sober minds choosing,
> We've pledged ourselves never to spree.

The most popular antialcohol tract of the era was T. S. Arthur's melodramatic novel, *Ten Nights in a Barroom and What I Saw There* (1854). It described in shocking detail how a once-happy village was ruined by Sam Slade's tavern. The book was second only to Stowe's *Uncle Tom's Cabin* as a best-seller in the 1850s, and it enjoyed a highly successful run on the stage. Its touching theme song began with the words of a little girl:

> Father, dear father, come home with me
>   now,
> The clock in the belfry strikes one.

The Perils of Drink *Among the many evils of alcohol, reformers fulminated especially against its corrupting effects on family life, as shown in this prohibitionist tract of the 1820s, entitled* The Drunkard's Progress. *(American Antiquarian Society, Worcester, Massachusetts.)*

Early foes of Demon Drink adopted two major lines of attack. One was to stiffen the individual's will to resist the wiles of the little brown jug. The moderate reformers thus stressed "temperance" rather than "teetotalism," or the total elimination of intoxicants. But less patient zealots gradually came to believe that temptation should be removed by legislation. Prominent among this group was Neal S. Dow of Maine, a bluenosed reformer who, as a mayor of Portland and an employer of labor, had often witnessed the debauching effect of alcohol.

Dow—the "Father of Prohibition"—sponsored the so-called Maine Law of 1851, which supplanted an earlier effort in 1846. This drastic new statute, hailed as "the law of Heaven Americanized," prohibited the manufacture and sale of intoxicating liquor. Other states in the

North followed Maine's example, and by 1857 about a dozen had passed various prohibitory laws. But these figures are deceptive, for within a decade some of the statutes were repealed or declared unconstitutional, if not openly flouted.

It was clearly impossible to legislate thirst out of existence, especially in localities where public sentiment was hostile. Yet on the eve of the Civil War the prohibitionists had registered inspiriting gains. There was much less drinking among women than earlier in the century and probably much less per capita consumption of hard liquor.

Women in Revolt

Sexual differences were strongly emphasized in nineteenth-century America—largely because the burgeoning market economy was increasingly separating women and men into sharply distinct economic roles. Women were thought to be physically and emotionally weak, but also artistic and refined. Endowed with finely tuned moral sensibilities, they were the keepers of society's conscience, with special responsibility to teach the young how to be good and productive citizens of the Republic. Men were considered strong but crude, always in danger of slipping into some savage or beastly way of life if not guided by the gentle hands of their loving ladies.

But if sexual roles were sharply separated, men and women could still be regarded as equals. As a sign of the prestigious position of American women, French visitor Alexis de Tocqueville noted that in his native France rape was punished only lightly, while in America it was one of the few crimes punishable by death.

The home was a woman's special sphere. Even reformers like Catharine Beecher, who urged her sisters to seek employment as teachers, endlessly celebrated the role of the good homemaker. But some women increasingly felt that the glorified sanctuary of the home was in fact a gilded cage. They yearned to tear down the bars that separated the private world of women from the public world of men.

The clamorous female reformers gathered strength as the century neared its halfway point. Most of them were broad-gauge battlers; while demanding rights for women, they participated in the general reform movement of the age, fighting for temperance and the abolition of slavery. Like men, they had been touched by the evangelical spirit that offered the alluring promise of earthly reward for human endeavor. Neither foul eggs nor foul words, when hurled by disapproving men, could halt women heartened by these doctrines.

The woman's rights movement was mothered by some arresting characters. Prominent among them was Lucretia Mott, a sprightly Quaker whose ire had been aroused when she and her fellow female delegates to the London antislavery convention of 1840 were not recognized. Elizabeth Cady Stanton, a mother of seven who had insisted on leaving "obey" out of her marriage ceremony, shocked fellow feminists by going so far as to advocate suffrage for women. Quaker-reared Susan B. Anthony, a militant lecturer for woman's rights, exposed herself to rotten garbage and vulgar epithets. She became such a conspicuous advocate of female rights that progressive women everywhere were called "Suzy Bs."

Stellar Suffragists   *Elizabeth Cady Stanton (left) and Susan B. Anthony (right) were two of the most persistent battlers for women's rights. (Brown Brothers.)*

What It Would Be If Some Ladies Had Their Own Way The men are sewing, tending the baby, and washing clothes. This scene seemed absurd then, but not a century later. (Historical Pictures Service, Chicago.)

Other feminists challenged the man's world. Dr. Elizabeth Blackwell, a pioneer in a previously forbidden profession for women, was the first female graduate of a medical college. Precocious Margaret Fuller edited a transcendentalist journal, *The Dial*, and is remembered for having said, "I accept the universe." The talented Grimké sisters, Sarah and Angelina, spoke at antislavery gatherings and aroused the ire of conservatives. Lucy Stone retained her maiden name after marriage—hence, the latter-day "Lucy Stoners," who follow her example. Amelia Bloomer revolted against the current "street sweeping" female attire by donning a semimasculine short skirt with Turkish trousers—"bloomers," they were called—amid much bawdy ridicule about "Bloomerism" and "loose habits." A jeering male rhyme of the times jabbed:

> Gibbey, gibbey gab
> The women had a confab
> And demanded the rights
> To wear the tights
> Gibbey, gibbey gab.

Fighting feminists met at Seneca Falls, New York, in a memorable Woman's Rights Convention (1848). The defiant Stanton read a "Declaration of Sentiments," which in the spirit of the Declaration of Independence declared that "all men *and women* are created equal." One resolution formally demanded the ballot for females. The Seneca Falls meeting, which launched the modern woman's rights movement, not surprisingly became the object of scorn and denunciation from press and pulpit.

The crusade for woman's rights was eclipsed by that against slavery in the decade before the Civil War. Male idiots could still vote; women could not. Yet women were being gradually admitted to colleges, and some states, beginning with Mississippi in 1839, were even permitting wives to own property after marriage.

Wilderness Utopias

Bolstered by the utopian spirit of the age, various reformers, ranging from the high-minded to the "lunatic fringe," set up more than forty communities of a cooperative, communistic, or "communitarian" nature. Seeking human betterment, a wealthy and idealistic Scottish textile manufacturer, Robert Owen, established in 1825 a communal society of about a thousand persons at New Harmony, Indiana. Little harmony prevailed in the colony, which, in addition to hardworking visionaries, attracted a sprinkling of radicals, lazy theorists, and outright scoundrels. The enterprise sank in a morass of contradiction and confusion.

Brook Farm in Massachusetts, comprising two hundred acres of grudging soil, was started in 1841 with the brotherly cooperation of about twenty intellectuals. They prospered reasonably well until 1846, when they lost by fire a large new communal building shortly before its completion. The whole experiment in "plain living and high thinking" then collapsed in debt. Although a financial failure, Brook Farm was in some ways a social and educational success.

A more radical experiment was the Oneida Colony, founded in New York in 1848. It practiced free love ("complex marriage"), birth control, and the eugenic selection of parents to produce superior offspring. The leader finally fled to Canada to escape prosecution for adultery. This curious enterprise flourished for more than thirty years, largely because its craftsmen made superior steel traps and Oneida Community (silver) Plate. In 1879–1880 the group embraced monogamy and abandoned communism.

Various communistic experiments, mostly small-scale, have been attempted since Jamestown. But in competition with democratic free enterprise and free land, virtually all of them sooner or later failed or changed their methods. Perhaps the longest-lived sect has been the Shakers, who, beginning in 1776, set up the first of a score or so of religious communities. They attained a membership of about six thou-

Shakers in Dancing Ceremony

sand in 1840, but since they opposed both marriage and free love, they were virtually extinct by 1940.

The Dawn of Scientific Achievement

Early Americans, confronted with pioneering problems, were more interested in practical gadgets than in pure science. Thomas Jefferson, for example, was a gifted amateur inventor, who won a gold medal for a new type of plow. Noteworthy were the writings of the mathematician Nathaniel Bowditch (1733–1838) on practical navigation and of the oceanographer Matthew F. Maury (1806–1873) on ocean winds and currents. All these writers promoted safety, speed, and economy. But as far as basic science was concerned, Americans were best known for borrowing and adapting the findings of Europeans.

Yet the Republic was not without scientific talent. The most influential American scientist of the first half of the nineteenth century was Professor Benjamin Silliman (1779–1864), a pioneer chemist and geologist who taught and wrote brilliantly at Yale College for more than fifty years. Professor Louis Agassiz (1807–1873), a distinguished French-Swiss immigrant, served for a quarter of a century at Harvard College. As a path-breaking student of biology who sometimes carried snakes in his pockets, he insisted on original research and deplored the overemphasis on memory work. Professor Asa Gray (1810–1888) of Harvard College, the Columbus of American botany, published over 350 books, monographs, and papers. His textbooks set new standards for clarity and interest.

Lovers of American bird lore owed much to the French-descended John J. Audubon (1785–1851), who painted wild fowl in their natural habitat. His magnificently illustrated *Birds of America* attained considerable popularity. The Audubon Society for the protection of birds was named after him, although as a young man he shot much feathered game for sport.

Medicine in America, despite a steady growth of medical schools, was still primitive by mod-

Passenger Pigeons, by John Audubon (left) *An astute naturalist and a gifted artist, Audubon drew the birds of America in loving detail. Ironically, he had to go to England in the 1820s to find a publisher for his pioneering depictions of the unique beauty of American wildlife. (New-York Historical Society.)* **John J. Audubon** (right) *Born in Haiti and educated in France, he achieved fame as America's greatest ornithologist. (American Museum of Natural History.)*

ern standards. Bleeding remained a common remedy. Plagues of smallpox were still dreaded, and the terrible yellow fever epidemic of 1793 in Philadelphia took several thousand lives. "Bring out your dead!" was the daily cry of the drivers of the death wagons.

People everywhere complained of ill health—malaria, the "rheumatics," the "miseries," and the chills. Illness often resulted from improper diet, hurried eating, perspiring and cooling off too rapidly, and ignorance of germs and sanitation. "We was sick every fall, regular," wrote the mother of the future President Garfield. Life expectancy was still dismayingly short—about forty years for a white person born in 1850, and less for blacks. The suffering from decayed or

ulcerated teeth was enormous; tooth extraction was often practiced by the muscular village blacksmith.

An outbreak of cholera occurred in New York City in 1832, and a wealthy businessman, Philip Hone, wrote in his diary for the Fourth of July: "The alarm about the cholera has prevented all the usual jollification under the public authority. . . . The Board of Health reports to-day twenty new cases and eleven deaths since noon yesterday. The disease is here in all its violence and will increase. God grant that its ravages may be confined, and its visit short."

Early Advertising *Hawkers of patent medicines pioneered the techniques of modern advertising. Here a pain killer is promoted by invoking the totally irrelevant image of Molly Pitcher. The legendary subject of a poem by John Greenleaf Whittier, Pitcher reputedly took her fallen husband's place at a cannon during the Revolutionary War Battle of Monmouth in 1778. What this exploit had to do with anaesthetics is by no means clear, but it supposedly sold the product. (The Granger Collection.)*

Self-prescribed patent medicines were common (one dose for people, two for horses) and included Robertson's Infallible Worm Destroying Lozenges. Among home remedies was the rubbing of tumors with dead toads. The use of medicine by the regular doctors was often harmful, and Dr. Oliver Wendell Holmes declared in 1860 that if the medicines, as then employed, were thrown into the sea, humans would be better off and the fish worse off.

Victims of surgical operations were ordinarily tied down, often after a stiff drink of whiskey.

The surgeon then sawed or cut with breakneck speed, undeterred by the piercing shrieks of the patient. A priceless boon for medical progress came in the early 1840s, when several American doctors and dentists, working independently, successfully employed laughing gas and ether as anesthetics.

Artistic Achievements

Architecturally, America contributed little of note in the first half of the century. The rustic Republic, still under pressure to erect shelters in haste, was continuing to imitate European models. Public buildings and other important structures followed Greek and Roman lines, which seemed curiously out of place in a wilderness setting. A remarkable Greek revival came between 1820 and 1850, partly stimulated by the heroic efforts of the Greeks in the 1820s to wrest independence from the "terrible Turk." About midcentury strong interest developed in a revival of Gothic forms, with their emphasis on pointed arches and large windows.

Talented Thomas Jefferson, architect of revolution, was probably the ablest American architect of his generation. He brought a classical design to his Virginia hilltop home, Monticello—perhaps the most stately mansion in the nation (see p.160). The quadrangle of the University of Virginia at Charlottesville, another creation of Jefferson, remains one of the finest examples of classical architecture in America.

The art of painting continued to be handicapped. It suffered from the dollar grabbing of a raw civilization; from the hustle, bustle, and absence of leisure; from the lack of a wealthy class to sit for portraits—and then pay for them. Some of the earliest painters were forced to go to England, where they found both training and patrons. America exported artists and imported art.

Painting, like the theater, also suffered from the Puritan prejudice that art was a sinful waste of time—and often obscene. John Adams boasted that "he would not give a sixpence for a bust of Phidias or a painting by Raphael." When Edward Everett, the eminent Boston scholar and orator, placed a statue of Apollo in his home, he had its naked limbs draped.

Competent painters nevertheless emerged. Gilbert Stuart (1755–1828), a spendthrift Rhode Islander and one of the most gifted of the early group, wielded his brush in England in competition with the best artists. He produced several portraits of Washington, all of them somewhat idealized and dehumanized. Truth to tell, the famous general had by then lost his natural teeth and some of the original shape of his face. Charles Willson Peale (1741–1827), a Marylander, painted some sixty portraits of Washington, who patiently sat for about fourteen of them. John Trumbull (1756–1843), who had fought in the Revolutionary War, recaptured its scenes and spirit on scores of striking canvases.

During the nationalistic upsurge after the War of 1812, American painters of portraits turned increasingly from human landscapes to romantic mirrorings of local landscapes. The Hudson River school excelled in this type of art. At the same time, portrait painters gradually encountered some unwelcome competition from the invention of a crude photograph known as the daguerreotype, perfected about 1839 by a Frenchman, Louis Daguerre.

Music was slowly shaking off the restraints of colonial days, when the prim Puritans had frowned upon nonreligious singing. Rhythmic and nostalgic "darky" tunes, popularized by whites, were becoming immense hits by mid-century. Special favorites were the uniquely American minstrel shows, featuring white actors with blackened faces. "Dixie," later adopted by the Confederates as their battle hymn, was written in 1859, ironically in New York City by an Ohioan. The most famous black songs, also ironically, came from a white Pennsylvanian, Stephen C. Foster (1826–1864). His one excursion into the South occurred in 1852, after he had published "Old Folks at Home." Foster made a valuable contribution to American folk music by capturing the plaintive spirit of the slaves. An odd and pathetic figure, he finally lost both his art and his popularity and died in a charity ward after drowning his sorrows in drink.

The Blossoming of a National Literature

"Who reads an American book?" sneered a British critic in 1820. The painful truth was that the nation's rough-hewn, pioneering civilization gave little encouragement to "polite" literature. Much of the reading matter was imported or plagiarized from England.

Busy conquering a continent, the Americans poured most of their creative efforts into practical outlets. Praiseworthy were political essays, like *The Federalist* of Hamilton, Jay, and Madison; pamphlets, like Tom Paine's *Common Sense;* and political orations, like the masterpieces of Daniel Webster. In the category of nonreligious books published before 1820, Benjamin Franklin's *Autobiography* (1818) is one of the few that achieved genuine distinction. His narrative is a classic in its simplicity, clarity, and inspirational quality. Even so, it records only a fragment of "Old Ben's" long, fruitful, and amorous life.

A genuinely American literature received a strong boost from the wave of nationalism that followed the War of Independence and especially the War of 1812. By 1820 the older seaboard areas were sufficiently removed from tree-chopping so that literature could be supported as a profession. The Knickerbocker Group in New York blazed brilliantly across the literary heavens, thus enabling America for the first time to boast of a literature to match her magnificent landscapes.

Washington Irving (1783–1859), born in New York City, was the first American to win international recognition as a literary figure. Steeped in the traditions of New Netherland, he published in 1809 his *Knickerbocker's History of New York*, with its amusing caricatures of the Dutch. When the family business failed, Irving was forced to turn to the goose-feather pen. In 1819–1820 he published *The Sketch Book*, which brought him immediate fame at home and abroad. Combining a pleasing style with delicate charm and quiet humor, he used English as well as American themes and included such immortal Dutch-American tales as "Rip Van Winkle" and "The Legend of Sleepy

Hollow." Europe was amazed to find at last an American with a feather in his hand, not in his hair. Later turning to Spanish locales and biography, Irving did much to interpret America to Europe and Europe to America. He was, said the Englishman William Thackeray, "the first ambassador whom the New World of letters sent to the Old."

James Fenimore Cooper (1789-1851) was the first American novelist, as Washington Irving was the first general writer, to gain world fame and to make New World themes respectable. Marrying into a wealthy family, he settled down on the frontier of New York. Reading one day to his wife from an insipid English novel, Cooper remarked in disgust that he could write a better book himself. His wife challenged him to do so—and he did.

After an initial failure, Cooper launched out upon an illustrious career in 1821 with his second novel, *The Spy*—an absorbing tale of the American Revolution. His stories of the sea were meritorious and popular, but his fame rests most enduringly on the *Leatherstocking Tales*. A deadeye rifleman named Natty Bumppo, one of nature's noblemen, meets with Indians in stirring adventures like *The Last of the Mohicans*. James Fenimore Cooper's novels had a wide sale among Europeans, some of whom came to think of all American people as born with tomahawk in hand. Actually Cooper was exploring the viability and destiny of America's republican experiment, by contrasting the values of "natural men," children of the wooded wilderness, with the artificiality of modern civilization.

A third member of the Knickerbocker group in New York was the belated Puritan William Cullen Bryant (1794–1878), transplanted from Massachusetts. At age sixteen he wrote the meditative and melancholy "Thanatopsis" (published in 1817), which was one of the first high-quality poems produced in the United States. Critics could hardly believe that it had been written on "this side of the water." Although Bryant continued with poetry, he was forced to make his living by editing the influential New York *Evening Post*. For over fifty years he set a model for journalism that was dignified, liberal, and high-minded.

Trumpeters of Transcendentalism

A golden age in American literature dawned in the second quarter of the nineteenth century, when an amazing outburst shook New England. One of the mainsprings of this literary flowering was transcendentalism, especially in the Boston area, which preened itself as "the Athens of America."

The transcendentalist movement of the 1830s resulted in part from a liberalizing of the straitjacket Puritan theology. It also owed much to foreign thinkers, including the German romantic philosophers. The transcendentalists rejected the prevailing theory, derived from John Locke, that all knowledge comes to the mind through the senses. Truth, rather, "transcends" the senses: it cannot be found by observation alone. Every person possesses an inner light that can illuminate the highest truth and put him or her in direct touch with God, or the "Oversoul."

These mystical doctrines of transcendentalism defied precise definition, but they underlay concrete beliefs. Foremost was a stiff-backed individualism in matters religious as well as social. Closely associated was a commitment to self-reliance, self-culture, and self-discipline. These traits naturally bred hostility to authority and to formal institutions of any kind, as well as to all conventional wisdom. Finally came exaltation of the dignity of the individual, whether black or white—the mainspring of a whole array of humanitarian reforms.

Best known of the transcendentalists was Boston-born Ralph Waldo Emerson (1803–1882). Tall, slender, and intensely blue-eyed, he mirrored serenity in his noble features. Trained as a Unitarian minister, he early forsook his pulpit and ultimately reached a wider audience by pen and platform. He was a never-failing favorite as a lyceum lecturer and for twenty years took a western tour every winter. Perhaps his most thrilling public effort was a Phi Beta Kappa address, "The American Scholar," delivered at Harvard College in 1837. This brilliant appeal was an intellectual Declaration of Independence, for it urged American writers to throw off European traditions and delve into the riches of their own backyards.

Hailed as both a poet and a philosopher, Emerson was not of the highest rank as either. He was more influential as a practical philosopher and through his fresh and vibrant essays enriched countless thousands of humdrum lives. Catching the individualistic mood of the Republic, he stressed self-reliance, self-improvement, self-confidence, optimism, and freedom. The secret of Emerson's popularity lay largely in the fact that his ideals reflected those of an expanding America. Among his most quoted observations are: "Whoso would be a man, must be a non-conformist"; "A foolish consistency is the hobgoblin of little minds"; "God offers to every mind its choice between truth and repose."

Ralph Waldo Emerson (1803–1882) *Emerson's philosophical observations include such statements as: "The less government we have, the better—the fewer laws, and the less confided power"; "To be great is to be misunderstood"; "Every hero becomes a bore at last"; "Shallow men believe in luck"; "When you strike a king, you must kill him." (Courtesy, Concord Free Public Library, gift of Mrs. Arthur Holland.)*

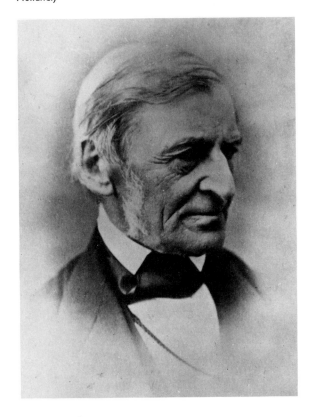

> *In 1849 Thoreau published* On the Duty of Civil Disobedience, *asserting "I heartily accept the motto, 'That government is best which governs least'; and I should like to see it acted up to more rapidly and systematically. Carried out, it finally amounts to this, which also I believe— 'That government is best which governs not at all'; and when men are prepared for it, that will be the kind of government which they will have. Government is at best an expedient; but most governments are sometimes, inexpedient."*

Henry David Thoreau (1817–1862) was Emerson's close associate—a poet, a mystic, a transcendentalist, and a nonconformist. Condemning a government that supported slavery, he refused to pay his Massachusetts poll tax and was jailed for a night.* A gifted prose writer, he is well known for *Walden: Or Life in the Woods* (1854). The book is a record of Thoreau's two years of simple existence in a hut that he built on the edge of Walden Pond, near Concord, Massachusetts. A stiff-necked individualist, he believed that he should reduce his bodily wants so as to gain time for a pursuit of truth through study and meditation. Thoreau's *Walden* and his essay on *Civil Disobedience* exercised a strong influence in furthering idealistic thought, both in America and abroad. His writings later encouraged Mahatma Gandhi to resist British rule in India and, still later, inspired the development of American civil rights leader Martin Luther King, Jr.'s thinking about nonviolence.

Bold, brassy, and swaggering was the open-collared figure of Brooklyn's Walt Whitman (1819–1892). In his famous collection of poems *Leaves of Grass* (1855), he gave free rein to his gushing genius with what he called a "barbaric yawp." Highly romantic, emotional, and unconventional, he dispensed with titles, stanzas,

---

*The story (probably apocryphal) is that Emerson visited Thoreau at the jail and asked, "Why are you here?" The reply came, "Why are you *not* here?"

Walt Whitman   *This portrait of the young poet appeared in the first edition of* Leaves of Grass *(1855). (Rare Book Division, New York Public Library, Astor, Lenox and Tilden Foundations.)*

rhymes, and at times even regular meter. He handled sex with shocking frankness, although he laundered his verses in later editions, and his book was banned in Boston.

Whitman's *Leaves of Grass* was at first a financial failure. The only three enthusiastic re-

> In 1876 the **London Saturday Review** *referred to Whitman as the author of a volume of "so-called poems which were chiefly remarkable for their absurd extravagances and shameless obscenity, and who has since, we are glad to say, been little heard of among decent people." In 1888 Whitman wrote: "I had my choice when I commenced. I bid neither for soft eulogies, big money returns, nor the approbation of existing schools and conventions. . . . I have had my say entirely my own way, and put it unerringly on record—the value thereof to be decided by time."*

views that it received were written by the author himself—anonymously. But in time the once-withered *Leaves of Grass*, revived and honored, won for Whitman an enormous following in both America and Europe. His fame increased immensely among "Whitmaniacs" after his death.

Leaves of Grass gained for Whitman the informal title "Poet Laureate of Democracy." Singing with transcendental abandon of his love for the masses, he caught the exuberant enthusiasm of an expanding America that had turned her back on the Old World:

> All the Past we leave behind;
> We debouch upon a newer, mightier world,
>   varied world;
> Fresh and strong the world we seize—world
>   of labor and the march—
> Pioneers! O Pioneers!

Here at last was the native art for which critics had been crying.

Glowing Literary Lights

Certain other literary giants were not actively associated with the transcendentalist movement, though not completely immune to its influences. Professor Henry Wadsworth Longfellow (1807–1882), who for many years taught modern languages at Harvard College, was one of the most popular poets ever produced in America. Handsome and urbane, he lived a generally serene life, except for the tragic deaths of two wives, the second of whom perished before his eyes when her dress caught fire. Writing for the genteel classes, he was adopted by the less cultured masses. His wide knowledge of European literature supplied him with many themes, but some of his most admired poems were based on American traditions—"Evangeline," "Hiawatha," and "The Courtship of Miles Standish." Immensely popular in Europe, Longfellow was the only American ever to be honored with a bust in the Poets' Corner of Westminster Abbey.

A fighting Quaker, John Greenleaf Whittier (1807–1892), with piercing dark eyes and swarthy complexion, was the uncrowned poet laureate of the antislavery crusade. Less talented as a craftsman than Longfellow, he was vastly more important in influencing social action. His poems cried aloud against inhumanity, injustice, and intolerance, against

> The outworn rite, the old abuse,
> The pious fraud transparent grown.

Undeterred by insults and the stonings of mobs, Whittier helped arouse a calloused America on the slavery issue. A great conscience rather than a great poet or intellect, Whittier was one of the moving forces of his generation, whether moral, humanitarian, or spiritual. Gentle and lovable, he was preeminently the poet of human freedom.

Many-sided James Russell Lowell (1819–1891), who succeeded Professor Longfellow at Harvard, ranks as one of America's better poets. He was also a distinguished essayist, literary critic, editor, and diplomat—a diffusion of talents that hampered his poetical output. He is remembered as a political satirist in his *Biglow Papers,* especially those of 1846 dealing with the Mexican War. Written partly as poetry in the Yankee dialect, the *Papers* condemned in blistering terms the alleged slavery-expansion designs of the Polk administration.

Slender Dr. Oliver Wendell Holmes (1809–1894), who taught anatomy with a sparkle at Harvard Medical School, was a prominent poet, essayist, novelist, lecturer, and wit. A nonconformist and a fascinating conversationalist, he shone among a group of literary lights who regarded Boston as "the hub of the universe." His poem "The Last Leaf," in honor of the last "white Indian" of the Boston Tea Party, came to apply to himself. Dying at age eighty-five, he was the "last leaf" among his distinguished contemporaries.*

The most noteworthy literary figure produced by the South before the Civil War, unless Edgar Allan Poe is regarded as a southerner, was nov-

---

*Oliver Wendell Holmes had a son with the same name who became a distinguished justice of the Supreme Court (1902–1932) and who lived to be ninety-four, less two days.

elist William Gilmore Simms (1806–1870). Quantitatively, at least, he was great: eighty-two books flowed from his ever-moist pen, winning for him the title "the Cooper of the South." His themes dealt with the southern frontier in colonial days and with the South during the Revolutionary War. But he was neglected by his own section, even though he married into the socially elite and became a slaveowner. The high-toned planter aristocracy would never accept the son of a poor Charleston storekeeper.

Literary Individualists and Dissenters

Not all writers in these years believed so keenly in human goodness and social progress. Edgar Allan Poe (1809–1849), who spent much of his youth in Virginia, was an eccentric genius. Orphaned at an early age, cursed with ill health, and married to a child-wife of fourteen who fell fatally ill of tuberculosis, he suffered hunger, cold, poverty, and debt. Failing at suicide, he took refuge in the bottle and dissipated his talent early. Poe was a gifted lyric poet, as "The Raven" attests. A master stylist, he also excelled in the short story, especially of the horror type, in which he shared his alcoholic nightmares with fascinated readers. If he did not invent the modern detective novel, he at least set new high standards in tales like "The Gold Bug."

Poe was fascinated by the ghostly and ghastly, as in "The Fall of the House of Usher" and other stories. He reflected a morbid sensibility distinctly at odds with the usually optimistic tone of American culture. Partly for this reason, Poe has perhaps been even more prized by Europeans than by his own countrymen. His brilliant career was cut short when he was found drunk in a Baltimore gutter and shortly thereafter died.

Two other writers reflected the continuing Calvinist obsession with original sin and with the never-ending struggle between good and evil. In somber Salem, Massachusetts, writer Nathaniel Hawthorne grew up in an atmosphere heavy with the memories of his Puritan forebears and the tragedy of his father's premature death on an ocean voyage. His masterpiece

Hazardous Whaling   Moby Dick *gives a vivid firsthand picture of whaling which proved to be an important industry from colonial times to the end of the nineteenth century. (From* Etchings of a Whaling Cruise, *by John Ross Browne, 1846. Stanford University Libraries.)*

was *The Scarlet Letter* (1850), which described the Puritan practice of forcing an adultress to wear a scarlet *A* on her clothing.* The tragic tale chronicles the psychological effects of sin on the guilty heroine and her secret lover (the father of her baby), a minister of the gospel in Puritan Boston. In *The Marble Faun* (1860), Hawthorne dealt with a group of young American artists who witness a mysterious murder in Rome. He thus explored the concepts of the omnipresence of evil and the dead hand of the past weighing upon the present.

Herman Melville (1819–1891), an orphaned and ill-educated New Yorker, went to sea as a youth and served eighteen adventuresome months on a whaler. "A whale ship was my Yale College and my Harvard," he wrote. Jumping ship in the South Seas, he lived among cannibals, from whom he providentially escaped uneaten. His fresh and charming tales of the South Seas were immediately popular, but his masterpiece, *Moby Dick* (1851), was not. This epic novel was a complex allegory of good and evil, told in terms of the conflict between a

---

*This was how Hester Prynne got her *A* in the *The Scarlet Letter.* An *H* stood for heresy and an *I* for incest.

whaling captain, Ahab, and a giant white whale, Moby Dick. Captain Ahab, who lost a leg to the marine monster, swore revenge. His pursuit finally ended when Moby Dick rammed and sank Ahab's ship, leaving only one survivor. The whale's exact identity and Ahab's motives remained obscure. In the end the sea, like the terrifyingly impersonal and unknowable universe of Melville's imagination, simply rolled on.

Moby Dick was widely ignored at the time of its publication; people were accustomed to more straightforward and upbeat prose. A disheartened Melville continued to write unprofitably for some years, part of the time eking out a living as a customs inspector, and then died in relative obscurity and poverty. Ironically, his brooding masterpiece about the mysterious white whale had to wait until the more jaded twentieth century for readers and for proper recognition.

Portrayers of the Past

A distinguished group of American historians was emerging at the same time that other writers were winning distinction. Energetic George

Bancroft (1800–1891), who as secretary of the navy helped found the Naval Academy at Annapolis in 1845, has deservedly received the title "Father of American History." He published a spirited, superpatriotic history of the United States to 1789 in six (originally ten) volumes (1834–1876), a work that grew out of his vast researches in dusty archives in Europe and America.

Two other historians are read with greater pleasure and profit today. William H. Prescott (1796–1859), who accidentally lost the sight of an eye while in college, conserved his remaining weak vision and published classic accounts of the conquest of Mexico (1843) and Peru (1847). Francis Parkman (1823–1893), whose eyes were so defective that he wrote in darkness with the aid of a guiding machine, penned a brilliant series of volumes, beginning in 1851. In epic style he chronicled the struggle between France and England in colonial times for the mastery of North America.

Early American historians of prominence were almost without exception New Englanders, largely because the Boston area provided well-stocked libraries and a stimulating literary tradition. These writers numbered abolitionists among their relatives and friends and hence were disposed to view unsympathetically the slavery-cursed South. The writing of American history for generations to come was to suffer from an antisouthern bias perpetuated by this early "made in New England" interpretation.

Varying Viewpoints

Early chronicles of the antebellum period universally lauded the reformers, portraying them as disinterested, idealistic persons intent on improving American society. After World War II, however, historians began searching for selfish motivations underlying the apparent benevolence of the reformers. This view described the advocates of reform as conservative, upper-class women and men who felt threatened by the ferment of life in antebellum America. The pursuit of reforms like prohibition, asylums, and mandatory education represented a means of asserting "social control." In this vein, David H. Donald identified one reform movement as "the anguished protest of an aggrieved class against a world they never made." The wave of reform activity in the 1960s coincided with a resurgence in the reputation of antebellum reformers. Recent interpretations stress the religious commitments of reformers and especially the participation of women, who sought various social improvements as an extention of their role as protectors of the home and family.

Select Readings

Primary Source Documents

On the women's movement, see the "Seneca Falls Manifesto"* (1848), which set the stage for later feminist agitation. Henry D. Thoreau's *Walden* * is a classic of the period, as is Ralph Waldo Emerson's "The American Scholar," in *Collected Works of Ralph Waldo Emerson* (1971), edited by Robert E. Spiller.

Secondary Sources

General intellectual histories are Merle Curti, *The Growth of American Thought* (3d ed., 1964), and Ralph H. Gabriel, *The Course of American Democratic Thought* (2d ed., 1956). See also Perry Miller's *Life of the Mind in America: From the Revolution to the Civil War* (1965). Also of general interest are

Daniel Boorstin, *The Americans: The National Experience* (1965), and Fred Somkin, *Unquiet Eagle: Memory and Desire in the Idea of American Freedom, 1815–1860* (1967). Ronald Walters summarizes *American Reformers, 1815–1860* (1978). An older but still useful discussion of reform is Alice F. Tyler, *Freedom's Ferment* (1944). For particular subjects, consult David Rothman, *The Discovery of the Asylum* (1971), and Gerald Grob, *Mental Institutions in America: Social Policy to 1875* (1973); on juvenile delinquency, Joseph Hawes, *Children in Urban Society* (1971); and on prohibition, Ian Tyrrell, *Sobering Up: From Temperance to Prohibition in Antebellum America* (1979). Women's history for this period has recently blossomed in a number of fine studies, including Ellen Carol Dubois, *Feminism and Suffrage* (1978); Barbara J. Berg, *The Remembered Gate: Origins of American Feminism—The Woman and the City, 1800–1860* (1977); Ruth Bordin, *Women and Temperance* (1981); Estelle B. Freedman, *Their Sisters' Keepers: Women's Prison Reform in America, 1830–1930* (1981); Keith E. Melder, *The Beginnings of Sisterhood* (1977); and emphasizing intellectual and literary history, Ann Douglas, *The Feminization of American Culture* (1977). F. O. Mathiessen's masterful *American Renaissance* (1941) is indispensable on the writers of the 1840s and 1850s, as is Alfred Kazin's *An American Procession* (1984). D. H. Lawrence, *Studies in Classic American Literature* (1923), is a classic in its own right. See also Neil Harris's imaginative *Artist in American Society: The Formative Years, 1790–1860* (1968) and Barbara Novak's stimulating *Nature and Culture: American Landscape Painting, 1825–1875* (1980.)

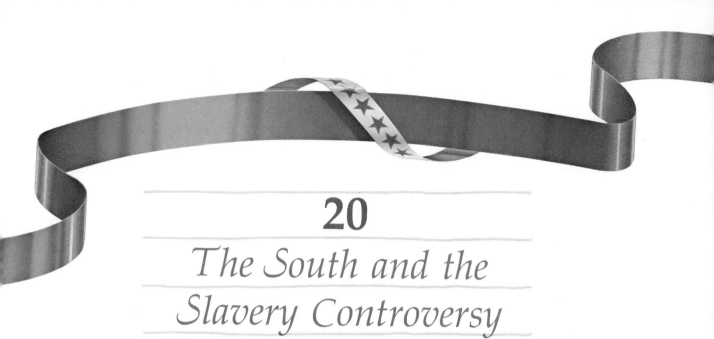

20

The South and the Slavery Controversy

If you put a chain around the neck of a slave, the other end fastens itself around your own.

Ralph Waldo Emerson, 1841

"Cotton Is King!"

When George Washington first took the presidential oath, the economic wheels of the South were creaking badly. They were burdened with depressed prices, unmarketable products, overcropped lands, and the dead weight of an unprofitable slave system. Some southern statesmen, including Thomas Jefferson, were talking openly of freeing their slaves and confidently predicting that slavery would gradually die of economic anemia.

But the introduction of Whitney's cotton gin in 1793 changed the scene. The newly popularized short-staple cotton, which brought a premium price, gradually became the dominant southern crop, eclipsing tobacco, rice, and sugar. Slavery was reinvigorated, with the slave

being chained to the gin, and the planter being chained to the slave.

As time passed, the Cotton Kingdom developed into a huge agricultural factory, pouring out avalanches of the fluffy fiber. Quick profits drew planters to the virgin bottomlands of the gulf states. As long as the soil was still vigorous, the yield was bountiful and the rewards were high. Caught up in an economic spiral, the planters bought more slaves and land to grow more cotton, so as to buy still more slaves and land.

Northern shippers reaped a large part of the profits from the cotton trade. They would load bulging bales of cotton at southern ports, transport them to England, sell them for pounds sterling, and buy needed manufactured goods for sale in the United States. To a large degree

Cotton as King *In this Northern Civil War cartoon, the Confederacy appears as a lighted bomb.*

the prosperity of both North and South rested on the bent backs of southern slaves.

Cotton accounted for half the value of all American exports after 1840. The South produced more than half of the entire world's supply of cotton—a fact that held foreign nations in partial bondage. Britain was then the leading industrial power. Its most important single manufacture in the 1850s was cotton cloth, from which about one-fifth of its population, directly or indirectly, drew its livelihood. About 80 percent of this precious supply of fiber came from the white-carpeted acres of the South.

Southern leaders were fully aware that England was tied to them by cotton threads, and this dependence gave them a heady sense of power. In their eyes "Cotton was King," the gin was his throne, and the black bondsmen were his henchmen. If war should ever break out between North and South, northern warships would presumably cut off the outflow of cotton.

Fiber-famished British factories would then close their gates, starving mobs would force the London government to break the blockade, and the South would triumph. Cotton was a powerful monarch indeed.

The Planter "Aristocracy"

Before the Civil War the South was in some respects not so much a democracy as an oligarchy—or a government by the few, in this case heavily influenced by a planter aristocracy. In 1850 only 1,733 families owned more than 100 slaves each, and this select group provided the cream of the political and social leadership of the section and nation. Here was the mint-julep South of the tall-columned and white-painted plantation mansion—the "big house," where dwelt the "cottonocracy."

The planter aristocrats, with their blooded horses and Chippendale chairs, enjoyed a lion's share of southern wealth. They could educate their children in the finest schools, often in the North or abroad. Their money provided the leisure for study, reflection, and statecraft, as was notably true of men like John C. Calhoun (a Yale graduate) and Jefferson Davis (a West Point graduate). They felt a keen sense of obligation to serve the public. It was no accident that Virginia and its southern sisters produced a higher proportion of front-rank statesmen before 1860 than the "dollar-grubbing" North.

But even in its best light, dominance by a favored aristocracy was basically undemocratic. It widened the gap between rich and poor. It hampered tax-supported public education, because

Thomas Jefferson wrote in 1782: "The whole commerce between master and slave is a perpetual exercise of the. . . . most unremitting despotism on the one part, and degrading submissions on the other. . . . Indeed I tremble for my country when I reflect that God is just; that his justice cannot sleep forever." Unlike Washington, Jefferson did not free his slaves in his will; he had fallen upon distressful times.

Harvesting Cotton *This Currier and Ives print shows slaves of both sexes harvesting cotton, which is then "ginned," baled, carted to the riverbank, and taken by paddlewheeler downriver to New Orleans. (The Granger Collection.)*

the rich planters could and did send their children to private institutions.

Southern gentry were high-strung, though generally soft-spoken, courteous, hospitable, and chivalrous. Jealous of their honor, they clung to dueling long after it had died out in the North. They carried on the somewhat spurious "cavalier" tradition of early Virginia and developed a martial spirit that is still reflected in high-quality southern military academies like The Citadel (Charleston) and the Virginia Military Institute (Lexington).

A favorite author of southerners was Sir Walter Scott, whose manors and castles, graced by brave Ivanhoes and fair Rowenas, roughly mirrored their own semifeudal society. Southern aristocrats, who sometimes staged jousting tournaments, strove to perpetuate a type of medievalism that had died out in Europe—or was rapidly dying out.* Mark Twain later accused Sir Walter Scott of having had a hand in start-

ing the Civil War. The British novelist, Twain said, aroused the southerners to fight for a decaying social structure—"a sham civilization."

Slaves of the Slave System

Unhappily the moonlight-and-magnolia tradition concealed much that was worrisome, distasteful, and sordid. Plantation agriculture was wasteful, largely because King Cotton and his money-hungry subjects despoiled the good earth. Quick profits led to excessive cultivation, or "land butchery," which in turn caused a heavy leakage of population to the West and Northwest.

The economic structure of the South became increasingly monopolistic. As the land wore thin, many small farmers sold their holdings to more prosperous neighbors and went north or west. The big got bigger and the small smaller. When the Civil War finally broke, a large percentage of southern farms had passed from the hands of the families that had originally cleared them.

---

*Oddly enough, by legislative enactment jousting became the official state sport of Maryland in 1962.

*Southern Cotton
Production, 1820*

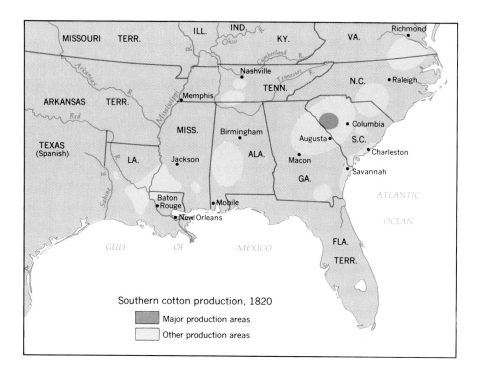

Southern cotton production, 1820

■ Major production areas

□ Other production areas

Another cancer in the bosom of the South was the financial instability of the plantation system. The temptation to overspeculate in land and slaves caused many planters, including Andrew Jackson in his later years, to plunge in beyond their depth. Although the black bondsmen might in extreme cases be fed for as little as ten cents a day, there were other expenses. The slaves represented a heavy investment of capital, perhaps $1,200 each in the case of prime field hands; and they might deliberately injure themselves or run away. An entire slave quarter might be wiped out by disease or even by lightning, as happened in one instance to twenty luckless blacks.

Dominance by King Cotton likewise led to a dangerous dependence on a one-crop economy, whose price level was at the mercy of world conditions. The whole system discouraged a healthy diversification of agriculture and particularly of manufacturing.

Southern planters resented watching the North grow fat at their expense. They were pained by the heavy outward flow of commissions and interest to northern middlemen, bankers, agents, and shippers. True sons of the South, especially by the 1850s, deplored the fact that when born they were wrapped in Yankee-made swaddling clothes and that they spent the rest of their lives in servitude to Yankee manufacturing. When they died, they were laid in coffins held together with Yankee nails and

Basil Hall, an Englishman, visited part of the cotton belt on a river steamer (1827–1828). Noting the preoccupation with cotton, he wrote: "All day and almost all night long, the captain, pilot, crew, and passengers were talking of nothing else; and sometimes our ears were so wearied with the sound of cotton! cotton! cotton! that we gladly hailed a fresh inundation of company in hopes of some change—but alas! . . . 'What's cotton at?' was the first eager inquiry. 'Ten cents [a pound].' 'Oh, that will never do!' From the cotton in the market they went to the crops in the fields—the frost which had nipped their shoots—the hard times—the overtrading—and so round to the prices and prospects again and again."

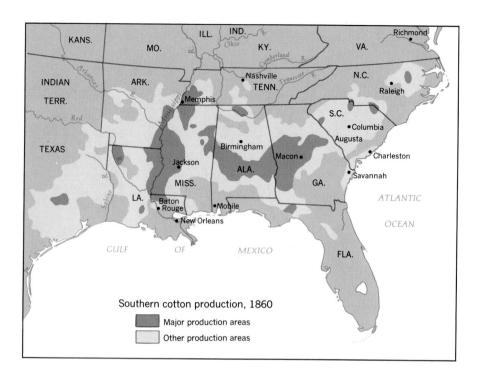

Southern Cotton Production, 1860

Southern cotton production, 1860

▮ Major production areas

▯ Other production areas

were buried in graves dug with Yankee shovels. The South furnished the corpse and the hole in the ground.

The Cotton Kingdom also repelled large-scale European immigration, which added so richly to the manpower and wealth of the North: In 1860 only 4.4 percent of the southern population was foreign-born, as compared with 18.7 percent for the North. German and Irish immigration to the South was generally discouraged by the competition of slave labor, by the high cost of fertile land, and by European ignorance of cotton growing. The diverting of non-English immigration to the North caused the white South to become the most Anglo-Saxon section of the nation.

The White Majority

Only a handful of southern whites lived in Grecian-pillared mansions. Below those 1,733 families in 1850 who owned a hundred or more slaves were the less wealthy slaveowners. They

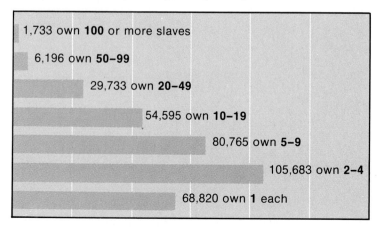

1,733 own **100** or more slaves

6,196 own **50–99**

29,733 own **20–49**

54,595 own **10–19**

80,765 own **5–9**

105,683 own **2–4**

68,820 own **1** each

Slaveowning Families, 1850 The philosopher Ralph Waldo Emerson, a New Englander, declared in 1856: "I do not see how a barbarous community and a civilized community can constitute a state. I think we must get rid of slavery or we must get rid of freedom."

Distribution of Slaves, 1820

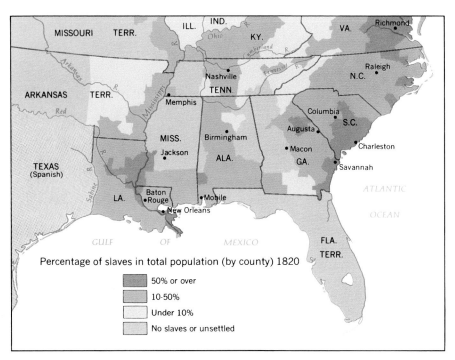

Percentage of slaves in total population (by county) 1820

- 50% or over
- 10-50%
- Under 10%
- No slaves or unsettled

totaled in 1850 some 345,000 families, representing about 1,725,000 white persons. Over two-thirds of these families—255,268 in all—owned fewer than ten slaves each. All told, only about one-fourth of white southerners owned slaves or belonged to a slaveowning family.

The smaller slaveowners did not own a majority of the slaves, but they made up a majority of masters. These lesser masters were typically small farmers. With the striking exception that their household contained a slave or two, or perhaps an entire slave family, the style of their lives probably resembled that of small farmers in the North more than it did that of the southern planter aristocracy. They lived in modest farmhouses and sweated beside their bondsmen in the cotton fields, laboring callus for callus just as hard as their slaves.

Beneath the slaveowners was the great body of whites who owned no slaves at all. By 1860 their numbers had swelled to 6,120,825 persons—three-quarters of the southern white population. Shouldered off the richest bottomlands by the mighty planters, they scratched a simple living from the thinner soils of the backcountry and the mountain valleys. To them, the riches

of the Cotton Kingdom were a distant dream, and they often sneered at the lordly pretensions of the cotton "snobocracy." These red-necked yeomen participated in the market economy scarcely at all. As subsistence farmers, they raised corn and hogs, not cotton, and lived often isolated lives, punctuated periodically by extended socializing and sermonizing at religious camp meetings.

Some of the least prosperous nonslaveholding whites were scorned even by slaves as "poor white trash." Known also as "hillbillies," "crackers," or "clay eaters," they were often described as listless, shiftless, and misshapen. Later investigations have revealed that many of them were not simply lazy, but sick, suffering from malnutrition and parasites, especially hookworm.

All these whites without slaves had no direct stake in the preservation of slavery, yet they were among the stoutest defenders of the slave system. Why? The answer is not far to seek.

The carrot on the stick ever dangling before their eyes was the hope of buying a slave or two and of parlaying their holdings into riches—all in accord with the "American dream" of upward

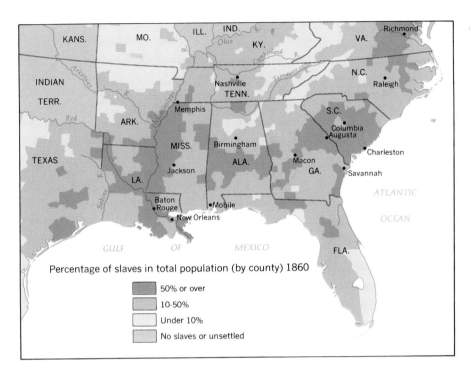

Percentage of slaves in total population (by county) 1860

- 50% or over
- 10-50%
- Under 10%
- No slaves or unsettled

social mobility. They also took fierce pride in their presumed racial superiority, which would be watered down if the slaves were freed. Many of the poorer whites were hardly better off economically than the slaves; some, indeed, were not so well off. But even the most wretched whites could take perverse comfort from the knowledge that they outranked someone in status: the still more wretched Afro-American bondsman. Thus did the logic of economics join with the illogic of racism in buttressing the slave system.

In a special category among white southerners were the mountain whites, more or less marooned in the valleys of the Appalachian range that stretched from western Virginia to northern Georgia and Alabama. Civilization had largely passed them by, and they still lived under spartan frontier conditions. They were a kind of living ancestry, for some of them retained Elizabethan speech forms and habits that had long since died out in England.

As independent small farmers, hundreds of miles distant from the heart of the cotton kingdom and rarely if ever in sight of a slave, these mountain whites had little in common with the whites of the flatlands. Many of them, including future president Andrew Johnson of Tennessee, hated both the haughty planters and their gangs of blacks. They looked upon the impending strife between North and South as "a rich man's war but a poor man's fight."

When the war came, the tough-fibered mountain whites constituted a vitally important peninsula of Unionism jutting down into the secessionist Southern sea. They ultimately played a significant role in crippling the Confederacy. Their attachment to the Union party of Abraham Lincoln was such that, for generations after the Civil War, the only concentrated Republican strength in the solid South was to be found in the southern highlands.

Free Blacks: Slaves Without Masters

Precarious in the extreme was the standing of the South's free blacks, who numbered about 250,000 by 1860. In the upper South, the free black population traced its origins to a wavelet of emancipation inspired by the idealism of Revolutionary days. In the deeper South, many free blacks were mulattoes, usually the emancipated children of a white planter and his black mistress. Throughout the South were some free blacks who had purchased their freedom with earnings from labor after hours. Many free blacks owned property, especially in New Orleans, where a sizable mulatto community prospered. Some, such as William T. Johnson, the "barber of Natchez," even owned slaves. He was the master of fifteen bondsmen; his diary records that in June 1848 he flogged two slaves and a mule.

The free blacks in the South were a kind of "third race." They were prohibited from certain occupations and forbidden from testifying against whites in court. They were always vulnerable to being highjacked back into slavery by unscrupulous slave traders. As free men and women they were walking examples of what might be achieved by emancipation and hence were resented and detested by defenders of the slave system.

Free blacks were also unpopular in the North, where about another 250,000 of them lived. Several states forbade their entrance, most denied them the right to vote, and some barred blacks from public schools. In 1835 New Hampshire farmers hitched their oxen to a small schoolhouse that had dared to enroll fourteen black children and dragged it into a swamp. Northern blacks were especially hated by the pick-and-shovel Irish immigrants, with whom they competed for menial jobs. Much of the agitation in the North against the spread of slavery into the new territories in the 1840s and 1850s grew out of race prejudice, not humanitarianism.

Antiblack feeling was in fact frequently stronger in the North than in the South. The gifted and eloquent former slave Frederick Douglass, an abolitionist and self-educated orator of rare power, was several times mobbed and beaten by northern rowdies. It was sometimes observed that white southerners, who were often suckled and reared by black nurses, liked the black as an individual but despised the race. The white northerner, on the other hand, often professed to like the race but disliked individual blacks.

Plantation Slavery

In society's basement in the South of 1860 were nearly 4 million black human chattels. Their numbers had quadrupled since the dawn of the century, as the booming cotton economy created a seemingly unquenchable demand for slave labor. Legal importations of African slaves into America ended in 1808, when Congress nailed up the bars. But the price of "black ivory" was so high in the years before the Civil War that uncounted thouands of blacks were smuggled into the South, despite the death penalty for slavers. Though several were captured, only one slave trader was ever executed, N. P. Gordon, and this took place in New York in 1862, the second year of the Civil War. Yet the huge bulk of the increase in the slave population came not from imports but instead from natural reproduction—a fact that distinguished slavery in America from other New World societies and that implied much about the tenor of the slave regime and the conditions of family life under slavery.

***Slave Deck of the Slaver* Wildfire**   *Captured by the U.S. Navy, this slave ship was brought into Key West, Florida, in April 1860. The blacks were freed. (From a daguerreotype [photograph] published in* Harper's Weekly, *June 2, 1860.)*

The Cruelty of Slavery (left) *Held captive in a net, a slave sits on the Congo shore, waiting to be sold and shipped (Collection Photothèque Musée de 'Homme) (above) The device was riveted around a slave's neck. Its attached bells, like a cow bell, made it impossible for the wearer to hide from his or her owner.*

Above all, the planters regarded the slaves as investments, into which they had sunk nearly $2 billion of their capital by 1860. Slaves were the primary form of wealth in the South, and as such they were cared for as any asset is cared for by a prudent capitalist. Accordingly, they were sometimes, though by no means always, spared dangerous work, like putting a roof on a house. If a neck was going to be broken, the master preferred it to be that of a wage-earning Irish laborer rather than that of a prime field hand, worth $1,800 by 1860 (a price that had quintupled since 1800). Tunnel blasting and swamp draining were often consigned to itinerant gangs of expendable Irishmen because the labor was "death on niggers and mules."

Slavery was profitable for the great planters, though it hobbled the economic development of the region as a whole. The profits from the cotton boom sucked ever more slaves from the upper to the lower South, so that by 1860 the Deep South states of South Carolina, Florida, Mississippi, Alabama, and Louisiana each had a majority or near-majority of blacks and accounted for about half of all slaves in the South.

Breeding slaves in the way that cattle are bred was not openly encouraged. But thousands of blacks from the soil-exhausted slave states of the Old South, especially tobacco-depleted Virginia, were "sold down the river" to toil as field-gang laborers on the cotton frontier of the lower Mississippi Valley. Women who bore thirteen or fourteen babies were prized as "rattlin' good breeders," and some of these fecund females were promised their freedom when they had produced ten. White masters, all too frequently, would force their attentions on female slaves, fathering a sizable mulatto population, most of which remained enchained.

Slave auctions were brutal sights. The open selling of human flesh under the hammer, sometimes with cattle and horses, was among the most revolting aspects of slavery. On the auction block families were separated with distressing frequency, usually for economic reasons such as bankruptcy or the division of "property" among heirs. The sundering of families in this fashion was perhaps slavery's greatest psychological horror. Abolitionists decried the practice, and Harriet Beecher Stowe seized on the emotional power of this theme by putting it at the heart of the plot of *Uncle Tom's Cabin*.

Life Under the Lash

White southerners often romanticized about the happy life of their singing, dancing, banjo-strumming, joyful "darkies," but how did the slaves actually live? There is no simple answer to this question. Conditions varied greatly from region to region, from large plantation to small farm, and from master to master. Everywhere, of course, slavery meant hard work, ignorance, and oppression. The slaves—both men and women—usually toiled from dawn to dusk in the fields, under the watchful eyes and ready whip-hand of a white overseer or black "driver." They had no civil or political rights, other than minimal protection from arbitrary murder or unusually cruel punishment. Some states offered further protections, such as banning the

sale of a child under the age of ten away from his or her mother. But all such laws were difficult to enforce, since slaves were forbidden to testify in court or even to have their marriages legally recognized.

CASH!

All persons that have SLAVES to dispose of, will do well by giving me a call, as I will give the

HIGHEST PRICE FOR

Men, Women, & CHILDREN.

Any person that wishes to sell, will call at Hill's tavern, or at Shannon Hill for me, and any information they want will be promptly attended to.

Thomas Griggs.

Charlestown, May 7, 1835.

PRINTED AT THE FREE PRESS OFFICE, CHARLESTOWN.

A Slave Auction   Abraham Lincoln said in 1865, "Whenever I hear anyone arguing for slavery, I feel a strong impulse to see it tried on him personally." (above *The Library of Congress*; below *The Chicago Historical Society*.)

Floggings were common, for the whip was the substitute for the wage-incentive system and the most visible symbol of the planter's mastery. Strong-willed slaves were sometimes sent to "breakers," whose technique consisted mostly in lavish laying on of the lash. As an abolitionist song of the 1850s lamented:

> To-night the bond man, Lord
> Is bleeding in his chains;
> And loud the falling lash is heard
> On Carolina's plains!

But savage beatings made sullen laborers, and lash marks hurt resale values. There are, to be sure, sadistic monsters in any population, and the planter class contained its share. But for financial as well as humane reasons, the typical planter did not customarily go out and beat to death a valuable field hand before breakfast.

By 1860 most slaves were concentrated in the "black belt" of the Deep South that stretched from South Carolina and Georgia into the new southwest states of Alabama, Mississippi, and Louisiana. This was the region of the southern frontier, into which the explosively growing Cotton Kingdom had burst in a few short decades. As on all frontiers, life was often rough and raw, and in general the lot of the

Flogging Slaves　*An example of antislavery propaganda, 1838. (Courtesy, American Antiquarian Society.)*

slave was harder here than in the more settled areas of the Old South.

A majority of blacks lived on larger plantations that harbored communities of twenty or more slaves. In some counties of the Deep South, especially along the lower Mississippi River, blacks accounted for more than 75 percent of the population. There the family life of slaves tended to be relatively stable, and a distinctive Afro-American slave culture developed. Forced separations of spouses, parents, and children were evidently more common on smaller plantations and in the upper South.

The Slave Quarters　*This Civil War–era photograph shows the stark simplicity of black family life in the South. South Carolina Senator Hammond declared in 1858: "In all social systems there must be a class to do the mean duties. . . . It constitutes the very mudsills of society. . . . Fortunately for the South, she found a race adapted to that purpose. . . . We use them for that purpose and call them slaves." (Library of Congress.)*

Slave marriage vows sometimes proclaimed, "Until death or *distance* do you part."

With impressive resilience, blacks managed to sustain family life in slavery, and most slaves were raised in stable two-person households. Continuity of family identity across generations was evidenced in the widespread practice of naming children for grandparents or adopting the surname not of a current master, but of a forebear's master. Afro-Americans also displayed their African cultural roots when they avoided marriage between first cousins, in contrast to the frequent intermarriage of close relatives among the ingrown planter aristocracy.

African roots were also visible in slave religious practices. Though heavily Christianized by the itinerant evangelists of the Second Great Awakening, blacks in slavery molded their own distinctive religious forms from a mixture of Christian and African elements. They emphasized those aspects of the Christian heritage that seemed most pertinent to their own situation—especially the captivity of the Israelites in Egypt. One of their most haunting spirituals implored:

> Tell old Pharaoh
> "Let my people go."

And another lamented:

> Nobody knows de trouble I've had
> Nobody knows but Jesus

African practices also persisted in the "responsorial" style of preaching, in which the congregation frequently punctuates the minister's remarks with assents and *amen*s—an adaptation of the give-and-take between caller and dancers in the African ringshout dance.

The Burdens of Bondage

Slavery was intolerably degrading to the victims. They were deprived of the dignity and sense of responsibility that come from independence and the right to make choices. They were denied an education, because reading brought ideas, and ideas brought discontent. Many states passed laws forbidding their instruction,

and perhaps nine-tenths of adult slaves at the beginning of the Civil War were totally illiterate. For all slaves—indeed for all blacks, slave or free—the "American dream" of bettering one's lot through study and hard work was a cruel and empty mockery.

Not surprisingly, victims of the "peculiar institution" devised countless ways to throw sand in its gears. When workers are not voluntarily hired and adequately compensated, they can hardly be expected to work with alacrity. Accordingly, slaves often slowed the pace of their labor to the barest minimum that would spare them the lash, thus fostering the myth of black "laziness" in the minds of whites. They filched food from the "big house" and other goods that had been produced by their labor. They sabotaged expensive equipment, stopping the work routine altogether until repairs were accomplished. Occasionally, they even put poison in their master's food.

The slaves also universally pined for freedom. Many took to their heels as runaways, frequently in search of a separated family member. A black girl, asked if her mother was dead, replied, "Yassah, massah, she is daid, but she's free." Others rebelled, though never successfully. In 1800 an armed insurrection led by a slave named Gabriel in Richmond, Virginia, was foiled by informers, and its leaders were hanged. Denmark Vesey, a free black, led another ill-fated rebellion in Charleston in 1822. Also betrayed by informers, Vesey and more than thirty followers were publicly strung from the gallows. In 1831 the semiliterate Nat Turner, a visionary black preacher, led an uprising that slaughtered about sixty Virginians, mostly women and children. Reprisals were swift and bloody.

The dark taint of slavery also left its mark on the whites. It fostered the brutality of the whip, the bloodhound, and the branding iron. White southerners increasingly lived in a state of imagined siege, surrounded by potentially rebellious blacks inflamed by abolitionist propaganda from the North. Their fears bolstered an intoxicating theory of biological racial superiority and turned the South into a reactionary backwater in an era of progress—one of the last bastions of

Early Emancipation in the North

slavery in the Western world. The defenders of slavery were forced to degrade themselves, along with their victims. As Booker T. Washington, a distinguished black leader and former slave, later observed, whites could not hold blacks in a ditch without getting down there with them.

Early Abolitionism

The inhumanity of the "peculiar institution" gradually caused antislavery societies to sprout forth. The first stirrings of abolitionist sentiment occurred at the time of the Revolution, especially among Quakers. Because of the widespread loathing of blacks, some of the earliest abolitionist efforts focused on transporting the blacks bodily back to Africa. The American Colonization Society was founded for this purpose in 1817, and in 1822 the Republic of Liberia, on the fever-stricken West African coast, was established for former slaves. Its capital, Monrovia, was named after President Monroe. Some 15,000 freed blacks were transported over the next four decades. But most blacks had no wish to be transplanted into a strange civilization after becoming partially Americanized. By 1860 virtually all southern slaves were no longer Africans, but native-born Afro-Americans, with their own distinctive history and culture. Yet the colonization idea appealed to some antislav-

eryites, including Abraham Lincoln, down to the time of the Civil War.

In the 1830s the abolitionist movement took on new energy and momentum, mounting to the proportions of a crusade. American abolitionists took heart in 1833 when their British counterparts unchained the slaves in the West Indies. Most important, the religious spirit of the Second Great Awakening now inflamed the hearts of many abolitionists against the sin of slavery. Prominent among them was lanky, tousle-haired Theodore Dwight Weld, who had been evangelized by Charles Grandison Finney in New York's Burned-Over District in the 1820s. Self-educated and simple in manner and speech, Weld appealed with special power and directness to his rural audiences of untutored farmers.

Spiritually inspired by Finney, Weld was materially aided by two wealthy and devout New York merchants, the brothers Arthur and Lewis Tappan. In 1832 they paid his way to Lane Theological Seminary in Cincinnati, Ohio, which was presided over by the formidable Lyman Beecher, father of a remarkable brood, including novelist Harriet Beecher Stowe, feminist Catharine Beecher, and preacher-abolitionist Henry Ward Beecher. Expelled along with several other students in 1834 for organizing an eighteen-day debate on slavery, Weld and his fellow "Lane Rebels"—full of the energy and idealism of youth—fanned out across the Old

Northwest preaching the antislavery gospel. Humorless and deadly earnest, Weld also assembled a potent propaganda pamphlet, *American Slavery As It Is* (1839). It was among the most effective abolitionist tracts and greatly influenced Harriet Beecher Stowe's *Uncle Tom's Cabin.*

Radical Abolitionism

On New Year's Day, 1831, a shattering abolitionist blast came from the bugle of William Lloyd Garrison, a mild-looking reformer of twenty-six. The emotionally high-strung son of a drunken father and a spiritual child of the Second Great Awakening, Garrison published in

"Am I Not a Woman and a Sister?" *A popular appeal. (Garrison's* Liberator.*)*

William Lloyd Garrison (1805–1879) *The most conspicuous and most hated of the abolitionists, Garrison was a nonresistant pacifist and a poor organizer. He favored northern secession from the South and antagonized both sections with his intemperate language. (The Bettman Archive.)*

Boston the first issue of his militantly antislavery newspaper *The Liberator.* With this mighty paper broadside Garrison triggered a thirty-year war of words and in a sense fired one of the opening guns of the Civil War.

Stern and uncompromising, Garrison nailed his colors to the masthead of his weekly. He proclaimed in strident tones that under no circumstances would he tolerate the poisonous weed of slavery but would stamp it out at once, root and branch:

> I will be as harsh as truth and as uncompromising as justice . . . I am in earnest—I will not equivocate—I will not excuse—I will not retreat a single inch—and I WILL BE HEARD!

Other dedicated abolitionists rallied to Garrison's standard, and in 1833 they founded the American Anti-Slavery Society. Prominent among them was Wendell Phillips, a Boston patrician and renowned orator who came to be known as "abolition's golden trumpet." A man of strict principle, he would eat no cane sugar and wear no cotton cloth, since both were produced by southern slaves.

Black abolitionists distinguished themselves as living monuments to the cause of Afro-American freedom. Their ranks included David

Walker, whose incendiary *Appeal to the Colored Citizens of the World* (1829) advocated a bloody end to white supremacy. Also noteworthy were Sojourner Truth, a freed black woman in New York who fought tirelessly for black emancipation and women's rights, and Martin Delaney, one of the few black leaders to take seriously the notion of mass recolonization of Africa. In 1859 he visited West Africa's Niger Valley seeking a suitable site for relocation.

The greatest of the black abolitionists was Frederick Douglass. Escaping from bondage in 1838 at the age of twenty-one, Douglass was "discovered" by the abolitionists three years later when he gave a stunning impromptu speech at an antislavery meeting in Massachusetts. Thereafter he lectured widely for the

Frederick Douglass (c. 1817–1895) *Born a slave in Maryland, Douglass escaped to the North and became the most prominent black abolitionist. Gifted as an orator, writer, and editor, he continued to battle for the civil rights of his people after emancipation. Near the end of a distinguished career, he served as U.S. minister to Haiti. (Library of Congress.)*

Sojourner Truth *Also known simply as "Isabella," she held audiences spellbound with her deep, resonant voice and the religious passion with which she condemned the sin of slavery. This photo was taken about 1870. (National Portrait Gallery, Smithsonian Institution, Washington, D.C.)*

cause, despite frequent beatings and threats against his life. In 1845 he published his classic autobiography, *Narrative of the Life of Frederick Douglass*. It depicted his remarkable origins as the son of a black slave woman and a white father, his struggle to learn to read and write, and his eventual escape to the North.

Douglass was as flexibly practical as Garrison was stubbornly principled. Garrison often appeared to be more interested in his own righteousness than in the substance of the slavery evil itself. He repeatedly demanded that the "virtuous" North secede from the "wicked" South. Yet he did not explain how the creation of an independent slave republic would bring an end to the "damning crime" of slavery. Renouncing politics, on the Fourth of July, 1854, he publicly burned a copy of the Constitution as "a covenant with death and an agreement with hell" (a phrase he borrowed from a Shaker

> *Frederick Douglass, the remarkable ex-slave, told of Mr. Covey, a white owner who bought a single female slave "as a breeder." She gave birth to twins at the end of the year. "At this addition to the human stock Covey and his wife were ecstatic with joy. No one dreamed of reproaching the woman or finding fault with the hired man, Bill Smith, the father of the children, for Mr. Covey himself had locked the two up together every night, thus inviting the result."*

condemnation of marriage). Critics, including some of his former supporters, charged that Garrison was cruelly probing the moral wound in America's underbelly but offering no acceptable balm to ease the pain.

Douglass, on the other hand, along with other abolitionists, increasingly looked to politics to end the blight of slavery. These political abolitionists backed the Liberty party in 1840, the Free Soil party in 1848, and eventually the Republican party in the 1850s. In the end, most abolitionists, including even the pacifistic Garrison himself, followed out the logic of their beliefs and supported a frightfully costly fratricidal war as the price of emancipation.

High-minded and courageous, the abolitionists were men and women of goodwill and various colors who faced the cruel choice that people in many ages have had thrust upon them: When is evil so enormous that it must be denounced, even at the risk of precipitating bloodshed and butchery?

The South Lashes Back

Antislavery sentiment was not unknown in the South, and in the 1820s antislavery societies were more numerous south of Mason and Dixon's line than north of it. But after about 1830 the voice of white southern abolitionism was silenced. In a last gasp of southern questioning of slavery, the Virginia legislature debated and eventually defeated various emancipation proposals in 1831–1832. That debate marked a turning point. Thereafter all the slave states tightened their slave codes and moved to prohibit emancipation of any kind, voluntary or compensated. Nat Turner's rebellion in 1831 sent a wave of hysteria sweeping over the snowy cotton fields, and planters in growing numbers slept with pistols by their pillows. Although Garrison had no demonstrable connection with the Turner conspiracy, his *Liberator* appeared at about the same time, and he was bitterly condemned as a terrorist and an inciter of murder. The state of Georgia offered $5,000 for his arrest and conviction.

The nullification crisis in 1832 further implanted haunting fears in white southern minds, conjuring up nightmares of black incendiaries and abolitionist devils. Jailings, whippings, and lynchings now greeted rational efforts to discuss the slavery problem in the South.

Pro-slavery whites responded by launching a massive defense of slavery as a positive good. In doing so, they forgot their own section's previous doubts about the morality of the "peculiar institution." Slavery, they claimed, was supported by the authority of the Bible and the wisdom of Aristotle. It was good for the Africans, who were lifted from the barbarism of the jungle and clothed with the blessings of Christian civilization. Slavemasters did indeed encourage religion in the slave quarters. A catechism for blacks contained such passages as:

Q. Who gave you a master and a mistress?
A. God gave them to me.
Q. Who says that you must obey them?
A. God says that I must.

White apologists also pointed out that master-slave relationships really resembled those of a family. On many plantations, especially those in the Old South of Virginia and Maryland, this argument had a certain plausibility. A slave's tombstone bore this touching inscription:

JOHN:
A faithful servant
  and true friend:
Kindly, and considerate:
Loyal, and affectionate:
The family he served
Honours him in death:
But, in life they gave him love:
For he was one of them

A Two-Way Proslavery Cartoon *Published in New York, the cartoon shows a chilled and rejected free black in the North (left) disconsolately passing a grogshop, while (right) a happy southern slave enjoys life with a fishing rod in the company of a white youth.*

Southern whites were quick to contrast the "happy" lot of their "servants" with that of the overworked northern wage slaves, including sweated women and stunted children. The blacks mostly toiled in the fresh air and sunlight, not in dark and stuffy factories. They did not have to worry about slack times or unemployment, as did the "hired hands" of the North. Provided with a jail-like form of Social Security, they were cared for in sickness and old age, unlike northern workers, who were turned adrift.

These curious proslavery arguments only widened the chasm between a backward-looking South and a forward-looking North—and indeed much of the rest of the Western world. The southerners reacted to the pressure of their own fears and the merciless nagging of the northern abolitionists. Increasingly the white South turned in upon itself and grew hotly intolerant of any embarrassing questions about the status of slavery.

Regrettably, also, the controversy over free people endangered free speech in the entire country. Piles of petitions poured in upon Congress from the antislavery reformers; and in 1836 sensitive southerners drove through the House the so-called gag resolution. It required all such antislavery appeals to be tabled without debate. This attack on the right of petition aroused the sleeping lion in an aged ex-president, Representative John Quincy Adams, and he waged a successful eight-year fight for its repeal.

Southern whites likewise resented the flooding of their mails with incendiary abolitionist literature. Even if the blacks could not read, they could interpret the inflammatory drawings, such as those that showed masters knocking the teeth out of their slaves with clubs. In 1835 a mob in Charleston, South Carolina, looted the local post office and burned a pile of abolitionist propaganda. Capitulating to southern pressures, the Washington government in the 1830s ordered southern postmasters to destroy abolitionist material and called on southern state officials to arrest federal postmasters who did not comply. Such was "freedom of the press" as guaranteed by the Constitution.

Lovejoy's Press Destroyed

The Abolitionist Impact in the North

Abolitionists—especially the extreme Garrisonians—were for a long time unpopular in many parts of the North. Northerners had been brought up to revere the Constitution and to regard the clauses on slavery as a lasting bargain. The ideal of Union, hammered home by the thundering eloquence of Daniel Webster and others, had taken deep root; and Garrison's wild talk of secession grated harshly on northern ears.

The North also had a heavy economic stake in Dixieland. By the late 1850s the southern planters owed northern bankers and other creditors about $300 million, and much of this immense sum would be lost—as, in fact, it later was—should the Union dissolve. New England textile mills were fed with cotton raised by the slaves, and a disrupted labor system might cut off this vital supply and bring unemployment. The Union during these critical years was partly bound together with cotton threads, tied by lords of the loom in collaboration with the so-called lords of the lash. It was not surprising that strong hostility developed in the North against the boat-rocking tactics of the radical antislaveryites.

Repeated tongue-lashings by the extreme abolitionists provoked many mob outbursts in the North, some led by respectable gentlemen. A gang of young toughs broke into Lewis Tappan's New York house in 1834 and demolished its interior, while a crowd in the street cheered. In 1835 Garrison, with a rope tied around him, was dragged through the streets of Boston by the so-called Broadcloth Mob but escaped almost miraculously. Reverend Elijah P. Lovejoy, of Alton, Illinois, not content to assail slavery, impugned the chastity of Catholic women. His printing press was destroyed four times, and in 1837 he was killed by a mob, thus becoming "the martyr abolitionist." So unpopular were the antislavery zealots that ambitious politicians, like Lincoln, usually avoided the taint of Garrisonian abolition like the plague.

Yet by the 1850s the abolitionist outcry had made a deep dent in the northern mind. Many citizens had come to see the South as the land of the unfree and the home of a hateful institution. Few northerners were prepared to abolish slavery outright, but a growing number, including Abraham Lincoln, opposed extending it to the territories in the West. People of this stamp, commonly called "free-soilers," swelled their ranks as the Civil War approached.

Varying Viewpoints

Ulrich Bonnell Phillips made three key arguments in his landmark study *American Negro Slavery* (1918). First, he claimed that slavery was a dying economic institution, unprofitable to the slaveowner and an obstacle to the economic development of the South as a whole. Second, Phillips contended that slavery was a rather benign institution and that the planters, contrary to abolitionist charges of ruthless exploitation, treated their chattels with kindly paternalism. Third, Phillips reflected the dominant racial attitudes of his time in his belief that slaves were passive and dim by nature and did not abhor the institution.

For more than half a century, historians have debated these assertions, sometimes heatedly. More sophisticated economic analysis has refuted Phillips' claim that slavery would have withered away without a war. Economic historians have demonstrated that slavery was a viable, profitable, expanding economic system and that slaves constituted a good investment. The price of a prime field hand rose dramatically, even in the 1850s.

No such definitive conclusion has yet been reached in the disputes over slave treatment and slave personality. Beginning in the late 1950s, historians came increasingly to emphasize the harshness of the slave system. One study, Stanley Elkins' *Slavery,* went so far as to compare the "peculiar institution" to the Nazi concentration camps. Both were "total institutions," Elkins contended, which "infantilized" their victims. Recently, scholars such as Eugene Genovese have criticized both views. Without diminishing the deprivations and pains of slavery, these students of the "peculiar institution" concede that slavery embraced a strange form of paternalism, a system that reflected not the benevolence of southern slaveholders but their need to protect and coax work out of their often recalcitrant "investment."

The revised conceptions of the master-slave relationship also spilled over into the debate over slave personality. Some historians, like Kenneth Stampp, denied Phillips' portrait of the slave as a passive "Sambo." They stressed the frequency and variety of violent and peaceful slave resistance. Others, like Elkins, accepted the Sambo stereotype but saw it as a consequence of slavery rather than a natural attribute of the slave. A third view sees the Sambo character as an act, an image that slaves used to confound their masters without incurring punishment. Adherents of the latter view, conspicuously including Herbert Gutman and Lawrence Levine, also emphasize the tenacity with which slaves maintained their own culture, despite the hardships of bondage.

The reputation of the abolitionists, both moderate and extreme, has greatly improved, reflecting the changed atmosphere generated by the civil rights struggles of the 1960s and 1970s. Once vilified as irresponsible provokers of a needless war, they are now commonly hailed as champions of human rights.

Select Readings

Primary Source Documents

Two influential abolitionist documents are Theodore Dwight Weld, *American Slavery As It Is** (1839), and the inaugural editorial of William Lloyd Garrison's *The Liberator** (1831). Roy P. Basler, ed., *The Collected Works of Abraham Lincoln* (1933), contains the Great Emancipator's assessment of abolitionism in 1854. For southern perspectives, see James Henry Hammond's famous "Cotton Is King" speech, *Congressional Globe,* 36 Cong., 1 sess. p 961 (March 3, 1858).*

Secondary Sources

A good introduction to southern history is Clement Eaton, *A History of the Old South: The Emergence of a Reluctant Nation* (1975). Wilbur J. Cash, *The Mind of the South* (1941), is an engagingly written classic. Always incisive is C. Vann Woodward, *The Burden of Southern History* (1960) and *American Counterpoint* (1971). Frank L. Owsley, *Plain Folk of the Old South* (1949), illuminates the lives of non-slaveholding whites. Owsley's views are challenged in Eugene Genovese, *The Political Economy of Slavery* (1965), and Genovese and Elizabeth Fox-Genovese, *Fruits of Merchant Capital* (1983). Genovese also discusses *The World the Slaveholders Made* (1970), which should be supplemented by James Oakes, *The Ruling Race: A History of American Slaveholders* (1982). Gavin Wright, *The Political Economy of the Cotton South* (1978), is particularly thoughtful. Catherine Clinton examines *The Plantation Mistress* (1982). The literature on slavery and Afro-Americans is enormous; the best place to start is John Hope Franklin, *From Slavery to Freedom* (5th ed., 1980), and consult also Nathan Irving Huggins' sometimes lyrical *Black Odyssey* (1977). The modern debate on slavery began with Ulrich B. Phillips' classic *American Negro Slavery* (1918); a darker view of the same subject is found in Kenneth M. Stampp, *The Peculiar Institution* (1956). Consult also Stanley Elkins' stimulating essay, *Slavery* (2d ed., 1968), which also has interesting observations on the abolitionists. More recently, considerable furor has surrounded the publication of Robert Fogel and Stanley Engerman, *Time on the Cross: The Economics of American Slavery* (2 vols., 1974). For contrasting views and rebuttals, see John W. Blassingame, *The Slave Community* (rev. ed., 1979); Herbert Gutman, *Slavery and the Numbers Game* (1975); the same author's *The Black Family in Slavery and Freedom, 1750–1925* (1976); Paul David, *Reckoning with Slavery* (1976); Eugene Genovese, *Roll, Jordan, Roll* (1974); and Carl N. Degler's comparison of slavery and race relations in Brazil and the United States, *Neither Black nor White* (1971). Robert Starobin examines *Industrial Slavery in the Old South* (1970), and Ira Berlin tells the story of free blacks in *Slaves without Masters* (1975), which should be supplemented by Michael P. Johnson and James L. Roark, *Black Masters: A Free Family of Color in the Old South* (1984), and their *No Chariot Let Down: Charleston's Free People of Color on the Eve of the Civil War* (1984). See also Leon Litwack, *North of Slavery* (1961), for the situation of blacks outside the South. David B. Davis provides indispensable background to the history of abolitionism in *The Problem of Slavery in Western Culture* (1966) and *The Problem of Slavery in the Age of Revolution* (1975). The best brief history of the abolitionists is James B. Stewart, *Holy Warriors* (1976). Aileen Kraditor is favorably disposed toward Garrison in *Means and Ends in American Abolitionism: Garrison and His Critics* (1967). Consult also Lewis Perry, *Radical Abolitionists* (1973). Benjamin Quarles examines *Black Abolitionists* (1969), as do Jane H. and William H. Pease in *They Who Would Be Free: Blacks Search for Freedom, 1830–1861* (1974). Arna Bontemps presents the life of Frederick Douglass, the most prominent black abolitionist, in *Free at Last* (1971). White attitudes can be studied in Winthrop Jordan's masterful *White over Black* (1968) and George Frederickson's insightful *The Black Image in the White Mind* (1971).

21
Renewing the Sectional Struggle, 1848–1854

> *Secession! Peaceable secession! Sir, your eyes and mine are never destined to see that miracle.*
>
> Daniel Webster,
> Seventh of March speech, 1850

The Popular Sovereignty Panacea

The year 1848, highlighted by a rash of revolutions in Europe, was filled with unrest in America. The Treaty of Guadalupe Hidalgo had officially ended the war with Mexico, but it had initiated a new and perilous round of political warfare in the United States. The vanquished Mexicans had been forced to relinquish an enormous tract of real estate, including Texas, California, and all the area between. The acquisition of this huge domain raised anew the burning issue of extending slavery into the territories. Northern antislaveryites had rallied behind the Wilmot Proviso, which flatly prohibited slavery in any territory acquired in the Mexican War. Southern senators had blocked the passage of the proviso, but the issue would not die

(see p. 287). Ominously, debate over slavery in the area of the Mexican Cession threatened to disrupt the ranks of both Whigs and Democrats and split national politics along North-South sectional lines.

Each of the two great political parties was a vital bond of national unity, for each enjoyed powerful support in both North and South. If they should be replaced by two purely sectional groupings, the Union would be in peril. To politicians, the wisest strategy seemed to be to sit on the lid of the slavery issue and ignore the boiling beneath. Even so, the cover bobbed up and down ominously in response to the agitation of zealous northern abolitionists and hot-headed southern "fire-eaters."

Anxious Democrats were forced to seek a new standard-bearer in 1848. President Polk, broken in health by overwork and chronic diarrhea, had pledged himself to a single term. The Democratic National Convention at Baltimore turned to an aging leader, General Lewis Cass, a veteran of the War of 1812. Though a senator and diplomat of wide experience and considerable ability, he was sour-visaged and somewhat pompous. His enemies dubbed him General "Gass" and quickly noted that *Cass* rhymed with *jackass*. The Democratic platform, in line with the lid-sitting strategy, was silent on the burning issue of slavery in the territories.

But Cass himself had not been silent. His views on the extension of slavery were well known, because he was the reputed father of "popular sovereignty." This was the doctrine that stated that the sovereign people of a territory, under the general principles of the Constitution, should themselves determine the status of slavery.

Popular sovereignty had a persuasive appeal. The public liked it because it accorded with the democratic tradition of self-determination. Politicians liked it because it seemed a comfortable compromise between a ban on slavery in the territories and southern demands that Congress protect slavery in the territories. Popular sovereignty tossed the slavery problem into the laps of the people in the various territories. Advocates of the doctrine thus hoped to dissolve the most stubborn national issue of the day into a series of local issues. Yet popular sovereignty had one fatal defect: it might serve to spread the blight of slavery.

Political Triumphs for General Taylor

The Whigs, meeting in Philadelphia, cashed in on the "Taylor fever." They nominated frank and honest Zachary Taylor, the "Hero of Buena Vista," who had never held civil office or even voted for president. Henry Clay, the living embodiment of Whiggism, should logically have been nominated. But he had made too many speeches—and too many enemies.

As usual, the Whigs pussyfooted in their platform. Eager to win at any cost, they dodged all troublesome issues and merely extolled the homespun virtues of their candidate. The self-reliant old frontier fighter had not committed himself on the issue of slavery extension. But as a wealthy resident of Louisiana, living on a sugar plantation, he owned scores of slaves.

Ardent antislavery men in the North, distrusting both Cass and Taylor, organized the Free-Soil party. Aroused by the conspiracy of silence in the Democratic and Whig platforms, the Free-Soilers made no bones about their own stand. They came out foursquare for the Wilmot Proviso and against slavery in the territories. Going beyond other antislavery groups, they broadened their appeal by advocating federal aid for internal improvements and by urging free government homesteads for settlers.

The new party assembled a strange assortment of people in the same political bed. It attracted industrialists miffed at Polk's reduction

General Zachary Taylor *This Democratic campaign cartoon of 1848 charges that Taylor's reputation rested on Mexican skulls. (Courtesy of The New-York Historical Society, New York City.)*

of protective tariffs. It appealed to Democrats resentful of Polk's settling for part of Oregon while insisting on all of Texas—a disparity that suggested a menacing southern dominance in the Democratic party. It harbored many northerners whose hatred was directed not so much at slavery as at blacks and who gagged at the prospect of sharing the virgin western territories with Afro-Americans. It also contained a large element of "conscience Whigs," heavily influenced by the abolitionist crusade, who condemned slavery on moral grounds. The Free-Soilers trotted out wizened former President Van Buren and marched into the fray, shouting "Free soil, free speech, free labor, and free men." As the first widely inclusive party organized around the issue of slavery and confined to a single section, the Free-Soil party foreshadowed the emergence of the Republican party six years later.

With the slavery issue officially shoved under the rug by the two major parties, the politicians on both sides opened fire on personalities. The amateurish Taylor had to be carefully watched, lest his indiscreet pen puncture the reputation won by his sword. His admirers puffed him up as a gallant knight and a Napoleon, and sloganized his remark, allegedly uttered during the Battle of Buena Vista, "General Taylor never surrenders." Taylor's wartime popularity pulled him through. He harvested 1,360,967 popular and 163 electoral votes, as compared with Cass's 1,222,342 popular and 127 electoral votes. Free-Soiler Van Buren, although winning no state, polled 291,263 ballots and apparently diverted enough Democratic strength from Cass in the crucial state of New York to throw the election to Taylor.

"Californy Gold"

Tobacco-chewing President Taylor—with his stumpy legs, rough features, heavy jaw, black hair, ruddy complexion, and squinty gray eyes—was a military square peg in a political

Placer Miners in California *Cheap but effective, placer mining consisted of literally "washing" the gold out of surface deposits. No deep excavation was required. This crew of miners in California in 1852 was using a "long tom" sluice that washed relatively large quantities of ore. (California State Library.)*

California Gold Rush Country *Miners from all over the world swarmed over the rivers that drained the western slope of California's Sierra Nevada mountains. Their nationalities and religions, their languages and their ways of life, are recorded in the colorful place names they left behind.*

ing was even sent as far away as the Hawaiian Islands for washing.

The overnight inpouring of tens of thousands of people into the future Golden State completely overwhelmed the one-horse government of California. A distressingly high proportion of the newcomers were lawless men, accompanied or followed by virtueless women. A contemporary song ran:

> Oh what was your name in the States?
> Was it Thompson or Johnson or Bates?
> Did you murder your wife,
> And fly for your life?
> Say, what was your name in the States?

An outburst of crime inevitably resulted from the presence of so many outcasts. Robbery, claim jumping, and murder were commonplace; and such violence was only partly discouraged by rough vigilante justice. In San Francisco, from 1848 to 1856, there were scores of lawless killings but only three semilegal hangings.

A majority of the Californians, as decent and law-abiding citizens needing protection, grappled earnestly with the problem of erecting an adequate state government. Privately encouraged by President Taylor, they drafted a constitution in 1849 that excluded slavery and then boldly applied to Congress for admission. California would thus bypass the usual territorial stage, thwarting southern congressmen seeking to block free soil. Southern politicians, alarmed by this "impertinent" stroke for freedom, arose in violent opposition. Would California prove to be the golden straw that broke the back of the Union?

round hole. He would have been spared much turmoil if he could have continued to sit on the slavery lid. But the discovery of gold in California, early in 1848, blew the cover off.

A horde of adventurers poured into the valleys of California. Singing "O Susannah!" and shouting "Gold! Gold! Gold!" they began tearing frantically at the yellow-graveled streams and hills. A fortunate few of the bearded miners "struck it rich" at the "diggings." But the luckless many, who netted blisters instead of nuggets, probably would have been money well ahead if they had stayed at home unaffected by the "gold fever," which was often followed by more deadly fevers. The most reliable profits were made by those who mined the miners, notably by charging outrageous rates for laundry and other personal services. Some soiled cloth-

Sectional Balance and the Underground Railroad

The South of 1850 was relatively well off. It then enjoyed, as it had from the beginning, more than its share of the nation's leadership. It had seated in the White House the war hero Zachary Taylor, a Virginia-born, slaveowning planter from Louisiana. It had a majority in the cabinet and on the supreme bench. If outnumbered in the House, the South had equality in

Blacksmith Shop *Completed in the last third of the nineteenth century, this painting is attributed to Francis A. Beckett. This blacksmith shop in gold rush California was exceptionally well outfitted. The leather-aproned owner sports a stovepipe hat, while his assistants wear mere derbies. Note the massive bellows suspended from the high ceiling. It could heat the fire to blast-furnace temperatures. (National Gallery of Art, Washington, Gift of Edgar William and Bernice Chrysler Garbisch.)*

the Senate, where it could hope to exercise a veto voice. Its cotton fields were expanding, and the price of the snowy fiber was profitably high. Few sane people, North or South, believed that slavery was seriously threatened where it already existed below the Mason-Dixon line.* The fifteen slave states could easily veto any proposed constitutional amendment.

Yet the South was deeply worried, as it had been for several decades, by the ever-tipping political balance. There were then fifteen slave states and fifteen free states. The admission of California would destroy the delicate equilibrium in the Senate, perhaps forever. Potential

slave territory under the American flag was running short, if it had not already disappeared. Agitation had already developed in the territories of New Mexico and Utah for admission as nonslave states. The fate of California might well establish a precedent for the rest of the Mexican Cession territory—an area purchased largely with southern blood.

The idea that many ne'er-do-wells went west is found in Ralph Waldo Emerson's Journals (January 1849): "If a man is going to California, he announces it with some hesitation; because it is a confession that he has failed at home."

---

*Originally the southern boundary of colonial Pennsylvania.

Texas and the Compromise of 1850

Texas nursed an additional grievance of its own. It claimed a huge area east of the Rio Grande and north to the forty-second parallel, embracing in part about half the territory of present New Mexico. The federal government

was proposing to detach this prize, while hot-blooded Texans were threatening to descend upon Santa Fe and seize what they regarded as rightfully theirs. The explosive quarrel foreshadowed shooting.

Many southerners were also angered by the nagging agitation in the North for the abolition of slavery in the District of Columbia. They looked with alarm on the prospect of a ten-mile-square oasis of free soil, thrust between slaveholding Maryland and slaveholding Virginia.

Even more disagreeable to the South was the loss of runaway slaves, many of whom were assisted north by the Underground Railroad. It consisted of an informal chain of "stations" (antislavery homes), through which scores of "passengers" (runaway slaves) were spirited by "conductors" (usually white and black abolitionists) from the slave states to the free-soil sanctuary of Canada.

The most amazing of these "conductors" was an illiterate runaway slave from Maryland, fearless Harriet Tubman. During nineteen forays into the South, she rescued more than three hundred slaves, including her aged parents, and deservedly earned the title "Moses." Lively imaginations later exaggerated the role of the Underground Railroad and its "station masters," but its existence was a fact.

Resurrection of Henry Box Brown *Brown, a slave, was shipped to Philadelphia abolitionists from Virginia in a box. (Library of Congress.)*

Harriet Tubman, Premier Assistant of Runaway Slaves *John Brown called her "General Tubman" for her effective work in helping slaves escape to Canada. During the Civil War she served as a Union spy behind Confederate lines. Herself illiterate, she worked after the war to bring education to the freed slaves in North Carolina. (Library of Congress.)*

By 1850 southerners were demanding a new and more stringent fugitive-slave law. The old one, passed by Congress in 1793, had proved inadequate to cope with runaways, especially since unfriendly state authorities failed to provide needed cooperation. Unlike cattle thieves, the abolitionists who ran the Underground Railroad did not gain personally from their lawlessness. But to the slaveowners the loss was infuriating, whatever the motives. The moral judgments of the abolitionists seemed, in some ways, more galling than outright theft. They reflected not only a holier-than-thou attitude but a refusal to obey the laws solemnly passed by Congress.

Estimates indicate that the South in 1850 was losing perhaps 1,000 runaways a year, out of its total of some 4 million slaves. In fact, more blacks probably gained their freedom by self-purchase or voluntary emancipation than ever escaped. But the principle weighed heavily with the slavemasters. They rested their argument on the Constitution, which protected slavery, and on the laws of Congress, which provided for slave-catching.

Twilight of the Senatorial Giants

Southern fears were such that Congress was confronted with catastrophe in 1850. Free-soil California was banging on the door for admission, and "fire-eaters" in the South were voicing ominous threats of secession. The crisis brought into the congressional forum the most distinguished assemblage of statesmen since the Constitutional Convention of 1787—the Old Guard of the dying generation and the young gladiators of the new. That "immortal trio"— Clay, Calhoun, and Webster—appeared together for the last time on the public stage.

Henry Clay, now seventy-three years of age, played a crucial role. The "Great Pacificator" had come to the Senate from Kentucky to engineer his third great compromise. The once-glamorous statesman—though disillusioned, enfeebled, and racked by a cruel cough—was still eloquent, conciliatory, captivating. He proposed and skillfully defended a series of compromises. He was ably seconded by thirty-seven-year-old Senator Stephen A. Douglas of Illinois, the "Little Giant" (5 feet 4 inches; 1.62 meters), whose role was less spectacular but even more important. Clay urged with all his persuasiveness that the North and South both make concessions and that the North partially yield by enacting a more effective fugitive-slave law.

Senator John C. Calhoun, then sixty-eight and dying of tuberculosis, championed the South in his last formal speech. Too weak to deliver it himself, he sat bundled up in the Senate chamber, his eyes glowing within a stern face, while a younger colleague read his fateful words. Although approving the purpose of Clay's proposed concessions, Calhoun rejected them as not providing adequate safeguards. His impassioned plea was to leave slavery alone, return runaway slaves, give the South its rights as a minority, and restore the political balance. He had in view, as was later revealed, an utterly unworkable scheme of electing two presidents, one from the North and one from the South, each wielding a veto.

Calhoun died in 1850, before the debate was over, uttering the sad words, "The South! The South! God knows what will become of her!" Appreciative fellow citizens in Charleston erected to his memory an imposing monument, which bore the inscription "Truth, Justice, and the Constitution." Calhoun had labored to preserve the Union and had taken his stand on the Constitution, but his proposals in their behalf almost undid both.

Daniel Webster next took the Senate spotlight to uphold Clay's compromise measures in his last great speech, a three-hour effort. Now sixty-eight years old and suffering from a liver complaint aggravated by high living, he had lost some of the fire in his magnificent voice. Speaking deliberately and before overflowing galleries, he urged all reasonable concessions to the South, including a new fugitive-slave law with teeth.

As for slavery in the territories, asked Webster, why legislate on the subject? To do so was an act of sacrilege, for Almighty God had already passed the Wilmot Proviso. The good Lord had decreed—through climate, topography, and geography—that a plantation economy, and hence a slave economy, could not profitably exist in the Mexican Cession territory.* Webster sanely concluded that compromise, concession, and sweet reasonableness would provide the only solutions. "Let us not be pygmies," he pleaded, "in a case that calls for men."

---

*Webster was wrong here; within one hundred years California had become one of the great cotton-producing states of the Union.

> *Ralph Waldo Emerson, the philosopher and moderate abolitionist, was outraged by Webster's support of concessions to the South in the Fugitive Slave Act. In February 1851 he wrote in his Journal: I opened a paper to-day in which he [Webster] pounds on the old strings [of liberty] in a letter to the Washington Birthday feasters at New York. 'Liberty! liberty!' Pho! Let Mr. Webster, for decency's sake, shut his lips once and forever on this word. The word liberty in the mouth of Mr. Webster sounds like the word love in the mouth of a courtesan."*

Webster's famed Seventh of March speech, 1850, was his finest, if measured by its immediate effects. It helped turn the tide in the North toward compromise. The clamor for printed copies became so great that Webster mailed out more than 100,000, remarking that 200,000 would not satisfy the demand. His tremendous effort visibly strengthened Union sentiment. It was especially pleasing to the banking and commercial centers of the North, which stood to lose millions of dollars by secession. One prominent Washington banker canceled two notes of Webster's, totaling $5,000, and sent him a personal check for $1,000 and a message of congratulations.

But the abolitionists, who had regarded Webster as one of themselves, upbraided him as a traitor, worthy of bracketing with Benedict Arnold. The poet Whittier lamented.

> So fallen! so lost! the light withdrawn
>   Which once he wore!
> The glory from his gray hairs gone
>   For evermore!

These reproaches were most unfair. Webster, who had long regarded slavery as evil but disunion as worse, despised the abolitionists and never joined their ranks.

Deadlock and Danger on Capitol Hill

The stormy congressional debate of 1850 was not finished, for the Young Guard from the North were yet to have their say. This was the group of newer leaders who, unlike the aging Old Guard, had not grown up with the Union. They were more interested in purging and purifying it than in patching and preserving it.

William H. Seward, the wiry and husky-throated freshman senator from New York, was the able spokesman for many of the younger northern radicals. A strong antislaveryite, he came out flat-footedly against concession. He seemed not to realize that compromise had brought the Union together and that when the sections could no longer compromise, they would have to part company.

Seward argued earnestly that Christian legislators must obey God's moral law as well as man's mundane law. He therefore appealed, with reference to excluding slavery in the territories, to an even "higher law" than the Constitution. This alarming phrase, wrenched from its context, may have cost him the presidential nomination and the presidency in 1860.

As the great debate in Congress ran its heated course, deadlock seemed certain. Blunt old President Taylor, who had allegedly fallen under the influence of men like "Higher Law" Seward, seemed bent on vetoing any compromise passed by Congress. His military ire was aroused by the threats of Texas to seize Santa Fe. He appeared to be doggedly determined to "Jacksonize" the dissenters, if need be, by leading an army against the Texans in person and hanging all "damned traitors." If troops had begun to march, the South probably would have rallied to the defense of her sister state, and the Civil War might have erupted in 1850.

A Seward Caricature   *He later became Lincoln's foremost rival for the presidency, and still later his secretary of state.*

Compromise of 1850

CONCESSIONS TO THE NORTH	CONCESSIONS TO THE SOUTH
California admitted as a free state	The remainder of the Mexican Cession area to be formed into the territories of New Mexico and Utah, without restriction on slavery, hence open to popular sovereignty
Territory disputed by Texas and New Mexico to be surrendered to New Mexico	Texas to receive $10 million from the federal government as compensation
Abolition of the slave trade (but not slavery) in the District of Columbia	A more stringent Fugitive Slave Law, going beyond that of 1793

Breaking the Congressional Logjam

At the height of the controversy in 1850, President Taylor unknowingly helped the cause of concession by dying suddenly, probably of an acute intestinal disorder. Portly, round-faced Vice-President Millard Fillmore, a colorless and conciliatory New York lawyer-politician, took over the reins. As presiding officer of the Senate, he had been impressed with the arguments for conciliation, and he gladly signed the series of compromise measures that passed Congress after seven long months of stormy debate. The balancing of interests in the Compromise of 1850 was delicate in the extreme.

The struggle to get these measures accepted by the country was hardly less heated than in Congress. In the northern states, "Union savers" like Senators Clay, Webster, and Douglas orated on behalf of the compromise. The ailing Clay himself delivered more than seventy speeches, as a powerful sentiment for acceptance gradually crystallized in the North. It was strengthened by a growing spirit of goodwill, which sprang partly from a feeling of relief and partly from an upsurge of prosperity enriched by California gold.

But the "fire-eaters" of the South were still violently opposed to concessions. One extreme South Carolina newspaper avowed that it loathed the Union and hated the North as much as it did Hell itself. A movement in the South to boycott northern goods gained some headway, but in the end the southern Unionists, assisted by the warm glow of prosperity, prevailed.

In mid-1850 an assemblage of southern extremists had met in Nashville, Tennessee, ironically near the burial place of Andrew Jackson. The delegates not only took a strong position in favor of slavery but condemned the compromise measures then being hammered out in Congress. Meeting again later in the year after the bills had passed, the convention proved to be a dud. By that time southern opinion had reluctantly accepted the verdict of Congress.

Like the calm after a storm, a second Era of Good Feelings dawned. Disquieting talk of secession subsided. Reasonable people, both North and South, were determined that the compromises should be a "finality" and that the explosive issue of slavery should be buried. But this reign of reason proved all too brief.

Balancing the Compromise Scales

Who got the better of the compromise of 1850?

The answer is clearly the North. California, as a free state, tipped the Senate balance permanently against the South. The territories of New Mexico and Utah were open to slavery on

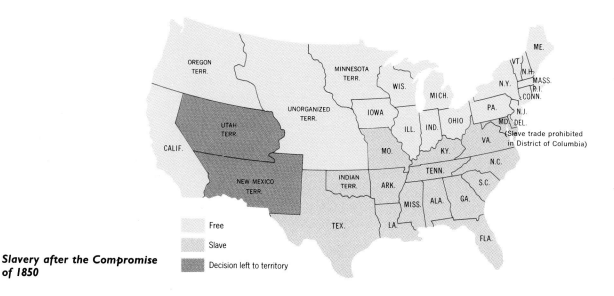

Slavery after the Compromise of 1850

Free

Slave

Decision left to territory

A Ride for Liberty *This famous painting by New England artist Eastman Johnson brilliantly evokes the anxiety of fleeing slaves. (The Brooklyn Museum. Gift of Miss Gwendolyn O.L. Conkling.)*

the basis of popular sovereignty. But the iron law of nature—the "highest law" of all—had loaded the dice in favor of free soil. The southerners urgently needed more slave territory to restore the "sacred balance." If they could not carve new states out of the recent conquests from Mexico, where else would they get them?

Even the apparent gains of the South rang hollow. Disgruntled Texas was to be paid $10 million toward discharging its indebtedness, but in the long run this was a modest sum. The immense area in dispute had been torn from the side of slaveholding Texas and was almost certain to be free. The South had halted the drive toward abolition in the District of Colum-

bia, at least temporarily, by permitting the outlawing of the slave traffic. But even this move was an entering wedge toward complete emancipation in the nation's capital.

Most alarming of all, the drastic new Fugitive Slave Law—"the Bloodhound Bill"—stirred up a storm of opposition in the North. The fleeing slaves could not testify in their own behalf, and they were denied a jury trial. These harsh practices threatened to create dangerous precedents for the whites. The federal commissioner who handled the case of a fugitive would receive five dollars if the runaway were freed and ten dollars if not—an arrangement that strongly resembled a bribe. Freedom-loving northerners

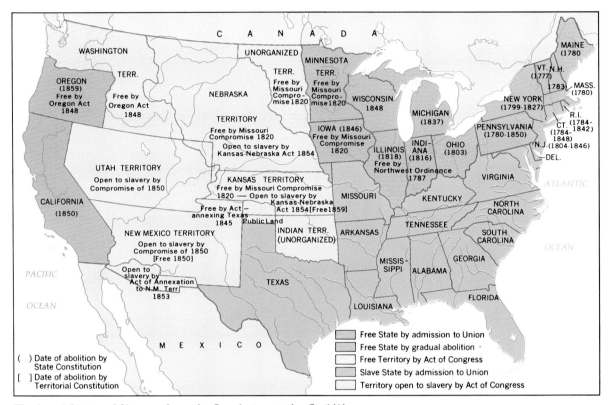

The Legal Status of Slavery, from the Revolution to the Civil War

who aided the slave to escape were liable to heavy fines and jail sentences. They might even be ordered to join the slave-catchers, and this possibility rubbed salt into old sores.

So savage was this "Man-Stealing Law" that it touched off an explosive chain reaction in the North. Many shocked moderates, hitherto passive, were driven into the swelling ranks of the abolitionists. Cried one poet:

> Lashed with her hounds, must we
> Run down the poor who flee
> From Slavery's hell?

The Underground Railroad stepped up its timetable, while infuriated northern mobs rescued slaves from their pursuers. Massachusetts, in a move toward nullification suggestive of South Carolina in 1832, made it a penal offense for any state official to enforce the new federal statute. Other states passed "personal liberty laws," which denied local jails to federal officials and otherwise hampered enforcement. The abolitionists rent the heavens with their protests against the man-stealing statute. A meeting presided over by Garrison in 1851 declared, "We execrate it, we spit upon it, we trample it under our feet."

Beyond question, the Fugitive Slave Law was an appalling blunder on the part of the South.

Regarding the Fugitive Slave Act of 1850, Ralph Waldo Emerson declared (May 1851) at Concord, Massachusetts: "The act of Congress . . . is a law which every one of you will break on the earliest occasion—a law which no man can obey, or abet the obeying, without loss of self-respect and forfeiture of the name of gentleman." Privately he wrote in his Journal: "This filthy enactment was made in the nineteenth century, by people who could read and write. I will not obey it, by God" (July 1851).

No single irritant of the 1850s was more persistently galling to both sides, and none did more to awaken in the North a spirit of antagonism against the South. The southerners in turn were embittered because the northerners would not in good faith execute the law—the one real and immediate "gain" from the Great Compromise. Slave-catchers, with some success, redoubled their efforts.

Should the shooting showdown have come in 1850? From the standpoint of the secessionists, yes; from the standpoint of the Unionists, no. Time was fighting for the North. With every passing decade this huge section was forging further ahead in population and wealth—in crops, factories, foundries, ships, and railroads.

Delay also added immensely to the moral strength of the North—to its will to fight for the Union. In 1850 countless thousands of northern moderates were unwilling to pin the South to the rest of the nation with bayonets. But the inflammatory events of the 1850s did much to bolster the Yankee will to resist secession, whatever the cost. This one feverish decade gave the North time to accumulate the physical and moral strength that provided the margin of victory. Thus, the Compromise of 1850, from one point of view, won the Civil War for the Union.

Defeat and Doom for the Whigs

Meeting in Baltimore, the Democratic nominating convention of 1852 startled the nation. Hopelessly deadlocked, it finally stampeded to the second "dark horse" candidate in American history, an unrenowned lawyer politician, Franklin Pierce, from the hills of New Hampshire. The Whigs tried to jeer him back into obscurity with the cry, "Who is Frank Pierce?" Democrats replied, "The Young Hickory of the Granite Hills."

Pierce, though handsome, was a weak and indecisive figure. Youngish, militarily erect, smiling, and convivial, he had served without real distinction in the Mexican War. As a result of a painful groin injury that caused him to fall off a horse, he was known as the "Fainting General," though scandalmongers pointed to a fondness for alcohol. But he was enemyless because he had been inconspicuous, and as a prosouthern northerner he was acceptable to the slavery wing of the Democratic party. His platform came out emphatically for the finality of the compromise of 1850, Fugitive Slave Law and all.

The Whigs, also convening in Baltimore, missed a splendid opportunity to capitalize on their record in statecraft. Able to boast of a praiseworthy achievement in the Compromise of 1850, they might logically have nominated President Fillmore or Senator Webster, both of whom were associated with it. But having won in the past only with military heroes, they turned to another, "Old Fuss and Feathers" Winfield Scott, perhaps the ablest American general of his generation. Although he was a huge and impressive figure, his manner bordered on haughtiness. His personality not only repelled the masses but eclipsed his genuinely statesmanlike achievements. The Whig platform praised the Compromise of 1850 as a lasting arrangement, though less enthusiastically than the Democrats.

With slavery and sectionalism to some extent soft-pedaled, the campaign again degenerated into a dull and childish attack on personalities. Democrats ridiculed Scott's pomposity; Whigs charged that Pierce was the hero of "many a well-fought *bottle*." Democrats cried exultantly, "We Polked 'em in '44; we'll Pierce 'em in '52."

Luckily for the Democrats, the Whig party was hopelessly split. Antislavery Whigs of the North swallowed Scott as their standard-bearer

In assailing the candidacy of "Fuss and Feathers" Scott, James Buchanan, himself elected president some four years later, declared that to elevate generals would cause "aspiring officers" to favor "foreign wars, as the best means of acquiring military glory. . . . Napoleon was endeared to his army by his designation of 'the little Corporal'; General Jackson, by that of 'Old Hickory'; and General Taylor was 'Rough and Ready'; but what shall we say to 'Fuss and Feathers'?"

but deplored his platform, which endorsed the hated Fugitive Slave Law. The current phrase ran, "We accept the candidate but spit on the platform." Southern Whigs, who doubted Scott's loyalty to the Compromise of 1850 and especially to the Fugitive Slave Law, accepted the platform but spat on the candidate. More than five thousand Georgia Whigs—"finality men"—futilely voted for Webster, although he had died nearly two weeks before the election.

General Scott, victorious on the battlefield, met defeat at the ballot box. His friends remarked whimsically that he was not used to "running." Actually, he was stabbed in the back by his fellow Whigs, notably in the South. The pliant Pierce won in a landslide, 254 electoral votes to 42, though the popular count was closer, 1,601,117 to 1,385,453.

The election of 1852 was fraught with frightening significance, though it may have seemed tame at the time. It marked the effective end of the disorganized Whig party and, within a few years, its complete death. The Whigs were governed at times by the crassest opportunism, and they won only two presidential elections (1840, 1848) in their colorful career, both with war heroes. They finally choked to death trying to gag down the Fugitive Slave Law. But their great contribution—and a noteworthy one indeed—was to help implant and uphold the ideal of Union through leaders like Clay and Webster. Both of these statesmen, by unhappy coincidence, died during the campaign. But the good that they had done lived after them and contributed powerfully to the preservation of a united United States.

President Pierce the Expansionist

At the outset the Pierce administration displayed vigor. The new president, standing confidently before some fifteen thousand people on inauguration day, delivered from memory a clear-voiced inaugural address. His cabinet contained aggressive southerners, including as secretary of war one Jefferson Davis, future president of the Confederacy. The people of Dixie were determined to acquire more slave territory, and the compliant Pierce was prepared to be their willing tool.

The intoxicating victories of the Mexican War stimulated the spirit of Manifest Destiny, especially among "slaveocrats" lusting for new

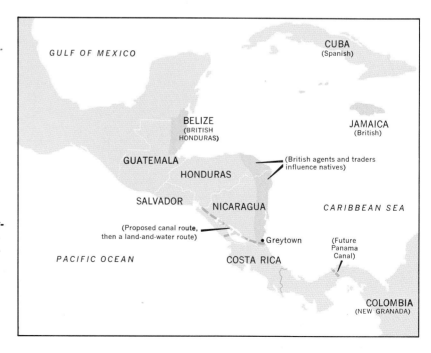

Central America, c. 1850, Showing British Possessions and Proposed Canal Routes *Until President Theodore Roosevelt swung into action with his big stick in 1903, a Nicaraguan canal, closer to the United States, was generally judged more desirable than a canal across Panama.*

slave territory. The conquest of a Pacific frontage, and the discovery of gold on it, aroused lively interest in the trans-isthmian land routes of Central America, chiefly in Panama and Nicaragua. Many Americans were looking even further ahead to potential canal routes and to the islands flanking them, notably Spain's Cuba.

Nicaragua was of vital concern to Great Britain, the world's leading maritime and commercial power. Fearing that the grasping Yankees would monopolize the trade arteries there, the British made haste to secure a solid foothold at Greytown, the eastern end of the proposed Nicaraguan canal route. This challenge to the Monroe Doctrine forthwith raised the ugly possibility of an armed clash. The crisis was surmounted in 1850 by the Clayton-Bulwer Treaty, which stipulated that neither America nor Britain would fortify or secure exclusive control over any future isthmian waterway. This agreement, at the time, seemed necessary to halt the British, but to American canal promoters in later years, it proved to be a ball and chain.

America had become a Pacific power with the acquisition of California and Oregon, both of which faced the Orient. The prospects of a rich trade with the Far East now seemed rosier. Americans had already established contacts with China, and shippers were urging Washington to push for commercial intercourse with Japan. The mikado's empire, after some disagreeable experiences with the European world, had withdrawn into a cocoon of isolationism and had remained there for over two hundred years. But by 1853, as events proved, Nippon was ready to emerge, partly because of the Russian menace.

The Washington government was now eager to pry open the bamboo gates of Japan. It dispatched a fleet of awesome, smoke-belching warships, commanded by Commodore Matthew C. Perry, brother of the hero of the Battle of Lake Erie in 1813. By a judicious display of force and tact, he persuaded the Japanese in 1854 to sign a memorable treaty. It provided for only a commercial foot in the door, but it was the beginning of an epochal relationship between the Land of the Rising Sun and the Western world. Ironically, this achievement at-tracted little notice at the time, partly because Perry devised no memorable slogan.

Coveted Cuba: Pearl of the Antilles

Sugar-rich Cuba, lying off the nation's southern doorstep, was the prime objective of Manifest Destiny in the 1850s. Supporting a large population of enslaved blacks, it was coveted by the South as the most desirable slave territory available. Carved into several states, it would once more restore the political balance in the Senate.

Cuba was a kind of heirloom—the most important remnant of Spain's once-mighty New World empire. Polk, the expansionist, had taken steps to offer $100 million for it, but the sensitive Spaniards had replied that they would see it sunk into the ocean before they would sell it to the Americans at any price. With purchase completely out of the question, seizure was apparently the only way to pluck the ripening fruit.

Private adventurers from the South now undertook to shake the tree of Manifest Destiny. During 1850–1851 two filibustering expeditions, each numbering several hundred armed men, descended upon Cuba. Both feeble efforts were repelled, and the last one ended in tragedy when the leader and fifty followers—some of them from the "best families" of the South—were summarily shot or strangled. So outraged were the southerners that an angry mob sacked Spain's consulate in New Orleans.

Spanish officials in Cuba rashly forced a showdown in 1854, when they seized an American steamer, *Black Warrior,* on a technicality. Now was the time for President Pierce, dominated as he was by the South, to provoke a war with Spain and seize Cuba. The major powers of Europe—England, France, and Russia—were about to become bogged down in the Crimean War and hence were unable to aid Spain.

An incredible cloak-and-dagger episode followed. The secretary of state instructed the American ministers in Spain, England, and France to prepare confidential recommendations for the acquisition of Cuba. Meeting initially at Ostend, Belgium, the three envoys drew

Cuban Discomfort *"Master Jonathan tries to smoke a Cuba, but it doesn't agree with him!" English chortle over America's Cuban blunder. (Punch, 1850.)*

up a top-secret dispatch, soon known as the Ostend Manifesto. This startling document urged that the administration offer $120 million for Cuba. If Spain refused, and if its continued ownership endangered American interests, the United States would "be justified in wresting" the island from the Spanish.

The secret Ostend Manifesto quickly leaked out. Northern free-soilers, already angered by the Fugitive Slave Law and other gains for slavery, rose in an outburst of wrath against the "manifesto of brigands." Confronted with disruption at home, the red-faced Pierce administration was forced to drop its brazen schemes for Cuba.

Clearly the slavery issue, like a two-headed snake with the heads at cross purposes, deadlocked territorial expansion in the 1850s. The North, flushed with Manifest Destiny, was developing a renewed appetite for Canada. The South coveted Cuba. Neither section would permit the other to get the apple of its eye, so neither got either. The shackled black hands of Harriet Beecher Stowe's Uncle Tom, who had already aroused the North, held the South back from Cuba. The internal distresses of the United States were such that, for once, it could not take advantage of Europe's distresses—in this case the Crimean War.

The first platform of the newly born (antislavery) Republican party in 1856 lashed out at the Ostend Manifesto, with its transparent suggestion that Cuba be seized. The plank read:

Resolved, That the highwayman's plea, that 'might makes right,' embodied in the Ostend Circular, was in every respect unworthy of American diplomacy, and would bring shame and dishonor upon any Government or people that gave it their sanction."

Pacific Railroad Promoters and the Gadsden Purchase

Acute transportation problems were another legacy of the Mexican War. The newly acquired prizes of California and Oregon might just as well have been islands some eight thousand miles (thirteen thousand kilometers) west of the nation's capital. The sea routes to and from the isthmus, to say nothing of those around South America, were too long. Covered-wagon travel past bleaching animal bones was possible, but slow and dangerous. A popular song recalled:

They swam the wide rivers and crossed the
  tall peaks,
And camped on the prairie for weeks upon
  weeks.
Starvation and cholera and hard work and
  slaughter,
They reached California spite of hell and high
  water.

Feasible land transportation was imperative—or the newly won possessions on the
Pacific Coast might break away. Camels were
even proposed as the answer. Several score of
these temperamental beasts—"ships of the
desert"—were imported from the Near East, but
mule-driving Americans did not adjust to them.
A transcontinental railroad was clearly the only
real solution to the problem.

Railroad promoters, both North and South,
had projected many drawing-board routes to the
Pacific Coast. But the estimated cost in all cases
was so great that for many years there could obviously be only one line. Should its terminus be
in the North or in the South? The favored section would reap rich rewards in wealth, population, and influence. The South, losing the economic race with the North, was eager to extend
a railroad through adjacent southwestern territory all the way to California.

Another chunk of Mexico now seemed desirable, because the campaigns of the recent war
had shown that the best railway route ran
slightly south of the Mexican border. Secretary
of War Jefferson Davis, a Mississippian, arranged to have James Gadsden, a prominent
South Carolina railroad man, appointed minister to Mexico. Finding Santa Anna in power for
the sixth and last time, and as usual in need of
money, Gadsden made gratifying headway. He
negotiated a treaty in 1853, which ceded to the
United States the Gadsden Purchase area for
$10 million. The transaction aroused much crit-
icism among northerners, who objected to paying a huge sum for a cactus-strewn desert
nearly the size of Gadsden's South Carolina.
Undeterred, the Senate approved the pact after
shortsightedly eliminating a window on the
Gulf of California.

No doubt the Gadsden Purchase enabled the
South to claim the coveted railroad with even
greater insistence. A southern track would be
easier to build, because the mountains were
less high and because the route, unlike the proposed northern lines, would not pass through
unorganized territory. Texas was already a state
at this point, and New Mexico (with the Gadsden Purchase added) was a formally organized
territory, with federal troops available to provide
protection against marauding tribes of Indians.
Any northern or central railroad line would have
to be thrust through the unorganized territory
of Nebraska, where the buffalo and Indians
roamed.

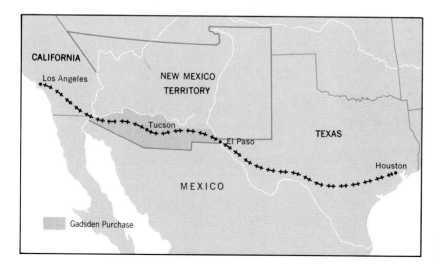

Gadsden Purchase, 1853 *Future
Southern Pacific Railroad (completed
1882) is shown.*

Northern railroad boosters quickly replied that if organized territory were the test, then Nebraska should be organized. Such a move was not premature, because thousands of land-hungry pioneers were already poised on the Nebraska border. But all schemes proposed in Congress for organizing the territory were greeted with apathy or hostility by many southerners. Why should the South help create new free-soil states and thus cut its own throat by facilitating a northern railroad?

Stephen A. Douglas (1813–1861) *Despite having stirred up sectional bitterness, Douglas was so devoted to the Union that he warmly supported his rival, Lincoln, when war broke out. He attended the inauguration and reportedly held Lincoln's stovepipe hat while the president spoke. (National Portrait Gallery, Smithsonian Institution, Washington, D.C.)*

Douglas's Kansas-Nebraska Scheme

At this point in 1854 Senator Stephen A. Douglas of Illinois delivered a counterstroke to offset the Gadsden thrust for southern expansion westward. A squat, bull-necked, and heavy-chested figure, the "Little Giant" radiated the energy and breezy optimism of the self-made man. An ardent booster for the West, he longed to break the North-South deadlock over westward expansion and stretch a line of settlements across the continent. He had also invested heavily in Chicago real estate and in railway stock and was eager to have the Windy City become the eastern terminus of the proposed Pacific railroad. He would thus endear himself to the voters of Illinois, benefit his section, and enrich his own purse.

A veritable "steam engine in breeches," Douglas threw himself behind a legislative scheme that would enlist the support of a reluctant South. The proposed Territory of Nebraska would be carved into two territories, Kansas and Nebraska. Their status regarding slavery would be settled by popular sovereignty—a democratic concept to which Douglas and his western constituents were deeply attached. Kansas, which lay due west of slaveholding Missouri, would presumably choose to become a slave state. But Nebraska, lying west of free-soil Iowa, would presumably become a free state.

Douglas's Kansas-Nebraska scheme ran headlong into a formidable political obstacle. The Missouri Compromise of 1820 had forbidden slavery in the Nebraska Territory, which lay north of the sacred 36°30′ line; and the only way to open the region to popular sovereignty was to repeal the ancient compact outright. This bold step Douglas was prepared to take, even at the risk of shattering the uneasy truce patched up by the Great Compromise of 1850.

Many southerners, who had not conceived of Kansas as slave soil, rose to the bait. Here was a chance to gain one more slave state. The pliable President Pierce, under the thumb of southern advisers, threw his full weight behind the Kansas-Nebraska Bill.

But the Missouri Compromise, now thirty-four years old, could not be brushed aside lightly. Whatever Congress passes it can repeal, but by this time the North had come to regard the sectional pact as almost as sacred as the Constitution itself. Free-soil members of Congress struck back furiously. They met their match in the violently gesticulating Douglas, who was the ablest rough-and-tumble debater of his generation. Employing twisted logic and oratorical fireworks, he rammed the bill through Congress, with strong support from many southerners. So heated were political passions that bloodshed was barely averted. Some members carried a concealed revolver or a bowie knife—or both.

Douglas's motives in prodding anew the snarling dog of slavery have long puzzled historians. His personal interests have already been mentioned. In addition, his foes accused him of angling for the presidency in 1856. Yet his admirers have argued plausibly in his defense that if he had not championed the ill-omened bill, someone else would have.

The truth seems to be that Douglas acted somewhat impulsively and recklessly. His heart did not bleed over the issue of slavery, and he declared repeatedly that he did not care whether it was voted up or down in the territories. What he failed to perceive was that hundreds of thousands of his fellow countrymen in the North *did* feel deeply on this moral issue. They regarded the repeal of the Missouri Compromise as an intolerable breach of faith, and they would henceforth resist to the last trench all future Southern demands for slave territory.

Genuine leaders, like skillful chess players, must foresee the possible effects of their moves. Douglas predicted a "hell of a storm," but he grossly underestimated its proportions. His critics in the North, branding him a "Judas" and a "traitor," greeted his name with frenzied boos, hisses, and "three groans for Doug." But he still enjoyed a high degree of popularity among his following in the Democratic party, especially in Illinois, a stronghold of popular sovereignty.

Congress Legislates a Civil War

The Kansas-Nebraska Act—a curtain raiser to a terrible drama—was one of the most momentous measures ever to pass Congress. By one

Douglas Hatches a Slavery Problem   *Note the already hatched Missouri Compromise, Squatter Sovereignty, and Filibustering (in Cuba), and the about-to-hatch Free Kansas and Dred Scott decision. So bitter was the outcry against Douglas at the time of the Kansas-Nebraska controversy that he claimed with exaggeration that he could have traveled from Boston to Chicago at night by the light from his burning effigies. (Republican cartoon.)*

way of reckoning, it led directly down the slippery slope to Civil War.

Antislavery northerners were angered by what they condemned as an act of bad faith by the "Neb-rascals" and their "Nebrascality." All future compromise with the South would be immeasurably more difficult, and without compromise there was bound to be conflict.

Henceforth the Fugitive Slave Law of 1850, previously enforced in the North only halfheartedly, was a dead letter. The Kansas-Nebraska Act wrecked two compromises: that of 1820, which it repealed specifically, and that of 1850, which northern opinion repealed indirectly. Emerson wrote, "The Fugitive [Slave] Law did much to unglue the eyes of men, and now the Nebraska Bill leaves us staring." Northern abolitionists and southern "fire-eaters" alike were stirred to new outbursts. The growing legion of antislaveryites gained numerous recruits, who resented the grasping move by the "slavocracy" for Kansas. The southerners, in turn, became

Kansas and Nebraska, 1854 *Future Union Pacific Railroad (completed 1869) is shown. Note the Missouri Compromise line of 36°30' (1820).*

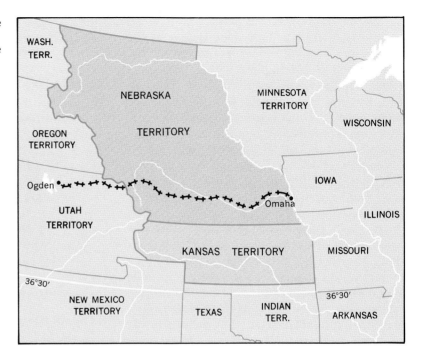

inflamed when the free-soilers tried to control Kansas, contrary to the presumed "deal."

The proud Democrats—a party now over half a century old—were shattered by the Kansas-Nebraska Act. They managed to elect a president two years later, but he was the last one they were to boost into the White House for twenty-eight long years.

Undoubtedly the most durable offspring of the Kansas-Nebraska blunder was the new Republican party. It sprang up spontaneously in the Middle West, notably in Wisconsin and Michigan, as a mighty moral protest against the gains of slavery. Gathering together dissatisfied elements, it soon included disgruntled Whigs (among them Abraham Lincoln), Democrats, Free-Soilers, Know-Nothings, and other foes of the Kansas-Nebraska Act. The hodgepodge party spread eastward with the rapidity of a prairie fire and with the zeal of a religious crusade. Unheard of and unheralded at the beginning of 1854, it elected a Republican Speaker of the House of Representatives within two years. Never really a third-party movement, it erupted with such force as to become almost overnight the second major political party—and a purely sectional one at that.

At long last the dreaded sectional rift had appeared. The new Republican party would not be allowed south of the Mason-Dixon line. Countless southerners subscribed wholeheartedly to the sentiment that it was "a nigger stealing, stinking, putrid, abolition party." The Union was in dire peril.

Varying Viewpoints

Historical analysts of the 1850s have long been preoccupied with the mounting controversy over slavery. Why, they have asked, did the long-simmering slavery issue finally boil to a head in the decade of the 1850s, eventually exploding in the brutal Civil War of 1861–1865? Many scholars, most notably David M. Potter, have argued that the irreconcilable differences between free and slave societies—moral, political, economic, and social—increasingly eroded the ties between the sections and inexorably set the United States on the road to Civil War. In this process, no event was more important than the breakdown of the Jacksonian party system. When the slavery issue tore both the Democratic and Whig parties apart, the last ligaments binding the nation together were dissolved, and the war inevitably came.

In recent years, historians of the "ethnocultural" school, especially Michael Holt, have challenged this traditional view. They note that the two great national parties had focused attention on issues like the tariff, banking, and internal improvements, thereby muting sectional differences over slavery. In this view, the demise of the "second-party system" is blamed not on growing differences over slavery but on a temporary *consensus* between the two parties on almost all national issues *other* than slavery. In this peculiar political atmosphere, the slavery issue was shoved to the fore, encouraging the emergence of Republicans in the North and secessionists in the South. In the absence of regular, national, two-party conflict over economic issues, purely regional parties (like the Republicans) coalesced. They identified their opponents not simply as competitors for power but as threats to their way of life, even to the life of the Republic itself. This approach thus suggests an answer to the question of why the Civil War came when it did: sectional strife had existed at least since the Missouri Compromise, but, paradoxically, it was only with the collapse of traditional partisan conflict in the 1850s that it led to war.

Select Readings

Primary Source Documents

The *Congressional Globe* for 1850 contains the dramatic orations of a dying generation of American statesmen on the Compromise of 1850. See the speeches by Webster,* Calhoun,* and Clay (in Richard Hofstadter, ed., *Great Issues in American History*). The debate on the Kansas-Nebraska Bill can be found in the 1854 volume of the same source, which includes addresses by Stephen A. Douglas* and his Republican opponent, Salmon P. Chase.*

Secondary Sources

The best account of the events of the 1850s is David M. Potter's masterful *The Impending Crisis, 1848–1861* (1976). Sketchy but penetrating is Roy F. Nichols, *The Stakes of Power, 1845–1877* (1961); see also his more detailed *The Disruption of American Democracy* (1948). Comprehensive treatments may be found in James G. Randall and David Donald, *The Civil War and Reconstruction* (rev. ed., 1969), and Allan Nevins, *Ordeal of the Union* (2 vols., 1947). See also Avery O. Craven, *The Coming of the Civil War* (2d ed., 1957), his *Civil War in the Making* (1959), and his *Growth of Southern Nationalism* (1953). David Potter also offers illuminating insights in *The South and the Sectional Conflict* (1968). The standard work is Holman Hamilton, *Prologue to Conflict: The Crisis and Compromise of 1850* (1964). The emergence of the Republican party can be studied in Eric Foner's brilliant discussion of ideology, *Free Soil, Free Labor, Free Men* (1970); William Gienapp, *The Origins of the Republican Party*

(1985); and Michael Holt's perceptive *Forging a Majority: The Formation of the Republican Party in Pittsburgh* (1969). Foner's ideas can be pursued further in his *Politics and Ideology in the Age of the Civil War* (1980), while Holt has developed his views in *The Political Crisis of the 1850s* (1978), an unusually provocative book. Party politics are treated in Thomas B. Alexander, *Sectional Stress and Party Strength: A Computer Analysis of Roll-Call Voting Behavior in the United States House of Representatives, 1836–1860* (1967), and two books by Joel H. Silbey, *The Shrine of Party: Congressional Voting Behavior, 1841–1852* (1967) and his unorthodox *Partisan Imperative: The Dynamics of American Politics before the Civil War* (1985). Richard H. Sewell, *Ballots for Freedom: Antislavery Politics in the United States, 1837–1860* (1976), is a standard work.

22

Drifting toward Disunion, 1854–1861

A house divided against itself cannot stand. I believe this government cannot endure permanently half slave and half free.

Abraham Lincoln, 1858

Stowe and Helper: Literary Incendiaries

Sectional tensions were further strained in 1852, and later, by an inky phenomenon. Harriet Beecher Stowe, a wisp of a woman and the mother of a half-dozen children, published her heartrending novel *Uncle Tom's Cabin.* Dismayed by the passage of the Fugitive Slave Law, she was determined to awaken the North to the wickedness of slavery by laying bare its terrible inhumanity, especially the cruel splitting of families. Her book, though lacking high literary quality, was distinguished by powerful imagery and touching pathos. "God wrote it," she explained in later years—a reminder that the sources of her antislavery sentiments lay in the evangelical religious crusades of the Second Great Awakening.

The success of the novel at home and abroad was sensational. Several hundred thousand copies were published in the first year, and the totals soon ran into the millions as the tale was translated into more than a score of languages. It was also put on the stage in "Tom shows" for lengthy runs. No other novel in American history—perhaps in all history—can be compared with it as a political force. To millions of people it made slavery appear almost as evil as it really was.

When Mrs. Stowe was introduced to President Lincoln in 1862, he reportedly remarked

Harriet Beecher Stowe (1811–1896)   *She was a remarkable woman whose pen helped to change the course of history. (The Metropolitan Museum of Art, gift of I. N. Phelps Stokes, Edward S. Hawes, Alice Mary Hawes, and Marion Augusta Hawes, 1937.)*

"The Book that Made this Great War"   *Lincoln's celebrated remark to author Harriet Beecher Stowe reflected the enormous emotional impact of her impassioned novel. (The Granger Collection.)*

with twinkling eyes, "So you're the little woman who wrote the book that made this great war." The truth is that *Uncle Tom's Cabin* helped start the Civil War—and win it. The South condemned that "vile wretch in petticoats" when it

> In the closing scenes of Stowe's novel, Uncle Tom's brutal master, Simon Legree, orders the $1,200 slave savagely beaten (to death) by two fellow slaves. Through tears and blood Tom exclaims: "No! no! no! my soul an't yours Mas'r! You haven't bought it—ye can't buy it! It's been bought and paid for by One that is able to keep it. No matter, no matter, you can't harm me!" "I can't" said Legree, with a sneer; "we'll see—we'll see! Here, Sambo, Quimbo, give this dog such a breakin' in as he won't get over this month!"

learned that hundreds of thousands of fellow Americans were reading and believing her "unfair" indictment. Mrs. Stowe had never witnessed slavery at first hand in the Deep South, but she had seen it briefly during a visit to Kentucky, and she had lived for many years in Ohio, a center of Underground Railway activity.

Uncle Tom, endearing and enduring, left a profound impression on the North. Uncounted thousands of readers swore that henceforth they would have nothing to do with the enforcement of the Fugitive Slave Law. The tale was devoured by millions of impressionable youths in the 1850s—the later Boys in Blue who volunteered to fight the Civil War through to its grim finale. The memory of a beaten and dying Uncle Tom helped sustain them in their determination to wipe out the plague of slavery.

The novel was immensely popular abroad, especially in England and France. Countless readers wept over the kindly Tom and the angelic Eva, while deploring the brutal Simon Legree. When the guns in America finally began to boom, the common people of England sensed that the triumph of the North would spell the end of the black curse. The governments in London and Paris seriously considered intervening in behalf of the South, but they were sobered by the realization that many of their own people, aroused by the "Tom-mania," might not support them.

Another trouble-brewing book appeared in 1857, five years after the debut of Uncle Tom. Entitled *The Impending Crisis of the South,* it was written by Hinton R. Helper, a nonaristocratic white from North Carolina. Hating both slavery and blacks, he attempted to prove by an array of statistics that indirectly the nonslaveholding whites were the ones who suffered most from the millstone of slavery. Unable to secure a publisher in the South, he finally managed to find one in the North.

Helper's influence was negligible among the poorer whites to whom he addressed his message. His book, with its "dirty allusions," was banned in the South, where book-burning parties were held. But in the North countless thousands of copies, many in condensed form, were distributed as campaign literature by the Republicans. Southerners were further embittered when they learned that their northern brethren were spreading these wicked "lies." Thus did southerners, reacting much as they did to *Uncle Tom's Cabin,* become increasingly unwilling to sleep under the same federal roof with their hostile Yankee bedfellows.

The North-South Contest for Kansas

The rolling plains of Kansas had meanwhile been providing a horrible example of the workings of popular sovereignty, although admittedly under abnormal conditions.

Newcomers who ventured into Kansas were a motley lot. Most of the northerners were just ordinary westward-moving pioneers in search of richer lands beyond the sunset. But a small part of the inflow was financed by groups of northern abolitionists or free-soilers. The most famous of these antislavery organizations was the New England Emigrant Aid Company, which sent about two thousand persons to the troubled area to forestall the South—and also to make a profit. Shouting "Ho for Kansas," many of them carried the deadly new breech-loading Sharps rifles, nicknamed "Beecher's Bibles" after the Reverend Henry Ward Beecher (Harriet Beecher Stowe's brother), who had helped raise money for their purchase. Many of the Kansas-bound pioneers sang Whittier's marching song (1854):

> We cross the prairie as of old
> The pilgrims crossed the sea,
> To make the West, as they the East,
> The homestead of the free!

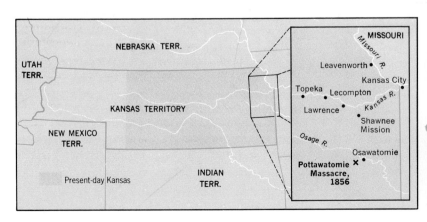

Bleeding Kansas, 1854–1860
Abolitionist newspapers had a field day reporting Kansas "atrocities" hatched by the proslavery party. Where facts were lacking, imaginations took over. Victims were portrayed as law-abiding, antislavery citizens, while aggressors were invariably "border ruffians" or "hired henchmen," maddened by whiskey. One notorious murder was later proved to have resulted from a purely personal quarrel between two men, both of whom were free-soilers.

Southern spokesmen, now more than ordinarily touchy, raised furious cries of betrayal. They had supported the Kansas-Nebraska scheme of Douglas with the informal understanding that Kansas would become slave and Nebraska free. The northern "Nebrascals," allegedly by foul means, were now apparently out to "abolitionize" *both* Kansas and Nebraska.

A few southern hotheads, quick to respond in kind, attempted to "assist" small groups of well-armed slaveowners to Kansas. Some carried banners proclaiming:

> Let Yankees tremble, abolitionists fall,
> Our motto is, "Give Southern Rights to All."

But planting blacks on Kansas soil was a losing game. Slaves were valuable and volatile property, and foolish indeed were owners who would take them where bullets were flying and where the soil might be voted free under popular sovereignty. The census of 1860 found only 2 slaves among 107,000 souls in all the territory and only 15 in Nebraska. There was much force in the charge that the whole quarrel over slavery in the territories revolved around "an imaginary Negro in an impossible place."

Crisis conditions in Kansas rapidly worsened. When the day came in 1855 to elect members of the first territorial legislature, proslavery "border ruffians" poured in from Missouri to vote early and often. The slavery supporters triumphed and then set up their own puppet government at Shawnee Mission. The free-soilers, unable to stomach this fraudulent conspiracy, established an extralegal regime of their own in Topeka. The confused Kansans thus had their choice between two governments—one based on fraud, the other on illegality.

Tension mounted as settlers also feuded over conflicting land claims. The breaking point came in 1856 when a gang of proslavery raiders, alleging provocation, shot up and burned a part of the free-soil town of Lawrence. This outrage was but the prelude to a bloodier tragedy.

John Brown (1800–1859) *A militant abolitionist, Brown became perhaps the most sung-about man up to that time, except Jesus. From a primitive photograph (daguerreotype) taken in 1856. (Courtesy Kansas Historical Society.)*

Kansas in Convulsion

The fanatical figure of John Brown now stalked upon the Kansas battlefield. Spare, gray-bearded, iron-willed, and narrowly ignorant, he was dedicated to the abolitionist cause. The power of his glittering gray eyes was such, so he claimed, that his stare could force a dog or cat to slink out of a room. Becoming involved in dubious dealings, including horse stealing, he moved to Kansas from Ohio with a part of his large family. Brooding over the recent attack on Lawrence, "Old Brown" of Osawatomie led a band of his followers to Pottawatomie Creek, in May 1856. There they literally hacked to pieces five surprised men, allegedly proslaveryites. This fiendish butchery, clearly the product of a deranged mind, besmirched the free-soil cause and brought vicious retaliation from the proslavery forces.

Civil war in Kansas, which thus flared forth in 1856, continued intermittently until it merged with the large-scale Civil War of

> John Brown, an avid reader of the Old Testament, evidently believed in the principle of an eye for an eye, and a hand for a hand. A surviving son of one of his victims later testified under oath that "I found my father and one brother, William, lying dead in the road . . . I saw my other brother lying dead on the ground . . . in the grass, near a ravine, his fingers were cut open; there was a hole in his breast. William's head was cut open, and a hole in his jaw . . . and a hole was also in his side. My father was shot in the forehead and stabbed in the breast."

was a compromise that, in effect, submitted the *entire* Lecompton Constitution to a popular vote. The free-soil voters thereupon thronged to the polls and snowed it under. But Kansas was denied statehood until 1861, when the southern secessionists left Congress.

President Buchanan, by antagonizing the numerous Douglas Democrats in the North, hopelessly divided the once-powerful Democratic party. Until then, it had been the only remaining *national* party, for the Whigs were dead and the Republicans were sectional. With the disruption of the Democrats came the snapping of one of the last important strands in the rope that was barely binding the Union together.

1861–1865. Altogether, the Kansas conflict destroyed millions of dollars' worth of property, paralyzed agriculture in certain areas, and cost scores of lives.

Yet by 1857 Kansas had enough people, chiefly free-soilers, to apply for statehood on a popular-sovereignty basis. The proslavery forces, then in the saddle, devised a tricky document known as the Lecompton Constitution. The people were not allowed to vote for or against the constitution as a whole, but for the constitution either "with slavery" or "with no slavery." If they voted against slavery, one of the remaining provisions of the constitution would protect the owners of slaves already in Kansas. So whatever the outcome, there would still be black bondage in Kansas. Many free-soilers, infuriated by this trick, boycotted the polls. Left to themselves, the slaveryites approved the constitution with slavery late in 1857.

The scene next shifted to Washington. President Pierce had been succeeded by the no-less-pliable James Buchanan, who was also strongly under southern influence. Blind to sharp divisions within his own Democratic party, Buchanan threw the weight of his administration behind the notorious Lecompton Constitution. But Senator Douglas, who had championed true popular sovereignty, would have none of this semipopular fraudulency. Deliberately tossing away his strong support in the South for the presidency, he fought courageously for fair play and democratic principles. The outcome

"Bully" Brooks and His Bludgeon

"Bleeding Kansas" also splattered blood on the floor of the United States Senate in 1856. Senator Charles Sumner of Massachusetts, a tall and imposing figure, was a leading abolitionist—one of the few prominent in political life. Highly educated but cold, humorless, intolerant, and egotistical, he had made himself one of the most disliked men in the Senate. Brooding over the turbulent miscarriage of popular sovereignty, he delivered a blistering speech entitled "The Crime against Kansas." Sparing few epithets, he condemned the proslavery men as "hirelings picked from the drunken spew and vomit of an uneasy civilization." He also referred insultingly to South Carolina and to its white-haired Senator Butler, one of the best-liked members of the Senate.

Hot-tempered Congressman Brooks, of South Carolina, now took vengeance into his own hands. Ordinarily gracious and gallant, he resented the insults to his state and to its senator, a distant cousin. His code of honor called for a duel, but in the South one fought only with one's social equals. And had not the coarse language of the Yankee, who probably would reject a challenge, dropped him to a lower order? To Brooks, the only alternative was to chastise the senator as one would beat an unruly dog. On May 22, 1856, he approached Sumner, then sitting at his Senate desk, and pounded the orator with an eleven-ounce cane

Sumner Beaten by Brooks   *Note that the cartoonist has two of the senators smiling or laughing and one of them preventing interference with his cane. Note also that Sumner is defending himself with a quill pen while Brooks is wielding a club. (Courtesy the New York Public Library, Astor, Lenox, and Tilden Foundations.)*

SOUTHERN CHIVALRY — ARGUMENT versus CLUB'S.

until it broke. The victim fell bleeding and unconscious to the floor, while several nearby senators refrained from interfering.

Sumner had been provocatively insulting, but this counteroutrage put Brooks in the wrong. The House of Representatives could not muster enough votes to expel the Carolinian, but he resigned and was triumphantly reelected. Southern admirers deluged Brooks with

---

Regarding the Brooks assault on Sumner, one of the more moderate antislavery journals (Illinois State Journal) declared, "Brooks and his Southern allies have deliberately adopted the monstrous creed that any man who dares to utter sentiments which they deem wrong or unjust, shall be brutally assailed. . . . " One of the milder southern responses came from the Petersburg (Virginia) Intelligencer: "Although Mr. Brooks ought to have selected some other spot for the altercation than the Senate chamber, if he had broken every bone in Sumner's carcass it would have been a just retribution upon this slanderer of the South and her individual citizens."

---

canes, some of them gold-headed, to replace the one that had been broken. The injuries to Sumner's head and nervous system were serious. He was forced to leave his seat for three and a half years and go to Europe for treatment that was both painful and costly. Meanwhile Massachusetts defiantly reelected him, leaving his seat eloquently empty. Bleeding Sumner was thus joined with bleeding Kansas as a political issue.

The free-soil North was mightily aroused against the "uncouth" and "cowardly" "Bully" Brooks. Copies of Sumner's abusive speech, otherwise doomed to obscurity, were sold by the tens of thousands. Every blow that struck the senator doubtless made thousands of Republican votes. The South, although not unanimous in approving Brooks, was angered not only because Sumner had made such an intemperate speech but because it had been so extravagantly applauded in the North.

The Sumner-Brooks clash and the ensuing reactions revealed how dangerously inflamed passions were becoming, North and South. It was ominous that the cultured Sumner should have used the language of a barroom bully and that the gentlemanly Brooks should have employed the tactics and tools of a thug. Emotion was displacing thought. The blows rained on

Sumner's head were, broadly speaking, among the first blows of the Civil War.

"Old Buck" versus "The Pathfinder"

With bullets whining in Kansas, the Democrats met in Cincinnati to nominate their presidential standard-bearer of 1856. They shied away from both the weak-kneed President Pierce and the dynamic Douglas. Each was too heavily blackened by the Kansas-Nebraska Act. The delegates finally chose James Buchanan (pronounced by many *Buck*-anan), who was muscular, white-haired, and tall (6 feet; 1.83 meters), with a short neck and a protruding chin. Because of an eye defect, he carried his head cocked to one side. A well-to-do Pennsylvania lawyer, he had been serving as minister to London during the recent Kansas-Nebraska uproar. He was therefore "Kansasless," and hence relatively enemyless. But in a crisis that called for giants, "Old Buck" Buchanan was mediocre, irresolute, confused.

Delegates of the fast-growing Republican party met in Philadelphia with bubbling enthusiasm. "Higher Law" Seward was their most conspicuous leader, and he probably would have arranged to win the nomination had he been confident that this was a "Republican year." The final choice was Captain John C. Frémont, the so-called Pathfinder of the West—a dashing but erratic explorer-soldier-surveyor who was supposed to find the path to the White House. The black-bearded and flashy young adventurer was virtually without political experience, but like Buchanan he was not tarred with the Kansas brush. The Republican platform came out vigorously against the extension of slavery into the territories, while the Democrats declared no less emphatically for popular sovereignty.

An ugly dose of antiforeignism was injected into the campaign, even though slavery extension loomed largest. The recent horde of immigrants from Ireland and Germany had alarmed "nativists," as many old-stock Protestants were called. They organized the American party, known also as the Know-Nothing party because

of its secretiveness, and in 1856 nominated the lackluster ex-President Fillmore. Antiforeign and anti-Catholic, these superpatriots adopted the slogan "Americans Must Rule America." Remnants of the dying Whig party likewise endorsed Fillmore, and they and the Know-Nothings threatened to cut into Republican strength.

Republicans fell in behind Frémont with the zeal of crusaders. Shouting "We Follow the Pathfinder" and "We Are Buck Hunting," they organized glee clubs which sang (to the tune of the "Marseillaise"):

> Arise, arise ye brave!
> And let our war-cry be,
> Free speech, free press, free soil, free men,
> Fré-mont and victory!

Frémont, the Explorer, in Heroic Pose *It was said with exaggeration that from the ashes of his campfires have sprung cities. Actually he was a pathmarker as much as a pathfinder; a great deal of the land he explored had already been traversed by fur-seeking "mountain men." (Library of Congress.)*

"And free love," sneered the Buchanan supporters ("Buchaneers").

Mudslinging bespattered both candidates. "Old Fogy" Buchanan was assailed because he was a bachelor: the fiancée of his youth had died after a lovers' quarrel. Frémont was reviled because of his illegitimate birth, for his young mother had left her elderly husband, a Virginia planter, to run away with a French adventurer. In due season she gave birth to John in Savannah, Georgia—further to shame the South. More harmful to Frémont was the allegation, which alienated many bigoted Know-Nothings and other "nativists," that he was a Roman Catholic.

The Electoral Fruits of 1856

A bland Buchanan, although polling less than a majority of the popular vote, won handily. His tally in the Electoral College was 174 to 114 for Frémont, with Fillmore garnering 8. The popular vote was 1,832,955 for Buchanan to 1,339,932 for Frémont, with 871,731 for Fillmore.

Why did the aroused Republicans go down to defeat? Frémont lost much ground because of grave doubts as to his honesty, capacity, and sound judgment. Perhaps more damaging were

> *Spiritual overtones developed in the Frémont campaign, especially over slavery. The* Independent, *a foremost religious journal, saw in Frémont's nomination "the good hand of God." As election day neared it declared: "Fellow-Christians! Remember it is for Christ, for the nation, and for the world that you vote at this election! Vote as you pray! Pray as you vote!"*

the violent threats of the southern "fire-eaters" that the election of a sectional "Black Republican" would be a declaration of war on them, forcing them to secede. Many northerners, anxious to save both the Union and their profitable business connections with the South, were thus intimidated into voting for Buchanan. Innate conservatism triumphed, assisted by so-called southern bullyism.

It was probably fortunate for the Union that secession and civil war did not come in 1856, following a Republican victory. Frémont, an ill-balanced and second-rate figure, was no Abraham Lincoln. And in 1856 the North was more willing to let the South depart in peace than in 1860. Dramatic events from 1856 to 1860 were to arouse hundreds of thousands of still-apathetic northerners to a fighting pitch.

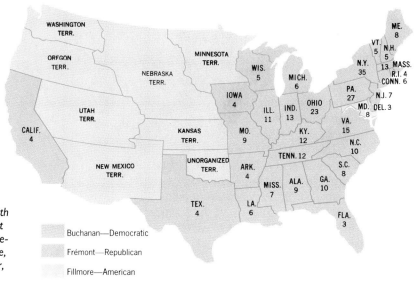

Presidential Election of 1856 *(with electoral vote by state) The fateful split of 1860 was here foreshadowed. The regional polarization in 1856, shown here, was to be even sharper four years later, as illustrated by the maps on p. 407.*

Buchanan—Democratic

Frémont—Republican

Fillmore—American

Yet the Republicans in 1856 could rightfully claim a "victorious defeat." The new party—a mere two-year-old infant—had made an astonishing showing against the well-oiled Democratic machine. Whittier exulted:

> Then sound again the bugles,
>   Call the muster-roll anew;
> If months have well-nigh won the field,
>   What may not four years do?

The election of 1856 cast a long shadow forward, and politicians, North and South, peered anxiously toward 1860.

The Dred Scott Bombshell

The Dred Scott decision, handed down by the Supreme Court on March 6, 1857, abruptly ended the two-day presidential honeymoon of the unlucky bachelor, James Buchanan. This pronouncement was one of the opening paper-gun blasts of the Civil War.

Basically, the case was simple. Dred Scott, a black slave, had lived with his master for five years in Illinois and Wisconsin Territory. Backed by interested abolitionists, he sued for freedom on the basis of his long residence on free soil.

The Supreme Court proceeded to turn a simple legal case into a complex political issue. It ruled, not surprisingly, that Dred Scott was a black slave and not a citizen, and hence could not sue in federal courts.* The tribunal could then have thrown out the case on these technical grounds alone. But a majority decided to go further, under the leadership of emaciated Chief Justice Taney from the slave state of Maryland. A sweeping judgment on the larger issue of slavery in the territories seemed desirable, particularly to forestall arguments by two free-soil members who were preparing dissenting opinions. The prosouthern majority evidently hoped in this way to lay the vexed question to rest.

Taney's thunderclap rocked the free-soilers back on their heels. A majority of the Court had decreed that because a slave was private property, he or she could be taken into *any* territory

---

*This part of the ruling, denying blacks their citizenship, seriously menaced the precarious position of the South's quarter-million free blacks.

and held there. The reasoning was that the Fifth Amendment clearly forbade Congress to deprive persons of their property without due process of law. The Court, to be consistent, went further. The Missouri Compromise, banning slavery north of 36°30', had been repealed three years earlier by the Kansas-Nebraska Act. But its spirit was still venerated in the North. Now the Court had ruled that the Compromise of 1820 had been unconstitutional all along: Congress had no power to ban slavery from the territories, regardless even of what the territorial legislatures themselves might want.

A cry of delight broke from southern throats over this unexpected victory. Champions of popular sovereignty were aghast, including Senator Douglas and a host of northern Democrats. Another lethal wedge was thus driven between the northern and southern wings of the once-united Democratic party.

Wall Street During the Panic of 1857   *The financial crisis further burdened President Buchanan, already reeling from the armed clashes in Kansas and the controversy over the Dred Scott decision. (Museum of the City of New York.)*

Taney's decision, in the case of Dred Scott, referred to the status of slaves when the Constitution was adopted: "They had for more than a century before been regarded as beings of an inferior order; and altogether unfit to associate with the white race, either in social or political relations; and so far inferior that they had no rights which the white man was bound to respect. . . . This opinion was at that time fixed and universal in the civilized portion of the white race." Taney's statement was historically sound as it related to the United States, but highly offensive to antislaveryites when applied to conditions in 1857.

Foes of slavery extension, especially the Republicans, were infuriated by the Dred Scott setback. Their chief rallying cry had been the banishing of bondage from the territories. They now insisted that the ruling of the Court was merely an opinion, not a decision, and just as binding as the views of a "southern debating society." Republican defiance of the exalted tribunal was intensified by an awareness that a majority of its members were southerners and by the conviction that it had debased itself—"sullied the ermine"—by wallowing in the gutter of politics.

Southerners in turn were inflamed by all this defiance. They began to wonder anew how much longer they could remain married to a section that refused to honor the Supreme Court, to say nothing of the constitutional compact that had established it.

The Financial Crash of 1857

Bitterness caused by the Dred Scott decision was deepened by hard times, which dampened a period of feverish prosperity. Late in 1857 a panic burst about Buchanan's harassed head. The storm was not so bad economically as the panic of 1837, but psychologically it was probably the worst of the nineteenth century.

What caused the crash? Inpouring California gold played its part by helping to inflate the currency. The demands of the Crimean War had overstimulated the growing of grain, while frenzied speculation in land and railroads had further ripped the economic fabric. When the collapse came, over five thousand businesses failed within a year. Unemployment, accompanied by hunger meetings in urban areas, was widespread. "Bread or Death" stated one desperate slogan.

The North, including the grain growers, was hardest hit. The South, enjoying favorable cotton prices abroad, rode out the storm with flying colors. Panic conditions seemed further proof that cotton *was* king and that its economic kingdom was stronger than that of the North. This fatal delusion helped drive the overconfident southerners closer to a shooting showdown.

Financial distress in the North, especially in agriculture, gave a new vigor to the demand for free farms of 160 acres from the public domain. For several decades interested groups had been urging the federal government to abandon its ancient policy of selling the land for revenue. Instead, the argument ran, acreage should be given outright to the sturdy pioneers as a reward for risking health and life to develop it.

A scheme to make outright gifts of homesteads encountered two-pronged opposition. Eastern industrialists had long been unfriendly to free land; some of them feared that their underpaid workers would be drained off to the West. The South was even more bitterly opposed, partly because gang-labor slavery could not flourish on a mere 160 acres. Free farms would merely fill up the territories more rapidly with free-soilers and further tip the political balance against the South. In 1860, after years of debate, Congress finally passed a homestead act—one that made public lands available at a nominal sum of twenty-five cents an acre. But it was stabbed to death by the veto pen of Buchanan, near whose elbow sat leading southern sympathizers.

The panic of 1857 also created a clamor for higher tariff rates. Several months before the crash, Congress, embarrassed by a large Treasury surplus, had enacted the Tariff of 1857. The new law, responding to pressures from the South, reduced duties to about 20 percent on dutiable goods—the lowest point since the War of 1812. Hardly had the revised rates been placed on the books when financial distress descended like a black pall. Northern manufacturers, many of them Republicans, noisily blamed their misfortunes on the low tariff. As the surplus melted away in the Treasury, industrialists in the North pointed to the need for higher duties. But what really concerned them was their desire for increased protection. Thus, the panic of 1857 gave the Republicans two surefire issues for the election of 1860: protection for the unprotected and farms for the farmless.

An Illinois Rail-Splitter Emerges

The Illinois senatorial election of 1858 now claimed the national spotlight. Senator Douglas's term was about to expire, and the Republicans decided to run against him a rustic Springfield lawyer, one Abraham Lincoln. The candidate—6 feet 4 inches (1.93 meters) in height and 180 pounds (81.7 kilograms) in weight—presented an awkward but arresting figure. Lincoln's legs, arms, and neck were grotesquely long; his head was crowned by coarse, black, and unruly hair; and his face was sad, sunken, and weather-beaten.

Lincoln was no silver-spoon child of destiny. Born in a Kentucky log cabin to impoverished

In 1832, when Lincoln became a candidate for the Illinois legislature, he delivered a speech at a political gathering: "I presume you all know who I am. I am humble Abraham Lincoln. I have been solicited by many friends to become a candidate for the Legislature. My [Whiggish] politics are short and sweet, like the old woman's dance. I am in favor of a national bank. I am in favor of the internal-improvement system, and a high protective tariff. These are my sentiments and political principles. If elected, I shall be thankful; if not, it will be all the same." He was elected two years later.

parents, he attended a frontier school for not more than a year; being an avid reader, he was mainly self-educated. All his life he said, "git," "thar," "heered." Though narrow-chested and somewhat stoop-shouldered, he shone in his frontier community as a wrestler and weight lifter, and spent some time, among other pioneering pursuits, as a splitter of logs for fence rails. A superb teller of earthy and amusing stories, he would oddly enough plunge into protracted periods of melancholy.

Lincoln's private and professional life was not especially noteworthy. He married "above himself" socially, into the influential Todd family of Kentucky; and the temperamental outbursts of his high-strung wife, known by her enemies as the "she wolf," helped to school him in patience and forbearance. After reading a little law, he gradually emerged as one of the dozen or so better-known trial lawyers in Illinois, although still accustomed to carrying important papers in his stovepipe hat. He was widely referred to as

Abraham Lincoln, a Most Uncommon Common Man *Early photograph (daguerreotype) by Matthew B. Brady, distinguished photographer of the era.*

"Honest Abe," partly because he would refuse cases that he could not conscientiously defend.

The rise of Lincoln as a political figure was less than rocketlike. After making his mark in the Illinois legislature as a Whig politician of the logrolling variety, he served one undistinguished term in Congress, 1847–1849. Until 1854, when he was forty-five years of age, he had done nothing to establish a claim to statesmanship. But the passage of the Kansas-Nebraska Act in that year lighted within him unexpected fires. After mounting the Republican bandwagon, he emerged as one of the foremost politicians and orators of the Northwest. At the Philadelphia convention of 1856, where John Frémont was nominated, Lincoln actually received 110 votes for the vice-presidential nomination.

The Great Debate: Lincoln versus Douglas

Lincoln, as Republican nominee for the Senate seat, boldly challenged Douglas to a series of joint debates. This was a rash act, because the stumpy senator was probably the nation's most devastating debater. Douglas promptly accepted the challenge, and seven meetings were arranged from August to October 1858.

At first glance, the two contestants seemed ill matched. The well-groomed and polished Douglas, with stocky figure and bullish voice, presented a striking contrast to the lanky Lincoln, with his baggy clothes and unshined shoes. Moreover, "Old Abe," as he was called in both affection and derision, had a piercing, high-pitched voice and was often ill at ease when he began to speak. But as he threw himself into an argument, he seemed to grow in height, while his glowing eyes lighted up a rugged face. He relied on logic rather than on table-thumping.

The most famous of the forensic clashes came at Freeport, Illinois, where Lincoln nearly impaled his opponent on the horns of a dilemma. Suppose, he queried, the people of a territory should vote slavery down? The Supreme Court in the Dred Scott decision had decreed that they could not. Who would prevail, the Court or the people?

Lincoln and Douglas Debate, 1858 *Thousands of persons attended each of the seven Lincoln-Douglas debates. Douglas is shown here sitting to Lincoln's right in the debate at Charleston, Illinois, in September. On one occasion, Lincoln quipped that Douglas's logic would prove that a horse chestnut was a chestnut horse. (Illinois State Historical Library.)*

Legend to the contrary, Douglas and some southerners had already publicly answered the Freeport question. The "Little Giant" therefore did not hesitate to meet the issue head on, honestly and consistently. He replied that no matter how the Supreme Court ruled, slavery would stay down if the people voted it down. Laws to protect slavery would have to be passed by the territorial legislatures. These would not be forthcoming in the absence of popular approval, and black bondage would soon disappear. Douglas, in truth, had American history on his side. Where public opinion does not support the federal government, as in the case of Jefferson's embargo, the law is almost impossible to enforce.

The upshot was that Douglas defeated Lincoln for the Senate seat. The "Little Giant's" loyalty to popular sovereignty, which still had a powerful appeal in Illinois, probably was decisive. Senators were then chosen by state legislatures; and in the general election that followed

Lincoln expressed his views on the relation of the black and white races in 1858, in a debate with Stephen A. Douglas: "I, as well as Judge Douglas, am in favor of the race to which I belong, having the superior position. I have never said anything to the contrary, but I hold that notwithstanding all this, there is no reason in the world why the negro is not entitled to all the natural rights enumerated in the Declaration of Independence, the right to life, liberty, and the pursuit of happiness. I hold that he is as much entitled to those rights as the white man. I agree with Judge Douglas he is not my equal in many respects—certainly not in color, perhaps not in moral or intellectual endowment. But in the right to eat the bread, without leave of anybody else, which his own hand earns, he is my equal and the equal of Judge Douglas, and the equal of every living man." (First Lincoln-Douglas Debate, Ottawa, Illinois, August 21, 1858.)

the debates, more pro-Douglas members were elected than pro-Lincoln members. Yet thanks to inequitable apportionment, the districts carried by Douglas supporters represented a smaller population than those carried by the Lincoln supporters. "Honest Abe" thus won a clear moral victory.

Lincoln possibly was playing for larger stakes than just the senatorship. Although defeated, he had shambled into the national limelight in company with the most prominent northern politicians. Newspapers in the East published detailed accounts of the debates, and Lincoln began to emerge as a potential Republican nominee for president. But Douglas, in winning Illinois, hurt his chances of winning the presidency, while further splitting his splintering party. After his opposition to the Lecompton Constitution for Kansas and his further defiance of the Supreme Court at Freeport, southern Democrats were determined to break up the party (and the Union) rather than accept him. The Lincoln-Douglas debate platform thus proved to be one of the preliminary battlefields of the Civil War.

"A Premature Movement" *John Brown hands the pike to the slave and says "Follow me!" but the startled black protests that they have not finished seeding "at our house." Brown had made the fatal error of not earlier asking the slaves in question if they were willing to rise. (Harper's Weekly, 1859.)*

John Brown: Murderer or Martyr?

The gaunt, grim figure of John Brown of Kansas fame now appeared again in a more terrible way. His crackbrained scheme was to invade the South secretly with a handful of followers, call upon the slaves to rise, furnish them with arms, and establish a kind of black free state as a sanctuary. Brown secured several thousand dollars for firearms from northern abolitionists and finally arrived in hilly western Virginia with some twenty men, including several blacks. At scenic Harpers Ferry he seized the federal arsenal in October 1859, incidentally killing seven innocent people, including a free black, and injuring ten or so more. But the slaves, largely ignorant of Brown's strike, failed to rise, and the wounded Brown and the remnants of his tiny band were quickly captured.

"Old Brown" was convicted of murder and treason, after a hasty but legal trial. His presumed insanity was supported by affidavits

from seventeen friends and relatives, who were trying to save his neck. Actually thirteen of his near relations were regarded as insane, including his mother and grandmother. Governor Wise of Virginia would have been most wise, so his critics say, if he had only clapped the culprit into a lunatic asylum.

But Brown—"God's angry man"—was given every opportunity to pose and to enjoy martyrdom. Though probably of unsound mind, he was clever enough to see that he was worth much more to the abolitionist cause dangling from a rope than in any other way. His demeanor during the trial was dignified and courageous, his last words were to become a classic, and he marched up the scaffold steps without flinching. His conduct was so exemplary, his devotion to freedom so inflexible, that he took on an exalted character, however deplorable his previous record may have been. So the hangman's trap was sprung, and Brown plunged not into oblivion but into world fame. A memorable marching song of the impending Civil War ran:

> John Brown's body lies a-mould'ring in the grave,
> His soul is marching on.

The effects of Harpers Ferry were calamitous. In the eyes of the South, already embittered, "Osawatomie Brown" was a wholesale murderer and an apostle of treason. Many southerners asked how they could possibly remain in the Union while a "murderous gang of abolitionists" were financing armed bands to "Brown" them. Moderate northerners, including Republican leaders, openly deplored this mad exploit. But the South naturally concluded that the violent abolitionist view was shared by the entire North, dominated by "Brown-loving" Republicans.

Abolitionists and other ardent free-soilers were infuriated by Brown's execution. Many of them were ignorant of his bloody past and his even more bloody purposes, and they were outraged because the Virginians had hanged so earnest a reformer who was working for so righteous a cause. On the day of his execution, free-soil centers in the North tolled bells, fired guns, half-masted flags, and held mass meetings. Some spoke of "Saint John" Brown, while the serene Ralph Waldo Emerson compared the new martyr-hero with Jesus. The gallows became a cross. E. C. Stedman wrote:

> And Old Brown,
> Osawatomie Brown,
> May trouble you more than ever,
>   when you've nailed his coffin down!

The ghost of the martyred Brown would not be laid to rest.

The Disruption of the Democrats

Beyond question the presidential election of 1860 was the most fateful in American history. On it hung the issue of peace or civil war.

Deeply divided, the Democrats met in Charleston, South Carolina, with Douglas the leading candidate of the northern wing of the party. But the southern "fire-eaters" regarded him as a traitor, as a result of his unpopular stand on the Lecompton Constitution and the Freeport Doctrine. After a bitter wrangle over the platform, the delegates from most of the cotton states walked out. When the remainder could not scrape together the necessary two-thirds vote for Douglas, the entire body dissolved in confusion. The first tragic secession was the secession of southerners from the Democratic National Convention. It became habit-forming.

The Democrats tried again in Baltimore. This time the Douglas Democrats, chiefly from the North, were firmly in the saddle. Many of the cotton-state delegates again took a walk, and the rest of the convention enthusiastically nominated their hero. The platform came out squarely for popular sovereignty and, as a sop to the South, against obstruction of the Fugitive Slave Law by the states.

Angered southern Democrats promptly organized a rival convention in Baltimore, in which many of the northern states were unrepresented. They selected as their leader the stern-jawed vice-president, John C. Breckinridge, a man of moderate views from the border state of Kentucky. The platform favored the extension of slavery into the territories and the annexation of slave-populated Cuba.

A middle-of-the-road group, fearing for the Union, hastily organized the Constitutional Union party, sneered at as the "Do Nothing" or "Old Gentleman's" party. It consisted mainly of former Whigs and Know-Nothings, a veritable "gathering of graybeards." Desperately anxious to elect a compromise candidate, they met in Baltimore and nominated for the presidency John Bell of Tennessee. They went into battle ringing hand bells for Bell and voicing the slogan "The Union, the Constitution, and the Enforcement of the Laws."

A Rail-Splitter Splits the Union

Elated Republicans were presented with a heaven-sent opportunity. Scenting victory in the breeze as their opponents split hopelessly, they gathered in Chicago in a huge, boxlike wooden structure called the Wigwam. William H. Seward was by far the best known of the contenders. But his radical utterances, including his "irrepressible conflict" speech at Rochester in 1858, had fatally injured his prospects.* His numerous enemies coined the slogan "Success Rather than Seward." Lincoln, the favorite son of Illinois, was definitely a "Mr. Second Best," but he was a stronger candidate because he had made fewer enemies. Overtaking Seward on the third ballot, he was nominated amid scenes of the wildest excitement.

The Republican platform had a seductive appeal for just about every important nonsouthern group. For the free-soilers, nonextension of slavery; for the northern manufacturers, a protective tariff; for the immigrants, no abridgment of rights; for the Northwest, a Pacific railroad; for the West, internal improvements at federal expense; and for the farmers, free homesteads from the public domain. Seductive slogans were

"Vote Yourselves a Farm" and "Land for the Landless."

Southern secessionists promptly served notice that the election of the "baboon" Lincoln—the "abolitionist" rail-splitter—would split the Union. "Honest Abe," though hating slavery, was no abolitionist. But he saw fit, perhaps mistakenly, to issue no statements to quiet southern fears. He had already put himself on record; and fresh statements might stir up fresh antagonisms.

As the election campaign ground noisily forward, Lincoln enthusiasts staged roaring rallies and parades, complete with pitch-dripping torches and oilskin capes. They extolled "High Old Abe," the "Woodchopper of the West," and the "Little Giant Killer," while groaning dismally for "Poor Little Doug." Enthusiastic "Little Giants" and "Little Dougs" retorted with "We want a statesman, not a rail-splitter, as President." Douglas himself waged a vigorous speaking campaign, even in the South, and threatened to put the hemp with his own hands around the neck of the first secessionist.

The returns, breathlessly awaited, proclaimed a sweeping victory for Lincoln (see the table on page 408).

The Electoral Upheaval of 1860

Awkward "Abe" Lincoln had run a curious race. To a greater degree than any other holder of the nation's highest office (except J. Q. Adams), he was a minority president. Sixty percent of the voters preferred some other candidate. He was also a sectional president, for in ten southern states, where he was not allowed on the ballot, he polled no popular votes. The election of 1860 was virtually two elections: one in the North, the other in the South. South Carolinians rejoiced over Lincoln's victory; they now had their excuse to secede. In winning the North the "rail-splitter" had split off the South.

Douglas, though scraping together only twelve electoral votes, made an impressive showing. He drew important strength from all sections and ranked a fairly close second in the popular-vote column. In fact, the Douglas

---

*Seward had referred to an "irrepressible conflict" between slavery and freedom, though not necessarily a bloody one.

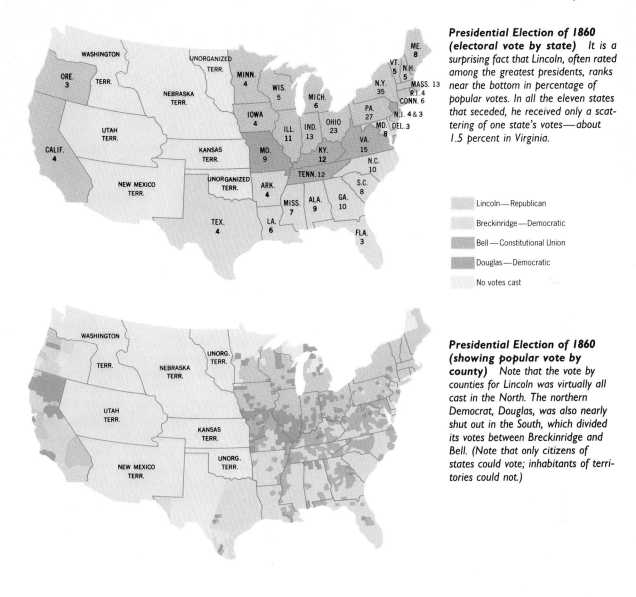

Presidential Election of 1860 (electoral vote by state) *It is a surprising fact that Lincoln, often rated among the greatest presidents, ranks near the bottom in percentage of popular votes. In all the eleven states that seceded, he received only a scattering of one state's votes—about 1.5 percent in Virginia.*

Lincoln—Republican

Breckinridge—Democratic

Bell—Constitutional Union

Douglas—Democratic

No votes cast

Presidential Election of 1860 (showing popular vote by county) *Note that the vote by counties for Lincoln was virtually all cast in the North. The northern Democrat, Douglas, was also nearly shut out in the South, which divided its votes between Breckinridge and Bell. (Note that only citizens of states could vote; inhabitants of territories could not.)*

Democrats and the Breckinridge Democrats together amassed 366,484 more votes than did Lincoln.

A myth persists that if the Democrats had only united behind Douglas, they would have triumphed. Yet the cold figures tell a different story. Even if the "Little Giant" had received all the electoral votes cast for all three of Lincoln's opponents, the "rail-splitter" would have won, 169 to 134, instead of 180 to 123. Lincoln still would have carried the populous states of the North and the Northwest. On the other hand, if the Democrats had not broken up, they could have entered the campaign with higher enthusiasm and better organization and might have won.

Significantly, the verdict of the ballot box did not indicate a strong sentiment for secession. Breckinridge, while favoring the extension of slavery, was no disunionist. Although the candidate of the "fire-eaters," in the slave states he polled fewer votes than the combined strength of his opponents, Douglas and Bell. He even failed to carry his own Kentucky.

Election of 1860

CANDIDATE	POPULAR VOTE	PERCENTAGE OF POPULAR VOTE	ELECTORAL VOTE
Lincoln	1,865,593	39.79%	180 (every vote of the free states except for 3 of New Jersey's 7 votes)
Douglas	1,382,713	29.40	12 (only Missouri and 3 of New Jersey's 7 votes)
Breckinridge	848,356	18.20	72 (all the cotton states)
Bell	592,906	12.61	39 (Virginia, Kentucky, Tennessee)

President Jefferson Davis (1808–1889) *Faced with grave difficulties, he was probably as able a man for the position as the Confederacy could have chosen. The Davis family had moved south from Kentucky; the Lincoln family, north. If the migrations had been reversed, the presidential roles might have been reversed, as some have speculated. (Library of Congress.)*

Yet the South, despite its electoral defeat, was not badly off. It still had a five-to-four majority on the supreme bench. Although the Republicans had elected Lincoln, they controlled neither the Senate nor the House of Representatives. The federal government could not touch slavery in those states where it existed except by a constitutional amendment, and such an amendment could be defeated by one-fourth of the states. The fifteen slave states numbered nearly one-half of the total—a fact not fully appreciated by southern hotheads.

The Secessionist Exodus

A tragic chain reaction of secession now began to explode. South Carolina, which had threatened to go out if the "sectional" Lincoln came in, was as good as its word. Four days after the election of the "Illinois baboon" by "insulting" majorities, its legislature voted unanimously to call a special convention. Meeting at Charleston in December 1860, it unanimously voted to secede. During the next six weeks, six other states of the lower South, though somewhat less united, followed South Carolina over the precipice. Four more were to join them later, bringing the total to eleven.

With the eyes of destiny upon them, the seven seceders, formally meeting at Montgomery, Alabama, created a government known as the Confederate States of America. As their

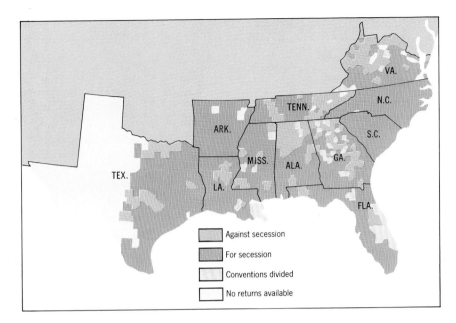

Southern Opposition to Secession, 1860–1861 (showing vote by county) *This county vote shows the opposition of the antiplanter, antislavery mountain whites in the Appalachian region. There was also considerable resistance to secession in Texas, where Governor Sam Houston, who led the Unionists, was deposed by secessionist hotheads.*

Map legend:
- Against secession
- For secession
- Conventions divided
- No returns available

president they chose Jefferson Davis, a dignified and austere recent member of the United States Senate from Mississippi. He was a West Pointer and a former cabinet member with wide military and administrative experience; but he suffered from chronic ill-health, as well as from a frustrated ambition to be a Napoleonic strategist.

The crisis, already critical enough, was deepened by the "lame duck"* interlude. Lincoln, although elected president in November 1860, could not take office until four months later, March 4, 1861. During this period of protracted uncertainty, when he was still a private citizen in Illinois, seven of the eleven deserting states pulled out of the Union.

President Buchanan, the aging incumbent, has been blamed for not holding the seceders in the Union by sheer force—for wringing his hands instead of secessionist necks. Never a vigorous man and habitually conservative, he was now nearly seventy, and although devoted to the Union, he was surrounded by prosouthern advisers. As an able bachelor-lawyer wedded to the Constitution, he did not believe that the southern states could legally secede. Yet he could find no authority in the Constitution for stopping them with guns.

"Oh for one hour of Jackson!" cried the advocates of strong-arm tactics. But "Old Buck" Buchanan was not "Old Hickory," and he was faced with a far more complex and serious problem. One important reason why he did not resort to force was that the tiny standing army of

Three days after Lincoln's election, Horace Greeley's influential New York *Tribune* (November 9, 1860) had declared: "If the cotton States shall decide that they can do better out of the Union than in it, we insist on letting them go in peace. The right to secede may be a revolutionary one, but it exists nevertheless. . . . Whenever a considerable section of our Union shall deliberately resolve to go out, we shall resist all coercive measures designed to keep it in. We hope never to live in a republic, whereof one section is pinned to the residue by bayonets." After the secession movement got well under way, Greeley's *Tribune* changed its tune.

---

*The "lame duck" period was shortened to ten weeks in 1933 by the Twentieth Amendment (see the Appendix).

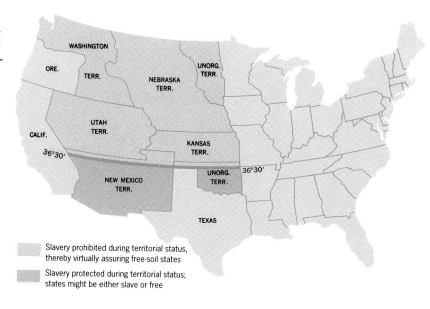

Proposed Crittenden Compromise, 1860 *Stephen A. Douglas claimed that "if the Crittenden proposition could have been passed early in the session [of Congress], it would have saved all the States, except South Carolina." But Crittenden's proposal was doomed—Lincoln opposed it, and Republicans cast not a single vote in its favor.*

Slavery prohibited during territorial status, thereby virtually assuring free-soil states

Slavery protected during territorial status; states might be either slave or free

some fifteen thousand men, then widely scattered, was urgently needed to control the Indians in the West. Public opinion in the North, at that time, was far from willing to unsheathe the sword. Fighting would merely shatter all prospects of adjustment, and until the guns began to boom, there was still a flickering hope of reconciliation rather than a contested divorce. The weakness lay not so much in Buchanan as in the Constitution and in the Union itself. Ironically, when Lincoln became president, he continued essentially Buchanan's wait-and-see policy.

The Collapse of Compromise

Impending bloodshed spurred final and frantic attempts at compromise—in the American tradition. The most promising of these efforts was sponsored by Senator Crittenden of Kentucky, on whose shoulders had fallen the mantle of a fellow Kentuckian, Henry Clay.

The proposed Crittenden amendments to the Constitution were designed to appease the South. Slavery in the territories was to be prohibited north of 36°30′, but south of that line it was to be given federal protection in all territories existing or "hereafter to be acquired" (such

as Cuba). Future states, north or south of 36°30′, could come into the Union with or without slavery, as they should choose. In short, the slavery supporters were to be guaranteed full rights in the southern territories, as long as they were territories, regardless of the wishes of the majority under popular sovereignty. Federal protection in a territory south of 36°30′ might conceivably, though improbably, turn the entire area permanently to slavery.

Lincoln flatly rejected the Crittenden scheme, which offered some slight prospect of success, and all hope of compromise fled. For

One reason why the Crittenden Compromise failed in December 1860 was the prevalence of an attitude reflected in a private letter of Senator Hammond of South Carolina on April 19: "I firmly believe that the slave-holding South is now the controlling power of the world—that no other power would face us in hostility. Cotton, rice, tobacco, and naval stores command the world; and we have sense to know it, and are sufficiently Teutonic to carry it out successfully. The North without us would be a motherless calf, bleating about, and die of mange and starvation."

this refusal he must bear a heavy responsibility. Yet he had been elected on a platform that opposed the extension of slavery, and he felt that as a matter of principle he could not afford to yield, even though gains for slavery in the territories might be only temporary. Larger gains might come later in Cuba and Mexico.

As for the supposedly spineless "Old Fogy" Buchanan, how could he have prevented the Civil War by starting a civil war? No one has yet come up with a satisfactory answer. If he had used force on South Carolina in December 1860, the fighting almost certainly would have erupted three months sooner than it did, and under less favorable circumstances for the Union. The North would have appeared as the heavy-handed aggressor. And the crucial Border States, so vital to the Union, probably would have been driven into the arms of their "wayward sisters."

Farewell to Union

Secessionists who parted company with their sister states left for a number of avowed reasons, mostly relating in some way to slavery. They were alarmed by the inexorable tipping of the political balance against them—"the despotic majority of numbers." The "crime" of the North, observed James Russell Lowell, was the census returns. Southerners were also dismayed by the triumph of the new sectional Republican party, which seemed to threaten their rights as a slaveholding minority. They were weary of free-soil criticism, abolitionist nagging, and northern interference, ranging from the Underground Railroad to John Brown's raid. "All we ask is to be let alone," declared president Jefferson Davis in an early message to his congress.

Many southerners supported secession because they felt sure that their departure would be unopposed, despite "Yankee yawp" to the contrary. They were confident that the clodhopping and codfishing Yankee would not or could not fight. They believed that northern manufacturers and bankers, so heavily dependent on southern cotton and markets, would not dare to cut their own economic throats with their own swords. But should war come, the immense debt owed to northern creditors by the South—happy thought—could be promptly repudiated, as it later was.

Southern leaders regarded secession as a golden opportunity to cast aside their generations of "vassalage" to the North. An independent Dixieland could develop its own banking

"Wretched Condition of the Old Party at the White House"
Buchanan is hard-pressed between southern threats of violence and northern reminders of his obligation to uphold the Constitution. (Harper's Weekly, 1861.)

> *James Russell Lowell, the northern poet and essayist, wrote in the* Atlantic Monthly *shortly after the secessionist movement began:* "The fault of the free States in the eyes of the South is not one that can be atoned for by any yielding of special points here and there. Their offence is that they are free, and that their habits and prepossessions are those of freedom. Their crime is the census of 1860. Their increase in numbers, wealth, and power is a standing aggression. It would not be enough to please the Southern States that we should stop asking them to abolish slavery: what they demand of us is nothing less than that we should abolish the spirit of the age. Our very thoughts are a menace."

and shipping, and trade directly with Europe. The low Tariff of 1857, passed largely by southern votes, was not in itself menacing. But who could tell when the "greedy" Republicans would win control of Congress and drive through their own oppressive protective tariff? For decades there had been this fundamental friction between the North, with its manufacturing plants, and the South, with its agrarian economy.

Worldwide impulses of nationalism—then stirring in Italy, Germany, Poland, and elsewhere—were fermenting in the South. This huge area, with its distinctive culture, was not so much a section as a subnation. It could not view with complacency the possibility of being lorded over, then or later, by what it regarded as a hostile nation of northerners.

The principles of self-determination—of the Declaration of Independence—seemed to many southerners to apply perfectly to them. Few, if any, of the seceders felt that they were doing anything wrong or immoral. The thirteen original states had voluntarily entered the Union, and now seven—ultimately eleven—southern states were voluntarily withdrawing from it.

Historical parallels ran even deeper. In 1776, thirteen American colonies, led by the rebel George Washington, had seceded from the British Empire by throwing off the yoke of King George. In 1860–1861, eleven American states, led by the rebel Jefferson Davis, were seceding from the Union by throwing off the yoke of "King" Abraham Lincoln. With that burden gone, the South was confident that it could work out its own peculiar destiny more quietly, happily, and prosperously.

Varying Viewpoints

Few issues have generated as much heat among American historians as the causes of the War for Southern Independence. The very names chosen to describe the conflict—notably *Civil War* or *War Between the States*—reveal much about various authors' points of view. Opinions have naturally differed according to section, but in general the appraisals of the war have gone through four phases.

The so-called nationalist school in the late nineteenth century found slavery and Union to be the fundamental causes of the bloodletting and approved the war because it ended slavery and preserved the Union. In the early twentieth century, some writers, notably Charles Beard, argued that the war was not about slavery per se, but about the basic economic conflict between an industrial North and an agricultural South.

After the disappointing results of World War I, some historians argued that the Civil War itself had been a great mistake, traceable not to any fundamentally "irreconcilable conflict," whether racial or economic, but to the breakdown of political institutions and the ineptitude of a blundering generation of leaders. But since World War II, a "neo-nationalist" view has generally prevailed. It pictures the Civil War as an all-but-inevitable clash between two cultures and two sets of social values, ending in victory for the forces of virtue and progress.

Select Readings

Primary Source Documents

Harriet Beecher Stowe's *Uncle Tom's Cabin* (1852) and Hinton R. Helper's *Impending Crisis of the South** (1857) are vivid and important. The Lincoln-Douglas debates* (1858) frame the issues of the 1850s and remain classics of American oratory.

Secondary Sources

Refer to the previous chapter for the titles by Roy F. Nichols, James G. Randall and David Donald, and A. O. Craven. Richly detailed is Allan Nevins, *The Emergence of Lincoln* (2 vols., 1950). David Donald, *Charles Sumner and the Coming of the Civil War* (1960), is an outstanding biography. See also his able *Charles Sumner and the Rights of Man* (1970). Lincoln's rise is developed in Don E. Fehrenbacher's *Prelude to Greatness* (1962) and in Carl Sandburg's *Abraham Lincoln: The Prairie Years* (2 vols., 1926). The explosive Kansas issue is dealt with in James A. Rawley, *Race and Politics: "Bleeding Kansas" and the Coming of the Civil War* (1969). On the Lincoln-Douglas debates see Harry V. Jaffa, *Crisis of the House Divided* (1959). Don E. Fehrenbacher bril-

liantly and thoroughly dissects *The Dred Scott Case* (1978). The final moments before fighting began are scrutinized in David M. Potter, *Lincoln and His Party in the Secession Crisis* (1942), and in Kenneth M. Stampp, *And the War Came* (1950). The southern side of the question appears in Steven A. Channing, *Crisis of Fear: Secession of South Carolina* (1970); William L. Barney, *The Secessionist Impulse: Alabama and Mississippi* (1974); William J. Evitts, *A Matter of Allegiances: Maryland from 1850 to 1861* (1974); and Ralph A. Wooster, *The Secessionist Convention of the South* (1962). See also Michael P. Johnson, *Toward a Patriarchal Republic: The Secession of Georgia* (1977); J. Mills Thornton III, *Power and Politics in a Slave Society: Alabama 1820–1860* (1978); and Marc W. Kruman, *Parties and Politics in North Carolina, 1836–1865* (1983). Stephen B. Oates paints a vivid portrait of John Brown in *To Purge This Land with Blood* (1970). Thomas J. Pressley reviews the copious literature about the war in *Americans Interpret Their Civil War* (1954). George Forgie offers a psychoanalytic explanation of the coming of the war in *Partricide in the House Divided: A Psychological Interpretation of Lincoln and His Age* (1979).

23

The War for Southern Independence

My paramount object in this struggle is to save the Union, and is not either to save or to destroy slavery.

Abraham Lincoln, 1862

President of the Disunited States of America

Abraham Lincoln solemnly took the oath of office on March 4, 1861, after having slipped into Washington at night, partially disguised to thwart assassins. He thus became president, not of the *United* States of America, but of the disunited states of America. Seven had departed; eight more were teetering on the edge. The girders of the unfinished Capitol dome loomed nakedly in the background, as if to symbolize the imperfect state of the Union.

Lincoln's inaugural address was firm yet conciliatory: there would be no conflict unless the South provoked it. Secession, the president declared, was wholly impracticable, because "Physically speaking, we cannot separate."

Here Lincoln put his finger on a profound geographical truth. The North and South were Siamese twins, bound inseparably together. If they had been divided by the Pyrenees Mountains or the Danube River, a sectional divorce would have been more feasible. But the Appalachian Mountains and the mighty Mississippi River both ran the wrong way.

Uncontested secession would create new controversies. What share of the national debt should the South be forced to take with it? What portion of the jointly held federal territories, if any, should the Confederate states be allotted—areas so largely purchased with Southern blood? How would the fugitive-slave issue be dealt with? The Underground Railroad would certainly redouble its activity, and it would have to transport its passengers only across the Ohio River, not all the way to Canada. Was it conceivable that all such problems could have been solved without ugly armed clashes?

A united United States had hitherto been the top-dog republic in the Western Hemisphere. If this powerful democracy should break into two hostile parts, the European nations would be delighted. They could gleefully transplant to America their hoary concept of the balance of power. Playing the no less hoary game of divide and conquer, they could incite one snarling fragment of the dis-United States against the other. The colonies of the European powers in the New World, notably those of Britain, would thus be made safer against the rapacious Yankees. And European imperialists, with no unified republic to stand across their path, could the more easily defy the Monroe Doctrine and seize territory in the Americas.

Lincoln's Contentious Cabinet

A greedy horde of hungry office seekers, elbowing for the patronage gravy trough, overwhelmed Lincoln at the very outset. At a time when he needed a clear mind for pressing affairs of state, he was forced to worry about the "postmastership at Podunk." There were, in his earthy phrase, "too many hogs for the tits."

The cabinet was dominated by Lincoln's former rivals for the presidential nomination. Headstrong and egotistical William H. Seward,

Secretary William H. Seward (1801–1872) *Seward was a senator, a secretary of state, and the purchaser of Alaska ("Seward's Folly"), where both a peninsula and a city were named after him. (National Archives.)*

Secretary of State Seward entertained the dangerous idea that if the North picked a fight with one or more European nations, the South would once more rally around the flag. On April Fool's Day, 1861, he submitted to Lincoln a memorandum recommending "I would demand explanations from Spain and France, categorically, at once. I would seek explanations from Great Britain and Russia. . . .And, if satisfactory explanations are not received from Spain and France . . . would convene Congress and declare war against them." Lincoln quietly but firmly quashed Seward's scheme.

the front-running contender at Chicago in 1860, was of necessity made secretary of state. He regarded himself as a kind of prime minister, but after some difficulty Lincoln tactfully put him in his place. Happily, Seward turned out to be one of the abler secretaries of state.

Other cabinet members were likewise problem children. The secretary of the treasury was a leading abolitionist, Salmon P. Chase of Ohio. A massive, handsome man, he was self-righteous, opinionated, and constantly stung by the presidential bee buzzing in his bonnet. The original secretary of war, Simon Cameron, became involved in graft and was succeeded by bulldoglike Edwin M. Stanton, stocky, black-haired, and asthmatic. Though tireless and decisive, he was arrogant, irascible, vindictive, and double-dealing. A Democrat and a more distinguished lawyer than Lincoln, Stanton had savagely criticized the "imbecility" of his future chief, whom he dubbed the "original gorilla."

Unhappily the cabinet was never completely harmonious or loyal to the president. A minor civil war within his official family was but one of the many crosses that Lincoln had to bear while prosecuting the larger Civil War.

South Carolina Assails Fort Sumter

The plight of the federal forts had meanwhile partially overshadowed political squabbles. As the seceding states left, they had seized the United States arsenals, mints, and other public property within their borders. When Lincoln took office, only two significant forts in the South still flew the Stars and Stripes. The more important of the pair was square-walled Fort

"A House Divided against Itself Cannot Stand"
Contemporary cartoon of Lincoln.

Sumter, in Charleston Harbor, with fewer than 100 men.

Ominously, the choices presented to Lincoln by Fort Sumter were all bad. This stronghold had provisions that would last only a few weeks—until the middle of April 1861. If no supplies were forthcoming, its commander would have to surrender without firing a shot. Lincoln, quite understandably, did not feel that such a weak-kneed course squared with his obligation to protect federal property. But if he sent reinforcements, the South Carolinians would undoubtedly fight back; they could not tolerate a federal fort blocking the mouth of their most important Atlantic seaport.

After agonizing indecision, Lincoln adopted a middle-of-the-road solution. He notified the South Carolinians that an expedition would be sent to *provision* the garrison, though not to *reinforce* it. But in Southern eyes "provision" spelled "reinforcement."

A Union naval force was next started on its way to Fort Sumter—a move that the South regarded as an act of aggression. On April 12, 1861, the cannons of the Carolinians opened fire on the fort, while crowds in Charleston applauded and waved handkerchiefs. After a thirty-four-hour bombardment, which took no life, the dazed garrison surrendered.

The firing on the fort electrified the North, which at once responded with cries of "Remember Fort Sumter" and "Save the Union." Hitherto countless Northerners had been saying that if the Southern states wanted to go, they should not be pinned to the rest of the nation with bayonets. "Wayward sisters, depart in peace" was a common sentiment, expressed even by the commander of the army, war hero General Winfield Scott, now so old at seventy-five that he had to be boosted onto his horse.

But the assault on Fort Sumter provoked the North to a fighting pitch: the fort was lost, but the Union was saved. Lincoln had contrived to win a great strategic victory. Southerners had wantonly fired upon the glorious Stars and Stripes, and honor demanded an armed response. Lincoln promptly (April 15) issued a call to the states for seventy-five thousand mili-

> James L. Petigru, a South Carolinian, was one of the few prominent citizens of the state to oppose secession. When asked by a stranger in December 1860 where the insane asylum could be found, he pointed out the Baptist church, in which the secession convention had gathered. "It looks like a church," he said, "but it is now a lunatic asylum; go right there and you will find one hundred and sixty-four maniacs within." They voted unanimously for secession.

tiamen; and volunteers sprang to the colors in such enthusiastic numbers that many were turned away—a mistake not often repeated. On April 19 and 27 the president proclaimed a leaky blockade of Southern seaports.

The call for troops, in turn, aroused the South much as the attack on Fort Sumter had aroused the North. Lincoln was now waging war—from the Southern view an aggressive war—on the Confederacy. Virginia, Arkansas, and Tennessee, all of which had earlier voted down secession, reluctantly joined their embattled sister states, as did North Carolina. Thus the seven states became eleven as the "submissionists" and "Union shriekers" were overcome. Richmond, Virginia, replaced Mont-

gomery, Alabama, as the Confederate capital— too near Washington for strategic comfort on either side.

Brothers' Blood and Border Blood

The only slave states left were the crucial Border States. This group consisted of Missouri, Kentucky, Maryland, Delaware, and later West Virginia—the "mountain white" area that somewhat illegally tore itself from the side of Virginia in mid-1861. If the North had fired the first shot, some or all of these doubtful states probably would have seceded, and the South might well have succeeded. The border group actually boasted a white population more than half that of the entire Confederacy. Lincoln reportedly said that he hoped to have God on his side, but he had to have Kentucky.

In dealing with the Border States, the president did not rely solely on moral suasion but successfully used methods of dubious legality. In Maryland he declared martial law where needed and sent in troops, because this state threatened to cut off Washington from the North. He also deployed Union soldiers in western Virginia and notably in Missouri, where they fought beside Unionists in a local civil war within the larger Civil War.

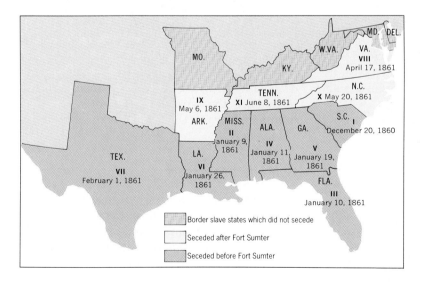

Seceding States (with dates and order of secession) Note the long period of time between the secession of South Carolina, the first state to go, and that of Tennessee, the last state to leave the Union. These six months were a time of terrible trial for moderate Southerners. When a Georgia statesman pleaded for restraint and negotiations with Washington, he was rebuffed with the cry: "Throw the bloody spear into this den of incendiaries!"

Any official statement of the North's war aims was profoundly influenced by the teetering Border States. At the very outset, Lincoln was obliged to declare publicly that he was not fighting to free the blacks. An antislavery declaration would no doubt have driven the Border States into the welcoming arms of the South. Lincoln had to insist repeatedly—even though weakening his moral cause—that his primary purpose was to preserve the Union at all costs. Thus, the war began not as one between slave soil and free soil, but one for the Union with slaveholders on both sides.

Unhappily, the conflict between "Billy Yank" and "Johnny Reb" was a brothers' war. There were many Northern volunteers from the Southern states and many Southern volunteers from the Northern states. The "mountain whites" of the South sent north some 50,000 men, and the loyal slave states contributed some 300,000 soldiers to the Union. In many a family of the Border States, one brother rode north to fight with the Blue, another south to fight with the Gray. Senator Crittenden of Kentucky, who fathered the abortive Crittenden Compromise, fathered two sons: one became a general in the Union army, the other a general in the Confederate army.

Europe's Aristocracy Sticks Together

Confederates were inspirited by the open sympathy of Europe's ruling classes, with the conspicuous exception of Russia. The South could reasonably hope for mediation or armed intervention, which almost came. At the very least, it could expect the sale of weapons, warships, and supplies, all of which did come.

Why were the upper classes of Western Europe so favorably disposed to the Confederacy? They had from the beginning abhorred the incendiary example of the American democratic experiment and were overjoyed to see the long-smoking chimney at last "take fire." Moreover, the semifeudal, aristocratic elements, especially in England, had long cherished something of a fellow feeeling for the semifeudal, aristocratic society of the South. The Foreign Offices of

Regarding the Civil War, the London Times *(November 7, 1861) editorialized: "The contest is really for empire on the side of the North, and for independence on that of the South, and in this respect we recognize an exact analogy between the North and the Government of George III, and the South and the Thirteen Revolted Provinces."*

both Britain and France, reflecting these pro-Southern sentiments, naturally welcomed the breakup of the fast-growing and ever-threatening United States.

Leaders of British industrial and commercial life likewise hailed the newly born Confederacy. For one thing, it would provide the long-coveted independent cotton supply. For another, it would increase the opportunities of British shippers and manufacturers to make profits from the South, without the hurdle of a Yankee protective tariff.

On the other hand, countless workingpeople in England, and to some extent in France, were pulling or praying for the North. Many of them had read *Uncle Tom's Cabin,* and they sensed that a victory for the Union would result in freeing the slaves. The ending of human bondage anywhere would further dignify free labor everywhere.

The common folk in Britain could not yet cast the ballot, but they could cast the brick. Their certain hostility to any official intervention on behalf of the South evidently had a sobering effect on the British cabinet. Thus, the dead hands of Uncle Tom helped Uncle Sam by restraining the British and French ironclads from breaking the Union blockade.

Confederate Assets

Both North and South were unready for war, as Americans are inclined to be. Each gained valuable experience from the other, and this fact partly explains why they battled so long on relatively even terms.

The South had only to fight defensively, behind interior lines, and hence needed fewer troops. The North had to invade the Confederacy, conquer it, and drag it back bodily into the Union—a prodigious task involving an area about as large as all Western Europe south of Scandinavia. Indeed, the South did not have to win the war to win its independence; it had merely to repulse or discourage the invader. A draw would be a victory. The Confederate states would then be left independent—and this was all they really wanted.

Until the emancipation proclamations of 1862–1863, many observers conceded to the South the superior moral cause, despite the dark stain of slavery. It was fighting for self-determination, for self-government, for its peculiar social structure, for hearth and home, for fundamental freedoms (for whites, not slaves). Favorite slogans were "Death before Dishonor" and "For Our Altars and Our Firesides."

The South not only had talented officers but had them from the beginning. Conspicuous among the dozen or so first-rate leaders was General Robert E. Lee, with his florid face, graying hair, and knightly bearing. In poise, magnanimity, and sense of honor he embodied the Southern ideal. President Lincoln had unofficially offered him the command of the armies of the North, but when Virginia seceded, Lee felt honor-bound to go along with his native state. Lee's chief lieutenant was the black-bearded and unpretentious young Thomas J. ("Stonewall") Jackson, a somewhat eccentric teacher of tactics and philosophy at the Virginia Military Institute. With his "foot cavalry," "Stonewall" Jackson was a master of speed and deception.

The North was much less fortunate. It was forced to use costly trial-and-error methods until it uncovered a general, in the person of Ulysses Simpson Grant, who would crunch his way to victory. The Union was further handicapped by numerous political officers, including the pompously incompetent General Benjamin F. ("Beast Ben") Butler, who aroused a storm by threatening harsh measures against the defiant women of New Orleans. His famous "woman order" decreed that females insulting his soldiers were to be jailed as common prostitutes. Their misbehavior stopped quickly.

Southern men were of a fighting breed. Accustomed to managing horses and bearing arms from boyhood, they made excellent cavalrymen and foot soldiers. They were supremely self-confident, and their high-pitched "rebel yell" ("Yeeeahhhh") was designed to strike terror into the hearts of fuzz-chinned Yankee recruits, known as "fresh fish." Yet the Northern "shopkeepers" and "clodhoppers" adjusted themselves surprisingly well to the rugged demands of military life. They may have been short on dash, but they were long on discipline and determination.

Confederate Chances

The South, as primarily an immense farm, was severely hampered by the scarcity of its factories. Yet it seized the weapons stored in federal arsenals when it seceded and managed to sneak through the Union blockade an impressive mass of munitions. Displaying remarkable resourcefulness, the Southerners developed ironworks which, though limited, turned out much artillery. "Yankee ingenuity" was not confined to Yankees.

As the war dragged on, grave shortages developed among the Southerners in such necessities as shoes, uniforms, and blankets. There were immense stores of food in the South but the civilians and soldiers often went hungry. "Forward, men! They have cheese in their haversacks," was the reported cry of one Southern officer as he attacked the Yankees. Much of the hunger was caused by a breakdown of transportation, especially where the railroads were cut or destroyed by the Northern invader.

Formidable though all these handicaps were, the chances for Southern independence were unusually favorable. This was true even though the Confederates had to start from scratch in building a government, an army, and a navy. As one Southern general remarked, never was a major revolution undertaken with better prospects of success. Certainly the thirteen colonies in 1776 had faced more hazardous odds.

Tredegar Iron Works, Richmond, Virginia *This was by far the most important of the Confederate iron works. Using skilled slave labor, this plant equipped the army with nearly twelve hundred scarce cannons. Without these works, the Confederacy probably would have collapsed. Their presence in Richmond helps to explain why the South fought so hard to keep the city. (The Granger Collection.)*

The might-have-beens are fascinating. *If* the Border States had seceded, *if* the uncertain states of the upper Mississippi Valley had turned against the Union, *if* a wave of Northern defeatism had demanded an armistice, and *if* England and/or France had broken the blockade, the South probably would have won. All of these possibilities came close to realities, but none of them happened. Successful revolutions, including the American Revolution of 1776, have generally succeeded because of foreign intervention. The South counted on it, did not get it, and lost.

Yankee Advantages

The North was not only a huge farm but a sprawling factory as well—and wars were already being fought with both smokestacks and guns. Yankees boasted about three-fourths of

Manufacturing by Sections, 1860

SECTION	NUMBER OF ESTABLISHMENTS	CAPITAL INVESTED	AVERAGE NUMBER OF LABORERS	ANNUAL VALUE OF PRODUCTS	PERCENTAGE OF TOTAL VALUE
New England	20,671	$ 257,477,783	391,836	$ 468,599,287	24%
Middle states	53,387	435,061,964	546,243	802,338,392	42
Western states	36,785	194,212,543	209,909	384,606,530	20
Southern states	20,631	95,975,185	110,721	155,531,281	8
Pacific states	8,777	23,380,334	50,204	71,229,989	3
Territories	282	3,747,906	2,333	3,556,197	1
	140,533	$1,009,855,715	1,311,246	$1,885,861,676	

the nation's wealth, including overwhelming superiority in manufacturing, shipping, and banking. The Union also possessed nearly three-fourths of the thirty thousand miles (forty-eight thousand kilometers) of railroads. Not only did it have longer and better trackage, but it had abundant facilities for repair and replacement, all of which the South sorely lacked.

Additionally the North controlled the sea. With its vastly superior navy, it established a blockade that choked off the bulk of Southern exports and imports. This stoppage not only hampered the South economically and militarily but finally shattered its morale. While strangling the Confederacy with one hand, the North could simultaneously keep open the sea-lanes to Europe. It was thus able to exchange huge quantities of grain for munitions, and in this way it used European factories to supplement its own. During the early months of the war, the North imported many more firearms from abroad than it was able to manufacture at home.

Union forces likewise enjoyed a much larger reservoir of manpower. The loyal states had a population of some 22 million; the seceding states, 9 million. This latter figure included about 3.5 million slaves. The population advantage of the North was somewhat greater than 2 to 1, and the estimated enlistments ran 1,556,000 to 1,082,000. Manpower odds against General Lee were ordinarily about 3 to 2, sometimes 3 to 1. Such superior numbers usually gave the North the advantage of choosing the point of attack.

Lieutenant Porter and Soldiers   *Union soldiers of the Fourth Michigan Infantry. (Library of Congress.)*

A broad stream of European immigrants continued to pour into the North, thanks to Northern control of the seas. Though slowed down a bit by the war, especially during the first two years, the inflow totaled over 800,000 newcomers of both sexes from 1861 through 1865—far more than the total casualties in the armed

Immigration to United States, 1860–1866

YEAR	TOTAL	BRITAIN	IRELAND	GERMANY	ALL OTHERS
1860	153,640	29,737	48,637	54,491	20,775
1861	91,918	19,675	23,797	31,661	16,785
1862	91,985	24,639	23,351	27,529	16,466
1863	176,282	66,882	55,916	33,162	20,322
1864	193,418	53,428	63,523	57,276	19,191
1865*	248,120	82,465	29,772	83,424	52,459
1866	318,568	94,924	36,690	115,892	71,062

*Only the first three months of 1865 were war months.

services of the North. The bulk of new arrivals were British, Irish, and German; and large numbers of them were induced to enlist in the Union armies. Tens of thousands of earlier immigrants, inspired by a love of freedom and gratitude to their adopted land, likewise joined the colors. Altogether, about one-fifth of the Union forces were foreign-born. In one division, commands were given in four different languages; and some German units even had guttural-accented officers of their own nationality. Southerners branded foreign enlistees as "Hessians" or "Yankee Hessians."

Blacks Battle Bondage

Altogether about 180,000 blacks served in the Union armies, most of them from the slave states but many from the free-soil North. Blacks accounted for about 10 percent of the total enlistments in the Union forces, on land or sea, and included two Massachusetts regiments raised largely through the efforts of the ex-slave Frederick Douglass.

Black volunteers were at first rejected. Race prejudice, fear of arming blacks, and a feeling that whites should fight their own war raised a forbidding hand. But as manpower ran low and emancipation was proclaimed, black enlistees

> The two most prominent German-American generals, Franz Sigel and Carl Schurz, were both refugees from the German revolutions of 1848. Sigel did yeoman work in saving Missouri, with its large German population, for the Union. Both generals suffered reverses, but Schurz, through no fault of his own, was routed. German-speaking soldiers, when asked whom they were serving with, would reply, "I fights mit Sigel and I runs mit Schurz."

were welcomed, although at first they were not paid as well as the whites. Strangely enough, the blacks had to fight for the privilege of fighting for freedom.

Black fighting men unquestionably had their hearts in a war against slavery. They participated in about five hundred engagements, major and minor, and received twenty-two Congressional Medals of Honor—the highest military award. Their casualties were extremely heavy; over thirty-eight thousand died, whether from battle, sickness, or reprisals by vengeful masters. A few were put to death as slaves in revolt, for not until 1864 did the South recognize them as prisoners of war. In later years many white Southerners blamed their defeat on the "unfair" use of blacks and foreigners.

Black Union Soldiers *These former slaves, recruited into the Union army in Tennessee, helped to man an artillery battery during the battle of Nashville. (Library of Congress.)*

> In August 1863 Lincoln wrote to Grant that enlisting black soldiers "works doubly, weakening the enemy and strengthening us." In December 1863 he announced that "it is difficult to say they are not as good soldiers as any." In August 1864 he said, "Abandon all the posts now garrisoned by black men, take 150,000 [black] men from our side and put them in the battlefield or cornfield against us, and we would be compelled to abandon the war in three weeks."

For reasons of pride, prejudice, and principle, the Confederacy could not bring itself to enlist slaves until a month before the war ended, and then it was too late. Meanwhile tens of thousands were impressed into labor battalions, the building of fortifications, the supplying of armies, and other war-connected activities. Slaves moreover were "the stomach of the Confederacy," for they kept the farms going while the white men fought.

Ironically, the great mass of Southern slaves did little to help their Northern liberators, white or black. A thousand scattered torches in the hands of a thousand slaves would have brought the Southern soldiers home, and the war would have ended. Through the "grapevine," the blacks learned of Lincoln's Emancipation Proclamation. Yet the bulk of them, whether because of fear, loyalty, lack of leadership, or strict policing, did not cast off their chains. But tens of thousand revolted "with their feet," when they abandoned their plantations upon the approach or arrival of Union armies, with or without emancipation proclamations. About twenty-five thousand joined Sherman's march through Georgia in 1864, and their presence in such numbers created problems of supply and discipline.

Rallying to the Flag of the Union

The ideal of Union was a tremendous asset to the North. This ideal was compounded largely of pride in the flag, in the past, and in the future. America could not hope to shame its monarchical critics and achieve its Manifest Destiny if it divided. The teachings of Webster and Clay had been driven home, as indicated by such popular Northern watchwords as "Union Forever" and "What God Hath Joined Let No Man Put Asunder." A rousing Northern song, widely sung since the 1850s, proudly proclaimed:

> The union of lakes, the union of lands,
>   The union of States none can sever,
> The union of hearts, the union of hands,
> And the flag of our union forever.*

Devotion to the Union aroused the North with unexpected fury against the "flag of disunion" and helped to hold the Border States in line. The concept infused in the North the will to fight and retained the Southerner-infiltrated states of the upper Mississippi Valley. Finally, the ideal provided the Northerners with the inspiring war cry of Union, until such time as the moral issue of slavery could be brought out into the open, as it was late in 1862.

Dethroning King Cotton

Textile mills in Britain were fatally dependent on Southern cotton, and the Confederates were supremely confident that the British fleet would be forced to break the blockade. Why did King Cotton fail them?

English manufacturers had on hand, when the shooting started in 1861, a heavy oversupply of fiber. The real pinch did not come until about a year and a half later, when thousands of hungry operatives were thrown out of work. But by this time Lincoln had announced his slave-emancipation policy, and the "wage slaves" of England were not going to demand a war for the slaveowners of the South.

The direst effects of the "cotton famine" in England were relieved in several ways. Hunger among unemployed workers was partially eased when certain kindhearted Americans sent over several cargoes of foodstuffs. As Union armies penetrated the South, they captured or bought

---

*George P. Morris, "The Flag or Our Union."

> As the Civil war neared the end of its third year, the London *Times* (January 7, 1864) could boast: "We are as busy, as rich, and as fortunate in our trade as if the American war had never broken out, and our trade with the States had never been disturbed. Cotton was no King, notwithstanding the prerogatives which had been loudly claimed for him."

considerable supplies of cotton and shipped them to England; and the Confederates also ran a limited quantity through the blockade. In addition, the cotton growers of Egypt and India, responding to high prices, increased their output. Finally, booming war industries in England, which supplied both North and South, relieved unemployment.

King Wheat and King Corn—of the Northern agricultural royalty—proved to be more potent potentates than King Cotton. During these war years the North, blessed with ideal weather, produced bountiful crops of grain and harvested them with McCormick's mechanical reaper. In the same period the British suffered a series of bad harvests. They were forced to import huge quantities of grain from America, which happened to have the cheapest and most abundant supply. If the British had broken the blockade to get cotton, they would have provoked the North to war and would have cut off this precious granary. Unemployment for some seemed better than hunger for all. Hence, one Yankee journal could exult:

> Wave the stars and stripes high o'er us,
> Let every freeman sing . . .
> Old King Cotton's dead and buried:
>   brave young Corn is King.

President Davis versus President Lincoln

The Confederate government, like King Cotton, betrayed fatal weaknesses. Its constitution, borrowing liberally from that of the Union, had one deadly defect. Created by secession, it could not

logically deny future secession to its states. Jefferson Davis, while making his bow to states' rights, had in view a well-knit central government. But determined states' rights supporters fought him bitterly to the end. The Richmond regime even encountered difficulty in persuading certain state troops to serve outside their own borders. Governor Brown of Georgia, a belligerent states' righter, at times seemed ready to secede from the secession and fight both sides. States' rights were no less damaging to the Confederacy than Yankee sabers.

Sharp-featured President Davis—tense, humorless, legalistic, stubborn—was repeatedly in hot water. Though an eloquent orator and an able administrator, he at no time enjoyed real personal popularity and was often at loggerheads with his congress. At times there was serious talk of impeachment. Unlike Lincoln, Davis was somewhat imperious and inclined to

President Davis, the Acrobat, on Rope of Cotton
The "Confederacy" is a fuse bomb; the flag reads, "Let Us Alone," a Davis theme. The cotton rope is unraveling.

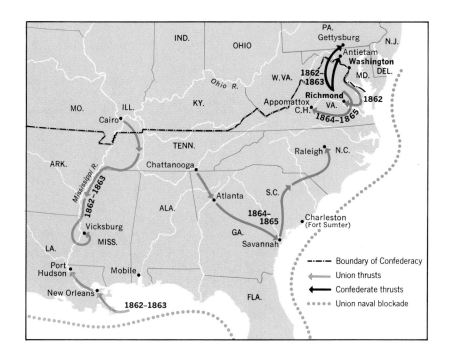

Main Thrusts, 1861–1865
*Northern strategists at first
believed that the rebellion
could be snuffed out quickly by
a swift, crushing blow. But the
stiffness of Southern resistance
to the Union's early probes revealed that the conflict would
be a war of attrition, long and
bloody.*

defy rather than lead public opinion. Suffering acutely from neuralgia and other nervous disorders (including a tic) he overworked himself with the details of both civil government and military operations. No one could doubt his courage, sincerity, integrity, and devotion to the South, but the task proved beyond his powers. It was probably beyond the powers of any mere mortal.

Lincoln also had his troubles, but on the whole they were less prostrating. The North enjoyed the prestige of a long-established government, financially stable and fully recognized both at home and abroad. Lincoln, the inexperienced prairie politician, proved superior to the more experienced but less flexible Jefferson Davis. Able to relax with droll stories at critical times, "Old Abe" grew as the war dragged on. Tactful, quiet, patient, yet firm, he developed a genius for interpreting and leading a fickle public opinion. Holding aloft the banner of Union with inspiring utterances, he revealed charitableness toward the South and forbearance toward backbiting colleagues. "Did [Secretary] Stanton say I was a damned fool?" he reportedly replied to a talebearer. "Then I dare say I must

be one, for Stanton is generally right and he always says what he means."

Strangulation of the South by Sea

As finally developed, the general plan of Northern attack had four phases. First, slowly suffocate the South by blockading its coasts. Second, cut it in half by seizing control of the Mississippi River backbone. Third, chop it to pieces (a later idea) by sending troops through Georgia and then north into the Carolinas. Fourth, strangle it by capturing its capital (Richmond) and by pounding its remaining armies into submission. The overall strategy called for slowly beating down the enemy rather than delivering a knockout punch.

The blockade started leakily: it was not clamped down all at once but was extended by degrees. An airtight patrol of some 3,500 miles (5,635 kilometers) of coast was impossible for the hastily improvised Northern navy, which consisted partly of converted yachts and ferryboats. But blockading was simplified by concentrating on the principal ports and inlets. Only at

---

*When news reached Washington that the Mer-
rimack had sunk two wooden Yankee warships
with ridiculous ease, President Lincoln, much
"excited," summoned his advisers. Secretary of
the Navy Welles records: "The most frightened
man on that gloomy day. . .was the Secretary
of War [Stanton]. He was at times almost frantic. . . . The Merrimack, he said, would destroy
every vessel in the service, could lay every city
on the coast under contribution, could take
Fortress Monroe. . . . Likely the first movement
of the Merrimack would be to come up the Potomac and disperse Congress, destroy the Capital and public buildings."*

---

such places were dock facilities available for
loading bulky bales of cotton.

How was the blockade regarded by the naval
powers of the world? Ordinarily, they probably
would have defied it, for it was never completely
effective and was especially sievelike at the outset. But England, the greatest maritime nation,
recognized it as binding and warned its shippers that they ignored it at their peril. An explanation is easy. Blockade happened to be the
chief offensive weapon of Britain, which was
still Mistress of the Seas. Britain plainly did not
want to tie its hands in a future war by insisting
that Lincoln maintain impossibly high blockading standards.

Blockade-running soon became riskily
profitable, as the growing scarcity of Southern
goods drove prices skyward. The most successful runners were swift, gray-painted steamers,
scores of which were specially built in Scotland.
A leading rendezvous was the West Indian port
of Nassau, in the British Bahamas, where at
one time thirty-five of the speedy ships were
counted. The low-lying craft would take on cargoes of arms brought in by tramp steamers from
England, leave with fraudulent papers for
"Halifax" (Canada), and return a few days later
with a cargo of cotton. The risks were great, but
the profits would mount to 700 percent and
more for lucky gamblers. Two successful voyages might well pay for capture on a third. The
lush days of blockade-running finally passed as

Union squadrons gradually pinched off the
leading Southern ports, from New Orleans to
Charleston.

The Northern navy enforced the blockade
with high-handed practices. Yankee captains,
for example, would seize British freighters on
the high seas, if laden with war supplies for the
tiny port of Nassau and other halfway stations.
The justification was that obviously these shipments were "ultimately" destined, by devious
routes, for the Confederacy.

London, although not happy, acquiesced in
this disagreeable doctrine of "ultimate destination" or "continuous voyage." British blockaders
might find such a farfetched interpretation
highly useful in a future war—as in fact they
did in the World War of 1914–1918.

The most alarming Confederate threat to the
blockade came in 1862. Resourceful Southerners raised and reconditioned a former wooden
United States warship, the *Merrimack,* and
plated its sides with old iron railroad rails. Renamed the *Virginia,* this clumsy but powerful
monster easily destroyed two wooden ships of
the Union navy in the Virginia waters of
Chesapeake Bay; it also threatened catastrophe
to the entire Yankee blockading fleet. (Actually
the homemade ironclad was not a seaworthy
craft.)

A tiny Union ironclad, the *Monitor,* built in
about 100 days, arrived on the scene in the nick
of time. For four hours, on March 9, 1862, the
little "Yankee cheesebox on a raft" fought the
wheezy *Merrimack* to a standstill. Britain and
France had already built several powerful ironclads, but the first battle-testing of these new
craft heralded the doom of wooden warships. A
few months after the historic battle, the Confederates destroyed the *Merrimack* to keep her
from the grasp of advancing Union troops.

The Runners of Bull Run

By the summer of 1861, a Union army of some
thirty thousand men was being drilled near
Washington. It was ill prepared for battle, but
Northern newspaper editors, eager to end the
war in a hurry, raised the cry "On to Rich-

Battle of the Merrimack and the Monitor, March 9, 1862. *(Library of Congress.)*

mond!" Proddings by the press and public finally forced action, contrary to the better judgment of some of the generals. This was a classic example of the dangerous pressure that can be exerted by an ill-informed public.

Preliminaries of the clash at Bull Run, on July 21, 1861, seemed like those of a sporting event. The raw Yankee recruits marched or straggled from the capital, accompanied by congressmen, ladies, and others riding out with lunch baskets to see the fun. The ill-trained Union force encountered a smaller Confederate army at Bull Run (Manassas Junction), some thirty miles (forty-eight kilometers) southwest of Washington. At first the battle went well for the Yankees. But "Stonewall" Jackson's gray-clad warriors stood like a stone wall (here he won his nickname), and Confederate reinforcements arrived unexpectedly. Panic suddenly seized the weary Union soldiers, many of whom fled in disgraceful confusion. The Confederates, too exhausted or too disorganized to pursue effectively, feasted on captured lunches.

The "military picnic" at Bull Run, though not decisive militarily, was significant psychologically. Defeat was better than victory for the Union, because it dispelled all illusions of a one-punch war and caused the Northerners to buckle down to the staggering task at hand. Conversely, the victory was worse than a defeat for the South, because it inflated an already dangerous overconfidence. Many of the Southern soldiers deserted, some boastfully to display their trophies, others feeling sure that the war was now over. Southern enlistments fell off sharply, and preparations for a protracted conflict slackened.

"Tardy George" McClellan

Northern hopes brightened later in 1861, when General George B. McClellan was given command of the Army of the Potomac, as the major Union force near Washington was now called. Red-haired and red-mustached, strong and stocky, McClellan was a brilliant, thirty-four-year-old West Pointer. As a serious student of warfare who was dubbed "Young Napoleon," he had seen plenty of fighting, first in the Mexican

War and then as an observer of the Crimean War in Russia.

Cocky George McClellan embodied a curious mixture of virtues and defects. He was a superb organizer and drillmaster, and he injected splendid morale into the Army of the Potomac. Hating to sacrifice his troops, he was idolized by his men, who affectionately called him "Little Mac." But he was a perfectionist who seems not to have realized that an army is never ready to the last button and that wars cannot be won without running some risks. He consistently but erroneously believed that the enemy outnumbered him, partly because his intelligence reports from the head of Pinkerton's Detective Agency were unreliable. He was overcautious—Lincoln once accused him of having "the slows"—and he addressed the president in an arrogant tone which a less forgiving person would never have tolerated. Privately the general referred to his chief as a "baboon."

As McClellan discreetly continued to drill his army without moving it toward Richmond, the derisive Northern watchword became "All Quiet along the Potomac." The song of the hour was

Lincoln treated McClellan's demands for reinforcements and his excuses for inaction with infinite patience. One exception came when the general complained that his horses were tired. Lincoln wrote: "I have just read your dispatch about sore-tongued and fatigued horses. Will you pardon me for asking what the horses of your army have done since the battle of Antietam that fatigues anything?" (October 24, 1862.)

"Tardy George" (McClellan). After threatening to "borrow" the army if it was not going to be used, Lincoln finally issued firm orders to move.

A reluctant McClellan decided upon a waterborne flanking approach to Richmond. Choosing the route up the peninsula formed by the James and York Rivers, he warily advanced toward the city in the spring of 1862 with about 100,000 men. After taking a month to capture historic Yorktown, which bristled with imitation wooden cannons, he finally came within sight of the spires of Richmond. Then General Lee

"Masterly Inactivity, or Six Months on the Potomac"
McClellan and his Confederate foe view each other cautiously, while their troops engage in visiting, marrying, and sports. (Frank Leslie's Illustrated Newspaper, 1862.)

Peninsular Campaign, 1862

suddenly struck with about 70,000 troops. Brilliantly assisted by "Stonewall" Jackson, he slowly drove McClellan back to his base on Chesapeake Bay. Although the Union army was still in fighting shape, the whole Peninsular Campaign was abandoned as a costly failure.

McClellan was now given a less active command, amid a storm of controversy. His enemies accused "Mac the Unready" of having moved too timorously. His defenders claimed that he would have captured Richmond if Lincoln had not withdrawn troops for the defense of Washington, which had been jeopardized by the lightning feints of General Jackson in the Shenandoah Valley. It is worth noting that McClellan was never decisively defeated and that after the war Lee rated him the ablest of his many opponents.

A Union army near Washington, strengthened by units from McClellan's command, was now entrusted to overconfident General Pope. A handsome, dashing, soldierly figure, he boasted that in the western theater, from which he had come, he had seen only the backs of the enemy. He quickly got a front view, for General Lee, at the Second Battle of Bull Run (August 29–30, 1862), furiously attacked him and inflicted a crushing defeat. Gloom once more enshrouded the North.

The Antietam Pivotal Point

Lee now undertook a daring thrust into Maryland. He hoped to win a victory that would not only encourage foreign intervention, but also seduce this wavering Border State and her sisters from the Union. The Confederate troops sang lustily:

> Thou wilt not cower in the dust,
>   Maryland! my Maryland!
> Thy gleaming sword shall never rust,
>   Maryland! my Maryland!

But the Marylanders did not respond to the siren song. The presence among the invaders of so many blanketless, hatless, and shoeless soldiers dampened the state's ardor.

Events finally shaped up for a critical battle at Antietam Creek, Maryland. Lincoln, responding to popular pressure, hastily restored "Little Mac" to active command of the main Northern army. The soldiers tossed their caps into the air and hugged his horse as they hailed his return. At Antietam, on September 17, 1862, McClellan succeeded in halting Lee in one of the bitterest and bloodiest days of the war.

Antietam was more or less a draw militarily. But Lee, finding his thrust parried, retired across the Potomac. McClellan, from whom much more had been hoped, was removed from his field command for the second and final time. His numerous critics, condemning him for not having boldly pursued the ever-dangerous Lee, finally got his scalp.

The landmark Battle of Antietam was one of the decisive engagements of world history—probably the most decisive of the Civil War. Jefferson Davis was perhaps never again so near victory as on that fateful summer day. The British and French governments were on the verge of diplomatic mediation, a species of interference sure to be angrily resented by the North. An almost certain rebuff by Washington might well have spurred Paris and London into

Confederate Corpses at Antietam *Unknown to Lee, who had dangerously divided his army, McClellan had somehow obtained a copy of the Confederate battle plan. The Union forces thus had a great tactical advantage, and the result was appalling slaughter. The twelve-hour fight at Antietam Creek ranks as the bloodiest day of the war, with more than ten thousand Confederate casualties and even more on the Union side. "At last the sun went down and the battle ended," one historian wrote, "smoke heavy in the air, the twilight quivering with the anguished cries of thousands of wounded men." (Library of Congress.)*

armed intervention. But both capitals cooled off when the Union displayed unexpected power at Antietam, and their chill deepened with the passing months.

Bloody Antietam was also the long-awaited "victory" that Lincoln needed for launching his Emancipation Proclamation. The abolitionists had long been clamoring for action: Wendell Phillips was denouncing the president as a "first-rate second-rate man." By midsummer of 1862, with the Border States safely in the fold, Lincoln was ready to move. But he believed that to issue such an edict on the heels of a series of military disasters would be folly. It would seem like a confession that the North, unable to conquer the South, was forced to call upon the slaves to murder their masters. Lincoln therefore decided to wait for the outcome of Lee's invasion.

Antietam served as the needed emancipation springboard. The halting of Lee's offensive was just enough of a victory to justify Lincoln's issuing, on September 23, 1862, the preliminary Emancipation Proclamation. This hope-giving document announced that on January 1, 1863, the president would issue a final proclamation.

On the scheduled date he fully redeemed his promise, and the Civil War became more of a moral crusade.

A Proclamation without Emancipation

Lincoln's Emancipation Proclamation of 1863 declared "forever free" the slaves in those Confederate states still in rebellion. The blacks in the loyal Border States were not affected, nor were those in specific conquered areas in the South—all told, about 800,000. The tone of the document was dull and legalistic: there was no clarion call for a holy war to achieve freedom. Lincoln in fact is on record as late as February of 1865 as favoring cash compensation to the owners of all slaves.

The presidential pen did not formally strike the shackles from a single slave. Where Lincoln could presumably free the slaves—that is, in the loyal Border States—he refused to do so, lest he spur disunion. Where he could not—that is, in the Confederate states—he tried to. In short, where he *could* he would not, and where he *would* he could not. Thus, the Emancipation

Proclamation was stronger on proclamation than emancipation.

Yet much unofficial do-it-yourself liberation did take place. Thousands of jubilant slaves, learning of the proclamation, flocked to the invading Union armies, stripping already rundown plantations of their work force. In this sense the Emancipation Proclamation was heralded by the patter of running feet. But many fugitives would have come anyhow, as they had from the war's outset. Actually, Lincoln did not go so far as legislation already passed by Congress for freeing enemy-owned slaves. His immediate goal was not so much to liberate the slaves as to strengthen the moral cause of the Union at home and abroad. This he succeeded in doing. At the same time, Lincoln's proclamation, though of dubious constitutionality, clearly foreshadowed the ultimate doom of slavery. This was legally achieved by action of the individual states and by their ratification of the Thirteenth Amendment in 1865, eight months after the Civil War had ended. (For text, see the Appendix.)

Public reactions to the long-awaited proclamation of 1863 were varied. "God bless Abraham Lincoln," exulted the antislavery editor

> *Many of the British aristocrats were unfriendly to the North, and the London Spectator sneered at Lincoln's so-called Emancipation Proclamation: "The Government liberates the enemy's slaves as it would the enemy's cattle, simply to weaken them in the coming conflict. . . . The principle asserted is not that a human being cannot justly own another, but that he cannot own him unless he is loyal to the United States."*

Horace Greeley in his New York *Tribune*. But many ardent abolitionists complained that Lincoln had not gone far enough. On the other hand, formidable numbers of Northerners, especially in the Old Northwest and the Border States, felt that he had gone too far. A Democratic rhymester sneered:

Honest old Abe, when the war first began,
Denied abolition was part of his plan;
Honest old Abe has since made a decree,
The war must go on till the slaves are all free.
As both can't be honest, will some one tell how,
If honest Abe then, he is honest Abe now?

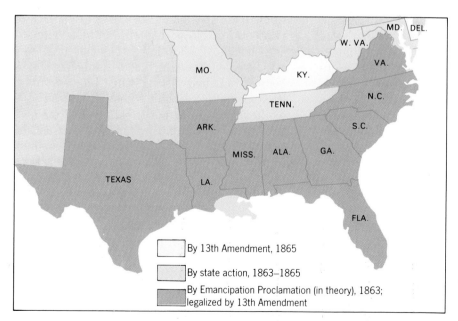

Emancipation in the South President Lincoln believed that compensated emancipation of the slaves would be fairest to the South. He formally proposed such an amendment to the Constitution in December 1862. What finally emerged was the Thirteenth Amendment of 1865, which freed all slaves without compensation.

By 13th Amendment, 1865

By state action, 1863–1865

By Emancipation Proclamation (in theory), 1863; legalized by 13th Amendment

Lincoln Plays His Last Card
Lincoln's last card was the Emancipation Proclamation, shown as a black spade. (London Punch, 1862.)

Opposition mounted in the North against supporting an "abolition war"; ex-President Pierce and others felt that emancipation should not be "inflicted" on the slaves. Many Boys in Blue, especially from the Border States, had volunteered to fight for the Union, not against slavery. Desertions increased sharply. The crucial congressional elections in the autumn of 1862 went heavily against the administration, particularly in New York, Pennsylvania, and Ohio. Democrats even carried Lincoln's Illinois, although they did not secure control of Congress.

The Emancipation Proclamation caused an outcry to rise from the South that "Lincoln the fiend" was trying to stir up the "hellish passions" of a slave insurrection. Aristocrats of Europe, noting that the proclamation applied only to rebel slaveholders, were inclined to sympathize with Southern protests. But the Old World working classes, especially in England, reacted otherwise. They sensed that the proclamation spelled the ultimate doom of slavery, and many laborers were more determined than ever to oppose intervention. Gradually the diplomatic position of the Union improved.

The North now had much the stronger moral cause. In addition to preserving the Union, it had committed itself to freeing the slaves. The moral position of the South was correspondingly weakened.

Bisecting the Confederacy

Luckily the spectacular rise of Ulysses S. Grant provided Lincoln at last with an able general—and one who did not have to be shelved after every reverse. As a mediocre student at West Point, Grant had distinguished himself only in horsemanship, although he did fairly well in mathematics. After participating with credit in the Mexican War, he was stationed at isolated frontier posts, where boredom and loneliness drove him to drink. Resigning from the army to avoid a court martial for drunkenness, he failed at various business ventures, and when war came, he was working in his father's leather store in Illinois at $50 a month.

Grant did not cut much of a figure. The shy and silent shopkeeper was short, stooped, awkward, stubble-bearded, and sloppy in dress. He managed with some difficulty to secure a colonelcy in the volunteers. From then on his military experience—combined with boldness, resourcefulness, and doggedness—brought a meteoric rise.

Grant's first signal success came in the northern Tennessee theater. After heavy fighting, he succeeded in capturing Fort Henry and Fort Donelson on the Tennessee and Cumberland rivers in February 1862. When the Confederate commander at Fort Donelson asked for terms, Grant bluntly demanded "an unconditional and immediate surrender."

This triumph in Tennessee was of major significance. Kentucky was riveted more securely to the Union, and the gateway was opened to the rest of Tennessee as well as to Georgia and the heart of the South. Grant's exploit also captured the imagination of the victory-starved North and infused badly needed life into the Union cause.

"Unconditional Surrender" Grant was caught napping several weeks later at Shiloh, in southern Tennessee, April 6–7, 1862. But he finally managed to beat off the enemy on one of the goriest fields of the war. Lincoln resisted all demands for his removal by saying, "I can't spare

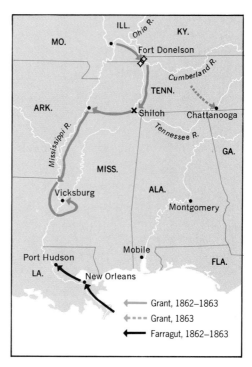

The Mississippi River and Tennessee, 1862–1863

A Civil War Observation Balloon, 1862 This Mathew Brady photograph, taken during the Peninsular Campaign of 1862, shows a Union observer aloft watching the battle of Fair Oaks. Despite such technological innovations, the Union armies failed to reach their objective of Richmond. (Library of Congress.)

this man, he fights." When talebearers later told Lincoln that Grant drank too much, the president allegedly replied, "Find me the brand, and I'll send a barrel to each of my other generals." There is no evidence that Grant's drinking habits had a seriously adverse effect on his performance.

Other Union thrusts were in the making. In the spring of 1862, a flotilla commanded by David G. Farragut joined with a Northern army to strike the South a staggering blow by seizing New Orleans. With Union gunboats both ascending and descending the Mississippi, the eastern part of the Confederacy was left with a precarious back door. Through this narrowing entrance, between Vicksburg and Port Hudson, flowed herds of vitally needed cattle and quantities of other provisions from Louisiana and Texas. The fortress of Vicksburg, located on a hairpin turn of the Mississippi, was the South's sentinel protecting the lifeline to the western sources of supply.

General Grant was now given command of the Union forces attacking Vicksburg and in the teeth of grave difficulties displayed rare skill and daring. This was his best-fought campaign of the war. Vicksburg at length surrendered, on July 4, 1863, with the garrison reduced to eating mules and rats. Five days later came the fall of Port Hudson, the last Southern bastion on the Mississippi. The spinal cord of the Confederacy was now severed and, in Lincoln's quaint phrase, the Father of Waters at last flowed "unvexed to the sea."

Sherman Scorches Georgia

General Grant, the victor of Vicksburg, was now transferred to the east Tennessee theater, where Confederates had driven Union forces from the battlefield at Chickamauga into the city of Chattanooga, to which they then laid siege. Grant won a series of desperate engagements in November 1863 in the vicinity of besieged Chattanooga; including Missionary Ridge and Lookout Mountain ("the Battle above the Clouds"). Chattanooga was liberated, the state was cleared of Confederates, and the way

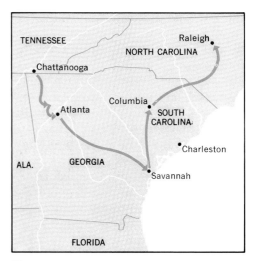

Sherman's March, 1864–1865

was thus opened for an invasion of Georgia. Grant was rewarded by being made general-in-chief.

The conquest of Georgia was entrusted to General William Tecumseh Sherman. Red-haired and red-bearded, grim-faced and ruthless, he captured and burned Atlanta in September 1864. He then daringly undertook to cut loose from his base of supplies, live off the country for some 250 miles (402 kilometers), and emerge at Savannah on the sea. As a rousing Northern song ("Marching through Georgia") put it:

"Sherman's dashing Yankee boys will never reach the coast!"
So the saucy rebels said—and 't was a handsome boast.

But Sherman's hated "Blue Bellies," sixty thousand strong, cut a sixty-mile (ninety-seven-kilometer) swath of destruction through Georgia. They burned buildings, leaving only the blackened chimneys ("Sherman's Sentinels"). They tore up railroad rails, heated them red-hot, and twisted them into "iron doughnuts" and "Sherman's hairpins." They bayoneted family portraits and ran off with valuable "souvenirs." "War . . . is all hell," admitted Sherman later, and he proved it by his efforts to "make Georgia howl." One of his major purposes was to destroy supplies destined for the Confederate army and

> A letter picked up on a dead Confederate in North Carolina and addressed to his "deer sister" concluded that it was "dam fulishness" trying to "lick shurmin." He had been getting "nuthin but hell & lots uv it" ever since he saw the "dam yanks," and he was "tirde uv it." He would head for home now, but his old horse was "plaid out." If the "dam yankees" had not got there yet, it would be a "dam wunder." They were thicker than "lise on a hen and a dam site ornerier."

to weaken the morale of the men at the front by waging war on their homes.

Sherman was a pioneer practitioner of "total war." His success in "Shermanizing" the South was attested by increasing numbers of Confederate desertions. Although his methods were brutal, he probably shortened the struggle and hence saved lives. But there can be no doubt that the discipline of his army at times broke down, as roving riffraff (Sherman's "bummers") engaged in an orgy of pillaging. "Sherman the Brute" was universally damned in the South.

After seizing Savannah as a Christmas present for Lincoln, Sherman's army veered north into South Carolina, where the destruction was even more vicious. Many Union soldiers believed that this state, the "hell-hole of secession," had wantonly provoked the war. The capital city, Columbia, burst into flames, in all probability the handiwork of the Yankee invader. Crunching northward, Sherman's conquering army had rolled deep into North Carolina by the time the war ended.

Lee's Last Lunge

After Antietam, Lincoln replaced McClellan as commander of the Army of the Potomac with General A. E. Burnside, whose ornate side-whiskers came to be known as "burnsides" or "sideburns." Protesting his unfitness for this responsibility, Burnside proved it when he launched a rash frontal attack on Lee's strong position at Fredericksburg, Virginia, on December 13, 1862. A chicken could not have lived in the line of fire, remarked one Confederate officer. More than ten thousand Northern soldiers were killed or wounded in "Burnside's Slaughter Pen."

A new slaughter pen was prepared when General Burnside yielded his command to "Fighting Joe" Hooker, an aggressive officer but a headstrong subordinate. At Chancellorsville, Virginia, May 2–4, 1863, Lee daringly divided his numerically inferior force and sent "Stonewall" Jackson to attack the Union flank. The strategy worked. Hooker, temporarily dazed by a near hit from a cannonball, was badly beaten but not crushed. This victory was probably Lee's most brilliant, but it was dearly bought. Jackson was mistakenly shot by his own men in the gathering dusk and died a few days later. "I have lost my right arm," lamented Lee. Southern folklore relates how Jackson outflanked the angels while getting into Heaven.

Lee now prepared to follow up his brilliant victory by invading the North again, this time through Pennsylvania. A decisive blow would add strength to the peace movement in the North, and would also encourage foreign intervention. Three days before the battle was

Lee's Chief Battles, December 1862–July 1863

joined, General George G. Meade—scholarly, unspectacular, abrupt—was aroused from his sleep at 2 A.M. with the unwelcome news that he would replace Hooker. The high tide of the Confederacy was at hand.

Quite by accident Meade took his stand on the green rolling hills near quiet little Gettysburg, Pennsylvania. There his ninety-two thousand men in blue locked in furious combat with Lee's seventy-six thousand gray-clad warriors. The battle seesawed throughout three days, July 1–3, 1863, and the outcome was in doubt until almost the very end. The failure of General Pickett's magnificent but bloodily futile charge finally broke the back of the Confederates.

Lee's defeat was his worst to date, but he took full responsibility for it, even though some of his subordinates had failed him. From now on the Southern cause was doomed, for Vicksburg had surrendered on the day after the reverse at Gettysburg. Yet the men of Dixie fought on, through sweat, blood, and weariness of spirit. The Confederacy was like a cut flower—outwardly blooming but slowly dying.

Later in that dreary autumn of 1863, with the graves still fresh, Lincoln journeyed to Gettysburg to dedicate the cemetery. He read a two-minute address, following a two-hour speech by the orator of the day. Lincoln's noble remarks were branded by the London *Times* as "ludicrous" and by Democratic editors as "dishwatery" and "silly." The address attracted relatively little attention at the time, but the president was speaking for the ages.

Grant Outlasts Lee

Grant was now brought in from the West over Meade, who was blamed for failing to pursue the defeated but always dangerous Lee. Lincoln needed a general who, employing the superior resources of the North, would have the intestinal stamina to drive straight ahead, regardless of casualties. A soldier of bulldog tenacity, Grant was the man for this meat-grinder type of warfare. His overall basic strategy was to assail the enemy's armies simultaneously, so that they could not assist one another and hence could be

destroyed piecemeal. His personal motto was "When in doubt, fight." Lincoln urged him "to chew and choke, as much as possible."

A grimly determined Grant, with more than 100,000 men, struck for Richmond. He engaged Lee in a series of furious battles in the Wilderness of Virginia, during May and June of 1864, notably in the leaden hurricane of the "Bloody Angle" and "Hell's Half Acre." In this Wilderness Campaign Grant suffered about 50,000 casualties, or nearly as many men as Lee had at the start. But Lee lost about as heavily in proportion.

In a ghastly gamble, on June 3, 1864, Grant ordered a frontal assault on the impregnable position of Cold Harbor. The Union soldiers advanced to almost certain death with papers pinned on their backs bearing their names and addresses. In a few minutes, about seven thousand men were killed or wounded.

Public opinion in the North was appalled by this "blood and guts" type of fighting. Critics cried that "Grant the Butcher" had gone insane. But his basic strategy of hammering ahead seemed brutally necessary; he could trade two men for one and still beat the enemy to its

Grant's Virginia Campaign, 1864–1865

General Ulysses S. Grant and General Robert E. Lee   *Trained at West Point, Grant (left) proved to be a better general than a president. Oddly, he hated the sight of blood and recoiled from rare beef. Lee (right), a gentlemanly general in an ungentlemanly business, remarked when the Union troops were bloodily repulsed at Fredericksburg. "It is well that war is so terrible, or we should get too fond of it." (Left and right, National Archives.)*

knees. "I propose to fight it out on this line," he wrote, "if it takes all summer." It did—and it also took all autumn, all winter, and a part of the spring.

Early in 1865 the Confederates, tasting the bitter dregs of defeat, tried desperately to negotiate for peace between the "two countries." But Lincoln could accept nothing short of Union, and the Southerners could accept nothing short of independence. So the war had to grind on— amid smoke and agony—to its terrible climax.

The end came with dramatic suddenness. Rapidly advancing Northern troops captured Richmond and cornered Lee at Appomattox Court House in Virginia, in April 1865. Grant— stubble-bearded and informally dressed—met with Lee on Palm Sunday and granted generous terms of surrender. Among other concessions, the hungry Confederates were allowed to keep their own horses for spring plowing.

Tattered Southern veterans—"Lee's Ragamuffins"—wept as they took leave of their beloved commander. The elated Union soldiers cheered, but they were silenced by Grant's stern admonition, "The war is over; the rebels are our countrymen again." Unfortunately, as the tragic sequel proved, this soldierly forgiveness was not shared by all Northern hearts.

Varying Viewpoints

Why did the North win the Civil War? The usual answer is that superior industry and transportation tipped the scales in the Union's favor. This line of reasoning leads to the conclusion that the Civil War was the first "modern" war, in which victory turned at least as much on home-front economic mobilization as on battlefield prowess.

Another approach focuses on military strategy. Historians of this persuasion argue that Union successes in the western theater more than compensated for the early debacles in Virginia. Victories in the West allowed the emergence of tacticians like Grant and Sherman, who were better equipped to wage a modern total war than the valiant but old-fashioned Confederate generals.

A third answer emphasizes political leadership. In this view, the Lincoln administration was able to maintain control at home and prevent unfavorable foreign intervention in the conflict. The government of Jefferson Davis had no such domestic or diplomatic success. One historian has even suggested that if the North and South had traded presidents, the Confederacy would have won its independence. Even today, heated debate continues over the relative importance of battlefront and behind-the-lines factors in accounting for the North's crushing victory.

Select Readings

Primary Source Documents

Abraham Lincoln's reply in 1862 to Horace Greeley's "Prayer of Twenty Millions"* (*Collected Works of Abraham Lincoln,* edited by Roy P. Basler, 1953) is an early statement of the president's war aims. See also, in the same collection, the Emancipation Proclamation (1863). Reminiscences of the military struggle include Eliza Andrews, *The War-Time Journal of a Georgia Girl**(1908): *Memoirs of General William T. Sherman** (1887); and C. Vann Woodward, ed., *Mary Chestnut's Civil War* (rev. ed., 1981). See also Stephen Crane's classic war novel *The Red Badge of Courage* (1895).

Secondary Sources

An able survey is James G. Randall and David Donald, *The Civil War and Reconstruction* (rev. ed., 1969); greater detail appears in James G. Randall, *Lincoln the President* (4 vols., 1945–1955). Capable one-volume studies are Peter J. Parish, *The American Civil War* (1975), and James M. McPherson, *Ordeal by Fire: The Civil War and Reconstruction* (1982). See also the multi-volume study by Shelby Foote, *The Civil War* (3 vols., 1958–1974), and Allan Nevins' monumental *Ordeal of the Union* (8 vols., 1947–1971). Bruce Catton has a series of a dozen or so books on aspects of the Civil War, all readable and knowledgeable, including *A Stillness at Appomattox* (1953) and *This Hallowed Ground* (1956). Russell T. Weigley, *The American Way of War* (1973), puts military history in a broader context. Richard N. Current, *Lincoln and the First Shot* (1963), partially exculpates Lincoln. See also T. Harry Williams, *Lincoln and His Generals* (1952). Herman Hattaway and Archer Jones discuss *How the North Won* (1983). An intriguing analysis of Confederate strategy is Grady McWhiney and Perry D. Jamison, *Attack and Die* (1982). Bell I. Wiley's descriptions of common soldiers, *The Life of Johnny Reb* (1943) and *The Life of Billy Yank* (1952), are classics. See also Benjamin Quarles, *The Negro in the Civil War* (1953), and James M. McPherson's collection of documents, *The Negro's Civil War* (1965). Emancipation is treated in Louis Gerteis, *From Contraband to Freedmen: Federal Policy toward Southern Blacks, 1861–1865*

(1973); Herman Belz, *Emancipation and Equal Rights: Politics and Constitutionalism during the Civil War Reconstruction* (1978); and LaWanda Cox, *Lincoln and Black Freedom* (1981). On the abolitionists' role in securing emancipation, see James M. McPherson, *The Struggle for Equality* (1964). The Southern response is discussed in Robert Durden, *The Gray and the Black: The Confederate Debate on Emancipation* (1973). The two leading Civil War generals are masterfully treated in Douglas S. Freeman, *R. E. Lee* (4 vols., 1934–1935), and William S. McFeely, *Grant* (1981).

24

Behind the Lines: North and South

> *Long experience has shown that armies can not be maintained unless desertion shall be punished by the severe penalty of death. . . . [But] must I shoot a simple-minded soldier boy who deserts, while I must not touch a hair of a wily agitator who induces him to desert?*
>
> Abraham Lincoln, 1863

Diplomatic Warriors Abroad

America's diplomatic front, ordinarily second fiddle in wartime, has seldom been so critical as during the Civil War. The attitude of the major European countries, particularly France and Britain, was crucial. Both nations had formidable ironclads in their navies, and if either power had decided to intervene, it probably could have smashed the wooden blockading fleet of the Union with terrifying ease—at least in the early years of the war. If this had happened, the South almost certainly would have won its independence. An infuriated North might well have turned its bayonets against British Canada, there to seek vengeance and compensation.

Napoleon III, the slippery dictator of France, was openly unfriendly to the North. Behind the smoke screen of the Civil War, he was attempting to prop up his puppet, the Austrian nobleman Maximilian, on the throne of Mexico. The success of this hazardous venture depended on the collapse of the Union. Napoleon had the naval strength to break the Northern blockade, but because he did not have the nerve to attempt this venture alone, he sought the support of Britain. The London government saw fit to restrain the ambitious dictator, so intervention never came.

British officialdom, heavily tinged with aristocracy, was personally more friendly to the aristocratic South than to the "shopkeeping" North. But the common folk of Britain had grown increasingly intolerant of slavery. The London government therefore proclaimed an official neutrality and observed it rather well—at least as well as it could with its leaky neutrality laws.

The first real crisis with Britain came over the *Trent* affair, late in 1861. A Union warship cruising on the high seas north of Cuba stopped a British mail steamer, the *Trent,* and forcibly removed from it two Confederate diplomats who were on their way to England. The American captain was guilty of a serious error: he should have brought the entire ship to port for proper judicial judgment.

An outburst of rejoicing arose from the Northerners. They had as yet won no important military victory, and they regarded the seizure of these two eminent envoys as a brilliant stroke. Many loyal Unionists feared that if the diplomats had continued on their journey, they might have persuaded Britain and France to break the blockade. Besides, patriotic citizens, remembering the impressment days of 1812, thought it great sport to give John Bull a dose of his own medicine. Americans were now dragging men from the decks of British ships for a change.

Britons were outraged: upstart Yankees could not do this sort of thing to the Mistress of the Seas. War preparations buzzed, and redcoated troops embarked for Canada, with bands blaring "I Wish I Was in Dixie." The London Foreign Office forthwith prepared an ultimatum, demanding a surrender of the prisoners and a proper apology.

Luckily the *Trent* crisis was surmounted, but only with grave difficulty. The recently laid Atlantic cable had gone dead, and the delays caused by slow steamship communication gave passions on both sides a chance to cool. Lincoln gradually perceived that the North had on its hands two "white elephants," and despite the popularity of their seizure, he reluctantly decided to release them. Secretary of State Seward was at pains to sweeten the pill for the Ameri-

Outraged by the outcome of the Trent *affair,* Representative Lovejoy of Illinois, who "literally wept tears of vexation," proclaimed on the floor of Congress: "I hate the British government. . . . I now here publicly avow and record my inextinguishable hatred. . . . I mean to cherish it while I live, and to bequeath it as a legacy to my children when I die. And if I am alive when war with England comes, as sooner or later it must, for we shall never forget this humiliation, and if I can carry a musket in that war I will carry it."

can public. In a clever note he in effect congratulated the British on having accepted, at long last, the views for which the Republic had futilely fought them in the War of 1812.

Destructive Confederate "Pirates"

A dangerous development for the United States came in the autumn of 1862. The British cabinet, yielding to the urgings of Napoleon III, seemed about to join France in mediating between North and South, with consequent dangers of shooting. The Union "victory" at Antietam came as a bucket of cold water to such schemes, for Canada was vulnerable to Union bayonets and British shipping was exposed to Yankee privateers.

A new major crisis in Anglo-American relations arose over the unneutral building in England of Confederate commerce-raiders, notably the *Alabama*. These vessels were not warships within the meaning of loopholed British law, because they left their shipyards unarmed and picked up their guns elsewhere. The *Alabama* escaped in 1862 to the Portuguese Azores and there took on weapons and a crew from two English ships that followed her. Although flying the Confederate flag and officered by Confederates, she was manned by Britons and never entered a Confederate port. England was thus the chief naval base of the Confederacy.

The *Alabama* lighted the skies from Europe to the Far East with the burning hulks of the

Yankee merchantmen. In all, this "British pirate" captured over sixty vessels. Competing British shippers were delighted, while an angered North had to divert naval strength from its blockade for wild-goose chases. The barnacled *Alabama* finally accepted a challenge from a stronger Union cruiser off the coast of France in 1864 and was quickly destroyed. A picture of the battle, widely sold in the North, bore the words: "Built of English oak in an English yard, armed with English guns, manned by an English crew, and sunk in the English Channel."

As time passed, the shortsighted officials in London began to develop twinges of conscience. They were given no peace by the American minister, Charles Francis Adams, who persistently presented lists of sinkings and bills for damages by the British-built raider. The Foreign Office gradually perceived that it was sanctioning a dangerous precedent that might one day be used against Britain by a future foe—perhaps one without a navy (Ireland?) or even one without a seacoast. Fearing that provocation might push the Americans too far, London took drastic action in 1863. It openly violated its own leaky laws when it seized another raider being built for the South. Its action was clear evidence of a new determination to be truly neutral.

Confederate commerce-destroyers, chiefly British-built, captured in all more than 250 Yankee ships, including many whalers. The owners of several hundred others, fearing destruction, transferred them to foreign flags. Under existing federal laws, these could not be transferred back to American registry. Fortunately for the North, the *Alabama*s did not cripple the war effort, because British and other neutral shipping was available. But the American merchant marine, only recently the proud challenger of England, was riddled, and never fully recovered. Earnest citizens, deeply angered, talked openly of securing both revenge and recompense by seizing Canada when the war was over.

Charles Francis Adams (1807–1886) *Son of President John Quincy Adams, grandson of President John Adams, and father of author Henry Adams, he was himself widely regarded as of presidential timber, especially in 1872. His chief claim to distinction was his bold and dignified diplomacy in London during the Civil War. (Courtesy of the Fogg Art Museum, Harvard University.)*

Foreign Flare-Ups

A final Anglo-American crisis was touched off in 1863 by the Laird rams—two Confederate warships being constructed in Great Britain. Designed to destroy the wooden ships of the Union navy with their iron rams and large-caliber guns, they were far more dangerous than the swift and lightly armed *Alabama*. If delivered to the South, they probably would have sunk the blockading squadrons and then brought Northern cities under their fire. In angry retaliation, the North doubtless would have invaded Canada, and a full-dress war with Britain would have erupted.

There were no legal grounds for detaining the Laird rams, for their fraudulent papers indicated a non-Confederate purchaser. But Minister Adams took a hard line, warning that "this is war" if the rams were released. At the last minute the London government relented and bought the two ships for the Royal Navy. Everyone seemed satisfied—except the disappointed Confederates. Britain also eventually repented its sorry role in the *Alabama* business. It agreed in 1871 to submit the *Alabama* dispute to arbitration and in 1872 paid American claimants $15.5 million for damages caused by wartime commerce-raiders. On the London Foreign Office wall was hung the canceled draft for $15.5 million, as a warning to future ministries to be more careful.

American anger was also directed at Canada, where despite the vigilance of British authorities, Southern agents plotted to burn Northern cities. One Confederate raid into Vermont left three banks plundered and one American citizen dead. Hatred of England burned especially fiercely among Irish-Americans, and they unleashed their fury on Canada. A secret Irish brotherhood, the Fenians, raised several tiny "armies" of a few hundred green-shirted men and launched invasions of Canada, notably in the years 1866 and 1870. The Fenians' objective was to wring Irish freedom from the British by capturing Canada as their hostage. The Canadians condemned the Washington government for permitting such violations of neutrality, but the administration was hampered by the presence of so many Irish-American voters.

As fate would have it, two great nations emerged from the fiery furnace of the American Civil War. One was a reunited United States, the other was a united Canada. The British Parliament established the Dominion of Canada in 1867. It was partly designed to bolster the Canadians, both politically and psychologically, against the possible vengeance of the United States.

Still scheming to find a new French foothold in the New World, haughty Emperor Napoleon III of France dispatched a French army to occupy Mexico City in 1863. On the ruins of a crushed republic the following year, he enthroned an Austrian tool, the Archduke Maximilian, as emperor of Mexico. Both sending the army and installing Maximilian were done in flagrant violation of the Monroe Doctrine.

The North, as long as it was convulsed by war, pursued a walk-on-eggs policy toward France. But when the shooting stopped, Secretary of State Seward, speaking with the authority of nearly a million bayonets, prepared to march south. Napoleon realized that his costly gamble was doomed. He reluctantly took "French leave" of his ill-starred puppet in 1867, and Maximilian soon crumpled ingloriously before a Mexican firing squad. With his death the Monroe Doctrine took on new life.

Volunteers and Draftees: North and South

Ravenous, the gods of war demanded men—lots of men. Northern armies were at first manned solely by volunteers, with each state assigned a quota based on population. But in 1863, after volunteering had slackened off, Congress passed a federal conscription law for the first time on a nationwide scale in the United States. The provisions were grossly unfair to the poor. Rich boys, including young John D. Rockefeller, could hire substitutes to go in their places or purchase exemption outright by paying $300. "Three-hundred-dollar men" was the scornful epithet applied to these slackers. Draftees who did not have the necessary cash complained that their banditlike government demanded "three hundred dollars or your life."

The draft was especially damned in the Democratic strongholds of the North, notably in New York City. A frightful riot broke out in 1863, touched off largely by underprivileged and antiblack Irish-Americans who shouted, "Down with Lincoln!" and "Down with the draft!" For several days the city was at the mercy of a burning, drunken, pillaging mob,

The New York Draft Riot, 1863   Irish workers resented competition for jobs by "nagurs." The free blacks in turn called the Irish "white niggers." (Museum of the City of New York.)

and scores of lives were lost, including many lynched blacks. Elsewhere in the North conscription met with resentment and an occasional minor riot.

More than 90 percent of the Union troops were volunteers, since social and patriotic pressures to enlist were strong. As able-bodied men became scarcer, generous bounties for enlistment were offered by federal, state, and local authorities. An enterprising and moneywise volunteer might legitimately pocket more than $1000.

With money flowing so freely, an unsavory crew of "bounty brokers" and "substitute brokers" sprang up, at home and abroad. They combed the poorhouses of the British Isles and Western Europe; and many an Irishman or German was befuddled with whiskey and induced to enlist. A number of the slippery "bounty boys" deserted, volunteered elsewhere, and netted another handsome haul. The records reveal that one "bounty jumper" repeated his profitable operation thirty-two times. But desertion was by no means confined to "bounty jumpers." The rolls of the Union army recorded about 200,000 deserters of all classes, and the Confederate authorities were plagued with a problem of similar dimensions.

Like the North, the South relied mainly on volunteers. But since the Confederacy was much less populous, it scraped the bottom of its manpower barrel much more quickly. Quipsters observed that any man who could see lightning and hear thunder was judged fit for service. The Richmond regime, robbing both "cradle and grave" (ages 17 to 50), was forced to resort to conscription as early as April 1862, nearly a year earlier than the Union.

Confederate draft regulations also worked serious injustices. As in the North, a rich man could hire a substitute or purchase exemption. Slaveowners or overseers with twenty slaves might also claim exemption. These special privileges, later modified, made for bad feeling among the less prosperous, many of whom complained that this was a "a rich man's war but a poor man's fight." Why sacrifice one's life to save slavery? No large-scale draft riots broke out in the South, as in New York City. But the Confederate conscription agents often found it prudent to avoid those areas inhabited by sharpshooting mountain whites, who were branded "Tories," "traitors," and "Yankee-lovers."

Number of Men in Uniform at Date Given

DATE	UNION	CONFEDERATE
July 1861	186,751	112,040
January 1862	575,917	351,418
March 1862	637,126	401,395
January 1863	918,121	446,622
January 1864	860,737	481,180
January 1865	959,460	445,203

The Dollar Goes to War

Blessed with a lion's share of the wealth, the North rode through the financial breakers much more smoothly than the South. Excise taxes on tobacco and alcohol were substantially increased by Congress. An income tax was levied for the first time in the nation's experience; and although the rates were painlessly low by later standards, they netted millions of dollars.

Customs receipts likewise proved to be important revenue-raisers. Early in 1861, after enough antiprotection Southern members had seceded, Congress passed the Morrill Tariff Act, superseding the low Tariff of 1857. It increased the existing duties some 5 to 10 percent, boosting them to about the moderate level of the Walker Tariff of 1846. But these modest rates were soon pushed sharply upward by the necessities of war. The increases were designed partly to raise additional revenue and partly to provide more protection for the prosperous manufacturers who were being plucked by the new internal taxes. A protective tariff thus became identified with the Republican party, as American industrialists, predominantly Republicans, waxed fat on these welcome benefits.

The Washington Treasury also issued greenbacked paper money, totaling nearly $450 million at face value. This printing-press currency was inadequately supported by gold, and hence its value was determined by the nation's credit. Greenbacks thus fluctuated with the fortunes of Union arms and at one low point were worth only 39 cents on the gold dollar. The holders of the notes, victims of creeping inflation, were indirectly taxed as the value of the currency slowly withered in their hands.

Yet borrowing far outstripped both greenbacks and taxes as a money-raiser. The Federal Treasury netted $2,621,916,786 through the sale of bonds, which bore interest and which were payable at a later date. The modern technique of selling these issues to the people directly through "drives" and payroll deductions had not yet been devised. Accordingly, the Treasury was forced to market its bonds through the private banking house of Jay Cooke

and Company, which received a commission of three-eighths of 1 percent on all sales. With both profits and patriotism at stake, the bankers succeeded in making effective appeals to citizen purchasers.

A financial landmark of the war was the National Banking System, authorized by Congress in 1863. Launched partly as a stimulant to the sale of government bonds, it was also designed to establish a standard bank-note currency. (The country was then flooded with depreciated "rag money" issued by unreliable bankers.) Banks that joined the National Banking System could buy government bonds and issue sound paper money backed by them. The war-born National Banking Act thus turned out to be the first significant step taken toward a unified banking network since 1836, when the "monster" Bank of the United States was killed by Andrew Jackson. Spawned by the war, this new system continued to function for fifty years.

Taxation by Inflation

An impoverished South was beset by different financial problems. Customs duties were choked off as the coils of the Union blockade tightened. Large issues of Confederate bonds were sold at home and abroad, amounting to nearly $400 million. The Richmond regime also increased taxes sharply and imposed a 10 percent levy on farm produce. But in general the states' rights Southerners were vigorously opposed to heavy direct taxation by the central authority: only about 1 percent of the total income was raised in this way.

As revenue began to dry up, the Confederate government was forced to print blue-backed paper money with complete abandon. "Runaway inflation" occurred as Southern presses continued to grind out the poorly backed treasury notes, totaling in all more than $1 billion. One breakfast for three in Richmond in 1864 cost $141. The Confederate paper dollar finally sank to the point where it was worth only 1.6 cents when Lee surrendered. The extent to which the Southern currency melted away in the pockets

A contemporary (October 22, 1863) Richmond diary portrays the ruinous effects of inflation: "A poor woman yesterday applied to a merchant in Carey Street to purchase a barrel of flour. The price he demanded was $70. 'My God!' exclaimed she, 'how can I pay such prices? I have seven children; what shall I do?' 'I don't know, madam,' said he coolly, 'unless you eat your children.'"

of its holders was the extent to which those citizens were taxed in a roundabout way by their government. Tens of millions of dollars were thus quietly filched from Confederate wallets. Yet inflation did not ruin the South, as was commonly believed. Rather, an inflation of the currency, together with the levy on farm produce, kept the Confederacy going to the end.

"Shoddy" Millionaires in the North

Wartime prosperity in the North was little short of miraculous. The marvel is that a divided nation could fight a costly conflict for four long years and then emerge seemingly more prosperous than ever before. It is true that the early months after secession, with the stoppage of cotton imports and other dislocations, brought temporary depression. But the clouds soon gave way to the sunshine of military orders and warborn civilian prosperity.

New factories, sheltered by the friendly umbrella of the new protective tariffs, mushroomed forth. Soaring prices, resulting from inflation, unfortunately pinched the day laborer and the white-collar worker to some extent. But the manufacturers and businesspeople raked in "the fortunes of war."

The Civil War spawned a millionaire class for the first time in American history, though a few individuals of extreme wealth could have been found earlier. Many of these newly rich were noisy, gaudy, brassy, and given to extravagant living. Their emergence merely illustrates the truth that some gluttony and greed always mar

the devotion and self-sacrifice called forth by war. The story of speculators and peculators was roughly the same in both camps. But graft was more flagrant in the North than in the South, partly because there was more to steal.

Yankee "sharpness" appeared at its worst. Dishonest agents, putting profits above patriotism, palmed off aged and blind horses on government purchasers. Unscrupulous Northern manufacturers supplied shoes with cardboard soles and fast-disintegrating uniforms of reprocessed or "shoddy" wool, rather than virgin wool. Hence, the reproachful term "shoddy millionaires." One profiteer reluctantly admitted that his profits were "painfully large."

Newly invented laborsaving machinery enabled the North to expand economically, even though the cream of its manpower was being drained off by the fighting front. The sewing machine wrought wonders in fabricating uniforms and military footwear. Clattering mechanical reapers, which numbered about 250,000 by 1865, proved hardly less potent than thundering guns. They not only released tens of thousands of farm boys for the army but fed

"Nightmare of a War Profiteer" *A dead soldier forces on him the same poisonous food and drink with which he supplied the army. (Vanity Fair, 1861.)*

them while there. They produced vast surpluses of grain which, when sent abroad, helped dethrone King Cotton. They provided profits with which the North was able to buy munitions and supplies from abroad. They contributed to the feverish prosperity of the North—a prosperity that enabled the Union to weather the war with flying colors.

Other industries were humming. The discovery of petroleum gushers in 1859 had led to a rush of "Fifty-Niners" to Pennsylvania. The result was the birth of a new industry, with its "petroleum plutocracy" and "coal oil Johnnies." Pioneers continued to push westward during the war, altogether an estimated 300,000 souls. Major magnets were free gold nuggets and free land under the Homestead Act of 1862. Strong propellants were the federal draft agents. The only major Northern industry to suffer a crippling setback was the ocean-carrying trade, which fell prey to the *Alabama* and its sister raiders.

A Crushed Cotton Kingdom

Dismally different was the plight of the South, which had fought to exhaustion. The suffocation caused by the blockade, together with the destruction by invaders, took a terrible toll. Transportation collapsed. The South was even driven to the economic cannibalism of pulling up rails from the less-used lines to repair the main ones. Window weights were melted down into bullets; gourds replaced dishes; pins became so scarce that they were loaned with reluctance.

To the brutal end, the South revealed remarkable resourcefulness and spirit. Women buoyed up their menfolk, many of whom had seen enough of war at first hand to be heartily sick of it. A proposal was made by a number of women that they cut off their long hair and sell it abroad. But the project was not adopted, partly because of the blockade. The self-sacrificing women took pride in denying themselves the silks and satins of their Northern sisters. The chorus of a song, "The Southern Girl," touched a cheerful note:

The blockade produced acute shortages, including morphine for the wounded. One North Carolinian recalled his boyhood: "There was a poppy bed in every garden planted for this purpose, and when I was seven years old I worked daily for the soldiers, scraping the inspissated juice of the poppy from the bulbar ovaries which had been punctured a few days before, and, like everyone else, I worked under the eternal mandate, 'Don't taste it!' On some fifty poppy heads it was a morning's work to get a mass about as big as a small peanut."

So hurrah! hurrah! For Southern Rights, hurrah!
Hurrah! for the homespun dress the Southern ladies wear.

The Northern Captains of Industry had conquered the Southern Lords of the Manor. A crippled South left the capitalistic North free to work its own way, with high tariffs and other benefits. The industrial giants of the North, ushering in the full-fledged industrial revolution, were destined for increased dominance over American economic and political life. Hitherto the agrarian "slavocracy" of the South, by using sectional alliances, had partially checked the rising plutocracy of the North. Now cotton capitalism had lost out to industrial capitalism. The South of 1865 was rich in little but amputees, war heroes, ruins, and memories.

Limitations on Wartime Liberties

"Honest Abe" Lincoln, when inaugurated, laid his hand on the Bible and swore a solemn oath to uphold the Constitution. Then, driven by sheer necessity, he proceeded to tear a few holes in that hallowed document. He sagely concluded that if he did not do so, and patch the parchment later, there might not be a Constitution of a *united* United States to mend. The "rail-splitter" was no hairsplitter.

But such infractions were not, in general, sweeping. Congress, as is often true in time of crisis, generally accepted or confirmed the president's questionable acts. Lincoln, though accused of being a "Simple Susan Tyrant," did not believe that his ironhanded authority would continue, once the Union was preserved. As he pointedly remarked in 1863, a man suffering from "temporary illness" would not persist in feeding on bitter medicines for "the remainder of his healthful life."

Congress was not in session when war erupted, so Lincoln gathered the reins into his own hands. Brushing aside legal objections, he boldly proclaimed a blockade. (His action was later upheld by the Supreme Court.) He arbitrarily increased the size of the federal army—something that only Congress can do under the Constitution (see Art. I, Sec. VIII, para. 12). (Congress later approved.) He directed the secretary of the treasury to advance $2 million without appropriation or security to three private citizens for military purposes—a grave irregularity contrary to the Constitution (see Art.

> Lincoln, Kentucky-born like Jefferson Davis, was aware of Kentucky's crucial importance. In September 1861 he remarked: "I think to lose Kentucky is nearly the same as to lose the whole game. Kentucky gone, we cannot hold Missouri, nor, I think, Maryland. These all against us, and the job on our hands is too large for us. We would as well consent to separation at once, including the surrender of this capital [Washington]."

I, Sec. IX, par. 7). He suspended the precious privilege of the writ of habeas corpus, so that anti-Unionists might be summarily arrested. In taking this step, he defied a ruling by the chief justice that the safeguards of habeas corpus could be set aside only by authorization of Congress, as provided in the Constitution (see Art. I, Sec. IX, para. 2). Nearly two years later, in 1863, Congress acquiesced in the suspension.

Lincoln's regime was guilty of many other high-handed acts. For example, it arranged for "supervised" voting in the Border States. There the intimidated citizen, holding a colored ballot indicating his party preference, had to march between two lines of armed troops. The federal officials also ordered the suspension of certain newspapers and the arrest of their editors on grounds of obstructing the war.

Jefferson Davis was less able than Lincoln to exercise arbitrary power, mainly because of confirmed states' righters who revealed an intense spirit of localism. To the very end of the conflict the owners of horse-drawn vans in Petersburg, Virginia, prevented the joining of the incoming and outgoing tracks of a militarily vital railroad. The South seemed willing to lose the war before it would surrender local rights—and it did.

The Yankee Guy Fawkes *Lincoln is represented as destroying American liberties by the draft, the suspension of habeas corpus, and the Emancipation Proclamation. (London Fun, 1863.)*

The Curse of Copperheadism

Hundreds of Northern citizens were arrested by the military authorities, chiefly on charges of hindering the Union cause by preaching defeatism or peace-at-any-price-ism. Many were seized without a warrant and were held for pro-

The Copperhead Party *The cartoon shows the party in favor of a vigorous prosecution of peace. (Harper's Weekly, 1863.)*

longed periods without trial, as in czarist Russia. A large percentage of the persons thus abused were so-called Copperhead Democrats. The Copperheads were partisans who obstructed the war effort by disloyal talk—or worse—and they were named after the poisonous snake, which strikes without a warning rattle. Dubbed members of the "White Feather Party," the Copperheads accused the Lincolnites of urging "War to the knife, and the knife to the hilt" in this uncivil Civil War.

Notorious among the victims of autocratic arrest was a prominent Copperhead, Clement L. Vallandigham. This tempestuous character was an Ohio ex-congressman who possessed brilliant oratorical gifts and unusual talents for stirring up trouble. A Southern partisan, he publicly demanded an end to the "wicked and cruel" war. The civil courts in Ohio were open, and he should have been tried in them. But he was convicted by a military tribunal in 1863 for treasonable utterances and was then sentenced to prison. Lincoln decided that if Vallandigham liked the Confederates so much, he ought to be banished to their lines. This was done.

Vallandigham was not so easily silenced. Working his way to Canada, he ran for the governorship of Ohio on foreign soil and polled a substantial but insufficient vote. He returned to his own state before the war ended, and although he defied "King Lincoln" and spat upon a military decree, he was not further prosecuted. The strange case of Vallandigham inspired Edward Everett Hale to write his moving but fictional story of Philip Nolan, "The Man without a Country" (1863), which was immensely popular in the North and which helped stimulate devotion to the Union. Nolan was a young army officer found guilty of participation in the Aaron Burr plot of 1806. He had cried out in court, "Damn the United States! I wish I may never hear of the United States again!" For this outburst he was condemned to a life of complete exile on American warships.

Considering the hatreds aroused, civil liberties and constitutional rights fared rather well. Some of the power usurped by the chief executive was retained, but most of it was gradually restored to the courts and Congress after the shooting stopped. Wartime penalties on the whole were mild and pardons speedy. Thousands of unterrified and unmolested Copperhead Democrats openly denounced Lincoln as "the Illinois Ape," demanded an end to the "Nigger War," discouraged enlistments, and encouraged desertions.

Salmon P. Chase (1808–1873) *Chase was so conspicuously identified with antislavery in Ohio that he was known as "the Attorney General for Fugitive Slaves." He served with distinction during the Civil War as secretary of the treasury, in which capacity he inaugurated the National Banking System. (The Union League Club, New York.)*

Politics as Usual in 1864

Political infighting in the North added greatly to Lincoln's cup of woe. Factions within his own party, distrusting his ability, sought to tie his hands. Conspicuous among these critics was the group led by the overambitious Secretary of the Treasury Chase. The masterstroke of the anti-Lincoln Republicans was the creation of the meddlesome Congressional Committee on the Conduct of the War, which may have stirred up about as much trouble as it smoothed over. The extreme abolitionists, in addition, clamored for an immediate freeing of the slaves, regardless of the political and military consequences.

Most dangerous of all were the Northern Democrats. Deprived of the brains that had departed with the Southern wing, they were left with the taint of association with the seceders. A tragedy befell the Democrats—and the Union—when their gifted leader, Stephen A. Douglas, died of typhoid fever seven weeks after war began. Unshakably devoted to the Union, he probably could have kept much of his following on the straight and narrow path of loyalty.

Lacking a leader, the Democrats became badly divided. A large group of so-called War Democrats patriotically supported the Lincoln administration, but tens of thousands of Peace Democrats and regular Democrats did not. Many of the dissenters were outright Copperheads. They ranged all the way from those who wished the enemy Godspeed to those who favored a restored Union—but one restored by negotiation, not war.

Lincoln's precarious authority depended on his retaining Republican control of Congress. His majority was menaced by the Copperheads, who were especially strong in Ohio, Indiana, and Illinois, all of which contained many Southerners. Only with difficulty did the war governors of these states manage to keep them cooperating with Washington.

Lincoln Defeats McClellan at the Polls

Presidential elections come by the calendar and not by the crisis. As fate would have it, the election of 1864 fell most inopportunely in the midst of war.

The Republican party, fearing defeat, executed a clever maneuver. Joining with the War Democrats, it proclaimed itself to be the Union party. Thus the Republican party passed temporarily out of existence.

Lincoln's renomination at first encountered surprisingly strong opposition. Hostile factions whipped up considerable agitation to shelve homely "Old Abe" in favor of handsome Secretary of the Treasury Chase. Lincoln was accused of lacking force, of being overready to compromise, of not having won the war, and of having shocked many sensitive souls by his ill-timed and earthy jokes. ("Prince of Jesters," one

NORTHERN DEMOCRATS			REPUBLICANS
COPPER-HEADS	PEACE DEMO-CRATS	WAR DEMO-CRATS	

Union Party, 1864 *The shaded area represents the Union Party.*

journal called him.) But the "ditch Lincoln" move collapsed, and he was nominated by the Union party without serious dissent.

Lincoln's running mate was ex-tailor Andrew Johnson, a loyal War Democrat from Tennessee who had been a small slaveowner when the conflict began. He was placed on the Union party ticket to "sew up" the election by attracting War Democrats and the voters in the Border States, and not with proper regard for the possibility that Lincoln might die in office. Southerners and Copperheads alike condemned both candidates as birds of a feather: two ignorant, third-rate, boorish, backwoods politicians born in log cabins.

Embattled Democrats—regular and Copperhead—nominated the deposed and overcautious war hero, General McClellan. The Copperheads managed to force into the Democratic platform a plank denouncing the prosecution of the war as a failure. But McClellan, who could not otherwise have faced his old comrades-in-arms, repudiated this defeatist declaration.

The ensuing campaign was noisy and heated. The Democrats cried, "Old Abe removed McClellan. We'll now remove Old Abe." They also sang, "Mac Will Win the Union Back." The Union party supporters shouted for "Uncle Abe and Andy" and urged, "Vote as you shot." Their most effective slogan, growing out of a remark by Lincoln, was: "Don't swap horses in the middle of the river."

Lincoln's reelection was at first gravely in doubt. The war was going badly, as "Butcher" Grant continued to be bogged down in the Wilderness of Virginia. Lincoln himself gave way to despondency, fearing that political defeat was imminent. The anti-Lincoln Republicans, taking heart, started a new movement to "dump" Lincoln in favor of someone else.

But the atmosphere of gloom was changed electrically, as balloting day neared, by a succession of Northern victories. Admiral Farragut captured Mobile, Alabama, after defiantly shouting the now famous, "Damn the torpedoes! Go ahead." General Sherman seized

A Lincoln-Johnson Campaign Poster, 1864 *(New-York Historical Society.)*

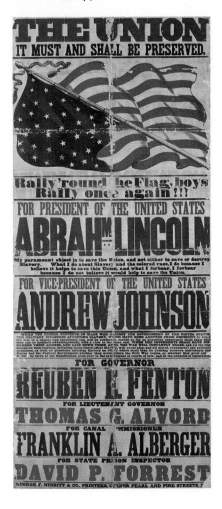

Presidential Election of 1864 (showing popular vote by county) *Lincoln also carried California, Oregon, and Nevada, but there was a considerable McClellan vote in each.*

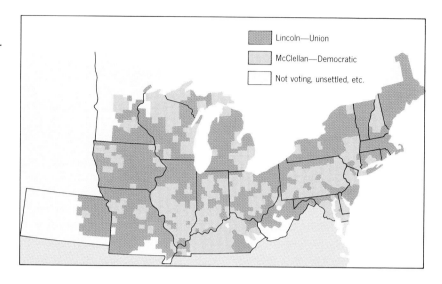

Lincoln—Union

McClellan—Democratic

Not voting, unsettled, etc.

Atlanta. General ("Little Phil") Sheridan laid waste the verdant Shenandoah Valley of Virginia so thoroughly that in his words "a crow could not fly over it without carrying his rations with him."

The president pulled through, but nothing more than necessary was left to chance. At election time many Northern soldiers were furloughed home to support Lincoln. One Pennsylvania veteran voted forty-nine times—once for himself and once for each absent member of his company. Other soldiers were permitted to cast their ballots at the front.

Lincoln, bolstered by the so-called "bayonet vote," vanquished General McClellan by 212 electoral votes to 21, with the loss of only Kentucky, Delaware, and New Jersey. But "Little Mac" ran a much closer race than the electoral count indicates. He netted a surprising 45 percent of the popular vote, 1,803,787 to Lincoln's 2,206,938, piling up much support in the Southerner-infiltrated states of the Old Northwest, in New York, and also in his native state of Pennsylvania.

One of the most crushing defeats suffered by the South was the defeat of the Northern Democrats in 1864. The removal of Lincoln was the last real hope for a Confederate victory, and the Southern soldiers would wishfully shout, "Hurrah for McClellan!" When Lincoln triumphed, desertions from the sinking Southern ship increased sharply.

The Martyrdom of Lincoln

On the night of April 14, 1865 (Good Friday), only five days after Lee's surrender, Ford's Theater in Washington witnessed its most sensational drama. A half-crazed, fanatically pro-Southern actor, John Wilkes Booth, slipped behind Lincoln as he sat in his box and shot him in the head. After lying unconscious all night, the Great Emancipator died the following morning. "Now he belongs to the ages," remarked the once-critical Secretary Stanton—probably the finest thing he ever said.

Lincoln expired in the arms of victory, at the very pinnacle of his fame. From the standpoint of his reputation, his death could not have been better timed if he had hired the assassin. A large number of his countrymen had not suspected his greatness, and many others had even doubted his ability. But his dramatic death helped to erase the memory of his shortcomings and caused his nobler qualities to stand out in clearer relief.

The full impact of Lincoln's death was not at once apparent to the South. Hundreds of bedraggled ex-Confederate soldiers cheered, as did some Southern civilians and Northern Copperheads, when they learned of the assassination. This reaction was only natural, because Lincoln had kept the war grinding on to the bitter end. If he had only been willing to stop the shooting, the South would have won.

As time wore on, increasing numbers of Southerners perceived that Lincoln's death was a calamity for them. Belatedly they recognized that his kindliness and moderation would have been the most effective shields between them and vindictive treatment by the victors. The assassination unfortunately increased the bitterness in the North, partly because of the fantastic rumor that Jefferson Davis had plotted it.

A few historians have argued that Andrew Johnson, now president-by-bullet, was crucified for Lincoln. The implication is that if the "railsplitter" had lived, he would have run into serious trouble, perhaps impeachment, at the hands of the embittered members of his own party who demanded harsh treatment of the South.

The crucifixion thesis does not stand up under scrutiny. Lincoln no doubt would have clashed with Congress; in fact, he had already found himself in some hot water. The legislative branch normally struggles to win back the power that has been wrested from it by the executive in time of crisis. But the surefooted and

The powerful London Times, *voice of the upper classes, had generally criticized Lincoln during the war, especially after the Emancipation Proclamation of 1862. He was then condemned as "a sort of moral American Pope" destined to be "Lincoln the Last." When the president was shot, the* Times *reversed itself (April 29, 1865): "Abraham Lincoln was as little of a tyrant as any man who ever lived. He could have been a tyrant had he pleased, but he never uttered so much as an ill-natured speech. . . . In all America there was, perhaps, not one man who less deserved to be the victim of this revolution than he who has just fallen."*

experienced Lincoln could hardly have blundered into the same quicksands that engulfed Johnson. Lincoln was a victorious president, and there is no arguing with victory. Enjoying battle-tested powers of leadership, Lincoln possessed in full measure tact, sweet reasonableness, and an uncommon amount of common

The Burning of Richmond, April, 1865   *The proud Confederate capital, after holding out against repeated Union assaults, was evacuated and burned in the final days of the war. (Library of Congress.)*

sense. Andrew Johnson, hot-tempered and impetuous, lacked all of these priceless qualities.

Ford's Theater, with its tragic murder of Lincoln, set the stage for the terrible ordeal of Reconstruction.

The Aftermath of the Nightmare

The Civil War took a grisly toll in gore, about as much as all of America's subsequent wars combined. Over 600,000 men died in action or of disease, and in all over a million were killed or seriously wounded. To its lasting hurt, the white South lost the cream of its young manhood and potential leadership. In addition, tens of thousands of babies went unborn because potential fathers were at the front.

Direct monetary costs of the conflict totaled about $15 billion. But this colossal figure does not include continuing expenses, such as pensions and interest on the national debt. The intangible costs—dislocations, disunities, wasted energies, lowered ethics, blasted lives, bitter memories, and burning hates—cannot be calculated.

The greatest constitutional decision of the century, in a sense, was written in blood and handed down at Appomattox Court House, near which Lee surrendered. The extreme states' righters were crushed. The national government, rewelded in the fiery furnace of war, emerged unbroken. Nullification and secession, those twin nightmares of previous decades, were laid to rest.

Beyond doubt the Civil War—the nightmare of the Republic—was the supreme test of American democracy. It finally answered the question, in the words of Lincoln at Gettysburg, whether a nation dedicated to such principles "can long endure." The preservation of democratic ideals, though not an officially announced war aim, was subconsciously one of the major objectives of the North.

Prisoners from the Front   *This celebrated painting of 1866 by Winslow Homer reflected the painter's first-hand observations of the war. He brilliantly captured the enduring depths of sectional animosity. The Union officer somewhat disdainfully asserts his command of the situation; the beaten and disarmed Confederates exhibit an out-at-the-elbows pride and defiance. (The Metropolitan Museum of Art. Gift of Mrs. Frank B. Porter, 1922.)*

Victory for Union arms also provided inspiration to the champions of democracy and liberalism the world over. The great English Reform Bill of 1867, under which Britain became a true political democracy, was passed two years after the Civil War ended. American democracy had proved itself, and its success was an additional argument used by the disfranchised British masses in securing similar blessings for themselves.

The "Lost Cause" of the South was lost, but few Americans today would argue that the end result was not for the best. America was again united physically, though for many years still divided spiritually by the passions of war. With the shameful cancer of slavery sliced away by the sword, free labor was further dignified by the removal of servile competition. Grave dangers were averted, including constant friction and conflict between North and South, each bristling with guns. The Monroe Doctrine, as foreigners could readily observe, took on more muscle. A strong and united nation was thus left free to fulfill its destiny as the overshadowingly powerful Republic of the hemisphere— and ultimately of the world.

Varying Viewpoints

When the Civil War ended, slavery was officially defunct, secession was a dead issue, and industrial growth was surging forward. Charles Beard later hailed the war as the "Second American Revolution," because it had transformed the legal and institutional structure of government and placed the levers of power firmly in the hands of a new business class.

But did the bloody conflict neatly bisect the nation's history? In recent years many scholars have questioned the concept that the war constituted a dramatic turning point. Slavery may have formally disappeared, but blacks remained a scandalously subordinated social group. Regional differences persisted, even down to the present day. Thomas Cochran has even argued that the Civil War may have *retarded* overall industrialization. As for the rising commercial class of the postwar "Gilded Age," many historians now point to its antecedents in both the Whig and Jacksonian movements. History, it seems, is a mighty stream, which in time partially submerges even momentous events like the Civil War beneath the surface of its relentless flow.

Select Readings

Primary Source Documents

The Constitution of the Confederacy* (1861) makes an interesting contrast to the United States Constitution. Two diaries that describe life behind the Confederate lines are those of John B. Jones, published as Earl S. Miers, ed., *A Rebel War Clerk's Diary** (1958), and Paul B. Barringer, *The Natural Bent** (1949). Lincoln's Gettysburg Address (1863) (in Henry Steele Commager, *Documents of American History*) poetically proclaims the president's highest war aims, as does his Second Inaugural Address (1865), in Roy P. Basler, ed., *The Collected Works of Abraham Lincoln* (1953), Vol. VIII, pp. 332–333.

Secondary Sources

See the references for the previous chapter, especially those by James M. McPherson and Allan Nevins. The best one-volume biography is Stephen B. Oates, *With Malice toward None: The Life of*

Abraham Lincoln (1977). Home-front politics are treated in James A. Rawley, *The Politics of Union* (1974), and in Joel Silbey, *A Respectable Minority: The Democratic Party in the Civil War Era* (1977). See also Jean H. Baker, *Affairs of Party: The Political Culture of the Northern Democrats in the Mid–Nineteenth Century* (1983). Lincoln's problems are analyzed in LaWanda Cox, *Lincoln and Black Freedom* (1981); William B. Hesseltine, *Lincoln and the War Governors* (1948); and T. Harry Williams, *Lincoln and the Radicals* (1941). For a different view of the same subject, see Hans L. Trefousse, *The Radical Republicans: Lincoln's Vanguard for Racial Justice* (1969). Richard N. Current, *The Lincoln Nobody Knows* (1958), and David Donald, *Lincoln Reconsidered* (1956), offer interesting insights. Eugene C. Murdoch analyzes the military draft in the North in *One Million Men* (1971), while Adrian Cook treats an important by-product of the draft, the New York City riots, in *Armies of the Street* (1974). Mary E. Massey presents the interesting story of women in the Civil War in *Bonnet Brigades* (1966); that topic also figures in Anne Firor Scott's *The Southern Lady* (1970). On the Confederacy, see Charles P. Roland, *The Confederacy* (1960), and Emory M. Thomas, *The Confederate Nation, 1861–1865* (1979). Economic matters are handled in Ralph L. Andreano, ed., *The Economic Impact of the American Civil War* (1962), and David T. Gilchrist and W. David Lewis, eds., *Economic Change in the Civil War Era* (1965). Two useful anthologies are David Donald, ed., *Why the North Won the Civil War* (1960), and Robert P. Swierenga, ed., *Beyond the Civil War Synthesis: Political Essays on the Civil War Era* (1975). The war's literary legacy is keenly analyzed in Edmund Wilson's classic *Patriotic Gore* (1962) and in Daniel Aaron's *The Unwritten War: American Writers and the Civil War* (1973). For a fascinating discussion of Northern intellectuals and the conflict, consult George M. Frederickson, *The Inner Civil War* (1965).

25

The Ordeal of Reconstruction

> With malice toward none, with charity for all, with firmness in
> the right as God gives us to see the right, let us strive on to
> finish the work we are in, to bind up the nation's wounds, to
> care for him who shall have borne the battle and for his widow
> and orphan, to do all which may achieve and cherish a just
> and lasting peace among ourselves and with all nations.
>
> Abraham Lincoln, Second Inaugural, March 4, 1865

The Problems of Peace

The battle was done, the buglers silent. Bone-weary and bloodied, the American people, North and South, now faced the staggering challenges of peace. Four questions loomed large. How would the South, physically devastated by war and socially revolutionized by emancipation, be rebuilt? How would the liberated blacks fare as free men and women? How would the Southern states be reintegrated into the Union? And who would direct the process of Reconstruction—the Southern states themselves, the president, or the Congress?

Other questions also clamored for answers. What should be done with the captured Confederate ringleaders, all of whom were liable to charges of treason? During the war a popular Northern song had been "Hang Jeff Davis to a Sour Apple Tree," and even innocent children had lisped it. Davis was temporarily clapped into irons during the early days of his two-year imprisonment. But he and his fellow "conspirators" were finally released, partly because the odds were that no Virginia jury would convict them. All rebel leaders were finally pardoned by President Johnson as sort of a Christmas present in 1868. But Congress did not remove all

Richmond Devastated *Charleston, Atlanta, and other Southern cities looked much the same, resembling bombed-out Berlin and Munich in 1945. (Library of Congress.)*

remaining civil disabilities until thirty years later and only posthumously restored Davis's citizenship more than a century later.

Dismal indeed was the picture presented by the war-racked South when the rattle of musketry faded. Not only had an age perished, but a civilization had collapsed, in both its economic and its social structure. The moonlight-and-magnolia Old South, largely imaginary in any case, had forever gone with the wind.

Handsome cities of yesteryear, such as Charleston and Richmond, were rubble-strewn and weed-choked. An Atlantan returned to his once-fair hometown and remarked, "Hell has laid her egg, and right here it hatched."

Economic life had creaked to a halt. Banks and business houses had locked their doors, ruined by runaway inflation. Factories were smokeless, silent, dismantled. The transportation system had broken down completely. Before the war, five different railroad lines had converged on Columbia, South Carolina; now the nearest connected track was 29 miles (47 kilometers) away. Efforts to untwist the rails corkscrewed by Sherman's soldiers proved bumpily unsatisfactory.

Agriculture—the economic lifeblood of the South—was almost hopelessly crippled. Once-white cotton fields now yielded a lush harvest of nothing but green weeds. Seed was scarce, and livestock had been driven off by plundering Yankees. Pathetic instances were reported of men hitching themselves to plows, while women and children gripped the handles. Not until 1870 did the seceded states produce as large a cotton crop as that of the fateful year 1860, and much of that came from new acreage in the Southwest.

A "Jeff Davis Necktie" *A twisted iron rail after having been heated in a Yankee bonfire.*

The princely planter aristocrats were humbled by the war—at least temporarily. Reduced to proud poverty, they faced charred and gutted mansions, lost investments, and almost worthless land. Their investment of more than $2 billion in slaves, their primary form of wealth, had evaporated with emancipation.

Beaten but unbent, many high-spirited white Southerners remained dangerously defiant. They cursed the "damnyankees" and spoke of "your government" in Washington, instead of "our government." One Southern bishop refused to pray for President Andrew Johnson, though Johnson proved to be in sore need of divine guidance. Conscious of no crime, these former Confederates continued to believe that their view of secession was correct and that the "lost cause" was still a just war. One popular anti-Union song ran:

> I'm glad I fought agin her, I only wish we'd
> won,
> And I ain't axed any pardon for anything I've
> done.

Such attitudes boded ill for the prospects of painlessly binding up the Republic's wounds.

Unfettered Freedmen

Confusion abounded in the still-smoldering South about the precise meaning of "freedom" for blacks. Emancipation took effect haltingly and unevenly in different parts of the conquered Confederacy, and in some regions planters stubbornly protested that slavery was legal until state legislatures or the Supreme Court might act. Newspapers in Mississippi earnestly discussed *gradual* emancipation. For many bondsmen, the shackles of slavery were not struck off in a single mighty blow; long-suffering blacks often had to struggle out of their chains link by link.

The variety of responses to emancipation, by whites as well as blacks, illustrated the sometimes startling complexity of the master-slave relationship. Unbending loyalty to "ole Massa" prompted many slaves to help their owners resist the liberating Union armies. Blacks blocked the door of the "big house" with their bodies or stashed the plantation silverware under mattresses in their own humble huts, where it would be safe from the plundering "bluebellies." On other plantations, pent-up bitterness burst violently forth on the day of liberation. A group of Virginia slaves laid twenty lashes on the back of their former master—a painful dose of his own favorite medicine. Newly emancipated slaves sometimes eagerly accepted the invitation of Union troops to join in the pillaging of their master's possessions. One freedman said that he felt entitled to steal a chicken or two, since the whites had robbed him of his labor and his children.

Emancipation followed by re-enslavement, or worse, was the bewildering lot of many blacks, as Union armies marched in and out of various localities. A North Carolina slave estimated that

> Carl Schurz described a Fourth of July affair in Savannah, Georgia, in 1865: "The colored firemen of this city desired to parade their engine on the anniversary of our independence. . . . In the principal street of the city the procession was attacked with clubs and stones by a mob . . . and by a crowd of boys swearing at the d———d niggers. The colored firemen were knocked down, some of them severely injured, their engine was taken away from them, and the peaceable procession dispersed."

he had celebrated emancipation about twelve times. As blacks in one Texas county flocked to the free soil of the liberated county next door, their owners bushwacked them with rifle fire as they swam for freedom across the river that marked the county line. The next day, trees along the riverbank were bent with swinging corpses—a grisly warning to others dreaming of liberty.

Prodded by the bayonets of Yankee armies of occupation, all masters were eventually forced to recognize their slaves' permanent freedom. The once-commanding planter would assemble his former human chattels in front of the porch of the "big house" and announce their liberty. This "Day of Jubilo" was the occasion of wild rejoicing. Tens of thousands of blacks naturally took to the roads. They sought long-separated loved ones, as formalizing a "slave marriage" was the first goal of many newly free men and women. Others traveled in search of economic opportunity in the towns or in the still-wild West. Many moved simply to test their new freedom.

Desperately trying to bootstrap themselves up from slavery, blacks assembled in "Conventions of Freedmen" to fight to make their freedom a reality. Led by ministers of God and freeborn blacks from the North, these conventions expressed surprisingly moderate views. But moderation could not guarantee a warm reception by embittered white Southerners. The freed blacks were going to need all the friends—and the power—they could find in Washington.

The Freedmen's Bureau

Abolitionists had long preached that slavery was a degrading institution. Now the emancipators had to face the brutal truth that the former slaves were in many ways indeed degraded. The freedmen were overwhelmingly unskilled, unlettered, without property or money, and with scant knowledge of how to survive as free persons. To cope with this problem throughout the conquered South, Congress created the Freedmen's Bureau in 1865.

On paper at least, the bureau was intended to be a kind of primitive welfare agency. It was to provide food, clothing, and education both to

Free at Last   *A black family in South Carolina photographed just after emancipation. Three generations are apparently present here, suggesting the cohesiveness and endurance of the Afro-American family, despite the harshness of slavery. (Library of Congress.)*

Primary School for Freedmen in Vicksburg, Mississippi, 1866 *Note the wide range of ages. (The Granger Collection.)*

freedmen and to white refugees. It was also authorized to distribute up to forty acres of abandoned or confiscated land to black settlers. Heading the bureau was a warmly sympathetic friend of the blacks, Union General Oliver O. Howard, who later founded and served as president of Howard University in Washington, D.C.

The bureau achieved its greatest successes in education. It taught an estimated 200,000 black folk how to read. Many former slaves had a passion for learning, partly because they wanted to close the gap between themselves and the whites and partly because they longed to read the Word of God. In one elementary class in North Carolina sat four generations of the same family, ranging from a six-year-old tot to a seventy-five-year-old grandmother.

But in other areas the Bureau's accomplishments were meager—or even mischievous. It distributed virtually no land. Its local administrators often collaborated with planters in expelling blacks from towns and cajoling them into signing labor contracts to work for their former masters. Yet the white South resented the bureau as a meddlesome federal interloper that threatened to upset white racial dominance. President Andrew Johnson, who shared the white-supremacist views of most white Southerners, repeatedly tried to kill it, and it expired in 1872.

Johnson: The Tailor President

Few presidents have ever been faced with a more perplexing sea of troubles than that confronting Andrew Johnson. What manner of man was this medium-built, dark-eyed, black-haired Tennessean, now chief executive by virtue of the bullet that killed Lincoln?

No citizen, not even Lincoln, has ever reached the White House from humbler beginnings. Born to impoverished parents in North Carolina and early orphaned, Johnson never attended school but was apprenticed to a tailor at age ten. Ambitious to get ahead, he taught himself to read, and later his wife taught him to write and do simple arithmetic. Like many another self-made man, he was inclined to overpraise his maker.

President Andrew Johnson (1808–1875) An "accidental president," Andrew Johnson was the only chief executive to be impeached by the House, though narrowly acquitted by the Senate. A former U.S. senator from Tennessee, he was reelected in 1875 to the Senate that had formally tried him seven years earlier. As he said in a public speech in 1866: "I love my country. Every public act of my life testifies that is so. Where is the man who can put his finger upon one act of mine . . . to prove the contrary." (Library of Congress.)

Democrats and other pro-Southern elements, and Johnson, a Democrat, seemed to be the ideal man. Unfortunately, he appeared at the vice-presidential inaugural ceremonies the following March in a scandalous condition. He had recently been afflicted with typhoid fever, and although not known as a heavy drinker, he was urged by his friends to take a stiff bracer of whiskey. This he did—with disgraceful results.

"Old Andy" Johnson was no doubt a man of parts—unpolished parts. He was intelligent, able, forceful, and gifted with homespun honesty. Steadfastly devoted to duty and to the people, he was a dogmatic champion of states' rights and the Constitution. He would often present a copy of the document to visitors, and he was buried with one as a pillow.

Yet the man who had raised himself from the tailor's bench to the president's chair was a misfit. A Southerner who did not understand the North, a Tennessean who had earned the distrust of the South, a Democrat who had

Johnson as a Parrot He was constantly invoking the Constitution. (Harper's Weekly.)

Johnson early became identified with politics in Tennessee, to which he had moved when seventeen years old. He shone as an impassioned champion of the poor whites against the planter aristocrats, although he himself ultimately owned a few slaves. He excelled as a two-fisted stump speaker before angry and heckling crowds, among whom on occasion he could hear a pistol being cocked. Elected to Congress, he attracted much favorable attention in the North (but not the South) when he refused to secede with his own state. After Tennessee was partially "redeemed" by Union armies, he was appointed war governor and served courageously in an atmosphere of danger.

Destiny next thrust Johnson into the vice-presidency. Lincoln's Union party in 1864 needed to attract support from the War never been accepted by the Republicans, a president who had never been elected to the office, he was not at home in a Republican White House. Hotheaded, contentious, and stubborn, he was the wrong man in the wrong place at the wrong time. A Reconstruction policy devised by the angels might well have failed in his tactless hands.

Presidential Reconstruction

Even before the shooting war had ended, the political war over Reconstruction had begun. Abraham Lincoln believed that the Southern states had never legally withdrawn from the Union. Their formal restoration to the Union would therefore be relatively simple. Accordingly, Lincoln in 1863 proclaimed his "10 percent" Reconstruction plan. It decreed that a state could be reintegrated into the Union when 10 percent of its voters in the presidential election of 1860 had taken an oath of allegiance to the United States and pledged to abide by emancipation. The next step would be formal erection of a state government. Lincoln would then recognize the purified regime.

Lincoln's proclamation provoked a sharp reaction in Congress, where Republicans feared the restoration of the planter aristocracy to power and the possible re-enslavement of the blacks. Republicans therefore rammed through Congress in 1864 the Wade-Davis Bill, which required that 50 percent of a state's voters take the oath of allegiance and demanded stronger safeguards for emancipation than Lincoln's as the price of readmission. Lincoln "pocket-vetoed" this bill by refusing to sign it after Congress had adjourned. Republicans were outraged. They refused to seat delegates from Louisiana after that state had reorganized its government in accordance with Lincoln's 10 percent plan in 1864.

The controversy surrounding the Wade-Davis Bill had revealed deep differences between the president and Congress. Unlike Lincoln, many in Congress insisted that the seceders had indeed left the Union—had "committed suicide" as republican states—and

had therefore forfeited all their rights. They could be readmitted only as "conquered provinces" on such conditions as Congress should decree.

This episode further revealed differences among Republicans. Two factions were emerging. The majority moderate group tended to agree with Lincoln that the seceded states should be restored to the Union as simply and swiftly as reasonable—though on Congress's terms, not the president's. The minority radical group believed that the South should suffer more severely for its sins. Before the South should be restored, the radicals wanted its social structure uprooted, the haughty planters punished, and the helpless blacks protected by federal power.

Some of the radicals were secretly pleased when the assassin's bullet felled Lincoln, for the martyred president had shown tenderness toward the South. Spiteful "Andy" Johnson, who shared their hatred for the planter aristocrats, would presumably also share their desire to reconstruct the South with a rod of iron.

Johnson soon disillusioned them. He agreed with Lincoln that the seceded states had never legally been outside the Union. Thus, he quickly recognized several of Lincoln's 10 percent governments, and on May 29, 1865, he issued his own Reconstruction proclamation. It disfranchised certain leading Confederates, in-

Before President Johnson softened his Southern policy, his views were radical. Speaking on April 21, 1865, he declared: "It is not promulgating anything that I have not heretofore said to say that traitors must be made odious, that treason must be made odious, that traitors must be punished and impoverished. They must not only be punished, but their social power must be destroyed. If not, they will still maintain an ascendancy, and may again become numerous and powerful; for, in the words of a former Senator of the United States, 'When traitors become numerous enough, treason becomes respectable.'"

cluding those with taxable property worth more than $20,000, though they might petition him for personal pardons. It called for special state conventions, which were required to repeal the ordinances of secession, repudiate all Confederate debts, and ratify the slave-freeing Thirteenth Amendment. States that complied with these conditions, Johnson declared, would be readmitted.

Johnson, savoring his dominance over the high-toned aristocrats who now begged his favor, granted pardons in abundance. Bolstered by the political resurrection of the planter elite, the recently rebellious states moved rapidly in the second half of 1865 to organize governments. But as the pattern of the new governments became clear, Republicans of all stripes grew furious.

The Baleful Black Codes

Among the first acts of the new Southern regimes sanctioned by Johnson was the passage of the iron-toothed Black Codes. These laws were designed to regulate the affairs of the emancipated blacks, much as the slave statutes had done in pre–Civil War days. The Black Codes aimed, first of all, to ensure a stable labor supply. The crushed Cotton Kingdom could not

Black Huts at the Trent River Settlement, North Carolina *(Harper's Weekly, June 9, 1866.)*

Early in 1866 one congressman quoted a Georgian: "The blacks eat, sleep, move, live, only by the tolerance of the whites, who hate them. The blacks own absolutely nothing but their bodies; their former masters own everything, and will sell them nothing. If a black man draws even a bucket of water from a well, he must first get the permission of a white man, his enemy. . . . If he asks for work to earn his living, he must ask it of a white man; and the whites are determined to give him no work, except on such terms as will make him a serf and impair his liberty."

rise from its weeds until the fields were once again put under hoe and plow—and many whites feared that black field hands and plow drivers would not work unless forced to do so.

Severe penalties were therefore imposed by the codes on blacks who "jumped" their labor contracts, which usually committed them to work for the same employer for one year, and generally at pittance wages. Violators could be made to forfeit back wages or could be forcibly dragged back to work by a paid "Negro-catcher." In Mississippi the captured freedmen could be fined and then hired out to pay their fines—an arrangement that closely resembled slavery itself.

The codes also sought to restore as nearly as possible the pre-emancipation system of race relations. Freedom was legally recognized, as were some other privileges, such as the right to marry. But all the codes forbade a black to serve on a jury; some even barred blacks from renting or leasing land. A black could be punished for "idleness" by being sentenced to work on a chain gang. Nowhere were blacks allowed to vote.

These oppressive laws mocked the ideal of freedom, so recently purchased by buckets of blood. The Black Codes imposed terrible burdens on the unfettered blacks, struggling against ignorance and poverty to make their way as free persons. Thousands of impoverished former slaves began to slip into the status of sharecrop farmers, as did many of the landless whites. The luckless sharecroppers gradually sank into a morass of virtual peonage and remained there for generations. Formerly slaves to masters, countless blacks as well as poorer whites became virtual slaves to the soil and to their creditors.

The Black Codes made an ugly impression in the North. If the former slaves were being re-enslaved, people asked one another, had not the Boys in Blue spilled their blood in vain? Had the North really won the war?

Congressional Reconstruction

These questions grew more insistent when the congressional delegations from the newly reconstituted Southern states presented themselves in the Capitol in December 1865. To the shock and disgust of the Republicans, many former Confederate leaders were on hand to claim their seats.

The appearance of these ex-rebels was a natural but costly blunder. Voters of the South, seeking able representatives, had turned instinctively to their experienced statesmen. But most of the Southern leaders were tainted by active association with the "lost cause." Among them were four former Confederate generals, five colonels, and various members of the Richmond cabinet and Congress. Worst of all, there was the shrimpy but brainy Alexander Stephens, ex-vice-president of the Confederacy, still under indictment for treason.

The presence of these "whitewashed rebels" infuriated the Republicans in Congress. The war had been fought to restore the Union, but not on these kinds of terms. The Republicans were in no hurry to embrace their former enemies—virtually all of them Democrats—in the chambers of the Capitol. While the South had been "out" from 1861 to 1865, the Republicans in Congress had enjoyed a relatively free hand. They had passed much legislation that favored the North, such as the Morrill Tariff, the Pacific Railroad Act, and the Homestead Act. Now many Republicans balked at giving up this political advantage. On the first day of the congressional session, December 4, 1865, they banged shut the door in the face of the newly elected Southern delegations.

Looking to the future, the Republicans were alarmed to realize that a restored South would be stronger than ever in national politics. Before the war a black slave had counted as three-fifths of a person in apportioning congressional representation. Now the slave was five-fifths of a person. Eleven Southern states had seceded and been subdued by force of arms. But now, owing to full counting of free blacks, the rebel states were entitled to twelve more votes in Congress, and twelve more presidential electoral votes, than they had previously enjoyed. Again, angry voices in the North raised the cry: Who won the war?

Republicans had good reason to fear that ultimately they might be elbowed aside. Southerners might join hands with Democrats in the North and win control of Congress or maybe even the White House. If this happened, they could perpetuate the Black Codes, perhaps even formally re-enslave the blacks. They could dismantle the economic program of the Republican party by lowering tariffs, rerouting the transcontinental railroad, repealing the free-farm Homestead Act, possibly even repudiating the national debt. President Johnson thus deeply provoked the congressional Republicans when he announced on December 6, 1865, that the recently rebellious states had satisfied his conditions and that in his view the Union was now restored.

Johnson Clashes with Congress

A clash between president and Congress was now inevitable. It exploded into the open in February 1866, when the president vetoed a bill (later repassed) extending the life of the controversial Freedmen's Bureau.

Aroused, the Republicans swiftly struck back. In March 1866 they passed the Civil Rights Bill, which conferred on the blacks the privilege of American citizenship and struck at the Black Codes. President Johnson resolutely vetoed this forward-looking measure on constitutional grounds, but in April congressmen

An Inflexible President *This Republican cartoon shows Johnson knocking blacks out of the Freedmen's Bureau by his veto. (Thomas Nast,* Harper's Weekly, *1866.)*

gress assumed the dominant role in running the government. One critic called Johnson "the dead dog of the White House."

The Republicans now undertook to rivet the principles of the Civil Rights Bill into the Constitution as the Fourteenth Amendment. They feared that the Southerners might one day win control of Congress and repeal the hated law. The proposed amendment, as approved by Congress and sent to the states in June 1866, was sweeping. It (1) conferred civil rights, including citizenship but excluding the franchise, on the freedmen; (2) reduced proportionately the representation of a state in Congress and in the Electoral College if it denied the blacks the ballot; (3) disqualified from federal and state office former Confederates who as federal officeholders had once sworn "to support the Constitution of the United States"; and (4) guaranteed the federal debt, while repudiating all Confederate debts. (See text of Fourteenth Amendment in the Appendix.)

The radical faction was disappointed that the Fourteenth Amendment did not grant the right to vote, but all Republicans were agreed that no state should be welcomed back into the Union fold without first ratifying the Fourteenth Amendment. Yet President Johnson advised the Southern states to reject it, and all of the "sinful eleven," except Tennessee, defiantly spurned the amendment. Their spirit was reflected in a Southern song:

> And I don't want no pardon for what I was or
> am,
> I won't be reconstructed and I don't give a
> damn.

steamrollered it over his veto—something they repeatedly did henceforth. The hapless president, dubbed "Sir Veto" and "Andy Veto," had his presidential wings clipped short, as Con-

Principal Reconstruction Proposals and Plans

YEAR	PROPOSAL OR PLAN
1864–1865	Lincoln's 10 percent proposal
1865–1866	Johnson's version of Lincoln's proposal
1866–1867	Congressional plan: 10 percent plan with Fourteenth Amendment
1867–1877	Congressional plan of military Reconstruction: Fourteenth Amendment plus black suffrage, later established nationwide by Fifteenth Amendment

The Reconstruction Dose   This Republican cartoon shows Johnson as a bad boy urging the South to reject the medicine with which Dr. Congress, backed up by Mrs. Columbia, is trying to restore her health. (Frank Leslie's Illustrated Newspaper, 1867.)

Swinging 'Round the Circle with Johnson

As 1866 lengthened, the battle grew between the Congress and the president. The root of the controversy was Johnson's "10-percent" governments that had passed the most severe Black Codes. Congress had tried to temper the worst features of the codes by extending the life of the embattled Freedmen's Bureau and passing the Civil Rights Bill. Both measures Johnson had vetoed. Now the issue was whether Reconstruction was to be carried on with or without the drastic Fourteenth Amendment. The Republicans would settle for nothing less.

The crucial congressional elections of 1866—more crucial than some presidential elections—were fast approaching. President Johnson was naturally eager to escape from the clutch of Congress by securing a majority favorable to his soft-on-the-South policy. Invited to dedicate a Chicago monument to Stephen A. Douglas, he undertook to speak at various cities en route in support of his views.

Johnson's famous "swing around the circle," beginning in the late summer of 1866, was a seriocomedy of errors. The president delivered a series of "give 'em hell" speeches, in which he accused the radicals in Congress of having planned large-scale antiblack riots and murder in the South. As he spoke, hecklers hurled insults at him. Reverting to his stump-speaking days in Tennessee, he shouted back angry retorts, amid cries of "You be damned" and "Don't get mad, Andy." The dignity of his high office sank to a new low, as the old charges of drunkenness were revived.

As a vote-getter, Johnson was highly successful—for the opposition. His inept speechmaking heightened the cry "Stand by Congress" against the "Tailor of the Potomac." When the ballots were counted, the Republicans had rolled up more than a two-thirds majority in both Houses of Congress.

Republican Principles and Programs

The Republicans now had a veto-proof Congress and virtually unlimited control of Reconstruction policy. But moderates and radicals still disagreed over the best course to pursue in the South.

The radicals in the Senate were led by the courtly and principled idealist Charles Sumner, now recovered from his prewar caning on the Senate floor, who tirelessly labored not only for black freedom but for racial equality. In the House the most powerful radical was Thaddeus Stevens, crusty and vindictive congressman from Pennsylvania. Seventy-four years old in 1866, he was a curious figure, with a protruding lower lip, a heavy black wig covering his bald head, and a deformed foot. An unswerving friend of blacks, he had defended runaway slaves without fee and, before dying, insisted on burial in a black cemetery. His affectionate

Representative Thaddeus Stevens, in a congressional speech on January 3, 1867, urged the ballot for blacks out of concern for them and out of bitterness against the whites: "I am for Negro suffrage in every rebel state. If it be just, it should not be denied; if it be necessary, it should be adopted; if it be a punishment to traitors, they deserve it."

devotion to blacks was matched by his vitriolic hatred of rebellious white Southerners. A masterly parliamentarian with a razor-sharp mind and withering wit, Stevens was a leading figure on the Joint (House-Senate) Committee on Reconstruction.

Still opposed to rapid restoration of the Southern states, the radicals wanted to keep them out as long as possibe and apply federal power to bring about a drastic social and economic transformation in the South. But moderate Republicans, more attuned to time-honored Republican principles of states' rights and self-government, recoiled from the full implications of the radical program. They preferred policies that restrained the states from abridging citizens' rights, rather than policies that directly involved the federal government in individual lives. The actual policies adopted by Congress showed the influence of both these schools of thought, though the moderates, as the majority faction, had the upper hand. And one thing both groups agreed on by 1867 was the necessity to enfranchise black voters, even if it took federal troops to do it.

Reconstruction by the Sword

Against a backdrop of vicious and bloody race riots that had erupted in several Southern cities, Congress passed the Military Reconstruction Act of March 2, 1867. Supplemented by later measures, this drastic legislation divided the South into five military districts, each commanded by a Union general and policed by blue-clad soldiers, about twenty thousand all

Thaddeus Stevens (1792–1868) *Stevens, who regarded the seceded states as "conquered provinces," promoted much of the major Reconstruction legislation, including the Fourteenth (civil rights) Amendment. He was among the foremost in the impeachment of President Johnson. (Library of Congress.)*

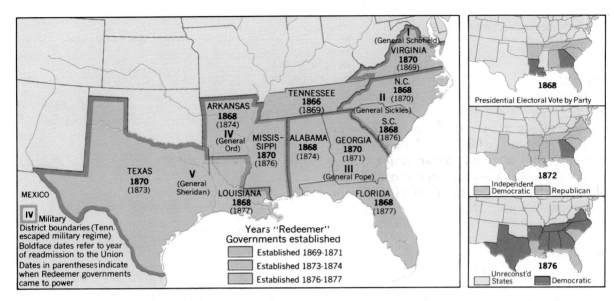

Military Reconstruction, 1867 (five districts and commanding generals)
For many white Southerners, military Reconstruction amounted to turning the knife in the wound of defeat. An often-repeated story of later years had a Southerner remark, "I was sixteen years old before I discovered that damnyankee was two words."

disfranchised?

told. The act also temporarily disfranchised tens of thousands of former Confederates.

Congress additionally laid down stringent conditions for the readmission of the seceded states. The wayward sisters were required to ratify the Fourteenth Amendment, giving the former slaves their rights as citizens. The bitterest pill of all to white Southerners was the stipulation that they guarantee in their state constitutions full suffrage for their former adult male slaves. Yet the act, reflecting moderate sentiment, stopped short of giving the freedmen land or education at federal expense. The overriding purpose of the moderates was to create an electorate in Southern states that would vote those states back into the Union on acceptable terms and thus free the federal government from direct responsibility for the protection of black rights. As later events would demonstrate, this approach proved woefully inadequate to the cause of justice for the blacks.

The radical Republicans were still worried. The danger loomed that once the unrepentant states were readmitted, they would amend their constitutions so as to withdraw the ballot from the blacks. The only ironclad safeguard was to incorporate black suffrage in the federal Constitution. This goal was finally achieved by the Fifteenth Amendment, passed by Congress in 1869 and ratified by the required number of states in 1870. (For text, see the Appendix.)

Military Reconstruction of the South not only usurped certain functions of the president as commander in chief but set up a martial regime of dubious legality. The Supreme Court had already ruled, in the case *Ex parte Milligan* (1866), that military tribunals could not try civilians, even during wartime, in areas where the civil courts were open. Peacetime military rule seemed starkly contrary to the spirit of the Constitution. But the circumstances were extraordinary in the Republic's history, and for the time being the Supreme Court avoided giving offense to the Republican Congress.

Prodded into line by federal bayonets, the Southern states got on with the task of constitution making. By 1870 all of them had reorganized their governments and had been accorded full rights. The hated "bluebellies" were withdrawn from police work only when the new regimes—usually called "radical" regimes—seemed to be firmly entrenched. Finally, in

Southern Reconstruction by State

STATE	READMITTED TO REPRESENTATION IN CONGRESS	HOME RULE (DEMOCRATIC REGIME) REESTABLISHED	COMMENTS
Tennessee	July 24, 1866		Ratified Fourteenth Amendment in 1866 and hence avoided military Reconstruction.*
Arkansas	June 22, 1868	1874	
North Carolina	June 25, 1868	1870	
Alabama	June 25, 1868	1874	
Florida	June 25, 1868	1877	
Louisiana	June 25, 1868	1877	Federal troops restationed in 1877, as result of Hayes-Tilden electoral bargain.
South Carolina	June 25, 1868	1877	Same as above.
Virginia	January 26, 1870	1869	
Mississippi	February 23, 1870	1876	
Texas	March 30, 1870	1874	
Georgia	[June 25, 1868] July 15, 1870	1872	Readmitted June 25, 1868, but returned to military control after expulsion of blacks from legislature.

*For many years Tennessee was the only state of the secession to observe Lincoln's birthday as a legal holiday. Many Southern states still observe the birthdays of Jefferson Davis and Robert E. Lee.

1877, the last federal muskets were removed from state politics.

The Realities of Radical Reconstruction in the South

The blacks now had freedom, of a sort. Their friends in Congress had only haltingly and somewhat belatedly secured the franchise for them. Both Presidents Lincoln and Johnson had proposed to give the ballot gradually to selected blacks who qualified for it through education, property ownership, or military service. Moderate Republicans and even many radicals at first hesitated to bestow suffrage on the freedmen. The Fourteenth Amendment, in many ways the heart of the Republican program for Reconstruction, had fallen short of guaranteeing the right to vote. But by 1867 hesitation had given way to a hard determination to enfranchise the former slaves wholesale and immediately, while thousands of white Southerners were being denied the vote. By glaring contrast most of the Northern states, before ratification of the Fifteenth Amendment in 1870, withheld the ballot from their tiny black minorities. White Southerners naturally concluded that the Republi-

A white Virginian wrote from his deathbed: "Now with what will be my lastest breath, I here repeat and would willingly proclaim my unmitigated hatred to Yankee rule . . . and all connections with Yankees, and the perfidious, malignant and vile Yankee race." A Virginia woman noted at about the same time: "I have this morning witnessed a procession of nearly a thousand children belonging to colored schools. . . .When I thought that the fetters of ignorance were broken, and that they might not be forced from their parents and sold at auction to the highest bidder, my heart went up in adoring gratitude to the great God; not only on their account, but that we white people were no longer permitted to go on in such wickedness, heaping up more and more wrath of God upon our devoted heads."

Freedmen Voting, Richmond, Virginia, 1871 *The exercise of democratic rights by former slaves constituted a political and social revolution in the South, and was bitterly resented by whites. (The Granger Collection.)*

cans were hypocritical in insisting that blacks in the South be allowed to vote.

How well did the radical regimes rule? In five states—Alabama, Florida, Louisiana, Mississippi, and South Carolina—the black voters enfranchised by the new state constitutions made up a majority of the electorate. But only in South Carolina did blacks predominate in the lower house of the legislature. No state senate had a black majority, and there were no black governors during what the whites called "black reconstruction." Many of the newly elected black legislators were literate and able; more than a few came from the ranks of the prewar free blacks who had acquired considerable education. More than a dozen black congressmen and two black United States senators, Hiram Revels and Blanche K. Bruce, both of Mississippi, did creditable work in the national capital.

Yet in many Southern capitals, former slaves held offices ranging from doorkeeper up to Speaker, to the bitter resentment of their one-time masters. Some untutored blacks fell under the control of white "scalawags" and "carpetbaggers," who used the blacks as political henchmen. The "scalawags" were Southerners, sometimes former Unionists and Whigs. By collaborating in creating the new regimes, they earned the undying enmity of the former Confederates, who accused them, often with wild exaggeration, of plundering the treasuries of the Southern states through their political influence in the radical governments. "Carpetbaggers" were mainly Northerners who supposedly had packed all their worldly goods into a single carpet-bag suitcase at war's end and had come South to seek their fortune.

In many radical regimes, graft did indeed run rampant. This was especially true in South Carolina and Louisiana, where conscienceless promoters and other pocket-padders used politically inexperienced blacks as cat's-paws. The

Black Reconstruction *A composite portrait of the first black senators and representatives in the 41st and 42nd congresses. Senator Hiram Revels, on the left, was elected in 1870 to the seat that had been occupied by Jefferson Davis when the South seceded. (The Granger Collection.)*

worst "black-and-white" legislatures purchased, as "legislative supplies," such "stationery" as hams, perfumes, suspenders, bonnets, corsets, champagne, and a coffin. One "thrifty" carpetbag governor in a single year "saved" $100,000 from a salary of $8,000. Yet this sort of corruption was by no means confined to the South in these postwar years. The crimes of the Reconstruction governments were no more outrageous than the scams and felonies being perpetrated in the North at the same time, especially in Boss Tweed's New York.

The radical legislatures also passed much desirable legislation and introduced many badly needed reforms. For the first time in Southern history, steps were taken toward establishing adequate public schools. Tax systems were streamlined; public works were launched; and property rights were guaranteed to women. Many of these reforms were so welcome that they were retained by the all-white "redeemer" governments that later returned to power.

Knights of the White Sheet

Deeply embittered, some Southern whites resorted to savage measures against "radical" rule. Many whites resented the success and ability of black legislators as much as they resented alleged "corruption." A number of secret organizations mushroomed forth, the most notorious of which was the "Invisible Empire of the South," or Ku Klux Klan, founded in Tennessee in 1866. Besheeted night riders, their horses' hoofs muffled, would approach the cabin of an "upstart" black and hammer on the door. In ghoulish tones one thirsty horseman would demand a bucket of water. Then, under pretense of drinking, he would pour it into a rubber attachment concealed beneath his mask and gown, smack his lips, and declare that this was

---

In a 1900 speech Senator Tillman of South Carolina brutally boasted: "We preferred to have a United States army officer rather than a government of carpetbaggers and thieves and scallywags and scoundrels who had stolen everything in sight and mortgaged posterity . . . by issuing bonds. When that happened we took the government away. We stuffed the ballot boxes. We shot them. We are not ashamed of it."

the first water he had tasted since he was killed at the Battle of Shiloh. If fright did not produce the desired effect, force was employed.

Such tomfoolery and terror proved partially effective. Many ex-bondsmen and white "carpetbaggers," quick to take a hint, shunned the polls. Those stubborn souls who persisted in their "upstart" ways were flogged, mutilated, or even murdered. In one Louisiana parish in 1868, the whites in two days killed or wounded two hundred victims; a pile of twenty-five bodies was found half-buried in the woods. By such atrocious practices were blacks "kept in their place"—that is, down. The Klan became a refuge for numerous bandits and cutthroats. Any scoundrel could don a sheet.

Congress, outraged by this night-riding lawlessness, passed the harsh Force Acts of 1870 and 1871. Federal troops were able to stamp out much of the "lash law," but by this time the "Invisible Empire" had already done its work of intimidation. Many of the outlawed groups continued their tactics in the guise of "dancing clubs," "missionary societies," and "rifle clubs," though the net effect of all the hooded terrorists has probably been exaggerated. Economic reprisals were often more effective, especially when causing blacks to lose their jobs.

Attempts to empower the blacks politically failed miserably. The white South, for many decades, openly flouted the Fourteenth and Fifteenth Amendments. Wholesale disfranchisement of the blacks, starting conspicuously about 1890, was achieved by intimidation, fraud, and trickery. Among various underhanded schemes were the literacy tests, un-

The Ku Klux Klan *A contemporary view of the Klan. (Archives of Rutherford B. Hayes Library.)*

The following excerpt is part of a pathetic appeal to Congress in 1871 by a group of Kentucky blacks:

"We believe you are not familiar with the description of the Ku Klux Klans riding nightly over the country, going from county to county, and in the county towns, spreading terror wherever they go by robbing, whipping, ravishing, and killing our people without provocation, compelling colored people to break the ice and bathe in the chilly waters of the Kentucky River.

"The [state] legislature has adjourned. They refused to enact any laws to suppress Ku-Klux disorder. We regard them [the Ku-Kluxers] as now being licensed to continue their dark and bloody deeds under cover of the dark night. They refuse to allow us to testify in the state courts where a white man is concerned. We find their deeds are perpetrated only upon colored men and white Republicans. We also find that for our services to the government and our race we have become the special object of hatred and persecution at the hands of the Democratic Party. Our people are driven from their homes in great numbers, having no redress only [except] the United States court, which is in many cases unable to reach them."

Persons in United States Lynched
[by race], 1882–1970*

YEAR	WHITES	BLACKS	TOTAL
1882	64	49	113
1885	110	74	184
1890	11	85	96
1895	66	113	179
1900	9	106	115
1905	5	57	62
1910	9	67	76
1915	13	56	69
1920	8	53	61
1925	0	17	17
1930	1	20	21
1935	2	18	20
1940	1	4	5
1945	0	1	1
1950	1	1	2
1965	0	0	0

*There were no lynchings in 1965–1970. In every year from 1882 (when records were first kept) to 1964, the number of lynchings corresponded roughly to the figures here given. The worst year was 1892, when 161 blacks and 69 whites were lynched (total 230); the next worst was 1884, when 160 whites and 51 blacks were lynched (total 211).

fairly administered by whites to the advantage of illiterate whites. In the eyes of white Southerners, the goal of white supremacy fully justified dishonorable devices.

Johnson Walks the Impeachment Plank

Radicals meanwhile had been sharpening their hatchets for President Johnson. Annoyed by the obstruction of the "drunken tailor" in the White House, they falsely accused him of maintaining there a harem of "dissolute women." Not content with curbing his authority, they decided to remove him altogether by constitutional processes.* Under existing law the president pro tempore of the Senate, the unscrupulous and

---

*For impeachment, see Art. I, Sec. II, para. 5; Art. I, Sec. III, paras. 6, 7; Art. II, Sec. IV, in the Appendix.

rabidly radical "Bluff Ben" Wade of Ohio, would then become president.

As an initial step, Congress in 1867 passed the Tenure of Office Act—as usual over Johnson's veto. Contrary to precedent, the new law required the president to secure the consent of the Senate before he could remove his appointees once they had been approved by that body. One purpose was to freeze into the cabinet the secretary of war, Edwin M. Stanton, a holdover from the Lincoln administration. Though outwardly loyal to Johnson, he was secretly serving as a spy and informer for the radicals. Another purpose was to goad Johnson into breaking the law and thus establish grounds for his impeachment.

An aroused Johnson was eager to get a test case before the Supreme Court, for he believed the Tenure of Office Act to be unconstitutional. (That slow-moving tribunal finally ruled indirectly in his favor fifty-eight years later.) Expecting reasonable judicial speed, Johnson abruptly dismissed the two-faced Stanton early in 1868. The president did not believe that the law applied to Lincoln's holdovers, even though the radicals insisted otherwise.

A radical-influenced House of Representatives struck back swiftly. By a count of 126 to 47, it voted to impeach Andrew Johnson for "high crimes and misdemeanors," as called for by the Constitution. Most of the specific accusations grew out of the president's so-called violation of the ("unconstitutional") Tenure of Office Act. Two additional articles related to Johnson's verbal assaults on the Congress, involving "disgrace, ridicule, hatred, contempt, and reproach."

A black leader protested to whites in 1868: "It is extraordinary that a race such as yours, professing gallantry, chivalry, education, and superiority, living in a land where ringing chimes call child and sire to the Gospel of God—that with all these advantages on your side, you can make war upon the poor defenseless black man."

U.S. SENATE

No.

U.S. SENATE

To be taken up at MAIN ENTRANCE

U.S. SENATE

Impeachment OF THE President

ADMIT THE BEARER

MARCH 13. 1868

Geo. T. Brown
Sergeant-at-Arms.

Philp & Solomons, Wash. D.C.

Impeachment Drama
The impeachment proceedings against President Andrew Johnson, among the most severe constitutional crises in the Republic's history, were high political theater, and tickets were in sharp demand. (The Granger Collection.)

A Not-Guilty Verdict for Johnson

With evident zeal, the radical-led Senate now sat as a court to try Johnson on the dubious impeachment charges. The House conducted the prosecution. The trial aroused intense public interest and, with one thousand tickets printed, proved to be the biggest show of 1868. Johnson kept his dignity and sobriety and maintained a discreet silence. His battery of attorneys was extremely able, while the House prosecutors, including oily-tongued Benjamin F. Butler and embittered Thaddeus Stevens, bungled their flimsy case.

On May 16, 1868, the day for the first voting in the Senate, the tension was electric, and heavy breathing could be heard in the galleries. By a margin of only one vote, the radicals failed to muster the two-thirds majority for Johnson's removal. Seven independent-minded Republican senators, courageously putting country above party, voted "not guilty."

The radicals were infuriated. "The country is going to the Devil!" cried the crippled Stevens as he was carried from the hall. President-to-be Wade had even chosen his cabinet, with the unscrupulous Benjamin F. Butler as secretary of state. But the nation, though violently aroused, accepted the verdict with a good temper that did credit to its political maturity. In a less stable republic, an armed uprising might have erupted against the president.

The nation thus narrowly avoided a bad precedent that would have gravely weakened one of the three branches of the federal government. Johnson was clearly guilty of bad speeches, bad judgment, and bad temper, but not of "high crimes and misdemeanors." From the standpoint of the radicals, his greatest crime had been to stand inflexibly in their path.

The Purchase of Alaska

Johnson's administration, though largely reduced to a figurehead, achieved its most enduring success in the field of foreign relations.

The Russians by 1867 were in a mood to sell the vast and chilly expanse now known as Alaska. They had already overextended themselves in North America, and they saw that in the likely event of another war with England, they probably would lose their defenseless province to the sea-dominant British. Alaska, moreover, had been ruthlessly "furred out" and was a growing economic liability. The Russians were therefore eager to unload their "frozen asset" on the Americans, and they put out seductive feelers in Washington. They preferred the United States to any other purchaser, primarily

Alaska and the Lower Forty-Eight States (a size comparison)

because they wanted to strengthen further the Republic as a barrier against their ancient enemy, Britain.

In 1867 Secretary of State Seward, an ardent expansionist, signed a treaty with Russia that transferred Alaska to the United States for the bargain price of $7.2 million. But Seward's enthusiasm for these frigid wastes was not shared by his ignorant or uninformed countrymen, who jeered at "Seward's Folly," "Seward's Icebox," "Frigidia," and "Walrussia." The American people, still preoccupied with Reconstruction and other internal vexations, were economy-minded and antiexpansionist.

Then why did Congress and the American public sanction the purchase? For one thing

The Alaska Purchase Satirized It is pilloried as a scheme to get votes for the Johnson administration. Ursus, a polar bear, is hailed as the bears' candidate. (American Antiquarian Society.)

Russia, alone among the powers, had been conspicuously friendly to the North during the recent Civil War. Americans did not feel that they could offend their great and good friend, the czar, by hurling his walrus-covered icebergs back into his face. Besides, the territory was rumored to be teeming with furs, fish, and gold, and it might yet "pan out" profitably—as it later did with natural resources, including oil and gas. So Congress and the country accepted "Seward's Polar Bear Garden," somewhat wryfacedly and derisively but nevertheless hopefully.

The Heritage of Reconstruction

Many white Southerners regarded Reconstruction as a more grievous wound than the war itself. It left an angry scar that would take generations to heal. They resented the upending of their social and racial system, the humiliation of being ruled by blacks, and the insult of federal intervention in their local affairs. Yet few rebellions have ended with the victors sitting down to a love feast with the vanquished. Given the explosiveness of the issues that had caused the war, and the bitterness of the fighting, the wonder is that Reconstruction was not far harsher than it was. The fact is that Lincoln, Johnson, and most Republicans had no clear picture at war's end of what federal policy toward the South should be. Policymakers groped their way, influenced as much by Southern responses to defeat and emancipation as by any plans of their own to impose a specific program on the South.

The Republicans acted from a mixture of idealism and political expediency. They wanted both to protect the freed slaves and to promote the fortunes of the Republican party. In the end, their efforts backfired badly. Republican Reconstruction conferred only fleeting benefits

> The remarkable ex-slave Frederick Douglass wrote in 1882: "Though slavery was abolished, the wrongs of my people were not ended. Though they were not slaves, they were not yet quite free. No man can be truly free whose liberty is dependent upon the thought, feeling, and action of others, and who has himself no means in his own hands for guarding, protecting, defending, and maintaining that liberty. Yet the Negro after his emancipation was precisely in this state of destitution. . . . He was free from the individual master, but the slave of society. He had neither money, property, nor friends. He was free from the old plantation, but he had nothing but the dusty road under his feet. He was free from the old quarter that once gave him shelter, but a slave to the rains of summer and the frosts of winter. He was, in a word, literally turned loose, naked, hungry, and destitute, to the open sky."

on the blacks, envenomed the whites, and virtually extinguished the Republican party in the South for nearly one hundred years.

In the light of hindsight, the Republican Reconstruction program seems too narrowly conceived. Moderate Republicans in particular never appreciated the efforts necessary to make the freed slaves completely independent citizens, nor the lengths to which Southern whites would go to preserve their system of racial dominance. Had Thaddeus Stevens' radical program of drastic economic reforms and heftier protection of political rights been enacted, things might well have been different. But ingrained American resistance to tampering with property rights and violating the principle of local self-government, combined with spreading indifference in the North to the plight of the blacks, formed too formidable an obstacle.

Varying Viewpoints

Few topics have triggered as much intellectual warfare as the "dark and bloody ground" of Reconstruction. The period provoked questions—sectional, racial, and constitutional—about which people felt deeply and remain deeply divided even today. Scholarly argument goes back conspicuously to a Columbia University historian, William A. Dunning, whose students, in the early years of the twentieth century, published a series of histories of the Reconstruction South. Dunning and his disciples were influenced by the turn-of-the-century spirit of sectional reconciliation as well as by current theories about black racial inferiority. Sympathizing with the white South, they wrote about Reconstruction as a kind of national disgrace, foisted upon a prostrate region by vindictive, self-seeking radical Republican politicians. If the South had wronged the North by seceding, the North had wronged the South by reconstructing. For a long time this persuasive view held sway, reinforced by a widespread suspicion in the 1920s and 1930s that the Civil War itself had been a tragic and unnecessary blunder. Black historian W. E. B. Du Bois' *Black Reconstruction,* in 1935, represented virtually the only serious attack on the "Dunning school" until World War II.

After the Second World War, two developments in American culture encouraged a new examination of the Dunning approach. One was the spread of a more egalitarian attitude toward racial questions, especially following the agitation of the 1960s. The other factor was the growing conviction that ideals counted for a great deal in this controversy. Consequently, many historians now showed much more interest in the real problems of the black freedmen, more admiration for the "helpful" radical Republicans as genuine idealists rather than as self-seeking politicians, and less sympathy for the beaten and defiant white South. Kenneth Stampp's *Era of Reconstruction* (1965) probably best summarizes these newer views.

Recent trends in Reconstruction scholarship have reinforced this "revisionist" view. First, historians have concentrated on the earliest stages of Reconstruction, concluding that Lincoln was more sympathetic to the radicals than was Johnson and would probably have pursued a vigorous policy. Second, economic analyses have lent credence to the radicals' claim that only a drastic transformation of Southern society could have secured fair treatment for the freedmen.

Select Readings

Primary Source Documents

Booker T. Washington's classic autobiography *Up from Slavery* (1901) records one freedman's experiences. Contemporary comments on the process of Reconstruction include the laments of editor Edwin L. Godkin, *The Nation* (December 7, 1871, p. 364),* and Frederick Douglass, *Life and Times of Frederick Douglass* (1882), as well as the debates in the *Congressional Globe* (1867–1868)* between radicals like Thaddeus Stevens and moderates like Lyman Trumbull.

Secondary Sources

Overall accounts may be found in James G. Randall and David Donald, *The Civil War and Reconstruction* (rev. ed., 1969), and James McPherson, *Ordeal By Fire: The Civil War and Reconstruction* (1981), perhaps the best brief introduction. Lincoln's early efforts at Reconstruction are handled in Peyton McCrary, *Abraham Lincoln and Reconstruction* (1978); LaWanda Cox, *Lincoln and Black Freedom* (1981); and Herman Belz, *Emancipation and Equal Rights* (1978). Willie Lee Rose engagingly describes a *Re-*

hearsal for Reconstruction: The Port Royal Experiment* (1964). Otis A. Singletary discusses *The Negro Militia and Reconstruction* (1957). Dan Carter, *When the War Was Over: The Failure of Self-Reconstruction in the South, 1865–1867* (1985), charts the first years of the period. Following up the story of national politics is Eric L. McKitrick, *Andrew Johnson and Reconstruction: Principle and Prejudice, 1865–1866* (1963). Sympathetic to the radical Republicans are James M. McPherson, *The Struggle for Equality* (1964), and Hans L. Trefousse, *The Radical Republicans* (1969). See also David Montgomery, *Beyond Equality: Labor and the Radical Republicans, 1862–1872* (1967). Siding with the radicals in the impeachment fight are Michael L. Benedict, *The Impeachment and Trial of Andrew Johnson* (1973), and Hans L. Trefousse, *Impeachment of a President* (1975). Conditions in the South are analyzed in W. E. B. Du Bois' controversial classic *Black Reconstruction* (1935) and in Leon F. Litwack's brilliantly evocative *Been in the Storm So Long* (1979), a revealing study of the initial responses, by both blacks and whites, to emancipation. It can be usefully supplemented by Roger Ransom and Richard L. Sutch, *One Kind of Freedom: The Economic Consequences of Emancipation* (1977). See also James Roark, *Masters without Slaves: Southern Planters in the Civil War and Reconstruction* (1977), and Lawrence Powell, *New Masters: Northern Planters during the Civil War and Reconstruction* (1980). Roger Shugg, *Origins of Class Struggle in Louisiana* (1968), Dwight Billings, *Planters and the Making of a "New South": Class, Politics and Development in North Carolina, 1865–1900* (1979), and Jonathan Wiener, *Social Origins of the New South: Alabama, 1860–1885* (1978), elucidate the political economy of the postbellum South. Race relations are the subject of Joel Williamson, *After Slavery: The Negro in South Carolina during Reconstruction* (1965). Consult also Thomas Holt, *Black over White: Negro Political Leadership in South Carolina during Reconstruction* (1977). C. Vann Woodward's *The Strange Career of Jim Crow* (rev. ed., 1974) is a classic study of the origins of segregation. His views have drawn criticism in Harold O. Rabinowitz, *Race Relations in the Urban South, 1865–1890* (1977). See also the same author's *Southern Black Leaders of the Reconstruction Era* (1982). Special studies of value are William P. Vaughn, *Schools for All* (1974); William S. McFeely, *Yankee Stepfather: General O. O. Howard and the Freedmen* (1968); William C. Gillette, *The Right to Vote: Politics and the Passage of the 15th Amendment* (1965); Stanley I. Kutler, *Judicial Power and Reconstruction Politics* (1968); Harold M. Hyman, *A More Perfect Union: The Impact of the Civil War and Reconstruction on the Constitution* (1973). New scholarship is presented in Kenneth M. Stampp and Leon Litwack, eds., *Reconstruction: An Anthology of Revisionist Writings* (1969), and Robert P. Swierenga, ed., *Beyond the Civil War Synthesis* (1975). Eric Foner looks at emancipation in a comparative perspective in *Nothing but Freedom* (1983). A comprehensive study of the climax of this troubled period is William Gillette, *Retreat from Reconstruction, 1869–1879* (1979).

---

* An asterisk indicates that the document, or an excerpt from it, can be found in Thomas A. Bailey and David M. Kennedy, eds., *The American Spirit: United States History as Seen by Contemporaries*, 6th ed. (Lexington, Mass.: D. C. Heath and Company, 1987).

26

Politics in the Gilded Age, 1869–1889

> *Grant . . . had no right to exist. He should have been extinct for ages. . . . That, two thousand years after Alexander the Great and Julius Caesar, a man like Grant should be called—and should actually and truly be—the highest product of the most advanced evolution, made evolution ludicrous. . . . The progress of evolution, from President Washington to President Grant, was alone evidence enough to upset Darwin. . . . Grant . . . should have lived in a cave and worn skins.*
>
> Henry Adams, The Education of Henry Adams, 1907

The "Bloody Shirt" Elects Grant

Disillusionment ran deep among idealistic Americans in the era after the Civil War. They had spilled their blood for Union, emancipation, and Abraham Lincoln, who had promised "a new birth of freedom." Instead, they got a bitter dose of corruption, petty politics, and Ulysses S. Grant, a great soldier but a baby politician.

Wrangling between Congress and Andrew Johnson soured the people on professional politicians, and the notion still prevailed that a good general was bound to make a good president. Stubbily bearded General Grant, with his slightly stooped body measuring a shade over 5 feet 8 inches (1.72 meters), was by far the most popular Northern hero to emerge from the war. Grateful citizens of Philadelphia, Washington, and his home town of Galena, Illinois, passed the hat around and in each place presented him with a house. New Yorkers tendered him a check for $105,000. The general, silently puffing on his cigar, accepted these gifts with open arms, as if the Republic owed them to him for having rescued the Union.

Unfortunately, this hard-riding soldier was a toddler in the political woods. He had almost no political experience, and his one presidential vote had been cast for the Democratic ticket in 1856. A better judge of horseflesh than of human beings, his cultural background was breathtakingly narrow. He once reportedly remarked that Venice (Italy) would be a fine city if only it were drained.

The Republicans, now freed from the Union party coalition of war days, enthusiastically nominated Grant for the presidency in 1868. The party's platform sounded a clarion call for continued Reconstruction of the South under the glinting steel of federal bayonets. Yet Grant, always a man of few words, struck a highly popular note in his letter of acceptance when he said "Let us have peace." This noble sentiment became a leading campaign slogan and was later engraved on his tomb beside the Hudson River.

Expectant Democrats, meeting in their own nominating convention, denounced military Reconstruction but could agree on little else. Wealthy eastern delegates demanded a plank promising that federal bonds, issued during the war, would be redeemed in gold—even though many of the bonds had been purchased with badly depreciated paper greenbacks. Poorer middle western delegates answered with the "Ohio Idea," forcing a "repudiation" plank into the platform. It called for redemption in greenbacks to the maximum extent possible. Down-on-their-luck agrarian Democrats thus hoped to keep more money in circulation, which would make loans less costly and easier to find.

The midwestern delegates got the platform but not the candidate, who turned out to be the conservative former governor of New York, Horatio Seymour. He promptly repudiated the "repudiation" plank, thereby sinking the Democrats' scant hopes for success at the polls. Republicans whipped up enthusiasm for Grant by energetically "waving the bloody shirt"—that is, reviving gory memories of the Civil War—which became for the first time a prominent feature of a presidential campaign.* "Vote as

You Shot" was a powerful Republican slogan aimed at Union army veterans.

Grant won, with 214 electoral votes to 80 for Seymour. But despite his great popularity, the former general scored a majority of only 300,000 in the popular vote (3,013,421 to 2,706,829). Most white voters apparently supported Seymour, and the ballots of three still-unreconstructed southern states were not counted. An estimated 500,000 former slaves gave Grant his margin of victory. To remain in power, the Republican party had somehow to continue to control the South—and to keep the ballot in the hands of the grateful freedmen. Republicans could not take future victories "for Granted."

The Era of Good Stealings

The population of the Republic continued to vault upward by vigorous leaps, despite the awful bloodletting of the Civil War. Census takers reported over 39 million souls in 1870, a gain of 26.6 percent over the previous decade, as the immigrant tide surged again. The United States was now the third largest nation of the Western world, ranking behind Russia and France.

But the moral stature of the Republic fell regrettably short of its physical stature. The war and its aftermath bred waste, extravagance, speculation, and graft. When so much money is thrown about with wild abandon, a great deal sticks to the wrong fingers.

A few skunks can pollute a large area. Although the great majority of businesspeople and government officials conducted their affairs with decency and honor, the whole atmosphere was fetid. The Man in the Moon, it was said, had to hold his nose when passing over America. Railroad promoters sometimes left gullible bond buyers with only "two streaks of rust and a right of way." Unscrupulous stock-market manipulators were a cinder in the public eye. Too many judges and legislators put their power up for hire. Cynics defined an honest politician as one who, when bought, would stay bought.

Notorious in the financial world were two millionaires, "Jubilee Jim" Fisk and Jay Gould. The corpulent Fisk—bold, impudent, unprinci-

---

*The expression is said to have derived from a speech by Representative Benjamin F. Butler, who allegedly waved before the House the bloodstained nightshirt of a Klan-flogged carpetbagger.

pled—often paraded in public with "cuddlesome women" behind a span of fast horses. He provided the "brass," and the undersized and cunning Gould provided the brains of the combination. The crafty pair concocted a plot in 1869 to "corner" the gold market. Their slippery game would work only if the federal Treasury refrained from selling gold. The conspirators worked on President Grant directly and also through his brother-in-law, who received $25,000 for his complicity. On "Black Friday" (September 24, 1869), Fisk and Gould madly bid the price of gold skyward, while scores of honest businesspeople were driven to the wall. The bubble finally broke when the Treasury, contrary to Grant's supposed assurances, was compelled to release gold. A congressional probe concluded that Grant had done nothing crooked, though he had acted stupidly and indiscreetly.

The infamous Tweed Ring in New York City vividly displayed the ethics (or lack of ethics) typical of the age. Burly "Boss" Tweed—240 pounds (109 kilograms) of rascality—employed bribery, graft, and fraudulent elections to milk the metropolis of as much as $200 million. He adopted the cynical rule: "Addition, division, and silence." The books once recorded a payment of $138,000 to a plasterer for two days of labor. Honest citizens were cowed into silence. Protestors found their tax assessments raised.

Tweed's luck finally ran out. *The New York Times* secured damning evidence in 1871 and courageously published this, though offered $5 million not to do so. A gifted cartoonist, Thomas Nast, pilloried Tweed mercilessly, after spurning a heavy bribe to desist. The portly thief reportedly complained that his illiterate followers could not help seeing "them damn pictures." A New York attorney, Samuel J. Tilden, headed the prosecution and gained fame that later paved the path to his presidential nomination. Unbailed and unwept, Tweed died behind bars.

Boss Tweed Manipulates Ballots
Another Nast cartoon had Tweed ask, "as long as I count the votes, what are you going to do about it?" (Thomas Nast in Harper's Weekly, *1871.)*

In a famous series of newspaper interviews in 1905, George Washington Plunkitt, a political "boss" in the same Tammany Hall "machine" that had spawned William Marcy Tweed, candidly described his ethical and political principles: "Everybody is talkin' these days about Tammany men growin' rich on graft, but nobody thinks of drawin' the distinction between honest graft and dishonest graft. There's all the difference in the world between the two. Yes, many of our men have grown rich in politics. I have myself. I've made a big fortune out of the game, and I'm gettin' richer every day, but I've not gone in for dishonest graft—blackmailin' gamblers, saloonkeepers, disorderly people, etc.—and neither has any of the men who have made big fortunes in politics.

"There's an honest graft, and I'm an example of how it works. I might sum up the whole thing by sayin': 'I seen my opportunities and I took 'em.'

"Just let me explain by examples. My party's in power in the city, and it's goin' to undertake a lot of public improvements. Well, I'm tipped off, say, that they're going to lay out a new park at a certain place.

"I see my opportunity and I take it. I go to that place and I buy up all the land I can in the neighborhood. Then the board of this or that makes its plan public, and there is a rush to get my land, which nobody cared particular for before.

"Ain't it perfectly honest to charge a good price and make a profit on my investment and foresight? Of course, it is. Well, that's honest graft."

A Carnival of Corruption

With the atmosphere so badly contaminated, it was small wonder that the easygoing Grant apparently failed to scent some of the worst evil-doing in public life. His cabinet was a nest of grafters and incompetents, with one notable exception, Secretary of State Hamilton Fish. Favor seekers haunted the White House, often plying Grant with cigars, wines, and horses. His election was a godsend to his in-laws of the Dent family, several dozen of whom attached themselves to the public payroll.

Grant was tarred by the Crédit Mobilier scandal, though the dirtiest work had been done in 1867–1868, before he took office. The Crédit Mobilier was a railroad construction company, formed by the insiders of the transcontinental Union Pacific Railway. They cleverly hired themselves to build the line and sometimes paid themselves as much as $50,000 a mile for construction that cost $30,000 a mile. In one year the Crédit Mobilier paid dividends of 348 percent. Fearing that Congress might blow the whistle, the company furtively distributed shares of its valuable stock to key congressmen.

A New York newspaper finally exposed the scandal in 1872, and a congressional investigation confirmed some of the worst charges. Two members of Congress were formally censured, and the vice-president of the United States was shown to have accepted twenty shares of stock and some dividends.

The breath of scandal in Washington also reeked of alcohol. In 1875 the public learned that a sprawling Whiskey Ring had robbed the

"All Smoke" *Cartoonist Thomas Nast makes light of the Grant scandals. Grant was a heavy cigar smoker, who reportedly smoked twenty cigars a day; he died of cancer of the throat. (Harper's Weekly, 1872.)*

Treasury of millions in excise-tax revenues. "Let no guilty man escape," insisted President Grant. But when his own private secretary turned up among the culprits, the president speedily changed his views. He volunteered a written statement to the jury, with all the weight of his exalted office behind it, and the thief escaped. News of further rottenness in the Grant administration broke in 1876, when Secretary of War Belknap was shown to have pocketed some $24,000 by selling the privilege of disbursing supplies—often junk—to the Indians. The House voted unanimously to impeach him. Belknap resigned the same day, thus avoiding conviction by the Senate. Grant, ever loyal to his crooked cronies, accepted his resignation "with great regret."

The Liberal Republican Revolt of 1872

By 1872 a powerful wave of disgust with Grantism was beginning to build up throughout the nation, even before some of the worst scandals had been exposed. Reform-minded citizens banded together in the Liberal Republican party. Voicing the slogan "Turn the Rascals Out," they urged purification of the Washington administration and an end to military Reconstruction.

The Liberal Republicans muffed their chance when their Cincinnati nominating convention, heavily studded with starry-eyed reformers, fell into the hands of amateurish newspapermen and scheming politicians. This "conclave of cranks" now astounded the country by nominating the brilliant but erratic Horace Greeley for the presidency. Greeley was a mind-boggling choice. Though he was a fearless editor of the *New York Tribune*, he was dogmatic, emotional, petulant, and notoriously unsound in his political judgments.

More astonishing still was the action of the office-hungry Democrats, who endorsed Greeley's candidacy. In swallowing Greeley, the Democrats "ate crow" in large gulps, for the eccentric editor had long blasted them as traitors, slave whippers, saloon keepers, horse thieves, and idiots. Yet Greeley pleased the Democrats,

Greeley and the Democrats "Swallow" Each Other   *A Republican jibe at the forced alliance between these former foes. General W. T. Sherman wrote from Paris to his brother: "I feel amazed to see the turn things have taken. Grant who never was a Republican is your candidate; and Greeley who never was a Democrat, but quite the reverse, is the Democratic candidate." (Thomas Nast in* Harper's Weekly, *1872.)*

North and South, when he pleaded for a clasping of hands across "the bloody chasm." The Republicans dutifully renominated Grant, and the voters were thus presented with a choice between two candidates who had made their careers in fields other than politics, and who were both eminently unqualified, by temperament and lifelong training, for high political office.

Much mud was spattered along the campaign trail in 1872. Greeley was denounced as an atheist, a communist, a free-lover, a vegetarian, a brown-bread eater, and a cosigner of Jefferson Davis's bail bond, which in fact he had signed. "Grant beat Davis—Greeley bailed him," ran the slogan. The much-defamed Greeley was heard to wonder if he were running for the presidency or the penitentiary. Grant, in turn, was derided as an ignoramus, a drunkard, and a swindler. But the regular Republicans, chanting "Grant us another term," pulled the president through. The count in the electoral column was 286 to 66, in the popular column 3,596,745 to 2,843,446.

For Greeley, the outcome was tragic. Within a month he lost the election, his wife, his job, his mind, and his life. Liberal Republican agitation frightened the regular Republicans into cleaning their own house before they were thrown out of it. The Republican Congress in 1872 passed a general amnesty act, removing political disabilities from all but some five hundred former Confederate leaders. Congress also moved to reduce high Civil War tariffs and to fumigate the Grant administration with mild civil-service reform. Like many American third parties, the Liberal Republicans left some enduring footprints, even in defeat.

Depression Doldrums in the Seventies

The evil repute of the scandal-scarred Grant years was worsened by the paralyzing panic that broke in 1873. Bursting with startling rapidity, the crash was one of those periodic plummets that roller-coastered the economy in this age of unbridled capitalist expansion. Overreaching promoters had laid more railroad track, sunk more mines, erected more factories, and cleared more grainfields than existing mar-

"Substance and Shadow" *The metallic (specie) dollar is the substance; the depreciated paper greenback is the shadow. (Harper's Weekly, 1875.)*

kets could bear. Bankers, in turn, had made too many imprudent loans to finance those enterprises. When profits failed to materialize, loans went unpaid, and the whole credit-based house of cards fluttered down.

The first severe shock came with the failure of the New York banking firm of Jay Cooke & Company, headed by the fabulously rich Jay Cooke, financier of the Civil War. Boom times became gloom times as more than fifteen thousand businesses went bankrupt; and in New York City an army of unemployed riotously battled police.

Hard times breathed new life into the issue of greenbacks. During the war $450 million of the "folding money" had been issued, but it had depreciated under a cloud of popular mistrust and dubious legality.* By 1868 the Treasury had already withdrawn $100 million of the "battle-born currency" from circulation, and

---

*The Supreme Court in 1870 declared the Civil War Legal Tender Act unconstitutional. With the concurrence of the Senate, Grant thereupon added to the bench two justices who could be counted on to help reverse that decision, which happened in 1871. This is how the Court grew to its current size of nine justices.

"hard-money" people everywhere looked forward to its complete disappearance. But now afflicted agrarian and debtor groups—"cheap-money" supporters—clamored for a reissuance of the greenbacks. With a crude but essentially accurate grasp of monetary theory, they reasoned that more money meant cheaper money and, hence, rising prices and easier-to-pay debts. Creditors, of course, reasoning from the same premises, advocated precisely the opposite policy.

The "hard-money" advocates carried the day in 1874 when they persuaded the confused Grant to veto a bill to print more paper money. They scored another victory in the Resumption Act of 1875, which pledged the government to the further withdrawal of greenbacks from circulation and to the redemption of all paper currency in gold at face value, beginning in 1879.

Down but not out, debtors now looked for relief to another precious metal, silver. The "sacred white metal," they claimed, had received a raw deal. In the early 1870s, the Treasury stubbornly and unrealistically maintained that an ounce of silver was worth only 1/16 as much as an ounce of gold, though open-market prices for silver were higher. Silver miners thus stopped offering their shiny product for sale to the federal mints. With no silver flowing into the federal coffers, Congress formally dropped the coinage of silver dollars in 1873. Fate then played a sly joke when new silver discoveries later in the 1870s shot production up and forced silver prices down. Westerners from silver-mining states joined with debtors in assailing the "Crime of '73," demanding a return to the "Dollar of Our Daddies." This demand, like the demand for more greenbacks, was essentially a call for inflation. Republicans resisted this call and counted on Grant to hold the line against it. He did not disappoint them.

Grant's name continued to be associated with sound money, though not with sound government. The Treasury began to accumulate gold stocks against the appointed day for resumption of metallic-money payments. Coupled with the reduction of greenbacks, this policy was called "contraction." It had a noticeable deflationary effect—the amount of money per capita in circulation actually *decreased* between 1870 and 1880, from $19.42 to $19.37. Contraction probably worsened the impact of the depression. But the new policy did restore the government's credit rating, and it brought the embattled greenbacks up to their full face value. When Redemption Day came in 1879, few greenback holders bothered to exchange the lighter and more convenient bills for gold.

The fate of silver disappointed the friends of easy money. "Soft-money" advocates continued to clamor for the unlimited coinage of all silver mined at the old value-ratio of 16 to 1. "Sound-money" champions scornfully rejected the coinage of any silver at all. A compromise was struck with the Bland-Allison Act of 1878, masterminded by Representative Richard P. ("Silver Dick") Bland of Missouri. The law instructed the Treasury to buy and coin between $2 million and $4 million worth of silver bullion each month. But the government dampened the hopes of inflationists when it stuck steadfastly to a policy of buying only the legal minimum.

Republican "hard-money" policy had a political backlash. It helped elect a Democratic House of Representatives in 1874, and in 1878 it spawned a Greenback Labor Party that polled over a million votes and elected fourteen members of Congress.

Pallid Politics in the Gilded Age

The political seesaw was delicately balanced throughout most of the Gilded Age (a sarcastic name given to the post–Civil War era by Mark Twain in 1873). Even a slight nudge could tip the teeter-totter to the advantage of the opposition party. Every presidential election was a squeaker, and the majority party in the House of Representatives switched six times in the eleven sessions between 1869 and 1891. Wobbling in such shaky equilibrium, politicians were not inclined to take bold, firm stands. They tended, instead, to tiptoe timidly, producing a political record that was often trivial and petty.

Few significant economic issues separated the major parties. Democrats and Republicans saw very nearly eye-to-eye on major questions like the tariff, currency, and civil-service reform. Yet despite their rough agreement on these national matters, the two parties were ferociously competitive with each other. They were tightly and efficiently organized, and they commanded fierce loyalty from their partisans. Voter turnouts reached heights unmatched before or since. Nearly 80 percent of eligible voters cast their ballots in presidential elections in the three decades after the Civil War. On Election Days, droves of the party faithful tramped behind marching bands to the polling places, and "ticket splitting," or failing to vote the straight party line, was as rare as a silver dollar.

How can this apparent paradox of political consensus and partisan fervor be explained? The answer lies in the sharp ethnic and cultural differences in the membership of the two parties—in distinctions of style and tone, and especially of religious sentiment. Republican voters tended to adhere to those creeds that traced their lineage to Puritanism. They stressed strict codes of personal morality and believed that government should play a role in regulating both the economic and the moral affairs of the community as a whole. Democrats, among whom immigrant Lutherans and Roman Catholics figured heavily, were more likely to adhere to faiths that took a less stern view of human weakness. Their religions professed toleration of differences in an imperfect world, and they spurned government efforts to impose a single moral standard on the entire society. These differences in temperament and religious values often produced raucous political contests at the local level, where issues like prohibition and education loomed large.

Democrats, still somewhat cursed with the charge of wartime Copperheadism, had a solid electoral base in the South. They also ran well in the northern industrial cities, which were packed with immigrants and controlled by well-oiled political machines. Republicans could usually count on winning the Midwest and the rural and small-town Northeast, still populous enough to swing the northeastern states regularly into the Republican column. Grateful freedmen in the South contributed significant numbers of votes to the Republicans. Another important bloc of Republican ballots came from the members of the Grand Army of the Republic (GAR)—a politically potent fraternal organization of several hundred thousand Union veterans of the Civil War. The initials *GAR* were humorously interpreted to mean "Generally All Republicans." The lifeblood of both parties was patronage—disbursing jobs by the bucketful in return for votes, kickbacks, and party service. In this postwar era of vastly expanded government employment—especially in the postal service—the old practice of awarding the spoils to the victors had mushroomed into a big business. Reformers increasingly assailed the spoils system as both the nemesis of efficient public administration and the nutrient of rampant corruption.

Boisterous infighting beset the Republican party in the 1870s and 1880s. A "Stalwart" faction, led by the handsome and imperious Roscoe ("Lord Roscoe") Conkling, United States senator from New York, unblushingly embraced the time-honored system of swapping civil-service jobs for votes. Once needled by a rival as having a "turkey gobbler strut," Conkling was forever after portrayed by cartoonists as a gobbling turkey, with the curl that he affected in the middle of his forehead. Opposed to the Conklingites were the so-called "Half-Breeds," who flirted coyly with civil-service reform, but whose real quarrel with the Stalwarts was over who should grasp the ladle that dished out the spoils. The champion of the Half-Breeds was James G. Blaine, a radiantly personable congressman from Maine. Gifted with a photographic memory for names and faces, he was a politician's politician. He had a fine physical presence, flashing eyes, a thrilling speaking voice, and an elastic conscience. A perennial contender for the presidency, Blaine was inclined to demagoguery in his pursuit of the office. He would twist the British lion's tail for Irish votes and wave the bloody shirt for veterans' votes. The fact that he himself had not heard the whine of Confederate bullets led to the jibe, "Invisible in war, invincible in peace." But despite all the color of their personalities,

Conkling and Blaine succeeded for the most part only in stalemating each other and deadlocking their party.

The Hayes-Tilden Standoff, 1876

Hangers-on around Grant, like fleas urging their ailing dog to live, begged the "Old Man" to try for a third term in 1876. The general, blind to his own ineptitudes, showed a disquieting willingness. But the House of Representatives, by a lopsided bipartisan vote of 233 to 18, spiked the third-term boom. It passed a resolution that sternly reminded the country—and Grant—of the antidictator implications of the two-term tradition.

With Grant out of the running, and with the Conklingites and Blaineites checkmating each other, the Republicans turned to a compromise candidate, Rutherford B. Hayes, who was ob-

President Rutherford B. Hayes (1822–1893) *Henry Adams wrote that Hayes "is a third-rate nonentity, whose only recommendation is that he is obnoxious to no one." (Library of Congress.)*

scure enough to be dubbed "The Great Unknown." Of medium build, he displayed a high-domed forehead above a heavy reddish beard. Wounded several times as an officer in the Civil War, he appealed to veterans. His foremost qualification was the fact that he hailed from the electorally doubtful but potent state of Ohio, where he had served three terms as governor. So crucial were the "swing" votes of Ohio in the cliff-hanging presidential contests of the day that the state produced more than its share of presidential candidates. A political saying of the 1870s went:

> Some are born great,
> Some achieve greatness,
> And some are born in Ohio.

Pitted against the humdrum Hayes was the Democratic nominee, Samuel J. Tilden, who had risen to fame as the man who bagged Boss Tweed in New York. Boyish-faced and smooth-shaven (unusual in that bewhiskered age), Tilden was slightly built, nervous, droopy-eyed, and weak-voiced ("Whispering Sammy"). Campaigning against Republican scandal and for sweeping civil-service reform, Tilden racked up 184 electoral votes of the needed 185, with 20 votes in four states doubtful because of irregular returns (see map). Surely Tilden could pick up at least one of these, especially in view of the fact that he had polled 247,448 more popular votes than Hayes, 4,284,020 to 4,036,572.

Both parties scurried to send "visiting statesmen" to the contested southern states of Louisiana, South Carolina, and Florida. All three disputed states submitted two sets of returns, one Democratic and one Republican. As the weeks drifted by, the paralysis tightened. Here were the makings of an epochal constitutional crisis. The Constitution merely specifies that the electoral returns from the states shall be sent to Congress, and in the presence of the House and Senate they shall be *opened* by the president of the Senate (see the Twelfth Amendment). But who should *count* them? On this point the Constitution was silent. If counted by the president of the Senate (a Republican), the Republican returns would be selected. If counted by the Speaker of the House (a Democrat), the Democratic returns would be chosen.

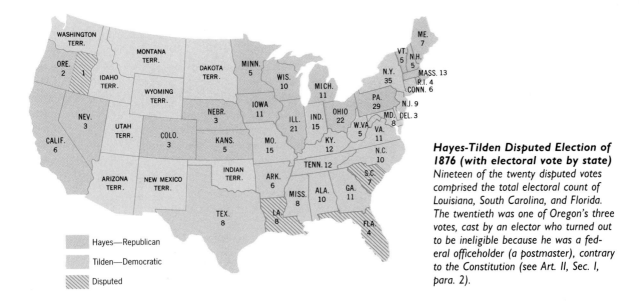

Hayes-Tilden Disputed Election of 1876 (with electoral vote by state) *Nineteen of the twenty disputed votes comprised the total electoral count of Louisiana, South Carolina, and Florida. The twentieth was one of Oregon's three votes, cast by an elector who turned out to be ineligible because he was a federal officeholder (a postmaster), contrary to the Constitution (see Art. II, Sec. I, para. 2).*

The Compromise of 1877

Clash or compromise was the stark choice. The danger loomed that there would be no president on Inauguration Day, March 4, 1877. "Tilden or Blood!" cried Democratic hotheads, and some of their "Minute Men" began to drill with arms. But behind the scenes frantically laboring statesmen gradually hammered out an agreement in the Henry Clay tradition—the Compromise of 1877.

The election deadlock itself was to be broken by the Electoral Count Act, which passed Congress early in 1877. It set up an electoral commission consisting of fifteen men selected from the Senate, the House, and the Supreme Court. The fifteenth member of the commission, according to Democratic schemes, was to have been the giant-sized Justice David Davis, an independent—with Democratic leanings. But at the last moment he resigned from the bench to go to the Senate, and the only remaining members of the Supreme Court were Republicans. One Republican rhymester chortled at the Democrats:

> They digged a pit, they digged it deep,
> They digged it for their brother;
> But through their sin they did fall in
> The pit they digged for t' other.

In February 1877, about a month before Inauguration Day, the Senate and House met together in an electric atmosphere to settle the dispute. The roll of the states was tolled off alphabetically. When Florida was reached—the first of the three southern states with two sets of returns—the disputed documents were referred to the electoral commission, which sat in a nearby chamber. After prolonged discussion the members agreed, by the partisan vote of eight Republicans to seven Democrats, to accept the Republican returns. Outraged Democrats in Congress, smelling defeat, undertook to launch a filibuster "until hell froze over."

Renewed deadlock was avoided by the rest of the complex Compromise of 1877, already partially concluded behind closed doors. The Democrats reluctantly agreed that Hayes might

Composition of the Electoral Commission, 1877

MEMBERS	REPUBLICANS	DEMOCRATS
Senate (Republican majority)	3	2
House (Democratic majority)	2	3
Supreme Court	3	2
TOTAL	8	7

Thomas Nast Favors a Truce   (Harper's Weekly, 1877)

take office in return for his withdrawing intimidating federal troops from the two states in which they remained, Louisiana and South Carolina. Among various concessions, the Republicans assured the Democrats a place at the presidential patronage trough and support for a bill subsidizing the Texas and Pacific Railroad's construction of a southern transcontinental line. Not all of these promises were kept in later years, including the Texas and Pacific subsidy. But the deal held together long enough to break the dangerous electoral standoff. The Democrats permitted Hayes to receive the remainder of the disputed returns—all by the partisan vote of 8 to 7. So close was the margin of safety that

Troop Removal in South Extracts Aching Bayonet Tooth   *Contemporary cartoon.*

the explosive issue was settled only three days before the new president was officially sworn into office.

The compromise bought peace at a price. Violence was averted by sacrificing the black freedmen in the South. With the Hayes-Tilden deal, the Republican party quietly abandoned its commitment to black equality. That commitment had been weakening, in any case. The Civil Rights Act of 1875 was in a sense the last feeble gasp of the congressional radical Republicans. The act supposedly guaranteed equal accommodations in public places and prohibited racial discrimination in jury selection, but the law was born toothless and stayed that way for nearly a century. Hayes clinched the bargain soon after his inauguration, when he appointed former Confederate general D. M. Key as postmaster general. Hayes also withdrew the last federal troops that were propping up carpetbag governments, and the bayonet-backed Republican regimes collapsed as the blue-clad soldiers departed. The solid Democratic South speedily solidified and speedily suppressed the now friendless blacks. Reconstruction, for better or worse, was officially ended.

Cold-Water Integrity on the Potomac

Rutherford ("Rutherfraud") B. Hayes took office with a cloud over his title. Newspapers pilloried him as "Old 8-to-7" and "His Fraudulency," and cartoonists sketched him with "Fraud" on his honest brow. All this cut him deeply. A man of unsullied honor and high ideals—a "Queen Victoria in breeches"—he believed himself rightfully elected. Lucy Webb Hayes, his wife and childhood sweetheart, was a kindred spirit. Family prayers were offered daily; and because both the president and Mrs. Hayes were temperance advocates, "Lemonade Lucy" served no alcohol. The "cold-water administration" swept the fetid, smoke-laden atmosphere out of the wineless White House.

Hayes's years in office were turbulent. Labor disturbances rumbled throughout the country during his term. The explosive atmosphere was largely a by-product of the long years of depression and deflation following the panic of 1873.

Mass disorders convulsed a number of major eastern cities in 1877. The paralyzing railroad strikes of that year, which verged on civil war in places like Baltimore and Pittsburgh, forced Hayes to call out the federal troops. Order was restored only after scores of rioters had been killed or injured.

Economic unrest swept to California and included hardworking Chinese laborers among its victims. By 1880 the Golden State counted seventy-five thousand of these Oriental newcomers, about 9 percent of its entire population. In San Francisco, Irish-born demagogue Denis Kearney incited his followers to violent abuse of the hapless Chinese. The Kearneyites, many of whom were recently arrived immigrants from Europe, fiercely resented the competition of cheap labor from the still more recently arrived Chinese. The beef-eater, they claimed, had no chance against the rice-eater in a life-and-death struggle for jobs and wages. The present tens of thousands of Chinese "coolies" were regarded as a menace; the prospective millions, as a calamity. Taking to the streets, gangs of Kearneyites terrorized the Orientals by shearing off precious pigtails. Some Chinese victims were murdered outright.

Congress finally responded to all this uproar in 1879, when it passed a bill severely restricting the influx of Chinese immigrants. But Hayes, ever the man of honor, vetoed this discriminatory measure on the grounds that it violated the existing treaty with China. Angry Californians burned the president in effigy. Once the scrupulous Hayes was out of the way, in 1882, Congress slammed the door on Chinese laborers, and it stayed slammed until 1943.

Hayes accomplished little that was lasting—except writing "finished" to Reconstruction. His legislative record was negligible, and his political record was a disaster. As the presidential campaign of 1880 approached, Hayes was a man without a party. Denounced as "Granny" Hayes and a "Goody Two-Shoes" reformer, he was openly repudiated by the old-line politicians. He had earlier declared himself to be a single-termer, and this decision proved to be a face-saver because he probably could not have won renomination in any event.

The Garfield Interlude

Deadlocked for thirty-five ballots by the usual Stalwart–Half-Breed standoff, the Republicans finally broke the impasse when they nominated for the presidency in 1880 a "dark-horse" candidate, James A. Garfield of Ohio. Broad-shouldered and tall (6 feet; 1.83 meters), Garfield enjoyed many political assets. Born in a log cabin in the electorally powerful state of Ohio, "Boatman Jim" had struggled up from poverty

**Campaign Banner, Election
of 1880** *(Smithsonian Institution, Division of Political History.)*

by driving mules along the towpaths of the Ohio
Canal. He had served honorably as a Civil War
officer, rising to the rank of major general.

Crestfallen spoilsmen received some slight
consolation. The delegates chose for the vice-
presidency a notorious Stalwart, Senator Conkling's henchman Chester A. Arthur of New
York. The platform declared emphatically for
the protective tariff and somewhat feebly for reform of the civil service, sneeringly labeled the
"snivel service" by those who plundered it for
their own political gain. One Republican delegate from Texas blurted out, "What are we here
for except the offices?"

Wrathful Democrats, still seething over having been robbed of the presidency in 1876,
nominated another former Civil War general,
Winfield S. Hancock. He appealed to veterans
as a hero wounded at Gettysburg, and he was
popular in the South, where he had fair-mind-
edly headed one of the military Reconstruction
districts. The Democratic platform called for
civil-service reform and a "tariff for revenue
only."

The campaigners shunned real controversy
like leprosy, as happened in so many electoral
contests during this politically cautious era.
Turning their backs on the festering problems
of debt-burdened farmers and powerless laborers, Republicans strove desperately to wring another president from the bloody shirt by verbally
refighting the Civil War. They drenched Indiana with Republican money ("soap"), helping to
grease it into the Republican column. Energetic
Democrats, equally oblivious to deepening economic and social injustices, harped on Garfield's alleged receipt of $329 in stock dividends
in the Crédit Mobilier scandal. They chalked
those telltale figures on buildings, walls, and
fences.

Garfield, "the Canal Boy," barely scraped
across the electoral reefs. He polled only 39,213
more votes than Hancock—4,453,295 to
4,414,082—but his margin in the electoral
column was a comfortable 214 to 155. The new
president was an able and generous man and a
devoted son who turned and kissed his mother
after taking the inaugural oath. But he had one
serious weakness. He hated to hurt people's
feelings by saying "no."

Office-hungry Republicans besieged the
White House. "My God!" exclaimed an exasper-

ated Garfield, "What is there in this place that a man should ever want to get into it?" He rewarded his chief political benefactor, James G. Blaine, with the prize plum of the secretaryship of state. The Half-Breed Blaine immediately set out to persuade the president to clip the wings of his perennial Stalwart nemesis, the "turkey-gobbler" Senator Roscoe Conkling of New York. Conkling, a colossus of conceit, fought back bitterly, especially when the president appointed a staunch anti-Conklingite to the coveted office of collector of the port of New York.

Then, as the political battle was raging, tragedy struck. A disappointed and mentally deranged office seeker, Charles J. Guiteau, shot President Garfield in the back in a Washington railroad station. The victim lingered in agony for eleven weeks and died on September 19, 1881. Guiteau, when seized, reportedly cried: "I am a Stalwart. Arthur is now President of the United States." The implication was that now the Conklingites would all get good jobs. At his trial, Guiteau went so far as to ask all those who had benefited politically by the assassination to contribute to his defense fund. The appeal availed little, as he was found guilty of murder and hanged.

Statesmen are dead politicians, the saying goes, and Garfield's "martyrdom" undoubtedly enhanced his reputation. Brutal though the thought is, Garfield's greatest single service to his country probably was to die when he did and as he did. An unwitting martyr to the evils of spoils seeking, he departed this life in such a way as to shock public servants into taking action to correct flagrant abuses. The nation might well bow its head in shame when it was a case of "an office—or your life."

President James A. Garfield (1831–1881) *He was the second President to be killed by an assassin's bullet. He may have had a premonition; two days before the shooting he called in Lincoln's son for an hour of recollection of the 1865 assassination. (Culver Pictures, Inc.)*

Chester Arthur Takes Command

Garfield's death was rendered all the more shocking by the low repute of his successor. Arthur had no apparent qualifications for the presidency, though he was well endowed in other ways. The new president was a wealthy, handsome widower who enjoyed a richly stocked wine cellar and a wardrobe that included eighty pairs of trousers. He could wear his clothes to advantage, for he was tall (6 feet 2 inches; 1.88 meters), well proportioned, and sported a mustache with billowing sideburns. His previous political experience consisted almost entirely of faithful service as a spoilsman in Conkling's sprawling political machine.

Disgust with the circumstances of Garfield's murder churned the public's clamor for civil-service reform into an irresistible wave, and Arthur commendably threw his influence behind the movement. The Republican party itself began to reveal a previously undetected enthusiasm for reform. Republicans lost control of the House in the midterm elections of 1882, and they rightly feared further political hemorrhaging if they failed to find a cure for the ravages that the spoils system was inflicting on the body politic.

The Pendleton Act of 1883—the so-called Magna Charta of civil-service reform—was the medicine finally applied to the long-suffering organs of the federal government. It prohibited, at least on paper, financial assessments on jobholders, including lowly scrubwomen. It established a merit system of making appointments to office on the basis of aptitude rather than "pull." It set up a Civil Service Commission, charged with administering open competitive examinations to applicants for posts in the classified service. Offices not "classified" by the president remained the fought-over footballs of politics.

Ironically, the success of the new antispoilsmen law depended largely on the cooperation of a seasoned former spoilsman, President Arthur. Fortunately, he cooperated with vigor. By 1884 he had classified nearly 14,000 federal offices,

The Office Makes the Man   *Besieged by his former New York cronies, Arthur tries to assert the dignity of his new presidential office. ("The Proper Thing," James A. Wales, as printed in* Judge, *November 19, 1881. Courtesy, Harvard College Library.)*

But observers at first underestimated Arthur. He proved to have unsuspected reserves of intelligence, idealism, and integrity. A Phi Beta Kappa graduate of Union College, he had served as a lawyer for the abolitionist cause while a young man in New York. Now the responsibilities of the highest office in the land lifted "Prince" Arthur to new, unexpected heights. He prosecuted with vigor certain post-office frauds and gave his former Conklingite cronies a frosty reception when they came seeking favors. "For the vice-presidency, I was indebted to Mr. Conkling," he declared, "but for the presidency of the United States my debt is to the Almighty."

Theodore Roosevelt, an ardent civil-service reformer, condemned the patronage system as "tending to degrade American politics. . . . The men who are in office only for what they can make out of it are thoroughly unwholesome citizens, and their activity in politics is simply noxious. . . . Decent private citizens must inevitably be driven out of politics if it is suffered to become a mere selfish scramble for plunder, where victory rests with the most greedy, the most cunning, the most brazen. The whole patronage system is inimical to American institutions; it forms one of the gravest problems with which democratic and republican government has to grapple."

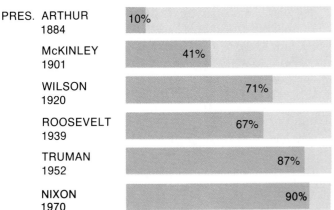

Growth of Classified Civil Service
(subject to competitive requirements)

PRES.			
ARTHUR 1884	10%	13,780 offices out of 131,208	
McKINLEY 1901	41%	106,205 offices out of 256,000	
WILSON 1920	71%	497,603 offices out of 691,116	
ROOSEVELT 1939	67%	662,832 offices out of 920,310	
TRUMAN 1952	87%	2,278,446 offices out of 2,603,267	
NIXON 1970	90%	2,393,000 offices out of 2,645,000	

or about 10 percent of the total. A century later, about 90 percent of federal offices were classified.

Civil-service reform was a necessary idea whose time had come. Yet like many well-intentioned reforms, it bred unintended problems of its own. The law skimmed off much of the cream of federal patronage and put it safely beyond the reach of grasping politicians. They were now forced to look elsewhere for money, "the mother's milk of politics." Increasingly, they turned to the bulging coffers of the big corporations. A new breed of "boss" emerged—less skilled at mobilizing small armies of immigrants and other voters on election day, but more adept at milking dollars from manufacturers and lobbyists. The Pendleton Act partially divorced politics from patronage, but it helped drive politicians into "marriages of convenience" with big-business leaders.

One good term deserves another, and President Arthur's surprising display of integrity deserved to be rewarded with a presidential nomination "in his own right." But his reforms had offended too many powerful Republicans. His ungrateful party turned him out to pasture, and in 1886 he died of a cerebral hemorrhage.

The Blaine-Cleveland Mudslingers of 1884

James G. Blaine's persistence in pursuit of the presidential nomination finally paid off in 1884. The dashing Down-Easter, blessed with almost

Congressman James G. Blaine *His very political adroitness during a long public career ironically cast doubts on his moral integrity and helped to deny him the presidency. (Courtesy of the National Archives.)*

New York political "boss" Roscoe Conkling denounced the civil-service reformers in the New York World (1877): "[The reformers'] vocation and ministry is to lament the sins of other people. Their stock in trade is rancid, canting self-righteousness. They are wolves in sheep's clothing. Their real object is office and plunder. When Dr. Johnson defined patriotism as the last refuge of a scoundrel, he was unconscious of the then undeveloped capabilities and uses of the word "Reform."

Little Lost Mugwumps Who Had Gone Astray
James G. Blaine, depicted as Little Bo Peep, tries to woo the errant Mugwump reformers back into the Republican fold in 1884. (The Granger Collection.)

every political asset except a reputation for honesty, was the clear choice of the Republican Convention in Chicago. But many reform-minded Republicans gagged on Blaine's candidacy. They referred contemptuously to Blaine as the "tattooed man"—tattooed with countless political villainies. Blaine's enemies publicized the fishy-smelling "Mulligan letters," written by Blaine to a Boston businessman and linking the powerful politician to a corrupt deal involving federal favors to a southern railroad. At least one of the damning documents ended with the furtive warning "Burn this letter." Some reformers, unable to swallow Blaine, bolted to the Democrats. They were sneeringly dubbed *Mugwumps*, a word of Indian derivation apparently meaning "great man" or "holier than thou."*

Victory-starved Democrats, scenting their own success in the nomination of a tainted Republican, turned enthusiastically to a noted reformer, Grover Cleveland. A burly bachelor with a soup-straining mustache and a taste for chewing tobacco, Cleveland was a solid but not brilliant lawyer of forty-seven. He had rocketed

from the mayor's office in Buffalo to the governorship of New York and the presidential nomination in three short years. He enjoyed a well-deserved reputation for probity in office, gained especially by his veto, while governor, of a popular bill reducing fares on New York City's elevated railroads. Moralistic Americans, hungry for a candidate whose character they could applaud, seemed to have found their man at last in "Grover the Good."

Unfortunately, Cleveland's admirers soon got something of a shock. Resolute Republicans, digging for dirt in the past of bachelor Cleveland, unearthed the report that he had been involved in an amorous affair with a Buffalo widow, to whom an illegitimate son had been born, now eight years old. Although several other men had been attentive to her at the same time, Cleveland had forthrightly assumed full responsibility and had made financial provision for the unwelcome offspring. Democratic elders, who had launched the campaign on a high moral plane, were demoralized. They hurried to Cleveland and urged him to lie like a gentleman, but their ruggedly honest candidate insisted, "Tell the truth."

The campaign of 1884 sank to perhaps the lowest level in American experience, as the two parties grunted and shoved for the hog trough

---

*Latter-day punsters jibed that the Mugwumps were priggish politicians who sat on the fence with their "mugs" on one side and their "wumps" on the other.

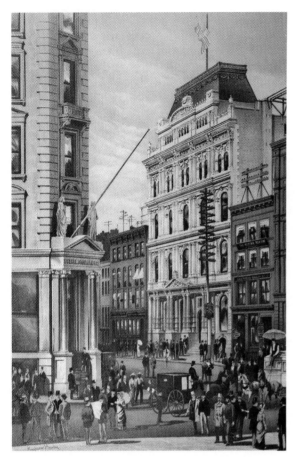

The New York Stock Exchange, c. 1884 *The New York financial community usually supported Republican candidates, but in 1884 many Wall Streeters, including money mogul J. P. Morgan, whose office is shown here on the left, backed Grover Cleveland because of his "sound-money" views. (Eno Collection, New York Public Library.)*

of office. Few fundamental differences separated them. Even the bloody shirt had faded to a pale pink.* Personalities, not principles, claimed the headlines. Enormous crowds of Democrats surged through city streets, chanting—to the rhythm of left, left, left, right, left—"Burn, burn, burn this letter!" Republicans taunted in re-

---

*Neither Blaine nor Cleveland had served in the Civil War. Cleveland had hired a substitute to go in his stead while he supported his widowed mother and two sisters. Blaine was the only candidate nominated by the Republicans from Grant through McKinley (1868 to 1900) who had not been a Civil War officer.

turn: "Ma, ma, where's my pa?" Defiant Democrats shouted back, "Gone to the White House, ha, ha, ha!"

The contest hinged on the state of New York, where Blaine blundered badly in the closing days of the campaign. A witless Republican clergyman damned the Democrats in a speech as the party of "Rum, Romanism, and Rebellion"—insulting at one stroke the race, the faith, and the patriotism of New York's numerous Irish-American voters. Blaine was present at the time but lacked the presence of mind to repudiate the statement immediately. The pungent phrase, shortened to "RRR," stung and stuck. Blaine's silence seemed to give consent, and the wavering Irishmen who deserted his camp helped to account for Cleveland's paper-thin plurality of about a thousand votes in New York State.

Cleveland swept the solid South and squeaked into office with 219 to 182 electoral votes and 4,879,507 to 4,850,293 popular votes. Basically, the issue narrowed down to a choice between public dishonesty and private immorality. The desertion of the Mugwumps and Blaine's mishaps in New York were the deciding factors.

"I Want My Pa!"
Malicious anti-Cleveland cartoon. (Puck.)

A Banner from Cleveland's First Presidential Campaign *This elaborate, fringed banner was typical of the ornate style of the Gilded Age. (Smithsonian Institution.)*

"Old Grover" Takes Over

Bull-necked Cleveland in 1885 was the first Democrat to take the oath of presidential office since Buchanan, twenty-eight years earlier. Huge question marks hung over his portly frame (5 feet 11 inches, 250 pounds; 1.8 meters, 113 kilograms). Could the "party of disunion" be trusted to govern the Union? Would desperate Democrats, ravenously hungry after twenty-four years of exile, trample the frail sprouts of civil-service reform in a stampede to the patronage trough? Could Cleveland restore a measure of respect and power to the maligned and enfeebled presidency?

Cleveland was not a suave or skillful political leader. Inclined to put his foot down rather than slide it down, he could not work well in party harness. His fame had been built on his vetoes, and he at first showed little stomach for taking bold political initiatives. A staunch apostle of the hands-off creed of *laissez-faire*, the new president caused the hearts of businesspeople and bankers to beat with contentment. He summed up his political philosophy in 1887 when he vetoed a bill to provide seeds for drought-ravaged Texas farmers. "Though the people support the government," he declared, "the government should not support the people." As tactless as a mirror and as direct as a bulldozer, he was outspoken, unbending, and profanely hot-tempered.

At the outset, Cleveland calmed the disquiet of some of his critics. He narrowed the North-South chasm by naming to his cabinet two former Confederates, but he stopped far short of handing over the government to ex-rebels. As

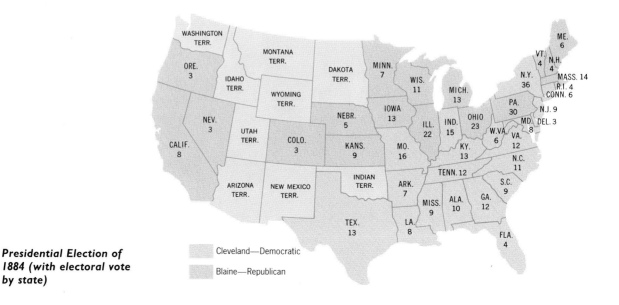

Presidential Election of 1884 (with electoral vote by state)

Cleveland—Democratic

Blaine—Republican

BETWEEN SCYLLA AND CHARYBDIS.

Grover Cleveland (1837–1908) *A strong supporter of civil service reform and tariff reduction, president-elect Cleveland was also the country's most eligible bachelor. In this cartoon of 1884, he is shown struggling to avoid office-seekers on the one side and potential mothers-in-law on the other. (*Puck, *November 26, 1884.)*

for the civil service, Cleveland was whipsawed between the demands of the Democratic faithful for jobs and the demands of the Mugwumps, who had helped elect him, for reform. Believing in the merit system, Cleveland at first favored the cause of the reformers; but he eventually caved in to the carpings of Democratic bosses and fired almost two-thirds of the 120,000 federal employees, including 40,000 incumbent (Republican) postmasters.

Military pensions gave Cleveland some of his most painful political headaches. The Union had tried to treat its veterans generously, but by the 1880s the pension legislation contained gaping loopholes and was aggressively abused. The prospect of easy access to Treasury dollars attracted grafters as honey attracts flies. Slippery pension attorneys ferreted out able-bodied veterans and induced them to file fraudulent claims. If the Pension Bureau proved uncompliant, the claimant might appeal to his congressman, who, mindful of the politically powerful GAR, would often introduce a special bill.

Hundreds of private pension bills were thus logrolled through Congress and sent to the White House. Handouts were granted to deserters, to bounty jumpers, to men who never served, and to former soldiers who in later years had incurred disabilities in no way connected with war service. Cleveland, a slave to his conscience, read the bills carefully, vetoed several hundred of them, and then laboriously penned individual veto messages for Congress. Sometimes he waxed sarcastic, as when referring to one man's "terrific encounter with the measles." A Democrat and a nonveteran, Cleveland was in a vulnerable position when it came to fighting the pension-grabbers. Yet he showed real courage in taking them on. His fortitude was well displayed in 1887 when he risked the retribution of the GAR and vetoed a bill adding several hundred thousand new pensioners to the rolls.

Cleveland Files Rough Edges from Tariff
(Harper's Weekly, 1888.)

Cleveland Battles for a Lower Tariff

During the Civil War, tariff schedules had been jacked up to new high levels, partly to raise revenues for the insatiable military machine. American industry, which was preponderantly in Republican hands, had profited from this protection and hated to see the sheltering benefits reduced in peacetime. But the high duties continued to pile up revenue at the customshouses, and by 1881 the Treasury was running an annual surplus amounting to an embarrassing $145 million. Most of the government's income, in those pre–income tax days, came from the tariff.

Congress could reduce the vexatious surplus in two ways. One was to squander it on pensions and "pork-barrel" bills and thus curry favor with veterans and other self-seeking groups. The other was to lower the tariff—something that the big industrialists vehemently opposed.

Grover Cleveland, the rustic Buffalo attorney, had known little and cared less about the tariff before entering the White House. But as he studied the subject, he was much impressed by the arguments for downward revision of the tariff schedules. Lower barriers would mean lower prices for consumers and less protection for monopolies. Most important, they would mean an end to the Treasury surplus, a standing mockery of Cleveland's professed belief in fiscal orthodoxy and small-government frugality. After much hesitation, Cleveland saw his duty and overdid it.

Rejecting the advice of Democratic politicians, Cleveland decided to prod the hornet's nest of the tariff issue. "What's the use," he insisted, "of being elected or reelected unless you stand for something?" With his characteristic bluntness, Cleveland tossed an appeal for lower tariffs like a bombshell into the lap of Congress in late 1887. The annual message of the president had always been devoted to a review of the year's events, but Cleveland concentrated his fire solely on the tariff.

The response was electric. Cleveland succeeded admirably in smoking the issue out into the open. Democrats were deeply depressed at the obstinacy of their chief. Republicans rejoiced at his apparent recklessness. The old warrior Blaine gloated that "There's one more President for us in [tariff] protection." For the first time in years, a real issue divided the two parties and would dominate the upcoming presidential election of 1888.

Harrison Ousts Cleveland in 1888

Dismayed Democrats, seeing no alternative, somewhat dejectedly nominated Cleveland in their St. Louis convention. Eager Republicans turned to Benjamin Harrison, whose grandfather was former President William Henry ("Tippecanoe") Harrison. The grandson, "Little Ben," was joyously hailed as "Young Tippecanoe" and was pictured wearing his grandfather's military hat. Democrats maliciously cartooned the pint-sized Indianan as rattling around ridiculously in the oversize martial headgear.

The campaign proceeded on a fairly high level, despite some feeble flapping of the bloody shirt and some further probing of Cleveland's private life. The "Beast of Buffalo," who had married his beautiful twenty-one-year-old ward (twenty-seven years his junior) during his second year in the White House, was absurdly accused of beating his wife during drunken fits. But the tariff was the prime issue. The two parties flooded the country with some 10 million pamphlets on the subject.

The British lion's tail came in for some energetic twisting, especially when a California man claiming English birth wrote to the British minister in Washington, Sir Lionel Sackville-West, for advice on how to vote. The foolish diplomat replied, in effect, that a vote for Cleveland, with his low-tariff policies, was a vote for England, the champion of "free trade." Republicans jubilantly trumpeted the indiscreet letter and made it a front-page sensation. The crucial Irish vote in New York, normally Democratic, began to slip away. Cleveland was forced to send the "damned Englishman" packing off to England. Crowds of gleeful Republicans tramped through New York chanting:

> West, West, Sackville-West
> He didn't want to go home
> But Cleveland thought it best.

The specter of a lowered tariff spurred the Republicans to frantic action. In an impressive demonstration of the post–Pendleton Act politics of alliances with big business, they raised a war chest of some $3 million—the lushest yet—largely by "frying the fat" out of nervous industrialists. The money was widely used to line up corrupt "voting cattle" known as "repeaters" and "floaters." In Indiana, always a crucial "swing" state, votes were shamelessly purchased for as much as $20 each.

On election day, Harrison nosed out Cleveland, 233 to 168 electoral votes. A change of about 7,000 ballots in New York would have reversed the outcome. Cleveland actually polled more popular votes, 5,537,857 to 5,447,129. Such are the curiosities of the Electoral College.

Grover Cleveland, the first sitting president to be voted out of his chair since Martin Van Buren in 1840, could count some noteworthy

On the night before the inauguration of Harrison, a crowd of jubilant Republicans tauntingly serenaded the darkened White House with a popular campaign ditty directed at Grover Cleveland:
> Down in the cornfield
> Hear that mournful sound;
> All the Democrats are weeping—
> Grover's in the cold, cold ground!

But Grover was to rise again and serve as president for four more years.

achievements during his four-year term. Two legislative landmarks in 1887 were the Dawes Act, designed to control the Indians (see p. 562), and the Interstate Commerce Act (see p. 512), designed to curb the railroads. Cleveland's administration also retrieved for the government some 81 million acres of the public domain in the West—land that in many cases had been improperly acquired by the "cattle barons" or the railroad "octopus" (see pp. 504–505).

A "Campaign Ball" Used in Harrison's Campaign, 1888 Ball-rolling, torchlight parades and rallies, and similar sorts of hoopla were common features of political campaigns in the late nineteenth century. (Library of Congress.)

But for the most part, Cleveland, despite his gruff integrity and occasional courage, was tied down in office by the same threads that held all presidents of the day to Lilliputian levels. Grant, Hayes, Garfield, Arthur, and Harrison are often called the "forgettable presidents." Bearded and bland in person, they left mostly blanks—or blots—on the nation's political record. In this dull galaxy even such a dim light as Cleveland shone like a bright star. What little political vitality existed was found in local settings, or in Congress, which overshadowed the White House during most of the Gilded Age.

As the nineteenth century drew to a close, observers were asking "Why are the 'best men' not in politics?" One answer was that they had been lured away from public life by the lusty attractions of the booming industrial economy. Talented men ached for profits, not the presidency; they dreamed of controlling corporations, not Congress. What the nation lost in political leadership, it gained in an astounding surge of economic growth. Though still in many ways a political dwarf, the United States was about to stand up before the world as an industrial colossus.

Varying Viewpoints

Historians have long been harsh in their appraisal of the Gilded Age political system. Taking their cue from contemporary satirical commentaries such as Henry Adams' *Democracy* and Mark Twain and Charles Dudley Warner's *The Gilded Age*, they have condemned the politicians of the era as petty, corrupt, and self-serving. Such a view is conspicuous in Charles and Mary Beard's *The Rise of American Civilization* (4 vols., 1927–1942), perhaps the most influential American history textbook ever written. It is equally evident in Vernon Louis Parrington's classic literary history *Main Currents of American Thought* (3 vols., 1927–1930), where the entire era is contemptuously dismissed as the time of "The Great Barbecue."

The Beards and Parrington were leaders of the so-called progressive school of historical writing that flourished in the early years of the twentieth century. Progressive historians, many of whom had reached intellectual maturity in the late nineteenth century, shared Henry Adams' disillusionment that the Civil War had failed to generate a rebirth of American idealism. Their political sympathies were fiercely antibusiness and warmly prolabor, profarmer, and proreform. All these attitudes deeply colored their scholarship and encouraged their conclusion that the Gilded Age was a terrible time in the Republic's history, a time when politicians were irresponsibly preoccupied with irrelevant and distracting issues like the tariff, the civil service, and the money question.

Yet the generation of political leaders from Grant to Cleveland, whatever their faults, succeeded in largely healing the terrible wounds of the Civil War and presided over an unprecedented burst of economic expansion. These were no small achievements, even if one recognizes that they were purchased at a high price (such as the abandonment of the freedmen and the exploitation of industrial workers). Moreover, the late nineteenth century witnessed an unparalleled degree of mass political participation, as "army-style" parties mobilized millions of citizens to take part in the electoral process.

Recently, "ethnocultural" historians like Richard Jensen and Paul Kleppner have explained the high level of political participation by citing the cultural values aroused by local issues like prohibition and education. Yet they have not fully explained the relation between the passions supposedly stirred by these "cultural" questions and the persistence of the major parties in focusing on bread-and-butter economic issues at the national level. The shadow of progressive historiography still lies long across the American historical imagination, preventing a sympathetic, comprehensive appraisal of the genuine accomplishments of the Gilded Age political system, in both the local and national arenas.

Select Readings

Primary Source Documents

Henry Adams penned some perceptive and sour observations on the era in his autobiographical *Education of Henry Adams* (1907) and in his novel *Democracy* (1880). See also the classic satire by Mark Twain and Charles Dudley Warner, *The Gilded Age* (1873).

Secondary Sources

The scandal-rocked Grant era is treated with brevity in James G. Randall and David Donald, *The Civil War and Reconstruction* (rev. ed., 1969), and at greater length in William Gillette, *Retreat from Reconstruction* (1979), and James M. McPherson, *Ordeal by Fire* (1981). Consult also William McFeely, *Grant* (1981). Southern politics is detailed in Otto H. Olsen, *Reconstruction and Redemption in the South* (1980); Terry L. Seip, *The South Returns to Congress* (1983); Michael Perman, *The Road to Redemption* (1984); and J. Morgan Kousser, *The Shaping of Southern Politics* (1974). William Gillette, *The Right to Vote* (1965); Dale Baum, *The Civil War Party System: The Case of Massachusetts, 1848–1876* (1984); and James C. Mohr, *The Radical Republicans and Reform in New York during Reconstruction* (1973), discuss the North. Mark W. Summers analyzes *Railroads, Reconstruction and the Gospel of Prosperity* (1984). On the party systems, see Paul Kleppner, *The Third Electoral System, 1835–1892* (1979); Morton Keller, *Affairs of State: Public Life in Nineteenth-Century America* (1977); Samuel McSeveney, *The Politics of Depression: Political Behavior in the Northeast, 1893–1896* (1972); and Richard Jensen, *The Winning of the Mid-West* (1971). Administrative history is handled in Leonard D. White, *The Republican Era, 1869–1901* (1958). Money questions are treated in Irwin Unger, *The Greenback Era* (1964); Walter T. K. Nugent, *Money and American Society, 1865–1880* (1968); and Allen Weinstein's account of the "Crime of '73," *Prelude to Populism* (1970); C. Vann Woodward sharply analyzes the Compromise of 1877 in *Reunion and Reaction* (rev. ed., 1956). California receives special attention in Alexander Saxton, *The Indispensable Enemy: Labor and the Anti-Chinese Movement in California* (1975).

27

Industry Comes of Age,
1865–1900

The Iron Colt Becomes an Iron Horse

The feverish years after the Civil War witnessed an unparalleled outburst of railroad construction. When Lincoln was shot in 1865, there were only 35,000 miles (56,350 kilometers) of steam railways in the United States, mostly east of the Mississippi. By 1900 the figure had spurted up to 192,556 miles (310,115 kilometers), or more than that for all of Europe combined.

Transcontinental railroad building was so costly and risky as to require governmental subsidies. The extension of rails into thinly peopled regions was unprofitable until the areas could be built up; and private promoters were unwilling to suffer heavy initial losses. Congress, impressed by arguments supporting military and postal needs, began to advance liberal money loans to two favored cross-continent companies in 1862 and added enormous donations of acreage paralleling the tracks. All told, Washington rewarded the railroads with 155,504,994 acres, while the western states contributed 49 million more—a total area larger than Texas.

Grasping railroads tied up even more land than this for a number of years. Land grants were made in broad belts along the proposed route. Within these belts, the railroads were allowed to choose *alternate* mile-square sections in checkerboard fashion (see map). But until they determined the precise location of their tracks and decided which sections were the choicest selections, the railroads withheld *all* the land from other users. President Cleveland put an end to this foot-dragging practice in

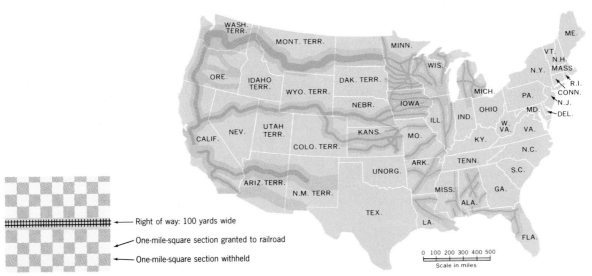

Right of way: 100 yards wide

One-mile-square section granted to railroad

One-mile-square section withheld

Federal Land Grants to Railroads *The color portions indicate areas within which the railroads might be given specific parcels of land. The heavy green lines are in proportion to the land finally granted to the railroads. As shown at left, lands were reserved in belts of various widths on either side of a railroad's right of way. Until the railroad selected the individual mile-square sections it chose to possess, all such sections within the belt were withdrawn from eligibility for settlement.*

1887 and threw open to settlement the still-unclaimed public portions of the land-grant areas.

Noisy criticism, especially in later years, was leveled at the "giveaway" of so valuable a birthright to greedy corporations. But the government did receive beneficial returns, including long-term preferential rates for postal service and military traffic. Granting land was also a "cheap" way to subsidize a much-desired transportation system, because it avoided new taxes for direct cash grants. The railroads could turn the land into gold by using it as collateral for loans or, later, by selling it. This they often did, at an average price of $3 an acre. Critics were also prone to overlook the fact that the land did not have even that relatively modest value until the railroads had ribboned it with steel.

Frontier villages touched by the magic wand of the iron rail became flourishing cities; those that were bypassed often withered away as "ghost towns." Little wonder that communities fought one another for the privilege of playing host to the railroads. Ambitious towns custom-arily held out monetary and other attractions to the builders who sometimes blackmailed them into contributing more generously.

Spanning the Continent with Rails

Deadlock in the 1850s over the proposed transcontinental railroad was broken when the South seceded, leaving the field to the North. In 1862, the year after the guns first spoke at Fort Sumter, Congress made provision for starting the much-talked-about line. One weighty argument for action was the urgency of bolstering the Union, already disrupted, by binding the Pacific Coast more securely to the rest of the Republic.

The *Union* Pacific Railroad—note the word *Union*—was thus commissioned by Congress to thrust westward from Omaha, Nebraska. For each mile (1.6 kilometers) of track constructed, the company was granted 20 square miles (51.8 square kilometers) of land, alternating in 640-acre sections on either side of the track. For each mile the builders were also to receive a generous federal loan, ranging from $16,000 on the flat prairie land to $48,000 for mountainous country. The laying of rails began in earnest after the Civil War ended in 1865; and with juicy loans and land grants available, the "groundhog" promoters made all possible haste.

Sweaty construction gangs, containing many Irish "Paddies" (Patricks) who had fought in the Union armies, worked at a frantic pace. On one record-breaking day, a sledge-and-shovel army of some five thousand men laid 10 miles (16 kilometers) of track. A favorite song was:

> Then drill, my Paddies, drill;
> Drill, my heroes, drill;
> Drill all day,
> No sugar in your tay,
> Workin' on the U. P. Railway.

When hostile Indians attacked, the laborers would drop their picks and seize their rifles. Scores of men lost their lives as they built the line with one hand and fended off the attacking Indians with the other. Relaxation and convivi-ality were provided by the tented towns, known as "hells on wheels," that sprang up at rail's end, sometimes numbering as many as ten thousand men and a sprinkling of painted prostitutes. The fabulous profits of the huge enterprise were reaped by the insiders of the Crédit Mobilier construction company. They slyly pocketed $73 million for some $50 million worth of breakneck construction, while bribing congressmen to look the other way.

Rail laying at the California end was undertaken by the Central Pacific Railroad. This line pushed boldly eastward from boom-town Sacramento, over and through the towering, snow-clogged Sierra Nevada. Four farseeing men—the so-called Big Four—were the chief financial backers of the enterprise. The quartet included the heavyset, enterprising ex-Governor Leland Stanford of California, who had useful political connections, and the burly, energetic Collis P. Huntington, an adept lobbyist. The Big Four cleverly operated through two construction companies, and although they pocketed tens of

Westward Ho *A busy railroad construction camp in the pioneer days of transcontinental railroad building. (Brown Brothers.)*

Leland Stanford (1824–1893) *Multimillionaire railroad builder, California governor, and U.S. senator, he founded Stanford University as a memorial to his only son, who died as a youth. (Stanford University.)*

(golden) spike, with ex-Governor Stanford clumsily wielding a silver sledgehammer.* In all, the Union Pacific built 1,086 miles (1,739 kilometers); the Central Pacific, 689 miles (1,110 kilometers).

Completion of the transcontinental line—a magnificent engineering feat for that day—was one of America's most impressive peacetime undertakings. It spiked the West Coast more firmly to the Union and facilitated a flourishing trade with the Orient. It penetrated the arid barrier of the deserts, paving the way for the phenomenal growth of the Great West. Americans compared this electrifying achievement with the Declaration of Independence and the emancipation of the slaves; jubilant Philadelphians again rang the cracked bell of Independence Hall.

---

*The spike was promptly removed and is now exhibited at the Stanford University Museum. There were two other gold ceremonial spikes.

millions in profits they kept their hands relatively clean by not becoming involved in the bribery of congressmen.

The Central Pacific, which was granted the same princely subsidies as the Union Pacific, had the same incentive to haste. Some ten thousand pigtailed Chinese laborers, with picturesque basket hats and flapping pantaloons, proved to be cheap, efficient, docile, and expendable (hundreds lost their lives in premature explosions and other mishaps). The rocky Sierra Nevada presented a formidable barrier; and the nerves of the Big Four were strained when their workers could chip only a few inches a day through rocky tunnels, while the Union Pacific was sledgehammering westward across the plains.

A "wedding of the rails" was finally consummated near Ogden, Utah, in 1869, as two locomotives gently kissed cowcatchers. The colorful ceremony included the breaking of champagne bottles and the driving of a last ceremonial

Promoting the Union Pacific Railroad, 1869 *(Union Pacific Railroad.)*

Early Pacific Railway Lines (with completion dates) The Great Northern line claimed several distinctions: it was the last-built of the major transcontinental roads, the only one constructed without lavish federal subsidies, and the most northerly. Its larger-than-life promoter, James J. Hill, once declared: "You can't interest me in any proposition in any place where it doesn't snow. . . . No man on whom the snow does not fall ever amounts to a tinker's dam."

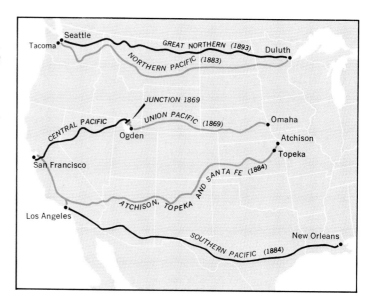

Binding the Country with Railroad Ties

With the westward trail now blazed, four other transcontinental lines were completed before the century's end. None of them secured monetary loans from the federal government, as did the Union Pacific and the Central Pacific. But all of them except the Great Northern received generous grants of land.

The Northern Pacific Railroad, stretching from Lake Superior to Puget Sound, reached its terminus in 1883. The Atchison, Topeka, and Santa Fe, stretching through the southwestern

deserts to California, was completed in 1884. The Southern Pacific ribboned from New Orleans to San Francisco and was consolidated in the same year.

The last spike of the last of the five transcontinental railroads of the nineteenth century was hammered home in 1893. The Great Northern, which ran from Duluth to Seattle north of the Northern Pacific, was the creation of a far-visioned Canadian-American, James J. Hill, a bearlike man who was probably the greatest railroad builder of all. Endowed with a high sense of public duty, he perceived that the prosperity of his railroad depended on the prosperity of the area that it served. He ran agricultural demonstration trains through the "Hill Country" and imported from England blooded bulls, which he distributed to the farmers. His enterprise was so soundly organized that it rode through later financial storms with flying colors.

Yet the romance of the rails was not without its sordid side. Pioneer builders were often guilty of gross overoptimism. Avidly seeking land bounties and pushing into areas that lacked enough potential population to support a railroad, they sometimes laid down rails that led "from nowhere to nothing." When prosperity failed to smile upon their coming, they went into bankruptcy, carrying down with them the

In 1892 General Weaver, nominee of the Populists, wrote regarding the railroad magnates: "In their delirium of greed the managers of our transportation systems disregard both private right and the public welfare. Today they will combine and bankrupt their weak rivals, and by the expenditure of a trifling sum possess themselves of properties which cost the outlay of millions. Tomorrow they will capitalize their booty for five times the cost, issue their bonds, and proceed to levy tariffs upon the people to pay dividends upon the fraud."

savings of trusting investors. Many of the large railroads in the post–Civil War decades passed through seemingly endless bankruptcies, mergers, or reorganizations.

Railroad Consolidation and Mechanization

The success of the western lines was facilitated by welding together and expanding the older eastern networks, notably the New York Central. The moving genius in this enterprise was "Commodore" Cornelius Vanderbilt—burly, boisterous, white-whiskered. Having made his millions in steamboating, he daringly turned, in his late sixties, to a new career in railroading. Though ill educated, ungrammatical, coarse, and ruthless, he was clear-visioned. Offering superior service at lower rates, he amassed a fortune of $100 million. His name is perhaps best remembered through his contribution of $1 million to the founding of Vanderbilt University in Tennessee.

Two significant new improvements proved a boon to the railroads. One was the steel rail, which Vanderbilt helped popularize when he replaced the old iron tracks of the New York Central with the tougher metal. Steel was safer and more economical because it could bear a heavier load. A standard gauge of track width likewise came into wide use during the postwar years, thus eliminating the expense and inconvenience of numerous changes from one line to another.

Other refinements played a vital role in railroading. The Westinghouse air brake, generally adopted in the 1870s, was a marvelous contribution to efficiency and safety. The Pullman Palace Cars, advertised as "gorgeous traveling hotels," were introduced on a considerable scale in the 1860s. Alarmists condemned them as "wheeled torture chambers" and potential funeral pyres, for the wooden cars were equipped with swaying kerosene lamps. Appalling accidents continued to be almost daily tragedies, despite safety devices like the telegraph ("talking wires"), double-tracking, and (later) the block signal.

Cornelius Vanderbilt (1794–1877) *Vanderbilt established a shipping-land transit line across Nicaragua, in response to the California gold rush. In 1873 he was the first to connect New York and Chicago by rail. (The Granger Collection.)*

Revolution by Railways

Metallic fingers of the railroads touched intimately countless phases of American life. For the first time, a sprawling nation became united in a physical sense, bound with ribs of iron and steel. By stitching North America together from sea to sea, the transcontinental lines created an enormous domestic market for American raw materials and manufactured goods—probably the largest integrated national market area in the world. This huge empire of commerce beckoned to foreign and domestic investors alike, as well as to businesspeople who could now dare

**Traveling First Class,
c. 1899** *The sumptuously
appointed dining car of a
crack train, the Chicago Great
Western Limited. (Library of
Congress.)*

to dream on a continental scale. The very concept of time was altered, as chugging railroad engines tracked the transit of the sun across the heavens, necessitating the creation of distinct "time zones" from coast to coast.

More than any other single factor, the railroad network spurred the amazing industrialization of the post–Civil War years. The puffing locomotives opened up fresh markets for manufactured goods and sped raw materials to the factory. The forging of the rails themselves provided the largest single backlog for the adolescent steel industry.

The screeching iron horse likewise stimulated mining and agriculture, especially in the West. It took farmers out to their land, carried the fruits of their toil to market, and brought them their manufactured necessities. Clusters of farm settlements paralleled the railroads, just as earlier they had followed the rivers.

Railways boomed the cities and played a leading role in the great cityward movement of the last decades of the century. The iron monsters could feed enormous concentrations of people and at the same time ensure them a livelihood by providing both raw materials and markets.

Railroad companies also stimulated the mighty stream of immigration. Seeking settlers to whom their land grants might be sold at a profit, they advertised seductively in Europe and sometimes offered to transport the newcomers free to their farms.

Finally, the railroad, more than any other single factor, was the maker of millionaires. A raw new aristocracy, consisting of "lords of the rail," replaced the old southern "lords of the lash." The multiwebbed lines became the playthings of Wall Street; and colossal wealth was amassed by stock speculators and railroad wreckers.

Wrongdoing in Railroading

Corruption lurks nearby when fabulous fortunes can be amassed overnight. The fleecings administered by the railroad construction companies, such as the Crédit Mobilier, were but the first of the bunco games that the railroad promoters learned to play. Methods soon became more refined, as fast-fingered financiers executed multimillion-dollar maneuvers beneath the noses of a bedazzled public. Jay Gould was the most adept of these ringmasters of rapacity. For nearly thirty years he boomed and busted the stocks of the Erie, the Kansas Pacific, the Union Pacific, and the Texas and Pacific in an incredible circus of speculative skullduggery.

One of the favorite devices of the moguls of manipulation was *stock watering.* The term originally referred to the practice of making cattle thirsty by feeding them salt and then having them bloat themselves with water before they were weighed in for sale. Thus, railroad stock promoters grossly inflated their claims about a given line's assets and profitability and sold stocks and bonds far in excess of the railroad's actual value. "Promoters' profits" often were the tail that wagged the iron horse itself. Railroad managers were forced to charge extortionate rates and wage ruthless competitive battles in order to pay off the exaggerated financial obligations with which they were saddled.

The public interest was frequently trampled underfoot as the railroad titans waged their brutal wars. Crusty old Cornelius Vanderbilt, when told that the law stood in his way, reportedly exclaimed: "Law! What do I care about the law? Hain't I got the power?" On another occasion he supposedly threatened some associates: "I won't sue you, for the law is too slow. I'll ruin you." His son, William H. Vanderbilt, when asked in 1883 about the discontinuance of a fast mail train, reportedly snorted, "The public be damned!"

While abusing the public, the railroaders blandly bought and sold people in public life. They bribed judges and legislatures, employed arm-twisting lobbyists, and elected their own "creatures" to high office. They showered free passes on journalists and politicians in profusion. One railroad man noted in 1885 that in the West "no man who has money, or official position, or influence thinks he ought to pay anything for riding on a railroad."

Railroad kings were, for a time, virtual industrial monarchs. As manipulators of a huge natural monopoly, they exercised more direct control over the lives of more people than did the presi-

The Public Be Damned!   *Wealthy William H. Vanderbilt traveling in one of his palace cars. (New York* Daily Graphic.)

dent of the United States—and their terms were not limited to four years. They increasingly shunned the crude bloodletting of cutthroat competition and began to cooperate with one another to rule the railroad dominion. Sorely pressed to show at least some returns on their bloated investments, they entered into defensive alliances to protect precious profits.

The earliest form of combination was the "pool"—an agreement to divide the business in a given area and share the profits. Other rail barons granted secret rebates or kickbacks to powerful shippers in return for steady and assured traffic. Often they slashed their rates on competing lines, but they more than made up the difference on noncompeting ones, where they might actually charge more for a short haul than for a long one.

Government Bridles the Iron Horse

It was not healthy that so many people should be at the mercy of so few. Impoverished farmers, especially in the Middle West, began to wonder if the nation had not escaped from the slavery power only to fall into the hands of the money power, as represented by the railroad plutocracy.

But the American people, though quick to respond to political injustice, were slow to combat

"Uncle Sam's Wild West Show" The new Interstate Commerce Commission cautiously sets about lassoing refractory railroads under Uncle Sam's watchful eye. (Harper's Weekly, 1887.)

economic injustice. Dedicated to free enterprise and to the principle that competition is the soul of trade, they cherished a traditionally keen pride in progress. They remembered that Jefferson's ideals were hostile to governmental interference with business. Above all, there shimmered the "American dream": the hope that in a catch-as-catch-can economic system, anyone might become a millionaire.

The depression of the 1870s finally goaded the farmers into protesting against being "railroaded" into bankruptcy. Under pressure from organized agrarian groups like the Grange (Patrons of Husbandry), many midwestern legislatures tried to regulate the railroad monopoly.

These scattered state efforts came to a screeching halt in 1886. The Supreme Court, in the famed *Wabash* case, decreed that individual states had no power to regulate *inter*state commerce. If the mechanical monster were to be corralled, the Washington government would have to do the job.

Stiff-necked President Cleveland did not look kindly on effective regulation. But Congress ignored his grumbling indifference and passed the epochal Interstate Commerce Act in 1887. It prohibited rebates and pools and required the railroads to publish their rates openly. It also forbade unfair discrimination against shippers and outlawed charging more for a short haul than for a long one over the same line. Most important, it set up the Interstate Commerce Commission (ICC) to enforce and administer the new legislation.

Despite acclaim, the Interstate Commerce Act emphatically did not represent a popular victory over corporate wealth. One of the leading corporation lawyers of the day, Richard Olney, shrewdly noted that the new commission "can be made of great use to the railroads. It satisfies the popular clamor for a government supervision of railroads, at the same time that such supervision is almost entirely nominal. . . . The part of wisdom is not to destroy the Commission, but to utilize it."

What the new legislation did do was to provide an orderly forum where competing business interests could resolve their conflicts in peaceable ways. The country could now avoid ruinous rate wars among the railroads and outraged, "confiscatory" attacks on the lines by pitchfork-prodded state legislatures. This was a modest accomplishment but by no means an unimportant one. The Interstate Commerce Act tended to stabilize, not revolutionize, the existing business system.

Yet the act still ranks as a red-letter law. It was the first large-scale attempt by Washington to regulate business in the interest of society at large. It heralded the arrival of a series of independent regulatory commissions in the next century, which would massively commit the government to monitoring and directing the private economy. It foreshadowed the doom of freewheeling, buccaneering business practices and served full notice that there was a public interest in private enterprise that the government was bound to protect.

Miracles of Mechanization

Postwar industrial expansion, partly a child of the railroad network, rapidly began to assume gigantic proportions. When Lincoln was elected in 1860, the Republic ranked only fourth among the manufacturing nations of the world. By 1894 it had bounded into first place; and it has never relinquished that leadership. Why the sudden upsurge?

Liquid capital, previously scarce, was now becoming abundant. The word *millionaire* had not been coined until the 1840s, and in 1861 only a handful of individuals were in this class. But the Civil War, partly through profiteering, created immense fortunes; and these accumulations could now be combined with the customary borrowings from foreign capitalists.

The amazing natural resources of the nation were now about to be fully exploited, including coal, oil, and iron. For example, the Minnesota–Lake Superior region, which had yielded some iron ore by the 1850s, contributed the rich deposits of the Mesabi Range by the 1890s. This priceless bonanza, where mountains of red-rusted ore could be scooped up by steam-shovels, ultimately became a cornerstone of a vast steel empire.

Unskilled labor, both homegrown and imported, was now cheap and plentiful. Steel, the keystone industry, came to be based largely on the sweat of low-priced immigrant labor, working in two twelve-hour shifts, seven days a week.

American ingenuity at the same time played a vital role in the second American industrial revolution. Techniques of mass production, pioneered by Eli Whitney, were being perfected by the captains of industry. American inventiveness flowered luxuriantly in the postwar years: between 1860 and 1890 some 440,000 patents were issued. Business operations were facilitated by the cash register, the stock ticker, and the typewriter ("literary piano"), which attracted home-confined women to industry. Urbanization was speeded by the refrigerator car, the electric dynamo, and the electric railway, which displaced animal-drawn cars.

One of the most ingenious inventions was the telephone, introduced by Alexander Graham Bell in 1876. A teacher of the deaf who was given a dead man's ear to experiment with, he remarked that if he could make the dumb talk, he could make iron speak. America was speedily turned into a nation of "telephoniacs," as a gigantic system was erected on his invention. The social impact of this instrument was further revealed when an additional army of "number please" women was attracted from the home into industry. Telephone boys were at first employed at switchboards, but their profanity shocked patrons.

The most versatile inventor of all was Thomas A. Edison, who as a boy had been considered so dull-witted that he was taken out of school. This "Wizard of the Wires" ran a veritable invention factory in New Jersey. He is perhaps best known for his perfection in 1879 of the electric light, which he unveiled after trying some six thousand filaments. So deaf that he was not easily distracted, he displayed sleepless energy and a flair for practical money-making schemes rather than pure science. He invented, perfected, or did useful exploratory work on the phonograph, the mimeograph, the dictaphone,

> Regarding the exploitation of immigrant labor, Ralph Waldo Emerson wrote in 1860: "The German and Irish millions, like the Negro, have a great deal of guano in their destiny. They are ferried over the Atlantic, and carted over America, to ditch and to drudge, to make corn cheap, and then to lie down prematurely to make a spot of green grass on the prairie."

THE EDISON "CONCERT" PHONOGRAPH

Advertisement for the New Edison Phonograph
(Harper's Weekly.)

and the moving picture. "Genius," he said, "is one percent inspiration and ninety-nine percent perspiration."

The Trust Titan Emerges

Despite pious protests to the contrary, competition was the bogeyman of most business leaders of the day. Tycoons like Andrew Carnegie, the steel king, John D. Rockefeller, the oil baron, and J. Pierpont Morgan, the bankers' banker, exercised their genius in devising ways to circumvent competition. Carnegie integrated every phase of his steel-making operation. His miners scratched the ore from the earth in the Mesabi Range; Carnegie ships floated it across the Great Lakes; Carnegie railroads delivered it to the blast furnaces at Pittsburgh. When the molten metal finally poured from the glowing crucibles into the waiting ingot molds, no other hands but those in Carnegie's employ had touched the product. Carnegie thus pioneered the creative entrepreneurial tactic of "vertical integration," combining into one organization all phases of manufacturing from mining to marketing. His goal was to improve efficiency by making supplies more reliable, controlling the quality of the product at all stages of production, and eliminating middlemen's fees.

Less justifiable on grounds of efficiency was the technique of "horizontal integration," which simply meant consolidating with competitors to monopolize a given market. Rockefeller was a master of this strategem. He perfected a device for controlling bothersome rivals—the "trust." Stockholders in various smaller oil companies assigned their stock to the board of directors of Rockefeller's Standard Oil Company. It then consolidated and concerted the operations of the previously competing enterprises. "Let us prey" was said to be Rockefeller's unwritten motto. Ruthlessly wielding vast power, Standard Oil soon cornered virtually the entire world petroleum market. Weaker competitors, left out of the trust agreement, went to the wall. Rockefeller's stunning success inspired many imitators, and the word *trust* came to be generally used to describe any large-scale business combination.

The imperial Morgan devised still other schemes for eliminating wasteful competition. The depression of the 1890s drove into his welcoming arms many bleeding businesspeople, wounded by cutthroat competition. His prescribed remedy was to consolidate rival enterprises and to ensure future harmony by placing officers of his own banking syndicate on their various boards of directors. These came to be known as "interlocking directorates."

J. P. Morgan (1837–1913) *As the most influential banker of his day, he symbolized to many people the power and arrogance of "finance capitalism." (Library of Congress.)*

The Supremacy of Steel

"Steel is king!" might well have been the exultant war cry of the new industrialized generation. The mighty metal ultimately held together the new steel civilization, from skyscrapers to coal scuttles, while providing it with food, shelter, and transportation. Steel making, notably rails for railroads, typified the dominance of "heavy industry," which concentrated on making "capital goods," as distinct from the production of "consumer goods" such as clothes and shoes.

Now taken for granted, steel was a scarce commodity in the wood-and-brick America of Abraham Lincoln. Considerable iron went into railroad rails and bridges, but steel was expensive and was used largely for products like cutlery. The early iron horse snorted exclusively (and dangerously) over iron rails; and when in the 1870s "Commodore" Vanderbilt of the New York Central began to use steel rails, he was forced to import them from England.

Yet within an amazing twenty years, the United States had outdistanced all foreign competitors and was pouring out more than one-third of the world's supply of steel. By 1900 the Americans were producing as much as England and Germany combined.

What wrought the transformation? Chiefly the invention in the 1850s of a method of making cheap steel—the Bessemer process. It was named after a derided British inventor, although an American had stumbled on it a few years earlier. William Kelly, a Kentucky manufacturer of iron kettles, discovered that cold air blown on red-hot iron caused the metal to become white-hot by igniting the carbon and thus eliminating impurities. He tried to apply the new "air boiling" technique to his own product, but his customers decried "Kelly's fool steel," and his business declined. Gradually the Bessemer-Kelly process won acceptance, and these two "crazy men" ultimately made possible the present steel civilization.

A revolutionary steel-fabricating process was not the whole story. America was one of the few places in the world where one could find relatively close together abundant coal for fuel, rich iron ore for smelting, and other essential ingredients for making steel. The nation also boasted an abundant labor supply, guided by industrial know-how of a high order. The stage was set for miracles of production.

Carnegie and Other Sultans of Steel

Kingpin among steelmasters was Andrew Carnegie, an undersized, charming Scotsman. As a towheaded lad, he was brought to America by his impoverished parents in 1848 and got a job as a bobbin boy at $1.20 a week. Mounting the ladder of success so fast that he was said to have scorched the rungs, he forged ahead by working hard, doing the extra chore, cheerfully assuming responsibility, and smoothly cultivating influential people.

After accumulating some capital, Carnegie entered the steel business in the Pittsburgh area. A gifted organizer and administrator, he achieved success by picking high-class associates and by eliminating many of the middlemen. Although inclined to be tough-fisted in business, he was not a monopolist and disliked monopolistic trusts. His remarkable organization was a partnership that involved, at its maximum, about forty "Pittsburgh millionaires." By 1900 Carnegie was producing one-fourth of the nation's Bessemer steel, and the partners were dividing profits of $40 million a year, with the "Napoleon of the Smokestacks" himself receiving a cool $25 million. These were the pre–income tax days, when millionaires were really rich, and profits represented take-home pay.

Into the picture now stepped the financial giant of the age, J. Pierpont Morgan. "Jupiter" Morgan had made a legendary reputation for himself and his Wall Street banking house by financing the reorganization of railroads, insurance companies, and banks. An impressive figure of a man, with massive shoulders, shaggy brows, piercing eyes, and a bulbous, acne-cursed red nose, he had established an enviable reputation for integrity. He did not believe that "money power" was dangerous, except when in dangerous hands—and he did not regard his own hands as dangerous.

The force of circumstances brought Morgan and Carnegie into collision. By 1900 the canny

Carnegie Presents the Trust as a Trustworthy Beast *Steel, oil, coal, lumber, sugar, and salt are all represented.* (Harper's Weekly.)

little Scotsman, weary of turning steel into gold, was eager to sell his holdings. Morgan had meanwhile plunged heavily into the manufacture of steel pipe tubing. Carnegie, cleverly threatening to invade the same business, was ready to ruin his rival if he did not receive his price. The steelmaster's agents haggled with the imperious Morgan for eight agonizing hours, and the financier finally agreed to buy out Carnegie for over $400 million. Fearing that he would die "disgraced" with so much wealth, Carnegie dedicated the remaining years of his

> Carnegie wrote in 1889: "The man who dies leaving behind him millions of available wealth, which was his to administer during life, will pass away 'unwept, unhonored, and unsung,' no matter to what uses he leaves the dross which he cannot take with him. Of such as these the public verdict will then be: 'The man who dies thus rich dies disgraced.'"

life to giving away money for public libraries, pensions for professors, and other such philanthropic purposes—in all disposing of about $350 million.

Morgan moved rapidly to expand his new industrial empire. He took the Carnegie holdings, added others, "watered" the stock liberally, and in 1901 launched the enlarged United States Steel Corporation. Capitalized at $1.4 million, it was America's first billion-dollar corporation—a larger sum than the total estimated wealth of the nation in 1800. The industrial revolution, with its hot Bessemer breath, had at last come into its own.

Rockefeller Grows an American Beauty Rose

A sudden emergence of the oil industry was one of the most striking developments of the years during and after the Civil War. Traces of oil found on streams had earlier been bottled for back-rub and other patent medicines, but not until 1859 did the first well in Pennsylvania—"Drake's Folly"—pour out its liquid "black gold." Almost overnight an industry was born that was to take more wealth from the earth—and more useful wealth at that—than all of the gold extracted by the forty-niners and their western successors. The soaring popularity of kerosene as an illuminant for lamps struck a crippling blow at the old whale-oil business.

John D. Rockefeller—lanky, shrewd, ambitious, abstemious (he neither drank, smoked, nor swore)—came to dominate the oil industry. Born to a family of precarious income, he became a successful businessman at age nineteen. One upward stride led to another, and in 1870 he organized the Standard Oil Company of Ohio, nucleus of the great trust formed in 1882. Locating his refineries in Cleveland, he sought to eliminate the middlemen and squeeze out competitors.

Pious and parsimonious, Rockefeller flourished in an era of completely free enterprise. So-called piratical practices were employed by "corsairs of finance," and business ethics were distressingly low. Rockefeller, operating "just to the windward of the law," pursued a policy of rule or ruin. "Sell all the oil that is sold in your district" was the hard-boiled order that went out to his local agents. By 1877 Rockefeller controlled 95 percent of all the oil refineries in the country.

Rockefeller—"Reckafellow," as Carnegie had once called him—showed little mercy. A kind of primitive savagery prevailed in the jungle world of big business, where only the fittest survived. Or so Rockefeller believed. His son later explained that the giant American Beauty rose could be produced "only by sacrificing the early buds that grew up around it." His father pinched off the small buds with complete ruthlessness. Employing spies and extorting secret rebates from the railroads, he even forced the lines to pay him rebates on the freight bills of his competitors!

Rockefeller thought he was simply obeying a law of nature. "The time was ripe" for aggressive consolidation, he later reflected. "It had to come, though all we saw at the moment was the need to save ourselves from wasteful conditions. . . . The day of combination is here to stay. Individualism has gone, never to return."

Washington as Seen by the Trusts   *"What a funny little government,"* John D. Rockefeller observes in this satirical cartoon. His own wealth and power are presumed to dwarf the resources of the federal government. *(The Verdict, January 22, 1900. New York Public Library.)*

On the other side of the ledger, Rockefeller's oil monopoly did turn out a superior product at a relatively cheap price. It achieved important economies, both at home and abroad, by its large-scale methods of production and distribution. This, in truth, was the tale of the other trusts, as well. The efficient use of expensive machinery called for bigness, and consolidation proved more profitable than ruinous price wars.

Other trusts blossomed along with the American Beauty of oil. These included the sugar trust, the tobacco trust, the leather trust, and the harvester trust, which amalgamated some two hundred competitors. The meat industry arose on the backs of bawling western herds, and meat kings like Gustavus F. Swift and Philip Armour took their place among the new royalty. Wealth was coming to dominate the commonwealth.

These untrustworthy trusts, and the "pirates" who captained them, were disturbingly new. They eclipsed an older American aristocracy of modestly successful merchants and professionals. An arrogant class of "new rich" was now elbowing aside the patrician families in the mad scramble for power and prestige. Not surprisingly, the ranks of the antitrust crusaders were frequently spearheaded by the "best men"—genteel old-family do-gooders who were not radicals but conservative defenders of their own vanishing influence.

The Gospel of Wealth

Monarchs of yore invoked the divine right of kings, and America's industrial plutocrats took a somewhat similar stance. Some candidly credited heavenly help. "Godliness is in league with riches," preached the Episcopal bishop of Massachusetts, and hardfisted John D. Rockefeller piously acknowledged that "the good Lord gave me my money." But most defenders of wide-open capitalism relied more heavily on the survival-of-the-fittest theories of Charles Darwin. "The millionaires are a product of natural selection," concluded Yale Professor William Graham Sumner. "They get high wages and live in luxury, but the bargain is a good one for society."

Despite plutocracy and deepening class divisions, the captains of industry provided material progress.

Self-justification by the wealthy inevitably involved contempt for the poor. Many of the rich, especially the newly rich, had pulled themselves up by their own bootstraps; hence, they concluded that those who stayed poor must be lazy and lacking in enterprise. The Reverend Russell Conwell of Philadelphia became rich by delivering his lecture "Acres of Diamonds" thousands of times. In it he said, "There is not a poor person in the Unied States who was not made poor by his own shortcomings." Such attitudes were a formidable roadblock to social reform.

Plutocracy, like the earlier slavocracy, took its stand firmly on the Constitution. The clause that gave Congress sole jurisdiction over interstate commerce was a godsend to the monopolists; their high-priced lawyers used it time and again to thwart controls by the state legislatures. Giant trusts likewise sought refuge behind the Fourteenth Amendment, which had been originally designed to protect the rights of the ex-slaves as persons. The courts ingeniously interpreted a corporation to be a legal "person" and decreed that, as such, it could not be deprived of its property by a state without "due process of law" (see Art. XIV, para. 1). There is some questionable evidence that slippery corporation lawyers deliberately inserted this loophole when the Fourteenth Amendment was being fashioned in 1866.

Great industrialists likewise sought to incorporate in "easy states," like New Jersey, where the restrictions on big business were mild or

> Industrial millionaires were condemned in the Populist platform of 1892: "The fruits of the toil of millions are boldly stolen to build up colossal fortunes for a few . . . and the possessors of these, in turn despise the Republic and endanger liberty. From the same prolific womb of governmental injustice we breed the two great classes—tramps and millionaires."

The New Rich and the New Immigrants   A well-to-do family out for a jaunt (above) and a tenement family doing "piecework" at home—shelling nuts for commercial use (below). The young girl at the table seems to be "snitching" some nuts for herself. The apparently growing gulf between the super-rich and the squalid poor deeply worried reformers in the late nineteenth century. They feared that democracy could not survive in the face of such gross inequality. (Above, Brown Brothers; below, International Museum of Photography at George Eastman House.)

nonexistent. For example, the Southern Pacific Railroad, with much of its trackage in California, was incorporated in Kentucky.

The increasing concentration of capital, through trusts and other combines, was astounding. By 1890 the value of all property in the United States was estimated at $65 billion, of which $25 billion represented the assets of corporations. Cynics sneered that *USA* meant United Syndicates of America.

Government Tackles the Trust Evil

At long last the masses of the people began to mobilize against monopoly. They first tried to control the trusts through state legislation, as they had earlier attempted to curb the railroads. Failing here, as before, they were forced to appeal to Congress. After prolonged pulling and hauling, the Sherman Anti-Trust Act of 1890 was finally signed into law.

The Sherman Act flatly forbade combinations in restraint of trade, without any distinction between "good" trusts and "bad" trusts. Bigness, not badness, was the sin. The law proved ineffective, largely because it had only baby teeth or no teeth at all, and because it contained legal loopholes through which clever corporation lawyers could wriggle. But the new act was unexpectedly effective in one respect. Contrary to its original intent, it was used to curb labor unions or labor combinations that were deemed to be restraining trade.

Early prosecutions of the trusts by the Justice Department under the Sherman Act of 1890, as it turned out, were neither vigorous nor successful. The decisions in seven of the first eight cases presented by the attorney general were adverse to the government. More new trusts were formed in the 1890s under President McKinley than during any other like period. Not until 1914 were the paper jaws of the

Sherman Act fitted with reasonably sharp teeth. Until then, there was some question whether the government would control the trusts or the trusts the government.

But the iron grip of monopolistic corporations was being threatened. A revolutionary new principle had been written into the law books by the Sherman Anti-Trust Act of 1890, as well as by the Interstate Commerce Act of 1887. Private greed must henceforth be subordinated to public need.

The South in the Age of Industry

The industrial tidal wave that washed over the North after the Civil War caused only feeble ripples in the backwater of the South. The plantation system had degenerated into a pattern of absentee land ownership. White and black sharecroppers now tilled the soil for a share of

American Industry in 1900 *By the end of the nineteenth century once-rural America boasted the world's largest industrial output—a development with enormous consequences for politics, diplomacy, and family life.*

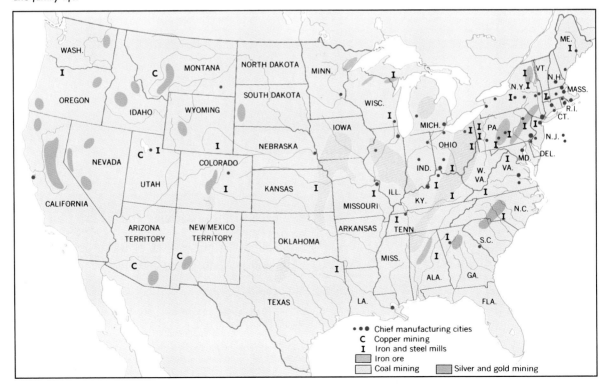

the crop, or they became tenants, in bondage to their landlords who controlled needed credit and supplies.

Southern agriculture received a welcome boost in the 1880s, when machine-made cigarettes replaced the roll-your-own variety and tobacco consumption shot up. James Buchanan Duke took full advantage of the new technology to mass-produce the dainty "coffin nails." In 1890, in what was becoming a familiar pattern, he absorbed his main competitors into the American Tobacco Company. The cigarette czar later showed such generosity to Trinity College, near his birthplace in Durham,

North Carolina, that the trustees gratefully changed its name to Duke University.

Industrialists tried to coax the agricultural South out of the fields and into the factories, but with only modest success. The region remained overwhelmingly rural. Prominent among the boosters of a "new South" was silver-tongued Henry W. Grady, editor of the Atlanta *Constitution*. He tirelessly exhorted the ex-Confederates to become "Georgia Yankees" and outplay the North at the commercial and industrial game.

Yet formidable obstacles lay in the path of southern industrialization. One was the paper barrier of regional rate-setting systems imposed by the northern-dominated railroad interests. Railroads gave preferential rates to manufactured goods moving southward from the north, but in the opposite direction they discriminated in favor of southern raw materials. The net effect was to keep the South in a kind of "third world" servitude to the Northeast—as a supplier of raw materials to the manufacturing metropolis, unable to develop a substantial industrial base of its own.

A bitter example of this economic discrimination against the South was the "Pittsburgh plus" pricing system in the steel industry. Rich deposits of coal and iron ore near Birmingham, Alabama, worked by low-wage southern labor, should have given steel manufacturers there a

SPINDLES IN NEW ENGLAND (by thousands)		SPINDLES IN COTTON STATES (by thousands)
8,632	1880	561
10,934	1890	1,570
13,171	1900	4,368
15,735	1910	10,494
18,287	1920	15,231
11,351	1930	18,586
5,279	1940	17,641
3,739	1950	17,673
269	1980	16,795

Cotton Manufacturing Moves South Textile manufacturing usually looms large in the early stages of industrial development. In later stages, it gives way to higher-technology businesses. This trend can be seen here, both in the migration of textile manufacturing to the southern United States and in the decline in the number of spindles in the United States as a whole since the 1930s, as developing Third World countries became major textile producers.

competitive edge, especially in southern markets. But the steel lords of Pittsburgh brought pressure to bear on the compliant railroads. As a result, Birmingham steel, no matter where it was delivered, was charged a fictional fee, as if it had been shipped from Pittsburgh. This stunting of the South's natural economic advantages throttled the growth of the Birmingham steel industry.

In manufacturing cotton textiles, the South fared considerably better. Southerners had long resented shipping their fiber to New England, and now their cry was "Bring the mills to the cotton." Beginning about 1880, northern capital began to erect cotton mills in the South, largely in response to tax benefits and the prospect of cheap and nonunionized labor. Many smokestacks now pricked the southern skyline, but as late as 1900 the South still produced a smaller percentage of the nation's manufactured goods than it had before the Civil War. (See chart on p. 521.)

The Impact of the New Industrial Revolution on America

Economic miracles wrought during the decades after the Civil War enormously increased the wealth of the Republic. The standard of living rose sharply, and well-fed American workers enjoyed more physical comforts than their coworkers in any other powerful nation. Urban centers mushroomed as the insatiable factories demanded more American labor and as immigrants swarmed like honeybees to the new jobs.

Early Jeffersonian ideals were withering before the smudgy blasts from the smokestacks. As agriculture declined in relation to manufacturing, America could no longer aspire to be a nation of small freehold farms. Jefferson's concepts of free enterprise, with neither help nor hindrance from Washington, were being thrown out the factory window. Tariffs had already provided assistance, but the long arm of federal authority was now committed to decades of corporation curbing and "trust-busting."

Older ways of life also wilted in the heat of the factory furnaces. The very concept of time was revolutionized. Rural American migrants and peasant European immigrants, used to living by the languid clock of nature, now had to regiment their lives by the factory whistle. The seemingly arbitrary discipline of industrial labor did not come easily and sometimes had to be forcibly taught. One large corporation simultaneously instructed its Polish immigrant workers in the English language and in the obligations of factory work schedules:

> I hear the whistle. I must hurry.
> I hear the five-minute whistle.
> It is time to go into the shop. . . .
> I change my clothes and get ready to work.
> The starting whistle blows.
> I eat my lunch.
> It is forbidden to eat until then. . . .
> I work until the whistle blows to quit.
> I leave my place nice and clean.
> I put all my clothes in the locker.
> I must go home.

Probably no single group was more profoundly affected by the new industrial age than women. Sucked into industry by recent inventions, chiefly the typewriter and the telephone switchboard, millions of stenographers and "hello girls" achieved a new economic and social independence. Careers for women also meant delayed marriages and smaller families.

The clattering machine age likewise accentuated class division. "Industrial buccaneers" flaunted bloated fortunes, while their rags-to-riches spouses displayed glittering diamonds. Such extravagances evoked bitter criticism. Some of it was envious, but much of it rose from the small and increasingly vocal group of socialists and other radicals, many of whom were recent European immigrants. The existence of an oligarchy of money was amply demonstrated by the fact that by 1900 about one-tenth of the people owned and controlled nine-tenths of the nation's wealth.

Finally, strong pressures for foreign trade developed as the tireless industrial machine threatened to flood the domestic market. American products radiated out all over the world—notably the five-gallon kerosene can of the Standard Oil Company. The flag follows trade, and empire tends to follow the flag—a harsh lesson that America was soon to learn.

In Unions There Is Strength

Sweat of the laborer lubricated the vast new industrial machine. Yet the wageworkers did not share proportionately with their employers in the benefits of the age of big business.

The worker, suggestive of the Roman galley slave, was becoming a lever-puller in a giant mechanism. Individual originality and creativeness were being stifled, and less value than ever before was being placed on manual skills. Before the Civil War the worker might have toiled in a small plant, whose owner hailed the employee in the morning by first name and inquired after the family's health. But now the factory hand was employed by a corporation—depersonalized, bodiless, soulless, and often conscienceless. The directors knew the worker not; and in fairness to their stockholders they did not feel that they could engage in large-scale private philanthropy.

As new machines were invented, many of the regular employees were thrown out of work. In the long run more jobs were created than destroyed, but in the short run the manual worker was often hard hit. Labor is the most perishable of all commodities. A pair of shoes unsold may be sold tomorrow, but today's labor not sold today is lost forever.

A glutted labor market, moreover, severely handicapped the wage earners. The vast new railroad network could shuttle unemployed workers, including blacks and immigrants, into areas where wages were high and thus beat standards down. Inpouring Europeans further worsened conditions. During the 1880s and

The Reverend Henry Ward Beecher of Brooklyn (1813–1887), the most distinguished (and notorious) clergyman of the era after the Civil War, said: "The trade union, which originated under the European system, destroys liberty. I do not say a dollar a day is enough to support a working man, but it is enough to support a man. Not enough to support a man and five children if a man insists on smoking and drinking beer."

1890s and later, the labor market had to absorb several hundred thousand unskilled workers a year.

Individual workers were powerless to battle single-handedly against giant industry. Forced to organize and fight for basic rights, they found the dice heavily loaded against them. The corporation could dispense with the individual worker much more easily than the worker could dispense with the corporation. Employers could pool vast wealth through thousands of stockholders, retain high-priced lawyers, buy up the local press, and put pressure on the politicians. They could import strikebreakers ("scabs") and employ thugs to beat up labor organizers. In 1886 Jay Gould reputedly boasted, "I can hire one-half of the working class to kill the other half."

Corporations had still other weapons in their arsenals. They could call upon the federal courts—presided over by well-fed and conservative judges—to issue injunctions ordering the strikers to cease striking. If defiance and disorders ensued, the company could request the state and federal authorities to bring in troops. Employers could lock their doors against rebellious workers—a process called the "lockout"—and then starve them into submission. They could compel them to sign "ironclad oaths" or "yellow dog contracts," both of which were solemn agreements not to join a labor union. They could put the names of agitators on a "black list" and circulate it among fellow employers. A corporation might even own the "company town," with its high-priced grocery stores and "easy" credit. Oftentimes the worker sank into perpetual debt—a status that strongly resembled serfdom. Countless thousands of blackened coal miners were born in a company house, nurtured by a (high-priced) company store, and buried in a company graveyard—prematurely dead.

The public, annoyed by recurrent strikes, grew deaf to the outcry of the worker. American wages were perhaps the highest in the world, although a dollar a day for pick-and-shovel labor does not now seem excessive. Carnegie and Rockefeller had battled their way to the top, and the view was common that the laborer could do likewise. Somehow the strike seemed like a

The Strike *1886, by Robert Koehler (1850–1917).* *Scenes like this were becoming more typical of American life in the late nineteenth century, as industrialism advanced spectacularly and sometimes ruthlessly. Here an entire community of men, women, and children—many of them apparently immigrant newcomers—challenges the power of the "boss." The scene is tense but orderly, though violence seems to be imminent, as one striker reaches for a rock. (Collection of Lee Baxandall.)*

foreign importation—socialistic and hence unpatriotic. Big business might combine into trusts to raise prices, but the worker must not combine into unions to raise wages. Unemployment seemed to be an act of God, who somehow would take care of the laborer.

Labor Limps Along

Labor unions, which had been few and disorganized in 1861, were given a strong boost by the Civil War. This bloody conflict, with its drain on human resources, put more of a premium on labor; and the mounting cost of living provided an urgent incentive to unionization. By 1872 there were several hundred thousand organized workers and thirty-two national unions, including such crafts as bricklayers, typesetters, and shoemakers. They were not concerned with the sweet by-and-by but with the bitter here and now.

The National Labor Union, organized in 1866, represented a giant bootstride by the workers. It lasted six years and attracted the impressive total of some 600,000 members, including the skilled, unskilled, and farmers. Its keynote was social reform, although it agitated for such specific goals as the eight-hour day and the arbitration of industrial disputes. It finally succeeded in winning an eight-hour day for government workers, but the devastating depression of the 1870s dealt it a knockout blow. Labor was generally rocked back on its heels during these hectic years. Wage reductions in 1877 touched off a series of strikes on the railroads which were so violent as to verge on civil war.

A new organization—the Knights of Labor—seized the torch dropped by the defunct National Labor Union. Officially known as The Noble and Holy Order of the Knights of Labor, it began inauspiciously in 1869 as a secret society, with a private ritual, passwords, and a grip.

Secrecy, which continued until 1881, would forestall possible reprisals by employers.

The Knights of Labor, like the National Labor Union, sought to include all workers in "one big union." Their slogan was: "An injury to one is the concern of all." A welcome mat was rolled out for the skilled and unskilled, for men and women, for whites and underprivileged blacks, some 90,000 of whom joined. The Knights excluded only liquor dealers, professional gamblers, lawyers, bankers, and stockbrokers.

Setting up broad goals, the embattled Knights refused to thrust their lance into politics. Instead, they campaigned for economic and social reform, including producers' cooperatives and codes for safety and health. Voicing the war cry "Labor is the only creator of values and capital," they frowned upon industrial warfare while fostering industrial arbitration. The ordinary workday was then ten hours or more, and the Knights waged a determined campaign for the eight-hour stint. A favorite song of these years ran:

> Hurrah, hurrah, for labor,
>   it is mustering all its powers,
> And shall march along to victory
>   with the banner of eight hours.

Under the eloquent but often erratic leadership of Terence V. Powderly, an Irish-American of nimble wit and fluent tongue, the Knights won a number of strikes for the eight-hour day. By 1886, though their claim of a million members was evidently exaggerated, they were clearly a force to be reckoned with.

Unhorsing the Knights of Labor

Despite their outward success, the Knights were riding for a fall. They became involved in a number of May Day strikes in 1886, about half of which failed. A focal point was Chicago, which contained about 80,000 Knights. The city was also honeycombed with a few hundred anarchists, many of them foreign-born, who were advocating a violent overthrow of the American government.

Tensions rapidly built up to the bloody Haymarket Square episode. Labor disorders had broken out, and on May 4, 1886, the Chicago police advanced on a meeting called to protest alleged brutalities by the authorities. Suddenly a dynamite bomb was thrown which killed or injured several dozen persons, including police.

Hysteria swept the Windy City. Eight anarchists were rounded up, although nobody proved that they had anything to do directly with the bomb. But the judge and jury held that since they had preached incendiary doctrines, they could be charged with conspiracy. Five were sentenced to death, one of whom committed suicide, and the other three were given stiff prison terms.

Agitation for clemency mounted. In 1892, some six years later, John P. Altgeld, a German-born Democrat of strong liberal tendencies, was elected governor of Illinois. After studying the Haymarket case exhaustively, he pardoned the three survivors. Violent abuse was showered on him by conservatives, unstinted praise by those who thought the men innocent. He was defeated for reelection and died a few years later in relative obscurity, "The Eagle Forgotten." Whatever the merits of the case, Altgeld displayed courage in opposing what he regarded as a gross injustice.

The Haymarket Square bomb helped blow the props from under the Knights of Labor. They were associated in the public mind, though mistakenly, with the anarchists. The eight-hour movement suffered correspondingly, and subsequent strikes by the Knights met with scant success. The right to choose to strike carried with it the right to lose the strike.

Another fatal handicap of the Knights was their inclusion of both skilled and unskilled workers. Unskilled labor could easily be replaced by strikebreaking "scabs." High-class

> Henry George, the tax reformer, observed in 1879, "The methods by which a trade union can alone act are necessarily destructive; its organization is necessarily tyrannical."

craft unionists, who enjoyed a semimonopoly of skills, could not readily be supplanted and hence enjoyed a superior bargaining position. They finally wearied of sacrificing this advantage on the altar of solidarity with their unskilled coworkers and sought refuge in a federation of exclusively skilled craft unions—the American Federation of Labor. The desertion of the skilled craft unionists dealt the Knights a body blow. By the 1890s they had melted away to 100,000 members, and these gradually fused with other protest groups of that decade.

The AF of L to the Fore

The elitist American Federation of Labor, born in 1886, was largely the brainchild of squat, square-jawed Samuel Gompers. This colorful Jewish cigar maker, born in a London tenement and removed from school at age ten, was

Samuel Gompers (1850–1924) *Samuel Gompers declared, "Show me the country in which there are no strikes and I'll show you that country in which there is no liberty." In later years this was notably true of authoritarian countries. (National Archives.)*

brought to America when thirteen. Taking his turn at reading informative literature to fellow cigar makers in New York, he was pressed into overtime service because of his strong voice. Rising spectacularly in the labor ranks, he was elected president of the American Federation of Labor every year except one from 1886 to 1924.

Significantly, the American *Federation* of Labor was just what it called itself—a federation. It consisted of an association of self-governing national unions, each of which kept its independence, with the AF of L unifying overall strategy. No individual laborer as such could join the central body.

Gompers adopted a down-to-earth approach, soft-pedaling attempts to engineer sweeping social reform. A bitter foe of socialism, he kept the federation squarely on the cautious path of conservatism. He had no quarrel with capitalism as such, but he wanted labor to win its fair share. All he wanted, he said simply, was "more." His objectives were better wages and hours, as well as other improved conditions for the worker. Another major goal of Gompers was the "trade agreement" authorizing the "closed shop"—or all-union labor. His chief weapons were the walkout and the boycott, enforced by "We don't patronize" signs. The stronger craft unions of the federation, by pooling funds, were able to amass a war chest that would enable them to ride out prolonged strikes.

The AF of L thus established itself on solid but narrow foundations. Although attempting to speak for all workers, it fell far short of being representative of them. Composed of skilled crafts, like the carpenters and the bricklayers, it was willing to let unskilled laborers, including women and especially blacks, shift for themselves. Though hard-pressed by big industry, the federation was basically nonpolitical. But it did attempt to persuade members to reward friends and punish foes at the polls. The AF of L weathered the panic of 1893 reasonably well, and by 1900 it could boast a membership of 500,000. Critics referred to it, with questionable accuracy, as "the labor trust."

Labor disorders continued throughout the years from 1881 to 1900, during which there was an alarming total of over 23,000 strikes. These disturbances involved 6,610,000 workers, with a total loss to both employers and employees of $450 million. The strikers lost about half their strikes, and won or compromised the remainder. Perhaps the gravest weakness of organized labor was that it still embraced only a small minority of all working people—about 3 percent in 1900.

But attitudes toward labor had begun to change perceptibly by 1900. The public was beginning to concede the right of workers to organize, to bargain collectively, and to strike. As a sign of the times, Labor Day was made a legal holiday by act of Congress in 1894. A few enlightened industrialists had come to perceive the wisdom of avoiding costly economic warfare by bargaining with the unions and signing agreements. But the vast majority of employers continued to fight organized labor, which achieved its grudging gains only after recurrent strikes and frequent reverses. Nothing was handed to it on a silver platter. Management still held the whip hand, and several trouble-fraught decades were to pass before labor was to gain a position of relative equality with capital. If the age of big business had dawned, the age of big labor was still some distance from the horizon.

Varying Viewpoints

The capitalists who forged an industrial America in the late nineteenth century were once called *captains of industry*—a respectful title that bespoke the awe due their wondrous material accomplishments. But these economic innovators have never been universally admired. During the Great Depression of the 1930s, when the entire industrial order they had created seemed to have collapsed utterly, it was fashionable to speak of them as *robber barons*—a term implying scorn for their high-handed methods. This sneer came often to the lips and pens of left-wing critics like Matthew Josephson, who sympathized with the working classes that were allegedly brutalized by the factory system.

Criticism has also come from writers nostalgic for a preindustrial past. These critics see in industrialization a stripping away of the traditions, values, and pride of native farmers and immigrant craftspeople. Conceding that economic development elevated the standard of living for working Americans, this interpretation contends that the industrial revolution diminished their "quality of life." Accordingly, historians like Herbert Gutman and David Montgomery portray labor's struggle for control of the workplace as the central drama of industrial expansion.

In recent years, as attention has focused on problems of economic development in the "Third World," American industrialization in the nineteenth century has come to be regarded as relatively painless and commendably successful. The reputation of the leading capitalists responsible for that process has risen accordingly.

Select Readings

Primary Source Documents

Andrew Carnegie's "Wealth",* *North American Review* (June 1889), gives the philosophy of the Gilded Age's greatest entrepreneur. Henry Grady's Boston speech (1889), in Joel C. Harris, *Life of Henry W. Grady* (1890), dramatizes the plight of the South. Samuel Gompers penned his "Letter on Labor in Industrial Society," an open letter to Judge Peter Grossup, in 1894 (in Richard Hofstadter, *Great Issues in American History*). William Dean Howell's novel *The Rise of Silas Lapham* (1885) treats the moral impact of the new business culture on one New England businessman and his family.

Secondary Sources

A penetrating survey is Samuel P. Hays, *The Response to Industrialism, 1885–1914* (1957). Other useful general accounts include Ray Ginger, *Age of Excess* (1965), and John A. Garraty, *The New Commonwealth* (1968). Stuart Bruchey puts the period in context in *The Growth of the Modern Economy* (1975). Consult also Robert Higgs, *The Transformation of the American Economy, 1865–1914* (1971), and W. Elliot Brownlee, *Dynamics of Ascent: A History of the American Economy* (1974). Business is the subject of Alfred D. Chandler, Jr., *The Visible Hand: The Managerial Revolution in American Business* (1978), and Saul Engelbourg, *Power and Morality: American Business Ethics, 1840–1914* (1980). The thought and attitudes characteristic of the new industrial age are examined by Richard Hofstadter, *Social Darwinism in American Thought* (rev. ed., 1955); Daniel T. Rodgers, *The Work Ethic in Industrial America, 1850–1920* (1978); and John G. Cawelti, *Apostles of the Self-Made Man: Changing Concepts of Success in America* (1965). On the railroads, see George R. Taylor and Irene D. Neu, *The American Railroad Network, 1861–1890* (1956); Robert Fogel, *The Union Pacific Railroad* (1960); and the same author's provocative *Railroads and American Economic Growth* (1964). C. Vann Woodward has provided a masterful analysis of *Origins of the New South, 1877–1913* (1951), which can be profitably supplemented by Jonathan M. Wiener, *Social Origins of the New South* (1978), and Dwight Billings, *Planters and the Making of a "New South"* (1979). Labor is the subject of S. B. Kaufman, *Samuel Gompers and the Origins of the American Federation of Labor* (1973); Gerald Grob, *Workers and Utopia* (1961); and David Montgomery's innovative *Workers' Control in America: Studies in the History of Work, Technology, and Labor Struggles* (1979). Especially stimulating is Herbert Gutman, *Work, Culture, and Society in Industrializing America* (1976). On female workers, see David Katzman, *Seven Days a Week: Women and Domestic Service in Industrializing America* (1978); Philip Foner, *Women and the American Labor Movement* (1979); Alice Kessler-Harris, *Out to Work: A History of Wage-Earning Women in the United States* (1982); and Milton Cantor and Bruce Laurie, eds., *Class, Sex, and the Woman Worker* (1977).

28

America Moves to the City, 1865–1900

What shall we do with our great cities? What will our great cities do with us . . . ? [T]he question . . . does not concern the city alone. The whole country is affected . . . by the condition of its great cities.

Lyman Abbott, 1891

The Urban Frontier

Born in the country, America moved to the city in the post–Civil War decades. By 1900 the nation's upsurging population nearly doubled from its level of some 40 million souls enumerated in the census of 1870. Yet in the same period the population of American cities *tripled*. By the end of the nineteenth century, 4 out of 10 Americans were city dwellers, in striking contrast to the rustic population of stagecoach days.

This cityward drift affected not only the United States, but most of the Western world. European peasants, pushed off the land in part by competition from cheap American foodstuffs, were pulled into cities—in both Europe and America—by the new lure of industrial jobs. A revolution in agriculture thus fed the industrial and urban revolutions.

The growth of American metropolises was spectacular. In 1860 no city in the United States could boast a million inhabitants; by 1890 New York, Chicago, and Philadelphia had spurted past the million mark. By 1900 New York, with some 3.5 million people, was the second largest city in the world, outranked only by London.

Cities grew both up and out. The cloud-brushing skyscraper allowed more people and workplaces to be packed onto a parcel of land. Appearing first as a ten-story building in Chicago in 1885, the skyscraper was made usable by the perfecting of the electric elevator. An opinionated Chicago architect, Louis Sullivan (1856–1924), contributed formidably to the further development of the skyscraper with his famous principle that "form follows function." Nesting loftily above city streets in the new

Cliff Dwellers, by George Bellows *Bellows was a leading artist of the so-called Ashcan School, a group of painters who depicted in realistic detail the squalor and teeming vitality of turn-of-the-century city life. (Los Angeles County Museum of Art, Los Angeles County Funds.)*

steel-skeleton high-rises that Sullivan helped to make popular, many Americans were becoming modern cliff dwellers.

Americans were also becoming commuters, carted daily between home and job on the mass-transit lines that radiated out from central cities to surrounding suburbs. Electric trolleys, powered by wagging antennae from overhead wires, pushed city limits explosively outward. The compact and communal "walking city," its boundaries fixed by the limits of leg-power, gave way to the immense and impersonal megalopolis, carved into distinctly different districts for business, industry, and residential neighborhoods—which were segregated by race, ethnicity, and social class.

Rural America could not compete with the siren song of the city. Industrial jobs, above all, drew country folks off the farms and into factory centers. But the urban life-style also held powerful attractions. The predawn milking of cows had little appeal when compared with the late-night glitter of city lights. Electricity, in-

door plumbing, and telephones—whose numbers leapt from some 50,000 in 1880 to over 1 million in 1900—all made life in the big city more alluring. Engineering marvels like the skyscraper and New York's awesome Brooklyn Bridge, a harplike suspension span dedicated in 1883, further added to the seductive glamour of the gleaming cities.

But the jagged skyline of America's perpendicular civilization could not fully conceal the canker sores of a feverish growth. Criminals flourished like lice in the teeming asphalt jungles. Sanitary facilities could not keep pace with the mushrooming population explosion. Impure water, uncollected garbage, unwashed bodies, and droppings from draft animals enveloped many cities in a satanic stench. Baltimore was described as smelling like a billion polecats.

The cities were monuments of contradiction. They represented "humanity compressed," remarked one observer, "the best and the worst combined, in a strangely composite community." They harbored merchant princes and mis-

erable paupers, stately banks and sooty factories, green-grassed suburbs and treeless
ghettos, towering skyscrapers and stinking tenements. The glaring contrasts that assaulted
the eye in New York reminded one visitor of "a
lady in ball costume, with diamonds in her ears,
and her toes out at the boots."

Worst of all were the human pigsties known
as slums. They seemed to grow ever more
crowded, more filthy, and more rat-infested, especially after the perfection in 1879 of the
"dumbbell" tenement. So named because of the
outline of its floor plan, the dumbbell was usually seven or eight stories high, with shallow,
sunless, and ill-smelling air shafts providing
minimal ventilation. Several families were sardined onto each floor of the barrackslike structures, and they shared a malodorous toilet in
the hall. In these fetid warrens, conspicuously
in New York's "Lung Block," hundreds of un-

The Shift to the City   *Percentage of total population living in cities of twenty-five hundred or more. Note the slowing
of the cityward trend in the 1970s.*

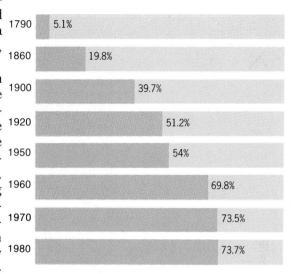

Year	Percentage
1790	5.1%
1860	19.8%
1900	39.7%
1920	51.2%
1950	54%
1960	69.8%
1970	73.5%
1980	73.7%

Lower Broadway, 1875   *Horses still abounded in New York and other cities when this lithograph
was made, but they would soon be displaced by street railways and automobiles. (Library of Congress.)*

fortunate urbanites coughed away their lives. "Flophouses" abounded where the half-starved and unemployed might sleep for a few cents on verminous mattresses. Small wonder that slum dwellers strove mightily to escape their wretched surroundings—as many of them did. The slums remained foul places, inhabited by successive waves of newcomers, but to a remarkable degree hardworking people moved up and out of them. The most successful families left the inner city altogether and headed for the semirural suburbs. These leafy "bedroom communities" eventually ringed the brick-and-concrete cities with a greenbelt of affluence.

The New Immigration

The powerful pull of the American urban magnet was felt even in faraway Europe. A brightly colored stream of immigrants continued to pour in from the old "mother continent." In each of the three decades from the 1850s through the 1870s, more than 2 million migrants had stepped onto America's shores. By the 1880s the stream had swelled to a rushing torrent, as more than 5 million cascaded into the country. A new high for a single year was reached in 1882, when 788,992 arrived—or more than 2,100 a day.

Until the 1880s, most immigrants had come from the British Isles and Western Europe, chiefly Germany and Scandinavia. They were typically fair-skinned Anglo-Saxon and Teutonic types; and they were usually Protestant, except for the Catholic Irish and many Catholic Germans. Many of them boasted a comparatively high rate of literacy and were accustomed to some kind of representative government. Their Old Country ways of life were such that they fitted relatively easily into American society, especially when they took up farms, as many did.

But in the 1880s the character of the immigrant stream changed drastically. The so-called New Immigrants came from Southern and Eastern Europe. Among them were swarthy Italians, Croats, Slovaks, Greeks, and Poles; many of them worshiped in Orthodox churches or synagogues. They came from countries with little history of democratic government, where people had grown accustomed to cringing before despotism. They were heavily illiterate and impoverished. And they flooded into the jam-packed cities rather than move out to farms.

These new peoples totaled only 19 percent of the inpouring immigrants in the 1880s; but by the first decade of the next century, they constituted an astonishing 66 percent of the total inflow. They hived together in cities like New York and Chicago, where the "Little Italys" and "Little Polands" soon claimed more inhabitants than many of the largest cities of the same nationality in the Old World. Some Americans

Annual Immigration, 1860–1984

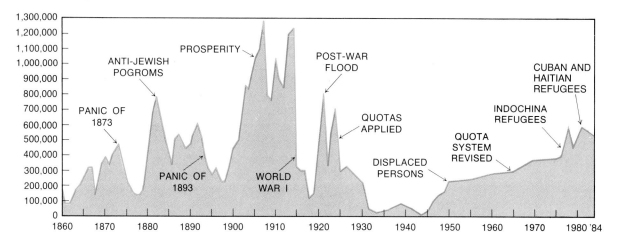

who had arrived earlier were asking if the nation had become a melting pot, a stew kettle, or a dumping ground.

Southern Europe Uprooted

Why were these bright-shawled and quaint-jacketed strangers hammering on the gates? In part, they left their old countries because Europe seemed to have no room for them. The population of the Old World was growing vigorously. It nearly doubled in the century after 1800, thanks in part to abundant supplies of fish and grain from America and to the widespread cultivation in Europe of that humble New World transplant, the potato. American food imports and the galloping pace of European industrialization shook the peasantry loose from its ancient habitats and customary occupations, creating a vast, footloose army of the unemployed. Europeans by the millions drained out of the countryside and into European cities. Most stayed there, but some kept moving and left Europe altogether. About 60 million Europeans abandoned the Old Continent in the nineteenth and early twentieth centuries. More than half of them moved to the United States, but that striking fact should not obscure the important truth that masses of people were already in motion in Europe before they felt the tug of the American magnet. Immigration to America was, in many ways, a by-product of the urbanization of Europe.

"America fever" proved highly contagious in Europe. The United States was often painted as a land of fabulous opportunity in the "America letters" of friends and relatives already transplanted—letters that were soiled by the hands of many readers. "We eat here every day," wrote one jubilant Pole, "what we get only for Easter in our [native] country." The land of the free was also blessed with freedom from military conscription and religious persecution.

Profit-seeking Americans trumpeted throughout Europe the attractions of the new promised land. Industrialists wanted low-wage labor, railroads wanted buyers for their land grants, states wanted more population, and steamship lines wanted more human cargo for their holds. In

> Mary Antin, who came to America from Russian Poland in 1894, when thirteen years of age, later wrote in The Promised Land (1912): "So at last I was going to America! Really, really going, at last! The boundaries burst. The arch of heaven soared. A million suns shone out for every star. The winds rushed in from outer space, roaring in my ears, 'America! America!'"

fact, the ease and cheapness of steam-powered shipping greatly accelerated the transoceanic flood.

As the century lengthened, savage persecution of minorities in Europe drove many shattered souls to American shores. In the 1880s the Russians turned violently upon their own Jews, chiefly in the Polish areas. Tens of thousands of these battered refugees, fleeing their burning homes, arrived in seaboard cities of the Atlantic Coast, notably New York. Virtually unique among the New Immigrants, Jews often had experience with city life in Europe, and many of them brought their urban skills of tailoring or shopkeeping with them when they landed in American cities. Too poor to move further, they huddled together in the already stinking slums, where they were allegedly difficult to "Americanize."

Many of the immigrants never intended to become Americans in any case. A large number of them were single men who worked in the United States for several months or years and then returned home with their hard-earned roll of American dollars. Some 25 percent of the nearly 20 million persons who arrived between 1820 and 1900 were "birds of passage" who eventually returned to their country of origin. For them the grip of the American magnet was never strong.

Even those who stayed in America struggled heroically to preserve their traditional culture. Catholics expanded their parochial-school system, and Jews established Hebrew schools. Foreign-language newspapers abounded. Yiddish theaters, kosher food stores, Polish parishes, Greek restaurants, and Italian social clubs all attested to the desire to keep old ways alive. Yet time took its toll on these efforts to conserve the customs of the Old World in the New. The children of the immigrants grew up speaking fluent English, sometimes mocking the broken grammar of their parents. They often rejected the old country manners of their mothers and fathers in their desire to plunge headlong into the mainstream of American life.

Reactions to the New Immigration

America's governmental system, nurtured in wide-open spaces, was ill suited to the cement forests of the great cities. Beyond minimal checking to weed out criminals and the insane, the federal government did virtually nothing to

Jane Addams (1860–1935) *Though she never married, she "mothered" hundreds of youngsters like this one at Hull House, the Chicago settlement house she founded in 1889. (Jane Addams Memorial Collection, University of Illinois at Chicago, the Library.)*

ease the assimilation of immigrants into American society. State governments, usually dominated by rural representatives, did even less. City governments, overwhelmed by the sheer scale of rampant urban growth, proved woefully inadequate to the task. By default, the business of ministering to the immigrants' needs fell to the unofficial "governments" of the urban political machines, led by "bosses" like New York's notorious Boss Tweed.

Taking care of the immigrants was big business, indeed. Trading jobs and services for votes, a powerful boss might claim the loyalty of thousands of followers. In return for their support at the polls, the boss provided employment on the city's payroll, found housing for new arrivals, tided over the needy with gifts of food and clothing, patched up minor scrapes with the law, and helped get schools, parks, and hospitals built in immigrant neighborhoods. Reformers gagged at this cynical exploitation of the immigrant vote, but the political boss provided valuable assistance that was forthcoming from no other source.

The nation's social conscience, slumbering since the antislavery crusade, gradually awakened to the plight of the cities, and especially their immigrant masses. Prominent in this awakening were several Protestant clergymen, who sought to apply the lessons of Christianity to the slums and factories. Noteworthy among them was Walter Rauschenbusch, who in 1886 became pastor of a German Baptist church in New York City. Also conspicuous was Washington Gladden, who took over a Congregational church in Columbus, Ohio, in 1882. Preaching the "social gospel," they both insisted that the churches tackle the burning social issues of the day. The Sermon on the Mount, they declared, was the science of society, and many social gospelers predicted that socialism would be the logical outcome of Christianity. These "Christian socialists" did much to prick calloused middle-class consciences, thus preparing the path for the progressive reform movement after the turn of the century.

One middle-class woman who was deeply dedicated to uplifting the urban masses was Jane Addams (1860–1935). Born into a prosperous Illinois family, Addams was one of the first generation of college-educated women. Upon her graduation, she sought other outlets for her large talents than could be found in teaching or charitable volunteer work, then the only permissible occupations for a young woman of her social class. Inspired by a visit to England, in 1889 she acquired the decaying Hull mansion in Chicago. There she established Hull House, the most prominent (though not the first) American settlement house.

Soft-spoken but tenacious, Jane Addams became a kind of urban American saint in the eyes of many admirers. The philosopher William James told her: "You utter instinctively the truth we others vainly seek." She was a broad-gauge reformer who courageously condemned war as well as poverty, and she eventually won the Nobel Peace Prize in 1931. But her pacifism also earned her the enmity of some Americans, including the Daughters of the American Revolution, who choked on her antiwar views and expelled her from membership in their august organization.

Located in a poor immigrant neighborhood of Greeks, Italians, Russians, and Germans, Hull House offered instruction in English, counseling to help newcomers cope with American big-city life, child-care services for working mothers, and cultural activities of all kinds for neighborhood residents. Following Jane Addams' lead, women founded settlement houses in other cities as well. Conspicuous among the houses was Lillian Wald's Henry Street Settlement in New York, which opened its doors in 1893.

The settlement houses became centers of women's activism and of social reform. The women of Hull House successfully lobbied in 1893 for an Illinois antisweatshop law that protected women workers and prohibited child labor. They were led in this case by the black-clad Florence Kelley, a guerrilla warrior in the urban jungle. Armed with the insights of socialism and endowed with the voice of an actress, Kelley was a lifelong battler for the welfare of women, children, blacks, and consumers. She later moved to the Henry Street Settlement in New York and served for three decades as general secretary of the National Consumers League.

The pioneering work of Addams, Wald, and Kelley helped blaze the trail that many women—and some men—later followed into careers in the new profession of social work. These reformers vividly demonstrated the truth that the city was the frontier of opportunity for women, just as the wilderness had been the frontier of opportunity for men. The urban frontier opened boundless new possibilities for women—as social workers and secretaries, store clerks and seamstresses, telephone operators and bookkeepers. More than a million women joined the work force in the single decade of the 1890s. As America moved to the city, women moved nearer to economic independence.

Narrowing the Welcome Mat

Antiforeignism, or "nativism," earlier touched off by the Irish and German arrivals in the 1840s and 1850s, bared its ugly face in the 1880s with fresh ferocity. The New Immigrants had come for much the same reasons as the Old—to escape the poverty and squalor of Europe and to seek new opportunities in America. But "nativists" viewed the Eastern and Southern Europeans as culturally and religiously exotic hordes and often gave them a rude reception. The newest newcomers aroused widespread alarm. Their high birthrate, common among people with a low standard of living and sufficient youth and vigor to pull up stakes, raised worries that the original Anglo-Saxon stock would soon be outbred and outvoted. Still more horrifying was the prospect that it would be mongrelized by a mixture of "inferior" South European blood and that the fairer Anglo-Saxon

Sociologist E. A. Ross wrote in 1914: "Observe immigrants . . . in their gatherings. You are struck by the fact that from ten to twenty per cent are hirsute, low-browed, big-faced persons of obviously low mentality. . . . They . . . clearly belong in skins, in wattled huts at the close of the Great Ice Age. These oxlike men are descendants of those who always stayed behind."

Looking Backward *Older immigrants, trying to keep their own humble arrival in America "in the shadows," sought to close the bridge that carried them and their ancestors across the Atlantic. (The New York Public Library, Prints Division, Astor, Lenox and Tilden Foundations.)*

types would disappear. One New England writer cried out in anguish:

> O Liberty, white Goddess! is it well
> To leave the gates unguarded?

"Native" Americans voiced additional fears. They blamed the immigrants for the degradation of urban government. Trade unionists assailed the alien arrivals for their willingness to work for "starvation" wages that seemed to them like princely sums and for importing in their intellectual baggage such dangerous doctrines as socialism, communism, and anarchism. Many business leaders, who had welcomed the flood of cheap manual labor, began to fear that they had embraced a Frankenstein's monster.

Antiforeign organizations, reminiscent of the "Know-Nothings" of antebellum days, were now revived in a different guise. Notorious among them was the American Protective Association

(APA), which was created in 1887 and soon claimed a million members. In seeking its nativist goals, the APA urged voting against Roman Catholic candidates for office and sponsored the publication of lustful fantasies about runaway nuns.

Organized labor was quick to throw its growing weight behind the move to choke off the rising tide of foreigners. Frequently used as strikebreakers, the wage-depressing immigrants were hard to unionize because of the language barrier. Labor leaders argued, not illogically, that if American industry was entitled to protection from foreign goods, the American worker was entitled to protection from foreign laborers.

Congress finally nailed up partial bars against the inpouring immigrants. The first restrictive law, in 1882, banged the gate in the faces of paupers, criminals, and convicts, all of whom had to be returned at the expense of the greedy or careless shipper. Congress further responded to pained outcries from organized labor when in 1885 it prohibited the importation of workers under contract—usually for substandard wages.

In later years other federal laws lengthened the list of undesirables to include the insane, polygamists, prostitutes, alcoholics, anarchists, and persons carrying contagious diseases. A proposed literacy test, long a favorite of nativists because it favored the Old Immigrants over the New, met vigorous opposition. It was not enacted until 1917, after three presidents had vetoed it on the grounds that literacy was more a measure of opportunity than of intelligence.

The year 1882, in addition to the first federal restrictions on immigration, brought forth a law to bar completely one ethnic group—the Chinese (see p. 491). Hitherto America had gathered to her ample breast the oppressed and underprivileged of all races and creeds. Hereafter the gates would be padlocked against defective undesirables—plus the Chinese.

Four years later, in 1886, the Statue of Liberty arose in New York harbor, a gift from the people of France. On its base were inscribed the words of Emma Lazarus:

> Give me your tired, your poor
> Your huddled masses yearning to breathe free,
> The wretched refuse of your teeming shore.

President Cleveland declared in 1897: "It is said . . . that the quality of recent immigration is undesirable. The time is quite within recent memory when the same thing was said of immigrants who, with their descendants, are now numbered among our best citizens."

To many nativists, those noble words described only too accurately the "scum" washed up by the New Immigrant tides. Yet the uprooted immigrants, unlike "natives" lucky enough to have had parents who caught an earlier ship, became American citizens the hard way. They stepped off the boat, many of them full-grown and well muscled, ready to put their shoulders to the nation's industrial wheels. The Republic owes much to these latercomers—for their brawn, their brains, their courage, and the yeasty diversity they brought to American society.

Churches Confront the Urban Challenge

The swelling size and changing character of the urban population posed sharp challenges to American churches, which, like other national

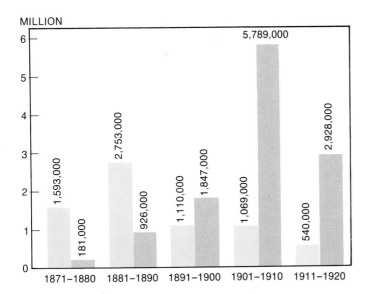

MILLION

Old and New Immigration (by decade)
In the 1970s, the sources of immigration to the United States shifted yet again. The largest number of immigrants came from Latin America (especially Mexico), the next largest from Asia. The old "mother continent" of Europe accounted for only 10 percent of the immigrants to America in the 1980s.

Leading nations of the Old Immigration: England, Ireland, Germany

Leading nations of the New Immigration: Italy, Austria–Hungary, Russia

Values by decade:
- 1871–1880: 1,593,000 / 181,000
- 1881–1890: 2,753,000 / 926,000
- 1891–1900: 1,110,000 / 1,847,000
- 1901–1910: 1,069,000 / 5,789,000
- 1911–1920: 540,000 / 2,928,000

Lady Liberty Being Readied for Travel *A centennial "birthday present" from the French people, the Statue of Liberty arrived from France in 1886. (Cliché: Musées de la Ville de Paris.)*

institutions, had grown up in the country. Protestant churches, in particular, suffered heavily from the shift to the city, where many of their traditional doctrines and pastoral approaches seemed irrelevant. Some of the larger houses of worship, with their stained-glass windows and thundering pipe organs, were tending to become merely sacred diversions or amusements. Reflecting the wealth of their prosperous parishioners, many of the old-line churches were distressingly slow to raise their voices against social and economic vices. John D. Rockefeller was a pillar of the Baptist church; J. Pierpont Morgan, of the Episcopal church. Trinity Episcopal Church in New York actually owned some of the city's worst slum property. Cynics remarked that the Episcopal church had

become "the Republican party at prayer." Some religious leaders began to worry that in the age-old struggle between God and the Devil, the Wicked One was registering dismaying gains. The mounting emphasis was on materialism; too many devotees worshipped "the bitch-goddess success." Money was the accepted measure of achievement, and the new gospel of wealth proclaimed that God caused the righteous to prosper.

Into this spreading moral vacuum stepped a new generation of urban revivalists. Most conspicuous was a former Chicago shoe salesman, Dwight Lyman Moody. Like many of those to whom he preached, Moody was a country boy who had made good in the big city. Proclaiming a gospel of kindness and forgiveness, Moody was a modern urban circuit rider who took his message to countless American cities in the 1870s and 1880s. Clad in a dark business suit, the bearded and rotund Moody held huge audiences spellbound. When he preached in Brooklyn, special trolley tracks had to be laid to carry the crowds who wanted to hear him. Moody contributed powerfully to adapting the old-time religion to the facts of city life. The Moody Bible Institute in Chicago carried on his work after his death in 1899.

Simultaneously, the Roman Catholic and Jewish faiths were gaining enormous strength from the New Immigration. By 1900 the Roman Catholics had increased their lead as the largest single denomination, numbering nearly 9 million communicants. Roman Catholic and Jewish groups kept the common touch better than many of the leading Protestant churches. Cardinal Gibbons (1834–1921), an urban Catholic leader devoted to American unity, was immensely popular with Roman Catholics and Protestants alike. Acquainted with every president from Johnson to Harding, he employed his liberal sympathies to assist the American labor movement.

By 1890 the variety-loving American could choose from 150 religious denominations, 2 of them newcomers. One was the band-playing Salvation Army, whose soldiers without swords invaded America from England in 1879 and established a beachhead on the street corners. Appealing frankly to the down-and-outers, the so-called Starvation Army did much practical good, especially with free soup.

The other important new faith was the Church of Christ, Scientist (Christian Science), founded by Mary Baker Eddy in 1879, after she had suffered much ill health. Preaching that the true practice of Christianity heals sickness, she set forth her views in a book entitled *Science and Health with Key to the Scriptures* (1875), which sold an amazing 400,000 copies before her death. A fertile field for converts was found in America's hurried, nerve-racked, and urbanized civilization, to which Mrs. Eddy held out the hope of relief from discords and diseases through prayer as taught by Christian Science. By the time she passed on in 1910, she had founded an influential church that embraced several hundred thousand devoted worshipers.

Darwin Disrupts the Churches

The old-time religion received many blows from modern trends, including a booming sale of books on comparative religion and on historical criticism as applied to the Bible. Most unsettling of all was *On the Origin of Species*, a highly controversial volume published in 1859, on the eve of the Civil War, by the English naturalist Charles Darwin. He set forth in lucid form the sensational theory that humans had slowly evolved from lower forms of life—a theory that was soon summarized to mean "the survival of the fittest." In American minds the struggle for the survival of the Union eclipsed for a time that for the survival of the fittest, and the real impact of Darwinism was delayed until the postwar years.

Evolution cast serious doubt on a literal interpretation of the Bible, which relates how God created the heaven and the earth in six days. The Conservatives, or "Fundamentalists," stood firmly on the Scripture as the inspired and infallible Word of God, and they condemned what they thought was the "bestial hypothesis" of the Darwinians. "Modernists" parted company with the "Fundamentalists" and flatly refused to accept the Bible in its entirety as either history or science.

Mary Baker Eddy (1821–1910) Her Science and Health *declared: "We classify disease as error, which nothing but Truth or Mind can heal, and this Mind must be divine, not human." (Used with permission © 1929, renewed 1957, The Christian Science Publishing Society. All rights reserved.)*

This furious battle over Darwinism created rifts in the churches and colleges of the post–Civil War era. "Modernist" clergymen were removed from their pulpits; teachers of biology who embraced evolution were dismissed from their chairs. But as time wore on, an increasing number of liberal thinkers were able to reconcile Darwinism with Christianity. They heralded the revolutionary theory as a newer and grander revelation of the ways of the Almighty.

Darwin wrote in 1871: "Man is descended from a hairy, tailed quadruped, probably arboreal in its habits. . . . For my part I would as soon be descended from a baboon . . . as from a savage who delights to torture his enemies, . . . treats his wives like slaves, . . . and is haunted by the grossest superstitions."

> *A famous and vehement evangelist, Billy Sunday, declared in 1908: "I have studied the Bible from Genesis to Revelation, I have read everything that Bob Ingersoll ever spouted. . . . And if Bob Ingersoll isn't in hell, God is a liar and the Bible isn't worth the paper it is printed on."*

As one commentator observed:

> Some call it Evolution,
> And others call it God.

But Darwinism undoubtedly did much to loosen religious moorings and to promote unbelief among the gospel-glutted. The most bitterly denounced skeptic of the era was a golden-tongued orator, Colonel Robert G. Ingersoll, who lectured widely on "Some Mistakes of Moses" and "Why I Am an Agnostic." He might have gone far in public life if he had stuck to politics and refrained from attacking orthodox religion by "giving hell hell," as he put it.

The Lust for Learning

Public education continued its upward climb. The ideal of tax-supported elementary schools, adopted on a nationwide basis before the Civil War, was still gathering strength. Americans were accepting the truism that a free government cannot function successfully if the people are shackled by ignorance. Beginning about 1870, more and more states were making at least a grade-school education compulsory, and this gain, incidentally, helped check the frightful abuses of child labor.

Spectacular indeed was the spread of the high schools, especially by the 1880s and 1890s. Before the Civil War, private academies at the secondary level were common, and tax-supported high schools were rare, numbering only a few hundred. But the concept was now gaining impressive support that a high-school education, as well as a grade-school education, was the birthright of every citizen. By 1900 there were some six thousand high schools. In addition, free textbooks were being provided in increasing quantities by the taxpayers of the states during the last two decades of the century.

Other trends were noteworthy. Teacher-training schools, then called "normal schools," experienced a striking expansion after the Civil War. In 1860 there were only twelve of them; in 1910, over three hundred. Kindergartens, earlier borrowed from Germany, also began to gain strong support. The New Immigration in the 1880s and 1890s brought vast new strength to the private Catholic parochial schools, which were fast becoming a major pillar of the nation's educational structure.

Public schools, though showering benefits on children, excluded millions of adults. This deficiency was partially remedied by the Chautauqua movement, a successor to the lyceums, which was launched in 1874 on the shores of Lake Chautauqua, in New York. The organizers achieved gratifying success through nationwide public lectures, often held in tents and featuring well-known speakers, including the witty Mark Twain. In addition, there were extensive Chautauqua courses of home study, for which 100,000 persons enrolled in 1892 alone.

Crowded cities, despite their cancers, generally provided better educational facilities than the old one-room, one-teacher red schoolhouse. The success of the public schools is confirmed by the falling of the illiteracy rate from 20 percent in 1870 to 10.7 percent in 1900. Americans were developing a profound faith in formal education, often misplaced, as the sovereign remedy for their ills.

Booker T. Washington and Education for Black People

War-torn and impoverished, the South lagged far behind its sister states in public education, and the blacks suffered most severely. A staggering 44 percent of nonwhites were illiterate in 1900. Some help came from northern philanthropists, but the foremost champion of black education was an ex-slave, Booker T. Washington, who had slept under a board sidewalk to save pennies for his schooling. Called in 1881 to head the black normal and industrial school at Tuskegee, Alabama, he began with forty students in a tumbledown shanty. Undaunted by adversity, he succeeded in teaching his people useful trades so that they could gain self-respect and merit a position of economic equality with the whites. But he stopped short of advocating *social* equality.

A stellar member of the Tuskegee faculty, beginning in 1896, was slave-born George Washington Carver, who as an infant in Missouri was kidnaped and ransomed for a horse worth $300. He became an internationally famous agricultural chemist who helped the economy of the South by discovering hundreds of new uses for the lowly peanut (shampoo, axle grease), sweet potato (vinegar), and soybean (paints).

Other black leaders, notably Dr. W. E. B. Du Bois, asssailed Booker T. Washington as an "Uncle Tom," who was condemning their race to manual labor and perpetual inferiority. Born in Massachusetts, Du Bois was a mixture of African, French, Dutch, and Indian blood ("Thank God, no Anglo-Saxon," he would add). After a determined struggle, he earned a Ph.D. at Harvard, the first of his race to achieve this goal. He demanded full equality for the blacks, social as well as economic, and helped to found the National Association for the Advancement of Colored People in 1910. He was especially determined that the "talented tenth" of the black community be given the opportunity to develop their capacities so as to be able to help their race on its difficult upward path. An exceptionally talented historian, sociologist, and poet, he died as a self-exile in Africa in 1963, at the age of ninety-five.

The Hallowed Halls of Ivy

Colleges and universities also shot up like lusty young saplings in the decades after the Civil War. A college education increasingly seemed indispensable in the scramble for the golden apple of success. The educational battle for women, only partially won before the war, now turned into a rout of the masculine diehards.

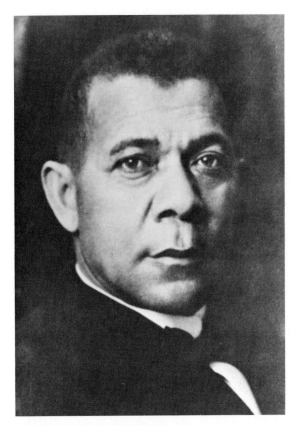

Booker T. Washington (1856–1915)   *In a famous speech in Atlanta, Washington accepted social separateness for blacks: "In all things that are purely social, we can be as separate as the fingers, yet one as the hand in all things essential to mutual progress." (Tuskegee Institute.)*

Women's colleges, like Vassar, were gaining ground; and universities open to both sexes were blossoming forth, notably in the Middle West. By 1900 every fourth college graduate was a woman.

The almost phenomenal growth of higher education owed much to the Morrill Act of 1862. This enlightened law, passed after the South had seceded, provided a generous grant of the public lands to the states for support of education. "Land-grant colleges," most of which became state universities, in turn bound themselves to provide certain services, such as military training. The Hatch Act of 1887, supplementing the Morrill Act, provided federal funds for the establishment of agricultural

Educational Levels, 1870–1985

YEAR	NUMBER GRADUATING FROM HIGH SCHOOL	NUMBER GRADUATING FROM COLLEGE	MEDIAN SCHOOL YEARS COMPLETED (YEARS)*
1870	16,000	9,371	
1880	23,634	10,353	
1890	43,731	15,539	
1900	94,883	27,410	
1910	156,429	37,199	8.1[†]
1920	311,266	48,622	8.2[†]
1930	666,904	122,484	8.4[†]
1940	1,221,475	186,500	8.6
1950	1,199,700	432,058	9.3
1960	1,864,000	389,183	10.6
1970	2,906,000	827,234	12.1
1980	2,747,700	929,000	12.5
1985	2,656,000	945,000	12.6

*Persons twenty-five years and over.
[†]1910–1930 based on retrogressions of 1940 data; 1940 was the first year measured. (Folger and Nam, *Education of the American Population*, a 1960 Census Monograph.)
(Sources: Updates from National Center for Education Statistics. *Digest of Education Statistics, 1983–1984* and *The Condition of Education 1985*.)

experiment stations in connection with the land-grant colleges.

Private philanthropy richly supplemented federal grants to higher education. Many of the new industrial millionaires, developing tender social consciences, donated immense fortunes to educational enterprises. A "philanthropist" was cynically described as "one who steals privately and gives publicly." In the twenty years from 1878 to 1898, these money barons gave away about $150 million. Noteworthy among the new private universities of high quality to open were Cornell (1865) and Leland Stanford Junior (1891), the latter founded in memory of the deceased fifteen-year-old only child of a builder of the Central Pacific Railroad. The University of Chicago, opened in 1892, speedily forged into a front-rank position, owing largely to the lubricant of Rockefeller's oil millions. A Chicago newspaper proclaimed:

> Let us then be up and doing,
> All becoming money kings;
> Some day we may be endowing
> Universities and things.

Rockefeller died at 97, after having given some $550 million for philanthropic purposes.

Significant also was the sharp increase in professional and technical schools, where modern laboratories were replacing the solo experiment performed by instructors in front of their classes. Towering among the specialized institutions was the Johns Hopkins University, opened in 1876, which maintained the nation's first high-grade graduate school. Several generations of American scholars, repelled by snobbish English cousins and attracted by painstaking Continental methods, had attended German universities. Johns Hopkins ably carried on the Germanic tradition of profusely footnoted tomes. Reputable scholars no longer had to go abroad for a gilt-edged graduate degree; and Dr. Woodrow Wilson, among others, received his Ph.D. from Johns Hopkins.

The March of the Mind

Cut-and-dried, the old classical curriculum in the colleges was on the way out, as the new industrialization brought insistent demands for "practical" courses and specialized training in the sciences. The elective system, which permitted students to choose more courses in cafeteria fashion, was gaining popularity. It received a powerful boost in the 1870s, when Dr. Charles W. Eliot, a vigorous young chemist, became president of Harvard College and embarked upon a lengthy career of educational statesmanship.

Winds of "dangerous doctrines" threatened to shipwreck freedom of teaching in the colleges. Disagreeable incidents involved the dismissal of professors who taught evolution or expressed hostility to high tariffs. For many years, some of the big business alumni of Yale vainly sought the bald scalp of the low-tariff economist and sociologist William Graham Sumner.

Medical schools and medical science after the Civil War were prospering. Despite the enormous sale of patent medicines and Indian remedies—"good for man or beast"—the new scientific gains were reflected in improved public health. Revolutionary discoveries abroad, such as those of the French scientist Louis Pasteur and the English physician Joseph Lister, left their imprint on America.* The popularity of heavy whiskers waned as the century ended; such hairy adornments were now coming to be regarded as germ traps. As a result of new health-promoting precautions, including campaigns against public spitting, life expectancy at birth was measurably increased.

One of America's most brilliant intellectuals, the slight and sickly William James (1842–1910), served for thirty-five years on the Harvard faculty. Through his numerous writings he made a deep mark on many fields. His *Principles of Psychology* (1890) helped to establish the modern discipline of behavioral psychology. In *The Will to Believe* (1897) and *Varieties of Religious Experience* (1902), he explored the philosophy and psychology of religion. In his most famous work, *Pragmatism* (1907), he colorfully described America's greatest contribution to the history of philosophy. The concept of pragmatism held that truth was to be tested, above all, by the practical consequences of an idea, by action rather than theories. This kind of reasoning aptly expressed the philosophical temperament of a nation of doers.

The Appeal of the Press

Books continued to be a major source of edification and enjoyment, for both juveniles and adults. Best-sellers of the 1880s were generally old favorites like *David Copperfield* and *Ivanhoe.*

Well-stocked public libraries—the poor man's university—were making encouraging progress, especially in Boston and New York. The magnificent Library of Congress building, which opened its doors in 1897, provided thirteen acres of floor space in the largest and costliest edifice of its kind in the world. A new era was inaugurated by the generous gifts of Andrew Carnegie. This openhanded Scotsman, book-starved in his youth, contributed $60 million for the construction of public libraries all over the country. By 1900 there were about nine thousand free circulating libraries in America, each with at least three hundred books.

Roaring newspaper presses, spurred by the invention of the linotype in 1885, more than kept pace with the demands of a word-hungry public. But the heavy investment in machinery and plant was accompanied by a growing fear of offending advertisers and subscribers. Bare-knuckle editorials were, to an increasing degree, being supplanted by feature articles and noncontroversial syndicated material. The day of slashing journalistic giants like Horace Greeley was passing.

Sensationalism, at the same time, was beginning to debase the public taste. The semiliterate immigrants, combined with straphanging urban commuters, created a profitable market for news that was simply and punchily written. Sex, scandal, and other human-interest stories burst into the headlines, as a vulgarization of the press accompanied the growth of circulation. Critics now complained in vain of these "presstitutes."

Two new journalistic tycoons emerged. Joseph Pulitzer, Hungarian-born and near-

---

*From Pasteur came the word *pasteurize*; from Lister came *Listerine.*

blind, was a leader in the techniques of sensationalism in St. Louis and especially with the New York *World.* His use of the colored comic supplements, featuring the "Yellow Kid," gave the name of *yellow journalism* to his lurid sheets. A close and ruthless competitor was youthful William Randolph Hearst, who had been expelled from Harvard College for a crude prank. Able to draw on his California father's mining millions, he ultimately built up a powerful chain of newspapers, beginning with the San Francisco *Examiner* in 1887.

Unfortunately, the overall influence of Pulitzer and Hearst was not altogether wholesome. Although both championed many worthy causes, both prostituted the press in their struggle for increased circulation; both "stooped, snooped, and scooped to conquer." Their flair for scandal and sensational rumor was happily somewhat offset by the introduction of syndicated material and by the strengthening of the news-gathering Associated Press, which had been founded in the 1840s.

Apostles of Reform

Magazines partially satisfied the public appetite for good reading, notably old standbys like *Harper's,* the *Atlantic Monthly,* and *Scribner's Monthly.* Possibly the most influential journal of all was the liberal and highly intellectual New York *Nation,* which was read largely by professors, preachers, and publicists as "the weekly Day of Judgment." Launched in 1865 by the Irish-born Edwin L. Godkin, a merciless critic, it crusaded militantly for civil-service reform, honesty in government, and a moderate tariff. The *Nation* attained only a modest circulation—about 10,000 in the nineteenth century—but Godkin believed that if he could reach the right 10,000 leaders, his ideas through them might reach the 10 millions.

Another journalist-author, Henry George, was an original thinker who left an enduring mark. Poor in formal schooling, he was rich in idealism and in the milk of human kindness. After seeing poverty at its worst in India, and land-grabbing at its greediest in California, he

> Henry George, in Progress and Poverty (1879), wrote: *"Our boasted freedom necessarily involves slavery, so long as we recognize private property in land. Until that is abolished, Declarations of Independence and Acts of Emancipation are in vain. So long as one man can claim the exclusive ownership of the land from which other men must live, slavery will exist, and as material progresses on, must grow and deepen!"*

took pen in hand. His classic treatise *Progress and Poverty* undertook to solve "the great enigma of our times"—"the association of progress with poverty." According to George, the pressure of growing population on a fixed supply of land unjustifiably pushed up property values, showering unearned profits on owners of land. A single 100 percent tax on those windfall profits would eliminate unfair inequalities and stimulate economic growth.

George soon became one of the most controversial figures of his age. His single-tax ideas were so horrifying to the propertied classes that his manuscript was rejected by numerous publishers. Finally brought out in 1879, the book gradually broke into the best-seller lists and ultimately sold some 3 million copies. George also lectured widely in America, where he influenced thinking about the maldistribution of wealth, and in Britain, where he left an indelible mark on English Fabian socialism.

Edward Bellamy, a quiet Massachusetts Yankee, was another journalist-reformer of remarkable power. In 1888 he published a socialistic novel, *Looking Backward,* in which the hero, falling into a hypnotic sleep, awakens in the year 2000. He "looks backward" and finds that the social and economic injustices of 1887 have melted away under an idyllic government, which has nationalized big business to serve the public interest. To a nation already alarmed by the trust evil, the book had a magnetic appeal and sold over a million copies. Scores of Bellamy Clubs sprang up to discuss this mild utopian socialism, and they definitely influenced American reform movements near the end of the century.

Postwar Writing

As literacy increased, so did book reading. Post–Civil War Americans devoured millions of "dime novels," usually depicting the wilds of the woolly West. Paint-bedaubed Indians and quick-triggered gunmen like "Deadwood Dick" shot off vast quantities of powder, and virtue invariably triumphed. These lurid "paperbacks" were frowned upon by parents, but goggle-eyed youths read them in haylofts or in schools behind the broad covers of geography books. The king of dime novelists was Harlan F. Halsey, who made a fortune by dashing off about 650 novels, often one in a day.

General Lewis Wallace—lawyer-soldier-author—was a colorful figure. Having fought with distinction in the Civil War, he sought to combat the prevailing wave of Darwinian skepticism with his novel *Ben Hur: A Tale of the Christ* (1880). A phenomenal success, the book sold an estimated 2 million copies in many languages, including Arabic and Chinese, and later appeared on stage and screen. It was the *Uncle Tom's Cabin* of the anti-Darwinists, who found in it support for the Holy Scriptures.

An even more popular writer was Horatio ("Holy Horatio") Alger, a Puritan-reared New Englander, who in 1866 forsook the pulpit for the pen. Deeply interested in New York newsboys, he wrote more than a hundred volumes of juvenile fiction that sold over 100 million copies. His stock formula was that virtue, honesty, and industry are rewarded by success, wealth, and honor—a kind of survival of the purest, especially nonsmokers, nondrinkers, nonswearers, and nonliars. Although Alger's own bachelor life was criticized, he implanted morality and the conviction that there is always room at the top (especially if one is lucky enough to save the life of the boss's daughter and marry her).

In poetry Walt Whitman was one of the few luminaries of yesteryear who remained active. Although shattered in health by service as a

Emily Dickinson (1830–1886) *A great American poet, she never married but pursued intense intellectual relationships with several men, including the abolitionist Thomas Wentworth Higginson. (Amherst College Library.)*

Civil War nurse, he brought out successive—and purified—revisions of his hardy perennial, *Leaves of Grass.* The assassination of Lincoln inspired him to write two of the most moving poems in American literature, "O Captain! My Captain!" and "When Lilacs Last in the Dooryard Bloom'd."

The curious figure of Emily Dickinson, one of America's most gifted lyric poets, did not emerge until 1886, when she died and her poems were discovered. A Massachusetts spinster and recluse, disappointed in love, she wrote over a thousand short lyrics on odd scraps of paper. Only two were published during her lifetime, and those without her consent. As she wrote:

> How dreary to be somebody!
> How public, like a frog
> To tell your name the livelong June
> To an admiring bog!

Among the lesser poetical lights was a tragic southerner, Sidney Lanier (1842–1881). He was oppressed by poverty and ill health, and torn between flute playing and poetry. Dying young of tuberculosis, he wrote some of his finest poems while afflicted with a temperature of 104 degrees Fahrenheit (40 degrees Celsius). He is perhaps best known for his "The Marshes of Glynn," a poem of faith inspired by the current clash between Darwinism and orthodox religion.

No other southern poet came as close as Lanier to the first rank in the postwar years of the nineteenth century. Undistinguished for literature before the Civil War, Dixieland had even less reason for distinction after it. But its literary star would rise again in the twentieth century.

Literary Landmarks

In novel writing, the romantic sentimentality of a youthful era was giving way to a rugged realism that reflected more faithfully the materialism of an industrial society. American authors now turned increasingly to the coarse human comedy of the world around them to find their subjects.

Mustachioed Mark Twain (1835–1910) had leapt to fame with *The Celebrated Jumping Frog of Calaveras County* (1867) and *The Innocents Abroad* (1869). He teamed up with Charles Dudley Warner in 1873 to write *The Gilded Age.* An acid satire on post–Civil War politicians and speculators, the book gave a name to an era. With his scanty formal schooling in frontier Missouri, Twain typified a new breed of American authors in revolt against the elegant refinements of the old New England school of writing. Christened Samuel L. Clemens, he served for a time as a Mississippi riverboat pilot and later took his pen name, Mark Twain, from the boatman's cry that meant two fathoms. After a brief stint in the armed forces, Twain journeyed westward to California, a trip he described, with a mixture of truth and tall tales, in *Roughing It* (1872).

Many other books flowed from Twain's busy pen. His *The Adventures of Tom Sawyer* (1876) and *The Adventures of Huckleberry Finn* (1884) rank among American masterpieces, though initially regarded as "trash" by snobbish Boston critics. His later years were soured by bankruptcy growing out of unwise investments,

Mark Twain (1835–1910) *Born Samuel Langhorne Clemens, he was not only America's most popular author, but also a renowned platform lecturer. (The Bettmann Archive.)*

In 1935 Ernest Hemingway wrote: "All modern American literature comes from one book by Mark Twain called Huckleberry Finn. . . . All American writing comes from that. There was nothing before. There has been nothing as good since."

and he was forced to take to the lecture platform and amuse what he called "the damned human race." A great tribute was paid to his self-tutored genius—and to American letters—when England's Oxford University awarded him an honorary degree in 1907. Journalist, humorist, satirist, and foe of social injustice, he made his most enduring contribution in recapturing frontier realism and humor in the authentic American dialect.

Another author who wrote out of the West and achieved at least temporary fame and fortune was Bret Harte (1836–1902). A foppishly dressed New Yorker, Harte struck it rich in California with gold-rush stories, especially "The Luck of Roaring Camp" and "The Outcasts of Poker Flat." Catapulted suddenly into notoriety by those stories, he never again matched their excellence or their popularity. He lived out his final years in London as little more than a hack writer.

William Dean Howells (1837–1920), a printer's son from Ohio, could boast of little schoolhouse education, but his busy pen carried him high into the literary circles of the East. In 1871 he became the editor in chief of the prestigious Boston-based *Atlantic Monthly* and was subsequently presented with honorary degrees from six universities, including Oxford. He wrote about ordinary people and about contemporary and sometimes controversial social themes. *A Modern Instance* (1882) deals with the once-taboo subject of divorce; *The Rise of Silas Lapham* (1885) describes the trials of a newly rich paint manufacturer caught up in the caste system of Brahmin Boston. *A Hazard of New Fortunes* (1890) portrays the reformers, strikers, and Socialists in Gilded Age New York.

Stephen Crane (1871–1900), the fourteenth son of a Methodist minister, also wrote about the seamy underside of life in urban, industrial America. His *Maggie: A Girl of the Streets* (1893), a brutal tale about a poor prostitute driven to suicide, was too grim to find a publisher. Crane had to have it printed privately. He rose quickly to prominence with *The Red Badge of Courage* (1895), the stirring story of a bloodied young Civil War recruit ("fresh fish") under fire. Crane himself had never seen a battle and wrote entirely from the printed Civil

> *Crane wrote in* The Red Badge of Courage: *"At times he regarded the wounded soldiers in an envious way. He conceived persons with torn bodies to be peculiarly happy. He wished that he, too, had a wound, a red badge of courage."*

War records. He died of tuberculosis in 1900, when only twenty-nine.

Henry James (1843–1916), brother of Harvard philosopher William James, was a New Yorker who turned from law to literature. Taking as his dominant theme the confrontation of innocent Americans with subtle Europeans, James penned a remarkable number of brilliant novels, including *Daisy Miller* (1879), *The Portrait of a Lady* (1881), and *The Wings of the Dove* (1902). In *The Bostonians* (1886) he wrote one of the first novels about the rising feminist movement. James frequently made women his central characters, exploring their inner reactions to complex situations with a deftness that marked him as a master of "psychological realism." Long resident in England, he became a British subject shortly before his death.

Candid portrayals of contemporary life and social problems were the literary order of the day by the turn of the century. Jack London (1876–1916), famous as a nature writer in such books as *The Call of the Wild* (1903), turned to depicting a possible fascistic revolution in *The Iron Heel* (1907). Frank Norris (1870–1902), like London a Californian, wrote *The Octopus* (1901), an earthy saga of the stranglehold of the railroad and corrupt politicians on California

> *Jack London, the Socialist who hated strikebreakers known as "scabs," said: "No man has a right to scab so long as there is a pool of water to drown his carcass in, or a rope long enough to hang his body with. Judas Iscariot was a gentleman compared with a scab. For betraying his master, he had character enough to hang himself. A scab has not."*

> *Dreiser's pessimism was reflected in* Sister Carrie: *"Our civilization is still in a middle stage, scarcely beast, in that it is no longer wholly guided by instinct; scarcely human, in that it is not yet wholly guided by reason."*

wheat ranchers. A sequel, *The Pit* (1903), dealt with the making and breaking of speculators on the Chicago wheat exchange.

Conspicuous among the new "social novelists" rising in the literary firmament was Theodore Dreiser (1871–1945), a homely, gangling writer from Indiana. He burst upon the literary scene in 1900 with *Sister Carrie*, a graphically realistic narrative of a poor working girl in Chicago and New York. She becomes one man's mistress, then elopes with another, and finally strikes out on her own to make a career on the stage. The fictional Carrie's disregard for prevailing moral standards so offended Dreiser's publisher that the book was soon withdrawn from circulation.

The New Morality

Victoria Woodhull, who was real flesh and blood, also shook the pillars of conventional morality when she publicly proclaimed her belief in free love in 1871. Woodhull was a beautiful and eloquent divorcée, sometime stockbroker, and tireless feminist propagandist. Together with her sister she published a far-out periodical, *Woodhull and Claflin's Weekly*. The sisters again shocked respectable society in 1872 when their journal struck a blow for the new morality by charging that Henry Ward Beecher, the most famous preacher of his day, had for years been carrying on an adulterous affair.

Pure-minded Americans sternly resisted these affronts to their moral principles. Their foremost champion was a portly crusader, Anthony Comstock, who made lifelong war on the "immoral." Armed after 1873 with a federal statute—the notorious "Comstock Law"—this self-appointed defender of sexual purity boasted that he had confiscated no fewer than 202,679 "obscene pictures and photos"; 4,185 "boxes of pills, powders, etc., used by abortionists"; and 26 "obscene pictures, framed on walls of saloons." His proud claim was that he had driven at least fifteen people to suicide.

The antics of the Woodhull sisters and Anthony Comstock exposed to daylight the battle going on in late nineteenth-century America over sexual attitudes and the place of women. Switchboards and typewriters in the booming cities became increasingly the tools of women's liberation. Economic freedom encouraged sexual freedom, and the "new morality" began to be reflected in soaring divorce rates, the spreading practice of birth control, and increasingly frank discussion of sexual topics. By 1913, said one popular magazine, the chimes had struck "sex o'clock in America."

Families and Women in the City

The new urban environment was hard on families. Not only fathers but mothers and even children as young as ten years old often worked, and usually in widely scattered locations. On the farm having many children meant having more hands to help with hoeing and harvesting; but in the city more children meant more mouths to feed, more crowding in sardine-tin tenements, and more human baggage to carry in the uphill struggle for social mobility. Not surprisingly, birthrates were still dropping and family size continued to shrink as the nineteenth century lengthened. Marriages were being delayed, and more couples learned the techniques of birth control. The decline in family size in fact affected rural Americans as well as urban dwellers, and old-stock "natives" as well as new immigrant groups.

Women were growing more independent in the urban environment, and in 1898 they heard the voice of a major feminist prophet, Charlotte Perkins Gilman. In that year the freethinking and original-minded Gilman published *Women and Economics*, a classic of feminist literature. A distant relative of Harriet Beecher Stowe and

Catharine Beecher, Gilman displayed the restless temperament and reforming zeal characteristic of the remarkable Beecher clan. Strikingly handsome, she shunned traditional feminine frills and instead devoted herself to a vigorous regimen of physical exercise and philosophical meditation.

In her masterwork of 1898, Gilman called on women to abandon their dependent status and contribute to the larger life of the community through productive involvement in the economy. Rejecting all claims that biology gave women a fundamentally different character from men, she argued that "our highly specialized motherhood is not so advantageous as believed." She advocated centralized nurseries and cooperative kitchens to facilitate women's participation in the work force—anticipating by more than half a century the day-care centers and convenience-food services of a later day.

Fiery feminists also continued to insist on the ballot. They had been demanding the vote since before the Civil War, but many high-minded female reformers had temporarily shelved the cause of women to battle for the rights of blacks. In 1890 militant suffragists formed the National American Women's Suffrage Associa-

Marriages and Divorces, 1890–1980

YEAR	MARRIAGES	DIVORCES	RATIO OF DIVORCES TO MARRIAGES
1890	570,000	33,461	1 : 17
1900	709,000	55,751	1 : 12
1910	948,166	83,045	1 : 11
1920	1,274,476	170,505	1 : 7
1930	1,126,856	195,961	1 : 5
1940	1,595,879	264,000	1 : 6
1950	1,667,231	385,144	1 : 4.3
1960	1,523,381	393,000	1 : 3.8
1970	2,159,000	708,000	1 : 3
1980	2,393,000	1,184,000	1 : 2

tion. Its founders included aging pioneers like Elizabeth Cady Stanton, who had helped organize the first woman's rights convention in 1848, and her long-time comrade Susan B. Anthony, the radical Quaker spitfire who had courted jail by trying to cast a ballot in the 1872 presidential election.

By 1900 a new generation of women had taken command of the suffrage battle. Their most effective leader was Carrie Chapman Catt,

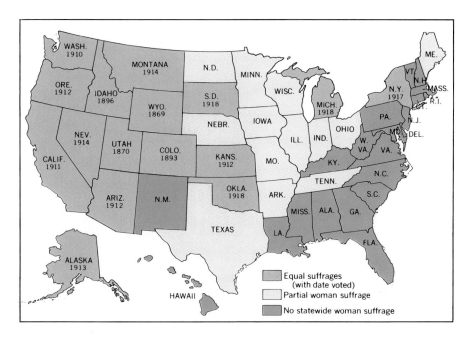

Woman Suffrage before the Nineteenth Amendment *Dates show when a state or territory adopted woman suffrage. Note the concentration of woman-suffrage states in the West.*

a pragmatic and businesslike reformer of relentless dedication. Significantly, under Catt the suffragists deemphasized the argument that women deserved the vote, as a matter of right, because they were in all respects the equals of men. Instead, Catt stressed the desirability of giving women the vote if they were to continue to discharge their traditional duties as homemakers and mothers in the increasingly public world of the city. Women had special responsibility for the health of the family and the education of children, the argument ran. On the farm, women could discharge these responsibilities in the separate sphere of the isolated homestead. But in the city, they needed a voice on boards of public health, police commissions, and school boards.

By thus linking the ballot to a traditional definition of women's role, suffragists registered encouraging gains as the new century opened, despite continuing showers of rotten eggs and the jeers of male critics who insisted that women were made for loving, not for voting. Women were increasingly permitted to vote in local elections, particularly on issues related to the schools. Wyoming Territory—later called "the Equality State"—granted the first unrestricted suffrage to women in 1869. This important breach in the dike once made, many states followed Wyoming's example. Paralleling these triumphs, most of the states by 1890 had passed laws to permit wives to own or control their property after marriage. City life also fostered the growth of a spate of women's organizations, including the General Federation of Women's Clubs, which counted some 200,000 members in 1900.

Prohibition of Alcohol and Social Progress

Alarming gains by Demon Rum spurred the temperance reformers to redoubled zeal. Especially obnoxious to them was the shutter-doored corner saloon, appropriately called "the poor man's club." It helped keep both him and his family poor. Liquor consumption had increased during the nerve-racking days of the Civil War; and immigrant groups, accustomed to alcohol

in the Old Country, were hostile to restraints. Whiskey-loving foreigners in Boston would rudely hiss temperance lecturers.

The National Prohibition party, organized in 1869, polled a sprinkling of votes in some of the ensuing presidential elections. Among the favorite songs of these sober souls were "I'll Marry No Man If He Drinks," "Vote Down the Vile Traffic," and "The Drunkard's Doom." Typical was:

> Now, all young men, a warning take,
> And shun the poisoned bowl;
> 'Twill lead you down to hell's dark gate,
> And ruin your own soul.

Carrie Nation Advertised as a Lecturer   *She holds her famous hatchet. Carrie Nation took her antidrink crusade to several universities, including Harvard and Yale, which she denounced as "hellholes." Predictably, the students greeted her with wild burlesque. (Courtesy Kansas Historical Society.)*

Militant ladies entered the alcoholic arena, notably when the Woman's Christian Temperance Union (WCTU) was organized in 1874. The white ribbon was its symbol of purity; the saintly Frances E. Willard—also a champion of planned parenthood—was its leading spirit. Less saintly was a muscular and mentally deranged "Kansas Cyclone," Carrie A. Nation, whose first husband had died of alcoholism. With her hatchet she boldly smashed saloon bottles and bars, and her "hatchetations" brought considerable disrepute to the prohibition movement by the violence of her one-woman crusade.

But rum was now on the run. The potent Anti-Saloon League was formed in 1893, with its members singing "The Saloon Must Go" and "Vote for Cold Water, Boys." Female supporters sang "The Lips That Touch Liquor Must Never Touch Mine." Statewide prohibition, which had made surprising gains in Maine and elsewhere before the Civil War, was sweeping new states into the "dry" column. The great triumph—but only a temporary one—came in 1919, when the national prohibition amendment (Eighteenth) was attached to the Constitution.

Banners of other social crusaders were aloft. The American Society for the Prevention of Cruelty to Animals was created in 1866, after its founder had witnessed brutality to horses in Russia. The American Red Cross was launched in 1881, with the dynamic 5-foot (1.52-meter) Clara Barton, an "angel" of Civil War battlefields, as a leading spirit. Organized philanthropy, a forerunner of annual charity drives, was becoming popular, beginning with Buffalo in the 1870s, and was replacing the old haphazard methods of giving. More money went into salaries and other collection costs, but the recipients of charity also got more, despite a poet's protest against

> The organized charity, scrimped and iced,
> In the name of a cautious, statistical Christ.

Artistic Triumphs

America still lacked artists to match her magnificent mountains. Art had been of sickly growth in the rustic years of the Republic,

Clara Barton (1821–1912)   *A shy Massachusetts school teacher, she was afflicted with attacks of nervous prostration during the first half of her life. She established the American National Red Cross, which she headed from 1881 to 1904. (Brown Brothers.)*

largely because of an absence of leisure and wealth. The nation now had both, but the results were unspectacular. Perhaps the roar of the industrialized civilization repelled the delicate muses; perhaps art itself was becoming mechanized. Roll-film cameras, popularized by George Eastman in the 1880s, enabled all people to be their own artists.

Yet several portrait painters of distinction emerged, notably James Whistler (1834–1903). This eccentric and quarrelsome Massachusetts Yankee had earlier been dropped from West Point after failing chemistry. "Had silicon been a gas," he later jested, "I would have been a major general." Moving to Europe, he did much of his work in England, including the celebrated portrait of his mother. Another gifted portrait painter, likewise self-exiled in England, was John Singer Sargent (1856–1925). His flattering but somewhat superficial likenesses of the British nobility were highly prized.

Other brush wielders, no less talented, brightened the artistic horizon. Self-taught George Inness (1825–1894) looked like a fanatic with his long hair and piercing gaze, but he became America's leading landscapist. Thomas Eakins (1844–1916) attained a high degree of realism in his paintings, a quality not appreciated by portrait sitters who wanted their moles overlooked. Boston-born Winslow Homer (1836–1910), who as a youth had secretly drawn sketches in school, was perhaps the greatest painter of the group. Earthily American and largely resistant to foreign influences, he revealed rugged realism and boldness of conception. His canvases of the sea and of fisherfolk were masterly, and probably no American artist has excelled him in portraying the awesome power of the ocean.

Probably the most gifted sculptor yet produced by America was Augustus Saint-Gaudens (1848–1907). Born in Ireland of an Irish mother and a French father, he became an adopted American. Although he sculptured many noble statues, his most striking work is the "Adams Monument," a shrouded and enigmatic female figure representing grief or a kindred emotion. It was erected in a Washington cemetery by the historian Henry Adams in memory of his beloved wife, who had committed suicide.

Music, too, was gaining popularity. America of the 1880s and 1890s was assembling high-quality symphony orchestras, notably in Boston and Chicago. The famed Metropolitan Opera House of New York was erected in 1883. In its fabled "Diamond Horseshoe" the newly rich, often under the pretense of enjoying the imported singers, would flaunt their jewels, gowns, and

> Hamlin Garland, the well-known novelist and writer of short stories, was immensely impressed by the cultural value of the Chicago Columbian Exposition. He wrote to his aged parents on their Dakota farm: "Sell the cook stove if necessary and come. You must see this fair."

furs. A marvelous discovery was the reproduction of music by mechanical means. The phonograph, though a squeakily imperfect instrument when invented by the deaf Edison, had by 1900 reached over 150,000 homes. Americans were rapidly being dosed with "canned music," as the "sitting room" piano increasingly gathered dust.

In addition to skyscraper builder Louis Sullivan, the most famous American architect of the age was Henry H. Richardson. Born in Louisiana and educated at Harvard and in Paris, Richardson settled in Boston and from there spread his immense influence throughout the eastern half of the United States. He popularized a distinctive, ornamental style that came to be known as "Richardsonian." High-vaulted arches, like those on Gothic churches, were his trademark. His masterpiece and most famous work was the Marshall Field Building (1885) in Chicago. Enjoying his success, Richardson was noted for his capacity for champagne, his love of laughter, and the bright yellow vests he sported.

A revival of classical architectural forms—and a setback for realism—came with the great Columbian Exposition. Held in Chicago in 1893, it honored the four-hundredth anniversary of Columbus's first voyage. This so-called dream of loveliness, which was visited by 27 million people, did much to raise American artistic standards and promote city planning, although many of the spectators were attracted primarily by the torsal contortions of a hootchy-kootchy dancer, "Little Egypt."

The Business of Amusement

Fun and frolic were not neglected by the workaday American. The pursuit of happiness, heralded in the Declaration of Independence, had by century's end become a frenzied scramble. People sought their pleasures fiercely, as they had overrun their continent fiercely. And now they had more time to play.

Varied diversions beckoned. As a nation of "joiners" contemptuous of royalty, Americans inconsistently sought to escape from democratic equality in the aristocratic hierarchies of lodges. The legitimate stage still flourished, as appre-

The Circus Is Coming *Traveling shows like P. T. Barnum's were a major form of entertainment before the days of movies, radio, and television. (The Granger Collection.)*

ciative audiences responded to the lure of the footlights. Vaudeville, with its coarse jokes and graceful acrobats, continued to be immensely popular during the 1880s and 1890s.

The circus—high-tented and multiringed—finally emerged full-blown. Phineas T. Barnum, the master showman who had early discovered that "the public likes to be humbugged," joined hands with James A. Bailey in 1881 to stage the "Greatest Show on Earth."*

Colorful "Wild West" shows, first performed in 1883, were even more distinctively American. Headed by the knightly, goateed, and free-drinking William F. ("Buffalo Bill") Cody, the troupe included war-whooping Indians, live buffalo, and deadeye marksmen. Among them was the girlish Annie Oakley. Rifle in hand, at thirty paces she could perforate a tossed-up card half a dozen times before it fluttered to the

ground. (Hence, the term *Annie Oakley* for a punched ticket, later for a free pass.)

Baseball, already widely played before the Civil War, was clearly emerging as the national pastime, if not a national mania. A league of professional players was formed in the 1870s, and in 1888 an all-star baseball team toured the world, using the pyramids as a backstop while in Egypt.

A gladiatorial trend toward spectators' sports, rather than participants' sports, was well exemplified by football. This rugged game, with its dangerous flying wedge, had become popular well before 1889, when Yaleman Walter C. Camp chose his first "All American" team. The Yale-Princeton game of 1893 drew fifty thousand cheering spectators, while foreigners jeered that the nation was getting sports "on the brain."

Even pugilism, with its long background of bare-knuckle brutality, gained a new and gloved respectability in 1892. Agile "Gentleman Jim" Corbett, a scientific boxer, wrested the world

---

*Now Ringling Bros. and Barnum and Bailey Circus.

championship from the aging and alcoholic John L. Sullivan, the fabulous "Boston Strong Boy."

Two crazes swept the country in the closing decades of the century. Croquet became enormously popular, though condemned by moralists of the "naughty nineties" because it exposed feminine ankles and promoted flirtation. The low-framed "safety" bicycle came to replace the high-seated model. By 1893 a million bicycles were in use, and thousands of young ladies, jokesters remarked, were turning to this new "spinning wheel."

Basketball was invented in 1891 by James Naismith, a YMCA instructor in Springfield, Massachusetts. Designed as an active indoor sport that could be played during the winter months, it spread rapidly and enjoyed enormous popularity in the next century.

The land of the skyscraper was plainly becoming more standardized, owing largely to the new industrialization. To an increasing degree, Americans were falling into the ways of lockstep living—playing, reading, thinking, and talking alike. They were eating the same canned food and wearing the same ready-made clothes. But what they had lost in variety, they were gaining in efficiency. They were still inseparably wedded to the ideal of unlimited human progress, and they still glimpsed, with invincible optimism, the unexplored vistas that stretched into the future.

Varying Viewpoints

In addition to industrialization, three major developments seemed to alter the fabric of American life in the late nineteenth century: massive immigration, urbanization, and the further advance of the woman's movement. Historians have long concentrated on the innovative and transforming features of these processes. They have asked, for example, how America was changed by the great immigrant influx—or, alternatively, how migration changed the immigrants themselves. How did city life alter life-styles and political institutions? How did the "new woman" change the basis of family organization and sexual behavior? Increasingly, scholars have been answering "not so much as expected" to all these questions. Recent investigations tend to emphasize the persistence of ethnic identities among immigrants, the preservation of small-town or village values in the booming metropolitan centers, and even the modest dimensions of the nineteenth-century "sexual revolution." True revolutions are rare in history. Even the massive social upheavals of this fermenting era did not fully displace older customs and attitudes.

Select Readings

Primary Source Documents

Jacob Riis, *How the Other Half Lives** (1890), is a vivid account of life in America's slums. In *A Hazard of New Fortunes* (1890), William Dean Howells penned one of the first "urban novels" in American literature. Frances Willard's *Glimpses of Fifty Years** (1880) is the memoir of a leading prohibitionist. Victoria Woodhull, *The Scarecrows of Sexual Slavery** (1874), provocatively illustrates some changing ideas about women's role. Henry James' novel *The Bostonians* (1886) vividly portrays feminists and suffragists.

Secondary Sources

The Rise of the City, 1878–1898 (1933) is a classic study by Arthur M. Schlesinger. More recent are Gunther Barth, *City People: The Rise of Modern City Culture in Nineteenth-Century America* (1980); Blake McKelvey, *The Urbanization of America, 1860–1915* (1963); Howard Chudacoff, *The Evolution of American Urban Society* (1975); and Sam Bass Warner, Jr., *The Urban Wilderness* (1972). Specific cities are discussed in Warner's *The Private City: Philadelphia in Three Periods of Its Growth* (1968) and in his study of Boston, *Streetcar Suburbs* (1962). See also Edward K. Spann, *The New Metropolis: New York City, 1840–1857* (1981). Eric H. Monkkonen discusses *Police in Urban America, 1860–1920* (1981). On architecture, see Sherman Paul, *Louis Sullivan* (1962). Oscar Handlin introduced the study of immigrant communities in American cities with his *Boston's Immigrants* (rev. ed., 1959). More recent studies of the same topic include Thomas Kessner, *The Golden Door: Italian and Jewish Mobility in New York City, 1880–1915* (1977); Stephan Thernstrom, *The Other Bostonians* (1973); Virginia Yans-McLaughlin, *Family and Community: Italian Immigrants in Buffalo, 1880–1930* (1975); Dino Cinel, *From Italy to San Francisco: The Immigrant Experience* (1982); Humbert Nelli, *Italians of Chicago, 1880–1920* (1970); J. Barton, *Peasants and Strangers* (1975); C. Griffen and S. Griffen, *Natives and Newcomers* (1978); and Irving Howe's monumental and moving account of Jewish immigration, *World of Our Fathers* (1976). Maldwyn Jones, *American Immigration* (1960), is a well-written introduction, as is Thomas J. Archdeacon, *Becoming American* (1983). Oscar Handlin, *The Uprooted* (1951), is an imaginative account of the immigrant experience. John Higham examines the "nativist" reaction in *Strangers in the Land* (1955). On medicine consult Morris J. Vogel, *The Invention of the Modern Hospi-tal: Boston, 1870–1930* (1980), and Paul Starr, *The Social Transformation of American Medicine* (1982). On education see Lawrence Cremin, *The Transformation of the School* (1961), and Laurence Veysey, *The Emergence of the American University* (1965). Black history for this period is illuminated by three studies: August Meier, *Negro Thought in America, 1880–1915* (1963); Louis R. Harlan, *Booker T. Washington: The Making of a Black Leader, 1865–1901* (1972); and Elliot M. Rudwick, *W. E. B. Du Bois: A Study in Minority Group Leadership* (1960). On women and the family, consult Carl Degler, *At Odds: Women and the Family from the Revolution to the Present* (1980); Steven Mintz, *A Prison of Expectations: The Family in Victorian Culture* (1983); William Leach, *True Love and Perfect Union: The Feminist Reform of Sex and Society* (1980); Mari Jo Buhle, *Women and American Socialism, 1870–1920* (1981); Margaret W. Rossiter, *Women Scientists in America* (1982); Aileen Kraditor, *Ideas of the Women Suffrage Movement* (1965); Eleanor Flexner, *Century of Struggle* (1959); Elisabeth Griffith, *In Her Own Right: The Life of Elizabeth Cady Stanton* (1984); Rosalind Rosenberg, *Beyond Separate Spheres* (1982); Allen F. Davis, *American Heroine: The Life and Legend of Jane Addams* (1973); and Elaine May, *Great Expectations: Marriage and Divorce in Post-Victorian America* (1980). John L. Thomas considers *Alternative America: Henry George, Edward Bellamy, Henry Demarest Lloyd, and the Adversary Tradition* (1983). Bruce Kuklick examines Harvard's star-studded philosophy department in *The Rise of American Philosophy* (1977). Two fascinating studies document the rise of a "new" middle-class mentality: Burton J. Bledstein, *The Culture of Professionalism* (1976), and Thomas Haskell, *The Emergence of Professional Social Science* (1977). See also Alexandra Oleson and John Voss, eds., *The Organization of Knowledge in Modern America, 1860–1920* (1979).

29

The Great West and the Agricultural Revolution, 1865–1890

> Up to our own day American history has been in a large degree the history of the colonization of the Great West. The existence of an area of free land, its continuous recession, and the advance of American settlement westward, explain American development.
>
> Frederick Jackson Turner, 1893

The Indian Barrier to the West

When the Civil War crashed to a close, the frontier line was still wavering westward. A long fringe of settlement, bulging outward here and there, ran roughly north through central Texas and on to the Canadian border. Between this jagged line and the settled areas on the Pacific slope, there were virtually no white people. The only exceptions to mention were the islands of Mormons in Utah, occasional trading posts and gold camps, and a few scattered Spanish-Mexican settlements in the Southwest.

Sprawling in expanse, the Great West was a rough square that measured about 1,000 miles (1,600 kilometers) on each side. Embracing mountains, plateaus, deserts, and plains, it was the habitat of the Indian, the buffalo, the wild horse, the prairie dog, and the coyote. Twenty-five years later—that is, by 1890—the entire domain had been carved into states, except for four territories. Pioneers flung themselves greedily on this enormous prize, as if to ravish it. Never before in human experience, probably, had so huge an area been reduced so rapidly to a semblance of civilization.

The Indians, to their misfortune, stood in the path of the American settlers. Like the blades of mighty scissors, two lines of onward-moving pioneers were closing in simultaneously—one from the Pacific Coast, the other from the trans-Mississippi East. A clash was inevitable between an acquisitive civilization and a traditional culture, as the march of modernity crushed under its feet the hunting grounds and hence the food supply of the native inhabitants.

Tens of thousands of buffalo-hunting Indians roamed the spacious western plains in 1860. In three centuries the Spanish-introduced horse had transformed the culture of the Plains Indians, causing the tribes to become more nomadic and more warlike. The Plains Indians had become superbly skilled riders and fighters.

In 1851 the Washington government, yielding to expansionist pressures, determined to crack the great Indian barrier in the West and induce the tribes to "concentrate" in certain "inviolable" areas to the north and south of in-

> One disheartened Indian complained to the white Sioux Commission created by Congress: "Tell your people that since the Great Father promised that we should never be removed we have been moved five times. . . . I think you had better put the Indians on wheels and you can run them about wherever you wish."

tended white settlement. In the 1860s Washington intensified this policy and herded the Indians into still smaller confines. The Sioux were to be "guaranteed" the sanctuary of the Black Hills in Dakota Territory. Certain southern tribes were to be relocated in the "Indian territory" of present Oklahoma.

The Indians surrendered their ancestral lands only when they had received solemn promises from the Great White Father in Washington that they would be left alone and provided with food, clothing, and other supplies.

Cavalry Charge on the Southern Plains, by Frederic Remington *(Metropolitan Museum of Art, gift of Several Gentlemen, 1911.)*

Regrettably, the federal Indian agents were often corrupt. They palmed off moth-eaten blankets, spoiled beef, and other defective provisions on the friendless Indians. One of these cheating officials, on an annual salary of $1,500, returned home after four years with an estimated "savings" of $50,000.

Grasping white men were guilty of many additional provocations. They flagrantly disregarded treaty promises, openly seized the land of the Indians, wantonly slaughtered their game, and occasionally debauched their women. During the Civil War the Sioux of Minnesota, facing starvation and taking advantage of the sectional quarrel, went on the warpath and murdered several hundred settlers. The uprising was finally crushed by federal troops, and nearly forty of the Sioux Indians, after a summary trial, were hanged at a well-attended mass execution.

From 1868 to about 1890, almost incessant warfare raged in various parts of the West between Indians and whites. A printed list of the names of the engagements alone covers over a hundred pages. The fighting was fierce and harrowing, especially the winter campaigning in subzero weather. Many of the regular troops were veterans of the Civil War, and their ranks embraced four crack black units, including the famous Tenth Cavalry. All told, about one-fifth of all soldiers assigned to the frontier during these years were black. Generals Sherman, Sheridan ("the only good Indian is a dead Indian"), and Custer, all of whom had won their spurs in the Civil War, gathered further laurels in the West. They were matched against formidable adversaries, for the Indians of the

---

A young lieutenant told Colonel Chivington that to attack the Indians would be a violation of pledges. "His reply was, bringing his fist down close to my face, 'Damn any man who sympathizes with Indians.' I told him what pledges were given the Indians. He replied that he 'had come to kill Indians, and believed it to be honorable to kill Indians under any and all circumstances.'"

Plains, unlike those first encountered by the American colonists, rode swift ponies and enjoyed baffling mobility. To the disgust of the American soldiers, "the hostiles" were often better armed than the federal troops sent against them with clumsy muzzle-loaders. The War Department was perhaps not so much to blame as conscienceless white fur traders, who provided the Indians with the most modern repeating rifles.

Receding Native Population

Savagery was not all on the side of the Indians. Where fighting is protracted and uncivilized, the ethics of combat are ordinarily pulled down to a primitive level. Whites were often the immediate aggressors, and they sometimes shot peaceful Indians on sight, just to make sure they would give no trouble. At Sand Creek, Colorado, in 1864, Colonel J. M. Chivington's militia massacred in cold blood some four hundred Indians who apparently thought they had been promised immunity. Women were shot praying for mercy, children had their brains dashed out, and braves were tortured, scalped, and unspeakably mutilated. On several notorious occasions, innocent Indians were killed for outrages committed by their fellow tribesmen; sometimes they were shot just for "sport."

Unquestionably, the most spectacular of these clashes was the Sioux War of 1876–1877, touched off when a horde of gold-greedy miners rushed into the Black Hills of South Dakota during the stampede of 1875. The proud and warlike Sioux, their lands invaded despite treaty guarantees, took to the warpath. Conspicuous among their leaders was heavyset Sitting Bull, a medicine man as wily as he was influential.

Sioux braves were hotly pursued by impetuous George A. Custer, the buckskin-clad "boy general," now demoted to lieutenant colonel. Attacking what turned out to be a superior force of some 2,500 well-armed warriors near the Little Big Horn River in present Montana, the "White Chief with Yellow Hair" and his 264 officers and men were completely wiped out in 1876 when two supporting columns failed to come to their rescue.* (Sitting Bull sat out this battle, safely "making medicine" in his tent, while Crazy Horse played a stellar role.) But white reinforcements later arrived, and Sitting Bull and the remnants of his band were finally driven to Canada, where hunger forced them to return and surrender.

The Nez Percé Indians of Idaho were likewise goaded into warfare in 1877, when gold-crazed prospectors trespassed upon their beaver streams. Chief Joseph, a noble and unusually humane leader, established himself as a remarkable strategist when he undertook a roundabout retreat of 1,500 miles (2,400 kilometers) to Canada, only to be cornered 30 miles (48 kilometers) from safety.

Fierce Apache tribes of Arizona and New Mexico were the most difficult to subdue. Led by Geronimo, whose eyes blazed hatred of the whites, they were pursued into Mexico by federal troops using the sun-flashing heliograph, a communication device, which impressed the Indians as "big medicine." Scattered remnants of the braves were finally persuaded to surrender after their women had been exiled to Florida. The Apaches ultimately became successful farmers in Oklahoma, where they raised stock instead of raiding settlements.

This relentless fire-and-sword policy of the whites at last shattered the spirit of the Indians. The vanquished Native Americans were finally ghettoized in "human zoos," known as reservations, there to eke out a sullen existence as wards of the government. Their white masters had at last discovered that the Indians were much cheaper to feed than to fight. Even so, for many decades they were almost ignored to death.

The taming of the Indians was engineered by a number of factors. Of cardinal importance was the railroad, which shot an iron arrow through the heart of the West. Locomotives ("bad medicine wagons") could bring out unlimited numbers of troops, farmers, cattlemen,

Geronimo (c. 1829–1909) *He was the most famous Apache leader. (National Archives.)*

sheepherders, and settlers. The luckless Indians were also ravaged by the white people's diseases, to which they showed little resistance, and by their firewater, to which they showed almost no resistance. Above all, the virtual extermination of the buffalo resulted in the near-extermination of the Plains Indians.

Bellowing Herds of Bison

Tens of millions of buffalo—described by early Spaniards as "hunchback cows"—blackened the western prairies when the white Americans first arrived. These shaggy, lumbering animals were

---

*When the whites wiped out Indians, the engagement (in white history books) was usually a "battle"; when the Indians wiped out whites, it was a "massacre." "Strategy," when practiced by Indians, was "treachery."

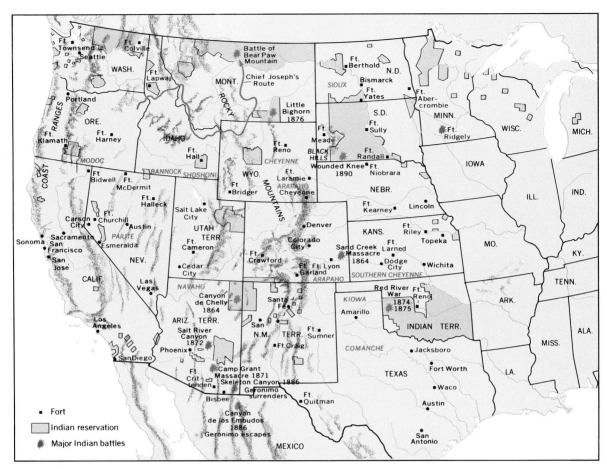

Indian Wars, 1860–1890   *Surrendering in 1877, Chief Joseph of the Nez Percé declared: "Our chiefs are killed. . . . The old men are all dead. . . . The little children are freezing to death. . . . I want to have time to look for my children. . . . Hear me, my chiefs. My heart is sick and sad. From where the sun now stands I will fight no more forever."*

the staff of life for the Indian. Their flesh provided food; their dried dung provided fuel ("buffalo chips"); their hides provided clothing, lariats, bowstrings, and harness.

When the Civil War closed, there were still some 15 million of these meaty beasts grazing on the western plains. In 1868 a Kansas Pacific locomotive had to wait eight hours for a herd to amble across the tracks; experience had shown that trying to smash through would produce only mangled flesh and derailment. Much of the food supply of the railroad construction gangs came from leathery buffalo steaks. "Buffalo Bill" Cody—sinewy, telescope-eyed, and a crack shot—killed over 4,000 animals in eighteen months while employed by the Kansas Pacific.

With the building of the railroad, the massacre of the herds began in deadly earnest. Most of the stupid creatures were slain for their hides and in response to the insatiable demand for buffalo robes, then highly fashionable. Others were felled merely for their tongues or a few other choice cuts, while the rest of the carcass was left to be picked by the vultures. Countless buffalo were shot with repeating rifles for sheer amusement. "Sportsmen" on lurching railroad trains would lean out the windows and blaze away at the brutes to satisfy their lust for slaughter or excitement.

Such wholesale butchery could have only one end. By 1885 fewer than a thousand buffalo were left, and the once-numerous quadrupeds were in danger of complete extermination. Somewhat like the Indians, a few thousand of the beefy animals have been kept alive, largely as living museum pieces. The whole story is a shocking example of the greed and waste that accompanied the conquest of the continent.

The End of the Trail

By the 1880s the national conscience began to stir uneasily against the policy of corralling and then exterminating the Indians. Helen Hunt Jackson, a Massachusetts writer of children's literature, pricked the moral sense of Americans in 1881, when she published *A Century of Dishonor*. The book chronicled the sorry record of governmental ruthlessness and chicanery in dealing with the Indians. Her later novel *Ramona* (1884), a love story of injustice to the California aborigines, sold some 600,000 copies and further inspired sympathy for the Indians.

Debate seesawed. Humanitarians wanted to treat the Indians kindly and persuade them thereby to "walk the white man's road." Yet hard-liners insisted on the current policy of forced containment and brutal punishment. Neither side showed much respect for traditional Indian culture. Christian reformers, who

The Buffalo Hunt 1890, by Frederic Remington (1861–1909)   *A New Yorker who first went west at the age of nineteen as a cowboy and ranch cook, Remington became the foremost artist of the vanishing way of life of the old Far West. Once a common sight on the high plains, the kind of buffalo kill that Remington records here was a great rarity by the time he painted this scene in 1890. The once vast herds of bison had long since been reduced to a pitiful few by the white man's rifles. (Detail, courtesy of the Buffalo Bill Historical Center, Cody, Wyoming.)*

often administered educational facilities on the reservations, sometimes withheld precious food to force the Indians to give up their tribal religion. In 1884 these zealous white souls joined with military men in successfully persuading the federal government to outlaw the sacred Sun Dance. When the "Ghost Dance" cult later spread to the Dakota Sioux, the army bloodily stamped it out in 1890 at the so-called Battle of Wounded Knee. In the fighting thus provoked, an estimated two hundred Indian men, women, and children were killed, as well as twenty-nine invading soldiers.

The misbegotten offspring of the movement to reform Indian policy was the Dawes Severalty Act of 1887. Reflecting the forced-civilization views of the reformers, the act dissolved many tribes as legal entities, wiped out tribal ownership of land, and set up individual Indian family heads with 160 free acres. If the Indians behaved themselves like "good white settlers," they would get full title to their holdings, as well as citizenship, in twenty-five years. The probationary period was later extended, but full citizenship was granted to all Indians in 1924.

The Dawes Act struck directly at the organization of the tribe and tried to make rugged individualists out of the Indians. Whatever its good intentions, this legislation did much to accelerate the already advanced decay of traditional Indian culture. The Dawes Act remained the government's official Indian policy until 1934, when the Indian Reorganization Act ("The Indian New Deal") reversed the individualistic approach and belatedly tried to restore the tribal basis of Indian life.

Under these new federal policies, defective though they were, the Indian population started to mount slowly. The total number had been reduced by 1887 to about 243,000—the result of bullets, bottles, and bacteria—but the census of 1980 counted nearly 1.5 million Indians, urban and rural.

Mining: From Dishpan to Ore-Breaker

The conquest of the Indians and the coming of the railroad were life-giving boons to the mining frontier. The golden gravel of California continued to yield "pay dirt," and in 1858 an electrifying discovery convulsed Colorado. Avid "fifty-niners" or "Pike's Peakers" rushed west to rip at the ramparts of the Rockies. But there were more miners than minerals; and many gold-grubbers, with "Pike's Peak or Bust" inscribed on the canvas of their covered wagons, creaked

Helena, Montana, 1865
Mining towns such as this one sprang up wherever gold- and silver-diggers thought they would strike it rich. They would abandon such towns as soon as the "diggings" were depleted, leaving "ghost towns" behind. (Montana Historical Society.)

wearily back with the added inscription, "Busted, by Gosh." Yet countless bearded fortune seekers stayed on, some to strip away the silver deposits, others to extract nonmetallic wealth from the earth in the form of golden grain.

"Fifty-niners" also poured feverishly into Nevada in 1859, after the fabulous Comstock Lode had been uncovered. A fantastic amount of gold and silver, worth more than $340 million, was mined by the "Kings of the Comstock" from 1860 to 1890. The scantily populated state of Nevada, "child of the Comstock Lode," was prematurely railroaded into the Union in 1864, partly to provide three electoral votes for President Lincoln.

Smaller "lucky strikes" drew frantic gold- and silver-seekers into Montana, Idaho, and other western states. Boom towns, known as "Helldorados," sprouted from the desert sands like magic. Every third cabin was a saloon, where sweat-stained miners drank adulterated liquor ("rotgut") in the company of accommodating women. Lynch law and hempen vigilante justice, as in early California, preserved a crude semblance of order in the towns. And when the "diggings" petered out, the gold-seekers decamped, leaving picturesque "ghost towns" silhouetted in the desert, such as Virginia City, Nevada. Begun with a boom, these towns ended with a whimper.

Once the loose surface gold was gobbled up, ore-breaking machinery was imported to smash the gold-bearing quartz. This operation was so expensive that it could ordinarily be undertaken only by corporations pooling the wealth of stockholders. Gradually the age of big business came to the mining industry. Dusty, bewhiskered miners, dishpans in hand, were replaced by the impersonal and beardless corporations, with their costly machinery and trained engineers. The once-picturesque gold-washer became just another day laborer, for it took gold to get gold.

Yet the mining frontier had played a vital role in subduing the continent. Magnetlike, it attracted population and wealth, while advertising the wonders of the Wild West. The amassing of precious metals helped finance the Civil War, facilitated the building of railroads, and forced attention to the Indian problem. The outpouring of silver and gold enabled the Treasury to resume specie payments in 1879 and injected the silver issue into American politics. "Silver Senators," representing the thinly peopled "acreage states" of the West, used their disproportionate influence to promote the interests of the silver miners. Finally, the mining frontier added to American folklore and literature, as the writings of Bret Harte and Mark Twain so colorfully attest.

Beef Bonanzas and the Long Drive

When the Civil War ended, the grassy plains of Texas supported several million tough, long-horned cattle. These scrawny beasts, whose horn spread sometimes reached 8 feet (2.4 meters), were killed primarily for their hides. There was no way of getting their meat profitably to market.

The problem of marketing was neatly solved when the transcontinental railroads thrust their iron fingers into the West. Cattle could now be shipped bodily to the stockyards, and under "beef barons" like the Swifts and Armours, the highly industrialized meat-packing business sprang into existence as a main pillar of the economy. Drawing upon the gigantic stockyards at Kansas City and Chicago, the meat packers could ship their fresh products to the East Coast in the newly perfected refrigerator cars.

A spectacular feeder of the new slaughterhouses was the "Long Drive." Texas cowboys—black, white, and Mexican—drove herds numbering from one thousand to ten thousand head slowly over the unfenced and unpeopled plains until they reached a railroad terminal. The bawling beasts grazed en route on the free government grass. Favorite terminal points were flyspecked "cow towns" like Dodge City—"the Bibulous Babylon of the Frontier"—and Abilene (Kansas), Ogallala (Nebraska), and Cheyenne (Wyoming). At Abilene, order was maintained by Marshal James B. ("Wild Bill") Hickok, a fabulous gunman who reputedly killed only in self-

The Long Drive *(Harper's Weekly, 1874.)*

Cattle Trails

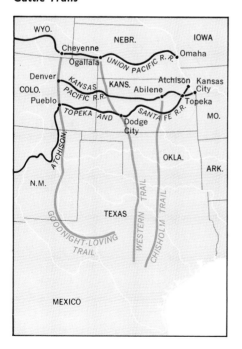

defense or in the line of duty and who was finally shot in the back while playing poker.*

As long as lush grass was available, the Long Drive proved profitable—that is, to the luckier cattlemen who escaped the Indians, stampedes, cattle fever, and other hazards. From 1866 to 1888 bellowing herds, totaling over 4 million steers, were driven northward from the beef bowl of Texas. In peak years the profits to some cattlemen would soar as high as 40 percent. The steer was king in a Cattle Kingdom richly carpeted with grass.

What the Lord giveth, the Lord also taketh away. The railroad made the Long Drive; the

---

*Frontier marshals like Hickok, Wyatt Earp, and "Bat" Masterson have been highly romanticized; some were little better than criminals who shot men from behind curtains: hooligans, not heroes. They were less "fast on the draw" and less accurate with their "six-guns" than commonly portrayed. A western saying was that God did not make all men equal; Colonel Colt did.

railroad unmade the Long Drive, primarily because the locomotives ran both ways. The same rails that bore the cattle from the open range to the kitchen range brought out the homesteader and the sheepherder. Both of these intruders, amid flying bullets, built barbed-wire fences that were too numerous to be cut down by the cowboys. Furthermore the terrible winter of 1886–1887, with blinding blizzards reaching 68 degrees below zero (−56 degrees Celsius), left thousands of dazed cattle starving and freezing. Overexpansion and overgrazing likewise took their toll, as the cowboys slowly gave way to ploughboys.

The only escape for the stockmen was to make cattle raising a big business and avoid the perils of overproduction. Breeders learned to fence their ranches, lay in winter feed, import blooded bulls, and produce fewer and meatier animals. They also learned to organize. The Wyoming Stock-Growers' Association, especially in the 1880s, virtually controlled the state and its legislature.

These were the days when cowboyhood was in flower. The equipment of the lone cowhand —from "shooting irons" and ten-gallon hat to chaps and high-heeled boots—served a useful, not an ornamental, function. A "genuwine" gun-toting cowpuncher, riding where men were men and smelled like horses, could justifiably boast of his toughness.

These bowlegged Knights of the Saddle, with colorful trappings and cattle-lulling songs, became an authentic part of American folklore. A substantial number of them were blacks, perhaps five thousand, who especially enjoyed the newfound freedom of the open range.

Free Land for Free Families

A new day dawned for western farmers with the Homestead Act of 1862—an epochal measure vigorously opposed by the South before secession. The law provided that a settler could acquire as much as 160 acres of land (a quarter-section) by living on it five years, improving it, and paying a nominal fee averaging about $30.00. As an alternative, land might be acquired after only six months' residence at $1.25

Homesteaders in Colorado, c. 1870   *This family had probably been creaking across the Great Plains for more than two months. (The Denver Public Library, Western History Department.)*

an acre. Lands acquired in either fashion were to be exempt from attachment for debt.

The Homestead Act marked a drastic departure from previous policy. Hitherto public land had been sold primarily for revenue; now it was to be given away to encourage a rapid filling of empty spaces and to provide a stimulus to the family farm—"the backbone of democracy." The new law was a godsend to a host of farmers who could not afford to buy large holdings; and during the forty years after its passage, about half a million families took advantage of the Homestead Act to carve out new homes in the vast open stretches. Yet five times that many families *purchased* their land from the railroads, the land companies, or the states.

The Homestead Act often turned out to be a cruel hoax. The standard 160 acres, quite adequate in the well-watered Mississippi basin, frequently proved pitifully inadequate on the rain-scarce Great Plains. Thousands of homesteaders, perhaps two out of three, were forced to give up the one-sided struggle against drought. Uncle Sam, it was said, bet 160 acres against ten dollars that the settlers could not live on their homesteads for five years. One of these unsuccessful gambles in Greer County, western Oklahoma, inspired a folk song:

> Hurrah for Greer County! The land of the free,
> The land of the bedbug, grasshopper, and flea;
> I'll sing of its praises, I'll tell of its fame,
> While starving to death on my government claim.

Naked fraud was spawned by the Homestead Act and sister laws. Perhaps ten times more of the public domain wound up in the clutches of land-grabbing promoters than in the hands of bona fide farmers. Unscrupulous corporations would use "dummy" homesteaders—often aliens bribed with cash or a bottle of beer—to grab the best properties containing timber, minerals, and oil. Settlers would later swear that they had "improved" the property by erecting a "twelve by fourteen" dwelling, which turned out to measure twelve by fourteen *inches*. In later years the Washington officials were only partially successful in unraveling the tangled skein

The Homesteader's Wife, by Harvey Dunn *Women as well as men toiled without shade or respite on the sun-scorched and wind-parched Great Plains. (South Dakota Memorial Art Center Collection.)*

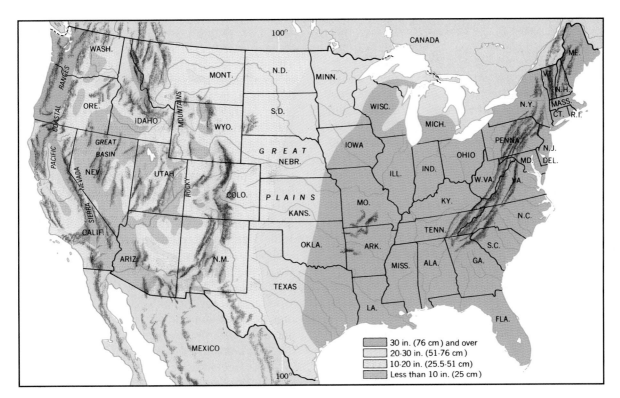

Average Annual Precipitation *In the northern hemisphere, storms usually circle the globe in a west-to-east direction. Much of the life-nourishing water in these storms is dumped as rainfall on the western slopes of the cloud-high Pacific Coastal ranges and the Rocky Mountains. This weather pattern creates deep, dry "rain-shadows" in the Great Basin and in the plains area immediately east of the Rockies.*

of deceit. So functioned the government's first big "giveaway" program.

Taming Western Deserts

The life-giving railways also played a major role in developing the agricultural West, largely through the profitable marketing of crops. In addition, some railroad companies induced Americans and European immigrants to buy the cheap lands earlier granted by the government. A leader in such "induced colonization" was the Northern Pacific Railroad, which at one time had nearly a thousand paid agents in Europe distributing roseate leaflets in various languages.

A shattering of the myth of the Great American Desert further opened the gateways to the agricultural West. The windswept prairies were for the most part treeless, and the tough sod had been pounded solid by millions of buffalo hooves. Pioneer explorers and trappers had assumed that the soil must be sterile, simply because it was not heavily watered and did not support immense forests. But once the prairie sod was broken—as was done in Kansas with special plows pulled by four powerful yokes of oxen—the earth proved to be astonishingly fruitful.

This boom in western farming was aided by additional stimulants. Improved irrigation techniques—"the miracle of water"—caused deserts to bloom, notably in Mormon Utah. Tough strains of wheat that were resistant to cold and drought were imported from Russia, and they blossomed into billowing yellow carpets. New flour-milling processes, which brought John S. Pillsbury of Minneapolis both fame and fortune, increased the demand for grain.

Wheat growers were lured out onto the poorer marginal lands, owing to the high prices in the 1870s resulting from crop failures in other parts of the world. The farmers rashly pushed beyond the 100th meridian as far west as the semiarid regions of eastern Colorado and Montana, where they developed the special techniques of "dry" farming, including frequent shallow cultivation. To the farmers' dismay, they were to discover in the next decade that dry farming is most successful in wet years and that dusty farms produce dust bowls. "Pioneering does not pay," observed the steelman Andrew Carnegie.

Barbed wire, hardly less than the railroad, bound together the Great West. Fences were necessary to contain livestock, as well as to enclose water holes. Wood was too scarce on the treeless prairies to be used for fencing, and ordinary wire would not hold a rampaging steer. In 1874 Joseph F. Glidden invented a superior type of barbed wire, and in 1883 the company using his patent was turning out 600 miles (966 kilometers) of the new product each day. Among other contributions, barbed wire gave the farmer greater protection against trespassing cattle, although further spelling the doom of the Long Drive.

"Boomers" in Oklahoma

The Far West Comes of Age

The Great West experienced a fantastic growth of population from the 1870s to the 1890s. A current quip was that one could not tell the truth about the West without lying. Confederate and Union veterans alike moved into the sunset with their families, as did a certain fraction of the inpouring immigrants.

A parade of new western states proudly joined their eastern sisters. Boom-town Colorado, offspring of the Pike's Peak gold rush, was greeted in 1876 as "the Centennial State." In 1889–1890 a Republican Congress, eagerly seeking more Republican electoral and congressional votes, admitted in a wholesale lot six new states: North Dakota, South Dakota, Montana, Washington, Idaho, and Wyoming. The Mormon church formally and belatedly banned polygamy in 1890, but not until 1896 was Utah deemed worthy of admission. Only Oklahoma, New Mexico, and Arizona remained to be lifted into statehood from contiguous territory on the mainland of North America.

In a last gaudy fling, the Washington government made available to settlers vast stretches of fertile plains formerly occupied by the Indians in the district of Oklahoma ("the Beautiful Land"). Scores of overeager and well-armed "sooners," illegally jumping the gun, had entered Oklahoma Territory. They had to be evicted repeatedly by federal troops, who on occasion would shoot the horses of intruders. On April 22, 1889, all was in readiness for the legal opening, and some 50,000 "boomers" were poised expectantly on the boundary line. At high noon the bugle shrilled, and a horde of "eighty-niners" poured in on lathered horses or careening vehicles. That night a lonely spot on the prairie had mushroomed into the tent city of Guthrie, with over 10,000 souls. By the end of the year Oklahoma boasted 60,000 inhabitants, and Congress made it a territory. In 1907 it became "the Sooner State."

The mad haste of the "boomers" underscored the fact that fertile free land was no longer abundant. In 1890—a watershed date—the superintendent of the census announced that for the first time in America's experience a frontier

Homesteads from the Public Lands *(acreage legally transferred to private ownership)*

line was no longer discernible. All the unsettled areas were now broken into by isolated bodies of settlement.

Actually, few Americans in 1890 realized that the fading frontier line had disappeared. The Homestead Act remained on the books—and still does—and more millions of acres were taken up after 1890 than between 1862 and 1890. But in general the new lands were less desirable, and many sterile or parched farms, though well watered with sweat, had to be abandoned. To this day the federal government, which owns nearly one-fourth of all American soil, has many millions of acres that may be homesteaded. But they are mostly grazing lands and other marginal areas incapable of sustaining a decent standard of living. From time to time, considerable acreage was rendered attractive for homesteading by the completion of irrigation or reclamation projects. In these ways the frontier survived its "death" by several decades.

As the nineteenth century neared its sunset, the westward-tramping American people were disturbed to find that their fabled free land was going or had gone. The secretary of war had prophesied in 1827 that five hundred years would be needed to fill the West. But when the nation learned that its land was not inex-

haustible, the seeds were planted in the public mind for the belated conservation movement of later decades.

The Folding Frontier

The frontier was more than a place: it was also a state of mind and a symbol of opportunity. Its passing ended a romantic phase of the nation's internal development and created new economic and psychological problems.

Traditionally footloose, Americans have been notorious for their mobility; the automobile trailer is a typically American vehicle. The nation's farmers, unlike the peasants of Europe, have seldom remained rooted to their soil. The land, sold for a profit as settlement closed in, was often the settler's most profitable crop.

Much has been said about the frontier as a "safety valve." The theory is that when hard times came, the unemployed who cluttered the city pavements merely moved west, took up farming, and prospered.

In truth, relatively few city dwellers, at least in the populous eastern centers, migrated to the frontier during depressions. Most of them did not know how to farm; few of them could raise enough money to transport themselves west and then pay for livestock and expensive machinery. The initial outlay for equipment had become so heavy by the 1880s and 1890s that the West was decreasingly a land of opportunity for farmers, though it might be for ranchers, miners, and day laborers. A large proportion of the settlers who moved west came from farms on the older frontier, which was within striking distance of the new frontier.

But the "safety-valve" theory does have some validity. For one thing, free acreage lured westward a host of immigrant farmers. Many of these newcomers would have stayed in the eastern cities to worsen the problems of the festering slums. The frontier also drew off some restless spirits and no doubt exercised a powerful psychological influence. Even though easterners seldom pulled up stakes and moved west, in theory they could always flee to the frontier. This prospect often gave a lift to these drooping spirits—and perhaps also a lift to the wages paid by their employers.

Once the fertile and well-watered free lands were gone, farmers could no longer move west in significant numbers. They had to stand and fight, and consequently they voiced their grievances more and fled from them less. Some farmers actually turned their backs upon the West and moved east. In fact, the vast cityward movement near the end of the century partially replaced the old westward movement.

American history cannot be properly understood unless it is viewed in the light of this westward-moving experience—an experience that was centuries long and soul-searing. Though raucous and raw, the frontier was the cradle of youthful and robust Americanism, and it left an enduring imprint on the older settlements. The Wild West, with its pistol-popping days, was about to disappear. But much of the frontier's distinctive flavor remained with the American people, among whom lingered its incurable optimism, its resilient toughness, its handyman resourcefulness, and its zestful eagerness for social and economic reform. These westering pioneers carried the seeds of civilization with them into the wilderness. The life we live, they dreamed of; the life they lived, we can only dream.

The Farm Becomes a Factory

The role of the American farmers, who had once been jacks-and-jills-of-all-trades, was rapidly changing. In colonial days they had lived on a kind of Robinson Crusoe's island; they had raised their own food, and the women had woven the clothing. But diversification of crops declined with the passing decades; and after the Civil War, if not earlier, the immense grain-producing areas of the Mississippi Valley found themselves in the throes of an agricultural revolution. Prices were so favorable that the farmers were concentrating on a single money-crop, such as wheat or corn. They could use their profits to buy their foodstuffs at the country store, instead of raising them themselves. They could secure their manufactured goods in town or by mail order, perhaps from the Chicago firm of Aaron Montgomery Ward, established in 1872, with its first catalog a single sheet.

Large-scale farmers were now both specialists and businesspeople. As cogs in the vast industrial machine, they were intimately tied in with banking, railroading, and manufacturing.

Harvesting the Wheat *Equipment like this enormous reaper was both efficient and expensive. The "skinner," or driver, had his hands full. (The Bettmann Archive, Inc.)*

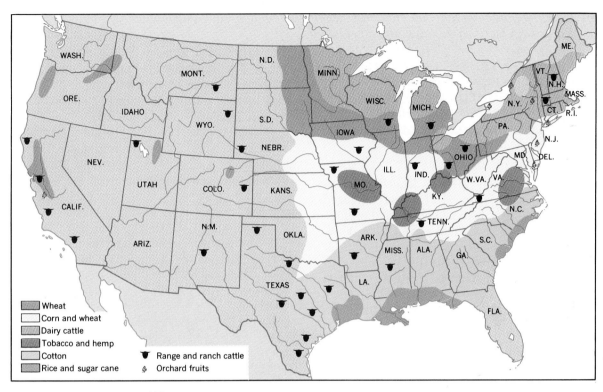

American Agriculture in 1900.

They had to buy expensive machinery to plant and to harvest their crops. A powerful steam engine could drag behind it simultaneously the plow, seeder, and harrow. The speed of harvesting wheat was immensely increased in the 1870s by the twine binder and then in the 1880s by the "combine"—the combined reaper-thresher, which was drawn by twenty to forty horses and which both reaped and bagged the grain. Widespread use of such costly equipment naturally called for first-class management. But the farmers, often unskilled as businesspeople, were inclined to blame the banks and railroads, rather than their own shortcomings, for their losses.

This amazing mechanization of agriculture in the postwar years was almost as striking as the mechanization of industry. In fact, the modernization of agriculture drove many marginal farmers off the land, thus swelling the ranks of the new industrial work force. As the rural population steadily decreased, those farmers who remained achieved miracles of production, making America the world's breadbasket and butcher shop. The farm was attaining the status of a factory—an outdoor grain factory. Bonanza wheat farms of the Minnesota–North Dakota area, for example, were enormous. By 1890 there were at least a half-dozen of them larger than fifteen thousand acres, with communication by telephone from one part to another. King Wheat was achieving an increasingly prominent position in the galaxy of agricultural potentates.

Deflation Dooms the Debtor

Once the farmers became chained to a one-crop economy—wheat or corn—they were in the same leaky boat with the southern cotton growers. As long as prices stayed high, all went well. But when they skidded in the 1880s, bankruptcy fell like a blight on the farm belts.

A contemporary farm protest song, "The Kansas Fool," ran:
>   The bankers followed us out west;
>   And did in mortgages invest;
>   They looked ahead and shrewdly planned,
>   And soon they'll have our Kansas land.

The grain farmers were no longer the masters of their own destinies. They were engaged in one of the most fiercely competitive of businesses, for the price of their product was determined in a world market by the world output. If the wheat fields of Argentina, Russia, and other foreign countries smiled, the price of the farmers' grain would fall and American sodbusters would face ruin, as they did in the 1880s and 1890s.

Low prices and a deflated currency were the chief worries of the frustrated farmers—North, South, and West. If a family had borrowed $1,000 in 1855, when wheat was worth about a dollar a bushel, they expected to pay back the equivalent of 1,000 bushels, plus interest, when the mortgage fell due. But if they let their debt run to 1890, when wheat had fallen to about fifty cents a bushel, they would have to pay back the price of 2,000 bushels for the $1,000 they had borrowed, plus interest. This unexpected burden struck them as unjust, though their steely-eyed creditors often branded the complaining farmers as slippery and dishonest rascals.

The deflationary pinch on the debtor flowed partly from the static money supply. There were simply not enough dollars to go around, and as a result, prices were forced down. In 1870 the currency in circulation for each person was $19.42; in 1890 it was only $22.67. Yet during these twenty years business and industrial activity, increasing manyfold, had intensified the scramble for available currency.

The forgotten farmers were caught on a treadmill. Despite unremitting toil, they operated year after year at a loss and lived off their fat as best they could. In a vicious circle, their farm machinery increased their output of grain, lowered the price, and drove them even deeper into debt. Mortgages engulfed homesteads at an alarming rate; by 1890 Nebraska alone reported more than 100,000 farms blanketed with mortgages. The repeated crash of the sheriff-auctioneer's hammer kept announcing to the world that another sturdy American husbandman had become landless in a landed nation.

Ruinous rates of interest, running from 8 to 40 percent, were charged on mortgages, largely by agents of eastern loan companies. The wind-burned sons and daughters of the sod, who felt that they deserved praise for developing the country, cried out in despair against the loan sharks and the Wall Street octopus.

Farm tenancy rather than farm ownership was spreading like stinkweed. The trend was especially marked in the sharecropping South, where cotton prices also sank dismayingly. By 1880 one-fourth of all American farms were operated by tenants. The United States was ready to feed the world, but under the new industrial feudalism the farmers were about to sink into a status suggesting Old World serfdom.

Unhappy Husbandmen

Even Dame Nature ceased smiling, as her powerful forces conspired against agriculture. Mile-wide clouds of grasshoppers, leaving "nothing but the mortgage," periodically ravaged prairie farms. The terrible cotton-boll weevil was also wreaking havoc in the South by the early 1890s.

The good earth was going sour. Floods added to the waste of erosion, which had already washed the topsoil off millions of once-lush southern acres. Expensive fertilizers were urgently needed. A long succession of droughts seared the trans-Mississippi West, beginning in the summer of 1887. Whole towns were abandoned. "Going home to the wife's folks" and "In God we trusted, in Kansas we busted" were typical laments of many impoverished farmers, as they fled their weather-beaten shacks and sun-baked sod houses. One irate "poet" proclaimed:

>   Fifty miles to water,
>   A hundred miles to wood,
>   To hell with this damned country,
>   I'm going home for good.

To add to their miseries, the soil-tillers were gouged by their government—local, state, and national. Their land was overassessed and they paid painful local taxes, while wealthy easterners concealed their stocks and bonds in safe-deposit boxes. Protective tariffs of these years, while pouring profits into the pockets of the manufacturer, imposed heavy burdens on agriculture, especially in the South. Cotton producers or grain growers had to sell their low-priced, unprotected product in a fiercely competitive world market, while buying high-priced manufactured goods in a protected home market.

The farmers were also "farmed" by the corporations and processors. They were at the mercy of the harvester trust, the barbed-wire trust, and the fertilizer trust, all of which could control output and raise prices to extortionate levels. Middlemen took a juicy "cut" from the selling price of the goods that the farmers bought, while storage rates for their grain at warehouses and elevators were pushed up by the operators.

In addition, the railroad octopus had the grain growers in its grip. Freight rates could be so high that the farmers sometimes lost less if they burned their corn for fuel than if they shipped it. If they raised their voices in protest, the ruthless railroad operators might let their grain spoil in damp places or refuse to provide them with cars when needed.

Farmers still made up nearly one-half the population in 1890, but they were hopelessly disorganized. The manufacturers and the railroad barons knew how to combine to promote their interests, and so, increasingly, did industrial workers. But the farmers were by nature independent and individualistic—dead set against consolidation or regimentation. No really effective Carnegie or Gompers arose among them to preach the gospel of economic integration and concentration. They never did organize successfully to restrict production until forced to by the Washington government nearly half a century later, in Franklin Roosevelt's New Deal days. Meanwhile they were slowly being goaded into a large-scale political uprising.

The Farmers Take Their Stand

Agrarian unrest had flared forth earlier, in the Greenback movement shortly after the Civil War. Prices sagged in 1868, and a host of farmers unsuccessfully sought relief from low prices and high indebtedness by demanding an inflation of the currency with paper money.

The National Grange of the Patrons of Husbandry—better known as the Grange—was organized in 1867. Its leading spirit was Oliver H. Kelley, a shrewd and energetic Minnesota

Pioneer Sod House in Nebraska, 1888 *Lumber was scarce. Note deer antlers on well top and mule-drawn grain mower at left. (S. D. Butcher Collection, Nebraska State Historical Society.)*

The Grange Awakening the Sleepers The farmer tries to arouse the apathetic public to the dangers of the onrushing railroad monopoly.

farmer then working as a clerk in Washington. A primary objective at first was to stimulate the minds of the farm folk by social, educational, and fraternal activities.

With picnics, music, and lecturers, the Grange had much colorful appeal. Kelley, a Mason, introduced a mumbo jumbo of passwords and secrecy, as well as a four-ply hierarchy, ranging (for men) from Laborer to Husbandman and (for women) from Maid to Matron. The movement was a godsend to the sun-bonneted and bony-handed womenfolk, who were cursed with loneliness in widely separated farmhouses. The Grange spread like an old-time prairie fire and by 1875 claimed 800,000 members, chiefly in the Middle West and South. Buzzing with gossip, these ginghamed and calloused folk often met in red schoolhouses around potbellied stoves.

The Grangers gradually raised their goals from self-improvement to improvement of the farmers' plight. In a determined effort to escape the clutches of the trusts, they established cooperatives for both consumers and producers. Their most ambitious experiment was an attempt to manufacture harvesting machinery, but this venture, partly as a result of mismanagement, ended in financial disaster.

Embattled Grangers also went into politics, enjoying their most gratifying success in the grain-growing regions of the upper Mississippi Valley, chiefly in Illinois, Wisconsin, Iowa, and Minnesota. There, through state legislation, they strove to regulate railway rates and the storage fees charged by railroads and by the operators of warehouses and grain elevators. Many of the state courts, notably in Illinois, were disposed to recognize the principle of public control of private business for the general welfare. But a number of the so-called Granger Laws were badly drawn, and they were bitterly fought through the high courts by the well-paid lawyers of the "interests." Following judicial reverses, most severely at the hands of the Supreme Court in the famous *Wabash Railroad* decision of 1886 (see p. 512), the Grangers faded rapidly in influence. But their organization has lived on as a vocal champion of farm interests, while brightening rural life with social activities.

Farmers' grievances likewise found a vent in the Greenback Labor party, which combined the inflationary appeal of the earlier Greenbackers with a program for improving the lot of labor. In 1878, the high-water mark of the movement, the Greenback-Laborites polled over a million votes and elected fourteen members of Congress. In the presidential election of 1880 the Greenbackers ran General James B. Weaver, an old Granger who was a favorite of the Civil War veterans and who possessed a remarkable voice and bearing. He spoke to perhaps a half-million citizens in a hundred or so speeches but polled only 3 percent of the total popular vote.

The Passionate Populist Crusade

A striking manifestation of rural discontent, cresting in the late 1880s, came through the Farmers' Alliances, North and South, white and black. Like the Grangers, these groups sponsored picnics and other social gatherings; they bestirred themselves in politics; they organized cooperatives of various kinds; and they sought to break the strangling grip of the railroads and manufacturers. By about 1890 the members of the Farmers' Alliances probably numbered about a million hard-bitten souls, many of

Mary E. Lease (1853–1933) *She was so eloquent as to be called a "Patrick Henry in Petticoats." (Courtesy of the Kansas Historical Society.)*

whom sang "Toilers Unite" and "Where Will the Farmer Be?"

A new grouping—the People's party—began to emerge spectacularly in the early 1890s. Better known as the Populists, and cynically dubbed the "Popocrats," these zealous folk attracted countless recruits from the Farmers' Alliances. The higher the foreclosure rate on mortgages, the deeper the anger of the farmers. Numerous whiskered prophets sprang forward to lead the Populists. Among these assorted characters loomed an eloquent red-haired "spellbinder," Ignatius Donnelly from the state of Minnesota, who was three times elected to Congress.

The queen of the "calamity howlers" was undeniably Mary Elizabeth ("Mary Yellin'") Lease, a tall, athletically built woman who was called "the Kansas Pythoness." In 1890 she made an estimated 160 speeches. Upbraiding the moneyed aristocracy and denouncing the government "of Wall Street, by Wall Street, and for Wall Street," she reportedly cried that the Kansans should raise "less corn and more hell." They did. The big-city New York *Evening Post* snarled, "We don't want any more states until we can civilize Kansas." To many easterners, complaint, not corn, was the chief crop of the westerners.

> Conservatives branded the Populists "Calamity Shouters," "Calamity Prophets," and "Calamity Howlers." In 1892 the Chicago *Tribune* much underestimated the appeal of the Populists when it sneered, "The calamity platform adopted by the Populists at Omaha might invite a limited measure of support in a droughty season or a grasshopper year."

Yet the Populists, despite their peculiarities, were not to be laughed aside. In deadly earnest, they were leading an impassioned crusade to relieve the misfortunes of the farmer. Smiles faded from Republican and Democratic faces alike as countless thousands of Populists sang, "Good-bye, My Party, Good-bye." Yawning eastern plutocrats would have done well to heed these western "hayseeds," for at long last the calloused and sun-baked sons and daughters of the prairies were marshaling their vast political strength. They would soon join their fellow farmers in the South in a ferocious attack on the northeastern citadels of power.

Varying Viewpoints

For at least two generations, historical writing about the American West was dominated by the Turner thesis. In a famous essay of 1893, "The Significance of the Frontier in American History," historian Frederick Jackson Turner argued that the American character had been uniquely shaped by the frontier experience. Europeans had been transformed into tough, inventive, and self-reliant Americans in the struggle to overcome the hazards of the wilderness, including distance, deserts, and Indians. Turner wrote just three years after the superintendent of the census had officially declared the frontier line to be no longer recognizable. Thus, in part, Turner's essay posed a provocative question: What forces might forge a distinctive national character now that the testing ground of the frontier had been plowed and tamed?

Turner's hypothesis is among the most important and stimulating yet proposed about the formative influences on American society. But as the frontier era recedes ever further into the past, scholars are less persuaded that the Turner thesis is an adequate explanation of the national identity. Americans are still different from Europeans and other peoples, even though Turner's frontier virtually disappeared nearly a century ago. The latest scholarship has also demonstrated that the West did not transform the rest of the country but rather was transformed by it, especially in its industrialization. Recent writers have also ceased to portray the Indians as just another obstacle for white civilization to overcome on its westward march. If any cultures were transformed by the American frontier experience, it was Indian cultures, which were altered almost beyond recognition by contact with the whites.

Select Readings

Primary Source Documents

Black Elk Speaks, edited by John G. Neihardt (1932), is an eloquent Indian statement about the Sioux experience. Theodore Roosevelt's *Hunting Trips of a Ranchman** (1885) offers the future president's views on the Indian question. Mary Lease's famous call to arms is recorded in William E. Connelley, ed., *History of Kansas, State and People** (1928).

Secondary Sources

Vivacious chapters appear in Ray A. Billington, *Westward Expansion* (rev. ed., 1974). Walter Prescott Webb, *The Great Plains* (1931), is a classic. Richard A. Bartlett describes *The New Country: A Social History of the American Frontier, 1776–1890* (1974). Native Americans are discussed in Wilcomb Washburn, *The Indian in America* (1975), and in Dee

Brown's popularly written *Bury My Heart at Wounded Knee: An Indian History of the American West* (1970). Consult also Washburn's *Red Man's Land, White Man's Law* (1971); Francis P. Prucha, *Americanizing the American Indian* (1973); and Thomas Berger's novel *Little Big Man* (1964). The military history of the "Indian Wars" is covered in S. L. A. Marshall, *Crimsoned Prairie* (1972). Two intriguing studies of cross-cultural perception are Robert F. Berkhofer, Jr., *The White Man's Indian* (1978), and Richard Drinnon, *Facing West: The Metaphysics of Indian Hating and Empire Building* (1980). Two special studies of interest are Allan G. Bogue, *Money at Interest: The Farm Mortgage on the Middle Border* (1955), and the same author's *From Prairie to Corn Belt: Farming on the Illinois and Iowa Prairies in the Nineteenth Century* (1963). For beef, see Lewis Atherton, *The Cattle Kings* (1961); Philip Durham and Everett L. Jones, *The Negro Cowboys* (1965); Robert Dykstra, *The Cattle Town* (1968); and Gene M. Gressley, *Bankers and Cattlemen* (1966). A powerful work on the farmers' protest is Lawrence Goodwyn, *Democratic Promise* (1976), abridged as *The Populist Moment* (1978). See also John D. Hicks' classic *The Populist Revolt* (1931); Walter T. K. Nugent, *The Tolerant Populists* (1963); Steven Hahn, *The Roots of Southern Populism* (1983); and Bruce Palmer, *"Man over Money": The Southern Populist Critique of American Capitalism* (1980). Henry Nash Smith, *Virgin Land: The American West as Symbol and Myth* (1950), is a landmark study of particular interest to students of literature.

30

The Revolt of the
Debtor, 1889–1900

You come to us and tell us that the great cities are in favor of the gold standard. We reply that the great cities rest upon our broad and fertile prairies. Burn down your cities and leave our farms, and your cities will spring up again as if by magic. But destroy our farms, and the grass will grow in the streets of every city in the country.

William Jennings Bryan, Cross of Gold Speech, 1896

The Republicans Return under Harrison

Benjamin Harrison—stocky, heavily bearded, and dignified—was inaugurated president under weeping heavens on March 4, 1889. The outgoing Grover Cleveland obligingly held an umbrella over him. The incoming president was an honest and earnest party man, but unhappily he was brusque and abrupt. He could charm a crowd of ten thousand people with his oratory, but he would chill them individually with a clammy handshake. He came to be known, rather unfairly, as "the White House Ice Chest."

After their four-year fast, Republicans panted hungrily for the fleshpots of federal office. Harrison gave the headstrong and still-ambitious "Plumed Knight," James G. Blaine, the secretaryship of state as a consolation prize for failing to attain the presidency. The new president also named to the Civil Service Commission a bespectacled and violently energetic New Yorker, Theodore Roosevelt, as a reward for the eager-beaver politician's oratory in the campaign.

Republicans in the House of Representatives could hardly expect smooth sailing; they had only three votes more than the necessary quorum of 163 members. If the Democrats continued their practice of refusing to answer roll calls, the Republicans could muster a quorum only with difficulty. The Democrats were also prepared to make numerous delaying motions. These included time-consuming demands for a roll call to determine the presence of a quorum, even though one was obviously present. For their part, the Republicans were eager to get on with squandering money and thus safeguard the high tariff that was producing a surplus.

Into this explosive cockpit stepped the new Republican Speaker of the House, Thomas B. Reed of Maine. A hulking figure who towered 6 feet 3 inches (1.91 meters), he had already made his mark as a masterful debater. Cool and collected, he spoke with a harsh nasal drawl and wielded a verbal harpoon of sarcasm. One congressman who had declaimed that he would "rather be right than President," like Henry Clay, was silenced by Reed's rasping sneer that he would "never be either." Opponents cringed at "the crack of his quip."

Early in 1890 the redoubtable Reed undertook single-handedly to change the House rules. He believed that the majority should legislate, in accord with democratic practices, and not be crippled by a filibustering minority. He therefore ignored Democratic speakers who sprang to their feet and sought to establish the absence of a quorum. In piecing out quorums, he counted as present certain Democrats in the chamber who had not answered the roll and who, rule book in hand, furiously denied that they were legally present. For three days pandemonium rocked the House, while Reed held his ground, reputedly counting as present congressmen who were in the barbershop or on trains headed for home.

The gavel rule of "Czar" Reed finally prevailed. The Fifty-first, or "Billion-Dollar," Congress*—the first in peacetime to appropriate approximately this sum—gave birth to a bumper crop of expensive legislative babies. When the Democrats won control of the House two years later, they paid Reed the compliment of adopting some of his reforms for speedier action.

---

*By the 1980s Congress was appropriating an average of more than a billion dollars *a day!*

President Harrison Disposes of Surplus (Puck, 1892.)

Political Gravy for All

President Harrison, himself a Civil War general, was disposed to deal generously with his old comrades-in-arms. He appointed as commissioner of pensions a Civil War amputee, who promised to drive a six-mule team through the Treasury and to wring "from the hearts of some the prayer, 'God help the surplus.'" He cut a wide swath, and a Treasury surplus has never been a problem since his day.

This "Billion-Dollar" Congress cooperated by opening wide the federal purse in the Pension Act of 1890. It showered pensions on all Union Civil War veterans who had served for ninety days and who were now unable to do manual labor. Between 1891 and 1895 the host of pensioners was thus raised from 676,000 to 970,000, and by the time Harrison left office in 1893, the annual bill had shot up from $81 million to $135 million. Thus was faintly foreshadowed the government-financed "welfare state" of the twentieth century.

This policy of liberality toward old soldiers had special attractions for Republican politicians. It helped to solve the problem of the

Treasury surplus—a problem that had bedeviled President Cleveland. It helped to save the protective tariff by making plausible, even necessary, the continuance of high customs duties. It helped to secure Republican votes, for the aging veterans of the GAR (Grand Army of the Republic) were grateful to the GOP (Grand Old Party) for its handouts.

"Czar" Reed's gavel, pounding imperiously, drove through Congress additional bills, conspicuous among which was the Sherman Anti-Trust Act of 1890. This pioneering law, though a feeble bludgeon, did something to quiet the mounting uproar against bloated corporations. (See pp. 519–520.)

Noteworthy also was the Sherman Silver Purchase Act of 1890. The western miners were acutely unhappy over the limited silver-purchase program under the Bland-Allison Law of 1878, and many of the silverites were demanding unrestricted government buying of the "beloved white metal." At the same time, many debt-burdened western and southern farmers were clamoring for the unlimited coinage of silver. They were convinced that the addition of an immense amount of metallic money would inflate the currency and thus make for higher prices and easier debt payments. The "Gold Bug" East looked with conservative horror on any such tampering with the money supply but hungered for the profits that might be reaped from a boost in the tariff schedules.

Thus, the stage was set for a huge logrolling operation. Western silver agitators agreed to support a protective tariff, which they detested; eastern protectionists agreed to support a silver bill, which they distrusted. As a part of the resulting Sherman Silver Purchase Act of 1890, the Treasury was to buy a total of 4.5 million ounces (127,800 kilograms) monthly—about all that was being mined—and pay for it in notes redeemable in either silver or gold. This new law, while boosting the price for the miners, would approximately double the minimum amount of silver that could be acquired under the old Bland-Allison Law.

High-tariff Republicans reaped their political reward with the McKinley Tariff Bill, which boosted rates to their highest peacetime level yet—an average of 48.4 percent on dutiable goods. Sponsored in the House by William McKinley of Ohio, the "high priest of high protection," the bill disposed of the troublesome surplus by giving a bounty of two cents a pound to American sugar producers. It also raised tariffs on agricultural products—a hollow gesture to farmers, because foreign growers could never compete with soil-rich Americans.

These new duties on manufactured goods, as fate would have it, actually brought new woes to the farmers. Some eastern manufacturers raised their prices even before the law went into effect. Tin peddlers—some reportedly in the pay of the Democrats—went systematically from house to house in the Middle West, displaying their wares to housewives. They would cleverly but dishonestly say that yesterday a pie pan sold for ten cents, but today for twenty-five cents—all because of the wicked Republican tariff.

Mounting discontent against "Bill" McKinley and his McKinley Bill caused voters to rise in wrath, especially in the midwestern farm belt. The congressional landslide of 1890 reduced the Republican membership of the House from 166 to a scant 88 members, as compared with 235 Democrats. Even the highly publicized McKinley lost his seat in the House. Ominously for conservatives, the new Congress also included nine members of the Farmers' Alliance, the militant organization of southern and western farmers.

Unhorsing President Harrison in 1892

Discontent over Republican high-tariff policies gave the Democrats high hopes as the presidential election of 1892 approached. Their man of destiny was portly but energetic former president Grover Cleveland. He had built up a profitable law practice in New York City and, after hobnobbing with his wealthy clientele, had become increasingly conservative. Yet his reputation was such that he was nominated in Chicago on the first ballot.

Gathering in Minneapolis, the Republicans renominated cold-fish President Harrison, even though he was cordially disliked by party bosses. With seemingly arrogant disregard for the political consequences, their platform championed the protective tariff.

Color was added to the campaign of 1892 by the newly formed People's Party (Populists), which arose out of the grievances of frustrated farmers in the West and South. Meeting in Omaha, the Populists adopted a scorching platform that denounced the "prolific womb of governmental injustice." It demanded free and unlimited coinage of silver at the ratio of sixteen to one, a graduated income tax, and government ownership of the telephone and telegraph, as well as the railroads. As their presidential candidate the Populists uproariously nominated the eloquent old Greenbacker, General James B. Weaver.

Except for the raucous protests of the Populists, the campaign of 1892 was clean, quiet, and creditable. A few faint appeals were made to the fast-fading bloody shirt. But the tariff, as in the preceding campaign, was the overshadowing issue.

An epidemic of strikes then sweeping the country proved damaging to Harrison's cause: they eloquently refuted the shopworn Republican argument that high protection meant high wages. The most notorious outburst flared forth at Carnegie's Homestead plant near Pittsburgh, following a pay slash for the steelworkers. Company officials called in three hundred armed Pinkerton detectives. Defiant strikers, armed with rifles and dynamite, forced their assailants to surrender after a vicious battle in which ten persons were killed and some sixty wounded. Troops were eventually summoned, and both the strike and the union were broken. But this unsavory episode—lead instead of bread—doubtless cost the Republicans thousands of votes.

With this unexpected boost from the Pinkerton Agency, Cleveland unhorsed Harrison. "Old Grover" polled 277 electoral votes to his opponent's 145, and 5,555,426 popular votes to 5,182,690. Cleveland, like Andrew Jackson, received a popular plurality three times, though he took office only twice.

The Populists made a remarkable showing. Singing "Good-bye, Party Bosses," they rolled up 1,029,846 popular votes and 22 electoral votes for General Weaver. They thus became one of the few third parties in American history to break into the electoral column. But their electoral votes came only from six middle western and western states, four of which (Kansas,

The Kansas Legislature, 1890 *Rifle-bearing Populists seized the Kansas capitol after the election of 1890, to make good their claim that they had won at the polls. Republicans disagreed and eventually prevailed when sergeants-at-arms, shown here, restored order. (The Kansas State Historical Society, Topeka.)*

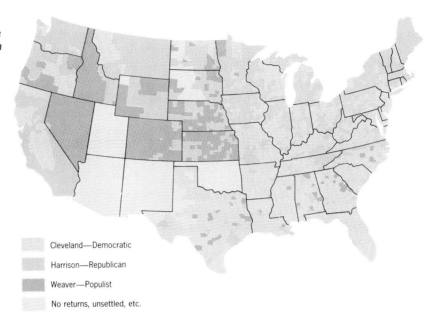

Presidential Election of 1892 (showing vote by county) Note the concentration of Populist strength in the semi-arid farming regions of the Western half of the country. (Compare with annual precipitation map on p. 567.)

Cleveland—Democratic

Harrison—Republican

Weaver—Populist

No returns, unsettled, etc.

Colorado, Idaho, and Nevada) fell completely into the Populist basket. The new party failed to gain valuable allies when the indebted white farmers of the solid South, though sorely tempted, refused to desert the Democratic camp in large numbers. They feared losing political power to the blacks, for there was even a segregated Colored Farmers' National Alliance that claimed more than a million members.

Southern blacks, tens of thousands of them attracted by Populist reforms, were heavy losers. When the white ruling class discovered that this vote could not be controlled, all remaining black suffrage in the South was virtually eliminated. More than a half-century was to pass before the blacks could again vote in considerable numbers. Accompanying this disfranchisement were more severe Jim Crow Laws, backed up by atrocious lynchings and designed primarily to keep blacks segregated in public places, including hotels and restaurants.

"Old Grover" Cleveland Again

Grover Cleveland took office once again in 1893, the only president ever reelected after defeat. He was the same old bull-necked and bull-headed Cleveland, with a little more weight, polish, conservatism, and self-assertiveness. But if it was the same old Grover Cleveland, it was not the same old country; the debtors were up in arms, and the advance shadows of panic were falling.

Hardly had Cleveland seated himself in the presidential chair when the depression of 1893 burst about his burly frame. Lasting for about four years, it was the most devastating economic downturn of the century. As the first large-scale depression in the new urban and industrial age, it brought unprecedented hardships to the masses in the cities. Contributing causes were the splurge of overbuilding and overspeculation, labor disorders, and the current agricultural depression. Free-silver agitation had also damaged American credit abroad, and the usual pinch on American finances had come when European banking houses, after

A popular protest song of the 1890s among western farmers was entitled "The Hayseed." One stanza ran:

I once was a tool of oppression,
And as green as a sucker could be,
And monopolies banded together
To beat a poor hayseed like me.

earlier failures, began to call in loans from the United States.

Distress was acute and widespread. About eight thousand American business houses collapsed in six months, and dozens of railroad lines went into the hands of receivers. Business executives "died like flies under the strain," wrote Henry Adams. Soup kitchens were set up for the unemployed, while gangs of hoboes ("tramps") wandered aimlessly about the country. Local charities did their feeble best, but the federal government, bound by the let-nature-take-its-course philosophy of the times, was unable to relieve the suffering masses.

Cleveland, who had earlier been bothered by a surplus, was now burdened with a deficit. Under the Sherman Silver Purchase Act, the Treasury was required to issue legal tender notes for the silver bullion that it bought. Owners of the paper currency would then present it for gold, and by law the notes had to be reissued. New holders would repeat the process, thus draining away gold in an "endless-chain" operation.

Alarmingly, the gold reserve in the Treasury dropped below $100 million, which was popularly regarded as the safe minimum for supporting about $350 million in outstanding paper money. Cleveland saw no alternative but to halt the bleeding away of gold by engineering a repeal of the Sherman Silver Purchase Act of 1890. For this purpose he summoned Congress into an extra session in the summer of 1893.

Unknown to the country, complications threatened from another quarter. A malignant growth had developed on the roof of Cleveland's mouth, and it had to be removed on a private yacht with extreme secrecy. If the president had died under the knife, his place would have been taken by the "soft money" vice-president, Adlai E. Stevenson—an eventuality that would have deepened the crisis.

In Congress the debate over the repeal of the silver act was meanwhile running its heated course. An eloquent young congressman from Nebraska, thirty-three-year-old William Jennings Bryan, held the galleries spellbound for three hours as he championed the cause of free silver. The friends of silver announced that "hell would freeze over" before Congress passed the repeal measure. But an angered Cleveland used

> In his special message to Congress (1893) Cleveland said: "Unless Government bonds are to be constantly issued and sold to replenish our exhausted gold, only to be again exhausted, it is apparent that the operation of the silver-purchase law now in force leads in the direction of the entire substitution of silver for the gold in the Government Treasury, and that this must be followed by the payment of all Government obligations in depreciated silver."

his office-giving power to break the filibuster in the Senate. He thus alienated the Democratic silverites and disrupted his party at the very outset of his administration.

Gold Shortages and Job Shortages

The hemorrhaging of gold from the Treasury was only partially stopped by the repeal of the Sherman Silver Purchase Act. Other currency was still being presented for redemption, and in February 1894, the gold reserve sank to a dismaying $41 million. The nation was in grave danger of going off the gold standard.

Again Cleveland was forced to act vigorously. As a champion of sound money, he could see no alternative but to sell government bonds for gold and deposit the proceeds in the Treasury. Two bond issues were floated in 1894, totaling over $100 million, but the "endless-chain" operations continued relentlessly.

Early in 1895 Cleveland turned in desperation to J. P. Morgan, "the bankers' banker," and a Wall Street syndicate. After tense negotiations at the White House, the bankers agreed to lend the government $65 million in gold. They were obviously in business for profit, so they charged a commission amounting to about $7 million. But they did make a significant concession when they agreed to obtain one-half of the gold abroad and take the necessary steps to dam it up in the leaky Treasury. The loan, at least temporarily, helped restore confidence in the nation's finances.

But the bond deal stirred up a storm. The Wall Street ogre, especially in the eyes of the

West and South Feed the Country While Wall Street Milks It *A cartoon of the 1890s highly popular with Democrats and Populists.*

silverites and other debtors, symbolized all that was wicked and grasping. Cleveland's secretive dealings with mighty "Jupiter" Morgan were savagely condemned as a "sellout" of the national government. But Cleveland was certain that he had done no wrong. Sarcastically denying that he was "Morgan's errand boy," he asserted: "Without shame and without repentance I confess my share of the guilt."

Ragged armies of the unemployed, victims of the depression, were meanwhile staging demonstrations. The most famous of these marches was that of "General" Jacob S. Coxey, a wealthy Ohio quarry owner, who started for Washington in 1894 with several score of supporters, accompanied by a swarm of newspaper reporters. His platform included a demand that the government relieve unemployment by an inflationary public works program, supported by some $500 million in legal tender notes to be issued by the Treasury. Coxey himself rode in a carriage with his wife and infant son, appropriately named Legal Tender Coxey, while his tiny "army" tramped along behind, singing:

> We're coming, Grover Cleveland,
>   500,000 strong,
> We're marching on to Washington
>   to right the nation's wrong.

The "Commonweal Army" of Coxeyites finally straggled into the nation's capital. But the "invasion" took on the aspects of a comic opera when "General" Coxey and his "lieutenants"

were arrested for walking on the grass. Other armies—"petitions in boots"—were less well behaved and accounted for considerable disorder and pillage.

Cleveland Crushes the Pullman Strike

Violent flare-ups accompanied labor protests, notably in Chicago. Most frightening was the crippling Pullman strike of 1894. Eugene V. Debs, an impetuous but personally lovable labor leader, had helped organize the American Railway Union of about 150,000 members. The Pullman Palace Car Company, which maintained a model town near Chicago for its employees, was hit hard by the depression and cut wages about one-third, while holding the line on rent for the company houses. The workers finally struck—in some places overturning Pullman cars—and paralyzed railway traffic from Chicago to the Pacific Coast.

This terrorism in Chicago was serious but not completely out of hand. At least this was the judgment of Governor Altgeld of Illinois, a friend of the downtrodden who had pardoned the Haymarket Square anarchists the year before (see p. 525). But Attorney General Olney, an arch-conservative and an ex–railroad attorney, urged the dispatch of federal troops. His legal grounds were that the strikers were interfering with the transit of the United States mail. Cleveland supported Olney with the ringing

The Pullman Strike, 1894 *These federal troops broke the back of the strike by force of arms.*
(Culver Pictures, Inc.)

declaration, "If it takes the entire army and navy to deliver a postal card in Chicago, that card will be delivered."

To the delight of conservatives, the Pullman strike was crushed by bayonet-supported intervention from Washington. Debs and his leading associates, who had defied a federal court injunction to cease striking, were sentenced to six months' imprisonment for contempt of court. Ironically, the lean labor agitator spent much of his enforced leisure reading radical literature, which had much to do with his later leadership of the Socialist movement in America.

Embittered cries of "government by injunction" now burst from organized labor. This was the first time that such a legal weapon had been used conspicuously by Washington to break a strike, and it was all the more distasteful because defiant laborites who were held in contempt could be imprisoned without jury trial. Signs multiplied that employers were striving to smash labor unions by court action. Nonlabor

> After the Pullman strike collapsed, Debs said, "No strike has ever been lost." In 1897 he declared: "The issue is Socialism versus Capitalism. I am for Socialism because I am for humanity."

elements of the country, including the Populists and other debtors, were likewise incensed. They saw in the brutal Pullman episode further proof of an unholy alliance between big business and the courts.

Democratic Tariff Tinkering

The McKinley Tariff of 1890 had been designed to keep protection high and the surplus low. It succeeded remarkably in achieving both goals. By 1894 the Treasury was faced with an alarming deficit of $61 million.

In Congress the Democrats undertook to frame a tariff that would provide adequate revenue with moderate protection, as they had promised in the Cleveland-Harrison campaign of 1892. A bill aimed at securing these objectives was introduced in the House. As a concession to the Populists and other foes of "plutocracy," the measure included a tax of 2 percent on incomes over $4,000. Joseph H. Choate, a wealthy lawyer, growled, "Communistic, socialistic."

When the new tariff bill reached the Senate, it ran afoul of a swarm of lobbyists in the pay of big industry. After much buttonholing and vote trading, the Wilson-Gorman Bill was drastically revamped by the addition of over 630 amendments. The sugar trust stirred up a scandal when it inserted benefits to itself worth a sweet $20 million a year. As a result of such back-stairs pressures, the Wilson-Gorman law of 1894 fell scandalously short of establishing a low tariff, even though it did reduce the existing McKinley rates from 48.4 percent to 41.3 percent on dutiable goods. (See Appendix.)

Cleveland was outraged by what he regarded as a gross betrayal of Democratic campaign pledges. In an angry outburst he denounced the bill as "party perfidy and party dishonor"—to the glee of the Republicans. But to veto the patchwork affair would leave the even higher McKinley Tariff on the books, so Cleveland grudgingly let the bill become law without his signature. The Wilson-Gorman hodgepodge at least had the redeeming feature of the income tax, which was highly popular among the masses.

But the income tax lasted less than a year. In 1895 the Supreme Court, by a five-to-four deci-

"He Must Be Kept Out" An anti-free silver cartoon, 1896. (The Granger Collection.)

Crying for Protection *Uncle Sam is called on in this 1896 cartoon to nurse so-called "infant industries"—some of which had in fact long since grown into vigorous adulthood. (The Granger Collection.)*

sion, struck down this part of the Wilson-Gorman Act.* The only popular feature of the unpopular tariff law thus perished under the judicial tomahawk. A chorus of denunciation rose from the Populists and other impoverished groups, who found further proof that the courts were only the tools of the plutocrats.

Democratic political fortunes naturally suffered. The tariff dynamite that had blasted the Republicans out of the House in 1890 now dislodged the Democrats, with a strong helping hand from the depression. Revitalized Republicans, singing "The Soup House" and "Times Are Mighty Hard," won the congressional elections of 1894 in a landslide and now had 244 votes to 105 for the Democrats. The prospects of the Republicans for 1896 seemed roseate. They were openly boasting that they had only to

---

*It violated the "direct tax" clause. See Art. I, Sec. IX, para. 4, Appendix. The Sixteenth Amendment to the Constitution, adopted in 1913, permitted an income tax.

nominate a "rag baby" or a "yaller dog," and they could put it in the White House. Such optimism misread the signs of the times.

Discontented debtors, especially the Populists, were turning in throngs to free silver as a cure-all. An enormously popular pamphlet, entitled *Coin's Financial School* (1894), was being distributed by the hundreds of thousands of copies. Written by William Hope Harvey, it was illustrated by clever woodcuts, one of which depicted the gold ogre beheading the beautiful silver maiden. In fiction parading as fact, the booklet showed how the "little professor"—"Coin" Harvey—overwhelmed the bankers and professors of economics with his brilliant sallies in behalf of free silver. The belief was gaining momentum among silverites and debtors that there was a foul conspiracy on foot, both nationally and internationally, to elevate gold above silver.

McKinley: Hanna's Fair-Haired Boy

The leading candidate for the Republican presidential nomination in 1896 was ex-congressman McKinley of Ohio, sponsor of the ill-starred tariff bill of 1890. He had established a creditable Civil War record, having risen to the rank of major; he hailed from the electorally potent state of Ohio; and he could point to long years of honorable service in Congress, where he had made many friends by his kindly and conciliatory manner. Rather small in stature (5 feet 7 inches; 1.7 meters), and with a high forehead and a prominent chin, he added to his inches by his dignity and by his resemblance to Napoleon Bonaparte—a characteristic seized upon by the cartoonists. He was widely hailed as "the Napoleon of Protection" and "the Advance Agent of Prosperity."

As a presidential candidate, McKinley was peculiarly the creation of a fellow Ohioan, Marcus Alonzo Hanna. The latter had made his fortune in the iron business, and he now coveted the role of president-maker. He was personally attracted to McKinley; "I love McKinley," he once said. When the overgenerous Ohio congressman faced bankruptcy after unwisely en-

Uncle Sam: "It Won't Work Without a New Wheel"
A specious argument for bimetallism. (W. H. Harvey, Coin's Financial School Up to Date, 1895.)

dorsing a friend's notes for about $100,000, Hanna and his wealthy associates paid off the obligation.

Hanna, as a wholehearted Hamiltonian, believed that a prime function of government was to aid business. Honest, earnest, rough, and direct, he became the personification of big industry in politics. He was often cartooned, quite unfairly, as a bloated bully in a loud chekered suit with a dollar sign on each checker. As a conservative in business, he was a confirmed "standpatter," content not to rock the boat. He believed that in some measure prosperity "trickled down" to the laborer, whose dinner pail was full when business flourished. Critics assailed this idea as equivalent to feeding the horses in order to feed the sparrows.

A hardfisted Hanna, although something of a novice in politics, organized his preconvention campaign for McKinley with consummate skill and with a liberal outpouring of his own money. The convention steamroller, well lubricated

Hanna: That man Clay was an ass. It's better to be President than to be right!

Hanna Lampooned This cartoon reflects Democratic and Populist resentment of the wealth and power of Republican Mark Hanna and his candidate, William McKinley. (Library of Congress.)

with Hanna's dollars, nominated McKinley on the first ballot at St. Louis in June 1896.

The Republican platform cleverly straddled the monetary question. It declared for the gold standard, even though McKinley's voting record in Congress had been embarrassingly friendly to silver. But the platform made a gesture toward the silverites when it came out for international bimetallism, or a worldwide gold-silver standard. The catch was that all the leading nations of the world would have had to agree to such a scheme, and this obviously they would not do. Additionally, the platform condemned hard times and Democratic incapacity, while pouring praise on the protective tariff.

Bryan: Silverite Messiah

Dissension riddled the Democratic camp. Cleveland no longer led his party; dubbed "the Stuffed Prophet," he was undeniably the most unpopular man in the country. Labor-debtor groups remembered too vividly the silver-purchase repeal, the Pullman strike, and the backstairs Morgan bond deal. Ultraconservative in finance, Cleveland was now more a Republican than a Democrat on the silver issue.

Rudderless, the Democratic convention met in Chicago in July 1896, with the silverites in command. Shouting insults at the absent Cleveland, they refused, by a suicidal vote of 564 to 357, to endorse their own administration. They had the enthusiasm and the numbers; all they lacked was a leader.

A new Moses suddenly appeared in the person of William Jennings Bryan of Nebraska. Then only thirty-six years of age and known as "the Boy Orator of the Platte,"* he stepped confidently onto the platform before fifteen thousand people. His masterful presence was set off by handsome features, a smooth-shaven jaw, and raven-black hair. He radiated honesty, sincerity, and energy. He had a good mind but not a brilliant one; he was less a student of books than of human nature; and he possessed broad human sympathies. His was a great heart rather than a great head; a great voice rather than a great brain.

In Chicago the setting was made to order for a magnificent oratorical effort. A hush fell over the convention as Bryan stood before it. With an organlike voice that rolled into the outer corners of the huge hall, he delivered a fervent plea for silver. Rising to supreme heights of eloquence, he thundered, "We will answer their demands for a gold standard by saying to them: 'You shall not press down upon the brow of labor this crown of thorns, you shall not crucify mankind upon a cross of gold.'"

The Cross of Gold speech was a sensation. Swept off its feet in a tumultuous scene, the Democratic convention nominated Bryan the next day on the fifth ballot. The platform declared for the unlimited coinage of silver at the ratio of 16 ounces of silver to 1 of gold, though

---

*One contemporary sneered that Bryan, like the Platte River, was "six inches deep and six miles wide at the mouth."

William Jennings Bryan on the Platform   *The most famous political orator of his age, he is speaking here at the Democratic Convention of 1896. (Left, The Bettmann Archive. Right, Underwood and Underwood.)*

the market ratio was about 32 to 1. This meant that the silver in a dollar would be worth about fifty cents.

Democratic "Gold Bugs," unable to swallow Bryan, bolted their party over the silver issue. Conservative Senator Hill of New York, when asked if he was a Democrat still, reportedly replied, "Yes, I am a Democrat still—*very* still." The Democratic minority, including Cleveland, charged that the Populist-silverites had stolen both the name and the clothes of their party. They nominated a lost-cause ticket of their own, and many of them, including Cleveland, hoped for a McKinley victory.

Populists were left out in the cold, for the Democratic majority had appropriated their main plank—"16 to 1," that "heaven-born ratio." The bulk of the confused "Popocrats," rather than submit to a hard-money McKinley victory,

endorsed Bryan in their convention. Singing "The Jolly Silver Dollar of the Dads," they became in effect the "Demo-Pop" party. But many of the original Populists refused to support Bryan and went down with their colors nailed to the mast.

Hanna Leads the "Gold Bugs"

Mark Hanna smugly assumed that he could make the tariff the focus of the campaign. But Bryan, a dynamo of energy, forced the free-trade issue into a back seat when he took to the stump in behalf of free silver. Sweeping through twenty-seven states and traveling 18,000 miles (29,000 kilometers), he made between five and six hundred speeches—thirty-six in one day—and even invaded the East, "the enemy's country." Vachel Lindsay caught the spirit of his oratorical orgy:

> Prairie avenger, mountain lion,
> Bryan, Bryan, Bryan, Bryan,
> Gigantic troubadour, speaking like a siege
> gun,
> Smashing Plymouth Rock with his
> boulders from the West.*

Free silver became almost as much a religious as a financial issue. Hordes of fanatical free-silverites hailed Bryan as the messiah to lead them out of the wilderness of debt. They sang, "We'll All Have Our Pockets Lined with Silver" and "No Crown of Thorns, No Cross of Gold."

William Jennings Bryan created panic among eastern conservatives with his threat of converting their holdings overnight into fifty-cent dollars. The "Gold Bugs" vented their alarm in abusive epithets, which ranged all the way from "fanatic" and "madman" to "traitor" and "murderer." "In God We Trust, with Bryan We Bust," the Republicans sneered, while one eastern clergyman cried, "That platform was made in Hell."

Widespread fear of Bryan and the "silver lunacy" enabled "Dollar Mark" Hanna, now chairman of the Republican National Committee, to shine as a money raiser. He "shook down" the trusts and plutocrats and piled up an enormous "slush fund" for a "campaign of education"—or of propaganda, depending on one's point of view. The Republicans amassed the most formidable political campaign chest thus far in American history. At all levels—national, state, and local—it amounted to about $16 million, as contrasted with about $1 million for the poorer Democrats (roughly "16 to 1"). With some justification, the Bryanites accused Hanna of "buying" the election and of floating McKinley into the White House on a tidal wave of greenbacks. The Republicans definitely had the edge in money and mud.

---

*Reprinted with permission of Macmillan Publishing Company, Inc., from *Collected Poems*, by Vachel Lindsay. Copyright 1920 by Macmillan Publishing Company, Inc., renewed 1948 by Elizabeth C. Lindsay.

Appealing to the Pocketbook Vote

With gold gushing into his money bags, Hanna waged a high-pressure campaign against silver. He distributed tens of millions of pamphlets, tracts, leaflets, and posters, many of them in the native languages of immigrant groups. He sent out hundreds of "spellbinders" onto the stump, where they engaged in the free and unlimited coinage of wordage. There was a maximum of shouting and a minimum of thinking, primarily because only a few trained economists were able to grasp fully the implications of silver-and-gold bimetallism—and even they disagreed. "The whole currency question," wrote the humorist "Mr. Dooley" (Finley Peter Dunne), "is a matter of lungs."

Republicans harped constantly on their promise of prosperity. Reminding the voters of Cleveland's "Democratic panic," they appealed to the "belly vote" with their prize slogan: "McKinley and the Full Dinner Pail." McKinley, though an effective orator, was no match for Bryan in the rough-and-tumble of stump speaking. He remained at his Ohio home, conducting a quiet and dignified "front-porch" campaign. Stressing prosperity, he read calm and confident little speeches to delegations of visiting Republicans.

Bryan's cyclonic campaign, launched with irresistible enthusiasm, began to lose steam as the weeks passed. Just before the election, the price of wheat rose sharply, owing largely to crop failures abroad. Hostility to the Republican party in the vast wheat belt began to wane, even though agriculture generally remained depressed.

Fear probably was the strongest ally of Hanna, the worst enemy of Bryan, who allegedly had "silver on the brain." Republican businesspeople placed contracts with manufacturers, contingent on the election of McKinley. A few factory owners, with thinly veiled intimidation, paid off their workers and told them not to come to work on Wednesday morning if Bryan won. Reports were also current that employers were threatening to pay their employees in fifty-cent pieces, instead of dollars, if Bryan triumphed. Such were some of the "dirty tricks" of the "Stop Bryan, Save America" crusade.

Class Conflict: Plowholders versus Bondholders

Hanna's campaign methods paid off, for on election day McKinley triumphed decisively. The vote was 271 to 176 in the Electoral College, and 7,102,246 to 6,492,559 in the popular column. Responding to fear, hope, and excitement, an unprecedented outpouring of voters flocked to the polls. McKinley ran strongly in the populous East, where he carried every county of New England, and in the upper Mississippi Valley. Bryan's states, concentrated in the debt-burdened South and the trans-Mississippi West, involved more acreage than McKinley's but less population—only the South and the desert, cynics said.

The free-silver election of 1896 was probably the most significant since Lincoln's victories in 1860 and 1864. Despite Bryan's strength in the South and West, the results vividly demonstrated his lack of appeal to the unmortgaged farmer and especially the eastern urban laborer. Many wage earners in the East voted for their jobs and full dinner pails, threatened as they were by free silver, free trade, and fireless factories. Living precariously on a fixed wage, the

> In gold-standard England there was much relief over McKinley's victory. The London Standard commented: "The hopelessly ignorant and savagely covetous waifs and strays of American civilization voted for Bryan, but the bulk of the solid sense, business integrity, and social stability sided with McKinley. The nation is to be heartily congratulated."

factory workers had no reason to favor inflation, which was the heart of the Bryanites' program.

The Bryan-McKinley battle heralded the advent of a new era in American politics. At first glance, the election seemed to be the age-old story of the underprivileged many against the privileged few, of the indebted backcountry against the wealthier seaboard, of the country against the city, of the agrarians against the industrialists, of Main Street against Wall Street, of the nobodies against the somebodies. Yet when Bryan made his evangelical appeal to all those supposed foes of the social order, there were simply not enough of them.

The outcome was instead a resounding victory for big business, the big cities, middle-class

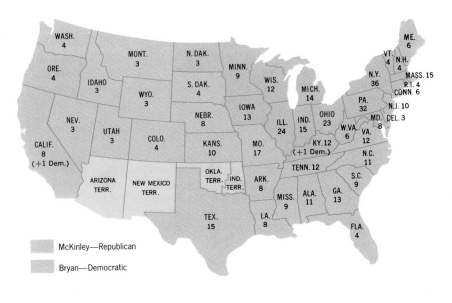

McKinley—Republican

Bryan—Democratic

Presidential Election of 1896 (with electoral vote by state) *This election tolled the death knell of the Gilded Age political system, with its razor-close elections, strong party loyalties, and high voter turnouts. For years after 1896 Republicans predominated, and citizens showed declining interest in either joining parties or voting.*

values, and financial conservatism. Bryan's defeat marked the last serious effort to win the White House with mostly agrarian votes. The future of presidential politics lay not on the farms, with their dwindling population, but in the mushrooming cities.

The smashing Republican victory of 1896 also ensured a Republican grip on the White House for sixteen consecutive years—indeed, for all but eight of the next thirty-six years. McKinley's election thus imparted a new character to the American political system. The long period of Republican dominance that it ushered in was accompanied by diminishing voter participation in elections, a weakening of party organizations, and the fading away of issues like the money question and civil-service reform, which came to be replaced by concern for industrial regulation and the welfare of labor. Scholars have dubbed this new political era the period of the "fourth party system."[*]

Republican Standpattism Enthroned

An eminently "safe" McKinley took the inaugural oath in 1897. Though a man of considerable ability, he was an ear-to-the-ground politician who seldom got far out of line with majority opinion. His cautious, conservative nature caused him to shy away from the flaming banner of reform. Business was given a free rein, and the trusts, which had trusted him in 1896, were allowed to develop more mighty muscles without serious restraints.

---

[*]The first party system, marked by doubts about the very legitimacy of parties, embraced the Federalist-Republican clashes of the 1790s and early 1800s. The second party system took shape with the emergence of mass-based politics in the Jacksonian era, pitting Democrats against Whigs. The third party system was characterized by the precarious equilibrium between Republicans and Democrats, as well as the high electoral participation, that lasted from the end of the Civil War to McKinley's election. The fourth party system is described above. The fifth party system emerged in Franklin Roosevelt's New Deal, which initiated a long period of Democratic ascendancy. Each of these "systems," except the fifth, has lasted about forty years. Debate continues as to whether the nation has now entered or is about to enter the era of the sixth party system.

McKinley, unlike Cleveland, was able to work smoothly in party harness. With impeccable white vest, he seemed never to perspire, even in cruelly muggy Washington. Able to get along well with Congress—he had served there for many years—he shone best at reconciling conflicting interests. Conciliatory and warmhanded, he would send an angry-faced caller away beaming, sometimes wearing a carnation from the presidential desk. McKinley continued to maintain intimate relations with Hanna, but he was by no means under the thumb of his mentor, despite Vachel Lindsay's cruel query:

> Where is McKinley, Mark Hanna's McKinley,
> His slave, his echo, his suit of clothes?

The tariff issue, which had played second fiddle to silver in the "Battle of '96," quickly forced itself to the fore. The current Wilson-Gorman law was not raising enough revenue to cover the annual Treasury deficits, and the Republican trusts had purchased additional protection by their lush contributions to Hanna's "slush fund."

In due course the Dingley Tariff Bill was jammed through the House in 1897, under the pounding gavel of the rethroned "Czar" Reed. The proposed new rates were high, but not high enough to satisfy the paunchy lobbyists, who once again descended upon the Senate. Over 850 amendments were tacked onto the overburdened bill. The resulting piece of patchwork finally established the average rates at 46.5 percent, substantially higher than the Democratic Wilson-Gorman Act of 1894 and in some categories even higher than the McKinley Act of 1890. (See the chart in the Appendix.)

Inflation without Silver

Prosperity, long lurking around the corner, began to return with a rush in 1897, the first year of McKinley. The depression of 1893 had run its course, and farm prices rose. Paint-thirsty middle western barns blossomed out in new colors, and the wheels of industry increased their hum. Republican politicians, like crowing roosters causing the sun to rise, claimed credit for bringing in the sunlight of prosperity.

The Gold Standard Act, loudly demanded by hard-moneyites, was not passed by the Republicans until 1900, when many silverites had left Congress. It provided that the paper currency was to be redeemed freely in gold. Last-ditch silverites fought the bill with bitterness but without success. The cries of the inflationists, further choked by returning prosperity, gradually died away. Thus ended some twenty years of paternalistic attempts to "do something" for the debtor.

In retrospect, a controlled expansion of American currency in the 1880s and 1890s was clearly desirable. Prices were depressed, money was tight, and the volume of currency in circulation lagged far behind the increasing volume of business. Agrarian debtors therefore had a good cause: relief from social and economic hardship through an inflation of the dollar supply. But free silver, which aroused exaggerated fears, was a poor sword. By brandishing this tinseled weapon, Bryan actually defeated his own ends. The free-silver fixation not only discredited the case for needed currency expansion but seriously set back the movement for agrarian reform.

Nature and science gradually provided an inflation that the "Gold Bug" East had fought so frantically to prevent. Electrifying discoveries of new gold deposits in Canada (Klondike), Alaska, South Africa, and Australia eased the pressure, as did the perfecting of the cheap cyanide process for extracting gold from low-grade ore. Moderate inflation thus took care of the currency needs of an explosively expanding nation, as its circulatory system greatly improved. The tide of "silver heresy" rapidly receded, and the "Popocratic" fish were left gasping high and dry on a golden-sanded beach.

Varying Viewpoints

Populism seemed to pose the only organized opposition to the new economic and political order that settled massively into place in the 1890s. Thus, the Populists became heroes to several generations of writers, who disliked that new order and looked back longingly at America's agrarian past. John D. Hicks, *The Populist Revolt* (1931), sympathetically portrayed the embattled farmers as last-ditch defenders of a passing way of life, doomed to go down to defeat with "Boy Bryan" in 1896.

Hicks' point of view was the dominant one until about 1955, when it was sharply challenged by Richard Hofstadter in *The Age of Reform*. Hofstadter charged that Hicks and other writers had romanticized the Populists, who were themselves simply "harassed little country businessmen," and not picturesque "calamity howlers" standing steadfast against the advance of commercial culture. More-

over, argued the city-born-and-bred Hofstadter, the Populist revolt was aimed not just at big business and high finance, but somewhat irrationally at urbanism, the East, and modernity itself.

Hofstadter thus exposed a "dark side" of populism, which contained elements of anti-intellectualism, self-deception, and even anti-Semitism. This view, in turn, has been vigorously attacked by Lawrence Goodwyn's *Democratic Promise: The Populist Moment in America* (1976). Focusing on the real grievances and organizational successes of farmers in the South, he sees populism as the last gasp of popular political participation, a democratic "moment" in American history. The ultimate absorption of the Populists into the Democratic party, in Goodwyn's view, resulted in a widespread alienation from politics that has persisted until the present day.

Select Readings

Primary Source Documents

William H. "Coin" Harvey's *Coin's Financial School** (1894) expounded the silverite position. It was answered by E. P. Wheeler in *Real Bi-Metallism, or True Coin versus False Coin** (1895). William Jennings Bryan's Cross of Gold speech* won him the Democratic nomination in 1896 and a hallowed place in the annals of American oratory.

Secondary Sources

Valuable background can be found in the books by Hicks, Hahn, and Goodwyn cited in the preceding chapter. A comprehensive account is Harold U. Faulkner, *Politics, Reform and Expansion, 1890–1900* (1959). Carl N. Degler, *The Age of Economic Revolution, 1876–1900* (1977), is a brief survey. Placing the period within a larger context are Robert H. Wiebe, *The Search for Order, 1877–1920* (1967), and Richard Hofstadter's stimulating *The Age of Reform* (1955). Paolo Coletta's biography of *William*

Jennings Bryan (3 vols., 1964–1969) is rich in detail. On politics, see H. Wayne Morgan, *From Hayes to McKinley* (1969); R. Hal Williams, *Years of Decision: American Politics in the 1890s* (1978); and Robert D. Marcus, *Grand Old Party: Political Structure in the Gilded Age* (1971). Recently a new school of historians has concentrated on local issues. Their works include Richard Jensen, *The Winning of the Midwest* (1971); Samuel T. McSeveney, *The Politics of Depression* (1972); and two works by Paul Kleppner, *The Cross of Culture* (1970) and *The Third Electoral System, 1853–1892* (1979). Charles Hoffman examines *The Depression of the Nineties* (1970), an issue given much attention in David P. Thelen, *The New Citizenship: Origins of Progressivism in Wisconsin, 1885–1900* (1972). The election of 1896 is examined in Robert F. Durden, *The Climax of Populism: The Election of 1896* (1965), and Stanley L. Jones, *The Presidential Election of 1896* (1964). Also informative are Paul W. Glad, *McKinley, Bryan and the People* (1964), and H. Wayne Morgan, *William McKinley and His America* (1963).

31

The Path of Empire

> We assert that no nation can long endure half republic and half empire, and we warn the American people that imperialism abroad will lead quickly and inevitably to despotism at home.
>
> Democratic National Platform, 1900

Imperialist Stirrings

From the end of the Civil War to the 1880s, the indifference of most Americans to the outside world was almost unbelievable. But then in the sunset decades of the nineteenth century, a momentous shift occurred in American foreign policy. The new diplomacy mirrored the far-reaching changes that were reshaping industry, agriculture, and the social structure.

The Republic was becoming increasingly outward-looking as exports of both manufactured goods and agricultural products shot up. Many Americans believed that the United States had to expand or explode. Their country was bursting with a new sense of power generated by the booming increase in population, wealth, and industrial production—and it was trembling from the hammer blows of labor violence and agrarian unrest. Overseas markets might provide a safety valve to relieve such pressures.

Other forces also stimulated overseas expansion. The lurid "yellow press" of Joseph Pulitzer and William Randolph Hearst whetted the popular taste for excitement abroad. Missionaries, inspired by books like the Reverend Josiah Strong's *Our Country: Its Possible Future and Its Present Crisis,* looked overseas for new vineyards to till. Strong trumpeted the superiority of Anglo-Saxon civilization and summoned Americans to spread their religion and their values to the "backward" peoples. He cast his seed on fertile ground. At the same time, virile Americans like Theodore Roosevelt and Congressman Henry Cabot Lodge were interpreting Darwinism to mean that the earth belonged to the strong and the fit—that is, to Uncle Sam. This view was strengthened as latecomers to the colonial scramble scooped up leavings from the banquet table of earlier diners. Africa, previously unexplored and mysterious, was partitioned by the Europeans in the 1880s in a pell-mell rush of colonial conquest. In the 1890s Japan, Germany, and Russia all extorted concessions from the anemic Chinese Empire. If America was to survive in the competition of modern nation-states, perhaps it, too, would have to become an imperial power.

The development of a new steel navy also focused attention overseas. Captain Alfred Thayer Mahan's book of 1890, *The Influence of Sea Power upon History, 1660–1783,* argued that control of the sea was the key to world dominance. Read by the English, Germans, and Japanese, as well as by his fellow Americans, Mahan helped to stimulate the naval race among the great powers that gained momentum around the turn of the century. Red-blooded Americans joined in the demands for a mightier navy and for an American-built isthmian canal between the Atlantic and the Pacific.

America's new international interest manifested itself in several ways. As secretary of state, first in the Garfield administration and later in the Harrison administration, James G. Blaine pushed his "Big Sister" policy. It aimed to rally the Latin American nations behind Uncle Sam's leadership and to open Latin American markets to Yankee traders. His efforts bore modest fruit in 1889, when he presided over the first Pan-American Conference in Washington, D.C. Though the frock-coated delegates did little more than open a crack in the door for economic cooperation through reciprocal tariff reduction, they blazed the way for a long and increasingly important series of inter-American assemblages.

A number of diplomatic crises or near-wars also marked the path of American diplomacy in the late 1880s and early 1890s. The American and German navies nearly came to blows in 1889 over the faraway Samoan Islands in the South Pacific. The lynching of eleven Italians in New Orleans in 1891 brought America and Italy to the brink of war, until the United States agreed to pay compensation. In the ugliest affair, American demands on Chile after the deaths of two American sailors in the port of Valparaiso in 1892 made hostilities between the two countries seem inevitable. The threat of attack by Chile's modern navy spread alarm on the Pacific Coast, until American power finally forced the Chileans to pay an indemnity. A simmering argument between the United States and Canada over seal hunting near the Pribilof Islands off the coast of Alaska was resolved by arbitration in 1893. The willingness of Americans to risk war over such distant and minor disputes demonstrated the aggressive new national mood.

Monroe's Doctrine and the Venezuelan Squall

America's anti-British feeling, which periodically came to a head, flared forth ominously in 1895–1896 over Venezuela. For more than a half-century the jungle boundary between British Guiana and Venezuela had been in dispute. The Venezuelans, whose claims on the whole were extravagant, had repeatedly urged arbitration. But the prospect of a peaceful settlement faded when gold was discovered in the contested area.

Secretary Olney's undiplomatic note to Britain read: "To-day the United States is practically sovereign on this continent, and its fiat is law upon the subjects to which it confines its interposition. . . . Its infinite resources combined with its isolated position render it master of the situation and practically invulnerable as against any or all other powers."

The Venezuela–British Guiana Boundary Dispute

President Cleveland—"mad clear through," as he put it—sent a bristling special message to Congress. He urged an appropriation for a commission of experts, who would run the line where it ought to go. Then, he implied, if the British would not accept this rightful boundary, the United States would fight for it.

The entire country, irrespective of political party, was swept off its feet in an outburst of hysteria. War seemed inevitable, even though Britain had thirty-two warships of the battleship class to only five for America.

Fortunately, sober second thoughts prevailed on both sides of the Atlantic. The British, though vastly annoyed by their upstart cousins, had no real urge to fight. Canada was vulnerable to yet-to-be-raised American armies, and Britain's rich merchant marine was vulnerable to American commerce raiders. The European atmosphere was menacing, for Britain's traditional policy of "splendid isolation" was bringing insecure isolation. Russia and France were unfriendly; and Germany, under the saber-rattling Kaiser Wilhelm II, was about to challenge British naval supremacy.

The German kaiser, blunderingly and unwittingly, increased chances of a peaceful solution

President Cleveland, a champion of righteousness and no lover of Britain, at length decided upon a strong protest. His no less pugnacious Secretary of State Olney was authorized to present to London a smashing note, which Cleveland later dubbed a "twenty-inch gun" blast. Olney declared in effect that the British, by attempting to dominate Venezuela in this quarrel and acquire more territory, were flouting the Monroe Doctrine. London should therefore submit the dispute to arbitration. Not content to stop here, Olney haughtily informed the number one naval power that the United States was now calling the tune in the Western Hemisphere.

British officials, unimpressed, took four months to prepare their reply. Preoccupied elsewhere, they were inclined to shrug off Olney's lengthy blast as just another twist of the lion's tail designed to elicit cheers from Irish-American voters. When London's answer finally came, it flatly denied the relevance of the Monroe Doctrine, while no less emphatically spurning arbitration. In short, the affair was none of America's business.

The Real British Lion *A widespread American concept in the 1890s. (New York* Evening World, *1895.)*

"The World's Plunderers" *(Thomas Nast,* Harper's Weekly, *1885.)*

to the Venezuelan crisis. An unauthorized British raiding party of six hundred armed men was captured by the Dutch-descended Boers in South Africa, and the kaiser forthwith cabled his congratulations to the victors. Overnight, British anger against America was largely deflected to Germany, and London consented to arbitrate the Venezuelan dispute. The final decision, ironically, awarded the British the bulk of what they had claimed from the beginning.

America had skated close to the thin ice of a terrible war, but the results on the whole were favorable. The prestige of the Monroe Doctrine was immensely enhanced. Europe was irked by Cleveland's claim to domination in this hemisphere, but he had made his claim stick. Many Latin American republics were pleased by the determination of the United States to protect them, and when Cleveland died in 1908, some of them lowered their flags to half-mast.

The chastened British, their eyes fully opened to the European peril, were now determined to cultivate Yankee friendship. They inaugurated an era of "patting the eagle's head," which replaced a century or so of America's "twisting the lion's tail." Growing numbers of Englishmen were willing to heed Alfred Lord Tennyson's earlier injunction:

> Be proud of those strong sons of thine
> Who wrench'd their rights from thee!

Spurning the Hawaiian Pear

Enchanted Hawaii had early attracted the attention of Americans. In the morning years of the nineteenth century, the breeze-brushed islands were a way station and provisioning point for Yankee shippers, sailors, and whalers. In 1820 came the first New England missionaries, who preached the twin blessings of Protestant Christianity and protective calico. They came to do good—and did well; their children did even better. In some respects Honolulu took on the earmarks of a typical New England town.

Americans gradually came to regard the Hawaiian Islands as a virtual extension of their own coastline. The State Department, beginning in the 1840s, sternly warned other powers to keep their grasping hands off. America's grip was further tightened in 1875 by a commercial reciprocity agreement and in 1887 by a treaty with the native government guaranteeing priceless naval-base rights at spacious Pearl Harbor.

But trouble, both economic and political, was brewing in the languid insular paradise. Sugar cultivation, which had become immensely profitable, went somewhat sour in 1890 when the McKinley Tariff raised barriers against the Hawaiian product. White planters, mostly Americans, were further alarmed by the increasingly autocratic tendencies of dusky Queen Liliuokalani, who insisted that native Hawaiians should control Hawaii. Desperate whites, though only a tiny minority, organized a successful revolt early in 1893. It was openly assisted by American troops, who landed under the unauthorized orders of the expansionist American minister in Honolulu. "The Hawaiian pear is now fully ripe," he wrote exultantly to his superiors in Washington, "and this is the golden hour for the United States to pluck it."

Hawaii, like Texas of earlier years, seemed ready for annexation—at least in the eyes of the ruling American whites. An appropriate treaty was rushed to Washington. But before it could be railroaded through the Senate, Republican President Harrison's term expired and Democratic President Cleveland came in. "Old Grover," who set great store by "national honesty," suspected that his powerful nation had gravely wronged the deposed Queen Liliuokalani.

Cleveland abruptly withdrew the treaty from the Senate early in 1893 and then sent a special investigator to Hawaii. The subsequent probe revealed the damning fact that a majority of the Hawaiian natives did not favor annexation at all. But the white revolutionists were firmly in the saddle, and Cleveland could not unhorse them without using armed force—a step American public opinion would not have tolerated.

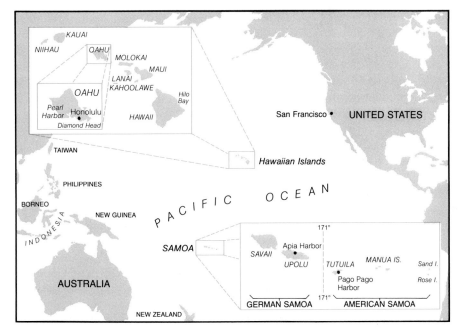

The Pacific *The enlargements show the Hawaiian Islands and the Samoas, both areas of American imperialistic activity in the late nineteenth century.*

Queen Liliuokalani (1838–1917) *She was the last reigning queen of Hawaii, whose opposition to reforms led to her dethronement. She wrote many songs, the most famous of which was Aloha Oe or Farewell to Thee, played countless times by Hawaiian bands for departing tourists. (Hawaii Public Archives.)*

Although the queen could not be reinstated, the surgarcoated move for annexation had to be abandoned temporarily—until 1898.

The question of annexing Hawaii touched off the first full-fledged imperialistic debate in American experience. Cleveland was savagely criticized for trying to stem the new Manifest Destiny, and a popular jingle ran:

> . . .Liliuokalani,
> Give us your little brown hannie.

But Cleveland's motives, in a day of international land-grabbing, were honorable both to himself and to his country. The Hawaiian pear continued to ripen for five more years.

Revolt in the Cuban Pesthouse

Cuba's masses, frightfully misgoverned, again rose against their Spanish oppressor in 1895. The roots of their revolt were partly economic, with partial origins in the United States. Sugar production—backbone of the island's prosperity—was crippled when the American tariff of 1894 restored high duties on the toothsome product.

Driven to desperation, the insurgents now adopted a scorched-earth policy. They reasoned that if they did enough damage, Spain might be willing to move out. Or the United States might move in and help the Cubans win their independence. In pursuance of this destructive strategy, the *insurrectos* put the torch to cane fields and sugar mills; they even dynamited passenger trains.

American sympathies, ever on the side of patriots fighting for freedom, went out to the Cuban underdogs. Aside from pure sentiment, the United States had an investment stake of about $50 million in Cuba and an annual trade stake of about $100 million. Moreover, Spanish misrule in Cuba menaced the shipping routes of the West Indies and the Gulf, and less directly the future isthmian canal.

Fuel was added to the Cuban conflagration in 1896 with the coming of the Spanish General ("Butcher") Weyler. He undertook to crush the rebellion by herding many civilians into barbed-wire reconcentration camps, where they could not give assistance to the armed *insurrectos*. Lacking proper sanitation, these enclosures turned into deadly pestholes, where the victims died like dogs.

An outraged American public demanded action. Congress in 1896 overwhelmingly passed a resolution that called upon President Cleveland to recognize the belligerency of the revolted Cubans. But as the government of the insurgents consisted of hardly more than a few fugitive leaders under palm trees, Cleveland—an antijingoist and anti-imperialist—refused to budge. He defiantly remarked that if Congress declared war, he would not, as commander in chief, issue the necessary order to mobilize the army.

The Mystery of the Maine *Explosion*

Atrocities in Cuba were made to order for the sensational new "yellow journalism." William R. Hearst and Joseph Pulitzer, then engaged in a titanic duel for circulation, attempted to outdo each other with screeching headlines and hair-raising "scoops." Lesser competitors zestfully followed suit.

Where atrocity stories did not exist, they were invented. Hearst sent the gifted artist Frederic Remington to Cuba to draw sketches, and when the latter reported that conditions were not bad enough to warrant hostilities, Hearst is alleged to have replied, "You furnish the pictures and I'll furnish the war." Among other outrages, Remington depicted Spanish customs officials brutally disrobing and searching an American woman. Most readers of Hearst's *Journal,* their indignation soaring, had no way of knowing that such tasks were performed by female attendants. "Butcher" Weyler was removed in 1897, yet conditions steadily worsened. There was some talk in Spain of granting the restive island a type of self-government, but such a surrender was so bitterly opposed by many Spaniards in Cuba that they engaged in furious riots. Early in the year 1898 Washington sent the battleship *Maine* to Cuba, ostensibly for a "friendly visit" but actually to protect and evacuate Americans if a dangerous flare-up should again occur.

This already explosive situation suddenly grew acute, on February 9, 1898, when Hearst sensationally headlined a private letter written by the Spanish minister in Washington, Dupuy de Lôme. The indiscreet epistle, which had been stolen from the mails, described President McKinley as an ear-to-the-ground politician who lacked good faith. The resulting uproar was so violent that Dupuy de Lôme was forced to resign.

A tragic climax came a few days later, on February 15, 1898, when the *Maine* mysteriously blew up in Havana harbor, with a loss of 260 officers and men. Two investigations of the iron coffin were undertaken, one by United States naval officers, and the other by Spanish officials, whom the Americans would not trust

Remington's Disrobing Propaganda *(New York Journal 1897.)*

near the wreck. The Spanish commission announced that the explosion had been internal and presumably accidental; the American commission reported that the blast had been caused by a submarine mine. Washington, not unmindful of popular indignation, spurned Spanish proposals of arbitration.

Various theories have been advanced as to how the *Maine* was blown up. The least convincing explanation of all is that the Spanish

> *Many Spaniards felt that accusations about their blowing up the Maine reflected on Spanish honor. One Madrid newspaper spoke up: "The American jingoes . . . imagine us capable of the most foul villainies and cowardly actions. Scoundrels by nature, the American jingoes believe that all men are made like themselves. What do they know about noble and generous feelings? . . . We should not in any way heed the jingoes: they are not even worth our contempt, or the saliva with which we might honor them in spitting at their faces."*

The Explosion of the Maine, February 15, 1898   *Encouraged and amplified by the "yellow press," the outcry over the tragedy of the Maine helped to drive the country into an impulsive war against Spain. (Chicago Historical Society.)*

The Spanish Brute   *(From Judge.)*

officials in Cuba were guilty, for they were under the American gun and Spain was far away. Not until 1976 did Admiral H. G. Rickover, under U.S. Navy auspices, give what appears to be the final answer. He presented overwhelming evidence that the initial explosion had resulted from spontaneous combustion in one of the coal bunkers adjacent to a powder magazine. Ironically, this is essentially what the Spanish commission had concluded in 1898.

Red-blooded Americans, now war-mad, blindly accepted the least likely explanation. Lashed to fury by the yellow press, they leapt to the conclusion that the Spanish government had been guilty of intolerable treachery. The battle cry of the hour became:

> Remember the *Maine!*
> To hell with Spain!

Nothing would do but to hurl the "dirty" Spanish flag from the hemisphere.

McKinley Unleashes the Dogs of War

The national war fever burned higher, even though American diplomats had already gained Madrid's agreement to Washington's two basic demands: a revocation of reconcentration and an armistice with Cuban rebels. The cautious McKinley did not want hostilities. The hesitant chief executive was condemned by jingoes as "Wobbly Willie" McKinley, while fight-hungry Theodore Roosevelt reportedly snarled that the "white-livered" occupant of the White House did not have "the backbone of a chocolate éclair." The president, whose shaken nerves required sleeping pills, was even being hanged in effigy. Many critics did not realize that backbone was needed to stay out of war, not to plunge into it.

McKinley's private desires clashed sharply with the public demands of the people. He did not want hostilities, for he had seen enough bloodshed as a major in the Civil War. Mark Hanna and Wall Street did not want war, for business might be unsettled. But a frenzied public, prodded by the "yellow press," clamored for war to free the abused Cubans. The president, recognizing the inevitable, finally yielded and gave the people what they wanted.

But public pressures did not fully explain McKinley's course. He had no faith in Spain's promises regarding Cuba; it had made them and broken them before. He was certain that there would have to be a showdown sooner or later. He believed in the democratic principle that the people should rule, and he hesitated to deny the American masses what they demanded—even if it was not good for them. He also perceived that if he stood out against war, the Democrats would make political capital out of his stubbornness. Bryan might sweep into the presidency two years later under a banner inscribed "Free Cuba and Free Silver." Gold-standard McKinley was a staunch party man, and to him it seemed better to break up the remnants of Spain's once-glorious empire than to break up the Grand Old Party—especially since war seemed inevitable.

On April 11, 1898, McKinley sent his war message to Congress, urging armed interven-

President William McKinley (1843–1901)
Traditionally regarded as a pliant tool of Mark Hanna and Republican big business, he is now rated by historians as a reasonably able President. He was notably considerate toward his long-ailing wife, who suffered embarrassing seizures at state dinners. He would graciously cover her contorted face with a handkerchief. (Library of Congress.)

tion to free the oppressed Cubans. The legislators responded uproariously with what was essentially a declaration of war. In a burst of self-righteousness, they likewise adopted the hand-tying Teller Amendment. This proviso proclaimed to the world that when the United States had overthrown Spanish misrule, it would give the Cubans their freedom—a declaration that caused imperialistic Europeans to smile skeptically.

Dewey's May Day Victory at Manila

The American people plunged into the war lightheartedly, like schoolchildren off to a picnic. Bands blared incessantly "There'll Be a Hot Time in the Old Town Tonight" and "Hail, Hail, the Gang's All Here," thus leading foreigners to believe that those were national anthems.

But such jubilation seemed premature to European observers. The regular army, which was commanded by corpulent Civil War oldsters, was unprepared for a war under tropical skies. It numbered only 2,100 officers and 28,000 men, as compared with some 200,000 Spanish troops in Cuba. The American navy, at least to transatlantic experts, seemed slightly less powerful than Spain's. European powers, moreover, were generally friendly to their Old World associate. The only conspicuous exception was the ally-seeking British, who were ardently wooing their giant daughter in the west.

Yet in one important respect Spain's apparent superiority was illusory. Its navy, though formidable on paper, was in wretched condition. It labored under the added handicap of having to operate thousands of miles from its home base. But the new American steel navy, now fifteen years old and ranking about fifth among the fleets of the world, was in fairly good trim, though the war was to lay bare serious defects.

The readiness of the navy owed much to two men: the easygoing Secretary Long and his bellicose subordinate, Assistant Secretary Theodore Roosevelt. The secretary hardly dared leave his desk for fear that his overzealous underling would stir up a hornet's nest. On February 25, 1898, while Long was away for a weekend, Roosevelt had cabled Commodore George

Dewey's Route in the Philippines, 1898

Dewey, commanding the American Asiatic Squadron at Hong Kong, to descend upon Spain's Philippines in the event of war. McKinley subsequently confirmed these instructions, even though an attack in the distant Far East seemed like a strange way to free nearby Cuba.

Dewey carried out his orders magnificently on May 1, 1898. Sailing boldly with his six warships at night into the fortified harbor of Manila, he trained his guns the next morning on the ten-ship Spanish fleet, one of whose craft was only a moored hulk without functioning engines. The entire collection of antiquated and overmatched vessels was quickly destroyed, with a loss of nearly four hundred Spaniards killed and wounded, and without the loss of a single life in Dewey's fleet. An American consul who was there wrote that all the American sailors needed was cough drops for throats made raw by cheers of victory.

Unexpected Imperialistic Plums

George Dewey, quiet and taciturn, became a national hero overnight. He was promptly promoted to the rank of admiral, as the price of flags rose sharply. An amateur poet blossomed forth with:

> Oh, dewy was the morning
> Upon the first of May,
> And Dewey was the Admiral,
> Down in Manila Bay.
> And dewy were the Spaniards' eyes,
> Them orbs of black and blue;
> And dew we feel discouraged?
> I dew not think we dew!

Yet Dewey was in a perilous position. He had destroyed the enemy fleet, but he could not storm the forts of Manila with his sailors. His nerves frayed, he was forced to wait in the steaming-hot bay while troop reinforcements were slowly assembled in America.

Foreign warships meanwhile had begun to gather in the harbor, ostensibly to safeguard their nationals in Manila. The Germans sent five vessels—a naval force more powerful than Dewey's—and their haughty admiral defied the American blockade regulations. After several disagreeable incidents, Dewey lost his temper and threatened the arrogant German with war "as soon as you like." Happily, the storm blew over. The British commander, by contrast, was conspicuously successful in carrying out London's new policy of friendliness. A false tale consequently spread that the British dramatically interposed their ships to prevent the Germans from blowing the Americans out of the water.

Long-awaited American troops, finally arriving in force, captured Manila on August 13, 1898. They collaborated with the Filipino insurgents, commanded by their well-educated, part-Chinese leader, Emilio Aguinaldo. Dewey, to his later regret, had brought this shrewd and magnetic revolutionist from exile in Asia, so that he might weaken Spanish resistance.

These thrilling events in the Philippines had meanwhile focused attention on Hawaii. An impression spread that America needed the archipelago as a coaling and provisioning way station, in order to send supplies and reinforcements to Dewey. The truth is that the United States could have used these island "Crossroads of the Pacific" without annexing them, so eager was the white-dominated Honolulu government to compromise its neutrality and risk the vengeance of Spain. But an appreciative American public would not leave Dewey in the lurch. A joint resolution of annexation was rushed through Congress and approved by McKinley on July 7, 1898.

The residents of Hawaii were granted American citizenship with annexation and received full territorial status in 1900. These events in the idyllic islands, though seemingly sudden, were but the culmination of nearly a century of Americanization by sailors, whalers, traders, and missionaries.

The Confused Invasion of Cuba

Shortly after the outbreak of war, the Spanish government ordered a fleet of warships to Cuba. It was commanded by Admiral Cervera, who protested that his wretchedly prepared ships were flirting with suicide. Four armored cruisers finally set forth (one without its main battery of guns). They were accompanied by six

Emilio Aguinaldo (c. 1869–1964) Leader of the Philippine insurrection against American rule, Aguinaldo never became completely reconciled to America's role in his native land. After all his brushes with death, he died in Manila in 1964 in his ninety-fifth year. (The Bettmann Archive.)

torpedo boats, three of which had to be abandoned en route.

Panic seized the eastern seaboard of the United States. American vacationers abandoned their seashore cottages, while nervous investors moved their securities to inland depositories. Demands for protection poured in on Washington from nervous citizens, and the Navy Department was forced to dispatch some useless old Civil War ships to useless places for morale purposes. Cervera finally found refuge in bottle-shaped Santiago harbor, Cuba, where he was blockaded by the much more powerful American fleet.

Sound strategy seemed to dictate that an American army be sent in from the rear to drive out Cervera. Command of the invading force was entrusted to the grossly overweight General

Colonel Theodore Roosevelt with Some of the "Rough Riders" *Roosevelt later described his first encounter with the Spanish enemy: "Soon we came to the brink of a deep valley. There was a good deal of cracking of rifles way off in front of us, but as they used smokeless powder we had no idea as to exactly where they were, or who they were shooting at. Then it dawned on us that we were the target. The bullets began to come overhead, making a sound like the ripping of a silk dress, with sometimes a kind of pop. . . . We advanced, firing at them, and drove them off." (Library of Congress.)*

William R. Shafter, a leader so blubbery and gout-stricken that he had to be carried about on a door. The ill-prepared American conquerors were unequipped for war in tropics; they had been amply provided with heavy woolen underwear and uniforms designed for subzero operations against the Indians.

The "Rough Riders," a part of the invading army, now charged onto the stage of history. This colorful regiment of volunteers, short on discipline but long on dash, consisted largely of western cowboys and other hardy characters, with a sprinkling of ex-polo players and ex-convicts. Commanded by Colonel Leonard Wood, the group was organized principally by the glory-hungry Roosevelt, who had resigned from the Navy Department to serve as lieutenant colonel. Though totally without military experi-

ence, he used his strong political "pull" to secure his commission and to bypass physical standards. He was so nearsighted that as a safeguard he took along a dozen pairs of spectacles, cached in handy spots on his person or nearby.

About the middle of June a bewildered American army of seventeen thousand men finally embarked at congested Tampa, Florida, amid scenes of indescribable confusion. The "Rough Riders," fearing that they would be robbed of glory, rushed one of the transports and courageously held their place for almost a week in the broiling sun. About half of them finally got to Cuba without most of their horses, and the bowlegged regiment then came to be known as "Wood's Weary Walkers."

Shafter's landing near Santiago, Cuba, was made without serious opposition. Defending

Spaniards, even more disorganized than the Americans, were unable to muster at this spot more than two thousand men. Brisk fighting broke out on July 1 at El Caney and San Juan Hill, up which Colonel Roosevelt and his horseless "Rough Riders" charged, with strong support from two crack black regiments. They suffered heavy casualties, but the colorful colonel, having the time of his life, shot a Spaniard with his revolver, and rejoiced to see his victim double up like a jackrabbit. He later wrote a book on his exploits, which, "Mr. Dooley" remarked, ought to have been entitled *Alone in Cubia* [*sic*].

> With a mixture of modesty and immodesty, Colonel Roosevelt wrote privately in 1903 of his "Rough Riders": "In my regiment nine-tenths of the men were better horsemen than I was, and probably two-thirds of them better shots than I was, while on the average they were certainly hardier and more enduring. Yet after I had had them a very short while they all knew, and I knew too, that nobody else could command them as I could."

Curtains for Spain in America

The American army, fast closing in on Santiago, spelled doom for the Spanish fleet. Admiral Cervera, again protesting against suicide, was flatly ordered to fight for the honor of the flag. The odds against him were heavy: the guns of the U.S.S. *Oregon* alone threw more metal than his four armored cruisers combined. After a running chase, on July 3, the foul-bottomed Spanish fleet was entirely destroyed, as the wooden decks caught fire and the blazing infernos were beached. About five hundred Spaniards were killed, as compared with one for the Americans. "Don't cheer, men," admonished

The Rough Riders Charge up San Juan Hill *Theodore Roosevelt thought it a "bully fight."*
From a painting by Frederic Remington. (Remington Art Museum, Ogdensburg, New York.)

The Cuban Campaign, 1898

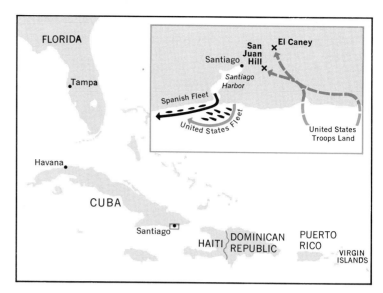

Captain Philip of the *Texas*, "the poor devils are dying." Shortly thereafter Santiago surrendered.

Hasty preparations were now made for a descent upon Puerto Rico before the war should end. The American army, commanded by the famed Indian-fighter General Nelson A. Miles, met little resistance, as most of the population greeted the invaders as liberating heroes. "Mr. Dooley" was led to refer to "Gin'ral Miles' Gran' Picnic an' Moonlight Excursion." By this time Spain had satisfied its honor, and on August 12, 1898, it signed an armistice.

If the Spaniards had held out a few months longer in Cuba, the American army might have melted away. The inroads of malaria, typhoid, dysentery, and yellow fever became so severe that hundreds were incapacitated—"an army of convalescents." Others suffered from odorous canned meat known as "embalmed beef." Fiery and insubordinate Colonel Roosevelt, who had no regular military career to jeopardize, was a ringleader in making "round-robin"* demands on Washington that the army be moved before it perished. About twenty-five thousand men,

---

*A "round-robin" is signed in circular form around the edges of a document so that no one person can be punished as the first signer.

80 percent of them ill, were transferred to chilly Long Island, where their light summer clothing finally arrived.

One of the worst scandals of the war was the high death rate from sickness, especially typhoid fever. This disease was rampant in the unsanitary training camps located in the United States. All told, nearly four hundred men lost their lives to bullets; over five thousand to bacteria and other causes.

McKinley Heeds Duty, Destiny, and Dollars

Late in 1898 the Spanish and American negotiators met in Paris, there to begin heated discussions. McKinley had sent five commissioners, including three senators, who would have a final vote on their own handiwork. War-racked Cuba, as expected, was freed from its Spanish overlords. The Americans had little difficulty in securing the remote Pacific island of Guam, which they had captured early in the conflict from astonished Spaniards who, lacking a cable, had not known that a war was on. They also picked up Puerto Rico, the last crumb of Spain's once magnificent American empire. It was to prove a difficult morsel for Uncle Sam to digest.

Knottiest of all was the problem of the Philippines, a veritable apple of discord. These lush islands not only embraced an area larger than the British Isles but also contained a completely alien population of some 7 million souls. McKinley was confronted with a devil's dilemma. He did not feel that America could honorably give the islands back to Spanish misrule, especially after it had fought a war to free Cuba. And America would be turning its back upon its responsibilities in a cowardly fashion, he believed, if it simply pulled up anchor and sailed away.

Other alternatives open to McKinley were trouble-fraught. The ill-prepared native Filipinos, if left to govern themselves, might fall into anarchy. One of the major powers might then try to seize them, possibly aggressive Germany, and the result might be a world war into which the United States would be sucked. Seemingly the least of the evils consistent with national honor and safety was to acquire all the Philippines and then perhaps give "the little brown brothers" their freedom later.

President McKinley, ever sensitive to public opinion, kept a carefully attuned ear to the ground. The rumble that he heard seemed to call for the entire group of islands. Zealous Protestant missionaries were eager for new converts from Spanish Catholicism*; and the in-

*The Philippines were substantially Christianized by Catholics before the founding of Jamestown in 1607.

valid Mrs. McKinley, to whom her husband was devoted, expressed deep concern about the welfare of the Filipinos. Wall Street had generally opposed the war; but awakened by the booming of Dewey's guns, it was clamoring for profits in the Philippines. "If this be commercialism," cried Mark Hanna, then "for God's sake let us have commercialism."

A tormented McKinley, so he was later reported as saying, finally went down on his knees seeking divine guidance. An inner voice seemed to tell him to take all the Philippines and Christianize and civilize them. This solution apparently coincided with the demands of the American people as well as with the McKinley-Hanna outlook. The mixture of things spiritual and material in McKinley's reasoning was later slyly summarized by a historian: "God directs us—perhaps it will pay." Profits thus joined hands with piety.

Fresh disputes broke out with the Spanish negotiators in Paris, once McKinley had reached the thorny decision to keep the Philippines. Manila had been captured the day *after* the armistice was signed, and the islands could not properly be listed among the spoils of war. The deadlock was broken when the Americans at length agreed to pay Spain $20 million for

Uncle Sam's White Elephant   *(New York Herald, 1898.)*

this Philippine liability—one of the best bargains the Spaniards ever drove and their last great haul from the New World. Ex-Speaker "Czar" Reed sneered at America's having acquired millions of Malays, at three dollars a head, "in the bush."

America's Course (Curse?) of Empire

The signing of the pact of Paris—a trouble-fraught document—touched off one of the most impassioned debates of American history. Except for glacial Alaska and coral-reefed Hawaii, the Republic had hitherto acquired only contiguous territory on the continent. All previous acquisitions had been thinly peopled and capable of ultimate statehood. But in the Philippines the nation had on its hands a distant tropical area, thickly populated by Asiatics of alien race, tongue, religion, and governmental institutions.

An Anti-Imperialist League sprang into being to fight the McKinley administration's expansionist moves. The organization counted among its members some of the most prominent people in America, including the presidents of Stanford and Harvard universities, the philosopher William James, and the novelist Mark Twain. The anti-imperialist blanket even stretched over such strange bedfellows as the labor leader Samuel Gompers and the steel titan Andrew Carnegie. "Goddamn the United States for its vile conduct in the Philippine Isles!" burst out the usually mild-mannered Professor James. The Harvard philosopher could not believe that the United States could "puke up its ancient soul in five minutes without a wink of squeamishness."

Anti-imperialists had still other arrows in their quiver. The Filipinos panted for freedom; and to annex them would violate the "consent of the governed" philosophy in the Declaration of Independence. Despotism abroad might well beget despotism at home. Finally, annexation would propel the United States into the political and military cauldron of the Far East.

Yet the expansionists or imperialists could sing a seductive song. They appealed to patriotism and to the glory of annexation—"don't let any dastard dishonor the flag by hauling it down." Stressing the opportunities for exploiting the islands, they played up possible trade profits. Manila, in fact, might become another Hong Kong. The richer the natural resources of the islands appeared to be, the less capable of self-government the Filipinos seemed to be.

Imperial Uncle Sam
Tailored by William McKinley, an overstuffed Uncle Sam dismisses the anti-imperial protests of reformers Carl Schurz and Oswald Ottendorfer, as well as New York World publisher Joseph Pulitzer. (Library of Congress.)

Rudyard Kipling, the British poet laureate of imperialism, urged America down the slippery path:

> Take up the White Man's burden—
> Ye dare not stoop to less—
> Nor call too loud on Freedom
> To cloak your weariness.

In short, the wealthy Americans must help to uplift (and exploit) the underprivileged, underfed, and underclad of the world.

In the Senate the Spanish treaty ran into such heated opposition that it seemed doomed to defeat. But at this juncture the silverite Bryan unexpectedly sallied forth as its champion. As a Democratic volunteer colonel whom the Republicans had kept out of Cuba, he apparently had no reason to help the McKinley administration out of a hole. But free silver was dead as a political issue. Bryan's foes assumed that he was preparing to fasten the stigma of imperialism on the Republicans and then to sweep into the presidency in 1900 under the flaming banner of anti-imperialism.

Bryan could support the treaty on plausible grounds. He argued that the war would not officially end until America had ratified the pact. It already had the islands on its hands, and the sooner it accepted the document, the sooner it could give the Filipinos their independence. After Byran had used his personal influence with certain Democratic senators, the treaty was approved, on February 6, 1899, with only one vote to spare. But the responsibility, as Bryan had foreseen, rested primarily with the Republicans.

Perplexities in Puerto Rico and Cuba

Puerto Rico was a poverty-stricken island, the fertility of whose million inhabitants, including many blacks, outran that of their soil. By the Foraker Act of 1900 Congress accorded the Puerto Ricans a limited degree of popular government and in 1917 granted them United States citizenship. Although the American regime worked wonders in education, sanitation, good roads, and other physical improvements, many of the inhabitants continued to clamor for independence. Many ultimately moved to New York City, where they added to the complexity of the melting pot.

A thorny legal problem was posed by the question: Did the Constitution follow the flag? Did American laws, including tariff laws, apply with full force to the newly acquired possessions, chiefly the Philippines and Puerto Rico?

Beginning in 1901 with the insular cases, a badly divided Supreme Court decreed, in effect, that the flag did outrun the Constitution, and that the outdistanced document did not necessarily extend with full force to the new windfalls. The Congress was therefore left with a free hand to determine the degree of applicability.

Cuba, scorched and chaotic, presented another headache. An American military government, set up under the administrative genius of General Leonard Wood of Rough Rider fame, wrought miracles in government, finance, education, agriculture, and public health. Under his leadership a frontal attack was launched on yellow fever. Spectacular experiments were performed by Dr. Walter Reed and others upon American soldiers, who volunteered as human guinea pigs; and the stegomyia mosquito was proved to be the lethal carrier. A cleanup of breeding places for mosquitoes wiped out yellow fever in Havana, while removing the recurrent fear of epidemics in cities of the South and the Atlantic seaboard.

The United States, honoring its self-denying Teller Amendment of 1898, withdrew from Cuba in 1902. Old World imperialists could scarcely believe their eyes. But the Washington government could not turn this rich and strategic island completely loose on the international sea; a grasping power like Germany might secure dangerous lodgment near America's soft underbelly. The Cubans were therefore forced to write into their own constitution of 1901 the so-called Platt Amendment.

The hated restriction placed a severe hobble on the Cubans. They bound themselves not to impair their independence by treaty or by contracting a debt beyond their resources. They further agreed that the United States might intervene with troops to restore order and to provide mutual protection. Finally, the Cubans promised to sell or lease needed coaling or naval stations, ultimately two and then only one (Guantanamo), to their powerful "benefactor." The United States is still there on about twenty-eight thousand acres under an agreement that can be revoked only by the consent of both parties.

New Horizons in Two Hemispheres

In essence the Spanish-American War was a kind of gigantic coming-out party. Despite a common misconception, the conflict did not cause the United States to become a world power. Dewey's thundering guns merely advertised the fact that the nation was already a world power.

The war itself was short (113 days), spectacular, low in casualties, and uninterruptedly successful—despite the bungling. American prestige rose sharply, and the European powers grudgingly accorded the Republic more respect. In Germany, Prince Bismarck reportedly growled that there was a special Providence that looked after drunkards, fools, and the United States of America. At times it seemed as though not only Providence but the Spaniards were fighting on the side of the Yankees. So great, in fact, was America's good fortune that rejoicing citizens found in the victories further support—misleading support—for their indifference to adequate preparedness.

An exhilarating new spirit thrilled America. National pride was touched and cockiness was increased by what John Hay called a "splendid little war."* Enthusiasm over these triumphs made easier the rush down the thorny path of empire. America did not start the war with imperialistic motives, but after falling through the cellar door of imperialism in a drunken fit of idealism, it wound up with imperialistic and colonial fruits in its grasp. The much-criticized British imperialists were pleased, partly because of the newfound friendship, partly because misery loves company. But America's German rival was envious, and Latin American neighbors were deeply suspicious of Yankee greed.

By taking on the Philippine liability, the United States became a full-fledged Far Eastern power. Hereafter these distant islands were to be a "heel of Achilles"—a kind of indefensible hostage given to Japan, as the event proved in 1941. With singular shortsightedness, the

---

*Anti-imperialist William James called it "our squalid war with Spain."

Americans assumed dangerous commitments that they were later unwilling to defend by proper naval and military outlays.

But the lessons of unpreparedness were not altogether lost. Captain Mahan's big-navyism seemed vindicated, and pride in the exploits of the navy brought popular support for more and better battleships. A masterly organizer, Elihu Root, took over the reins at the War Department. He established a general staff and founded the War College in Washington. His genius later paid dividends when the United States found itself involved in the World War of 1914–1918.

One of the happiest results of the conflict was the further closing of the "bloody chasm" between North and South. Thousands of patri-

Three years after the Spanish-American War ended, a foreign diplomat in Washington remarked, "I have seen two Americas, the America before the Spanish American War and the America since."

otic southerners had flocked to the Stars and Stripes, and the gray-bearded General Joseph ("Fighting Joe") Wheeler—a Confederate cavalry hero of about a thousand Civil War skirmishes and battles—was given a command in Cuba. He allegedly cried, in the heat of battle "To hell with the Yankees! Dammit, I mean the Spaniards."

Varying Viewpoints

Imperialism has long been an embarrassing topic for students of American history, largely because of the Republic's own revolutionary origins and anticolonial tradition. Many writers discuss the dramatic overseas expansion of the 1890s as some kind of aberration—a sudden, singular, and short-lived departure from time-honored American principles and practices. Various excuses have been offered to explain this spasmodic lapse: the irresponsible behavior of the "yellow press"; the political strains imposed by the depression of the 1890s and the Populist upheaval; and the contagious scramble for imperial possessions by European powers during these years.

But recently some historians, notably William Appleman Williams and Walter LaFeber, have sought to ascribe American imperialism to deep-lying economic causes, especially the hunger for overseas markets. These scholars try to link the two most striking developments of the age: the amazing industrialization of America and the Republic's emergence as a great world power. They conclude that the explanation of expansion abroad is to be found in economic expansion at home. In essence, this approach takes a backward step toward the old-fashioned concept of the "age of the robber barons" and seeks to apply that concept to foreign policy. Such a "revisionist" interpretation has been sharply challenged by scholars who argue that foreign policy is much too complex to be explained by economic factors alone.

Select Readings

Primary Source Documents

Examples of "yellow journalism" include Joseph Pulitzer's New York *World* and William R. Hearst's New York *Journal.* Particularly interesting is the editorial in the *World* of February 13, 1897,* and the article by Charles Duval in the *Journal* of October 10, 1897.* McKinley's War Message,* James D. Richardson, ed., *Messages and Papers of the Presidents* (1899), vol. X, pp. 139ff., outlines the American rationale for intervention. The anti-imperialist answer can be found in Charles E. Norton's article in *Public Opinion* June 23, 1898, pp. 775–776.*

Secondary Sources

Main outlines are sketched in Foster Rhea Dulles, *America's Rise to World Power, 1898–1954* (1955); in the relevant chapters of Thomas A. Bailey, *Diplomatic History of the American People* (10th ed., 1980); and in Thomas G. Paterson, *American Foreign Policy: A Brief History* (2d ed., 1983). Two general (and quite contrasting) interpretations of modern American foreign policy are George F. Kennan, *American Diplomacy* (1951), and William Appleman Williams, *The Tragedy of American Diplomacy* (1959). Consult also Williams' *The Roots of the Modern American Empire* (1961); as well as Ernest R. May, *Imperial Democracy* (1961), and his *American Imperialism: A Speculative Essay* (1968); and Walter

LaFeber, *The New Empire* (1963). Thoughtful perceptions can be found in Robert Seager II, *Alfred Thayer Mahan* (1977); James L. Abrahamson, *America Arms for a New Century* (1981); and John A. S. Grenville and George B. Young, *Politics, Strategy, and American Diplomacy: Studies in Foreign Policy, 1873–1917* (1966). On the war itself, see Frank Freidel, *The Splendid Little War* (1958), and David F. Trask, *The War with Spain in 1898* (1981). Fascinating reading is Hyman G. Rickover, *How the Battleship* Maine *Was Destroyed* (1976). Helpful studies of the opponents of expansion are Robert L. Beisner, *Twelve against Empire: The Anti-Imperialists, 1898–1900* (1968); E. Berkeley Tompkins, *Anti-Imperialism in the United States: The Great Debates, 1890–1920* (1970); and Kendrick A. Clements, *William Jennings Bryan: Missionary Isolationist* (1983). Thomas McCormick sees a design for "informal" imperialism in *The China Market* (1967). David F. Healey examines *The United States in Cuba, 1898–1902* (1963), while Leon Wolff paints a grim picture of American involvement in the Philippines in *Little Brown Brother* (1961). For more on the Philippine imbroglio, see Peter W. Stanley, *A Nation in the Making: The Philippines and the United States, 1899–1921* (1975); Richard E. Welch, Jr., *Response to Imperialism: The United States and the Philippine-American War, 1899–1902* (1979); and Stuart C. Miller, *"Benevolent Assimilation": The American Conquest of the Philippines, 1899–1903* (1982).

32

America on the World Stage, 1899–1909

I never take a step in foreign policy unless I am assured that I shall be able eventually to carry out my will by force.

Theodore Roosevelt, 1905

"Little Brown Brothers" in the Philippines

Unhappily, the liberty-loving Filipinos were tragically deceived. They had assumed that they, like the Cubans, would be granted their freedom after the war. A clear-cut pledge by Congress to this effect probably would have averted the sorry sequel, but the Senate by the narrowest of margins refused to pass such a resolution. Bitterness toward the American troops continued to mount and finally erupted into open insurrection on February 4, 1899, under Emilio Aguinaldo.

The war with the Filipinos, unlike the "splendid" little set-to with Spain, was sordid and prolonged. It involved more savage fighting, more soldiers killed, and far more scandal.

Anti-imperialists redoubled their protests. In their view the United States, having plunged into war with Spain to free Cuba, was now fighting 10,000 miles (16,000 kilometers) away to rivet shackles on a people who asked for nothing but liberty—in the American tradition.

As the ill-equipped Filipino armies were defeated, they melted into the jungle to wage a vicious guerrilla warfare. Many of the outgunned Filipinos used barbarous methods, and inevitably the infuriated American troops responded in kind. A brutal soldier song betrayed inner feelings:

> Damn, damn, damn the Filipinos!
> Cross-eyed kakiak ladrones [thieves]!
>   Underneath the starry flag
>   Civilize 'em with a Krag [rifle],
> And return us to our own beloved homes.

Liberty Halts American Butchery in the Philippines (Life, 1899.)

Atrocity tales shocked and rocked the United States, for such methods did not reflect America's better self. Uncle Sam's soldiers were goaded to such extremes as the painful "water cure"—that is, forcing water down victims' throats until they yielded information or died. Reconcentration camps were even established which strongly suggested those of "Butcher" Weyler in Cuba. America, having begun the Spanish war with noble ideals, now dirtied its hands. One New York newspaper published a reply to Rudyard Kipling's famous poem:

> We've taken up the white man's burden
> Of ebony and brown;
> Now will you kindly tell us, Rudyard,
> How we may put it down?

The backbone of the Filipino insurrection was finally broken in 1901, when Aguinaldo was captured by a clever if unsporting ruse. But sporadic fighting dragged on for many dreary months.

The problem of a government for the conquered islanders worried President McKinley, who, in 1899, appointed a Philippine Commission to make appropriate recommendations. In its second year this body was headed by future President William H. Taft, an able and amiable lawyer-judge from Ohio who weighed about 350 pounds (159 kilograms). Forming a strong attachment for the Filipinos, he called them his "little brown brothers" and danced light-footedly with their tiny women. But among the American soldiers, sweatily combing the jungles, a different view of the insurgent prevailed:

> He may be a brother of Big Bill Taft,
> But he ain't no brother of mine.

McKinley's "benevolent assimilation" of the Philippines proceeded with painful slowness. Millions of American dollars were poured into the islands to improve roads, sanitation, and public health. Important economic ties, including trade in sugar, developed between the two peoples. American teachers—"pioneers of the blackboard"—set up an unusually good school system and helped make English a second language. But all this vast expenditure, which profited America little, was ill received. The Filipinos, who hated compulsory Americanization, preferred less sanitation and more liberty. Like caged hawks, they beat against their gilded bars until they finally got their freedom, on the Fourth of July, 1946.

John Hay Defends China (and U.S. Interests)

Exciting events had meanwhile been brewing in faraway and enfeebled China. Following its defeat by Japan in 1894–1895, the imperialistic European powers, notably Russia and Germany, moved in. Like vultures descending upon a stranded whale, they began to tear away valuable leaseholds and economic spheres of influence from the Manchu government.

A growing group of Americans viewed the vivisection of China with alarm. Churches were worried about their missionary vineyards; manufacturers and exporters feared that Chinese markets would be monopolized by Europeans. An alarmed American public, openly prodded by the press and unofficially prodded by certain free-trade Britons, demanded that Washington

John Hay (1838–1905) *This gifted writer, poet, novelist, historian, and wit first attained some prominence as assistant private secretary to President Lincoln. He became a headline-catching secretary of state under President McKinley, notably with the Open Door. (Library of Congress.)*

do something. Secretary of State John Hay, a quiet but witty poet-novelist-diplomat with a flair for capturing the popular imagination, finally decided upon a dramatic move.

In the summer of 1899 Hay dispatched to all the great powers a communication soon known as the Open Door note. He urged them to announce that in their leaseholds or spheres of influence they would respect certain Chinese rights and the ideal of fair competition. In short, in their dealings with foreign traders the intruding powers would observe the Open Door. The principle was not new, for America had tried repeatedly to make it the basis of its commercial dealings with China in the nineteenth century. But the phrase *Open Door* quickly caught the public fancy and gained wide acceptance.

Hay's proposal of this self-denying policy caused much squirming in the leading capitals of the world. It was like asking all those who do not have thieving designs to stand up and be counted. Italy alone accepted the Open Door

The commercial interests of both Britain and America were imperiled by the power grabs in China, and a close understanding between the two powers would have helped both. Yet as Secretary Hay wrote privately in June 1900: "Every Senator I see says, 'For God's sake, don't let it appear we have any understanding with England.' How can I make bricks without straw? That we should be compelled to refuse the assistance of the greatest power in the world [Britain], in carrying out our own policy, because all Irishmen are Democrats and some [American] Germans are fools—is enough to drive a man mad."

unconditionally; it was the only major power that had no leasehold or sphere of influence in China. Britain, Germany, France, and Japan all accepted, but subject to the condition that the others acquiesce unconditionally. Russia, with covetous designs on China's Manchuria, in effect politely declined. But John Hay, rather than run the risk of a flat rejection, cleverly interpreted the Russian refusal as an acceptance and proclaimed that the Open Door was in effect. Under such dubious midwifery was the infant born, and no one should have been surprised when the child proved to be sickly and relatively short-lived.

Hinging the Open Door in China

Open Door or not, patriotic Chinese did not care to be used as a mat by the Europeans. In 1900 a superpatriotic group known as the "Boxers" broke loose with the cry "Kill Foreign Devils." Over two hundred missionaries and other luckless whites were murdered, and a number of foreign diplomats were besieged in the capital, Beijing (Peking).

A rescue force of some eighteen thousand soldiers, hastily assembled, arrived in the nick of time. This multination contingent consisted of Japanese, Russian, British, French, German, and American troops, with the American contribution some twenty-five hundred men. Such participation in a joint military operation, especially in Asia, was plainly contrary to the nation's time-honored principles of nonentanglement and noninvolvement. But America had not been a Far Eastern power in the days of the Founding Fathers.

The victorious allied invaders acted angrily and vindictively. They assessed prostrate China an excessive indemnity of $333 million, of which America's share was to be $24.5 million. When Washington discovered that this sum was much more than enough to pay damages and expenses, it remitted about $18 million. The Beijing government, appreciating this gesture of goodwill, set aside the money to educate a selected group of Chinese students in the United States. These bright young scholars

later played a significant role in the westernization of the Orient.

Secretary Hay now let fly another paper broadside, for he feared that the triumphant powers might use the Boxer outrages as a pretext for carving up China outright. His new circular note to the powers in 1900 announced that henceforth the Open Door would embrace the territorial integrity of China, in addition to its commercial integrity. Hay remembered his previous rebuff; this time he did not ask for formal acceptances.

Defenseless China was spared partition during these troubled years. But its salvation was probably not due to Hay's fine phrases, which the American people were reluctant to back up with fighting forces. China owed its preserva-

The Boxer Rebellion, 1900 *United States troops fought alongside other western armies against the Chinese nationalistic uprising in Beijing. (Collier's, September 22, 1900.)*

tion far more to the strength of the competing powers; none of them could trust the others to gain an advantage.

Kicking "Teddy" Roosevelt Upstairs

President McKinley's renomination by the Republicans in 1900 was a foregone conclusion. He had piloted the country through a victorious war; he had acquired rich, though burdensome, real estate; he had established the gold standard; and he had brought the promised prosperity of the full dinner pail. "We'll stand pat!" was the poker-playing counsel of Mark Hanna, since 1897 a senator from Ohio. McKinley was renominated at Philadelphia on a platform that smugly endorsed prosperity, the gold standard, and overseas expansion.

An irresistible vice-presidential boom had developed for "Teddy" Roosevelt (TR), the cowboy-hero of San Juan Hill. Capitalizing on his war-born popularity, he had been elected governor of New York, where the local political bosses had found him headstrong and difficult to manage. They therefore devised a scheme to kick the colorful colonel upstairs into the vice-presidency.

This plot to railroad Roosevelt worked beautifully. Gesticulating wildly, he attended the nominating convention, where his western-style cowboy hat made him stand out like a white crow. He had no desire to die of slow rot in the vice-presidential "burying ground," but he was eager to prove that he could get the nomination if he wanted it. He finally gave in when, to the accompaniment of cries of "We want Teddy," he received a unanimous vote, except for his own. A frantic Hanna reportedly moaned that there would be only one heartbeat between that wild-eyed "madman"—"that damned cowboy"—and the presidency of the United States.

William Jennings Bryan was the odds-on choice of the Democrats, meeting at Kansas City. The free-silver issue was now as dead as an abandoned mine, but Bryan, a slave to consistency, forced a silver plank down the throats of his protesting associates. He thus helped crucify himself on a cross of silver. The Democratic

Roosevelt and McKinley, 1900   *The flamboyant vice-presidential candidate dwarfed the mild-mannered McKinley in the eyes of this cartoonist, and of many other Americans. (The New-York Historical Society.)*

platform proclaimed, as did Bryan, that the "paramount" issue was Republican overseas imperialism.

Imperialism or Bryanism in 1900?

Campaign history partially repeated itself in 1900. McKinley, the soul of dignity, sat safely on his front porch, as before. Bryan, also as before, took to the stump in a cyclonic campaign, assailing both imperialism and Republican-fostered trusts.

The superenergetic, second-fiddle Roosevelt out-Bryaned Bryan. He toured the country with revolver-shooting cowboys, and his popularity cut heavily into Bryan's support in the Middle West. Flashing his magnificent teeth and pounding his fist fiercely into his palm, Roosevelt denounced all dastards who would haul down Old Glory.

Bryanites loudly trumpeted their "paramount" issue of imperialism. Lincoln, they charged, had abolished slavery for 3.5 million Africans; McKinley had reestablished it for 7 million Malayans. But the question of imperialism was actually stale; it had been agitating the novelty-loving American people for more than two years. The Republic had the Philippines on its hands anyhow, and the real question was not "Should it keep them?" but "What should it do with them in the future?" Besides, anti-imperialists like Bryan were merely encouraging the Filipinos to resist.

Republicans responded by charging that "Bryanism," not imperialism, was the paramount issue. By this accusation they meant that Bryan would rock the boat of prosperity, once he got into office with his free-silver lunacy and other dangerous ideas. The voters were much less concerned about imperialism than about "Four Years More of the Full Dinner Pail" and "Let Well Enough Alone." Prosperity at home seemed more important than freedom abroad. When the smoke cleared off, McKinley had triumphed by a much wider margin than in 1896; 7,218,491 to 6,356,734 popular votes, and 292 to 155 electoral votes.

Victory for the Republicans was not a mandate for or against imperialism, legend to the contrary. The confused voters were not asked to decide this issue but, basically, to select either McKinley or Bryan. Many citizens who favored Bryan's anti-imperialism feared his free silver; many who favored McKinley's "sound money" hated his imperialism. One citizen wrote to ex-President Cleveland: "It is a choice between evils, and I am going to shut my eyes, hold my nose, vote, go home and disinfect myself." If there was any mandate at all it was for the two *P*s: prosperity and protection. Content with good times, the country anticipated four more years of a full dinner pail crammed with fried chicken. "Boss" Platt of New York gleefully looked forward to Inauguration Day, when he would see Roosevelt "take the veil" as vice-president.

TR: Brandisher of the Big Stick

Kindly William McKinley had scarcely served another six months when, in September 1901, he was murdered by a deranged anarchist. Roosevelt became president at age forty-two, the youngest thus far in American history. Knowing he had a reputation for impulsiveness and radicalism, he sought to reassure the country by proclaiming that he would carry out the policies of his predecessor. Cynics sneered that he would indeed carry them out—to the garbage heap.

What manner of man was Theodore Roosevelt, the red-blooded blue blood? Born into a wealthy and distinguished New York family, he had fiercely built up his spindly, asthmatic body by a stern and self-imposed routine of exercise. Graduating from Harvard with Phi Beta Kappa honors, he published at the age of twenty-four the first of some thirty volumes of muscular prose. Then came busy years, which involved duties as a ranch owner and bespectacled cowboy ("Four Eyes") in the Dakotas, followed by various political posts. When fully developed, he was a barrel-chested 5 feet 10 inches (1.76 meters), with prominent teeth, squinty eyes, droopy mustache, and piercing voice.

The Rough Rider's high-voltage energy was electrifying. Believing that it was better to wear out than to rust out, he would shake the hands of some six thousand persons at one stretch or ride horseback many miles in a day as an example for portly cavalry officers. Not surprisingly, he gathered about him a group of athletic, tennis-playing cronies, who were popularly dubbed "the tennis cabinet."

Incurably boyish and bellicose, Roosevelt loved to fight—"an elegant row." He never ceased to preach the virile virtues and to denounce civilized softness, with its pacifists and other "flubdubs" and "mollycoddles." An ardent champion of military and naval preparedness, he adopted as his pet proverb, "Speak softly and carry a big stick, [and] you will go far." If statesmen had the big stick, they could work their will among foreign nations without shouting; if they lacked it, shouting would do no good. TR had both a big stick and a shrill voice.

Wherever Roosevelt went, there was a great stir. At a wedding he eclipsed the bride; at a funeral, the corpse. Shockingly unconventional, he loved to break hoary precedents—the hoarier the better. He was a colossal egoist, and his self-confidence merged with self-righteousness. So sure was he of the correctness of his convictions that he impetuously branded people liars who disagreed with him. As a true cosmopolite, he loved people and mingled with those of all ranks, from Catholic cardinals to professional prizefighters, one of whom blinded a Rooseveltian eye in a White House bout.

An outspoken moralizer and reformer, Roosevelt preached righteousness from the White House pulpit. One British author found him an interesting combination of St. Paul and St. Vitus. Yet he was an opportunist who would compromise rather than butt his head against a stone wall. He was, in reality, much less radical than his blustery actions would indicate. A middle-of-the-roader, he stood just a little left of center and bared his mulelike molars at liberals and reactionaries alike.

Roosevelt rapidly developed into a master politician with an idolatrous personal following. TR—as he was called—had an enormous popular appeal, partly because the common people saw in him a fiery champion. A magnificent showman, he was always front-page copy; and his cowboyism, his bear shooting, his outsize teeth, and his pince-nez glasses were ever the delight of the cartoonist. Though a staunch party man, he detested many of the dirty-handed bosses; but he learned, as Cleveland never did, to hold his nose and work with them.

Above all, Roosevelt was a direct-actionist. He believed that the president should lead; and although he made mistakes, he kept things noisily moving—generally forward. Never a lawyer, he condemned the law and the courts as too slow. He had no real respect for the delicate checks and balances among the three branches of the government. Finding the Constitution too rigid, he would on occasion ignore it; finding Congress too rebellious, he tried a mixture of coercion and compromise on it. The president, he felt, may take any action in the general interest that is not specifically forbidden by the laws and the Constitution. As one poet noted:

> The Constitution rides behind
> And the Big Stick rides before,
> (Which is the rule of precedent
> In the reign of Theodore.)*

---

*From "The Ballad of Grizzly Gulch," in *At the Sign of the Dollar* (1903).

Theodore Roosevelt *Roosevelt gives a speech in North Carolina in 1902. (The Bettmann Archive.)*

Colombia Blocks the Canal

Foreign affairs absorbed much of Roosevelt's bullish energy. Having traveled extensively in Europe, he enjoyed a far more intimate knowledge of the outside world than most of his predecessors.

The Spanish-American War had emphasized the need for constructing the long-talked-about canal, through which only printer's ink had ever flowed. Anxious Americans had learned a dramatic object lesson when the battleship *Oregon*, stationed on the Pacific Coast at the outbreak of hostilities, made a full-speed dash around South America to join the fleet in Cuban waters. Alarmists speculated on what might have happened if it had not arrived in time for the Battle of Santiago and if the Spanish fleet had been stronger. An isthmian canal would plainly augment the strength of the navy by increasing its mobility. Such a waterway would also make easier the defense of such recent acquisitions as Puerto Rico, Hawaii, and the Philippines, while facilitating the operations of the American merchant marine.

Initial obstacles in the path of the canal builders were legal rather than geographical. By the terms of the ancient Clayton-Bulwer Treaty, concluded with Britain in 1850, the United States could not secure exclusive control over such a route. But by 1901 America's British cousins were willing to yield ground. Confronted with an unfriendly Europe and bogged down in the South African Boer War, they conceded the Hay-Pauncefote Treaty in 1901. It not only gave the United States a free hand to build the canal but conceded the right to fortify it as well.

Legal barriers now removed, the next question was: Where should the canal be dug? Many American experts favored the Nicaraguan route, but the agents of the old French Canal Company were eager to salvage something from the costly failure at S-shaped Panama. Represented by a young, energetic, and unscrupulous engineer, Philippe Bunau-Varilla, the New Panama Canal Company suddenly dropped the price of its holdings from $109 million to the fire-sale price of $40 million.

The Nicaragua-versus-Panama issue was hotly debated in Congress, where a serious objection to Nicaragua was its volcanic activity. Providentially for Bunau-Varilla, Mount Pelée, on the West Indian island of Martinique, blew its top in May 1902 and wiped out some thirty thousand souls. The clever Frenchman hastily secured ninety Nicaraguan postage stamps, each bearing a picture of the country's most fearsome volcano, and sent one to each senator. Hanna delivered a persuasive Senate speech, in which he stressed the engineering advantages of the Panama route. In June 1902 Congress finally accepted his views.

The scene now shifted to Colombia, of which Panama was an unwilling part. A treaty highly favorable to the United States was negotiated in Washington with the agent of the Colombian government in Bogotá. It granted the lease of a 6-mile-wide (9.66-kilometer) zone in perpetuity, in return for $10 million and an annual payment of $250,000. But when the pact was submitted to the Bogotá Senate, it was unanimously rejected. The isthmian strip was regarded as one of Colombia's most valuable natural assets, and many Colombians felt that they were not getting enough money. Evidence later unearthed indicates that if Washington had been willing to pay an additional $15 million, the pact would have been approved.

Roosevelt was infuriated by his setback at the hands of what he called those "dagoes." Frantically eager to be elected president "in his own right" in 1904, he was anxious to "make the dirt fly" to impress the voters. "Damn the law," he reportedly cried in private, "I want the canal built!" He assailed "the blackmailers of Bogotá" who, like armed highwaymen, were blocking the onward march of civilization. He failed to point out that the Senate of the United States also rejects treaties.

Uncle Sam Creates Puppet Panama

Impatient Panamanians, who had rebelled numerous times, were ripe for another revolt. They had counted on a wave of prosperity to follow construction of the canal, and they feared that the United States would now turn to the Nicaraguan route. Scheming Bunau-Varilla was no less disturbed by the prospect of losing the company's $40 million. Working hand in glove with the Panama revolutionists, he raised a tiny "patriot" army consisting largely of members of the Panamanian fire department, plus five hundred "bought" Colombian troops—for a reported price of $100,000.

The Panama revolution occurred on November 3, 1903, with the incidental killing of a Chinese civilian and a donkey. Colombian troops were gathered to crush the uprising, but American naval forces would not let them cross the isthmus. Roosevelt justified this highly questionable interference by a strained interpretation of the treaty of 1846 with Colombia. (This pact obligated Washington to maintain the "perfect neutrality" of the isthmus, obviously against outsiders.)

Roosevelt moved rapidly to make steamy Panama a virtual outpost of the United States.

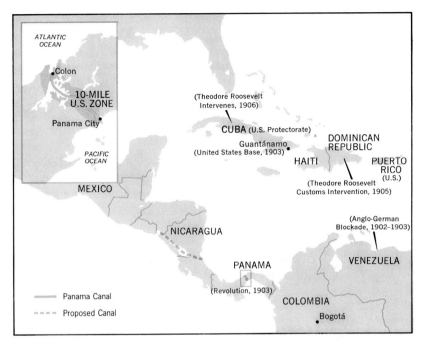

ATLANTIC OCEAN

Colon

10-MILE U.S. ZONE

Panama City

PACIFIC OCEAN

MEXICO

(Theodore Roosevelt Intervenes, 1906)

CUBA (U.S. Protectorate)

Guantánamo (United States Base, 1903)

DOMINICAN REPUBLIC

HAITI

PUERTO RICO (U.S.)

(Theodore Roosevelt Customs Intervention, 1905)

(Anglo-German Blockade, 1902–1903)

NICARAGUA

PANAMA

VENEZUELA

(Revolution, 1903)

COLOMBIA

Bogotá

——— Panama Canal

- - - - Proposed Canal

Big Stick in the Caribbean
In 1901 Roosevelt declared: "If a man continually blusters . . . a big stick will not save him from trouble; and neither will speaking softly avail, if back of the softness there does not lie strength, power. . . . If the boaster is not prepared to back up his words his position becomes absolutely contemptible."

Three days after the uprising, he hastily extended the right hand of recognition. Fifteen days later, Bunau-Varilla, who was now the Panamanian minister despite his French citizenship, signed the Hay–Bunau-Varilla treaty in Washington. The price of the canal strip was left the same, but the zone was widened from 6 to 10 miles (9.66 to 16 kilometers). The French company gladly pocketed its $40 million from the United States Treasury.

Roosevelt, it seems clear, did not actively plot to tear Panama from the side of Colombia. But the conspirators knew of his angrily expressed views, and they counted on his using the big stick to prevent Colombia from intervening. Yet the Rough Rider became so indiscreetly involved in the Panama affair as to create the impression that he had been a secret party to the intrigue.

Unhappily, the United States suffered a black eye as a result of Roosevelt's "cowboy diplomacy." European imperialists, who were old hands at this sort of thing, could now raise their eyebrows sneeringly at America's superior moral pretensions—and they did.

Completing the Canal and Appeasing Colombia

The so-called rape of Panama marked an ugly downward lurch in Uncle Sam's relations with Latin America. Much fear had already been aroused by the recent seizure of Puerto Rico and by the Yankee stranglehold on Cuba. The fate of Colombia, when it dared defy the Colossus of the North, indicated that its weak sister republics were not safe. The era of the bullying "Big Brother" policy was brazenly launched.

Roosevelt heatedly defended himself against all charges of evildoing. He claimed that he had received a "mandate from civilization" to start the canal and that Colombia had wronged the United States by not permitting itself to be benefited. To deal with these "blackmailers," he insisted, was like "nailing currant jelly to the wall."

But TR was not completely candid. He failed to point out that the Nicaragua route was about equally feasible and that it was available without a revolution. Yet this alternative would have

TR Intervenes in Panama *(The Bettmann Archive.)*

project was completed at an initial cost of about $400 million, just as World War I was breaking out. The whole enterprise, in the words of the English writer James Bryce, was "the greatest liberty Man has ever taken with Nature."

TR's Perversion of Monroe's Doctrine

Latin American debt defaults created the conditions for further Rooseveltian involvement in affairs south of the border. Nations such as Venezuela and the Dominican Republic were chronically in arrears in their payments to European creditors, particularly Britain and Germany. Seeking to force payment, German warships sank two Venezuelan gunboats and bombarded a town in early 1903.

This ironfisted intervention aroused Roosevelt. He feared that if the Germans or British

involved some delay, and the presidential election of 1904 was fast approaching.

Active work was begun on "making the dirt fly" in 1904, but grave difficulties were encountered, ranging from labor troubles to landslides. The organization was finally perfected under an energetic but autocratic West Point engineer, Colonel George Washington Goethals. At the outset, sanitation proved to be more important than excavation. Colonel William C. Gorgas, the quiet and determined exterminator of yellow fever in Havana, ultimately made the Canal Zone "as safe as a health resort."

Americans finally succeeded where the French had failed. In 1914 the colossal canal

In 1911 Roosevelt made a costly boast in a speech in Berkeley, California: "I am interested in the Panama Canal because I started it. If I had followed traditional, conservative methods I would have presented a dignified state paper . . . to Congress and the debates on it would have been going on yet; but I took the Canal Zone and let Congress debate; and while the debate goes on the Canal does also."

Roosevelt in Panama *He visited the Panama Canal construction site in 1906 to see "the dirt fly." He was the first president to leave the United States for foreign soil. (Theodore Roosevelt Collection, Harvard College Library.)*

got their foot in the door as bill collectors, they might remain in Latin America, in flagrant violation of the Monroe Doctrine. Roosevelt therefore devised a devious policy of "preventive intervention," better known as the Roosevelt corollary of the Monroe Doctrine. He declared that in the event of future financial malfeasance by the Latin American nations, the United States itself would intervene, take over the customshouses, pay off the debts, and keep the troublesome powers on the other side of the Atlantic. The United States had a moral obligation to do so, Roosevelt argued, because it would not permit the European nations themselves to intervene in the bankrupt banana republics. In short, no outsiders could push the Latin nations around except Uncle Sam, Policeman of the Caribbean.

This new brandishing of the big stick in the Caribbean became effective in 1905. It was formalized by a Dominican treaty two years later, giving the United States supervisory powers over Dominican tariff collections. Dominican officials, who had raked in much juicy graft, were not happy over such interference, and they acquiesced only after some strenuous arm-twisting from Washington. But from a debt-collecting point of view, the customshouse intervention was a success.

Roosevelt's corollary, though tacked onto the Monroe Doctrine, bore only a strained relation to the original dictum of 1823. Monroe had in effect said to the European powers, "Thou shalt not intervene." TR changed this warning to mean, "We shall intervene to prevent you from intervening." The Roosevelt doctrine was actually so radical as to be a completely new policy, but it gained readier acceptance by being associated with the honored name of Monroe. Yet in its own right the corollary had considerable merit as a preemptive stroke.

Roosevelt's rewriting of Monroe's doctrine had its dark side. It probably did more than any other single step to promote the "Bad Neighbor" policy begun in these years. As time wore on,

Roosevelt wrote to a correspondent in February 1904: "I have been hoping and praying for three months that the Santo Domingans would behave so that I would not have to act in any way. I want to do nothing but what a policeman has to do. . . . As for annexing the island, I have about the same desire to annex it as a gorged boa-constrictor might have to swallow a porcupine wrong-end-to."

Theodore Roosevelt and his Big Stick in the Caribbean, 1904   *Roosevelt's policies seemed to be turning the Caribbean into a Yankee pond. (The Granger Collection.)*

the new corollary was used to justify wholesale interventions and repeated landings of the marines, all of which helped turn the Caribbean into a "Yankee lake." Latin Americans mistakenly cursed the unoffending Monroe, when they should have cursed the offending Roosevelt. To them it seemed as though the Monroe Doctrine, far from providing a shield, was a cloak behind which the United States sought to strangle them.

The shadow of the big stick likewise fell on Cuba in 1906. Revolutionary disorders brought an appeal from the Cuban president, and "necessity being the mother of intervention," United States Marines were landed. These police forces were withdrawn temporarily in 1909, but in Latin American eyes the episode was but another example of the creeping power of the Colossus of the North.

Roosevelt on the World Stage

Booted and spurred, Roosevelt charged into international affairs far beyond Latin America. The outbreak of war between Russia and Japan in 1904 gave him a chance to perform as a global statesman. The Russian bear, having lumbered across Asia, was seeking to bathe its frostbitten paws in the ice-free ports of China's Manchuria, particularly Port Arthur. In Japanese eyes Manchuria and Korea in czarist hands were pistols pointed at Japan's strategic heart. Russian troops had invaded Manchuria during the Boxer outburst of 1900 and, despite solemn promises, were not withdrawing. The czar was obviously stalling until his trans-Siberian railroad could be finished, as it would be in a few months. With the clock ticking against them, the Japanese suddenly began war in 1904 with a devastating surprise pounce on the Russian fleet at Port Arthur. They proceeded to administer a humiliating series of beatings to the inept Russians—the first serious military setback to a European power by a non-European force since the Turkish invasions of the sixteenth century. But as the war dragged on, Japan began to run short of men and yen—a weakness she did not want to betray to the enemy. Tokyo officials therefore approached Roosevelt in the deepest secrecy, and asked him to help sponsor peace negotiations.

Roosevelt agreed and shepherded the delegates of the two sides together at Portsmouth, New Hampshire, in 1905. The Japanese presented stern demands for a huge indemnity and the entire strategic island of Sakhalin, while the Russians stubbornly refused to concede the depths of their defeat. Blustering at both sides behind the scenes, Roosevelt forced through an accord in which the Japanese received no indemnity and only the southern half of Sakhalin.

Far East, 1904–1905

For achieving this agreement, as well as for helping arrange an international conference at Algeciras, Spain, in 1906 to mediate North African disputes, Roosevelt received the Nobel

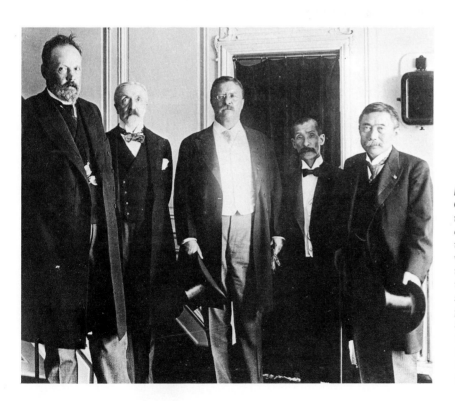

Roosevelt at Portsmouth Conference *TR meets with the two Russian and two Japanese delegates, 1905. Roosevelt wrote that dealing with U.S. senators was a tough job, but dealing with these peace envoys was even tougher. He had to be "polite and sympathetic and patient in explaining for the hundredth time something perfectly obvious . . . when I really want to give utterance to whoops of rage and jump up and knock their heads together." (The Bettmann Archive.)*

There is a curious modernity about what Roosevelt wrote to a British friend in May 1905: "I like the Russian people, but abhor the Russian system of government and I cannot trust the word of those at the head."

"Isn't It a Daisy?"   Uncle Sam admires his battleship fleet. (Philadelphia Record.)

Peace Prize in 1906. But the price of TR's diplomatic glory was high for American foreign relations. Two historic friendships withered on the windswept plains of Manchuria. American relations with Russia, once friendly, soured as the Russians implausibly accused Roosevelt of robbing them of military victory. Revelations about this time of savage massacres of Russian Jews further poisoned American feeling against Russia. Japan, once America's protégé, felt robbed of its indemnity. Both newly powerful, Japan and America now became rivals in Asia, as fear and jealousy between the two nations grew. To many Americans, the Nipponese were getting too big for their kimonos.

Japanese Laborers in California

The population of America's Pacific Coast was directly affected by the Russo-Japanese War. A new restlessness swept over the rice paddies of Japan, largely as a result of the dislocations and tax burdens caused by the recent conflict. Numerous Japanese laborers, with their wives and children, began to pour into the spacious valleys of California. By 1906 approximately seventy thousand Japanese dwelt along the Pacific Coast. Nervous Californians, confronted by another "yellow peril," feared being drowned in an Oriental sea.

A showdown on the Japanese influx came in 1906. Following the frightful earthquake and fire of that year in San Francisco, the local school authorities, pressed for space, decreed that Oriental children should attend a special school.

Instantly, the Japanese school incident brewed an international crisis. The people of Japan, who were highly sensitive on questions of race, regarded this discrimination as an insult to them and their beloved children. On both sides of the Pacific, irresponsible war talk sizzled in the "yellow press"—the real "yellow peril." Roosevelt, who as a Rough Rider had relished shooting, was less happy over the prospect that California might stir up a war that all the other states would have to fight. He therefore invited the entire San Francisco Board of Education, headed by a bassoon-playing mayor under indictment for graft, to come to the White House.

TR finally broke the deadlock, but not until he had brandished his big stick and bared his big teeth. The Californians were induced to repeal the offensive school order and to accept what came to be known as the "Gentlemen's Agreement." This secret understanding was worked out, during 1907–1908, by an exchange of diplomatic notes between Washington and Tokyo. The Japanese, for their part, agreed to stop the flow of laborers to the American mainland by withholding passports. Caucasian Californians, their fears allayed, henceforth slept more easily.

Roosevelt worried that his intercession between California and Japan might be interpreted in Tokyo as prompted by fear of the Nipponese. Accordingly, he hit upon a dramatic scheme to impress the Japanese with the heft of his big stick. He daringly decided to send the entire battleship fleet on a highly visible voyage around the world.

Late in 1907 sixteen sparkling-white, smoke-belching battleships started from Virginia waters. Their commander pointedly declared that he was ready for "a feast, a frolic, or a fight." The Great White Fleet—to the accompaniment of cannonading champagne corks—received tumultuous welcomes in Latin America, Hawaii, New Zealand, and Australia.

As events turned out, an overwhelming reception in Japan was the high point of the trip. Tens of thousands of kimonoed schoolchildren had been trained to wave tiny American flags and sing "The Star-Spangled Banner"—reportedly in English. In the warm diplomatic atmosphere created by the visit of the fleet, the Root-Takahira agreement of 1908 was reached with Japan. The United States and Japan solemnly pledged themselves to respect each other's territorial possessions in the Pacific and to uphold the Open Door in China. The once fight-thirsty Roosevelt, who thus went out of his way to avoid a war with Japan, regarded the battleship cruise as his most important contribution to peace. The voyage of the white fleet also gave Uncle Sam a new recruiting slogan: "Join the Navy and See the World."

Varying Viewpoints

Disagreement marks historical appraisals of America's emergence as a great power at the turn of the twentieth century. On the one hand, historians have praised the maturing of the Republic, which was now able to take its place among the arbiters of the world's destinies. On the other hand, many writers have tried to define America's new role in distinctive terms. They argue that the United States did not enter the great power game as just another player but introduced a new style of diplomatic play and perhaps even a new set of rules.

Judgments clash about these alleged innovations. An older school of thought stresses the idealism that America brought to the world arena. More recently, "New Left" revisionists have charged that America's contribution to international life was the self-serving notion of "informal empire," typified by a worldwide Open Door doctrine. This strategy shunned formal territorial possession but sought economic dominance of foreign raw materials, markets, and investments.

Historians disagree further about the motivating impulses of American diplomacy. Recent "revisionists" have tended almost exclusively to emphasize domestic economic factors in explaining American foreign policy. The United States sought foreign markets, the argument goes, to solve the problems of domestic overproduction and recurring business depressions. Other scholars respond that international politics can only be properly understood in an international context. They argue that Theodore Roosevelt, for example, acted not for narrow domestic reasons but because he realistically perceived that if the United States did not hold its own against the other powers, it would soon risk being eclipsed on the world stage, and even being pushed around in its own hemisphere, despite the Monroe Doctrine.

Select Readings

Primary Source Documents

Theodore Roosevelt's "corollary"* to the Monroe Doctrine, in *A Compilation of the Messages and Papers of the Presidents*, vol. XVI, pp. 7053–7054, found its first expression in 1904. *The Annual Report* of the secretary of commerce and labor for 1908 contains the "Gentlemen's Agreement" with Japan. For the intrigue surrounding the independence of Panama and the building of the canal, see *Foreign Relations of the United States** (1903) and Theodore Roosevelt to Albert Shaw, October 10, 1903,* in *The Letters of Theodore Roosevelt*, edited by Elting E. Morison (1951), vol. 3, p. 628.

Secondary Sources

Broad outlines appear in Foster Rhea Dulles, *America's Rise to World Power* (1955). More detailed is Howard K. Beale, *Theodore Roosevelt and the Rise of America to World Power* (1956). Analytical and sympathetic are John M. Blum, *The Republican Roosevelt*

(new ed., 1977), and G. Wallace Chessman, *Theodore Roosevelt and the Politics of Power* (1969). Especially good on the youthful TR are Edmund Morris, *The Rise of Theodore Roosevelt* (1979), and David McCullough, *Mornings on Horseback* (1981). For the Open Door, consult A. Whitney Griswold, *The Far Eastern Policy of the United States* (1938), and Marilyn B. Young, *The Rhetoric of Empire: America's China Policy, 1895–1901* (1968). On relations with Japan, see Charles E. Neu, *An Uncertain Friendship: Theodore Roosevelt and Japan, 1906–1909* (1967), and his *The Troubled Encounter: The United States and Japan* (1975). Also valuable are two books by Akira Iriye, *Across the Pacific* (1967), and *Pacific Estrangement: Japanese and American Expansion, 1897–1911* (1972). James Reed discusses *The Missionary Mind and American East Asian Policy, 1911–1915* (1983). On the treatment of the Japanese in the United States, see Roger Daniels, *The Politics of Prejudice* (1962). The canal issue is analyzed in David McCullough, *The Path between the Seas* (1977), and Walter LaFeber, *The Panama Canal* (1978).

33

Progressivism and the Republican Roosevelt

> When I say I believe in a square deal I do not mean . . . to give every man the best hand. If the cards do not come to any man, or if they do come, and he has not got the power to play them, that is his affair. All I mean is that there shall be no crookedness in the dealing.
>
> Theodore Roosevelt, 1905

Progressive Roots

Nearly 76 million Americans greeted the new century in 1900. Of them, almost 1 in 7 was foreign-born. In the fourteen years of peace that remained before the Great War of 1914 engulfed the globe, 13 million more migrants would carry their bundles down the gangplanks to the land of promise.

Hardly had the twentieth century dawned on the ethnically and racially mixed American people than they were convulsed by a reform movement, the like of which the nation had not seen since the 1840s. The new crusaders, who called themselves "progressives," waged war on many evils, notably monopoly, corruption, inefficiency, and social injustice. The progressive

army was large, multicolored, and widely deployed, but it had a single battle cry: "Strengthen the State." The "real heart of the movement," explained one of the progressive reformers, was "to use the government as an agency of human welfare."

The ground swell of the new reformist wave went far back—to the Greenback Labor party of the 1870s and the Populists of the 1890s, to the mounting unrest throughout the land as grasping industrialists concentrated more and more power in fewer and fewer hands. An outworn philosophy of hands-off individualism seemed increasingly out of place in the modern machine age. Social and economic problems were now too complex for the designedly feeble Jeffersonian organs of government. Progressive

Becoming American *Flooded with immigrant children, many of whom could scarcely speak English, schools like this one in New York in 1892 cultivated loyalty to the immigrants' adopted land by teaching courses in "civics" and encouraging patriotic rituals like the pledge of allegiance to the flag. (Jacob A. Riis Collection, Museum of the City of New York.)*

theorists were insisting that society could no longer afford the luxury of a limitless "let-alone" policy (*laissez-faire*). The people, through government, must substitute mastery for drift.

Well before 1900 perceptive politicians and writers had begun to pinpoint targets for the progressive attack. Bryan, Altgeld, and the Populists loudly branded the "bloated trusts" with the stigma of corruption and wrongdoing. In 1894 Henry Demarest Lloyd charged headlong into the Standard Oil Company with his book entitled *Wealth against Commonwealth*. Eccentric Thorstein Veblen assailed the new rich with his prickly pen in *The Theory of the Leisure Class* (1899), a savage attack on "predatory wealth" and "conspicuous consumption."

Other pen-wielding knights likewise entered the fray. The keen-eyed and keen-nosed Danish immigrant Jacob A. Riis, a reporter for the New York *Sun*, shocked middle-class Americans in 1890 with *How the Other Half Lives*. His account was a damning indictment of the dirt, disease, vice, and misery of the rat-gnawed human rookeries known as New York slums. The book deeply influenced a future New York City police commissioner, Theodore Roosevelt. Novelist Theodore Dreiser used his blunt prose to batter promoters and profiteers in *The Financier* (1912) and *The Titan* (1914).

Socialists, now swelling in numbers, must take high rank among the caustic critics of existing injustices. Many of them were European immigrants who decried "bloody capitalism," and they began to register appreciable strength at the ballot boxes as the new century dawned. They received much of their inspiration from abroad, where countries like Germany were launching daring experiments in state social-

Life on the Lower East Side of New York City "Street Arabs" often slept wherever they could. Many families counted themselves lucky to share a single room, no matter how squalid. (Jacob A. Riis Collection, Museum of the City of New York.)

ism. In faraway Australia and New Zealand, Socialist reforms were also being undertaken that attracted much notice in America.

High-minded messengers of the social gospel also contributed mightily to the upsurging wave of reform, as did the ever-growing women's movement. Feminists in multiplying numbers added social justice to suffrage on their list of needed reforms. With urban pioneers like Jane Addams blazing the way, women entered the fight to clean up corrupt city governments, to protect women on the clanging factory floor, to keep children out of the smudgy mills and sooty mines, and to ensure that only safe food products found their way to the family table. Much of progessivism reflected the new public concerns of women, born of their changing role in the still-stretching cities.

Raking Muck with the Muckrakers

Beginning about 1902 the exposing of evil became a flourishing industry among American publishers. A group of aggressive ten- and fifteen-cent popular magazines surged to the front, notably *McClure's*, *Cosmopolitan*, *Col-*

lier's, and *Everybody's*. Waging fierce circulation wars, they dug deep for the dirt that the public loved to hate. Enterprising editors financed extensive research and encouraged pugnacious writing by their bright young reporters, whom President Roosevelt branded as "muckrakers" in 1906. Annoyed by their excess of zeal, he compared the mudslinging magazine dirt-diggers to the figure in Bunyan's *Pilgrim's Progress* who was so intent on raking manure that he could not see the celestial crown dangling overhead.

Hester Street, c. 1900 *Crowded tenement-dwellers took to the streets on hot summer days, as in this heavily Italian neighborhood in turn-of-the-century New York. (Brown Brothers.)*

Despite presidential scolding, these muckrakers boomed circulation, and some of their most scandalous exposures were published as best-selling books. The reformer-writers ranged far, wide, and deep in their crusade to lay bare the muck of iniquity in American society. In 1902 a brilliant New York reporter, Lincoln Steffens, launched a series of articles in *McClure's* entitled "The Shame of the Cities." He fearlessly unmasked the corrupt alliance between big business and municipal government. Steffens was followed in the same magazine by Ida M. Tarbell, a pioneering woman journalist who published a devastating but factual exposé of the Standard Oil Company. (Her father had been ruined by the oil interests.) Fearing legal reprisals, the muckraking magazines went to great pains and expense to check their material—paying as much as three thousand dollars to verify a single Tarbell article.

Muckrakers fearlessly tilted their pen-lances at varied targets. They assailed the malpractices of life insurance companies and tariff lobbies. They roasted the beef trust, the "money trust," the railroad barons, and the corrupt amassing of American fortunes. Thomas W. Lawson, an erratic speculator who had himself made $50 million on the stock market, laid bare the practices of his accomplices in "Frenzied Finance." This series of articles, appearing in 1905–1906, rocketed the circulation of *Everybody's*. Lawson, by fouling his own nest, made many enemies among his rich associates, and he died a poor man.

David G. Phillips shocked an already startled nation by his series in *Cosmopolitan* entitled "The Treason of the Senate" (1906). He boldly charged that seventy-five of the ninety senators did not represent the people at all but the railroads and trusts. This withering indictment, buttressed by facts, impressed President Roosevelt. Phillips continued his slashing attacks through novels and was fatally shot in 1911 by a deranged young man whose family he had allegedly maligned.

Some of the most effective fire of the muckrakers was directed at social evils. The ugly list included the immoral "white slave" traffic in women, the rickety slums, and the appalling number of industrial accidents. The sorry subjugation of America's 9 million blacks—of whom 90 percent still lived in the South, and one-third were illiterate—was spotlighted in Ray Stannard Baker's *Following the Color Line*

In his muckraker speech (1906), Roosevelt said: "Now, it is very necessary that we should not flinch from seeing what is vile and debasing. There is filth on the floor and it must be scraped up with the muck-rake; and there are times and places where this service is the most needed of all the services that can be performed. But the man who never does anything else, who never thinks or speaks or writes, save of his feats with the muck-rake, speedily becomes, not a help to society, not an incitement to good, but one of the most potent forces for evil."

Child Workers   *Two young girls tend a thread-winding machine. The boy is already a veteran coal miner. (Left, Library of Congress; right, International Museum of Photography at George Eastman House.)*

(1908). The abuses of child labor were brought luridly to light by John Spargo's *The Bitter Cry of the Children* (1906).

Vendors of potent patent medicines (often heavily spiked with alcohol) likewise came in for bitter criticism. These conscienceless vultures sold incredible quantities of adulterated or habit-forming drugs, while "doping" the press with lavish advertising. Muckraking attacks in *Collier's* were ably reinforced by Dr. Harvey W. Wiley, chief chemist of the Department of Agriculture, who with his famous "Poison Squad," performed experiments on himself.

Full of sound and fury, the muckrakers signified much about the nature of the progressive reform movement. They were long on lamentation and short on sweeping remedies. To right social wrongs they counted on publicity and an aroused public conscience, not drastic political change. They sought not to overthrow capitalism but to cleanse it. The cure for the ills of American democracy, they earnestly believed, was more democracy.

Political Progressivism

Progressive reformers were mainly middle-class men and women who felt themselves squeezed from above and below. They sensed pressure from the new giant corporations, the restless immigrant hordes, and the aggressive labor unions. The progressives simultaneously sought two goals: to use state power to curb the trusts and to stem the Socialist threat by generally improving the common person's conditions of life and labor. Progressives emerged in both major parties, in all regions, and at all levels of government. The truth is that progressivism was less a minority movement and more a majority mood.

One of the first objectives of progressives was to regain the power that had slipped from the hands of the people into those of the "interests." These ardent reformers pushed for direct primary elections so as to undercut power-hungry party bosses. They favored the "initiative" so that voters could directly propose legislation themselves, thus bypassing the boss-bought

> *Ex-President Roosevelt wrote of reform in 1913: "It is vitally necessary to move forward and to shake off the dead hand, often a fossilized dead hand, of the reactionaries; and yet we have to face the fact that there is apt to be a lunatic fringe among the votaries of any forward movement."*

state legislatures. Progressives also agitated for the "referendum." This device would place laws on the ballot for final approval by the people, especially laws that had been railroaded through a compliant legislature by free-spending agents of big business. The "recall" would enable the voters to remove faithless elected officials, particularly those who had been bribed by bosses or lobbyists.

Rooting out graft also became a prime goal of earnest progressives. A number of the state legislatures passed corrupt-practices acts, which limited the amount of money that candidates could spend for their election. Such legislation also restricted huge gifts from corporations, for which the donors would expect special favors. The secret Australian ballot was likewise being introduced more widely in the states to counteract boss rule. Bribery was less feasible when bribers could not tell if they were getting their money's worth from the bribed.

Direct election of United States senators became a favorite goal of progressives, especially after the muckrakers had exposed the scandalous tie-in between greedy corporations and Congress. By 1900 the Senate had so many rich men that it was often sneered at as the "Millionaires' Club." Too many of the prosperous solons, elected as they then were by trust-dominated legislatures, heeded the voice of their "masters" rather than that of the masses.

A constitutional amendment to bring about the popular election of senators had rough sledding in Congress, for the plutocratic members of the Senate were happy with existing methods. But a number of states established primary elections in which the voters expressed their preferences for the Senate. The local legislatures, when choosing senators, found it politically wise to heed the voice of the people. Partly as a result of such pressures, the Seventeenth Amendment to the Constitution, approved in 1913, established the direct election of senators. (See the Appendix.) But the expected improvement in caliber was slow in coming.

"Suffragettes" Put the Pressure on Washington *Success finally crowned their effort with the ratification of the Nineteenth Amendment in 1920. (UPI/ Bettmann Newsphotos.)*

In 1908 President Roosevelt wrote prophetically: "Personally I believe in woman's suffrage, but I am not an enthusiastic advocate of it, because I do not regard it as a very important matter. I am unable to see that there has been any special improvement in the position of women in those states in the West that have adopted woman's suffrage, as compared with those states adjoining them that have not adopted it. I do not think that giving the women suffrage will produce any marked improvement in the condition of women. I do not believe that it will produce any of the evils feared, and I am very certain that when women as a whole take any special interest in the matter they will have suffrage if they desire it."

Woman suffrage, the goal of feminists for many decades, likewise received powerful new support from the progressives early in the 1900s. The political reformers believed that women's votes would elevate the political tone; foes of the saloon felt that they could count on the support of enfranchised females. The "suffragists," crying "Votes for Women" and "Equal Suffrage for Men and Women," protested bitterly against "Taxation without Representation." Many of the states, especially the more liberal ones in the West, gradually extended the vote to women. But by 1910 nationwide female suffrage was still a decade away; and a suffragist could still be sneeringly defined as "One who has ceased to be a lady and has not yet become a gentleman."

Progressivism in the Cities and States

Progressives scored some of their most impressive gains in the cities. Frustrated by the inefficiency and corruption of machine-oiled city government, many localities followed the pioneering example of Galveston, Texas. In 1901 it had appointed expert-staffed commissions to manage urban affairs. Other communities adopted the city-manager system, also designed to take politics out of municipal administration. Some of these "reforms" obviously valued efficiency more highly than democracy, as control of civic affairs was further removed from the hands of the people.

Urban reformers likewise attacked "slumlords," juvenile delinquency, and wide-open prostitution (vice-at-a-price), which flourished in red-light districts unchallenged by bribed police. Public-spirited city-dwellers also moved to halt the corrupt sale of franchises for streetcars and other public utilities.

Progressivism naturally bubbled up to the state level, notably in Wisconsin, which became a yeasty laboratory of reform. The governor of the state, pompadoured Robert M. ("Fighting Bob") La Follette, was an undersized but overengined crusader who emerged as the most militant of the progressive Republican leaders. After a desperate fight with entrenched monopoly, he reached the governor's chair in 1901. Routing the lumber and railroad "interests," he wrested considerable control from the crooked corporations and returned it to the people. He also perfected a scheme for regulating public utilities, while laboring in close association with experts on the faculty of the state university at Madison.

Other states marched steadily toward the progressive camp, as they undertook to regulate railroads and trusts, chiefly through public utilities commissions. Oregon was not far behind Wisconsin, and California made giant bootstrides under the stocky Hiram W. Johnson. Elected Republican governor in 1910, this dynamic prosecutor of grafters helped break the dominant grip of the Southern Pacific Railroad on California politics and then, like La Follette, set up a political machine of his own. Heavily whiskered Charles Evans Hughes, the able and fearless reformist Republican governor of New York, had earlier gained national fame as an investigator of malpractices by gas and insurance companies and by the coal trust.

In these and other states, fired-up progressives tackled head-on a whole array of social problems. One of the most remarkable features of this era was the energy and confidence with which reformers did battle with a host of evils. They finally secured the enactment of safety and sanitation codes for industry and closed certain harmful trades to juveniles. Progressives

Temperance Women Sing Outside Saloon (Frank Leslie's Illustrated Newspaper, Feb. 21, 1874. By permission of the Houghton Library, Harvard University.)

further protected the toiler with workmen's compensation laws, thus relieving the injured laborer from the burden of lawsuits to prove negligence on the part of the employer. The reformers also secured laws setting maximum hours and minimum wages.

Steaming and unsanitary sweatshops were a public scandal in many cities. The issue was thrust into the public eye in 1911, when a fire at the Triangle Shirtwaist Company in New York City incinerated 146 women workers, mostly girls. Lashed by the public outcry, the legislature of New York and later other legislatures passed laws regulating the hours and conditions of toil in such firetraps. Prisons and "reform" schools likewise came under sharp scrutiny, as the public increasingly accepted the view that these penal institutions were primarily for reformation rather than punishment.

But crusaders for these humane measures did not always have smooth sailing. One dismaying setback came in 1905, when the Supreme Court invalidated a New York law establishing a ten-hour day for bakers. Yet the reformist progressive wave finally washed up into the judiciary, and in 1917 the Court upheld a ten-hour law for factory workers. Gradually, the concept of the employer's responsibility to soci-

ety was replacing the old dog-eat-dog philosophy of unregulated free enterprise.

Corner saloons, with their shutter doors, naturally attracted the ire and fire of progressives. Alcohol was intimately connected with prostitution in red-light districts, with the drunken voter, with crooked city officials dominated by "booze" interests, and with the blowsy "boss" who counted poker chips by night and miscounted ballots by day (including the "cemetery vote"). By 1900 cities like New York and San Francisco had one saloon for about every two hundred people.

Antiliquor campaigners received powerful support from several militant organizations, notably the Women's Christian Temperance Union (WCTU). Pious Frances E. Willard, one of its founders, would fall on her knees in prayer on saloon floors. She found a vigorous ally in the Anti-Saloon League, which was aggressive, well organized, and well financed.

Caught up in the crusade, some states and numerous counties passed "dry" laws, which controlled, restricted, or abolished alcohol. The big cities were generally "wet," for they had a large immigrant vote accustomed in the Old Country to the free flow of wine and beer. When World War I erupted in 1914, nearly one-half of the population lived in "dry" territory, and nearly three-fourths of the total area had outlawed the saloon. Demon Rum was groggy, and he was to be floored—temporarily—by the Eighteenth Amendment in 1919.

TR's Square Deal for Labor

Theodore Roosevelt, though something of an imperialistic busybody abroad, was touched by the progressive wave at home. Like other reformers, he feared that the "public interest" was being submerged in the drifting seas of indifference. Everybody's interest was nobody's interest. Roosevelt decided to make it his. His sportsman's instincts spurred him into demanding a "Square Deal" for capital, labor, and the public at large. Broadly speaking, his program embraced three *C*s: control of the corporations, consumer protection, and conservation of natural resources.

The Square Deal for labor received its acid test in 1902, when a crippling strike broke out in the anthracite coal mines of Pennsylvania. Some 140,000 besooted workers, many of them illiterate immigrants, had long been frightfully exploited and accident-plagued. They demanded, among other improvements, a 20 percent increase in pay and a reduction of the working day from ten to nine hours.

Unsympathetic mine owners, confident that a chilled public would react against the miners, refused to arbitrate or even negotiate. One of their spokesmen, multimillionaire George F. Baer, reflected the high-and-mighty attitude of certain ungenerous employers. Workers, he wrote, would be cared for "not by the labor agitators, but by the Christian men to whom God in His infinite wisdom has given the control of the property interests of this country." Closed minds meant closed mines.

As coal supplies dwindled, factories and schools were forced to shut down, and even hospitals felt the icy grip of winter. Desperately seeking a solution, Roosevelt summoned representatives of the striking miners and the mine owners to the White House. He was vastly annoyed by the "extraordinary stupidity and bad

temper" of the "wooden-headed gentry" who operated the mines. As he later confessed, if it had not been for the dignity of his high office, he would have taken one of them "by the seat of the breeches" and "chucked him out of the window."

Roosevelt finally resorted to his trusty big stick when he threatened to seize the mines and operate them with federal troops. Faced with this first-time-ever threat to use federal bayonets against capital, rather than labor, the owners grudgingly consented to arbitration. A compromise decision ultimately gave the miners a 10 percent pay boost and a working day of nine hours. But their union was not officially recognized as a bargaining agent.

Keenly aware of the mounting antagonisms between capital and labor, Roosevelt urged Congress to create a new Department of Commerce and Labor. This goal was achieved in 1903. (Ten years later the agency was split in two.) An important arm of the newly born Department of Commerce and Labor was the Bureau of Corporations, which was authorized to probe businesses engaged in interstate commerce. The bureau was highly useful in helping to break the stranglehold of monopoly and in clearing the road for the era of "trust-busting."

TR Corrals the Corporations

The many-webbed railroads sorely needed restraint. The Interstate Commerce Commission, created in 1887 as a feeble sop to the public, had proved woefully inadequate. Railroad barons could simply appeal the commission's decisions on rates to the federal courts—a process that might take ten years.

Spurred by the former-cowboy president, Congress passed effective railroad legislation, beginning with the Elkins Act of 1903. This curb was aimed primarily at the rebate evil. Heavy fines could now be imposed both on the railroads that gave rebates and on the shippers that accepted them.

Still more effective was the Hepburn Act of 1906. Free passes, with their hint of bribery, were severely restricted. The once-infantile

The Sherman Anti-Trust Law Returns from the Dead
(Bartholomew in the Minneapolis Journal.)

Interstate Commerce Commission was expanded, and its reach was extended to include express companies, sleeping-car companies, and pipelines. For the first time, the commission was given real molars when it was authorized, on complaint of shippers, to nullify existing rates and stipulate maximum rates.

Railroads also provided Roosevelt with an opportunity to brandish his antitrust bludgeon. *Trusts* had come to be a fighting word in the progressive era. Roosevelt believed that these industrial behemoths, with their efficient means of production, had arrived to stay. He concluded that there were "good" trusts, with public consciences, and "bad" trusts, which lusted greedily for power. He was determined to respond to the popular outcry against the trusts yet not to throw out the baby with the bathwater by indiscriminately smashing all large businesses.

Roosevelt, as a trustbuster, first burst into the headlines in 1902 with an attack on the Northern Securities Company, a railroad holding company organized by financial titan J. P. Morgan and empire builder James J. Hill. These Napoleonic moguls of money sought to achieve a virtual monopoly of the railroads in the Northwest. Roosevelt was therefore challenging the most regal potentates of the industrial aristocracy.

The railway promoters appealed to the Supreme Court, which in 1904 upheld Roosevelt's antitrust suit and ordered the Northern Securities Company to be dissolved. The decision jolted Wall Street and angered big business but greatly enhanced Roosevelt's reputation as a trust smasher.

Roosevelt's big stick crashed down on other giant monopolies, as he initiated over forty legal proceedings against them. The Supreme Court in 1905 declared the beef trust illegal, and the heavy fist of justice fell upon monopolists controlling sugar, fertilizer, harvesters, and other key products.

Much mythology has inflated Roosevelt's reputation as a trustbuster. The Rough Rider understood the political popularity of monopoly-smashing, but he did not consider it sound economic policy. Combination and integration, he felt, were the hallmarks of the age, and to try to stem the tide of economic progress by political means he considered the rankest folly. Bigness was not necessarily badness; so why punish success? Roosevelt's real purpose in assaulting the Goliaths of industry was symbolic: to prove conclusively that the government, not private business, ruled the country. He believed in regulating, not fragmenting, the big business combines. The threat of dissolution, he felt, might make the sultans of the smokestacks more amenable to federal regulation—as it did.

In truth, Roosevelt never swung his trust-crushing stick with maximum force. In many ways, the huge industrial behemoths were healthier—though perhaps more "tame"—at the end of Roosevelt's reign than they had been before. His successor, William Howard Taft,

> Roosevelt preached: "The man who advocates destroying the trusts by measures which would paralyze the industries of the country is at least a quack, and at worst an enemy to the Republic."

actually "busted" more trusts than TR did. In one celebrated instance in 1907, Roosevelt even gave his personal blessing to J. P. Morgan's plan to have U.S. Steel absorb the Tennessee Coal and Iron Company, without fear of antitrust reprisals. When Taft then launched a suit against U.S. Steel in 1911, the political reaction from TR was explosive.

Caring for the Consumer

Roosevelt backed a noteworthy measure in 1906 that benefited both corporations and consumers. Big meat packers were being shut out of certain European markets because some American meat—from the small packinghouses, claimed the giants—had been found to be tainted. Foreign governments were even threatening to ban all American meat imports by throwing out the good beef with the bad botulism.

At the same time, American consumers hungered for safer canned products. Their appetite for reform was whetted by Upton Sinclair's sensational novel *The Jungle*, published in 1906. Sinclair intended his revolting tract to focus attention on the plight of the workers in the big canning factories, but instead he appalled the public with his description of disgustingly unsanitary food products. (As he put it, he aimed for the nation's heart, but hit its stomach.) The book described in noxious detail the filth, disease, and putrefaction in Chicago's damp, ill-ventilated slaughterhouses. Many readers, including Roosevelt, were so sickened that for a time they found meat unpalatable. The president was moved by the loathsome mess in Chicago to appoint a special investigating commission, whose cold-blooded report almost outdid Upton Sinclair's novel. It related how piles of poisoned rats, rope ends, splinters, and other debris were scooped up and canned as potted ham. A cynical jingle ran:

> Mary had a little lamb,
>   And when she saw it sicken,
> She shipped it off to Packingtown,
>   And now it's labeled chicken.

Backed by a nauseated public, Roosevelt induced Congress to pass the Meat Inspection Act of 1906. It decreed that the preparation of meat shipped over state lines would be subject to federal inspection from corral to can. Although the

Sausage-Making, c. 1906   *White-jacketed inspectors like these on the right made some progress in cleaning up the septic slaughterhouses after the passage of the Meat Inspection Act in 1906. (Brown Brothers.)*

largest packers resisted certain features of the act, they grudgingly accepted it as an opportunity to drive their smaller, fly-by-night competitors out of business. At the same time, they could receive the government's seal of approval on their exports. As a companion to the Meat Inspection Act, the Pure Food and Drug Act of 1906 was designed to prevent the adulteration and mislabeling of foods and drugs.

Earth Control

Wasteful Americans, assuming that their natural resources were inexhaustible, had looted and polluted their incomparable domain with unparalleled speed and greed. Westerners were

> In his annual message to Congress (1907), Roosevelt declared prophetically: "We are prone to speak of the resources of this country as inexhaustible; this is not so. The mineral wealth of the country, the coal, iron, oil, gas, and the like, does not reproduce itself, and therefore is certain to be exhausted ultimately; and wastefulness in dealing with it to-day means that our descendants will feel the exhaustion a generation or two before they otherwise would."

especially eager to accelerate the destructive process, for they panted to build up the country, and the environmental consequences be hanged. But even before the end of the nineteenth century, far-visioned leaders saw that such a squandering of the nation's birthright would have to be halted or America would sink from resource richness to despoiled squalor.

A first feeble step toward conservation had been taken with the Desert Land Act of 1877, under which the federal government sold arid land cheaply on condition that the purchaser irrigate the thirsty soil within three years. More successful was the Forest Reserve Act of 1891, authorizing the president to set aside public forests as national parks and other reserves. Under this statute some 46 million acres of magnificent trees were rescued from the lumberman's saw in the 1890s and preserved for posterity. The Carey Act of 1894 distributed federal land to the states on condition that it be irrigated and settled. The law led to the cultivation of about a million barren acres, in a happy marriage of desert and water.

A new day in the history of conservation dawned with the advent of Roosevelt. Huntsman, naturalist, rancher, lover of the great outdoors, he was appalled by the pillaging of timber and mineral resources. Other dedicated conservationists, notably Gifford Pinchot, head of the federal Division of Forestry, had broken important ground before him. But Roosevelt seized the banner of leadership and charged into the fray with all the weight of his prestige, his energy, his firsthand knowledge, and his slashing invective.

High Point for Conservation *Conservationist Roosevelt and famed naturalist-conservationist John Muir visit Glacier Point, on the rim of Yosemite Valley, California. In the distance is Yosemite Falls; a few feet behind Roosevelt is a sheer drop of 3,254 feet. (Historical Pictures Service, Chicago.)*

Sunrise, Yosemite Valley, by Albert Bierstadt *A German-born artist, Bierstadt romanticized the already awesome beauty of the American West. (Courtesy Amon Carter Museum, Fort Worth, Texas.)*

The thirst of the desert still unslaked, Congress responded to the whip of the Rough Rider by passing the Newlands Act of 1902. Washington was authorized to collect money from the sale of public lands in the sun-baked western states and then use these funds for the development of irrigation projects. Settlers repaid the cost of reclamation from their now-productive soil, and the money was put into a revolving fund to finance more such enterprises. The giant Roosevelt Dam, constructed on Arizona's Salt River, was appropriately dedicated by Roosevelt in 1911. Thanks to this epochal legislation, dozens of dams were thrown across virtually every major western river in the ensuing decades.

Roosevelt pined to preserve the nation's shrinking forests. By 1900 only about a quarter of the once-vast virgin timberlands remained standing. Lumbermen had already logged off most of the first-growth timber from Maine to Michigan, and the sharp thud of their axes was beginning to split the silence in the great fir forests of the Pacific slope. Roosevelt proceeded to set aside in federal reserves some 125 million acres, or almost three times the acreage thus

Gifford Pinchot, a foremost conservationist in the Roosevelt administration, wrote: "The object of our forest policy is not to preserve the forests because they are refuges for the wild creatures of the wilderness, but the making of prosperous homes. Every other consideration comes as secondary. . . . The test of utility . . . implies that no lands will be permanently reserves which can serve the people better in any other way."

Loggers in the State of Washington, 1912 *It took the sweat and skill of many men to conquer a giant Douglas fir like this one. An ax-wielding "sniper" had rounded the edges of this log so that a team of oxen, driven by a "bullwhacker," could more easily drag it out of the woods along a "skid road." Skid road (sometimes corrupted as skid row) was also a name for the often-sleazy sections of logging towns, where loggers spent their time in the off-season. (Culver Pictures, Inc.)*

saved from the saw by his three predecessors. He similarly earmarked millions of acres of coal deposits, as well as water resources useful for irrigation and power. To set a shining example, in 1902 he banned Christmas trees from the White House.

> Campaigning in Kansas in 1910, ex-President Roosevelt said: *"Of all the questions which can come before this nation, short of its existence in a great war, there is none which compares in importance with the great central task of leaving this land even a better land for our descendants than it is for us, and training them into a better race to inhabit the land and pass it on. Conservation is a great moral issue, for it involves the patriotic duty of insuring the safety and continuance of the nation."*

Conservation, including reclamation, may have been Roosevelt's most enduring tangible achievement. The superactive president took conservation out of the conversation stage, threw the force of his colorful personality behind it, dramatized it, and aroused public opinion to a constructive crusade. Conservation under Roosevelt became almost a religion; its more truly scientific stages were to come in later decades.

But the dynamic TR's concept of conservation went beyond the simple sentiment of "woodman-spare-that-tree." Intelligent use, not esthetic preservation, was Roosevelt's first priority. Under him, professional foresters and engineers developed a policy of multiple-use resource management. They sought to combine recreation, sustained-yield logging, watershed protection, and summer stock-grazing on the same expanse of federal land.

Rational use of resources meant large-scale

and long-term planning, as well as efficient administrative techniques. Roosevelt's conservation program, like many of his business policies, meant working hand in glove with the biggest resource users. The one-man-and-a-mule logger, or the one-man-and-a-dog sheepherder, could not be counted upon to cooperate with the new resources bureaucracy. The little fellow was inevitably shouldered aside, in the interests of efficiency, by the combined strength of big business and big government.

The "Roosevelt Panic" of 1907

Roosevelt was handily elected president "in his own right" in 1904 and entered his new term buoyed up by his enormous personal popularity—the cuddly "teddy bear" honored one of his bear-hunting exploits (when he saved the life of a cub), and children piped vigorously on whistles modeled on his famous teeth. Yet the conservative Republican bosses considered him as dangerous and unpredictable as a rattlesnake. They grew increasingly restive as Roosevelt in his second term called ever more loudly for regulating the corporations, taxing incomes, and protecting workers. Roosevelt, meanwhile, had partly defanged himself after his election in 1904 by announcing that under no circumstances would he be a candidate for a third term. This was a tactical blunder, for the power of the king wanes when the people know he will be dead in four years.

Roosevelt suffered a sharp setback in 1907, when a short but punishing panic descended on Wall Street. The financial flurry featured frightened "runs" on banks, suicides, and criminal indictments against speculators.

The financial world hastened to blame Roosevelt for the storm. It cried that this "quack" had unsettled industry with his boat-rocking tactics. Conservatives damned him as "Theodore the Meddler" and branded the current distress the "Roosevelt panic." The hot-tempered president lashed back at his critics when he accused "certain malefactors of great wealth" of having deliberately engineered the monetary crisis to force the government to relax its assaults on trusts.

Fortunately, the panic of 1907 paved the way for long-overdue fiscal reforms. Precipitating a currency shortage, the flurry laid bare the need for a more elastic medium of exchange. In a crisis of this sort, the hard-pressed banks were unable to increase the volume of money in circulation, and those with ample reserves were reluctant to lend to their less fortunate sisters. Congress in 1908 responded by passing the Aldrich-Vreeland Act, which authorized national banks to issue emergency currency backed by various kinds of collateral. The path was thus smoothed for the epochal Federal Reserve Act of 1913.

The Rough Rider Thunders Out

Still warmly popular in 1908, Roosevelt could easily have won a second presidential nomination and almost certainly the election. But he felt bound by his impulsive postelection promise after his victory in 1904.

The departing president thus naturally sought a successor who would carry out "my policies." The man of his choice was amiable, ample-girthed, and huge-framed (6 feet tall; 1.83 meters) William Howard Taft, secretary of

Taft Campaigning *A powerful voice was a political necessity in the pre-electronic age. (United Press International Photo.)*

TR Engineers Taft's Nomination at Chicago
(Harding in the Brooklyn Eagle, 1908.)

war and a mild progressive. As an heir apparent, he had often been called upon in Roosevelt's absence to "sit on the lid"—all 350 pounds (159 kilograms) of him. At the Republican convention of 1908 in Chicago, Roosevelt used his control of the party machinery—the "steamroller"—to push through Taft's nomination on the first ballot. Three weeks later, in mile-high Denver, in the heart of silver country, the Democrats nominated twice-beaten William Jennings Bryan.

The dull campaign of 1908 featured the rotund Taft and the now-balding "Boy Orator" both trying to claim the progressive Roosevelt mantle. The solid Judge Taft read cut-and-dried speeches while Bryan griped that Roosevelt had stolen his policies from the Bryanite camp. The prosperous voters chose stability with Roosevelt-endorsed Taft, who polled 321 electoral votes to 162 for Bryan. The victor's popular count was 7,675,320 to 6,412,294. The election's only surprise came from the Socialists,

who amassed 420,793 votes for Eugene V. Debs, the hero of the Pullman strike of 1894.

Roosevelt, ever in the limelight, left soon after the election for a lion hunt in Africa. His numerous enemies clinked glasses while toasting "Health to the lions," and a few irreverently prayed that some lion would "do its duty." But TR survived, still bursting with energy at the age of fifty-one in 1909.

Roosevelt was branded by his adversaries as a wild-eyed radical, but his reputation as an eater of errant industrialists now seems inflated. He fought many a sham battle, and the number of laws that he inspired was certainly not in proportion to the amount of noise he emitted. He was often under attack from the reigning business lords, but the more enlightened of them knew that they had a friend in the White House. Roosevelt should be remembered first and foremost as the cowboy who started to tame the bucking bronco of adolescent capitalism, thus ensuring it a long adult life.

TR's enthusiasm and perpetual youthfulness, like an overgrown Boy Scout's, appealed to the young of all ages. "You must always remember," a British diplomat cautioned his colleagues, "that the president is about six." He served as a political lightning rod to protect capitalists against popular indignation—and against socialism, which Roosevelt regarded as "ominous." He strenuously sought the middle road between unbridled individualism and paternalistic collectivism.

Several other contributions of Roosevelt lasted beyond his presidency. First, he greatly enlarged the power and prestige of the presidential office—and masterfully developed the technique of using the big stick of publicity as a political bludgeon. Second, he helped to shape the progressive movement and beyond it the liberal reform campaigns later in the century. His Square Deal, in a sense, was the grandfather of the New Deal later launched by his fifth cousin, Franklin D. Roosevelt.

Finally, to a greater degree than any of his predecessors, TR opened the eyes of Americans to the fact that they shared the world with other nations. As a great power they had fallen heir to responsibilities—and had been seized by ambitions—from which there was no escaping.

Taft: A Round Peg in a Square Hole

William Howard Taft, with his ruddy complexion and upturned mustache, at first inspired widespread confidence. "Everybody loves a fat man," the saying goes, and the jovial Taft, with "mirthquakes" of laughter bubbling up from his abundant abdomen, was personally popular. He had graduated second in his class at Yale and had established an enviable reputation as a lawyer and judge, though widely regarded as hostile to labor unions. He had been a trusted administrator under Roosevelt—in the Philippines, at home, and in Cuba, where he had served capably as a troubleshooter.

But "good old Will" suffered from lethal political handicaps. Roosevelt had led the conflicting elements of the Republican party by the sheer force of his personality. Taft, in contrast, had none of the arts of a dashing political leader and none of Roosevelt's zest for the fray. Recoiling from the clamor of controversy, he generally adopted an attitude of passivity toward Congress. He was a poor judge of public opinion, and his candor made him a chronic victim of "foot-in-mouth" disease.

"Peaceful Bill" was no doubt a mild progressive, but at heart he was more wedded to the status quo than to change. Significantly, his cabinet did not contain a single representative of the party's "insurgent" wing, which was on fire for reform of current abuses, especially the tariff.

President William H. Taft (1857–1930) *A conservative lawyer-judge, Taft was handicapped by following the dominating Theodore Roosevelt. About two weeks after taking over the presidency, he wrote to "My dear Theodore," that "When I am addressed as 'Mr. President,' I turn to see whether you are not at my elbow." (Brown Brothers.)*

The Dollar Goes Abroad as a Diplomat

The brand of "dollar diplomacy" was stamped, somewhat unfairly, on the foreign policy of the Taft administration. This concept had two sides: (1) using foreign policy to protect Wall Street dollars invested abroad and (2) using Wall Street dollars to uphold foreign policy. The first aspect was grossly overplayed by Taft's critics; the second aspect was widely misunderstood.

Though ordinarily lethargic, Taft bestirred himself to use the lever of American investments to boost American diplomacy. Washington warmly encouraged Wall Street bankers to sluice their surplus dollars into foreign areas of strategic concern to the United States, especially in the Far East and in the regions that might menace the Panama Canal. Otherwise, investors from rival powers, such as Germany, might take advantage of financial chaos and secure a lodgment inimical to Uncle Sam's interests, both physical and commercial. New York bankers would thus strengthen American defenses and foreign policies, while bringing further prosperity to their homeland—and to themselves. The almighty dollar thereby supplanted the big stick.

China's Manchuria was the object of Taft's most spectacular effort to inject the reluctant dollar into the Far Eastern theater. Newly ambitious Japan and imperialistic Russia, recent foes, controlled the railroads of this strategic province. President Taft saw in the Manchurian railway monopoly a possible strangulation of Chinese economic interests and a consequent slamming of the Open Door in the faces of United States merchants. In 1909 Secretary of State Knox blunderingly proposed that a group of American and foreign bankers buy the Manchurian railroads and then turn them over to China under a self-liquidating arrangement. Both Japan and Russia, unwilling to be jockeyed out of their dominant position, bluntly rejected Knox's overtures. Taft was showered with ridicule.

Another dangerous new trouble spot was the revolution-riddled Caribbean—now virtually a Yankee lake. Hoping to head off trouble, Washington urged Wall Street bankers to pump dollars into the financial vacuums in Honduras and Haiti to keep out foreign funds. The United States, under the Monroe Doctrine, would not permit foreign nations to intervene, and consequently it had some moral obligation to interfere financially to prevent economic and political chaos.

Again necessity was the mother of armed Caribbean intervention. Sporadic disorders in palm-fronded Cuba, Honduras, and the Dominican Republic brought American forces to these countries to restore order. A revolutionary upheaval in Nicaragua, perilously close to the nearly completed canal, resulted in the landing of twenty-five hundred marines in 1912. (See map, p. 661.)

Taft the Trustbuster

Taft managed to gain some fame as a smasher of monopoly. The ironic truth is that the colorless Taft brought 90 suits against the trusts during his 4 years in office, as compared with some 44 for Roosevelt in 7 1/2 years.

By fateful happenstance the most sensational judicial actions during the Taft regime came in 1911. In that year the Supreme Court ordered the dissolution of the mighty Standard Oil Company, which was judged to be a combination in restraint of trade in violation of the Sherman Anti-Trust Act of 1890. At the same time, the Court handed down its famous "rule of reason." This doctrine held that only those combinations that "unreasonably" restrained trade were illegal. This fine-print proviso ripped a huge hole in the government's antitrust net.

Even more explosively, in 1911 Taft decided to press an antitrust suit against the United States Steel Corporation. This initiative infuriated Roosevelt, who had personally been involved in one of the mergers that prompted the suit. Once Roosevelt's protégé, President Taft was increasingly taking on the role of his antagonist. The stage was being set for a bruising confrontation.

Taft Splits the Republican Party

Lowering the barriers of the high protective tariff—the "Mother of Trusts"—was high on the agenda of the progressive members of the Republican party, and they at first thought they had a friend and ally in Taft. True to his campaign promises to reduce tariffs, Taft called Congress into special session in March 1909. The House proceeded to pass a moderately reductive bill, but senatorial reactionaries, led by Senator Aldrich of Rhode Island, tacked on hundreds of upward tariff revisions. Only such items as hides, sea moss, and canary-bird seed were left on the duty-free list.

After much handwringing, Taft signed the Payne-Aldrich Bill, thus betraying his campaign promises and outraging the progressive wing of his party, heavily drawn from the Midwest. Taft rubbed salt in the wound by proclaiming it "the best bill that the Republican party ever passed."

Taft revealed a further knack for shooting himself in the foot in his handling of conservation. The portly president was a dedicated conservationist, and his contributions actually equaled or surpassed those of Roosevelt. He set up the Bureau of Mines to control mineral resources, rescued millions of acres of western coal lands from exploitation, and protected water-power sites from private development.

But those praiseworthy accomplishments were largely erased in the public mind by the noisy Ballinger-Pinchot quarrel that erupted in 1910. When Secretary of the Interior Ballinger opened public lands in Wyoming, Montana, and Alaska to corporate development, he was sharply criticized by Gifford Pinchot, chief of the Agriculture Department's Division of Forestry and a stalwart Rooseveltian. When Taft dismissed Pinchot on the narrow grounds of insubordination, a storm of protest arose from conservationists and from Roosevelt's friends, who were legion. The whole unsavory episode further widened the growing rift between the president and the former president, one-time bosom friends.

The reformist wing of the Republican party was now up in arms. It had been aroused mostly by the unpopular Payne-Aldrich Tariff and by White House support for Ballinger. Taft was being pushed increasingly into the embrace of the standpat Old Guard. When he deserted the progressives in their attack on the

Taft the Golfer Hits Tariff Ball *Actually, he flubbed the ball. Contemporary cartoon.*

Taft Pleads for Lower Tariff
TR glares from the wall, and the Big Stick gathers cobwebs. One congressman wrote that Taft was "a well-meaning man who was born with two left feet." (Johnson in the Philadelphia North American, 1909.)

> *Roosevelt, who preached the doctrine of the "strenuous life," practiced it until almost the end. In 1913 he sent a political message on a still-preserved phonograph recording to the Boy's Progressive League: "Don't flinch, don't foul, and hit the line hard."*

leading Old Guard mouthpiece in the House of Representatives, the coarse and profane Speaker, "Uncle Joe" Cannon, the breach was complete.

By the spring of 1910, the Grand Old Party was split wide open, owing largely to the clumsiness of Taft. A suspicious TR returned triumphantly to New York in June 1910 and shortly thereafter stirred up a tempest. Unable to keep silent, he took to the stump at Osawatomie, Kansas, and shocked the Old Guard with a flaming speech. The doctrine that he proclaimed—popularly known as the "New Nationalism"—urged the national government to increase its power to remedy economic and social abuses.

Weakened by these internal divisions, the Republicans lost badly in the congressional elections of 1910. In a victory of landslide proportions, the Democrats emerged with 228 seats, leaving the once-dominant Republicans with only 161. In a further symptom of the reforming temper of the times, a Socialist representative, Austrian-born Victor L. Berger, was elected from Milwaukee.* The Republicans, by virtue of holdovers, retained the Senate, 51 to 41, but the insurgents in their midst were numerous enough to make that hold precarious.

The Taft-Roosevelt Rupture

The insurgent uprising in Republican ranks had now blossomed into a full-fledged revolt. Early in 1911 the National Progressive Republican League was formed, with the fiery, white-maned Senator La Follette of Wisconsin its

---

*He was eventually denied his seat in 1919, during a wave of antired hysteria.

leading candidate for the Republican presidential nomination. The assumption was that Roosevelt, an anti–third termer, would not permit himself to be "drafted."

But the restless Rough Rider began to change his views about third terms as he saw Taft, hand in glove with the hated Old Guard, discard "my policies." In February 1912 Roosevelt formally wrote to seven state governors that he was willing to accept the Republican nomination. His reasoning was that the third-term tradition applied to three *consecutive elective* terms. Exuberantly he cried, "My hat is in the ring!" and "The fight is on and I am stripped to the buff!"

Roosevelt forthwith seized the Progressive banner, while La Follette, who had served as a convenient pathbreaker, was protestingly elbowed aside. Girded for battle, the Rough Rider clattered into the presidential primaries then being held in many states. He shouted through half-clenched teeth that the president had fallen under the thumb of the reactionary bosses and that, although Taft "means well, he means well feebly." The once-genial Taft, now in a fighting mood, retorted by branding Roosevelt supporters "emotionalists and neurotics."

"Where Will He Land?" (Steele in the Denver *Post,* February, 1912.)

Roosevelt the Take-Back Giver   *(Knecht in the Evansville [Indiana] Courier.)*

A Taft-Roosevelt explosion was near in June 1912, when the Republican convention met in Chicago. The Rooseveltites, who were about 100 delegates short of winning the nomination, challenged the right of some 250 Taft delegates to be seated. Most of these contests were arbitrarily settled in favor of Taft, whose supporters held the throttle of the convention steamroller.

The Roosevelt adherents, crying "fraud" and "naked theft," in the end refused to vote, and Taft triumphed.

Roosevelt, the good sportsman, proved to be a poor loser. Having tasted for once the bitter cup of defeat, he was now on fire to lead a third-party crusade.

Varying Viewpoints

Debate about progressivism has revolved around a question that is simple to ask but devilishly difficult to answer: Who were the progressives? It was once taken for granted that progressive reformers were simply the heirs of the Jeffersonian-Jacksonian-Populist reform tradition; they were the oppressed and downtrodden common people who finally erupted in wrath and demanded their due. In his influential *Age of Reform*, Richard Hofstadter debunked that view. Progressive leaders, he argued, were middle-class people whose pocketbooks were not threatened by emerging industrialism but whose social status was jeopardized. "Status anxiety" thus prompted these people to become reformers, and their psychological motivation tended to render many of their efforts quirky and ineffectual.

By contrast, "New Left" writers, notably Gabriel Kolko, argue that progressivism was dominated by older business elites who successfully perverted "reform" to their own conservative ends. Still other scholars, such as Samuel P. Hays and Robert H. Wiebe, suggest that the progressives were members of a newly emergent social class possessed of the new techniques of scientific expertise and organizational know-how. In this view, progressivism was not a struggle of the people *versus* the "interests," nor a confused campaign by status-threatened reformers, nor a conservative coup d'état. The movement was simply an effort to rationalize and modernize many social institutions ("reform without a fight"). Yet the argument that progressives paved the way to a scientific, bureaucratic future is severely qualified by Otis Graham's study showing that less than half the surviving progressives approved the later reforms of the New Deal. Where did the progressives—and progressivism—go?

Select Readings

Primary Source Documents

Lincoln Steffens' *The Shame of the Cities** (1904) is an exemplary muckraking document, as is Upton Sinclair's notorious novel *The Jungle* (1906). For a less than gracious assessment of the muckrakers, see Theodore Roosevelt, "The Man with the Muckrake," *Putnam's Monthly and The Critic*, vol. I (October 1906), pp. 42–43.* A revealing account of municipal politics is George Washington Plunkitt's *Plunkitt of Tammany Hall** (1905). See also the decision of the Supreme Court on state bakery regulations in *Lochner* v. *New York*, 198 U.S. 45 (1905). Oliver Wendell Holmes, Jr.'s thundering dissent in the *Lochner* case is reprinted in Richard Hofstadter, *Great Issues in American History*.

Secondary Sources

A brief introduction is John W. Chambers, *The Tyranny of Change: America in the Progressive Era, 1900–1917* (1980). Perceptive interpretations are Samuel P. Hays, *The Response to Industrialism, 1885–1914* (1957); Robert H. Wiebe, *The Search for Order* (1967); and Richard Hofstadter, *The Age of Reform* (1955). Valuable analyses of progressivism at the state level include George Mowry's *The California Progressives* (1951); Richard McCormick's exceptionally good *From Realignment to Reform: Political Change in New York State, 1893–1910* (1981); and David Thelen's study of Wisconsin, *The New Citizenship* (1972). David Chalmers analyzes *The Muckrake Years* (1974). Especially provocative are James Weinstein, *The Corporate Ideal in the Liberal State* (1968), and Gabriel Kolko, *The Triumph of Conservatism* (1963). Consult also Robert Wiebe, *Businessmen and Reform* (1962), and Alfred D. Chandler, Jr., *The Visible Hand* (1977). On pure food and drugs,

see Oscar E. Anderson, Jr., *The Health of a Nation: Harvey H. Wiley and the Fight for Pure Food* (1958), and James H. Young, *Toadstool Millionaires* (1961). Other social issues of importance are treated in James H. Timberlake, *Prohibition and the Progressive Movement* (1963); David J. Rothman, *Conscience and Convenience: The Asylum and Its Alternatives in Progressive America* (1980); Roy Lubove, *The Progressives and the Slums* (1962); Allen F. Davis, *Spearheads for Reform: The Social Settlements and the Progressive Movement, 1890–1914* (1967); James Patterson, *America's Struggle against Poverty, 1900–1980* (1981); David B. Tyack, *The One Best System: A History of American Urban Education* (1974); and Jack Hall, *Juvenile Reform in the Progressive Era* (1971). Municipal reform is the subject of Martin J. Schiesl, *The Politics of Efficiency* (1977); and two useful anthologies, Bruce Stave, ed., *Urban Bosses, Machines and Progressive Reformers* (1972), and Blaine A. Brownell and Warren E. Stickle, eds., *Bosses and Reformers* (1973). On conservation see Samuel P. Hays, *Conservation and the Gospel of Efficiency* (1959); Elmo Richardson, *The Politics of Conservation* (1962); and James Penick, Jr., *Progressive Politics and Conservation* (1968). Socialism is discussed in Nick Salvatore, *Eugene V. Debs: Citizen and Socialist* (1982); James Weinstein, *The Decline of Socialism in America, 1912–1925* (1967); and Mari Jo Buhle, *Women and American Socialism, 1897–1920* (1981). Another perspective on women in this period is given in Rosalind Rosenberg, *Beyond Separate Spheres* (1982). The Taft era is summarized in Paolo Coletta, *The Presidency of William Howard Taft* (1973). See also Norman Wilensky, *Conservatives in the Progressive Era* (1965), and James Holt, *Congressional Insurgents and the Party System, 1909–1916* (1968). Otis Graham traces the progressive legacy in *Encore for Reform: The Old Progressives and the New Deal* (1967).

34
Wilsonian Progressivism at Home and Abroad

> This is not a day of triumph; it is a day of dedication. Here muster not the forces of party, but the forces of humanity. . . . I summon all honest men, all patriotic, all forward-looking men, to my side. God helping me, I will not fail them, if they will but counsel and sustain me!
>
> Thomas Woodrow Wilson, Inaugural Address, 1913

The Emergence of Dr. Thomas Woodrow Wilson

Office-hungry Democrats—the "outs" since 1897—were jubilant over the disruptive Republican brawl at Chicago. If they could come up with an outstanding reformist leader, they had an excellent chance to win the White House. Such a leader appeared in Dr. Woodrow Wilson, once a mild conservative but now a militant progressive. Beginning professional life as a brilliant academic lecturer on government, he had risen in 1902 to the presidency of Princeton University, where he had achieved some sweeping educational reforms.

Wilson entered politics in 1910 when New Jersey bosses, needing a respectable "front"

candidate for the governorship, offered him the nomination. They expected to lead the academic novice by the nose, but to their surprise, Wilson waged a passionate reform campaign in which he assailed the "predatory" trusts and promised to return state government to the people. Riding the crest of the progressive wave, the "Schoolmaster in Politics" was swept into office.

Once in the governor's chair, Wilson drove through the legislature a sheaf of forward-looking measures that made reactionary New Jersey one of the more liberal states. Filled with righteous indignation, Wilson revealed irresistible reforming zeal, burning eloquence, superb powers of leadership, and a refreshing habit of appealing over the heads of the scheming bosses to the sovereign people. Now a figure of national eminence, Wilson was being widely mentioned for the presidency.

When the Democrats met at Baltimore in 1912, Wilson was nominated on the forty-sixth ballot, aided by William Jennings Bryan's switch to his side. The Democrats gave Wilson a strong reform platform to run on, including calls for antitrust legislation, monetary changes, and tariff reductions.

The "Bull Moose" Campaign of 1912

Surging events had meanwhile been thrusting Roosevelt to the fore as a candidate for the presidency on a third-party Progressive Republican ticket. The fighting ex-cowboy, angered by his recent rebuff, was eager to lead the charge. A pro-Roosevelt Progressive convention, with about two thousand delegates from forty states, assembled in Chicago during August 1912. Dramatically symbolizing the rising political status of women, as well as Progressive support for the cause of social justice, settlement-house pioneer Jane Addams placed Roosevelt's name in nomination for the presidency. Roosevelt was applauded tumultuously as he cried in a vehement speech, "We stand at Armageddon, and we battle for the Lord!" The hosanna spirit of a religious revival meeting suffused the convention, as the hoarse delegates sang "Onward, Christian Soldiers" and "Battle Hymn of the Republic." William Allen White, the caustic Kansas journalist, later wrote, "Roosevelt bit me and I went mad."

Fired-up Progressives entered the campaign with righteousness and enthusiasm. Roosevelt boasted that he felt "as strong as a bull moose," and, the bull moose took its place with the jackass and the elephant in the American political zoo. As one poet whimsically put it:

> I want to be a Bull Moose,
> And with the Bull Moose stand
> With antlers on my forehead
> And a Big Stick in my hand.

Roosevelt and Taft were bound to slit each other's political throats; by dividing the Republican vote, they guaranteed a Democratic victory. The two antagonists tore into each other as only former friends can. "Death alone can take me out now," cried the once-jovial Taft, as he branded Roosevelt a "dangerous egotist" and a "demagogue." Roosevelt, fighting mad, assailed Taft as a "fathead" with the brain of a "guinea pig."

Beyond the clashing personalities, the overshadowing question of the 1912 campaign was which of two varieties of progressivism would prevail—Roosevelt's New Nationalism or Wilson's New Freedom. Both men favored a more active governmental role in economic and social affairs, but they disagreed sharply over specific strategies. Roosevelt preached the theories spun out by the progressive thinker Herbert Croly in his book *The Promise of American Life* (1910). Croly and TR both favored continued consolidation of trusts and labor unions, paralleled by the growth of powerful regulatory agencies in Washington. Roosevelt and his "bull moosers" also campaigned for woman suffrage and a broad program of social welfare, including mini-

GOP Divided by Bull Moose Equals Democratic Victory (Puck, 1912.)

Woodrow Wilson Campaigning, 1912 *A magnificent orator, Wilson used his speaking skills to advantage in the three-way race for the White House in 1912. (Brown Brothers.)*

mum-wage laws and "socialistic" social insurance. Clearly the Progressives looked forward to the kind of activist welfare state that Franklin Roosevelt's New Deal would one day make a reality.

Wilson's New Freedom, by contrast, favored small enterprise, entrepreneurship, and the free functioning of unregulated and unmonopolized markets. The Democrats shunned social-welfare proposals and pinned their economic faith on competition—on the "man on the make," as Wilson put it. The keynote of Wilson's campaign was not regulation but fragmentation of the big industrial combines, chiefly by means of vigorous enforcement of the antitrust laws. The election of 1912 thus offered the voters a choice not merely of policies but of political and economic philosophies—a rarity in United States history.

The heat of the campaign cooled a bit when, in Milwaukee, Roosevelt was shot in the chest by a fanatic. The Rough Rider suspended active campaigning for more than two weeks after delivering, with bull moose gameness and a bloody shirt, his scheduled speech.

Woodrow Wilson: A Minority President

Former professor Wilson won handily, with 435 electoral votes and 6,296,547 popular votes. The "third-party" candidate, Roosevelt, finished second, receiving 88 electoral votes and 4,118,571

The Presidential Vote, 1912

CANDIDATE	PARTY	ELECTORAL VOTE	POPULAR VOTE	APPROXIMATE PERCENTAGE
Woodrow Wilson	Democratic	435	6,296,547	41%
Theodore Roosevelt	Progressive	88	4,118,571	27
William H. Taft	Republican	8	3,486,720	23
Eugene V. Debs	Socialist	—	900,672	6
E. W. Chafin	Prohibition	—	206,275	1
A. E. Reimer	Socialist-Labor	—	28,750	.2

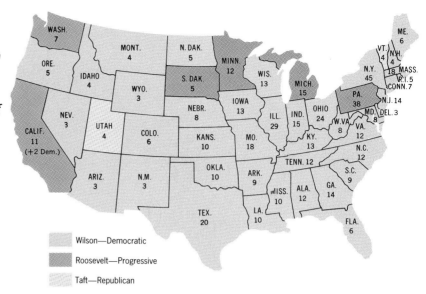

Presidential Election of 1912 (with electoral vote by state) The Republican split surely boosted Wilson to victory, as he failed to win a clear majority in any state outside the old Confederacy. The election gave the Democrats solid control of the White House and both houses of Congress for the first time since the Civil War.

popular votes. Taft won only 8 paltry electoral votes and 3,486,720 popular votes.

The election figures are fascinating. Wilson, with only 41 percent of the popular vote, was clearly a minority president, though his party won a majority in Congress. His popular total was actually smaller than Bryan had amassed in any of his three defeats, despite the increase in population. Taft and Roosevelt together polled over a million and a quarter more votes than the Democrats. Progressivism rather than Wilson was the runaway winner. Though the Democratic total obviously included many conservatives in the solid South, still the combined progressive vote for Wilson and Roosevelt exceeded the tally of the more conservative Taft. To the progressive tally must be added some support for the Socialist candidate, hardy Eugene V. Debs, who rolled up 900,672 votes, or more than twice as many as he had netted four years earlier. Starry-eyed Socialists dreamed of being in the White House within eight years.

Roosevelt's lone-wolf course was tragic both for himself and for his former Republican associates. Perhaps, to rephrase William Allen White, he had bitten himself and gone mad. The Progressive party, which was primarily a one-man show, had no future because it had elected few candidates to state and local offices.

Without patronage plums to hand out to the faithful workers, death by slow starvation was inevitable. Yet the Progressives made a tremendous showing for a hastily organized third party and helped spur the enactment of many of their pet reforms by the Wilsonian Democrats.

As for the Republicans, they were thrust into unaccustomed minority status in Congress for the next six years and were frozen out of the White House for eight years. Taft himself had a fruitful old age. He taught law for eight pleasant years at Yale University and in 1921 became chief justice of the United States Supreme Court—a job for which he was far more happily suited than the presidency.

Wilson: The Idealist in Politics

(Thomas) Woodrow Wilson, the second Democratic president since 1861, looked like the ascetic intellectual he was, with his clean-cut features, pinched-on eyeglasses, and trim figure (5 feet 11 inches and 179 pounds; 1.8 meters, 81.2 kilograms). Born in Virginia shortly before the Civil War, and reared in Georgia and the Carolinas, the professor-politician was the first man from one of the seceded southern states to

Wilson and Taft *The outgoing President greets the incumbent at Wilson's inauguration, 1913. (Library of Congress.)*

reach the White House since Zachary Taylor, sixty-four years earlier.

The impact of Dixieland on young "Tommy" Wilson was profound. He sympathized with the Confederacy's gallant attempt to win its independence, a sentiment that partly inspired his ideal of self-determination for minority peoples in other countries. Steeped in the traditions of Jeffersonian democracy, he shared Jefferson's faith in the masses—if they were properly informed.

Son of a Presbyterian minister, Wilson was reared in an atmosphere of fervent piety. He later used the presidential pulpit to preach his inspirational political sermons. A moving orator, Wilson could rise on the wings of spiritual power to soaring eloquence. Skillfully using a persuasive voice, he relied not on arm-waving but on sincerity and moral appeal. As a lifelong student of finely chiseled words, he turned out to be a "phraseocrat" who coined many noble epigrams. Someone has remarked that he was born halfway between the Bible and the dictionary, and never got away from either.

A profound student of government, Wilson believed that the chief executive should play a

dynamic role. He was convinced that Congress could not function properly unless the president, like a kind of prime minister, got out in front and provided leadership. He enjoyed dramatic success, both as governor and as president, in appealing over the heads of legislators to the sovereign people.

Splendid though Wilson's intellectual equipment was, he suffered from serious defects of personality. Though jovial and witty in private, he could be cold and standoffish in public. Incapable of unbending and acting the showman, like "Teddy" Roosevelt, he lacked the common touch. He loved humanity in the mass rather than the individual in person. His academic background caused him to feel the most at home with scholars, although he had to work

President Woodrow Wilson (1856–1924) *A realist-idealist, Wilson wrote some six years before coming to the White House: "The President is at liberty, both in law and conscience, to be as big a man as he can." Fighting desperately later for the League of Nations and breaking himself down, he said: "I would rather fail in a cause that I know some day will triumph than to win in a cause that I know some day will fail." (The White House Historical Association.)*

with politicians. An austere and somewhat arrogant intellectual, he looked down his nose through pince-nez glasses upon lesser minds, including journalists. He was especially intolerant of stupid senators, whose "bungalow" minds made him "sick."

Wilson's burning idealism—especially his desire to reform ever-present wickedness—drove him forward faster than lesser spirits were willing to go. His sense of moral righteousness was such that he often found compromise difficult; black was black, wrong was wrong, and one should never compromise with wrong. President Wilson's Scotch Presbyterian ancestors had passed on to him an inflexible stubbornness. When convinced that he was right, he would break before he would bend, unlike Theodore Roosevelt.

Wilson Tackles the Tariff

Few presidents have arrived at the White House with a clearer program than Wilson's or one destined to be so completely achieved. The new president called for an all-out assault on what he called "the triple wall of privilege": the tariff, the banks, and the trusts.

He tackled the tariff first, summoning Congress into special session in early 1913. In a precedent-shattering move, he did not send his presidential message over to the Capitol to be read loudly by a bored clerk, as had been the custom since Jefferson's day. Instead, he appeared in person before a joint session of Congress and presented his appeal with stunning eloquence and effectiveness.

Moved by Wilson's aggressive leadership, the House swiftly passed the Underwood Tariff Bill, which provided for a substantial reduction of rates. When a swarm of lobbyists descended on the Senate, seeking to disembowel the bill, Wilson promptly issued a fighting message to the people, urging them to hold their elected representatives in line. The tactic worked. The force of public opinion, aroused by the president's oratory, secured final approval late in 1913 of the bill Wilson wanted.

The new Underwood tariff substantially reduced import fees. It also was a landmark in tax legislation. Under authority granted by the recently ratified Sixteenth Amendment, Congress enacted a graduated income tax, beginning with a modest levy on incomes over $3,000 (then considerably higher than the average family's income). By 1917 revenue from the income tax shot ahead of receipts from the tariff. This gap has since been vastly widened.

Wilson Battles the Bankers

A second bastion of the "triple wall of privilege" was the antiquated and inadequate banking and currency system, long since outgrown by the Republic's lusty economic expansion. The country's financial structure, still creaking along under the Civil War National Banking Act, revealed glaring defects. Its most serious shortcoming, as exposed by the panic of 1907, was the inelasticity of the currency. Banking reserves were heavily concentrated in New York and a handful of other large cities and could not be mobilized in times of financial stress into areas that were badly pinched.

In 1908 Congress had authorized an investigation headed by a mossback banker, Republican Senator Aldrich. Three years later Aldrich's special commission recommended a gigantic bank with numerous branches—in effect, a third Bank of the United States.

For their part, Democratic banking reformers heeded the findings of a House committee chaired by Congressman Arsene Pujo, which traced the tentacles of the "money monster" into the hidden vaults of American banking and business. President Wilson's confidant, progressive-minded Massachusetts attorney Louis D. Brandeis, further fanned the flames of reform with his incendiary though scholarly book *Other People's Money and How the Bankers Use It* (1914).

In June 1913, in a second dramatic personal appearance before both houses of Congress, the president delivered a stirring plea for sweeping reform of the banking system. He ringingly endorsed Democratic proposals for a decentralized bank in government hands, as opposed to Republican demands for a huge private bank with fifteen branches.

Again appealing to the sovereign people, Wilson scored another triumph. In 1913 he signed the epochal Federal Reserve Act, the most important piece of economic legislation between the Civil War and the New Deal. The new Federal Reserve Board, appointed by the president, oversaw a nationwide system of twelve regional reserve districts, each with its own central bank. Though these regional banks were actually bankers' banks, owned by member financial institutions, the final authority of the Federal Reserve Board guaranteed a substantial measure of public control. The board was also empowered to issue paper money—"Federal Reserve Notes"—backed by commercial paper, such as the promissory notes of businesspeople. Thus, the amount of money in circulation could be swiftly increased as needed for the legitimate requirements of business.

The Federal Reserve Act was a red-letter achievement. It carried the nation with flying banners through the financial crises of the World War of 1914–1918. Without it, the Republic's progress toward the modern economic age would have been seriously retarded.

The President Tames the Trusts

Without pausing for breath, Wilson pushed toward the last remaining rampart in the "triple wall of privilege"—the trusts. Early in 1914 he

"Vindicated," 1914 *(Fitzpatrick in the St. Louis* Post-Dispatch.*)*

Organization of Holding Companies *It should be borne in mind that the voting stock of a corporation is often only a fraction of the total stock.*

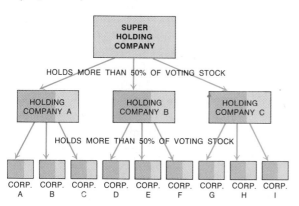

again went before Congress in a personal appearance that still carried drama.

Nine months and thousands of words later, Congress responded with the Federal Trade Commission Act of 1914. The new law empowered a presidentially appointed commission to turn a searchlight on industries engaged in interstate commerce, such as the meat packers. The commissioners were expected to crush monopoly in the cradle by rooting out unfair trade practices, including unlawful competition, false advertising, mislabeling, adulteration, and bribery.

The knot of monopoly was further cut by the Clayton Anti-Trust Act of 1914. It lengthened the shopworn Sherman Act's list of business practices that were deemed objectionable, including price discrimination and interlocking directorates (whereby the same individuals served as directors of supposedly competing firms).

The Clayton Act also conferred long-overdue benefits on labor. Conservative courts had unexpectedly been ruling that trade unions fell under the antimonopoly restraints of the Sherman Act. A classic case involved striking hatmakers in Danbury, Connecticut, who were assessed triple damages of more than $250,000, which resulted in the loss of their savings and homes. The Clayton Act therefore sought to exempt labor and agricultural organizations from antitrust prosecution, while explicitly legalizing strikes and peaceful picketing.

Union leader Samuel Gompers hailed the act as the Magna Charta of labor because it legally lifted human labor out of the category of "a commodity or article of commerce." But the rejoicing was premature, as conservative judges in later years continued to clip the wings of the union movement.

"Too Cowed [Proud] to Fight," 1916 *Congress passes Adamson Eight-Hour Act. (Harding in the Brooklyn Eagle.)*

Wilsonian Progressivism at High Tide

Energetically scaling the "triple wall of privilege," Woodrow Wilson had treated the nation to a dazzling demonstration of vigorous presidential leadership. He proved nearly irresistible in his first eighteen months in office. For once, a political creed was matched by deed, as the progressive reformers racked up victory after victory.

Standing at the peak of his powers at the head of the progressive forces, Wilson pressed ahead with further reforms. The Federal Farm Loan Act of 1916 made credit available to farmers at low rates of interest—as long demanded by the Populists. The Warehouse Act of 1916 authorized loans on the security of staple crops—another Populist idea. Other laws benefited rural America by providing for highway construction and the establishment of agricultural extension work in the state colleges.

Sweaty laborers also made gains as the progressive wave foamed forward. Sailors, treated brutally from cat-o'-nine-tails days onward, were given relief by the La Follette Seamen's Act of 1915. It required decent treatment and a living wage on American merchant ships. One unhappy result of this well-intentioned law was the crippling of America's merchant marine, as shippers recoiled from the high-wage freight rates on American vessels.

Wilson further helped the workers with the Workingmen's Compensation Act of 1916, granting assistance to federal civil-service employees during periods of disability. In the same year the president approved an act restricting child labor on products flowing into interstate commerce, though the standpat Supreme Court soon invalidated the law. Railroad workers, numbering about 1.7 million, were not sidetracked. The Adamson Act of 1916 established an eight-hour day for all employees on trains in interstate commerce, with extra pay for overtime.

Wilson earned the enmity of businesspeople and bigots but endeared himself to progressives when in 1916 he nominated for the Supreme Court the prominent reformer Louis D. Brandeis—the first Jew to be called to the high bench. Yet even Wilson's progressivism had its limits, and it clearly stopped short of better treatment for blacks. The southern-bred Wilson actually presided over accelerated segregation in the federal bureaucracy. When a delegation of black leaders personally protested to him, the schoolmasterish president virtually froze them out of his office.

Despite these limitations, Wilson knew that to be reelected in 1916, he needed to identify himself clearly as the candidate of progressivism. He appeased businesspeople by making conservative appointments to the Federal Reserve Board and the Federal Trade Commission, but he devoted most of his energies to cultivating progressive support. Wilson's election in 1912 had been something of a fluke, owing largely to the Taft-Roosevelt split in Republican ranks. To remain in the White House, he would have to woo the bull moose voters into the Democratic fold.

New Directions in Foreign Policy

In one important area, Wilson chose not to answer the trumpet call of the bull moosers. In contrast to Roosevelt and even Taft, Wilson recoiled from an aggressive foreign policy. Hating imperialism, he was repelled by TR's big stickism. Suspicious of Wall Street, he detested the so-called dollar diplomacy of Taft.

In office only a week, Wilson declared war on dollar diplomacy. He proclaimed that the government would no longer offer special support to American investors in Latin America and China. Shivering from this Wilsonian bucket of cold water, American bankers pulled out of the Taft-engineered six-nation loan to China the next day.

In a similarly self-denying vein, Wilson persuaded Congress in early 1914 to repeal the Panama Canal Tolls Act of 1912, which had exempted American coastwise shipping from tolls and thereby provoked sharp protests from injured Britain. The president further chimed in with the anti-imperial song of Bryan and other Democrats when he signed the Jones Act in 1916. It granted to the Philippines the boon of territorial status and promised independence as soon as a "stable government" could be established. That happy day came thirty years later, on July 4, 1946.

Wilson also partially defused a menacing crisis with Japan in 1913. The California legislature, still seeking to rid the Golden State of Japanese settlers, prohibited them from owning land. Tokyo, understandably irritated, lodged

The United States in the Caribbean *This map explains why many Latin Americans accused the United States of turning the Caribbean Sea into a Yankee lake. It also suggests that Uncle Sam was much less "isolationist" in his own back yard than he was in faraway Europe or Asia.*

A New Sentry in the Caribbean Sea," 1916 *Uncle Sam sits on the three main Virgin Islands. (Courtesy of Dayton News.)*

In 1917 Wilson purchased from Denmark the Virgin Islands, in the West Indies, tightening the grip of Uncle Sam in these shark-infested waters. Increasingly the Caribbean Sea, with its vital approaches to the now-completed Panama Canal, was taking on the earmarks of a Yankee preserve.

Moralistic Diplomacy in Mexico

Rifle bullets whining across the southern border served as a constant reminder that all was not quiet in Mexico. For decades Mexico had been sorely exploited by foreign investors in oil, railroads, and mines. By 1913 American capitalists had sunk about a billion dollars into the underdeveloped but richly endowed country, and about fifty thousand United States citizens had taken up residence south of the Rio Grande.

But if Mexico was rich, the Mexicans were poor. Fed up with their miserable lot, they at last revolted. Their revolution took an ugly turn in 1913, when a conscienceless clique murdered the popular new revolutionary president and installed General Huerta, a full-blooded Indian, in the president's chair. All this chaos accelerated a massive migration of Mexicans to the United States. More than a million Spanish-speaking newcomers tramped across the southern border in the first three decades of the twentieth century. Settling mostly in Texas, New Mexico, Arizona, and California, they swung picks building highways and railroads or followed the fruit harvests as pickers. Though

vigorous protests. At Fortress Corregidor, in the Philippines, American gunners were put on around-the-clock alert. But when Wilson dispatched Secretary of State William Jennings Bryan to plead with the California legislature to soften its stand, tensions eased somewhat.

Revolution-rent Haiti soon forced Wilson to eat some of his anti-imperialist words. The climax of the disorders came in 1914–1915, when an outraged populace literally tore to pieces the brutal Haitian president. Wilson reluctantly dispatched marines to protect American lives and property. In 1916 he stole a page from Roosevelt's corollary to the Monroe Doctrine and concluded a treaty with Haiti providing for United States supervision of finances and the police. In the same year, he sent the leather-necked marines to the riot-rocked Dominican Republic, and that debt-cursed land came under the shadow of the American eagle's wings.

Congressman Humphrey voiced Republican complaints against Wilson's Mexican policy in 1916: "It is characterized by weakness, uncertainty, vacillation, and uncontrollable desire to intermeddle in Mexican affairs. He has not had the courage to go into Mexico nor the courage to stay out. . . . I would either go into Mexico and pacify the country or I would keep my hands entirely out of Mexico. If we are too proud to fight, we should be too proud to quarrel. I would not choose between murderers."

often segregated in Spanish-language enclaves, they helped to create a unique borderland culture that blended Mexican and American folkways.

The revolutionary bloodshed also menaced American lives and property in Mexico. Cries for intervention burst from the lips of American jingoes. Prominent among those chanting for war was the influential chain-newspaper publisher William Randolph Hearst, whose views presumably were colored by his ownership of a Mexican ranch larger than Rhode Island. Yet President Wilson stood firm against demands for intervention. It was "perilous," he declared, to determine foreign policy, "in the terms of material interest."

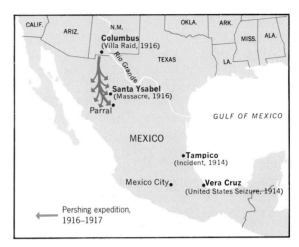

The United States and Mexico, 1914–1917

Uncle Sam Refuses Huerta's Blood-Drenched Hand
Republican journalist George Harvey wrote: "What legal or moral right has a President of the United States to say who shall or shall not be President of Mexico?" (New York Daily Tribune, 1913.)

But though he refused to intervene, Wilson also refused to recognize officially the murderous government of "that brute" Huerta, even though most foreign powers acknowledged Huerta's bloody-handed regime. "I am going to teach the South American republics to elect good men," the former schoolmaster declared. He put his munitions where his mouth was in 1914, when he allowed American arms to flow to Huerta's principal rivals, white-bearded Venustiano Carranza and swarthy Francisco ("Pancho") Villa.

The Mexican volcano erupted at the Atlantic seaport of Tampico in April 1914, when a small party of American sailors was arrested. The Mexicans promptly released the captives and apologized, but they refused the hotheaded American admiral's demand for a salute of twenty-one guns. Wilson, heavy-hearted but stubbornly determined to eliminate Huerta, asked Congress for authority to use force against Mexico. Before Congress could act, Wilson ordered the navy, which was seeking to intercept a German ship bearing arms to Huerta, to seize the Mexican port of Vera Cruz. Huerta as well as Carranza hotly condemned this high-handed Yankee intervention.

Just as a full-dress shooting conflict seemed inevitable, Wilson was rescued by an offer of mediation from the ABC Powers—Argentina, Brazil, and Chile. Huerta collapsed in July 1914 under pressure from within and without. He was succeeded by his arch-rival, Venustiano Carranza, still fiercely resentful of Wilson's military meddling. The whole sorry episode did not augur well for the future of United States–Mexican relations.

The sinister figure of "Pancho" Villa had meanwhile stolen the spotlight. A bloodthirsty combination of bandit and Robin Hood, he emerged as the chief rival of President Carranza, whom Wilson reluctantly supported with arms and diplomatic recognition. Villa displayed his hatred of the gringos in January 1916, when his followers killed eighteen United States citizens in cold blood at Santa Ysabel, Mexico. The culminating outrage occurred in March 1916, when Villistas shot up Columbus, New Mexico, leaving behind seventeen dead Americans.

General John J. ("Black Jack")* Pershing, a grim-faced and ramrod-erect veteran of the Cuban and Philippine campaigns, was ordered to break up the bandit band. His hastily organized force of several thousand horse-borne troops penetrated deep into rugged Mexico with surprising speed. They clashed with Carranza's forces and mauled the Villistas but missed capturing Villa himself. As the threat of war with Germany loomed larger, the invading army was withdrawn in January 1917.

Thorny Problems in Mexico *President Huerta clung to power for more than a year in 1913–1914, despite Woodrow Wilson's strong disapproval of his regime. (New York Public Library.)*

Thunder across the Sea

Europe's powder magazine, long smoldering, blew up in the summer of 1914, when the flaming pistol of a Serb patriot killed the heir to the throne of Austria-Hungary. An outraged Vienna government, backed by Germany, forthwith presented a stern ultimatum to neighboring Serbia.

An explosive chain reaction followed. Tiny Serbia, backed by its powerful Slav neighbor Russia, refused to bend the knee sufficiently. The Russian czar began to mobilize his ponderous war machine, menacing Germany on the east, even as his ally, France, confronted Germany on the west. In alarm, the Germans struck suddenly at France through unoffending Belgium; their objective was to knock their ancient enemy out of action so that they would have a free hand to repel Russia. Great Britain, its coastline jeopardized by the assault on Belgium, was sucked into the conflagration on the side of France.

Almost overnight most of Europe was locked in a fight to the death. On one side were arrayed the Central Powers: Germany and Austria-Hungary, and later Turkey and Bulgaria. On the other side were the Allies, principally

---

*So called from his earlier service as an officer with the crack black Tenth Cavalry.

Pancho Villa with His Rag-Tag Army in Mexico, c. 1916 *His daring, impetuosity, and horsemanship made Villa a hero to the masses of northern Mexico. Yet he proved to be a violent and poorly directed force against social abuses, and he was assassinated in 1923. (Brown Brothers.)*

France, Britain, and Russia, and later Japan and Italy.

Americans thanked God for the ocean moats and self-righteously congratulated themselves on having had ancestors wise enough to have abandoned the hell pits of Europe. America felt strong, snug, smug, and secure—but not for long.

A Precarious Neutrality

Peaceloving President Wilson, his grief over the war's outbreak compounded by the recent death of his wife, sorrowfully issued the routine neutrality proclamation and called on Americans to be neutral in thought as well as deed. But such scrupulous evenhandedness proved difficult.

Both sides wooed the United States, the great neutral in the West. The British enjoyed the boon of close cultural, linguistic, and economic ties with America and had the added advantage of controlling most of the transatlantic cables. Their censors sheared away war stories harmful to the Allies and drenched the United States with tales of German bestiality.

The Germans and the Austro-Hungarians counted on the natural sympathies of their transplanted countrymen in America. Including persons with at least one foreign-born parent,

people with blood ties to the Central Powers numbered some 11 million in 1914. Some of these recent immigrants expressed noisy sympathy for the fatherland, but most were simply grateful to be so distant from the fray.

Most Americans were anti-German from the outset. With his villainous upturned mustache, Kaiser Wilhelm II seemed the embodiment of

"The Great Wall," 1914 *The Monroe Doctrine is depicted as a protective shield. (Courtesy of Nashville Tennessean.)*

The Kaiser Ravishes Belgium *He had little to do with the so-called atrocities, but propagandists made him the arch-villain of the war. (New York* World, *1914.)*

arrogant autocracy, an impression strengthened by Germany's ruthless strike at neutral Belgium. German and Austrian agents further tarnished the image of the Central Powers in American eyes when they resorted to violence in American factories and ports. When a German operative in 1915 absentmindedly left his briefcase on a New York elevated car, its documents detailing plans for industrial sabotage were quickly discovered and publicized. American opinion, already ill disposed, was further inflamed against the kaiser and his fatherland. Yet the great majority of Americans earnestly hoped to stay out of the horrible war.

America Earns Blood Money

When Europe burst into flames in 1914, the United States was bogged down in a worrisome business recession. But as fate would have it, British and French war orders soon pulled American industry out of the morass of hard times and onto a peak of war-born prosperity. Part of this boom was financed by American bankers, notably the Wall Street firm of J. P. Morgan and Company, which eventually advanced to the Allies the enormous sum of $2.3 billion during the period of American neutrality. The Central Powers protested bitterly against the immense trade between America and the Allies, but this traffic did not in fact violate the international neutrality laws. Germany was technically free to trade with the United States. It was prevented from doing so not by American policy but by geography and the British navy. Trade between Germany and America had to move across the surface of the Atlantic; but

Principal Foreign Elements in the United States (Census of 1910; Total U.S. Population: 91,972,266)

COUNTRY OF ORIGIN		FOREIGN-BORN	NATIVES WITH TWO FOREIGN-BORN PARENTS	NATIVES WITH ONE FOREIGN-BORN PARENT	TOTAL
Central Powers	Germany	2,501,181	3,911,847	1,869,590	8,282,618
	Austria-Hungary	1,670,524	900,129	131,133	2,701,786
Allied Powers	Great Britain	1,219,968	852,610	1,158,474	3,231,052
	(Ireland)*	1,352,155	2,141,577	1,010,628	4,504,360
	Russia	1,732,421	949,316	70,938	2,752,675
	Italy	1,343,070	695,187	60,103	2,098,360
TOTAL (for all foreign countries, including those not listed)		13,345,545	12,916,311	5,981,526	32,243,282

*Ireland was not yet independent.

U.S. Exports to Belligerents, 1914–1916

BELLIGERENT	1914	1915	1916	PERCENTAGE RELATION OF 1916 FIGURE TO 1914 FIGURE
Britain	$594,271,863	$911,794,954	$1,526,685,102	257%
France	159,818,924	369,397,170	628,851,988	393
Italy*	74,235,012	184,819,688	269,246,105	364
Germany	344,794,276	28,863,354	288,899	0.08

*Italy joined the Allies in April 1915.

the British controlled the sea-lanes, and they threw a noose-tight blockade of mines and ships across the North Sea, gateway to German ports. Over the unavailing protests of American shippers, farmers, and manufacturers, the British began forcing American vessels off the high seas and into their ports. This harassment of American shipping proved highly effective, as trade between Germany and the United States virtually ceased.

Hard-pressed Germany did not tamely consent to being starved out. In retaliation for the British blockade, in February 1915 Berlin announced a submarine war area around the British Isles. The submarine was a weapon so new that existing international law could not be made to fit it. The old rule that a warship must stop and board a merchantman could hardly apply to submarines, which could easily be rammed or sunk if they surfaced.

The cigar-shaped marauders posed a dire threat to the United States—so long as Wilson insisted on maintaining America's neutral rights. Berlin officials declared that they would try not to sink *neutral* shipping, but they

The Fatherland, *the chief German-American propaganda newspaper in the United States, cried: "We [Americans] prattle about humanity while we manufacture poisoned shrapnel and picric acid for profit. Ten thousand German widows, ten thousand orphans, ten thousand graves bear the legend 'Made in America.'"*

warned that mistakes would probably occur. Wilson now determined on a policy of calculated risk. He would continue to claim profitable neutral trading rights, while hoping that no high-seas incident would force his hand to grasp the sword of war. Setting his peninsular jaw, he emphatically warned Germany that it would be held to "strict accountability" for any attacks on American vessels or citizens.

The German U-boats meanwhile began their deadly work. In the first months of 1915, they

British Military Area (declared November 3, 1914), and German Submarine War Zone (declared February 4, 1915)

Advertisement from the New York Herald, May 1, 1915 *Six days later the Lusitania was sunk. Note the German warning. (The Granger Collection.)*

sank about ninety ships in the war zone. Then the submarine issue became acute when the British passenger liner *Lusitania* was torpedoed and sank off the coast of Ireland on May 7, 1915, with the loss of 1,198 lives, including 128 Americans.

The *Lusitania* was carrying forty-two hundred cases of small-arms ammunition, a fact the Germans used to justify the sinking. But Americans were swept by a wave of shock and anger

A German U-Boat *This deadly new weapon rendered useless the existing rules of naval warfare and eventually forced the United States into declaring war against Germany in 1917. (UPI/Bettmann Newsphotos.)*

OCEAN STEAMSHIPS.

CUNARD

EUROPE VIA LIVERPOOL
LUSITANIA

Fastest and Largest Steamer
now in Atlantic Service Sails
SATURDAY, MAY 1, 10 A. M.
Transylvania, Fri., May 7, 5 P.M.
Orduna, - - Tues.,May 18, 10 A.M.
Tuscania, - - Fri., May 21, 5 P.M.
LUSITANIA, Sat., May 29, 10 A.M.
Transylvania, Fri., June 4, 5 P.M.

Gibraltar—Genoa—Naples—Piraeus
S.S. Carpathia, Thur., May 13, Noon

ROUND THE WORLD TOURS
Through bookings to all principal Ports
of the World.
Company's Office, 21-24 State St., N. Y.

NOTICE!

TRAVELLERS intending to embark on the Atlantic voyage are reminded that a state of war exists between Germany and her allies and Great Britain and her allies; that the zone of war includes the waters adjacent to the British Isles; that, in accordance with formal notice given by the Imperial German Government, vessels flying the flag of Great Britain, or of any of her allies, are liable to destruction in those waters and that travellers sailing in the war-zone on ships of Great Britain or her allies do so at their own risk.

IMPERIAL GERMAN EMBASSY

WASHINGTON, D. C., APRIL 22, 1915.

at this act of "mass murder" and "piracy." The eastern United States, closer to the war, seethed with talk of fighting, but the rest of the country showed a strong distaste for hostilities. The peaceloving Wilson had no stomach for leading a disunited nation into war. He well remembered the mistake in 1812 of his fellow Princetonian, James Madison. Instead, by a series of increasingly strong notes, Wilson attempted to bring the German warlords sharply to book. Even this measured approach was too much for Secretary of State Bryan, who resigned rather than sign a protest note that might spell shooting. But Wilson resolutely stood his ground. "There is such a thing," he said, "as a man being too proud to fight." This kind of talk incensed war-thirsty Theodore Roosevelt. The Rough Rider assailed the "flubdubs" and "mollycoddles" who heeded the "weasel words" of the pacifistic professor in the White House.

Yet Wilson, sticking to his verbal guns, made some diplomatic progress. After another British liner, the *Arabic*, was sunk in August 1915, with the loss of two American lives, Berlin reluctantly agreed not to sink unarmed and unresisting passenger ships *without warning*.

This pledge appeared to be violated in March 1916, when the Germans torpedoed a French passenger steamer, the *Sussex*. The infuriated Wilson informed the Germans that unless they renounced the inhuman practice of sinking merchant ships without warning, he would break diplomatic relations—an almost certain prelude to war.

Germany reluctantly knuckled under to President Wilson's *Sussex* ultimatum, agreeing not to sink passenger ships and merchant vessels without giving warning. But the Germans attached a long string to their *Sussex* pledge: the United States would have to persuade the Allies to modify what Berlin regarded as their illegal blockade. This, obviously, was something that Washington could not do. Wilson promptly accepted the German pledge, without accepting the "string." He thus won a temporary but precarious diplomatic victory—precarious because Germany could pull the string whenever it chose, and the president might suddenly find himself hauled over the cliff of war.

The President Leads a Preparedness Parade *After the Lusitania sinking in May 1915, Wilson dropped his opposition to an American military buildup. In 1916 he toured the country to urge support for preparedness. (Brown Brothers.)*

Wilson Wins Reelection in 1916

Against this ominous backdrop, the presidential campaign of 1916 gathered speed. Both the bull moose Progressives and the Republicans met in Chicago. The Progressives uproariously renominated Theodore Roosevelt, but the Rough Rider, who loathed Wilson and all his works, had no stomach for splitting the Republicans again and ensuring the reelection of his hated rival. In refusing to run, he sounded the death knell of the Progressive party.

Roosevelt's Republican admirers also clamored for "Teddy," but the Old Guard detested the renegade who had ruptured the party in 1912. Instead, they drafted Supreme Court Justice Charles Evans Hughes, a cold intellectual who had achieved a solid liberal record when he was governor of New York. The Republican platform condemned the Democratic tariff, assaults on the trusts, and Wilson's wishy-washiness in dealing with both Mexico and Germany.

The richly bewhiskered Hughes ("an animated feather duster") left the bench for the campaign stump, where he was not at home. In anti-German areas of the country, he assailed Wilson for not standing up to the kaiser, while

A Wilson Campaign Truck, 1916 *The reelected President would soon have to eat the slogan about keeping out of war. (UPI/Bettmann Newsphotos.)*

in isolationist areas he took a softer line. This fence-straddling operation led to the jeer, "Charles Evasive Hughes."

Hughes was further plagued by Roosevelt, who was delivering a series of skin-'em-alive speeches against "that damned Presbyterian hyprocrite Wilson." Frothing for war, TR privately sneered at Hughes as a "whiskered Wilson"; the only difference between the two, he said, was "a shave."

Wilson, nominated by acclamation at the Democratic convention in St. Louis, ignored Hughes on the theory that one should not try to murder a man who is committing suicide. His campaign was built on the slogan "He Kept Us Out of War."

Democratic orators warned that by electing Charles Evans Hughes, the nation would be electing a fight—with a certain frustrated Rough Rider leading the charge. A Democratic

Presidential Election of 1916 (with electoral vote by state) *Wilson was so worried about being a lame-duck President in a time of great international tensions that he drew up a plan whereby Hughes, if victorious, would be appointed Secretary of State, Wilson and the Vice-President would resign, and Hughes would thus succeed immediately to the Presidency.*

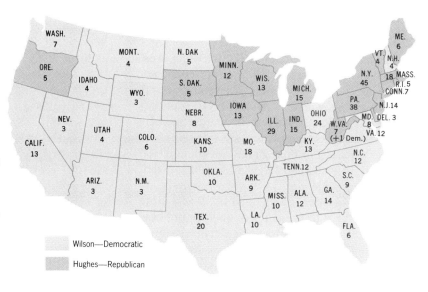

advertisement appealing to the American workingpeople read:

> You are Working;
> —Not Fighting!
> Alive and Happy;
> —Not Cannon Fodder!
> Wilson and Peace with Honor?
> or
> Hughes with Roosevelt and War?

On election day Hughes swept the East and looked like a surefire winner. Wilson went to bed that night prepared to accept defeat, while the New York newspapers displayed huge portraits of "The President-Elect—Charles Evans Hughes."

But the rest of the country turned the tide. Midwesterners and westerners, attracted by Wilson's progressive reforms and antiwar policies, flocked to the polls for the president. The final result, in doubt for several days, hinged on California, which Wilson carried by some 3,800 votes out of about a million cast.

Wilson barely squeaked through, with a final vote of 277 to 254 in the Electoral College, and

During the 1916 campaign J. A. O'Leary, the head of a pro-German and pro-Irish organization, sent a scorching telegram to Wilson condemning him for having been pro-British in approving war loans and ammunition traffic. Wilson shot back an answer: "Your telegram received. I would feel deeply mortified to have you or anybody like you vote for me. Since you have access to many disloyal Americans and I have not, I will ask you to convey this message to them." President Wilson's devastating and somewhat insulting response probably won for him more votes than it lost.

9,127,695 to 8,533,507 in the popular column. The prolabor Wilson had received strong support from the working class and from ex–bull moosers, whom Republicans failed to lure back into their camp. Wilson had not specifically promised to keep the country out of war, but probably enough voters relied on such implicit assurances to ensure his victory. Their hopeful expectations were soon rudely shattered.

Varying Viewpoints

Wilson's achievement in realizing his New Freedom reforms in 1913 and 1914 undeniably constitutes one of the most noteworthy examples of presidential leadership. Yet the precise character of Wilson's accomplishment remains something of a puzzle. Some historians conclude that Wilson, having beaten Roosevelt in the election, proceeded to implement Roosevelt's program. These scholars point especially to the New Nationalist flavor of the Federal Reserve Act and the Federal Trade Commission. Other analysts claim that the Clayton Anti-Trust Act was faithful in following Wilson's campaign pledges and reflected his "real" political beliefs. Still other critics, noting especially Wilson's appointment of businesspeople to the new governmental bodies, charge that the rhetoric of progressive reform was simply a cloak for the consolidation of conservative rule. This dispute again illustrates the difficulty of defining *progressive*.

No issue, however, reveals the ambiguity of that term as well as the debate over the nation's entry into World War I. Was Wilson's conduct of foreign policy consistent with the principles of his "New Freedom"? Was United States intervention in the brutal European war a repudiation of the progressive program or the logical culmination of it? These questions continue to spark controversy today.

Select Readings

Primary Source Documents

Theodore Roosevelt's "Acceptance Speech"* at the Progressive convention of 1912, and Woodrow Wilson's collection of campaign speeches, *The New Freedom** (1913), give the substance and flavor of the critical 1912 campaign. Louis D. Brandeis, *Other People's Money and How the Bankers Use It** (1914), expresses the philosophy of a key Wilson adviser. On the *Lusitania* incident, see *Foreign Relations of the United States*, 1915, Supplement, pp. 394–395, 420.*

Secondary Sources

See the titles by John W. Chambers, Samuel P. Hays, Richard Hofstadter, and Robert H. Wiebe cited in Chapter 33. John M. Cooper, Jr.'s, *The Warrior and the Priest* (1983) deftly contrasts Wilson and Theodore Roosevelt. Biographies of Wilson include Arthur Link's five-volume *Wilson* (1947–1965) and John M. Blum's *Woodrow Wilson and the Politics of Morality* (1956). Particularly interesting is Alexander and Juliette George's psychological study, *Woodrow Wilson and Colonel House* (1956). For a sharply contrasting view, see Edwin A. Weinstein, *Woodrow Wilson: A Medical and Psychological Biography* (1981). The road to World War I finds comprehensive treatment in Ernest May, *The World War and American Isolation, 1914–1917* (1959), and Daniel M. Smith, *The Great Departure: The United States and World War I, 1914–1920* (1965). Consult also Ross Gregory, *The Origins of American Intervention in the First World War* (1971); John M. Cooper, Jr., *The Vanity of Power: American Isolation and the First World War, 1914–1917* (1969); and Patrick Devlin, *Too Proud to Fight: Woodrow Wilson's Neutrality* (1975). Special studies of value include Thomas A. Bailey and Paul B. Ryan, *The Lusitania Disaster* (1975); Jeffrey J. Safford, *Wilsonian Maritime Diplomacy* (1978); Ronald Radosh, *American Labor and Foreign Policy* (1969); and Burton I. Kaufman, *Efficiency and Expansion* (1974). For the European background see Laurence Lafore, *The Long Fuse* (1965), and Fritz Fisher, *Germany's Aims in the First World War* (1967). Social and intellectual currents are described in Henry F. May, *The End of American Innocence: A Study of the First Years of Our Own Time, 1912–1917* (1959).

35
The War to End War,
1917–1918

> The world must be made safe for democracy. Its peace must be planted upon the tested foundations of political liberty. We have no selfish ends to serve. We desire no conquest, no dominion. We seek no indemnities for ourselves, no material compensation for the sacrifices we shall freely make.
>
> Woodrow Wilson, War Message, April 2, 1917

War by Act of Germany

Destiny dealt cruelly with Woodrow Wilson. The lover of peace, as fate would have it, was forced to lead a hesitant and peaceloving nation into war. As the last days of 1916 slipped through the hourglass, the president made one final futile attempt to mediate between the embattled belligerents. On January 22, 1917, he delivered one of his most moving addresses, realistically declaring that only a negotiated "peace without victory" would prove durable.

Germany's warlords responded with a blow of the mailed fist. On January 31, 1917, they announced to an astonished world that they intended to wage *unlimited* submarine warfare, sinking *all* ships, including America's, in the war zone.

The Germans thus jerked viciously on the string they had attached to their *Sussex* pledge in 1916. Wilson, his bluff now called, broke diplomatic relations but refused to move toward war unless the Germans undertook "overt" acts against American lives and property. To defend American interests short of war, the president asked Congress for authority to arm American merchant ships. When a band of midwestern senators launched a filibuster to block the measure, Wilson denounced them as a "little group of willful men" who were rendering a great nation "helpless and contemptible." But their obstruction was a powerful reminder of the continuing strength of American isolationism.

"All the News That's Fit to Print."

The New York Times.

THE WEATHER
Fair, colder today; tomorrow warmer, probably rain; wind northwest.
For full weather report see Page 24.

VOL. LXVI...NO. 21,619.   ...   NEW YORK, TUESDAY, APRIL 3, 1917.—TWENTY-FOUR PAGES.   ONE CENT In New York City. | TWO CENTS New England and Middle States. | THREE CENTS Elsewhere.

PRESIDENT CALLS FOR WAR DECLARATION, STRONGER NAVY, NEW ARMY OF 500,000 MEN, FULL CO-OPERATION WITH GERMANY'S FOES

War! The depredations of the submarine finally forced Wilson's hand, and he asked Congress for a declaration of war on April 2, 1917. Four days later, after considerable debate and with 56 dissenting votes, Congress obliged the president. (The Granger Collection.)

Meanwhile, the sensational Zimmerman note was intercepted and published on March 1, 1917, to the outraged howls of Americans, especially westerners. German foreign secretary Zimmerman had secretly proposed a German-Mexican alliance, holding out to anti-Yankee Mexico the inducement of recovering Texas, New Mexico, and Arizona.

On the heels of this provocation came the long-dreaded "overt" acts in the Atlantic, where German U-boats sank four unarmed American merchant vessels in the first two weeks of March. As one Philadelphia newspaper observed, the "difference between war and what we have now is that now we aren't fighting back." Simultaneously came the rousing news that a revolution in Russia had toppled the cruel regime of the czars. America could now fight foursquare for democracy on the side of the Allies, without the black sheep of Russian despotism in the Allied fold.

Subdued and solemn, Wilson at last stood before a hushed joint session of Congress on the evening of April 2, 1917, and asked for a declaration of war. He had lost his gamble that America could pursue the profits of neutral trade without being sucked into the ghastly maelstrom. A myth developed in later years that America was dragged unwittingly into war by munitions makers and Wall Street bankers, desperate to protect their profits and loans. Yet the weapons merchants and financiers were already thriving, unhampered by wartime government restrictions and heavy taxation. Their slogan might well have been "Neutrality Forever." The simple truth is that British harassment of Amer-

ican commerce had been galling but endurable; Germany had resorted to the mass killing of civilians. The difference was like that between a gang of thieves and a gang of murderers. President Wilson had drawn a clear, if risky,

"I Dare You To Come Out" The Kaiser defies American rights, national honor, freedom of the seas, and international law. (Richards in the Philadelphia North American, 1917.)

line against the depredations of the submarine. The German people, in a last desperate throw of the dice, chose to cross it. In a figurative sense, America's war declaration of April 6, 1917, bore the unambiguous trademark "Made in Germany."

Wilsonian Idealism Enthroned

"It is a fearful thing to lead this great peaceful people into war," Wilson said in his war message. It was fearful indeed, not least of all because of the formidable challenge it posed to Wilson's leadership skills. Ironically, it fell to the scholarly Wilson, deeply respectful of American traditions, to shatter one of the most sacred of those traditions by entangling America in a distant European war.

How could the president arouse his countrymen to shoulder this unprecedented burden? For more than a century, they had prided themselves on their isolation from the periodic outbursts of militarized violence that afflicted the Old World. Since 1914 their pride had been reinforced by the lush profits gained through neutrality. German U-boats had now roughly shoved a wavering America into the abyss, but ominously, no fewer than six senators and fifty representatives (including the first congresswoman, Jeannette Rankin of Montana) had voted against the war resolution. Wilson could whip up no enthusiasm, especially in the landlocked Middle West, by fighting to make the world safe from the submarine. To unify his country, Wilson would have to proclaim more glorified aims.

Wilson's burning idealism led him instinctively to an inspired decision. Radiating the spiritual fervor of his Presbyterian ancestors, he declared the twin goals of "a war to end war" and a crusade "to make the world safe for democracy." Flourishing the sword of righteousness, Wilson virtually hypnotized the nation with his lofty ideals. He contrasted the selfish war aims of the other belligerents, Allied and enemy alike, with America's shining altruism. America, he preached, did not fight for the sake of riches or territorial conquest. The Republic sought only to shape an international or-

der in which democracy could flourish without fear of power-crazed autocrats and militarists.

In Wilsonian idealism, the personality of the president and the necessities of history were perfectly matched. The high-minded Wilson genuinely believed in the principles he so eloquently intoned. And probably no other appeal could have successfully converted the American people from their historic hostility to involvement in European squabbles. Americans, it seemed, could be either isolationists or crusaders, but nothing in between.

Wilson's appeal worked—perhaps too well. Holding aloft the torch of idealism, the president fired up the public mind to a fever pitch. "Force, force to the utmost, force without stint or limit," he cried, while the country responded less elegantly with "Hang the Kaiser." Lost on the gale was Wilson's earlier plea for "peace without victory."

Fourteen Potent Wilsonian Points

Wilson quickly came to be recognized as the moral leader of the Allied cause. He scaled a summit of inspiring oratory on January 8, 1918, when he delivered his famed Fourteen Points Address to an enthusiastic Congress. Though one of his primary purposes was to keep reeling Russia in the war, Wilson's eloquence inspired all the drooping Allies to make mightier efforts and demoralized the enemy governments by holding out alluring promises to their dissatisfied minorities.

The first five of the Fourteen Points were broad in scope. ① A proposal to abolish secret treaties pleased liberals of all countries. ② Freedom of the seas appealed to the Germans, as well as to Americans who distrusted British sea power. ③ A removal of economic barriers among nations was comforting to Germany, which feared postwar vengeance. ④ Reduction of armament burdens was gratifying to taxpayers everywhere. ⑤ An adjustment of colonial claims in the interests of both native peoples and the colonizers was reassuring to the anti-imperialists.

Other points among the fourteen proved to be no less seductive. They held out the promise of independence ("self-determination") to op-pressed minority groups, such as the Poles, millions of whom lay under the heel of Germany and Austria-Hungary. The capstone point, number fourteen, foreshadowed the League of Nations—an international organization that Wilson hoped would provide a system of collective security. Wilson earnestly prayed that this new scheme would effectively guarantee the political independence and territorial integrity of all countries, whether large or small.

Yet Wilson's appealing points, though raising hopes the world over, were not everywhere applauded. Certain leaders of the Allied nations, with an eye to territorial booty, were less than enthusiastic. Hard-nosed Republicans at home grumbled, and some of them openly sneered at the "fourteen commandments" of "God Almighty Wilson."

Anti-German Propaganda   *(Trustees of the Imperial War Museum, London.)*

Creel Manipulates Minds

Mobilizing the mind for war, both in America and abroad, was an urgent task facing the Washington authorities. For this purpose, the Committee on Public Information was created. It was headed by a youngish journalist, George Creel, who, though outspoken and tactless, was gifted with zeal and imagination. His job was to sell America on the war and sell the world on Wilsonian war aims.

The Creel organization, employing some 150,000 workers at home and overseas, proved that words were indeed weapons. It sent out an army of 75,000 "four-minute men"—often longer-winded than that—who delivered countless speeches containing much "patriotic pep."

Creel's propaganda took varied forms. Posters were splashed on billboards in the "Battle of the Fences," as artists "rallied to the colors." Millions of leaflets and pamphlets, which contained the most pungent Wilsonisms, were showered like confetti upon the world. Propaganda booklets with red-white-and-blue covers were printed by the millions.

Hang-the-Kaiser movies, carrying such titles as *The Kaiser, the Beast of Berlin* and *To Hell with the Kaiser*, revealed the "Hun" in his bloodiest colors. Arm-waving conductors by the thousands led huge audiences in songs that poured scorn on the enemy and glorified the "boys" in uniform.

The entire nation, catching the frenzied spirit of a religious revival, burst into song. This was undoubtedly America's singingest war. Most memorable was George M. Cohan's spine-tingling "Over There":

> Over there, over there
> Send the word, send the word over there,
> That the Yanks are coming, the Yanks are coming,
> The drums rum-tumming ev'rywhere.

Creel typified American war mobilization, which relied more on aroused passion and voluntary compliance than on formal laws. But he rather oversold the ideals of Wilson and led the world to expect too much. When the president proved to be a mortal and not a god, the result-

Hanging the Kaiser—A Favorite Sport *(Life, 1918.)*

ing disillusionment at home and abroad was disastrous.

Enforcing Loyalty and Stifling Dissent

German-Americans numbered over 8 million, counting those with at least one parent foreign-born, out of a total population of 100 million. On the whole they proved to be gratifyingly loyal. Yet rumormongers were quick to spread tales of spying and sabotage: even trifling epidemics of diarrhea were blamed on German agents. A few German-Americans were tarred, feathered, and beaten; in one extreme case a German Socialist in Illinois was lynched by a drunken mob.

As emotion mounted, hate hysteria swept the nation against Germans and things Germanic. Orchestras found it unsafe to present German-composed music, like that of Wagner or Beethoven. The teaching of the German language was shortsightedly discontinued in many high schools and colleges. Sauerkraut became "liberty cabbage," and hamburger became "liberty steak."

Both the Espionage Act of 1917 and the Sedition Act of 1918 reflected current fears about Germans and antiwar Americans. Especially visible among the nineteen hundred prosecutions undertaken under these laws were antiwar Socialists and members of the radical union Industrial Workers of the World (IWWs). Kingpin Socialist Eugene V. Debs was convicted under the Espionage Act in 1918 and sentenced to ten years in a federal penitentiary. IWW leader William D. ("Big Bill") Haywood and ninety-nine associates were similarly convicted. There was also mild press censorship, and some papers such as *The Masses* were denied mailing privileges.

These prosecutions form an ugly chapter in the history of American civil liberty. With the dawn of peace, presidential pardons were rather freely granted, like that given to Eugene Debs by President Harding in 1921. Yet a few victims lingered behind bars into the 1930s.

The Nation's Factories Go to War

Victory was no foregone conclusion, especially since the Republic, despite ample warning, was caught flat-footedly unready for its leap into global war. The pacifistic Wilson had only belatedly backed some mild preparedness measures beginning in 1915, including the creation of a civilian Council of National Defense to study problems of economic mobilization. He had also launched a shipbuilding program (as much to capture the belligerents' war-disrupted foreign trade as to anticipate America's possible entry into the war) and endorsed a modest beefing-up of the army, which with 100,000 regulars then ranked about fifteenth among the armies of the world, in the same category with Persia. It would take a herculean effort to mobilize America's daunting but disorganized resources and throw them into the field quickly enough to bolster the Allied war effort.

Towering obstacles confronted economic mobilizers. Sheer ignorance was among the biggest roadblocks. No one knew precisely how much steel or explosive powder the country was capable of producing. Old ideas also proved to be liabilities, as traditional fears of big government hamstrung efforts to orchestrate the economy from Washington. States' rights Democrats and businesspeople alike balked at federal economic controls, even though the embattled nation could ill afford the freewheeling, hit-or-miss chaos of the peacetime economy.

Late in the war, and after some bruising political battles, Wilson succeeded in imposing some order on this economic confusion. In March 1918 he appointed lone-eagle stock speculator Bernard Baruch to head the War Industries Board. But the War Industries Board never had more than feeble formal powers, and it was disbanded within days after the armistice. Even in a globe-girdling crisis, the American preference for *laissez-faire* and for a weak central government proved amazingly strong.

Perspiring workers were urged to put forth their best efforts, spurred by the slogan "Labor Will Win the War." Women were encouraged to enter industry and also agriculture, where they were called "farmerettes." Women's war work at

last prompted the president to endorse woman suffrage as "a vitally necessary war measure." Nearly a century of struggle was crowned with success when women received the right to vote with the passage of the Nineteenth Amendment in 1920. (For text, see the Appendix.) Tens of thousands of southern blacks were drawn to the North by the magnet of war industries—the large-scale beginnings of a migration of immense sociological significance. A "work or fight" rule, requiring all able-bodied males to be regularly employed in some useful occupation, was issued by the War Department in 1918. Fortunately for the Allied cause, Samuel Gompers and his powerful American Federation of Labor gave loyal support to the war effort.

Yet labor harbored grievances. Admittedly, the wages of 1914 had nearly doubled by 1918, but inflationary prices, boosted by war, feverishly kept pace with the wage scale. (Prices, too, nearly doubled between 1916 and 1920.) Not even the call of patriotism and Wilsonian idealism could stifle all labor disputes; during the conflict there were some six thousand strikes. The National War Labor Board, with

Women and War *The first World War created many new jobs for women, as in this factory producing artillery shells. But the war ended too quickly for many women to secure a permanent foothold in the workforce. (Photoworld.)*

Suffragists Picket the White House, 1917 *Militant feminists sometimes handcuffed themselves to the White House fence to dramatize their appeal to the President. (Library of Congress.)*

former President Taft as cochairman, was finally established as the supreme court for labor disputes. More than a thousand cases came before it.

Some of the most crippling labor sabotage was engineered by the left-wing IWWs, popularly known as the "I Won't Works" or "Wobblies." As transient laborers in such industries as fruit and lumber, the "Wobblies" were victims of some of the worst working conditions in the country. When they protested, many of the "Wobblies" were arrested, beaten up, or run out of town.

Forging a War Economy

Mobilization relied more on the heated emotions of patriotism than on the cool majesty of the laws. The largely voluntary and somewhat haphazard character of economic war organization testified eloquently to ocean-insulated

Food Administration Poster *(Hoover Institution, Stanford University, California.)*

America's safe distance from the fighting—as well as to the still-modest scale of government power in the progressive-era Republic.

As the larder of democracy, America had to feed itself and its allies. By a happy inspiration, the man chosen to head the Food Administration was the Quaker-humanitarian Herbert C. Hoover. He was already considered a hero because he had successfully led a massive charitable drive to feed the starving people of war-racked Belgium.

In common with other American war administrators, Hoover preferred to rely on voluntary compliance rather than on formal edicts. He deliberately rejected issuing ration cards, a practice used in Europe. Instead, he waged a whirlwind propaganda campaign through posters, billboards, newspapers, pulpits, and movies. To save food for export, Hoover proclaimed wheatless Wednesdays and meatless Tuesdays—all on a voluntary basis. Even children, when eating apples, were urged to be "patriotic to the core."

Food surpluses were piled up in still other ways. The country soon broke out in a rash of vegetable "victory gardens," as perspiring patriots hoed their way to victory in backyards or on vacant lots. Congress severely restricted the use of foodstuffs for manufacturing alcoholic beverages, and the war-born spirit of self-denial helped accelerate the wave of prohibition that was sweeping the country. Many leading brewers were German-descended, and this taint made the drive against alcohol all the more popular. The reformers' dream of a saloonless nation was finally achieved—temporarily—in 1919, with the passage of the Eighteenth Amendment, prohibiting all alcoholic drinks.

Thanks to the superheated patriotic wartime spirit, Hoover's voluntary approach worked, as farm production increased by one-fourth, and food exports to the Allies tripled in volume. Hoover's methods were widely imitated in other war agencies. The Fuel Administration exhorted Americans to save fuel with "heatless Mondays," "lightless nights," and "gasless Sundays." The Treasury Department sponsored monster parades and invoked slogans like "Halt the Hun" to promote four great Liberty Loan drives, followed by a Victory Loan campaign in 1919. Together, these efforts netted the then-fantastic sum of about $21 billion, or two-thirds of the current cost of the war to the United States. The remainder was raised by increased taxes, which, unlike the loan subscriptions, were obligatory. (The ultimate bill, including interest and veterans' benefits, mounted to some $112 billion.)

Pressures of various kinds, patriotic and otherwise, were used to sell bonds. The unfortunate German-American who could not display a Liberty Bond button might find his or her house bedaubed with yellow paint. A number of reluctant investors in war bonds were roughly handled, and there was at least one instance of a man who signed for a bond with a rope around his neck.

Despite the Wilson administration's preference for voluntary means of mobilizing the economy, the government on occasion reluctantly exercised its sovereign formal power, notably when it took over the nation's railroads following indescribable traffic snarls in late 1917. Washington also bestirred itself formidably to get its hands on ships. It seized enemy merchant vessels trapped in America's harbors and orchestrated a gigantic drive to construct new

"Making His Dollars Fight," 1917 *A German-American is forced to buy bonds. (Courtesy Baltimore American.)*

Miracles in Shipbuilding *(BBC Hulton Picture Library.)*

uphold freedom of the seas. It would continue to ship war materials to the Allies and supply them with loans, which finally totaled nearly $10 billion. But in April and May of 1917, the European associates laid their cards on the table. They confessed that they were scraping the bottom not only of their money chests but, more ominously, of their manpower barrels. A huge American army would have to be raised, trained, and transported, or the whole western front would collapse.

Conscription was the only answer to the need for raising an immense army with all possible speed. Wilson disliked a draft, as did many other Americans with Civil War memories; but he eventually accepted and eloquently supported conscription as a disagreeable and temporary necessity.

The proposed draft bill immediately ran into a barrage of criticism in Congress. A congress-

Navy Recruiting Poster, World War I *(The Granger Collection.)*

tonnage. A few concrete vessels were launched, including one appropriately named *Faith*. A wooden-ship program was undertaken, though after months of war, birds were still nesting in the trees from which the vessels were to be hammered.

The shipbuilding program eventually got into high gear, but it was largely too late to make a substantial contribution. More than half of the American troops who made it to Europe were transported on foreign ships. Once they went into battle, they fired mostly British and French artillery pieces and flew almost exclusively in British and French aircraft. Only in the next world war did the United States become the arsenal of democracy. In 1917–1918 the great gifts of America the Unready to the Allied cause were food, money, and above all, men.

Making Plowboys into Doughboys

Most citizens, at the outset, did not dream of sending a mighty force to France. As far as fighting went, America would use its navy to

A Universal Draft *The pre-war song "I Didn't Raise My Boy To Be a Soldier" was changed to "I Didn't Raise My Boy To Be a Slacker," which in turn inspired the cruel parody: "I Didn't Raise My Dog To Be a Sausage." (Chopin in the San Francisco* Examiner, *1917.)*

man from Missouri, deploring compulsion, cried out in protest that there was "precious little difference between a conscript and a convict." Prophets of doom predicted that on draft-registration day the streets would run red with blood. At length Congress—six weeks after declaring war—grudgingly got around to passing conscription.

The draft act required the registration of all males between the ages of eighteen and forty-five. No "draft dodger" could purchase his exemption or hire a substitute, as in the easygoing days of the Civil War, though there were many exemptions for men in key industries, such as shipbuilding.

The draft machinery, on the whole, worked effectively. Registration day proved to be a day of patriotic pilgrimages to flag-draped registra-

tion centers, and there was no shedding of blood, as some had gloomily predicted. Despite precautions, some 337,000 "slackers" escaped the draft, and about 4,000 conscientious objectors were excused.

Within a few frantic months the army was increased from about 200,000 men to over 4 million. For the first time women were admitted to the armed forces; some 11,000 to the navy and 269 to the marine corps.

Recruits were supposed to receive six months of training in America and two more months overseas. But so great was the urgency that many doughboys were swept swiftly into battle scarcely knowing how to handle a rifle, much less a bayonet.

Fighting in France—Belatedly

Russia's collapse underscored the need for haste. The communistic Bolsheviks, after seizing power, ultimately removed their beaten country from the "capitalistic" war early in 1918. This sudden defection released hundreds of thousands of battle-tested Germans for the front in France, where, for the first time in the war, they were developing a dangerous superiority in manpower.

Berlin's calculations as to American tardiness were surprisingly accurate. Germany had counted on knocking out Britain six months after the declaration of unlimited submarine warfare, long before America could get into the struggle. No really effective American fighting force reached France until about a year after Congress declared war. Berlin had also reckoned on the inability of the Americans to transport their army, assuming that they were able to raise one. Here again the German predictions were not far from the mark as shipping shortages plagued the Allies.

France gradually began to bustle with American "doughboys." The first trainees to reach the front were used as replacements in the Allied armies and were generally deployed in quiet sectors with the British and French. The newcomers soon made friends with the French girls—or tried to—and one of the most sung-

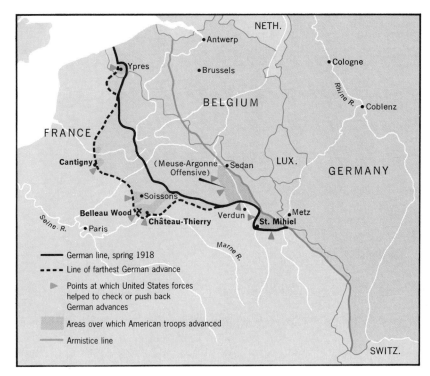

Major U.S. Operations in France, 1918 One "doughboy" recorded in his diary his baptism of fire at St. Mihiel: "Hiked through dark woods. No lights allowed, guided by holding on the pack of the man ahead. Stumbled through underbrush for about half mile into an open field where we waited in soaking rain until about 10:00 P.M. We then started on our hike to the St. Mihiel front, arriving on the crest of a hill at 1:00 A.M. I saw a sight which I shall never forget. It was the zero hour and in one instant the entire front as far as the eye could reach in either direction was a sheet of flame, while the heavy artillery made the earth quake."

about women in history was the fabled "Mademoiselle from Armentières." One of the printable stanzas ran:

> She was true to me, she was true to you,
> She was true to the whole damned army, too.

American operations were not confined solely to France; small detachments fought in Belgium, Italy, and notably Russia. The United States, hoping to keep stores of munitions from falling into German hands when Bolshevik Russia quit fighting, contributed some 5,000 troops to an Allied invasion of northern Russia at Archangel. Wilson likewise sent nearly 10,000 troops to Siberia as part of an Allied expedition, which included more than 70,000 Japanese. Major American purposes were to prevent Japan from getting a stranglehold on Siberia, to rescue some 45,000 marooned Czechoslovak troops, and to snatch military supplies from red Bolshevik control. Sharp fighting at Archangel and in Siberia involved casualties on both sides, including several hundred Americans. The Communist rulers of Soviet Russia have never allowed their people to forget these "capitalistic" interventions.

America Helps Hammer the "Hun"

The dreaded German drive on the western front exploded in the spring of 1918. Spearheaded by about half a million troops, the enemy rolled forward with terrifying momentum. So dire was the peril that the Allied nations for the first time united under a supreme commander, the quiet French Marshal Foch, whose axiom was: "To make war is to attack." Until then the Allies had been fighting imperfectly coordinated actions.

At last the ill-trained "Yanks" were coming— and not a moment too soon. Late in May 1918, the forward-rolling Germans, smashing to within 40 miles (64 kilometers) of Paris, threatened to knock out France. Newly arrived American troops, numbering fewer than 30,000, were thrown into the breach at Chateau-Thierry, right in the teeth of the German advance. This was a historic moment—the first

Over There *American troops ("doughboys") man a machine gun in a bomb-blasted forest. (UPI/Bettmann Newsphotos.)*

significant engagement of American troops in a European war. Battle-fatigued French soldiers watched incredulously as the roads filled with endless truckloads of American "doughboys," singing New World songs at the top of their voices, a seemingly inexhaustible flood of fresh and gleaming youth. With their arrival, it was clear that a new American giant had arisen in the West to replace the dying Russian titan in the East.

American weight in the scales was now being felt. By July 1918 the awesome German drive had spent its force, and keyed-up American boys participated in a Foch counteroffensive in the Second Battle of the Marne. This engagement marked the beginning of a German withdrawal that was never effectively reversed. In September 1918 nine American divisions (about 243,000 men) joined four French divisions to push the Germans from the St. Mihiel salient, a German dagger in France's flank.

The Americans, dissatisfied with merely bolstering the British and French, had meanwhile been demanding a separate army. General John J. ("Black Jack") Pershing was finally assigned a front of 85 miles (137 kilometers), stretching northwestward from the Swiss border to meet the French lines.

As a part of the last mighty Allied assault, involving several million men, Pershing's army undertook the Meuse-Argonne offensive, from September 26 to November 11, 1918. One objective was to cut the German railroad lines feeding the western front. This battle, the most titanic thus far in American history, lasted forty-seven days and engaged 1.2 million American troops. With especially heavy fighting in the rugged Argonne Forest, the killed and wounded mounted to 120,000, or 10 percent of the Americans involved. The slow progress and severe losses from machine guns resulted in part from inadequate training, in part from dashing open-

Gassed *This painting by noted artist John Singer Sargent captures the horror of trench warfare in World War I. The enemy was often distant and unseen, and death came impersonally from gas or artillery fire. American troops, entering the line only in the war's final days, were only briefly exposed to this kind of brutal fighting. (Trustees of the Imperial War Museum.)*

field tactics, with the bayonet liberally employed. Tennessee-bred Alvin C. York, a member of an antiwar religious sect, became a hero when he single-handedly killed 20 Germans and captured 132 more.

Victory was in sight—and fortunately so. The slowly advancing American armies in France were eating up their supplies so rapidly that they were in grave danger of running short. But the battered Germans were ready to raise their arms and cry "Kamerad" ("Comrade"). Their allies were deserting them; the British blockade was causing critical food shortages; and the German armies were reeling under the sledgehammer blows of the Allies. Propaganda leaflets, containing seductive Wilsonian promises, were raining upon their crumbling lines from balloons, shells, and rockets.

The Fourteen Points Disarm Germany

Berlin was now ready to hoist the white flag. Warned of imminent defeat by the generals, it turned to the presumably softhearted Wilson in October 1918, seeking a peace based on the Fourteen Points. In stern responses, the president made it clear that the kaiser must be thrown overboard before an armistice could be negotiated. War-weary Germans, whom Wilson had been trying to turn against their "military masters," took the hint. The kaiser was forced to flee to Holland, where he lived out his remaining twenty-three years, "Unwept, unhonored, and unhung."

The exhausted Germans were through. They laid down their arms at eleven o'clock on the eleventh day of the eleventh month of 1918, and an eerie, numbing silence fell over the western front. War-taut America burst into a

Approximate Comparative Losses in World War I

Men Killed in Battle

1,700,000	Russia
1,600,000	Germany
1,385,000	France
900,000	British Empire
800,000	Austria
462,000	Italy
49,000	United States

German "Repentance" *A prophetic reflection of the view that the failure to smash Germany completely would lead to another world war. (Dallas* News, *1918.)*

delirium of around-the-clock rejoicing, as streets were jammed with laughing, whooping, milling, dancing masses. The war to end wars had ended.

Wilson Steps Down from Olympus

Woodrow Wilson had helped to win the war. What role would he now play in shaping the peace? Expectations ran extravagantly high. As the fighting in Europe crashed to a close, the American president towered at the peak of his popularity and power. In lonely huts in the mountains of Italy, candles burned before poster-portraits of the revered American prophet. In Poland starry-eyed university students would meet on the streets, clasp hands, and utter only one word, "Wilson." No other man had ever occupied so dizzy a pinnacle as moral leader of the world. Wilson also had behind him the prestige of victory and the economic resources of the mightiest nation on earth. But at this fateful moment, his sureness

Armistice Celebration, November 11, 1918 *The whole world rejoiced. (Whitney Museum of American Art.)*

of touch deserted him, and he began to make a series of tragic fumbles.

Under the slogan "Politics Is Adjourned," partisan political strife had been kept below the surface during the war crisis. Hoping to strengthen his hand at the Paris peace table, Wilson broke the truce by personally appealing for a Democratic victory in the congressional elections of November 1918. But the maneuver backfired when voters instead returned a narrow Republican majority to Congress. Having staked his personal prestige on the outcome, Wilson went to Paris as a diminished leader. Unlike all the parliamentary statesmen at the table, he did not command a legislative majority at home.

Wilson's decision to go in person to Paris to help make the peace infuriated Republicans. At that time no president had traveled to Europe, and Wilson's journey looked to his critics like flamboyant grandstanding. He further ruffled Republican feathers when he snubbed the Senate in making up his peace delegation and neglected to include a single Republican senator in his official party. The logical choice was the new chairman of the Senate Committee on Foreign Relations, slender and aristocratically bewhiskered Henry Cabot Lodge of Massachusetts, a Harvard Ph.D. But including Lodge would have been problematic for the president. The senator's mind, quipped one critic, was like the soil of his native New England: "naturally barren but highly cultivated." Wilson loathed him, and the feeling was warmly reciprocated. An accomplished author, Lodge had been known as "the scholar in politics" until Wilson

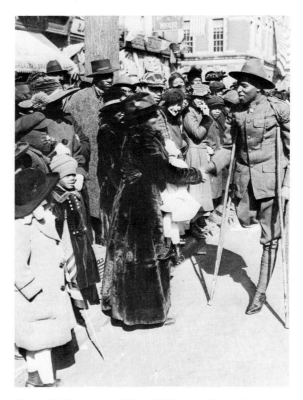

Black Soldier Hero of World War I *(United Press International photo.)*

came on the scene. The two men were at dagger points personally and politically.

An Idealist Battles the Imperialists in Paris

Woodrow Wilson, the great prophet arisen in the West, received tumultuous welcomes from the masses of France, England, and Italy late in 1918 and early in 1919. They saw in his idealism the promise of a better world. But the statesmen of France and Italy were careful to keep the new messiah at arm's length from worshipful crowds. He might so arouse the people as to prompt them to overthrow their leaders and upset finespun imperialistic plans.

Almost from the outset, the Paris Conference of great and small nations fell into the hands of an inner clique, known as the Big Four. Wilson,

Theodore Roosevelt, *referring to Wilson's practice of drafting diplomatic notes on his own typewriter, telegraphed several senators (October 24, 1918):* "Let us dictate peace by the hammering guns and not chat about peace to the accompaniment of clicking typewriters. The language of the fourteen points and the subsequent statements explaining or qualifying them are thoroughly mischievous." *Roosevelt favored the Germans' unconditional surrender.*

Wilson in Dover, England, 1919 *Hailed by many Europeans in early 1919 as the Savior of the Western world, Wilson was a fallen idol only a few months later, when his own countrymen repudiated the peace treaty he had helped to craft. (National Archives.)*

representing the richest and freshest great power, more or less occupied the driver's seat. He was joined by genial Premier Vittorio Orlando of Italy and by the brilliant Prime Minister David Lloyd George of Britain. Perhaps the most realistic of the quartet was cynical, hard-bitten Premier Georges Clemenceau of France, the seventy-eight-year-old "organizer of victory" known as "the Tiger."

Speed was urgent when the conference opened on January 18, 1919. Europe seemed to be slipping into anarchy; the red tide of communism was licking westward from Bolshevist Russia.

> *Grave concern was expressed by General Bliss, one of the five American peace commissioners (December 18, 1918): "I am disquieted to see how hazy and vague our ideas are. We are going to be up against the wiliest politicians in Europe. There will be nothing hazy or vague about their ideas."*

Wilson's ultimate goal was a world parliament to be known as the League of Nations, but he first bent his energies to preventing any cynical parceling out of the former colonies and protectorates of the vanquished powers. He forced through a compromise between naked imperialism and Wilsonian idealism. The victors would not receive the conquered territory outright, but only as trustees of the League of Nations. Strategic Syria, for example, was awarded to France, and oil-rich Iraq went to Britain. But in practice this half-loaf solution was little more than the old prewar colonialism, thinly disguised.

Meanwhile, Wilson had been serving as midwife for the League of Nations, which he envisioned as containing an Assembly with seats for all nations and a Council to be controlled by the great powers. He gained a signal victory over the skeptical Old World diplomats in February 1919, when they agreed to make the League Covenant, Wilson's brainchild, an integral part of the final peace treaty. At one point he spoke so eloquently for his plan that even the hard-boiled newspaper reporters forgot to take notes.

Hammering Out the Treaty

Domestic duties now required Wilson to make a quick trip to America, where ugly storms were brewing in the Senate. Certain Republican solons, led by Senator Lodge, were sharpening their knives for Wilson. To them the League was either a useless "sewing circle" or an overpotent "super-state." They were joined by a dozen or so isolationists, led by Senators William Borah of Idaho and Hiram Johnson of California, who were known as "irreconcilables" or "the Battalion of Death."

Thirty-nine Republican senators or senators-elect—enough to defeat the treaty—proclaimed that the Senate would not approve the League of Nations in its existing imperfect form. These difficulties delighted Wilson's Allied adversaries in Paris. They were now in a stronger bargaining position, because Wilson would have to beg them for changes in the covenant that would safeguard the Monroe Doctrine and other American interests dear to the senators.

As soon as Wilson was back in Paris, hard-headed Premier Clemenceau pressed French demands for the German-inhabited Rhineland and the Saar Valley, a rich coal area. Faced with fierce Wilsonian opposition to this violation of self-determination, France settled for a compromise whereby the Saar Basin would remain under the League of Nations for fifteen years and then a popular vote would determine its fate.* In exchange for dropping its demands for the Rhineland, France got a Security Treaty in which both Britain and America pledged to come to its aid in the event of another German invasion. The French later felt betrayed when this pact was quickly pigeonholed by the United States Senate, which shied away from all entangling alliances.

Wilson's next battle was with Italy over Fiume, a valuable seaport inhabited by both Italians and Yugoslavs. When Italy demanded Fi-

"Seein' Things" (*Brooklyn* Eagle, *1919.*)

ume, Wilson insisted that the seaport go to Yugoslavia and appealed over the heads of Italy's leaders to the country's masses. The maneuver fell flat. The Italian delegates went home in a huff, while the Italian masses turned savagely against Wilson.

Another crucial struggle was with Japan over China's Shantung peninsula and the German islands in the Pacific, which the Japanese had seized during the war. Japan was conceded the strategic Pacific islands under a League of Nations mandate,* but Wilson fiercely opposed Japanese control of Shantung as a violation of self-determination for its 30 million Chinese residents. But when the Japanese threatened to walk out, Wilson reluctantly accepted a compromise whereby Japan kept Germany's economic holdings in Shantung and pledged to return the peninsula to China at a later date. The Chinese were outraged by this imperialistic solution, while Clemenceau jeered that Wilson "talked like Jesus Christ and acted like Lloyd George."

---

*The Saar population voted overwhelmingly to rejoin Germany in 1935.

---

*In due time the Japanese illegally fortified these islands—the Marshalls, Marianas, and Carolines—and used them as bases against the United States in World War II.

The Peace Treaty That Bred a New War

A completed Treaty of Versailles, after more weeks of wrangling, was handed to the Germans in June 1919—almost literally on the point of a bayonet. They had given up their arms on the strength of assurances that they would be granted a peace based on the Fourteen Points. A careful analysis of the treaty shows that only about four of the twenty-three original Wilsonian points and subsequent principles were fully honored. Loud and bitter cries of betrayal burst from German throats—charges that Adolf Hitler vehemently reiterated during his meteoric rise to power.

Wilson, of course, was guilty of no conscious betrayal. But the Allied powers were torn by conflicting aims, many of them sanctioned by secret treaties. There had to be compromise at

"Pilgrim Landing in America, 1919" *(Harding in the* Brooklyn *Eagle, 1919.)*

Paris—or there would be no agreement. Faced with hard realities, Wilson was forced to compromise away some of his less cherished Fourteen Points in order to salvage the more precious League of Nations. He was much like the mother who had to throw her sickly younger children to the pursuing wolves in order to save her sturdy firstborn child.

A troubled Wilson was not happy with the results. Greeted a few months earlier with frenzied acclaim in Europe, he was now a fallen idol, condemned alike by disillusioned liberals and frustrated imperialists. He was keenly aware of some of the injustices that had been forced into the treaty. But he was hoping that the League of Nations—a potent League with America as a leader—would iron out the inequities.

Yet the richly condemned treaty had much to commend it. Not least among its merits was its liberation of millions of minority peoples, such as the Poles, from the yoke of an alien dynasty. Disappointing though Wilson's handiwork was, he saved the pact from being an old-time peace of imperialism. His critics to the contrary, the settlement was almost certainly a fairer one because he had gone to Paris.

The Domestic Parade of Prejudice

At home in America, breakers loomed. Superpatriots, with their strong isolationist convictions, raised a furious outcry against entanglement. Revering the memory of Washington, Jefferson, and Monroe, they were hostile to a newfangled "League of Notions."

The Treaty of Versailles was showered with brickbats from all sides. Rabid Hun-haters, regarding the pact as not harsh enough, voiced their discontent. Professional liberals, like the editors of the New York *Nation,* thought it too harsh—and a gross betrayal to boot. German-Americans, Italian-Americans, and other "hyphenated" Americans were aroused because the peace settlement was not sufficiently favorable to their native lands.

Irish-Americans, traditional twisters of the British lion's tail, denounced the League. They felt that with the additional votes of the five dominions, it gave Britain undue influence; and they feared that it could be used to force the United States to crush any rising for Irish independence. Crowds of Irish-American zealots hissed and booed Wilson's name.

Wilson's Tour and Collapse (1919)

Despite mounting discontent, the president had reason to feel optimistic. When he brought home the treaty, with the "Wilson League" firmly riveted in as Part I, a strong majority of the people still seemed favorable. At this time—early July 1919—Senator Lodge had no real hope of defeating the pact. His strategy was merely to amend it in such a way as to "Americanize," "Republicanize," or "senatorialize" it. The Republicans could then claim political credit for the changes.

Lodge effectively used delay to confuse and divide public opinion. He read the entire 264-page treaty aloud in the Senate Foreign Relations Committee and held protracted hearings in which people of various nationalities aired their grievances.

Wilson fretted increasingly as the hot summer of 1919 wore on. The bulky pact was bogged down in the Senate, while the nation was drifting into confusion and apathy. He therefore decided to go to the country in a spectacular speechmaking tour. He would appeal over the heads of the Senate to the sovereign people—as he often had in the past.

The strenuous barnstorming campaign was undertaken in the face of protests by physicians and friends. Wilson had never been robust; he had entered the White House nearly seven years before with a stomach pump and with headache pills for his neuritis. His frail body had begun to sag under the strain of partisan strife, a global war, and a hectic peace conference. But he declared that he was willing to die, like the "doughboys" he had sent into battle, for the sake of the new world order.

The presidential tour, begun in September 1919, got off to a rather lame start. The Middle West received Wilson lukewarmly, partly because of strong German-American influence. Trailing after him like bloodhounds came two "irreconcilable" senators, Borah and Johnson, who spoke in the same cities a few days later. Hat-tossing crowds answered their attacks on Wilson, crying, "Impeach him, impeach him!"

But the reception was different in the Rocky Mountain region and on the Pacific Coast. These areas, which had elected Wilson in 1916, welcomed him with heartwarming outbursts. The high point—and the breaking point—of the return trip was at Pueblo, Colorado, September 25, 1919. Wilson, with tears coursing down his cheeks, pleaded for the League of Nations as the only real hope of preventing future wars. That night he collapsed from physical and nervous exhaustion.

Wilson and His Advisers, c. 1920 *After his stroke in 1919, the sickly Wilson met only occasionally with his cabinet. (The Bettmann Archive.)*

Wilson was whisked back in the "funeral train" to Washington, where several days later a stroke paralyzed one side of his body. During the next few weeks he lay in a darkened room in the White House, as much a victim of the war as the unknown soldier buried at Arlington. For 7 1/2 months he did not meet his cabinet.

Wilson Rejects the Lodge Reservations

Senator Lodge, coldly calculating, was now at the helm. After failing to amend the treaty outright, he finally came up with fourteen formal reservations to it—a sardonic slap at Wilson's Fourteen Points. These safeguards reserved the rights of the United States under the Monroe Doctrine and the Constitution and otherwise sought to protect American sovereignty. Senator Lodge and other critics were especially alarmed by Article X of the League because it *morally* bound the United States to aid any member vic-

timized by external aggression. A jealous Congress wanted to reserve to itself the constitutional war-declaring power.

Wilson, hating Lodge, saw red at the mere suggestion of the *Lodge* reservations. He was quite willing to accept somewhat similar reservations sponsored by his faithful Democratic followers, but he insisted that the Lodge reservations "emasculated" the entire pact.

Though too feeble to lead, Wilson was still strong enough to obstruct. When the day finally came for the voting in the Senate, he sent word to all true Democrats to vote *against* the treaty with the odious Lodge reservations attached. Wilson hoped that when these were cleared away, the path would be open for ratification without reservations or with only mild Democratic reservations.

Loyal Democrats in the Senate, on November 19, 1919, blindly did Wilson's bidding. Combining with the "irreconcilables," mostly Republicans, they rejected the treaty with the Lodge reservations appended, 55 to 39.

Defeat through Deadlock

The nation was too deeply shocked to accept the verdict as final. About four-fifths of the senators professed to favor the treaty, with or without reservations, yet a simple majority could not agree on a single proposition. So strong was public indignation that the Senate was forced to act a second time. In March 1920 the treaty was brought up again, with the Lodge reservations tacked on.

There was only one possible path to success. Unless the Senate approved the pact with the Lodge reservations, the entire document would be rejected. But the sickly Wilson, still sheltered behind drawn curtains and blind to disagreeable realities, again sent word to all loyal Democrats to vote down the treaty with the obnoxious Lodge reservations. He thus signed the death warrant of the treaty as far as America was concerned. On a fateful March 19, 1920, the treaty netted a simple majority but failed of the necessary two-thirds majority by a count of 49 yeas to 35 nays.

Who defeated the treaty? The Lodge-Wilson personal feud, traditionalism, isolationism, disillusionment, and partisanship all contributed to the confused picture. But Wilson himself must bear a substantial share of the responsibility. He asked for all or nothing—and got nothing. One Democratic senator angrily charged that the president had strangled his own brainchild with his own palsied hands rather than let the Senate straighten its crooked limbs. Isolationist Re-

publicans jeeringly rewrote the 1916 slogan to read: "He Kept Us Out of Peace."

The "Solemn Referendum" of 1920

Wilson had his own pet solution for the deadlock, and this partly explains why he refused to compromise on Lodge's terms. He proposed to settle the treaty issue in the forthcoming presidential campaign of 1920 by appealing to the people for a "solemn referendum." This was sheer folly, for a true mandate on the League in the noisy arena of politics was clearly an impossibility.

Jubilant Republicans gathered in Chicago in June 1920 with wayward bull moosers back in the camp and the senatorial Old Guard back in the saddle. The convention devised a masterfully ambiguous platform that could appeal to both pro-League and anti-League sentiment in the party. The nominee would run on a teeter-totter rather than a platform.

As the leading presidential contestants killed one another off, the political weather vane began to veer toward genial Senator Warren G. Harding of Ohio. A group of Senate bosses, meeting rather casually in the historic "smoke-filled" Room 404 of the Hotel Blackstone, informally decided on the affable and malleable Ohioan. Their fair-haired boy was a prosperous, backslapping, small-town newspaper editor of the "folksy" type, quite the opposite of Wilson, who had earlier noted the senator's "disturbingly dull" mind. For vice-president the party nominated frugal, grim-faced Governor Calvin ("Silent Cal") Coolidge of Massachusetts, who had attracted conservative support by breaking a police strike in Boston.

Meeting in San Francisco, Democrats nominated earnest Governor James M. Cox of Ohio, who strongly supported the League. His running mate was assistant navy secretary Franklin D. Roosevelt, a young, handsome, vibrant New Yorker.

Democratic attempts to make the campaign a referendum on the League were thwarted by Senator Harding, who issued muddled and contradictory statements on the issue from his front porch. Pro-League and anti-League

Senator Hitchcock, the Democratic leader, later told of one of his brief visits to Wilson and his suggestion of compromise with Lodge.

" 'Let Lodge compromise,' he replied.

'Well, of course,' I added, 'he must compromise also, but we might well hold out the olive branch.'

'Let Lodge hold out the olive branch,' he retorted, and that ended it for that day, for he was too sick a man to argue with in the presence of his anxious doctor and his more anxious wife."

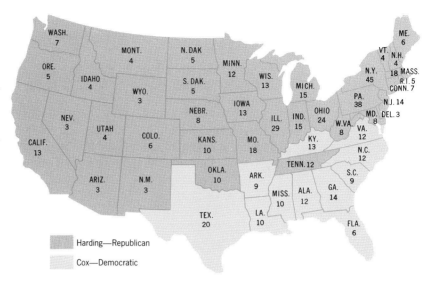

Presidential Election of 1920 (with electoral vote by state) *Cox rashly claimed that "traitors" would vote Republican. But Harding and Coolidge ran successfully as small-town boys who had made good. Harding celebrated his 55th birthday on election day, and the voters presented him with the largest victory margin to date in an American presidential election.*

Republicans both claimed that Harding's election would advance their cause, while the candidate suggested that if elected he would work for a vague Association of Nations—*a* league but not *the* League.

With newly enfranchised women swelling the vote totals, Harding was swept into power with a prodigious plurality of over 7 million votes—16,143,407 to 9,130,328 for Cox. The electoral count was 404 to 127. Eugene V. Debs, federal prisoner number 9653 at the Atlanta Penitentiary, rolled up the largest vote ever for the left-wing Socialist party—919,799.

Public desire for a change found vent in a resounding repudiation of "high and mighty" Wilsonism. People were tired of professional highbrowism, star-reaching idealism, bothersome do-goodism, moral overstrain, and constant self-sacrifice. Eager to lapse back into "normalcy," they were willing to accept a second-rate president—and they got a third-rate one.

Although the election could not be considered a true referendum, Republican isolationists successfully turned Harding's victory into a death sentence for the League. Politicians increasingly shunned the League as they would a leper. When the legendary Wilson died in 1924, admirers knelt in the snow outside his Washington home. His "great vision" of a league for peace had died long before.

The Betrayal of Great Expectations

America's spurning of the League was tragically shortsighted. The Republic had helped to win a costly war, but it blindly kicked the fruits of victory under the table. Whether a strong international organization would have averted World War II in 1939 will always be a matter of dispute. But there can be no doubt that the orphaned League of Nations was undercut at the start by the refusal of the mightiest power on the globe to join it. The Allies themselves were largely to blame for the new world conflagration that flared up in 1939, but they found a convenient justification for their own shortcomings by pointing an accusing finger at Uncle Sam.

The ultimate collapse of the Treaty of Versailles must be laid, at least in some degree, at America's doorstep. This complicated pact, tied in with the four other peace treaties through the League Covenant, was a top-heavy structure designed to rest on a four-legged table. The fourth leg, the United States, was never put into place. This rickety structure teetered crazily for over a decade and then crashed in ruins—a debacle that played into the hands of the German demagogue Adolf Hitler.

No less ominous events were set in motion when the Senate spurned the Security Treaty with France. The French, fearing that a new generation of Germans would follow in their fathers' goose steps, undertook to build up a powerful military force. Predictably resenting the presence of strong French armies, Germany began to rearm illegally. The witches' cauldron of uncertainty and suspicion brewed an intoxicant that helped inflame the fanatical following of dictator Hitler.

The United States, as the tragic sequel proved, hurt its own cause when it buried its head in the sands. Granted that the conduct of its Allies had been disillusioning, it had its own ends to serve by carrying through the Wilsonian program. It would have been well advised if it had forthrightly assumed its war-born responsibilities and had resolutely played the role of global leader into which it had been thrust by the iron hand of destiny. In the interests of its own security, if for no better reason, the United States should have used its enormous strength to shape world-shaking events. Instead, it per-

Interlocking Treaty Structure

mitted itself to drift along aimlessly and dangerously toward the abyss of a second and even more bloody international disaster.

Varying Viewpoints

Was Woodrow Wilson a starry-eyed idealist or a hard-nosed realist? For more than half a century, this question has hung over discussions of the president's wartime diplomacy and peacemaking, especially his proposal for a League of Nations. Wilson's detractors charge that the American leader naively tried to impose his own high-minded legal and moral concepts on international affairs, which often do not operate according to the rules of law and morality. Some "New Left" writers have claimed that Wilson's diplomacy revealed an objectionable purpose of another kind: a thrust to open the world to American economic penetration.

Wilson's defenders usually emphasize that his lofty principles were tempered by pragmatism. They stress the give-and-take char-

acter of some of his proposals, such as the mandates for former colonial territories. Apologists also point out that the League did embody the modern, and presumably "realistic," concept of "collective security." Recently, writers such as Arno Mayer and N. Gordon Levin, Jr., have attempted to rehabilitate Wilson. They credit him with an immensely sophisticated grasp of the way certain "ideals"—such as free trade, reduced armaments, and political stability—would benefit both the world and the profit margins of American businesspeople. To them Woodrow Wilson now appears to be a farseeing visionary who perceived the compatibility of his high principles with this country's own material interests.

Select Readings

Primary Source Documents

John J. Pershing, *My Experiences in the World War**
(1931), recounts American fighting tactics. Wilson's
"Fourteen Points Address" to Congress on January 8,
1918* (*Congressional Record*, 65 Cong., 2 sess.,
p. 691), defined the nation's war aims. The dealings
at the Versailles Conference are described in the
words of Wilson's personal adviser, *The Intimate Papers of Colonel House** (1928). William E. Borah,
"*Speech on the League of Nations*" (1919), in Richard
Hofstadter, *Great Issues in American History*, reveals the isolationist position. Ernest Hemingway's *A
Farewell to Arms* (1929) is an outstanding war novel.

Secondary Sources

The home front is emphasized in David M. Kennedy,
*Over Here: The First World War and American Soci-
ety* (1980). Economic mobilization is covered in
Robert Cuff, *The War Industries Board* (1973);
Daniel R. Beaver, *Newton D. Baker and the Ameri-
can War Effort* (1966); and Charles Gilbert, *Ameri-
can Financing of World War I* (1970). On labor, see
Frank L. Grubbs, Jr., *The Struggle for Labor Loyalty*
(1968); and David Brody, *Labor in Crisis: The Steel
Strike of 1919* (1965). Politics are treated in Seward
Livermore, *Politics Is Adjourned: Woodrow Wilson
and the War Congress, 1916–1918* (1966). American
propaganda efforts are colorfully portrayed in James
R. Mock and Cedric Larson, *Words That Won the
War* (1939), and Stephen L. Vaughn, *Holding Fast
the Inner Lines: Democracy, Nationalism, and the
Committee on Public Information* (1980). The abuse
of civil liberties is luridly described in H. C. Peterson
and Gilbert C. Fite, *Opponents of War, 1917–1918*
(1957), and is more soberly analyzed in Harry N.
Scheiber, *The Wilson Administration and Civil Liberties, 1917–1921* (1960), and Paul L. Murphy,
*World War I and the Origin of Civil Liberties in the
United States* (1979). Military matters are handled in

Edward M. Coffman, *The War to End All Wars: The
American Military Experience in World War I*
(1968), and Arthur E. Barbeau and Florette Henri,
*Unknown Soldiers: Black American Troops in World
War One* (1974). The war experiences of women are
captured in Maurine W. Greenwald, *Women, War,
and Work* (1980). Gerd Hardach, *The First World
War, 1914–1918* (1977), is a broad economic history.
On Wilson's foreign economic policies, see Jeffrey J.
Safford, *Wilsonian Maritime Diplomacy* (1978), and
Burton I. Kaufman, *Efficiency and Expansion: Foreign Trade Organization in the Wilson Administration* (1974). The postwar international economic position of the United States is discussed in Carl
Parrini, *Heir to Empire* (1969); Michael Hogan, *Informal Entente* (1977); and Joan Hoff Wilson, *American Business and Foreign Policy, 1920–1933* (1973).
Paul P. Abrahams examines *The Foreign Expansion
of American Finance and Its Relationship to the Foreign Economic Policies of the United States,
1907–1921* (1976). Works of cultural history include
Stanley Cooperman, *World War I and the American
Novel* (1966); Stuart Rochester, *American Liberal
Disillusionment in the Wake of World War I* (1977);
and Paul Fussell, *The Great War and Modern Memory* (1975). On the peace, see Arthur S. Link,
Woodrow Wilson: Revolution, War, and Peace
(1979), and two studies by Thomas A. Bailey,
Woodrow Wilson and the Lost Peace (1944) and
Woodrow Wilson and the Great Betrayal (1945).
Consult also N. Gordon Levin, Jr., *Woodrow Wilson
and World Politics* (1968); Arno J. Mayer, *Politics
and Diplomacy of Peacemaking* (1967); and Arthur
Walworth, *America's Moment: 1918* (1977). Lodge is
somewhat rehabilitated in John A. Garraty, *Henry
Cabot Lodge* (1953), and especially in William C.
Widenor, *Henry Cabot Lodge and the Search for an
American Foreign Policy* (1980). The end of this
troubled period is sketched in Burl Noggle, *Into the
Twenties: The U.S. from Armistice to Normalcy*
(1974).

36

American Life in the "Roaring Twenties"

America's present need is not heroics but healing; not nostrums but normalcy; not revolution but restoration; . . . not surgery but serenity.

Warren G. Harding, 1920

Insulating America from the Radical Virus

Bloodied by the war and disillusioned by the peace, Americans turned inward in the 1920s. Shunning diplomatic commitments to foreign countries, they also denounced "radical" foreign ideas, condemned "un-American" life-styles, and clanged shut the immigration gates against foreign peoples. They partly sealed off the domestic economy from the rest of the world and plunged headlong into a dizzying decade of homegrown prosperity.

Hysterical fears of red Russia continued to color American thinking for several years after the Bolshevik revolution of 1917, which spawned a tiny Communist party in America.

Tensions were heightened by an epidemic of strikes that convulsed the Republic at war's end, many of them the result of high prices and frustrated union-organizing drives. Upstanding Americans jumped to the conclusion that labor troubles were fomented by bomb-and-whisker Bolsheviks. A general strike in Seattle in 1919, though modest in its demands and orderly in its methods, prompted a call from the mayor for federal troops, to head off "the anarchy of Russia." Fire-and-brimstone evangelist "Billy" Sunday struck a responsive chord when he described a Bolshevik as "a guy with a face like a porcupine and a breath that would scare a pole cat. . . . If I had my way, I'd fill the jails so full of them that their feet would stick out the window."

Bolsheviks Hide under the Stars and Stripes
(*Philadelphia* Inquirer, *1919.*)

The "big red scare" of 1919–1920 resulted in a nationwide crusade against left-wingers whose Americanism was suspect. Attorney General A. Mitchell Palmer, who perhaps "saw red" too easily, earned the title of the "Fighting Quaker" by his excess of zeal in rounding up suspects. They ultimately totaled about six thousand. This drive to root out radicals was redoubled in June 1919, when a bomb shattered both the nerves and the Washington home of Palmer. The "Fighting Quaker" was thereupon dubbed the "Quaking Fighter."

Other events highlighted the red scare. Late in December 1919, a shipload of 249 alleged alien radicals was deported on the *Buford* ("Soviet Ark") to the "workers' paradise" of Russia. One zealot cried, "My motto for the Reds is S.O.S.—ship or shoot." Hysteria was temporar-ily revived in September 1920, when a still-unexplained bomb blast in Wall Street killed thirty-eight persons and wounded several hundred others.

Various states joined the pack in the outcry against radicals. In 1919–1920 a number of legislatures, reflecting the anxiety of "solid" citizens, passed criminal syndicalism laws. These antired statutes, some of which were born of the war, made unlawful the mere *advocacy* of violence to secure social change. Critics protested that mere words were not criminal deeds, that there was a great gulf between throwing fits and throwing bombs, and that "free screech" was for the nasty as well as the nice. Violence was done to traditional American concepts of free speech as IWWs and other radicals were vigorously prosecuted. The hysteria went so far that in 1920 five members of the New York legislature, all lawfully elected, were denied their seats simply because they were Socialists.

The red scare was a godsend to conservative businesspeople, who used it to break the backs of the fledgling unions. Labor's call for the "closed," or all-union, shop was denounced as "Sovietism in disguise." Employers, in turn, hailed their own antiunion campaign for the "open" shop as "the American plan."

Antiredism and antiforeignism were reflected in a notorious case regarded by liberals as a "judicial lynching." Nicola Sacco, a shoe-factory worker, and Bartolomeo Vanzetti, a fish peddler, were convicted in 1921 of the murder of a Massachusetts paymaster and his guard. The jury and judge were probably prejudiced in some degree against the defendants because they were Italians, atheists, anarchists, and draft dodgers.

Liberals and radicals the world over rallied to the defense of the two aliens doomed to die. The case dragged on for six years until 1927, when the condemned men were electrocuted. Communists and other radicals were thus presented with two martyrs in the "class struggle," while many American liberals hung their heads. The evidence against the accused, though damaging, betrayed serious weaknesses. If the trial had been held in an atmosphere less surcharged with antiredism, the outcome might well have been only a prison term.

An author-soldier (Guy Empey) applauded the "deportation delirium" when he wrote: "I believe we should place them [the Reds] all on a ship of stone, with sails of lead, and that their first stopping place should be hell."

Hooded Hoodlums of the KKK

A new Ku Klux Klan, spawned by the postwar reaction, mushroomed fearsomely in the early 1920s. Despite the familiar sheets and hoods, it more closely resembled the antiforeign "nativist" movements of the 1850s than the antiblack night riders of the 1860s. It was antiforeign, anti-Catholic, antiblack, anti-Jewish, antipacifist, anti-Communist, anti-internationalist, antievolutionist, antibootlegger, antigambling, antiadultery, and anti–birth control. It was also pro–Anglo Saxon, pro–"native" American, and pro-Protestant. In short, the besheeted Klan betokened an extremist, ultraconservative uprising against many of the forces of diversity and modernity that were transforming American culture.

As reconstituted, the Klan spread with astonishing rapidity, especially in the Middle West and the "Bible Belt" South. At its peak in the mid-1920s, it enrolled about 5 million duespaying members and wielded potent political influence. It capitalized on the typically American love of excitement, adventure, and joining, to say nothing of the adolescent love for secret ritual. "Knights of the Invisible Empire" included among their officials Imperial Wizards, Grand Goblins, King Kleagles, and other horrendous "kreatures." The most impressive displays were "konclaves" and huge flag-waving parades. The chief warning was the burning of the fiery cross. The principal weapon was the lash, supplemented by tar and feathers. Rallying songs were "The Fiery Cross on High," "One Hundred Percent American," and "The Ku Klux Klan and the Pope" (against kissing the Pope's toe). One brutal slogan was "Kill the Kikes, Koons, and Katholics."

This reign of hooded horror, so repulsive to the best American ideals, collapsed rather suddenly in the late 1920s. Decent people at last recoiled from the orgy of ribboned flesh and terrorism, while scandalous embezzling by Klan officials launched a congressional investigation. The bubble was punctured when the movement was exposed, not as a crusade, but as a vicious racket based on a ten-dollar initiation fee. At bottom, the KKK was an alarming manifestation of the intolerance and prejudice so com-

KKK Parade of 40,000 Men in Washington, 1925
(United Press International photo.)

mon in the anxiety-plagued minds of the 1920s. America needed no such cowardly apostles, whose white sheets concealed dark purposes.

Stemming the Foreign Flood

Isolationist America of the 1920s, ingrown and provincial, had little use for the immigrants who began to flood into the country again as peace settled soothingly on the war-torn world. Some 800,000 stepped ashore in 1920–1921, about two-thirds of them from southern and eastern Europe. The "one-hundred-percent Americans," gagging at the sight of this resumed "New Immigration," once again cried that the famed poem at the base of the Statue of Liberty was all too literally true: they claimed that a sickly Europe was indeed vomiting on America "the wretched refuse of its teeming shore."

Congress temporarily plugged the breach with the Emergency Quota Act of 1921. Newcomers from Europe were restricted in any given year to a definite quota, which was set at 3 percent of the persons of their nationality who

Annual Immigration and the Quota Laws

	Immigrants from N. and W. Europe	Immigrants from Other Countries, Principally S. and E. Europe
Average annual inflow, 1907–1914	176,983	685,531
Quotas under Act of 1921	198,082	158,367
Quotas under Act of 1924	140,999	21,847
Quotas under National-Origins Provision of 1929	132,323	20,251
Quotas under McCarran-Walter Act of 1952	125,165	29,492

had been living in the United States in 1910. This national-origins system was relatively favorable to the immigrants from southern and eastern Europe, for by 1910 immense numbers of them had already arrived.

This stopgap legislation of 1921 was replaced, after more mature reflection, by the Immigration Act of 1924. Quotas for foreigners were cut from 3 percent to 2 percent. The national-origins base was shifted from the census of 1910 to that of 1890, when comparatively few South Europeans had arrived.* Great Britain and Northern Ireland, for example, could send 65,721 a year as against 5,802 for Italy. South Europeans bitterly condemned the device as unfair and discriminatory—a triumph for the "nativist" belief that blue-eyed and fair-haired North Europeans were of better blood. The purpose was clearly to freeze America's existing racial composition, which was largely North European. A flagrantly discriminatory section of the Immigration Act of 1924 slammed the door absolutely against Japanese immigrants. Mass "Hate America" rallies erupted in Japan, and one Japanese superpatriot expressed his outrage by committing suicide near the American Embassy in Tokyo. Exempt from the quota system were Canadians and Latin Americans.

The quota system effected an epochal departure in American policy. It recognized that the nation was filling up and that a "No Vacancy" sign was needed. Immigration henceforth died down to a comparative trickle. By 1931, probably for the first time in American experience, more foreigners left than arrived. Quotas thus

The Only Way to Handle It   *(Library of Congress.)*

EUROPE

GATE 3%

---

*Five years later the Act of 1929, using 1920 as the quota base, virtually cut immigration in half by limiting the total to 152,574 a year. In 1965 Congress abolished the national-origins quota system.

> A recognized expert on American immigration, Henry P. Fairchild, wrote in 1926, "The typical immigrant of the present does not really live in America at all, but, from the point of view of nationality, in Italy, Poland, Czecho-Slovakia, or some other foreign country."

caused America to sacrifice something of its tradition of freedom and opportunity, as well as much of its color and variety.

The Prohibition "Experiment"

One of the last peculiar spasms of the progressive reform movement was prohibition, loudly supported by crusading churches and by women. The arid new order was authorized in 1919 by the Eighteenth Amendment (for text, see the Appendix), as implemented by the Volstead Act passed by Congress later that year. Together these laws made the world "safe for hypocrisy."

The legal abolition of alcohol was fairly popular in the Middle West, and especially so in the South. Southern whites were eager to keep stimulants out of the hands of the blacks, lest they burst out of "their place." But despite the overwhelming ratification of the "dry" amendment, strong opposition persisted in the larger eastern cities. Concentrated colonies of "wet" foreign-born peoples hated to abandon their Old World drinking habits. Yet most Americans assumed that prohibition had come to stay. Everywhere there were last wild flings, as the nation prepared to enter upon a permanent "alcoholiday."

Prohibition Blues   The Lafayette Hotel, shown here in John Sloan's 1928 painting, was one of the few fine hotels in New York to survive the era of closed bars and dry dining rooms. (The Metropolitan Museum of Art, Gift of Friends of John Sloan, 1928.)

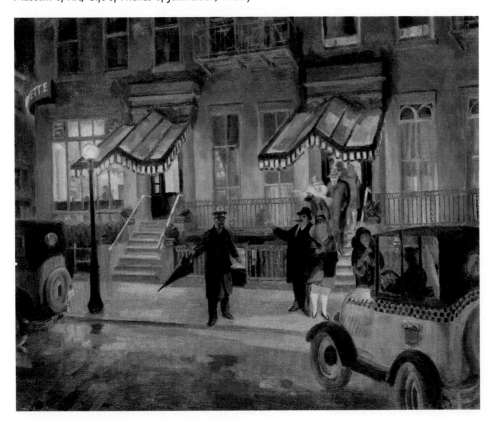

But prohibitionists were naive in the extreme. They overlooked the tenacious American tradition of strong drink and of weak control by the central government, especially over private lives. They forgot that the federal authorities had never satisfactorily enforced a law where the majority of the people—or a strong minority—were hostile to it. They ignored the fact that one cannot make a crime overnight out of something that millions of people have never regarded as a crime. Lawmakers could not legislate away a thirst.

Peculiar conditions hampered the enforcement of prohibition. Profound disillusionment over the aftermath of the war raised serious questions as to the wisdom of further self-denial. Slaking thirst became a cherished personal liberty, and many ardent wets believed that the way to bring about repeal was to violate the law on a large enough scale. Hypocritical, hip-flasked legislators spoke or voted dry while privately drinking wet. ("Let us strike a blow for liberty" was an ironic toast.) Frustrated soldiers, returning from France, complained that prohibition had been "put over" on them while they were "over there." Grimy workers bemoaned the loss of their cheap beer, while pointing out that the idle rich could buy all the illicit alcohol they wanted. Flaming youth of the jazz age thought

it "smart" to swill bootleg liquor—"liquid tonsillectomies." Millions of older citizens likewise found forbidden fruit fascinating, especially when they engaged in "bar hunts."

Prohibition might have started off on a better foot if there had been a larger army of enforcement officials. But the state and federal agencies were understaffed, and their snoopers, susceptible to bribery, were underpaid. The public was increasingly distressed as scores of persons, including innocent bystanders, were killed by quick-triggered dry agents.

Prohibition simply did not prohibit. The old-time "men only" corner saloons were replaced by thousands of "speakeasies," each with its tiny grilled window through which the thirsty spoke softly before the barred door was opened. Hard liquor, especially the cocktail, was drunk in staggering volume by both sexes. Largely because of the difficulties of transporting and concealing bottles, beverages of high alcoholic content were popular. Foreign rumrunners, often from the West Indies, had their inning, and countless cases of liquor leaked down from Canada. The zeal of American prohibition agents on occasion strained diplomatic relations with Uncle Sam's northern neighbor.

"Home brew" and "bathtub gin" became popular, as law-evading adults engaged in "alky cooking" with toy stills. The worst of the homemade "rotgut" produced blindness, even death. The affable bootlegger worked in silent partnership with the friendly undertaker.

Yet the "noble experiment" was not entirely a failure. Bank savings increased, and absenteeism in industry decreased, presumably because of the newly sober ways of formerly soused barflies. On the whole, probably less liquor was consumed than in the days before prohibition, though strong drink continued to be available. As the legendary tippler remarked, prohibition was "a darn sight better than no liquor at all."

The Golden Age of Gangsterism

Prohibition spawned shocking crimes. The lush profits of illegal alcohol led to bribery of the police, many of whom were induced to see and

Federal Agents Destroy Booze in Brooklyn *(The Bettmann Archive, Inc.)*

smell no evil. Violent gang wars broke out in the big cities between rivals seeking to corner the rich market in booze. Rival triggermen used their sawed-off shotguns and chattering "typewriters" (machine guns) to "erase" bootlegging competitors who were trying to "muscle in" on their "racket." In the gang wars of the 1920s in Chicago, about five hundred low characters were murdered. Arrests were few and convictions were even fewer, as the button-lipped gangsters covered for one another with the underworld's code of silence.

Chicago was by far the most spectacular example of lawlessness. In 1925 "Scarface" Al Capone, a grasping and murderous booze distributor, began six years of gang warfare which netted him millions of blood-spattered dollars. He zoomed through the streets in an armor-plated car with bulletproof windows. A Brooklyn newspaper quipped:

> And the pistols' red glare,
> Bombs bursting in air
> Give proof through the night'
> That Chicago's still there.

Capone, though branded "Public Enemy Number One," could not be convicted of the cold-blooded massacre, on St. Valentine's Day in 1929, of seven disarmed members of a rival gang. But after serving most of an eleven-year sentence in a federal penitentiary for income-tax evasion, he was released as a syphilitic wreck.

Gangsters rapidly moved into other profitable and illicit activities: prostitution, gambling, and narcotics. Honest merchants were forced to pay "protection money" to the organized thugs; otherwise their windows would be smashed, their trucks overturned, or their employees or themselves beaten up. Racketeers even invaded the ranks of local labor unions as organizers and promoters. Organized crime had come to be one of the nation's most gigantic businesses. By 1930 the annual "take" of the underworld was estimated to be from $12 billion to $18 billion—several times the income of the Washington government.

Criminal callousness sank to new depths in 1932 with the kidnapping for ransom, and eventual murder, of the infant son of aviator-

"The King Still Reigns," 1930 *Gangster Al Capone, headquartered in Chicago, was reported as saying: "Everybody calls me a racketeer. I call myself a businessman. When I sell liquor, it's bootlegging. When my patrons serve it on a silver tray on Lake Shore Drive, it's hospitality." (Courtesy of Baltimore Sun.)*

hero Charles A. Lindbergh. The entire nation was inexpressibly shocked and saddened, causing Congress in 1932 to pass the so-called Lindbergh Law, making interstate abduction in certain circumstances a death-penalty offense.

Monkey Business in Tennessee

Education in the 1920s continued to make giant bootstrides. More and more states were requiring young people to remain in school until age sixteen or eighteen, or until graduation from high school. The proportion of seventeen-year-olds who finished high school almost doubled in the 1920s, to more than one in four.

The most revolutionary contribution to educational theory during these yeasty years was made by mild-mannered Professor John Dewey, who was on the faculty of Columbia University from 1904 to 1930. By common consent one of America's few front-rank philosophers, he set forth the principles of "learning by doing" that formed the foundation of so-called progressive education, with its greater "permissiveness." He believed that the workbench was as essential as the blackboard, and that "education for life" should be a primary goal of the teacher.

This new emphasis on creating socially useful adults rendered many schools more attractive. No longer was the schoolhouse a kind of juvenile jail, from which the pupils burst at the end of the year chanting, as young Dewey had when a youngster in Vermont, "Good-bye school, good-bye teacher, damned old fool."

Science also scored wondrous advances in these years. A massive public-health program, launched by the Rockefeller Foundation in the South in 1909, had virtually wiped out the ancient affliction of hookworm by the 1920s. Better nutrition and health care helped to increase the life expectancy of a newborn infant from fifty years in 1901 to fifty-nine years in 1929.

Hiram Wesley Evans, imperial wizard of the Ku Klux Klan, in 1926 movingly described the cultural grievances that inspired the Klan and lay behind much of the Fundamentalist revolt against "Modernism": "Nordic Americans for the last generation have found themselves increasingly uncomfortable and finally deeply distressed. . . . One by one all our traditional moral standards went by the boards, or were so disregarded that they ceased to be binding. The sacredness of our Sabbath, of our homes, of chastity, and finally even of our right to teach our own children in our own schools fundamental facts and truths were torn away from us. Those who maintained the old standards did so only in the face of constant ridicule. . . . We found our great cities and the control of much of our industry and commerce taken over by strangers. . . . We are a movement of the plain people, very weak in the matter of culture, intellectual support, and trained leadership. . . . This is undoubtedly a weakness. It lays us open to the charge of being 'hicks' and 'rubes' and 'drivers of second-hand Fords.'"

The Fundamentalist Outcry Radicalism and science are both condemned. (The King's Business, May, 1925, p. 197.)

Yet both science and progressive education in the 1920s were subjected to unfriendly fire from Fundamentalists. These old-time religionists charged that the teaching of Darwinian evolution was destroying faith in God and the Bible, while contributing to the moral breakdown of youth in the jazz age. Numerous attempts were made to secure laws prohibiting the teaching of evolution, "the bestial hypothesis," in the public schools, and three southern states adopted such shackling measures. The trio included Tennessee, in the heart of the so-called Bible Belt South, where the spirit of evangelical religion was still robust.

The stage was set for the memorable "Monkey Trial" at the hamlet of Dayton, eastern Tennessee, in 1925. A likable high-school biology teacher, John T. Scopes, was indicted for teaching evolution. Batteries of newspaper reporters, armed with notebooks and cameras, descended upon the quiet town to witness the spectacle. Scopes was defended by nationally

**The Ford Assembly Line:
Making the Model T, 1914**
*First introduced in 1913, Ford's
"assembly line system" was based
on the principle of "taking the
work to the man," rather than
moving workers and tools around
on the factory floor. By 1914 this
revolutionary technique had cut
the average labor time needed to
build a Model T chassis from
twelve and one-half to one and
one-half hours. (Courtesy of Ford
Motor Company.)*

known attorneys, while William Jennings Bryan, an ardent Presbyterian Fundamentalist, joined the prosecution. Taking the stand as an expert on the Bible, Bryan was made to appear foolish by the famed criminal lawyer, Clarence Darrow. Five days after the trial was over, Bryan died of a stroke, no doubt brought on by the heat and strain.

This historic clash between theology and biology proved inconclusive. Scopes, the forgotten man of the drama, was found guilty and fined $100. But the supreme court of Tennessee, while upholding the law, set aside the fine on a technicality.* The Fundamentalists at best won only a hollow victory, for the absurdities of the trial cast ridicule on their cause. Yet even though increasing numbers of Christians were coming to reconcile the revelations of religion with the findings of modern science, Fundamentalism, with its emphasis on literal reading of the Bible, remained a vibrant force in American spiritual life. It was especially strong in the Baptist church and in the rapidly growing Churches of Christ, organized in 1906.

---

*The Tennessee law was not formally repealed until 1967.

The Mass-Consumption Economy

Prosperity—real, sustained, and widely shared—put much of the "roar" into the twenties. The economy kicked off its war harness in 1919, faltered a few steps in the recession of 1920–1921, and then sprinted forward for nearly seven years. Both the recent war and Treasury Secretary Andrew Mellon's tax policies favored the rapid expansion of capital investment. Ingenious machines, powered by relatively cheap energy from newly tapped oil fields, dramatically increased the productivity of the laborer. Assembly-line production reached such perfection in Henry Ford's famed Rouge River plant near Detroit that a finished automobile emerged every ten seconds.

Great new industries suddenly sprouted forth. Supplying electrical power for the humming new machines became a giant business in

> The bombastic Fundamentalist evangelist
> W. A. ("Billy") Sunday declared in 1925, "If a
> minister believes and teaches evolution, he is a
> stinking skunk, a hypocrite, and a liar."

"Babe" Ruth: The "Sultan of Swat" *(Brown Brothers.)*

the 1920s. Above all, the automobile, once the horseless chariot of the rich, now became the carriage of the common citizen. By 1930 Americans owned almost 30 million cars.

The nation's deepening "love affair" with the automobile headlined a momentous shift in the character of the economy. American manufacturers seemed to have mastered the problems of production; their worries now focused on consumption. Could they find the mass markets for the goods they had contrived to spew forth in such profusion?

Responding to this need, a new arm of American commerce came into being: advertising. By persuasion and ploy, allure and sexual suggestion, advertisers sought to make Americans be chronically discontented with their paltry possessions and want more, more, more. A founder of this new "profession" was Bruce Barton, prominent New York partner in a Madison Avenue firm. In 1925 Barton published a bestseller, *The Man Nobody Knows,* setting forth the seductive thesis that Jesus Christ was the greatest adman of all time. "Every advertising man ought to study the parables of Jesus," Barton preached. "They are marvelously condensed, as all good advertising should be." Barton even had a good word to say for Christ's

executive ability: "He picked up twelve men from the bottom ranks of business and forged them into an organization that conquered the world."

In this commercialized atmosphere, even sports were becoming a big business. Ballyhooed by the "image makers," home-run heroes like George H. ("Babe") Ruth were far better known than most statesmen. The fans bought tickets in such numbers that "Babe's" hometown park, Yankee Stadium, became known as "the house that Ruth built." In 1921 the slugging heavyweight champion, Jack Dempsey, knocked out the dapper French light heavyweight, Georges Carpentier. The Jersey City crowd in attendance had paid more than a million dollars—the first in a series of million-dollar "gates" in the golden 1920s.

Buying on credit was another innovative feature of the postwar economy. "Possess today and pay tomorrow" was the message directed at buyers. Once-frugal descendants of Puritans went ever deeper into debt to own all kinds of newfangled marvels—refrigerators, vacuum cleaners, and especially cars and radios—now. Prosperity thus accumulated an overhanging cloud of debt, and the economy became increasingly vulnerable to disruptions of the credit structure.

Putting America on Rubber Tires

A new industrial revolution slipped into high gear in America in the 1920s. Thrusting out steel tentacles, it changed the daily life of the people in unprecedented ways. Machinery was the new messiah—and the automobile was its principal prophet.

Of all the inventions of the era, the automobile cut the deepest mark. It heralded an amazing new industrial system, based on assembly-line methods and mass-production techniques.

Americans adapted rather than invented the gasoline engine; Europeans can claim the original honor. By the 1890s a few daring American inventors and promoters, including Henry Ford and Ransom E. Olds (Oldsmobile), were developing the infant automotive industry. By 1910 there were sixty-nine companies, with a total annual production of 181,000 units. The early contraptions were neither speedy nor reliable. Many a stalled motorist, profanely cranking a balky car, had to endure the jeer "Get a horse" from the occupants of a passing dobbin-drawn carriage.

An enormous industry sprang into being, as Detroit became the motorcar capital of America. The mechanized colossus owed much to the stopwatch efficiency techniques of Frederick W. Taylor, a prominent inventor, engineer, and tennis player, who sought to eliminate wasted motion. His epitaph reads: "Father of Scientific Management."

Best known of the new crop of industrial wizards was Henry Ford, who more than any other individual put America on rubber tires. His high and hideous Model T ("Tin Lizzie") was cheap, rugged, and reasonably reliable, though rough and clattering. The parts of Ford's "flivver" were highly standardized, but the behavior of this "rattling good car" was so individualized that it became the butt of numberless jokes.

Lean and silent Henry Ford, who was said to have wheels in his head, erected an immense personal empire on the cornerstone of his mechanical genius, though his associates provided much of the organizational talent. Ill educated, this multimillionaire mechanic was socially and culturally narrow; "History is bunk," he once testified. But he dedicated himself with one-track devotion to the gospel of standardization. After two early failures, he grasped and applied fully the techniques of assembly-line production—"Fordism." He is supposed to have re-

Henry Ford in His First Car, Built in 1896
He has been called "Father of the Traffic Jam."
(Courtesy of Ford Motor Company.)

Efficient Henry Ford was accused of invading privacy in 1922, when this notice was posted in his Detroit factory: "From now on it will cost a man his job . . . to have the odor of beer, wine or liquor on his breath, or to have any of these intoxicants on his person or in his home. The Eighteenth Amendment is a part of the fundamental laws of this country. It was meant to be enforced. Politics has interfered with the enforcement of this law, but so far as our organization is concerned, it is going to be enforced to the letter."

marked that the purchaser could have his automobile any color he desired—just as long as it was black. So economical were his methods that in the mid-1920s he was selling the Ford roadster for $260—well within the purse of a thrifty worker.

The flood of Fords was phenomenal. In 1914 the "Automobile Wizard" turned out his five hundred thousandth Model T. By 1930 his total had risen to 20 million, or, on a bumper-to-bumper basis, more than enough to encircle the globe. A national newspaper and magazine poll conducted in 1923 revealed Ford to be the people's choice for the presidential nomination in 1924. By 1929, when the great bull market collapsed, there were 26 million motor vehicles

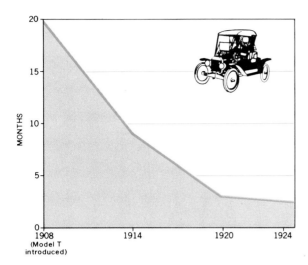

The Cost of a Model T Ford, 1908–1924   *Henry Ford's mass production techniques cut the costs of production dramatically, and put the automobile within reach of the workingperson's purse. (Cost is shown in months of labor for an employee at the average national wage.)*

registered in the United States. This figure, averaging 1 for every 4.9 Americans, represented far more automobiles than existed in all the rest of the world.

The Advent of the Gasoline Age

The impact of the self-propelled carriage on various aspects of American life was tremendous. A gigantic new industry emerged, dependent on steel, but displacing steel from its kingpin role. Employing directly or indirectly about 6 million people by 1930, it was a major prop of the nation's prosperity. Thousands of new jobs, moreover, were created by supporting industries. The lengthening list would include rubber, glass, and fabrics, to say nothing of highway construction and thousands of service stations and garages. America's standard of living, responding to this infectious prosperity, rose to an enviable level.

New industries boomed lustily; older ones grew sickly. The petroleum business experienced an explosive development. Hundreds of oil derricks shot up in California, Texas, and

Oklahoma, as these states expanded wondrously and the new frontier became an industrial frontier. The once-feared railroad octopus, on the other hand, was hard hit by the competition of passenger cars, buses, and trucks. An age-old story was repeated: one industry's gains were another industry's pains.

Other effects were widely felt. Speedy marketing of perishable foodstuffs, such as fresh fruits, was accelerated. A new prosperity enriched outlying farms, as city dwellers were provided with produce at attractive prices. Countless new roads ribboned out to meet the demand of the American motorist for smoother and faster highways, often paid for by taxes on gasoline. The era of mud ended as the nation made haste to construct the finest network of hard-surfaced roadways in the world. Lured by new seductiveness in advertising, and encouraged by the perfecting of installment-plan buying, countless Americans with shallow purses acquired the habit of riding as they paid.

Zooming motorcars were agents of social change. At first a luxury, they rapidly became a necessity. Essentially devices for needed transportation, they soon developed into a badge of freedom and equality—a necessary prop for self-respect. To some, ostentation seemed more important than transportation. Leisure hours could now be spent more pleasurably, as tens of thousands of cooped-up souls responded to the call of the open road on joyriding vacations. Women were further freed from clinging-vine dependence on men. Isolation among the sections was broken down, while the less attractive states lost population at an alarming rate. By the late 1920s, Americans owned more automobiles than bathtubs. "I can't go to town in a bathtub," one housewife explained.

Other social by-products of the automobile were visible. Autobuses made possible the consolidation of schools and to some extent of churches. The sprawling suburbs spread out still farther from the urban core, as America became a nation of commuters.

The demon machine, on the other hand, exacted a terrible toll by catering to the American mania for speed. Citizens were becoming statistics. Not counting the hundreds of thousands of injured and crippled, the one millionth American had died in a motor vehicle accident by 1951—more than all those killed on all the battlefields of all the nation's wars to that date. "The public be rammed" seemed to be the motto of the new age.

Virtuous home life partially broke down as joyriders of all ages forsook the ancestral hearth for the wide-open spaces. The morals of flaming youth sagged correspondingly—at least in the judgment of their elders. Even the disgraceful crime waves of the 1920s and 1930s were partly stimulated by the motorcar, for gangsters could now make quick getaways.

Yet no sane American would plead for a return of the old horse and bugy, complete with fly-breeding manure. The automobile contributed notably to improved air and environmental quality, despite its later notoriety as a polluter. Life might be cut short on the highways, and smog might poison the air, but the automobile brought more convenience, pleasure, and excitement into people's lives than almost any other single invention.

A Farewell to the Horse as Early as 1899 New York City was home to some 150,000 horses at the turn of the century. Each creature produced several pounds of manure a day. Horse "dumplings" littered nearly every street, attracting flies and emitting stench. In dry weather the traffic ground the manure to dust, which blew in sickening clouds about the city. (Davenport in the New York Journal.)

Humans Develop Wings

Gasoline engines also provided the power that enabled man to fulfill the age-old dream of sprouting wings. After near-successful experiments by others with heavier-than-air craft, the Wright brothers, Orville and Wilbur, performed "the miracle at Kitty Hawk," North Carolina. On a historic day—December 17, 1903—Orville Wright took aloft a feebly engined plane that stayed airborne for 12 seconds and 120 feet (37 meters). Thus, the air age was launched by two obscure bicycle repairmen.

As aviation gradually got off the ground, the world slowly shrank. The public was made increasingly air-minded by unsung heroes—often martyrs—who appeared as stunt fliers at fairs and other public gatherings. Airplanes—"flying coffins"—were used with marked success for various purposes during the Great War of 1914–1918. Shortly thereafter private companies began to operate passenger lines with airmail contracts, which were in effect a subsidy from Washington. The first transcontinental airmail route was established from New York to San Francisco in 1920.

In 1927 modest and skillful Charles A. Lindbergh, the so-called Flyin' Fool, electrified the world by the first solo west-to-east conquest of the Atlantic. Seeking a prize of $25,000, the lanky stunt flier courageously piloted his single-engined plane, the *Spirit of St. Louis,* from New York to Paris in a grueling thirty-three hours and thirty-nine minutes.

Lindbergh and His "Spirit of St. Louis"   *(National Archives.)*

Lindbergh's exploit swept Americans off their feet. Fed up with the cynicism and debunking of the jazz age, they found in this wholesome and handsome youth a genuine hero. They clasped the fluttering "Lone Eagle" to their hearts much more warmly than the bashful young man desired. "Lucky Lindy" received an uproarious welcome in the "hero canyon" of lower Broadway, as eighteen hundred tons of ticker tape and other improvised confetti showered upon him. Lindbergh's achievement—it was more than a "stunt"—did much to dramatize and popularize flying, while giving a strong boost to the infant aviation industry.

The impact of the airship was tremendous. It provided the soaring American spirit with yet another dimension. At the same time, it gave birth to a giant new industry. Unfortunately, the accident rate in the pioneer stages of aviation was high, though hardly more so than on the early railroads. But by the 1930s and 1940s, travel by air on regularly scheduled airlines was

markedly safer than on many overcrowded highways.

Humanity's new wings also increased the tempo of an already breathless civilization. The floundering railroad received another sharp setback through the loss of passengers and mail. A lethal new weapon was given to the gods of war; and with the coming of city-busting aerial bombs, people could well debate whether the conquest of the air was a blessing or a curse. The Atlantic was shriveling to about the size of the Aegean Sea in the days of Socrates, while isolation behind ocean moats was becoming a bygone dream.

The Radio Revolution

The speed of the airplane was far eclipsed by the speed of radio waves. Guglielmo Marconi, an Italian, invented wireless telegraphy in the 1890s, and his brainchild was used for long-range communication during World War I.

Next came the voice-carrying radio, a triumph of many minds. A red-letter day was posted in November 1920, when the Pittsburgh station KDKA broadcast the news of the Harding landslide. Later miracles were achieved in transatlantic wireless photographs, radiotelephones, and television. In harmony with American free enterprise, radio programs were generally sustained by bothersome "commercials," as contrasted with the drabber government-owned systems of Europe.

Like other marvels, the radio not only created a new industry but added richness to the fabric of American life. More joy was given to leisure hours, and many children who had been lured from the fireside by the automobile were brought back by the radio. The nation was better knit together. Various sections heard Americans with standardized accents, and countless millions "tuned in" on perennial comedy favorites like "Amos 'n' Andy." Advertising was further perfected as an art.

Educationally and culturally, the radio made a significant contribution. Sports were further stimulated. Politicians had to adjust their speaking techniques to the new medium, and mil-

> Radio came in with a bang in the winter of 1921–1922. A San Francisco newspaper reported a discovery that countless citizens were making: "There is radio music in the air, every night, everywhere. Anybody can hear it at home on a receiving set, which any boy can put up in an hour."

Radio Listeners and Lookers in the 1920s (Brown Brothers.)

lions rather than thousands of voters heard their pleas. A host of listeners swallowed the gospel of their favorite newscaster or were even ringside participants in world-shaking events. Finally, the music of famous artists and symphony orchestras was beamed into countless homes.

Hollywood's Filmland Fantasies

The flickering movie was the fruit of numerous geniuses, including Thomas A. Edison. As early as the 1890s this novel contraption, though still in crude form, had attained some popularity in the naughty peep-show penny arcades. The real birth of the moving picture came in 1903, when the first story sequence reached the screen. This breathless melodrama—*The Great Train Robbery*—was featured in the five-cent theaters, popularly called "nickelodeons." Spectacular among the first full-length classics was D. W. Griffith's *The Birth of a Nation* (1915), which glorified the Ku Klux Klan of Reconstruction days and defamed the blacks. White southerners would fire their six-shooters at the silver screen during the attempted "rape" scene.

A fascinating industry was thus launched. Hollywood, in southern California, quickly became the movie capital of the world, for it enjoyed a maximum of sunshine and other advantages. Early producers featured nudity and heavy-lidded female vampires ("vamps"), and an outraged public forced the screen magnates to set up their own rigorous code of censorship. The motion picture really arrived during the World War of 1914–1918, when it was used as an engine of anti-German propaganda. Specially prepared "hang the kaiser" films aided powerfully in selling war bonds and in boosting morale.

A new era began in 1927 with the success of the first "talkie"—*The Jazz Singer*, starring the white performer Al Jolson in blackface. The age of the "silents" was ushered out as theaters everywhere were "wired for sound." At about the same time, reasonably satisfactory color films were being produced.

> In the face of protests against sex in the movies, the industry appointed a "movie czar," Will H. Hays, who issued the famous "Hays Code" in 1934. As he stated in a speech, "This industry must have toward that sacred thing, the mind of a child, toward that clean virgin thing, that unmarked slate, the same responsibility, the same care about the impressions made upon it, that the best clergyman or the most inspired teacher of youth would have."

Movies eclipsed all other new forms of amusement in the phenomenal growth of their popularity. Tens of thousands of actors and "extras" were employed in the cardboard cities behind Hollywood's high wooden fences, to say nothing of additional thousands engaged in exhibiting the films and selling noisy popcorn. Movie "stars" of the first pulchritude commanded much larger salaries than the president of the United States, in some cases as much as $100,000 for a single picture. Many actors and actresses were far more widely known than the nation's political leaders.

The "movie habit" rapidly created a nation of "cinemaniacs." By 1930 weekly admissions totaled 100 million—a large number of them "repeaters"—in a population of 122,775,000. Many of the moviegoers were openmouthed children, much of whose education, not all of it

A New Frontier for the New Woman   *The typewriter revolutionized women's employment opportunities in the early twentieth century just as dramatically as the mechanical reaper had revolutionized agriculture in the preceding century. (International Museum of Photography at George Eastman House.)*

wholesome, was derived from this new type of textbook.

Other social consequences of the silver screen were incalculable. Attendance at movie "palaces" provided an escape from drab reality; filmland became the standard for taste, styles, songs, and morals. Newsreels, travelogues, and other informative "shorts" offered infinite possibilities for education, but they constituted only a tiny part of the total offering. Two by-products of the industry were the cheap movie magazine and the no less cheap keyhole commentator, both unduly concerned with the foibles and "sex-capades" of the "stars."

Nor did the influence of the moving picture end here. It almost exterminated vaudeville and robbed the footlighted theater of much patronage. It no doubt hurt attendance at religious services. Like the radio and the motorcar, it contributed to the further standardization of America, for the mass of the people idolized the same actors and heard the same "hit" tunes. Hollywood dominated not only the domestic but the foreign movie market and provided potent anti-American propaganda. Moviemakers placed an unwholesome overemphasis on the idle rich, the plush boudoir, the glowering gangster, and the quick-shooting cattle rustler.

The Delirious Decade

Far-reaching changes in life-styles and values paralleled the dramatic upsurge of the economy. The census of 1920 revealed that for the first time a majority of Americans no longer lived in the countryside but in urban areas. Women continued to find opportunities for employment in the booming cities, though they tended to cluster in a few low-paying jobs (such as retail clerking and office typing) that quickly became classified as "women's work." An organized birth-control movement, led by fiery feminist Margaret Sanger, openly championed the use of contraceptives. A National Women's Party began in 1923 to agitate for an Equal Rights Amendment to the Constitution.* To

---

*The campaign for an Equal Rights Amendment (ERA) was still stalled short of success over six decades later.

some defenders of traditional ways, it seemed that the world had suddenly gone mad.

Even the churches were affected. The Fundamentalist champions of the old-time religion lost ground to the Modernists, who liked to think that God was a "good guy" and the universe a pretty chummy place.

Some churchmen tried to fight the Devil with worldly weapons. Competing with joyriding automobiles and golf links, they turned to quality entertainment of their own, including wholesome moving pictures for young people. One uptown house of the Lord in New York advertised on a billboard: "Come to Church: Christian Worship Increases Your Efficiency."

Even before the war, one observer thought the chimes had "struck sex o'clock in America," and the 1920s witnessed what many old-timers regarded as a veritable erotic eruption. Advertisers exploited sexual allure to sell everything from soap to car tires. Once-modest maidens now proclaimed their new freedom as "flappers" in bobbed tresses and dresses. Young women appeared with hemlines elevated, stockings rolled, breasts taped flat, cheeks rouged, and lips a "crimson gash" that held a dangling cigarette. Thus did the "flapper" symbolize a

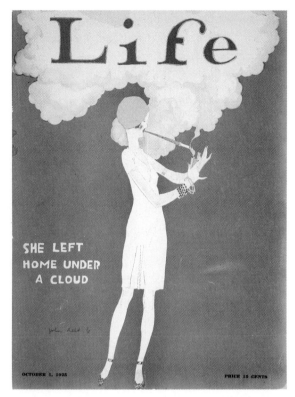

Changing Lifestyles *The woman smoker is lampooned in this magazine cover of 1925. (The Granger Collection.)*

The Guardian of Morality *Women's new one-piece bathing suits were a sensation in the 1920s. Here a check is carefully made to ensure that not too much leg is showing. (Library of Congress.)*

King Oliver's Creole Jazz Band, Early 1920s *Joseph ("Joe") King Oliver arrived in Chicago from New Orleans in 1918. His band became the first important black jazz ensemble and made Chicago's Royal Garden Cafe a magnet for jazz lovers. Left to right: Honoré Dutrey, trombone; Baby Dodds, drums; King Oliver, cornet; Lil Hardin, piano; Bill Johnson, banjo; and Johnny Dodds, clarinet. Kneeling in the foreground is the young Louis Armstrong. (Historical Pictures Service, Chicago.)*

yearned-for and devil-may-care independence (some said wild abandon) in American women. Still more adventuresome females shocked their elders when they sported the new one-piece bathing suits.

Justification for this new sexual frankness could be found in the recently translated writings of Dr. Sigmund Freud. This Viennese physician appeared to argue that sexual repression was responsible for a variety of nervous and emotional ills. Thus not pleasure alone, but health, demanded sexual gratification and liberation.

Many taboos flew out the window as sex-conscious Americans let themselves go. As unknowing Freudians, teenagers pioneered the sexual frontiers. Glued together in syncopated embrace, they danced to jazz music squeaking from phonographs. In an earlier day a kiss had been the equivalent of a proposal of marriage. But in the new era exploratory young folk sat in darkened movie houses or took to the highways and byways in automobiles—branded "houses of prostitution on wheels" by straitlaced elders. There, the youthful "neckers" and "petters" poached upon the forbidden territory of each other's bodies.

If the flapper was the goddess of the "era of wonderful nonsense," jazz was its sacred music. With its virtuoso wanderings and tricky syncopation, jazz moved up from New Orleans along with the migrating blacks during World War I. Tunes like W. C. Handy's "St. Louis Blues" became instant classics, as the wailing saxophone became the trumpet of the new era. Blacks gave birth to jazz, but the entertainment industry soon spawned all-white bands—notably Paul Whiteman's. Caucasian impresarios cornered the profits, though not the creative soul, of America's most native music.

Literary Liberation

Likewise in literature an older era seemed to have ground to a halt with the recent war. By the dawn of the 1920s, most of the custodians of an aging genteel culture had died—Henry James in 1916, Henry Adams in 1918, and William Dean Howells (the "Dean of American literature") in 1920. A few novelists who had been popular in the previous decades lingered on, notably the well-to-do, cosmopolitan New Yorker Edith Wharton and the Virginia-born Willa Cather, esteemed for her stark but sympathetic portrayals of pioneering on the prairies.

But in the decade after the war, a new generation of writers burst upon the scene. Many of them hailed from ethnic and regional backgrounds different from that of the Protestant New Englanders who traditionally had dominated American cultural life. The newcomers exhibited the energy of youth, the ambition of excluded outsiders, and in many cases, the smoldering resentment of ideals betrayed. They bestowed on American literature a new vitality, imaginativeness, and artistic quality.

A patron saint of many young authors was Henry L. Mencken, the "Bad Boy of Baltimore," who admired their critical attitude toward American society. But few went so far in their faultfinding as Mencken himself. Little escaped his acidic wit. In the pages of his green-covered monthly *American Mercury*, he wielded a slashing rapier as much as a pen. He assailed marriage, patriotism, democracy, prohibition, Rotarians, and the middle-class American "booboisie." The South he contemptuously dismissed as "the Sahara of the Bozart" (a bastardization of *beaux arts*, French for the "fine arts"), and he scathingly attacked do-gooders as "Puritans." Puritanism, he jibed, was "the haunting fear that someone, somewhere, might be happy."

The war had jolted many young writers out of their complacency about traditional values and literary standards. With their pens they probed for new codes of morals and understanding, as well as fresh forms of expression. F. Scott Fitzgerald, a handsome Minnesota-born Princetonian then only twenty-four years old, became an overnight celebrity when he published *This Side of Paradise* in 1920. The book became a kind of Bible for the young. It was eagerly devoured by aspiring flappers and their ardent wooers, many of whom affected an air of bewildered abandon toward life. Catching the spirit of the hour (often about 4 A.M.), Fitzgerald found "All gods dead, all wars fought, all faiths in man shaken." He followed this melancholy success with *The Great Gatsby* (1925), a brilliant evocation of the glamour and cruelty of an achievement-oriented society. Theodore Dreiser's masterpiece of 1925 explored much the same theme: *An American Tragedy* dealt with the murder of a pregnant working girl by her socially ambitious young lover.

F. Scott Fitzgerald and His Wife, Zelda   *They are shown here in the early days of their marriage. (Historical Pictures Service, Chicago.)*

Ernest Hemingway, who had seen action on the Italian front in 1917, was among the writers most affected by the war. He responded to pernicious propaganda and the overblown appeal to patriotism by devising his own lean, word-sparing style. Hemingway spoke with a voice that was to have many imitators but no real equals. In *The Sun Also Rises* (1926), he told of disillusioned, spiritually numb American expatriates in Europe. In *A Farewell to Arms* (1929), he crafted one of the finest novels in any language about the war experience. A troubled soul, he finally blew out his brains with a shotgun blast in 1961.

Other writers turned to a critical probing of American small-town life. Sherwood Anderson dissected various fictional personalities in *Winesburg, Ohio* (1919), finding them all in some way warped by their cramped psychological surroundings. But the chief chronicler of midwestern life was spindly, red-haired, heavy-drinking Sinclair Lewis, a hotheaded journalistic product of Sauk Centre, Minnesota. A master of satire, he sprang into prominence in 1920 with *Main Street*, the story of one woman's unsuccessful war against provincialism. In *Babbitt* (1922) he affectionately pilloried George F. Babbitt, a prosperous, vulgar, middle-class real estate broker who slavishly conformed to the respectable materialism of his group. The word *Babbittry* was quickly coined to describe his all-too-familiar life-style.

William Faulkner, a dark-eyed, pensive Mississippian, penned a bitter war novel in 1926, *Soldier's Pay*. He then turned his attention to a fictional chronicle of an imaginary, history-rich Deep South county. In powerful books like *The Sound and the Fury* (1929) and *As I Lay Dying* (1930), Faulkner peeled back layers of time and consciousness from the constricted souls of his ingrown southern characters.

Nowhere was innovation in the 1920s more obvious than in poetry. Ezra Pound, a brilliantly erratic Idahoan who deserted America for Europe, rejected what he called "an old bitch civilization, gone in the teeth" and proclaimed his doctrine: "Make It New." Pound strongly influenced the Missouri-born and Harvard-educated T. S. Eliot, who took up residence in England. In "The Waste Land" (1922), Eliot produced one of the most impenetrable but

influential poems of the century. Robert Frost, a San Francisco–born poet, wrote hauntingly about his adopted New England. The most daringly innovative of all was e. e. cummings, who relied on unorthodox diction and peculiar typesetting to produce startling poetical effects.

On the stage, Eugene O'Neill, a New York dramatist and Princeton dropout of globe-trotting background, laid bare Freudian notions of sex in plays like *Strange Interlude* (1928). A prodigious playwright, he authored more than a dozen productions in the 1920s and won the Nobel Prize in 1936.

O'Neill arose from New York's Greenwich Village, which before and after the war was a seething cauldron of writers, painters, musicians, actors, and other would-be artists. After the war, a black cultural renaissance also took root uptown in Harlem, led by such gifted writers as Claude McKay and Langston Hughes, and jazz artists like Louis Armstrong. They proudly exulted in their black culture. Although many whites frequented the black jazz joints, black writers were yet to win a wide audience among white readers.

Architecture also married itself to the new materialism and functionalism. Long-range city planning was being intelligently projected, and architects like Frank Lloyd Wright were advancing the theory that buildings should grow from their sites and not slavishly imitate Greek and Roman importations. The machine age outdid itself in New York City when it thrust upward the cloud-brushing Empire State Building, 102 stories high. Dedicated in 1931, the "Empty State Building" towered partially vacant during the depressed 1930s.

Wall Street's Big Bull Market

The boom of the golden twenties showered genuine benefits on Americans. Their incomes and living standards assuredly rose, but there always seemed to be something fantastic about it all. People sang, somewhat incredulously:

> My sister she works in the laundry,
> My father sells bootlegger gin,
> My mother she takes in the washing,
> My God! how the money rolls in!

Signals abounded that the economic joyride might end in a crash; even in the best years of the 1920s several hundred banks failed annually. This something-for-nothing craze was well illustrated by real estate speculation, especially the fantastic Florida boom that culminated in 1925. Numerous underwater lots were sold to eager purchasers for preposterous sums. The whole wildcat scheme collapsed when the peninsula was devastated by a West Indian hurricane, which belied advertisements of a "soothing tropical wind."

The stock exchange provided even greater sensations. Speculation ran wild, and an orgy of boom-or-bust trading pushed the bull market up to dizzy peaks. "Never sell America short" and "Be a bull on America" were favorite catchwords, as Wall Street gamblers gored one another and fleeced greedy lambs. The stock market became a veritable gambling den.

As the 1920s lurched forward, everybody seemed to be buying stocks "on margin"—that is, with a small down payment. Barbers, stenographers, and elevator boys cashed in on "hot tips" picked up while on duty. One valet was reported to have parlayed his wages into a quarter of a million dollars. "The cash register crashed the social register" as rags-to-riches Americans eagerly worshiped at the altar of the ticker-tape machine. So powerful was the intoxicant of quick profits that few heeded the voices raised in certain quarters to warn that this kind of tinsel prosperity could not last forever.

Little was done by Washington to curb money-mad speculators. In the wartime days of Wilson, the national debt had rocketed from the 1914 figure of $1,188,235,400 to the 1921 peak of $23,976,250,608. Conservative principles of money management pointed to a diversion of surplus funds to reduce this financial burden.

A businesslike move toward economic sanity was made in 1921, when a Republican Congress created the Bureau of the Budget. Its director was to assist the president in preparing

Calvin Coolidge Presides over the "Jazz Age" *His hands-off policies were sweet music to big business. (Culver Pictures.)*

careful estimates of receipts and expenditures for submission to Congress as the annual budget. This reform, long overdue, was designed in part to prevent haphazardly extravagant appropriations.

The burdensome taxes inherited from the war were especially distasteful to Secretary of the Treasury Mellon, as well as to his fellow millionaires. Their theory was that such high levies forced the rich to invest in tax-exempt securities rather than in the factories that provided prosperous payrolls. The Mellonites also argued, with considerable persuasiveness, that high taxes not only discouraged business but, in so doing, also brought a smaller net return to the Treasury than moderate taxes.

Seeking to succor the "poor" rich people, Mellon helped engineer a series of tax reductions from 1921 to 1926. Congress followed his lead by repealing the excess-profits tax, abolishing the gift tax, and reducing excise taxes, the surtax, the income tax, and estate taxes. In 1921 a wealthy person with an income of $1 million had paid $663,000 in income taxes; in 1926 the same person paid about $200,000. Mellon's spare-the-rich policies thus shifted much of the tax burden from the wealthy to the middle-income groups.

Mellon, the "greatest secretary of the treasury since Hamilton," remains a controversial figure. True, he reduced the national debt by $10 billion—from about $26 billion to $16 billion. But foes of the emaciated multimillionaire charged that he should have bitten a larger chunk out of the debt, especially while the country was pulsating with prosperity. He was also accused of indirectly encouraging the bull market. If he had absorbed more of the national income in taxes, there would have been less money left for frenzied speculation. His refusal to do so typified the single-mindedly probusiness regime that dominated the political scene throughout the postwar decade.

Varying Viewpoints

Many historians have depicted the 1920s as a great watershed in the history of American culture, seeing it as the "first decade of modern America." Frederick Lewis Allen's immensely popular book, *Only Yesterday* (1931), probably did more than any other single work to project the image of the 1920s as a decade that witnessed what Allen called a "revolution in manners and morals." The census finding in 1920 that a majority of Americans now lived in urban areas, the seeming "defeat" of religious Fundamentalism at the Scopes trial, the emergence of the "flapper," and the shift from a capital-goods to a consumer-goods economic base are often cited as evidence of this social transformation. The advertising executive at the wheel of a Ford seemed to have replaced the farmer behind a plow as the typical American.

But the modern, transformative character of the 1920s has perhaps been exaggerated. The Great Depression amply demonstrated that familiar problems of the business cycle remained. Mounting evidence points to the persistence of ethnic identities and immigrant and minority cultural traits. Changes in sexual behavior and the roles of women had roots deep in the industrializing, urbanizing era of the nineteenth century. Folklore to the contrary, prohibition *did* diminish the consumption of alcohol by Americans. Recent events have demonstrated the continued vitality of "old-time religion." And rural culture, manifested in widespread suspicion of cities and the popularity of "country western" music, still lives.

Select Readings

Primary Source Documents

For the fallout from the red scare, see Walter Lippmann's eloquent plea for the lives of the Italian-American radicals Sacco and Vanzetti in the New York *World** (August 19, 1927). The life of automaker and business magnate Henry Ford is told in his *My Life and Work** (1922). For caustic fictional versions of those conditions, see the novels of Sinclair Lewis, *Babbit* (1922), *Arrowsmith* (1925), and *Main Street* (1920).

Secondary Sources

The best introduction to the 1920s is William Leuchtenburg, *The Perils of Prosperity, 1914–1932* (1958). Frederick Lewis Allen, *Only Yesterday* (1931), is an evocative recollection of the texture of life in the decade. Equally informative are Robert S. Lynd and Helen M. Lynd's classic sociological studies, *Middletown* (1929) and *Middletown in Transition* (1937). Robert K. Murray, *Red Scare* (1955), is authoritative; on the same subject, see Stanley Coben, *A. Mitchell Palmer* (1963). Immigration restriction is dealt with in John Higham, *Strangers in the Land* (1955). Paul A. Carter, *Another Part of the Twenties* (1977), also deals with immigration and ethnicity. The standard work on the revived Klan is David M. Chalmers, *Hooded Americanism* (rev. ed., 1981). Also valuable is Kenneth T. Jackson, *The Ku Klux Klan in the City, 1915–1930* (1967). The changing experiences of women are discussed in Winnifred Wandersee, *Women's Work and Family Values, 1920–1940* (1981); Lois Scharf and Joan M. Jensen, eds., *Decades of Discontent: The Women's Movement, 1920–1940* (1983); and the final chapters of Lois Banner's *American Beauty* (1983). Prohibition is handled in Andrew Sinclair, *Era of Excess: A Social History of the Prohibition Movement* (1962),

and Norman H. Clark's highly readable *Deliver Us from Evil* (1976). On a related subject, see Humbert S. Nelli, *The Business of Crime* (1976). Revealing on the Scopes trial are Ray Ginger, *Six Days or Forever?* (1958), and Lawrence W. Levine's sensitive study of William Jennings Bryan, *Defender of the Faith* (1965). On the economy, see George H. Soule, *Prosperity Decade* (1947); Alfred D. Chandler, Jr., *Strategy and Structure: Chapters in the History of Industrial Enterprise* (1962); Irving Bernstein, *The Lean Years: A History of the American Worker, 1920–1933* (1960); and Daniel Nelson, *Frederick Winslow Taylor and the Rise of Scientific Management* (1980). On advertising, consult Stuart Ewen, *Captains of Consciousness* (1976), and Daniel Pope, *The Making of Modern Advertising* (1983). Movies are featured in Lary May, *Screening Out the Past: The Birth of Mass Culture and the Motion Picture Industry* (1980), and in Robert Sklar, *Movie-Made America* (1975). The "youth culture" is the subject of Paula Fass, *The Damned and the Beautiful: American Youth in the 1920s* (1977). Changing sexual attitudes are analyzed in David M. Kennedy, *Birth Control in America: The Career of Margaret Sanger* (1970). Gilbert Osofsky describes the background of the "Harlem renaissance" in *Harlem: The Making of a Ghetto, 1890–1930* (1966). See also David Lewis, *When Harlem Was in Vogue* (1981). William M. Tuttle, *Race Riot: Chicago in the Red Summer of 1919* (1970), describes the violent side of race relations in the 1920s. Three stimulating literary histories are Frederick J. Hoffman, *The Twenties: American Writing in the Postwar Decade* (1955); Alfred Kazin, *On Native Grounds* (1942); and Daniel J. Singal, *The War Within: From Victorian to Modernist Thought in the South, 1919–1945* (1982). David M. Kennedy, *Over Here: The First World War and American Society* (1980), pays special attention to the literature that emerged from the war experience.

37

The Politics of Boom and Bust, 1920–1932

We in America today are nearer to the final triumph over poverty than ever before in the history of any land. We have not yet reached the goal—but . . . we shall soon, with the help of God, be in sight of the day when poverty will be banished from this nation.

Herbert Hoover, 1928

The Republican "Old Guard" Returns

Handsome President Harding—with erect figure (6 feet; 1.83 meters), broad shoulders, high forehead, bushy eyebrows, and graying hair—was one of the best-liked men of his generation. An easygoing, warm-handed first-namer, he exuded graciousness and love of people. So kindly was his nature that he would brush off ants rather than crush them.

Yet the amiable, smiling exterior concealed a weak, flabby interior. With a mediocre mind, Harding quickly found himself beyond his depth in the presidency. "God! What a job!" was his anguished cry on one occasion.

Harding, like Grant, was unable to detect moral halitosis in his evil associates, and he was soon surrounded by his poker-playing, shirt-sleeved cronies of the "Ohio Gang." "A good guy," Harding was "one of the boys." He hated to hurt people's feelings, especially those of his friends, by saying "no"; and designing political leeches capitalized on this weakness. The difference between George Washington and Warren Harding, ran a current quip, was that while Washington could not tell a lie, Harding could not tell a liar. He "was not a bad man," said one Washington observer. "He was just a slob."

Candidate Harding, who admitted his scanty mental furnishings, had promised to gather about him the "best minds" of the party. Charles Evans Hughes—masterful, imperious, incisive, brilliant—brought to the secretaryship of state a dominating if somewhat conservative leadership. The new secretary of the treasury was a lean and elderly Pittsburgh aluminum king, Andrew W. Mellon, multimillionaire collector of the paintings that are now displayed in Washington as his gift to the nation. Chubby-faced Herbert Hoover, famed feeder of the Belgians and Food Administrator, became secretary of commerce. An energetic businessman and engineer, he raised his second-rate cabinet post to first-rate importance, especially in drumming up foreign trade for American manufacturers.

But the "best minds" of the cabinet were largely offset by two of the worst. Senator Albert B. Fall of New Mexico, a scheming anticonservationist, was appointed secretary of the interior. As guardian of the nation's natural resources, he resembled the wolf hired to protect the sheep. Harry M. Daugherty, a small-town lawyer but a big-time crook in the "Ohio Gang," was supposed to prosecute wrongdoers as attorney general.

President Warren G. Harding (1865–1923) *Harding's father was rumored to have said that if Warren had been born a girl, she would have been "in trouble" much of the time because of an inability to say "no." (Brown Brothers.)*

GOP Reaction at the Throttle

Well intentioned but weak-willed, Harding was a perfect "front" for enterprising industrialists. A McKinley-style old order settled heavily back into place at war's end, crushing the reform seedlings that had sprouted in the progressive era. A blowsy, nest-feathering crowd moved into Washington and proceeded to hoodwink Harding, whom many regarded as an "amiable boob."

This new Old Guard hoped to improve on the old business doctrine of *laissez-faire*. Their plea was not simply for government to keep hands off business but for government to help guide business along the path to profits. They subtly and effectively achieved their ends by putting the courts and the administrative bureaus into the safekeeping of fellow standpatters. Harding initiated these practices and set the tone of Republican economic policies for the rest of the decade.

The Supreme Court was a striking example of this trend. Harding lived less than three years as president, but to him fell the task of appointing four of the nine justices. Several of his choices were or became deep-dyed reactionaries, and they held the dike against popular currents for nearly two decades. Harding's fortunate choice for chief justice was ex-President Taft, who not only performed his duties ably but surprisingly was more liberal than some of his cautious associates.

In the first years of the 1920s, the Supreme Court axed progressive legislation. It killed a federal child-labor law, stripped away many of labor's hard-won gains, and rigidly restricted governmental intervention in the economy. In the landmark case of *Adkins* v. *Children's Hospital* (1923), the Court invalidated a minimum-wage law for women. Its strained ruling was that because females now had the vote (Nineteenth Amendment), they could no longer be protected by special legislation.

> Mr. Justice Holmes, wryly dissenting in the Adkins *case, said: "It would need more than the Nineteenth Amendment to convince me that there are no differences between men and women, or that legislation cannot take those differences into account."*

Corporations, under Harding, could once more relax and expand. Antitrust laws were often ignored, circumvented, or feebly upheld by friendly prosecutors in the attorney general's office. The Interstate Commerce Commission, to single out one agency, came to be dominated by men who were personally sympathetic to the managers of the railroads. Harding reactionaries might well have boasted, "We care not what laws the Democrats pass as long as we are permitted to administer them."

Big industrialists, striving to lessen competition, now had a free hand to set up trade associations. Cement manufacturers, for example, would use these agencies to agree upon standardization of product, publicity campaigns, and a united front in dealing with the railroads and labor. Although many of these associations ran counter to the spirit of existing antitrust legislation, their formation was encouraged by Secretary Hoover. His sense of engineering efficiency was shocked by the waste resulting from cutthroat competition.

The Aftermath of War

Wartime government controls on the economy were swiftly dismantled. The War Industries Board disappeared with almost indecent haste. With its passing, progressive hopes for more government regulation of big business evaporated.

Washington likewise returned the railroads to private management in 1920. Reformers had hoped that wartime government operation of the lines might lead to their permanent nationalization. Instead, Congress passed the Esch-Cummins Transportation Act of 1920, which encouraged private consolidation of the railroads and pledged the Interstate Commerce Commission to guarantee their profitability. The new philosophy was not to save the country from the railroads, as in the days of the Populists, but to save the railroads for the country.

The federal government also tried to pull up anchor and get out of the shipping business. The Merchant Marine Act of 1920 authorized the Shipping Board, which controlled about fifteen hundred vessels, to dispose of much of the hastily built wartime fleet at bargain-basement prices. The board operated the remaining vessels without conspicuous success. Under the LaFollette Seaman's Act of 1915, American shipping could not thrive in competition with foreigners, who all too often provided their crews with wretched food and starvation wages.

Labor, suddenly deprived of its wartime crutch of friendly government support, limped along badly in the postwar decade. A bloody strike in the steel industry was ruthlessly broken in 1919, partly by exploiting ethnic and racial divisions among the steelworkers and partly by branding the strikers as dangerous "reds." The Railway Labor Board, a successor body to the wartime labor boards, ordered a wage cut of 12 percent in 1922, provoking a two-month strike. It ended when Attorney General Daugherty, who fully shared Harding's big-business bias, clamped on the strikers one of the most sweeping injunctions in American history. Unions wilted in this hostile political environment, and membership dropped by nearly 30 percent between 1920 and 1930.

Vicious race riots also rocked the Republic in the years following the Great War. The prospect of fat pay envelopes in smoking war plants had sucked thousands of blacks out of the South into such northern industrial cities as New York and Chicago. The war thus kicked off a historic exodus that redistributed America's black population, with lasting social and political effects. But in the immediate postwar period, blacks were brutally taught that the North was not a promised land. A racial reign of terror descended on Chicago in the summer of 1919, leaving twenty-three blacks and fifteen whites dead. Clashes also inflamed Knoxville, Omaha, Washington, and other cities.

Needy veterans were among the few non-business groups to reap lasting gains from the war. Congress in 1921 generously created the Veterans' Bureau, authorized to operate hospitals and provide vocational rehabilitation for the disabled.

Veterans quickly organized into pressure groups. The American Legion was founded in Paris in 1919 by Colonel Theodore Roosevelt, Jr. Legionnaires met periodically to renew old hardships and let off steam in good-natured horseplay. The Legion soon became distinguished for its militant patriotism, rock-ribbed conservatism, and zealous anti-radicalism.

The Legion also became notorious for its aggressive lobbying for veterans' benefits. The chief grievance of the former "doughboys" was monetary—they wanted their "dough." The former servicemen demanded "adjusted compensation" to make up for the wages they had "lost" when they turned in their work clothes for military uniforms during the Great War.

Critics denounced this demand as a holdup "bonus," but the millions of veterans deployed heavy political artillery. They browbeat Congress into passing a bonus bill in 1922, which Harding promptly vetoed. Re-forming their lines, the repulsed veterans gathered for a final attack. In 1924 Congress again hoisted the white flag and passed the Adjusted Compensation Act. It gave every former soldier a paid-up insurance policy due in twenty years—adding about $3.5 billion to the total cost of the war. Penny-pinching Calvin Coolidge sternly vetoed the measure, but Congress overrode him, leaving the veterans with their loot.

America Seeks Benefits without Burdens

Making peace with the fallen foe was the most pressing problem left on Harding's doorstep. The United States, having rejected the Treaty of Versailles, was still technically at war with Germany, Austria, and Hungary nearly three years after the armistice. Peace was finally achieved by lone-wolf tactics. In July 1921 Congress passed a simple joint resolution that declared the war officially ended.

Isolation was enthroned in Washington. The Harding administration, with the Senate "irreconcilables" holding a hatchet over its head, continued to regard the League of Nations as a thing unclean. Harding at first refused even to support the League's world health program. But the new world body was much too important to be completely ignored. "Unofficial observers" were sent to its seat in Geneva, Switzerland, to hang around like detectives shadowing a suspected criminal.

Harding could not completely turn his back on the outside world, especially the Middle East, where a sharp rivalry developed between America and Britain for oil-drilling concessions. Remembering that the Allies had floated to victory on a flood of oil, experts recognized that liquid "black gold" was to be as necessary as blood in the battles of tomorrow. Secretary Hughes at length secured for American oil companies the right to share in the exploitation of the sandy region's oil riches.

Disarmament was one international issue on which Harding, after much indecision, finally seized the initiative. He was prodded by businesspeople unwilling to dig deeper into their pockets for money to finance the ambitious naval building program started during the war. A deadly contest was shaping up with Britain and Japan, which watched with alarm as the oceans filled with American vessels. Britain still commanded the world's largest navy, but the clatter of American riveters proclaimed that the United States would soon overtake it. Tensions ran especially high in the Far East, where the Japanese were growing increasingly restive. Anxieties were further heightened by a long-standing Anglo-Japanese alliance (signed in 1902), which apparently obligated the British to join with Japan in the event of war between Japan and the United States.

Ship-Scrapping at the Washington Conference

Public agitation in America, fed by these worries, brought about the headline-making Washington "Disarmament" Conference in 1921–1922. Invitations went to all the major naval powers—except Bolshevik Russia, whose government the United States refused officially to recognize. The double agenda included naval disarmament and the situation in the Far East.

At the outset, Secretary Hughes startled the delegates, who were expecting the usual diplomatic fence-straddling, with a comprehensive, concrete plan for declaring a ten-year "holiday" on construction of battleships and even for scrapping some of the huge dreadnoughts already built or being built. He proposed that the scaled-down navies of America and Britain should enjoy parity in battleships and aircraft carriers, with Japan on the small end of a 5–5–3 ratio. This arrangement sounded to the sensitive Japanese ambassador like "Rolls-Royce, Rolls-Royce, Ford."

Complex bargaining followed in the wake of Hughes's proposals. The Five-Power Naval Treaty of 1922 embodied Hughes's ideas on ship ratios, but only after face-saving compensation was offered to the insecure Japanese. The British and Americans both conceded that they would refrain from fortifying their Far Eastern possessions, including the Philippines. The Japanese were not subjected to such restraints in their possessions. In addition, a four-power treaty replaced the Anglo-Japanese alliance. The new pact bound Britain, Japan, France, and the United States to preserve the status quo in the Pacific—another concession to the jumpy Japanese. Finally, the Washington Conference gave chaotic China—"the Sick Man of the Far East"—a shot in the arm with the Nine-Power Treaty of 1922, whose signatories agreed to nail wide open the Open Door in China.

When the final gavel banged, the Harding-ites boasted with much fanfare—and some justice—of their globe-shaking achievement in disarmament. But their satisfaction was somewhat illusory. No restrictions had been placed on small warships, and the other powers churned ahead with the construction of cruisers, destroyers, and submarines, while penny-pinching Uncle Sam lagged dangerously behind. Congress also pointedly declared that it was making no commitment to the use of armed force or any kind of joint action when it ratified the Four-Power Treaty. These reservations, in effect, rendered the treaty a dead letter. Ominously, the American people seemed content to rely for their security on words and wishful thinking rather than on weapons and hard-headed realism.

A similar sentimentalism welled up later in the decade, when Americans clamored for the "outlawry of war." The conviction spread that if quarreling nations would only take the pledge to foreswear war as an instrument of national policy, swords could be beaten into plowshares. Calvin Coolidge's secretary of state, Frank B. Kellogg, who later won the Nobel Peace Prize for his role, was lukewarm about the idea. But after petitions bearing more than 2 million signatures cascaded into Washington, he signed with the French foreign minister in 1928 the famed Kellogg-Briand Pact. Officially known as the Pact of Paris, it was ultimately ratified by sixty-two nations.

	Battleships	Battleship Tonnage	Aircraft Carrier Tonnage
U. S.	18	525,000	135,000
Britain	22	525,000	135,000
Japan	10	315,000	81,000
France	7	175,000	60,000
Italy	6	175,000	60,000

Limits Imposed by Washington Conference *The pledge of the British and Americans to refrain from fortifying their Far Eastern possessions, while Japan was allowed to fortify its, was the key to the naval limitation treaty. The United States and Great Britain thus won a temporary victory but later paid a horrendous price when they had to dislodge the well-entrenched Japanese from the Pacific in World War II.*

As for the burdens of armament, the New York Independent, *a prominent magazine, noted in January 1921 that the country was "more afraid of the tax collector than of any more distant foe."*

This new parchment peace was delusory in the extreme. Defensive wars were still permitted, and what scheming aggressor could not cook up an excuse of self-defense? Lacking both muscles and teeth, the pact was a diplomatic derelict—and virtually useless in a showdown. Yet it accurately—and dangerously—reflected the American mind in the 1920s, which was all too ready to be lulled into a false sense of security. This mood took even deeper hold in the ostrichlike neutralism of the 1930s.

Hiking the Tariff Higher

A comparable lack of realism afflicted foreign economic policy in the 1920s. Businesspeople, shortsightedly obsessed with the dazzling prospects in the prosperous home market, sought to keep that market to themselves by flinging up high, virtually unclimbable, tariff walls around the United States. They were spurred into action by their fear of a flood of cheap goods from recovering Europe, especially in the brief but sharp recession of 1920–1921.

In 1922 Congress passed the comprehensive Fordney-McCumber Tariff Law. Glib lobbyists once more descended upon Washington and helped boost schedules from the average of 27 percent under Wilson's Underwood Tariff of 1913 to an average of 38.5 percent, which was almost as high as Taft's Payne-Aldrich Tariff of 1909. (See the Appendix.) Duties on farm produce were increased, and the principle was proclaimed that the general rates were designed to equalize the cost of American and foreign production. A promising degree of flexibility was introduced for the first time, when the president was authorized, with the advice of the fact-finding Tariff Commission, to reduce or increase duties by as much as 50 percent.

Presidents Harding and Coolidge, true to their big-industry sympathies, were far more friendly to tariff increases than to reductions. In six years they authorized thirty-two upward changes, including on their list vital commodities like dairy products, chemicals, and pig iron. During the same period the White House ordered only five reductions. These included mill feed and such trifling items as bobwhite quail, paintbrush handles, phenol, and cresylic acid.

The high-tariff course thus charted by the Republican regimes set off an ominous chain reaction. European producers felt the squeeze, for the American tariff walls prolonged the postwar chaos. An impoverished Europe needed to sell its manufactured goods to the United States, particularly if it hoped to achieve economic recovery and to pay its huge war debt to Washington. America needed to give foreign nations a chance to make a profit from it so that they could buy its manufactured articles and repay debts. International trade, Americans were slow to learn, is a two-way street. In general, they could not sell to others in quantity unless they bought from them in quantity—or lent them more American dollars.

"It Works Both Ways," 1921 *(Courtesy of Dallas News.)*

Erecting tariff walls was a game that two could play. The American example spurred European nations, throughout the feverish 1920s, to pile up higher barriers themselves. These artificial obstacles were doubly bad: they hurt not only American-made goods but the products of neighboring European countries as well. The whole vicious circle further deepened the international economic distress, providing one more rung on the ladder by which Adolf Hitler scrambled to power.

The Stench of Scandal

Loose morality and get-rich-quickism of the Harding era manifested themselves spectacularly in a series of scandals.

Early in 1923 Colonel Charles R. Forbes, onetime deserter from the army, was caught with his hand in the till and resigned as head of the Veterans' Bureau. An appointee of the gullible Harding, he and his accomplices looted the government to the tune of about $200 million, chiefly in connection with the building of veterans' hospitals. He was sentenced to two years in a federal penitentiary.

Most shocking of all was the Teapot Dome scandal, an affair that involved priceless naval oil reserves at Teapot Dome (Wyoming) and Elk Hills (California). In 1921 the slippery secretary of the interior, Albert B. Fall, induced his careless colleague, Secretary of the Navy Denby, to transfer these valuable properties to the Interior Department. Harding indiscreetly signed the secret order. Fall then quietly leased the lands to oilmen Harry F. Sinclair and Edward L. Doheny, but not until he had received a bribe ("loan") of $100,000 from Doheny and about three times that amount in all from Sinclair.

Teapot Dome, no tempest in a teapot, finally came to a whistling boil. Details of the crooked transaction gradually began to leak out in March 1923, two years after Harding took office. Fall, Sinclair, and Doheny were indicted the next year, but the case dragged through the courts until 1929. Finally Fall was found guilty of taking a bribe and was sentenced to one year in jail. By a curious quirk of justice, the two bribe givers were acquitted while the bribe taker was convicted, although Sinclair served several months in jail for having "shadowed" jurors and for refusing to testify before a Senate committee.

The oily smudge from Teapot Dome polluted the prestige of the Washington government. Right-thinking citizens wondered what was going on when public officials could sell out the nation's vital resources, especially those reserved for the United States Navy. The acquittal of Sinclair and Doheny undermined faith in the courts, while giving further currency to the cynical sayings, "You can't put a million dollars in jail" and "In America everyone is assumed guilty until proven rich."

Others scandals erupted, two of them involving suicides. Persistent reports as to the underhanded doings of Attorney General Daugherty brought a Senate investigation in 1924 of the illegal sale of pardons and liquor permits. Forced to resign, the accused official was tried in 1927 but was released after a jury twice failed to agree. During the trial, Daugherty hid behind the trousers of the now-dead Harding by implying that persistent probing might uncover crookedness in the White House.

Harding was mercifully spared the full revelation of these iniquities, though his worst suspicions were aroused. While the scandals were beginning to break, he embarked upon a speechmaking tour across the country all the way to Alaska. On the return trip he died in San Francisco, on August 2, 1923, of pneumonia and thrombosis. His death may have been hastened by a broken heart resulting from the disloyalty of designing friends. Mourning millions, not yet fully aware of the graft in Washington, expressed genuine sorrow.

The brutal fact is that Harding was not a big enough man for the presidency—as he himself privately admitted. Such was his weakness that he tolerated persons and conditions that subjected the Republic to its worst disgrace since the days of President Grant.

Calvin Coolidge: A Yankee in the White House

News of Harding's death was sped to Vice-President Coolidge, then visiting at the New England farmhouse of his father. By the light of two kerosene lamps the elder Coolidge, a justice of the peace, used the old family Bible to administer the presidential oath to his son.

This homespun setting was symbolic of Coolidge. Quite unlike Harding, the stern-faced Vermonter, with his thin nose and tightly set lips, embodied the New England virtues of honesty, morality, industry, and frugality. As a youth, his father reported, he seemed to get more sap out of a maple tree than did any of the other boys. Practicing a rigid economy in both money and words, "Silent Cal" came to be known in Washington conversational circles for his brilliant flashes of silence. His dour, serious visage prompted the acid observation that he had been "weaned on a pickle."

Coolidge seemed to be a crystallization of the commonplace. A painfully shy individual of average height (5 feet 10 inches; 1.77 meters), he was blessed with only mediocre powers of leadership. He would occasionally display a dry wit in private; but his speeches, delivered in a nasal New England twang, were invariably boring. A staunch apostle of the status quo, he was no

Farm-Bred Coolidge Revisits Vermont   *(Harvard College Library.)*

The Cash Register Chorus   *Business croons its appreciation of "Coolidge prosperity." (Courtesy, St. Louis Post-Dispatch and the State Historical Society of Missouri.)*

THE CASH REGISTER CHORUS.

knight in armor riding forth to tilt at wrongs. His only horse, in fact, was an electric-powered steed on which he took his exercise. True to Republican philosophy, he became the "high priest of the great god Business." He believed that "the man who builds a factory builds a temple" and the "the man who works there worships there."

The hands-off temperament of "Cautious Cal" Coolidge suited the times perfectly. His thrifty, cheese-paring nature caused him to sympathize fully with Secretary of the Treasury Mellon's efforts to reduce both taxes and debts. No foe of industrial bigness, he let business have its head. "Coolidge luck" held during his 5 1/2 prosperity-blessed years.

Ever a profile in caution, Coolidge slowly gave the Harding regime a badly needed moral fumigation. Teapot Dome had scalded the Republican party badly, but so transparently honest was the vinegary Vermonter that the scandalous oil did not rub off on him. The public, though at first shocked by scandal, quickly simmered down; and an alarming tendency developed in certain quarters to excuse some of the wrongdoers on the grounds that "they had gotten away with it." Some critics even condemned the government prosecutors for continuing to rock the boat. America's moral sense was evidently being dulled by prosperity.

Mechanizing Agriculture
Just as the automobile replaced the horse on city streets, so did the gas-engine tractor replace horses and mules on the nation's farms in the 1920s. American farmers owned ten times more tractors in 1930 than they had owned in 1920. The smoke-belching tractors bolstered productivity—and also increased the farmers' debt burden, as the depression made tragically clear. (Library of Congress.)

Have you placed a Sentimental Value on your Horses out of proportion to the work they are able to perform?

BAILOR MOTOR CULTIVATORS

Frustrated Farmers

Sun-bronzed farmers were caught squarely in a boom-or-bust cycle in the postwar decade. While the fighting had raged, they had raked in money hand over gnarled fist; by the spring of 1920 the price of wheat had shot up to an incredible three dollars a bushel. But peace brought an end to government-guaranteed high prices and to massive purchases by other nations, as foreign production reentered the stream of world commerce.

Machines also threatened to plow the farmers under an avalanche of their own overabundant crops. The gasoline-engine tractor was working a revolution on American farms. This steel mule was to cultivation and sowing what the McCormick reaper was to harvesting. Blue-denimed husbandmen no longer had to plod after the horse-drawn plow with high-footed gait. They could sit erect on their chugging mechanical chariots and turn under and harrow many acres in a single day. They could grow bigger crops on larger areas, using fewer horses and hired hands. The wartime boom had encouraged them to bring vast new tracts under cultivation, especially in the "wheat belt" of the up-

per Midwest. But such improved efficiency and expanded agricultural acreage helped to pile up more price-dampening surpluses. A withering depression swept through agricultural districts in the 1920s, when one farm in four was sold for debt or taxes.

As a plaintive song of the period ran:

> No use talkin', any man's beat,
> With 'leven-cent cotton and forty-cent meat.

Schemes abounded for bringing relief to the hard-pressed farmers. A bipartisan "farm bloc" from the agricultural states sprouted up in Congress in 1921 and succeeded in driving through some helpful laws. Noteworthy was the Capper-Volstead Act, which exempted farmers' marketing cooperatives from antitrust prosecution. The farm bloc's favorite proposal was the McNary-Haugen Bill, pushed energetically from 1924 to 1928. It sought to keep agricultural prices high by authorizing the government to buy up surpluses and sell them abroad. Losses to the government were to be made up by a special tax on the farmers. Congress twice passed the bill, but frugal Calvin Coolidge twice vetoed it. Farm prices stayed down, and the farmers' political temperatures stayed high, reaching fever pitch in the election of 1924.

A Three-Way Race for the White House in 1924

Self-satisfied Republicans, chanting "Keep Cool and Keep Coolidge," nominated "Silent Cal" for the presidency at their convention in Cleveland in the simmering summer of 1924. Squabbling Democrats had more difficulty choosing a candidate when they met in New York's sweltering Madison Square Garden. Reflecting many of the cultural tensions of the decade, the party was hopelessly split between "wets" and "drys," urbanites and farmers, Fundamentalists and Modernists, northern liberals and southern standpatters, immigrants and old-stock Americans. In one symptomatic spasm of discord, the conventioneers failed by just one vote to pass a resolution condemning the Ku Klux Klan.

Deadlocked for an unprecedented 102 ballots, the convention at last turned wearily, sweatily, and unenthusiastically to John W. Davis. A wealthy corporation lawyer connected with the Wall Street banking house of J. P. Morgan and Company, the polished nominee was no less conservative than cautious Calvin Coolidge.

The field was now wide open for a liberal candidate. The white-pompadoured Senator ("Fighting Bob") LaFollette from the state of Wisconsin, perennial aspirant to the presidency and now sixty-nine years of age, sprang forward to lead a new Progressive grouping. He gained the endorsement of the American Federation of Labor and enjoyed the support of the shrinking Socialist party, but his major constituency was made up of the price-pinched farmers. LaFollette's new Progressive party, fielding only a presidential ticket, with no candidates for local office, was a head without a body. It proved to be only a shadow of the robust Progressive coalition of prewar days. Its platform called for government ownership of railroads and relief for farmers, lashed out at monopoly and antilabor injunctions, and urged a constitutional amendment to limit the Supreme Court's power to invalidate laws passed by Congress.

LaFollette turned in a respectable showing, polling nearly 5 million votes. But "Cautious Cal" and the oil-bespattered Republicans slipped easily back into office, overwhelming Davis, 15,718,211 votes to 8,385,283. The electoral count stood at 382 for Coolidge, 136 for Davis, and 13 for LaFollette, all from his home state of Wisconsin. As the so-called conscience of the calloused 1920s, LaFollette injected a badly needed liberal tonic into a decade

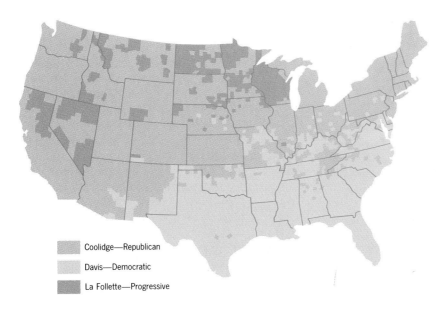

- Coolidge—Republican
- Davis—Democratic
- La Follette—Progressive

Presidential Election of 1924 (showing popular vote by county) *Note the concentration of LaFollette's votes in the old Populist strongholds of the Middle West and the mountain states. His ticket did especially well in the grain-growing districts battered by the postwar slump in agricultural prices.*

drugged on prosperity. But times were too good for too many for his reforming message to carry the day.

Foreign-Policy Flounderings

Isolation continued to reign in the Coolidge era. Despite presidential proddings, the Senate proved unwilling to allow America to adhere to the World Court—the judicial arm of the still-suspect League of Nations. Coolidge only half-heartedly—and unsuccessfully—pursued further naval disarmament after the loudly trumpeted agreements worked out at the Washington Conference in 1922.

A glaring exception to Uncle Sam's inward-looking indifference to the outside world was his armed interventionism in the Caribbean and Central America. American troops were withdrawn (after an eight-year stay) from the Dominican Republic in 1924, but they remained in Haiti from 1914 to 1934. President Coolidge in 1925 briefly removed American bayonets from troubled Nicaragua, where they had glinted intermittently since 1909, but in 1926 he sent

"Harmony in Europe," 1932   *(Courtesy of Detroit News.)*

them back, five thousand strong, and they stayed until 1933. American oil companies clamored for a military expedition to Mexico in 1926 when the Mexican government began to assert its sovereignty over oil resources. Coolidge kept cool and defused the Mexican crisis with some skillful diplomatic negotiating. But his mailed-fist tactics elsewhere bred sore resentments south of the Rio Grande, where critics loudly assailed "*yanqui* imperialism."

Overshadowing all other foreign-policy problems in the 1920s was the knotty issue of international debts, a complicated tangle of private loans, Allied war debts, and German reparations payments. Almost overnight, World War I had reversed the international financial position of the United States. In 1914 America had been a debtor nation in the sum of about $4 billion; by 1922 it had become a creditor nation in the sum of about $16 billion. The almighty dollar rivaled the pound sterling as the financial giant of the world. American investors loaned some $10 billion to foreigners in the 1920s, though even this huge river of money could not fully refloat the war-shelled world economy. Americans, bewitched by lucrative investment opportunities in their domestic economy, did not lend nearly so large a fraction of their national income overseas as had the British in the prewar period.

The key knot in the debt tangle was the $10 billion that the United States Treasury had loaned to the Allies during and immediately after the war. Uncle Sam held their IOU's—and he wanted to be paid. The Allies, in turn, protested that the demand for repayment was grossly unfair. The French and the British pointed out, with much justice, that they had held up a wall of flesh and bone against the common foe until America the Unready had finally entered the fray. America, they argued, should write off its loans as war costs, just as the Allies had been tragically forced to write off the lives of millions of young men. The debtors also complained that the real effect of their borrowed dollars had been to fuel the boom in the already roaring wartime economy in America, where nearly all their purchases had been made. And the final straw, protested the Europeans, was that America's postwar tariff walls made it almost impossible for them to sell the goods to earn the dollars to pay their debts.

Unraveling the Debt Knot

Uncle Sam's tightfisted insistence on getting his money back helped to harden the hearts of the Allies against conquered Germany. The French and the British demanded that the Germans make enormous reparations payments, totaling some $32 billion, as compensation for war-inflicted damages. The Allies hoped to settle their debts to America with the money received from Germany. The French, seeking to extort lagging reparations payments, sent troops into Germany's industrialized Ruhr Valley in 1923. Berlin responded by permitting its currency to inflate astronomically. At one point in October 1923, a loaf of bread cost 480 million marks, or about $120 million in preinflation money. German society teetered on the brink of mad anarchy, and the whole international house of financial cards threatened to flutter down in colossal chaos.

Sensible statesmen now urged that war debts and reparations alike be drastically scaled down or even canceled outright. But to Americans such proposals smacked of "welshing" on a debt. "We went across, but they won't come across," cried a prominent politician. Scrooge-like, Calvin Coolidge turned aside suggestions

> Pundit Walter Lippmann wrote in the New York World (1926): "International debts are like bills submitted to pay for the damage done on a wild party by one's grandfather. The payment seems to the debtor like pure loss, and when it is paid by one nation to another it seems like tribute by the conquered to the conqueror. Money borrowed to build a railroad earns money to pay for itself. But money borrowed to fight a war produces nothing."

of debt cancellation with a typically terse question: "They hired the money, didn't they?" The Washington administration proved especially unrealistic in its dogged insistence that there was no connection whatever between debts and reparations.

Reality finally was partly recognized in the Dawes Plan of 1924. Negotiated largely by Charles Dawes, about to be nominated as Coolidge's running mate, it rescheduled German reparations payments and opened the way for further American private loans to Germany. The whole financial cycle now became still more complicated, as American bankers loaned money to Germany, Germany paid reparations to France and Britain, and the former Allies paid war debts to the United States. Clearly the source of this monetary merry-go-round was the

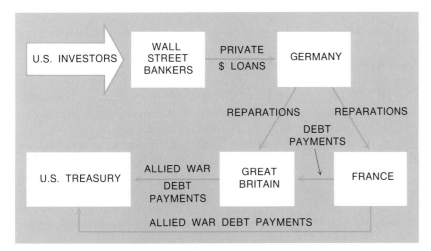

Aspects of the Financial Merry-go-round, 1921–1933 *Great Britain, with a debt of over $4 billion owed to the U.S. Treasury, had a huge stake in proposals for inter-Allied debt cancellation, but France's stake was even larger. Less prosperous than Britain in the 1920's, and more battered by the war, which had been fought on its own soil, France owed nearly $3.5 billion to the United States and additional billions to Britain.*

flowing well of American credit. When that well dried up after the great crash in 1929, the tangled jungle of international finance quickly turned into a desert. President Herbert Hoover declared a one-year debt moratorium in 1931, and before long all the debtors had defaulted—except "honest little Finland," which struggled along making payments until the last of her debt was erased in 1976.

Uncle Sam never did get his money, but he harvested a lush crop of ill will. Irate French crowds on occasion attacked American tourists, and throughout Europe Uncle Sam was caricatured as Uncle Shylock, greedily whetting his knife for the last pound of Allied flesh. The bad taste left in American mouths by the whole sorry episode contributed powerfully to the storm-cellar neutrality legislation passed by Congress in the 1930s.

The Triumph of Herbert Hoover, 1928

Poker-faced Calvin Coolidge, the tight-lipped "Sphinx of the Potomac," apparently bowed himself out of the 1928 presidential race when he tersely announced: "I do not choose to run." His logical successor was super-Secretary (of Commerce) Herbert Hoover, unpopular with the political bosses but the much-admired darling of the masses, who asked "Hoo but Hoover?" He was nominated on a platform that clucked contentedly over both prosperity and prohibition.

Still-squabbling Democrats nominated Alfred E. Smith, four-time governor of New York and one of the most colorful personalities in American politics. He was a wisecracking, glad-handing liberal who suffered from fatal political handicaps. "Al(cohol)" Smith was soakingly and drippingly "wet" at a time when the country was still devoted to the "noble experiment" of prohibition. To a nation that had only recently moved to the city, native New Yorker Smith seemed too abrasively urban. He was a Roman Catholic in an overwhelmingly Protestant—and unfortunately prejudiced—land. Many dry, rural, and Fundamentalist Democrats gagged

on his candidacy, and they saddled the wet Smith with a dry running mate and a dry platform. Jauntily sporting a brown derby and a big cigar, Smith, "the Happy Warrior," tried to carry alcohol on one shoulder and water on the other. But his effort was doomed from the start.

Radio figured prominently in this campaign for the first time, and it helped Hoover more than Smith. The New Yorker had more personal sparkle, but he could not project it through the radio (which in his Lower East Side twang he pronouned "radd-dee-o," grating on the ears of many listeners). Iowa-born Hoover, with his double-breasted dignity, came out of the microphone better than he went in. Decrying un-American "socialism" and preaching "rugged individualism," he sounded both grass-rootish and statesmanlike.

Chubby-faced, ruddy-complexioned Herbert Hoover, with his painfully high starched collar, was a living example of the American success story and an intriguing mixture of two centuries. As a poor orphan boy who had worked his way through Stanford University, he had absorbed the nineteenth-century copybook maxims of industry, thrift, and self-reliance. As a fabulously successful mining engineer and a brilliant businessman, he had honed to a high degree the efficiency doctrines of the progressive era.

A small-town boy from Iowa and Oregon, he had traveled and worked abroad extensively. Long years of self-imposed exile had deepened his determination, abundantly supported by national tradition, to avoid foreign entanglements. His experiences abroad had further strengthened his faith in American individualism, free enterprise, and small government.

With his unshaken dignity, Hoover was a far cry from the ordinary backslapping politician. Though a citizen of the world and loaded down with international honors, he was quite shy, standoffish, and stiff. Personally colorless in public, he had been accustomed during much of his life to giving orders to subordinates and not to soliciting votes. Never before elected to public office, he was thin-skinned in the face of criticism, and he did not adapt himself readily to the necessary give-and-take of political ac-

Herbert Hoover on the Road *"Whistle-stop" campaigns, with candidates speaking from the rear platforms of trains, were a standard feature of American politics before the advent of television. Herbert Hoover here speaks to a crowd in Akron, Ohio, during the 1932 campaign. (UPI/Bettmann Newsphotos; print from the collection of the Herbert Hoover Presidential Library.)*

commodation. His real power lay in his integrity, his humanitarianism, his passion for assembling the facts, his efficiency, his talents for administration, and his ability to inspire loyalty in close associates. They called him "the Chief."

As befitted America's newly mechanized civilization, Hoover was the ideal businessperson's candidate. A millionaire in his own right, he recoiled from anything suggesting socialism, paternalism, or "planned economy." Yet as secretary of commerce, he had exhibited some progressive instincts. He endorsed labor unions and supported federal regulation of the new radio broadcasting industry. He even flirted for a time with the idea of government-owned radio, similar to the British Broadcasting Corporation (BBC).

As bands blared Smith's theme song, "The Sidewalks of New York," the campaign sank into the sewers beneath the sidewalks. Despite the best efforts of Hoover and Smith, below-the-belt tactics were employed to a disgusting degree by lower-level campaigners. Religious bigotry raised its hideous head over Smith's Catholicism. An irresponsible whispering campaign claimed that "A Vote for Al Smith Is a Vote for the Pope" and that the White House, under Smith, would become a branch of the Vatican—complete with "Rum, Romanism, and Ruin." Hoover's attempts to quash such "smears" were in vain.

The proverbially solid South—"100 percent American" and a stronghold of Protestant Ku Klux Klanism—shied away from "city slicker" Al Smith. It might have accepted a Catholic, or a wet, or the descendant of Irish grandparents, or an urbanite. But a mixture of Catholicism, wettism, foreignism, and liberalism brewed on the sidewalks of New York was too bitter a dose for southern stomachs. Smith's theme song was a constant and rasping reminder that his upbringing had not been convincingly American.

Hoover triumphed in a landslide. He bagged 21,391,993 popular votes to 15,016,169 for his embittered opponent, while rolling up an electoral count of 444 to 87. A huge Republican majority was returned to the House of Representatives. Tens of thousands of dry southern Democrats—"Hoovercrats"—rebelled against Al Smith, and Hoover proved to be the first Republican candidate in fifty-two years, except for Harding's Tennessee victory in 1920, to carry a

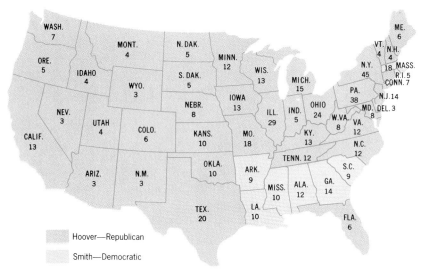

Presidential Election of 1928 (with electoral vote by state)
Smith, despite his defeat, managed to poll almost as many votes as the victorious Coolidge had in 1924. By attracting to the party an immense urban or "sidewalk" vote, the breezy New Yorker foreshadowed Roosevelt's New Deal victory in 1932, when the Democrats patched together the solid South and the urban North. A cruel joke had Smith cabling the Pope a single word after the election: "Unpack."

Hoover—Republican

Smith—Democratic

state that had seceded. He swept five states of the former Confederacy, as well as all the Border States.

President Hoover's First Moves

Prosperity in the late 1920s smiled broadly as the Hoover years began. Soaring stocks on the bull market continued to defy the laws of financial gravitation. But two immense groups of citizens were not getting their share of the riches flowing from the national horn of plenty: the unorganized wage earners and especially the disorganized farmers.

Hoover's administration, in line with its philosophy of promoting self-help, responded to the outcry of the farmers with legislative aspirin. The Agricultural Marketing Act, passed by Congress in June 1929, was designed to help the farmers help themselves, largely through producers' cooperatives. It set up a Federal Farm Board, with a revolving fund of half a billion dollars at its disposal. Money was lent generously to farm organizations seeking to buy, sell, and store agricultural surpluses.

In 1930 the Farm Board itself created both the Grain Stabilization Corporation and the Cotton Stabilization Corporation. The prime goal was to bolster sagging prices by buying up surpluses. But the two agencies were soon suffocated by an avalanche of farm produce, as wheat dropped to fifty-seven cents a bushel and cotton to five cents a pound.

Farmers had meanwhile clutched at the tariff as a possible straw to help keep their heads above the waters of financial ruin. During the recent presidential campaign, Hoover, an amateur in politics, had been stampeded into a politically unwise pledge. He had promised to call Congress into special session to consider agricultural relief and, specifically, to bring about "limited" changes in the tariff. These hope-giving assurances no doubt won many votes for Hoover in the middle western farm belt.

The Hawley-Smoot Tariff of 1930 followed the well-worn pattern of legislative horse trading. It started out in the House as a fairly reasonable protective measure, designed to assist the farmers. But by the time the high-pressure lobbyists had pushed it through the Senate, it had acquired about a thousand amendments. It thus turned out to be the highest protective tariff in the nation's peacetime history. The average duty on nonfree goods was raised from 38.5 percent, as established by the Fordney-McCumber Act of 1922, to nearly 60 percent.

To angered foreigners, the Hawley-Smoot Tariff was a blow below the trade belt. It seemed like a declaration of economic warfare on the entire outside world. It reversed a promising worldwide trend toward reasonable tariffs and widened the yawning trade gaps. It plunged both America and other nations deeper into the terrible depression which had already begun. It increased international financial chaos and forced the United States further into the bog of economic isolationism. And economic isolationism, both at home and abroad, was playing directly into the hands of a wild-eyed German demagogue, Adolf Hitler.

The Great Crash
Ends the Golden Twenties

When Herbert Hoover confidently took the presidential oath on March 4, 1929, there were few black clouds on the economic horizon. The "long boom" seemed endless, with the painful exception of the debt-blanketed farm belt. America's productive colossus—stimulated by the automobile, radio, movie, and other new industries—was roaring along at a dizzy speed that suggested a permanent plateau of prosperity. Few people sensed that it might smother its own fires by pouring out too much.

The speculative bubble was actually near the bursting point. Prices on the stock exchange continued to spiral upward and create a fool's paradise of paper profits, despite Hoover's early but fruitless efforts to curb speculation through the Federal Reserve Board. A few prophets of disaster were bold enough to raise warning voices, but they were drowned out by the mad chatter of the ticker-tape machine.

Selected Stock Prices, September–November 1929

STOCKS	ADJUSTED HIGH PRICE SEPT. 3, 1929	LOW PRICE NOV. 13, 1929
American Can	$181 7/8	$ 86 1/8
General Electric	396 1/4	168 1/8
Montgomery Ward	137 7/8	49 1/4

A catastrophic crash came in October 1929. It was partially triggered by the British, who raised their interest rates in an effort to bring back capital lured abroad by American investments. Foreign investors and wary domestic speculators began to dump their "insecurities," and an orgy of selling followed. Tension built up to the panicky "Black Tuesday" of October 29, 1929, when 16,410,030 shares of stocks were sold in a save-who-may scramble. Wall Street became a wailing wall as gloom and doom replaced boom, and suicides increased alarmingly. A "sick joke" of the time had hotel room clerks ask registrants, "For sleeping or jumping?"

Losses, even in blue-chip securities, were fantastic. By the end of 1929—two months after the initial crash—stockholders had lost $40 billion in paper values, or more than the total cost of World War I to the United States. Typical

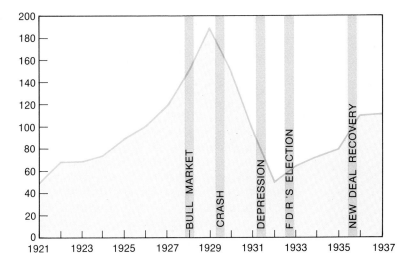

Index of Common Stock Prices
(1926 = 100)

prices of stocks are given in the accompanying table.

The stock-market collapse heralded a business depression, at home and abroad, that was the most prolonged and withering in American or world experience. No other industrialized nation suffered so severe a setback. By the end of 1930 more than 4 million workers in the United States were jobless; two years later the figure had about tripled. Hungry and despairing workers pounded pavements in search of nonexistent jobs ("We're firing, not hiring"). Where employees were not discharged, wages and salaries were often slashed. A current jingle ran:

> Mellon pulled the whistle,
> Hoover rang the bell
> Wall Street gave the signal
> And the country went to hell.

The misery and gloom were incalculable, as forests of dead chimneys stood starkly against the sky. Over five thousand banks collapsed in the first three years of the depression, carrying down with them the life savings of tens of thousands of widows and retired citizens. Countless thousands of honest, hardworking people lost their homes and farms to the forecloser's hammer. Bread lines formed, soup kitchens dispensed food, and apple sellers stood shivering on street corners trying to peddle their wares for five cents. Families felt the stress, as jobless fathers nursed their guilt and shame at not being able to provide for their households. Mothers meanwhile nursed fewer babies, as hard times reached even into the nation's bedrooms, precipitating a decade-long dearth of births. As cash registers gathered cobwebs, the song "My God, How the Money Rolls In" was replaced with "Brother, Can You Spare a Dime?"

Hooked on the Horn of Plenty

What caused the Great Depression? One basic explanation was overproduction by both farm and factory. Ironically, the depression of the 1930s was one of abundance, not want. It was the "great glut" or the "plague of plenty."

The nation's ability to produce goods had clearly outrun its capacity to consume or pay for them. Too much money was going into the hands of a few wealthy people, who in turn invested it in factories and other agencies of production. Not enough was going into salaries and wages, where revitalizing purchasing power could be more quickly felt.

Other maladies were at work. Overexpansion of credit through installment-plan buying overstimulated production. Paying on so-called easy terms caused many consumers to plunge in beyond their depth. Normal technological unemployment, resulting from new laborsaving machines, also added its burden to the abnormal unemployment of the "threadbare thirties."

This already bleak picture was further darkened by economic anemia abroad. Britain and the Continent had never fully recovered from the upheaval of World War I. Depression in America was given a further downward push by a chain-reaction financial collapse in Europe, following the failure in 1931 of a prominent Vienna banking house. A drying up of international trade, moreover, had been hastened by the shortsighted Hawley-Smoot Tariff of 1930. European uncertainties over reparations, war debts, and defaults on loans owed to America caused tensions that reacted unfavorably on the United States. Many of these conditions had been created or worsened by Uncle Sam's own narrow-visioned policies, but it was now too late to unscramble the omelet.

As if man-made disasters were not enough, a terrible drought scorched the Mississippi Valley

---

Shivering men sold apples on the street corners of the big cities at five cents apiece. Hoover, in his Memoirs *(1952), claimed that the apple growers shrewdly and profitably capitalized on "the sympathy of the public for the unemployed." He further stated, with obvious exaggeration: "Many persons left their jobs for the more profitable one of selling apples. When any left-winger wishes to indulge in scathing oratory, he demands, 'Do you want to return to selling apples?'"*

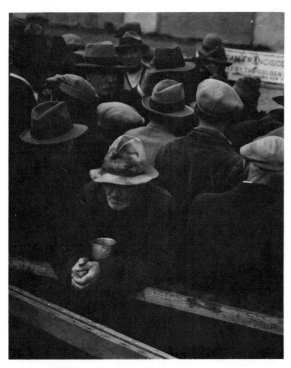

A San Francisco Bread Line in 1933   *(Dorothea Lange Collection, The Oakland Museum.)*

newspapers), fought over the contents of garbage cans, or cooked their findings in old oil drums in tin-and-paper shantytowns cynically named "Hoovervilles." The very foundations of America's social structure trembled.

Rugged Times for Rugged Individualists

Hoover's exalted reputation as a wonder-worker and efficiency engineer crashed about as dismally as the stock market. He doubtless would have shone in the prosperity-drenched Coolidge years, when he had foreseen the abolition of poverty and poorhouses. But damming the Great Depression proved to be a task beyond his engineering talents.

The perplexed president was impaled on the horns of a cruel dilemma. As a deservedly famed humanitarian, he was profoundly distressed by the widespread misery about him. Yet as a "rugged individualist," deeply rooted in an earlier era of free enterprise, he shrank from the heresy of government handouts. Convinced that industry, thrift, and self-reliance were the virtues that had made America great, President Hoover feared that a government doling out

in 1930. Thousands of farms were sold at auction for taxes, though in some cases kind neighbors would intimidate prospective buyers, bid one cent, and return the property to its original owner. Farm tenancy or rental—a species of peonage—was spreading at an alarming rate among both whites and blacks.

By 1930 the depression had become a national calamity. Through no fault of their own, a host of industrious citizens had lost everything. They wanted to work—but there was no work. The blighting effect of all this dazed despair on the spirit was incalculable and long-lasting. America's "uniqueness" no longer seemed so unique or its Manifest Destiny so manifest. Hitherto the people had grappled with storms, trees, stones, and other physical obstacles. But the depression was a baffling wraith they could not grasp. Initiative and self-respect were stifled, as panhandlers begged for food or "charity soup." In extreme cases "ragged individualists" slept under "Hoover blankets" (old

Blaming Hoover   *The once-popular president became an object of ridicule after 1929. (The Bettmann Archive, Inc.)*

Rainy Night, by Charles Burchfield   *This painting of downtown Buffalo in 1930 captures the somber, down-and-out mood of depression-era America. (Fine Arts Gallery of San Diego.)*

doles would weaken, perhaps destroy, the national fiber.

Hoover had deep faith in the efficiency of the industrial machine, which itself was undamaged by depression. From time to time he would attempt to encourage the public by issuing optimistic statements, which often were followed by a fresh decline. He was accused of saying, although he did not use these precise words, that prosperity was hovering just around the corner. "Hoovering," critics jibed.

As the depression nightmare steadily worsened, relief by local government agencies broke down. Hoover was finally forced to turn reluctantly from his doctrine of log-cabin individualism and accept the proposition that the welfare of the people in a nationwide depression is a direct concern of the national government.

The president at last worked out a compromise between the old hands-off philosophy and the "soul-destroying" direct dole then being used in England. He would assist the hard-pressed railroads, banks, and rural credit corporations, in the hope that if financial health were restored at the top of the economic pyramid, unemployment would be relieved at the bottom on a trickle-down basis.

Partisan critics sneered at the "Great Humanitarian"—he who had fed the faraway Belgians but would not use federal funds to feed

Hoover spoke approvingly in a campaign speech in 1928 of "the American system of Rugged Individualism." In 1930 he referred to Cleveland's 1887 veto of a bill to appropriate seed grain for the drought-stricken farmers of Texas: "I do not believe that the power and duty of the General Government ought to be extended to the relief of individual suffering. . . . The lesson should be constantly enforced that though the people support the Government the Government should not support the people."

needy Americans. Hostile commentators remarked that he was willing to lend government money to the big bankers, who allegedly had plunged the country into the mess. He would likewise lend money to agricultural organizations to feed pigs—but not people. Pigs, the cynics of the time noted, had no character to undermine.

Much of this criticism was unfair. Though continued suffering seemed to mock the effectiveness of Hoover's measures, his efforts probably prevented a more serious collapse than did occur. And his expenditures for relief, revolutionary for that day, paved the path for the enormous federal outlays of his New Deal successor, Franklin Roosevelt. Hoover proved that the old bootstrap-pulling techniques would no longer work in a crisis of this magnitude, especially where people lacked boots.

Herbert Hoover: Pioneer for the New Deal

President Hoover, in line with his "trickle-down" philosophy, at last recommended that Congress vote immense sums for useful public works. Though at heart an antispender, he secured from Congress appropriations totaling $2.25 billion for such projects. To alarmists, the Washington ship of state seemed in danger of sinking in a red-ink sea of unbalanced budgets and mounting debts. Hoover warned, "Prosperity cannot be restored by raids on the public treasury."

Most imposing of the public enterprises was the gigantic Hoover Dam on the Colorado River. Voted by Congress in the days of Coolidge, it was begun in 1930 under Hoover and completed in 1936 under Roosevelt. It succeeded in

Home Relief Station, by Louis Ribak *Destitute and despairing, millions of hard-working Americans like these had to endure the degradation and humiliation of going on relief as the pall of depression descended over the land. (Whitney Museum of American Art.)*

creating a huge man-made lake for purposes of irrigation, flood control, and electric power.

But Hoover sternly fought all schemes that he regarded as being "socialistic." Conspicuous among them was the Muscle Shoals Bill, designed to dam the Tennessee River and ultimately embraced by Franklin Roosevelt's Tennessee Valley Authority. Hoover emphatically vetoed this measure, primarily because he opposed the government's selling electricity in competition with its own citizens in private companies.

Early in 1932 Congress, responding to Hoover's belated appeal, established the Reconstruction Finance Corporation (RFC). With an initial working capital of half a billion dollars, this agency became a government lending bank. It was designed to provide indirect relief by assisting insurance companies, banks, agricultural organizations, railroads, and even hard-pressed state and local governments. But to preserve individualism and character, there would be no loans to individuals from this "billion-dollar soup kitchen."

"Pump-priming" loans by the RFC were no doubt of widespread benefit, though the organization was established many months too late for maximum usefulness. Projects that it supported were largely self-liquidating, and the government as a banker actually profited to the tune of many millions of dollars. Giant corporations so obviously benefited from this assistance that the RFC was dubbed—rather unfairly—"the millionaires' dole." The irony is that the thrifty and individualistic Hoover had sponsored the project, though with initial reluctance. It actually had a strong New Dealish flavor.

Hoover's administration also provided some indirect benefits for labor. After stormy debate, Congress passed the Norris–La Guardia Anti-Injunction Act in 1932, and Hoover signed it. The measure outlawed "yellow dog" (antiunion) contracts and forbade the federal courts to issue injunctions to restrain strikes, boycotts, and peaceful picketing.

The truth is that Herbert Hoover, despite criticism of his "heartlessness," did inaugurate a significant new policy. In previous panics the masses had been forced to "sweat it out." Slow though Hoover was to abandon this nineteenth-century bias, by the end of his term he had traveled a long way toward government assistance for needy citizens—a road that Franklin Roosevelt was to take all the way.

Hoover's woes were increased by a hostile Congress. At critical times during his first two years, the Republican majority proved highly uncooperative. Friction worsened during his last two years. A depression-cursed electorate, rebelling in the congressional elections of 1930, so reduced the Republican majority that Democrats controlled the new House and almost controlled the Senate. Insurgent Republicans could—and did—combine with opposition Democrats to harass Hoover. Some of the president's troubles were deliberately manufactured by Congress who, in his words, "played politics with human misery."

Routing the Bonus Army in Washington

Many veterans of World War I were numbered among the hard-hit victims of the depression. Industry had secured a "bonus"—though a dubious one—in the Hawley-Smoot Tariff. So the thoughts of the former "doughboys" naturally turned to what the government owed them for their services in 1917–1918, when they had "saved" democracy. A drive developed for the premature payment of the deferred bonus voted by Congress in 1924 and payable in 1945.

Thousands of impoverished veterans, both of war and of unemployment, were now prepared to move on to Washington, there to demand of Congress the immediate payment of their *entire* bonus. The "Bonus Expeditionary Force" (BEF), which mustered about twenty thousand souls, converged on the capital in the summer of 1932. These supplicants promptly set up unsanitary public camps and erected shacks on vacant lots—a gigantic "Hooverville." They thus created a menace to the public health, while attempting to intimidate Congress by their presence in force. After the pending bonus bill had failed in Congress by a narrow margin, Hoover arranged to pay the return fare of about six thousand bonus marchers. The rest refused to decamp, though ordered to do so.

Following riots that cost two lives, Hoover responded to the demands of the Washington authorities by ordering the army to evacuate the unwanted guests. Though Hoover charged that the "Bonus Army" was led by reds and riffraff, in fact only a sprinkling of them were former convicts and Communist agitators. The eviction was carried out by General Douglas MacArthur with bayonets and tear gas, and with far more severity than Hoover had planned. A few of the former soldiers were injured as the torch was put to their pathetic shanties in the inglorious "Battle of Anacostia Flats." An eleven-month-old "bonus baby" allegedly died from exposure to tear gas.

This brutal episode brought down additional condemnation on the once-popular Hoover, who by now was the most loudly booed man in the country. The Democrats, not content with Hoover's vulnerable record, employed professional "smear" artists to drive him from office. Cynics sneered that the "Great Engineer" had in a few months "ditched, drained, and damned the country." The existing panic was unfairly branded "the Hoover depression." In truth, Hoover had been oversold as a superman—and the public grumbled when his magician's wand failed to produce rabbits. The time was ripening for the Democratic party—and Franklin D. Roosevelt—to cash in on Hoover's calamities.

Japanese Militarists Attack China

The Great Depression, which brewed enough distress at home, added immensely to difficulties abroad.

Rampaging Japan stole the Far Eastern spotlight. In September 1931 the Japanese imperialists, noting that the Western world was badly mired down in depression, lunged into Manchuria. Alleging provocation, they rapidly overran the coveted Chinese province and proceeded to bolt shut the Open Door in the conquered area.

Peaceful peoples were stunned by this act of naked aggression. It was a flagrant violation

"The Light of Asia," 1933 *Japan sets fire to treaty commitments. (Reprinted with permission of the Washington Daily News.)*

of the League of Nations covenant, as well as of various other international agreements solemnly signed by Tokyo. Far-visioned observers feared that unless the major powers, acting through the League of Nations, could force Japan to disgorge, the League would perish. Failure would kill collective security and wipe out the best hope of averting another global conflagration.

Meeting in Geneva, the League was eager to strengthen itself by luring Uncle Sam into its camp. In response to an urgent invitation, an American sat for the first time, though unofficially, with the Council of the League during its discussions of the Manchurian crisis. An American also served on the firsthand investigating commission appointed by the League.

But intervention by the League availed nothing. Its five-man commission of probers reported in 1932 that the Japanese incursion was unjustified. But this condemnation, instead of driving Japan out of Manchuria, merely drove Japan out of the League. Another nail was thus hammered into the coffin of collective security.

Numerous red-blooded Americans, though by no means a majority, urged strong measures,

> Hoover later wrote of his differences with Secretary Stimson over economic boycotts: "I was soon to realize that my able Secretary was at times more of a warrior than a diplomat. To him the phrase 'economic sanctions' was the magic wand of force by which all peace could be summoned from the vasty deep. . . . Ever since Versailles I had held that 'economic sanctions' meant war when applied to any large nation."

ranging from boycotts to blockades. Possibly a tight blockade by the League, backed by the United States, would have brought Japan sharply to book. But Hoover reflected the isolationist sentiments of most Americans, who wanted no part of the Far Eastern mess. One newspaper remarked that America did not "give a hoot in a rain barrel" about who controlled Manchuria.

The League was handicapped in taking two-fisted action by the nonmembership of the United States. Washington flatly rebuffed initial attempts in 1931 to secure American cooperation in applying economic pressure. But Secretary of State Stimson, who was much more internationalist-minded than Hoover, indicated that the United States probably would not interfere with a League embargo. The next year Stimson was more eager to take vigorous steps, but the president cautiously restrained him.

Washington in the end decided to fire only paper bullets at the Japanese aggressors. The so-called Hoover-Stimson doctrine, proclaimed in 1932, declared that the United States would not recognize any territorial acquisitions that were achieved by force. Righteous indignation—or a preach-and-run policy—would substitute for vigorous initiatives.

This verbal slap on the wrist from America did not deter the march of the Japanese militarists. Smarting under a Chinese boycott, they bombed Shanghai in 1932, with shocking losses to the civilians. Outraged Americans launched informal boycotts of Japanese goods, chiefly dime-store knickknacks. But there was no real sentiment for armed intervention among a de-pression-ridden people who remained strongly isolationist during the 1930s. President Hoover, who fully shared their views, believed that boycotts and embargoes spelled bayonets and bombs.

In a broad sense, collective security died and World War II was born in 1931 on the windswept plains of Manchuria. The League members had the economic and naval power to halt Japan but lacked the courage to act. One reason—though not the only one—was that they could not count on America's support. Even so, the Republic came closer to stepping into the chill waters of internationalism than American prophets would have dared to predict in the early 1920s.

Hoover Pioneers for the Good Neighbor Policy

Hoover's arrival at the White House brought a more hopeful turn to relations with America's southern neighbors. The new president was deeply interested in the colorful lands below the Rio Grande; shortly after his election in 1928 he had undertaken a goodwill tour of Latin America—on a U.S. battleship.

World depression gave birth to a less aggressive attitude in the United States toward weak Latin neighbors. Following the stock-market collapse of 1929, Americans had less money to invest abroad. As millions of dollars' worth of investments in Latin America went sour, many Yankees felt as though they were more preyed upon than preying. Economic imperialism—so called—became much less popular in the United States than it had been in the golden twenties.

As an advocate of international goodwill, Hoover strove to abandon the interventionist twist given to the Monroe Doctrine by Theodore Roosevelt. In 1932 he negotiated a new treaty with the French-speaking republic of Haiti, and this pact, later supplanted by an executive agreement, provided for the complete withdrawal of American bayonets by 1934. Further pleasing omens came early in 1933, when the last marine "leathernecks" sailed away from the banana republic of Nicaragua after an almost continuous stay of some twenty years.

Herbert Hoover, the engineer in politics, thus happily engineered the foundation stones of the "Good Neighbor" policy. Upon them rose an imposing edifice in the days of his successor, Franklin Roosevelt.

Varying Viewpoints

Many American historians have been "liberals," and this political preference has strongly colored writing about the 1920s. The decade is often depicted as a rude interruption of the supposedly continuous reform surge that pulsated from progressivism to the New Deal. In this view, Harding's "normalcy" was not normal at all, and the conservatism of Coolidge and Hoover appeared as some kind of aberration. The three Republican presidents are seen as constituting a reactionary interlude in the forward march of liberal reform that is supposedly the main theme of American society in the present century. Such an interpretation is conspicuous in John D. Hick's *Republican Ascendancy*.

Yet in recent years many questions have been raised about this judgment. As historians increasingly distinguish progressivism from the New Deal, they naturally ask what, if anything, the 1920s "interrupted." And when "New Left" critics in the 1960s pooh-poohed the reform character of progressivism and of the New Deal itself, they implicitly suggested that the 1920s carried forward the essentially *conservative* course of modern American history.

Herbert Hoover's changing historical reputation illustrates these trends. He was widely criticized, for four decades after his presidency, as a callous incompetent and a head-in-the-sand, doctrinaire, *laissez-faire* conservative. But Hoover was partly rehabilitated in the 1970s when skepticism about big, activist government spread in the wake of Vietnam and the Watergate scandals. Hoover's historical standing will probably continue to serve as a kind of barometer of attitudes toward government. And debate continues as to whether the 1920s represented the last chapter in the history of a dying conservative order or simply another episode, however dramatic, in the ongoing saga of a highly individualistic, business-oriented society.

Select Readings

Primary Source Documents

Herbert Hoover, *American Individualism* (1922), contains the philosophy of the man and his times. See also Hoover's "Rugged Individualism" speech (1928), in Richard Hofstadter, *Great Issues in American History*. As the Great Depression descended, Hoover fought to maintain his principles in a noteworthy speech at New York's Madison Square Garden. *(*The New York Times,* November 1, 1932.) On foreign affairs, see the "Stimson Doctrine" (1931), in Henry Steele Commager, ed., *Documents of American History*.

Secondary Sources

A lively introduction to the postwar decade is Burl Noggle, *Into the Twenties: The United States from Armistice to Normalcy* (1974). On Harding see Robert K. Murray's balanced *The Harding Era* (1969); consult also his *Politics of Normalcy: Government Theory and Practice in the Harding-Coolidge Era* (1973). Burl Noggle looks at the chief scandal of the period in *Teapot Dome* (1962). David M. Kennedy, *Over Here: The First World War and American Society* (1980), discusses postwar race relations and demobilization, as well as the international economic aftermath of the war, a subject treated at greater length in Joan Hoff Wilson, *American Business and Foreign Policy, 1920–1933* (1971). For background on the Washington disarmament conference, consult Roger Dingman, *Power in the Pacific: The Origins of Naval Arms Limitation, 1914–1922* (1976). For the conference itself, see Thomas H. Buckley, *The United States and the Washington Conference, 1921–1922* (1970). The Democratic party is analyzed in David Burner, *The Politics of Provincialism* (1967). The complicated international financial tangle of the 1920s is deftly discussed in Herbert Feis, *The Diplomacy of the Dollar* (1950), and in the early chapters of Charles Kindleberger, *The World in Depression* (1973). The drama of the 1928 election is captured in Allan J. Lichtman, *Prejudice and the Old Politics: The Presidential Election of 1928* (1979), and in Oscar Handlin, *Al Smith and His America* (1958). The election is placed in a larger context in Samuel Lubell's classic *The Future of American Politics* (1952) and in Paul Kleppner, *Who Voted?: The Dynamics of Electoral Turnout, 1870–1980* (1982). The best brief biography of Hoover is Joan Hoff Wilson, *Herbert Hoover, Forgotten Progressive* (1975). Brilliantly unsympathetic toward Hoover is Arthur M. Schlesinger, Jr., *The Crisis of the Old Order, 1919–1933* (1957). More favorable is David Burner, *Herbert Hoover: A Public Life* (1979). On the depression itself, consult John K. Galbraith's breezy *The Great Crash, 1929* (1955); Peter Temin's trenchant *Did Monetary Factors Cause the Great Depression?* (1976); Robert McElvaine, *The Great Depression* (1984); and Lester V. Chandler's comprehensive *America's Greatest Depression* (1970).

38

The Great Depression and the New Deal

> The country needs and . . . demands bold, persistent experimentation. It is common sense to take a method and try it. If it fails, admit it frankly and try another. But above all, try something.
>
> Franklin D. Roosevelt, 1932 campaign speech

FDR: A Politician in a Wheelchair

Voters were in an ugly mood as the presidential campaign of 1932 neared. Countless factory chimneys remained ominously cold, while more than 11 million unemployed workers and their families sank ever deeper into the pit of poverty. The "chicken in every pot" of 1928 had seemingly laid a discharge slip in every pay envelope.

Herbert Hoover, sick at heart, was renominated by the Republican convention in Chicago without great enthusiasm. The platform indulged in extravagant praise of Republican antidepression policies, while halfheartedly promising to repeal national prohibition and return control of liquor to the states.

The rising star in the Democratic firmament was Governor Franklin Delano Roosevelt of New York, a fifth cousin of Theodore Roosevelt. Like the Rough Rider, he had been born to a wealthy New York family, had graduated from Harvard, had been elected as a kid-gloved politician to the New York legislature, had served as governor of the Empire State, had been nominated for the vice-presidency (though not elected), and had served capably as assistant secretary of the navy. Though both men were master politicians, adept with the colorful phrase, FDR was suave and conciliatory, while TR was pugnacious and denunciatory.

Infantile paralysis, while putting steel braces on Franklin Roosevelt's legs, put additional steel into his soul. Until 1921, when the dread disease struck, young Roosevelt—tall (6 feet 2 inches; 1.88 meters), athletic, classic-featured, and as handsome as a Greek god—impressed observers as charming and witty yet at times a superficial and arrogant "lightweight." But suffering humbled him and brought him down to the level of common clay. In courageously fighting his way back from complete help-lessness to a hobbling mobility, he schooled himself in patience, tolerance, compassion, and strength of will. He once remarked that after trying for two years to wiggle one big toe, all else seemed easy.

Another of Roosevelt's great personal and po-litical assets was his wife, Eleanor. The niece of Theodore Roosevelt, she was Franklin Roo-sevelt's distant cousin as well as his spouse. Tall, ungainly, and toothy, she overcame the

> In his successful campaign of 1928 for the gov-ernorship of New York, Roosevelt had played down alleged Democratic "socialism": "We of-ten hear it said that government operation of anything under the sun is socialistic. If that is so, our postal service is socialistic, so is the parcel post which has largely taken the place of the old express companies; so are the public highways which took the place of the toll roads."

misery of an unhappy childhood and emerged as a champion of the dispossessed—and ulti-mately, as the "conscience of the New Deal." FDR's political career was as much hers as it was his own; she traveled countless miles with him or on his behalf in all his campaigns, be-ginning with his run for the New York legisla-ture before World War I. She was to become the most active First Lady in history. Through her lobbying of her husband, her speeches, and her syndicated newspaper column, she powerfully influenced the policies of the national govern-ment. Always, she battled for the impoverished and the oppressed. At one meeting in Birming-ham, Alabama, she confounded local authorities and flouted the segregation statutes by deliber-ately straddling the aisle separating the black and white seating sections. Sadly, her personal relationship with her husband was often rocky, due to his occasional infidelity. Condemned by conservatives and loved by liberals, she was one of the most controversial—and consequential—public figures of the twentieth century.

Roosevelt's political appeal was amazing. His commanding presence and his golden speaking voice, despite a sophisticated accent, combined to make him the premier American orator of his generation. He could turn on charm in private conversations as one would turn on a faucet. As a popular depression governor of New York, he had sponsored heavy state spending to relieve human suffering. Though favoring frugality, he believed that money, rather than humanity, was expendable. He revealed a deep concern for the plight of the "forgotten man"—a phrase he used in a 1932 speech—although he was assailed by the rich as a "traitor to his class."

Eleanor Roosevelt   *She was America's most active First Lady, and commanded enormous popularity and influence during the Roosevelt presidency. Here she emerges, miner's cap in hand, from an Ohio coal mine. (A.P./Wide World.)*

Exuberant Democrats met in Chicago in June 1932 and speedily nominated Roosevelt. Al Smith felt entitled to a second chance; and a beautiful friendship wilted when he was elbowed aside for Franklin Roosevelt. The Democratic platform came out more forthrightly than the Republican for repeal of prohibition, assailed the so-called Hoover depression, and promised not only a balanced budget but sweeping social and economic reforms. Roosevelt flew daringly through stormy weather to Chicago, where he smashed precedent by accepting the nomination in person. He electrified the delegates and the public with these words: "I pledge you, I pledge myself to a new deal for the American people."

Presidential Hopefuls of 1932

In the campaign that followed, Roosevelt seized the offensive with a slashing attack on the Republican Old Dealers. He was especially eager to prove that he was not an invalid ("Roosevelt Is Robust") and to display his magnificent torso and radiant personality to as many voters as possible.

Roosevelt consistently preached a New Deal for the "forgotten man," but he was annoyingly vague and somewhat contradictory. Many of his speeches were "ghostwritten" by the "Brains Trust" (popularly the "Brain Trust"), a small group of reform-minded intellectuals. They were predominantly youngish college professors, who, as a kind of kitchen cabinet, later authored much of the New Deal legislation. Roosevelt rashly promised a balanced budget and berated heavy Hooverian deficits, amid cries of "Throw the Spenders Out!" and "Out of the Red with Roosevelt." All this was to make ironical reading in later months.

The high spirits of the Democrats found vent in the catchy air "Happy Days Are Here Again." This theme song fitted FDR's indestructible smile, his jauntily angled cigarette holder, his breezy optimism, and his promises to do something, even at the risk of bold experimentation.

Grim-faced Herbert Hoover remained in the White House, conscientiously battling the depression through short lunches and long hours.

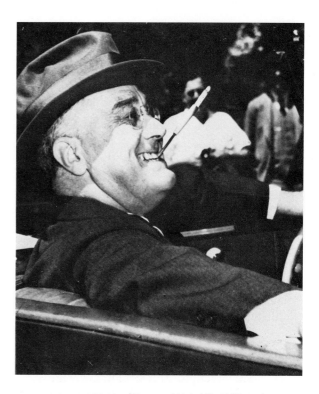

Roosevelt and Happy Days   *(Wide World Photos.)*

Out on the firing line his supporters halfheartedly cried, "The Worst Is Past," "It Might Have Been Worse," and "Prosperity Is Just around the Corner." Hoover never ceased to insist that the uncertainty and fear produced by Roosevelt's impending victory plunged the nation deeper into the depression.

With the campaign going badly for the Republicans, a weary and despondent Hoover was persuaded to take to the stump. He stoutly reaffirmed his faith in American free enterprise and individual initiative, and gloomily predicted that if the Hawley-Smoot Tariff were repealed, the grass would grow "in the streets of a hundred cities." Such down-at-the-mouthism contrasted sharply with Roosevelt's tooth-flashing optimism and sparkling promises.

The Humiliation of Hoover in 1932

Hoover had been swept into office on the rising tide of prosperity; he was swept out of office by the receding tide of depression. The flood of votes totaled 22,809,638 for Roosevelt and 15,758,901 for Hoover; the electoral count stood at 472 to 59. In all, the loser carried only six rock-ribbed Republican states.

One striking feature of the election was the beginning of a heavy shift of blacks, traditionally grateful to the Republican party of Lincoln, over to the Roosevelt camp. As the "last hired and first fired," black Americans had been among the worst sufferers from the depression. Beginning with the election of 1932, they became, notably in the great urban centers of the North, a vital element in the Democratic party.

Hard times unquestionably ruined the Republicans, for the electoral upheaval in 1932 was as much anti-Hoover as it was pro-Roosevelt. Democrats had only to harness the national grudge and let it pull them to victory. An overwhelming majority appear to have voiced a demand for change: *a* new deal rather then *the* New Deal, for the latter was only a gleam in the eyes of its sponsors. Any upstanding Democratic candidate probably could have won.

The preinauguration "lame duck" period now ground slowly to an end. Hoover, though defeated and repudiated, continued to be president for four long months, until March 4, 1933. But he was helpless to embark upon any long-range policies without the cooperation of Roosevelt—and the victorious president-elect proved rather uncooperative. Hoover at length succeeded in arranging two meetings with him to discuss the war-debt muddle. But Roosevelt, who airily remarked to the press, "It's not my baby," fought shy of assuming responsibility without authority. As Hoover privately confessed, he was trying to bind his successor to an anti-inflationary policy that would have made impossible many of the later New Deal experiments. But in politics the winner, not the loser, calls the tune.

With Washington deadlocked, the vast and vaunted American economic machine clanked to a virtual halt. One worker in four tramped the streets, feet weary and hands idle. Banks were locking their doors all over the nation, as people nervously stuffed paper money under their mattresses. Hooverites, then and later, accused Roosevelt of deliberately permitting the depression to worsen, so that he could emerge the more spectacularly as a savior.

FDR and the Three R's: Relief, Recovery, Reform

Great crises often call forth gifted leaders; and the hand of destiny tapped Roosevelt on the shoulder. On a dreary Inauguration Day, March 4, 1933, his vibrant voice, broadcast nationally from a bulletproof stand, provided the American people with inspirational new hope. He denounced the "money changers" who had brought on the calamity and declared that the government must wage war on the Great Depression as it would wage war on an armed foe. His clarion note was: "Let me assert my firm belief that the only thing we have to fear is fear itself."

Roosevelt moved decisively. Now that he had full responsibility, he boldly declared a nationwide banking holiday, March 6–10, as a prelude to opening the banks on a sounder basis. He then summoned the overwhelmingly Democratic Congress into special session to cope with the national emergency. Members stayed at their task for the so-called Hundred Days (March 9–June 16, 1933), hastily grinding out an unprecedented basketful of remedial legislation. Some of it derived from earlier progressivism, but mostly these new measures sought to deal with a desperate emergency.

Roosevelt's New Deal programs aimed at three *R*'s—relief, recovery, and reform. Short-range goals were relief and immediate recovery, especially in the first two years. Long-range goals were permanent recovery and reform of current abuses, particularly those that had produced the boom-or-bust catastrophe. The three-*R* objectives often overlapped and got in one another's way. But amid all the haste and topsy-turviness, the gigantic New Deal program lurched forward.

Firmly ensconced in the driver's seat, President Roosevelt cracked the whip. A green Congress so fully shared the panicky feeling of the country that it was ready to rubber-stamp bills drafted by White House advisers—measures

Principal New Deal Acts During Hundred Days Congress, 1933*
(Items in parentheses indicate secondary purposes)

RECOVERY	RELIEF	REFORM
FDR closes banks, March 6, 1933		
Emergency Banking Relief Act, March 9, 1933		
(Beer Act)	(Beer Act)	Beer and Wine Revenue Act, March 22, 1933
(CCC)	Unemployment Relief Act, March 31, 1933, creates Civilian Conservation Corps (CCC)	
FDR orders gold surrender, April 5, 1933		
FDR abandons gold standard, April 19, 1933		
(FERA)	Federal Emergency Relief Act, May 12, 1933, creates Federal Emergency Relief Administration (FERA)	
(AAA)	Agricultural Adjustment Act (AAA), May 12, 1933	
(TVA)	(TVA)	Tennessee Valley Authority Act (TVA), May 18, 1933 Federal Securities Act, May 27, 1933
Gold-payment clause repealed, June 5, 1933		
(HOLC)	Home Owners' Refinancing Act, June 13, 1933, creates Home Owners' Loan Corporation (HOLC)	
National Industrial Recovery Act, June 16, 1933, creates National Recovery Administration (NRA), Public Works Administration (PWA)	(NRA, PWA)	(NRA)
(Glass-Steagall Act)	(Glass-Steagall Act)	Glass-Steagall Banking Reform Act, June 16, 1933, creates Federal Deposit Insurance Corporation

*For later New Deal measures, see p. 753.

"The Galloping Snail" A jeer at the "assembly-line" bills rammed through Congress. (Thomas in the Detroit News. Reprinted with permission.)

that Roosevelt called "must legislation." More than that, Congress gave the president extraordinary blank-check powers: some of the laws that it passed expressly delegated legislative authority to the chief executive. One senator complained that if FDR asked Congress "to commit suicide tomorrow, they'd do it."

Roosevelt was delighted to accept executive leadership, and Congress responded to it, although he did not always know precisely where he was going. He was inclined to do things by intuition—off the cuff. He was like the quarterback, as he put it, whose next play depends on the success of the previous play. So desperate was the mood of an action-starved public that movement, even in the wrong direction, seemed better than no movement at all.

The frantic Hundred Days Congress passed many essentials of the New Deal "three *R*s," though important long-range measures were added in later sessions. These reforms owed much to the legacy of the pre–World War I progressive movement. Many of them were long overdue, sidetracked by the war in Europe and the Old Guard reaction of the 1920s. The New Dealers, sooner or later, embraced such pro-

gressive ideas as unemployment insurance, old-age insurance, minimum-wage regulations, conservation and development of natural resources, and restrictions on child labor. A few such reforms had already made limited gains in some of the states. Many of these forward-looking measures had been adopted a generation or so earlier by the more advanced countries of Western Europe. In the area of social welfare, the United States, in the eyes of many Europeans, remained a "backward nation."

Roosevelt Tackles Money and Banking

Banking chaos cried aloud for immediate action. Congress pulled itself together and in an incredible eight hours had the Emergency Banking Relief Act of 1933 ready for Roosevelt's busy pen. The new law clothed the president with power to regulate banking transactions and foreign exchange and to reopen solvent banks.

Roosevelt, the master showman, next turned to the radio to deliver the first of his thirty famous "fireside chats." As some 35 million people hung on his soothing words, he gave assurances that it was now safer to keep money in a reopened bank than "under the mattress." Confidence returned with a gush, and the banks began to unlock their doors.

The Emergency, or Hundred Days, Congress buttressed public reliance on the banking system by enacting the memorable Glass-Steagall Banking Reform Act. This measure provided for the Federal Deposit Insurance Corporation, which insured individual deposits up to $5,000 (later raised). Thus ended the disgraceful epidemic of bank failures, which dated back to the "wildcat" days of Andrew Jackson.*

Roosevelt moved swiftly elsewhere on the financial front, seeking to protect the melting gold reserve and to prevent panicky hoarding. He ordered all private holdings of gold to be sur-

---

*When FDR was inaugurated in 1933, not a single Canadian bank had failed.

Year	Failures
1920	167
1925	618
1930	1352
1931	2294
1932	1456
1933	4004
1934	57
1945	0

rendered to the Treasury in exchange for paper currency and then took the nation off the gold standard. The Emergency Congress responded to his recommendation by canceling the gold-payment clause in all contracts and authorizing repayment in paper money. A "managed currency" was well on its way.

Early in 1934 Roosevelt reduced the value of the gold content of the dollar to 59.06 cents, in accordance with authority granted by Congress. His theory was that this tinkering with the currency would stimulate business through controlled inflation. Prices did rise somewhat, but not in proportion to the change in the value of the currency. Alarmed conservatives, like the now "unhappy warrior" Al Smith, assailed "the baloney dollar" and accused the government of robbing the people of 40 cents on every dollar they owned. Actually, the purchasing power of the newly shrunken dollar was not substantially inferior to that of the old, except in purchases from foreigners.

Creating Jobs for the Jobless

Overwhelming unemployment, even more than banking, clamored for prompt remedial action. One out of every four workers was jobless when FDR took his inaugural oath—the highest level of unemployment in the nation's history, before or since. Roosevelt had no hesitancy about using federal money to assist the unemployed and at the same time to "prime the pump" of industrial recovery. (A farmer has to pour a little water into a dry pump—that is, "prime" it—to start the flow.)

The Hundred Days Congress responded to Roosevelt's spurs when it created the Civilian Conservation Corps (CCC), which proved to be perhaps the most popular of all the New Deal "alphabetical agencies." This law provided employment in fresh-air government camps for about 3 million uniformed young men, many of whom might otherwise have been driven into criminal habits. Their work was useful—including reforestation, fire fighting (forty-seven lost their lives), flood control, and swamp drainage. The recruits were required to help the old folks by sending home most of their pay. Both human resources and natural resources were thus conserved, though there were minor complaints of "militarizing" the nation's youth. Critics charged that CCC "soldiers" would later claim pensions for exposure to poison ivy.

The first major effort of the new Congress to grapple with the millions of adult unemployed was the Federal Emergency Relief Act. Its chief aim was immediate relief rather than long-range recovery. The resulting Federal Emergency Relief Administration (FERA) was handed over to zealous Harry L. Hopkins, a pauper-thin, shabbily dressed, chain-smoking New York social worker who had earlier won Roosevelt's friendship and who became one of his most influential advisers. Hopkins' agency

Reliefers Receive Free Federal Potatoes in Cleveland   *(Wide World Photos.)*

make-work tasks, which were dubbed "boondoggling." As this kind of labor put a premium on shovel-leaning slow motion, the scheme was widely criticized. "The only thing we have to fear," scoffers remarked, "is work itself."

Direct relief from Washington to needy families helped pull the nation through the ghastly winter of 1933–1934. But the disheartening persistence of unemployment and suffering demonstrated that emergency relief measures must be not only continued but supplemented. One danger signal was the appearance of various demagogues, notably a magnetic "microphone messiah," Father Coughlin, a Catholic priest in Michigan who began broadcasting in 1930 and whose slogan was "Social Justice." His anti–New Deal harangues to some 40 million radio fans finally became so anti-Semitic, fascistic, and demagogic that he was silenced in 1942 by his superiors.

Also notorious among the new brood of agitators were those who capitalized on popular discontent to make pie-in-the-sky promises. Most conspicuous of these individuals was a United States senator, Huey P. ("Kingfish") Long of Louisiana, who was said to have more brass than a government mule. He used his abundant rabble-rousing talents to publicize his "Share Our Wealth" program, which promised to make "Every Man a King." Every family was to receive $5,000, supposedly at the expense of the prosperous. H. L. Mencken called Long's chief lieutenant, former clergyman Gerald L. K. Smith, "the gutsiest, goriest, loudest and lustiest, the deadliest and damndest orator ever heard on this or any other earth, the champion

finally granted about $3 billion to the states for direct dole payments or preferably for wages on work projects.*

Immediate relief was also given two large and hard-pressed special groups by the Hundred Days Congress. One section of the Agricultural Adjustment Act made available many millions of dollars to help farmers meet their mortgages. Another law created the Home Owners' Loan Corporation (HOLC). Designed to refinance mortgages on nonfarm homes, it ultimately assisted about a million badly pinched households. The agency not only bailed out mortgage-holding banks, it also bolted the political loyalties of relieved middle-class homeowners securely to the Democratic party.

Harassed by the continuing plague of unemployment, FDR himself established the Civil Works Administration (CWA) late in 1933. As a branch of the Federal Emergency Relief Administration, it also fell under the direction of Hopkins. Designed to provide purely temporary jobs during the cruel winter emergency, it served a useful purpose. Tens of thousands of jobless were employed at leaf raking and other

---

*A boast attributed to Hopkins in 1938 was: "We will spend and spend, tax and tax, and elect and elect."

Farm Foreclosures and Defaults, 1929–1945

PER THOUSAND FARMS

Later Major New Deal Measures, 1933–1939
(Items in parentheses indicate secondary purposes)

RECOVERY	RELIEF	REFORM
(CWA)	FDR establishes Civil Works Administration (CWA), November 9, 1933	
Gold Reserve Act, January 30, 1934, authorizes FDR's devaluation, January 31, 1934		
		Securities and Exchange Commission (SEC) authorized by Congress, June 6, 1934
(Reciprocal Trade Agreements)	(Reciprocal Trade Agreements)	Reciprocal Trade Agreements Act, June 12, 1934
(FHA)	National Housing Act, June 28, 1934, authorizes Federal Housing Administration (FHA)	(FHA)
(Frazier-Lemke Act)	Frazier-Lemke Farm Bankruptcy Act, June 28, 1934	
(Resettlement Administration)	FDR creates Resettlement Administration, April 30, 1935	
(WPA)	FDR creates Works Progress Administration (WPA), May 6, 1935, under act of April 8, 1935	
(Wagner Act)	(Wagner Act)	(Wagner) National Labor Relations Act, July 5, 1935
		Social Security Act, August 14, 1935
		Public Utility Holding Company Act, August 26, 1935
(Soil Conservation Act)	Soil Conservation and Domestic Allotment Act, February 29, 1938	
(USHA)	(USHA)	U.S. Housing Authority (USHA) established by Congress, September 1, 1937
(Second AAA)	Second Agricultural Adjustment Act, February 16, 1936	
(Fair Labor Standards)	(Fair Labor Standards)	Fair Labor Standards Act, June 25, 1938
		Reorganization Act, April 3, 1939
		Hatch Act, August 2, 1939

Frances Perkins (1882–1965)   *The first woman cabinet member, she served as secretary of labor under Roosevelt. She was subjected to much undeserved criticism from male businessmen, laborites, and politicians. They sneered that FDR kept her in labor for many years. (Print from Franklin D. Roosevelt Library; owned by UPI.)*

boob-bumper of all time." Fear of Long's becoming a Fascist dictator ended when he was shot by an assassin in the Louisiana state capitol in 1935.

Another Pied Piper was gaunt Dr. Francis E. Townsend of California, a retired physician whose savings had recently been wiped out. He attracted the pathetic support of perhaps 5 million "senior citizens" with his fantastic plan. Each oldster sixty years of age or over was to receive $200 a month, provided that the money be spent within the month. One estimate had the scheme costing one-half of the national income.

Partly to quiet the ground swell of unrest produced by such crackbrained proposals, Congress authorized the Works Progress Administration (WPA) in 1935. The objective was employment on useful projects. Launched under the supervision of the ailing but energetic Hopkins, this remarkable agency ultimately spent about $11 billion on thousands of public build-

ings, bridges, and hard-surfaced roads. It controlled crickets in Wyoming and built a monkey pen in Oklahoma City. Critics sneered that WPA meant "We Provide Alms," but the fact is that over a period of eight years nearly 9 million persons were given jobs, not handouts.

Agencies of the WPA also found part-time occupations for needy high-school and college students and for such unemployed white-collar workers as actors, musicians, and writers. John Steinbeck, future Nobel Prize novelist, counted dogs in his California county. Cynical taxpayers condemned lessons in tap dancing, as well as the painting of scenes on post office walls. But much precious talent was nourished, self-respect was preserved, and more than a million pieces of art were created, many of them publicly displayed.

A Helping Hand for Industry and Labor

A daring attempt to stimulate a nationwide comeback was initiated when the Emergency Congress authorized the National Recovery Administration (NRA). This ingenious scheme was by far the most complex and far-reaching effort by the New Dealers to combine immediate relief with long-range recovery and reform. Triple-barreled, it was designed to assist industry, labor, and the unemployed.

Individual industries—over two hundred in all—were to work out codes of "fair competition," under which hours of labor would be reduced so that employment could be spread over more people. A ceiling was placed on the maximum hours of labor; a floor was placed under wages to establish minimum levels.

Labor, under the NRA, was granted additional benefits. Workers were formally guaranteed the right to organize and bargain collectively through representatives *of their own choosing*—not through handpicked agents of the company's choosing. The hated "yellow dog," or antiunion, contract was expressly forbidden, and certain safeguarding restrictions were placed on the use of child labor.

Industrial recovery through the NRA "fair competition" codes would at best be painful, for

Hooray for NRA   *Eight thousand school children formed this "blue eagle" in a San Francisco ball park. Techniques like these were used to rally support for the NRA "fair competition" codes. (UPI/ Bettmann Newsphotos.)*

these called for self-denial by both management and labor. Patriotism was appealed to by mass meetings and monster parades, which included 200,000 marchers on New York City's Fifth Avenue. A handsome blue eagle was designed as the symbol of the NRA, and merchants subscribing to a code displayed it in their windows with the slogan "We Do Our Part." A newly formed professional football team was christened the Philadelphia Eagles. Such was the enthusiasm for the NRA that for a brief period there was a marked upswing of business activity, although Roosevelt had warned, "We cannot ballyhoo our way to prosperity."

But the high-flying blue eagle gradually fluttered to earth. Too much self-sacrifice was expected of labor, industry, and the public for such a scheme to work. Critics began to brand NRA "National Run Around" and "Nuts Running America," symbolized by what Henry Ford called "that damn Roosevelt buzzard." A new "age of chiselry" dawned as certain unscrupu-

lous businesspeople ("chiselers") publicly displayed the blue bird on their windows but secretly violated the codes. Complete collapse was imminent when, in 1935, the Supreme Court shot down the dying eagle in the famed *Schechter* "sick chicken" decision. The learned justices unanimously held that Congress could not "delegate legislative powers" to the executive. They further declared that congressional control of interstate commerce could not properly apply to a local fowl business, like that of the Schechter brothers in Brooklyn and New York. Roosevelt was incensed by this "horse and buggy" interpretation of the Constitution, but actually the Court helped him out of a bad jam.

The same act of Congress that hatched the blue-eagled NRA also authorized the Public Works Administration (PWA), likewise intended both for industrial recovery and for unemployment relief. The agency was headed by the secretary of the interior, acid-tongued Harold L. Ickes, a free-swinging former bull mooser.

Long-range recovery was the primary purpose of the new agency, and in time over $4 billion was spent on some thirty-four thousand projects, which included public buildings, highways, and parkways. One spectacular achievement was the Grand Coulee Dam on the Columbia River—the largest structure erected by man since the Great Wall of China. Speed was essential if the jobless were to be put back to work, but "Honest Harold" Ickes was so determined to prevent waste and extravagance that he blocked maximum relief.

Special stimulants aided the recovery of one segment of business—the liquor industry. The imminent repeal of the prohibition amendment afforded an opportunity to raise needed federal revenue and at the same time to provide some employment. Prodded by Roosevelt, the Hundred Days Congress, in one of its earliest acts, legalized light wine and beer with an alcoholic content (presumably nonintoxicating) not exceeding 3.2 percent by weight, and levied a tax of five dollars on every barrel so manufactured. Disgruntled drys, unwilling to acknowledge the breakdown of law and order begotten by bootlegging, damned Roosevelt as "a 3.2 percent American." Prohibition was officially repealed by the Twenty-first Amendment late in 1933 (see Appendix)—and the saloon returned.

Paying Farmers Not to Farm

Ever since the war-boom days of 1918, the horny-handed farmers had suffered from low prices and overproduction, especially in grain. During the depression these conditions became desperate as countless mortgages were foreclosed, as corn was burned for fuel, and as embattled bands of farmers tried to prevent shipment of crops to glutted markets. In Iowa several counties had to be placed under martial law.

A radical new approach to farm recovery was embraced when the Emergency Congress established the Agricultural Adjustment Administration (AAA). Through "artificial scarcity" this agency was to establish "parity prices" for basic commodities. "Parity" was the price set for a product that gave it the same real value, in purchasing power, that it had enjoyed during the period from 1909 to 1914. The AAA would eliminate price-depressing surpluses by paying growers to reduce their crop acreage. The millions of dollars needed for these payments were to be raised by taxing processors of farm products, such as flour millers, who in turn would shift the burden to consumers.

Unhappily, the AAA got off to a wobbly start. It was begun after much of the cotton crop for 1933 had been planted, and balky mules, trained otherwise, were forced to plow under countless young plants. Several million squealing pigs were purchased and slaughtered. Much of their meat was distributed to persons on relief, but some of it was used for fertilizer. This "sinful" destruction of food, at a time when thousands of citizens were hungry, increased condemnation of the American economic system by many left-leaning critics.

"Subsidized scarcity" did have the effect of raising farm income, but the whole confused enterprise met with acid criticism. Farmers, food processors, consumers, and taxpayers were all in some degree unhappy. Paying the farmers not to farm actually increased unemployment, at a time when other New Deal agencies were striving to decrease it. When the Supreme Court finally killed the AAA in 1936 by declaring its regulatory taxation provisions unconstitutional, loud rejoicing was heard among foes of the plow-under program.

Quickly recovering from this blow, the New Deal Congress hastened to pass the Soil Conservation and Domestic Allotment Act of 1936. The withdrawal of acreage from production was now achieved by paying farmers to plant soil-

---

Novelist Steinbeck relates that when the "Okies" and "Arkies" reached California, they found the big growers unwilling to pay more than twenty-five cents an hour for work in the fields. One owner is made to say, "A Red is any son-of-a-bitch that wants thirty cents an hour when we're paying twenty-five!"

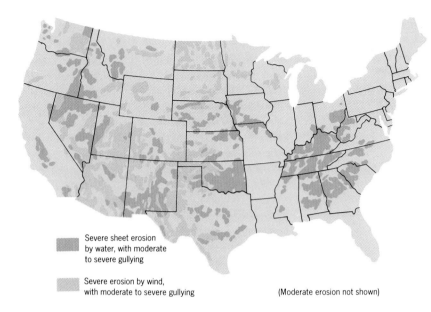

The Extent of Erosion, 1934
Note the extensive wind erosion in the Southwest, which was dubbed the "dust bowl" in the 1930s. Mechanized farmers had "busted" the sod of the southern plains so thoroughly that they literally broke the back of the land. Tons of dust blew out of the dust bowl in the 1930s and blotted the sun from the skies as far away as New York. A Kansas newspaperman reported in 1935 that in his dust-darkened town "Lady Godiva could ride through streets without even the horse seeing her."

Severe sheet erosion by water, with moderate to severe gullying

Severe erosion by wind, with moderate to severe gullying

(Moderate erosion not shown)

conserving crops, like soybeans, or to let their land lie fallow. With the emphasis thus on conservation, the Supreme Court placed the stamp of its approval on the revamped scheme.

The Second Agricultural Adjustment Act of 1938, passed two years later, was a more comprehensive substitute, although it continued conservation payments. If growers observed acreage restrictions on specified commodities like cotton and wheat, they would be eligible for parity payments. Other provisions of the new AAA were designed to give farmers not only a fairer price but a more substantial share of the national income. Both goals were partially achieved.

Dust Bowls and Black Blizzards

Dame Nature meanwhile had been providing some unplanned scarcity. Late in 1933 a prolonged drought struck the states of the trans-Mississippi Great Plains. Rainless weeks were followed by furious, whining winds, while the sun was darkened by millions of tons of powdery topsoil torn from once-fertile areas. Despondent citizens sat on front porches with protective masks on their faces, watching the

farms swirl by. Some of the dust darkened faraway Boston.

Burned and blown out of the dust bowl, tens of thousands of refugees fled their ruined acres. In five years about 350,000 Oklahomans and Arkansans—"Okies" and "Arkies"—trekked to southern California in "junkyards on wheels."

Dust Bowl Refugees　*Family of "Okies" in California. (Library of Congress.)*

The Dust Bowl *A combination of stingy nature and exploitative agricultural practices laid waste much of the southern Great Plains in the 1930s. In* Drought Stricken Area *artist Alexandre Hogue rendered this grim depiction of the damage done by the desolating dust storms. (Dallas Museum of Art, Dallas Art Association Purchase.)*

The dismal story of these human tumbleweeds was realistically portrayed in John Steinbeck's best-selling novel *The Grapes of Wrath* (1939), which proved to be the *Uncle Tom's Cabin* of the dust bowl.

Zealous New Dealers, sympathetic toward the soil-tillers, made various other efforts to relieve their burdens. The Frazier-Lemke Farm Bankruptcy Act, passed in 1934, made possible a suspension of mortgage foreclosures for five years, but it was voided the next year by the Supreme Court. A revised law, limiting the grace period to three years, was unanimously upheld. In 1935 the president set up the Resettlement Administration, charged with the task of removing near-farmless farmers to better land. And more than 200 million young trees were successfully planted on the bare prairies as windbreaks by the young men of the Civilian Conservation Corps, even though one governor jeered at trying to "grow hair on a bald head."

Battling Bankers and Big Business

Reformist New Dealers were determined from the outset to curb the "money changers" who had played fast and loose with gullible investors before the Wall Street crash of 1929. The Hundred Days Congress passed the "Truth in Securities Act" (Federal Securities Act), which required promoters to transmit to the investor sworn information regarding the soundness of their stocks and bonds. An old saying was thus reversed to read, "Let the seller beware," although the buyer might never read the fine print.

In 1934 Congress took further steps to protect the public against fraud, deception, and inside manipulation. It authorized the Securities and Exchange Commission (SEC), which was designed as a watchdog administrative agency. Stock markets henceforth were to operate more as trading marts and less as gambling casinos.

New Dealers likewise directed their fire at public utility holding companies, those super-supercorporations. Citizens had seen one of these incredible colossi collapse during the spring of 1932, when the Chicagoan Samuel Insull's multibillion-dollar financial empire crashed. Possibilities of controlling, with a minimum of capital, a half-dozen or so pyramided layers of big business suggested to Roosevelt "a ninety-six-inch dog being wagged by a four-inch tail." The Public Utility Holding Company Act of 1935 finally delivered a "death sentence" to this type of fatty growth, except where it might be deemed economically needful.

The TVA Harnesses the Tennessee River

Inevitably, the sprawling electric-power industry attracted the fire of New Deal reformers. Within a few decades it had risen from nothingness to a behemoth with an investment of $13 billion. As a public utility, it reached directly and regularly into the pocketbooks of millions of consumers for vitally needed services. Ardent New Dealers accused it of gouging the public with excessive rates, especially since it owed its success to having secured, often for a song, priceless waterpower sites from the public domain.

The tempestuous Tennessee River provided New Dealers with a rare opportunity. With its

> In flooding the Tennessee valleys to build the dams, the TVA authorities had to provide new houses for the lowland poor folk. According to one account: "When Ezra Hill saw the plans for the home which was to replace his old one in the flood area, he pointed to the place on the print showing the circles and ovals of bathroom fixtures. 'What's all this? . . . I won't have it! I guess a privy [outside] is still good enough for me.'"

tributaries, the river drained a badly eroded area about the size of England, and one containing some 2.5 million of the most poverty-stricken people in America. The federal government already owned valuable properties at Muscle Shoals, where it had erected plants for needed nitrates in World War I. By developing the hydroelectric potential of the entire area, Washington could combine the immediate advantage of putting thousands of people to work with a long-term project for reforming the power monopoly.

An act creating the Tennessee Valley Authority (TVA) was passed in 1933 by the Hundred Days Congress. This far-ranging enterprise was largely a result of the steadfast vision and unflagging zeal of Senator George W. Norris of Nebraska, after whom one of the mighty dams was named. From the standpoint of "planned economy," the TVA was by far the most revolutionary of all the New Deal schemes.

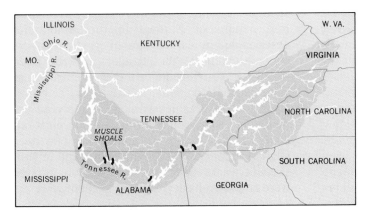

TVA Area *Only the nine dams on the Tennessee River are shown here. There are more than twenty on the tributaries.*

This new agency was determined to discover precisely how much the production and distribution of electricity cost, so that a "yardstick" could be set up to test the fairness of rates charged by private companies. Utility corporations lashed back at this entering wedge of governmental control, charging that the low cost of TVA power was due to dishonest bookkeeping and the absence of taxes. Critics complained that the whole dream was "creeping socialism in concrete."

But the New Dealers, shrugging off such outcries, pointed a prideful finger at the amazing achievements of the TVA. The gigantic project had brought to the area not only full employment and the blessings of cheap electric power, but low-cost housing, abundant cheap nitrates, the restoration of eroded soil, reforestation, improved navigation, and flood control. Rivers ran blue instead of brown; and a once-poverty-cursed area was being transformed into one of the most flourishing regions in the United States. Foreigners were greatly impressed with the possibilities of similar schemes in their own lands, and exulting New Dealers agitated for parallel enterprises in the valleys of the Columbia and Missouri rivers. But the conservatives in Congress, growing bolder, confined this particular type of socialism to the Tennessee Valley.

Housing Reform and Social Security

Gratifying beginnings had meanwhile been made by the New Deal in housing construction. To speed recovery and better homes, Roosevelt set up the Federal Housing Administration (FHA) as early as 1934. The building industry was to be stimulated by small loans to householders, both for improving their dwellings and for completing new ones. So popular did the FHA prove to be that it was one of the few "alphabetical agencies" to outlast the age of Roosevelt.

Congress bolstered the program in 1937 by authorizing the United States Housing Authority (USHA)—an agency designed to lend money to states or communities for low-cost construction. Though units for about 650,000 low-income persons were started, new building fell tragically short of needs. New Deal efforts to expand the project ran head-on into vigorous opposition from real estate promoters, builders, and landlords ("slumlords"), to say nothing of anti–New Dealers who attacked what they considered down-the-rathole spending. Nonetheless, for the first time in a century the slum areas in America ceased growing and even shrank.

Incomparably more important was the success of New Dealers in the field of unemployment insurance and old-age pensions. Their greatest victory was the epochal Social Security Act of 1935—one of the most complicated and far-reaching laws ever to pass Congress. To cushion future depressions, the measure provided for federal-state unemployment insurance. To provide security for old age, specified categories of retired workers were to receive regular payments from Washington. These payments ranged from $10 to $85 a month (later raised) and were financed by a payroll tax on both employers and employees. Provision was also made for the blind, the physically handicapped, delinquent children, and other dependents.

Republican opposition to the sweeping new legislation was bitter. "Social Security," insisted Hoover, "must be builded upon a cult of work, not a cult of leisure." The GOP national chairman falsely charged that every worker would have to wear a metal dog tag for life.

Social Security was largely inspired by the example of some of the more highly industrialized nations of Europe. In the agricultural America of an earlier day, there had always been farm chores for all ages, and the large family had cared for its own dependents. But in an urbanized economy, at the mercy of boom-or-bust cycles, the government was now recognizing its responsibility for the welfare of its citizens. By 1939 over 45 million persons were eligible for Social Security benefits, and in subsequent years further categories of workers were added and the payments to them were periodically increased.

A New Deal for Unskilled Labor

The NRA blue eagles, with their call for collective bargaining, had been a godsend to organized labor. As New Deal expenditures brought some slackening of unemployment, labor began to feel more secure and hence more self-assertive. A rash of walkouts occurred in the summer of 1934, including a paralyzing general strike in San Francisco (following a "Bloody Thursday"), which was broken only when outraged citizens resorted to vigilante tactics.

When the Supreme Court axed the blue eagle, a Congress sympathetic to labor unions undertook to fill the vacuum. The fruit of its deliberations was the Wagner, or National Labor Relations Act of 1935. This trailblazing law created a powerful new National Labor Relations Board for administrative purposes and reasserted the right of labor to engage in self-organization and to bargain collectively through representatives of its own choice. The Wagner Act proved to be one of the real milestones on

John L. Lewis (1880–1969) *Lewis became a miner and worked his way up to the presidency of the United Mine Workers of America. He once remarked of strikebreaking soldiers, "You can't dig coal with bayonets."*

"The Great Divide," 1936 *Steel industry as a factor in splitting labor. Note the industrial unions going left, the craft unions, right. (Fitzpatrick in the St. Louis* Post-Dispatch.)

the rocky road of the American labor movement.

Under the encouragement of a highly sympathetic National Labor Relations Board, a host of unskilled workers began to organize themselves into effective unions. The leader of this drive was beetle-browed, domineering, and melodramatic John L. Lewis, boss of the United Mine Workers. In 1935 he succeeded in forming the Committee for Industrial Organization (CIO) within the ranks of the skilled-craft American Federation of Labor. But skilled workers, ever since the days of the ill-fated Knights of Labor in the 1880s, had shown only lukewarm sympathy for the cause of unskilled labor, especially blacks. In 1936, following inevitable friction with the CIO, the older federation suspended the upstart unions associated with the newer organization. (The CIO transformed itself into

General Motors Sit-down Strikers, Flint, Michigan, 1937 *Strikers like these sometimes kept their spirits up with the song "Sit Down":*
> *When the boss won't talk*
> *Don't take a walk;*
> *Sit down, sit down.*
(United Press International photo.)

the fully independent *Congress* of Industrial Organizations in 1938.)

Nothing daunted, the rebellious CIO moved on a concerted scale into the huge automobile industry. Late in 1936 the workers resorted to a revolutionary technique (earlier used in both Europe and America) known as the sit-down strike: they refused to leave the factory buildings of General Motors at Flint, Michigan, and thus prevented the importation of strikebreakers. Conservative respecters of private property were scandalized. The CIO finally won a resounding victory when its union, after heated negotiations, was recognized by General Motors as the sole bargaining agency for its employees.

Roosevelt's "Coddling" of Labor

Unskilled workers now pressed their advantage. The United States Steel Company, hitherto an impossible nut for labor to crack, averted a costly strike when it voluntarily granted rights of unionization to its CIO-organized employees. But the "little steel" companies fought back savagely. Citizens were shocked in 1937 by the Memorial Day massacre at the plant of the Republic Steel Company in South Chicago. There, in a bloody fracas, police fired upon pickets and

workers, leaving the area strewn with several score dead and wounded.

A better deal for labor continued when Congress, in 1938, passed the memorable Fair Labor Standards Act (Wages and Hours Bill). Industries involved in interstate commerce were to set up minimum-wage and maximum-hour levels. Though not immediately established, the specific goals were forty cents an hour (later raised) and a forty-hour week. Labor by children under sixteen was forbidden; under eighteen, if the occupation was dangerous. These reforms were bitterly though futilely opposed by many industrialists, especially by those southern textile manufacturers that had profited from low-wage labor.

In later New Deal days, labor unionization flourished like crabgrass; "Roosevelt wants you to join a union" was the rallying cry of professional organizers. The president received valuable support at ballot-box time from labor leaders and many appreciative working men and women. One mill worker remarked that Roosevelt was "the only man we ever had in the White House who would know that my boss is a s.o.b."

The CIO surged forward, breaking completely with the AF of L in 1938. On that occasion the *Committee* for Industrial Organization

TOTAL NONFARM LABOR FORCE

1900
4.4% Organized   95.6% Unorganized

1954
34.7% Organized   65.3% Unorganized

1984
18% Organized   82% Unorganized

(C I O and A F of L merged in 1955)

CIO

AF of L
and
CIO

AF of L

INDEPENDENT UNIONS

MILLIONS OF MEMBERS

1900 1905 1910 1915 1920 1925 1930 1935 1940 1945 1950 1955 1960 1965 1970 1975 '80 '82 '85

The Rise of Organized Labor, 1900–1982 *The percentage of the total labor force that was organized increased until 1954, and it has declined ever since.*

was formally reconstituted as the *Congress* of Industrial Organizations (the new CIO), under the high-handed presidency of John L. Lewis. By 1940 the CIO could claim about 4 million members in its constituent unions, including some 200,000 black members. Nevertheless, bitter and annoying jurisdictional feuding, involving strikes, continued with the AF of L. At times labor seemed more bent on costly civil war than on its age-old war with management.

Landon Challenges "the Champ" in 1936

As the presidential campaign of 1936 neared, the New Dealers were on top of the world. They had achieved considerable progress, and millions of "reliefers" were grateful to their bountiful government. The exultant Democrats, meeting in Philadelphia, pushed through the renomination of Roosevelt in a brief rubber-stamp ceremony. Their platform stood squarely on the record of the New Deal years.

The Republicans, assembling in Cleveland, were hard pressed to find someone to feed to "the Champ." They finally settled on the colorless and mildly liberal Governor Alfred M. Landon of the Sunflower State of Kansas, a wealthy oilman, whose chief claim to distinction was that he had balanced the budget of his state in an era of unbalanced budgets. The Republican platform, though promising relief benefits that would cost many millions, condemned the New Deal of Franklin "Deficit" Roosevelt—its radicalism, experimentation, confusion, and "frightful waste." Popular watchwords were "Defeat the New Deal and Its Reckless Spending," "Let's Get Another Deck," "Life, Liberty, and Landon," and "Let's Make It a Landon-Slide."

Landon—"the Kansas Coolidge"—was honest, sincere, homespun, "commonsensical," and as American as cherry pie. But he had a poor radio voice and seemed schoolboyish on the stump. Surrounded by imitation Kansas sunflowers, Landon stressed "deeds, not deficits" and condemned New Deal high-handedness. Though opposing the popular Social Security Act, he advocated just enough reform to cause

> Three days before the 1936 election Roosevelt sounded positively dictatorial in his speech at New York's Madison Square Garden: "I should like to have it said of my first Administration that in it the forces of selfishness and of lust for power met their match. I should like to have it said of my second Administration that in it these forces met their master."

the Democrats to retort that he would continue the New Deal—a secondhand New Deal—in his own way. He was, they sneered, "the poor man's Hoover."

Democrats denounced the GOP as the party of big moneyed interests and the big depression and amid loud choruses of boos cried, "Remember Hoover!" The embittered ex-president called for "a holy crusade for liberty." A group of wealthy Republicans and conservative Democrats had in 1934 formed the American Liberty League to fight "socialistic" New Deal schemes, and they vented their reactionary spleen against "that man" Roosevelt, "the New Dealocrat." But they hurt their own cause by becoming a made-to-order target for FDR. Angry enough to stretch sheet iron, Roosevelt took to the stump and denounced the "economic royalists" who sought to "hide behind the flag and the Constitution." "I welcome their hatred," he proclaimed.

A landslide overwhelmed Landon, as the demoralized Republicans carried only two states, Maine and Vermont. This dismal showing caused political wiseacres to make the old adage read: "As Maine goes, so goes Vermont."* The popular vote was 27,752,869 to 16,674,665; the electoral count was 523 to 8—the most lopsided in 116 years. Democratic majorities, riding in on Roosevelt's magic coattails, were again returned to Congress. Jubilant Democrats could now claim more than two-thirds of the seats in the House and a like proportion in the Senate.

---

*Maine, which traditionally held its state elections in September, was long regarded as a political weather vane. Hence the expression "As Maine goes, so goes the nation."

The battle of 1936, perhaps the most bitter since Bryan's defeat in 1896, partially bore out Republican charges of class warfare. Even more than in 1932, the needy economic groups were lined up against the so-called greedy economic groups. CIO units contributed generously to FDR's campaign chest. Many left-wingers turned to Roosevelt, as the customary third-party protest vote sharply declined. Blacks, several million of whom had also enjoyed welcome relief checks, had by now largely shaken off their traditional allegiance to the Republican party. To them, Lincoln was "finally dead."

FDR won primarily because he appealed to the "forgotten man," whom he never forgot. Some of the president's support was only pocketbook-deep: "reliefers" were not going to bite the hand that doled out the government checks. No one, as Al Smith remarked, "shoots at Santa Claus." But Roosevelt in fact had forged a powerful and enduring coalition of the South, the blacks, the urbanites, and the poor. He proved especially effective in marshaling the support of the multitudes of "New Immigrants"—mostly the Catholics and Jews who had been clogging the great cities since the turn of the century. These once-scorned newcomers, with their now-numerous sons and daughters, had at last come politically of age.

Nine Old Men on the Supreme Bench

Bowing his head to the sleety blasts, Roosevelt took the presidential oath on January 20, 1937, instead of the traditional March 4. The Twentieth Amendment to the Constitution had been ratified in 1933. (See the Appendix.) It swept away the post-election "lame duck" session of Congress and shortened by six weeks the awkward period before inauguration.

Flushed with victory, Roosevelt interpreted his reelection as a mandate to continue New Deal reforms. But in his eyes the cloistered old men on the supreme bench, like fossilized stumbling blocks, stood stubbornly in the pathway of progress. In nine major cases involving the New Deal, the Roosevelt administration had been defeated seven times. The Court was ultraconservative, and six of the nine oldsters in black were over seventy. As luck would have it, not a single member had been appointed by FDR in his first term.

Roosevelt—his "Dutch up"—viewed with mounting impatience what he regarded as the obstructive conservatism of the Court. Some of these Old Guard appointees were hanging on with a senile grip, partly because they felt it their patriotic duty to curb the "socialistic" tendencies of that radical in the White House. Roosevelt believed that the voters in three successive elections—the presidential elections of 1932 and 1936 and the midterm congressional elections of 1934—had returned a smashing verdict in favor of his program of reform. Democracy, in his view, meant rule by the people. If the American way of life was to be preserved, Roosevelt argued, the Supreme Court ought to get in line with the supreme court of public opinion.

Roosevelt finally hit upon a Court scheme that he regarded as "the answer to a maiden's prayer." When he sprang it on a shocked nation, early in 1937, he caught the country and Congress completely by surprise. Roosevelt bluntly asked Congress for legislation to permit him to add a new justice to the Supreme Court for every member over seventy who would not retire. The maximum membership could then be fifteen. Roosevelt pointed to the necessity of injecting vigorous new blood, for the Court, he alleged, was far behind in its work. This charge, which turned out to be false, brought heated accusations of dishonesty. At best, Roosevelt was

The Supreme Court under Pressure   FDR regarded the justices as horse-and-buggy legalists. (Seibel in the Richmond Times-Dispatch, 1937.)

headstrong and not fully aware of the fact that the Court, in popular thinking, had become something of a sacred cow.

> In a radio address (March 1937), Roosevelt expressed some startling thoughts about the Supreme Court: "We have . . . reached the point . . . where we must take action to save the Constitution from the Court and the Court from itself. We must find a way to take an appeal from the Supreme Court to the Constitution itself. We want a Supreme Court which will do justice under the Constitution—not over it."

The Court Changes Course

Congress and the nation were promptly convulsed over the scheme to "pack" the Supreme Court with a "dictator bill," which one critic called "too damned slick." Franklin "Double-crossing" Roosevelt was savagely condemned for attempting to break down the delicate checks and balances among the three branches of the government. He was accused of grooming himself as a dictator by trying to browbeat the judiciary. In the eyes of countless citizens, mostly Republicans but including many Democrats, basic liberties seemed to be in jeopardy.

"God Bless the Supreme Court" was a fervent prayer.

The Court had meanwhile seen the ax hanging over its head. Whatever his motives, Justice Roberts, formerly regarded as conservative, began to vote on the side of his liberal colleagues. "A switch in time saves nine" was the classic witticism inspired by this change. By a five to four decision the Court, in March 1937, upheld the principle of a state minimum wage for women, thereby reversing its stand on a different case a year earlier. In succeeding decisions a Court more sympathetic to the New Deal upheld the National Labor Relations Act (Wagner Act) and the Social Security Act. Roosevelt's "Court-packing" scheme was further undermined when Congress voted full pay for justices over seventy who retired, whereupon one of the oldest conservative members resigned, to be replaced by a New Dealer, Justice Black.

Congress finally passed a court reform bill, but this watered-down version applied only to lower courts. Roosevelt, the master politician, thus suffered his first major legislative defeat at the hands of his own party in Congress. Americans have never viewed lightly a tampering with the Supreme Court by the president, no matter how popular their chief executive may be. Yet in losing this battle, Roosevelt incidentally won his campaign. The Court, as he had hoped, became markedly more friendly to New Deal reforms. Furthermore, a succession of deaths and resignations enabled him to make nine appointments to the tribunal—more than any of his predecessors since George Washington. Father Time "unpacked" the Court.

Yet in a sense FDR lost both the Court battle and the war. He so aroused conservatives of both parties in Congress that few New Deal reforms were passed after 1937, the year of the fight to "pack" the Supreme Court.

The Twilight of the New Deal

From 1933 to 1937 the country had been gradually inching its way out of the depression, largely because of the billions of dollars injected by Congress into the economic bloodstream. Although millions of dejected souls remained unemployed, gratifying gains had been registered. "We planned it that way," remarked Roosevelt cheerily.

But in 1937 a sharp recession set in, which hit bottom in 1938. The president's critics, branding this setback "the Roosevelt depression," asserted that if FDR could plan upward spirals, he must also have planned the downward dip. This particular recession was due to an overrapid cutting back of "pump-priming" spending by Washington.

Undiscouraged, Roosevelt had meanwhile been pushing the remaining measures of the New Deal. Early in 1937 he urged Congress—a Congress growing more conservative—to authorize a sweeping reorganization of the national administration in the interests of streamlined efficiency. But the issue became tangled up with his presumed dictatorial ambitions in regard to the Supreme Court, and he suffered another stinging defeat. Two years later, in 1939, Congress partially relented and in the Reorganization Act gave him limited powers for administrative reforms, including the key new Executive Office in the White House.

The New Dealers were accused of having the richest campaign chest in history; and in truth government relief checks had a curious habit of coming in bunches just before ballot time. To remedy such practices, which tended to make a farce of free elections, Congress adopted the much-heralded Hatch Act of 1939. It debarred federal administrative officials, except the highest policy-making officers, from active political campaigning and soliciting. It also forbade the use of government funds for political purposes as well as the collection of campaign contributions from persons receiving relief payments. The Hatch Act was broadened in 1940 to place limits on campaign contributions and expenditures, but such clever ways of getting around it were found that on the whole the legislation proved disappointing.

By 1938 the New Deal had clearly lost most of its early momentum. Magician Roosevelt could find few spectacular new reform rabbits to pull out of his tall silk hat. In the congressional elections of 1938 the Republicans, for the first time, cut heavily into the unwieldy New Deal majorities in Congress, though failing to gain control of either house. The international crisis that came to a boil in 1938–1939 shifted public attention away from domestic reform and no doubt helped save the political hide of the Roosevelt "spendocracy." The New Deal, for all practical purposes, had shot its bolt.

New Deal or Raw Deal?

Foes of the New Deal condemned its alleged waste, incompetence, confusion, contradictions, and cross-purposes, as well as the chiseling and graft in the alphabetical agencies—"alphabet soup," sneered Al Smith. Roosevelt had done nothing, cynics said, that an earthquake could not have done better. Critics deplored the employment of "crackpot" college professors, leftist "pinkos," and outright Communists. Such subversives, it was charged, were trying to make America over in the Bolshevik-Marxist image under "Rooseveltski." The Hearst newspapers assailed

> The Red New Deal with a Soviet seal
> Endorsed by a Moscow hand, The strange
>   result of an alien cult
> In a liberty-loving land.

Roosevelt was further accused by conservatives of being Jewish ("Rosenfield") and of tapping too many bright young Jewish leftists ("The Jew Deal") for his "Drain Trust."

Hardheaded businesspeople, who "had met a payroll," were shocked by the leap-before-you-look, try-anything-once spirit of Roosevelt, the jolly improviser. They accused him of confusing

"Keeping It Out of Balance," 1935   *(Fitzpatrick in the* St. Louis *Post-Dispatch.)*

> A basic objective of the New Deal was featured in Roosevelt's second inaugural address (1937): "I see one-third of a nation ill-housed, ill-clad, ill-nourished. . . . The test of our progress is not whether we add more to the abundance of those who have much; it is whether we provide enough for those who have too little."

noise and movement with progress. Humorist Will Rogers, the rope-twirling "poet lariat" of the era, remarked that if Roosevelt were to burn down the Capitol, people would say, "Well, we at least got a fire started, anyhow."

"Bureaucratic meddling" and "regimentation" were also bitter complaints of anti–New Dealers; and in truth, bureaucracy did blossom. The federal government, with its hundreds of thousands of employees, became incomparably the largest single business in the country, as the states faded further into the background.

Promises of budget balancing, to say nothing of other promises, had flown out the window—so foes of the New Deal pointed out. The national debt had skyrocketed from the already enormous figure of $19,487,000,000 in 1932 to $40,440,000,000 by 1939. America was becoming, its critics charged, a "handout state" trying to squander itself into prosperity—*U*.S. stood for "unlimited spending." Such lavish benefactions

Nat. Debt

were undermining the old virtues of thrift and initiative. Ordinary Americans, once self-reliant citizens, were getting a bad case of the "gimmies": their wishbones were becoming larger than their backbones. In the nineteenth century, hard-pressed workers went West; now they went on relief.

Business was bitter. Accusing the New Deal of fomenting class strife, conservatives insisted that the laborer and the farmer—especially the big operator—were being pampered. Why "soak the successful"? Countless businesspeople, especially Republicans, declared that they could pull themselves out of the depression if they could only get the federal government—an interventionist big government—off their backs. Private enterprise, they charged, was being stifled by "planned economy," "planned bankruptcy," "creeping socialism," and the philosophy "Washington can do it better," with a federal pill for every ill. States' rights were being ignored, while the government was competing in business with its own citizens, under a "dictatorship of do-gooders."

The aggressive leadership of Roosevelt—"one-man supergovernment"—also came in for denunciation. Heavy fire was especially directed at his attempts to browbeat the Supreme Court and to create a "dummy Congress." He had even tried in the 1938 elections, with backfiring results, to "purge" members of Congress who would not lockstep with him. The three sena-

tors whom he publicly opposed were all triumphantly reelected.

The most damning indictment of the New Deal was that it had failed to cure the depression. Afloat in a sea of red ink, it had merely administered aspirin, sedatives, and Band-Aids. Many economists believed that better results would have been achieved by much greater deficit spending. Despite some $20 billion poured out in six years of deficit spending and lending, of leaf raking and pump priming, the gap was not closed between production and consumption. There were even more mountainous farm surpluses under Roosevelt than under Hoover. Millions of dispirited men and women were still unemployed in 1939, after six years of drain, strain, and pain. Not until World War II blazed forth in Europe with Hitler—the greatest pump primer of all—was the unemployment headache solved. The sensational increase in the national debt was caused by World War II, not the New Deal. The national debt was only $40 billion in 1939 but $258 billion in 1945.

FDR's Balance Sheet

New Dealers staunchly defended their record. Admitting that there had been some waste, they pointed out that relief—not economy—had been the primary object of their multifront war on the depression. Conceding also that there had

Unemployment, 1929–1942 These cold figures can only begin to suggest the widespread human misery caused by mass unemployment. One man wrote to a newspaper in 1932: "I am forty-eight; married twenty-one years; four children, three in school. For the last eight years I was employed as a Pullman conductor. Since September, 1930, they have given me seven months part-time work. Today I am an object of charity. . . . My small, weak, and frail wife and two small children are suffering and I have come to that terrible place where I could easily resort to violence in my desperation."

Employment Agency, by Isaac Soyer *Millions of jobless Americans felt the despair Soyer captured in this painting, as depression-era unemployment reached levels never seen before or since in American history. (Whitney Museum of American Art.)*

been some graft, they argued that it had been trivial in view of the immense sums spent and the obvious need for haste.

Apologists for Roosevelt further declared that the New Deal had relieved the worst of the crisis in 1933. It promoted the philosophy of "balancing the human budget" and accepted the principle that the federal government was morally bound to prevent mass hunger and starvation by "managing" the economy. The Washington regime was to be used, not feared. America's economic system was kept from collapse; a fairer distribution of the national income was achieved; and the citizens were enabled to retain their self-respect. "Nobody is going to starve" was Roosevelt's promise.

Though hated by business tycoons, FDR should have been their patron saint, so his admirers claimed. He deflected popular resentments against business and may have saved the American system of free enterprise. Roosevelt's

quarrel was not with capitalism but with capitalists; he purged American capitalism of some of its worst abuses so that it might be saved from itself. He may even have headed off a more radical swing to the left by a mild dose of what was mistakenly condemned as "socialism." The head of the American Socialist party, when once asked if the New Deal had carried out the Socialist program, reportedly replied that it had indeed—on a stretcher.

Roosevelt, like Jefferson, provided reform without a bloody revolution—at a time in history when some foreign nations were suffering armed uprisings and when many Europeans

A grim quip of the times was: "Roosevelt doesn't hate rich men. He only wants to skin them."

were predicting either communism or fascism for America. He was upbraided by the left-wing radicals for not going far enough; by the right-wing radicals for not going too far. Choosing the middle road, he has been called the greatest American conservative since Hamilton. He was in fact Hamiltonian in his espousal of big government, but Jeffersonian in his concern for the "forgotten man." Demonstrating anew the value of powerful presidential leadership, he exer-cised that power to relieve the erosion of the nation's greatest physical resource—its people. He helped preserve democracy in America at a time when democracies abroad were disappearing down the sinkhole of dictatorship. And in playing this role, he unwittingly girded the nation for its part in the titanic war that hung on the horizon—a war in which democracy the world over would be at stake.

Varying Viewpoints

The New Deal has stirred hot debate since its beginnings in 1933. Some contemporaries like Herbert Hoover, and some historians like Edgar E. Robinson, condemned Roosevelt's program as a "socialistic" break from American traditions. But until recently, the great majority of historians have approved the political values of the New Deal and have praised its accomplishments.

Arthur M. Schlesinger, Jr., portrays the New Deal as a dramatic climax to a reform tradition reaching back through progressivism and populism to the age of Jackson. In an equally sympathetic but different vein, Richard Hofstadter views the New Deal as a bold response to a severe crisis and hence a triumphant departure from the old reform tradition. Another pro-Roosevelt scholar has dubbed the New Deal the "Third American Revolution."

In the last two decades, several younger "New Left" historians have challenged this orthodox interpretation. They see the New Deal as neither bold nor innovative, but simply as a conservative holding action to shore up sagging capitalism. The Roosevelt program, one of these scholars charges, did not promote recovery, redistribute wealth, improve race relations, or reform American business.

The consensus seems to be somewhere in the middle. As William Leuchtenburg has put it, the New Deal engineered a "half-way revolution." It was neither outright radical nor simply conservative but did initiate changes in the party system, labor relations, and the economic and social role of the federal government that significantly transformed American life.

Select Readings

Primary Source Documents

James Agee and Walker Evans, *Let Us Now Praise Famous Men* (1940), brilliantly evokes the misery of the depression in words and photographs. Franklin D. Roosevelt's dramatic "First Inaugural Address" (1933), in Henry Steele Commager, ed., *Documents of American History*, captured the imagination of the distressed nation. Less successful was Roosevelt's "Radio Address on Supreme Court Reform" (1937), in Richard Hofstadter, *Great Issues in American History*. See also Dorothy Thompson's attack on the Court plan in the Washington *Star*, February 10, 1937.* Clifford Odets' play *Waiting for Lefty* (1935) and John Steinbeck's novel *The Grapes of Wrath* (1939) exemplify the literature stimulated by the Great Depression.

Secondary Sources

A masterly summation is William E. Leuchtenburg, *Franklin D. Roosevelt and the New Deal, 1932–1940* (1963). Briefer and more critical of the limitations of reform is Paul Conkin, *The New Deal* (rev. ed., 1975). A readable biography is James MacGregor Burns, *Roosevelt: The Lion and the Fox* (1956). More detailed is Frank Freidel, *Franklin D. Roosevelt* (4 vols., 1952–1973). A sympathetic and perceptive family portrait is Joseph P. Lash, *Eleanor and Franklin* (1971). Brilliantly pro-FDR are the three volumes of Arthur M. Schlesinger, Jr.'s *Age of Roosevelt: The Crisis of the Old Order* (1957), *The Coming of the New Deal* (1959), and *The Politics of Upheaval* (1960). Less favorable is Edgar Eugene Robinson, *The Roosevelt Leadership* (1955). See also Richard Hofstadter, *The Age of Reform* (1955). John M. Blum, *From the Morgenthau Diaries* (3 vols., 1959–1967), gives the perspective of an important New Deal insider. The views of other contemporaries may be found in Frances Perkins, *The Roosevelt I Knew* (1946); Rexford G. Tugwell, *In Search of Roosevelt* (1972); and Raymond Moley, *After Seven Years* (1939). On the relation of the old progressives to the New Deal, consult Otis L. Graham, Jr., *An Encore for Reform* (1967), and Ronald L. Feinman, *Twilight of Progressivism: The Western Republican Senators and the New Deal* (1981). The social impact of the depression is vividly etched in Studs Terkel, *Hard Times* (1970), and in Ann Banks, *First Person America* (1980). Of special interest are Lois Sharf, *To Work and to Wed: Female Employment, Feminism, and the Great Depression* (1980), and Susan Ware, *Beyond Suffrage: Women in the New Deal* (1981). Alan Brinkley brilliantly chronicles *Voices of Protest: Huey Long, Father Coughlin, and the Great Depression* (1982). Labor is dealt with in Irving Bernstein, *Turbulent Years* (1970); and Ronald Schatz, *The Electrical Workers* (1983). Ellis Hawley, *The New Deal and the Problem of Monopoly* (1966), is a superb analysis of the conflicting currents of economic policy in the Roosevelt administration. A comprehensive assessment by several noted scholars is Harvard Sitkoff, ed., *Fifty Years Later: The New Deal Evaluated* (1985). James Patterson, *The New Deal and the States* (1969), examines the local impact of the Roosevelt measures, as does Charles H. Trout, *Boston, the Great Depression, and the New Deal* (1977). Indians receive special attention in Graham D. Taylor, *The New Deal and American Indian Tribalism* (1980), and Kenneth R. Philip, *John Collier's Crusade for Indian Reform* (1977). On blacks, see Harvard Sitkoff, *A New Deal for Blacks* (1978), and Nancy J. Weiss, *Farewell to the Party of Lincoln: Black Politics in the Age of FDR* (1983). Richard Lowitt analyzes *The New Deal and the West* (1984). See also James Cobb and Michael Namaroto, eds., *The New Deal and the South* (1984). Especially good on intellectual history are Richard H. Pells, *Radical Visions and American Dreams: Culture and Social Thought in the Depression Years* (1973), and Daniel Aaron, *Writers on the Left* (1961).

39

Franklin D. Roosevelt and the Shadow of War

The epidemic of world lawlessness is spreading. When an epidemic of physical disease starts to spread, the community approves and joins in a quarantine of the patients in order to protect the health of the community against the spread of the disease. . . .There must be positive endeavors to preserve peace.

Franklin D. Roosevelt,
Chicago Quarantine Speech, 1937

The London Conference and Soviet Recognition

The sixty-six-nation London Economic Conference, meeting in the summer of 1933, revealed how intimately Roosevelt's early foreign policy was entwined with his schemes for domestic recovery. This distinguished assemblage, to which America sent delegates, had as its major purpose a frontal attack on the global depression. It was particularly eager to stabilize national currencies on a worldwide front; and to such a course Washington had apparently committed itself in advance.

But Roosevelt began to have second thoughts. He evidently believed that his gold-juggling policies were stimulating faint blushes of returning prosperity. An international agreement on currency might tie his hands; and as an astute politician, he was unwilling to sacrifice probable recovery at home for possible recovery abroad. While vacationing on a cruiser in the North Atlantic, he dashed off a radio message to London, scolding the conference for trying to stabilize currencies and urging it to turn to more basic economic ills.

Roosevelt's bombshell message blew the rug from under the London Conference. The delegates adjourned empty-handed, amid cries of American bad faith. The conference, in any event, probably would have failed to produce a wonder drug for the world's economic maladies. But the Devil-take-the-hindmost attitude of Roosevelt plunged the world even deeper into the morass of narrow isolationism and extreme nationalism. This unfortunate trend, as fate would have it, played directly into the hands of power-mad dictators.

Less spectacular than Roosevelt's torpedoing of the London Conference was his formal recognition of the Soviet Union, late in 1933. Disagreeable though the thought might be to conservative Americans, the Bolshevik government had fastened itself securely on the backs of the Russian masses and had won recognition from other great powers. There was a certain unreality in America's refusing to recognize, after sixteen long years, the official existence of the Moscow government—a regime representing 160 million people and holding sway over one-sixth of the earth's land surface. Washington's cold-shoulder treatment, moreover, had not caused the Soviet Union to collapse or induced the Bolsheviks to abandon their insidious propaganda for world revolution.

Why did Roosevelt extend the right hand of recognition? He was first of all an outspoken liberal, not bound by the conservatism of his Republican predecessors. Hitler was on the rise in Germany, land-hungry Japan was on the rampage in the Far East, and many Americans believed that the recognition of Moscow might bolster the Russians against the Nipponese. Finally, a depression-ridden United States was willing to gamble that an enriching trade would develop with the Soviet Union. Profits promote partnerships.

Horse-trading negotiations with the Russians were concluded in Washington during November 1933. The Soviets formally promised, among other assurances, to refrain from revolutionary propaganda in America. They promptly broke this pledge. Large-scale trade with the U.S.S.R. did not develop, primarily because a huge American loan, which the Russians had expected, was not granted. Russia was regarded as a poor credit risk. Uncle Sam was to some

"Just Another Customer," 1933 The United States recognizes Russia. (Courtesy of the Dallas News.)

extent duped by Moscow, but at least he was now on official speaking terms—or name-calling terms—with the rulers of the largest and most populous of the European nations. Roosevelt remarked that while Russia was not yet "housebroken," it was still a good breed of dog. Dissenting conservatives condemned "Bolshevik butchers" and "profits stained with blood."

Freedom for (from?) the Filipinos

The Great Depression, otherwise a blight, actually brightened hopes for Philippine independence. McKinley's imperialistic dream bubble in the Far East had burst, and American taxpayers were eager to throw overboard their expensive tropical liability. Organized labor clamored for the exclusion of low-wage Filipinos, while American producers of sugar and other products were eager to restrict competition from the Philippines.

In 1934 Congress, remembering its earlier promises of Philippine independence, responded to the prodding of such self-seeking groups. It passed a bill under which the potentially rich islands were to become free, but only after a ten-year period of economic and political tutelage. Uncle Sam's military establishments were to be relinquished, but naval bases were to be reserved for future discussion—and retention.

Rather than freeing the Philippines, the American people tried to free themselves *from* the Philippines. With a selfish eye to their own welfare, they imposed upon the Filipinos economic terms so ungenerous as to threaten the islands with prostration. American isolationists, moreover, rejoiced to be rid of this Far Eastern heel of Achilles—so vulnerable to Japanese attack. Yet these turn-tail-and-run tactics, though applauded by anticolonialists in Eastern Asia, cost America "face" in the Far East. Abandoning the Filipinos did nothing to discourage the barefaced aggressions of the Japanese militarists.

Good Neighborism under FDR

A refreshing new era in relations with Latin America was heralded when Roosevelt ringingly proclaimed in his inaugural address, "I would dedicate this nation to the policy of the Good Neighbor."

Old-fashioned intervention by bayonet in the Caribbean had not paid off, except in an evil harvest of resentment, suspicion, and fear. The Great Depression had cooled off Yankee economic aggressiveness, as thousands of investors in Latin American "securities" became sackholders rather than stockholders. There were now fewer dollars to be protected by the rifles of the hated marines.

With war-thirsty dictators seizing power in Europe and Asia, Roosevelt was eager to line up the Latin Americans to help defend the Western Hemisphere. Embittered neighbors would be potential tools of transoceanic aggressors. President Roosevelt made clear at the outset that he was going to renounce armed intervention, particularly the vexatious corollary of the Monroe Doctrine devised by his cousin Theodore Roosevelt. Late in 1933, at the Seventh Pan-American Conference in Montevideo, the United States delegation formally accepted nonintervention.

Deeds followed words. The last marines embarked from Haiti in 1934. In the same year restive Cuba was released from the hobbles of the Platt Amendment, under which Uncle Sam had been free to intervene, although the naval base at Guantanamo was retained. The tiny country of Panama received a similar uplift in 1936, when the leading strings of Washington were partially unfastened.

The hope-inspiring Good Neighbor policy, with the accent on consultation and nonintervention, received its acid test in Mexico. A seizure of Yankee oil properties in 1938, under the constitution of 1917, brought vehement demands for armed intervention from American investors. But Roosevelt successfully resisted the clamor, and a settlement was finally threshed out in 1941, even though the oil companies lost much of their original stake.

Spectacular success crowned Roosevelt's Good Neighbor policy. His earnest attempts to inaugurate a new era of friendliness, though hurting some Yankee bondholders, paid rich dividends in goodwill among the peoples to the south. No other citizen of the United States has ever been held in such high esteem in Latin America during his lifetime. Roosevelt was cheered with tumultuous enthusiasm when, as a "traveling salesman for peace," he journeyed to the special Inter-American Conference at Buenos Aires in 1936. The Colossus of the North now seemed less a vulture and more an eagle.

Secretary Hull's Reciprocal Trade Agreements

Intimately associated with Good Neighborism, and also popular in Latin America, was the reciprocal trade policy of the New Dealers. Its chief architect was high-domed Secretary of State Cordell Hull, a homespun Tennessean of the low-tariff school. Like Roosevelt, he believed that trade was a two-way street; that a nation can sell abroad only as it buys abroad; that tariff barriers choke off foreign trade; and that trade wars beget shooting wars.

Responding to the Hull-Roosevelt leadership, Congress passed the Reciprocal Trade Agreements Act in 1934. Designed in part to lift American export trade from the depression doldrums, this far-visioned measure was aimed at both relief and recovery. At the same time, it would put into active operation the low-tariff policies of the New Dealers. (See tariff chart in the Appendix.)

The Trade Agreements Act avoided the dangerous uncertainties of a wholesale tariff revision; it merely whittled down the most objectionable schedules of the Hawley-Smoot law by amending them. Roosevelt was empowered to lower existing rates by as much as 50 percent, provided that the other country involved was willing to respond with similar reductions. The resulting pacts, moreover, were to become effective without the formal approval of the Senate. This novel feature not only ensured speedier action but sidestepped the twin evils of logrolling and high-pressure lobbying in Congress.

Secretary Hull, whose zeal for reciprocity was unflagging, succeeded in negotiating pacts with twenty-one countries by the end of 1939. During these same years American foreign trade increased appreciably, all presumably in part as a result of the Hull-Roosevelt policies. Trade agreements undoubtedly bettered economic and political relations with Latin America and proved to be an influence for peace in a war-bent world.

The Reciprocal Trade Agreements Act, with modifications, was renewed periodically by Congress—but invariably in the teeth of heated protests from high-tariff Republicans. James G. Blaine, Republican secretary of state of yesteryear, had fathered the reciprocal trade policy. But dyed-in-the-wool Republicans were inclined to shun the Blaine baby in Democratic diapers. Manufacturers were not alone in their opposition; they were joined by many middle western farmers who were hurt by lowered duties on

"One of Our Quaint Ideas about Foreign Trade"
(Fitzpatrick in the St. Louis Post-Dispatch.)

meat and other foreign imports. But a majority of the New Deal Congress felt that the interests of special groups, however important, should be sacrificed to those of the nation as a whole.

Impulses toward Storm-Cellar Isolationism

Post-1918 chaos in Europe, followed by the Great Depression, fostered the ominous concept of totalitarianism. The individual was nothing; the state was everything. Communist Russia led the way, with the crafty and ruthless Joseph Stalin finally emerging as dictator. Blustery Benito Mussolini, a swaggering Fascist, seized the reins of power in Italy during 1922. And Adolf Hitler, a fanatic with a toothbrush mustache, plotted and harangued his way into control of Germany in 1933 with liberal use of the "big lie."

Hitler was the most immediately dangerous, because he combined tremendous power with

Dictatorial Duo *Benito Mussolini of Italy (left) and Adolf Hitler of Germany (right) shared a fascistic political philosophy and together plotted the conquest of Europe. (The Granger Collection.)*

impulsiveness. A frustrated Austrian painter, with hypnotic talents as an orator and a leader, he had secured control of the Nazi party by making political capital of the Treaty of Versailles and the depression-spawned unemployment. He was thus a misbegotten child of the shortsighted postwar policies of the victorious Allies, including the United States. The desperate German people had fallen in behind the new Pied Piper, for they saw no other hope of escape from the plague of economic chaos and national disgrace. In 1936 the Nazi Hitler and the Fascist Mussolini allied themselves in the Rome-Berlin Axis.

International gangsterism was likewise spreading in the Far East, where the Nipponese were on the make. Like Germany and Italy, Japan was a so-called have-not power. Like them, it resented the ungenerous Treaty of Versailles. Like them, it demanded additional space

for its teeming millions, condemned to a potted-plant existence.

Japanese navalists were not to be denied. Determined to find a place in the Asiatic sun, Tokyo gave notice in 1934 of the termination of the twelve-year-old Washington Naval Treaty. A year later at London, the Japanese torpedoed all hope of effective naval disarmament. Upon being denied complete parity, they walked out on the multipower conference and accelerated their construction of giant battleships.

Jut-jawed Mussolini, seeking both glory and empire in Africa, brutally attacked Ethiopia in 1935 with bombers and tanks. The brave defenders, armed with spears and ancient firearms, were speedily crushed. Members of the League of Nations could have caused Mussolini's war machine to creak to a halt—if they had only dared to embargo oil. But when the League quailed rather than risk global hostilities, it merely signed its own death warrant.

Isolationism, long festering in America, received a strong boost from these alarms abroad. Though disapproving of the dictators, Americans still believed that their encircling seas conferred a kind of mystic immunity. They were continuing to suffer the disillusionment born of their participation in World War I, which they now regarded as a colossal blunder. They likewise cherished bitter memories of the ungrateful and defaulting debtors. As early as 1934 a spiteful Congress had passed the Johnson Debt Default Act, which prevented debt-dodging nations from borrowing further in the United States. If attacked again by aggressors, these delinquents could "stew in their own juice."

Mired down in the Great Depression, Americans had no real appreciation of the revolution-

---

Mussolini's thirst for national glory in primitive Ethiopia is indicated by his remark in 1940, "To make a people great it is necessary to send them to battle even if you have to kick them in the pants." (The Italians were notoriously unwarlike.) In 1934 Mussolini proclaimed in a public speech, "We have buried the putrid corpse of liberty."

ary forces being harnessed by the dictators. The "have-not" powers were out to become "have" powers. Americans were not so much afraid that totalitarian aggression would cause trouble as they were fearful that they might be drawn into it. Strong nationwide agitation welled up for a constitutional amendment to forbid a declaration of war by Congress—except in case of invasion—unless there was first a favorable popular referendum. With a mixture of seriousness and frivolity, a group of Princeton University students began to agitate in 1936 for a bonus to be paid to the Veterans of Future Wars (VFWs) while still alive.

Congress Legislates Neutrality

As the gloomy 1930s lengthened, an avalanche of lurid articles and books poured from American presses condemning the munitions manufacturers as war-fomenting "merchants of death." A Senate committee, headed by Senator Nye of North Dakota, was appointed in 1934 to investigate the "blood business." By sensationalizing evidence regarding America's entry into World War I, the senatorial probers tended to shift the blame away from the German submarines onto the American bankers and arms manufacturers. As the munitions makers had obviously made money out of the war, many a naive soul leaped to the illogical conclusion that these soulless scavengers had caused the war in order to make money. This kind of reasoning suggested that if the profits could only be removed from the arms traffic—"one hell of a business"—the country could keep out of any world conflict that might erupt in the future.

Responding to overwhelming popular pressure, Congress made haste to legislate the nation out of war. Action was spurred by the danger that Mussolini's Ethiopian assault would plunge the world into a new bloodbath. The Neutrality Acts of 1935, 1936, and 1937, taken together, stipulated that *when the president proclaimed* the existence of a foreign war, certain restrictions would automatically go into effect. No American could legally sail on a belligerent ship, or sell or transport munitions to a belligerent, or make loans to a belligerent.

This head-in-the-sand legislation marked in effect an abandonment of the traditional policy of freedom of the seas—a policy for which America had professedly fought two full-fledged wars and several undeclared wars. The Neutrality Acts, so called, were specifically tailored to keep the nation out of a conflict like World War I. If they had been in effect at that time, America probably would not have been sucked in—at least not in April 1917. Congress was one war too late with its legislation. What had seemed dishonorable to Wilson seemed honorable and desirable to a later disillusioned generation.

Storm-cellar neutrality proved to be tragically shortsighted. America falsely assumed that the decision for peace or war lay in its own hands, not in those of the satanic forces already unleashed in the world. Prisoner of its own fears, it failed to recognize that it should have used its enormous power to control international events in its own interest. Instead, it remained at the mercy of events controlled by the dictators.

Statutory neutrality, though of undoubted legality, was of dubious morality. America served notice that it would make no distinction whatever between brutal aggressors and innocent victims. By striving to hold the scales even, it actually overbalanced them in favor of the dictators, who had armed themselves to the teeth. By declining to use its vast industrial strength to aid its democratic friends and defeat its totalitarian foes, it helped spur the aggressors along their blood-spattered path of conquest.

America Dooms Loyalist Spain

The Spanish Civil War of 1936–1939—a proving ground and dress rehearsal in miniature for World War II—was a painful object lesson in the folly of neutrality-by-legislation. Spanish rebels, who rose against the left-leaning republican government in Madrid, were headed by Fascistic General Francisco Franco. Generously aided by his fellow conspirators, Hitler and Mussolini, he undertook to overthrow the established Loyalist regime, which in turn was assisted on a smaller scale by the Soviet Union. This pipeline from Communist Moscow chilled

> Claude Bowers, the U.S. ambassador in Spain, deplored neutrality and favored support for the defeated Loyalists. When he returned to America and met with Roosevelt, the president's first words were: "We've made a mistake. You've been right all along." At least this is what Bowers states in his memoirs.

the natural sympathies of many Americans, especially those of Roman Catholic faith.

Washington continued official relations with the Loyalist government. In accordance with previous American practice, this regime should have been free to purchase desperately needed munitions in the United States. But Congress, with the encouragement of Roosevelt and with only one dissenting vote, amended the existing neutrality legislation so as to apply an arms embargo to both Loyalists and rebels. "Roosevelt," remarked dictator Franco, "behaved in the manner of a true gentleman." FDR later regretted being so gentlemanly.

Uncle Sam thus sat on the sidelines while Franco, abundantly supplied with arms and men by his fellow dictators, strangled the republican government of Spain. The democracies, including the United States, were so determined to stay out of war that they helped to condemn a fellow democracy to death. In so doing, they further encouraged the dictators to take the dangerous road that led over the precipice of World War II.

Such peace-at-any-price-ism was further cursed with illogic. While determined to stay out of war, America declined to build up its armed forces to a point where it could deter the aggressors. In fact, it allowed its navy to decline in relative strength. It had been led to believe that huge fleets cause huge wars; it was also trying to spare the complaining taxpayer during the grim days of the Great Depression. When President Roosevelt repeatedly called for preparedness, he was branded a warmonger. Not until 1938, the year before World War II exploded, did Congress come to grips with the problem when it passed a billion-dollar naval construction act. The calamitous story was repeated of too little—and that too late.

Appeasing Japan and Germany

Sulfurous war clouds had meanwhile been gathering in the tension-taut Far East. In 1937 the Japanese militarists, at the Marco Polo Bridge near Beijing (Peking), touched off the explosion that led to a full-dress invasion of China. In a sense this attack was the curtain raiser of World War II.

Roosevelt declined to invoke the recently passed neutrality legislation, noting that the so-called China incident was not an officially declared war. If he had put the existing restrictions into effect, he would have cut off the trickle of munitions on which the Chinese were desperately dependent. The Japanese, of course, could continue to buy mountains of war supplies in the United States.

In Chicago—unofficial isolationist "capital" of America—Roosevelt delivered his sensational "Quarantine Speech" in the autumn of 1937. Alarmed by the recent aggressions of Italy and Japan, he called for "positive endeavors" to "quarantine" the aggressors—presumably by economic embargoes. One immediate result was a cyclone of protest from isolationists and other foes of involvement; they feared that a moral quarantine would lead to a shooting quarantine. Startled by this angry response, Roosevelt retreated and sought less direct means to curb the dictators.

America's isolationist mood deepened, especially in regard to China. In December 1937 Japanese aviators bombed and sank an American gunboat, the *Panay*, in Chinese waters, with a loss of two killed and thirty wounded. In the days of 1898, when the *Maine* went down, this outrage might have provoked war. But after Tokyo hastened to make the necessary apologies and pay a proper indemnity, Americans breathed a deep sigh of relief. Japanese militarists were thus encouraged to vent their anger against the "superior" white race by subjecting American civilians in China, both male and female, to humiliating slappings and strippings.

More immediately menacing was Adolf Hitler. In 1935 he had openly flouted the Treaty of Versailles by introducing compulsory military service in Germany. The next year he brazenly marched into the demilitarized German Rhineland, likewise contrary to the detested treaty, while France and Britain looked on in an agony of indecision. Lashing his following to a frenzy, Hitler undertook to persecute and then liquidate the Jewish population in the areas under his control. In the end, he wiped out about 6 million innocent victims, mostly in gas chambers. Calling upon his people to sacrifice butter for guns, he whipped the new German air force and mechanized ground divisions into the most devastating military machine the world had yet seen.

Suddenly, in March 1938, Hitler bloodlessly occupied German-speaking Austria, his birthplace. The democratic powers, wringing their hands in despair, prayed that this last grab would satisfy his passion for conquest.

But like a drunken reveler calling for madder music and stronger wine, Hitler could not stop. Intoxicated by his recent gains, he began to make bullying demands for the German-inhabited Sudetenland of his neighbor, tiny Czechoslovakia. The leaders of Britain and France, eager to appease Hitler, sought frantically to bring the dispute to the conference table. President Roosevelt, also deeply alarmed, kept the wires hot with personal messages, to both Hitler and Mussolini, urging a peaceful settlement.

A conference was finally held in Munich, Germany, in September of 1938. The Western European democracies, badly unprepared for war, betrayed Czechoslovakia to Germany when they consented to the shearing away of the Sudetenland. They hoped—and these hopes were shared by the American people—that the concessions at the conference table would slake Hitler's thirst for power and bring "peace in our time." Indeed, Hitler publicly promised that the Sudetenland "is the last territorial claim I have to make in Europe."

"Appeasement" of the dictators, symbolized by the ugly word *Munich* turned out to be merely surrender on the installment plan. It was like giving a cannibal a finger in the hope

What Next?   *The Western European democracies looked on helplessly as Nazi Germany swallowed up Austria and part of Czechoslovakia in 1938, and Hitler's juggernaut seemed unstoppable. (Fitzpatrick in the St. Louis **Post-Dispatch**, September 25, 1938.)*

of saving an arm. In March 1939, scarcely six months later, Hitler suddenly erased the rest of Czechoslovakia from the map, contrary to his solemn promises. The democratic world was again stunned.

Hitlerian Belligerency and U.S. Neutrality

Joseph Stalin, the sphinx of the Kremlin, was a key to the peace puzzle. In the summer of 1939 the British and French were busily negotiating with Moscow, hopeful of securing a mutual-defense treaty that would halt Hitler. But mutual suspicions proved insuperable. Almost overnight the Soviet Union astounded the watching world by signing, on August 23, 1939, a nonaggression treaty with the German dictator.

The notorious Hitler-Stalin pact meant that the Nazi German leader now had a green light to make war on Poland and the Western democracies, without fearing a stab in the back from Russia—his Communist arch-foe. Consternation struck those wishful thinkers in Western Europe who had fondly hoped that Hitler might be egged upon Stalin so that the twin menaces would bleed each other to death. It was as plain as the mustache on Stalin's face that the wily Soviet dictator was plotting to turn his German accomplice against the Western democracies. The two warring camps would then kill each other off—and leave Stalin bestriding Europe like a colossus.

World War II was only hours away. Hitler, intensifying the pressure, demanded from neighboring Poland a return of the areas wrested from Germany after World War I. Failing to secure satisfaction, he sent his mechanized divisions crashing into Poland at dawn on September 1, 1939.

Britain and France, honoring their commitments to Poland, promptly declared war. At long last they perceived the folly of continued appeasement. But they were powerless to aid Poland, which succumbed in three weeks to Hitler's smashing strategy of terror. Stalin, as prearranged secretly in his fateful pact with Hitler, came in on the kill for his share of old Russian Poland. Long-dreaded World War II was now fully launched, and the long truce of 1919–1939 had ended.

President Roosevelt speedily issued the routine proclamations of neutrality. Americans were overwhelmingly anti-Nazi and anti-Hitler; they fervently hoped that the democracies would win; they fondly believed that the forces of righteousness would triumph, as in 1918. But they were desperately determined to stay out: they were not going to be "suckers" again.

Neutrality promptly became a heated issue in the United States. Ill-prepared Britain and France urgently needed American airplanes and other weapons, but the Neutrality Act of 1937 raised a sternly forbidding hand. Roosevelt summoned Congress in special session, shortly after the invasion of Poland, to consider a lifting of the arms embargo. After six hectic weeks of debate, a makeshift law emerged.

European War Narrows the Atlantic   *(Courtesy of the Washington Star.)*

The Neutrality Act of 1939 provided that henceforth the European democracies might buy American war materials, but only on a "cash-and-carry" basis. This meant that they would have to transport the munitions in their own ships, after paying for them in cash. America would thus avoid loans, war debts, and the torpedoing of American arms-carriers. While Congress thus loosened former restrictions in response to interventionist cries, it added others in response to isolationist fears. Roosevelt was now authorized to proclaim danger zones into which American merchant ships would be forbidden to enter.

This unneutral neutrality law clearly favored the democracies against the dictators—and was so intended. As the British and French navies controlled the Atlantic, the European aggressors could not send their ships to buy America's munitions. The United States not only improved its moral position but simultaneously helped its economic position. An overseas demand for war goods brought a sharp upswing from the recession of 1937–1938 and ultimately solved the decade-long unemployment crisis. (See chart, p. 768.)

Aftermath of the Fall of France

The months following the collapse of Poland, while France and Britain marked time, were known as the "phony war." An ominous silence fell on Europe, as Hitler shifted his victorious divisions from Poland for a knockout blow at France. Inaction during this anxious period was relieved by the Soviets, who wantonly attacked neighboring Finland in an effort to secure strategic buffer territory. The debt-paying Finns, who had a host of admirers in America, were speedily granted $30 million by an isolationist Congress for *nonmilitary* supplies. But despite heroic resistance, Finland was finally flattened by the Russian steamroller.

An abrupt end to the "phony war" came in April 1940, when Hitler, again without warning, overran his weaker neighbors Denmark and Norway. Hardly pausing for breath, the next month he launched an unannounced as-

> In 1924, while briefly imprisoned, Hitler prepared a remarkable book, Mein Kampf (My Struggle), which brazenly set forth his objectives and techniques. He was a past master of the "big lie." As he wrote: "The primitive simplicity of their minds [the masses] renders them a more easy prey to a big lie than a small one, for they themselves often tell little lies but would be ashamed to tell big ones." He also said, "The victor will never be asked if he told the truth," and "Success is the sole earthly judge of right and wrong."

sault on Holland and Belgium, followed by a paralyzing blow at France. By late June, France was forced to surrender, but not until Mussolini had pounced on its rear for a jackal's share of the loot. Only by the so-called miracle of Dunkirk did the British manage to evacuate to England the bulk of their shattered and partially disarmed army. The crisis providentially brought forth an inspired leader in Prime Minister Winston Churchill, the bulldog-jawed orator who nerved his people to fight off the fearful air bombings of their cities.

France's sudden collapse shocked Americans out of their daydreams. Stouthearted Britons, singing "There'll Always Be an England," were all that stood between Hitler and the end in Europe of constitutional government. If Britain went under, Hitler would have at his disposal the workshops, shipyards, and slave labor of Western Europe. He might even have the powerful British fleet as well. This frightening possibility, which seemed to pose a dire threat to American security, steeled the American people to a tremendous effort.

Roosevelt moved with electrifying energy and dispatch. He called upon an already debt-burdened nation to build huge airfleets and a two-ocean navy, which could also check Japan. Congress, jarred out of its apathy toward preparedness, within a year appropriated the astounding sum of $37 billion. This figure was more than the total cost of fighting World War I.

Pro-British Propaganda This patriotic poster was put out by the Committee to Defend America by Aiding the Allies. (Trustees of the Imperial War Museum, London.)

and unneutral assistance to Britain before it fell under the heel of Hitler. Neutrality quickly went into the ash can.

Roosevelt at first arranged to transfer surplus federal arms to private American concerns ("dummies"), through which the weapons could be sent to bomb-blasted Britain. Airplanes, rifles, mortars, artillery, and ammunition were thus shipped in a technically legal way.

Advocates of aid to England formed propaganda groups, the most potent of which was the Committee to Defend America by Aiding the Allies. Its argument was double-barreled. To interventionists, it could appeal for direct succor to the British by such slogans as "Britain Is Fighting Our Fight." To the isolationists, it could appeal for assistance to the democracies by "All Methods Short of War," so that the terrible conflict would be kept in faraway Europe.

The isolationists, both numerous and sincere, were by no means silent. Determined to avoid

Congress also passed a conscription law, approved September 6, 1940. Under this measure—America's first peacetime draft—provision was made for training each year 1.2 million troops and 800,000 reserves. The act was later adapted to the requirements of a global war.

The Latin American bulwark likewise needed bolstering. Holland, Denmark, and France, all crushed under the German jackboot, had orphaned colonies in the New World. Would these fall into German hands? At the Havana Conference of 1940 the United States, by implication, agreed to share with its twenty sister republics the responsibility of upholding the Monroe Doctrine. This ancient dictum, hitherto unilateral, had been a bludgeon brandished only by the hated Yankee colossus. Now multilateral, it was to be wielded by twenty-one pairs of American hands—at least in theory.

Bolstering Britain with the Destroyer Deal (1940)

Before the fall of France, Washington had generally observed a technical neutrality. But now Americans had to choose between neutrality

Just So There'll Be No Misunderstanding" Hitler and Mussolini are warned not to seize orphaned colonies in America. (Ray in the Kansas City *Star.*)

bloodshed at all costs, they organized the America First Committee and proclaimed, "England Will Fight to the Last American." They contended that America should concentrate what strength it had to defend its own shores, lest a victorious Hitler, after crushing Britain, successfully assault it. Their basic philosophy was "The Yanks Are Not Coming," and their most effective speechmaker was the famed aviator Colonel Charles A. Lindbergh, who, ironically, had narrowed the Atlantic in 1927.

Britain was in critical need of destroyers, for German submarines were again threatening to starve it out with attacks on shipping. Roosevelt moved boldly when, on September 2, 1940, he agreed to transfer to Great Britain fifty old-model, four-funnel destroyers left over from World War I. In return, the British promised to hand over to the United States eight valuable defensive base sites, stretching from Newfoundland to South America. These strategically located outposts were to remain under the Stars and Stripes for ninety-nine years.

Transferring fifty destroyers to a foreign navy was a highly questionable disposal of government property, despite a strained interpretation of existing legislation. The exchange was achieved by a simple presidential agreement, without so much as a "by your leave" to Congress. Applause burst from the aid-to-Britain advocates, many of whom had been urging such a step. But condemnation arose from "America Firsters" and other isolationists, as well as from antiadministration Republicans. Some of them approved the transfer but decried Roosevelt's secretive and high-handed methods. Yet so grave was the crisis that the president was unwilling to submit the scheme to the uncertainties and delays of a full-dress debate in the Congress.

Shifting warships from a "neutral" United States to a belligerent Britain was, beyond question, a flagrant violation of neutral obligations— at least neutral obligations that had existed before Hitler's barefaced aggressions rendered dangerous such old-fashioned concepts of fair play. Public-opinion polls demonstrated that a majority of Americans were determined, even at the risk of armed hostilities, to provide the battered British with "all aid short of war."

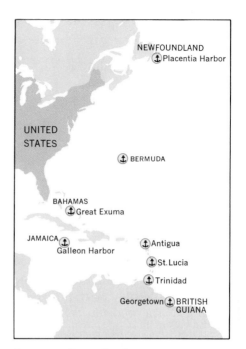

Destroyer-Bases Deal

FDR Shatters the Two-Term Tradition (1940)

A distracting presidential election, as fate decreed, came in the midst of this crisis. The two leading Republican aspirants were round-faced and flat-voiced Senator Robert A. Taft of Ohio, son of the ex-president, and an energetic boy wonder, lawyer-prosecutor Thomas E. Dewey of New York. But in one of the miracles of American political history, the Philadelphia convention was swept off its feet by a colorful latecomer, Wendell L. Willkie, a German-descended son of Hoosier Indiana. This dynamic lawyer—tousled-headed, long-lipped, broadfaced, and large-framed—had until recently been a Democrat and the head of a huge public utilities corporation. A complete novice in politics, he had rocketed from political nothingness in a few short weeks. His great appeal lay in his personality, for he was magnetic, transparently sincere, and honest in a homespun, Lincolnesque way.

With the galleries in Philadelphia wildly chanting "We Want Willkie," the delegates

A Campaign Poster from the Election of 1940
Roosevelt emerged as the only president ever to break the two-term tradition. (Franklin Delano Roosevelt Library.)

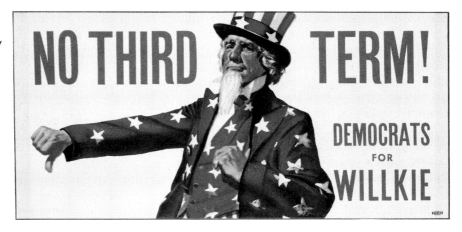

finally accepted this political upstart as the only candidate who could possibly beat Roosevelt. The Republican platform condemned FDR's alleged dictatorship, as well as the costly and confusing zigzags of the New Deal. Willkie, an outstanding liberal, was opposed not so much to the New Deal as to its extravagances and inefficiencies. Democratic critics branded him "the rich man's Roosevelt" and "the simple barefoot Wall Street lawyer."

While the rumor pot boiled, Roosevelt delayed to the last minute the announcement of his decision to challenge the sacred two-term tradition. Despite what he described as his personal yearning for retirement, he avowed that in so grave a crisis he owed his experienced hand to the service of his country and humanity. The Democratic delegates in Chicago, realizing that only with "the Champ" could they defeat Willkie, drafted him by a technically unanimous vote. "Better a Third Term Than a Third-Rater" was the war cry of many Democrats.

The old-line Republican bosses were not happy over having a recent Democrat head their ticket. Ex-Senator James Watson reportedly told Willkie to his face: "You have been a Democrat all your life. I don't mind the church converting a whore, but I don't like her to lead the choir the first night."

Burning with sincerity and energy, Willkie launched out upon a whirlwind, Bryanesque campaign in which he delivered over five hundred speeches. At times his voice became a hoarse croak. The country was already badly split between interventionists and isolationists, and Willkie might have widened the breach dangerously by a violent attack on Roosevelt's aid-to-Britain policies. But seeing eye-to-eye with FDR on the necessity of bolstering the democracies, he refrained from assailing the president's interventionism, though objecting to his methods.

In the realm of foreign affairs, there was not much to choose between the two candidates. Both promised to stay out of the war; both promised to strengthen the nation's defenses. Yet Willkie, with a mop of black hair in his eyes, hit hard at Rooseveltian "dictatorship" and the third term. His enthusiastic followers cried, "Win with Willkie," "No Fourth Term Either," and "There's No Indispensable Man."

Roosevelt, busy at his desk with mounting problems, made only a few speeches. Stung by taunts that he was leading the nation by the back door into the European slaughterhouse, he repeatedly denied any such intention. His most specific statement was at Boston, where he emphatically declared, "Your boys are not going to be sent into any foreign wars"—a pledge that later came back to plague him. He and his henchmen vigorously defended the New Deal as well as all-out preparations for the defense of America and aid to the Allies.

Roosevelt triumphed, although Willkie ran a strong race. The popular total was 27,307,819 to 22,321,018, and the electoral count was 449 to 82. This contest was much less of a walkaway than in 1932 or 1936; Democratic majorities in Congress remained about the same.

Jubilant Democrats hailed their triumph as a mandate to abolish the two-term tradition. But the truth is that Roosevelt won in spite of the third-term handicap. Voters generally felt that, should war come, the experienced hand of the tried leader was needed at the helm. Less appealing was the completely inexperienced hand of the well-intentioned Willkie, who had never held public office.

The hoary argument that one should not change horses in the middle of a stream was strong, especially in an era of war-spawned prosperity. Roosevelt might not have won if there had not been a war crisis. On the other hand, he probably would not have run if foreign perils had not loomed so ominously. In a sense, his opponent was Adolf Hitler, not Willkie.

Congress Passes the Landmark Lend-Lease Law

By late 1940 embattled Britain was nearing the end of its financial tether; its credits in America were being rapidly consumed by insatiable war orders. But Roosevelt, who had bitter memories of the wrangling over the Allied debts of World War I, was determined, as he put it, to eliminate "the silly, foolish, old dollar sign." He finally hit on the scheme of lending or leasing American arms to the reeling democracies. When the shooting was over, to use his comparison, the guns and tanks could be returned, just as one's next-door neighbor would return a length of garden hose when a threatening fire was put out. But isolationist Senator Taft (who was reputed to have the finest mind in Washington until he made it up) retorted that lending arms was like lending chewing gum: "You don't want it back." Who wants a chewed-up tank?

The lend-lease bill, patriotically numbered 1776, was entitled "An Act Further to Promote the Defense of the United States." Sprung on the country after the election was safely over, it was praised by the administration as a device that would keep the nation out of the war rather than get it in. The underlying concept was "Send guns, not sons" or "Billions, not bodies." America, so Roosevelt promised, would be the "arsenal of democracy." It would send a limitless supply of arms to the victims of aggression, who in turn would finish the job and keep the war on their side of the Atlantic. Accounts would be settled by returning the used weapons or their equivalents when the war was ended.

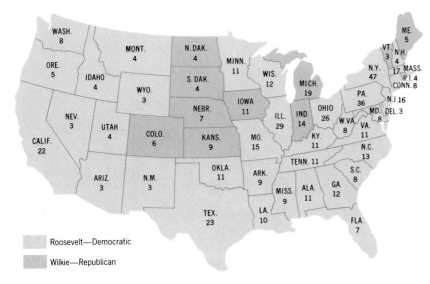

Presidential Election of 1940 (with electoral vote by state) Willkie referred to Roosevelt only as "the third-term candidate." On election eve, FDR hinted that Communists and Fascists were among Willkie's supporters. Despite these campaign conflicts, the two men respected each other. FDR later asked Willkie to serve as his emissary abroad and even suggested that they run together on a coalition ticket in 1944.

Main Flow of Lend-Lease Aid (width of arrows indicates relative amount) *The proud but desperate British prime minister, Winston Churchill, declared in early 1941: "Give us the tools and we will finish the job." Lend-lease eventually provided the British and other Allies with $50 billion worth of "tools."*

Lend-lease was heatedly debated throughout the land and in Congress. Most of the opposition came, as might be expected, from isolationists and anti-Roosevelt Republicans. The scheme was assailed as "the blank-check bill" and, in the words of isolationist Senator Wheeler, as "the new Triple-A [Agricultural Adjustment Act] bill"—a measure designed to "plow under every fourth American boy." Nevertheless lend-lease was finally approved in March 1941 by sweeping majorities in both houses of Congress.

Lend-lease was one of the most momentous laws ever to pass Congress; it was a challenge

No to Lend-Lease *These protesting mothers feared that America's increasing involvement with the Allied cause would eventually draw their sons into battle—as it did, despite President Roosevelt's assurances to the contrary. (A.P./Wide World Photos.)*

hurled squarely into the teeth of the Axis dictators. America pledged itself, to the extent of its vast resources, to bolster those nations that were indirectly defending it by fighting aggression. When the gigantic operation ended in 1945, America had sent about $50 billion worth of arms and equipment—much more than the cost to it of World War I—to those nations fighting aggressors. The passing of lend-lease was in effect an economic declaration of war; now a shooting declaration could not be very far around the corner.

By its very nature, the lend-lease bill marked the abandonment of any pretense of neutrality. It was no destroyer deal arranged privately by President Roosevelt. The bill was universally debated, over drugstore counters and cracker barrels, from California all the way to Maine; and the sovereign citizen at last spoke through convincing majorities in Congress. Most people probably realized that they were tossing the old concepts of neutrality out the window. But they also recognized that they would play a suicidal game if they bound themselves by the oxcart rules of the nineteenth century—especially while the aggressors themselves openly spurned international obligations. Lend-lease would admittedly involve a grave risk of war, but most Americans were prepared to take that chance rather than see Britain collapse and then face the dictators alone.

Lend-lease had the somewhat incidental result of gearing the nation's own factories for all-out war production. The enormously increased capacity thus achieved helped to save America's own skin when, at long last, the shooting war burst around its head.

Hitler himself evidently recognized lend-lease as an unofficial declaration of war. Until then, Germany had avoided attacking American ships; memories of Uncle Sam's decisive intervention in 1917–1918 were still fresh in German minds. But after the passing of lend-lease, there was less point in trying to curry favor with the United States. On May 21, 1941, the *Robin Moor*, an unarmed American merchantman, was torpedoed and destroyed by a German submarine in the South Atlantic, outside a war zone. The sinkings had started, but on a limited scale.

Hitler's Assault on Russia Spawns the Atlantic Charter

Two globe-shaking events marked the course of World War II before the assault on Pearl Harbor in 1941. One was the fall of France; the other was Hitler's invasion of Russia.

The scheming dictators, Hitler and Stalin, had been uneasy yoke-fellows under the ill-begotten pact of 1939. As masters of the double cross, neither trusted the other. They engaged in prolonged dickering in a secret attempt to divide potential territorial spoils between them, but Stalin gagged on dominant German control of the Balkans. Hitler thereupon decided to crush his coconspirator, seize the oil and other resources of Russia, and then have a free hand to snuff out Britain. He assumed that his all-conquering armies would subdue the "Mongol half-wits" of Russia in a few short weeks.

Out of a clear sky, on June 22, 1941, Hitler launched a devastating attack on his Soviet neighbor. This timely assault was an incredible stroke of good fortune for the democratic world—or so it seemed at the time. The two menaces could now slit each other's throats on the icy steppes of Russia. Or they would if the Soviets did not speedily collapse, as many military experts predicted.

Sound American strategy seemed to dictate speedy aid to Russia while it was still afloat. Roosevelt immediately promised assistance and backed up his words by making some military supplies available. Several months later, interpreting the lend-lease law to mean that the defense of Russia was essential for the defense of the United States, he extended $1 billion in lend-lease—the first installment on an ultimate

> Senator Harry S Truman (later president) expressed a common reaction to Hitler's invasion of Russia in 1941: "If we see that Germany is winning, we ought to help Russia, and if we see Russia is winning, we ought to help Germany, and that way let them kill as many as possible."

"Unexpected Guest," 1941   *Russia joins the democracies, Britain and America. (Courtesy Detroit* News.)

total of $11 billion. Meanwhile the valor of the Red Army, combined with the white paralysis of an early Russian winter, had halted the Hitlerian invaders at the gates of Moscow.

With the collapse of the Soviets still a dread possibility, the drama-charged Atlantic Conference was held in August 1941. British Prime Minister Winston Churchill, with cigar embedded in his cherubic face, secretly met with Roosevelt on a warship off the foggy coast of Newfoundland. This was the first of a series of history-making conferences between the two statesmen for the discussion of common problems, including the menace of Japan in the Far East.

The most memorable offspring of this get-together was the eight-point Atlantic Charter. It was formally accepted by Roosevelt and Churchill and endorsed by the Soviet Union later that year. Suggestive of Wilson's Fourteen Points, the new covenant outlined the aspirations of the democracies for a better world at war's end.

Surprisingly, the Atlantic Charter was rather specific. While opposing imperialistic annexations, it promised that there would be no territorial changes contrary to the wishes of the inhabitants (self-determination). It further affirmed the right of a people to choose their own form of government and, in particular, to regain the governments abolished by the dictators. Among various other goals, the charter declared for disarmament and a peace of security, pending "a permanent system of general security" (a new League of Nations).

Liberals the world over took heart from the Atlantic Charter, as they had taken heart from Wilson's comparable Fourteen Points. It was especially gratifying to subject populations, like the Poles, who were then ground under the iron heel of a conqueror. But the agreement was roundly condemned in the United States by isolationists and others hostile to Roosevelt. What right, they charged, had "neutral" America to confer with belligerent Britain on common policies? Such critics missed the point: the nation was no longer neutral.

U.S. Destroyers and Hitler's U-Boats Clash

Lend-lease shipments of arms to Britain on British ships were bound to be sunk by German wolf-pack submarines. If the intent was to get the munitions to England, not to dump them into the ocean, the freighters would have to be escorted by American warships. Britain simply did not have enough destroyers. The dangerous possibility of being "convoyed into war" had been mentioned in Congress during the lengthy debate on lend-lease, but administration spokespersons had brushed the idea aside. Their strategy was to make only one commitment at a time.

The fateful decision to convoy was taken in July 1941. Roosevelt, by virtue of his authority as commander in chief of the armed forces, issued orders to the navy to escort lend-lease shipments to Iceland. The British would then shepherd them the rest of the way.

Inevitable clashes with submarines ensued on the Iceland run, even though Hitler's orders were to strike American warships only in self-defense. In September 1941 the U.S. destroyer *Greer,* provocatively trailing a German U-boat, was attacked by the undersea craft, without damage to either side. Roosevelt then proclaimed a shoot-on-sight policy. On October 17 the escorting destroyer *Kearny,* while engaged in a battle with U-boats, lost eleven men when it was crippled but not sent to the bottom. Two weeks later the destroyer *Reuben James* was torpedoed and sunk off southwestern Iceland, with the loss of more than a hundred officers and men.

Neutrality was still inscribed on the statute books, but not in American hearts. Congress, responding to public pressures and confronted with a shooting war, voted in mid-November 1941 to pull the teeth from the now-useless Neutrality Act of 1939. Merchant ships could henceforth be legally armed, and they could enter the combat zones with munitions for Britain. Americans braced themselves for wholesale attacks by Hitler's submarines.

Heading for the Surprise Assault at Pearl Harbor

The blowup came, not in the Atlantic, but in the faraway Pacific. This explosion should have surprised no close observer, for Japan, since September of 1940, had been a formal military ally of Nazi Germany—America's shooting foe in the North Atlantic.

Japan's position in the Far East had grown more perilous by the hour. It was still mired down in the costly and exhausting "China incident," from which it could extract neither honor nor victory. Its war machine was fatally dependent on immense shipments from the United States of steel, scrap iron, oil, and aviation gasoline. Such assistance to the Japanese aggressor was highly unpopular in America. But Roosevelt had resolutely held off an embargo, lest he goad the Tokyo warlords into a descent upon the oil-rich and weakly defended Dutch East Indies.

Washington, late in 1940, finally imposed the first of its embargoes on Japan-bound supplies. This blow was followed in mid-1941 by a "freezing" of Nipponese assets in the United States and a cessation of all shipments of gasoline and other sinews of war. As the oil gauge dropped, the squeeze on Japan grew steadily more nerve-racking. Protracted delay was on the side of the United States. Japanese leaders were faced with two painful alternatives. They could either knuckle under to the Americans or break out of the embargo ring by a desperate attack on the oil supplies and other riches of Southeast Asia. The ticking of the clock, while soothing to American ears, drove the Japanese to madness.

Final tense negotiations with Japan took place in Washington during November and early December of 1941. The State Department insisted that the Japanese clear out of China but, to sweeten the pill, offered to renew trade relations on a limited basis. Japanese imperialists, after waging a bitter war against the Chinese for more than four years, were unwilling to lose face by withdrawing at the behest of the United States. Faced with capitulation or continued conquest, they chose the sword. They had to put up or shut up, as the American press noted. They put up, believing that the war had been forced on them.

Officials in Washington, having "cracked" the top-secret code of the Japanese, knew that Tokyo's decision was for war. But the United States, as a democracy committed to public debate and action by Congress, could not shoot first. Roosevelt, misled by Japanese ship movements in the Far East, evidently expected the blow to fall on British Malaya or perhaps on the Philippines. No one in high authority in Washington seems to have believed that the Japanese were either strong enough or foolhardy enough to lash out at Hawaii.

But the paralyzing blow struck Pearl Harbor, while Tokyo was deliberately prolonging negotiations in Washington. Japanese bombers, winging in from distant aircraft carriers, attacked without warning on the "Black Sunday" morning of December 7, 1941. It was a date, as Roosevelt told Congress, "which will live in infamy." About three thousand casualties were inflicted on American personnel; many aircraft were destroyed; the battleship fleet was virtually wiped out when all eight of the craft were

The Battleship West Virginia *Wrecked at Pearl Harbor* (U.S. Navy photo.)

sunk or otherwise immobilized; and numerous small vessels were damaged or destroyed. Fortunately for America, the three priceless aircraft carriers happened to be outside the harbor.

An angered Congress, the next day, officially recognized the war that had been "thrust" upon the United States. The roll call in the Senate and House lacked only one vote of unanimity. Germany and Italy, allies of Japan, spared Congress the indecision of debate by declaring war on December 11, 1941. This challenge was formally accepted on the same day by a unanimous vote of both Senate and House. The unofficial war, of many months' duration, was now official.

America's Transformation from Bystander to Belligerent

Japan's hara-kiri gamble in Hawaii paid off only in the short run. True, the Pacific fleet was largely destroyed or immobilized, but the sneak attack aroused and united America as almost nothing else could have done. To the very day of the blowup, a strong majority of Americans still wanted to keep out of war. But the bombs that pulverized Pearl Harbor blasted the isolationists into silence. The only thing left to do,

growled isolationist Senator Wheeler, was "to lick hell out of them."

But Pearl Harbor was not the full answer to the question of why the United States went to war. This treacherous attack was but the last explosion in a long chain reaction. Following the fall of France, Americans were confronted with a devil's dilemma. They desired above all to stay out of the conflict; yet they did not want Britain to be knocked out. They wished to halt Japan's conquests in the Far East—conquests that menaced not only American trade and security but international peace as well. To keep Britain from collapsing, the Roosevelt administration felt compelled to extend the unneutral aid that invited attacks from German submarines. To keep Japan from expanding, Washington undertook to cut off vital Japanese supplies and invite possible retaliation. Rather than let democracy die and dictatorship rule supreme, a strong majority of citizens were evidently determined to support a policy that might lead to war. It did.

Clearheaded Americans had come to the conclusion that no nation was safe in an era of international anarchy. Appeasement—the tactic of throwing the weaker persons out of the sleigh to the pursuing wolves—had been tried, but it had merely whetted dictatorial appetites. Power-drunk dictators had flouted international law and decency. Asserting the philosophy that might makes right, they had cynically negotiated nonaggression treaties with their intended victims, merely to lull them into a false sense of security. Most Americans were determined to stand firm—and let war come if it must—because they were convinced that with ruthless dictators on the loose, the world could not long remain half-enchained and half-free.

Roosevelt's war message to Congress began with these famous words: "Yesterday, December 7, 1941—a date which will live in infamy—the United States of America was suddenly and deliberately attacked by naval and air forces of the Empire of Japan."

Varying Viewpoints

After World War II ended in 1945, many historians were convinced that tragedy could have been averted if only the United States had awakened earlier from its isolationist illusions. These scholars condemned the policies and attitudes of the 1930s as a "retreat from responsibility." Much historical writing about the 1930s in the postwar period contained the strong flavor of medicine to ward off another infection by the isolationist virus. Yet in the wake of the Vietnam disaster, some historians began to suspect that there had been an overdose of the internationalist tonic—or that the prescription had been adulterated.

The appeasement "lessons" of the 1930s could not properly be applied to any and all subsequent situations. Ho Chi Minh was not Hitler and Vietnam was not Nazi Germany, yet American policymakers frequently defended their actions in Southeast Asia by making dubious comparisons with the pre–World War II decade. The reaction to this use (or misuse) of history has not spawned a "new isolationism" among historians but has prompted a renewed effort to understand the 1930s on their own terms, rather than construing the events of those years as timeless lessons for posterity.

Select Readings

Primary Source Documents

Franklin D. Roosevelt's "Quarantine the Aggressors" speech (1937), in Richard Hofstadter, *Great Issues in American History*, revealed what would become the goal of the president's foreign policy in succeeding years. See also Roosevelt's "Press Conference on Lend-Lease" (1940), in *The Public Papers and Addresses of Franklin D. Roosevelt, 1940 Volume* (1941), pp. 606–608.* For opposition to lend-lease, see the speech of January 12, 1941, by Montana Senator Burton K. Wheeler, *Congressional Record*, 77 Cong., 1 sess., Appendix, pp. 178–179.* Charles A. Lindbergh elaborated the isolationist position in *The New York Times*, April 24, 1941, p. 12.*

Secondary Sources

Indispensable and comprehensive is Robert Dallek, *Franklin D. Roosevelt and American Foreign Policy, 1932–1945* (1979). A useful brief survey is John E. Wiltz, *From Isolation to War, 1931–1941* (1968). More specialized is Lloyd Gardner, *Economic Aspects of New Deal Diplomacy* (1964). Isolationism is ably handled in Manfred Jonas, *Isolationism in America, 1935–1941* (1966); Thomas Guinsburg, *The Pursuit of Isolationism in the United States Senate from Versailles to Pearl Harbor* (1982); and Robert A. Divine, *The Reluctant Belligerent* (1965). Sympathetic to the isolationists is Wayne S. Cole, *Roosevelt and the Isolationists, 1932–1945* (1983). See also his *Charles A. Lindbergh and the Battle against American Intervention in World War II* (1974). On Good Neighborism consult Bryce Wood, *The Making of the Good Neighbor Policy* (1961), and Irwin F. Gellman, *Good Neighbor Diplomacy* (1979). The Spanish problem is dealt with in Allen Guttmann, *The Wound in the Heart: America and the Spanish Civil War* (1962). For the Far East, see Dorothy Borg, *The United States and the Far Eastern Crisis of 1933–1938* (1964); P. W. Schroeder, *The Axis Alliance and Japanese-American Relations, 1941* (1958); and Robert J. C. Butow, *Tojo and the Coming of the War* (1961). Warren F. Kimball analyzes *The Most Unsordid Act: Lend Lease, 1939–1941* (1969). David L. Porter examines *The Seventy-Sixth Congress and World War II, 1939–1940* (1979). The Japanese attack is considered in Roberta Wohlstetter, *Pearl Harbor: Warning and Decision* (1962), and in Gordon W. Prange, *At Dawn We Slept* (1981). A provocative analysis of the reasons of (or lack of them) for United States entry into the conflict is Bruce Russett, *No Clear and Present Danger* (1972).

40

America in World War II

Never before have we had so little time in which to do so much.

Franklin D. Roosevelt, 1942

The Allies Trade Space for Time

America was plunged into the inferno of World War II with the most stupefying and humiliating military defeat in its history. In the dismal months that ensued, the democratic world teetered on the edge of disaster.

Japan's fanatics forgot that whoever stabs a king must stab to kill. A wounded but still potent American giant pulled itself out of the mud of Pearl Harbor, grimly determined to avenge the bloody treachery. "Get Hirohito first" was the cry that rose from millions of infuriated Americans, especially on the Pacific Coast. These outraged souls regarded America's share in the global conflict as a private war of vengeance in the Pacific, with the European front a kind of holding operation.

But Washington, cooperating with the British, had earlier and wisely adopted the grand strategy of "getting Hitler first." If America diverted its main strength to the Pacific, Hitler might crush both Russia and Britain and then emerge unconquerable in Fortress Europe. But if Germany was knocked out first, the combined Allied forces could be concentrated on Japan, and its daring game of conquest would be up. Meanwhile, enough American strength would be sent to the Pacific to prevent the Nipponese from digging in too deeply.

The get-Hitler-first strategy was retained. But it encountered much ignorant criticism from two-fisted Americans who thirsted for revenge against Japan. Aggrieved protests were also registered by shorthanded American commanders in the Pacific and by Chinese and Aus-

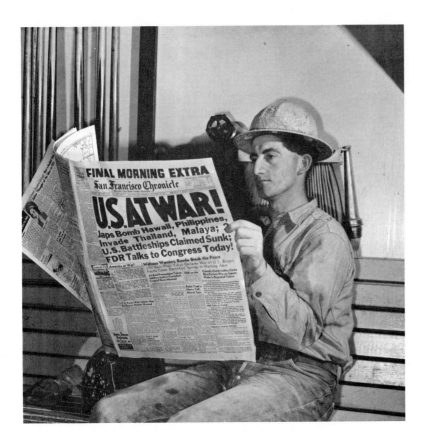

tralian allies. But Roosevelt, a competent strategist in his own right, resisted these pressures.

Given time, the Allies seemed bound to triumph. But would they be given time? True, they had on their side the great mass of the world's population, but the wolf is never frightened by the number of the sheep. The United States was the mightiest military power on earth—potentially. But wars are won with bullets, not blueprints. Indeed, America came perilously close to losing the war to the well-armed aggressors before it could begin to throw its full weight into the scales.

Time, in a sense, was the most needed munition. Expense was no limitation. The overpowering problem confronting America was to retool itself for all-out war production, while praying that the dictators would not meanwhile crush the democracies. Haste was all the more imperative because the highly skilled German scientists might turn up with unbeatable secret weapons—including atomic arms—as they almost did.

America's task was far more complex and back-breaking than during World War I. It had to feed, clothe, and arm itself, as well as transport its forces to regions as far separated as Britain and Burma. More than that, it had to send a vast amount of food and munitions to its hard-pressed allies, who stretched all the way from Russia to Australia. Could the American people, reputedly "gone soft," measure up to this colossal responsibility? Was democracy "rotten" and "decadent," as the dictators sneeringly proclaimed?

The Shock of War

National unity was no worry, thanks to the electrifying blow by the Japanese at Pearl Harbor. American Communists had denounced the

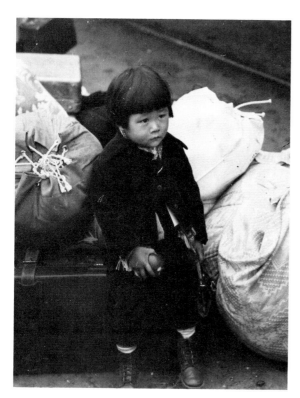

American Citizen of Japanese Ancestry Awaits Relocation *(Library of Congress.)*

many ethnic groups into American society. Immigration had been choked off for almost two decades before 1941, and America's ethnic communities were now composed of well-settled members, whose votes were crucial to Franklin Roosevelt's Democratic party. Consequently, there was virtually no governmental witch-hunting of minority groups, as had happened in World War I.

A painful exception was provided by the plight of some 110,000 Japanese-Americans, concentrated on the Pacific Coast. The Washington top command, fearing that they might act as saboteurs for the mikado in case of invasion, forcibly herded them together in concentration camps, though about two-thirds of them were American-born Americans. This brutal precaution was both unnecessary and unfair, as the loyalty and combat record of the Japanese-American proved to be admirable. But a wave of post–Pearl Harbor hysteria, backed by the long historical swell of anti-Japanese prejudice on the West Coast, temporarily robbed many Americans of their good sense—and their sense of justice. Partial financial compensation after the war only meagerly consoled these uprooted Americans for their hundreds of millions of dollars in property losses and their years of suffering and indignity.

The war prompted other changes in the American mood. Many programs of the once-popular New Deal—including the Civilian Conservation Corps, the Works Progress Administration, and the National Youth Administration—were wiped out by the conservative Congress elected in 1942. President Roosevelt declared in 1943 that "Dr. New Deal" was going into retirement, to be replaced by "Dr. Win-the-War." His announcement acknowledged not only the urgency of the war effort but the power of the revitalized conservative forces in the country. The era of New Deal reform was over.

World War II was no idealistic crusade, as World War I had been. The Washington government did make some effort to propagandize at home and abroad with the Atlantic Charter, but the accent was on action. Opinion polls in 1942 revealed that nine out of ten Americans could cite no provisions of the Atlantic Charter.

Anglo-French "imperialist" war before Hitler attacked Stalin in 1941, but they now clamored for an all-out assault on the Axis powers. The handful of strutting pro-Hitlerites in the United States melted away, while millions of Italian-Americans and German-Americans loyally supported the nation's war program. In contrast to World War I, when the patriotism of millions of new immigrants was hotly questioned, World War II actually speeded the assimilation of

American song titles aimed at the Japanese after Pearl Harbor were "Goodby, Mamma, I'm Off to Yokohama," "We Are the Sons of the Rising Guns," "Oh, You Little Son of an Oriental," "To Be Specific, It's Our Pacific," and "The Sun Will Soon Be Setting on the Land of the Rising Sun."

A majority then, and a near-majority two years later, confessed to having "no clear idea what the war is about." All Americans knew was that they had a dirty job on their hands and that the only way out was forward. They went about their bloody task with astonishing efficiency.

Building the War Machine

The war crisis made the drooping American economy snap to attention. Massive military orders—over $100 billion in 1942 alone—almost instantly soaked up the idle industrial capacity of the still-lingering Great Depression. Orchestrated by the War Production Board, American factories poured forth an avalanche of weaponry: 40 billion bullets, 300,000 aircraft, 76,000 ships, 86,000 tanks, and 2.6 million machine guns. Miracle-man shipbuilder Henry J. Kaiser was dubbed "Sir Launchalot" for his prodigies of ship construction; one of his ships was fully assembled in fourteen days, complete with life jackets and coat hangers.

The War Production Board halted manufacture of nonessential items such as passenger cars. It assigned priorities for transportation and access to raw materials. When the Japanese invasion of British Malaya and the Dutch East Indies snapped America's lifeline of natural rubber, the government imposed a national speed limit and gasoline rationing in order to conserve rubber and built fifty-one synthetic-rubber plants. By war's end they were far outproducing the prewar supply.

Farmers, too, rolled up their sleeves and increased their output. The armed forces drained the farms of manpower, but heavy new investment in agricultural machinery and improved

A young Japanese-American recorded in his diary on May 3, 1942, some of his first impressions of his hastily thrown-together "detention center": "I saw a soldier in a tall guardhouse near the barbed wire and did not like it because it reminds me of a concentration camp."

OURS...to fight for

Freedom of Speech   *Freedom of Worship*

Freedom from Want   *Freedom from Fear*

The Four Freedoms   *In his speech to Congress of January 6, 1941, requesting Lend-Lease aid to the Allies, President Roosevelt spoke eloquently of the "four freedoms" then threatened by Nazi and Japanese aggression. They are here given pictorial representation by Norman Rockwell, probably the most popular and well-loved American artist of the time. (National Archives.)*

fertilizers more than made up the difference. In 1944 and 1945 blue-jeaned husbandmen hauled in record-breaking billion-bushel wheat harvests.

These wonders of production also brought economic strains. Full employment and scarce consumer goods fueled a sharp inflationary surge in 1942. The Office of Price Administration eventually brought ascending prices under control with extensive regulations. Rationing held down the consumption of critical goods such as meat and butter, though some "black

Wartime Rationing *Unlike World War I, the Second World War forced the United States to resort to food rationing—though the system still allowed for considerable freedom of choice. Consumers received ration booklets with coupons worth so many "points," which were then exchanged, along with money, for the desired commodity. As this well-stocked butcher's shelf suggests, however, most foodstuffs were never in critically short supply. (Library of Congress.)*

marketeers" and "meatleggers" cheated the system. The War Labor Board (WLB) imposed ceilings on wage increases.

Labor unions, whose membership grew from about 10 million to more than 13 million workers during the war, fiercely resented the government-dictated wage ceilings. Despite the no-strike pledges of most of the major unions, a rash of labor walkouts plagued the war effort. Prominent among the strikers were the United Mine Workers, who several times were called off the job by their crusty and iron-willed chieftain, John L. Lewis.

Threats of lost production through strikes became so worrisome that Congress, in June 1943, passed the Smith-Connally Anti-Strike Act. It authorized the federal government to seize and operate tied-up industries. Strikes against any government-operated industry were made a criminal offense. Under the Smith-Con-

nally Act, Washington took over the coal mines and, for a brief period, the railroads. Yet work stoppages, while dangerous, actually accounted for less than 1 percent of the total working hours of the nation's wartime laboring force—a record better than blockaded Britain's. American workers, on the whole, were commendably committed to the war effort.

Manpower and Womanpower

The armed services enrolled nearly 15 million men in World War II—and some 216,000 women, who were employed for noncombat duties. Best known of these "women in arms" were the WAACS (Army), WAVES (Navy), and SPARS (Coast Guard). As the draft net was tightened after Pearl Harbor, millions of young men were plucked from their homes and clothed in "GI" (government issue) outfits. As the arsenal of democracy, the United States exempted certain key categories of industrial and agricultural workers from the draft, in order to keep its mighty industrial machine humming.

But even with these exemptions, the draft left the nation's farms and factories so drained of manpower that new workers had to be found. An agreement with Mexico in 1942 brought thousands of Mexican agricultural workers, called *braceros*, across the border to harvest the fruit and grain crops of the West. The *bracero* program outlived the war by some twenty years, becoming a fixed feature of the agricultural economy in many western states.

Even more dramatic was the march of women onto the factory floor. More than 6 million women took up jobs; over half of them had never before worked for wages. Many of them were mothers, and the government was obliged to set up some 3,000 day-care centers to care

> *Poster appeals and slogans urging women to enlist in the WAACs (Women's Army Auxiliary Corps) were "Speed Them Back, Join the WAAC," "I'd Rather Be with Them—than Waiting for Them," "Back the Attack, Be a WAAC! For America Is Calling," and (a song throwback to World War I) "The WAACs and WAVES Will Win the War, Parlez Vous."*

for "Rosie the Riveter's" children while she drilled the fuselage of a heavy bomber or joined the links of a tank track. When the war ended, Rosie and many of her sisters were in no hurry to put down their tools. They wanted to keep on working and often did. The war thus powerfully contributed to a revolution in the roles of women in American society.

Women at War   *More than 6 million women—3 million of them housewives who had never before worked for wages—entered the workforce during World War II. In contrast to the experience of women workers in World War I, many of these newly employed women continued as wage workers after the war. (Left, National Archives; right, Historical Picture Service, Inc., Chicago.)*

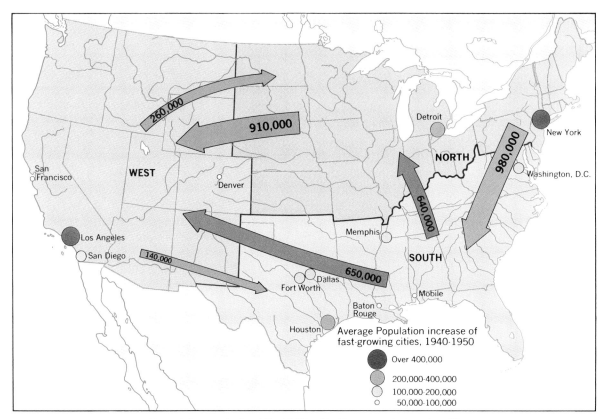

Internal Migration in the United States during World War II *Few events in American history have moved the American people about so massively as World War II. The West and the South boomed, and several war-industry cities grew explosively. A majority of migrants from the South were blacks. (Source: United States Department of Labor Bureau of Labor Statistics.)*

The war also proved to be a demographic cauldron, churning and shifting the American population. Many of the 15 million men and women in uniform, having seen new sights and glimpsed new horizons, chose not to go home again at war's end. War industries sucked people into boomtowns like Los Angeles, Detroit, Seattle, and Baton Rouge. California's population grew by nearly 2 million. The South experienced especially dramatic changes. Franklin Roosevelt had called the South "the nation's number one economic problem" in 1938; when war came, he seized the opportunity to accelerate the region's economic development. The states of the old Confederacy received a disproportionate share of defense contracts, including nearly $6 billion of federally financed industrial

facilities. Here were the origins of the postwar boom in the "Sunbelt."

Despite this economic stimulus in the South, some 1,000,000 blacks left the land of their ancient enslavement to seek jobs in the war plants of the West and North. Forever after, race relations constituted a national, not a regional, issue. Explosive tensions developed over employment, housing, and segregated facilities. Black leader A. Philip Randolph, head of the Brotherhood of Sleeping Car Porters, threatened a massive "Negro March on Washington" in 1941 to demand equal opportunities for blacks in war jobs and in the armed forces. Roosevelt's response was to issue an executive order forbidding discrimination in defense industries. In addition, the president established the Fair Employment Practices Commission (FEPC) to monitor compliance with his edict. Blacks were also drafted into the armed forces, though they were still generally assigned to service branches rather than combat units and subjected to petty degradations such as segregated blood banks for the wounded. But in general the war helped to embolden blacks in their long struggle for equality. Membership in the National Association for the Advancement of Colored People (NAACP) shot up almost to the half-million mark, and a new militant organization, the Congress of Racial Equality (CORE), was founded in 1942.

The sudden rubbing against one another of unfamiliar peoples produced some distressingly violent friction. In 1943 young "zoot-suit"-clad Mexicans and Mexican-Americans in Los Angeles were viciously attacked by Anglo sailors who cruised the streets in taxicabs, searching for victims. Order was restored only after the Mexican ambassador made an emotional plea, pointing out that such outbreaks were grist for Nazi propaganda mills. At almost the same time, an even more brutal race riot that killed twenty-five blacks and nine whites erupted in Detroit.

Holding the Home Front

Despite these ugly episodes, Americans on the home front suffered little from the war, compared to the peoples of the other fighting nations. By war's end much of the planet was a smoking ruin. But in America the war invigorated the economy and lifted the country out of a decade-long depression. Gross national product vaulted from less than $100 billion in 1940 to more than $200 billion in 1945. Corporate profits rose from about $6 billion in 1940 to almost twice that amount four years later. ("If you are going to try to go to war in a capitalist country," said Secretary of War Stimson, "you have to let business make money out of the process, or business won't work.") Despite wage ceilings, overtime pay fattened pay envelopes. Disposable personal income, even after payment of wartime taxes, more than doubled. On

Black Fighter Group *Virtually all military units were racially segregated in World War II, including this fighter squadron, composed entirely of blacks. (National Archives.)*

The Federal Budget, 1930–1985
British economist John Maynard Keynes had urged massive deficit spending by the government as a cure for the Great Depression. Never really tried in the 1930s, deficit spending prompted by World War II proved a sure-fire tonic for depression-spawned unemployment. The federal budget remained in chronic deficit in the post-World War II years, and mounted to staggering sums in the 1980s. (Sources: Historical Statistics of the United States *and* Statistical Abstract of the United States, *relevant years.)*

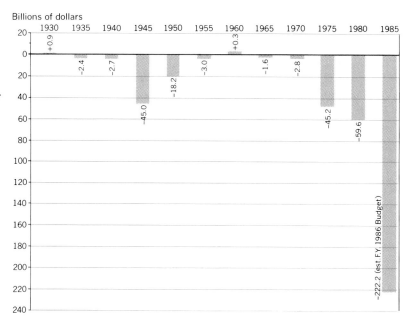

December 7, 1944, the third anniversary of Pearl Harbor, Macy's department store rang up the biggest sales day in its history. Americans had never had it so good—and they wanted it a lot better. When price controls were finally lifted in 1946, the American people's pent-up lust to consume pushed prices up 33 percent in less than two years. The rest of the world,

meanwhile, was still clawing its way out from under the rubble of war.

The hand of government touched more American lives more intimately during the war than ever before. The war, perhaps even more than the New Deal, pointed the way to the post-1945 era of big-government interventionism. Every household felt the constraints of the ra-

The National Debt 1930–1985 *Inflation and continuing budget deficits sent the national debt level over $1 trillion in the 1980s, when more than 9 percent of federal expenditures went for interest payments on that huge sum. But as this chart clearly shows, World War II provided the first massive boost to the mushrooming debt. (Sources:* Historical Statistics of the United States *and* Statistical Abstract of the United States, *relevant years.)*

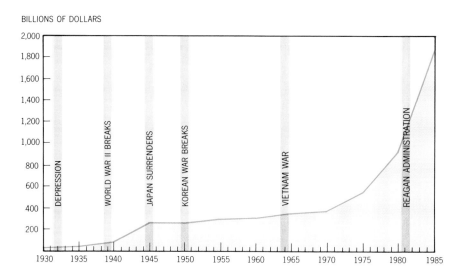

tioning system. Millions of men and women worked for Uncle Sam in the armed forces. Millions more worked for him in the defense industries, where their employers and unions were monitored by the FEPC and the WLB, and their personal needs were cared for by government-sponsored housing projects, day-care facilities, and health plans. The Office of Scientific Research and Development channeled hundreds of millions of dollars into university-based scientific research, establishing the partnership between the government and universities that underwrote America's technological and economic leadership in the postwar era.

The flood of war dollars—not the relatively modest rivulet of New Deal spending—at last swept the plague of unemployment from the land. War, not enlightened social policy, cured the depression. As the postwar economy continued to depend dangerously on military spending for its health, many observers saw in the years 1941–1945 the origins of a "warfare-welfare state."

The conflict was phenomenally expensive. The wartime bill amounted to more than $330 billion—ten times the direct cost of World War I and twice as much as *all* previous federal spending since 1776. Roosevelt would have preferred to follow a pay-as-you-go policy to finance the war, but the costs were simply too gigantic. The income-tax net was expanded to catch about four times as many people as before, and maximum tax rates rose as high as 90 percent. But despite such drastic measures, only about two-fifths of the war costs were paid from current revenues. The remainder was borrowed. The national debt skyrocketed from $49 billion in 1941 to $259 billion in 1945. When production finally slipped into high gear, the war was costing about $10 million an hour. This was the price of victory over such implacable enemies.

The Rising Sun in the Pacific

Early successes of the efficient Japanese militarists were breathtaking: they realized that they would have to win quickly or lose slowly. Seldom, if ever, has so much territory been conquered so rapidly with so little loss.

Simultaneously with the assault on Pearl Harbor, the Japanese launched widespread and uniformly successful attacks on various Far Eastern bastions. These included the American outposts of Guam, Wake, and the Philippines. In a dismayingly short time, the Nipponese invader seized not only the British-Chinese port of Hong Kong but also British Malaya, with its critically important supplies of rubber and tin.

Nor did the Nipponese tide stop there. The overambitious soldiers of the emperor, plunging into the snake-infested jungles of Burma, cut the famed Burma road. This was the route over which the United States had been trucking a trickle of munitions to the armies of the Chinese Generalissimo Jiang Jieshi (Chiang Kai-shek), who was still resisting the Japanese invader in China. Thereafter, intrepid American aviators were forced to fly a handful of war supplies to Jiang "over the hump" of the towering Himalaya Mountains from the India-Burma theater. Meanwhile, the Japanese had lunged southward against the oil-rich Dutch East Indies. The jungle-matted islands speedily fell to the assailant, after the combined British, Australian, Dutch, and American naval and air forces had been smashed at an early date by their numerically superior foe.

Better news came from the Philippines, which succeeded dramatically in slowing down the mikado's warriors for five months. The Japanese promptly landed a small but effective army, and General Douglas MacArthur, the eloquent and egotistical American commander, withdrew to a strong defensive position at Bataan, not far from Manila. There about twenty thousand American troops, supported by a much larger force of ill-trained Filipinos, held off violent Japanese attacks until April 9, 1942. The defenders, reduced to eating mules and monkeys, heroically traded their lives for time in the face of hopeless odds. They grimly joked while vainly hoping for reinforcements:

> We're the battling bastards of Bataan;
> No Mamma, no Papa, no Uncle Sam. . . .

Before the inevitable American surrender, General MacArthur was ordered by Washington to depart secretly for Australia, there to head the resistance against the Japanese. Leaving by

Corregidor–Bataan

motorboat and airplane, he proclaimed, "I shall return." After the battered remnants of his army had hoisted the white flag, they were treated with vicious cruelty in the infamous 85-mile (137-kilometer) Bataan death march. The island fortress of Corregidor, in Manila Harbor, held out until May 6, 1942, when it surrendered and left Japanese forces in complete control of the Philippine archipelago.

Japan's High Tide at Midway

The aggressive warriors from Nippon, making hay while the Rising Sun shone, pushed relentlessly southward. They invaded the turtle-shaped island of New Guinea, north of Australia, and landed on the Solomon Islands, from which they threatened Australia itself. Their onrush was finally checked by a crucial naval battle fought in the Coral Sea, in May 1942. An American carrier task force, with Australian support, inflicted heavy losses on the victory-flushed Nipponese. For the first time in history the fighting was all done by carrier-based aircraft, and neither fleet saw or fired a shot directly at the other.

Japan next undertook to seize Midway Island, more than 1,000 miles (1,600 kilometers) northwest of Honolulu. From this strategic base, it could launch devastating assaults on Pearl Harbor and perhaps force the weakened American Pacific fleet into destructive combat. An epochal naval battle was fought near Midway, June 3–6, 1942. Admiral Chester W. Nimitz, a high-grade naval strategist, directed a smaller but skillfully maneuvered carrier force, under Admiral Raymond A. Spruance, against the powerful invading fleet. The fighting was all done by aircraft, and the Japanese broke off action after losing four vitally important carriers.

The smashing success at Midway, combined with the Battle of the Coral Sea, turned the tide of Japan's conquest. But the thrust of the Nipponese into the eastern Pacific did net them America's fog-girt islands of Kiska and Attu, in the Aleutian archipelago, off Alaska. This easy conquest aroused fear of an invasion of the United States from the northwest. Much American strength was consequently diverted to the defense of Alaska, including the construction of the "Alcan" highway through Canada.

Yet the Japanese imperialists, overextended in 1942, suffered from "victory disease." Their appetites were bigger than their stomachs. If they had only dug in and consolidated their gains, they would have been much more difficult to dislodge.

American Leapfrogging toward Tokyo

Following the heartening victory at Midway, the United States for the first time was able to seize the initiative in the Pacific. In August 1942 American ground forces gained a toehold on Guadalcanal Island, in the Solomons, in an effort to protect the lifeline from America to Australia through the Southwest Pacific. An early naval defeat inflicted by the Japanese shortened American supplies dangerously, and for weeks the United States troops held onto the malarial island only by their fingernails. After four desperate sea battles for naval control, the Japanese troops evacuated Guadalcanal in February 1943.

Direct Hit on the Yorktown *Flying through a maelstrom of antiaircraft fire, Japanese pilots mortally wounded the aircraft carrier* Yorktown *during the Battle of Midway in early June 1942. A Japanese submarine later finished it off. (The Bettmann Archive.)*

American and Australian forces, under General MacArthur, meanwhile had been hanging on grimly to the southeastern tip of New Guinea, the last buffer protecting Australia. The scales of war gradually began to tip as the American navy, including submarines, inflicted lethal losses on Japanese supply ships and troop carriers. Conquest of the north coast of New Guinea was completed by August 1944, after General MacArthur had fought his way westward through green jungle hells. This hard-won victory was the first leg on the long return journey to the Philippines.

The United States Navy, with marines and army divisions doing the meat-grinder fighting, had meanwhile been "leapfrogging" the Japanese islands in the Pacific. Old-fashioned strategy dictated that the American forces, as they drove toward Tokyo, should reduce the fortified Japanese outposts on their flank. This course would have taken many bloodstained months,

for the holed-in defenders were prepared to die to the last man in their caves. The new strategy of island hopping called for bypassing some of the most heavily fortified Japanese posts, capturing nearby islands, setting up airfields on them, and then neutralizing the enemy bases through heavy bombing. Deprived of essential supplies from the homeland, the mikado's outposts would slowly wither on the vine—as they did.

Brilliant success crowned the American attacks on the Japanese island strongholds in the Pacific, where Admiral Nimitz skillfully coordinated the efforts of naval, air, and ground units. In May and August of 1943, Attu and Kiska in the Aleutians were easily retaken. In November 1943, "bloody Tarawa" and Makin, both in the Gilbert Islands, fell after suicidal resistance. In January and February 1944, the key outposts of the Marshall group succumbed after savage fighting.

United States Thrusts in the Pacific, 1942–1945
American strategists had to choose among four proposed plans for waging the war against Japan:
1. Defeating the Japanese in China by funneling supplies over the Himalayan "hump" from India.
2. Carrying the war into Southeast Asia (a proposal much favored by the British, who could thus regain Singapore).
3. Heavy bombing of Japan from Chinese air bases.
4. "Island hopping" from the South Pacific to within striking distance of the Japanese home islands. This strategy, favored by General Douglas MacArthur, was the one finally emphasized.

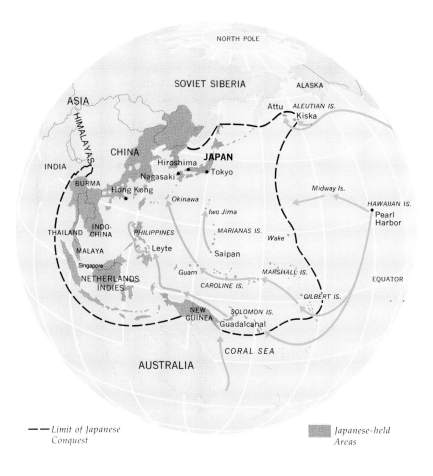

— — *Limit of Japanese Conquest*

Japanese-held Areas

Especially prized islands were the Marianas, of which America's conquered Guam was one. They were spacious enough to provide abundant airfields for American superbombers, and they were close enough to Japan to permit round-trip bombing. After fanatical resistance, the major islands fell to the American attackers in July and August 1944. With these unsinkable aircraft carriers now available, the first sustained air attacks on Japan were launched by giant bombers in November 1944.

The Allied Halting of Hitler

Early setbacks for America in the Pacific were paralleled in the Atlantic. Hitler had entered the war with a formidable fleet of ultramodern submarines, which ultimately operated in "wolf packs" with frightful effect, especially in the North Atlantic, the Caribbean, and the Gulf of Mexico. During ten months of 1942 more than 500 merchant ships were reported lost—111 in June alone—as ship destruction far outran construction.

The tide of subsea battle turned with agonizing slowness. Old techniques, such as escorting convoys of merchant vessels and dropping depth bombs from destroyers, were strength-

Prime Minister Churchill observed in a speech (May 1943): "The proud German Army has by its sudden collapse, sudden crumbling and breaking up . . . once again proved the truth of the saying, 'The Hun [German] is always either at your throat or at your feet.'"

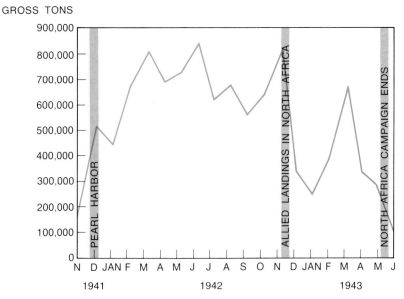

GROSS TONS

PEARL HARBOR

ALLIED LANDINGS IN NORTH AFRICA

NORTH AFRICA CAMPAIGN ENDS

N D JAN F M A M J J A S O N D JAN F M A M J
1941   1942   1943

Merchant Tonnage Sunk by U-Boats (November 1941–June 1943) *In early 1942, the U-boats stalked America's Atlantic coast. They picked off night-traveling, coast-hugging ships silhouetted againsts the lights from coastal cities that had failed to impose effective black-outs. Eventually the submarine menace was contained by electronic detection techniques (especially radar), and by airborne antisubmarine patrols operating from "baby flattops," small escort aircraft carriers.*

ened by air patrol, radar, and the bombing of submarine bases. "Keep 'Em Sailing" was the motto of oil-begrimed merchant seamen, hundreds of whom perished as unsung heroes in icy seas.

Not until the spring of 1943 did the Allies clearly have the upper hand against the U-boat. If they had not won the Battle of the Atlantic, Britain would have been forced under, and a second front could not have been launched from its island springboard. Victory over the undersea raiders was nerve-rackingly narrow. When the war ended, Hitler was about to mass-produce a fearsome new submarine—one that could remain underwater indefinitely and cruise at seventeen knots when submerged.

Meanwhile, the turning point of the land-air war against Hitler had come late in 1942. The British, who had launched a thousand-plane raid on Cologne in May, were now cascading bombs, with American help, on German cities. The Germans under Marshal Rommel—the "Desert Fox"—had driven across the hot sands of North Africa into Egypt, perilously close to the Suez Canal. A breakthrough would have spelled disaster for the Allies. But late in October 1942, British General Montgomery delivered a withering attack at El Alamein, west of Cairo. With the aid of several hundred hastily

shipped American Sherman tanks, he speedily drove the enemy back to Tunisia, more than 1,000 miles (1,600 kilometers) away.

On the Soviet front the unexpected successes of the red army gave a new lift to the Allied cause. In September 1942 the Russians halted the German steamroller at rubble-bestrewn Stalingrad, graveyard of Hitler's hopes. More than a score of invading divisions, caught

American Troops Entering Cologne, March 1945 *(H. Armstrong Roberts.)*

in an icy noose, later surrendered or were "mopped up." In November 1942 the resilient Russians unleashed a crushing counteroffensive, which was never seriously reversed. A year later, Stalin had regained about two-thirds of the blood-soaked Russian motherland wrested from him by the Teutonic invader.

The North African Second Front

Soviet leaders meanwhile had never ceased to clamor for an Anglo-American second front—a demand stridently supported by the few American Communists. Red divisions were doing practically all of the mud-and-blood fighting against Hitler's armies, and Moscow insisted that the Allies get into the war and drain off their fair share of the invader's strength. Russian officials did not regard the American operations in the Pacific as helpful, nor did they look upon the Allied aerial blasting of Germany as an adequate second front.

Many Americans were eager to begin a diversionary invasion of France in 1942 or 1943, while Russia was still afloat. They feared that the Soviets, unable to hold out against Germany, might make a separate peace, as they had in 1918, and leave the Western Allies to

face the fury of Hitler alone. But the British, remembering their fearful losses in 1914–1918, were not enthusiastic about a frontal assault on German-held France. It might end in complete disaster. They preferred to attack Hitler's Fortress Europe through the "soft underbelly" of the Mediterranean, while gathering strength for a cross-channel thrust.

An invasion of French-held North Africa was a compromise second front. It seemed less risky than a premature descent upon the coast of France, yet it would serve as a partial answer to the demands of the Russians for a diversion. If successful, it would open the Axis-dominated Mediterranean to lifeline communication with India and other parts of Asia.

The highly secret Allied attack on North Africa, launched in November 1942, was headed by a gifted and easy-smiling American general, Dwight D. ("Ike") Eisenhower, a master of organization and conciliation. As a joint Allied operation ultimately involving some 400,000 men (British, Canadian, French, and chiefly American), the invasion was the mightiest waterborne effort up to that time in history. About 850 ships of various sorts were employed.

At the outset, the surprise landing in North Africa was highly successful. The neutralized French, both anti-Hitler and pro-Ally, put up

Allied Thrusts in North Africa and Italy, 1942–1945 *Victory came fairly swiftly to the Allies in North Africa, but attacking the "soft underbelly" of Europe proved to be a delusion in Italy, where the rugged terrain favored the German defenders. They put up a bitter resistance on the landing beaches and made the Allies pay dearly for every yard gained as they retreated slowly up the mountainous spine of the Italian peninsula.*

only a token resistance. After savage fighting with the Germans, who inflicted a sharp setback on the green Americans at Kasserine Pass, the remnants of the German-Italian army were finally trapped in Tunisia. Some 266,000 dazed survivors surrendered in May 1943.

The North African campaign, though redeeming one continent, in itself was not conclusive. It was not the beginning of the end, but "the end of the beginning." Skeptical Russians scoffed at this second-rate second front, but valuable lessons were learned for the full-fledged invasion of France.

The Rough Road to Rome

New blows were now planned by the Allies. At Casablanca, in newly occupied French Morocco, President Roosevelt, who had boldly flown the Atlantic, met in a historic conference with Winston Churchill in January 1943. The Big Two agreed to step up the Pacific war, invade Sicily, increase pressure on Italy, and insist upon an "unconditional surrender" of the enemy—a phrase earlier popularized by General Grant during the Civil War. Such an unyielding policy would presumably hearten the ultrasuspicious Soviets, who professed to fear separate Allied peace negotiations. It would also forestall charges of broken armistice terms, such as had come after 1918.

Yet "unconditional surrender" proved to be one of the most controversial moves of the war. The main criticism was that it steeled the enemy to fight to a last-bunker resistance, while discouraging antiwar groups in Germany from revolting. Although there was no doubt some truth in these charges, no one can prove that "unconditional surrender" either shortened or lengthened the war. But by helping to destroy the German government utterly, the harsh policy immensely complicated the problems of reconstruction.

The victorious Allied forces—American, British, and Canadian—now turned against the not-so-soft underbelly of Europe. Sicily fell, in August 1943, after sporadic but sometimes bitter resistance. Shortly before the conquest of the island, Mussolini was deposed and a new Rome government was set up. Italy surrendered unconditionally early in September 1943, while Allied troops were pouring onto the toe of the Italian boot. President Roosevelt, referring to the three original Axis accomplices—Germany, Italy, and Japan—joked grimly that it was now one down and two to go. Two years later Mussolini, together with his attractive mistress, was brutally lynched by his own people. Both bodies were ingloriously hung up by the heels for public display.

But if Italy dropped out of the war, the Germans did not drop out of Italy. Hitler's well-trained troops resisted the Allied invaders with methodical and infuriating stubbornness. The luckless Italians, turning their coats, declared war on Germany in October 1943. "Sunny Italy" proceeded to belie its name, for in the snow-covered and mud-caked mountains of its elongated peninsula occurred some of the filthiest, bloodiest, and most frustrating fighting of the war.

For many months Italy appeared to be a dead end, as the Allied advance was halted by a seemingly impregnable German defense centered around the ancient monastery of Monte Cassino. After a touch-and-go assault on the Anzio beachhead, Rome was finally taken on June 4, 1944. Two days later, when the tremendous cross-channel invasion of France began, Italy became a kind of sideshow. But the Allies, with limited manpower, continued to fight their way slowly and painfully into northern Italy. On May 2, 1945, only five days before Germany's official surrender, several hundred thousand Axis troops in Italy laid down their arms and became prisoners of war.

The Italian campaign, though agonizingly slow, was by no means fruitless. It opened the Mediterranean, diverted some German divisions from the blazing Russian and French fronts, and provided air bases for bombing assaults on German Austria and southern Germany.

Eisenhower's D-Day Invasion of France

The Russians had never ceased their clamor for an all-out second front, and the time rapidly approached for Churchill, Roosevelt, and Stalin to meet in person to coordinate the promised effort. Marshal Joseph Stalin, with a careful eye on Russian military operations, balked at leaving the Soviet Union. President Roosevelt, who jauntily remarked in private, "I can handle that old buzzard," was eager to confer with him. The president seemed confident that Rooseveltian charm could woo the hardened conspirator of the Kremlin from his nasty Communist ways.

Teheran, the capital of Iran (Persia), was finally chosen as the meeting place. To this ancient city Roosevelt riskily flew, after a stopover conference in Cairo with Britain's Churchill and China's Jiang Jieshi regarding the war against Japan. At Teheran the discussions among Stalin, Roosevelt, and Churchill—from November 28 to December 1, 1943—progressed smoothly. Perhaps the most important achievement was agreement on broad plans, especially those for launching Russian attacks on Germany from the east simultaneously with the prospective Allied assault from the west.

Preparations for the cross-channel invasion of France were gigantic. Britain's fast-anchored isle virtually groaned with munitions, supplies, and troops, as nearly 3 million fighting men were readied. As the United States was to provide most of the Allied warriors, the overall command was entrusted to an American, General Eisenhower. He had already distinguished

Allies Landing in Normandy, June 6, 1944 Nine-foot ocean swells on invasion day made loading the assault landing craft, such as the one pictured here, treacherous business. Many men were injured or tossed into the sea as the bathtub-like amphibious vessels bobbed wildly up and down alongside the troop transports. As the vulnerable boats churned toward the beach, some officers led their tense, grim-faced troops in prayer. One major quoted from Shakespeare's Henry V:
 "He that outlives this day, and comes safe home
 Will stand a tip-toe when this day is named."
(The Bettmann Archive.)

Final Allied Thrusts in Europe, 1944–1945 *After breaking out of their D-Day beachhead in Normandy, Allied forces fought their way across German-occupied France, Belgium, and the Netherlands. They at last linked up inside Germany with Soviet troops advancing from the East. General Eisenhower held back his forces and permitted the oncoming Russians to capture Berlin, with the loss of about 100,000 Soviet soldiers. He argued with considerable force that because Roosevelt and Churchill had already assigned Berlin and its environs to the Soviets, American blood should not be shed unnecessarily.*

himself in the North African and Mediterranean campaigns, not only for his military capacity but also for his gifts as a conciliator of clashing Allied interests.

French Normandy, less heavily defended than other parts of the European coast, was pinpointed for the invasion assault. On D-Day, June 6, 1944, the enormous operation, which involved some forty-six hundred vessels, unwound. Stiff resistance was encountered from the Germans, who had been misled by a feint into expecting the blow to fall farther north. The Allies had already achieved mastery of the air over France. They were thus able to block reinforcements by crippling the railroads, while worsening German fuel shortages by bombing gasoline-producing plants.

The Allied beachhead, at first clung to with fingertips, was gradually enlarged, consolidated, and reinforced. After desperate fighting, the invaders finally broke out of the German iron ring at the base of the Normandy peninsula. Most spectacular were the lunges across France by American armored divisions, brilliantly commanded by blustery and profane General George S. ("Blood 'n' Guts") Patton. The retreat of the German defenders was hastened when an American-French force landed in August

1944 on the southern coast of France and swept northward. With the assistance of the French "underground," Paris was liberated in August 1944, amid exuberant manifestations of joy and gratitude.

Allied forces rolled irresistibly toward Germany, and many of the Americans encountered places, like Château-Thierry, familiar to their fathers in 1918. "Lafayette, we are here again," proclaimed some of the American soldiers jocosely. The first important German city (Aachen) fell to the Americans in October 1944, and the days of Hitler's "thousand-year *Reich*" were numbered.

FDR: The Fourth-Termite of 1944

The presidential campaign of 1944, which was bound to divert energy from the war program, came most awkwardly as the awful conflict roared to its climax. But the normal electoral processes continued to function, despite some loose talk of suspending them "for the duration."

Victory-starved Republicans met in Chicago with hopeful enthusiasm. They quickly nominated the short, mustached, and dapper

> *During the bitter campaign of 1944, Roosevelt's pre–Pearl Harbor policies came under sharp attack from Congresswoman Clare Boothe Luce (the "Blonde Bombshell"), who violently charged Roosevelt with having "lied us into war because he did not have the political courage to lead us into it."*

Thomas E. Dewey, popular vote-getting governor of New York. Regarded as a liberal, he had already made a national reputation as a prosecutor of grafters and racketeers in New York City. His shortness and youth—he was only forty-two—had caused one veteran New Dealer to sneer that the candidate had cast his diaper into the ring. To offset Dewey's mild internationalism, the convention nominated for the vice-presidency a strong isolationist, handsome and white-maned Senator John W. Bricker of Ohio. Yet the platform called for an unstinted prosecution of the war and for the creation of a new international organization to maintain peace.

Franklin Roosevelt, obviously aging under the strain, was the "indispensable man" of the Democrats. No other major figure was available, and the war was apparently grinding to its grand finale. He was nominated at Chicago on the first ballot by acclamation. But in a sense he was the "forgotten man" of the convention, for in view of his age, an unusual amount of attention was focused on the vice-presidency.

The scramble for the vice-presidential plum turned into something of a free-for-all. Henry A. Wallace, onetime "plow 'em under" secretary of agriculture, had served four years as vice-president and desired a renomination. But conservative Democrats distrusted him as an ill-balanced and unpredictable liberal. A "ditch Wallace" move developed tremendous momentum, despite the popularity of Wallace with large numbers of voters and many of the delegates. With Roosevelt's blessing, the vice-presidential nomination finally went to smiling and self-assured Senator Harry S Truman of Missouri ("the new Missouri Compromise"). Hitherto inconspicuous, he had recently attained national visibility

as the efficient chairman of a Senate committee conducting an investigation of wasteful war expenditures. Nobody had much against him or on him.

Roosevelt Defeats Dewey

A dynamic Dewey took the offensive, for Roosevelt was too busily involved in directing the war to spare much time for speechmaking. The vigorous young "crime buster," with his beautiful baritone voice and polished diction, denounced the tired and quarrelsome "old men" in Washington. He proclaimed repeatedly that after "twelve long years" of New Dealism, it was "time for a change." As for the war, Dewey would not alter the basic strategy but would fight it better—a type of "me-tooism" ridiculed by the Democrats. The fourth-term issue did not figure prominently, now that the ice had been broken by Roosevelt's third term. But "Dewey-eyed" Republicans, half-humorously, professed to fear fifth and sixth terms by the "lifer" in the White House.

In the closing weeks of the campaign, Roosevelt left his desk for the stump. He was stung by certain Republican charges, including alleged aspersions on his pet Scottie dog, Fala. He was also eager to show himself, even in chilling rains, to spike well-founded rumors of failing health.

Substantial assistance came from the new Political Action Committee of the CIO, which was organized to get around the law banning the direct use of union funds for political purposes. Zealous CIO members, branded as Communists by the Republicans, rang countless doorbells and asked, with pointed reference to the recent depression, "What were you doing in 1932?" At times Roosevelt seemed to be running again against Hoover. As in every one of his previous three campaigns, FDR was opposed by a majority of the newspapers, which were owned chiefly by Republicans. Roosevelt, as customary, won a sweeping victory: 432 to 99 in the Electoral College; 25,606,585 to 22,014,745 in the popular totals. Elated, he quipped that "the first twelve years are the hardest."

Battle of the Bulge

Roosevelt won primarily because the war was going well. A winning pitcher is not ordinarily taken out. Foreign policy was a decisive factor with untold thousands of voters, who concluded that Roosevelt's experienced hand was needed in fashioning a future organization for world peace. The dapper Dewey, cruelly dubbed "the little man on top of the wedding cake," had spoken smoothly of international cooperation, but his isolationist running mate, Bricker, had implanted serious doubts. The Republican party was still suffering from the taint of isolationism fastened on it by the Hardingites.

The Last Days of Hitler

By mid-December 1944, the month after Roosevelt's fourth-term victory, Germany seemed to be wobbling on its last legs. The Soviet surge had penetrated eastern Germany. Allied aerial "blockbuster" bombs, making the "rubble bounce" on an around-the-clock schedule, were falling like giant hailstones on cities, factories, and transportation arteries. The German western front seemed about to buckle under the

sledgehammer blows of the United States and its allies.

Hitler then staked everything on one last throw of his reserves. Secretly concentrating a powerful force, he hurled it, on December 16, 1944, against the thinly held American lines in the heavily befogged and snow-shrouded Ardennes forest. Caught off guard, the outmanned Americans were driven back, and the key Belgian port of Antwerp was menaced. The ten-day penetration was finally halted after the 101st Airborne Division had stood firm at the vital bastion of Bastogne. The commander, Brigadier General A. C. McAuliffe, defiantly answered the German demand for surrender with one word, "Nuts." Reinforcements were rushed up, and the last-gasp Hitlerian offensive was at length bloodily stemmed in the Battle of the Bulge.

In March 1945 forward-driving American troops reached Germany's Rhine River, where, by incredibly good luck, they found one strategic bridge undemolished. Pressing their advantage, General Eisenhower's troops reached the river Elbe in April 1945. There, a short distance south of Berlin, American and Russian advance guards dramatically clasped hands, amid cries of *"Amerikanskie tovarishchi"* (American comrades). The conquering Americans were

American and Russian Soldiers Meet in Germany, 1945 *Such friendly sights soon became rare as mutual suspicion deepened. (U.S. Army photo.)*

horrified to find blood-bespattered and still-stinking concentration camps, where the German Nazis had engaged in scientific mass murder of "undesirables," including an estimated 6 million Jews. The Washington government had long been informed about Hitler's campaign of genocide against the Jews and had been reprehensibly slow to take steps against it—such as bombing the rail lines that carried the victims to the camps. But until the war's end, the full dimensions of the "Holocaust" had not been known. When the details were revealed, the whole world was aghast.

The vengeful Russians, clawing their way forward from the east, reached Berlin in April 1945. After desperate house-to-house fighting, followed by an orgy of pillage and rape, they captured the bomb-shattered city. Adolf Hitler, after a hasty marriage to his mistress, committed suicide in an underground bunker, April 30, 1945.

Tragedy had meanwhile struck the United States. President Roosevelt, while relaxing at Warm Springs, Georgia, suddenly died from a massive cerebral hemorrhage on April 12, 1945. The crushing burden of twelve years in the White House had finally taken its toll. Knots of confused, leaderless citizens gathered to discuss the future anxiously, as a bewildered, unbriefed Vice-President Truman took the helm.

On May 7, 1945, what was left of the German government surrendered unconditionally. May 8 was officially proclaimed V-E Day—Victory in Europe Day—and was greeted with frenzied rejoicing in the Allied countries.

Japan Dies Hard

Japan's rickety bamboo empire meantime was tottering to its fall. American submarines—"the silent service"—were sending the Japanese

V-E Day, May 8, 1945   *These celebrants rejoiced in New York's Times Square as the Nazis collapsed. But months of bitter fighting against the Japanese still lay ahead for American forces in the Pacific. (National Archives.)*

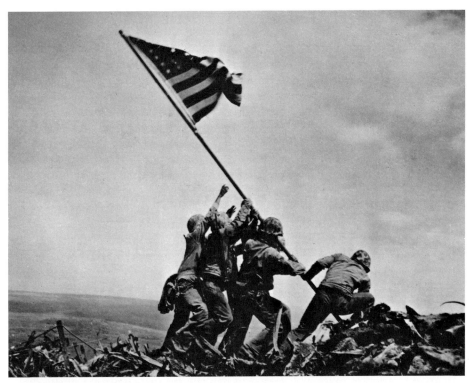

The Flag Raising at Iwo Jima *Atop Mt. Suribachi, press photographer Joe Rosenthal snapped this dramatic picture, probably the most famous of the war. (National Archives.)*

merchant marine to the bottom so fast they were running out of prey. All told, these underseas craft destroyed 1,042 ships, or about 50 percent of Nippon's entire life-giving merchant fleet.

Giant bomber attacks were more spectacular. Launched from Saipan and other captured Marianas, they were reducing the enemy's fragile cities to cinders. The massive fire-bomb raid on Tokyo, March 9–10, 1945, was annihilating. It destroyed over 250,000 buildings, gutted a quarter of the city, and killed an estimated 83,000 persons—a loss comparable to that later inflicted by atomic bombs.

General MacArthur was also on the move. Completing the conquest of jungle-draped New Guinea, he headed northwest for the Philippines, en route to Japan, with six hundred ships and 250,000 men. In a scene well staged for the photographers, he splashed ashore at Leyte Island, on October 20, 1944, with the summons:

"People of the Philippines, I have returned. . . . Rally to me."

Nippon's navy—still menacing—now made one last-chance effort to destroy MacArthur by wiping out his transports and supply ships. A gigantic clash at Leyte Gulf, fought on the sea and in the air, was actually three battles (October 23–26, 1944). The Americans won all of them, though the crucial engagement was almost lost when Admiral William F. ("Bull") Halsey was decoyed away by a feint.

Japan was through as a sea power: it had lost about sixty ships in the greatest naval battle of all time. American fleets, numbering more than four thousand vessels, now commanded Asiatic seas. Several battleships, raised from the mud of Pearl Harbor, were finding belated but sweet revenge.

Overrunning Leyte, MacArthur next landed on the main Philippine island of Luzon, in January 1945. Manila was his major objective; the ravaged city fell in March, but the Philippines were not conquered until July. Victory was purchased only after bitter fighting against holed-in Japanese, who took a toll of over sixty thousand American casualties.

America's steel vise was tightening mercilessly around Nippon. The tiny island of Iwo Jima, needed as a roosting place for damaged American bombers returning from Japan, was captured in March 1945. This desperate twenty-five-day assault cost over four thousand American dead.

Okinawa, a well-defended Japanese island, was next on the list: it was needed for closer bases from which to blast and burn enemy cities and industries. Fighting dragged on from April to June of 1945. Nipponese soldiers, fighting with cornered-rat courage from their caves, finally sold Okinawa for eighty thousand American casualties, while suffering far heavier losses themselves.

The American navy, which covered the invasion of Okinawa, sustained severe damage. Japanese suicide pilots, in an exhibition of mass hara-kiri for their god-emperor, crashed their bomb-laden planes onto the decks of the invading fleet. All told, they sank over thirty ships and badly damaged scores more.

Atomic Awfulness

Strategists in Washington were meanwhile planning an all-out invasion of the main islands of Japan—an invasion that presumably would cost hundreds of thousands of American (and Japanese) casualties. Tokyo, recognizing imminent defeat, had secretly sent peace feelers to Russia, which had not yet entered the Far Eastern war. The Americans, having broken the secret Japanese radio codes, knew of these feelers. But bomb-scorched Japan still showed no outward willingness to surrender *unconditionally.*

The Potsdam conference, held near Berlin in July 1945, sounded the death knell of the Japanese. There President Truman, still new on his job, met in a seventeen-day parley with Joseph Stalin and the British leaders. The con-

ferees issued a stern ultimatum to Japan: surrender or be destroyed. American bombers showered the grim warning on Japan in tens of thousands of leaflets, but no encouraging response was forthcoming.

America had a fantastic ace up its sleeve. Early in 1940, after Hitler's wanton assault on Poland, Roosevelt was persuaded by American and exiled scientists, notably German-born Albert Einstein, to push ahead with gigantic preparations for unlocking the secret of an atomic bomb. Congress, at Roosevelt's blank-check request, blindly made available nearly $2 billion. Many military minds were skeptical of this "damned professor's nonsense," but fear of well-known German scientific progress provided an additional spur.

The huge atomic project was pushed feverishly forward, as American know-how and industrial power were combined with the most advanced scientific knowledge. Much technical skill was provided by British and Continental scientists, some of whom, ironically, had been forced to flee the torture chambers of the dictators. Finally, in the desert near Alamogordo, New Mexico, on July 16, 1945, the experts detonated the first awesome atomic device.

With Japan still refusing to surrender, the Potsdam threat was fulfilled. On August 6, 1945, a lone American bomber dropped one atomic bomb on the military-base city of Hiroshima, Japan. In a blinding flash of death, followed by a funnel-shaped cloud, about 180,000 persons were left killed, wounded, or missing. Some 70,000 of them were dead or presumed dead.

Two days later, on August 8, Stalin entered the war against Japan, exactly on the deadline date previously agreed upon with his allies. Soviet armies speedily overran the depleted Japanese defenses in Manchuria and Korea in a six-day "victory parade" that involved several thousand Russian casualties. Stalin was evidently determined to be in on the kill, lest he lose a voice in the final division of Japan's holdings.

Fanatically resisting Japanese, though facing atomization, still did not surrender. American aviators, on August 9, dropped a second atomic bomb on the naval-base city of Nagasaki, home of the fictional "Madame Butterfly." The explosion took a horrible toll of about eighty thousand persons killed or missing.

Japan could endure no more. On August 10, 1945, Tokyo sued for peace on one condition: that Hirohito, the bespectacled Son of Heaven, be allowed to remain on his ancestral throne as nominal emperor. Despite their "unconditional surrender" policy, the Allies accepted this condition on August 14. The Japanese, though losing face, saved both their exalted ruler and what was left of their native land.

The formal end came, with dramatic force, on September 2, 1945. Official surrender ceremonies were conducted by General MacArthur on the battleship *Missouri* in Tokyo Bay. At the same time Americans at home hysterically celebrated V-J Day—Victory in Japan Day—after the most horrible war in history had ended in a mushrooming atomic cloud.

The Allies Triumphant

World War II proved to be terribly costly. American forces suffered some 1 million casualties, about one-third of which were deaths. Compared with other wars, the proportion killed by wounds and disease was sharply reduced, owing in part to the use of blood plasma and miracle drugs, notably penicillin. Yet heavy though American losses were, the Russian allies suffered casualties many times greater—perhaps 20 million persons killed.

America was fortunate in emerging with its mainland virtually unscathed. Two Japanese submarines, using shells and bombers, had rather harmlessly attacked the California and Oregon coast, and a few balloons, incendiary and otherwise, had drifted across the Pacific. But that was about all. Much of the rest of the world was bomb-pocked, rubble-strewn, and impoverished. America alone was untouched and healthy—oiled and muscled like a prize bull, standing astride the world's ruined landscape.

This complex conflict was the best-fought war in America's history. Though unprepared for it at the outset, the nation was better prepared than for the others, partly because it had begun to buckle on its armor about a year and a half before the war officially began. It was actually fighting German submarines in the Atlantic months before the final explosion in the Pacific at Pearl Harbor. In the end, it showed itself to

The Japanese Surrender   *Representatives of the Japanese government sign the surrender instrument on the deck of the battleship* Missouri *in Tokyo harbor, September 2, 1945. (AP/Wide World Photos.)*

be resourceful, tough, adaptable—able to accommodate itself to the tactics of an enemy who was relentless and ruthless.

American military leadership proved to be of the highest order. A new crop of war heroes emerged in brilliant generals like Eisenhower, MacArthur, and Marshall (chief of staff) and in imaginative admirals like Nimitz and Spruance. President Roosevelt and Prime Minister Churchill, as kindred spirits, collaborated closely in planning overall strategy. "It is fun to be in the same decade with you," FDR once cabled the British leader.

Industrial leaders were no less skilled, for marvels of production were performed almost daily. Assembly lines proved as important as battle lines; and victory went again to the side with the big smokestacks. The enemy was al-

most literally smothered by bayonets, bullets, bazookas, and bombs. Hitler and his Axis co-conspirators had chosen to make war with machines, and the ingenious Yankees could ask for nothing better. From 1940 to 1945, the output of American factories was simply phenomenal. As Winston Churchill remarked, "Nothing succeeds like excess."

Hermann Göring, a Nazi leader, had sneered, "The Americans can't build planes—only electric iceboxes and razor blades." Democracy had given its answer, as the dictators, despite long preparation, were overthrown and discredited. It is true that an unusual amount of direct control was exercised over the individual by the Washington authorities during the war emergency. But the American people preserved their precious liberties without serious impairment.

Varying Viewpoints

The United States emerged militarily triumphant in 1945, but one event threatened to tarnish the crown of moral victory: the atomic bombing of Japan. America is the only nation ever to have used an atomic weapon in war, and some critics noted cynically that the bomb was dropped, not on European enemies, but on people of a nonwhite race. A few scholars, notably Gar Alperovitz, have further charged that the holocaust at Hiroshima and Nagasaki was not the final shot of World War II but the first salvo in the Cold War. Alperovitz notes that the Japanese were already defeated in the summer of 1945 and were attempting to arrange a *conditional* surrender. President Truman ignored those attempts and unleashed his horrible new weapon, so the argument goes, not only to defeat Japan but also to frighten the Russians into less aggressive behavior.

Could the use of the atomic bomb have been avoided? The fact is that few policymakers even asked that question at the time, as Martin J. Sherwin's studies have made clear. American leaders wanted to end the war as quickly as possible, for a variety of reasons, and the bomb undoubtedly hastened the devastating conclusion. It also strengthened the American hand against the Russians, but that was not the *primary* reason for the fateful decision to proceed with the nuclear incineration of two Japanese cities. Nevertheless, remorse and misgivings about those horrible bomb-bursts continue to plague the nation's conscience.

Select Readings

Primary Source Documents

For background on the date that will live in infamy, see *Pearl Harbor Attack: Hearings before the Joint Committee on the Investigation of the Pearl Harbor Attack*, 79th Congress, 1st Session (1946).* Vivid portraits of the fighting are found in Ernie Pyle's *Here Is Your War* (1943) and *Brave Men* (1944). On the atomic bomb, consult the reactions of the *Nippon Times* (August 10, 1945)*, *The Christian Century* (August 29, 1945),* and President Truman's justification of the bombing in *Memoirs of Harry S Truman* (1955).*

Secondary Sources

A scholarly discussion of the home front is John M. Blum, *V Was for Victory: Politics and American Culture during World War II* (1976). Consult also Richard Polenberg, *War and Society: The United States, 1941–1945* (1972), and Harold G. Vatter, *The U.S. Economy in World War II* (1985). Studs Terkel has compiled an interesting oral history of the war experience in *The Good War* (1984). On women, see William H. Chafe, *The American Woman: Her Changing Social, Economic, and Political Roles, 1920–1970* (1972); on the internment of the Japanese-Americans, consult Roger Daniels, *Concentration Camps U.S.A.: Japanese-Americans and World War II* (1971), and Peter Irons, *Justice at War: The Story of the Japanese-American Internment Cases* (1983). On blacks, see Neil A. Wynn, *The Afro-Americans and the Second World War* (1976). Also interesting is Allan M. Winkler, *The Politics of Propaganda: The Office of War Information, 1942–1945* (1978). Nelson Lichtenstein examines *Labor's War at Home: The CIO in World War II* (1983). The military history of the war is capably handled in Albert Russell Buchanan, *The United States and World War II* (2 vols., 1964). The naval side is treated in Samuel E. Morison, *The Two-Ocean War* (1963), a condensation of his multivolume official history. See also Russell F. Weigley, *Eisenhower's Lieutenants: The Campaigns of France and Germany, 1944–1945* (1981). High strategy is developed in Kent R. Greenfield, *American Strategy in World War II* (1963). A good introduction to wartime diplomacy is Gaddis Smith, *American Diplomacy during the Second World War* (1965). More detailed are Herbert Feis's three volumes: *Churchill, Roosevelt, Stalin* (2d ed., 1967), *Between War and Peace: The Potsdam Conference* (1960), and *The Atomic Bomb and the End of World War II* (1966). Also valuable are Robert Dallek's work, cited in the preceding chapter; John L. Gaddis, *The United States and the Origins of the Cold War, 1941–1947* (1972); and two "revisionist" studies that are highly critical of American policy: Gabriel Kolko, *The Politics of War: The World and United States Foreign Policy, 1943–1945* (1968), and Lloyd Gardner, *Architects of Illusion: Men and Ideas in American Foreign Policy, 1941–1949* (1970). The war in Asia is covered in Jonathan Utley, *Going to War with Japan,* *1937–1941* (1985), and Akira Iriye, *Power and Culture: The Japanese-American War, 1941–1945* (1981). Consult also Christopher Thorne, *Allies of a Kind: The United States, Britain, and the War against Japan* (1978), and Ronald H. Spector's gracefully written *Eagle against the Sun: The American War with Japan* (1985). On the atomic bomb, see Richard G. Hewlett and Oscar E. Anderson Jr., *The New World* (1962); Martin J. Sherwin, *A World Destroyed: The Atomic Bomb and the Grand Alliance* (1975); and Gar Alperovitz's questionable critique of American nuclear strategy, *Atomic Diplomacy* (1965). Paul Boyer's *By the Bomb's Early Light* (1985) analyzes the bomb's impact on the American mind.

41

Harry S Truman and the Cold War

The attack upon Korea makes it plain beyond all doubt that Communism has passed beyond the use of subversion to conquer independent nations and will now use armed invasion and war.

Harry S Truman, June 27, 1950

Truman: The "Gutty" Man from Missouri

Trim and owlishly bespectacled Harry S Truman, with his graying hair and friendly, toothy grin, was called "the average man's average man." Even his height—5 feet 9 inches (1.75 meters)—was average. The first president in many years without a college education, he had farmed, served as an artillery officer in France during World War I, and failed as a haberdasher. He then tried his hand at precinct-level Missouri politics, through which he rose from a judgeship to the United States Senate. Though a protégé of a notorious political machine in Kansas City, he had managed to keep his own hands clean.

The roof caved in on Truman with Roosevelt's sudden death. Problems were overpowering, and the firm-mouthed new president approached his tasks with becoming humility. Gradually gaining confidence to the point of cockiness, he displayed courage, decisiveness, and a willingness to fight. Though amateurish as a public speaker at first, he finally developed into one of the most effective "give 'em hell" orators of his generation.

Yet by degrees the defects of Truman's common clay became painfully apparent. A smallish man suddenly thrust into an overwhelming job, he was inclined to go off half-cocked or stick mulishly to some wrongheaded notion. On occasion, he would dash off hot-tempered and highly indiscreet "s.o.b." letters. Worst of all,

President Harry S Truman (1884–1972) *When his Republican opponents complained that he was giving them "hell," he replied, "I don't give 'em hell, I just tell the truth and they think it's hell." (Copyrighted by the White House Historical Association, photo by the National Geographic Society.)*

President Truman permitted designing old associates of the "Missouri gang" to gather around him and, like Grant, was stubbornly loyal to them when they were caught with the cream on their whiskers. "To err is Truman" was a cynical explanation.

This was the man on whom Roosevelt's oversize mantle fell in April 1945, when victory over Hitler was in view. Truman's most pressing task was to follow through and win both the war and the peace. Fortunately, he developed a surprising capacity to seize the tiller with a bold hand in time of crisis. If he was sometimes small in the small things, he was often big in the big things. A motto on the White House desk read, "The buck stops here." A favorite saying of his was, "If you can't stand the heat, get out of the kitchen."

Yalta: Bargain or Betrayal?

Vast and silent, the Soviet Union continued to be the great enigma. The conference at Teheran in 1943, where Roosevelt had first met Stalin on a man-to-man basis, had done something to clear the air, but much had remained unresolved—especially questions about the postwar fates of Germany, Eastern Europe, and Asia.

A final fateful conference of the Big Three had taken place in February 1945 at Yalta. At this former czarist resort on the relatively warm shores of the Black Sea, Stalin, Churchill, and the fast-failing Roosevelt reached momentous agreements, after pledging their faith with vodka. Final plans were laid for smashing the buckling German lines and shackling the beaten Axis foe. Stalin agreed that Poland, with revised boundaries, should have a representative government based on free elections—a pledge that he soon broke. Bulgaria and Romania were likewise to have free elections—a promise also flouted. The Big Three further announced that they had decided to hold a multi-power conference, this time in San Francisco, for the purpose of fashioning a new international peacekeeping organization—the United Nations.

Of all the painful decisions at Yalta, the most controversial concerned the Far East. The atomic bomb had not yet been tested, and Washington strategists expected frightful American casualties in the projected assault on Japan. From Roosevelt's standpoint it seemed highly desirable that Stalin should enter the Asian war, pin down Japanese troops in Manchuria and Korea, and lighten American losses. But Russian casualties had already been enormous, and the Soviets presumably needed inducements to bring them into the Far Eastern conflagration.

Horse trader Stalin was in a position at Yalta to exact a high price. He agreed to attack Japan within three months after the collapse of Germany; and he later redeemed this pledge in full. In return, the Soviets were promised the southern half of Sakhalin Island, lost by Russia to Japan in 1905, and Japan's Kurile Islands as

The Big Three *From right to left, Churchill, Roosevelt, and Stalin take time out from their fateful meeting at Yalta in February 1945. (The Granger Collection.)*

well. The Soviet Union was also granted joint control over the railroads of China's Manchuria and, in a revival of czarist imperialism, received special privileges in the two key seaports of that area, Dairen and Port Arthur. These concessions evidently would give Stalin control over vital industrial centers of America's weakening Chinese ally.

Russia's last-minute entry into the war against Japan was hailed in the United States with delight. But critics quickly concluded that Stalin's aid had not been needed, and that in any case his desire to grab his share of the spoils would have brought him into the conflict without concessions. Foes of the dead Roosevelt charged angrily that he had sold Jiang Jieshi (Chiang Kai-shek) down the river when he conceded control of China's Manchuria to Stalin. The consequent undermining of Chinese morale, so the accusation ran, contributed powerfully to Jiang's overthrow by the Communists four years later. The critics also assailed the

"sellout" of Poland and other East European countries.

Defenders of the departed Roosevelt were not silent. They argued that if Stalin had kept his promise to support free elections in Poland and the liberated Balkans, the sorry sequel would have been different. Actually, Russian troops had then occupied much of Eastern Europe, and a war to throw them out was unthinkable. Apologists for Roosevelt also contended that Stalin, with his mighty red army, could have secured much more of China and that the Yalta conference really set limits to his ambitions.

The fact is that the Big Three at Yalta were not drafting a comprehensive peace settlement; at most they were sketching general intentions and testing one another's reactions. Later critics who howled about broken promises overlooked that fundamental point. In the case of Poland, Roosevelt admitted that the Yalta agreement was "so elastic that the Russians can stretch it all the way from Yalta to Washington without ever technically breaking it." More specific understandings among the wartime allies—especially the two emerging superpowers, the United States and the Soviet Union—awaited the arrival of peace.

The U.S.A. and the U.S.S.R.

History provided little hope that America and Russia would reach cordial understandings about the shape of the postwar world. Mutual suspicions were ancient, abundant, and deep. Communism and capitalism were historically hostile social philosophies. The United States had refused officially to recognize the Bolshevik revolutionary government in Moscow until it was sixteen years old, in 1933. Russian suspicions of the West were nourished by the British and American delays in opening up a second front against Germany, while the red army paid a ghastly price to roll the Nazi invaders back across Russia and Eastern Europe. Britain and America had also frozen their Soviet "ally" out of the project to develop atomic weapons, further feeding Stalin's mistrust. The Washington government rubbed salt in Soviet wounds when it abruptly terminated vital lend-lease aid to battered Russia in 1945 and spurned Moscow's plea for a $6 billion reconstruction loan—while approving a similar loan of $3.75 billion to Britain in 1946.

Different visions of the postwar world also separated the two superpowers. Stalin aimed above all to guarantee the security of the Soviet Union. Russia had twice in the twentieth century been stabbed in its heartland by attacks across the windswept plains of Eastern Europe. Stalin made it clear from the outset of the war that he was determined to have friendly governments along the Soviet western border, especially in Poland. By maintaining an extensive Soviet sphere of influence in Eastern and Central Europe, Moscow could protect Mother Russia and consolidate its revolutionary base as the world's leading Communist country.

To many Americans, that "sphere of influence" looked like an ill-gained "empire." Doubting that Soviet goals were purely defensive, they remembered the earlier Bolshevik call for

world revolution. Stalin's emphasis on "spheres" also clashed with Franklin Roosevelt's Wilsonian dream of an "open world," decolonized, demilitarized, and democratized, with a strong international organization to maintain global peace.

Even the ways in which the United States and the Soviet Union resembled each other were troublesome. Both countries had been largely isolated from world affairs before World War II—the United States through choice, the Russians through rejection by the other powers. Both nations had a history of conducting a kind of "missionary" diplomacy—of trying to export to all the world the political doctrines precipitated out of their respective revolutionary origins.

Unaccustomed to their great-power roles, unfamiliar with or even antagonistic to each other, and each believing in the universal applicability of its own particular ideology, America and Russia suddenly found themselves staring eyeball-to-eyeball over the prostrate body of battered Europe—a Europe that had been the traditional center of international affairs. In these circumstances, some sort of confrontation was virtually unavoidable. The wartime "Grand Alliance" of America, Russia, and Britain had been a misbegotten child of necessity, kept alive only until the mutual enemy was crushed. When the hated Hitler fell, suspicion and rivalry between Communistic, despotic Russia and capitalistic, democratic America were all but inevitable. In a fateful progression of events, marked often by misperceptions as well as by genuine conflicts of interest, the two powers provoked each other into a tense standoff known as the "Cold War."

Shaping the Postwar World

Despite these obstacles, the United States did manage at war's end to erect some of the structures that would support Roosevelt's vision of an open world. Meeting at Bretton Woods, New Hampshire, in 1944, the Western Allies established the International Monetary Fund (IMF) to encourage world trade by regulating currency exchange rates. They also founded the International Bank for Reconstruction and Development (World Bank), to promote economic growth in war-ravaged and underdeveloped areas. In contrast to its behavior after World War I, the United States took the lead in creating these important international bodies and supplied most of their funding. Ominously, the Soviets declined to participate.

As flags wept at half-mast, the United Nations Conference opened on schedule, April 25, 1945, despite Roosevelt's dismaying death thirteen days earlier. Unlike Woodrow Wilson, Roosevelt had displayed political tact by choosing both Republican and Democratic senators for the American delegation. Meeting at the San Francisco War Memorial Opera House, representatives from fifty nations fashioned a United Nations charter that strongly resembled the old League of Nations Covenant. It featured a Security Council dominated by the Big Five powers (the United States, Britain, Russia, France, and China), each of whom had the right of veto, and an Assembly that could be controlled by smaller countries. In contrast with the chilly American reception of the League in 1919, the U.S. Senate overwhelmingly approved the document on July 28, 1945, by a vote of eighty-nine to two.

The United Nations, setting up its permanent glass home in New York City, had some gratifying initial successes. It helped preserve peace in Iran, Kashmir, and other trouble spots. It played a large role in creating the new Jewish state of Israel. The U.N. Trusteeship Council guided former colonies to independence. Through such arms as UNESCO (United Nations Educational, Scientific, and Cultural Organization), FAO (Food and Agricultural Organization), and WHO (World Health Organization), the U.N. brought benefits to peoples the world over.

Far less heartening was the failure of the United Nations to control the fearsome new technology of the atom. United States delegate Bernard Baruch called in 1946 for a U.N. agency, free from the great-power veto, to inspect all nuclear facilities to prevent the manufacture of weapons. Fearful of giving up their veto, and suspicious of capitalist "spies" snooping around Mother Russia, the Soviets rejected the Baruch plan. A priceless opportunity to

> Bernard Baruch, in presenting his plan for the control of atomic energy to the United Nations, in June 1946, said: "We are here to make a choice between the quick and the dead. That is our business. Behind the black portent of the new atomic age lies a hope which, seized upon with faith, can work our salvation. If we fail, then we have damned every man to be the slave of fear. Let us not deceive ourselves; we must elect world peace or world destruction."

tame the nuclear monster in its infancy was forever lost. The atomic clock ticked ominously on, overshadowing all relations between the Soviet Union and the United States and casting a pall over the future of the human race.

The Problem of Germany

Hitler's ruined *Reich* posed especially thorny problems for all the wartime Allies. They agreed only that the cancer of nazism had to be cut out of the German body politic, which involved punishing Nazi leaders for war crimes. The Allies joined in trying twenty-two top culprits at Nuremberg, Germany, during 1945–1946. Accusations included committing crimes against the laws of war and humanity and plotting aggressions contrary to solemn treaty pledges.

Justice, Nuremberg-style, was harsh. Twelve of the accused Nazis swung from the gallows, and seven were sentenced to long jail terms. "Foxy Hermann" Göring, whose blubbery chest had once blazed with ribbons, cheated the hangman a few hours before his scheduled execution by swallowing a hidden cyanide capsule. The trials of several small-fry Nazis continued for years. Legal critics in America condemned these proceedings as judicial lynchings, because the victims were tried for offenses that had not been clear-cut crimes when the war began.

Beyond punishing the top Nazis, the Allies could agree on little about postwar Germany. Some American Hitler-haters, noting that an industrialized Germany had been a brutal aggressor, first wanted to dismantle German factories

"Witnesses for the Prosecution," 1945   (Fitzpatrick in the St. Louis Post Dispatch.)

healthy German economy was indispensable to the recovery of Europe. The Americans soon came to appreciate that fact. But the Soviets, deeply fearful of another Hitlerlike invasion, resisted all efforts to revitalize Germany.

Along with Austria, Germany had been divided at war's end into four military occupation zones, each assigned to one of the Big Four powers (France, Britain, America, and Russia). The Western Allies refused to allow Moscow to bleed their zones of the reparations that Stalin believed he had been promised at Yalta. They also began to promote the idea of a reunited Germany. The Communists responded by tightening their grip on their Eastern zone. Before long, it was apparent that Germany would remain permanently divided. West Germany eventually became an independent country, wedded to the West. East Germany, along with other Russian-dominated East European countries, such as Poland and Hungary, virtually disappeared from Western sight behind the "iron curtain" that Stalin clanged down across Europe from the Baltic to the Adriatic.

With Germany now split in two, there remained the problem of the rubble heap known as Berlin. Lying deep within the Soviet zone (see map, p. 824), this beleaguered isle in a red sea had been broken, like Germany as a whole, into sectors occupied by troops of each of the four victorious powers. In 1948, following angry

and reduce the fatherland to a potato patch. The Russians, denied American economic assistance, were determined to rebuild their shattered land by extracting enormous reparations from the Germans. Both these desires clashed headlong with the reality that an industrial,

Postwar Partition of Germany

controversies over German currency reform and four-power control, the Russians abruptly choked off all rail and highway access to Berlin. They evidently reasoned that the Allies would be starved out.

Berlin became a hugely symbolic issue for both sides. At stake was not only the fate of the city but a test of wills between Moscow and Washington. The Americans organized a gigantic airlift in the midst of hair-trigger tension. For nearly a year they ferried thousands of tons of supplies a day to the grateful Berliners, their former enemies. All Western Europeans took heart from this vivid demonstration of America's determination to honor its commitments in Europe. The Russians, their bluff dramatically called, finally lifted their blockade in May 1949. In the same year the governments of the two Germanies, East and West, were formally established. The Cold War had icily congealed.

Crystallizing the Cold War

A crafty Stalin also probed the West's resolve at other sensitive points, including oil-rich Iran. Seeking to secure oil concessions similar to those held by the British and Americans, Stalin in 1946 broke an agreement to remove his troops from Iran's northernmost province. Instead, he used them to aid a rebel movement. Truman sent off a stinging protest, and the Soviet dictator backed down.

Moscow's hard-line policies in Germany, Eastern Europe, and the Middle East wrought a psychological Pearl Harbor. The eyes of Americans were jarred wide open by the Kremlin's apparent unwillingness to continue the wartime partnership. Any remaining goodwill from the period of comradeship-in-arms evaporated in a cloud of dark distrust. "I'm tired of babying the Soviets," Truman remarked privately in 1946, as attitudes on both sides began to harden frostily.

Truman's piecemeal responses to various Soviet challenges took on intellectual coherence in 1947, with the formulation of the "containment doctrine." Crafted by a brilliant young diplomat and Soviet specialist, George F. Kennan, this concept held that Russia, whether czarist or

Berliners Watch Incoming U.S. Relief Airplane, 1948
(Walter Sanders, Life Magazine, © 1948 Time, Inc.)

Communist, was relentlessly expansionary. But the Kremlin was also cautious, Kennan argued, and the flow of Russian power into "every nook and cranny available to it" could be stemmed by "firm and vigilant containment."

Kennan's advice seemed to require a globe-girdling strategy of military and political preparedness. Truman embraced this advice when he formally and publicly adopted a "get-tough-with-Russia" policy in 1947. His first dramatic move was triggered by word that heavily burdened Britain could no longer bear the financial and military load of defending Greece against Communist pressures. If Greece fell, Turkey

> Former Prime Minister Churchill, in a highly controversial speech at Fulton, Missouri (March 1946), warned of Communist Russia's expansiveness: "From Stettin in the Baltic to Trieste in the Adriatic an iron curtain has descended across the Continent."

"Where To?"   *Truman Doctrine, 1947. (Courtesy of Rich-mond Times-Dispatch.)*

would presumably collapse and the strategic eastern Mediterranean would pass into the Soviet orbit.

In a surprise appearance, the president went before Congress, on March 12, 1947, and requested support for what came to be known as the Truman Doctrine. Specifically, he asked for $400 million to bolster Greece and Turkey, which Congress quickly granted. More generally, he declared that "it must be the policy of the United States to support free peoples who are resisting attempted subjugation by armed minorities or by outside pressures"—a sweeping and open-ended commitment of vast and worrisome proportions. Critics then and later charged that Truman had overreacted by promising unlimited support to any tinhorn despot who claimed to be resisting "Communist aggression." Critics also complained that the Truman Doctrine needlessly polarized the world into pro-Soviet and pro-American camps and unwisely construed the Soviet threat as primarily military in nature.

A threat of a different sort loomed in Western Europe—especially France, Italy, and Germany. These key nations were still suffering from the

Marshall Plan Tractors for France   *American-made tractors being unloaded in Le Havre, France, 1948. Aid of this sort helped war-ravaged Europe to revive economically and stabilize politically, while boosting sales of American manufacturing. (UPI/Bettmann Newsphotos.)*

hunger and economic chaos spawned by war. They were in grave danger of being taken over from the inside by Communist parties that could exploit these hardships.

Truman responded with a bold policy. In a commencement address at Harvard University on June 5, 1947, Secretary of State George C. Marshall invited the Europeans to get together and work out a *joint* plan for their economic recovery. If they did so, the United States would provide substantial financial assistance.

The democratic nations of Europe rose enthusiastically to the life-giving bait of the so-called Marshall Plan. They met in Paris in July 1947 to thrash out the details. The Soviets spurned a golden opportunity to share in the plan—or to snarl it hopelessly—when they walked out of the conference.

The Marshall Plan called for spending $12.5 billion over four years in sixteen cooperating countries. Congress at first balked at this huge sum. It looked even more huge when added to the nearly $2 billion the United States had already contributed to European relief through the United Nations Relief and Rehabilitation Administration (UNRRA) and the hefty American contributions to the United Nations, IMF, and World Bank. But a Soviet-sponsored Communist coup in Czechoslovakia finally spurred the legislators to action, and they voted the initial appropriations in April 1948.

Truman's Marshall Plan was a spectacular success. American dollars pumped reviving

Arrogant Capitalist *The Communists stereotyped Truman with moneybags and atomic bombs, defiantly backed by the West European capitalistic statesmen. (From the Soviet satirical magazine* Krokodil.*)*

blood into the economic veins of the anemic Western European nations. Within a few years most of them were exceeding their prewar outputs, as an "economic miracle" drenched Europe in prosperity. The Communist parties in

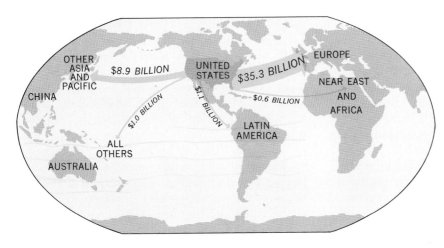

United States Foreign Aid, Military and Economic, 1945–1954 *Marshall Plan aid swelled the outlay for Europe. Note the emphasis on the "developed" world, with relatively little aid going to what are now called "third world" countries.*

"American Motor of the Latest Type" *The conquering Truman uses U.S. moneybags to induce dollar-hungry European nations to draw the U.S. capitalistic chariot. (From the Soviet satirical magazine* Krokodil.*)*

tion of the rising importance of air power). The uniformed heads of each service were brought together as the Joint Chiefs of Staff. Unification was a large and necessary step toward more efficient military management, but it did not end interservice rivalry, as reflected in the annual football contests between the academies at West Point, Annapolis, and Colorado Springs.

The National Security Act also established a National Security Council (NSC) to advise the president on security matters, and a Central Intelligence Agency (CIA) to coordinate the government's foreign fact-gathering. The "Voice of America," authorized by Congress in 1948, began beaming American radio broadcasts behind the iron curtain. In the same year, Congress enacted the nation's first peacetime, military draft, providing for the conscription of selected young men from nineteen to twenty-five years of age. The overshadowing presence of the Selective Service System shaped millions of young people's educational, marital, and career plans in the following quarter-century. One shoe at a time, a war-weary America was reluctantly returning to a war footing.

The Soviet threat was also forcing the divided democracies of Western Europe into an unforeseen degree of unity that was both economic and political. In 1948 Britain, France, Belgium, the Netherlands, and Luxembourg signed a path-breaking defensive alliance at Brussels. A security-seeking America, despite a deep-seated prejudice against peacetime entanglements, was drawn irresistibly toward the new grouping.

The alliance negotiations reached their climax in Washington. There, on April 4, 1949, the representatives of twelve nations, with white-tie pageantry, signed the historic North Atlantic Pact. It stipulated that an attack on one member by an aggressor would be an attack on all and that the signatories would then take such action as they deemed necessary, including "armed force."

Would the United States Senate, despite a strongly favorable public opinion, reject the treaty? Last-ditch isolationists insisted that the scheme was a dangerous involvement that would cause the Republic to become a kind of helpless tail to the European kite. But security

Italy and France lost ground, and these two keystone countries were saved from the westward thrust of communism.

America Begins to Rearm

The struggle to contain Soviet communism resulted in what came to be known as the "Cold War." It was not war, yet it was not peace. The standoff with the Kremlin banished the dreams of tax-fatigued Americans that guns could be beaten into automobiles.

The Soviet menace spurred the unification of the armed services as well as the creation of a huge new national security apparatus. Congress in 1947 passed the National Security Act, creating the Department of Defense. The department was to be housed in the sprawling Pentagon building on the banks of the Potomac and to be headed by a new cabinet officer, the secretary of defense. Under the secretary, but now without cabinet status, were the civilian secretaries of the navy, the army (replacing the old secretary of war), and the air force (a recognicame before tradition, and the Senate registered its approval, on July 21, 1949, by a vote of eighty-two to thirteen.

The pact was truly epochal. Uncle Sam did not assume a hard-and-fast commitment to rush to the aid of any one of the signatories assaulted by Soviet Russia—but there was clearly a moral commitment. Due notice was served on the government in Moscow that it attacked at its peril, and preparations were pushed by the North Atlantic Treaty Organization (NATO) to build up an army for defensive purposes. Membership was boosted to fourteen in 1952 by the inclusion of Greece and Turkey; to fifteen in 1955 by the addition of West Germany.

It seemed evident to Americans that the free nations would have to stand together, or they would be picked off one by one—in daisy-plucking fashion. A willingness to join a peacetime military alliance, despite ancient tradition, revealed a tormenting concern over Soviet aggressions. The Cold War had forced the nation to face cold facts.

Reconstruction and Revolution in Asia

Reconstruction in Japan was simpler than in Germany, primarily because it was largely a one-man show. The occupying American army, under the supreme Allied commander, five-starred General Douglas MacArthur, sat in the driver's seat. In the teeth of violent protests from the Soviet officials, he went inflexibly ahead with his program for the democratization of Japan. Following the pattern in Germany, top Japanese "war criminals" were tried in Tokyo from 1946 to 1948. Eighteen of them were sentenced to prison terms, and seven were hanged.

General MacArthur, as a kind of Yankee mikado, enjoyed stunning success. He made a tremendous impression on the Japanese with his aloof, Greek-god bearing; and the vanquished Nipponese cooperated with their conqueror to an astonishing degree. They were clever enough to see that good behavior and the adoption of democracy would speed the end of the occupation—as it did. A MacArthur-dictated constitution was adopted in 1946. It renounced militarism and introduced Western-style demo-

cratic government—paving the way for a phenomenal economic recovery that within a few decades made Japan one of the world's mightiest industrial powers.

If Japan was a success story for American policymakers, the opposite was true in China, where a bitter civil war had raged for years between Nationalists and Communists. Washington had halfheartedly supported the Nationalist government of Generalissimo Jiang Jieshi in his struggle with the Communists under Mao Zedong (Mao Tse-tung). But the generalissimo gradually began to forfeit the confidence of his people, owing to ineptitude and corruption within his regime. Communist armies swept south overwhelmingly, and late in 1949 Jiang was forced to flee with the remnants of his once-powerful force to the last-hope island of Formosa (Taiwan).

The collapse of Nationalist China was a depressing defeat for America and its allies in the Cold War—the worst to date. At one fell swoop nearly one-fourth of the world's population— some 500 million souls—was swept into the Communist camp. The Republicans, seeking "goats" who had "lost China," assailed President Truman and his bristly mustached, British-appearing secretary of state, Dean Acheson. They insisted that Democratic agencies, wormy with Communists, had deliberately withheld aid from Jiang Jieshi so that he would fall. Democrats heatedly replied that when a regime has forfeited the support of its people, no amount of outside help will save it. Truman, the

---

In August 1949 Secretary of State Acheson explained publicly why America had "dumped" Jiang Jieshi: "The unfortunate but inescapable fact is that the ominous result of the civil war in China was beyond the control of the government of the United States. Nothing that this country did or could have done within the reasonable limits of its capabilities could have changed that result; nothing that was left undone by this country has contributed to it. It was the product of internal Chinese forces, forces which this country tried to influence but could not."

argument ran, did not "lose" China because he never had China to lose. Jiang himself had never controlled all of China.

More bad news came in September 1949, when President Truman shocked the nation by announcing that the Soviets had exploded an atomic bomb—approximately three years earlier than many experts had thought possible. American strategists since 1945 had counted on keeping the Soviets in line by threats of a one-sided aerial attack with nuclear weapons. America's monopoly of this lethal weapon may in fact have restrained the Russians from launching out on a course of armed aggression. But atomic bombing was now a game that two could play.

Matched by the Russians in atomic weaponry, Truman ordered the development of the "H-bomb" (hydrogen bomb)—a city-smashing device many times more lethal than the atomic bomb. The United States exploded its first hydrogen device on a South Pacific atoll in 1952, despite warnings from some scientists that the H-bomb was so powerful that "it becomes a weapon which in practical effect is al-most one of genocide." Famed physicist Albert Einstein, whose theories had helped give birth to the atomic age, declared that "annihilation of any life on earth has been brought within the range of technical possibilities." The Russians exploded their first H-bomb in 1953, and the nuclear arms race entered a perilously competitive cycle. Nuclear "superiority" became a dangerous and delusive dream, as each side tried to overleap the other in the scramble to build more destructive weapons. If the Cold War should ever blaze into a hot war, there might be no world left for the Communists to communize or the democracies to democratize—a chilling thought that restrained both camps. Peace through mutual terror brought a shaky stability to the superpower standoff.

Truman on the Home Front

After the war ended with an atomic bang, America was again confronted with the familiar pattern of demobilization. Millions of men and

The Hydrogen Bomb *This test blast at Bikini Atoll in the Marshall Islands in 1954 was so power-ful that one Japanese fisherman was killed and all twenty-two of his crewmates were seriously injured by radioactive ash that fell on their vessel some eighty miles away. Fishing boats 1,000 miles from Bikini later brought in radioactively contaminated catches. (U.S. Air Force Photo.)*

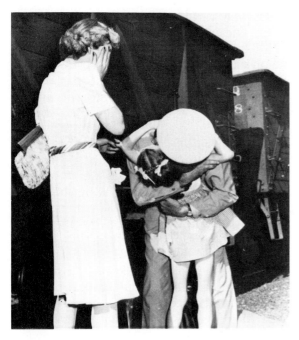

Daddy Comes Home   *(Wide World Photos, Inc.)*

women in the armed forces had to be put back into civilian clothes—a process that went forward fairly rapidly. Congress made generous financial provision for readjustment to nonmilitary life. Several million ex-servicemen and servicewomen, whose schooling in many instances had been interrupted, took advantage of the educational benefits provided by Congress in the so-called GI Bill of Rights. Colleges during the postwar years were crowded to the blackboards, as more than a million eager veterans entered halls of higher learning.

On other fronts, economic demobilization lurched forward. War factories and other installations owned by the government were disposed of at fire-sale prices, partly in the misplaced hope that there could never be another war. Price controls were removed, except for rents, although not until President Truman had waged a slam-bang losing fight with Congress for continued restrictions. Manufacturers and retailers were eager to get back to the old law of "supply and demand." When they did, inflationary pressures were irresistible, as prices giddily levitated by 33 percent in 1946–1947.

The G-I Bill   *Financed by the federal government, thousands of World War II veterans crowded into college classrooms in the 1940s. Here a fresh crop of ex-soldier-students lays in supplies for the new term (UPI/Bettmann Newsphotos.)*

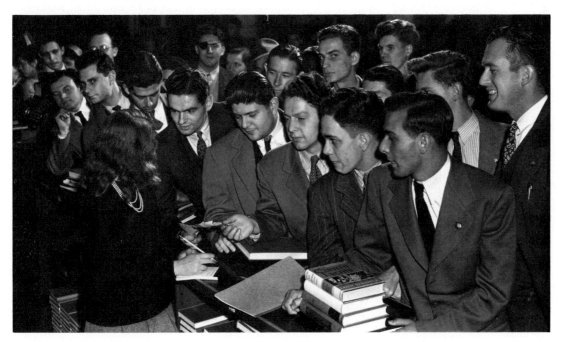

An epidemic of strikes swept the country, and during 1946 alone some 4.6 million laborers laid down their tools. Especially crippling were work stoppages in such industries as steel, motorcar manufacturing, and bituminous coal.

The growing power of the organized workers had meanwhile proved deeply disturbing to many conservatives. Asserting that big labor was now as much a menace as big business had ever been, die-hard industrialists demanded a showdown. The Republicans gained control of Congress in 1947, for the first time in fourteen years, and proceeded to call the tune. Balding, blunt-spoken Robert A. Taft of Ohio, son of the former president and one of the Republican big guns of the Senate, became cosponsor of a controversial new labor law known as the Taft-Hartley Act. It was passed in June 1947, over President Truman's vigorous veto.

"Where Does He Fit In?" *Doubts about the Taft-Hartley Act, 1949. (The Albany, New York,* Knickerbocker News. *By permission.)*

The new Taft-Hartley law promptly became a storm center. Partly designed to protect the public, this piece of legislation contained a number of provisions that caused labor leaders to condemn the entire act as a "slave labor law." Especially irksome were the provisions outlawing the closed (all-union) shop, while making unions liable for damages resulting from jurisdictional disputes among themselves. Union leaders were also required to take a non-Communist oath, though employers were not forced to do so. Despite labor's pained outcries, Taft-Hartleyism, while annoying, did not cripple the labor movement. The AF of L by 1950 could boast 8 million members and the CIO 6 million members.

Underprivileged black laborers, to an increasing degree, were sharing the war-spawned prosperity. Southern congressional representatives were blocking President Truman's recommendations for a national fair employment practices law and for civil rights legislation. But the plight of black "second-class citizens" was being generally improved by state legislation and changing public attitudes. Symptomatic of a new day for Afro-Americans was the breaking of the color bar in big-league baseball. Amid less controversy than predicted, the Brooklyn Dodgers led the way in 1947, when they signed a star black second baseman, Jack Roosevelt ("Jackie") Robinson.

Ferreting Out Alleged Communists

One of the most active Cold War fronts was at home, where a new anti-red chase was in full cry. Many nervous citizens feared that Communist spies, paid with Moscow gold, were undermining the government and treacherously misdirecting foreign policy. In 1947 Truman launched a massive "loyalty" program. The attorney general drew up a list of ninety supposedly disloyal organizations, none of which was given the right to prove its innocence. A Loyalty Review Board investigated more than 3 million federal employees, some 3,000 of whom either resigned or were dismissed, none under formal indictment.

Individual states likewise became intensely security-conscious. Loyalty oaths in increasing numbers were demanded of employees, especially teachers. Disagreeable incidents involving freedom of speech and teaching burst into the headlines. The gnawing question for many earnest Americans was: could the nation continue to enjoy traditional freedoms in a Cold War climate?

In 1949 eleven Communists were brought before a New York jury for violating the Smith Act of 1940, the first peacetime antisedition law since 1798. Hiding behind the very Constitution they were attempting to destroy, the defendants were convicted of advocating the overthrow of the American government by force and were sent to prison.

The House of Representatives in 1938 had established a Committee on Un-American Activities to investigate "subversion." In 1948 committee member Richard M. Nixon, an ambitious red-catcher, led the chase after Alger Hiss, a prominent ex–New Dealer and a distinguished member of the "eastern establishment." Accused of being a Communist agent in the 1930s, Hiss demanded the right to defend himself. He dramatically met his chief accuser before the Un-American Activities Committee in August 1948. Hiss denied everything but was

> In his inaugural address, January 1949, Truman said: "Communism is based on the belief that man is so weak and inadequate that he is unable to govern himself, and therefore requires the rule of strong masters. . . . Democracy is based on the conviction that man has the moral and intellectual capacity, as well as the inalienable right, to govern himself with reason and justice."

convicted of perjury in 1950 and sentenced to five years in prison.

In February 1950 Senator Joseph R. McCarthy, a Wisconsin Republican, spectacularly charged that there were scores of known Communists in the Department of State. He proved utterly unable to substantiate his accusation, and many Americans, including President Truman, began to fear that the red-hunt was turning into a witch-hunt. In 1950 Truman vetoed the McCarran Internal Security Bill, which among other provisions authorized the president to arrest and detain suspicious persons during an "internal security emergency." Critics protested that the bill smacked of police-state,

Feelings Run High over Communist Subversives Demonstrators for and against convicted atomic spies Julius and Ethel Rosenberg parade in front of the White House in 1953. For details, see p. 834. (United Press International photo.)

concentration-camp tactics. But the congressional guardians of the Republic's liberties enacted the bill over Truman's veto.

The stunning success of the Soviet scientists in developing an atomic bomb was presumably due, at least in part, to the cleverness of Communist spies in stealing American secrets. Notorious among those Americans and Britishers who had allegedly "leaked" atomic data to Moscow were two American citizens, Julius and Ethel Rosenberg. They were convicted in 1951 of espionage and, after prolonged appeals, went to the electric chair in 1953—the only people in American history ever executed in peacetime for espionage. Their sensational trial and electrocution, combined with fear of the A-bomb, rallied public support for look-under-the-bed congressional red-hunters.

Democratic Divisions in 1948

Attacking high prices and "High-Tax Harry" Truman, the Republicans had won control of Congress in the congressional elections of 1946. Their prospects had seldom looked rosier as they gathered in Philadelphia to choose their 1948 presidential candidate. They noisily renominated warmed-over New York Governor Thomas E. Dewey, still as debonair as if he had stepped out of a bandbox.

Also gathering in Philadelphia, Democratic politicos looked without enthusiasm on their hand-me-down president and sang, "I'm Just Mild about Harry." But their "dump Truman" movement collapsed when war hero Dwight D. Eisenhower refused to be drafted. The peppery president, unwanted but undaunted, was then chosen in the face of violent opposition by southern delegates. They were alienated by his strong stand in favor of civil rights for blacks, who now mustered many votes in the big-city ghettoes of the North.

Truman's nomination split the party wide open. Embittered southern Democrats from thirteen states, like their fire-eating forebears of 1860, next met in their own convention, in Birmingham, Alabama, with Confederate flags brashly in evidence. Amid scenes of heated defiance, these "Dixiecrats" nominated Governor J. Strom Thurmond of South Carolina on a States' Rights party ticket.

To add to the confusion within Democratic ranks, former Vice-President Henry A. Wallace threw his hat into the ring. Having parted company with the administration over its get-tough-with-Russia policy, he was nominated at Philadelphia by the new Progressive party—a bizarre collection of disgruntled former New Dealers, starry-eyed pacifists, progressives, well-meaning liberals, and Communist-fronters.

Wallace, a vigorous if misguided liberal, assailed Uncle Sam's "dollar imperialism" from the stump. This so-called Pied Piper of the Politburo took an apparently pro-Soviet line that earned him drenchings with rotten eggs in hostile cities. But to many Americans, Wallace raised the only hopeful voice in the deepening gloom of the Cold War.

With the Democrats deeply split three ways and the Republican congressional victory of 1946 just past, Dewey's victory seemed assured. Succumbing to overconfidence engendered by his massive lead in public-opinion polls, the cold, smug Dewey confined himself to dispensing soothing-syrup generalities like "Our future lies before us."

The seemingly doomed Truman, with little money and few active supporters, had to rely on his "gut-fighter" instincts and folksy personality. Whistle-stopping the country to deliver some three hundred "give 'em hell" speeches, he lashed out at the Taft-Hartley "slave labor" law and the "do-nothing" Republican Congress while whipping up support for his program of civil rights, improved labor benefits, and health insurance. "Pour it on 'em, Harry!" cried increasingly large and enthusiastic crowds, as the pugnacious president rained a barrage of verbal uppercuts on his opponent.

On election night the Chicago *Tribune* ran off an edition with the headline "DEWEY DEFEATS TRUMAN." But in the morning it turned out that "President" Dewey had embarrassingly snatched defeat from the jaws of victory. Truman had swept to a stunning triumph, to the complete bewilderment of politicians, pollsters, prophets, and pundits. Even though

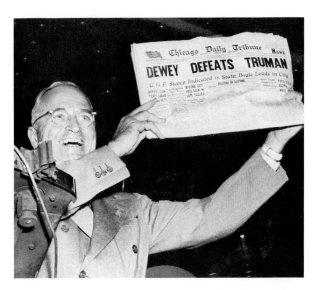

"That Ain't the Way I Heard It"! Truman Wins. (UPI/Bettmann Newsphotos.)

Thurmond took away 39 electoral votes in the South, Truman won 303 electoral votes, primarily from the South, Midwest, and West. Dewey's 189 electoral votes came principally from the East. The popular vote was 24,179,345 for Truman, 21,991,291 for Dewey, 1,176,125 for Thurmond, and 1,157,326 for Wallace. To make the victory sweeter, the Democrats regained control of Congress as well.

Truman's victory rested on farmers, workers, and blacks, all of whom saw threats from the Republicans. Republican overconfidence and Truman's lone-wolf, never-say-die campaign also won him the support of many Americans who admired his "guts." No one wanted him, someone remarked, except the people. Dewey, in contrast, struck many voters as arrogant, evasive, and wooden. When Dewey took the platform to give a speech, said one commentator, "he comes out like a man who has been mounted on casters and given a tremendous shove from behind."

Smilingly confident, Truman sounded a clarion note, in the fourth point of his inaugural address, when he called for a "bold new program" ("Point Four"). The plan was to lend American money and technical aid to underdeveloped lands to help them help themselves. Truman wanted to spend millions to keep underprivileged peoples from becoming Communists rather than spend billions to shoot them after they had become Communists. This farseeing program was officially launched in 1950, and it brought badly needed assistance to impoverished countries, notably in Latin America, Africa, the Near East, and the Far East.

At home, Truman outlined a sweeping "Fair Deal" program in his 1949 message to Congress. It called for badly needed housing, full employment, a higher minimum wage, better farm price supports, new TVAs, and an extension of Social Security. But most of the Fair Deal fell victim to Congressional opposition from Republicans and southern Democrats. The only major successes came in raising the minimum wage, providing for public housing in the Housing Act of 1949, and extending old-age insurance to many more beneficiaries in the Social Security Act of 1950.

The Korean Volcano Erupts (1950)

Korea, the Land of the Morning Calm, heralded a new and more ominous phase of the Cold War—a shooting phase—in June 1950.

When Japan collapsed in 1945, Russian troops had accepted the Japanese surrender north of the thirty-eighth parallel on the Korean peninsula, and American troops had done likewise south of that line. Both superpowers professed to want the reunification of Korea, but each helped to set up rival regimes above and below the parallel.

By 1949, when the Russians and Americans had both withdrawn their forces, the entire peninsula was a bristling armed camp, with two hostile regimes eyeing each other suspiciously. Secretary of State Acheson seemed to wash his hands of the dispute early in 1950, when he declared in a memorable speech that Korea was outside the essential United States defense perimeter in the Pacific.

The explosion came on June 25, 1950. Spearheaded by Soviet-made tanks, North Korean army columns rumbled across the thirty-eighth parallel. Caught flat-footed, the South Korean forces were shoved back southward to a dangerously tiny defensive area around Pusan, their weary backs to the sea.

President Truman sprang quickly into the breach, for he remembered that the old League of Nations had died from inaction. The invasion seemed to provide devastating proof of a fundamental premise in the "containment doctrine" that shaped Washington's foreign policy: that even a slight relaxation of America's guard was an invitation to Communist aggression somewhere.

The Korean invasion also provided the occasion for a vast expansion of the American military. Truman's National Security Council had recommended in a famous document of 1950 (known as National Security Council Memorandum Number 68, or NSC-68) that the United States should quadruple its defense spending. Buried at the time because it was considered politically impossible to implement, NSC-68 was resurrected by the Korean crisis. Truman now ordered a massive military buildup, well beyond what was necessary for the immediate purposes of the war. Soon the United States had 3.5 million men under arms and was spending $50 billion per year on the defense budget—some 13 percent of the gross national product.

Truman took full advantage of temporary Russian absence from the United Nations Security Council on June 25, 1950, when he obtained a unanimous condemnation of North Korea as an aggressor. The Council also called upon all U.N. members, including the United States, to "render every assistance" to restore peace. Two days later, without consulting Congress, Truman ordered American air and naval units to support South Korea. Before the week was out, he also ordered General Douglas MacArthur's Japan-based troops into action alongside the beleaguered South Koreans.

Officially, the United States was simply participating in a United Nations "police action." But in fact, the United States made up the overwhelming bulk of the U.N. contingents, and General MacArthur, appointed U.N. commander of the entire operation, took his orders from Washington, not from the Security Council.

The Military Seesaw in Korea

Rather than fight his way out of the southern Pusan perimeter, MacArthur launched a daring amphibious landing behind the enemy's lines at Inchon. This bold gamble, on September 15, 1950, succeeded brilliantly; within two weeks the North Koreans had retreated pell-mell behind the "sanctuary" of the thirty-eighth parallel. Truman's avowed intention was to restore South Korea to its former borders, but the pursuing South Koreans had already crossed the thirty-eighth parallel, and there seemed little point in permitting the North Koreans to regroup and come again. The U.N. Assembly tacitly authorized a crossing by MacArthur, whom President Truman ordered northward, provided that there was no intervention in force by the Chinese or Soviets.

The Americans thus raised the stakes in Korea, and in so doing, they quickened the fears of another potential player in this dangerous game. The Chinese Communists had publicly warned that they would not sit idly by and watch hostile troops approach the strategic Yalu River boundary between Korea and China. But MacArthur pooh-poohed all predictions of an effective intervention by the Chinese and reportedly boasted that he would "have the boys home by Christmas."

MacArthur guessed wrong. In November 1950 hordes of Chinese "volunteers" fell upon his rashly overextended lines and hurled the U.N. forces reeling back down the peninsula. The fighting now sank into a frostbitten stalemate on the icy terrain near the thirty-eighth parallel.

An imperious MacArthur, humiliated by this rout, pressed for drastic retaliation. He favored a blockade of the China coast and bombardment of Chinese bases in Manchuria. But Washington policymakers, with anxious eyes on Russia, refused to enlarge the already costly conflict. The chairman of the Joint Chiefs of Staff declared that a wider clash in Asia would be "the wrong war, at the wrong place, at the wrong time, and with the wrong enemy." Europe, not Asia, was the administration's first concern; and Russia, not China, loomed as the more threatening foe.

June 25, 1950   Sept. 14, 1950   Nov. 25, 1950   July 27, 1953

The Shifting Front in Korea

Two-fisted General MacArthur felt that he was being asked to fight with one hand tied behind his back. He sneered at the concept of a "limited war" and insisted that "there is no substitute for victory." When the general began to take issue publicly with presidential policies, Truman had no choice but to remove the insubordinate MacArthur from command (April 11, 1951). The imperious war hero, a legend in his own mind, returned to an uproarious welcome, while Truman was condemned as a "pig," an "imbecile," a "Judas," and an appeaser of "Communist Russia and Communist China." In July 1951 truce discussions began in a rude field tent near the firing line but were almost immediately snagged on the issue of prisoner exchange. They dragged on unproductively for nearly two years—while men continued to die.

The Advent of Eisenhower

Democratic prospects in the forthcoming presidential election of 1952 were blighted by the military deadlock, the clash with MacArthur, war-bred inflation, and the whiffs of scandal from the White House. Dispirited Democrats, convening in Chicago, nominated a reluctant Adlai E. Stevenson, the witty, eloquent, and idealistic governor of Illinois. Republicans headed

off a determined attempt by the isolationist wing of their party to nominate "Mr. Republican," Ohio Senator Robert A. Taft. Instead, they enthusiastically chose General Dwight D.

Truman Takes the Heat *(Courtesy,* Buffalo Courier Express; *photo by Barry Donahue.)*

The Republicans' Choice, 1952 *Nominee Eisenhower and his vice-presidential running mate Nixon greet the delegates. (Wide World Photos, Inc.)*

erywhere testified. His ruddy face, captivating grin, and glowing personality made him a perfect candidate in the dawning new age of television politics. He had an authentic hero's credentials as wartime supreme commander of the Allied forces in Europe, army chief of staff after the war, and the first supreme commander of NATO from 1950 to 1952. He had also been "civilianized" by a brief term as president of Columbia University, from 1948 to 1950.

Striking a grandfatherly, nonpartisan pose, Eisenhower left the rough campaigning to Nixon, who relished pulling no punches. The vice-presidential candidate lambasted his opponents with charges that they had cultivated corruption, caved in on Korea, and coddled Communists. He particularly blasted the intellectual ("egghead") Stevenson as "Adlai the appeaser," with a "Ph.D. from [Secretary of State] Dean Acheson's College of Cowardly Communist Containment."

Nixon himself faltered when reports surfaced of a secretly financed "slush fund" he had tapped while holding a seat in the Senate. Eisenhower seriously considered dropping him from the ticket, but a scared Nixon went on national television with a theatrical appeal filled with self-pity, during which he referred to the family cocker spaniel, Checkers. This "Checkers speech" was so heart-tugging as to save him his place on the ticket.

Eisenhower on the first ballot. As something of a concession to the hard-line anti-Communist Taft supporters, the convention selected as "Ike's" running mate California Senator Richard M. Nixon, who had distinguished himself as a relentless red-hunter.

Eisenhower was already the most popular American of his time, as "I Like Ike" buttons ev-

Presidential Election of 1952 (with electoral vote by state) *A Democrat quipped that "If the voters liked the Republicans the way they liked Ike, the two-party system would be in bad shape." Fortunately for Democrats, Eisenhower scored a personal, not a party, victory. Republicans won minuscule majorities in Congress, majorities that disappeared in the congressional elections two years later.*

Eisenhower—Republican

Stevenson—Democratic

Korean War Scene *Grief-stricken American soldier whose buddy has been killed is being comforted, while a medical corpsman fills out casualty tags. (U.S. Army photograph.)*

The outcome of the presidential election was never really in doubt. Given an extra prod by Eisenhower's last-minute pledge to go personally to Korea to end the war, the voters massively declared for "Ike." He garnered 33,963,234 votes to Stevenson's 27,314,992. He cracked the solid South wide open, ringing up 442 electoral votes to 89 for his opponent. "Ike" not only ran far ahead of his ticket but managed to pull enough Republicans into office on his military coattails to ensure GOP control of the new Congress by a paper-thin margin.

True to his campaign pledge, President-elect Eisenhower undertook a flying three-day visit to Korea in December 1952. But even a glamorous "Ike" could not immediately budge the peace negotiations off dead center. Seven long months later, after Eisenhower had threatened to use atomic weapons, an armistice was finally signed but was repeatedly violated in succeeding decades.

The brutal and futile fighting had lasted three years. About fifty-four thousand Americans lay dead, joined by perhaps more than a million Chinese, North Koreans, and South Koreans. Tens of billions of American dollars had been poured down the Asian sinkhole. Yet this terrible toll in blood and treasure bought only a return to the conditions of 1950; Korea remained divided at the thirty-eighth parallel. Americans took what little comfort they could from the fact that communism had been "contained" and that the bloodletting had been "limited" to something less than full-scale global war. The shooting had ended, but the Cold War remained frigidly unthawed.

Varying Viewpoints

Who was to blame for starting the Cold War? For nearly a generation after World War II, American historians generally agreed that the suspicious and grasping Soviets were almost solely responsible. This "orthodox" appraisal fitted comfortably with the traditional view of the United States as a God-blessed land with an idealistic foreign policy. But in the 1960s a revisionist interpretation began to flower, powerfully reinforced by revulsion against American atrocities in Vietnam. "New Left" revisionists attempted to reverse the orthodox view. They argued that the Soviets had understandably defensive intentions at the end of World War II and that the United States had behaved aggressively and irresponsibly. Some of these critics pointed an accusing finger at Truman. They alleged that he had abandoned Roosevelt's conciliatory approach and adopted a bullying attitude, emboldened by America's atomic monopoly. More radical revisionists like the Kolkos found the roots of American aggression before Truman's time in long-standing policies of economic expansion.

In the 1970s a "neoorthodox" interpretation emerged. Historians of this school, like John L. Gaddis, still place most of the blame for the Cold War on the Soviet Union, but they concede that American policies helped precipitate the conflict. They also note how the constraints of domestic politics and the miscalculations of American leaders led a nation in search of international security into a dangerous Cold War.

This historical debate over the origins of the Cold War has compelled the recognition that the United States did have vital interests at stake in postwar diplomacy, and that policymakers pursued those interests with vigor. But is self-interest necessarily immoral? Is security a one-way street? Can the blame ever be exclusively with one side in a complex international dispute? Some critics charge that the revisionist argument is stamped with its own brand of American provincialism, since it portrays the entire postwar world as shaped preponderantly by America's counterrevolutionary "imperialism." And so long as Soviet archives are closed, Russian intentions will remain a matter of conjecture.

Select Readings

Primary Source Documents

George F. Kennan's "long telegram," *Foreign Relations of the United States, 1946* (Vol. 6, 1969 pp. 696–709,* outlined the containment doctrine that would form the foundation of American foreign policy in the Cold War era. Harry S Truman first applied the containment doctrine when he enunciated the Truman Doctrine, *Congressional Record,* 80th Congress, 1st Session, p. 1981 (1947).* Joe McCarthy's vitriol can be found in his *McCarthyism: The Fight for America* (1952).*

Secondary Sources

See the titles cited in the preceding chapter by John L. Gaddis, Lloyd Gardner, Gar Alperovitz, Martin J. Sherwin, Herbert Feis, and Gabriel Kolko. Consult also Gaddis's *Strategies of Containment* (1982) and Joyce and Gabriel Kolko's *The Limits of Power: The World and United States Foreign Policy, 1945–1954* (1972), which roundly condemns Washington's actions. Useful surveys of the diplomatic history of the period, all of them in varying degrees critical of American policy, are Stephen Ambrose, *Rise to Globalism: American Foreign Policy since 1938* (rev. ed., 1983); Walter LaFeber, *America, Russia and the Cold War, 1945–1984* (5th ed., 1985); and Daniel Yergin, *Shattered Peace* (1977). Among the few useful books on the Russian side is Vojtech Mastny, *Russia's Road to the Cold War* (1979). Broader accounts that include discussion of domestic events are Donald R. McCoy, *The Presidency of Harry S Truman* (1984); Eric Goldman, *The Crucial Decade—*

and After: America, 1945–1960 (1961); Alonzo L. Hamby, *Beyond the New Deal: Harry S Truman and American Liberalism* (1973); Barton J. Bernstein, ed., *Politics and Policies of the Truman Administration* (1970); and Robert J. Donovan, *Conflict and Crisis: The Presidency of Harry S Truman* (1977). The implications of the election of 1948 are examined in Samuel Lubell's perceptive *The Future of American Politics* (1952). Various aspects of foreign policy are analyzed in Bruce Kuklick, *American Policy and the Division of Germany* (1972); Thomas A. Bailey, *The Marshall Plan Summer* (1978); James Tent, *Mission on the Rhine* (1983); and Timothy P. Ireland, *Creating the Entangling Alliance: The Origins of the North Atlantic Treaty Organization* (1981). The Asian side is treated in Akira Iriye, *The Cold War in Asia* (1974); Russell D. Buhite, *Soviet-American Relations in Asia, 1945–1954* (1982); and Robert M. Blum, *Drawing the4 Line: The Origins of the American Containment Policy in East Asia* (1982). Korea is discussed in David Rees, *Korea: The Limited War* (1964). On the "red scare" at home, see Richard M. Freeland, *The Truman Doctrine and the Origins of McCarthyism* (1971), and Thomas Reeves, *The Life and Times of Joe McCarthy* (1982), as well as David M. Oshinsky, *A Conspiracy So Immense: The World of Joe McCarthy* (1983). Daniel Bell, ed., *The Radical Right* (1963), places McCarthyism in a larger context. See also David W. Reinhard, *The Republican Right since 1945* (1983). Examinations of the impact of the Cold War on American culture include Victor Navasky, *Naming Names* (1980); Nora Sayre, *Running Time: The Films of the Cold War* (1982); Nancy Schwartz, *The Hollywood Writers' Wars* (1982); and Michael P. Rogin, *McCarthy and the Intellectuals* (1967). Valuable personal reflections by policymakers include Truman's own *Year of Decisions* (1955) and *Years of Trial and Hope* (1956); George F. Kennan, *Memoirs, 1925–1950* (1967); Dean Acheson, *Present at the Creation* (1969); and Charles Bohlen, *Witness to History* (1973).

42

The Eisenhower Era, 1953–1960

> *Every warship launched, every rocket fired signifies . . . a theft from those who hunger and are not fed, those who are cold and are not clothed.*
>
> Dwight D. Eisenhower, April 16, 1953

"Ike" Takes Command

In Dwight Eisenhower, the man and the hour apparently met. The nation sorely needed a respite from twenty years of depression and war. Yet the American people in the 1950s were unexpectedly dug into the front lines of the Cold War abroad and dangerously divided at home over the explosive issues of Communist subversion and civil rights. They longed for reassuring leadership, and "Ike" seemed ready to give it to them.

As a military commander, Eisenhower had cultivated a leadership style that self-consciously projected an image of sincerity, fairness, and optimism. He enjoyed remarkable success in harmonizing the efforts of potentially quarrelsome allies. He had been widely perceived during the war as an "unmilitary" general, and in the White House he similarly struck the pose of an "unpolitical" president, serenely above the petty partisan fray. He also shrewdly knew that his greatest "asset" was his enjoyment of the "affection and respect of our citizenry," as he confided to his diary in 1949.

"Ike" thus seemed ideally suited to soothe the anxieties of his troubled countrymen, much as a distinguished and well-loved grandfather brings stability to his family. He played this role well as he presided over a decade of shaky peace and shining prosperity. Yet critics charged that he unwisely hoarded the "asset" of his immense popularity, rather than spend it for a good cause, and that he cared more for social harmony than for social justice.

One of the first problems Eisenhower had to contend with was the swelling popularity and fearful power of Senator Joseph R. McCarthy, the anti-Communist "crusader." McCarthy had burst upon the national scene in February 1950, when he charged in a public speech that Secretary of State Dean Acheson was knowingly employing 205 Communist party members in the Department of State. Pressed to reveal the names, McCarthy at first conceded that there were only 57 genuine Communists and in the end failed to find even one. His Republican colleagues nevertheless realized the political usefulness of this kind of attack on the Democratic administration. Even the supposedly fair-minded Senator Robert Taft urged McCarthy, "If one case doesn't work, try another." Ohio's Senator John Bricker reportedly said, "Joe, you're a dirty s.o.b., but there are times when you've got to have an s.o.b. around, and this is one of them."

McCarthy flourished in the seething Cold War atmosphere of suspicion and fear. He was not the first nor even the most effective anti-red, but he was the most ruthless and did the most damage to American traditions of fair play and free speech. Elected to the Senate on the basis of a trumped-up war-hero record ("Con-

gress needs a tail-gunner"), McCarthy was just an obscure junior senator until he exploded his bombshell announcement in 1950 of Communists in the State Department. For the next four years "low-blow Joe" proved a master at manipulating the media and playing upon the anxieties of politicians and the public. The careers of countless officials, writers, actors, and others were ruined after McCarthy had "named" them, often unfairly, as Communists or Communist sympathizers.

As McCarthy's accusations spread ever more widely, his rhetoric grew bolder. Democrats, he charged, "bent to the whispered pleas from the lips of traitors." General George Marshall, former army chief of staff and ex–secretary of state, was denounced as "part of a conspiracy so immense and an infamy so black as to dwarf any previous venture in the history of man."

Politicians trembled in the face of such onslaughts, especially when opinion polls showed that a majority of the American people approved of McCarthy. Further, his intervention in certain key senatorial elections brought resounding defeat for his enemies. Eisenhower privately loathed McCarthy but publicly tried to stay out of his way, saying, "I will not get in the gutter with that guy." Trying to appease the brash demagogue from Wisconsin, Eisenhower allowed him, in effect, to control personnel policy at the State Department. One baleful result was

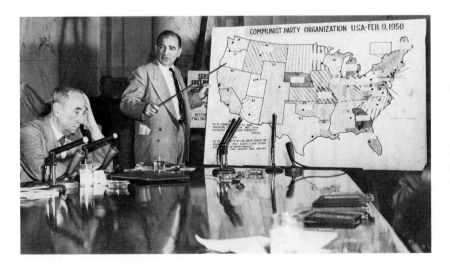

Exposing "Reds" *Senator McCarthy makes a point at the army-McCarthy hearings in 1954 while army counsel Joseph Welch ponders a reply. McCarthy declared in a speech in 1951: "Let me assure you that regardless of how high-pitched becomes the squealing and screaming of those left-wing, bleeding-heart, phony liberals, this battle is going to go on." (United Press International photo.)*

> Curiously, the Senate "condemned" McCarthy, not on the grounds that he assailed fellow Americans, but on the grounds that he failed to cooperate with a Senate investigating committee regarding matters that "affected the honor of the Senate and instead, repeatedly abused members who were trying to carry out assigned duties, thereby obstructing the constitutional processes of the Senate. . . ." On the other hand, a Fort Worth, Texas, newspaper wrote, "Joe McCarthy was slowly tortured to death by the pimps of the Kremlin."

severe damage to the morale and effectiveness of the professional foreign service.

McCarthy finally bent the bow too far. The nominal end of the Korean War partly cooled the feverish atmosphere in which he had thrived. When he attacked the United States Army, he at last met his match. The embattled military men fought back in thirty-five days of televised hearings in the spring of 1954. Up to 20 million Americans at a time watched in fascination as a boorish, surly McCarthy publicly cut his own throat by parading his essential meanness and irresponsibility. A few months later the Senate formally condemned him for "conduct unbecoming a member."

Three years later, unwept and unsung, McCarthy died. But *McCarthyism* has passed into the English language as a label for the dangerous forces of unfairness and fear that a democratic society can unleash only at its peril. The senator actually hurt his alleged cause by making Americans more afraid of the supposed Communists in their midst than of the real Communists in Moscow.

The Blacks Surge Forward

Black Americans had racked up only a few minor gains since New Deal days. Most still lived in the South, where state laws kept them strictly separated from whites in all public places—and most objectionably, in the schools. Only 20 percent of eligible southern blacks

were registered to vote. President Truman in 1948 had ended segregation in the federal service and had ordered "equality of treatment and opportunity" in the armed forces. The military brass had at first protested that "the army is not a sociological laboratory," but manpower shortages in Korea forced the integration of combat units, without the predicted loss of effectiveness. Yet Congress stubbornly resisted passing civil rights legislation, and President Eisenhower showed no real signs of interest in the racial issue. Within the government, initiative thus passed to the Supreme Court.

Breaking the path for civil rights advances was broad-jawed Chief Justice Earl Warren, former governor of California. Elevated to the supreme bench by Eisenhower, Warren shocked the president and other traditionalists with his active judicial intervention in previously taboo social issues. Publicly snubbed and privately criticized by President Eisenhower, Warren persisted in encouraging the Court to apply his straightforward populist principles to its interpretation of the Constitution: in short, legislation by the judiciary, in default of legislation by the Congress.

The unanimous decision of the Warren Court in *Brown* v. *Board of Education of Topeka, Kansas,* in May 1954 was epochal. In a forceful opinion, the learned justices ruled that segregation in the public schools was "inherently unequal" and thus unconstitutional. The uncompromising sweep of the decision startled conservatives like an exploding time bomb, for it reversed the Court's earlier declaration in *Plessy* v. *Ferguson* (1896) that "separate but equal" facilities were allowable under the Constitution. That doctrine was now dead. Desegregation, the justices insisted, must go ahead with "all deliberate speed."

The Border States generally made reasonable efforts to comply with this ruling, but in the Deep South diehards organized "massive resistance" against the Court's attack on the sacred principle of "separate but equal." More than a hundred southern congressional representatives and senators signed a "Declaration of Constitutional Principles" in 1956, pledging their unyielding resistance to desegregation. Several states diverted public funds to hastily created

In the desegregation decision of 1954, the Supreme Court quoted approvingly from a lower court: "Segregation of white and colored children in public schools has a detrimental effect upon the colored children. The impact is greater when it has the sanction of the law; for the policy of separating the races is usually interpreted as denoting the inferiority of the Negro group. A sense of inferiority affects the motivation of a child to learn. Segregation . . . has a tendency to retard the educational and mental development of Negro children. . . ."

"private" schools, for there the integration order was more difficult to apply. Throughout the South, white citizens' councils, sometimes with fire and hemp, thwarted attempts to make integration a reality. Ten years after the Court's momentous ruling, fewer than 2 percent of the eligible blacks in the Deep South states were sitting in classrooms with whites.

Crisis at Little Rock

President Eisenhower was little inclined toward promoting integration. He shied away from employing his vast popularity, and the prestige of his office, to educate white Americans about the need for racial justice. His personal attitudes may have helped to restrain him. He had grown up in an all-white town and spent his career in a segregated army. He had advised against integration of the armed forces in 1948 and had criticized Truman's call for a permanent Fair Employment Practices Commission. He complained that the Supreme Court's decision in *Brown* v. *Board of Education* had upset "the customs and convictions of at least two generations of Americans," and he steadfastly refused to issue a public statement endorsing the Court's conclusions. "I do not believe," he explained, "that prejudices, even palpably unjustifiable prejudices, will succumb to compulsion."

But in September 1957 "Ike" was forced to act. Orval Faubus, the governor of Arkansas,

Integration at Little Rock, 1957 *While white mobs jeered angrily at the first black students entering Central High School, federal troops, with bayonets fixed, enforced the law. (Left, Wide World Photos, Inc., right, UPI/Bettmann Archives.)*

Martin Luther King, Jr., and His Wife Coretta Arrested
King and his wife were arrested for the first time in Montgomery, Alabama, in 1955 while organizing a bus boycott. (Charles Moore, Black Star.)

mobilized the National Guard to prevent nine black students from enrolling in Little Rock's Central High School. Confronted with a direct challenge to federal authority, Eisenhower sent troops to escort the children to their classes.

In the same year, Congress passed the first Civil Rights Act since Reconstruction days. Eisenhower characteristically reassured a southern senator that the legislation represented "the mildest civil rights bill possible." It set up a permanent Civil Rights Commission to investigate violations of civil rights and authorized federal injunctions to protect voting rights.

Blacks meanwhile had been taking the civil rights movement into their own hands. On a historic day in December 1955, Mrs. Rosa Parks, a college-educated black seamstress, boarded a bus in Montgomery, Alabama, took a seat in the "whites only" section, and refused to give it up. The incident touched off a yearlong black boycott of the city buses, while catapulting to prominence the chief organizer, the Reverend Martin Luther King, Jr. The discipline and dignity of the boycotters, plus the inspirational leadership of Martin Luther King, Jr., heralded a new era of confidence and power for the South's restive blacks.

Eisenhower Republicanism at Home

The balding, sixty-two-year-old General Eisenhower had entered the White House in 1953 pledging his administration to a philosophy of "dynamic conservatism." "In all those things which deal with people, be liberal, be human," he advised. But when it came to "people's money, or their economy, or their form of government, be conservative." This balanced, middle-of-the-road course harmonized with the depression-haunted and war-weary mood of the times. Some critics called "Ike's" presidency a case of "the bland leading the bland."

Above all, Eisenhower strove to balance the federal budget and guard the Republic from what he called "creeping socialism." The former supreme allied commander put the brakes on Truman's enormous military buildup, though defense spending still soaked up some 10 percent of the gross national product. True to his small-government philosophy, Eisenhower supported the transfer of control over offshore oil fields from the federal government to the states. "Ike" also tried to curb the TVA by encouraging a private power company to build a generating plant to compete with the massive public utility spawned by the New Deal. Speaking of the TVA, Eisenhower reportedly said, "By God, if ever we could do it, before we leave here, I'd like to see us *sell* the whole thing, but I suppose we can't go that far." "Ike's" secretary of health, education, and welfare condemned free distribution of Salk antipolio vaccine as "socialized medicine." Secretary of Agriculture Ezra Taft Benson grappled manfully with the soaring costs of farm price supports. Yet prosperity remained beyond the next furrow for most farmers, despite mountains of surplus grain, bought by the government and stored in silo-shaped containers at a cost to taxpayers of nearly $2 million a day. Benson tried to get the government off the farm and return to "free-market" conditions—but he only succeeded in spending more money than any previous secretary of agriculture.

Eisenhower Republicans obviously could not unscramble all the eggs that had been fried by New Dealers and Fair Dealers for twenty long years. In many ways, "Ike" accepted and even advanced New Dealish programs. During his presidency, Social Security benefits were extended and the minimum wage raised to $1.00 an hour. In a public works project that dwarfed anything the New Deal had ever dreamed of, Eisenhower also backed a $27 billion plan to build 42,000 miles (67,600 kilometers) of sleek, fast interstate highways. The construction of these modern, multilane roads created countless construction jobs and speeded the suburbanization of America.

Despite his good intentions, Eisenhower managed to balance the budget only three times in his eight years in office, and in 1959 he incurred the biggest peacetime deficit thus far in American history. Yet critics blamed his fiscal timidity for aggravating several business recessions during the decade, especially the sharp downturn of 1957–1958, which left more than 5 million workers jobless. Economic troubles helped to revive the Democrats, who regained control of both houses of Congress in 1954. Unemployment jitters also helped to spark the merger of the AF of L and the CIO in 1955.

A "New Look" in Foreign Policy

Mere "containment" of communism was condemned in the 1952 Republican platform as "negative, futile and immoral." Incoming Secretary of State John Foster Dulles promised not merely to stem the red tide but to "roll back" its gains and "liberate captive peoples." At the same time, the new administration promised to balance the budget by cutting military spending.

How were these two contradictory goals to be reached? Dulles answered with a "policy of

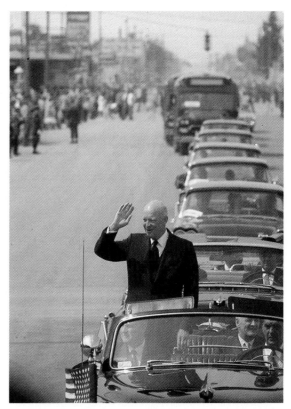

A Popular President *"Ike" exuded grandfatherly goodwill. (Wayne Miller/Magnum Photos, Inc.)*

boldness" in early 1954. The genial General Eisenhower would relegate the army and the navy to the back seat and build up an air fleet of superbombers with city-flattening nuclear bombs. These fearsome weapons would inflict "massive retaliation" on the Russians if they got out of hand. The advantages of this new policy were thought to be its paralyzing nuclear impact and its cheaper price tag when compared with conventional forces—"more bang for the buck."

Both aspects of the touted "new look" in foreign policy were delusions. In 1956 the Hungarians rose up against their Soviet masters and appealed in vain to the United States for aid. Embittered Hungarian freedom fighters naturally accused Uncle Sam of "welshing" when the chips were down. The truth was that America's mighty nuclear sledgehammer was too heavy a weapon to wield in such a relatively minor crisis. The rigid futility of the "massive retaliation" doctrine was thus starkly exposed. To his dismay, Eisenhower also discovered that the aerial and atomic hardware necessary for "massive retaliation" was staggeringly expensive. Military costs shot skyward. In 1960, as Eisenhower was about to leave office, he sagely but ironically warned against the dangerous growth of a "military-industrial complex" that his own policies had nurtured.

The Vietnamese Nightmare

Europe, thanks to the Marshall Plan and NATO, seemed reasonably secure by the early 1950s, but East Asia was a different can of worms. Nationalist movements had sought for years to throw off the French colonial yoke in Indochina. The Vietnamese leader, goateed Ho Chi Minh, had tried to appeal personally to Woodrow Wilson in Paris as early as 1919 to support self-determination for the peoples of Southeast Asia. Franklin Roosevelt had likewise inspired hope among Asian nationalists.

The Far East, 1955–1956

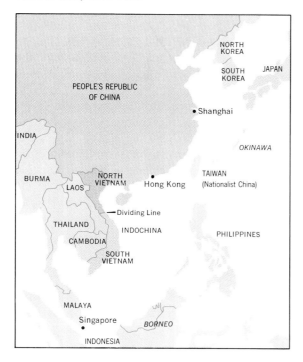

Cold War events dampened the dreams of anticolonial Asian peoples. Their leaders—including Ho Chi Minh—became increasingly Communist while the United States became increasingly anti-Communist. By 1954 American taxpayers were financing nearly 80 percent of the costs of a bottomless French colonial war in Indochina. Uncle Sam's share amounted to about $1 billion a year.

Despite this massive aid, French forces continued to crumble under guerrilla onslaughts. In March 1954 a key French garrison was trapped hopelessly in the fortress of Dien Bien Phu. The new "policy of boldness" was now put to the test. Secretary Dulles, Vice-President Nixon, and the chairman of the Joint Chiefs of Staff favored intervention with American bombers to help bail out the beleaguered French. But Eisenhower, correctly fearing British nonsupport, held back.

Dien Bien Phu fell, and a multination conference at Geneva roughly halved the two Vietnams at the seventeenth parallel, supposedly temporarily. The victorious Ho Chi Minh in the north consented to this arrangement on the assurance that Vietnam-wide elections would be held within two years. In the south, a pro-Western government under Ngo Dinh Diem was soon entrenched at Saigon. The Vietnamese never held the promised elections, primarily because the Communists seemed certain to win, and Vietnam remained a dangerously divided country.

Eisenhower promised economic and military aid to the conservative Diem regime, provided that it undertook certain social reforms. Change came at a snail's pace, but American aid continued, as Communist guerrillas heated up their campaign against Diem. The Americans had evidently backed a losing horse but could see no easy way to call off their bet. Secretary Dulles, in a vain attempt to prop up his shaky policy in Vietnam, engineered the creation of the eight-member Southeast Asia Treaty Organization (SEATO), including the United States, Britain, and France. Pieced together in late 1954, it was but a pale imitation of NATO and, as events were to prove, a frail prop on which to lean for the security of South Vietnam.

A False Lull in Europe

The United States had initially backed the French in Indochina, in part to win French approval of a plan to rearm Western Germany. Despite French fears, the Germans were finally welcomed into the NATO fold in 1955, with an expected contribution of half a million troops. In the same year, the East European countries and the Soviets signed the Warsaw Pact, creating a red military counterweight to the newly bolstered NATO forces in the West.

Despite these hardening military lines, the Cold War seemed to be thawing a bit. Eisenhower earnestly endeavored to cage the nuclear demon by negotiating arms-control agreements with Moscow, and early signs were encouraging. In May 1955 the Soviets rather surprisingly agreed to end the occupation of Austria, though only after exacting a stiff price. A summit conference in July produced little progress on the burning issues, but it bred a conciliatory "spirit of Geneva" that caused a modest blush of optimism to pass over the face of the Western world. Hopes rose further the following year when Soviet Communist party boss Nikita Khrushchev, a burly ex–coal miner, publicly denounced the bloody excesses of Joseph Stalin, the dictator dead since 1953.

Violent events late in 1956 ended the post-Geneva lull. When the liberty-loving Hungarians struck for their freedom, they were ruthlessly overpowered by Soviet tanks. While the Western world looked on in horror, Budapest was turned into a slaughterhouse, and thousands of refugees fled in panic for the Austrian border. The United States eventually altered its immigration laws to admit thirty thousand Hungarian fugitives.

Menaces in the Middle East

Increasing fears of Soviet penetration into the oil-rich Middle East spurred Washington to take audacious action. The government of Iran, supposedly influenced by the Kremlin, began to resist the power of the gigantic Western companies that controlled Iranian petroleum. In response, the American Central Intelligence Agency (CIA) engineered a coup in 1953 that installed the youthful shah of Iran as a kind of dictator. Though successful in the short run in securing Iranian oil for the West, the American intervention left a bitter legacy of resentment among many Iranians. More than two decades later, they took their revenge on the shah and his American allies.

The Suez crisis proved far messier than the swift stroke in Iran. President Nasser of Egypt, an ardent Arab nationalist, was seeking funds to build an immense dam on the upper Nile for urgently needed irrigation and power. America and Britain tentatively offered financial help, but when Nasser began to flirt openly with the Communist camp, Secretary of State Dulles dramatically withdrew the dam offer. Thus slapped in the face, Nasser promptly regained face by nationalizing the Suez Canal, owned chiefly by British and French stockholders.

Nasser's stroke placed a razor's edge at the jugular vein of Western Europe's oil supply. Secretary Dulles labored strenuously to ward off armed intervention, which was forbidden by the U.N. charter. But America's apprehensive British and French allies, after deliberately keeping Washington in the dark and coordinating their blow with one from Israel, staged a joint assault on Egypt late in October 1956. They were evidently determined to internationalize the canal and eliminate Nasser as a potential Middle Eastern Hitler.

For a breathless week the world teetered on the edge of the abyss. President Eisenhower, reluctantly siding against Britain and France, honored the nonaggression commitment of the U.N. charter and supported a cease-fire resolution. Russia, which for once voted with the Americans, threatened to pour "volunteers" into Egypt. Bending to such pressures, Britain, France, and Israel resentfully withdrew their troops, and for the first time in history a U.N. police contingent was sent to maintain order.

As the United Nations emerged with new laurels, the North Atlantic Treaty Organization (NATO) tottered. Britain and France were angered by America's willingness to turn against old friends and join the Soviet "butchers of

Budapest." The United States, irritated by the behind-the-back aggression of its NATO allies, rather grudgingly supplied them with oil during the five months when the Suez Canal was being cleared of sunken ships.

Increasing Communist pressures on the oil-rich Middle East prompted Washington to seek a new protective parasol. The instrument seized upon was the so-called Eisenhower Doctrine, approved overwhelmingly by Congress in March 1957. The Eisenhower Doctrine formally empowered the president to extend economic and military aid to the nations of the Middle East, provided that they desired it and were threatened by aggression from a Communist-controlled country.

Secretary Dulles, determined "to go to the brink," took a strong position in the Far East as well as in the Middle East in 1958. Chinese Communists began to shell the tiny Nationalist-held island of Quemoy, to which Jiang Jieshi (Chiang Kai-shek) had rashly committed about one-third of his entire Taiwanese army. Washington, brandishing the big stick of the Seventh Fleet, backed him in his determination to hang on. At the same time, Dulles partially quieted Communist fears by flying to Taiwan and inducing Jiang to renounce the use of force in regaining the Chinese mainland.

The Voters Still Like "Ike" in 1956

Blood-spattered Budapest and Suez provided the backdrop for the elections of 1956. Despite a heart attack in 1955 and a major abdominal operation in 1956, Eisenhower still enjoyed the public's confidence and affection. He and Vice-President Nixon were unanimously renominated by a jubilant Republican convention in San Francisco. Democrats, for their part, dutifully offered up Adlai Stevenson for a second time. Voters were thus presented with two warmed-over candidates—the first such matchup since 1900.

Democrats charged that the only order the magnetic ex-general had ever given was to mark time. They carped at Republican standpattism, at Eisenhower's shaky health (though Stevenson was to die first), and at the dubious moral character of "Tricky Dick" Nixon. In response, the GOP preened itself on being the party of peace, prosperity, and happiness. The biggest Republican asset remained "Ike's" irrepressible grin—described by one wartime colleague as "worth twenty divisions."

The election was a resounding personal endorsement of Eisenhower. He piled up an enormous majority of 35,590,472 votes to Stevenson's 26,022,752; in the Electoral College the

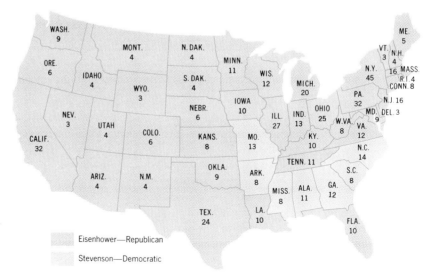

Presidential Election of 1956 (with electoral vote by state) *Eisenhower made even deeper inroads than he had in 1952 into the traditional bastion of Democratic strength, the once-solid South. Louisiana went Republican for the first time since Reconstruction days in 1876.*

Eisenhower—Republican

Stevenson—Democratic

count was 457 to 73. "Any jockey would look good riding Ike," crowed the GOP national chairman. But the general's coattails this time were not so stiff or so broad. He failed to win for his party either house of Congress—the first time since Zachary Taylor's election in 1848 that a winning president had left such a losing ticket behind him. The country remained heavily Democratic; but Eisenhower remained widely beloved. Voters were especially reluctant to abandon the old war-horse when events abroad threatened to spark off World War III at a push of the button.

Round Two for "Ike"

In fragile health, Eisenhower began his second term as a part-time president. Critics charged that he had his hands on his golf clubs, fly rod, and shotgun more often than on the levers of power. He seemed to rely more than ever on trusted lieutenants like Secretary of State Dulles and presidential assistant Sherman Adams, the tough-minded ex-governor of New Hampshire who had publicly condemned Democratic corruption.

Adams' chickens came home to roost in 1958, when a House investigation revealed that he had accepted expensive gifts from a Boston industrialist, on whose behalf he had thrice mildly interceded with federal agencies. Adams was forced to leave the White House under a dark cloud of scandal. Secretary Dulles, who had traveled half a million miles by air, died of cancer in 1959. His successor, Christian A. Herter, did not enjoy the president's confidence to the same degree. Shorn of his two most trusted aides, "Ike" in his last years did less golfing and more governing.

A key area in which the president bestirred himself was labor legislation. A drastic labor-reform bill in 1959 grew out of recurrent strikes in critical industries and scandalous revelations of gangsterism in high unionist echelons. In particular, fraud and brass-knuckle tactics tainted the Teamsters Union. The millionaire Teamster chief, "Dave" Beck, invoked the Fifth Amendment against self-incrimination 209

Above the Fray   *President Eisenhower was routinely criticized by liberals, as in this Herblock cartoon in the* Washington Post, *for his apparent indifference to many seething social problems of the day. His failure to employ his vast prestige on behalf of civil rights was especially conspicuous. (Herblock © 1957, The* Washington Post, *from Herblock's* Special for Today, *Simon and Schuster, 1958.)*

times before a Senate investigating committee in 1957 to avoid telling what he had done with $320,000. He was later sentenced to prison for embezzlement. When his union defiantly elected the tough-fisted James R. Hoffa as his successor, the AF of L–CIO expelled the Teamsters. The Senate committee reported that in fifteen years union officials had stolen or misappropriated some $10 million. Hoffa later was jailed for jury tampering, served part of his sentence, and disappeared—evidently the victim of the gangsters with whom he had consorted.

Legislation was clearly needed to prevent collective bargaining from becoming collective bludgeoning. Teamster boss Hoffa threatened to defeat for reelection those congressional representatives who dared to vote for a "tough" labor bill. Eisenhower responded with a dramatic television appeal, and Congress in 1959 passed the Landrum-Griffin Act. It was designed to bring labor leaders to book for financial shenanigans and to prevent bully-boy tactics. Seizing the opportune moment, antilaborites also forced into the bill prohibitions against "secondary boycotts" and certain kinds of picketing.

The Race with Russia into Space

Soviet scientists astounded the world on October 4, 1957, by lofting into orbit around the globe a beep-beeping "baby moon" (*Sputnik I*), weighing 184 pounds (83.5 kilograms). A month later they topped their own ace by sending aloft a larger satellite (*Sputnik II*), weighing 1,120 pounds (507 kilograms) and carrying a dog.

This amazing scientific breakthrough shattered American self-confidence. The Soviets had long been trying to convince the uncommitted nations that the shortcut to superior industrial production lay through communism—and the *Sputnik*s bolstered their claim. America had seemingly taken a back seat in scientific achievement. Envious "backward" nations laughed at Uncle Sam's discomfiture, all the more so because the Soviets were occupying outer space while American troops were occupying the high school in Little Rock.

Military implications of these man-made satellites proved sobering. If the Russians could fire heavy objects into outer space, they certainly could reach America with intercontinental ballistic missiles. Old-soldier Eisenhower, adopting a father-knows-best attitude toward the Soviet "gimmick," remarked that it should not cause "one iota" of concern. Others, chiefly Republicans, blamed the Truman administration for having spent more for supporting peanuts than for supporting a missile program at an early date. Agonizing soul-searching led to the conclusion that while the United States was well advanced on a broad scientific front, including color television, the Soviets had gone all out for rocketry. Experts testified that America's manned bombers were still a powerful deterrent, but heroic efforts were needed if the alleged "missile gap" was not to widen.

"Rocket fever" swept the nation. After humiliating and well-advertised failures (the Russians concealed theirs), the Americans regained some prestige four months after the initial Soviet triumph. They managed to put into orbit a grapefruit-sized satellite weighing 2.5 pounds (1.14 kilograms).

The *Sputnik* spur led to a critical comparison of the American educational system, already under fire as too easygoing, with that of the Soviet Union. A strong move developed to replace "frills" with solid subjects—to substitute square root for square dancing. Congress rejected demands for federal scholarships, but late in 1958 the National Defense and Education Act (NDEA) authorized $887 million in loans to needy college students and in grants for the improvement of teaching the sciences and languages. Exploring the space between the ears seemed necessary if the United States was going to catch up with the Russians in exploring outer space.

Nuclear Bombs, Lebanon, and Berlin

The fantastic race toward nuclear annihilation continued unabated. Emboldened by his *Sputnik*s, Premier Khrushchev boasted openly that he would shower rockets on America. Humanity-minded scientists urged that nuclear tests be stopped before the atmosphere became so polluted as to produce generations of deformed monsters. The Soviets, after completing an intensive series of exceptionally "dirty" tests, proclaimed a suspension in March 1958 and urged the Western world to follow. Beginning in October 1958, Washington did halt both underground and atmospheric testing. But all attempts to regularize such suspensions by proper inspection sank on the reef of mutual suspicions.

Thermonuclear suicide seemed nearer in July 1958, when both Egyptian and Communist plottings threatened to engulf Western-oriented Lebanon. After its president had called for aid under the Eisenhower Doctrine, the United States boldly landed several thousand troops (ultimately about fourteen thousand) and helped restore order without taking a single life.

This energetic action, in the teeth of Soviet condemnation and threats, served notice that Washington was unwilling to travel the well-rutted road to appeasement.

Khrushchev, no doubt feeling his missile-muscles, deliberately provoked an even more ominous crisis over Berlin—"a bone in the throat," he said—in November 1958. Annoyed by this pro-Western oasis in a Communist desert, he gave the three Western powers (Britain, France, the United States) six months to pull their troops out of West Berlin. The Soviet East German satellite would then take over, and if the West resisted, Moscow would rush to the aid of its puppet. This could only mean World War III. But Eisenhower and Dulles, again remembering the perils of appeasement, staunchly refused to yield well-established rights. The six-month deadline passed almost unnoticed.

Goodwill Diplomacy and the Spy Plane

Eisenhower took his cue from the highly publicized tours of Khrushchev when he embarked upon a whirlwind, eleven-nation goodwill trip in December 1959, all the way from Europe to India. Early in 1960 he staged a repeat performance in Latin America. Grinning his way through showers of confetti and shouts of "Eekay" (Ike), he scored a great personal triumph. He no doubt generated goodwill, but Democratic critics charged that stagecraft was no substitute for statecraft.

The burly Khrushchev, seeking new propaganda laurels, was eager to meet with Eisenhower and pave the way for a "summit conference" with Western leaders. Despite grave misgivings as to any tangible results, the president invited him to America in 1959. Arriving in New York, Khrushchev appeared before the U.N. General Assembly and dramatically resurrected the ancient Soviet proposal of complete disarmament. But he offered no practical means of achieving this end. He then journeyed out to the Pacific Coast and returned by way of Iowa, where he approvingly patted a prize pig. But the smiling, Kewpie-doll exterior concealed a steely,

bellicose interior, which occasionally erupted in bullying denunciations.

A noteworthy result of this tour was a meeting at Camp David, the president's rustic retreat in Maryland. Khrushchev emerged saying that his ultimatum for the evacuation of Berlin would be extended indefinitely. The relieved world gave prayerful but premature thanks for the "spirit of Camp David."

The Paris "summit conference," scheduled for May 1960, turned out to be an incredible fiasco. Both Moscow and Washington had publicly taken a firm stand on the burning Berlin issue, and neither could risk a public backdown. Then, on the eve of the conference, an American U-2 spy plane was shot down and its pilot captured deep in the heart of Russia. After bungling bureaucratic denials in Washington, "honest Ike" took the unprecedented step of assuming personal responsibility. Professing to be insulted by his "fishy friend," Khrushchev stormed into Paris filling the air with invective.

"What's So Funny?" *Premier Khrushchev gloats over "Ike's" spying discomfiture. (Copyright 1960 by Herblock in The Washington Post.)*

He demanded that Eisenhower not only apologize for the spy flights but punish those responsible for them. The president obviously would not punish himself, so the conference collapsed before it could get off the ground.

Khrushchev's "diplomacy by tantrum" virtually ended Eisenhower's "diplomacy by goodwill tour." Moscow abruptly canceled its invitation to Eisenhower to visit Russia. Violent demonstrations in Japan forced the president, with much loss of face, to abandon a trip to the Flowery Kingdom during his Far Eastern tour. America's slipping prestige thus received yet another body blow.

Cuba's Castroism Spells Communism

An ill-timed "goodwill" tour by Vice-President Nixon through South America in 1958 reaped a harvest of spit and spite. After being stoned, spat upon, and shouted down at Lima (Peru), Nixon narrowly escaped serious injury from a mob in Caracas (Venezuela). Decent Latin Americans were apologetic, but one of their leaders explained that since the masses could not vent their anger by spitting on the United States, they spat on the vice-president of the United States. Latin Americans bitterly resented Uncle Sam's lavishing billions of dollars on Europe, while doling out only millions to the poor relations to the south. They also chafed at Washington's continuing habit of intervening in Latin American affairs—as in a CIA-directed coup that ousted a leftist government in Guatemala in 1954. On the other hand, Washington continued to support—even decorate—bloody dictators who claimed to be combating Communists.

Most ominous of all was the Communist beachhead in Cuba. The ironfisted dictator Batista had encouraged huge investments of American capital, and Washington in turn had given him some support. When black-bearded Dr. Fidel Castro engineered a revolution early in 1959, he denounced the Yankee imperialists and began to expropriate valuable American properties in pursuing a land-distribution program. Washington, finally losing patience, released Cuba from "imperialistic slavery" by cutting off the heavy imports of Cuban sugar. Castro retaliated with further wholesale confiscations of Yankee property and in effect made his left-wing dictatorship an economic and military satellite of Moscow. Washington broke diplomatic relations with Cuba early in 1961.

Americans talked seriously of invoking the Monroe Doctrine before the Russians set up a Communist base only 90 miles (145 kilometers) from their shores. Khrushchev angrily proclaimed that the Monroe Doctrine was dead and indicated that he would shower missiles upon the United States if it attacked his good friend Castro.

The Cuban revolution, which Castro sought to "export" to his neighbors, brought other significant responses. At San Jose, Costa Rica, in August 1960, the United States induced the Organization of American States to condemn (unenthusiastically) Communist infiltration into the Americas. President Eisenhower, whom Castro dubbed "the senile White House golfer," hastily proposed a long-deferred "Marshall Plan" for Latin America. Congress responded to his recommendation with an initial authorization of $500 million. The Latin Americans had Castro to thank for attention that many of them regarded as too little and too late.

Kennedy Challenges Nixon for the Presidency

Republicans faced up to the presidential campaign of 1960 without great optimism, for they had taken a bad beating in the midterm congressional elections of 1958. Voters had been especially disturbed by the recession of 1957–1958, farm problems, and foreign tensions. Not only had the Republicans suffered the heaviest losses in the history of Senate elections, but the casualties were particularly severe among ultraconservative Republican senators. A crestfallen Eisenhower was dismayed that his "New Republicanism" had not taken root.

Vice-President Nixon was the Republican heir apparent. To many, he was a gifted party leader; to others, a ruthless opportunist. The "old" Nixon had been a no-holds-barred campaigner, especially in assailing Democrats and

The "Kitchen Debate"   *Vice-president Nixon, on a goodwill visit, and Soviet Premier Khrushchev wage an impromptu discussion on the nature of free government at the American exhibition in Moscow, 1959. (Photograph by Elliott Erwitt, Magnum Photos, Inc.)*

ballot triumph in Los Angeles over his closest rival, Senator Lyndon B. Johnson, the Senate majority leader from Texas. A disappointed South was not completely appeased when Johnson accepted second place on the ticket in an eleventh-hour marriage of convenience. Kennedy's challenging acceptance speech called upon the American people for sacrifices to achieve their potential greatness, which he hailed as the New Frontier.

The Presidential Issues of 1960

Bigotry, as was inevitable, showed its snarling face. Senator Kennedy was a Roman Catholic, the first to be nominated since Al Smith's ill-starred campaign in 1928. Smear artists revived the ancient charges about the Pope's controlling the White House. Kennedy pointed to his fourteen years of service in Congress, denied that he would be swayed by Rome, and asked if

John F. Kennedy Campaigning for the Presidency, 1960   *(Photograph by Henri Dauman, Magnum Photos, Inc.)*

left-wingers. The "new" Nixon was represented as a mature, seasoned statesman. More in the limelight than any earlier vice-president, he had shouldered heavy new responsibilities and had traveled globally as a "troubleshooter" in various capacities. He had vigorously defended American democracy in a famous "kitchen debate" with Khrushchev in Moscow in 1959. His supporters, flourishing a telling photograph of this finger-pointing episode, claimed that he alone knew how to "stand up to" the Russians.

Nixon was nominated unanimously on the first ballot in Chicago. His running mate was handsome Henry Cabot Lodge, Jr., of Massachusetts (grandson of Woodrow Wilson's archfoe), who had served conspicuously for seven years as American representative to the United Nations.

By contrast, the Democratic race for the presidential nomination started as a free-for-all. Supporters of Adlai Stevenson cried, "We're Madly for Adlai," but hardheaded politicians shied away from a two-time loser. John F. Kennedy—a tall (6 feet; 1.83 meters), youthful, dark-haired, and tooth-flashing millionaire senator from Massachusetts—won impressive victories in the primaries. He then scored a first-

Presidential Election of 1960 (with electoral vote by state) Kennedy owed his hairbreadth triumph to his victories in 26 of the 40 largest cities—and to Lyndon Johnson's strenuous campaigning in the South, where Kennedy's Catholic religion may have been a hotter issue than his stand on civil rights.

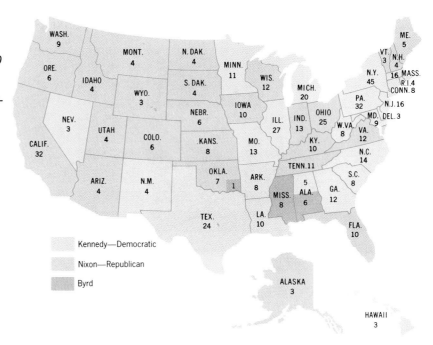

Kennedy—Democratic

Nixon—Republican

Byrd

some 40 million Catholic Americans were to be condemned to second-class citizenship from birth.

Kennedy's Catholicism aroused misgivings in the Protestant, Bible Belt South, which was ordinarily Democratic. "I fear Catholicism more than I fear communism," declaimed one Baptist minister in North Carolina. But the religious issue largely canceled itself out. If many southern Democrats stayed away from the polls because of Kennedy's Catholicism, northern Democrats in unusually large numbers supported Kennedy

Candidate Kennedy, in a speech to a Houston group of Protestant ministers (September 12, 1960), declared: "I believe in an America where the separation of church and state is absolute—where no Catholic prelate would tell the President, should he be a Catholic, how to act, and no Protestant minister would tell his parishioners for whom to vote . . . and where no man is denied public office because his religion differs from the President who might appoint him or the people who might elect him."

because of the bitter attacks on their Catholic faith.

Kennedy insisted that the Russians, with their nuclear bombs and *Sputnik*s, had gained on America in prestige and power. Nixon, forced to defend the dying administration, replied that the nation's prestige had not slipped, although Kennedy was causing it to do so by his unpatriotic talk.

Television may well have tipped the scales. Nixon agreed to meet Kennedy in four so-called debates. The contestants crossed words in millions of living rooms before audiences estimated at 60 million or more. Nobody "won" the debates. But Kennedy at least held his own and did not suffer by comparison with the more "experienced" Nixon. Many viewers found Kennedy's glamor and vitality far more appealing than Nixon's tired and pallid appearance.

Kennedy squeezed through by the rather comfortable margin of 303 electoral votes to 219, but with the breathtakingly close popular margin of only 118,574 votes out of over 68 million cast.* Like Franklin Roosevelt, Kennedy

---

*Six Democratic electors in Alabama, all eight unpledged Democratic electors in Mississippi, and one Republican elector in Oklahoma voted for Senator Harry F. Byrd.

ran well in the large industrial centers, where he had strong support from workers, Catholics, and blacks. (He had solicitously telephoned the pregnant Coretta King, whose husband, Martin Luther King, Jr., was then imprisoned in Georgia for a sit-in.)

Although losing a few seats, the Democrats swept both houses of Congress by wide margins. John Fitzgerald Kennedy—the youngest man and the first Catholic to be elected president—was free to set out for his New Frontier, provided that the die-hard conservatives in his party would join the wagon train.

An Old General Fades Away

President Eisenhower, the aging "dynamic" conservative, continued to enjoy extraordinary popularity to the final curtain. Despite Democratic jibes about "eight years of golfing and goofing," of "putting and puttering," Eisenhower was universally admired and respected for his dignity, decency, sincerity, goodwill, and moderation.

Pessimists had predicted that Eisenhower would be a seriously crippled "lame duck" during his second term, owing to the barrier against reelection erected by the Twenty-second Amendment, ratified in 1951. (See the Appendix.) In truth, he displayed more vigor, more political know-how, and more aggressive leadership during his last two years than ever before. For an unprecedented six years, from 1955 to 1961, Congress remained in Democratic hands, yet Eisenhower established unusual control over it. He wielded the veto 169 times, and only twice was he overridden by the required two-thirds vote.

America was fabulously prosperous in the Eisenhower years, despite pockets of poverty and unemployment, recurrent recessions, and perennial farm problems. To the north the vast

> In his Farewell Address on radio and television, January 17, 1961, Eisenhower warned against a potent new menace: "This conjunction of an immense military establishment and a large arms industry is new in the American experience. . . . In the councils of government, we must guard against the acquisition of unwarranted influence, whether sought or unsought, by the military-industrial complex."

St. Lawrence waterway project, constructed jointly with Canada and completed in 1959, had turned the cities of the Great Lakes into bustling ocean seaports.

"Old Glory" could now proudly display fifty stars. Alaska attained statehood in 1959, as did Hawaii. Alaska, though gigantic, was thinly populated and noncontiguous, but these objections were overcome in a Democratic Congress that expected Alaska to vote Democratic. Hawaii had ample population (largely of Oriental descent), advanced democratic institutions, and more acreage than Rhode Island, Delaware, or Connecticut.

Though a crusading general, Eisenhower as president mounted no moral crusade for civil rights. This was perhaps his greatest failing. Yet he was no bigot, and he had done far more than grin away problems and tread water. As a Republican president, he had further woven the reforms of the Democratic New Deal and Fair Deal into the fabric of national life. As a former general, he had exercised wise restraint in his use of military power and had soberly guided foreign policy away from countless threats to peace. He had ended one war and avoided all others. As the decades lengthened, appreciation of him grew.

Varying Viewpoints

Liberal historians, reflecting a Democratic bias that is widespread in academic circles, have portrayed the 1950s as the time of the "great postponement." These critics condemn Eisenhower as visionless and passive and lament the failure of the decade to carry forward vigorously the programs of the New Deal. But to other scholars the Eisenhower era has begun to appear in a more favorable light. Antidotes to the liberal conventional wisdom have come both from conservatives, who view Ike's presidency as an island of calm between the noisy clashes of the Truman years and the convulsive upheavals of the 1960s, and from radicals, who stress Eisenhower's restraint at the time of Dien Bien Phu and his desire to control the "military-industrial complex." In recent years some scholars, notably Fred I. Greenstein, have argued that Ike's public nonchalance masked decisive and adept behind-the-scenes leadership.

Select Readings

Primary Source Documents

Earl Warren's decision in *Brown* v. *Board of Education of Topeka,* 347 U.S. 492–495 (1954),* altered the course of race relations in the United States. It also sparked the opposition of one hundred southern congressmen, *Congressional Record,* 84th Congress, 2d Session, pp. 4515–4516 (1956).* Eisenhower's Farewell Address (1961)* warned of the dangers of the "military-industrial complex."

Secondary Sources

The era is surveyed readably in several works, including Eric F. Goldman, *The Crucial Decade—and After: America, 1945–1960* (1961); Richard Polenberg, *One Nation Divisible: Class, Race, and Ethnicity in the United States since 1938* (1980); William Leuchtenburg, *A Troubled Feast: American Society since 1945* (updated edition, 1983); William H. Chafe, *The Unfinished Journey: America since World War II* (1985); and more succinctly in Charles C. Alexander, *Holding the Line: The Eisenhower Era, 1952–1961* (1975). Eisenhower the man is the subject of Stephen Ambrose's two-volume biography, *Eisenhower: Soldier, General of the Army, President-Elect, 1890–1952* (1983) and *Eisenhower: The President* (1984). Eisenhower's own memoirs are rather bland: *Mandate for Change, 1953–1956* (1963) and *Waging Peace, 1956–1961* (1965). Fred I. Greenstein portrays Ike as the master of *The Hidden Hand Presidency* (1982). Gary W. Reichard, *The Reaffirmation of Republicanism: Eisenhower and the Eighty-third Congress* (1975), praises the president's political skills. Robert A. Divine, *Eisenhower and the Cold War* (1981), praises his diplomatic restraint. Various aspects of foreign policy are covered in Richard Immerman, *The CIA in Guatemala: The Foreign Policy of Intervention* (1982); Robert Schultzinger, *The Wise Men of Foreign Affairs: The History of the Council on Foreign Relations* (1984); Urs Schwarz, *American Strategy* (1966); Henry Kissinger, *Nuclear Weapons and Foreign Policy* (1957); and Herman Kahn's chilling *On Thermonuclear War* (1960). The background and consequences of the Supreme Court's 1954 desegregation decision are ably presented in Richard Kluger, *Simple Justice: The History of Brown v. Board of Education* (1976), and Raymond Wolters, *The Burden of Brown: Thirty Years of School Desegregation* (1984). For one man's experience of integration, see Jules Tygiel, *Baseball's Great Experiment: Jackie Robinson and His Legacy* (1983). See also Numan V. Bartley, *The Rise of Massive Resistance* (1969). Relevant memoirs and biographies include William O. Douglas, *The Court Years, 1939–1975* (1980); G. Edward White, *Earl Warren* (1982); Jerome E. Edwards, *Pat McCarran* (1982); John Bartlow Martin, *Adlai Stevenson* (2 vols., 1976–1977); and Townsend Hoopes, *The Devil and John Foster Dulles* (1973). On the election of 1960, see Theodore H. White's colorful *The Making of the President, 1960* (1961).

43

The Stormy Sixties

> *In the final analysis it is their war. They are the ones who have to win it or lose it . . . the people of Vietnam.*
>
> *John F. Kennedy, September 1963*

Kennedy's New Frontier Spirit

Hatless and topcoatless in the 22 degrees Fahrenheit chill (minus 5 degrees Celsius), youthful John F. Kennedy delivered a stirring inaugural address on January 20, 1961. Tall, elegantly handsome, speaking crisply and with staccato finger jabs at the air, Kennedy personified the glamor and vigor of the new administration. The youngest president ever elected, he assembled one of the youngest cabinets, including his thirty-five-year-old brother Robert as attorney general. "Bobby," the president quipped, would find the experience useful when he began to practice law. Business whiz Robert S. McNamara left the presidency of the Ford Motor Company to take over the Defense Department. Along with other youthful, talented advisers, they made up an inner circle of

"the best and the brightest" men around the president.

From the outset Kennedy inspired high expectations, especially among the young. His challenge of a "New Frontier" quickened patriotic pulses. He brought a warm heart to the Cold War when he proposed the Peace Corps, an army of idealistic and mostly youthful volunteers to bring American skills to underdeveloped countries. He summoned citizens to service with his clarion call to "ask not what your country can do for you: ask what you can do for your country."

Himself Harvard-educated, Kennedy and his Ivy League lieutenants (heavily from Harvard) radiated confidence in their abilities. The president's personal grace and wit won him the deep affection of many of his fellow citizens. In an unprecedented gesture, he invited white-maned

President and Mrs. John F. Kennedy *The young and vibrant first couple brought beauty, style, and grace to the White House. (Bettmann Newsphotos.)*

poet Robert Frost to speak at his inaugural ceremonies. The old Vermont versifier shrewdly took stock of the situation. "You're something of Irish and I suppose something of Harvard," he told Kennedy—and advised him to be more Irish than Harvard.

The New Frontier at Home

Kennedy came into office with narrow democratic majorities in Congress. Southern members of his own party threatened to team up with Republicans and lay the ax to New Frontier proposals such as medical assistance for the aged and increased federal aid to education. Kennedy won a first round in his campaign for a more cooperative Congress when he forced an

expansion of the all-important House Rules Committee, dominated by conservatives who could have bottled up his entire legislative program. Despite this victory, the New Frontier did not expand swiftly. Key medical and education bills remained stalled in Congress.

Another vexing problem was the economy. Kennedy had campaigned on the theme of "getting the country moving again" after the recessions of the Eisenhower years. While his advisers debated the best kind of economic medicine to apply, the president tried to hold the line against crippling inflation. His administration helped negotiate a noninflationary wage agreement in the steel industry in early 1962. The assumption was that the companies, for their part, would keep the lid on prices.

Almost immediately, steel management announced significant price increases, thereby seemingly demonstrating bad faith. The president erupted in wrath, remarking that his father had once said that "all businessmen were sons of bitches." He called the "big steel" men onto the White House carpet and unleashed his Irish temper. Overawed, the steel operators backed down, while displaying S.O.B. buttons, meaning "Sons of Business" or "Save Our Business."

The steel episode provoked fiery attacks by big business on the New Frontier, but Kennedy soon appealed to believers in free enterprise when he announced his support of a general tax cut bill. He rejected the advice of those who wished greater government spending and chose to stimulate the economy by slashing taxes and putting more money directly into private hands. When he announced his policy before a big business group, one observer called it "the most Republican speech since McKinley."

For economic stimulus, as well as for military strategy and scientific prestige, Kennedy also promoted a multibillion-dollar project to land an American on the moon. When skeptics objected that the money could best be spent elsewhere, Kennedy "answered" them in a speech at Rice University in Texas: "But why, some say, the moon? . . . And they may well ask, why climb the highest mountain? Why, thirty-five years ago, fly the Atlantic? Why does Rice play Texas?" Twenty-four billion dollars later, in

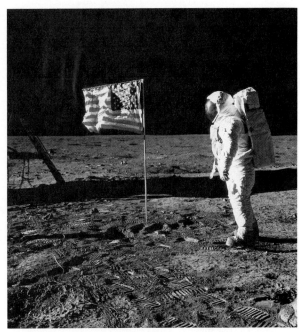

On the Moon　(left) *This moon's-eye view of Earth greeted the first men to land on the lunar surface. (right) Astronaut Aldrin poses with a stretched U.S. flag on the windless moon. His companion, Armstrong said, as he stepped from the spacecraft, "That's one small step for man; one giant leap for mankind." (Courtesy NASA.)*

1969, two American astronauts triumphantly planted human footprints on the moon's dusty surface.

Rumblings in Europe

A few months after settling into the White House, the new president met Soviet Premier Khrushchev at Vienna, in June 1961. Kennedy sought cooperation, but the tough-talking Russian adopted a belligerent attitude, threatening to make a treaty with East Germany and cut off Western access to Berlin. Visibly shaken, the president refused to be bullied. Upon returning, he requested an increase in the military budget and called up reserve troops for the possible defense of Berlin. The Soviets backed off from their most bellicose threats but suddenly began to construct the Berlin Wall in August 1961. A barbed-wire and concrete barrier, it was designed to plug the heavy population drain from East Germany to West Germany. But to the free

world the "Wall of Shame" looked like a gigantic enclosure around a concentration camp.

The Barbed-Wire-and-Brick Berlin Wall, 1962
(United Press International photo.)

Kennedy meanwhile turned his attention to Western Europe, now miraculously prospering after the tonic of Marshall Plan aid and the growth of the American-encouraged Common Market, or commercial union. He finally secured passage of the Trade Expansion Act in 1962, authorizing tariff cuts of up to 50 percent to promote trade with Common Market countries. This legislation led to the so-called Kennedy Round of tariff negotiations, concluded in 1967, and to a significant expansion of European-American trade.

But not all of Kennedy's ambitious designs for Europe were realized. American policymakers were dedicated to an economically and militarily united "Atlantic Community," with Uncle Sam the dominant partner. But they found their way blocked by towering, stiff-backed Charles de Gaulle of France. The Frenchman was suspicious of American intentions in Europe and on fire to recapture the *gloire* of Napoleonic France. With a haughty *"non"* he vetoed British application for Common Market membership in 1963. He likewise dashed cold water on an American proposal to develop a multinational nuclear arm within NATO. De Gaulle deemed the Americans unreliable in a crisis, so he tried to preserve French freedom of action by developing his own small atomic force ("farce," jibed his critics). Despite the perils of nuclear proliferation or Soviet domination, de Gaulle demanded an independent Europe, free of Yankee influence.

Foreign Flare-Ups and "Flexible Response"

Special problems for American foreign policy emerged from the worldwide decolonization of European overseas possessions after World War II. The African Congo received its independence from Belgium in 1960 and immediately exploded into violence. The United Nations sent in a peacekeeping force, to which Washington contributed much money but no manpower. Critics complained that increasingly Uncle Sam was picking up the tab for United Nations operations, while the organization itself was becoming dominated by the numerous newcomer nations from once-colonial Asia and Africa.

Sparsely populated Laos, freed of its French colonial overlords in 1954, was festering dangerously by the time Kennedy came into office. The Eisenhower administration had drenched this jungle kingdom with dollars but failed to cleanse the country of an aggressive Communist element. A red Laos, many observers feared, would be a river on which the influence of Communist China would flood into all of Southeast Asia.

As the Laotian civil war raged, Kennedy's military advisers seriously considered sending in American troops. But the president found that he had insufficient forces to put out the fire in Asia and still honor his commitments in Europe. Kennedy thus sought a diplomatic escape hatch in the fourteen-power Geneva conference, which agreed on the neutralization of Laos in 1962.

These "brushfire wars" intensified the pressure for a shift away from Secretary Dulles's dubious doctrine of "massive retaliation." Kennedy felt hamstrung by the knowledge that in a crisis he had the Devil's choice between humiliation or nuclear incineration. With Defense Secretary McNamara, he pushed the strategy of "flexible response"—that is, developing an array of military "options" that could be precisely matched to the scope and importance of the crisis at hand. To this end, Kennedy increased spending on conventional military forces and bolstered the Special Forces (Green Berets). They were an elite antiguerrilla outfit trained to survive on snake meat and to kill with scientific finesse.

Stepping into the Vietnam Quagmire

The doctrine of "flexible response" seemed sane enough, but it contained lethal logic. It potentially lowered the level at which diplomacy would give way to shooting. It also provided a mechanism for a progressive, and possibly endless, stepping-up of the use of force. Vietnam soon presented a grisly demonstration of these dangers.

Vietnam and Southeast Asia

far-off Asian slaughter pen. A graceful pullout was becoming increasingly difficult.

Cuban Confrontations

Uncle Sam regarded Latin America as his backyard, but his southern neighbors feared and resented the powerful Colossus of the North. Kennedy extended the hand of friendship with the Alliance for Progress (*Alianza para el Progreso*), hailed as a Marshall Plan for Latin America. A primary goal was to help the Good Neighbors close the gap between the calloused rich and the wretched poor, and thus quiet Communist agitation. But results were disappointing; there was little alliance and even less progress. American handouts had little positive impact on Latin America's social problems.

President Kennedy also struck below the border with the mailed fist. He had inherited from

The corrupt and conservative Diem government in Saigon, despite a deluge of American dollars, had ruled shakily since the partition of Vietnam in 1954. Anti-Diem agitation, spearheaded by the local Communist Viet Cong and encouraged by the red regime in the north, noisily threatened to topple the pro-American government from power. In a fateful decision late in 1961, Kennedy ordered a sharp increase in the number of "military advisers" (U.S. troops) in South Vietnam.

American forces had allegedly entered Vietnam to foster political stability—to help protect Diem from the Communists long enough to allow him to enact basic social reforms favored by the Americans. But the Kennedy administration eventually despaired of the reactionary Diem and encouraged a successful coup against him in November 1963. Ironically, the United States thus contributed to a long process of political disintegration that its original policy had meant to prevent. Kennedy still told the South Vietnamese that it was "their war," but he had made dangerously deep political commitments. By the time of his death, he had ordered more than fifteen thousand American men into the

"Backbone"   *United States supports South Vietnam.*
(By permission of Bill Mauldin and Wil-Jo Associates, Inc.)

the Eisenhower administration a CIA-backed scheme to topple Fidel Castro from power by invading Cuba with anti-Communist exiles. Trained and armed by Americans and supported by American air power, the invaders would trigger a popular uprising in Cuba and sweep to victory—or so the planners predicted.

On a fateful April 17, 1961, some twelve hundred exiles landed at Cuba's Bay of Pigs. Kennedy had decided from the outset against *direct* intervention, and the ancient aircraft of the anti-Castroites were no match for Castro's air force. In addition, no popular uprising greeted the invaders. With the invasion bogged down at the Bay of Pigs, Kennedy stood fast in his decision to keep hands off, and the bullet-riddled band of anti-Castroites surrendered. Most of the invaders rotted for two years in Cuban jails but were eventually "ransomed" for some $62 million worth of American drugs and other supplies. President Kennedy manfully assumed full responsibility for the failure, remarking that "victory has a hundred fathers, and defeat is an orphan."

The Bay of Pigs blunder naturally pushed Castro even further into the Soviet embrace. Wily Chairman Khrushchev lost little time taking full advantage of his Cuban comrade's position just 90 miles (145 kilometers) off Florida's coast. In October 1962 the aerial photographs of American spy planes revealed that the Russians were secretly and speedily installing nuclear-tipped missiles in Cuba. The Soviets evidently intended to use these devastating weapons to shield Castro and to blackmail the United States into backing down in Berlin and other trouble spots.

Kennedy and Khrushchev now began a nerve-racking game of "nuclear chicken." The president flatly rejected air force proposals for a "surgical" bombing strike against the missile-launching sites. Instead, on October 22, 1962, he ordered a naval "quarantine" of Cuba and demanded immediate removal of the threatening missiles. He also served notice on Khrushchev that any attack on the United States from Cuba would be regarded as coming from the Soviet Union and would trigger nuclear retaliation against the Russian heartland.

For an anxious week Americans waited while Soviet ships approached the patrol line established by the United States navy off the island of Cuba. Seizing or sinking a Russian vessel on the high seas would unquestionably be regarded by the Kremlin as an act of war. The world teetered breathlessly on the brink of global atomization.

In this tense eyeball-to-eyeball confrontation, Krushchev finally flinched. On October 28 he agreed to a partially face-saving compromise, by which he would pull the missiles out of Cuba. The United States in return agreed to end the quarantine and not invade the island.

Fallout from the Cuban missile crisis was considerable. A humiliated Khrushchev was ultimately hounded out of the Kremlin and became an "unperson." Hard-liners in Moscow, vowing never again to be humiliated in a nuclear face-off, launched an enormous program of military expansion. The Soviet buildup reached a crescendo in the next decade, stimulating, in turn, a vast American effort to "catch up with the Russians." The Democrats did better than expected in the midterm elections of November 1962—allegedly because the Republicans were "Cubanized." Kennedy, apparently sobered by the appalling risks he had just run, pushed harder for a nuclear test-ban treaty with the Soviet Union. After prolonged negotiations in Moscow, a pact prohibiting trial nuclear explosions in the atmosphere was signed in late 1963. Another barometer indicating a thaw in the Cold War was the installation (August 1963) of a Moscow-Washington "hot line," permitting immediate teletype communication in case of crisis.

Most significant was Kennedy's speech at the American University, Washington, D.C., in June 1963. The president urged Americans to abandon a view of Russia as a Devil-ridden land filled with fanatics and instead to deal with the world "as it is, not as it might have been had the history of the last eighteen years been different." Kennedy thus tried to lay the foundations for a realistic policy of peaceful coexistence with the Soviet Union. Here were the modest origins of the policy that later came to be known as "détente."

Martin Luther King Addresses the March on Washington, August 1963   *This was the occasion of King's famous "I Have a Dream" speech, in which he declared: "When the architects of our great republic wrote the magnificent words of the Constitution and the Declaration of Independence, they were signing a promissory note to which every American was to fall heir. This note was a promise that all men, yes, black men as well as white men, would be guaranteed the inalienable rights of life, liberty, and the pursuit of happiness." (Bettmann Newsphotos.)*

The Black Revolutionary Outburst

Kennedy had campaigned with a strong appeal to black voters, but he proceeded gingerly to redeem his promises. He had given a pledge to eliminate racial discrimination in federally funded housing projects "with a stroke of the pen." But it took him nearly two years to find the right pen.

Before long Kennedy was caught up in a convulsive racial revolution. Aroused blacks, impatient at the snail's pace of school desegregation in the Deep South, had begun to force the integration issue in new ways. A "sit-in" at a Woolworth lunch counter in Greensboro, North Carolina, in February 1960 had swelled into a wave of further sit-ins, lie-ins, wade-ins, and pray-ins to compel equal treatment for blacks in restaurants, transportation, employment, housing,

and voter registration. The most distinguished leader of this movement was the Reverend Martin Luther King, Jr., a young, bell-voiced clergyman from Atlanta. He preached Christian love and embraced the nonviolent tactics of India's Mohandas Gandhi. Not surprisingly, he was awarded the Nobel Peace Prize in 1964.

In the spring of 1963 King launched a campaign against discrimination in Birmingham, Alabama. A horrified world watched television screens as peaceful demonstrators were repeatedly repelled by the police with fire hoses, attack dogs, and electric cattle prods.

Integrating the southern universities almost brought wholesale slaughter. Some of them desegregated painlessly, but the University of Mississippi became a volcano. A twenty-nine-year-old air force veteran, James Meredith, encountered violent opposition when he attempted

"We Shall Overcome"
Martin Luther King, Jr., leads a peaceful demonstration from Selma to Montgomery in March 1965. (Photograph by Bruce Davidson, Magnum Photos, Inc.)

to register in October 1962. In the end President Kennedy was forced to send in four hundred federal marshals and three thousand troops. Two men died and scores were injured, but Meredith attended classes. He ultimately graduated—with a sheepskin that cost two lives and some 4 million taxpayer dollars.

In Alabama, Governor George Wallace stood in the doorway to prevent two black students from entering the State University in June 1963. "Segregation now! Segregation tomorrow! Segregation forever!" he shouted. But he soon yielded to federal pressures and let the students pass.

Jolted by these racial confrontations, President Kennedy went on television, June 11, 1963. In contrast to Eisenhower's cool aloofness from the racial issue, Kennedy called the situation a "moral crisis." He pleaded for new civil rights legislation to protect black citizens. In August, Martin Luther King, Jr., led 200,000 demonstrators, mostly black, on a peaceful "March on Washington" to demand more governmental action in the struggle for racial equality.

Still the violence continued. On the very night of Kennedy's stirring television appeal, a white gunman shot down Medgar Evers, a Mississippi civil rights worker. In September 1963 an explosion blasted a Baptist church in Birmingham, killing four black girls who had just finished their lesson called, "The Love That Forgives." By the time of Kennedy's death, his civil rights bill was making little legislative headway. Frustrated blacks were growing increasingly impatient.

The Killing of Kennedy

Violence haunted America in the mid-1960s, and it stalked grotesquely onto center stage on November 22, 1963. While riding in an open limousine in downtown Dallas, Texas, President Kennedy was shot in the brain by a concealed rifleman and died within seconds. As a stunned nation nursed its grief, the tragedy grew still more unbelievable. The alleged assassin, a furtive figure named Lee Harvey Oswald, was himself shot to death in front of the television cameras by a self-appointed avenger, Jack Ruby. So bizarre were the events surrounding the two murders that even an elaborate official investigation conducted by Chief Justice Warren could not quiet all doubts and theories about what had really happened.

Vice-President Johnson was promptly sworn in as president on a waiting airplane and flown back to Washington with Kennedy's body. Though he mistrusted "the Harvards," Johnson retained most of the bright Kennedy team. The new president managed a dignified and efficient transition, pledging continuity with his predecessor's policies.

For several days, the nation was steeped in sorrow. Not until then did many Americans realize how fully their young, vibrant president and his bewitching wife had cast a spell over them. Chopped down in his prime after only slightly more than a thousand days in the White House, he was acclaimed more for the ideals he had enunciated and the spirit he had kindled than for the concrete goals he had achieved. He had laid one myth to rest forever—that a Catholic could not be trusted with the presidency of the United States. Mass was celebrated only once in the White House—the day of his funeral.

The LBJ Brand on the Presidency

The torch had now passed to craggy-faced Lyndon Baines Johnson, a Texan who towered 6 feet 3 inches (1.91 meters). The new president hailed from the populist hill country of west Texas, whose people had first sent him to Washington as a twenty-nine-year-old congressman in 1937. Franklin D. Roosevelt was a political "Daddy" to him, Johnson claimed, and he had supported New Deal measures down the line. But when LBJ lost a Senate race in 1941, he learned the sobering lesson that liberal political beliefs did not necessarily win elections. He trimmed his sails to the right and squeezed himself into a Senate seat in 1948 with a questionable eighty-seven-vote margin—hence, the ironic nickname "Landslide Lyndon."

Entrenched in the Senate, Johnson developed into a legislative wheeler-dealer. He became the Democratic majority leader in 1954, wielding power second only to that of Eisenhower in the White House. He could move mountains or checkmate opponents as the occasion demanded, using what came to be known as the "Johnson treatment"—a flashing display of backslapping, flesh-pressing, and arm-twisting that overbore friend and foe alike.

Lyndon Johnson Sworn in on Air Force One
Kennedy's widow stands on Johnson's left in this dramatic scene just moments after the assassination. (Wide World Photos, Inc.)

As president, Johnson quickly shed the conservative coloration of his Senate years to reveal a still-living liberal underneath. He rammed Kennedy's stalled tax cut and civil rights bills through Congress and added proposals of his own for a billion-dollar "War on Poverty." Johnson voiced special concern for Appalachia, where the sickness of the soft-coal industry had left tens of thousands of mountain folk on the human slag heap.

Johnson's nomination by the Democrats in 1964 was a foregone conclusion; he was chosen by acclamation in Atlantic City as his birthday present. He had dubbed his domestic program the "Great Society"—a sweeping set of New Dealish economic and welfare measures aimed at transforming the American way of life.

Johnson Battles Goldwater in 1964

Thanks to the tall Texan, the Democrats stood foursquare on their most liberal platform since Truman's Fair Deal days. The Republicans, convening in San Francisco's Cow Palace, nominated box-jawed Senator Barry Goldwater of Arizona, a bronzed and bespectacled champion of rock-ribbed conservatism. The American stage was thus set for a historic clash of political principles.

Goldwater's forces had galloped out of the Southwest to ride roughshod over the moderate Republican "eastern establishment." Insisting that the GOP offer "a choice not an echo," Goldwater attacked the federal income tax, the Social Security system, the Tennessee Valley Authority, civil rights legislation, the nuclear test-ban treaty, and of course, the Great Society. His fiercely dedicated followers proclaimed: "In Your Heart You Know He's Right," which prompted the Democratic response, "In Your Guts You Know He's Nuts." Goldwater warmed right-wing hearts when he announced that "extremism in the defense of liberty is no vice. And . . . moderation in the pursuit of justice is no virtue."

Goldwater radiated sincerity and charm, but his aggressive "rightism" repelled millions of his own fellow Republicans. The Arizonan also habitually "shot from the lip," notably when he urged that American field commanders be given discretionary authority to use tactical nuclear weapons. Democrats gleefully exploited the image of Goldwater as a trigger-happy cowboy who would "Barry us" in the debris of World War III. This terrifying prospect loomed larger in the closing weeks of the campaign, when Russia's leader, Khrushchev, was sacked and Red China exploded its first nuclear bomb. In such a jittery atmosphere, voters shied away from the six-gun style of the Republican candidate.

Johnson cultivated the image of a resolute statesman by seizing upon the Tonkin Gulf episode early in August 1964. Unbeknownst to the American public or Congress, U.S. Navy ships had been cooperating with South Vietnamese gunboats in provocative raids along the coast of North Vietnam. Two of these American destroyers were reportedly fired upon by the North Vietnamese on August 2 and 4, although exactly what happened remains unclear. Johnson later reportedly quipped, "For all I know, the Navy was shooting at whales out there."

Johnson promptly called the attack "unprovoked" and moved swiftly to make political hay out of this episode. He ordered a "limited" retaliatory air raid against the North Vietnamese bases, proudly proclaiming that he sought "no wider war"—thus implying that the

Presidential Election of 1964
States are distorted according to the number of electoral votes indicated on each state. In New Orleans, toward the end of the campaign, a gutsy Johnson displayed his commitment to civil rights when he told a story about an old senator who once said of his Deep South constituents: "I would like to go back down there and make them just one more Democratic speech. . . . The poor old State, they haven't heard a Democratic speech in 30 years. All they hear at election time is Negro, Negro, Negro!" Johnson's open voicing of sentiments like this contributed heavily to his losses in the traditionally Democratic "solid South."

trigger-happy Goldwater did. Johnson also used the incident to spur congressional passage of the all-purpose Tonkin Gulf Resolution. With only two dissenting votes in both houses, the lawmakers virtually abdicated their war-declaring powers and handed the president a blank check to use further force in Southeast Asia.

The towering Texan rode to a spectacular victory in November 1964. The voters were herded into Johnson's column by fondness for the Kennedy legacy, faith in Great Society promises, and fear of Goldwater. A stampede of 43,129,566 Johnson votes trampled the Republican ticket with its 27,178,188 supporters. The tally in the Electoral College was 486 to 52. Goldwater carried only his native Arizona and five other states—all of them, significantly, in racially restless Dixieland. This cracking of the once solidly Democratic South afforded the Republicans about the only faint light in an otherwise bleak political picture. Johnson's record-breaking 61 percent of the popular vote swept lopsided Democratic majorities into both houses of Congress. The inept Goldwater proved to be not so much a candidate as a catastrophe, as some observers predicted that the Grand Old Party was stumbling down the road to the Federalist-Whig cemetery. (Yet sixteen years later Ronald Reagan would sail to victory on a Republican platform quite similar to Goldwater's.)

The Great Society Congress

Johnson's victory temporarily smashed the conservative coalition of southern Democrats and northern Republicans. A wide-open legislative road stretched before the Great Society programs, as the president skillfully ringmastered his two-to-one Democratic majorities. Congress poured out a flood of legislation, comparable only to the output of the New Dealers in the Hundred Days Congress of 1933. Fiscal orthodoxy flew out the window and planned deficits came in the door, as Johnson at last delivered on long-delayed Democratic promises of social reform. The Office of Economic Opportunity, the front line of the Great Society's War on Poverty, had its appropriation doubled to nearly $2 billion. Congress granted more than $1 bil-

An LBJ Speech *By the end of his term, he was so unpopular that he could find nonheckling audiences only on military bases or on navy ships. (Wally McNamee, photographer; the* Washington Post.*)*

lion to redevelop the gutted hills of Appalachia and voted a slightly greater amount for aid to elementary and secondary education. Yet the end results proved that poverty could not be papered over with greenbacks.

Johnson neatly avoided the thorny question of separation of church and state by channeling educational aid to students, not schools, thus allowing funds to flow to hard-pressed parochial institutions. (Catholic John F. Kennedy had not dared to touch this prickly issue.) With a keen eye for the dramatic, LBJ signed the education bill in the humble one-room Texas schoolhouse that he had attended as a boy. He also delighted in knowing that all "these Harvards" were working for him, a graduate of Southwest Texas State Teachers' College in San Marcos.

Other landmark laws flowed from Johnson's "hip-pocket Congress." Medicare for the elderly became a reality in 1965. Although it was a bitter pill for the American Medical Association to swallow, the system was welcomed by millions of older Americans who were being pushed into poverty by skyrocketing medical costs.

A tireless Johnson also prodded the Congress into creating two new cabinet offices: the Department of Transportation and the Department of Housing and Urban Development (HUD).

He named the first black cabinet member in the nation's history, noted economist Robert C. Weaver, to be secretary of housing and urban development. Other noteworthy laws established a National Endowment for the Arts and Humanities, designed to lift the level of American cultural life, and still other laws sweepingly reformed the long-criticized quota system for immigrants.

The Black Revolution Explodes

In Johnson's native South, the walls of segregation were crumbling, but not fast enough for long-suffering blacks. The Civil Rights Act of 1964 gave the federal government more muscle to enforce school-desegregation orders and to prohibit racial discrimination in all kinds of public accommodations and employment. But the problem of voting rights remained. In Mississippi, which had the largest black minority of any state, only about 5 percent of eligible blacks were registered to vote. The lopsided pattern was similar throughout the South. Ballot-denying devices like the poll tax, literacy tests, and barefaced intimidation still barred black people from the political process.

Beginning in 1964, opening up the polling booths became the chief goal of the black movement in the South. The Twenty-fourth Amendment, ratified in January 1964, abolished the poll tax in federal elections. (See the Appendix.) Blacks joined hands with white civil rights workers—many of them student volunteers from the North—in a massive voter-registration drive in Mississippi during the "Freedom Summer" of 1964. Singing "We Shall Overcome," they zealously set out to soothe generations of white anxieties and black fears.

But events soon blighted bright hopes. In late June 1964 one black and two white civil rights workers disappeared in Mississippi. Their badly beaten bodies were later found buried beneath an earthen dam. FBI investigators eventually arrested twenty-one white Mississippians in connection with the killings, including the local sheriff. But white juries refused to convict whites for these murders. In August an inte-

grated "Mississippi Freedom Democratic party" delegation was denied its seat at the national Democratic convention. Only a handful of black Mississippians had succeeded in registering to vote.

Early in 1965 Dr. Martin Luther King, Jr., resumed the voter-registration campaign in Selma, Alabama, where blacks made up 50 percent of the population but only 1 percent of the voters. State troopers with tear gas and whips assaulted King's demonstrators as they marched peacefully to the state capital at Montgomery. A Boston Unitarian minister was killed, and a few days later a white Detroit woman was shotgunned to death by Klansmen on the highway near Selma.

As the nation recoiled in horror before these violent scenes, President Johnson, speaking in soft southern accents, delivered a memorable address on television. What happened in Selma, he insisted, concerned all Americans, "who must overcome the crippling legacy of bigotry and injustice." Then, in a stirring adaptation of the anthem of the civil rights movement, the president concluded: "And we shall overcome." Following words with deeds, Johnson speedily shepherded through Congress the landmark Voting Rights Act of 1965, signed into law on August 6. It outlawed literacy tests and sent federal voter registrars into several southern states. Johnson later capped his legislative record on civil rights when he persuaded Congress in 1968 to pass the long-delayed Open Housing Bill, though the results were disappointing.

Black Rage

The Voting Rights Act of 1965 marked the end of an era in the troubled history of the black movement—the era of civil rights campaigns, focused on the South and led by peaceable moderates like Martin Luther King, Jr. Just five days after President Johnson signed the new voting law, a bloody riot exploded in Watts, a black ghetto in Los Angeles. Enraged blacks burned and looted their neighborhoods for nearly a week. When the smoke finally cleared, thirty-one blacks and three whites lay dead, more than a thousand persons had been injured, and hundreds of buildings stood charred and gutted.

Increasingly, violent voices began to be heard in the black movement, and its leadership divided dangerously between advocates of peaceful or militant tactics. Rising bitterness was highlighted by the career of Malcolm X, a brilliant Black Muslim preacher who favored black separatism and condemned the "blue-eyed white devils." In early 1965 he was cut down by black gunmen while speaking to a large crowd in New York City.

The moderation of Martin Luther King, Jr., came under heavy fire from younger black radicals in June 1966. King and Trinidad-born Stokely Carmichael of the Student Non-Violent Coordinating Committee (SNCC) vowed to resume a voter registration march through Mississippi, after its originator, James Meredith, had been gunned down along a Mississippi highway. (He was the same black man who had gained entrance to the University of Mississippi in 1962.) Sharp disagreements almost immediately flared forth, as Carmichael urged giving up peaceful demonstrations and pursuing "Black Power."

The phrase, "Black Power," frightened many whites, and their fears deepened when Stokely Carmichael was quoted as saying that Black Power "will smash everything Western civilization has created." Levelheaded advocates of Black Power intended the slogan to describe a broad-front effort to *exercise* the political rights gained by the civil rights movement. But for a time Black Power seemed to be simply a justification for pillage and arson. City-shaking riots erupted in Newark, New Jersey, in the summer of 1967, taking twenty-five lives, and in Detroit, Michigan, where federal troops restored order after forty-three people had died in the streets. Black rioters blindly burned down their own neighborhoods, attacking not so much white people as the symbols of white domination. These symbols of white domination included the landlord's property, police officers, and even firefighters, who had to battle blacks chanting "Burn, baby, burn."

James Meredith Shot during March to Jackson, Mississippi, 1966   *(Wide World Photos, Inc.)*

Riotous tactics angered white Americans, who now threatened to retaliate with their own "backlash" against ghetto arsonists and killers. Inner-city anarchy baffled many northerners, who had considered racial problems a purely "southern" question. But black concerns had moved North—as had nearly half the nation's black people. In the North the Black Power movement now focused less on civil rights and more on economic demands. Black unemployment, for example, was nearly double that for whites. These oppressive new problems seemed even less likely to be solved peaceably than the struggle for voting rights in the South.

Despair deepened when the magnetic and moderate voice of Martin Luther King, Jr., was forever silenced by a sniper's bullet in Memphis, Tennessee, on April 4, 1968. The killing of King cruelly robbed the American people of one of the most inspirational leaders in their history—at a time when they could least afford to lose him. This outrage triggered a nationwide orgy of ghetto-gutting and violence that cost over forty lives.

Rioters noisily made news, but thousands of other blacks quietly made history. Their voter registration in the South had shot upward, and by the late 1960s there were several hundred

"You Don't Understand Boy—You're Supposed to Just Shuffle Along" (From Straight Herblock, Simon and Schuster, 1964.)

black elected officials in the Old South. Cleveland, Ohio, and Gary, Indiana, had elected black mayors. By 1972 nearly half of the southern black children sat in integrated classrooms. Actually, more schools in the South were integrated than in the North. About a third of black families had risen economically into the ranks of the middle class—though an equal proportion remained below the "poverty line." King left a shining legacy of racial progress, but he was cut down when the job was far from completed.

Combating Communism in Two Hemispheres

Violence at home eclipsed Johnson's legislative triumphs, while foreign flare-ups threatened his political life. Discontented Dominicans rose in revolt against their military government in April 1965. Johnson speedily announced that the Dominican Republic was the target of a Castrolike coup by "Communist conspirators," and he dispatched American troops, ultimately some twenty-five thousand, to protect American lives and restore order. But the evidence of a Com-

munist takeover was fragmentary at best. Johnson was widely condemned, at home and in Latin America, for his temporary reversion to the officially abandoned "gunboat diplomacy." Critics charged that the two-fisted Texan was far too eager to back right-wing regimes with bayonets.

At about the same time, Johnson was floundering deeper into the monsoon mud of Vietnam. Viet Cong guerrillas attacked an American air base at Pleiku, South Vietnam, in February 1965. The president immediately ordered retaliatory bombing raids against military installations in North Vietnam and for the first time ordered attacking U.S. troops to land. By the middle of March 1965, the Americans had "Operation Rolling Thunder" in full swing—regular full-scale bombing attacks against North Vietnam. Before 1965 ended, some 184,000 American troops were involved, most of them slogging through the jungles and rice paddies of South Vietnam searching for guerrillas clad in black pajamas. When Barry Goldwater was asked what he would be doing differently in Vietnam if he were president, he replied that he would be doing the same thing—only "catching hell" for it. Many Americans complained that they had voted for Johnson but had got Goldwater.

Johnson had now taken the first fateful steps down a slippery path. He and his advisers believed that a fine-tuned, step-by-step increase in American force would drive the enemy to defeat with a minimum loss of life on both sides. But the president reckoned without due knowledge of the toughness, resiliency, and dedication of the local Viet Cong and their North Vietnamese allies. Aerial bombardment actually strengthened the Communists' will to resist. The enemy matched every increase in American firepower with more men and more wiliness in the art of guerrilla warfare.

The South Vietnamese themselves were meanwhile becoming spectators in their own war, as the fighting became increasingly Americanized. Corrupt and collapsible governments succeeded each other in Saigon with bewildering rapidity. Yet American officials continued to talk of defending a faithful democratic ally. Washington spokespersons also defended

The Mechanized War *High technology and modern equipment, such as this helicopter, gave the Americans in Vietnam a huge military advantage. But unaccompanied by a clear political purpose and a national will to win, that advantage was insufficient to achieve final victory. (U.S. Army photograph.)*

America's action as a test of Uncle Sam's "commitment" and of the reliability of his numerous treaty pledges to resist Communist encroachment. If the United States were to cut and run from Vietnam, claimed prowar "hawks," other nations would doubt America's word, crumble under Communist pressure, and drive America's first line of defense back to Waikiki Beach, in Hawaii, or even to the coast of California. Persuaded by such panicky thinking, Johnson steadily raised the military stakes in Vietnam. By 1968 he had poured more than half a million troops into Southeast Asia, and the annual bill for the war was exceeding $30 billion. Yet the end was nowhere in sight.

Vietnam Vexations

America could not defeat the enemy in Vietnam, but it seemed to be defeating itself. World opinion grew increasingly hostile; the blasting of an underdeveloped country by a mighty superpower struck many critics as obscene. Several nations expelled American Peace Corps volunteers. Disgusted European allies complained that they were being neglected militarily and punished economically, as America exported war-bred inflation to its trading partners.

Haughty Charles de Gaulle, ever suspicious of American reliability, ordered NATO off French soil in 1966.

Overcommitment in Southeast Asia also tied America's hands elsewhere. Capitalizing on American distractions in the Orient, the Soviet Union expanded its influence in the Mediterranean area, especially in Egypt. Tiny Israel humiliated the Russian-backed Egyptians in a devastating Six-Day War in June 1967, but the Middle East remained a packed powder keg that the war-plagued United States could not defuse.

The United States proved equally helpless when the North Koreans seized a U.S. intelligence ship, the *Pueblo*, in January 1968, evidently in international waters. They imprisoned the crew of some eighty men for eleven months. This humiliating episode angered red-blooded Americans, but it provoked no military response at a time when one Asiatic war was more than enough.

Domestic discontent also festered as the Vietnamese entanglement dragged on. Antiwar demonstrations had begun on a small scale with campus "teach-ins" in 1965, and gradually these protests mounted to tidal-wave proportions. As the long arm of the military draft dragged more and more young men off to the

Antiwar Demonstration in California   *Public opinion gradually but inexorably turned against the war. In 1965, polls showed that only 15 percent of Americans favored withdrawal from Vietnam. But by 1969, 69 percent of those interviewed indicated that they considered the war a "mistake," and by 1970, a majority supported withdrawal of U.S. troops. (Bob Fitch/ Black Star.)*

Asian slaughter pen, resistance stiffened. Thousands of draft registrants fled to Canada; others publicly burned their draft cards. Hundreds of thousands of marchers filled the streets of New York, San Francisco, and other cities, chanting

"Onward and Upward"   *Johnson's hopes for a Great Society were constantly dragged down by the grim demands of the Vietnam War. (Crawford for the NEA. Reproduced by permission of the Newspaper Enterprise Association.)*

"Hell no, we won't go," and "Hey, hey, LBJ, how many kids did you kill today?" Countless citizens felt the pinch of war-spawned inflation. Many Americans also felt pangs of conscience at the spectacle of their countrymen burning peasant huts and blistering civilians with ghastly napalm.

Opposition in Congress to the Vietnam involvement centered in the influential Senate Committee on Foreign Relations, headed by a former Rhodes scholar, Senator Fulbright of Arkansas. A constant thorn in the side of the president, he staged a series of widely viewed televised hearings in 1966 and 1967, during which prominent personages aired their views, largely antiwar. Gradually, the public came to feel that it had been lied to about the causes and "winnability" of the war. A yawning "credibility gap" opened between the government and the people. New flocks of antiwar "doves" were hatching daily.

Even within the administration, doubts were deepening about the wisdom of the war in Vietnam. When Defense Secretary McNamara expressed increasing discomfiture at the course of events, he was quietly eased out of the cabinet. President Johnson did announce "bombing halts" in early 1966 and early 1967, supposedly to lure the enemy to the peace table. But Washington did not pursue its "peace offensive" with much energy, and the other side did not respond with encouragement. Both sides used the bombing pauses to funnel more troops into South Vietnam.

By early 1968 the brutal and futile struggle had become the longest and most unpopular foreign war in the nation's history. The government had failed utterly to explain to the people what was supposed to be at stake in Vietnam. Many critics wondered if any objective could be worth the vast price, in blood and treasure, that America was paying. Casualties, killed and wounded, already exceeded 100,000. More bombs had been dropped on Vietnam than on all enemy territory in World War II. Evidence mounted that America had been entrapped in an Asian civil war, fighting against highly motivated rebels who were striving to overthrow an oppressive regime. Yet Johnson clung to his basic strategy of stepping up the pressure bit by bit. He stubbornly assured doubting Americans that he could see "the light at the end of the tunnel." But to growing numbers of Americans, it seemed that Johnson was bent on "saving" Vietnam by destroying it.

Vietnam Topples Johnson

Hawkish illusions that the struggle was about to be won were shattered by a blistering Communist offensive launched in late January 1968, during Tet, the Vietnamese New Year. At a time when the Viet Cong were supposedly licking their wounds, they suddenly and simultaneously mounted savage attacks on twenty-seven key South Vietnamese cities, including the capital, Saigon. Although eventually beaten off with heavy losses, they demonstrated anew that victory could not be gained by Johnson's strategy of gradual escalation. The Tet offensive ended in a military defeat but a political victory for the Viet Cong. With an increasingly insistent voice, American public opinion demanded a speedy end to the war. Opposition grew so vehement that President Johnson could feel the very foundations of government shaking under his feet.

American military leaders responded to the Tet attacks with a request for 200,000 more troops. The largest single increment yet, this addition would have swollen American troop strength in Vietnam to about the three-quarter-million mark. The size of the request staggered many policymakers. Former Secretary of State Dean Acheson reportedly advised the president that "the Joint Chiefs of Staff don't know what they're talking about." Johnson himself now began to doubt seriously the wisdom of continuing on his raise-the-stakes course.

The president meanwhile was being sharply challenged from within his own party. Eugene McCarthy, a little-known Democratic senator from Minnesota, had emerged as a contender for the 1968 Democratic presidential nomination. The soft-spoken McCarthy, a sometime poet and devout Catholic, gathered a small army of antiwar college students as campaign workers. Going "clean for Gene," with shaven faces and shortened locks, these idealistic recruits of the "Children's Crusade" invaded the key presidential primary state of New Hampshire to ring doorbells. On March 12, 1968, their efforts gave McCarthy an incredible 42 percent of the Democratic votes and twenty of the twenty-four convention delegates. President Johnson was on the same ballot, but only as a write-in candidate. Four days later Senator Robert F. Kennedy of New York, the murdered president's younger brother and by now himself

Justice on a Saigon Street, 1968 *South Vietnamese police chief executes suspected Viet Cong guerrilla. (Wide World Photos, Inc.)*

Robert F. Kennedy Campaigning *He is shown here running for Senator from New York in 1964. Wrapped in the Kennedy family mystique and exuding his own boyish charm, Kennedy excited partisan crowds to wildly adulatory outpourings. (Steve Schapiro/Black Star.)*

a "dove" on Vietnam, threw his hat into the ring. The charismatic Kennedy, heir to his fallen brother's mantle of leadership, stirred a passionate response among workers, blacks, Hispanics, and young people.

These startling events abroad and at home were not lost on LBJ. The country might explode in greater violence if he met the request of the generals for more troops. His own party was dangerously divided on the war issue. He might not even be able to win renomination after his relatively poor showing in New Hampshire. Yet he remained committed to victory in Vietnam. How could he salvage his blind-alley policy?

Johnson's answer came in a bombshell address on March 31, 1968. He announced on nationwide television that he would finally apply the brakes to the escalating war. He would freeze American troop levels and gradually shift more responsibility to the South Vietnamese themselves. Aerial bombardment of the enemy would be drastically scaled down. Then, in a dramatic plea to unify a dangerously divided nation, Johnson startled his vast audience by firmly declaring that he would not be a candidate for the presidency in 1968.

Johnson's "abdication" had the effect of preserving the military status quo. He had held the "hawks" in check, while offering himself as a sacrifice to the militant "doves." The United States could thus maintain the maximum *acceptable* level of military activity in Vietnam with one hand, while trying to negotiate a settlement with the other.

North Vietnam responded somewhat encouragingly three days later, when it expressed a willingness to talk about peace. After a month of haggling over the site, the adversaries agreed to meet in Paris. But progress was glacially slow, as prolonged bickering developed over the very shape of the conference table.

The Presidential Sweepstakes of 1968

Summer in 1968 was one of the hottest political seasons in the nation's history. Johnson's heir apparent for the Democratic nomination was his liberal vice-president, Hubert H. Humphrey, a former pharmacist, college teacher, mayor, and senator. Loyally supporting LBJ's Vietnam policies through thick and thin, he received the support of the party apparatus, dominated as it was by the White House. Senators McCarthy and Kennedy meanwhile dueled in several state primaries, with Kennedy's bandwagon gathering ever-increasing speed. But on June 5, 1968, the night of an exciting victory in the California primary, Kennedy was shot to death by a young Arab immigrant resentful of the candidate's pro-Israeli views.

Surrounded by bitterness and frustration, the Democrats met in Chicago in late August 1968. Angry antiwar zealots, deprived by an assassin's bullet of their leading candidate, streamed menacingly into Chicago. Mayor Daley responded by arranging for barbed-wire barricades around the convention hall ("Fort Daley"), as well as thousands of police and National Guard reinforcements. Many demonstrators baited the officers in blue as "pigs." Other militants, chanting "Ho, Ho, Ho Chi Minh," shouted obscenities and hurled bags and cans of human filth at the police lines. As people the world over watched on television, the exasperated "peace officers" broke into a "police riot," clubbing and manhandling innocent and guilty alike. Acrid tear gas fumes hung heavy over the city and

Democratic Presidential Hopeful Hubert Humphrey and Inquiring Reporters, 1968 *(Wide World Photos, Inc.)*

even drifted up to candidate Humphrey's hotel suite. Hundreds of people were arrested and scores hospitalized, but no one was killed—except, as cynics said, the Democratic party and its candidate.

Humphrey steamrollered to the nomination on the first ballot. The dovish McCarthyites failed even to secure an antiwar platform plank. Instead, the Humphrey forces, echoing the president, rammed through their own declaration that armed force would be relentlessly applied until the enemy showed more willingness to negotiate.

Scenting victory as the Democrats divided, the Republicans had jubilantly convened in plush Miami Beach, Florida, early in August 1968. Richard M. Nixon, the former vice-president whom John F. Kennedy had narrowly defeated eight years earlier, arose from his political grave to win the nomination. Nixon, with a "loser's image," was fighting history. Not since 1840 had a candidate won the presidency for a first term after a previous electoral defeat for that office. But Nixon had doggedly entered and won several Republican primaries. As a "hawk"

Richard Nixon on the Campaign Trail, 1968   (Raymond Depardon/Magnum Photos, Inc.)

on Vietnam and a right-leaning middle-of-the-roader on domestic policy, he could please the Goldwater conservatives and was acceptable to party moderates. He appealed to white Southern voters and to the "law and order" element when he tapped as his vice-presidential running mate Maryland's Governor Spiro T. Agnew, noted for his tough stands against blacks and dissidents. The Republican platform called for victory in Vietnam and a strong anticrime policy.

A "spoiler" third-party ticket—the American Independent party—added color and confusion to the campaign. It was headed by a scrappy ex-pugilist, George C. Wallace, former governor of Alabama. Wallace jabbed repeatedly at "pointy-headed bureaucrats," and he taunted hecklers as "bums" who needed a bath. Speaking behind a bullet-proof screen, he called for prodding the blacks into their place, with bayonets if necessary. He and his running mate, former air force General Curtis LeMay, also proposed smashing the North Vietnamese to smithereens by "bombing them back to the Stone Age."

Victory for Nixon

Vietnam proved a less crucial issue than expected. Between the positions of the Republicans and the Democrats, there was little to choose. Both candidates were committed to keeping on with the war until the enemy would settle for an "honorable peace," which seemed to mean an "American victory." The millions of "doves" had no place to roost, and many refused to vote at all. Humphrey, scorched by the LBJ brand, went down to defeat as a loyal prisoner of his chief's policies, despite Johnson's last-minute effort to bail him out by announcing a *total* bombing halt.

Nixon, who had lost a cliff-hanger to Kennedy in 1960, won one in 1968. He garnered 301 electoral votes, with 43.4 percent of the popular tally (31,785,480), as compared with 191 electoral votes and 42.7 percent of the popular votes (31,275,166) for Humphrey. Not since Woodrow Wilson in 1912 had the victor received so small a percentage. Nixon was also the first president-elect since 1848 not to bring

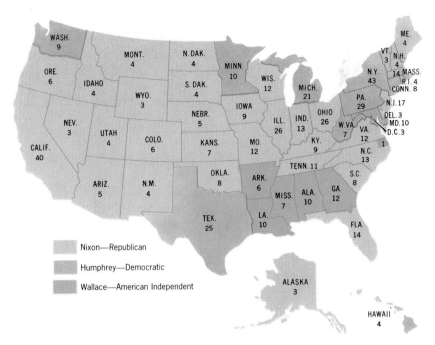

Presidential Election of 1968 (with electoral vote by state) *George Wallace won in five states, and he denied a clear majority to either of the two major-party candidates in twenty-five other states. A shift of some fifty thousand votes might well have thrown the election into the House of Representatives, giving Wallace the strategic bargaining position that he sought.*

Nixon—Republican

Humphrey—Democratic

Wallace—American Independent

in on his coattails at least one house of Congress for his party in an initial presidential election. He carried not a single major city, thus attesting to the continuing urban strength of the Democrats, who also won about 95 percent of the black vote. Nixon had received no clear mandate to do anything. He was a minority president who owed his election to divisions over the war and protest against the unfair draft, crime, and rioting.

Wallace did more poorly than expected. Yet he won an impressive 9,906,473 popular votes and 46 electoral votes, all from five states of the Deep South, four of which the Republican Goldwater had carried in 1964. Wallace remained a formidable force, for he had amassed the largest third-party popular vote in American history.

The Obituary of Lyndon Johnson

Talented but tragedy-struck Lyndon Johnson returned to his Texas ranch in January 1969 and died there four years later. His party was defeated, and his "me-too" Hubert Humphrey was repudiated. His popularity remained low in

the opinion polls, although it had risen somewhat after his "great renunciation"—ironically one of his most popular acts.

Yet Johnson's legislative leadership for a time had been remarkable. No president since Lincoln had worked harder or done more for civil rights. None had shown more compassion for the poor, the ill educated, and the black. Johnson seemed to suffer from a kind of inferiority complex about his own arid cultural background, and he strove furiously to prove that he could be a great "people's president" in the image of his idol, Franklin Roosevelt. His legislative achievements in his first three years in office indeed invited comparison with those of the New Deal.

But by 1966 Johnson was already sinking into the Vietnam quicksands. The Republicans had made gains in Congress, and a white "backlash" had begun to form against the black movement. Great Society programs began to wither on the vine, as soaring war costs sucked tax dollars into the military machine. Johnson had promised both guns and butter but could not keep that promise. Ever-creeping inflation blighted the prospects of prosperity, and the War on Poverty met resistance that was as stubborn as the Viet Cong and eventually went down to defeat. Great want persisted alongside great wealth.

Johnson had crucified himself on the cross of Vietnam. The Asian quagmire engulfed his noblest intentions. Committed to some degree by his two predecessors, he had chosen to defend the American foothold and enlarge the conflict rather than be run out. He was evidently persuaded by his brightest advisers, both civilian and military, that a "cheap" victory was possible. It would be achieved by massive aerial bombing and large, though limited, troop commitments. His decision not to escalate the fighting further offended the "hawks," and his refusal to back off altogether antagonized the "doves." Like the Calvinists of colonial days, luckless Lyndon Johnson was damned if he did and damned if he did not.

Varying Viewpoints

Why did the United States become so deeply immersed in the Vietnam quagmire? Three different explanations have been proposed. The first, appraising Vietnam in the context of the Cold War "containment" policy, portrays the Southeast Asian war as simply another instance of American response to the menace of the Communist "monolith." Had the United States refused to resist the enemy in Vietnam, other nations of the free world would have lost faith in America's will and would eventually have tumbled like "dominoes" into the Soviet bloc. A worldwide cycle of Communist aggression would thus have been encouraged, just as Hitler had been encouraged by the appeasers at Munich in 1938.

The second explanation does not question the anti-Communist thrust of American foreign policy but holds that Vietnam was a mistaken application of that policy. We should have known better, this argument goes, than to have taken over from the French their unwinnable war against a colonial people seeking to throw overboard Western control. Underrating of enemy strength, misguided military strategy, and the fear of appearing "soft on communism" have all been advanced as reasons why American policymakers pursued such an ill-advised course of action.

The third interpretation is the New Left revisionist perspective. It maintains that the Vietnam War was but the logical (and near-fatal) consequence of United States "imperialism." In this view, America feels that it must resist all left-leaning challenges to the existing world order so as to protect its access to overseas markets and raw materials. Significantly, this explanation bears some resemblance to the official defense of American policy. But New Left proponents reverse the official value judgment by holding that American economic domination, and even capitalism itself, are not worth preserving.

Select Readings

Primary Source Documents

Norman Mailer paints vivid portraits of the 1968 conventions in *Miami and the Siege of Chicago* (1968) and of the March on Washington in his *Armies of the Night* (1968). Martin Luther King's *Letter from Birmingham Jail* (1963)* eloquently defends the civil rights movement. The progress of the war in Vietnam is chronicled in *The Pentagon Papers* (1971).*

Secondary Sources

The tumultous decade of the sixties is treated in William L. O'Neill, *Coming Apart: An Informal His-*

tory of America in the 1960s (1971), and in Alan Matusow, *The Unraveling of America* (1984), as well as in the surveys cited in the last chapter. On Kennedy, see Theodore C. Sorenson, *Kennedy* (1965), and Arthur M. Schlesinger, Jr., *A Thousand Days* (1965), both appreciative accounts by insiders. More critical is Henry Fairlie, *The Kennedy Promise* (1973). Other useful biographies include Arthur M. Schlesinger, Jr., *Robert F. Kennedy and His Times* (1978); Warren I. Cohen, *Dean Rusk* (1980); and two books by Herbert Parmet: *Jack: The Struggles of John F. Kennedy* (1980) and *JFK: The Presidency of John F. Kennedy* (1983). Seymour Harris is informative on *Economics of the Kennedy Years* (1964), as is Jim F. Heath, *John F. Kennedy and the Business Community* (1969). The Cuban missile crisis is chronicled in Robert F. Kennedy, *Thirteen Days* (1969), and Graham Allison, *Essence of Decision* (1971). On the space program, consult Walter McDougall, *The Heavens and the Earth* (1985), and Clayton Koppes, *JPL (Jet Propulsion Laboratory) and the American Space Program* (1982). Kennedy's assassination is scrutinized, not entirely satisfactorily, in *The Official Warren Commission Report* (1964). Gripping reading is William Manchester, *Death of a President* (1967). Eric Goldman, *The Tragedy of Lyndon Johnson* (1969), is a sympathetic yet critical account of the Johnson presidency. In the same vein, with a psychoanalytic touch, is Doris Kearns, *Lyndon B. Johnson and the American Dream* (1976). Johnson's own memoir, *The Vantage Point* (1971), is marred by excessive self-justification. An equally unbalanced antidote is Robert Caro's *The Years of Lyndon Johnson: The Path to Power* (1982). The conditions that called forth the Great Society programs are movingly described in Michael Harrington, *The Other America: Poverty in the United States* (1962). James Patterson summarizes *America's Struggle against Poverty* (1981). The racial upheavals of the decade are discussed in Harvard Sitkoff, *The Struggle for Black Equality, 1954–1980* (1981); Clayborne Carson, *In Struggle: SNCC (Student Non-Violent Coordinating Committee) and the Black Awakening of the 1960s* (1981); Carl M. Bauer, *John F. Kennedy and the Second Reconstruction* (1977); and William H. Chafe, *Civilities and Civil Rights: Greensboro, North Carolina, and the Black Struggle for Freedom* (1980). See also Stephen B. Oates, *Let the Trumpet Sound: The Life of Martin Luther King, Jr.* (1982); Alex Haley, ed., *The Autobiography of Malcolm X* (1966); and Eldridge Cleaver, *Soul on Ice* (1968). On "New Left" radicals, consult Kirkpatrick Sale, *SDS (Students for a Democratic Society)* (1973); Sara Evans, *Personal Politics* (1979); Todd Gitlin, *The Whole World Is Watching: Mass Media in the Making and Unmaking of the New Left* (1980); and David Harris's personal memoir, *Dreams Die Hard* (1982). On Vietnam, consult Ronald Spector, *The United States Army in Vietnam* (1984), and Stanley Karnow's encyclopedic *Vietnam: A History* (1983). A concise account is George Herring, *America's Longest War* (1979). Presidential elections are described in continuing installments of Theodore H. White's *The Making of the President, 1964* (1965) and *The Making of the President, 1968* (1969).

44

The Stalemated Seventies

> *In all my years of public life, I have never obstructed justice.*
> *People have got to know whether or not their President is a*
> *crook. Well, I'm not a crook; I earned everything I've got.*
>
> *Richard Nixon, 1973*

Nixon "Vietnamizes" the War

Inaugurated on January 20, 1969, Richard Nixon urged the American people, torn with dissension over Vietnam and race relations, to "stop shouting at one another." Yet the new president seemed an unlikely conciliator of the clashing forces that appeared to be ripping American society apart. Solitary and suspicious by nature, he could be brittle and testy in the face of opposition. He also harbored bitter resentments against the "liberal establishment" that had cast him into the political darkness for much of the preceding decade. Yet Nixon brought one hugely valuable asset with him to the White House—his broad knowledge and thoughtful expertise in foreign affairs. With cal-

culating shrewdness, he applied himself to putting America's foreign-policy house in order.

The first burning need was to quiet the public uproar over Vietnam. President Nixon's announced policy—called "Vietnamization"—was to withdraw the 540,000 United States troops in South Vietnam over an extended period. The South Vietnamese—with American money, weapons, training, and advice—could then gradually take over the burden of fighting their own war.

The so-called Nixon Doctrine thus evolved. It proclaimed that the United States would honor its existing defense commitments but that in the future Asians and others would have to fight their own wars without the support of large bodies of American ground troops.

Nixon sought not to end the war but to win it by other means, without the further spilling of American blood. But even this much involvement was distasteful to the American "doves," many of whom demanded a withdrawal that was prompt, complete, unconditional, and irreversible. Antiwar protesters staged a massive national Vietnam moratorium in October 1969, as 100,000 people jammed the Boston Common and some 50,000 filed by the White House carrying lighted candles.

Undaunted, Nixon launched his own homefront counteroffensive. On November 3, 1969, he delivered a dramatic televised appeal to the great "silent majority," who presumably supported the war. Though ostensibly conciliatory, Nixon's appeal was in fact deeply divisive, as he sought to carve out a political constituency that would back his policies. His intentions soon became clear, when he unleashed tough-talking Vice-President Agnew for attacks on the "misleading" news media, as well as the "effete corps of impudent snobs" and the "nattering nabobs of negativism" who demanded quick withdrawal from Vietnam. Nixon himself in 1970 sneered at the student antiwar demonstrators as "bums."

By January 1970 the Vietnam conflict had become the longest in American history and, with 40,000 killed and over 250,000 wounded, the third most costly foreign war in the nation's experience. Disgust with the bloody mess in Vietnam was further deepened by shocking reports of the massacre of innocent women and

President Richard M. Nixon *Reversing Kennedy's inaugural plea to "bear any burden," Nixon told Congress in February 1970: "America cannot—and will not—conceive all the plans, design all the programs, execute all the decisions and undertake all the defense of the free nations of the world." (Costa Manos/Magnum Photos, Inc.)*

children by American troops in the village of My Lai. Even soldiers in the field shared the general disillusion, as drug abuse, mutiny, and sabotage reduced the army's effectiveness as a fighting force. Increasingly desperate for a

"Cold War? Not for Some" *(Brimrose in the Portland Oregonian by permission.)*

At a press conference in May 1970, President Nixon explained why he had called student rioters "bums." He stated that he had always upheld the right of nonviolent dissent, but "when students on university campuses burn buildings, when they engage in violence, when they break up furniture, when they terrorize their fellow students and terrorize the faculty, then I think 'bums' is perhaps too kind a word to apply to that kind of person."

quick end to the demoralizing conflict, Nixon widened the war in 1970 by attacking Vietnam's neighbor, Cambodia.

Cambodianizing the Vietnam War

For several years the North Vietnamese and Viet Cong had been using Cambodia, bordering South Vietnam on the west, as a springboard for troops, weapons, and supplies. Suddenly, on April 29, 1970, without consulting Congress, Nixon ordered American forces, joining with the South Vietnamese, to clean out these hornets' nests by invading Cambodia, which was officially neutral.

Restless students nationwide responded to the Cambodian invasion with rock throwing, window smashing, and arson. At Kent State University, in Ohio, members of the National Guard fired into an angry crowd, killing four and wounding many more; at Jackson State College, in Mississippi, the highway patrol discharged volleys at a student dormitory, killing two black students. The nation fell prey to turmoil as rioters and arsonists convulsed the land.

Nixon withdrew the American troops from Cambodia on June 29, 1970, after only two

The War at Home *Antiwar students clash with police in Ann Arbor, Michigan, in 1970. (Ken Hamblin, Black Star.)*

months. The president's supporters argued that the invasion had captured enemy supplies and given the South Vietnamese eight months to strengthen themselves. But the enemy bases were not eliminated, and Cambodian Communists soon overran large areas of the country.

In America the invasion deepened the bitterness between "hawks" and "doves," as right-wing groups physically assaulted leftists. Disillusionment with "whitey's war" increased ominously among blacks in the armed forces. The Senate (though not the House) overwhelmingly repealed the Gulf of Tonkin blank check that Congress had given Johnson in 1964 and sought ways to restrain Nixon. The youth of America, still aroused, were only slightly mollified when the government reduced draft calls and shortened the period of draftability, on a lottery basis, from eight years to one year. They were similarly pleased, though not pacified, when the twenty-sixth constitutional amendment, in 1971, lowered the voting age to eighteen.

In the spring of 1971, mass rallies and marches once more erupted from coast to coast. Belligerent "doves" attempted to shut down the government in Washington by blocking bridges, streets, and intersections. New combustibles fueled the fires of antiwar discontent in June 1971, when *The New York Times* published a top-secret Pentagon study of America's involvement in the Vietnam War. These Pentagon Papers, "leaked" to the *Times* by former Pentagon official Daniel Ellsberg, laid bare the blunders and deceptions of the Kennedy and Johnson administrations, especially the provoking of the 1964 North Vietnamese attack in the Gulf of Tonkin. As the antiwar firestorm flared ever higher, Nixon grew more daring in his search for an exit from Vietnam.

Nixon in Beijing (Peking) and Moscow

With bold insight, Nixon concluded that the road out of Vietnam ran through Beijing and Moscow. The two great Communist powers, Russia and China, were clashing bitterly over

"Henry Kissinger, Diplomat with a Global Vision"
Born in Germany, Kissinger never lost his German accent. A brilliant Harvard professor, he first served as Nixon's adviser on national security affairs and then as secretary of state. (Reprinted by permission of Chronicle Features, San Francisco.)

Nixon next traveled to Moscow in May 1972 to play his "China card" in a game of high-stakes diplomacy in the Kremlin. The Russians, hungry for American foodstuffs and haunted by the fear of intensified rivalry with an American-backed China, were ready to deal. Nixon's visit ushered in an era of relaxed tensions, called détente, and resulted in several significant agreements. One product of eased relations was the great grain deal of 1972—a three-year arrangement by which the food-rich United States agreed to sell the Russians at least $750 million worth of wheat, corn, and other cereals.

Far more important were efforts to stem the dangerously frantic competition in nuclear arms. The first major achievement was an anti–ballistic missile (ABM) treaty, which limited each nation to two clusters of defensive missiles. The second significant pact was an agreement, known as SALT (for Strategic Arms Limitation Talks), to freeze the numbers of long-range nuclear missiles for five years.

their rival interpretations of Marxism. Nixon astutely perceived that the Chinese-Russian tension afforded the United States an opportunity to play off one antagonist against the other—and to enlist the aid of both in pressuring North Vietnam into peace.

Nixon's thinking was reinforced by his national security adviser, Dr. Henry A. Kissinger. Bespectacled and German-accented, Kissinger had reached America as a youth when his parents fled Hitler's anti-Jewish persecutions. A former Harvard professor, in 1969 he had begun meeting secretly on Nixon's behalf with North Vietnamese officials in Paris to negotiate an end to the war in Vietnam. He was meanwhile preparing the president's path to Beijing and Moscow.

Nixon, heretofore an uncompromising anti-Communist, announced to a startled nation in July 1971 that he had accepted an invitation to visit China the following year. He made his historic journey in February 1972. Between glass-clinking toasts and walks on the fabled Great Wall of China, the president paved the way for improved relations between Washington and Beijing.

Balancing Act *Nixon treads delicately between the two Communist super-powers in 1973, holding some of the wheat with which he enticed both into détente. (© Ranan R. Lurie.)*

These accords constituted a long-overdue first step toward slowing the arms race. Yet even though the ABM treaty forbade elaborate defensive systems, the United States forged ahead with the development of "MIRVs" (Multiple Independently Targeted Reentry Vehicles), designed to overcome any defense by "saturating" it with large numbers of warheads, several to a rocket. Predictably, the Soviets proceeded to "MIRV" their own missiles, and the arms race ratcheted up to a still more perilous plateau, with over sixteen thousand nuclear warheads deployed by both sides in the 1980s.

Nixon's détente diplomacy was, on the whole, successful. By checkmating and co-opting the two great Communist powers, the president had cleverly set the stage for America's exit from Vietnam. But the concluding act in that wrenching tragedy still remained to be played.

A New Team on the Supreme Bench

Nixon had lashed out during the campaign at the "permissiveness" and "judicial activism" of the Supreme Court presided over by Chief Justice Earl Warren. Following his appointment in 1953, the jovial Warren had led the Court into a series of decisions that drastically affected civil rights, criminal law, the practice of religion, and the structure of political representation. The decisions of the Supreme Court under Warren reflected its deep concern for the individual, no matter how lowly.

In 1963 the Court held (*Gideon* v. *Wainwright*) that all defendants in serious criminal cases were entitled to legal counsel, even if they were too poor to afford it. More controversial were the rulings in two cases—*Escobedo* (1964) and *Miranda* (1966)—that ensured the right of the accused to remain silent and to enjoy other protections when accused of a crime. In this way safeguards were erected against confessions extorted under the rubber hose and other torture. Critics of these decisions were loud in their condemnation of "crook coddling" and demanded that the courts handcuff criminals, not the "cops."

Nor did the Court shy away from explosive religious issues. In two shocking decisions, in 1962 and 1963, it voted against required prayers and Bible reading in the public schools. These rulings were based on the First Amendment, which required the separation of church and state, but they seemed to put the justices in the same bracket with atheistic Communists. Cynics predicted that the "old goats in black coats" would soon be erasing "In God We Trust" from all coins.

Infuriating to many southerners was the determination of the Court, following the school-desegregation decision of 1954, to support black people in civil rights cases. Five southern state legislatures officially nullified the "sociological" Supreme Court decision, but they in turn were overruled by the high tribunal. In general, it held that the states could not deny to blacks the rights that were extended to white people. Conservatives complained bitterly that the Warren Court was not interpreting the Constitution but rewriting it, at the expense of states' rights. It was acting more like a legislature and not enough like a judicial body.

The Warren Court also struck at the overrepresentation in state legislatures of cow-pasture agricultural districts. Adopting the principle of

"You Mean These Apply to the Riff-Raff Too?" (From The Herblock Gallery, *Simon and Schuster, 1968.*)

one-man-one-vote, the Court in 1962 and 1964 ruled that the state legislatures, both upper and lower houses, would have to be reapportioned according to the human population, irrespective of cows. States' righters and assorted right-wingers raised anew the battle cry "Impeach Earl Warren." But the legislatures grudgingly went ahead with reapportionment.

From 1954 onward the Court came under endless criticism, the bitterest since New Deal days. Its foes made numerous but unsuccessful efforts to clip its wings through bills in Congress or through constitutional amendments. But the Court perhaps reflected not so much its own philosophy as the necessity of grappling with stubborn social problems spawned by mid-century tensions, even—or especially—if duly elected legislatures failed to do so.

Fulfilling campaign promises, President Nixon undertook to change the Court's philosophical complexion. Taking advantage of several vacancies, he sought appointees who would strictly interpret the Constitution, cease "meddling" in social and political questions, and not coddle radicals or criminals. The Senate in 1969 speedily confirmed his nomination of white-maned Warren E. Burger of Minnesota to succeed the retiring Earl Warren as chief justice. Before the end of 1971 the Court counted four conservative Nixon appointments out of nine members.

Nixon on the Home Front

Veto hatchet in hand, Nixon was frequently at odds with Congress. When the legislators passed what he regarded as "budget-busting" appropriations over his veto, he simply impounded (that is, refused to spend) the funds. Other presidents had occasionally failed to spend surplus money, but Nixon engaged in this practice repeatedly and on a large scale, despite court decisions overruling him. Impoundment was but one glaring example of his presidential expansion of constitutional powers at the expense of the legislative branch.

With Congress often in a balky mood, Nixon enjoyed scant success in his efforts to reform the welfare system. He fared better in his campaign for a "revenue-sharing" bill that provided for a return of $30 million in federal revenues to the states over a period of five years.

Worried about creeping inflation (then running at about 5 percent), Nixon overcame his distaste for economic controls and imposed a ninety-day wage-and-price freeze in 1971. Seeking to stimulate the nation's sagging exports, he next stunned the world by taking the United States off the gold standard and devaluing the dollar. These moves effectively ended the system of international currency stabilization that had functioned for more than a quarter of a century following World War II.

Congress worried about inflation, too, and in a fateful decision voted in 1972 to raise Social Security benefits and provide for automatic increases when the cost of living rose more than 3 percent in any year. Designed to protect the elderly and disabled against the ravages of inflation, this legislation actually helped to fuel the inflationary fire that raged out of control later in the decade.

Elected as a minority president, with only 43 percent of the vote in 1968, Nixon devised a clever but cynical plan—called the "southern strategy"—to achieve a majority in 1972. His Supreme Court nominations constituted an important part of this plan. He also courted white voters by soft-pedaling civil rights and openly opposing school busing to achieve racial balance. But as fate would have it, foreign policy dominated the presidential campaign of 1972.

The Nixon Landslide of 1972

Vietnam continued to be the burning issue. Nearly four years had passed since Nixon had promised, as a presidential candidate, to end the war and "win" the peace. Yet in the spring of 1972 the fighting escalated anew to alarming levels when the North Vietnamese, heavily equipped with foreign tanks, burst through the demilitarized zone (DMZ) separating the two Vietnams. Nixon reacted promptly by launching massive bombing attacks on strategic centers in North Vietnam, including Hanoi, the capital. Gambling heavily on foreign forbearance, he also ordered the dropping of contact mines to

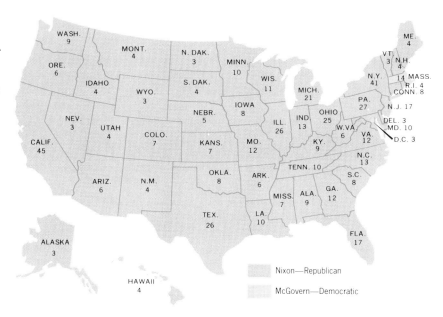

Presidential Election of 1972 (with electoral vote by state) Nixon buried McGovern in this election, but when his administration soon thereafter began to sink in a swamp of scandals, bumper stickers appeared in Boston proclaiming "Don't blame me, I'm from Massachusetts."

Nixon—Republican
McGovern—Democratic

blockade the principal harbors of North Vietnam. Either Russia or China or both could have responded explosively, but neither did, thanks to Nixon's shrewd diplomacy. The North Vietnamese offensive finally ground to a halt.

The continuing Vietnam conflict spurred the rise of South Dakota Senator George McGovern to the 1972 Democratic nomination. McGovern's promise to pull the remaining American troops out of Vietnam in ninety days earned him the backing of the large antiwar element in the party. But his appeal to racial minorities, feminists, leftists, and youth alienated the traditional working-class backbone of his party. Moreover, the discovery shortly after the convention that McGovern's running mate, Missouri Senator Thomas Eagleton, had undergone psychiatric care forced Eagleton's removal from the ticket and further doomed McGovern's candidacy.

Nixon's campaign emphasized that he had wound down the "Democratic war" in Vietnam from some 540,000 troops to about 30,000. His candidacy received an added boost just twelve days before the election when the high-flying Dr. Kissinger announced that "peace is at hand" in Vietnam and that an agreement would be settled in a few days.

Nixon won in a landslide. His lopsided victory encompassed every state except Massachu-

setts and the nonstate District of Columbia. He piled up 520 electoral votes to 17 and a popular majority of 47,169,911 votes to 29,170,383. McGovern had counted on a large number of young people's votes, but less than half the 18–21 age group even bothered to register. Nixon's claim that the election gave him an unprecedented mandate for his policies was weakened by Republican election losses in both the House and Senate.

Bombing North Vietnam to the Peace Table

The dove of peace, "at hand" in Vietnam just before the balloting, took flight after the election, when Nixon refused to be stampeded into accepting terms that had obvious loopholes. After the fighting on both sides had again escalated, he launched a furious two-week bombing of North Vietnam. To outsiders, this appeared to be an ironhanded effort to drive the North Vietnamese back to the conference table. This attack was the heaviest of the war and resulted in substantial losses of America's big B-52 bombers. But this merciless pounding drove the North Vietnamese negotiators to agree to cease-fire arrangements on January 23, 1973, nearly three months after peace was prematurely proclaimed.

President Nixon hailed the face-saving cease-fire agreements as "peace with honor," but the boast rang hollow. The United States was to withdraw its remaining 27,000 or so troops and could reclaim some 560 American prisoners of war. The government of South Vietnam would be permitted to continue receiving limited American support but no more American fighting forces. An election was eventually to be held to determine the future of the country. The North Vietnamese were allowed to keep some 145,000 troops in South Vietnam, where they could be used to spearhead a powerful new offensive when the time seemed ripe. Ominously, the North Vietnamese still occupied about 30 percent of South Vietnam. To many observers, the shaky "peace" seemed little more than a thinly disguised American retreat.

Watergate Woes

Nixon's electoral triumph was soon sullied by the so-called Watergate scandals. On June 17, 1972, some two months before his renomination, a bungled burglary had occurred in the Democratic headquarters, located in the Watergate apartment-office complex in Washington. Five men were arrested inside the building with electronic "bugging" equipment in their possession. They were working for the Republican Committee for the Re-election of the President—popularly known as CREEP—which had managed to raise tens of millions of dollars, often by secretive, unethical, or unlawful means. CREEP had also engaged in a "dirty tricks" campaign of espionage and sabotage, including faked documents, directed against Democratic candidates in the campaign of 1972.

The Watergate break-in proved to be only the tip of an iceberg in a slimy sea of corruption that made the Grant and Harding scandals look almost respectable. A number of prominently placed White House aides and advisers were forced to resign. Many were involved in a criminal obstruction of justice through tangled cover-ups or payment of hush money. By early

1974 twenty-nine people had been indicted, had pleaded guilty, or had been convicted of Watergate-related crimes.

The scandal in Washington also provoked the improper or illegal use of the Federal Bureau of Investigation and the Central Intelligence Agency. Even the Internal Revenue Service was called upon by Nixon's aides to audit or otherwise harass political opponents and others who had fallen into disfavor. A White House "enemies list" turned up that included innocent citizens who were to be hounded or prosecuted in various ways. In the name of national security, Nixon's aides had authorized a burglary of the files of Dr. Daniel Ellsberg's psychiatrist, so great was the determination to convict the man who had "leaked" the Pentagon Papers. This was the most notorious exploit of the White House "plumbers unit," created to plug up leaks of confidential information.

A select Senate committee, headed by the aging Senator Sam Ervin of North Carolina, conducted a prolonged and widely televised series

"The Ancient Mariner" Nixon troubled by Watergate albatross. (Courtesy SCRAWLS and the Palm Beach Post.)

of hearings in 1973–1974. John Dean III, a former White House lawyer with a remarkable memory, testified glibly and at great length as to the involvement of the top echelons in the White House, including the president, in the cover-up of the Watergate break-in. Dean in effect accused Nixon of the crime of obstructing justice, but the committee then had only the unsupported word of Dean against White House protestations of innocence.

The Great Tape Controversy

A bombshell exploded before Senator Ervin's committee in July 1973 when a former presidential aide reported the presence in the White House of "bugging" equipment, installed under the president's authority. President Nixon's conversations, in person or on the telephone, had been recorded on tape without notifying the other parties that electronic eavesdropping was taking place.

Nixon had emphatically denied prior knowledge of the Watergate burglary or involvement in the cover-up. Now Dean's sensational testimony could be checked against the White House tapes, and the Senate committee could better determine who was telling the truth. But for months Nixon flatly refused to produce the taped evidence. He took refuge behind various principles, including separation of powers and executive privilege (confidentiality). But all of them were at least constitutionally dubious, especially when used to cover up crime or obstruct justice.

The anxieties of the White House deepened when Vice-President Agnew, whom Nixon had lifted from relative obscurity in 1968, was forced to resign in October 1973, having been accused of taking bribes or "kickbacks" from Maryland contractors while governor and also as vice-president. President Nixon himself was now in danger of being removed by the impeachment route, so Congress invoked the Twenty-fifth Amendment (see the Appendix) to replace Agnew with a twelve-term congressman from Michigan, Gerald ("Jerry") Ford, whose record in public life was politically respectable and whose financial affairs proved to be above suspicion at a time when unquestioned honesty was in short supply.

Ten days after Agnew's resignation came the famous "Saturday Night Massacre" (October

"Tapeworm" Republican elephant suffers from a strange disease. (Reprinted by permission of Chronicle Features, San Francisco.)

20, 1973). Archibald Cox, a Harvard law professor appointed as a special prosecutor by Nixon in May, issued a subpoena for relevant tapes and other documents from the White House. Nixon thereupon fired Cox and then accepted the resignations of the attorney general and the deputy attorney general because they had refused to fire Cox.

The outraged public outcry brought such strident demands for impeachment or resignation that Nixon backed down. Although he agreed to comply with demands for tapes and documents from the new special prosecutor and the House Judiciary Committee, such materials were forthcoming only partially and after foot-dragging delays. Word gradually leaked out of the White House that some of the tapes were missing, that others had never been recorded, and that portions of key conversations had been mysteriously blotted out.

The Secret Bombing of Cambodia and the War Powers Act

As if Watergate were not enough, the constitutionality of Nixon's continued aerial battering of Cambodia came under increasing fire. In July 1973 America was shocked to learn that the U.S. Air Force had already secretly conducted some thirty-five hundred bombing raids against North Vietnamese positions in Cambodia. They had begun in March 1969 and had continued for some fourteen months prior to the open American incursion in May 1970. The most disturbing feature of these sky forays was that, while they were going on, American officials, including the president, were avowing that Cambodian neutrality was being respected. Countless Americans began to wonder what kind of representative government they had if they were fighting a war they knew nothing about.

Defiance followed secretiveness. After the Vietnam cease-fire in January 1973, Nixon openly carried on his large-scale bombing of Communist forces in order to help the rightist Cambodian government. This stretching of presidential war-making powers met furious opposition from the public and from a clear major-

The *Washington Post* (July 19, 1973) carried this news item: "American B-52 bombers dropped about 104,000 tons of explosives on Communist sanctuaries in neutralist Cambodia during a series of raids in 1969 and 1970. . . . The secret bombing was acknowledged by the Pentagon the Monday after a former Air Force major . . . described how he falsified reports on Cambodian air operations and destroyed records on the bombing missions actually flown."

ity in both houses of Congress, which repeatedly tried to stop the bombing by cutting off appropriations. But Nixon's vetoes of such legislation were always sustained by at least one-third-plus-one votes in the House. Finally, with appropriations running short, Nixon agreed to a compromise in June 1973 whereby he would end the Cambodian bombing six weeks later and seek congressional approval of any future action in that bomb-blasted country.

Congressional opposition to the expansion of presidential war-making powers by Johnson and Nixon led to the War Powers Act in November 1973. Passed over Nixon's veto, it required the president to report to Congress within forty-eight hours after committing troops to a foreign conflict or "substantially" enlarging American combat units in a foreign country. Such a limited authorization would have to end within sixty days unless Congress extended it for thirty more days.

Compelling Nixon to end the bombing of Cambodia in August 1973 was but one manifestation of what came to be called the "New Isolationism." The draft had ended in January 1973, although it was retained on a standby basis. Future members of the armed forces were to be well-paid volunteers—a change that greatly eased tensions among youth. Insistent demands arose in Congress for reducing American armed forces abroad, especially because some 300,000 remained in Europe more than a quarter of a century after Hitler's downfall. The argument often heard was that the Western European countries, with more population than the Soviet

Union, ought by now to be willing and able to provide for their own defense against the forces of communism. But President Nixon, fearful of a weakened hand in the high-stakes game of power politics, headed off all serious attempts at troop reduction.

The Arab Oil Embargo and the Energy Crisis

Adding to Nixon's problems, the long-rumbling Middle East erupted anew in October 1973, when the rearmed Syrians and Egyptians unleashed surprise attacks on Israel in an attempt to regain the territory they had lost in the Six-Day War of 1967. With the Israelis in desperate retreat, Kissinger, who had become secretary of state in September, hastily flew to Moscow in an effort to restrain the Soviets, who were supplying the attackers. Believing that the Russians were poised to fly combat troops to the Suez area, Nixon placed America's nuclear forces on alert and ordered a gigantic airlift of nearly $2 billion in war materials to the Israelis.

This assistance helped save the day, as the Israelis brilliantly turned the tide and threatened Cairo until American diplomacy brought about an uneasy cease-fire.

America's policy of backing Israel against its oil-rich neighbors exacted a heavy penalty. Late in October 1973, the Arab nations suddenly clamped an embargo on oil for the United States and other Israel-supporting countries. Americans, though abundantly forewarned by experts, overnight discovered that the age of cheap and abundant oil had ended. They suffered through a long winter of lowered thermostats and speedometers. Lines of automobiles at service stations lengthened as tempers shortened and a business recession deepened.

The "energy crisis" suddenly energized a number of long-deferred projects. The costly oil pipeline from northern to southern Alaska received congressional sanction in 1974, over the protests of conservationists and environmentalists. Congress enacted a national speed limit of fifty-five miles per hour in order to save fuel. Proposals multiplied for utilizing energy from the sun, wind, geothermal sources, and untapped coal deposits, of which the United

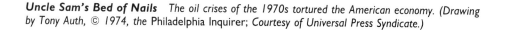

Uncle Sam's Bed of Nails *The oil crises of the 1970s tortured the American economy. (Drawing by Tony Auth, © 1974, the* Philadelphia Inquirer; *Courtesy of Universal Press Syndicate.)*

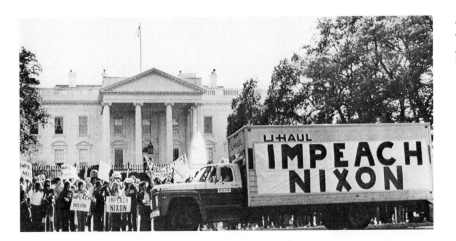

Pushing for Impeachment *An angry and disillusioned public grew increasingly impatient with the president's evasions in 1974. (United Press International photo.)*

States had more than half of the world's known reserves—or enough to last for an estimated several hundred years. Yet heavy coal consumption would increase air pollution. The result was that agitation mounted for relaxing standards for clean air and water, as well as pushing ahead with the construction of more nuclear power stations, despite their ever-present threat of catastrophic radioactivity.

The Arab "blackmail" embargo, partially leaky, was lifted in March 1974, after five months of anxiety and after the Egyptian-Israeli cease-fire had taken effect. Countless Americans, especially those in big, gas-gulping cars, reverted thoughtlessly to their speeding and other wasteful practices. The Middle Eastern sheiks had approximately quadrupled their price for crude oil, and their inevitable accumulation of tens of billions of dollars jeopardized the American balance of trade and payments. And despite the resumed flow of Middle Eastern oil, the country continued to be plagued in 1974 by double-digit inflation, high unemployment, and the growing realization that the cost of energy was headed ever upward.

The Unmaking of a President

Political tribulations added to the nation's cup of woe in 1974. The continuing impeachment inquiry cast damning doubts on Nixon's integrity. Responding to the House Judiciary Committee's demand for the Watergate tapes, Nixon agreed in the spring of 1974 to the publication of "relevant" portions of the tapes, declaring that these would vindicate him. But substantial sections of the wanted tapes were missing, while Nixon's "rough" language was excised with the phrase "expletive deleted." Confronted with demands for the rest of the material, Nixon flatly refused. On July 24, 1974, the president suffered a disastrous setback when the Supreme Court unanimously ruled that "executive privilege" gave him no right to withhold from the special prosecutor portions of tapes relevant to criminal activity. Skating on thin ice over hot water, Nixon reluctantly complied.

The House Judiciary Committee pressed ahead with its articles of impeachment. The key vote came late in July 1974, when the committee adopted the first article, which charged obstruction of "the administration of justice," including Watergate-related crimes. Two other articles were later approved by the committee accusing Nixon of having abused the powers of his office and of having shown contempt of Congress by ignoring lawful subpoenas for relevant tapes and other evidence.

Seeking to soften the impact of inevitable disclosure, Nixon voluntarily took a step, on August 5, 1974, that had a devastating effect on what remained of his credibility. He now made public three subpoenaed tapes of conversations with his chief aide on June 23, 1972. One of them had him giving orders, six days after the

Nixon, the Law-and-Order Man (Douglas Marlette, *the Charlotte* Observer.)

benefits; if he resigned, he could retain them—more than $150,000 a year—and retire in royal splendor.

Left with no better choice, Nixon choked back his tears and announced his resignation in a dramatic television appearance on August 8, 1974. Few presidents had flown so high, and none had been flung so low. In his Farewell Address Nixon admitted having made some "judgments" that "were wrong" but insisted that he had always acted "in what I believed at the time to be the best interests of the nation." Unconvinced, countless Americans would change the song "Hail to the Chief" to "Jail to the Chief."

The nation had survived a wrenching constitutional crisis, which proved that the impeachment machinery forged by the Founding Fathers could work when public opinion

The Last Good-bye Nixon boards a White House helicopter for the last time as president on August 9, 1974. (Wide World Photos, Inc.)

Watergate break-in, to use the Central Intelligence Agency to hold back an inquiry by the Federal Bureau of Investigation. Now Nixon's own tape-recorded words convicted him of having been an active party to the attempted cover-up, in itself the crime of obstructing justice. More than that, he had solemnly told the American people on television that he had known nothing of the Watergate cover-up until about nine months later.

The public backlash proved to be overwhelming. Republican leaders in Congress concluded that the guilty and unpredictable Nixon was a loose cannon on the deck of the ship of state. They frankly informed the president that his impeachment by the full House and removal by the Senate were foregone conclusions. They made it clear that he would best serve his nation, his party, and himself by resigning with honor, or a semblance of it. If convicted by the Senate, he would lose all his normal retirement overwhelmingly demanded that it be made to work. The principles were strengthened that no person is above the law and that presidents must be held to strict accountability for their acts. The United States of America, on the eve of its two-hundredth birthday as a republic, had given an impressive demonstration of self-discipline and self-government to the rest of the world.

The First Unelected President

Gerald Rudolph Ford, the first person to be made president solely by a vote of Congress, entered the blackened White House, in August 1974, with serious handicaps. He was widely—and unfairly—suspected of being little more than a dim-witted former college football player. President Johnson had sneered that "Jerry" was so lacking in brainpower that he could not walk and chew gum at the same time. Worse, Ford had been selected, not elected, vice-president, following Spiro Agnew's resignation in disgrace. An odor of illegitimacy hung about this president without precedent.

Then, out of a clear sky, Ford granted a complete pardon to Nixon for any crimes he may have committed as president, discovered or undiscovered. Democrats were outraged. They wanted iron-toothed justice, even vengeance. They heatedly charged, without persuasive evidence, that Ford was carrying out a "buddy deal" that had been cooked up when Nixon nominated him for the vice-presidency. Lingering suspicions about the pardon cast a dark shadow over Ford's prospects of being elected president in his own right in 1976.

Ford hit rough weather in the heavily Democratic Congress. A serious recession inspired several billion-dollar spending bills intended to reduce unemployment. Fearing the inflationary effects of these huge appropriations, Ford vetoed them. In all, he laid his veto ax to more than fifty bills during his brief term in office. Attacking the inflation problem, Ford launched a Whip Inflation Now campaign (complete with WIN buttons), but it failed to get off the ground. Inflation did drop from the double-digit

How Long Will Nixon Haunt the GOP? *Doubts about Ford's pardon of Nixon clouded his brief presidency. (Joseph A. Smith, as printed in* Newsweek, *September 23, 1974. Collection of the artist.)*

range of 12 percent to about 5 percent by the end of 1976, but the improvement turned out to be only temporary.

Ford's Foreign Affairs

The so-called détente with Russia that Nixon had crafted went haltingly forward. Hopes for a more civilized world rose modestly in July 1975 when President Ford joined leaders from thirty-four other nations in Helsinki, Finland, to sign several sets of historic accords. One group of agreements officially wrote an end to World War II by finally legitimizing the Soviet-dictated boundaries of Poland and other East European countries. In return, the Soviets put their signatures to a "third basket" of agreements, guaranteeing more liberal exchanges of people and information between East and West and protecting certain basic "human rights." The

Vietnam Refugees, 1975 *Thousands of South Vietnamese citizens who had supported the U.S. presence in the war against North Vietnam crowded onto every available form of transportation leaving the country. Fearing massive reprisals by the Communists, they were willing to abandon everything they owned and go anywhere, as long as it was out of the Communists' reach. (Official U.S. Navy photograph.)*

Helsinki accords helped to kindle small dissident movements in Eastern Europe and even in Russia itself, but the Soviets soon poured ice water on these sputtering flames of freedom. Russian restrictions on Jewish emigration had already, in December 1974, prompted the U.S. Congress to add punitive restrictions to a U.S.-Russian trade bill.

West Europeans, especially the West Germans, cheered the Helsinki conference as a milestone of détente, but in the United States, critics increasingly charged that détente was proving to be a one-way street, with American grain and technology flowing across the Atlantic to Russia and with little of comparable inportance flowing back. American conservatives cried that not only were the Soviet Communists preparing to "bury us" but that unwary Americans were supplying the shovels.

Détente was also conspicuously two-faced. Soviet ships and planes hauled great quantities of arms and military technicians to pro-Communist forces around the globe, while Cuba's Castro, with Moscow's blessing, dispatched thousands of troops to Africa. Such ill-concealed activity dashed hopes of establishing diplomatic relations with Cuba.

Despite these difficulties, Ford at first clung stubbornly to détente. But the American public's fury over Russian double-dealing so steadily mounted that by the end of his term the president was refusing even to pronounce the word *détente* in public. The thaw in the Cold War was threatening to prove chillingly brief.

Victory for North Vietnam

Early in 1975 the North Vietnamese gave full throttle to their long-expected drive southward. President Ford urged Congress to vote still more weapons for Vietnam, but his plea was in vain, and without the crutch of massive American aid, the South Vietnamese quickly and ingloriously collapsed.

The dam burst so rapidly that the remaining Americans had to be frantically evacuated by helicopter, the last of them on April 29, 1975. Also rescued were about 140,000 South Vietnamese, most of them so dangerously identified with the Americans that they feared a bloodbath by the victorious Communists. President Ford compassionately admitted these people to the United States, where they added further seasoning to the melting pot.

America's longest, most frustrating war thus ended, not with a bang, but with a whimper. In a technical sense the Americans had not lost the war; their client nation had. The United States had fought the North Vietnamese to a standstill and had then withdrawn its troops in 1973, leaving the Vietnamese to fight their own war, with generous shipments of costly American aircraft, tanks, and other munitions. President Thieu of South Vietnam complained bitterly that the United States had not done or sent enough. Yet the estimated cost to America was $118 billion in current outlays, together with some 56,000 dead and 300,000 wounded. The people of the United States had in fact provided just about everything, except the will to win—and that could not be injected by outsiders.

Technicalities aside, the United States had lost more than a war. It had lost face in the eyes of foreigners, pride in itself, confidence in its military prowess—and much of the economic muscle that had made possible its global leadership since World War II.

In mid-May 1975, about six weeks after the breakneck pullout from Vietnam, Washington applied some strong but strange medicine to its ailing foreign-policy image. Cambodian Communists provided the opportunity when they seized the *Mayaguez*, an unarmed American merchant ship, and captured its thirty-nine crew members. Scarcely pausing for clarification or negotiation, Ford dispatched American forces to free the sailors. The rescuers succeeded—but only after losing about as many lives as they presumably saved.

This swift, two-fisted strike proved a tonic to the U.S. public, who were still smarting from their recent rout in Vietnam, but its effects were short-lived. Americans reluctantly came to realize that their power as well as their pride had been wounded in Vietnam and that recovery would be slow and painful.

Passing the Buck *A cruel, satirical view of where responsibility for the Vietnam debacle should be laid. (© 1975, Jules Feiffer. Reprinted with permission of Universal Press Syndicate.)*

The Bicentennial Campaign and the Carter Victory

America's two-hundredth birthday, in 1976, fell during a presidential election year—a fitting coincidence for a proud democracy. Gerald Ford energetically sought nomination for the presidency in his own right and won the Republican nod at the Kansas City convention.

The Democratic standard-bearer was fifty-one-year-old James Earl Carter, Jr., a dark-horse candidate who galloped out of obscurity during the long primary-elections season. Carter, a peanut farmer from Plains, Georgia, had served as his state's governor from 1971 to 1975. Flashing a toothy smile and insisting on humble "Jimmy" as his first name, this born-again Baptist touched many people with his down-home sincerity. He ran against the memory of Nixon and Watergate as much as he ran against Ford, and his most effective campaign pitch was his promise that "I'll never lie to you." Untainted by ties with a corrupt and cynical Washington, he attracted voters as an outsider who would clean the disorderly house of "big government."

Carter squeezed out a narrow victory on election day, with 51 percent of the popular vote. The electoral count stood at 297 to 240. The winner swept every state except Virginia in his native South. Especially important were the votes of blacks, 97 percent of whom cast their ballots for Carter.

After the colorful inaugural ceremonies of January 20, 1977, Jimmy Carter waved off the official black limousine and walked, hand in hand with his wife Rosalyn, down Pennsylvania Avenue to his new home at the White House. This act symbolized his determination to maintain the common touch. The new president's popularity remained exceptionally high during his first few months in office, even when he courted public disfavor by courageously keeping his campaign promise to pardon ten thousand draft evaders of the Vietnam War era.

Carter also enjoyed hefty Democratic majorities in both houses of Congress. Hopes ran high that the stalemate of the Nixon-Ford years be-

President Jimmy Carter's Inaugural Walk, 1977 (Bettmann Newsphotos.)

tween a Republican White House and a Democratic Capitol Hill would now be ended. At first, Carter enjoyed notable political success. Congress granted his request to create a new cabinet-level Department of Energy. Calling the American tax system "a disgrace to the human race," Carter also proposed tax reform and reduction. Congress eventually obliged him, in part, with an $18 billion tax cut in 1978.

But Carter's honeymoon did not last long. An inexperienced outsider, he had campaigned against the Washington "establishment" and never quite made the transition to being an insider himself. He repeatedly rubbed congressional fur the wrong way, especially by failing to consult adequately with the leaders. Critics charged that he isolated himself in a shallow pool of fellow Georgians, whose ignorance of the ways of Washington compounded the problems of their greenhorn chief.

Carter's Humanitarian Diplomacy

As a committed Christian, President Carter displayed from the outset an overriding concern for "human rights" as the guiding principle of his foreign policy. He verbally lashed the dictatorial regimes of Cuba and Uganda, among others, and cut foreign aid to the repressive governments in Uruguay, Argentina, and Ethiopia. But he stopped short of punitive actions against other offending nations, such as South Korea or the Philippines, presumably because they were too vital to American security to risk insulting. In the African nations of Rhodesia (later Zimbabwe) and South Africa, Carter championed the oppressed black majority, whose cause was also eloquently defended by United Nations Ambassador Andrew Young.

The nightmarish nuclear arms race with the Soviet Union continued to cause jitters, especially because the limitations on intercontinental ballistic missiles, embodied in the SALT agreements signed by President Nixon, were due to expire in late 1977. Carter in February 1977 publicly called for renewing the SALT accords and extending them to include real reductions in nuclear armaments, not just limitations

Historical Double Take *Many Americans who looked back reverently to Roosevelt's "Rough Rider" diplomacy were outraged at the Panama "give-away." But the Carter administration, looking to the future, argued persuasively that relinquishing control of the canal would be healthy for U.S.–Latin American relations. (© Valtman/Rothco.)*

on their growth. The Soviets gave these proposals a frosty reception, though both sides agreed to honor the SALT treaty even after it formally expired.

Carter had better luck with two treaties designed to turn over to Panama complete ownership and control of the Panama Canal by the year 2000. But the president's most spectacular foreign-policy achievement came in September 1978 at Camp David, the woodsy presidential retreat in the Maryland highlands. By August 1978 relations between Egypt and Israel had deteriorated so far that another blowup in the misery-drenched Middle East seemed imminent. So grave was the danger that Carter courageously risked humiliating failure by inviting President Anwar Sadat of Egypt and Prime Minister Menachem Begin of Israel to a summit conference at Camp David.

The Signing of the Camp David Agreement, September 17, 1978   *Anwar Sadat of Egypt, Jimmy Carter of the United States, and Menachem Begin of Israel put their signatures to the historic accord that brought hopes of peace to the war-torn Middle East. (© Sygma.)*

Skillfully serving as go-between, Carter after thirteen days persuaded the two visitors to sign an accord (September 17, 1978) that held considerable promise of peace. Israel agreed in principle to withdraw from territory conquered in the 1967 war, and Egypt in return promised to respect Israel's borders. Both parties pledged themselves to sign a formal peace treaty within three months. The president crowned this diplomatic success by resuming full diplomatic relations with China in early 1979, after a nearly thirty-year interruption.

Despite these dramatic accomplishments, trouble stalked Carter's foreign policy. Overshadowing all international issues was the ominous reheating of the Cold War with Russia. Détente fell into disrepute as thousands of Cuban troops, assisted by Soviet advisers, appeared in Angola, Ethiopia, and elsewhere in Africa to support revolutionary factions. Negotiations with Moscow over the SALT II agreement remained stalled in the face of this Soviet military meddling. Also worrisome was the apparent confusion about foreign policy within the Carter administration. The dovish secretary of state, Cyrus Vance, seemed always at odds with the hawkish national security adviser, Polish-born Zbigniew Brzezinski. "Who's in charge here?" was a question repeatedly raised by the president's foreign-policy critics, whose numbers were growing.

Carter Tackles the Ailing Economy

Adding to Carter's mushrooming woes was the failing health of the economy. Prices had been rising feverishly, increasing at a rate of more than 10 percent a year by 1974 ("double-digit" inflation). Crippling oil-price hikes from the Organization of Petroleum Exporting Countries (OPEC) in that same year dealt the reeling economy another body blow. A stinging recession brought the inflation rate down temporarily during Gerald Ford's presidency, but virtually from the moment of Carter's inauguration, prices resumed their dizzying ascent. OPEC nearly doubled its petroleum charges in 1979, helping to drive American inflation well above 13 percent. The soaring bill for imported oil pushed America's balance of payments deeply into the red (an unprecedented $40 billion in

1978), as Americans paid more for foreign products than they were able to earn from selling their own goods overseas.

Yawning deficits in the federal budget, reaching nearly $60 billion in 1980, further aggravated the economy's inflationary ailments. Americans with fixed incomes—mostly elderly persons or workers without a strong union to go to bat for them—suffered from shrinking real incomes, as their dollars diminished in purchasing power. People with money to lend pushed interest rates ever higher, hoping to protect themselves from being repaid in badly depreciated dollars. The "prime rate" (the rate of interest that banks charged their very best customers) vaulted to an unheard-of 20 percent in early 1980. The high cost of borrowing money shoved small businesses to the wall and strangled the construction industry, heavily dependent on loans to finance new housing and other projects.

From the outset, Carter diagnosed America's economic disease as stemming primarily from the nation's costly dependence on foreign oil. Accordingly, one of the first acts of his presidency was a dramatic appeal to embark on an energy crusade that he called "the moral equivalent of war." He called for legislation to improve energy conservation, especially by curtailing the manufacture of large, gas-guzzling automobiles. But these proposals, in April 1977, ignited a blaze of indifference among the American people. They had already forgotten the long gasoline lines of 1973, when OPEC had first imposed an oil embargo. Public apathy and congressional hostility smothered President Carter's hopes of quickly initiating an energetic energy program.

Carter's Energy Woes

Events in faraway Iran jolted Americans out of their complacency about energy supplies in 1979. The imperious Mohammed Reza Pahlevi, shah of Iran, had long ruled his oil-rich land with a will of steel. His repressive regime finally provoked a backlash, and the shah was forced into globe-wandering exile in January 1979. Vi-

"Hello There, Have You Thought about the Energy Crisis Today?" *Carter opposes gas-guzzling cars. (Reprinted by permission of Chronicle Features, San Francisco.)*

olent revolution, spearheaded by Muslim fundamentalists, engulfed Iran in the wake of the shah's departure, and the crippling chaos soon spread to the country's oil fields. As Iranian oil stopped flowing into the stream of world commerce, petroleum prices resumed their steep rise, and shortages appeared. Americans once again found themselves waiting impatiently in long lines at their local gas stations or allowed to buy gasoline only on specified days.

The shock of rising oil prices and tightening oil supplies spurred inflation and threatened to stifle the economy. On the other hand, the suddenness and seriousness of the crisis vividly underscored the president's contention that the nation had to adopt a comprehensive energy program. Seeking to take political advantage of the calamity, Carter began in April 1979 to lift price controls from domestically produced oil, a move designed both to curtail consumption and to increase production. At the same time, he called for a massive "windfall profits" tax on the increased revenues that domestic oil producers would enjoy as a result of rising prices.

As the oil crisis deepened, President Carter sensed the rising temperature of popular discontent and sought ways to advance still further toward his energy goals. In July 1979 he retreated to the presidential mountain hideaway at Camp David, where he remained largely out of public view for ten days. Like a royal potentate of old, summoning the wise men of the realm for their counsel in a time of crisis, Carter called in over a hundred leaders from all walks of life to give him their views. Yet true to his folksy image, he ended his consultations by going to a nearby small town and soliciting the advice of some ordinary Americans in their modest living room. Meanwhile, the nation waited anxiously for the results of these extraordinary deliberations.

Carter came down from the mountaintop on July 15, 1979. He revealed his thoughts to the American people in a remarkable television address, which amounted to a kind of old-fashioned "jeremiad." He chided his fellow citizens for falling into a "moral and spiritual crisis" and for being too concerned with "material goods." He spoke somberly about the "malaise" afflicting the country. Finally, Carter arrived at his energy proposals. He boldly called for a ten-year, $140 billion federal program. Its centerpiece was to be a government-backed Energy Security Corporation, whose chief function would be to develop synthetic fuels ("synfuels") to replace costly foreign oil. Included also were proposals to impose limits on foreign oil imports and to encourage the substitution of coal for oil, especially by electric utility companies.

While Carter's address stunned and even perplexed the nation, he let drop another shoe a few days later. In a bureaucratic massacre of almost unprecedented proportions, he fired four cabinet secretaries. At the same time, he circled the wagons of his Georgian advisers more tightly about the White House by reorganizing and expanding the power of his personal staff. Critics began to wonder aloud whether Carter, the professed man of the people, was losing touch with the popular mood of the country.

Foreign Affairs and the Iranian Imbroglio

Hopes for a less dangerous world rose slightly in June 1979, when President Carter met with Soviet leader Leonid Brezhnev in Vienna to sign the long-stalled SALT II agreements, limiting

Two-Way SALT Talks *The grim specter of nuclear holocaust haunted the SALT II talks between Carter and Russian leader Leonid Brezhnev in Vienna in June 1979. (© Uluschak/Rothco.)*

the levels of lethal strategic weapons in the Russian and American arsenals. Yet from the outset Carter faced an uphill battle in trying to persuade the United States Senate to approve the SALT II treaty. Conservative critics of the president's defense policies remained deeply suspicious of the Soviet Union, which they regarded as the Wicked Witch of the East. These hard-liners unsheathed their long knives to carve up the SALT treaty when it came to the Senate for debate in the summer of 1979. Their hand was strengthened when news reports broke that a Soviet "combat brigade" was stationed in Castro's Cuba.

Political earthquakes in the petroleum-rich Persian Gulf region finally buried all hopes of ratifying the SALT treaty. The Western world depended heavily on the gulf nations for oil, the black milk from Mother Earth that nourishes all modern industrial economies. Yet this vital lifeline lay dangerously close to the Soviet Union. The prospect that political turmoil in the region might provide an excuse for the Soviet army to march in and seize control of essential oil supplies caused nightmares throughout the Western world.

Nightmare seemed to become reality on November 4, 1979, when a howling mob of rabidly anti-American Muslim militants stormed the United States Embassy in Teheran, Iran, and took all of its occupants hostage. The captors then demanded that the American authorities ship back to Iran the exiled shah, who had arrived in the United States two weeks earlier for medical treatment. The shaky Iranian government, barely visible through the smoke of revolution and religious upheaval then rocking the country, refused to intervene against the militants. Ayatollah Ruhollah Khomeini, the white-bearded Muslim holy man who inspired the revolutionaries, even accused the United States of masterminding an attack on the sacred Muslim city of Mecca.

World opinion hotly condemned the diplomatic felony in Iran, while Americans agonized over both the fate of the hostages and the stability of the entire Persian Gulf region. The Soviet army then aroused the West's worst fears on December 27, 1979, when it blitzed into the mountainous nation of Afghanistan, next door to Iran, and appeared to be poised for a thrust at the oil-jugular of the gulf.

President Carter reacted vigorously to these alarming events. He slapped an embargo on the export to Russia of grain and high-technology machinery and called for a boycott of the upcoming Olympic Games in Moscow. He proposed the creation of a "Rapid Deployment Force" to respond to suddenly developing crises in faraway places and requested that young

> *"History teaches, perhaps, very few clear lessons. But surely one such lesson learned by the world at great cost is that aggression, unopposed, becomes a contagious disease."* (President Jimmy Carter, addressing the nation on January 4, 1980, about the Soviet invasion of Afghanistan.)

people (including women) be made to register for a possible military draft. The president proclaimed that the United States would "use any means necessary, including force," to protect the Persian Gulf against Soviet incursions. He grimly conceded that he had misjudged the Russians, and the SALT treaty became a dead letter in the Senate. Meanwhile, the Soviet army met unexpectedly stiff resistance in Afghanistan and bogged down in a nasty guerrilla war that came to be called "Russia's Vietnam." But though the Russian bear was stalled in Afghanistan, the crisis in Iran ground on.

The Iranian Hostage Humiliation

The Iranian hostage episode was Carter's—and America's—bed of nails. The captured Americans languished in cruel captivity, while the

Blindfolded American Hostages Displayed by Iranian Militants, November 1979 *Humiliating scenes like this one were telecast on American television during the hostages' 444 days of captivity. (© 1981, Sipa Press from Black Star.)*

nightly news broadcasts in the United States showed humiliating scenes of Iranian mobs burning the American flag and spitting upon effigies of Uncle Sam.

Carter at first tried to apply economic sanctions and the pressure of world public opinion against the Iranians, while waiting for the emergence of a stable government with which to negotiate. But the political upheaval in Iran rumbled on endlessly, and the president's frustration grew. The Iranians released a few of the prisoners, but in April 1980 the Ayatollah Khomeini declared that the hotheaded militants, rather than the formal government, would retain custody of the fifty-two remaining hostages. Carter responded by giving the go-ahead to a daring rescue mission. A highly trained commando team penetrated deep into

Iran's sandy interior. Their plan required tick-tock-perfect timing to succeed, and when equipment failures prevented some members of the team from reaching their destination, the mission had to be scrapped. As the commandos withdrew in the dark desert night, two of their aircraft collided, killing eight of the would-be rescuers.

This disastrous failure of the rescue raid proved anguishing for Americans. The episode seemed to underscore the nation's helplessness and even incompetence in the face of a mortifying insult to the national honor. The stalemate with Iran dragged on throughout the rest of Carter's term in office, providing an embarrassing backdrop to the embattled president's struggle for reelection.

Varying Viewpoints

Richard Nixon may well be the most controversial political personality in recent American history. He built his career on the most inflammatory issues of the day, from red-chasing in the 1940s to the Vietnam War in the 1960s, and the Watergate episode ended his public life with the most explosive constitutional crisis in over a century. Ever combative and resourceful, he antagonized his enemies and cultivated his followers with unremitting energy and skill. Hence, there are few "objective" accounts of the Nixon years; passion still guides the pens of most writers (including Nixon himself), producing assessments that are either bitterly critical or aggressively apologetic. Thus it may be some time before historians can make a balanced appraisal of Nixon's role. The stain of Watergate, for example, has almost blotted from the record Nixon's initiatives in foreign policy, especially toward China. Whatever the final judgment, it seems that historians will be unforgiving of the wounds that Watergate inflicted on the American body politic. Trust in elected leaders is an essential but fragile ingredient in a democracy, and that trust was badly undermined by the Watergate revelations.

Select Readings

Primary Source Documents

Richard Nixon's vision of the international order is delineated in his *RN: The Memoirs of Richard Nixon* (1978.)* The articles of impeachment reported against Nixon can be found in *House of Representatives Report No. 93-1305,* 93d Congress, 2d Session, pp. 1–2 (1974).* Opposing opinions on the Panama Canal treaty were voiced by Cyrus Vance and Ronald Reagan, *Hearings before the Committee on Foreign Relations,* United States Senate, 95th Congress, 1st Session, pp. 10–15, 96–103 (1977).

Secondary Sources

Nixon's intriguing personality is examined in Gary Wills, *Nixon Agonistes: The Crisis of the Self-Made Man* (1970), and in Fawn Brodie, *Richard Nixon: The Shaping of His Character* (1981). Rowland Evans, Jr., and Robert D. Novak discuss *Nixon in the White House: The Frustration of Power* (1971). Theodore White continues his chronicle of presidential electioneering in *The Making of the President, 1972* (1973). Consult also Hunter S. Thompson's savagely masterful *Fear and Loathing on the Campaign Trail, 1972* (1973) and Timothy Crouse's insightful study of the political press, *The Boys on the Bus* (1973). Valuable background on American foreign policy in the Nixon years can be found in David P. Calleo and Benjamin Rowland, *America and the World Political Economy* (1973). On multinational corporations, see Richard J. Barnet and Ronald E. Muller, *Global Reach* (1974), and on monetary matters, John S. Odell, *U.S. International Monetary Policy* (1982). On the Paris peace negotiations, see Gareth Porter, *A Peace Denied* (1975). Retrospectives on Vietnam include George C. Herring, *America's Longest War* (1979); William Buckingham, *Operation Ranch Hand: The Air Force and Herbicides in Southeast Asia, 1961–1971* (1982); and William Shawcross's chilling account of Cambodia, *Sideshow* (2d ed., 1981). Shawcross is vigorously rebutted in Henry Kissinger's rich memoir, *White House Years* (1979). The Middle East is the focus of William B. Quandt, *Decade of Decisions: American Policy toward the Arab-Israeli Conflict, 1967–1976* (1977). The background to the oil crisis is charted in Michael B. Stoff, *Oil, War and American Security* (1980), and Irvine Anderson, *Aramco: The United States and Saudi Arabia* (1981). Arthur M. Schlesinger, Jr., traces the growth of *The Imperial Presidency* (1973). The Watergate crisis is vividly described in two books by Carl Bernstein and Robert Woodward, *All the President's Men* (1974) and *The Final Days* (1976). Jonathan Schell, *The Time of Illusion* (1976), as-

sesses the impact of the crisis on the nation's spirit and institutions. Many of the fallen president's former men have written of their involvement in the Watergate affair, including Jeb Stuart Magruder, John Dean, John Erlichman, and H. R. Haldeman. "Jerry" Ford, the first appointed president, is analyzed by his former press secretary in J. F. ter Horst, *Gerald Ford and the Future of the Presidency* (1974). For a sharply critical view, see Clark Mollenhoff, *The Man Who Pardoned Nixon* (1976). Consult also Richard Reeves, *A Ford, Not a Lincoln* (1975), and Ford's own *A Time to Heal: The Autobiography of Gerald Ford* (1979). Jimmy Carter wrote his autobiography, *Why Not the Best?* (1975), as did his wife, Rosalyn Carter, *First Lady from Plains* (1984). They should be supplemented by David Kucharsky, *The Man from Plains* (1976). Sharply critical are Clark R. Mollenhoff, *The President Who Failed: Carter Out of Control* (1980), and Joseph A. Califano, Jr. (whom Carter fired from the cabinet), *Governing America: An Insider's Report from the White House and the Cabinet* (1981). Other useful memoirs are Carter's own *Keeping Faith* (1982) and National Security Adviser Zbigniew Brzezinski's *Power and Principle* (1983). The debate on Panama spawned two noteworthy books: Walter LaFeber's prowithdrawal *The Panama Canal: The Crisis in Historical Perspective* (1978) and Paul B. Ryan's antiwithdrawal *The Panama Canal Controversy* (1977). On other aspects of Central American policy, see Richard Fagen, *The Nicaraguan Revolution* (1981), and LaFeber's *Inevitable Revolutions: The United States in Central America* (1983). On the SALT negotiations, see Thomas W. Wolfe, *The SALT Experience* (1979), and Strobe Talbott, *Endgame: The Inside Story of SALT II* (1979). The catastrophe in Iran is described in Michael Ledeen and William Lewis, *Debacle: The American Failure in Iran* (1981); Barry M. Rubin, *Paved with Good Intentions: The American Experience and Iran* (1980); and Pierre Salinger, *America Held Hostage* (1981).

45

Ronald Reagan and the Conservative Resurgence

> *It will be my intention to curb the size and influence of the federal establishment and to demand recognition of the distinction between the powers granted to the federal government and those reserved to the states or to the people.*
>
> Ronald Reagan, Inaugural Address, 1981

The Election of Ronald Reagan, 1980

Bedeviled abroad and becalmed at home, Carter's administration struck many Americans as bungling and befuddled. Frustrated critics bellyached loudly about the Georgian's alleged mismanagement of the nation's affairs. Accusations of ineptitude stung Carter deeply, for he had campaigned on a pledge to make the government "as competent as the American people." He had entitled his autobiography *Why Not the Best?*, to which his adversaries now responded, "We got the worst."

Disaffection with Carter ran deep even in his own Democratic party, where an "ABC" (Any-

body but Carter) movement gathered steam. The president's fiscal conservatism, as well as his removal of regulatory controls from major industries (such as the airlines), prompted the charge that he was a Republican wolf camouflaged as a Democratic sheep. The liberal inheritors of the Democratic New Deal tradition grew especially restless. They found their champion in Senator Edward Kennedy of Massachusetts, the last survivor of the assassin-plagued Kennedy brothers. In late 1979 Edward Kennedy declared his intention to contest Carter's renomination. But Kennedy was handicapped from the outset by lingering suspicions about his involvement in a 1969 automobile accident on Chappaquiddick Island, Massachusetts, in which a young woman assistant was drowned when his car plunged off a bridge.

While Kennedy and Carter noisily slugged it out in a series of bruising primary elections, delighted Republicans decorously proceeded to select their presidential nominee. Ronald Reagan, perennial darling of the right wing, easily outdistanced his rivals and secured the nomination he had sought for over a decade. Liberal Republican John Anderson, a well-groomed and well-spoken congressman from Illinois, proved unable to march rightward to the beat of Reagan's drum. He bolted the party to launch his own independent presidential bid. But his candidacy, aimed at voters slightly left of center, worried Carter much more than it did Reagan.

The hour of the conservative right seemed at last to have arrived. Census figures confirmed that the average American was older than in the stormy 1960s and much more likely to live in the South or West, the traditional bastions of the "old right." The conservative cause drew added strength from the emergence of a "new right," movement, partly in response to the "countercultural" protests of the 1960s. Spearheading the new right were evangelical Christian groups like the Moral Majority, which was composed of a dedicated minority of believers who enjoyed startling success as political fund-raisers and organizers. New right supporters tackled "social" issues such as abortion, the Equal Rights Amendment, pornography, and homosexual rights—all of which they passionately denounced. Together, the old and new right added up to a powerful political combination.

Ronald Reagan was well suited to lead this gathering conservative crusade. An actor turned politician, he enjoyed enormous popularity with his crooked grin and aw-shucks manner. He had grown up in a small Illinois town, the son of a ne'er-do-well, impoverished Irish father with a fondness for the bottle. Reagan got his start in life in the depressed 1930s as a sports announcer for an Iowa radio station. Good looks and a way with words landed him acting jobs in Hollywood, where he became a B-grade star in the 1940s. He displayed a flair for politics as

President Reagan   *The oldest man ever elected to the presidency, Reagan displayed youthful vigor both on the campaign trail and in office. (© 1980 Dennis Brack from Black Star.)*

president of the Screen Actors Guild in the McCarthy era of the early 1950s, when he helped to purge Communists and other suspected "reds" from the film industry. In 1954 he became a spokesman for the General Electric Corporation at a salary of some $150,000 per year. In that position he began to abandon his New Dealish political views and increasingly to preach a conservative, antigovernment line. Reagan's huge visibility and growing skill at promoting the conservative cause made him attractive to a group of wealthy California businessmen, who helped to launch his political career as governor of California from 1966 to 1974.

Memories of Chappaquiddick and the country's conservative mood killed Kennedy's candidacy. A badly battered Jimmy Carter, his party divided and in disarray, was left to do battle with Ronald Reagan. The Republican candidate

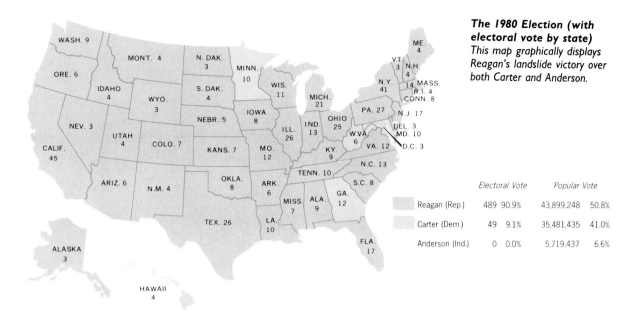

The 1980 Election (with electoral vote by state) *This map graphically displays Reagan's landslide victory over both Carter and Anderson.*

		Electoral Vote		Popular Vote	
	Reagan (Rep.)	489	90.9%	43,899,248	50.8%
	Carter (Dem.)	49	9.1%	35,481,435	41.0%
	Anderson (Ind.)	0	0.0%	5,719,437	6.6%

proved to be a formidable campaigner. He used his professional acting skills to great advantage in a series of televised "debates" with the colorless Carter. Reagan attacked the incumbent's fumbling performance in foreign policy and blasted the "big-government" philosophy of the Democratic party (a philosophy that Carter did not fully share). Carter countered ineffectively with charges that Reagan was a trigger-happy cold warrior who might push the country into nuclear war.

> One of Jimmy Carter's former speechwriters commented in 1979 on Carter's sometimes puzzling personality: The president, he said, displayed "a combination of arrogance, complacency, and—dread thought—insecurity at the core of his mind and soul. . . . He holds explicit, thorough positions on every issue under the sun . . . but he has no large view of the relations between them. . . . He fails to project a vision larger than the problem he is tackling at the moment. . . . [Yet] with his moral virtues and his intellectual skills, he is perhaps as admirable a human being as has ever held the job."

Carter's spotty record in office was no defense against Reagan's popular appeal. On election day the Republican rang up a spectacular victory, bagging over 51 percent of the popular vote, while 41 percent went to Carter and 7 percent to Anderson. The electoral count stood at 489 for Reagan and 49 for Carter (Anderson failed to gain a single electoral vote). Carter managed to win only six states and the District of Columbia, a defeat almost as crushing as George McGovern's loss to Richard Nixon in 1972. He was the first elected president to be unseated by the voters since Herbert Hoover was ejected from office in 1932. Equally startling, the Republicans gained control of the Senate for the first time in twenty-five years. Leading Democratic liberals who had been "targeted" for defeat by well-heeled new-right groups went down like dead timber in the conservative windstorm that swept the country.

Carter showed dignity in defeat, delivering a thoughtful Farewell Address that stressed his efforts to scale down the deadly arms race, to promote human rights, and to protect the environment. In one of his last acts in office, he signed a bill preserving some 100 million acres of Alaskan land for national parks, forests, and wildlife refuges. An unusually intelligent, articulate and well-meaning president, he had been hampered by his lack of managerial talent and had been badly buffeted by events beyond his control, such as the soaring price of oil and the galling insult of the continuing hostage crisis in Iran. If he was correct in believing that the country was suffering from a terrible "malaise," he never found the right medicine to cure the disease.

The Reagan Revolution

Reagan's arrival in Washington was triumphal. The Iranians contributed to the festive mood by releasing the hostages on Reagan's Inauguration Day, January 20, 1981, after 444 days of captivity. The new president, a hale and hearty sixty-nine-year-old, was devoted to fiscal fitness. He went vigorously into action on his first day in office by declaring a hiring freeze on federal employees, and soon after, he announced plans to slash some thirty-seven thousand jobs from the federal payrolls. Reagan also placed a freeze on implementing new economic regulations, which he believed throttled business and stifled economic growth.

Reagan assembled a conservative cabinet of the "best and the rightest." It included a highly controversial Coloradan, James Watt, as secre-

President Carter　*Hardworking and high-minded, Carter was beset by foreign and economic problems during his presidency. Defeated in 1980 by Ronald Reagan, Carter became the fifth president since Eisenhower's day to fail to serve two full terms in office. (Official White House photo.)*

tary of the interior. Watt was a product of the "Sagebrush Rebellion," a fiercely anti-Washington movement that had sprung up to protest federal control over the rich mineral and timber resources in the western states. Environmentalists howled loudly about Watt's schemes to hobble the Environmental Protection Agency and to permit oil drilling in scenic places. After bitter

The American Hostages Return from Iran, January 20, 1981　*In a pointed insult to Jimmy Carter, the Iranians released the hostages on the day he left office. (D. Goldberg/Sygma.)*

Republican conservatives scored a double victory in 1980, winning control of both the White House and the Senate. Aided by conservative Democratic "boll weevils," they also dominated the House of Representatives, and a new era of conservatism seemed to dawn in the nation's capital. (Reprinted with special permission of King Features Syndicate, Inc.)

protests, they succeeded in halting Watt's plan to allow oil exploration off the California coastline. Watt blithely rebuffed critics by saying that "I make lots of mistakes because I make lots of decisions." He made one mistake too many in 1983, when he thoughtlessly told an offensive ethnic joke in public and was forced to resign.

A major goal of Reagan's political career was to reduce the size of the government by shrinking the federal budget and slashing taxes. He declared, "Government is not the solution to our problem. Government is the problem." Years of New Deal–style tax-and-spend programs, he quipped, had created a federal government that

In his inaugural address, Ronald Reagan summoned Americans to "an era of national renewal." He explained that "it is not my intention to do away with the government. It is rather to make it work—work with us, not over us; to stand by our side, not ride on our back. . . . Can we solve the problems confronting us? The answer is an unequivocal and emphatic yes. To paraphrase Winston Churchill, I did not take the oath I have just taken with the intention of presiding over the dissolution of the world's strongest economy."

reminded him of the definition of a baby as a creature who was all appetite at one end, with no sense of responsibility at the other.

With near-religious zeal and remarkable effectiveness, Reagan set out to persuade Congress to legislate his policies into law. He proposed a new federal budget that necessitated cuts of some $35 billion, mostly in social programs like food stamps and federally funded job-training centers. Reagan worked naturally in harness with the Republican majority in the Senate, but to get his way in the Democratic House, he undertook some old-fashioned politicking. He especially wooed a group of mostly southern conservative Democrats (dubbed "boll weevils"), who abandoned their own party's leadership to follow the president.

Then on March 6, 1981, a deranged gunman shot the president as he was leaving a Washington hotel. A .22-caliber bullet penetrated beneath Reagan's left arm and collapsed his left lung. (Within one year, cranks or fanatics wounded or killed not only Reagan but also musician John Lennon, Egyptian President Anwar Sadat, and even Pope John Paul II.) With admirable courage and grace, and with impressive physical resilience for a man his age, Reagan recovered rapidly from his violent ordeal. Twelve days after the attack, he walked out of the hospital and returned to work. When he appeared a few days later on national television to address the Congress and the public on his budget, the outpouring of sympathy and support was enormous.

The Battle of the Budget

Swept along on a tide of presidential popularity, Congress swallowed Reagan's budget proposals, approving expenditures of some $695 billion, with a projected deficit of about $38 billion. To hit those financial targets, drastic surgery was required, and Congress plunged its scalpel deeply into America's social programs. Wounded Democrats wondered if the president's intention was to cut the budget or to gut the budget.

Reagan's triumph amazed political observers, especially defeated Democrats. The new president had descended upon Washington like an avenging angel of conservatism, kicking up a blinding whirlwind of political change. He sought nothing less than the dismantling of the welfare state and the reversal of the political evolution of the preceding half-century. His impressive performance demonstrated the power of the presidency with a skill not seen since Lyndon Johnson's day. Out the window went the textbooks that had concluded, largely on the basis of the stalemate of the 1970s, that the White House had been eclipsed by a powerful, uncontrollable Congress.

Reagan hardly rested to savor the sweetness of his victory. The second part of his economic program called for deep tax cuts, amounting to 25 percent across-the-board reductions over a period of three years. Once again, Reagan displayed his skill as a performer and a persuader in a highly effective television address in July 1981, when he pleaded for congressional passage of the tax-cut bill. Democrats, he quipped, "had never met a tax they didn't hike." Thanks largely to the continued defection of the "boll weevils" from the Democratic camp, the president again had his way. In August 1981 Congress approved a set of sweeping tax reforms that lowered individual tax rates, virtually eliminated federal estate taxes, and created new tax-free savings plans for small investors. Reagan's "supply-side" economic advisers assured him that the combination of budgetary discipline and tax reduction would stimulate new investment, boost productivity, and foster dramatic economic growth.

But at first "supply-side" economics seemed to be a beautiful theory mugged by a gang of brutal facts, as the economy slid into its deepest recession since the 1930s. Unemployment reached nearly 11 percent in 1982, businesses folded, and several bank failures jolted the nation's entire financial system. The automobile industry, once the brightest jewel in America's industrial crown, was turning in its dimmest performance in history. Battling against Japanese imports, major automakers reported losses in the hundreds of millions of dollars. Fuming and frustrated Democrats angrily charged that the president's budget cuts slashed especially cruelly at the poor and the handicapped and

WALLFLOWERS

Reagan's budget cuts fell almost exclusively on social programs, while the military outlay was scheduled to increase substantially. (© Mazzotta/Rothco.)

that his tax cuts favored the well-to-do. They accused Reagan of trying to make those Americans with the frailest shoulders carry the heaviest burden in the fight for fiscal reform.

Ignoring the yawping pack of Democratic critics, President Reagan and his economic advisers serenely waited for their supply-side economic policies ("Reaganomics") to produce the promised results. The supply-siders seemed to be vindicated when a robust economic recovery finally got under way in 1983. But other economists found the causes of the economic upturn not in the president's budget cutting and tax reforming but in his massive expenditures for the military. Reagan cascaded nearly 2 trillion budget dollars onto the Pentagon in the early and mid-1980s, asserting the need to close a "window of vulnerability" in the armaments race with the Soviet Union. Ironically, this conservative president thereby plunged the government into a red-ink bath of deficit spending that made the New Deal look stingy. Federal budget deficits topped $100 billion in 1982, and the government's books were nearly $200 billion out of balance in every year from 1983 to 1985. Massive government borrowing to cover those deficits kept interest rates high, and high interest rates in turn pushed the value of the dollar to record altitudes in the international money markets. The soaring dollar was good news for

American tourists and buyers of foreign cars, but it dealt crippling blows to American exporters, as the American international trade deficit approached $150 billion in 1985. The lords of international commerce and finance for a generation after World War II, Americans were in danger of becoming economic underlings and borrowers in the world economy of the 1980s.

Reagan's Tough Foreign Policy

Hard as nails toward the Soviet Union in his campaign speeches, Reagan saw no reason to change his tune after he arrived in the White House. In one of his first presidential news conferences, he claimed that the Soviets were "prepared to commit any crime, to lie, to cheat," in pursuit of their goal of world conquest. In a later speech he characterized Soviet Russia as the "focus of evil in the modern world." Critics wondered how the president could fulfill his promise to negotiate a new arms agreement with the Russians when he had publicly

painted them as so dishonest. Bafflement deepened when Reagan lifted Jimmy Carter's grain embargo against the offensive Soviets, even though they remained embattled in Afghanistan. In tones reminiscent of the Carter years, questioners asked if the Reagan administration even had a consistent foreign policy.

Europe flinched at the prospect of a reheated Cold War. Détente had brought both peace of mind and prosperity to West Europeans, and they turned a deaf ear to what they regarded as Reagan's outdated battle cry. A shudder ran through Western Europe in October 1981 when Reagan seemed to endorse the concept that the United States might fight the Russians in a "limited" nuclear war on European soil. Meanwhile, Soviet leaders talked alluringly of removing Soviet missiles from western Russia and of striking lucrative trade deals with the Europeans. Washington and Moscow entered into a tense war of nerves to capture the allegiance of Europe.

Relations with Russia further nose-dived in late 1981, when the government of Poland, needled for over a year by a popular movement of

Solidarity in Poland *Polish labor leader Lech Walesa addresses his supporters. (Bettmann Newsphotos.)*

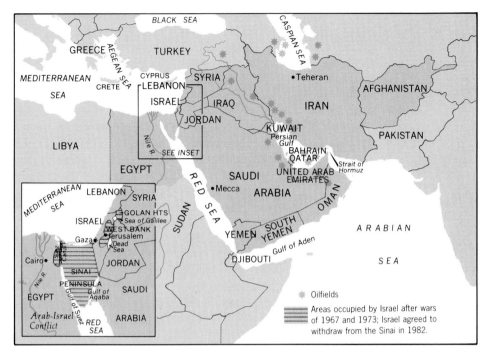

The Middle East *A combination of political instability and precious petroleum resources has made the region from Egypt to Afghanistan an "arc of crisis."*

working people organized into a massive union called "Solidarity," clamped martial law on the troubled country. Reagan saw the heavy fist of the Kremlin inside this Polish iron glove, and he imposed economic sanctions on Poland and Russia alike. This vigorous response further unsettled the West Europeans, who preferred more diplomatic—and less economically costly—means of aiding Poland. Notably absent from the mandated measures was a resumption of the grain embargo, which would have pinched the pocketbooks of too many American farmers.

The elegant Swiss city of Geneva became the chief arena in the Soviet-American contest over Europe. Seeking to stop the downward slide in America's relationship with its European allies, Reagan proposed new arms-control talks with the Russians at Geneva in late 1981. Discussions proceeded fitfully, slowed by the inertia and ill health of the aging oligarchs in the Kremlin.

Death swept away three Russian premiers between late 1982 and early 1985. Negotiations were further complicated when the Soviets, in September 1983, blasted from the skies a Korean passenger airliner that had inexplicably violated Russian airspace. Hundreds of civilians, including many Americans, plummeted to their deaths in the frigid Sea of Okhotsk. By the end of 1983, all arms-control negotiations with the Russians were broken off. The deepening chill in the Cold War was further felt in 1984, when Russian and Soviet-bloc athletes boycotted the Olympic Games in Los Angeles.

Troubles Abroad

The volatile Middle Eastern pot continued to boil ominously. Prospects for a peaceful resolution of the decades-old Arab-Israeli conflict were dealt a severe blow in October 1981 when extremist Egyptian nationalists gunned down the peace-seeking president of Egypt, Anwar Sadat. For its part, Israel badly strained its bonds of friendship with the United States by continuing to allow new settlements to be established in the occupied territory of the Jordan River's West Bank.

Israel further raised the stakes in the Middle East in June 1982 when it invaded neighboring Lebanon, seeking to suppress once and for all the guerrilla bases from which Palestinian fighters harassed beleaguered Israel. The Palestinians were bloodily subdued, but Lebanon, already pulverized by years of episodic civil war, was plunged into armed chaos. President Reagan was obliged to send American troops to Lebanon in 1983 as part of an international peacekeeping force, but their presence did not bring peace. A suicidal bomber crashed an explosives-laden truck into a United States Marine barracks on October 23, 1983, killing more than two hundred marines. President Reagan soon thereafter withdrew the remaining American troops, while miraculously suffering no political damage from this horrifying and humiliating attack. His mystified Democratic opponents began to call him a "Teflon president," to whom nothing hurtful could stick.

Central America, in the United States' own backyard, also rumbled menacingly in the early months of the Reagan administration. A leftist revolution had deposed the longtime dictator of Nicaragua in 1979. President Carter had tried to ignore the anti-American rhetoric of the revolutionaries, known as "Sandinistas," and to establish good diplomatic relations with them. But Reagan took their rhetoric at face value and hurled back at them some hot language of his own. He accused the Sandinistas of turning their country into a forward base for Soviet and Cuban military penetration of all of Central America. Brandishing photographs taken from high-flying spy planes, administration spokespersons claimed that Nicaraguan leftists were shipping weapons to revolutionary forces in tiny El Salvador, torn by violence since a coup in 1979.

Reagan sent military "advisers" to prop up the pro-American government of El Salvador. He also provided covert aid, including the CIA-engineered mining of harbors, to the "contra" rebels opposing the anti-American government of Nicaragua. Reagan also flexed his military muscles elsewhere in the turbulent Caribbean. In a dramatic display of American might, in 1983 he dispatched a heavy-firepower invasion force to the island of Grenada, where a military

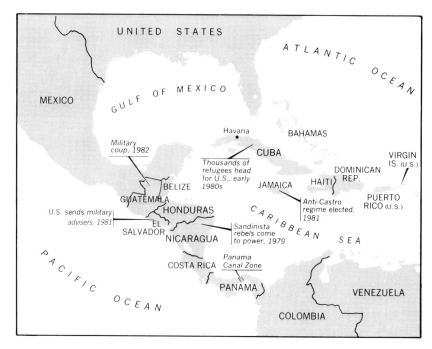

Central America and the Caribbean *This region of historical importance to the United States experienced dramatic political upheavals in the late 1970s and early 1980s.*

The Americans Invade Grenada, 1983   *United States forces easily overran the tiny Caribbean island-nation, thwarting a Marxist take-over. (Abbas/Magnum.)*

coup had killed the prime minister and brought Marxists to power. Swiftly overrunning the tiny island, American troops vividly demonstrated Reagan's determination to assert the dominance of the United States in the Caribbean, just as Theodore Roosevelt had done.

The Triumph of Reagan in 1984

A confident Ronald Reagan, bolstered by a buoyant economy at home and by the popularity of his muscular posture abroad, handily won renomination by the Republicans in 1984 for a second White House term. Democrats, divided as usual, noisily contested their party's nomination. The presumptive front-runner from the outset was Walter Mondale, former Minnesota senator and Jimmy Carter's vice-president, but he was sharply challenged by Colorado Senator Gary Hart. Youthful and handsome, Hart appealed to younger voters—especially those dubbed "yuppies," or "young upwardly mobile professionals"—when he called for "new ideas"

to revitalize the half-century-old New Dealish philosophy of the Democratic party. Black leader Jesse Jackson also ran hard for the Democratic nomination, trying to put together a "rainbow coalition" of minority groups that would add up to an electoral majority. But Mondale's strength in the old established Democratic bastions of labor and the South was too formidable, and he was nominated on the first ballot at the Democrats' San Francisco convention. Mondale made history by naming as his running mate Congresswoman Geraldine Ferraro of New York, the first woman ever to appear on a major-party presidential ticket.

President Reagan meanwhile had also advanced the feminist cause by nominating Sandra Day O'Connor to be a justice of the Supreme Court of the United States. A brilliant Stanford Law School graduate and public-spirited Arizona judge, O'Connor appealed to the president in part because she sympathized with his views on abortion, as he had taken care to ascertain. When she was sworn in on September 25, 1981, she became the 102d justice and

Geraldine Ferraro on the Campaign Trail   *The first woman to run on a major-party national ticket, Democratic vice-presidential candidate Ferraro is shown here campaigning in Madison, Wisconsin, in 1984. (A. Tannenbaum/Sygma.)*

the first woman to ascend to the high bench in the Court's 191-year history. Ironically, it had fallen to the most conservative president in half a century to appoint a woman to the Court, as

> Speaking to the National Association of Evangelicals, President Reagan said the following about abortion: "More than a decade ago, a Supreme Court decision [Roe v. Wade, 1973] literally wiped off the books of fifty states statutes protecting the rights of unborn children. Abortion on demand now takes the lives of up to 1 1/2 million unborn children a year. Human life legislation ending this tragedy will some day pass the Congress, and you and I must never rest until it does. Unless and until it can be proven that the unborn child is not a living entity, then its right to life, liberty, and the pursuit of happiness must be protected."

liberals had long desired. Reagan had also named two women to his cabinet and appointed another woman, Jeane Kirkpatrick, as ambassador to the United Nations.

The outcome of the 1984 presidential election was never really in doubt. Reagan's policies were too appealing, and his personal popularity too commanding, for Mondale seriously to threaten the president. On election day Reagan walked away with 525 electoral votes to Mondale's 13, winning everywhere except Minnesota and the District of Columbia. His popular vote margin was overwhelming—52,609,797 votes to 36,450,613 for Mondale.

A triumphant Ronald Reagan, reinvigorated by the election results, sought to secure his historical reputation as a man of peace by resuming arms-control talks with the Russians at Geneva in early 1985. Yet discussion again stalled, especially because the Russians balked at Reagan's determination to go ahead with a high-technology missile-defense research program officially called the Strategic Defense Initiative (SDI) but popularly known as "Star Wars." The plan, which Reagan unveiled in March 1983, called for orbiting battle stations in the heavens that could fire laser beams or other forms of concentrated energy to vaporize intercontinental missiles on lift-off. By emphasizing defense rather than offense, SDI upset four decades of strategic thinking about nuclear weaponry. Reagan regarded it as offering potential salvation from the nuclear nightmare, but many military experts remained deeply skeptical. They feared that "Star Wars" might be astronomically costly, ultimately unworkable, and fatally destabilizing to the distasteful but effective "balance of terror" that had kept the nuclear peace since World War II. For their part, the Soviets vigorously denounced "Star Wars," and scoffed at Reagan's startling suggestion that the United States might ultimately share its defensive technology with the Russians. Face-to-face talks between Reagan and new Soviet leader Mikhail Gorbachev at a Geneva summit meeting in November 1985 failed to break the arms-control impasse, and the menacing stockpiles of nuclear weapons continued to mount on both sides.

"WELL, IT'S ABOUT TIME"

The Justice is a Lady Herblock hails Sandra Day O'Connor's appointment to the Supreme Court, 1981. (© 1981 by Herblock in the Washington Post.)

Round Two for Reagan

A reelected Reagan pushed with renewed resolve to accomplish what he called the "second American revolution." Early in his second term he proposed a sweeping plan for overhauling the nation's much maligned tax system. Despite enormous budget deficits, the president remained robustly opposed to tax increases. His overall objective was to lower federal tax rates, and, by ending the exemption for state and local taxes, to force state governments to follow his lead in shrinking government activities of all kinds.

Staggering budget deficits, still in the $200-billion-a-year range, prompted Congress to pass a drastic piece of legislation in early 1986. The Gramm-Rudman-Hollings Act mandated a balanced budget by 1991. To reach that goal, the Act required automatic across-the-board spending cuts if Congress and the President could not

agree on a budget-balancing package. Given Reagan's notorious hostility to tax increases, the prospect loomed of continuing deep cuts in federal programs, including the president's favorite, "Star Wars" research.

"Reaganomics" received a powerful assist from plummeting world petroleum prices in 1986. A glut of oil helped to drown the ogre of inflation and sharply depress interest rates, giving the economy a strong boost. Yet many farmers remained regrettably immune to this economic medicine, as the worst farm crisis since the 1930s drove thousands of family farms out of business.

Reagan delivered on his promises to his conservative constituents by continuing to take up the cudgels for a variety of "social issues," including school prayer and restrictions on abortion. His administration also appeared to back

In a speech to the National Association of Evangelicals on March 8, 1983, President Reagan defined his stand on school prayer: "The Declaration of Independence mentions the Supreme Being no less than four times. 'In God We Trust' is engraved on our coinage. The Supreme Court opens its proceedings with a religious invocation. And the Members of Congress open their sessions with a prayer. I just happen to believe the school-children of the United States are entitled to the same privileges as Supreme Court Justices and Congressmen."

away from the federal government's two-decades-old commitment to affirmative action programs by supporting legal suits against hiring practices that favored minorities.

Dominating the political agenda at home, Reagan proved less able to control events abroad. Middle-East terrorists killed an American sailor during an airplane hijacking in June 1985, and four months later brutally murdered a wheel-chair-bound American citizen during the hijacking of an Italian cruise ship. Despite

sabre-rattling warnings from Washington about retaliation, the American government—like other governments afflicted by the plague of terrorism—seemed powerless to prevent such episodes, or even to capture and punish the perpetrators. A lightning air raid in April 1986 against Libya, a country accused by the Reagan administration of sponsoring many terrorist outrages felt good but unfortunately failed to stem the terrorist tide. The raid against Libya also strained relations with America's European allies. Many Europeans regarded the American attack as simply terrorism in reverse. The Europeans urged instead that Washington apply itself to curing what they regarded as the root cause of the terrorist disease—the continuing homelessness of thousands of Palestinians who were uprooted from their native land when the state of Israel was carved out of the Mediterranean desert in the 1940s.

The clash of racial violence in South Africa, where blacks stepped up their protests against the segregationist policies of "apartheid," also echoed noisily in America. The Reagan administration's policy of "constructive engagement" with the white South African regime struck many critics as morally bankrupt and politically

The Great Communicator
Ronald Reagan, an accomplished speaker, used television more effectively than any previous president. Here he displays his talent in his State of the Union Message, February 7, 1985. (AP/Wide World Photos.)

ineffective. In countless communities and colleges, concerned Americans debated the merits of withdrawing American business from the seething African nation.

The Reagan administration took credit in early 1986 for helping to topple the cruel dictator "Baby Doc" Duvalier in Haiti, and to oust the repressive despot Ferdinand Marcos from the Philippines. But skeptics wondered why it had taken the American government so long to detect the corruption of those flagrant autocrats. Skepticism deepened when Reagan on March 14, 1986, declared that henceforward the United States would oppose all dictators, both of the right and the left. The President's statement contradicted an earlier distinction, popular in administration circles, between "authoritarian" regimes—usually rightist and therefore acceptable—and "totalitarian" regimes—usually leftist and therefore reprehensible. To the president's critics, his announcement was simply an expedient ploy to cash in on the Haitian and Philippine events so as to gain support for his policies in Central America, especially Nicaragua.

The president turned up the heat on the Nicaraguan issue in a dramatic speech on March 16, 1986. The lava of Reagan's wrath flowed over the leftist Sandinista government as he appealed for authority to send arms to the "contra" rebel forces. But many people in the Congress and the country did not share Reagan's apocalyptic assessment of the stakes in Nicaragua. As the Central American timebomb ticked on, the fear grew that the stage was being set for another bloody American involvement resembling Vietnam.

At home and abroad, Ronald Reagan provided an example of vigorous leadership that had been strikingly lacking for more than a decade before his election in 1980. But whether the "Reagan revolution" would provide the permanent "national renewal" that the president sunnily promised was a question whose answer lay in the lap of historians still unborn.

Varying Viewpoints

The Reagan Era is only beginning to receive historical scrutiny, but debate has already crystallized around a single question—did Reagan's Presidency mark a revolutionary departure from the half-century-long course of American political and economic development that began with the New Deal? The affirmative view, shared by most administration partisans, holds that the "Reagan Revolution" halted the growth of the federal government, returned economic decision-making power to the private sector, and elevated the Republican Party to majority status in national politics. Other observers have expressed doubts about the extent of change under Ronald Reagan. Despite Reagan's early successes, these critics note, the federal budget grew at an unprecedented rate during Reagan's term of office, producing the largest budget deficits in the nation's history. The President's initiatives on tax reform and "social issues" were largely frustrated, and numerous public opinion polls suggested that the administration's program remained considerably less popular with the American people than the president himself. Republican dominance, if such surveys prove accurate, might not outlast Reagan's term.

Select Readings

Primary Source Documents

The debate over "Reaganomics" can be followed in Reagan's nationally televised address of July 27, 1981, *Weekly Compilation of Presidential Documents*, Vol. 17, no. 31* and in the critical response of *The New York Times*, August 2, 1981.* See also the comments of Budget Director David Stockman, in William Greider, *The Education of David Stockman and Other Americans* (1982). On arms control, see the pastoral letter of the National Council of Catholic Bishops, and the reply of Albert Wohlstetter in Charles Kegley and Eugene Wittkopf, eds., *The Nuclear Reader* (1985). On Central American policy, see Reagan's remarkable speech of March 16, 1986.*

Secondary Sources

Ronald Reagan is portrayed in Bill Boyarsky, *Reagan: His Life and Rise to the Presidency* (1981), Lou Cannon, *Reagan* (1982), Fred Greenstein, *The Reagan Presidency* (1983), and Robert Dallek, *Ronald Reagan: The Politics of Symbolism* (1984). Reagan's economic policies are discussed in Paul C. Roberts, *The Supply-Side Revolution* (1984), and are sharply criticized in David A. Stockman, *The Triumph of Politics: Why the Reagan Revolution Failed* (1986). Alternate views on the economy can be found in Lester Thurow, *The Zero-Sum Society* (1981), and Samuel Bowles et al., *Beyond the Wasteland* (1984). The debate over nuclear policy is covered in R. James Woolsey, *Nuclear Arms* (1984), and Strobe Talbott, *The Russians and Reagan* (1984), and Charles Kegley and Eugene Wittkopf, ed., *The Nuclear Reader* (1985). The neoconservative movement is best elucidated by the writings of its leaders. See Norman Pod-

horetz, *Breaking Ranks* (1979) and Irving Kristol, *Reflections of a Neoconservative* (1983). For a critical view, consult Peter Steinfels, *The Neoconservatives* (1979). Issues of special concern to the neoconservatives are treated by Charles Murray's *Losing Ground* (1984), an indictment of federal government social programs. Its conclusions are sharply contested by John E. Schwartz, *America's Hidden Success* (1983). This debate is put into historical perspective in James T. Patterson, *America's Struggle against Poverty, 1900–1980* (1981). Two studies of affirmative action are Allan P. Sindler, *Bakke, DeFinis and Minority Admissions* (1978) and J. Harvie Wilkinson, *From Brown to Bakke* (1979). A group of young Democrats has offered a "neo-liberal" response to the neoconservative challenge. See Gary Hart, *A New Democracy* (1983) and Paul Tsongas, *The Road from Here* (1981). The Presidential elections of the 1980s are chronicled by Jules Witcover and Jack Germond in two books, *Blue Smoke and Mirrors* (1981), and *Wake Us When It's Over: Presidential Politics of 1984* (1985). Reagan's election in 1980 is put into historical perspective in Theodore H. White, *America in Search of Itself* (1982). Kevin P. Phillips is also insightful about the implications of the conservative revival in *Post-Conservative America* (1982). Useful books on the role of religion in modern politics include Robert Booth Fowler, *A New Engagement: Evangelical Political Thought, 1966–1976* (1982); Robert Wuthrow, *The New Christian Right* (1983); and Richard John Neuhaus, *The Naked Public Square: Religion and Democracy in America* (1984). Critical of Reagan are William Leuchtenburg, *In the Shadow of FDR: From Harry Truman to Ronald Reagan* (1983); Paul D. Erickson, *Reagan Speaks: The Making of an American Myth* (1985); and especially Richard Reeves,*The Reagan Detour* (1985).

46

The American People since World War II

America stands at this moment at the summit of the world.

Winston Churchill, 1945

The Postwar Economic Boom

The American people, 140 million strong, cheered the blinding atomic climax of World War II in 1945. But when the shouting faded away, countless men and women began to worry about their future. Four fiery years of global war had not driven from their minds the painful memories of twelve desperate years of the Great Depression.

The decade of the 1930s had left deep scars. Joblessness and insecurity had pushed up the suicide rate and dampened the marriage rate. Babies went unborn as pinched budgets and sagging self-esteem wrought a sexual depression in countless American bedrooms. Breadless breadwinners had often felt a nagging sense of guilt about their helplessness, despite abundant evidence that the economic system, not individ-ual initiative, had broken down. Grim-faced observers were warning that the war had only temporarily lifted the pall of economic stagnation and that peace would bring the return of hard times. Homeward-bound GIs, so the gloomy predictions ran, would step out of the army's chow lines and back into the breadlines of the unemployed.

The faltering economy in the early postwar years threatened to confirm the worst predictions of the doomsayers who foresaw another Great Depression. Real gross national product (GNP) in 1946 and 1947 slumped sickeningly from its wartime peak and began to climb only haltingly in 1948. Then, beginning in 1950, the American economy surged onto a dazzling plateau of sustained growth. For the next two decades America's economic performance was the envy of the world. National income nearly

The Suburbanization of America   *After World War II, Americans by the millions moved to suburban housing developments like this one at Levittown, New York. Though criticized for their architectural monotony and cultural barrenness, the suburbs provided inexpensive and spacious housing for growing families seeking to escape the crowded confines of the cities. (Elliot Erwitt/Magnum Photos.)*

doubled in the 1950s and almost doubled again in the 1960s. It shot through the trillion-dollar mark in 1973. Americans, some 6 percent of the world's people, were enjoying about 40 percent of the planet's wealth. As the gusher of postwar prosperity poured forth its riches, Americans drank deeply from the gilded goblet. Millions of depression-deprived souls sought to make up for the sufferings of the 1930s. They determined to "get theirs" while the getting was good. A people who had once considered a chicken in every pot as the standard of comfort and security now hungered for two cars in every garage, swimming pools in their backyards, vacation homes, and gas-guzzling recreation vehicles.

What propelled this unprecedented economic explosion? World War II provided a powerful stimulus. While other countries had been ravaged by years of fighting, the United States had used the war crisis to fire up its smokeless factories and rebuild its depression-plagued economy. Invigorated by battle, America had almost effortlessly come to dominate the ruined global landscape of the postwar period. Yet perhaps the very ease of America's ascent to the summit of the world economy had unfitted it to stay there for long.

Ominously, much of the glittering prosperity of the 1950s and 1960s rested on the underpinnings of colossal military budgets, leading some critics to speak of a "permanent war economy."

Seven good reasons
for two FORDS

The Affluent Society *Growing families in the 1950s nourished a lusty demand for consumer goods like automobiles. This advertisement also underscores the sexual division of labor typical of families in the 1950s. It states that the husband needs a car for business, while the wife must have an automobile for "ferrying the family." (The Ford Motor Company from the J. Walter Thompson Company Archives.)*

The economic upturn of 1950 was fueled by massive appropriations for the Korean War, and defense spending accounted for some 10 percent of gross national product throughout the ensuing decade. Pentagon dollars primed the pumps of high-technology industries such as aerospace, plastics, and electronics—areas in which the United States reigned supreme. The military budget also financed much scientific research and development ("R and D"—hence the name of one of the most famous "think tanks," the Rand Corporation). More than ever before, unlocking the secrets of nature was the key to unleashing economic growth.

Cheap energy also fed the economic boom. American and European companies thoroughly dominated the international oil business. They controlled the flow of abundant petroleum from the sandy fields of the Middle East, and they kept prices low. Americans doubled their consumption of inexpensive and seemingly inexhaustible oil in the quarter-century after the war. Anticipating a limitless future of low-cost fuels, they flung out endless ribbons of highways, installed air-conditioning in their homes, and engineered a sixfold increase in the country's electrical-generating capacity between 1945 and 1970. Spidery grids of electrical cables carried the pent-up power of oil, gas, coal, and falling water to activate the tools of workers on the factory floor.

With the forces of nature thus increasingly harnessed in their hands, workers chalked up spectacular gains in productivity—the amount of output per hour of work. In the two decades after the outbreak of the Korean War, productivity increased at an average rate of more than 3 percent per year. Gains in productivity were also enhanced by the rising educational level of

National Defense Budget, 1940–1985

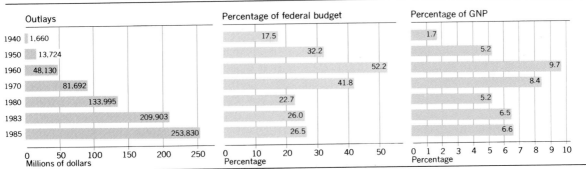

	Outlays (Millions of dollars)	Percentage of federal budget	Percentage of GNP
1940	1,660	17.5	1.7
1950	13,724	32.2	5.2
1960	48,130	52.2	9.7
1970	81,692	41.8	8.4
1980	133,995	22.7	5.2
1983	209,903	26.0	6.5
1985	253,830	26.5	6.6

(Source: Fiscal Year 1986, Budget, *Historical Tables.*)

the work force. By 1970 nearly 90 percent of the school-age population was enrolled in educational institutions—a dramatic contrast with the opening years of the century, when only half of this age group had attended school. Some 8 million veterans of World War II advanced their education by attending college at Uncle Sam's expense, thanks to the epochal "GI Bill of Rights" enacted at the end of the war. Better educated and better equipped, workers in 1970 could produce nearly twice as much in an hour's labor as they had in 1950.

Productivity was the key to prosperity. Rising productivity in the 1950s and 1960s had virtually doubled the average American's standard of living in the postwar quarter-century. Then, fatefully, productivity gains slowed to the vanishing point. The entire decade of the 1970s did not produce a productivity advance equivalent to even one year's gain in the preceding two decades. At this rate, it would take 500 more years to bring about another doubling of the average worker's standard of living.

The 1970s: End of an Economic Era?

What caused the sudden slump in productivity? Some observers cited the increasing presence in the work force of women and teenagers, who typically had fewer skills than male adult workers and were less likely to take the full-time, long-term jobs where skills might be developed. Other commentators blamed declining investment in new machinery, the heavy costs of compliance with government-imposed environmental and safety regulations, and the general shift of the economy from manufacturing to services, where productivity gains are more difficult to achieve. But whatever the explanation, it was clear that the postwar wave of robust economic growth had crested by the early 1970s.

Affluent Americans got the first glimpse of their diminishing economic prospects in 1971, when the Nixon administration executed some spectacular reversals in economic policy. Federal budget deficits were soaring, inflation was beginning to heat up, and the once almighty dollar was being pounded down and scorned in world markets, as the nation's balance of trade showed a distressing deficit for the first time since 1893. Faced with these sobering facts, Nixon announced a ninety-day freeze on wages and prices, devalued the dollar, and slapped a temporary surtax on imports.

These drastic measures briefly breathed life into the drooping economy, but worse shocks soon followed. Once a major oil exporter, the United States by the 1970s had become vulnerably dependent on imports of foreign oil. When the Organization of Petroleum Exporting Countries (OPEC) quadrupled oil prices in 1974 and tripled them again in 1979, it spelled the end of an era. Americans could no longer count on an ever-expanding stream of cheap, plentiful energy to fuel their economic growth. Nor could the United States ever again seriously consider a policy of economic isolation. For more than a century, foreign trade had accounted for less than 10 percent of American gross national product. Driven by the necessity to pay for huge foreign-oil bills, that figure rose rapidly in the 1970s, until by the mid-1980s some 25 percent of gross national product depended on foreign trade.

The first OPEC oil shock coincided with a breathtaking surge in the inflation rate, and many observers wrongly concluded that the oil crisis had caused inflation. In fact, the great inflation of the 1970s had its deepest roots in government policies of the 1960s—especially Lyndon Johnson's insistence on simultaneously fighting the war in Vietnam and funding his Great Society programs at home, all without a tax increase to finance the added expenditures that those policies required. Both military spending and welfare spending are inherently inflationary (in the absence of offsetting tax collections), because they put dollars in people's hands without adding to the supply of goods that those dollars can buy.

When too many dollars chase too few goods, prices rise—as they did astonishingly in the 1970s. The cost of living more than tripled from Richard Nixon's inauguration to Ronald Reagan's, in the longest and steepest inflationary cycle in the nation's history. One sorry implication of the huge military budget was thus distressingly revealed. At the same time, Americans began to see with a new clarity the real financial limits to the extension of the "welfare state."

Other weaknesses in the nation's economy were also laid bare by the abrupt reversal of America's financial fortunes in the 1970s. The competitive advantage of American business leaders had been so enormous after World War II that they had small incentive to modernize their plants and seek more efficient methods of production. The defeated German and Japanese people, meanwhile, had scratched their way out of the ruins of war and built wholly new factories with the most up-to-date technology and management techniques. By the 1970s their efforts paid handsome rewards, as they came to dominate industries like steel, automobiles, and consumer electronics—fields in which Uncle Sam had once been unchallengeable.

Americans were still prosperous in the 1980s. Median family income stood near $25,000. Even the several million Americans with incomes below the government's official "poverty level" enjoyed a standard of living higher than that of two-thirds of the rest of humankind. But

Median Money Incomes of Families, 1950–1983

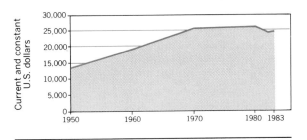

(Source: *Statistical Abstract of the United States*, 1985)

Americans were no longer the world's richest people. Citizens of several other countries boasted higher average per capita incomes. If affluent Americans wished to continue living in the style to which they had become accustomed—and to lift their own underprivileged countrymen out of poverty—they needed to solve the puzzle of increasing productivity, tame the inflationary tiger, refurbish their obsolescing industries, and regain their competitive edge in world markets.

Government Expenditures for Public Welfare, 1940–1980*

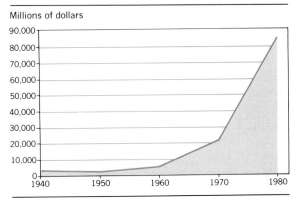

*Totals include both state and federal spending and reflect expenditures for such programs as Aid to Families with Dependent Children (AFDC), grants to the aged, blind, and disabled, food stamps, and various "anti-poverty" programs. Note the rapid growth of welfare spending in the 1960s, due to "Great Society" programs, and in the 1970s, due largely to inflation.
(Sources: *Historical Statistics of the United States* and *Statistical Abstract of the United States*, relevant years. Updates from Fiscal Year 1987, Budget, *Historical Tables*.)

New Economic Patterns

Underlying the prosperity-to-stagnation cycle of the postwar economy were some momentous changes in the nation's basic economic structure. Conspicuous was the accelerating shift of the work force out of agriculture, which achieved productivity gains virtually unmatched by any other economic sector. The family farm nearly became an antique artifact as consolidation produced giant agribusinesses able to employ costly machinery. Thanks largely to mechanization and to rich new fertilizers—as well as to government subsidies and price supports—one farmworker in the 1980s could produce food for over fifty people, compared with about fifteen people in the 1940s. Farmers whose forebears had busted sod with oxen or horses now plowed their fields in air-conditioned tractor cabs, listening on their stereophonic radios to weather forecasts or the latest Chicago commodities market quotations. Once the mighty backbone of the agricultural Republic, and still some 15 percent of the labor force at the end of

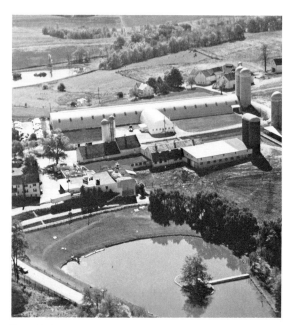

Bossy's New Home   *A large commercial dairy farm in Pennsylvania. (Grant Heilman Photography.)*

World War II, farmers made up less than 3 percent of the American population by the 1980s—yet they fed much of the world.

The booming economy created almost 40 million new jobs in the four post–World War II decades, but relatively few of them were on assembly lines. Employment in manufacturing grew only modestly and by the 1970s was actually shrinking in depressed "smokestack" industries like steel. The fastest-growing employment opportunities were in the service industries—notably information processing, medical care, communications, teaching, merchandising, and finance. Growing especially lustily was government, which by the 1980s employed nearly one in seven working Americans. Contrary to popular belief, federal payrolls held fairly steady, while the number of employees working for state and local governments more than tripled since World War II.

"Blue-collar" workers made up a strong majority of the work force in the 1950s. By the 1980s they accounted for only about 20 percent of American jobs. "White-collar" employees now constituted a majority. They proved far less inclined to join labor unions than their blue-collar

cousins, and by 1985 only about 19 percent of workers were unionized, down from a high point of nearly 35 percent in the 1950s. Organized labor withered along with the smokestack industries in which it had flourished.

Increasingly, America's economic future seemed to lie with high-technology industries like aerospace, biological engineering, and especially electronics. From its crude beginnings with Germany's "V-2" rockets at the end of World War II, rocketry had advanced to place astronauts on the moon in the 1960s, had produced a reusable Space Shuttle in the 1980s—and had equipped both the United States and the Soviet Union with bristling arsenals of intercontinental nuclear weapons. When scientists unlocked the secrets of molecular genetic structure in the early 1950s, the road lay open to breeding new strains of high-yield, bug- and weather-resistant crops; to curing hereditary diseases; and also, unfortunately, to unleashing genetic mutations that might threaten the fragile ecological balance in which humankind was delicately suspended. The development of the transistor in 1948 touched off an electronic revolution, especially in computers. Vast new technological complexes, such as California's "Silicon Valley" south of San Francisco, became hotbeds of entrepreneurship and invention.

U.S. Steel had been the flagship company of America's late-nineteenth-century industrial revolution, which emphasized heavy industry and the building of the nation's economic infrastructure. In turn, General Motors was the leading firm in the shift to an economy of mass consumerism in the 1920s. By the 1980s a new "postindustrial" economy was emerging in the United States, symbolized by the awesome rise of the International Business Machines Corporation (IBM), which specialized in serving the needs of the new "information society."

Economic Challenges

A rising tide lifts all boats, and the postwar river of riches lifted most Americans to new heights of consumption. But the golden flood of prosperity actually obscured persistent inequalities in American society. Even in the booming

The Electronic Revolution *This simple silicon wafer with computer chips lay at the heart of the postwar explosion of high-technology industries. (Dan McCoy/Rainbow.)*

1960s, some 20 percent of the American people lived a hand-to-mouth existence on paltry incomes below the official "poverty line." Lyndon Johnson's "War on Poverty," combined with continuing economic growth, substantially reduced that proportion by the 1980s. But tens of millions of Americans still remained mired in poverty—a depressing indictment of the inequities afflicting the world's richest superpower.

Other inequities lurked behind the glittering veil of America's wealth. The richest 20 percent of Americans in the 1980s still raked in nearly half the nation's income. This privileged position had changed little over the course of the

U.S. Population below the Poverty Line, 1959–1983

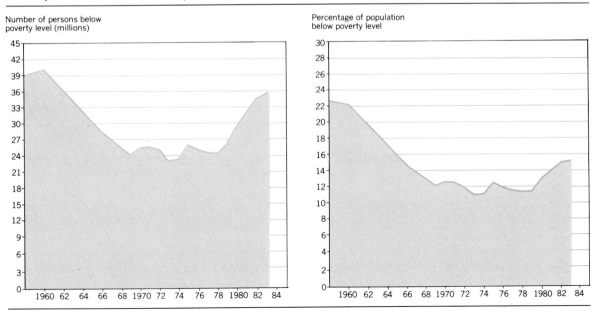

(Source: *Current Population Reports*, no. 138, p. 60.)

Manhattan's Lower East Side, 1977 *The persistence of poverty amidst plenty baffled policy-makers and angered critics in postwar America. (Bob Adelman.)*

century, despite progressive and New Deal reforms and the supposedly leveling influence of the income tax. Nor was there significant change in the relative position of the poorest 20 percent of Americans. They continued to receive less than 5 percent of the national income, just as they had before the 1930s. Hispanic families, on the whole, earned 34 percent less than white families; black families fared more poorly still, earning some 45 percent less than their white counterparts.

Critics also assailed the lopsided distribution of resources in moneyed America. They charged that the postwar explosion of prosperity had produced a troublesome combination of private opulence and public squalor. Americans had color televisions in their homes but garbage in their streets. They ate rich food but breathed foul air. Despite howls of protest from taxpayers, Americans gave a smaller percentage of their incomes to the tax collector than in almost any other advanced, industrialized nation.

The United States stubbornly remained the land of individualism, at least economically. The

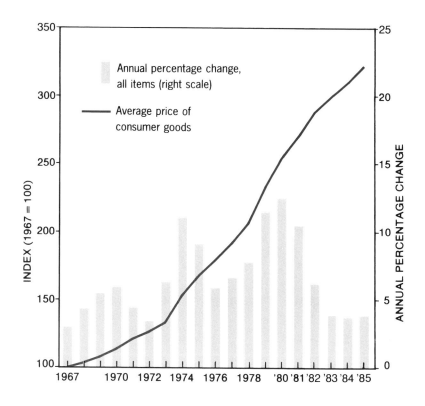

The History of the Consumer Price Index, 1967–1985 *This graph shows both the annual percentage of inflation and the absolute increase in 1967 dollars. (Statistical Abstract of the United States.)*

only public "service" for which Americans seemed willing to be taxed was national defense. When in 1973 the budget of the Department of Health, Education, and Welfare surpassed that of the Department of Defense, many citizens began to balk at paying the bills for further extension of government "benefits." After four decades of advancing New Deal and Great Society programs, a strong countercurrent took hold. Jimmy Carter campaigned successfully in 1976 against the allegedly bloated bureaucracy in Washington. Californians staged a "tax revolt" in 1978 (known by its official ballot title of "Proposition 13") that drastically slashed property taxes and forced painful cuts in government services. The California "tax quake" jolted other state capitals and even rocked the pillars of Congress in faraway Washington, D.C. Ronald Reagan rode the same political shock wave to presidential victory in 1980 and proceeded to rattle the "welfare state" to its very foundations. For the time being, at least, Americans apparently wanted more private goods and fewer public services.

The Smiling Sunbelt

The surging economic changes of the post-1945 period shook and shifted the American people,

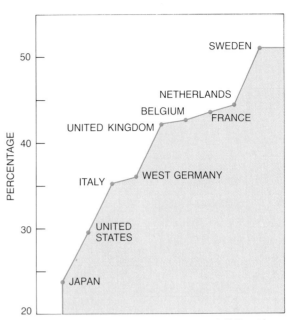

Comparative Tax Burdens   *Percentage of GNP paid as taxes in major industrial countries, 1980.*

amplifying the population redistribution set in motion by World War II. In the four decades after the war, the population of the North increased at only half the rate of the South and West. Especially striking was the growth of the "Sunbelt"—a fifteen-state area stretching in a smiling crescent from Virginia through Florida

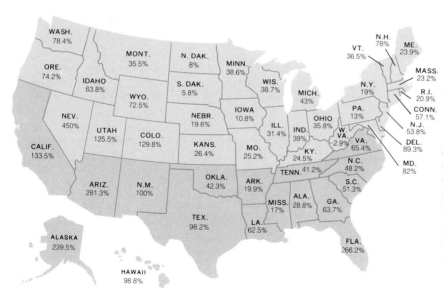

Population Increase in the Sunbelt States, 1950–1982
States with figures higher than 50 percent were growing faster than the national average. Note that "sunbelt" is a loose geographical concept, as some deep-South states had very little population growth, while the mountain and Pacific states were booming.

Sunbelt Prosperity *The old and the new West are evident in this view of booming Dallas. (Atlan/ Sygma.)*

and Texas to Arizona and California. In the 1950s California alone accounted for one-fifth of the nation's population growth and by 1963 had outdistanced New York as the most populous state—a position it still held in 1985 with some 26 million people.

The South and the Southwest were a new frontier for Americans after World War II. These modern pioneers came in search of jobs, a better climate, and lower taxes. Jobs they found in abundance, especially in the California electronics industry, in the aerospace complexes in Florida and Texas, and in the huge military installations that powerful southern congressional representatives secured for their districts.

A Niagara of federal dollars accounted for much of the Sunbelt's new prosperity, even though, ironically, southern and western politicians led the cry against government spending. In 1982 the South and West collected $75 billion more from the federal Treasury than they paid in, while the once-dominant Northeast (the "frostbelt") sent over $100 billion more to

Washington than it received. A new economic war between the states seemed to be shaping up. Northeasterners and their allies from the hard-hit heavy-industry region of the Ohio Valley (the "rustbelt") tried to rally political support with the sarcastic slogan "The North shall rise again."

The South still lagged behind the rest of the country in income and population, but it was rapidly closing the gap. Southern real wage rates reached near-equality with the national average by the mid-1970s. And black Americans, once hounded from the South by prejudice and poverty, were for the first time returning to the land of their ancient bondage. They came because of the improved racial climate after the civil rights successes of the 1960s and, like whites, because of the increasing availability of jobs.

These dramatic shifts of population and wealth further broke the historic grip of the North on the nation's political life. Every elected occupant of the White House since Kennedy's day has hailed from the Sunbelt, and the region's congressional representation is rising as its population grows. With their frontier ethic of unbridled individualism and their devotion to unregulated economic growth, the sunbelters were redrawing the Republic's political map.

Sick Cities and Sprawling Suburbs

Americans, as immigrants or westward-trekking pioneers, had always been a people on the move. But they were astonishingly footloose in the postwar era. For some three decades after 1945, an average of 30 million persons changed residences every year. Families especially felt the strain, as distance divided parents from children, and brothers and sisters from one another. Friendships were also harder to sustain in fluid neighborhoods. Mobility could exact a high human cost.

If they were white, these modern migrants tended to move to the suburbs, which expanded after World War II at a rate nearly double that of overall population growth and contained nearly half of all Americans by the 1980s. "White flight" left the inner cities—especially in the Northeast and Midwest—black, brown, and broke. Poorer residents, largely nonwhites, filled in behind the departing white middle class. Taxpaying businesses fled with their affluent customers from downtown shops to suburban shopping malls. The strapped city of Cleveland fell victim to these pressures in 1978 and defaulted on its debt payments. New York was rescued from a similar fate only by a federal bailout in 1975.

Despite black economic gains following the civil rights drives of the 1960s, the population of the green suburbs remained more than 90 percent white in the 1980s. About 80 percent of American blacks now lived in cities, in striking contrast to slavery days, while only about 28 percent of whites still inhabited the urban core. As the United States became a nation of black metropolises surrounded by white "greenbelts," a vivid and vexatious racial element was added to the age-old conflict between country and city.

America's "alabaster cities" of song and story grew more sooty and less safe in the era after World War II. Pollution, arson, and robbery were among the curses of urban life. Some observers claimed that breathing smoggy urban air was equivalent to smoking several packs of lung-blackening cigarettes daily. The rate of violent crimes committed in the cities increased threefold in the 1960s, though it slackened somewhat by the 1980s. Statistically, murder victims fell in 1983 at the rate of one every twenty-five minutes; burglaries occurred every ten seconds; two cars were stolen every minute; every seven minutes a woman was raped. By the 1980s, America imprisoned a larger fraction of its citizens than any country in the world except the Soviet Union and South Africa. Desperate citizens often set up vigilante patrols to protect their neighborhoods. Frightened urbanites cowered like nightly prisoners in their locked and bolted apartments. When New Yorker Bernhard Goetz, on December 22, 1984, gunned down four black youths who allegedly tried to mug him in a subway, he became a folk hero, and a court later exonerated him of assault charges. Americans in the 1980s were paying more for personal security systems and handguns than for all police departments—a perverse example of their preference for private means rather than public services.

The Postwar Baby Boom

Of all the changes in postwar America, none was more dramatic than the "baby boom"—the huge leap in the birthrate in the decade and a half after 1945. Confident young men and women tied the nuptial knot in record numbers at war's end, and they began immediately to fill the nation's empty cradles. They thus touched off a demographic explosion that added more than 50 million bawling babies to the nation's population by the end of the 1950s. The soaring birthrate finally crested in 1957 and was followed by a deepening birth dearth. By 1973 fertility rates had passed below the point necessary to maintain existing population figures. If the trend persisted, only further immigration would lift the American population above its 1985 level of some 239 million.

This boom-or-bust cycle of births begot a bulging wave along the American population curve. As the oversize postwar generation grew to maturity, it was destined—like the fabled pig passing through the python—to strain and distort many aspects of American life. Elementary-school enrollments, for example, swelled to nearly 34 million pupils in 1970. Then began a steady decline, as the onward-marching age group left in its wake closed schools and unemployed teachers.

The maturing babies of the postwar boom sent economic shock waves undulating through the decades. As tykes and toddlers in the 1940s and 1950s, they made up a lucrative market for manufacturers of canned food and other baby products. As teenagers in the 1960s, the same youngsters spent an estimated $20 billion a year for clothes and recorded rock music—and their sheer numbers laid the basis of the much-bally-hooed "youth culture" of that tumultuous decade. In the 1970s the consumer tastes of the aging baby-boomers changed again, and the most popular jeans maker began marketing pants with a fuller cut for those former "kids" who could no longer squeeze into their size-thirty Levi's. In the 1980s the horde of baby-boomers bumped and jostled one another in the job market, struggling to get a foothold on the crowded ladder of social mobility. Predictions were that the impact of the huge postwar generation would continue to ripple through American society until well into the next century, as its members passed eventually into retirement, placing enormous strains on the Social Security system.

The Graying of America

Retirement was increasingly likely to be a lengthier experience for Americans, who were living longer than ever before. A person born at the dawn of the century could expect to survive less than fifty years, but a white male born in the 1980s could anticipate a life span of nearly seventy-two years. His white female counter-part would probably outlive him by seven years. (The figures were slightly lower for nonwhites, reflecting differences in living standards, especially diet and health care.) The census of 1950 recorded that women for the first time made up a majority of Americans, thanks largely to greater feminine longevity. Miraculous medical advances lengthened and strengthened lives. Noteworthy were the development of antibiotics after 1940 and Dr. Jonas Salk's discovery in 1953 of a vaccine against a dreaded crippler, polio.

Longer lives spelled more older people. One American in nine was over sixty-five years of age in the 1980s, and projections were that one of every six people would be in the "sunset years" by 2030, as the median age rose toward forty. This aging of the population raised a host of political, social, and economic questions. Elderly persons formed a potent electoral bloc that successfully lobbied for governmental favors. In 1977 the "wrinkled radicals" scored a major victory when the California legislature abolished mandatory retirement at age sixty-five, and the following year the federal Congress passed similar legislation.

These triumphs for senior citizens symbolized the fading of the "youth culture" that had colored the American scene in the first three post–World War II decades. Medical gains also brought fiscal strains, especially in the Social Security system, established in 1935 to provide income for retired workers. When Social Security began, most of the labor force continued to work after age sixty-five. A half-century later, only 20 percent did, and a majority of the elderly population relied exclusively on Social Security checks for their living expenses. Benefits had risen so high, and the ratio of active workers to retirees had dropped so low, that drastic adjustments were necessary. The problem was intensified in the 1970s, when a compassionate Congress dramatically increased retirement benefits at a time when productivity growth was stalled.

Without greater productivity, larger payments to retirees could only mean smaller paychecks for workers. Many employees in the 1980s paid higher Social Security taxes (a maximum of $3,003 in 1986) than income taxes. Thanks to the political clout of the elderly, the share of gross national product spent on health care for people over sixty-five almost doubled in the twenty years after the enactment of Medicare legislation in 1965. This growth in medical payments for the old far outstripped the growth of educational expenditures for the young. A war between the generations loomed, as the ratio of workers to retirees, which stood at three to one in the 1980s, promised to fall to about two to one by the end of the century. Extending the working lifetime of still-active oldsters was one way of averting the crisis.

The New Immigration

Newcomers flooded into modern America. They washed ashore in waves that swelled in size after the Immigration and Nationality Act of 1965 had abolished the old quota system based on national origins (see p. 699–700). The new law made it easier for entire families to migrate and established "special categories" for political refugees. The result was a massive surge in immigration, which averaged over half a million legal entrants a year in the 1970s and 1980s. Probably an even larger number of "undocumented" migrants annually slipped across the United States border, and they may have added up to an astonishing 8 million persons by 1985. Legal and undocumented entrants together accounted for the heaviest inflow of immigrants in America's experience. In striking contrast to the historic pattern of immigration, Europe contributed far fewer people than did the teeming countries of Asia and Latin America, especially Mexico.

What prompted this new flocking to America? The truth is that the newest immigrants came for many of the same reasons as the old. They typically left countries where populations were growing rapidly and where agricultural and industrial revolutions were shaking people loose from old habits of life—conditions almost identical to those in nineteenth-century Europe. And they came to America, as previous immigrants had done, in search of jobs and economic opportunity.

The Newest Immigrants *Asia and Latin America replaced Europe as the main source of immigrants in the 1980s, as immigration, legal and illegal, reached the highest level ever in American history. (UPI/Bettmann Newsphotos.)*

The Southwest, from Texas to California, felt the immigrant impact especially sharply, as Mexican migrants concentrated heavily in that region. In 1984 Hispanics made up nearly 20 percent of the population in Texas, Arizona, and California and almost 40 percent in New Mexico—amounting to a demographic *reconquista* of the lands lost by Mexico in the war of 1846.

The size and geographic concentration of the Hispanic population in the Southwest had few precedents in the history of American immigration. Most previous groups had been so thinly scattered across the land that they had little choice but to learn English and make their way in the larger American society, however much they might have longed to preserve their Old Country language and customs. But Hispanic-Americans might succeed in creating a truly bicultural zone in the booming southwestern states. Many of them have championed bilingual education and stayed in close cultural contact with their mother country south of the border.

Old-stock Americans worried about the capacity of the modern United States to absorb this new immigrant mass. Yet foreign-born persons accounted for less than 10 percent of the American population in the 1980s—a far smaller proportion than the historical high point of 15 percent recorded in the census of 1910. Somewhat inconsistently, critics charged both that "illegal" immigrants robbed citizens of jobs and that they dumped themselves on the welfare rolls at the taxpayers' expense. In fact, studies showed that immigrants took jobs scorned by Americans and that they paid many times more dollars in taxes (withholding and Social Security taxes, as well as sales taxes) than they claimed for welfare payments. The real worry was that unscrupulous employers could take cruel advantage of undocumented workers, who were without recourse to legal protection. Legislation in Congress to choke off illegal entry by penalizing employers of undocumented aliens and by granting amnesty to many of those already here faltered repeatedly in the early 1980s. But some reform seemed inevitable, as the sheer volume of immigrants continued to grow.

Ethnic Pride

Thanks both to continued immigration and to their own high birthrate, Hispanic-Americans were becoming an increasingly important minority. The census of 1980 counted 14.6 million Hispanics. They included some 10 million Chicanos, or Mexican-Americans, mostly in the Southwest, as well as more than 2 million Puerto Ricans, chiefly in the Northeast, and about 1 million Cubans in Florida (where it was jokingly said that Miami had become the most "Anglo" city in Latin America).

Flexing their political muscles, Hispanics elected mayors of Miami, Denver, and San Antonio. After years of struggle, the United Farmworkers Organizing Committee (UFWOC), headed by soft-spoken and charismatic César Chávez, succeeded in improving work conditions for the mostly Chicano "stoop laborers" who followed the cycle of planting and harvesting across the American West. Hispanic influence seemed likely to grow, as suggested by the increasing presence of Spanish-language ballots and television broadcasts. Hispanic-Americans, newly confident and organized, might well become the nation's largest ethnic minority, outnumbering even blacks, by the turn of the century. Indeed, predictions were that the Chicano population of California would equal the "Anglo" population by the year 2000, when there would no longer be a single ethnic majority in the state, only a patchwork of minorities.

Other ethnic groups also grew more conscious of their unique identity in postwar America. The fire under the melting pot seemed to flicker out in the 1960s. Descendants of European immigrants, long thought to have been fused into the national amalgam, began to assert their unalloyed separateness. Ethnic stereotyping became a hazardous occupation, and dialect jokes fell into malodorous disrepute.

Asian-Americans made giant strides in the post–World War II era. Once feared and hated as the "yellow peril" and consigned to the most menial and degrading jobs, citizens of Japanese and Chinese ancestry were now counted among the most prosperous of Americans. By 1970

Henry Cisneros, Mayor of San Antonio, Texas
He symbolized the rising political power of Hispanic-Americans. (Bill Nation/Sygma.)

560), and held it for two months amid national publicity. Lawyers replaced warriors as various tribes sought, with some success, to regain long-lost fishing rights or to secure multimillion-dollar payments for land "stolen" by whites.

In Black America

Black Americans also scored notable advances in the postwar period, though they still had a long hill to climb before reaching full equality. Civil rights victories in the 1950s and 1960s made blatant segregation in public facilities a relic of the past, but patterns of residential segregation persisted. The number of black elected officials in the 1980s climbed over the five thousand mark, including hundreds in the Old South, twenty-one congresspersons, and the mayors of Chicago, Atlanta, Washington, and

The Oldest Americans *Indians demand justice. (Paul Fuscol/Magnum Photos, Inc.)*

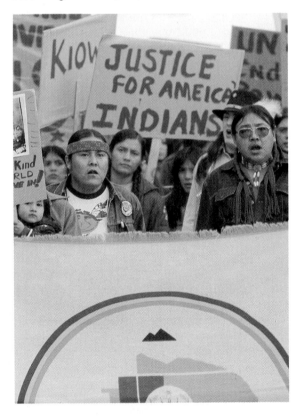

Japanese family income stood at 32 percent, and Chinese family income at 12 percent, above the national average. Asian-Americans graduated in Harvard's class of 1985 in numbers representing six times their proportion of the general population.

Indians, the original Americans, shared in the general awakening of "cultural nationalism." More than 1 million strong by the 1980s, they aggressively asserted their rich heritage and forced other Americans to recognize their desperate plight—often jobless, reservation-bound, and illiterate.

Militant members of the American Indian Movement (AIM) seized the Indian Bureau in Washington in 1972. The next year heavily armed Indians occupied the ghost-haunted village of Wounded Knee, South Dakota (see p.

Los Angeles. By 1970 the black-white income gap had noticeably narrowed, as black families earned on the average about 64 percent of the income of their white counterparts. But black economic gains had flowed in large part from general prosperity rather than from any basic redistribution of the nation's wealth or the permanent eradication of racism. When the economy faltered in the 1970s, the racial income gap began to widen again. Blacks once more suffered from the age-old stigma of being "the last hired and the first fired." Black unemployment in the 1980s was nearly double that of whites, and among black teenagers more than one in three found it almost impossible to land any kind of job.

Single women headed over half of black families, or almost four times the rate for whites. Understandably, a majority of these husbandless and jobless women depended on welfare to feed their children. As social scientists increasingly emphasized the importance of the home environment for success in school, it became clear that many fatherless, impoverished black children continued to suffer from educational handicaps that were difficult to overcome. Black youths in the 1980s still had about one year less schooling than whites of the

White Backlash *"Soiling of Old Glory." Anti-busing demonstration in Boston, April 1976. (Stanley Forman, Pulitzer Prize, 1977.)*

same age and were less than half as likely to earn college degrees.

Education remained the principal fighting front for blacks still struggling for their share of the American dream, and the North was soon transformed into the main educational battleground. There segregated schools often resulted not from overt discrimination but from segregated neighborhoods. Many white parents had moved to the suburbs to provide better schools for their children. Now they felt deeply threatened by court-ordered busing that seemed to deprive them unfairly of their hard-bought advantages. Violent confrontations shook cities like Boston, where school officials tried to achieve racial balance by busing. A new wave of "white flight" swept many metropolitan areas, as families fled not just to more distant suburbs but to private schools. In some northern cities the public-school system was being virtually abandoned to black pupils.

White anxiety about advancing minorities was also evident in higher education. Many colleges and professional schools initiated special admissions programs for minority members in the 1960s, and college enrollments of blacks shot up. But by the 1970s white students who had been denied admission raised to new heights the cry of "reverse discrimination." They charged that their rights had been violated by admissions officers who in some cases put more weight on racial or ethnic background than on ability or achievement.

One white Californian, Allan Bakke, made headlines in 1978 when the United States Supreme Court, by the narrowest margin (five to four), upheld his claim that his application to medical school had been turned down because of an admissions program that partially favored minority people. The Court declared that preference in admissions could not be given to members of any group, minority or majority, on the basis of ethnic or racial identity alone. Among the dissenters on the sharply divided bench was the Court's only black Justice, Thurgood Marshall. The judge warned in an impassioned opinion that the majority decision might sweep away years of progress by the civil rights movement.

Occupational Distribution of Working Women, 1900–1985 *

	1900	1920	1940	1960	1980	1985
Total White Collar Workers†	17.8	38.8	44.9	52.5	65.6	67.4
Clerical Workers	4.0	18.7	21.5	28.7	30.5	29.6
Manual Workers	27.8	23.8	21.6	18.0	14.8	11.5
Farm Workers	18.9	13.5	4.0	1.8	1.0	1.0
Service Workers‡	35.5	23.9	29.4	21.9	18.1	18.1

* Major categories; percent of women workers, ages 14 and older.
† Includes clerical, sales professional, and technical workers, managers and officials.
‡ Includes domestic servants.
(Sources: *Historical Statistics of the United States* and *Statistical Abstract of the United States,* relevant years.)

Civil rights supporters winced again in 1984 when the Supreme Court, in a case involving Memphis fire fighters, ruled that concern for racial equity could be subordinated to union rules about job seniority. The decision raised anew the old fear that last-hired blacks would be the first fired in an economic pinch.

Womanpower

Of all the beneficiaries of postwar prosperity, none reaped greater rewards than women. More than ever, urban offices and shops provided a bonanza of employment for female workers. During World War II, more than 6 million women took jobs vacated by departing GIs. To a remarkable extent, they kept working after the war. Women had made up less than 20 percent of the work force in the early part of the century, but at the conclusion of World War II, they accounted for 25 percent of the labor pool. In the next four decades, the great majority of new jobs went to women, thanks to the rapidly expanding service sector of the economy. By the mid-1980s, 44 percent of all wage earners were women, and 60 percent of working-age women held jobs. Most astonishing was the upsurge in employment of mothers. As recently as 1950, 90 percent of mothers with children under the age of six did not work for pay. But by the 1980s a majority of women with young children were wage earners.

Cynics claimed that women were the "new immigrants" into the work force—the latest cheap labor supply to be tapped by all-devouring capitalism. Women did receive lower wages than men in corresponding jobs, and they tended to be employed in a few low-skill, low-prestige occupations. Though they made up more than half the population, women in 1980 accounted for only 14 percent of lawyers (up from 5 percent in 1970), 13 percent of physi-

The New (Working) Woman *Many previously all-male occupations—and some brand-new ones—were opened to women in the 1960s and 1970s. (Photo: Suzanne Arms-Jeroboam.)*

Percentage of Working Married Women with Children, (Husband Present), 1948–1984

YEAR	TOTAL PERCENTAGE	NO CHILDREN UNDER 18	CHILDREN 6–17 ONLY	CHILDREN UNDER 6
1948	22.0	28.4	26.0	10.8
1950	23.8	30.3	28.3	11.9
1955	27.7	32.7	34.7	16.2
1960	30.5	34.7	39.0	18.6
1965	34.7	38.3	42.7	23.3
1970	40.8	42.2	49.2	30.3
1980	50.1	46.0	61.7	45.1
1984	52.8	47.1	65.4	51.8

cians (up from 10 percent in 1970), and 17 percent of judges (up from 6 percent in 1970).

Exploding employment opportunities for women set off a ground swell of social and psychological changes that mounted to tidal-wave proportions as the postwar era unfolded. When Betty Friedan in 1963 published *The Feminine Mystique*, which became a runaway best-seller,

Women in the Labor Force, 1900–1980

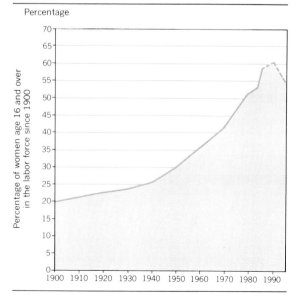

Percentage

Percentage of women age 16 and over in the labor force since 1900

* Percentages for 1990 and 1995 are projected.
(Sources: *Historical Statistics of the United States* and *Statistical Abstract of the United States*, relevant years. Updates from Bureau of Labor Statistics, *Handbook of Labor Statistics*, relevant years.

she spoke in rousing accents to millions of able, educated women who applauded her indictment of the stifling boredom of suburban housewifery. Many of those women were already working, though they struggled against the guilt and frustration of leading an "unfeminine" life—or griped that they had to bring home the bacon and then had to cook it, too.

Friedan gave focus and fire to these women's feelings, and the modern women's movement was launched. Traditional feminine roles were everywhere questioned. Women's liberationists ("libbers") picketed the Miss America pageant, burned their bras, condemned advertisements that demeaned women, and insisted that men help with the housework and baby-sitting. Some men feared, with exaggeration, that the hand that rocked the cradle was turning into the hand that cradled the rock.

Despite ridicule from "male chauvinists," the women's cause made notable headway. The Civil Rights Act of 1964 prohibited sexual discrimination by employers. President Johnson signed an executive order in 1965 that required employers on federal contracts to take "affirmative action" to ensure that more women and underprivileged minorities were hired. Within a few years several corporations, including American Telephone and Telegraph, were forced to provide back wages to female employees who had not been receiving equal pay for equal work and to abolish hiring and promotion practices that discriminated against women. Feminists pushed these gains still further in the 1980s,

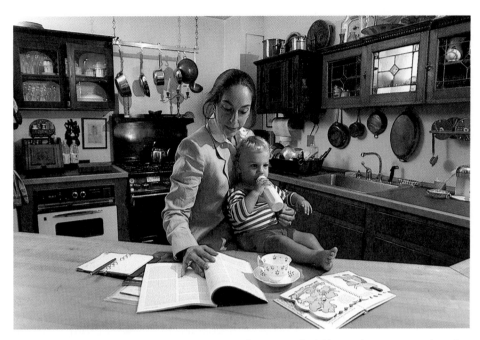

A Working Mother   By the 1980s, a majority of women with children at home were working for wages. Yet many of those mothers still had the primary responsibility for child-care and home-making. (Steve McCurry/Magnum Photos, Inc.)

when they introduced the concept called "comparable worth." They claimed that wage differentials between altogether different but "comparable" occupations (such as secretaries and streetsweepers) owed solely to sexual discrimination and should be abolished. Orthodox economists, who saw wage rates as fairly accurate reflections of free-market forces, were appalled at this "political" definition of equity.

In 1972 Congress sent the Equal Rights Amendment to the Constitution to the states for ratification. Commonly called ERA, the proposed amendment would guarantee sexual equality as part of the basic law of the land. Despite extraordinary efforts by feminists, the deadline for ratification passed without the required number of states having given their approval. But ardent supporters vowed to reintroduce the ERA in Congress and start the entire ratification process anew. Feminists received some satisfaction when the Supreme Court in 1973 (*Roe* v. *Wade*) upheld a woman's right to an abortion during the early months of pregnancy, provoking bitter criticism from Roman Catholics and various "right-to-life" groups.

Sally Ride, Astronaut   She was the first American woman in space. (NASA.)

Forward-looking feminists overturned the barriers that guarded many a citadel of masculinity. Numerous all-male strongholds, including Yale and Princeton, opened their doors to women students, and even West Point, Annapolis, and the Air Force Academy fell to the forces of the feminist revolution. In 1983 the armed services included nearly 200,000 enlisted women and some 27,000 female officers, including a handful of generals and admirals. Women were flying planes and orbiting in outer space; they governed states and cities, wrote Supreme Court decisions, and sat in both houses of the United States Congress. The emerging new role of women promised to add up to a revolution comparable to the coming of industrialism or the emancipation of the slaves.

The Fading Family

The family, once prized as the foundation of society and the nursery of the Republic, suffered heavy blows in postwar America. Divorce rates doubled in the decade after 1965, and by the 1980s two out of every five marriages ended in divorce. Seven times more children were affected by divorce than at the turn of the century, and kids who commuted between separated parents were becoming commonplace.

Families were not only falling apart at an alarming rate, they were also increasingly slow to form in the first place. The proportion of adults living alone tripled in the three decades after 1950, and by 1980 more than 20 percent of women aged twenty-five to twenty-nine had never been married. In 1960, 5 percent of all births were to unmarried women, but by 1980 one out of ten white babies and an astounding one out of two nonwhite babies were born to single mothers. Every fourth child in America was growing up in a household that lacked two parents.

Born and raised without the family support enjoyed by their forebears, Americans were also increasingly likely to be lonely in their later years. Most elderly people in the 1980s depended on the government, not on their loved ones, for their daily bread. The great majority of them drew their last breaths not in their own homes, but in hospitals and nursing facilities. From birth to death, the role of the family was dwindling.

Child-rearing, the family's foremost function, was being increasingly assigned to "parent-substitutes" at day-care centers or schools—or to television, the modern age's "electronic babysitter." Estimates were that the average child by age sixteen had watched up to fifteen thousand hours of TV—more time than was spent in the classroom.

Parents had become so uncertain as to how to raise their children in a rapidly changing world that many of them turned for advice to books, especially Dr. Benjamin Spock's *The Common Sense Book of Baby and Child Care*, first published in 1945. Millions of American youngsters in the following decades were raised on "the gospel according to Spock." The good doctor urged a natural, relaxed attitude toward child-rearing. In his book, Spock stressed parental "permissiveness" and de-emphasized strict rules and schedules for infants. Critics blamed him for breeding softness and disrespect for authority into an entire generation of American young people, including antiwar protesters in the Vietnam War era.

The Cultural Upheaval of the 1960s

Whatever the cause, a newly negative attitude toward all kinds of authority seemed to pervade much of postwar American society. Not only the family but other traditional institutions like the schools and the churches seemed to be losing their ability to define values and shape behavior. No matter what the topic, conventional wis-

Historian Theodore Roszak wrote in 1969: "It would hardly seem an exaggeration to call what we see arising among the young a 'counter culture': meaning, a culture so radically disaffiliated from the mainstream assumptions of our society that it scarcely looks to many as a culture at all, but takes on the alarming appearance of a barbarian intrusion."

dom and inherited ideas came under fire. "Trust no one over thirty" was a popular sneer in the heyday of the rebellious "youth culture" in the 1960s.

Skepticism about authority had deep historical roots in American culture, but it bloomed vigorously in the 1950s and burst into full flower in the 1960s. "Beat" poets like Allen Ginsberg and novelists like Jack Kerouac voiced dark disillusion with the materialistic beliefs of the complacent "establishment" in the Eisenhower era. The attractive young actor James Dean, in movies like *Rebel without a Cause* (1955), expressed the restless frustration of many young people.

The disillusion of the young reached crisis proportions in the tumultuous 1960s. Prompted by seething resentment against the war in Vietnam, many sons and daughters of the baby-boom generation turned to mind-bending drugs, tuned in to "acid rock," and dropped out of "straight" society. Some explored Oriental religions. Others "did their own thing" in communes or "alternate" institutions. Beflowered women in trousers and long-haired men with earrings heralded the rise of a self-conscious

> As a tough motorcycle-gang leader, Marlon Brando, in the film The Wild One (1954), summed up the anarchic impulses of the decade when he was asked, "What are you rebelling against?" His reply: "What d'ya got?"

"counterculture" mortally opposed to traditional American ways.

Straitlaced guardians of respectability denounced the self-indulgent romanticism of the "flower children" as the beginning of the end of modern civilization. Sympathetic observers hailed the "greening" of America—the replacement of materialism and imperialism by a new consciousness of human values. But the upheavals of the 1960s could be largely attributed to three *P*s: the youthful population bulge, protest against the Vietnam War, and the apparent permanence of prosperity. As the decade flowed into the 1970s, the flower children grew older and had children of their own, the war ended, and economic stagnation blighted the bloom of prosperity. Young people in the 1970s

The Counterculture
Clothes and hair-styles made political statements in the 1960s. (Henri Cartier-Bresson/ Magnum Photos, Inc.)

and 1980s seemed more concerned with finding a job in the system than with tearing the system down. The "counterculture" appeared in retrospect to be not the road to the future but a historical blind alley.

Beyond the 1960s

Yet some residues from the frothy 1960s remained. Opinion polls revealed that millions of Americans now regularly puffed marijuana, and the use of other "recreational drugs," especially cocaine, spread alarmingly. Sexual attitudes seemed drastically altered, as increasing numbers of men and women engaged in premarital intimacies. Legal sanctions against obscenity and pornography withered away, and nudity became almost obligatory on stage and screen. Even old taboos against homosexuality were crumbling as "gays" emerged from their closets and loudly demanded sexual tolerance. Yet by the 1980s the "sexual revolution" was seriously slowed by widening worries about genital herpes and AIDS (acquired immune deficiency syndrome).

A wave of religious fervor also seemed to roll out of the spiritually conscious 1960s. Church membership climbed toward record levels, and over 95 percent of adults in 1971 stated a religious preference. "Born-again" Christians abounded, including peanut-farmer Jimmy Carter of Georgia. The country was still predominantly Protestant, though the Roman Catholic Church counted some 52 million communicants in the early 1980s. Even among tradition-bound Roman Catholics, the liberal reforms launched in the 1960s endured. Clerics abandoned their Roman collars and Latin lingo, folk songs replaced Gregorian chants, and meatless Fridays became ancient history. But some cynics complained that changes like these proved that the churches, unable to defeat the Devil, had embraced him.

Modern America provided many diversions to compete with the churches for the national soul. At the close of World War II, less than half of American households were equipped with telephones; four decades later more than 95 percent had television sets, most of them color.

> *Speaking in 1961, Newton Minow urged his hearers to sit at length before a television screen. "I can assure you," he said, "that you will observe a vast wasteland. You will see a procession of game shows, violence, audience participation shows, formula comedies about totally unbelievable families, blood and thunder, mayhem, violence, sadism, murder, Western badmen, Western goodmen, private eyes, gangsters, more violence, and cartoons. And, endlessly, commercials—many screaming, cajoling and offending."*

Pre–World War II Americans had consistently mentioned reading as their favorite leisure-time activity. By the 1980s they overwhelmingly told pollsters that watching TV was their favorite indoor sport. Many newspapers folded as the public increasingly turned to the electronic eye for its view of the world. Some critics charged that Americans were not only reading less but also understanding less. The average television news broadcast emitted far fewer words than could be printed on a single newspaper page.

Politics also felt the impact of television, as the line between show business and the public business became blurred. Candidates who appeared to good advantage on the screen had a competitive edge. Some former film and sports stars even parlayed their media images into political careers, notably ex-actor Ronald Reagan of California. Political scientists argued that one especially troublesome tendency of the mass media was to obliterate local "intermediary" organizations, including political parties themselves, in favor of direct (usually one-way) communication between politicians and the public. Ominously, there was a direct relationship between the amount of money that candidates could raise and their effectiveness on television. These developments opened the door wide for demagoguery, deception, or the denial of a local voice in the political process.

Standard amusements also beguiled postwar Americans. Televised professional football grew so spectacularly in popularity that it came to rival baseball as the national sport, at least for spectators. Horse racing still attracted larger crowds than any other American sporting activity, followed far behind by collegiate football, now a big business. An increasing number of Americans shunned the spectator's role altogether. Seeking to "get away from it all" (and from each other), they flocked to the ski slopes, hiking trails, or jogging paths.

The Life of the Mind

Despite the mind-sapping chatter of the "boob tube," Americans in the postwar era were better educated than ever before. The GI Bill of Rights paid the college fees of millions of veterans in the 1940s and 1950s, thus stimulating a vast expansion of higher education. By the 1980s colleges were awarding nearly a million degrees a year, and one person in four in the twenty-five-to-thirty-four-year-old age group was a college graduate.

This expanding mass of educated persons lifted the economy to more advanced levels while creating consumers for "high culture." Americans annually made some 300 million visits to museums in the 1980s and boasted about a thousand opera companies and fifteen hundred symphony orchestras. Despite television, Americans bought books in record numbers, especially after the "paperback explosion" of the 1960s, when more than a million volumes a day were being sold. Increasingly, educated Americans read the lamentations of writers who protested against the affluent postwar society that had made possible these very gains in mass education and culture.

Harvard sociologist David Riesman criticized postwar Americans as conformists in *The Lonely Crowd* (1950), as did William H. Whyte, Jr., in *The Organization Man* (1956). Novelist Sloan Wilson explored a similar theme in *The Man in the Gray Flannel Suit* (1955). Harvard economist John Kenneth Galbraith questioned the relation between private enterprise and the public good in a series of books beginning with *The Affluent Society* (1958) and extending to *Economics and the Public Purpose* (1973). Collusion at the highest levels of the "military-industrial complex" was the subject of *The Power Elite* (1956), an influential piece of modern-day

> Yale psychiatrist Kenneth Keniston in 1971 said: "It is absolutely unprecedented in world history to have 75 percent of an age group with at least a high school education. We're very much into a kind of society that has never existed before. No one can guess the full impact of these wide educational gains. But they certainly mean that a large segment of society will be more literate, more capable of dealing with complexity, less attached to the traditional pieties. And social conflicts do flow from increased education. A person attached to traditional concepts accepts the idea of law and order, for instance. The college-educated person is more likely to ask, 'Is the law a just law?'"

muckraking by radical sociologist C. Wright Mills, who became a hero to the "New Left" in the 1960s. Futurologist Daniel Bell pointed to disturbing trends that might spell the doom of the postwar social and economic order in *The Coming of Post-Industrial Society* (1973) and *The Cultural Contradictions of Capitalism* (1976). Bell was sometimes linked with a small but influential group of intellectuals known as "neoconservatives." Their ranks included Norman Podheretz, editor of *Commentary* magazine, and Irving Kristol, editor of *The Public Interest*. Neoconservatives championed free-market capitalism liberated from government restraints, and they tended to take a tough stance in foreign policy. They also questioned liberal welfare programs and affirmative-action policies and called for a reaffirmation of traditional values of individualism and the centrality of the family. The neoconservatives' hour seemed to have arrived with the election of Ronald Reagan in 1980.

The Power of the Pen

In fiction writing some of the pre–World War II "realists" continued to ply their trade, notably Ernest Hemingway in *The Old Man and the Sea* (1952). A Nobel laureate in 1954, Hemingway was dead by his own duck gun in 1961. John

Steinbeck, another prewar writer who persisted in graphic portrayals of American society, received the Nobel Prize for literature in 1962, the seventh American to be so honored.

Brutal realism also characterized the earliest novels that portrayed soldierly life in World War II, such as Norman Mailer's *The Naked and the Dead* (1948) and James Jones's *From Here to Eternity* (1951). But as time passed, realistic writing fell from favor. Authors tended increasingly to write of the war and other topics in fantastic and even psychedelic prose. Joseph Heller's *Catch-22* (1961) dealt with the improbable antics and anguish of American airmen in the wartime Mediterranean. A savage satire, it made readers hurt when they laughed. The supercharged imagination of Kurt Vonnegut, Jr., poured forth works of puzzling complexity in sometimes impenetrably inventive prose.

Pennsylvania-born John Updike described the white middle class at bay in books like *Rabbit Run* (1960) and *Couples* (1968), as did Massachusetts-bred John Cheever in *The Wapshot Chronicle* (1957) and *The Wapshot Scandal* (1964). Louis Auchincloss wrote elegantly of upper-class New Yorkers. Gore Vidal contributed a series of intriguing historical novels as well as several impish and always iconoclastic works, including *Myra Breckinridge* (1968), about a reincarnated transsexual. Together, these writers constituted the rear guard of an older, WASP* elite that had long dominated American writing.

Writers on the Margin

The most striking development in postwar American letters was the rise of younger authors who represented the "marginal" regions and ethnic groups now coming into their own. The South boasted a literary renaissance, led by veteran Mississippi author William Faulkner, who was a Nobel recipient in 1950. Fellow Mississippians Walker Percy and Eudora Welty grasped the falling torch from the failing Faulkner, who died in 1962. Tennessean

Robert Penn Warren immortalized Louisiana politico Huey Long in *All the King's Men* (1946). Flannery O'Connor wrote perceptively of her native Georgia, and Virginian William Styron confronted the harsh history of his home state in a controversial fictional representation of an 1831 slave rebellion, *The Confessions of Nat Turner* (1967).

Books by black authors also made the best-seller lists, beginning with Richard Wright's chilling portrait of a black Chicago killer in *Native Son* (1940). Ralph Ellison depicted the black person's quest for personal identity in *Invisible Man* (1952), one of the most moving novels of the postwar era. James Baldwin won plaudits as a novelist and essayist, particularly for his sensitive reflections on the racial question in *The Fire Next Time* (1963). Black nationalist LeRoi Jones, who changed his name to Imamu Amiri Baraka, crafted powerful plays like *Dutchman* (1964). Toni Morrison and Alice Walker gave fictional voice to the experience of black women. Native Americans, too, achieved literary recognition, as Kiowa author N. Scott Momaday won a Pulitzer Prize for his portrayal of Indian life in *House Made of Dawn* (1968).

Women writers and women's themes forged to the fictional forefront as the feminist movement advanced. Californian Joan Didion explored the empty despair of contemporary life in works like *Play It as It Lays* (1970); and Joyce Carol Oates, in a series of novels, grotesquely portrayed the pervasive violence that afflicts modern America. John Irving made imaginative sport of the women's movement in *The World According to Garp* (1978).

Especially bountiful was the outpouring of books by Jewish novelists. Some critics quipped that a knowledge of Yiddish was becoming necessary to understand much of the dialogue presented in modern American novels. J. D. Salinger painted an unforgettable portrait of a sensitive, upper-class, Anglo-Saxon adolescent in *Catcher in the Rye* (1951), but other Jewish writers found their favorite subject matter in the experience of lower and middle-class Jewish immigrants. Philip Roth wrote comically about young New Jersey suburbanites in *Goodbye, Columbus* (1959) and penned an uproarious account of a sexually obsessed middle-aged New

---

*White Anglo-Saxon Protestant.

Yorker in *Portnoy's Complaint* (1969). Chicagoan Saul Bellow contributed masterful sketches of Jewish urban and literary life in landmark books like *The Adventures of Augie March* (1953), *Herzog* (1962), and *Humboldt's Gift* (1975). Bellow became the eighth American Nobel laureate for literature in 1977. Isaac Bashevis Singer emigrated to America from Poland in the 1930s and continued to write in Yiddish. He won the Nobel Prize for literature in 1978. E. L. Doctorow employed Old Testament themes in his fictional account of atomic spies Julius and Ethel Rosenberg, *The Book of Daniel* (1971), and imaginatively drew on other modern historical materials in books like *Ragtime* (1975) and *World's Fair* (1985).

Cultural Landmarks

Poetry also flourished in the postwar era, though poets, too, were often highly critical, even deeply despairing, about the shape of American life. Older poets were still active, including cantankerous Ezra Pound, jailed after the war in a U.S. Army detention center near Pisa, Italy, for alleged collaboration with the Fascist enemy. Connecticut insurance executive Wallace Stevens and New Jersey pediatrician William Carlos Williams continued after 1945 to pursue "second careers" as prolific poets. But younger poets were coming to the fore. Pacific northwesterner Theodore Roethke wrote lyrically about the land until his death by drowning in Puget Sound in 1963. Robert Lowell, descended from a long line of patrician New Englanders, sought to apply the wisdom of the Puritan past to the perplexing present in allegorical poems like *For the Union Dead* (1964). Troubled Sylvia Plath penned the moving verses of *Ariel* (1966) and a disturbing novel, *The Bell Jar* (1963), but her career was cut short when she took her own life in 1963. Another brilliant poet of the period, John Berryman, ended it all in 1972 by leaping from a Minneapolis bridge onto the frozen bank of the Mississippi River. Poetry seemed to be a dangerous occupation in modern America. The life of the poet, it was said, began in sadness and ended in madness.

Sam Shepard, Actor-Playwright *(John Bryson/Sygma.)*

Playwrights were also active, especially Tennessee Williams, with his series of sordid dramas about psychological misfits. Noteworthy were *A Streetcar Named Desire* (1947) and *Cat on a Hot Tin Roof* (1955). Arthur Miller brought to the stage searching probes of American values, notably in *Death of a Salesman* (1949). In the 1960s Edward Albee exposed the snarling underside of middle-class life in *Who's Afraid of Virginia Woolf?* (1962). The preeminent American playwright of the 1980s appeared to be Sam Shepard, who also gained recognition as a film actor.

New York became the art capital of the world after World War II, as well-heeled Americans supported a large number of painters and sculptors. The Ford Foundation also became a major patron of the arts, as did the federal government after the creation of the tax-supported National Foundation for the Arts in 1965. The open and

MECHA Mural, 1974, by student artists directed by Sergio O'Cadiz   *People have scribbled on walls since time immemorial, but in the 1960s and 1970s mural painting emerged as a new form of American folk art. Drab buildings and bare fences, often in minority inner-city neighborhoods, were turned into huge canvases. This mural incorporates many Mexican-American and Mexican themes, including the United Farm Workers' bird symbol and a skeleton, a frequent motif in Mexican art. (Courtesy of Rancho Santiago College, Preston Mitchell, photographer, La Mirada, CA.)*

tradition-free American environment seemed especially congenial to the experimental mood of much modern art. Jackson Pollock pioneered abstract expressionism in the 1940s and 1950s, flinging paint on huge canvases stretched on his studio floor. Realistic representation went out the window, as artists like Pollock and Willem de Kooning strove to create "action paintings" that expressed the painter's individuality and made the viewer a creative participant in defining the painting's "meaning." Pop artists in the 1960s, notably Andy Warhol, depicted everyday items of consumer culture, such as soup cans. Robert Rauschenberg made elaborate collages out of objects like cardboard boxes and newspaper clippings. Claes Oldenburg tried to stun viewers into a new visual awareness with unfamiliar versions of familiar objects, such as

giant plastic sculptures of pillow-soft telephones.

Architecture also benefited from the building boom of the postwar era. Old master Frank Lloyd Wright produced strikingly original designs, as in the round-walled Guggenheim Museum in New York. Louis Kahn employed stark geometric forms and basic building materials like brick and concrete to make beautiful, simple buildings. Eero Saarinen, the son of a Finnish immigrant, contributed a number of imaginative structures, including two Yale University residential colleges that evoked the atmosphere of an Italian hill town. In the 1970s Atlanta architect John Portman designed huge building complexes, such as Detroit's Renaissance Center, that suggested spaciousness even in the midst of crowded cities.

The American Prospect

The American spirit surged with vitality as the nation headed toward the last decade of the twentieth century, but grave problems still plagued the Republic. The economic growth that had made the American dream a near-reality for so many people seemed in danger of a permanent slowdown, despite the stimulus of the Reagan administration's economic policies. Energy costs remained high, and a new sensitivity to the environmental price of "progress" placed hobbles on business expansion. Some Americans, soured on the false satisfactions of wealth, welcomed the prospect of a "no-growth" economy. But enlarging the economic pie had historically been the American way of appeasing the appetites of various groups for a richer life. Because of fabulous growth, Americans had happily been spared bitter battles over the distribution of a relatively fixed supply of this world's goods. "No-growth" would change the rules of the political game, with consequences that no one could foresee. And for the great majority of the world's aspiring peoples who still plowed with oxen and nightly went to bed hungry, "no-growth" seemed a cruel joke perpetrated by the privileged few who had already grown fat and happy.

America was once a revolutionary force in a world of conservatism; it is now a conservative force in a world of revolutionism. This century has witnessed the Communist revolution, anti-

> Peter Passell and Leonard Ross, in The Retreat from Riches (1973), wrote: "The process of slowing growth is more likely to cause unnecessary ulcers than it is to alter our materialist values. . . . Twenty more years of growth could do for the poor what the Congress won't do. . . . Quite simply, growth is the only way in which America will ever reduce poverty."

colonial revolutions, and revolutions against ignorance, racism, sexism, and poverty. Everywhere, especially in the Third World, is the "revolution of rising expectations." The United States has resisted many of these movements in the outside world, and at home Americans thus far have managed to adjust to drastic social changes without undergoing shattering social upheavals. But as the human family grows at an alarming rate on a shrinking planet, the prospects for prolonged social peace may not be promising.

The task of steering a safe passage into a nuclearized future is the overshadowing mission confronting the American people in the closing years of the present century—in many ways "the American century." At the same time, new opportunities beckon in outer space, in the laboratory, and in the unending quest for social justice, individual fulfillment, and international peace. The challenges facing Americans are

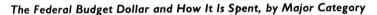

The Federal Budget Dollar and How It Is Spent, by Major Category

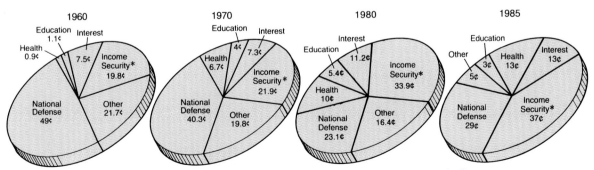

*Includes Social Security payments to the elderly and disabled, unemployment compensation, and welfare.
Note the shifting emphasis in the budget from defense spending to health and income security.
This shift was sharply checked by the Reagan administration.

formidable, at home and abroad, but so is the Republic. As the twentieth century approaches its sunset, the people of the United States can still proudly claim, in the words of Lincoln, that they and their heritage represent "the last best hope of earth."

Varying Viewpoints

No epoch in American history has witnessed so many bewildering changes as the era after World War II. Abundance has boosted millions of Americans into the comfortable ranks of the middle classes. At the same time, the spectacle of affluence has kindled the desires of the less privileged to share in a piece of the American pie. Wide margins of wealth have permitted the society to satisfy those desires, at least in part, without any paralyzing confrontations. But historical appraisals of these developments also include a negative aspect, as indicated in the titles of the books about the period by Carl Degler and William Leuchtenburg. Prosperity has been prodigious, but it seems to have spawned new social problems almost as rapidly as it has resolved old ones. It has fostered a consumer culture that is often too wasteful, too fast-paced, and too destructive of cherished values. It has perhaps promised more than can ever be delivered.

Many critics are claiming that the postwar epoch has already ended. They argue that as economic growth slows down and as the competition among groups for relatively scarce social goods becomes more intense, America will enter a new and unpredictable period in its history. That transformation will perhaps be comparable in its impact to the passing of the frontier phase in the late nineteenth century.

Select Readings

Primary Source Documents

On the changing family, consult Dr. Benjamin Spock, *Baby and Child Care* (1957),* and Betty Friedan, *The Feminine Mystique* (1963).* John Kenneth Galbraith criticizes the distribution of wealth in America in *The Affluent Society* (1958),* as does Michael Harrington's *The Other America* (1962).

Secondary Sources

Lucid overviews can be found in William H. Chafe, *The Unfinished Journey: America since World War II* (1986); Carl N. Degler, *Affluence and Anxiety: America since 1945* (2d ed., 1975); and William Leuchtenburg, *A Troubled Feast: American Society since 1945* (updated edition, 1983). The early postwar years are brought to life in Eric Goldman, *The Crucial Decade—and After: America, 1945–1960* (1961). The 1960s get special attention in William O'Neill, *Coming Apart: An Informal History of America in the 1960s* (1971). The problems of the cities are examined in Blake McKelvey, *The Emergence of Metropolitan America, 1915–1966* (1968). On crime, consult James Q. Wilson and Richard J. Hernstein, *Crime and Human Nature* (1986), and Elliott Currie, *Confronting Crime: An American Challenge* (1986). A provocative discussion may be found in Jane Jacobs, *The Death and Life of Great American Cities* (1961). Suburbia is the subject of Herbert J. Gans, *The Levittowners* (1967); Zane Miller, *Suburb* (1981); Carol O'Connor, *A Sort of Utopia: Scarsdale, 1891–1981* (1983); and Kenneth T. Jackson, *Crabgrass Frontier* (1986). Harold G. Vatter gives a valuable account of *The United States Economy in the 1950s* (1963). Edward Denison argues that improved education is the key to economic growth in *The Sources of Economic Growth in the United States* (1962). See the same author's *Accounting for United States Economic Growth, 1929–1969* (1974). America's international economic role is analyzed in David P. Calleo, *The Imperious*

Economy (1982). See also Richard J. Barnet, *The Alliance: America-Europe-Japan, Makers of the Postwar World* (1983). The southern economic boom is charted in Robert J. Newman, *Growth in the American South* (1984), and two books by James C. Cobb: *The Selling of the South* (1982) and *Industrialization and Southern Society* (1984). The rise of the "Sunbelt" is dramatically portrayed by Kirkpatrick Sale, *Power Shift* (1975), and Kevin Phillips, *The Emerging Republican Majority* (1970). George Masnick and Mary Jo Bane, *The Nation's Families: 1960–1990* (1980), is rich in statistical information. For a brilliant discussion of the same subject from an economic perspective, see Victor R. Fuchs, *How We Live* (1983). The evolving social participation of women is clearly spelled out by William H. Chafe in *The American Woman: Her Changing Social, Economic, and Political Roles, 1920–1970* (1972) and in the same author's more theoretical *Women and Equality: Changing Patterns in American Culture* (1977). Consult also Juanita Kreps, *Sex in the Marketplace* (1971), regarding women in the work force, and Gayle Graham Yates, *What Women Want: The Ideas of the Movement* (1975). See also Betty Friedan's *The Second Stage* (1981) and Robin Morgan's militant *Going Too Far* (1977). Several ethnic minority groups are examined in Daniel P. Moynihan and Nathan Glazer, *Beyond the Melting Pot* (1963), and in Thomas Sowell, *Ethnic America* (1981). Consult also Andrew Levison, *The Working-Class Majority* (1974). On blacks, see Harvard Sitkoff, *The Struggle for Black Equality, 1954–1980* (1981). Oscar Lewis movingly depicts the problems of Puerto Ricans in *La Vida* (1966). Regarding Indians, consult Alvin M. Josephy, *Now That the Buffalo Have Gone: A Study of Today's American Indians* (1982), and Vine DeLoria's *Custer Died for Your Sins* (1969). On Mexican-Americans, see Matt S. Meier and Feliciano Rivera, *The Chicanos* (1972), and Richard Rodriguez's poignant memoir, *Hunger of Memory* (1982). The newest immigrants are the subjects of David M. Reimers, *Still the Golden Door: The*

Third World Comes to America (1986). The emergence of a "youth culture" in the 1960s is illuminated in three studies by Kenneth Keniston: *The Uncommitted* (1965), *Young Radicals* (1968), and *Youth and Dissent* (1971). Popular books indicating the mood of the 1960s include Theodore Roszak, *The Making of a Counter-Culture* (1969), and Charles Reich, *The Greening of America* (1970). Also intriguing on the 1960s is Morris Dickstein, *The Gates of Eden: American Culture in the Sixties* (1977). A lucid survey of the intellectual history of the postwar era is Richard Pells, *The Liberal Mind in a Conservative Age* (1984). Sexual changes are scrutinized in Daniel Yankelovich, *The New Morality* (1974); Morton Hunt, *Sexual Behavior in the 1970s* (1974); and Paul Robinson, *The Modernization of Sex* (1976). John W. Aldridge, *After the Lost Generation* (1951), looks at the earliest post–World War II writers. On postwar literature in general, see Tony Tanner, *City of Words* (1971), and Alfred Kazin, *Bright Book of Life* (1973). On the arts, consult Edward Lucie-Smith, *Late Modern: The Visual Arts since 1945* (1969). On television, see David Marc, *Demographic Vistas: Television in American Culture* (1984). Long-term economic trends are interpreted in David F. Noble, *Forces of Production* (1984); Daniel Bell, *The Coming of Post-Industrial Society* (1973); and Charles F. Sabel and Michael J. Piore, *The Second Industrial Divide* (1984). For acid comment on the 1970s, see Christopher Lasch, *The Culture of Narcissism* (1979). On the baby boom and its implications, consult Richard A. Easterlin, *Birth and Fortune: The Impact of Numbers on Personal Welfare* (1980); Landon Y. Jones, *Great Expectations: America and the Baby Boom Generation* (1980); and Michael X. Delli Carpini, *Stability and Change in American Politics: The Coming of Age of the Generation of the 1960s* (1986). A sensitive and intriguing study of the values of modern Americans is Robert N. Bellah, *Habits of the Heart: Individualism and Commitment in American Life* (1985).

Appendix

Declaration of Independence

In Congress, July 4, 1776

The Unanimous Declaration of the Thirteen United States of America

[Bracketed material in color has been inserted by the authors. For adoption background, see pp. 112–113.]

When, in the course of human events, it becomes necessary for one people to dissolve the political bands which have connected them with another, and to assume, among the powers of the earth, the separate and equal station to which the laws of nature and of nature's God entitle them, a decent respect to the opinions of mankind requires that they should declare the causes which impel them to the separation.

We hold these truths to be self-evident: That all men are created equal; that they are endowed by their Creator with certain unalienable rights; that among these are life, liberty, and the pursuit of happiness; that, to secure these rights, governments are instituted among men, deriving their just powers from the consent of the governed; that whenever any form of government becomes destructive of these ends, it is the right of the people to alter or to abolish it, and to institute new government, laying its foundation on such principles, and organizing its powers in such form, as to them shall seem most likely to effect their safety and happiness. Prudence, indeed, will dictate that governments long established should not be changed for light and transient causes; and accordingly all experience hath shown that mankind are more disposed to suffer, while evils are sufferable, than to right themselves by abolishing the forms to which they are accustomed. But when a long train of abuses and usurpations, pursuing invariably the same object, evinces a design to reduce them under absolute despotism, it is their right, it is their duty, to throw off such government, and to provide new guards for their future security. Such has been the patient sufferance of these colonies; and such is now the necessity which constrains them to alter their former systems of government. The history of the present King of Great Britain is a history of repeated injuries and usurpations, all having in direct object the establishment of an absolute tyranny over these states. To prove this, let facts be submitted to a candid world.

He has refused his assent to laws, the most wholesome and necessary for the public good. [See royal veto, p. 92.]

He has forbidden his governors to pass laws of immediate and pressing importance, unless suspended in their operation till his assent should be obtained; and, when so suspended, he has utterly neglected to attend to them.

He has refused to pass other laws for the accommodation of large districts of people [by establishing new counties], unless those people would relinquish the right of representation in the legislature, a right inestimable to them, and formidable to tyrants only.

He has called together legislative bodies at places unusual, uncomfortable, and distant from the depository of their public records, for the sole purpose of fatiguing them into compliance with his measures. [E.g., removal of Massachusetts Assembly to Salem, 1774.]

He has dissolved representative houses repeatedly, for opposing, with manly firmness, his invasions on the rights of the people. [E.g., Virginia Assembly, 1765.]

He has refused for a long time, after such dissolutions, to cause others to be elected; whereby the legislative powers, incapable of annihilation, have returned to the people at large for their exercise; the state remaining, in the mean time, exposed to all the dangers of invasions from without and convulsions within.

He has endeavored to prevent the population [populating] of these states; for that purpose obstructing the laws for naturalization of foreigners; refusing to pass others to encourage their migration hither, and raising the conditions of new appropriations of lands. [E.g., Proclamation of 1763, p. 87.]

He has obstructed the administration of justice, by refusing his assent to laws for establishing judiciary powers.

He has made judges dependent on his will alone, for the tenure of their offices, and the amount and payment of their salaries. [See Townshend Acts, p. 97.]

He has erected a multitude of new offices, and sent hither swarms of officers to harass our people and eat out their substance. [See enforcement of Navigation Laws, p. 97.]

He has kept among us, in times of peace, standing armies, without the consent of our legislatures. [See pp. 94, 97.]

He has affected to render the military independent of, and superior to, the civil power.

He has combined with others to subject us to a jurisdiction foreign to our constitution, and unacknowledged by our laws, giving his assent to their acts of pretended legislation:

>   For quartering large bodies of armed troops among us [see Boston Massacre, p. 97];

>   For protecting them, by a mock trial, from punishment for any murders which they should commit on the inhabitants of these states [see 1774 Acts, pp. 100–101];

>   For cutting off our trade with all parts of the world [see Boston Port Act, p. 100];

>   For imposing taxes on us without our consent [see Stamp Act, p. 94];

>   For depriving us, in many cases, of the benefits of trial by jury;

>   For transporting us beyond seas, to be tried for pretended offenses;

>   For abolishing the free system of English laws in a neighboring province [Quebec], establishing therein an arbitrary government, and enlarging its boundaries, so as to render it at once an example and fit instrument for introducing the same absolute rule into these colonies [Quebec Act, p. 100];

>   For taking away our charters, abolishing our most valuable laws, and altering fundamentally the forms of our governments [E.g., in Massachusetts, p. 100];

>   For suspending our own legislatures, and declaring themselves invested with power to legislate for us in all cases whatsoever [see Stamp Act repeal, p. 96].

He has abdicated government here, by declaring us out of his protection and waging war against us. [Proclamation, p. 110.]

He has plundered our seas, ravaged our coasts, burned our towns, and destroyed the lives of our people. [E.g., the burning of Falmouth (Portland), p. 110.]

He is at this time transporting large armies of foreign mercenaries [Hessians, p. 110] to complete the works of death, desolation, and tyranny already begun with circumstances of cruelty and perfidy scarcely paralleled in the most barbarous ages, and totally unworthy the head of a civilized nation.

He has constrained our fellow-citizens, taken captive on the high seas [by impressment], to bear arms against their country, to become the executioners of their friends and brethren, or to fall themselves by their hands.

He has excited domestic insurrection among us [i.e., among slaves], and has endeavored to bring on the inhabitants of our frontiers the merciless Indian savages, whose known rule of warfare is an undistinguished destruction of all ages, sexes, and conditions.

In every stage of these oppressions we have petitioned for redress in the most humble terms; our repeated petitions have been answered only by repeated injury. [E.g., pp. 108–111.] A prince, whose character is thus marked by every act which may define a tyrant, is unfit to be the ruler of a free people.

Nor have we been wanting in our attentions to our British brethren. We have warned them, from time to time, of attempts by their legislature to extend an unwarrantable jurisdiction over us. We have reminded them of the circumstances of our emigration and settlement here. We have appealed to their native justice and magnanimity; and we have conjured them, by the ties of our common kindred, to disavow these usurpations, which would inevitably interrupt our connections and correspondence. They, too, have been deaf to the voice of justice and of consanguinity [blood relationship]. We must, therefore, acquiesce in the necessity which denounces [announces] our separation, and hold them, as we hold the rest of mankind, enemies in war, in peace friends.

We, therefore, the representatives of the United States of America, in General Congress assembled, appealing to the Supreme Judge of the world for the rectitude of our intentions, do, in the name and by the authority of the good people of these colonies, solemnly publish and declare, That these United Colonies are, and of right ought to be, FREE AND INDEPENDENT STATES; that they are absolved from all allegiance to the British crown, and that all political connection between them and the state of Great Britain is, and ought to be, totally dissolved; and that, as free and independent states, they have full power to levy war, conclude peace, contract alliances, establish commerce, and do all other acts and things which independent states may of right do. And for the support of this declaration, with a firm reliance on the protection of Divine Providence, we mutually pledge to each other our lives, our fortunes, and our sacred honor.

[Signed by]   JOHN HANCOCK [President]
                                                   [and fifty-five others]

Constitution of the United States of America

[Boldface headings and bracketed explanatory matter and marginal comments (both in color) have been inserted for the reader's convenience. Passages that are no longer operative are printed in italic type.]

PREAMBLE

On "We the people," see p. 247n.

We the people of the United States, in order to form a more perfect union, establish justice, insure domestic tranquillity, provide for the common defense, promote the general welfare, and secure the blessings of liberty to ourselves and our posterity, do ordain and establish this CONSTITUTION for the United States of America.

Article I. Legislative Department

Section I. Congress

Legislative power vested in a two-house Congress. All legislative powers herein granted shall be vested in a Congress of the United States, which shall consist of a Senate and a House of Representatives.

Section II. House of Representatives

1. The people elect representatives biennially. The House of Representatives shall be composed of members chosen every second year by the people of the several States, and the electors [voters] in each State shall have the qualifications requisite for electors of the most numerous branch of the State Legislature.

2. Who may be representatives. No person shall be a Representative who shall not have attained to the age of twenty-five years, and been seven years a citizen of the United States, and who shall not, when elected, be an inhabitant of that State in which he shall be chosen.

See 1787 compromise, p. 139.

See 1787 compromise, p. 139.

3. Representation in the House based on population; census. Representatives and direct taxes[1] shall be apportioned among the several States which may be included within this Union, according to their respective numbers, *which shall be determined by adding to the whole number of free persons, including those bound to service for a term of years* [apprentices and indentured servants], *and excluding Indians not taxed, three-fifths of all other persons* [slaves].[2] The actual enumeration [census] shall be made within three years after the first meeting of the Congress of the United States, and within every subsequent term of ten years, in such manner as they shall by law direct. The number of Representatives shall not exceed one for every thirty thousand, but each State shall have at least one Representative; *and until such enumeration shall be made, the State of New Hampshire shall be entitled to choose three, Massachusetts eight, Rhode Island and Providence Plantations one, Connecticut five, New York six, New Jersey four, Pennsylvania eight, Delaware one, Maryland six, Virginia ten, North Carolina five, South Carolina five, and Georgia three.*

---

[1] Modified in 1913 by the Sixteenth Amendment re income taxes (see p. 658).

[2] The word *slave* appears nowhere in the original, unamended Constitution. The three-fifths rule ceased to be in force when the Thirteenth Amendment was adopted in 1865 (see p. 43 and amendments below).

4. Vacancies in the House are filled by election. When vacancies happen in the representation from any State, the Executive authority [governor] thereof shall issue writs of election [call a special election] to fill such vacancies.

See Chase and Johnson trials, pp. 182, 474; Nixon trial preliminaries, pp. 893–894.

5. The House selects its Speaker; has sole power to vote impeachment charges (i.e., indictments). The House of Representatives shall choose their Speaker and other officers; and shall have the sole power of impeachment.

Section III.   Senate

1. Senators represent the states. The Senate of the United States shall be composed of two Senators from each State, *chosen by the legislature thereof,* [1] for six years; and each Senator shall have one vote.

2. One-third of senators chosen every two years; vacancies. *Immediately after they shall be assembled in consequence of the first election, they shall be divided as equally as may be into three classes. The seats of the Senators of the first class shall be vacated at the expiration of the second year, of the second class at the expiration of the fourth year, and of the third class at the expiration of the sixth year,* so that one-third may be chosen every second year; *and if vacancies happen by resignation or otherwise, during the recess of the legislature of any State, the Executive* [governor] *thereof may make temporary appointments until the next meeting of the legislature, which shall then fill such vacancies.* [2]

3. Who may be senators. No person shall be a Senator who shall not have attained to the age of thirty years, and been nine years a citizen of the United States, and who shall not, when elected, be an inhabitant of that State for which he shall be chosen.

4. The vice-president presides over the Senate. The Vice-President of the United States shall be President of the Senate, but shall have no vote, unless they be equally divided [tied].

5. The Senate chooses its other officers. The Senate shall choose their other officers, and also a President *pro tempore,* in the absence of the Vice-President, or when he shall exercise the office of President of the United States.

See Chase and Johnson trials, pp. 182, 474.

6. The Senate has sole power to try impeachments. The Senate shall have the sole power to try all impeachments. When sitting for that purpose, they shall be on oath or affirmation. When the President of the United States is tried, the Chief Justice shall preside:[3] and no person shall be convicted without the concurrence of two-thirds of the members present.

7. Penalties for impeachment conviction. Judgment in cases of impeachment shall not extend further than to removal from office, and disqualification to hold and enjoy any office of honor, trust or profit under the United States: but the party convicted shall nevertheless be liable and subject to indictment, trial, judgment and punishment, according to law.

Section IV.   Election and Meetings of Congress

1. Regulation of elections. The times, places and manner of holding elections for Senators and Representatives shall be prescribed in each State by the legislature thereof; but the Congress may at any time by law make or alter such regulations, except as to the places of choosing Senators.

---

[1] Repealed in favor of popular election in 1913 by the Seventeenth Amendment.
[2] Changed in 1913 by the Seventeenth Amendment.
[3] The vice-president, as next in line, would be an interested party.

2. Congress must meet once a year. The Congress shall assemble at least once in every year, and such meeting *shall be on the first Monday in December, unless they shall by law appoint a different day.*[1]

Section V.   Organization and Rules of the Houses

1. Each house may reject members; quorums. Each house shall be the judge of the elections, returns and qualifications of its own members, and a majority of each shall constitute a quorum to do business; but a smaller number may adjourn from day to day, and may be authorized to compel the attendance of absent members, in such manner, and under such penalties, as each house may provide.

See "Bully" Brooks case, pp. 395–396.

2. Each house makes its own rules. Each house may determine the rules of its proceedings, punish its members for disorderly behavior, and with the concurrence of two-thirds, expel a member.

3. Each house must keep and publish a record of its proceedings. Each house shall keep a journal of its proceedings, and from time to time publish the same, excepting such parts as may in their judgment require secrecy; and the yeas and nays of the members of either house on any question shall, at the desire of one-fifth of those present, be entered on the journal.

4. Both houses must agree on adjournment. Neither house, during the session of Congress, shall, without the consent of the other, adjourn for more than three days, nor to any other place than that in which the two houses shall be sitting.

Section VI.   Privileges of and Prohibitions upon Congressmen

1. Congressional salaries; immunities. The Senators and Representatives shall receive a compensation for their services, to be ascertained by law and paid out of the treasury of the United States. They shall in all cases except treason, felony and breach of the peace, be privileged from arrest during their attendance at the session of their respective houses, and in going to and returning from the same; and for any speech or debate in either house, they shall not be questioned in any other place [i.e., they shall be immune from libel suits].

2. A congressman may not hold any other federal civil office. No Senator or Representative shall, during the time for which he was elected, be appointed to any civil office under the authority of the United States, which shall have been created, or the emoluments whereof shall have been increased, during such time; and no person holding any office under the United States shall be a member of either house during his continuance in office.

Section VII.   Method of Making Laws

See 1787 compromise, p. 139.

1. Money bills must originate in the House. All bills for raising revenue shall originate in the House of Representatives; but the Senate may propose or concur with amendments as on other bills.

Nixon, more than any predecessors, "impounded" billions of dollars voted by Congress for specific purposes, because he disapproved of them. The courts generally failed to sustain him, and his impeachment foes regarded wholesale impoundment as a violation of his oath to "faithfully execute" the laws.

2. The president's veto power; Congress may override. Every bill which shall have passed the House of Representatives and the Senate, shall, before it become a law, be presented to the President of the United States; if he approve he shall sign it, but if not he shall return it with his objections to that house in which it shall have originated, who shall enter the objections at large on their journal, and proceed to reconsider it. If after such reconsideration two-thirds of that house shall agree to pass the bill, it shall be sent, together with the objections, to the other house, by which it shall likewise be recon-

---

[1] Changed in 1933 to January 3 by the Twentieth Amendment (see p. 764 and below).

sidered, and, if approved by two-thirds of that house, it shall become a law. But in all such cases the votes of both houses shall be determined by yeas and nays, and the names of the persons voting for and against the bill shall be entered on the journal of each house respectively. If any bill shall not be returned by the President within ten days (Sundays excepted) after it shall have been presented to him, the same shall be a law, in like manner as if he had signed it, unless the Congress by their adjournment prevent its return, in which case it shall not be a law [this is the so-called pocket veto].

3. All measures requiring the agreement of both houses go to president for approval. Every order, resolution, or vote to which the concurrence of the Senate and House of Representatives may be necessary (except on a question of adjournment) shall be presented to the President of the United States; and before the same shall take effect, shall be approved by him, or being disapproved by him, shall be repassed by two-thirds of the Senate and House of Representatives, according to the rules and limitations prescribed in the case of a bill.

Section VIII.   Powers Granted to Congress

Congress has certain enumerated powers:

1. It may lay and collect taxes. The Congress shall have power to lay and collect taxes, duties, imposts, and excises, to pay the debts and provide for the common defense and general welfare of the United States; but all duties, imposts and excises shall be uniform throughout the United States;

2. It may borrow money. To borrow money on the credit of the United States;

3. It may regulate foreign and interstate trade. To regulate commerce with foreign nations, and among the several States, and with the Indian tribes;

4. It may pass naturalization and bankruptcy laws. To establish an uniform rule of naturalization, and uniform laws on the subject of bankruptcies throughout the United States;

For 1798 naturalization, see p. 172.

5. It may coin money. To coin money, regulate the value thereof, and of foreign coin, and fix the standard of weights and measures;

6. It may punish counterfeiters. To provide for the punishment of counterfeiting the securities and current coin of the United States;

7. It may establish a postal service. To establish post offices and post roads;

8. It may issue patents and copyrights. To promote the progress of science and useful arts by securing for limited times to authors and inventors the exclusive right to their respective writings and discoveries;

9. It may establish inferior courts. To constitute tribunals inferior to the Supreme Court;

See Judiciary Act of 1789, p. 153.

10. It may punish crimes committed on the high seas. To define and punish piracies and felonies committed on the high seas [i.e., outside the three-mile limit] and offenses against the law of nations [international law];

11. It may declare war; authorize privateers. To declare war,[1] grant letters of marque and reprisal,[2] and make rules concerning captures on land and water;

---

[1] Note that presidents, though they can provoke war (see the case of Polk, p. 281) or wage it after it is declared, cannot declare it.

[2] Papers issued private citizens in wartime authorizing them to capture enemy ships.

12. It may maintain an army. To raise and support armies, but no appropriation of money to that use shall be for a longer term than two years;[1]

13. It may maintain a navy. To provide and maintain a navy;

14. It may regulate the army and navy. To make rules for the government and regulation of the land and naval forces;

See Whiskey Rebellion, p. 156.

15. It may call out the state militia. To provide for calling forth the militia to execute the laws of the Union, suppress insurrections, and repel invasions;

16. It shares with the states control of militia. To provide for organizing, arming, and disciplining the militia, and for governing such part of them as may be employed in the service of the United States, reserving to the States respectively the appointment of the officers, and the authority of training the militia according to the discipline prescribed by Congress;

17. It makes laws for the District of Columbia and other federal areas. To exercise exclusive legislation in all cases whatsoever, over such district (not exceeding ten miles square) as may, by cession of particular States, and the acceptance of Congress, become the seat of government of the United States,[2] and to exercise like authority over all places purchased by the consent of the legislature of the State, in which the same shall be, for the erection of forts, magazines, arsenals, dock-yards, and other needful buildings; —and

Congress has certain implied powers:

This is the famous "elastic clause"; see p. 155.

18. It may make laws necessary for carrying out the enumerated powers. To make all laws which shall be necessary and proper for carrying into execution the foregoing powers, and all other powers vested by this Constitution in the government of the United States, or in any department or officer thereof.

Section IX.   Powers Denied to the Federal Government

See 1787 slave compromise, p. 141.

1. Congressional control of slave trade postponed until 1808. *The migration or importation of such persons as any of the States now existing shall think proper to admit shall not be prohibited by the Congress prior to the year 1808; but a tax or duty may be imposed on such importation, not exceeding $10 for each person.*

See Lincoln's unlawful suspension, p. 448.

2. The writ of habeas corpus[3] may be suspended only in case of rebellion or invasion. The privilege of the writ of habeas corpus shall not be suspended, unless when in cases of rebellion or invasion the public safety may require it.

3. Attainders[4] and ex post facto laws[5] forbidden. No bill of attainder or ex post facto law shall be passed.

4. Direct taxes must be apportioned according to population. No capitation [head or poll tax] or other direct, tax shall be laid, unless in proportion to the census or enumeration herein before directed to be taken.[6]

5. Export taxes fobidden. No tax or duty shall be laid on articles exported from any State.

---

[1] A reflection of fear of standing armies earlier expressed in the Declaration of Independence.
[2] The District of Columbia, ten miles square, was established in 1791 with a cession from Virginia (see p. 154).
[3] A writ of habeas corpus is a document that enables a person under arrest to obtain an immediate examination in court to ascertain whether he or she is being legally held.
[4] A bill of attainder is a special legislative act condemning and punishing an individual without a judicial trial.
[5] An ex post facto law is one that fixes punishments for acts committed before the law was passed.
[6] Modified in 1913 by the Sixteenth Amendment (see p. 658, and amendments below).

6. Congress must not discriminate among states in regulating commerce. No preference shall be given by any regulation of commerce or revenue to the ports of one State over those of another; nor shall vessels bound to, or from, one State, be obliged to enter, clear, or pay duties in another.

See Lincoln's unlawful infraction, p. 448.

7. Public money may not be spent without congressional appropriation; accounting. No money shall be drawn from the treasury, but in consequence of appropriations made by law; and a regular statement and account of the receipts and expenditures of all public money shall be published from time to time.

8. Titles of nobility prohibited; foreign gifts. No title of nobility shall be granted by the United States: and no person holding any office of profit or trust under them, shall, without the consent of the Congress, accept of any present, emolument, office, or title, of any kind whatever, from any king, prince, or foreign state.

Section X.   Powers Denied to the States

Absolute prohibitions on the states:

On contracts, see Fletcher v. Peck, p. 223.

1. The states are forbidden to do certain things. No State shall enter into any treaty, alliance, or confederation; grant letters of marque and reprisal [i.e., authorize privateers]; coin money; emit bills of credit [issue paper money]; make anything but gold and silver coin a [legal] tender in payment of debts; pass any bill of attainder,[1] ex post facto,[1] or law impairing the obligation of contracts, or grant any title of nobility.

Conditional prohibitions on the states:

Cf. Confederation chaos, p. 132.

2. The states may not levy duties without the consent of Congress. No State shall, without the consent of the Congress, lay any imposts or duties on imports or exports, except what may be absolutely necessary for executing its inspection laws: and the net produce of all duties and imposts, laid by any State on imports or exports, shall be for the use of the treasury of the United States; and all such laws shall be subject to the revision and control of the Congress.

3. Certain other federal powers are forbidden the states except with the consent of Congress. No State shall, without the consent of Congress, lay any duty of tonnage [i.e., duty on ship tonnage], keep [nonmilitia] troops or ships of war in time of peace, enter into any agreement or compact with another State, or with a foreign power, or engage in war, unless actually invaded, or in such imminent danger as will not admit of delay.

Article II.   Executive Department

Section I.   President and Vice-President

1. The president is the chief executive; term of office. The executive power shall be vested in a President of the United States of America. He shall hold his office during the term of four years,[2] and, together with the Vice-President, chosen for the same term, be elected as follows:

See 1787 compromise, p. 140.

See 1876 Oregon case, p. 489.

2. The president is chosen by electors. Each State shall appoint, in such manner as the legislature thereof may direct, a number of electors, equal to the whole number of Senators and Representatives to which the State may be entitled in the Congress; but no Senator or Representative, or person holding an office of trust or profit under the United States, shall be appointed an elector.

---

[1] For definitions, see footnotes 4 and 5 on preceding page.
[2] No reference to reelection; for anti–third term Twenty-second Amendment, see below.

A majority of the electoral votes needed to elect a president. *The electors shall meet in their respective States, and vote by ballot for two persons, of whom one at least shall not be an inhabitant of the same State with themselves. And they shall make a list of all the persons voted for, and of the number of votes for each; which list they shall sign and certify, and transmit sealed to the seat of government of the United States, directed to the President of the Senate. The President of the Senate shall, in the presence of the Senate and House of Representatives, open all the certificates, and the votes shall then be counted. The person having the greatest number of votes shall be the President, if such number be a majority of the whole number of electors appointed; and if there be more than one who have such majority, and have an equal number of votes, then the House of Representatives shall immediately choose by ballot one of them for President; and if no person have a majority, then from the five highest on the list the said house shall in like manner choose the President. But in choosing the President the votes shall be taken by States, the representation from each State having one vote; a quorum for this purpose shall consist of a member or members from two-thirds of the States, and a majority of all the States shall be necessary to a choice. In every case, after the choice of the President, the person having the greatest number of votes of the electors shall be the Vice-President. But if there should remain two or more who have equal votes, the Senate shall choose from them by ballot the Vice-President.*[1]

See Burr-Jefferson disputed election of 1800, p. 175.

See Jefferson as vice-president in 1796, p. 168.

3. Congress decides time of meeting of Electoral College. The Congress may determine the time of choosing the electors and the day on which they shall give their votes; which day shall be the same throughout the United States.

To provide for foreign-born persons, like Alexander Hamilton, born in the British West Indies.

4. Who may be president. No person except a natural-born citizen, *or a citizen of the United States at the time of the adoption of this Constitution*, shall be eligible to the office of President; neither shall any person be eligible to that office who shall not have attained to the age of thirty-five years, and been fourteen years a resident within the United States [i.e., a legal resident]

Modified by Twentieth and Twenty-fifth Amendments below.

5. Replacements for president. In case of the removal of the President from office or of his death, resignation, or inability to discharge the powers and duties of the said office, the same shall devolve on the Vice-President, and the Congress may by law provide for the case of removal, death, resignation, or inability, both of the President and Vice-President, declaring what officer shall then act as President, and such officer shall act accordingly, until the disability be removed, or a President shall be elected.

6. The president's salary. The President shall, at stated times, receive for his services a compensation, which shall neither be increased nor diminished during the period for which he shall have been elected, and he shall not receive within that period any other emolument from the United States, or any of them.

7. The president's oath of office. Before he enter on the execution of his office, he shall take the following oath or affirmation:—"I do solemnly swear (or affirm) that I will faithfully execute the office of the President of the United States, and will to the best of my ability preserve, protect and defend the Constitution of the United States."

Section II.   Powers of the President

See cabinet evolution, p. 151.

1. The president has important military and civil powers. The President shall be commander in chief of the army and navy of the United States, and of the militia of the several States, when called into the actual service of the United States; he may require

---

[1] Repealed in 1804 by the Twelfth Amendment (for text, see amendments below).

the opinion, in writing, of the principal officer in each of the executive departments, upon any subject relating to the duties of their respective offices, and he shall have power to grant reprieves and pardons for offenses against the United States, except in cases of impeachment.[1]

For president's removal power, see pp. 474–475.

2. The president may negotiate treaties and nominate federal officials. He shall have power, by and with the advice and consent of the Senate, to make treaties, provided two-thirds of the Senators present concur; and he shall nominate, and by and with the advice and consent of the Senate, shall appoint ambassadors, other public ministers and consuls, judges of the Supreme Court, and all other officers of the United States, whose appointments are not herein otherwise provided for, and which shall be established by law: but the Congress may by law vest the appointment of such inferior officers, as they think proper, in the President alone, in the courts of law, or in the heads of departments.

3. The president may fill vacancies during Senate recess. The President shall have power to fill up all vacancies that may happen during the recess of the Senate, by granting commissions which shall expire at the end of their next session.

Section III.   Other Powers and Duties of the President

For president's personal appearances, see p. 658.

Messages; extra sessions; receiving ambassadors: execution of the laws. He shall from time to time give to the Congress information of the state of the Union, and recommend to their consideration such measures as he shall judge necessary and expedient; he may, on extraordinary occasions, convene both houses, or either of them, and in case of disagreement between them, with respect to the time of adjournment, he may adjourn them to such time as he shall think proper; he shall receive ambassadors and other public ministers; he shall take care that the laws be faithfully executed, and shall commission all the officers of the United States.

Section IV.   Impeachment

See Johnson's acquittal p. 475; also Nixon's near impeachment, pp. 893–894.

Civil officers may be removed by impeachment. The President, Vice-President and all civil officers[2] of the United States shall be removed from office on impeachment for, and on conviction of, treason, bribery, or other high crimes and misdemeanors.

Article III.   Judicial Department

Section I.   The Federal Courts

See Judicial Act of 1789, p. 153.

The judicial power belongs to the federal courts. The judicial power of the United States shall be vested in one Supreme Court, and in such inferior courts as the Congress may from time to time ordain and establish. The judges, both of the Supreme and inferior courts, shall hold their offices during good behavior, and shall, at stated times, receive for their services a compensation which shall not be diminished[3] during their continuance in office.

Section II.   Jurisdiction of Federal Courts

1. Kinds of cases that may be heard. The judicial power shall extend to all cases, in law and equity, arising under this Constitution, the laws of the United States, and treaties made, or which shall be made, under their authority; —to all cases affecting ambassa-

---

[1] To prevent the president's pardoning himself or his close associates, as was feared in the case of Richard Nixon. See pp. 893–894.
[2] I.e., all federal executive and judicial officers, but not members of Congress or military personnel.
[3] In 1978, in a case involving federal judges, the Supreme Court ruled that diminution of salaries by inflation was irrelevant.

dors, other public ministers and consuls; —to all cases of admiralty and maritime jurisdiction; —to controversies to which the United States shall be a party; —to controversies between two or more States; —*between a State and citizens of another State;*[1] —between citizens of different States; —between citizens of the same State claiming lands under grants of different States, and between a State, or the citizens thereof, and foreign states, citizens or subjects.

2. Jurisdiction of the Supreme Court. In all cases affecting ambassadors, other public ministers and consuls, and those in which a State shall be party, the Supreme Court shall have original jurisdiction.[2] In all the other cases before mentioned, the Supreme Court shall have appellate jurisdiction,[3] both as to law and fact, with such exceptions, and under such regulations, as the Congress shall make.

3. Trial for federal crime is by jury. The trial of all crimes, except in cases of impeachment, shall be by jury; and such trial shall be held in the State where the said crimes shall have been committed; but when not committed within any State, the trial shall be at such place or places as the Congress may by law have directed.

Section III.   Treason

See Burr trial, p. 189.

1. Treason defined. Treason against the United States shall consist only in levying war against them, or in adhering to their enemies, giving them aid and comfort. No person shall be convicted of treason unless on the testimony of two witnesses to the same overt act, or on confession in open court.

2. Congress fixes punishment for treason. The Congress shall have power to declare the punishment of treason, but no attainder of treason shall work corruption of blood, or forfeiture except during the life of the person attainted.[4]

Article IV.   Relations of the States to One Another

Section I.   Credit to Acts, Records, and Court Proceedings

Each state must respect the public acts of the others. Full faith and credit shall be given in each State to the public acts, records, and judicial proceedings of every other State.[5] And the Congress may by general laws prescribe the manner in which such acts, records, and proceedings shall be proved [attested], and the effect thereof.

Section II.   Duties of States to States

This stipulation is sometimes openly flouted. In 1978 Governor Jerry Brown of California, acting on humanitarian grounds, refused to surrender to South Dakota an American Indian, Dennis Banks, who was charged with murder in an armed uprising.

1. Citizenship in one state is valid in all. The citizens of each State shall be entitled to all privileges and immunities of citizens in the several States.

2. Fugitives from justice must be surrendered by the state to which they have fled. A person charged in any State with treason, felony, or other crime, who shall flee from justice, and be found in another State, shall on demand of the executive authority [governor] of the State from which he fled, be delivered up, to be removed to the State having jurisdiction of the crime.

---

[1] The Eleventh Amendment (see amendments below) restricts this to suits by a state against citizens of another state.
[2] I.e., such cases must originate in the Supreme Court.
[3] I.e., it hears other cases only when they are appealed to it from a lower federal court or a state court.
[4] I.e., punishment only for the offender; none for his or her heirs.
[5] E.g., a marriage valid in one is valid in all.

Basis of fugitive-slave laws; see pp. 374–375.

3. Slaves and apprentices must be returned. *No person held to service or labor in one State, under the laws thereof, escaping into another, shall, in consequence of any law or regulation therein, be discharged from such service or labor, but shall be delivered up on claim of the party to whom such service or labor may be due.* [1]

Section III.   New States and Territories

E.g., Maine (1820); see p. 219.

1. Congress may admit new states. New States may be admitted by the Congress into this Union; but no new State shall be formed or erected within the jurisdiction of any other State; nor any State be formed by the junction of two or more States, or parts of States, without the consent of the legislatures of the States concerned as well as of the Congress. [2]

2. Congress regulates federal territory and property. The Congress shall have power to dispose of and make all needful rules and regulations respecting the territory or other property belonging to the United States; and nothing in this Constitution shall be so construed as to prejudice any claims of the United States, or of any particular State.

Section IV.   Protection to the States

See Cleveland and the Pullman strike, pp. 584–585.

United States guarantees to states representative government and protection against invasion and rebellion. The United States shall guarantee to every State in this Union a republican form of government, and shall protect each of them against invasion; and on application of the legislature, or of the executive [governor] (when the legislature cannot be convened), against domestic violence.

Article V.   The Process of Amendment

The Constitution may be amended in four ways. The Congress, whenever two-thirds of both houses shall deem it necessary, shall propose amendments to this Constitution, or, on the application of the legislatures of two-thirds of the several States, shall call a convention for proposing amendments, which, in either case, shall be valid to all intents and purposes, as part of this Constitution, when ratified by the legislatures of three-fourths of the several States, or by conventions in three-fourths thereof, as the one or the other mode of ratification may be proposed by the Congress; provided *that no amendments which may be made prior to the year one thousand eight hundred and eight shall in any manner affect the first and fourth clauses in the ninth section of the first article;* [3] and that no State, without its consent, shall be deprived of its equal suffrage in the Senate.

Article VI.   General Provisions

This pledge honored by Hamilton, p. 153.

1. The debts of the Confederation are taken over. All debts contracted and engagements entered into, before the adoption of this Constitution, shall be as valid against the United States under this Constitution, as under the Confederation.

2. The Constitution, federal laws, and treaties are the supreme law of the land. This Constitution, and the laws of the United States which shall be made in pursuance thereof; and all treaties made, or which shall be made, under the authority of the United States, shall be the supreme law of the land; and the judges in every State shall be bound

---

[1] Invalidated in 1865 by the Thirteenth Amendment (for text see amendments below).
[2] Loyal West Virginia was formed by Lincoln in 1862 from seceded Virginia. This act was of dubious constitutionality and was justified in part by the wartime powers of the president. See pp. 417–418.
[3] This clause, re slave trade and direct taxes, became inoperative in 1808.

thereby, anything in the Constitution or laws of any State to the contrary notwithstanding.

3. Federal and state officers bound by oath to support the Constitution. The Senators and Representatives before mentioned, and the members of the several State legislatures, and all executive and judicial officers, both of the United States and of the several States, shall be bound by oath or affirmation to support this Constitution; but no religious test shall ever be required as a qualification to any office or public trust under the United States.

Article VII.   Ratification of the Constitution

See 1787 irregularity, p. 141.

The Constitution effective when ratified by conventions in nine states. The ratification of the conventions of nine States shall be sufficient for the establishment of this Constitution between the States so ratifying the same.

Done in Convention by the unanimous consent of the States present, the seventeenth day of September in the year of our Lord one thousand seven hundred and eighty-seven and of the Independence of the United States of America the twelfth. In witness whereof we have hereunto subscribed our names.

[Signed by]

G° WASHINGTON
Presidt and Deputy from Virginia
[and thirty-eight others]

AMENDMENTS TO THE CONSTITUTION

Amendment I.   Religious and Political Freedom

For background of Bill of Rights, see p. 152.

Congress must not interfere with freedom of religion, speech or press, assembly, and petition. Congress shall make no law respecting an establishment of religion,[1] or prohibiting the free exercise thereof; or abridging the freedom of speech, or of the press; or the right of the people peaceably to assemble, and to petition the government for a redress of grievances.

Amendment II.   Right to Bear Arms

The people may bear arms. A well-regulated militia being necessary to the security of a free State, the right of the people to keep and bear arms [i.e., for military purposes] shall not be infringed.[2]

Amendment III.   Quartering of Troops

See Declaration of Independence and British quartering above.

Soldiers may not be arbitrarily quartered on the people. No soldier shall, in time of peace, be quartered in any house without the consent of the owner, nor in time of war, but in a manner to be prescribed by law.

---

[1] In 1787 "an establishment of religion" referred to an "established church," or one supported by all taxpayers, whether members or not. But the courts have often acted under this article to keep religion, including prayers, out of the public schools.

[2] The courts, with "militia" in mind, have consistently held that the "right" to bear arms is a limited one.

Amendment IV. Searches and Seizures

A reflection of colonial grievances against crown.

Unreasonable searches are forbidden. The right of the people to be secure in their persons, houses, papers, and effects, against unreasonable searches and seizures, shall not be violated, and no [search] warrants shall issue but upon probable cause, supported by oath or affirmation, and particularly describing the place to be searched, and the persons or things to be seized.

Amendment V. Right to Life, Liberty, and Property

When witnesses refuse to answer questions in court, they routinely "take the Fifth Amendment."

The individual is guaranteed certain rights when on trial and the right to life, liberty, and property. No person shall be held to answer for a capital, or otherwise infamous crime, unless on a presentment [formal charge] or indictment of a grand jury, except in cases arising in the land or naval forces, or in the militia, when in actual service in time of war or public danger; nor shall any person be subject for the same offense to be twice put in jeopardy of life or limb; nor shall be compelled in any criminal case to be a witness against himself, nor be deprived of life, liberty, or property, without due process of law; nor shall private property be taken for public use [i.e., by eminent domain] without just compensation.

Amendment VI. Protection in Criminal Trials

See Declaration of Independence above.

An accused person has important rights. In all criminal prosecutions, the accused shall enjoy the right to a speedy and public trial, by an impartial jury of the State and district wherein the crime shall have been committed, which district shall have been previously ascertained by law, and to be informed of the nature and cause of the accusation; to be confronted with the witnesses against him; to have compulsory process [subpoena] for obtaining witnesses in his favor, and to have the assistance of counsel for his defense.

Amendment VII. Suits at Common Law

The rules of common law are recognized. In suits at common law, where the value in controversy shall exceed twenty dollars, the right of trial by jury shall be preserved, and no fact tried by a jury shall be otherwise re-examined in any court of the United States, than according to the rules of the common law.

Amendment VIII. Bail and Punishments

Excessive fines and unusual punishments are forbidden. Excessive bail shall not be required, nor excessive fines imposed, nor cruel and unusual punishments inflicted.

Amendment IX. Concerning Rights Not Enumerated

The Ninth and Tenth Amendments were bulwarks of southern states' rights before the Civil War.

The people retain rights not here enumerated. The enumeration in the Constitution, of certain rights, shall not be construed to deny or disparage others retained by the people.

Amendment X. Powers Reserved to the States and to the People

A concession to states' rights, p. 155.

Powers not delegated to the federal government are reserved to the states and the people. The powers not delegated to the United States by the Constitution, nor prohibited by it to the States, are reserved to the States respectively, or to the people.

Amendment XI.   Suits against a State

The federal courts have no authority in suits by citizens against a state. The judicial power of the United States shall not be construed to extend to any suit in law or equity, commenced or prosecuted against one of the United States by citizens of another State, or by citizens or subjects of any foreign state. [Adopted 1798.]

Amendment XII.   Election of President and Vice-President

Forestalls repetition of 1800 electoral dispute, p. 176.

See 1876 disputed election, p. 488.

See 1824 election, pp. 234–235.

1. Changes in manner of electing president and vice-president; procedure when no presidential candidate receives electoral majority. The electors shall meet in their respective States, and vote by ballot for President and Vice-President, one of whom, at least, shall not be an inhabitant of the same State with themselves; they shall name in their ballots the person voted for as President, and in distinct ballots the person voted for as Vice-President, and they shall make distinct lists of all persons voted for as President, and of all persons voted for as Vice-President, and of the number of votes for each, which lists they shall sign and certify, and transmit sealed to the seat of government of the United States, directed to the President of the Senate; —the President of the Senate shall, in the presence of the Senate and House of Representatives, open all the certificates and the votes shall then be counted; —the person having the greatest number of votes for President shall be the President, if such number be a majority of the whole number of electors appointed; and if no person have such majority, then from the persons having the highest numbers not exceeding three on the list of those voted for as President, the House of Representatives shall choose immediately, by ballot, the President. But in choosing the President, the votes shall be taken by States, the representation from each State having one vote; a quorum for this purpose shall consist of a member or members from two-thirds of the States, and a majority of all the States shall be necessary to a choice. And if the House of Representatives shall not choose a President whenever the right of choice shall devolve upon them, before *the fourth day of March*[1] next following, then the Vice-President shall act as President, as in the case of the death or other constitutional disability of the President.

2. Procedure when no vice-presidential candidate receives electoral majority. The person having the greatest number of votes as Vice-President shall be the Vice-President, if such number be a majority of the whole number of electors appointed; and if no person have a majority, then from the two highest numbers on the list the Senate shall choose the Vice-President; a quorum for the purpose shall consist of two-thirds of the whole number of Senators, and a majority of the whole number shall be necessary to a choice. But no person constitutionally ineligible to the office of President shall be eligible to that of Vice-President of the United States. [Adopted 1804.]

Amendment XIII.   Slavery Prohibited

For background, see pp. 430–431.

Slavery forbidden. 1. Neither slavery[2] nor involuntary servitude, except as a punishment for crime whereof the party shall have been duly convicted, shall exist within the United States, or any place subject to their jurisdiction.

2. Congress shall have power to enforce this article by appropriate legislation. [Adopted 1865.]

---

[1] Changed to January 20 by the Twentieth Amendment (for text, see amendments below).
[2] The only explicit mention of slavery in the Constitution.

Amendment XIV.   Civil Rights for Ex-slaves,[1] etc.

For background, see p. 465.

For corporations as "persons," see p. 519.

1. Ex-slaves made citizens; U.S. citizenship primary. All persons born or naturalized in the United States, and subject to the jurisdiction thereof, are citizens of the United States and of the State wherein they reside. No State shall make or enforce any law which shall abridge the privileges or immunities of citizens of the United States; nor shall any State deprive any person of life, liberty, or property, without due process of law; nor deny to any person within its jurisdiction the equal protection of the laws.

Abolishes three-fifths rule for slaves, Art. I, Sec. II, para. 3.

2. When a state denies citizens the vote, its representation shall be reduced. Representatives shall be apportioned among the several States according to their respective numbers, counting the whole number of persons in each State, excluding Indians not taxed. But when the right to vote at any election for the choice of Electors for President and Vice-President of the United States, Representatives in Congress, the executive and judicial officers of a State, or the members of the legislature thereof, is denied to any of the male inhabitants of such State, being twenty-one years of age and citizens of the United States, or in any way abridged, except for participation in rebellion, or other crime, the basis of representation therein shall be reduced in the proportion which the number of such male citizens shall bear to the whole number of male citizens twenty-one years of age in such State.[2]

Leading ex-Confederates denied office. See p. 463.

3. Certain persons who have been in rebellion are ineligible for federal and state office. No person shall be a Senator or Representative in Congress, or Elector of President and Vice-President, or hold any office, civil or military, under the United States, or under any State, who, having previously taken an oath, as a member of Congress, or as an officer of the United States, or as a member of any State legislature, or as an executive or judicial officer of any State, to support the Constitution of the United States, shall have engaged in insurrection or rebellion against the same, or given aid or comfort to the enemies thereof. But Congress may, by a vote of two-thirds of each house, remove such disability.

The ex-Confederates were thus forced to repudiate their debts and pay pensions to their own veterans, plus taxes for the pensions of Union veterans, their conquerors.

4. Debts incurred in aid of rebellion are void. The validity of the public debt of the United States, authorized by law, including debts incurred for payment of pensions and bounties for services in suppressing insurrection or rebellion, shall not be questioned. But neither the United States nor any State shall assume or pay any debt or obligation incurred in aid of insurrection or rebellion against the United States, or any claim for the loss or emancipation of any slave; but all such debts, obligations, and claims shall be held illegal and void.

5. Enforcement. The Congress shall have power to enforce, by appropriate legislation, the provisions of this article. [Adopted 1868.]

Amendment XV.   Suffrage for Blacks

For background, see p. 469.

Black males are made voters. 1. The right of citizens of the United States to vote shall not be denied or abridged by the United States or by any State on account of race, color, or previous condition of servitude.

2. The Congress shall have power to enforce this article by appropriate legislation. [Adopted 1870.]

---

[1] Occasionally an offender is prosecuted under the Thirteenth Amendment for keeping an employee or other person under conditions approximating slavery.
[2] The provisions concerning "male" inhabitants were modified by the Nineteenth Amendment, which enfranchised women. The legal voting age was changed from twenty-one to eighteen by the Twenty-sixth Amendment.

Amendment XVI.   Income Taxes

For background,
see pp. 585, 658.
Congress has power to lay and collect income taxes. The Congress shall have power to lay and collect taxes on incomes, from whatever source derived, without apportionment among the several States, and without regard to any census or enumeration. [Adopted 1913.]

Amendment XVII.   Direct Election of Senators

Senators shall be elected by popular vote. 1. The Senate of the United States shall be composed of two Senators from each State, elected by the people thereof, for six years; and each Senator shall have one vote. The electors in each State shall have the qualifications requisite for electors of [voters for] the most numerous branch of the State legislatures.

2. When vacancies happen in the representation of any State in the Senate, the executive authority of such State shall issue writs of election to fill such vacancies: Provided, that the Legislature of any State may empower the executive thereof to make temporary appointments until the people fill the vacancies by election as the Legislature may direct.

3. This amendment shall not be so construed as to affect the election or term of any Senator chosen before it becomes valid as part of the Constitution. [Adopted 1913.]

Amendment XVIII.   National Prohibition

For background,
see p. 702.
The sale or manufacture of intoxicating liquors is forbidden. 1. *After one year from the ratification of this article the manufacture, sale, or transportation of intoxicating liquors within, the importation thereof into, or the exportation thereof from the United States and all territory subject to the jurisdiction thereof, for beverage purposes, is hereby prohibited.*

2. *The Congress and the several States shall have concurrent power to enforce this article by appropriate legislation.*

3. *This article shall be inoperative unless it shall have been ratified as an amendment to the Constitution by the legislatures of the several States, as provided by the Constitution, within seven years from the date of the submission thereof to the States by the Congress.* [Adopted 1919; repealed 1933 by Twenty-first Amendment.]

Amendment XIX.   Woman Suffrage

For background,
see p. 678.
Women guaranteed the right to vote. 1. The right of citizens of the United States to vote shall not be denied or abridged by the United States or by any State on account of sex.

2. The Congress shall have power to enforce this article by appropriate legislation. [Adopted 1920.]

Amendment XX.   Presidential and Congressional Terms

Shortens lame-duck
periods by
modifying Art. I,
Sec. IV, para. 2.
1. Presidential, vice-presidential, and congressional terms of office begin in January. The terms of the President and Vice-President shall end at noon on the 20th day of January, and the terms of Senators and Representatives at noon on the 3d day of January, of the years in which such terms would have ended if this article had not been ratified; and the terms of their successors shall then begin.

2. New meeting date for Congress. The Congress shall assemble at least once in every year, and such meeting shall begin at noon on the 3d day of January, unless they shall by law appoint a different day.

3. Emergency presidential and vice-presidential succession. If, at the time fixed for the beginning of the term of the President, the President-elect shall have died, the Vice-President-elect shall become President. If a President shall not have been chosen before the time fixed for the beginning of his term, or if the President-elect shall have failed to qualify, then the Vice-President-elect shall act as President until a President shall have qualified; and the Congress may by law provide for the case wherein neither a President-elect nor a Vice-President-elect shall have qualified, declaring who shall then act as President, or the manner in which one who is to act shall be selected, and such persons shall act accordingly until a President or Vice-President shall have qualified.

4. The Congress may by law provide for the case of the death of any of the persons from whom the House of Representatives may choose a President whenever the right of choice shall have devolved upon them, and for the case of the death of any of the persons from whom the Senate may choose a Vice-President whenever the right of choice shall have devolved upon them.

5. Sections 1 and 2 shall take effect on the 15th day of October following the ratification of this article.

6. This article shall be inoperative unless it shall have been ratified as an amendment to the Constitution by the Legislatures of three-fourths of the several States within seven years from the date of its submission. [Adopted 1933.]

Amendment XXI.	Prohibition Repealed

For background, see p. 680.

1. Eighteenth Amendment repealed. The eighteenth article of amendment to the Constitution of the United States is hereby repealed.

2. Local laws honored. The transportation or importation into any State, Territory, or Possession of the United States for delivery or use therein of intoxicating liquors, in violation of the laws thereof, is hereby prohibited.

3. This article shall be inoperative unless it shall have been ratified as an amendment to the Constitution by conventions in the several States, as provided in the Constitution, within seven years from the date of the submission thereof to the States by the Congress. [Adopted 1933.]

Amendment XXII.	Anti–Third Term Amendment

Sometimes referred to as the anti–Franklin Roosevelt amendment.

Presidential term is limited. 1. No person shall be elected to the office of President more than twice, and no person who has held the office of President, or acted as President, for more than two years of a term to which some other person was elected President shall be elected to the office of President more than once. But this article shall not apply to any person holding the office of President when this article was proposed by the Congress [i.e., Truman], and shall not prevent any person who may be holding the office of President, or acting as President, during the term within which this article becomes operative [i.e., Truman] from holding the office of President or acting as President during the remainder of such term.

2. This article shall be inoperative unless it shall have been ratified as an amendment to the Constitution by the legislatures of three-fourths of the several States within seven years from the date of its submission to the States by the Congress. [Adopted 1951.]

Amendment XXIII.

Designed to give the District of Columbia three electoral votes and to quiet the century-old cry of "No taxation without representation." Yet the District of Columbia still has only one nonvoting member of Congress.

District of Columbia Vote

1. Presidential electors for the District of Columbia. The District, constituting the seat of government of the United States, shall appoint in such manner as the Congress may direct:

A number of electors of President and Vice-President equal to the whole number of Senators and Representatives in Congress to which the District would be entitled if it were a State, but in no event more than the least populous State; they shall be in addition to those appointed by the States, but they shall be considered for the purposes of the election of President and Vice-President, to be electors appointed by a State; and they shall meet in the District and perform such duties as provided by the twelfth article of amendment.

2. Enforcement. The Congress shall have the power to enforce this article by appropriate legislation. [Adopted 1961.]

Amendment XXIV.

Designed to end discrimination against blacks and other poor folk. An aspect of the civil rights crusade under President Lyndon Johnson. See p. 870.

Poll Tax

1. Payment of poll tax or other taxes not to be prerequisite for voting in federal elections. The right of citizens of the United States to vote in any primary or other election for President or Vice-President, for electors for President or Vice-President, or for Senator or Representative in Congress, shall not be denied or abridged by the United States or any State by reason of failure to pay any poll tax or other tax.

2. Enforcement. The Congress shall have the power to enforce this article by appropriate legislation. [Adopted 1964.]

Amendment XXV.

Presidential Succession and Disability

1. Vice-president to become president. In case of the removal of the President from office or of his death or resignation, the Vice-President shall become President.[1]

2. Successor to vice-president provided. Whenever there is a vacancy in the office of the Vice-President, the President shall nominate a Vice-President who shall take office upon confirmation by a majority vote of both Houses of Congress.

Gerald Ford was the first "appointed president." See pp. 890, 895.

3. Vice-president to serve for disabled president. Whenever the President transmits to the President pro tempore of the Senate and the Speaker of the House of representatives his written declaration that he is unable to discharge the powers and duties of his office, and until he transmits to them a written declaration to the contrary, such powers and duties shall be discharged by the Vice-President as Acting President.

4. Procedure for disqualifying or requalifying president. Whenever the Vice-President and a majority of either the principal officers of the executive departments or of such other body as Congress may by law provide, transmit to the President pro tempore of the Senate and the Speaker of the House of Representatives their written declaration that the President is unable to discharge the powers and duties of his office, the Vice-President shall immediately assume the powers and duties of the office as Acting President.

Thereafter, when the President transmits to the President pro tempore of the Senate and the Speaker of the House of Representatives his written declaration that no inability

---

[1] The original Constitution (Art. II, Sec. I, para. 5) was vague on this point, stipulating that "the powers and duties" of the president, but not necessarily the title, should "devolve" on the vice-president. President Tyler, the first "accidental president," assumed not only the powers and duties but the title as well.

exists, he shall resume the powers and duties of his office unless the Vice-President and a majority of either the principal officers of the executive department [s] or of such other body as Congress may by law provide, transmit within four days to the President pro tempore of the Senate and the Speaker of the House of Representatives their written declaration that the President is unable to discharge the powers and duties of his office. Thereupon Congress shall decide the issue, assembling within forty-eight hours for that purpose if not in session. If the Congress, within twenty-one days after receipt of the latter written declaration, or, if Congress is not in session, within twenty-one days after Congress is required to assemble, determines by two-thirds vote of both Houses that the President is unable to discharge the powers and duties of his office, the Vice-President shall continue to discharge the same as Acting President; otherwise, the President shall resume the powers and duties of his office. [Adopted 1967.]

Amendment XXVI.   Lowering Voting Age

A response to the current revolt of youth; see p. 884.

1. Ballot for eighteen-year-olds. The right of citizens of the United States, who are eighteen years of age or older, to vote shall not be denied or abridged by the United States or by any State on account of age.

2. Enforcement. The Congress shall have power to enforce this article by appropriate legislation. [Adopted 1971.]

An American Profile: The United States and Its People

Growth of U.S. Population and Area

CENSUS	POPULATION OF UNITED STATES	INCREASE OVER THE PRECEDING CENSUS		LAND AREA (SQ. MI.)	POP. PER SQ. MI.	PERCENT OF POP. IN URBAN AND RURAL TERRITORY	
		NUMBER	PERCENT			URBAN	RURAL
1790	3,929,214			867,980	4.5	5.1	94.9
1800	5,308,483	1,379,269	35.1	867,980	6.1	6.1	93.9
1810	7,239,881	1,931,398	36.4	1,685,865	4.3	7.2	92.8
1820	9,638,453	2,398,572	33.1	1,753,588	5.5	7.2	92.8
1830	12,866,020	3,227,567	33.5	1,753,588	7.3	8.8	91.2
1840	17,069,453	4,203,433	32.7	1,753,588	9.7	10.8	89.2
1850	23,191,876	6,122,423	35.9	2,944,337	7.9	15.3	84.7
1860	31,433,321	8,251,445	35.6	2,973,965	10.6	19.8	80.2
1870	39,818,449	8,375,128	26.6	2,973,965	13.4	24.9	75.1
1880	50,155,783	10,337,334	26.0	2,973,965	16.9	28.2	71.8
1890	62,947,714	12,791,931	25.5	2,973,965	21.2	35.1	64.9
1900	75,994,575	13,046,861	20.7	2,974,159	25.6	39.7	60.3
1910	91,972,266	15,997,691	21.0	2,973,890	30.9	45.7	54.3
1920	105,710,620	13,738,354	14.9	2,973,776	35.5	51.2	48.8
1930	122,775,046	17,064,426	16.1	2,977,128	41.2	56.2	43.8
1940	131,669,275	8,894,229	7.2	2,977,128	44.2	56.5	43.5
1950	150,697,361	19,028,086	14.5	2,974,726*	50.7	64.0	36.0
1960†	179,323,175	28,625,814	19.0	3,540,911	50.6	69.9	30.1
1970	203,235,298	23,912,123	13.3	3,536,855	57.5	73.5	26.5
1980	226,504,825	23,269,527	11.4	3,536,855	64.0	73.7	26.3
1985	239,000,000 (est.)						

*As remeasured in 1940; shrinkage offset by increase in water area.
†First year for which figures include Alaska and Hawaii.
Source: Census Bureau, *Historical Statistics of the United States*, updated by relevant *Statistical Abstract of the United States*.

Characteristics of the U.S. Population

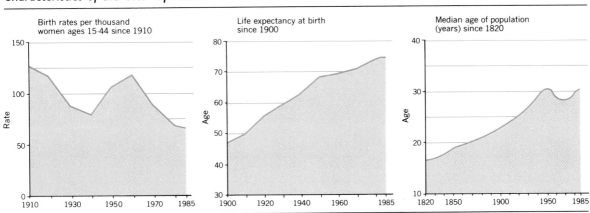

(Sources: *Historical Statistics of the United States* and *Statistical Abstract of the United States*, relevant years. Department of Health and Human Services, *Health, United States, 1985*.)

Changing Lifestyles in the Twentieth Century

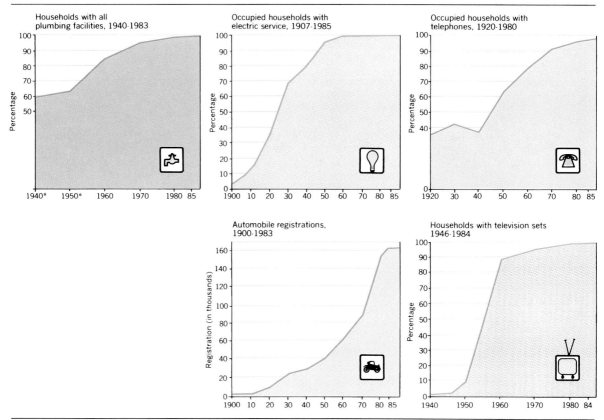

*Except for 1940 and 1950, figures are for "all plumbing facilities" (not defined in source). For 1940, figure is for flush toilet, inside structure, private use (64.7 percent had flush toilet, and private and/or shared inside structure, and 60.9 percent had installed bath or shower). For 1950, figure designates units with private toilet and bath, and hot running water (flush toilet, private or shared inside structure is 74.3 percent; installed bathtub or shower, 72.9 percent).
(Sources: *Historical Statistics of the United States* and *Statistical Abstract of the United States*, relevant years.)

Characteristics of the U.S. Labor Force

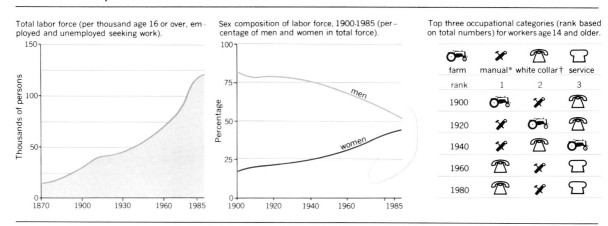

*Manual workers = operators, fabricators, and laborers plus precision production, craft, and repair.
†White collar workers = managerial and professional plus technical, sales, and administrative support.
(Sources: *Historical Statistics of the United States* and *Statistical Abstract of the United States*, relevant years, and Department of Labor Statistics, *Handbook of Labor Statistics*, relevant years.)

Leading Economic Sectors (Various Years)

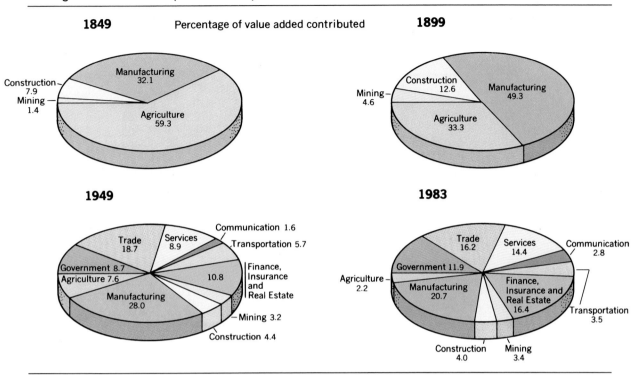

1849 Percentage of value added contributed **1899**

(Sources: *Historical Statistics of the United States* and *Statistical Abstract of the United States*, relevant years.)

Per Capita Disposable Personal Income in Constant (1982) Dollars, 1929–1985

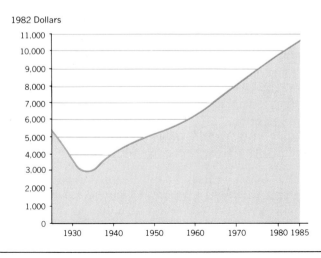

(Sources: *Historical Statistics of the United States* and *Statistical Abstract of the United States*.)

Value of Imports by Place of Origin (Millions of Dollars)

| YEAR | WESTERN HEMISPHERE | | EUROPE | | ASIA | | AUSTRALIA AND OCEANIA | AFRICA |
	TOTAL	CANADA	TOTAL	U.K.	TOTAL	JAPAN		
1900	224	39	441	160	146	33	29	11
1910	503	95	806	271	210	66	20	17
1920	2,424	612	1,228	514	1,397	415	80	150
1930	1,195	402	911	210	854	279	33	68
1940	1,089	424	390	155	981	158	35	131
1950	5,063	1,960	1,449	335	1,638	182	208	494
1960	6,864	2,901	4,268	993	2,721	1,149	266	534
1970	16,928	11,092	11,395	2,194	9,621	5,875	871	1,113
1980	78,687	41,459	48,039	9,842	80,299	30,714	3,392	34,410
1983	93,873	52,130	55,243	12,460	91,464	41,183	3,044	14,425

Value of U.S. Exports by Destination

| YEAR | WESTERN HEMISPHERE | | EUROPE | | ASIA | | AUSTRALIA AND OCEANIA | AFRICA |
	TOTAL	CANADA	TOTAL	U.K.	TOTAL	JAPAN		
1900	227	95	1,040	534	68	29	41	19
1910	479	216	1,136	506	78	22	34	19
1920	2,553	972	4,466	1,825	872	378	172	166
1930	1,357	659	1,838	678	448	165	108	92
1940	1,501	713	1,645	1,011	619	227	94	161
1950	4,902	2,039	3,306	548	1,539	418	151	376
1960	7,684	3,810	7,398	1,487	4,186	1,447	514	793
1970	15,612	9,079	14,817	2,536	10,027	4,652	1,189	1,580
1980	74,114	35,395	71,372	12,694	60,168	20,792	4,876	9,060
1983	63,970	38,244	58,871	10,621	63,813	21,894	4,827	8,788

Principal Exports, 1900–1985 (Leading Three Exports by Value in Dollars)

YEAR	FIRST	SECOND	THIRD
1900	cotton	wheat and wheat flour	meat products
1910	cotton	machinery	petroleum and products
1920	cotton	wheat and wheat flour	petroleum and products
1930	machinery	cotton	petroleum and products
1940	machinery	iron and steel mill products	petroleum and products
1950	machinery	cotton	automobiles*
1960	machinery	automobiles*	wheat and wheat flour
1970	machinery	automobiles*	wheat and wheat flour
1980	machinery	road motor vehicles*	metals and manufactures
1985	office machinery/automatic data processing	aircraft/space parts	electrical equipment

*includes parts

U.S. Foreign Trade, Ratio of Raw Materials to Manufactured Goods

YEAR	U.S. DOMESTIC EXPORTS		U.S. GENERAL IMPORTS	
	PERCENTAGE OF RAW MATERIALS	PERCENTAGE OF MANUFACTURED GOODS*	PERCENTAGE OF RAW MATERIALS	PERCENTAGE OF MANUFACTURED GOODS
1900	41.3	58.7	44.7	55.3
1910	40.0	60.0	46.4	53.6
1920	34.7	65.3	44.8	55.2
1930	26.7	73.3	45.8	54.2
1940	13.7	86.3	51.0	49.0
1950	26.8	73.2	47.7	52.3
1960	21.8	78.2	31.4	68.6
1970	17.2	82.8	16.8	83.2
1980	28.3	71.7	44.8†	55.2
1983	27.4	72.6	32.3	67.7
1985‡	17.3	82.7	34.1	65.9

*1985 figures based on most recent available month, April, 1985 (not seasonally adjusted)
†includes manufactured food
‡petroleum accounts for 70.7 percent of raw material imports and 31.7 percent of total imports

Value of Exports and Imports and Status of the Balance of Trade

(Sources for tables and graph: *Historical Statistics of the United States* and *Statistical Abstract of the United States*, relevant years.)

Tariff Levies on Dutiable Imports, 1821–1985 (Ratio of Duties to Value of Dutiable Imports)

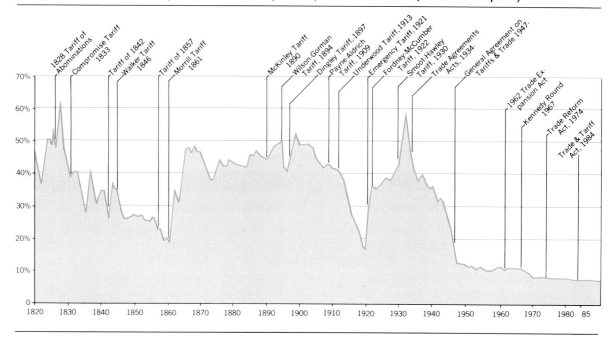

(Sources: *Historical Statistics of the United States* and *Statistical Abstract of the United States*, relevant years.)

Gross National Product in Current and Constant (1972) Dollars, 1900–1985

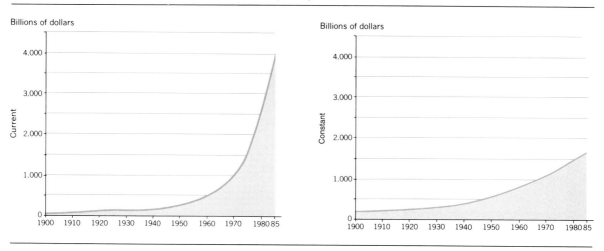

(Source: *1986 Economic Report of the President.*)

Presidential Elections*

ELECTION	CANDIDATES	PARTIES	POPULAR VOTE	ELECTORAL VOTE
1789	GEORGE WASHINGTON	No party designations		69
	JOHN ADAMS			34
	MINOR CANDIDATES			35
1792	GEORGE WASHINGTON	No party designations		132
	JOHN ADAMS			77
	GEORGE CLINTON			50
	MINOR CANDIDATES			5
1796	JOHN ADAMS	Federalist		71
	THOMAS JEFFERSON	Democratic-Republican		68
	THOMAS PINCKNEY	Federalist		59
	AARON BURR	Democratic-Republican		30
	MINOR CANDIDATES			48
1800	THOMAS JEFFERSON	Democratic-Republican		73
	AARON BURR	Democratic-Republican		73
	JOHN ADAMS	Federalist		65
	CHARLES C. PINCKNEY	Federalist		64
	JOHN JAY	Federalist		1
1804	THOMAS JEFFERSON	Democratic-Republican		162
	CHARLES C. PINCKNEY	Federalist		14
1808	JAMES MADISON	Democratic-Republican		122
	CHARLES C. PINCKNEY	Federalist		47
	GEORGE CLINTON	Democratic-Republican		6
1812	JAMES MADISON	Democratic-Republican		128
	DEWITT CLINTON	Federalist		89
1816	JAMES MONROE	Democratic-Republican		183
	RUFUS KING	Federalist		34
1820	JAMES MONROE	Democratic-Republican		231
	JOHN Q. ADAMS	Independent Republican		1
1824	JOHN Q. ADAMS (Min.)[†]	Democratic-Republican	108,740	84
	ANDREW JACKSON	Democratic-Republican	153,544	99
	WILLIAM H. CRAWFORD	Democratic-Republican	46,618	41
	HENRY CLAY	Democratic-Republican	47,136	37
1828	ANDREW JACKSON	Democratic	647,286	178
	JOHN Q. ADAMS	National Republican	508,064	83
1832	ANDREW JACKSON	Democratic	687,502	219
	HENRY CLAY	National Republican	530,189	49
	WILLIAM WIRT	Anti-Masonic ⎫	33,108	7
	JOHN FLOYD	National Republican ⎭		11
1836	MARTIN VAN BUREN	Democratic	765,483	170
	WILLIAM H. HARRISON	Whig ⎫		73
	HUGH L. WHITE	Whig ⎪	739,795	26
	DANIEL WEBSTER	Whig ⎬		14
	W. P. MANGUM	Whig ⎭		11
1840	WILLIAM H. HARRISON	Whig	1,274,624	234
	MARTIN VAN BUREN	Democratic	1,127,781	60
1844	JAMES K. POLK (Min.)[†]	Democratic	1,338,464	170
	HENRY CLAY	Whig	1,300,097	105
	JAMES G. BIRNEY	Liberty	62,300	

*Candidates receiving less than 1 percent of the popular vote are omitted. Before the Twelfth Amendment (1804), the Electoral College voted for two presidential candidates, and the runner-up became vice-president. Basic figures are taken primarily from *Historical Statistics of the United States, Colonial Times to 1970* (1975), pp. 1073–1074, and *Statistical Abstract of the United States,* appropriate years.

[†]"Min." indicates minority president—one receiving less than 50 percent of all popular votes.

ELECTION	CANDIDATES	PARTIES	POPULAR VOTE	ELECTORAL VOTE
1848	ZACHARY TAYLOR	Whig	1,360,967	163
	LEWIS CASS	Democratic	1,222,342	127
	MARTIN VAN BUREN	Free Soil	291,263	
1852	FRANKLIN PIERCE	Democratic	1,601,117	254
	WINFIELD SCOTT	Whig	1,385,453	42
	JOHN P. HALE	Free Soil	155,825	
1856	JAMES BUCHANAN (Min.)*	Democratic	1,832,955	174
	JOHN C. FRÉMONT	Republican	1,339,932	114
	MILLARD FILLMORE	American	871,731	8
1860	ABRAHAM LINCOLN (Min.)*	Republican	1,865,593	180
	STEPHEN A. DOUGLAS	Democratic	1,382,713	12
	JOHN C. BRECKINRIDGE	Democratic	848,356	72
	JOHN BELL	Constitutional Union	592,906	39
1864	ABRAHAM LINCOLN	Union	2,206,938	212
	GEORGE B. MCCLELLAN	Democratic	1,803,787	21
1868	ULYSSES S. GRANT	Republican	3,013,421	214
	HORATIO SEYMOUR	Democratic	2,706,829	80
1872	ULYSSES S. GRANT	Republican	3,596,745	286
	HORACE GREELEY	Democratic Liberal Republican	2,843,446	66
1876	RUTHERFORD B. HAYES (Min.)*	Republican	4,036,572	185
	SAMUEL J. TILDEN	Democratic	4,284,020	184
1880	JAMES A. GARFIELD (Min.)*	Republican	4,453,295	214
	WINFIELD S. HANCOCK	Democratic	4,414,082	155
	JAMES B. WEAVER	Greenback-Labor	308,578	
1884	GROVER CLEVELAND (Min.)*	Democratic	4,879,507	219
	JAMES G. BLAINE	Republican	4,850,293	182
	BENJAMIN F. BUTLER	Greenback-Labor	175,370	
	JOHN P. ST. JOHN	Prohibition	150,369	
1888	BENJAMIN HARRISON (Min.)*	Republican	5,447,129	233
	GROVER CLEVELAND	Democratic	5,537,857	168
	CLINTON B. FISK	Prohibition	249,506	
	ANSON J. STREETER	Union Labor	146,935	
1892	GROVER CLEVELAND (Min.)*	Democratic	5,555,426	277
	BENJAMIN HARRISON	Republican	5,182,690	145
	JAMES B. WEAVER	People's	1,029,846	22
	JOHN BIDWELL	Prohibition	264,133	
1896	WILLIAM MCKINLEY	Republican	7,102,246	271
	WILLIAM J. BRYAN	Democratic	6,492,559	176
1900	WILLIAM MCKINLEY	Republican	7,218,491	292
	WILLIAM J. BRYAN	Democratic; Populist	6,356,734	155
	JOHN C. WOOLLEY	Prohibition	208,914	
1904	THEODORE ROOSEVELT	Republican	7,628,461	336
	ALTON B. PARKER	Democratic	5,084,223	140
	EUGENE V. DEBS	Socialist	402,283	
	SILAS C. SWALLOW	Prohibition	258,536	
1908	WILLIAM H. TAFT	Republican	7,675,320	321
	WILLIAM J. BRYAN	Democratic	6,412,294	162
	EUGENE V. DEBS	Socialist	420,793	
	EUGENE W. CHAFIN	Prohibition	253,840	

*"Min." indicates minority president—one receiving less than 50 percent of all popular votes.

ELECTION	CANDIDATES	PARTIES	POPULAR VOTE	ELECTORAL VOTE
1912	WOODROW WILSON (Min.)*	Democratic	6,296,547	435
	THEODORE ROOSEVELT	Progressive	4,118,571	88
	WILLIAM H. TAFT	Republican	3,486,720	8
	EUGENE V. DEBS	Socialist	900,672	
	EUGENE W. CHAFIN	Prohibition	206,275	
1916	WOODROW WILSON (Min.)*	Democratic	9,127,695	277
	CHARLES E. HUGHES	Republican	8,533,507	254
	A. L. BENSON	Socialist	585,113	
	J. F. HANLY	Prohibition	220,506	
1920	WARREN G. HARDING	Republican	16,143,407	404
	JAMES M. COX	Democratic	9,130,328	127
	EUGENE V. DEBS	Socialist	919,799	
	P. P. CHRISTENSEN	Farmer-Labor	265,411	
1924	CALVIN COOLIDGE	Republican	15,718,211	382
	JOHN W. DAVIS	Democratic	8,385,283	136
	ROBERT M. LA FOLLETTE	Progressive	4,831,289	13
1928	HERBERT C. HOOVER	Republican	21,391,993	444
	ALFRED E. SMITH	Democratic	15,016,169	87
1932	FRANKLIN D. ROOSEVELT	Democratic	22,809,638	472
	HERBERT C. HOOVER	Republican	15,758,901	59
	NORMAN THOMAS	Socialist	881,951	
1936	FRANKLIN D. ROOSEVELT	Democratic	27,752,869	523
	ALFRED M. LANDON	Republican	16,674,665	8
	WILLIAM LEMKE	Union, etc.	882,479	
1940	FRANKLIN D. ROOSEVELT	Democratic	27,307,819	449
	WENDELL L. WILLKIE	Republican	22,321,018	82
1944	FRANKLIN D. ROOSEVELT	Democratic	25,606,585	432
	THOMAS E. DEWEY	Republican	22,014,745	99
1948	HARRY S TRUMAN (Min.)*	Democratic	24,179,345	303
	THOMAS E. DEWEY	Republican	21,991,291	189
	J. STROM THURMOND	States' Rights Democratic	1,176,125	39
	HENRY A. WALLACE	Progressive	1,157,326	
1952	DWIGHT D. EISENHOWER	Republican	33,936,234	442
	ADLAI E. STEVENSON	Democratic	27,314,992	89
1956	DWIGHT D. EISENHOWER	Republican	35,590,472	457
	ADLAI E. STEVENSON	Democratic	26,022,752	73
1960	JOHN F. KENNEDY (Min.)*†	Democratic	34,226,731	303
	RICHARD M. NIXON	Republican	34,108,157	219
1964	LYNDON B. JOHNSON	Democratic	43,129,566	486
	BARRY M. GOLDWATER	Republican	27,178,188	52
1968	RICHARD M. NIXON (Min.)*	Republican	31,785,480	301
	HUBERT H. HUMPHREY, JR.	Democratic	31,275,166	191
	GEORGE C. WALLACE	American Independent	9,906,473	46
1972	RICHARD M. NIXON	Republican	47,169,911	520
	GEORGE S. MC GOVERN	Democratic	29,170,383	17
1976	JIMMY CARTER	Democratic	40,828,657	297
	GERALD R. FORD	Republican	39,145,520	240
1980	RONALD W. REAGAN	Republican	43,899,248	489
	JIMMY CARTER	Democratic	35,481,435	49
	JOHN B. ANDERSON	Independent	5,719,437	0
1984	RONALD W. REAGAN	Republican	52,609,797	525
	WALTER MONDALE	Democratic	36,450,613	13

*"Min." indicates minority president—one receiving less than 50 percent of all popular votes.
†Six Democratic electors in Alabama, all eight unpledged Democratic electors in Mississippi, and one Republican elector in Oklahoma voted for Senator Harry F. Byrd.

Presidents and Vice-Presidents

TERM	PRESIDENT	VICE-PRESIDENT
1789–1793	George Washington	John Adams
1793–1797	George Washington	John Adams
1797–1801	John Adams	Thomas Jefferson
1801–1805	Thomas Jefferson	Aaron Burr
1805–1809	Thomas Jefferson	George Clinton
1809–1813	James Madison	George Clinton (d. 1812)
1813–1817	James Madison	Elbridge Gerry (d. 1814)
1817–1821	James Monroe	Daniel D. Tompkins
1821–1825	James Monroe	Daniel D. Tompkins
1825–1829	John Quincy Adams	John C. Calhoun
1829–1833	Andrew Jackson	John C. Calhoun (resigned 1832)
1833–1837	Andrew Jackson	Martin Van Buren
1837–1841	Martin Van Buren	Richard M. Johnson
1841–1845	William H. Harrison (d. 1841) John Tyler	John Tyler
1845–1849	James K. Polk	George M. Dallas
1849–1853	Zachary Taylor (d. 1850) Millard Fillmore	Millard Fillmore
1853–1857	Franklin Pierce	William R. D. King (d. 1853)
1857–1861	James Buchanan	John C. Breckinridge
1861–1865	Abraham Lincoln	Hannibal Hamlin
1865–1869	Abraham Lincoln (d. 1865) Andrew Johnson	Andrew Johnson
1869–1873	Ulysses S. Grant	Schuyler Colfax
1873–1877	Ulysses S. Grant	Henry Wilson (d. 1875)
1877–1881	Rutherford B. Hayes	William A. Wheeler
1881–1885	James A. Garfield (d. 1881) Chester A. Arthur	Chester A. Arthur
1885–1889	Grover Cleveland	Thomas A. Hendricks (d. 1885)
1889–1893	Benjamin Harrison	Levi P. Morton
1893–1897	Grover Cleveland	Adlai E. Stevenson
1897–1901	William McKinley	Garret A. Hobart (d. 1899)
1901–1905	William McKinley (d. 1901) Theodore Roosevelt	Theodore Roosevelt
1905–1909	Theodore Roosevelt	Charles W. Fairbanks
1909–1913	William H. Taft	James S. Sherman (d. 1912)
1913–1917	Woodrow Wilson	Thomas R. Marshall
1917–1921	Woodrow Wilson	Thomas R. Marshall
1921–1925	Warren G. Harding (d. 1923) Calvin Coolidge	Calvin Coolidge
1925–1929	Calvin Coolidge	Charles G. Dawes
1929–1933	Herbert C. Hoover	Charles Curtis
1933–1937	Franklin D. Roosevelt	John N. Garner
1937–1941	Franklin D. Roosevelt	John N. Garner
1941–1945	Franklin D. Roosevelt	Henry A. Wallace
1945–1949	Franklin D. Roosevelt (d. 1945) Harry S Truman	Harry S Truman
1949–1953	Harry S Truman	Alben W. Barkley
1953–1957	Dwight D. Eisenhower	Richard M. Nixon
1957–1961	Dwight D. Eisenhower	Richard M. Nixon
1961–1965	John F. Kennedy (d. 1963) Lyndon B. Johnson	Lyndon B. Johnson
1965–1969	Lyndon B. Johnson	Hubert H. Humphrey, Jr.

Presidents and Vice-Presidents

TERM	PRESIDENT	VICE-PRESIDENT
1969–1974	Richard M. Nixon	Spiro T. Agnew (resigned 1973); Gerald R. Ford
1974–1977	Gerald R. Ford	Nelson A. Rockefeller
1977–1981	Jimmy Carter	Walter F. Mondale
1981–1985	Ronald Reagan	George Bush
1985–1989	Ronald Reagan	George Bush

Admission of States

(See p. 144 for order in which the original thirteen entered the union.)

ORDER OF ADMISSION	STATE	DATE OF ADMISSION	ORDER OF ADMISSION	STATE	DATE OF ADMISSION
14	Vermont	Mar. 4, 1791	33	Oregon	Feb. 14, 1859
15	Kentucky	June 1, 1792	34	Kansas	Jan. 29, 1861
16	Tennessee	June 1, 1796	35	W. Virginia	June 20, 1863
17	Ohio	Mar. 1, 1803	36	Nevada	Oct. 31, 1864
18	Louisiana	April 30, 1812	37	Nebraska	Mar. 1, 1867
19	Indiana	Dec. 11, 1816	38	Colorado	Aug. 1, 1876
20	Mississippi	Dec. 10, 1817	39	N. Dakota	Nov. 2, 1889
21	Illinois	Dec. 3, 1818	40	S. Dakota	Nov. 2, 1889
22	Alabama	Dec. 14, 1819	41	Montana	Nov. 8, 1889
23	Maine	Mar. 15, 1820	42	Washington	Nov. 11, 1889
24	Missouri	Aug. 10, 1821	43	Idaho	July 3, 1890
25	Arkansas	June 15, 1836	44	Wyoming	July 10, 1890
26	Michigan	Jan. 26, 1837	45	Utah	Jan. 4, 1896
27	Florida	Mar. 3, 1845	46	Oklahoma	Nov. 16, 1907
28	Texas	Dec. 29, 1845	47	New Mexico	Jan. 6, 1912
29	Iowa	Dec. 28, 1846	48	Arizona	Feb. 14, 1912
30	Wisconsin	May 29, 1848	49	Alaska	Jan. 3, 1959
31	California	Sept. 9, 1850	50	Hawaii	Aug. 21, 1959
32	Minnesota	May 11, 1858			

Estimates of Total Costs and Number of Battle Deaths of Major U.S. Wars*

	TOTAL COSTS** (MILLIONS OF DOLLARS)	ORIGINAL COSTS	NUMBER OF BATTLE DEATHS
Vietnam Conflict	352,000	140,600	47,318[†]
Korean Conflict	164,000	54,000	33,629
World War II	664,000	288,000	291,557
World War I	112,000	26,000	53,402
Spanish-American War	6,460	400	385
Civil War { Union only	12,952	3,200	140,414
Civil War { Confederacy (est.)	N.A.	1,000	94,000
Mexican War	147	73	1,733
War of 1812	158	93	2,260
American Revolution	190	100	6,824

*Deaths from disease and other causes are not shown. In earlier wars especially, owing to poor medical and sanitary practices, non-battle deaths substantially exceeded combat casualties.

**The difference between total costs and original costs is attributable to continuing postwar payments for such items as veterans' benefits, interest on war debts, etc.

[†]1959–1983

Sources: *Historical Statistics of the United States, Statistical Abstract of the United States,* relevant years, and *The World Almanac and Book of Facts, 1986.*

Abbott, Lyman, 529

Abolitionism, 128, 238, 361–62; Douglass and, 356, 362–64; Garrison and, 362–64, 366; the North and, 356, 361–62, 366; radical, 362–64; reaction of the South to, 364–65; Underground Railroad and, 375. *See also* Slavery

Abortion, 916

Acadia (Nova Scotia), 79

Acheson, Dean, 829, 835, 843, 875

Act of Toleration (1649), 16

Adams, Abigail, 128

Adams, Charles Francis, 442, 443

Adams, Henry, 210, 480, 502, 583, 714

Adams, John, 57, 99, 102, 112, 130, 131, 138, 167, 181, 182, 195, 236; on education, 66; presidency of, 168–72, 175, 177; problems with France of, 169–72; quoted, 89; Treaty of Paris and, 122; as vice-president, 150

Adams, John Quincy, 206, 216, 224, 225, 227, 234–36; Canning proposal and, 227; death and funeral of, 242; land policy of, 237; Monroe Doctrine and, 228, 229; presidency of, 236–40; slavery and, 365; tariff issue and, 237–38

Adams, Samuel, 52, 54, 99, 114, 138, 142

Adams, Sherman, 851

Adamson Act of 1916, 660

Addams, Jane, 534–35, 633, 654

Adjusted Compensation Act (1924), 723

Adkins v. *Children's Hospital* (1923), 721

Adult education, 327–28, 540

Adventists, 322

Adventures of Augie March, The (Saul Bellow), 945

Adventures of Huckleberry Finn, The (Mark Twain), 546

Adventures of Tom Sawyer, The (Mark Twain), 546

Advertising, 706; exploitation in, 713; the radio and, 710

Affluent Society, The (John Kenneth Galbraith), 943

Afghanistan, Soviet invasion of, 903

AF of L, 526–27, 678, 761, 762–63, 832

AF of L–CIO, 847

Africa, 596; decolonization of European possessions in, 862; recolonization with slaves of, 361, 363; war campaign in North Africa, 806–7

African Congo, 862

Africans, in colonial America, 56

Agassiz, Louis, 338

Agnew, Spiro T., 878; resignation of, 890

Agricultural Adjustment Act, 752

Agricultural Adjustment Administration (AAA), 756–57

Agricultural Marketing Act (1929), 734

Agriculture: as Civil War casualty, 458–59; in colonial America, 59–60; expansion of the West and, 296; farming and threat of deflation, 571–72; foreign trade and farm products, 306; inventions to increase production, 296–97; Jefferson's attitude toward, 159; labor-saving machinery for, 446–47; mechanization of, 570–71. *See also* Farmers

Aguinaldo, Emilio, 605, 615

AIM, 935

Air brake, Westinghouse, 509

Aircraft carriers in World War II, 802, 804

Air force, superbombers for, 847

Alabama: Reconstruction in, 470, 471; slavery in, 357

Alabama (Confederate raider), 441, 442

Alamogordo, New Mexico, 814

Alaska, 226, 610; purchase of, 475–77; statehood for, 857; World War II defense of, 802

Albany Congress (1754), 140

Albee, Edward, 945

Alcohol: prohibition of, 550–51; reform campaign against, 318, 335–36

Aldrich, Nelson Wilmarth, 658

Aldrich-Vreeland Act (1908), 645

Aleutians, 803

Alexander I, Czar, 206

Alger, Horatio, 545

Algiers, Dey of, 136

Alien and Sedition Laws, 172–74, 180–81, 182

Allen, Ethan, 110

Allen, Frederick Lewis, 718

Alliance for Progress, 863

Allies (World War II), 792; halting of Hitler by, 804–6, 811–12; invasion of Italy by, 807; North African invasion by, 806–7; partition of Germany by, 823–25; triumph of, 815–16; war debts, 730–32

All the King's Men (Robert Penn Warren), 944

Alperovitz, Gar, 817

Altgeld, John P., 525

America First Committee, 783

American Anti-Slavery Society, 362

American Colonization Society, 361

American Federation of Labor, *see* AF of L

American Independent party, 878

American Indian Movement (AIM), 935

American Legion, 723

American Medical Association, 869

American Mercury, 715

American party, *see* Know-Nothing party

American Peace Society, 334

American Protective Association (APA), 536

American Railway Union, 584

American, Red Cross, 551

American Revolutionary War, 79; colonies' positions in, 104–6, 113–15; consequences of, 123–25; economic changes following, 129–30, 136–37; First Continental Congress and, 101–3; French aid in, 118–19; 122; Great Britain's strengths and weaknesses in, 103–4, 119–20; military campaigns in, 115–23; naval warfare in, 121–22; Patriots and Loyalists of, 113–15; roots of, 89–90, 93, 94–100; social changes after, 127–28; Treaty of Paris and, 123–25; as world war, 79, 119–20

"American Scholar, The" (Ralph Waldo Emerson), 333, 342

American Slavery as It Is (Theodore Dwight Weld), 362

American Society for the Prevention of Cruelty to Animals, 551

American System (1824), 214–15

American Temperance Society, 335

American Tobacco Company, 521

Ames, Fisher, 145, 168

Amusement, business of, 552–54

Anderson, John, 907

Anderson, Sherwood, 715

Andros, Sir Edmund, 29–30

Anesthetics, 340

Anglican church, *see* Church of England

Anglicans, in colonial America, 63

Anglo-Japanese alliance (1902), 723

Anne, Queen, 70, 79

Anthony, Susan B., 327, 336, 549

Antiballistic missile (ABM) treaty, 885–86

Antietam, Battle of (1862), 429–30, 435

Anti-Federalists, 141–42, 157, 159

Antiforeignism (nativism), 319–20, 535–37

Anti-Imperialist League, 610

Anti-Masonic party, 234, 254–55, 261

Antin, Mary, 533

Antinomianism, 26

Anti-Saloon League, 551, 638

Antislave societies, *see* Abolitionism

Antisweatshop law, 535

Antitrust laws, 722

APA, 536

Apache Indians, 7, 559

Appalachia, 867, 869

Appalachian Mountains, Proclamation of 1763 and, 87

Appomattox, 437

Arabic (ship), 669

Arab oil embargo, 892–93

Arawaks, 8

Architecture, 340, 552, 716, 946; in colonial America, 68

Aristocracy: first families of Virginia, 45–46; plantation, 350–51

Arkansas: Reconstruction in, 470; secession of, 417

Armed Neutrality (1780), 119, 120

Armour, Philip, 518

Armstrong, Louis, 716

Army, American: colonial, 105–6, 113–14, 130; Mexican War and, 286. *See also specific wars*

Arnold, Benedict, 110, 116–17, 118, 120, 122

"Aroostook War," 274
Art, 945–46
Arthur, Chester A., 492, 493–95, 502
Arthur, T. S., 335
Articles of Confederation (1777), 131–34, 137, 139, 145, 153; central government under, 142
Artists, 551–52
Arts, *see* Architecture; Literature; Music; Painting
Ashburton, Lord, 274
Asian-Americans, 934–35
Assembly-line production, 705–6
Associated Press, 544
Association, The, 102, 103
Astor, John Jacob, 305
Astronauts, 861
Atchison, Topeka, and Sante Fe, 508
Atlanta, Georgia, burning of, 434–35, 458
Atlanta *Constitution*, 521
Atlanta Monthly, 412
Atlantic, Battle of the, 805
Atlantic cable, 306–7
Atlantic Charter, 788, 794
Atlantic Conference (1941), 788
Atlantic Monthly, 544
Atomic bomb, 814–15, 830
Atomic energy, U.N. control of, 823
Attucks, Crispus, 98
Auchincloss, Louis, 944
Audubon, John J., 338
Audubon Society, 338
Austerlitz, Battle of (1805), 190
Austin, Stephen, 258, 259
Australian ballot, 636
Austria, 164, 824; Hitler's occupation of, 779
Austria-Hungary, World War I and, 664, 665
Austrian Succession, War of, 79, 80
Autobiography (Benjamin Franklin), 341
Automobile industry: assembly-line production in, 706; industrial revolution spawned by, 706–9; unions and, 762
Aviation, 709
Aztecs, 6

Babbittry, 716
Baby boom, postwar, 931–32
Bache, Benjamin Franklin, 168
Bacon, Nathaniel, 41–42
Bacon's Rebellion (1676), 41–42, 52
Baer, George F., 639
Bailey, James A., 553
Bailyn, Bernard, 106, 147
Baker, Ray Stannard, 634
Bakke, Allan, 936
Balboa, Vasco Núñez de, 8
Baldwin, James, 944
Baltimore, Lord (Cecelius Calvert), 15, 16
Baltimore, population of (1790), 149
Baltimore and Ohio Company, 301
Bancroft, George, 346–47
Banjos, 45
Bank of the United States, 213–14; Biddle and, 253–54, 255–56; Clay and, 253, 261; expansion of the West and, 217,

218; Hamilton and, 155–56; Jackson and, 252–54, 255–56; Jefferson and, 155, 181; loss of federal deposits by, 255–56; as a political football, 252–54; reestablishment of, 271–72
Banks and banking: Federal Reserve Act and, 659; F. Roosevelt presidency and, 750, 758–59; Wilson's attack on, 658–60
Banning, Lance, 161
Baptists, 66, 319, 321, 322; in colonial America, 63
Baraka, Imamu Amiri, 944
Barbados, 16, 23
Barbed wire, 568
Barnum, Phineas T., 325, 553
Barter system, 91
Barton, Bruce, 706
Barton, Clara, 551
Baruch, Bernard, 678, 823
Baseball, 325, 553
Basketball, 554
Bataan death march, 802
Bay of Pigs invasion, 864
Beans, 7
Beard, Charles, 147, 412, 455, 502
Beard, Mary, 502
Beavers, 76–77
Beck, "Dave," 851
Becker, Carl, 106
Beecher, Catharine, 329, 330, 336, 361
Beecher, Henry Ward, 361, 393, 523, 548
Beecher, Lyman, 361
Beef trust, 640
Beer, 318
BEF, 740–41
Begin, Menachem, 899
Behavioral psychology, 543
Beijing (Peking), 884–86
Belgium, 664, 666
Belknap, William W., 484
Bell, Alexander Graham, 513
Bell, Daniel, 943
Bell, John, 406, 407
Bellamy, Edward, 544
Bell Jar, The (Sylvia Plath), 945
Bellow, Saul, 945
Ben Hur: A Tale of the Christ (Lewis Wallace), 545
Bennett, James Gordon, 330
Bensen, Lee, 248
Benson, Ezra Taft, 846–47
Benton, Sen. Thomas H., 280
Berger, Victor L., 650
Berkeley, Governor (Virginia), 41–42
Berlin, U.S. airlift to, 824–25
Berlin Wall, 861
Berryman, John, 945
Bessemer process, 515
Bible reading in schools, 886
Bicycles, 554
Biddle, Nicholas, Bank of the United States and, 253–54, 255–56
Biglow Papers (James Russell Lowell), 345
"Big Sister" policy, 596
Bill of Rights, 152–53, 155; GI, 831, 924
Birbeck, Morris, 311

Birds of America (John J. Audubon), 338
Birmingham, Alabama, racial violence in, 865, 866
Birth control, 329, 548, 712
Birth of a Nation, The (film), 711
Bismarck, Otto von, 612
Black, Hugo, 766
Black Ball Line, 306
Black Codes, 464–65, 467
Blackfoot Indians, 7
"Black Friday," 482
Black Hawk (Indian chieftain), 257
Blacks: abolitionists among, 362–64; American Revolutionary War and, 98, 103, 128; Black Codes for, 464–65, 467; CIO and, 763; Civil Rights Act of 1875 and, 490; civil rights movement and, 844–45, 870–72; in Confederate army, 423; dishonorable devices used in South against, 471–74; Dred Scott decision and, 399–400; education for, 327, 540–41; freed slaves, 355–56; intimidation, fraud, and trickery practiced during Reconstruction on, 471–74; Irish immigrants and, 317; jazz music and, 714; Jim Crow laws and, 582; J. Kennedy and, 857; labor unions and, 525, 526; lynching of (1887–1970), 474; muckrakers on plight of, 634; 1920s cultural renaissance for, 716; population in thirteen colonies (1770–1775), 54; the Populists and, 582; postwar gains of, 935–37; professional sports and, 832; prohibition and, 701; racial violence against, 865–66; Reconstruction and, 457–61; 471–74; school desegregation for, 845–46; suffrage for, 466, 469, 470–72; switch to Democratic party by, 748, 764; in the president's cabinet, 870; in the Union armies, 422; voter-registration campaigns for, 870, 871–72; War of 1812 and, 204; Wilson presidency and, 661; World War I and, 678, 722; in World War II, 797–98. *See also* Slavery
"Black Tuesday" (October 29, 1929), 735
Black Warrior (steamer), 383–84
Blackwell, Dr. Elizabeth, 337
Blaine, James G., 487, 493, 495–97, 500, 578, 596, 775
Bland, Richard P., 486
Bland-Allison Act of 1878, 486, 580
Blockade-running, 426
Bloomer, Amelia, 337
"Blue laws," 36
Boer War, 622
Bolsheviks, 697–98
Bongo drums, 44
Bonomi, Patricia, 37
Bonus Bill of 1817, 215
Bonus Expeditionary Force (BEF), 740–41
Book of Daniel, The (E. L. Doctorow), 945
Books, 543
Boom towns, 563
Boone, Daniel, 87
Booth, Edwin T., 325
Booth, John Wilkes, 325, 452
Booth, Junius Brutus, 325

Borah, William, 689, 691
Border States, 417–18, 420, 423, 448
"Born-again" Christians, 942
Boston, 55, 95, 99, 110, 316; evacuation of, 111, 115; literary tradition of, 347; population of (1790), 149; religious persecution in, 320
Boston Associates, 293, 295
Boston *Columbian Centinel,* 217
Boston *Gazette,* 91
Bostonians, The (Henry James), 547
Boston Massacre (1770), 97–98
Boston Port Act (1774), 100, 101
Boston Tea Party (1773), 99–100
Bowditch, Nathaniel, 338
Bowers, Claude, 778
Bowie, James, 258–59
Boycotts, 526
Boys' Progressive League, 650
Braceros, 797
Braddock, General Edward, 83, 85
Bradford, William, 23, 29
"Brain Trust," 747
Brandeis, Louis D., 658, 660–61
Brando, Marlon, 941
Brandywine, Battle of (1777), 118
Brazil, 8, 31
Breckinridge, John C., 405–6, 407
Brezhnev, Leonid, 902
Bricker, John W., 810, 811, 843
British East India Company, 99
British Malaya, 795
British West Indies, 16, 237–38
Brock, Isaac, 202
Brook Farm (Massachusetts), 338
Brooklyn Bridge, 530
Brooks, Rep. P. S., 396–97
Brotherhood of Sleeping Car Porters, 797
Brown, John, 394, 404–5
Brown, Moses, 290
Brown University, 66, 67, 326
Brown v. Board of Education of Topeka, Kansas (1954), 844
Bruce, Blanche K., 471
Bryan, William Jennings, 578, 583, 646, 654, 662; imperialism issue and, 619–20; at "Monkey Trial," 705; the silver issue and, 588–91, 593; Spanish-American War and, 611
Bryant, William Cullen, 342
Bryce, James, 624
Brzezinski, Zbigniew, 900
Buchanan, James, 306, 381, 395, 397–98; secession and, 409, 411
Budget: military, 922–25; Reagan and, 910–12, 917. *See also* Economy
Budget, Bureau of the, 717–18
Buffalo (animals), 556; massacre of, 559–60
Buffalo, New York, 300, 303
Bulgaria, 664, 820, 822
Bulge, Battle of the, 811
Bull Run, battles of: first (1861), 427; second (1862), 429
Bunau-Varilla, Philippe, 622, 623
Bunker Hill, Battle of (1775), 110
Bunyan, Paul, 313

Burger, Warren E., 887
Burgoyne, General John, 116–18
Burke, Edmund, 93, 100
Burma, 801
Burnaby, Rev. Andrew, 86
"Burned-Over District," 322
Burnside, A. E., 435
Burr, Aaron, 175, 176, 189
Bushman, Richard, 72
Business organizations, 293–94
Butler, Benjamin F., 419, 475, 481n
Butler, Marion, 395
Buying: on credit, 706; installment-plan, 708, 736
Byrd, Harry F., 857n

Cabinet: formation of, 151–52; Kitchen, 245; Lincoln and, 414–15
Cablegrams, 306–7
Cadillac, Antoine, 77
Cajuns, 82
Calhoun, John C., 214, 216, 234, 237, 261, 350; break with Jackson of, 245–46, 248; Compromise of 1850 and, 375–76; tariffs and, 239, 251–52
California, 226, 279, 369; discovery of gold in, 372; gold mining in, 562; Japanese laborers in, 628–29; Mexican War and, 283–84, 285, 287; Oriental immigrants in, 491; purchase from Mexico of, 281, 282; railroads and, 506; statehood for, 372, 373, 375, 378, 383, 384
Callender, James, 173
Call of the Wild, The (Jack London), 547
Calvin, John, 21
Calvinism, 21–22, 320
Cambodia, secret bombing of, 891–92. *See also* Vietnam War
Cambodianizing the Vietnam War, 884
Cameras, 552
Cameron, Simon, 415
Camp, Walter C., 553
Camp David summit (1978), 899–900
Camp meetings, 320
Canada, 54; American-supported insurrection in, 273; attempts to invade, 110, 208, 215, 283, 443; as base of support for Indians, 199, 200; colonization by France of, 74–78, 86; established as dominion, 443; seal-hunting argument with, 596; War of 1812 and, 201–3, 209
Canals, 299–301, 303; federal funding for, 215, 236, 246
Canning, George, 227, 228
Canning proposal, 227
Capone, Al, 703
Capper-Volstead Act, 728
Carey Act of 1894, 642
Caribbean islands, 76
Carmichael, Stokely, 871
Carnegie, Andrew, 514–17, 523, 568, 610; contributions for public libraries made by, 543
Caroline (steamer), 273, 274
Carpentier, Georges, 706

Carpetbaggers, 471
Carranza, Venustiano, 663–64
Carroll, Charles, 301
Carter, James Earl, Jr., 898–904, 929; economy under, 900–901; election of, 898–99; energy issue and, 901–2; foreign affairs under, 899–900, 902–4; humanitarian diplomacy of, 899–900; loss to Reagan, 907–8
Cartwright, Peter, 321
Carver, George Washington, 541
Cass, Gen. Lewis, 370, 371
Castro, Fidel: CIA-backed plan to overthrow, 864; Cuban revolution and, 854
Catcher in the Rye (J. D. Salinger), 944
Catch-22 (Joseph Heller), 944
Cather, Willa, 714
Catherine the Great, Czarina, 120
Catholics (Catholicism), *see* Roman Catholics (Catholicism)
Cat on a Hot Tin Roof (Tennessee Williams), 945
Catt, Carrie Chapman, 549–50
Cattle raising, 563–65
Census, first official (1790), 149
Central America: Coolidge's intervention in, 730; Reagan's foreign policy in, 914, 919
Central High School (Little Rock, Arkansas), 846
Central Intelligence Agency (CIA), *see* CIA
Central Pacific Railroad, 506–7, 508
Century of Dishonor, A (Helen Hunt Jackson), 561
Champlain, Samuel de, 74
Charles I, King, 16, 22, 23, 27, 29
Charles II, King, 16, 27, 28, 29, 33
Charleston, South Carolina, 17, 55, 95, 458; American Revolutionary War and, 121; destruction of, 458; population of (1790), 149
Chase, Salmon P., 415, 450
Chase, Samuel, 182–83
Château-Thierry, Battle of, 683–84
Chautauqua movement, 540
Chávez, César, 934
Cheever, John, 944
Cherokee Indians, 256, 257; loss of land holdings by, 237
Chesapeake (frigate), 191–92, 201
Chiang Kai-shek, *see* Jiang Jieshi (Chiang Kai-shek)
Chicago, 300, 315, 386, 525–26, 529; gangsterism in, 703; New Immigrants to, 532–33; stockyards in, 563
Chicago, University of, 542
Chickasaw Indians, 257
Child-centered families, 330
Child labor, 292, 295, 635; antisweatshop laws for, 535
Child-rearing, 940
Chile, 596
China, 2, 596, 724; Boxer outrages in, 618–19; civil war in, 829–30; commercial trade with, 383; invasion by Japan of, 778; Korean War and, 836; nuclear

China (continued)
   bomb and, 868; Open Door policy in,
      617–19, 629; Yalta Conference and, 821
Chinese: federal restrictions against, 537;
   immigrants in California, 491
Chivington, J. M., 558
Choate, Joseph H., 585
Choctaw Indians, 257
Cholera epidemics, 339
Christians, "born-again," 942
Christian Science church, 539
Christmas Day, celebration of, 71
Churchill, Winston, 781, 788, 804, 807, 808,
   816; "Iron Curtain" speech of, 825;
   F. Roosevelt and, 788, 807, 816; at Yalta
   Conference, 820
Church of Christ, Scientist (Christian
   Science), 539, 705
Church of England (Anglican church), 22,
   23, 25, 30, 128; colonial America and,
   54–54
Church of Jesus Christ of Latter-Day Saints
   (Mormon church), 322–24
CIA: creation of, 828; Guatemala coup direc-
   ted by, 854; Iranian coup and, 849; plan
   to overthrow Castro, 864
Cigarettes, 521
Cincinnati, Ohio, 296
Circuses, 325, 553
Citadel, The (military academy), 351
Cities: economic inequalities of, 305; educa-
   tional facilities in, 540; effect on presi-
   dential politics of, 592; families and
   women in, 548–50; growth of, 314–16;
   immigrants and, 532–33; post–Civil War
   growth of, 529–32; social workers in,
   534–35; "white flight" from, 930. See
   also names of cities
City-manager system, 637
Civilian Conservation Corps (CCC), 751, 758
Civil rights, 870–72, 886; Eisenhower and,
   844, 845–46, 857; Johnson and, 870–72,
   879; J. Kennedy and, 865–66; Truman
   and, 832, 834
Civil Rights Act of 1875, 490
Civil Rights Act of 1964, 870, 938
Civil Rights Bill (1866), 465–66, 467
Civil Rights Commission, 846
Civil Service Commission, 494
Civil-service reform during the Arthur presidency, 494–95
Civil War, 355; blacks' participation in,
   422–23; casualties of, 454; Copperheadism during, 448–49; cost of, 454–55;
   cotton economy and, 423–24; Dred Scott
   decision and, 399–400; Emancipation
   Proclamation and, 430–32; European position toward, 415, 418, 419, 429, 432–34,
   436–37, 441–43; Fort Sumter and,
   416–17; influence of Uncle Tom's Cabin
   on, 392–93; Kansas-Nebraska Act and,
   387–88; Lee's surrender to Grant, 437;
   Mexican War as background for, 286–87;
   military campaigns of, 426–30, 432–37;
   mining of precious metals and, 563;
   Northern blockade of the Confederacy,

425–26; as supreme test of democracy,
   454–55; volunteers and draftees in,
   443–44
Civil War Legal Tender Act, 486n
Civil Works Administration (CWA), 752
Clark, George Rogers, 121, 125
Clark, William, 188
Class division, 522
Clay, Henry, 198, 314; Bank of the United
   States and, 253, 261; Compromise of
   1850 and, 375, 378; as leader of Whigs,
   261, 270, 271, 275, 278, 370; Missouri
   Compromise and, 219, 221; nationalism
   and, 214–15, 216; as presidential candi-
   date, 254–55; presidential election of
   1824 and, 234–36
Clayton Anti-Trust Act of 1914, 659–60
Clayton-Bulwer Treaty (1850), 383, 622
Clemenceau, Georges, 688, 689
Clemens, Samuel L., see Twain, Mark
Clermont (steamer), 299
Cleveland, Grover, 496–501, 578, 620; an-
   nexation of Hawaii and, 599–600; gold
   shortage and, 583–84; on immigration,
   537; Pullman strike and, 584–85; rail-
   roads and, 504–5, 512; revolution in
   Cuba and, 600; second presidency of,
   580, 582–87; silver issue and, 588; tariff
   bill and, 586; Venezuelan crisis and,
   597–98
Cleveland, Ohio, 300
Clinton, DeWitt, 299, 300
Clipper ships, 307–8
Closed shop, 526, 832
Clothing industry, 293
Coal mines, T. Roosevelt's Square Deal
   and, 639
Cobbett, William, 164
Cochran, Thomas, 455
Cody, William F. ("Buffalo Bill"), 553, 560
Cohan, George M., 676
Cohens v. Virginia (1821), 222
Coin's Financial School (William Hope
   Harvey), 587
Cold War, 822, 825–29, 834; Carter and, 900;
   Communist witch-hunt and, 832–34;
   Eisenhower and, 842; Korean War and,
   835–36; McCarthy and, 843–44; nuclear
   arms race and, 830; Truman and, 825–27
Collective bargaining, 754
Collective security, 741, 742
Colleges, 541–42; colonial, 67; liberal
   arts, 327
Collier's, 633, 635
Colombia, Panama Canal and, 622, 623
Colonial America: agriculture in, 59–60;
   clergy in, 58–59; committees of correspondence in, 98–99; culture in, 67–68;
   currency problems in, 91–92; education
   in, 48, 66–67; ethnic diversity of, 55–57;
   the Great Awakening in, 64–66; hardship of life in, 39–40; industry and commerce in, 59–62; intercolonial disunity
   in, 86; jurists (lawyers) in, 58–59; legislative systems of, 69–70; life-styles of,
   70–72, 324; mercantilism in, 92–93;

newspapers in, 69; physicians in, 58–59;
   population distribution in, 55; population
   growth in (1700–1775), 54; postal system in, 62; recruits in French and Indian War, 85–86; religion in, 62–66;
   slavery in, 14–15, 16, 42–45, 57, 58; social structure of, 45–48, 52, 57–58;
   strengths and weaknesses in Revolutionary War of, 104–6; thirteen original colonies of, 17; tobacco economy of, 40–41;
   transportation in, 62; women in, 39–40,
   46–47, 51, 61
Colorado, 188; mining in, 562–63; statehood
   of, 568
Colored Farmers' National Alliance, 582
Columbia College, 67
Columbian Exposition (1893), 552
Columbia River, 188, 276, 277, 278
Columbus, Christopher, 3–4, 7
"Combine" (reaper-thresher), 571
Coming of Post-Industrial Society, The
   (Daniel Bell), 943
Commerce and Labor, Department of,
   creation of, 639
Committee for Industrial Organization
   (CIO), 761, 762
Committee on Public Information, 676
Committee on Un-American Activities, 833
Committees of correspondence, 98–99
Committee to Defend America by Aiding the
   Allies, 782
Common Sense (Thomas Paine), 111, 112
Common Sense Book of Baby and Child
   Care, The (Benjamin Spock), 940
"Commonweal Army" of Coxeyites, 584
Commonwealth v. Hunt (1842), 296
Communal societies, 337–38
Communications: Atlantic cable, 306–7;
   Pony Express, 308; telegraphy, 293, 330
Communism: in China, 829–30; congressional
   witch-hunt for Communists, 833–34;
   in Cuba, 854; in Europe, 825–28; in
   Latin America, 872; McCarthy "crusade"
   against, 843–44; in Vietnam, 848–49
Communist party in the United States,
   697–98
Company town, 523
"Comparable worth," concept of, 939
Compromise of 1850 (Great Compromise),
   376–81, 386–87
Compromise of 1877, 489–90
Compulsory education, 540
Comstock, Anthony, 548
Comstock Law, 548
Comstock Lode, 563
Concentration camps, 812
Concord, Massachusetts, 103, 108
Conestoga wagons, 298
Confederacy (Confederate States of America):
   assets of, 418–19; blacks in Confederate
   army, 423; casualties of, 454; Davis as
   president of, 409, 411, 412, 424–25, 429,
   448; destroyer-raiders of, 441–42; eco-
   nomic blockade by North of, 425–26,
   434, 447; Emancipation Proclamation
   and, 432; European position toward, 418,

420, 421, 440, 441–42; financial aid for, 445–46; government weaknesses of, 424–25; handicaps of, 419–20; number of men in uniform (1861–1865), 444; secession from the Union and formation of, 408–9, 411–12; warships built by British for, 441–43

Confederate bonds, 445–46

Confederation: Congress of, 134–35; creation of, 131–32; economic instability under, 136–37; foreign relations and, 135–36

Confessions of Nat Turner, The (William Styron), 944

Congregationalists (Congregationalism), 63, 65, 128, 175, 319, 322; in colonial America, 63

Congress: Articles of Confederation and, 132–33; "Billion-Dollar" Congress, 579–80; civil rights legislation by, 846; of the Confederation, 134–35; Great Society program and, 869–70; Hoover presidency and, 740; Hundred Days Congress, 749–50, 751, 754, 756, 758; Kansas-Nebraska Act and, 387–88; League of Nations and, 689–92; National Banking System and, 445; neutrality legislation passed by, 777; official end of World War I and, 723; opposition to Vietnam War in, 874; Reconstruction and, 463, 465–70; Wilson and, 658, 660–61, 675–76

Congressional Committee on the Conduct of the War, 450

Congress of Industrial Organizations (CIO), 762–63; 1950 membership of, 832

Congress of Racial Equality (CORE), 798

Congress of Vienna (1814–1815), 206

Conkling, Roscoe, 487, 493–95

Connecticut, 136, 207; colonization of, 17, 27; established churches in (1775), 64; legislative system of, 69; state constitution for, 129

Conquistadores, 8–11

Conscription: during World War I, 681–82; during World War II, 782

Conservation of natural resources, 642–45, 650

Constitution: amendments to, 152–53; anti-federalists versus federalists and, 141–42; Articles of Confederation and, 131–34, 139; authority to interpret, 181–82, 247n; Bill of Rights of, 152–53, 155; central government under, 142; conservative safeguards in, 140–41; constitutional government and, 145–46; constitutional government and, 137–39; Crittenden Compromise and, 410, 418; drafting of, 129; Marshall on, 182; ratification of, 141–45; as a series of compromises, 139–40. *See also amendments to the Constitution*

Constitutional Convention, 137–39, 141

Constitutional Union party, 406

Constitution (superfrigate), 205

Continental Congress: First (1774), 101–3, 140; Second (1776), 108–9, 129, 138, 140

Contraction, 486

Convention of 1800, 171

Conwell, Russell, 518

Cooke, Jay, 485

Coolidge, Calvin, 693, 726–32; intervention in Central America by, 730; presidency of, 727–32; wartime debts and, 731

Cooper, James Fenimore, 212, 342

Copley, John S., 67

Copperhead Democrats (Copperheadism), 448–49, 450, 451, 452, 487

Coral Sea, Battle of, 802

Corbett, "Gentleman Jim," 553–54

CORE, 798

Cornbury, Lord, 70

Cornell University, 542

Corn (maize), 6, 7, 296

Cornwallis, Gen. Charles, 121, 122

Coronado, Francisco, 8

Corporations, Bureau of, 639

Corrupt-practices acts, 636

Cortés, Hernando, 9

Cosmopolitan, 633, 634

Cott, Nancy, 331

Cotton, 194; cotton gin and, 290, 292, 349; foreign trade and, 306; importance to British economy of, 290, 350, 423, 426; importance to the North's economy of, 349–50, 353; importance to the South's economy of, 290, 291, 349–50, 352, 353; machinery for fiber spinning, 290; New England textile factories and, 291–92; tariffs and, 238

Cotton, John, 25

Cotton-boll weevil, 572

Cotton gin, 290, 292, 349

Cotton mills, 522

Cotton Stabilization Board, 734

Coughlin, Father, 752

"Counterblast to Tobacco, A," 13

Country dances, 324

Couples (John Updike), 944

Covered wagons, 298; average rate of progress of, 277n

Cowboys, 565

Cox, Archibald, 891

Cox, James M., 693, 694

Coxey, "General" Jacob S., 584

Crane, Stephen, 547

Crawford, William H., 234, 235

Credit: buying on, 706; overexpansion of, 736

Crédit Mobilier Construction Company, 506, 510; scandal involving, 483, 492

Creek Indians, 7, 257

Creel, George, 676

CREEP, 889

Cresswell, Nicholas, 95

Crèvecoeur, Michel de, 55

Crime: automobiles and, 709; gangsterism and, 702–3

Crimean War, 335, 383, 384

Crimes of violence, 325

Criminal codes, 334

Crittenden, Sen. John J., 410, 418

Crittenden Compromise (1860), 410–11, 418

Croats, immigration of, 532

Crockett, Davy, 231, 258, 259

Croly, Herbert, 654

Cromwell, Oliver, 16

Croquet, 554

Crusades, 2

Cuba, 84, 383–84, 615, 648, 774; Bay of Pigs invasion, 864; independence of, 612; invasion of, 605–7, 626; missile crisis in, 864; revolution in, 600, 854; sugar production in, 500; troops to Africa from, 896

Cultural Contradictions of Capitalism, The (Daniel Bell), 943

Culture, post-1960s, 942–43

Cumberland Road (National Road), 218, 298–99

Cunningham, Noble E., 195

Currency: elastic, 658, 659; emergency, 645

Cushman, Charlotte, 325

Custer, George A., 558–59

Customs duties, 154–55

CWA, 752

Cyanide process for gold mining, 593

Cylindrical printing presses, 330

Czechoslovakia, 827; occupation of, 779

Da Gama, Vasco, 4

Daguerre, Louis, 341

Daisy Miller (Henry James), 547

Daley, Richard, 877

Dancing: in colonial America, 71; country dances, 324

Darrow, Clarence, 705

Dartmouth College, 66, 67

Dartmouth College v. *Woodward* (1819), 223

Darwin, Charles, 539–40

Darwinian evolution, 704–5

Darwinism, 539–40, 596

Daugherty, Harry M., 721

Daughters of Liberty, 96

Daughters of the American Revolution, 535

David Copperfield (Charles Dickens), 543

Davis, David, 489

Davis, Jefferson, 257, 350, 382, 383–85; imprisonment and pardoning of, 457–58; Lincoln's assassination and, 453; as president of the Confederacy, 409, 411, 412, 424–25, 429, 448

Davis, John W., 729

Dawes, Charles, 731

Dawes Plan of 1924, 731

Dawes Severalty Act of 1887, 501, 562

Day-care centers, 549

"Day of Doom" (Michael Wigglesworth), 25

D-Day invasion of France, 808–9

Dean, James, 941

Dean, John, III, 890

Death of a Salesman (Arthur Miller), 945

Debs, Eugene V., 584–85, 646, 656, 677, 694

Debt, national: Eisenhower presidency and, 847; Hamilton and, 153–54; 1914–1921, 717–18; 1932–1939; 767; 1939–1945, 768

Debts, wartime, Coolidge and, 731
Decatur, Stephen, 213
Declaration of Independence, 112–13, 115,
    118; ethnicity of signers of, 57; slavery
    and, 128
Declaration of Rights, 102
Declaration of the Rights of Man (French),
    113
Declaratory Act (1766), 96
Deere, John, 296
Deflation, grain farmers and, 571–73
De Gaulle, Charles, 862, 873
Deism, 320
Delaney, Martin, 363
Delaware, 417; colonization of, 17, 36; estab-
    lished churches in (1775), 64; legislative
    system of, 69
Delaware River, 36
De la Warr, Lord, 36
Delinquency, juvenile, 637
De Lôme, Dupuy, 601
Democracy: as the people's politics, 231–32;
    social, 314
Democracy in America (Alexis de Tocque-
    ville), 314
Democratic Jacksonianism, see Jacksonian
    Democrats
Democratic party, 266; anti-Lincoln faction
    in, 450; Dred Scott decision and, 400;
    1852 presidential election and, 381–82;
    1860 presidential election and, 405–6,
    407; ethnic and cultural difference
    between Republicans and, 486–88;
    evolution of, 161; Manifest Destiny and,
    278, 279; philosophy and policy of,
    267–68; presidential election of 1912
    and, 653, 654–55; the silver issue (1896)
    and, 588, 589
Democratic Republicans, see Jeffersonian
    Republicans
Demographics, see Population
Dempsey, Jack, 706
Denmark, 781
Depressions: of the 1890s, 514, 582,
    592–93; panic of 1819, 217, 221; panic
    of 1837, 263, 273; panic of 1857, 401
Desert Land Act of 1877, 642
De Soto, Hernando, 8–9
Destroyers for lend-lease convoys, 788–89
Détente, 885, 912; Helsinki accords and,
    895–96; J. Kennedy's policy of, 864
Detroit, 300, 707; race riots in, 871
Dewey, George, 604–5, 612
Dewey, John, 703–4
Dewey, Thomas E., 783, 810, 811, 834–35
Dial, The (transcendentalist journal), 337
Diaz, Bartholomeu, 4
Dickens, Charles, 273, 295
Dickinson, Emily, 545
Dictionaries, 327
Didion, Joan, 944
Diem, 863
Dien Bien Phu, 848
Dime novels, 545
Dingley Tariff Bill, 592
Diphtheria, 59

Diplomacy, dollar, 647–48
Disarmament, Harding presidency and,
    723–25
Discrimination, "reverse," 936
District of Columbia, see Washington, D.C.
"Divorce Bill," 263–64
Divorces, 548, 549, 940
Dix, Dorothea, 334
Doctorow, E. L., 945
Doheny, Edward L., 726
Dollar diplomacy, 647–48, 661
Domestic feminism, 329–30
Dominican Republic, 624, 648, 730, 872;
    marines sent to aid, 662
Dominion of New England (1686–1689), 29,
    140
Donald, David H., 347
Donnelly, Ignatius, 575
"Double-digit" inflation, 900
Douglas, Stephen A., 375, 378, 386–87, 395,
    397, 400, 450, 467; 1860 presidential
    election and, 405–7; Lincoln debates
    with, 402–4
Douglass, Frederick, 477; abolitionism and,
    356, 362–64; blacks in Union armies
    and, 422; on Reconstruction wrongs to
    blacks, 477
"Doves," 884
Dow, Neal S., 335
Drake, Francis, 11, 13
"Drake's Folly" (first oil well—Pennsylvania),
    517
Dred Scott decision (1857), 182n, 399–400
Dreiser, Theodore, 548, 632, 715
Drunkenness, 335–36
"Dry" farming, 568
"Dry" laws, 638–39
Du Bois, W. E. B., 478, 541
Dueling, 325; southern tradition of, 351
Duke, James Buchanan, 521
Duke University, 521
Dulles, John Foster, 847, 850, 851; Suez cri-
    sis and, 849; Vietnam policy of, 848
Dumbbell tenements, 531–32
Dunkirk, evacuation of British army from, 781
Dunning, William A., 478
Dutch East India Company, 30
Dutch East Indies, 795, 801
Dutch immigrants, 56
Dutchman (LeRoi Jones/Imamu Amiri Ba-
    raka), 944
Dutch Reformed church, 21; in colonial
    America, 63
Dutch West India Company, 31
Duty of Civil Disobedience, On the (Henry
    David Thoreau), 343
Duvalier, "Baby Doc," 919
Dwight, Timothy, 175
Dysentery, 39

Eagleton, Thomas, 888
Eakins, Thomas, 552
Earp, Wyatt, 565n
East Germany, 824–25
Eastman, George, 551
Eaton, John Henry, 235

Economics, "supply-side," 911, 917
Economics and the Public Purpose (John
    Kenneth Galbraith), 943
Economy: Carter and, 900–901; challenges
    to, 926–29; during 1970s, 924–25; Ei-
    senhower and, 846–47; mass-consump-
    tion, 705–6; new patterns in, 925–26;
    "no-growth," 947; post–World War II
    boom in, 921–24; prosperity of the
    1920s, 705–6, 717–18; World War II
    and, 799–801
Eddy, Mary Baker, 539
Edison, Thomas A., 513, 552, 711
Education: for blacks, 540–41; in colonial
    America, 48, 66–67; compulsory, 540;
    critical appraisal of American educational
    system, 852; elective system for, 542–43;
    German immigrants' influence on, 318;
    GI Bill of Rights and, 831; higher educa-
    tion, 327–28; influence of journalism on,
    330; levels of, 542; in the 1920s, 703–5;
    post–Civil War spread of, 540–43; public,
    540; public schools, 325–27; Roman
    Catholic system of, 319; school desegre-
    gation, 845–46, 870; segregation and,
    936; after World War II, 924, 943. See
    also names of colleges and universities
Education of Henry Adams, The (Henry Ad-
    ams), 480
Edwards, Jonathan, 65
Edward VI, King, 13
Egypt, Suez crisis in, 849–50. See also Mid-
    dle East
Eighteenth Amendment (1919), 141, 551,
    639, 680, 701
Eight-hour day, 524
Einstein, Albert, 814, 830
Eisenhower, Dwight D., 816, 834, 837–39;
    Camp David meeting with Khrushchev,
    853; civil rights movement and, 844,
    845–46, 857; Cold War and, 842; D-Day
    invasion and, 808–9; economic policies
    under, 846–47; foreign policy under,
    847–50; Korean War and, 839; labor leg-
    islation of, 851–52; McCarthy and,
    843–44; North African campaign and,
    806–7; presidency of, 842–57; quoted,
    842; space race and, 852; Vietnam policy
    of, 848; warning of "military-industrial"
    complex, 848, 857
Eisenhower Doctrine, 850, 852
El Alamein, 805
El Salvador, 914
Elastic currency, 658, 659
Election, presidential: of 1800, 174–76;
    of 1816, 215–16; of 1820, 221; of 1824,
    234–36; of 1828, 239–41; of 1832,
    253, 254–55; of 1836, 261–62; of 1840,
    264–66; of 1844, 278–79; of 1848,
    369–71; of 1852, 381–82; of 1856,
    397–98, 402; of 1860, 405–8; of 1864,
    450–52; of 1868, 480–81; of 1872,
    484–85; of 1876, 488–90; of 1884,
    495–97; of 1888, 500–501; of 1896, 587,
    590–92; of 1900, 619–20; of 1908, 646;
    of 1912, 653, 654–55; of 1916, 669–71;

of 1920, 693–94; of 1924, 729–30; of 1928, 732–33; of 1932, 745, 746–48; of 1936, 763–64; of 1940, 783–85; of 1944, 809–10; of 1948, 834–35; of 1952, 837–39; of 1956, 850–51; of 1960, 854–57; of 1964, 867–69; of 1968, 877–78; of 1972, 887–88; of 1976, 898–99; of 1980, 906–9; of 1984, 915–17

Elective system of education, 542–43
Electoral College, 140, 141
Electoral Count Act (1877), 489
Electric elevator, 529
Electricity, 529–30
Electric light, 513
Electric trolleys, 530
Elevator, electric, 529
Eliot, Charles W., 543
Eliot, T. S., 716
Elizabeth I, Queen, 11, 13
Elkins, Stanley, 367
Elkins Act of 1903, 639
Ellison, Ralph, 944
Ellsberg, Daniel, 884
Emancipation Proclamation (1863), 423, 430–31; public reaction to, 431–32
Embargo Act (1807), 192–94
Emergency Banking Relief Act of 1933, 750
Emergency currency, 645
Emergency Quota Act of 1921, 699–700
Emerson, Ralph Waldo, 103, 289, 311, 313, 314, 318, 333, 342–43, 373, 405; on immigrant labor, 513; on Quakers, 36; on slavery, 349, 376, 380, 387–88
Empey, Guy, 698
Empire State Building, 716
Empress of China (frigate), 130
Energy, Department of, 899
Energy, low-cost, 923
Energy crisis, 892–93; Carter and, 901–2
England, *see* Great Britain
Episcopalians, 128, 322
Equal Rights Amendment (ERA), 939; in the 1920s, 714
"Era of Good Feelings," 216, 217, 221
Erie Canal, 215, 299–300; railroads and, 302
Ervin, Sam, 889–90
Esch-Cummins Transportation Act of 1920, 722
Escobedo case, 886
Espionage Act of 1917, 677
Ether, 340
Ethiopia, 777
Ethnic pride, 934–35
European Common Market, 862
Evans, Hiram Wesley, 704
Everett, Edward, 340–41
Evers, Medgar, 866
Everybody's, 633, 634
Evolution, 539; teaching of, 704–5
Excess-profits tax, 718
Excise tax, 155, 156; repeal of, 181
Ex parte Milligan (1866), 469

Fabian socialism, 544
Factory system, 292–93; discipline of labor

in, 522; labor problems of, 194–96; workers' benefits (1805), 295–96, 306
Fad diets, 333
Fairchild, Henry P., 701
Fair Deal program, 835
Fair Employment Practices Commission, 798–99, 845
Fair Labor Standards Act (Wages and Hours Bill), 762
Fall, Albert B., 721, 726
Fallen Timbers, Battle of (1794), 166
"Fall of the House of Usher, The" (Edgar Allan Poe), 345
Falmouth, Massachusetts, 111
Families: black slave, 360; changes in (1790–1860), 328–30; in colonial America, 70–72; decline of, 940; in New England, 46–47
FAO (Food and Agriculture Organization), 823
Farmers, 925–26; deflation and, 572–73; "dry," 568; Grange and, 573–75; Great Depression and, 737; Homestead Act of 1862 and, 566–67; Hoover presidency and, 734; natural and business problems faced by, 572–73; 1920s boom-or-bust cycle for, 728–29; 1933 drought and, 757–58; the Populists and, 575–76; F. Roosevelt presidency and, 756–58; tenant, 572; western boom in farming, 567–68
Farmers' Alliance, 575, 580
Farming, *see* Agriculture
Farragut, David G., 434, 451
Fascist party, 776
Faubus, Orval, 845–46
Faulkner, William, 716, 944
Federal Deposit Insurance Corporation, 750
Federal Emergency Relief Act, 751
Federal Emergency Relief Administration (FERA), 751
Federal Farm Board, 734
Federal Farm Loan Act of 1916, 660
Federal Housing Administration (FHA), 760
Federalist, The (Alexander Hamilton, John Jay, and James Madison), 145, 153, 341
Federalists, 141–42, 157, 158; anti-Jefferson campaign of, 174–75; decline of, 177, 215–16; Hamilton and, 169; Jefferson presidency and, 180, 181; Louisiana Purchase and, 187, 189; War of 1812 and, 200–201
Federal Reserve Act of 1913, 645, 659
Federal Reserve Board, 659
"Federal Reserve notes," 659
Federal Reserve System, 264
Federal Securities Act, 758
Federal Trade Commission Act of 1914, 659
Feminine Mystique, The (Betty Friedan), 938
Feminism, 938–40
FERA, 751
Ferdinand, King, 4
Ferraro, Geraldine, 915
FHA, 760
Fields, Cyrus, 306–7
Fifteenth Amendment (1870), 469, 470, 473

Fifth Amendment, 400
Fifth party system, 592*n*
Fillmore, Millard, 378, 381, 397
Finland, invasion of, 781
Finney, Charles Grandison, 321, 361
Fire Next Time, The (James Baldwin), 944
Fireside chats, 750
First Amendment, 172
First Continental Congress (1774), 101–3, 140
First party system, 592*n*
Fish, Hamilton, 483
Fisheries, 224
Fishing, in colonial America, 60
Fisk, Jim, 481–82
Fitzgerald, F. Scott, 715
Five-Power Naval Treaty of 1922, 724
Flappers, 713, 714
Fletcher v. Peck (1810), 223
Flogging, of slaves, 359
Flophouses, 532
Florida, 84; Pinckney Treaty and, 167; Reconstruction in, 470, 471; slavery in, 357; as a Spanish colony, 17, 199, 224–25
Florida Purchase Treaty of 1819, 225, 276
Flour-milling processes, 567
Foch, Marshal, 683
Football, 553
Foraker Act of 1900, 611
Forbes, Charles R., 726
Force Acts (1870–1871), 473–74
Force Bill (1833), 252
Ford, Gerald R., 890; foreign affairs under, 895–96; inflation and, 895; loss to Carter, 898–99; *Mayaguez* incident and, 897; pardon of Nixon by, 895
Ford, Henry, 705–7
Fordney-McCumber Act of 1922, 725, 734
Foreign policy: of Carter, 899–900, 902–4; of Coolidge, 730–31; of Eisenhower, 847–50; of Ford, 895–96; of J. Kennedy, 862–64; in the late nineteenth century, 595–96; of Nixon, 882–86; of Reagan, 912–15, 918–19; of F. Roosevelt, 772–74; of Wilson, 661–65
Foreign trade, 306–7, 522; with China and Japan, 383; in colonial America, 60; embargoes and, 192–94, 197
Forest Reserve Act of 1891, 642
Formisano, Ronald, 268
Formosa (Taiwan), 829, 850
Forrest, Edwin, 325
Fort Donelson, 433
Fort Duquesne, 81–83
Fort Henry, 433
For the Union Dead (Robert Lowell), 945
Fort McHenry, 203
Fort Malden, 202
Fort Michilimackinac, 202
Fort Necessity, 82
Fort Sumter, 416–17
Fort Ticonderoga, 117
Foster, Stephen C., 341
"Fourteen Points" address, 675–76, 685–86
Fourteenth Amendment (1868), 466, 467, 469, 470, 473, 518

Fourth party system, 592n
France, 3; J. Adams presidency and, 169–72; American Revolutionary War and, 118–19, 122; Civil War and, 440, 441, 443; colonial war in Indochina of, 848–49; colonial wars with Britain, 78–79; colonization of Canada by, 74–78, 86; the Confederation and, 136; embargo on goods shipped to, 192–94, 197; French and Indian War and, 82, 83–84, 86; Jay's treaty with Britain and, 169; mercantilism and, 93; Napoleonic War, 79, 190; religious persecution in, 74; Texas war for independence and, 275; in World War I, 664–65, 682–83; in World War II, 780–82
Franco, Francisco, 777
Franco-American Treaty of 1778, 164, 168, 169
Franklin, Benjamin, 37, 65, 82–83, 104, 105, 113, 142; on J. Adams, 150; American Revolutionary War and, 114, 118; the Confederation and, 136; Constitutional Convention and, 139, 141; education and, 67, 69; quoted, 7, 58, 93; on religion, 64; scientific achievements of, 68; Treaty of Paris and, 123; writings of, 58, 68, 341
Franklin, William, 114
Frazier-Lemke Farm Bankruptcy Act of 1934, 758
Frederick the Great, 82
Freed blacks, 355–56
Freedmen's Bureau, 460–61, 465, 467
"Free incorporation" statutes, 293
Free love, 548
Freeport Doctrine, 405
Free-silver issue, 580, 588–91, 593, 611
"Free-soilers," 366, 388
Free-Soil party, 364, 370, 371
Frémont, John C., 284, 397–98
French and Indian War, 79, 81–86, 87
French Canal Company, 622
French Revolution, 79, 160, 226; impact of, 163–64
Freud, Sigmund, 714
Friedan, Betty, 938
From Here to Eternity (James Jones), 944
Frontier: preachers, 321–22; as symbol of opportunity, 569–70; wrestling, 312
Frost, Robert, 716
Fugitive Slave Law (1850), 375, 379–81, 382, 387, 391, 392
Fulbright, William, 874
Fuller, Margaret, 337
Fulton, Robert, 299
Fundamentalists, 539; progressive education and, 704–5
Fundamental Orders, 27
"Funding at par," 153
Fur trade, 76–77, 78

Gaddis, John L., 840
Gadsden, James, 385, 386
Gadsden Purchase (1853), 385

Galbraith, John Kenneth, 943
Gallatin, Albert, 181
Gambling, 313–14, 325
Gandhi, Mohandas, 343, 865
Gangsters, 702–3
GAR, see Grand Army of the Republic (GAR)
Garfield, James A., 301, 491–93, 502
Garland, Hamlin, 552
Garrison, William Lloyd, 380; abolitionism and, 362–64, 366
Gasoline engine, 706–7; aviation industry and, 709
Gasoline rationing, 795
Gates, Gen. Horatio, 118
Genêt, Citizen (Edmond Charles), 165, 168
General Federation of Women's Clubs, 550
General Incorporation Law (1848), 293
General Motors Corporation, 926
Genetic engineering, 296
Genovese, Eugene, 367
George, David Lloyd, 688
George, Henry, 525, 544
George I, King, 79
George II, King, 18, 79
George III, King, 68, 79, 150, 314; American colonies and, 96, 98, 103, 104; American Revolutionary War and, 110, 112, 113, 115, 122, 123, 125
Georgia, 90, 121, 136; colonization of, 17, 18–19; established churches in (1775), 64; eviction of Cherokee Indians from, 237; plantation economy of, 19; Reconstruction in, 470; Sherman's invasion of, 434–35; slavery in, 140
Germain, Lord George, 123
German-Americans, World War I hate hysteria against, 677, 680
German immigrants, 315, 318; in colonial America, 55; from 1860 to 1866, 421; influence on education of, 318
Germantown, Battle of (1777), 118
Germany: Allied partition of, 823–25; invasion of Soviet Union by, 805–6; Monroe Doctrine and, 227; rise of Hitler in, 775–76, 779; in World War I, 664, 665–69, 673–75, 682, 683–86; World War I reparation payments from, 731–32; in World War II, 811–12
Geronimo, 559
Gettysburg, Battle of (1863), 436
Ghent, Treaty of (1815), 206, 208, 209
Gibbons, Cardinal, 538
Gibbons v. Ogden (1842), 222
GI Bill of Rights, 831, 924
Gideon v. Wainwright (1963), 886
Gilbert, Felix, 177
Gilbert, Humphrey, 11, 13
Gilbert Islands, 803
Gilded Age, 486
Gilded Age, The (Mark Twain and Charles Dudley Warner), 546
Gilman, Charlotte Perkins, 549
Ginsberg, Allen, 941
Gladden, Washington, 534
Glass-Steagall Banking Reform Act, 750
Glidden, Joseph F., 568

Glorious (or Bloodless) Revolution (Great Britain—1688–1689), 30
Godey's Lady's Book, 328
Godkin, Edwin L., 544
Goethals, George Washington, 624
Goetz, Bernhard, 931
Gold, discovery in California of, 372
Gold mining, 562–63; new process for, 593
Gold reserve, 583–84; F. Roosevelt presidency and, 750–51
Gold Standard Act (1900), 593
Goldwater, Barry, 867–69, 872
Gompers, Samuel, 526, 610, 660, 678
Goodbye, Columbus (Philip Roth), 944
Good Neighbor policy, 774
Goodwyn, Lawrence, 594
Gorbachev, Mikhail, 917
Gordon, N. P., 356
Gorgas, William C., 624
Gorges, Sir Ferdinando, 27
Göring, Hermann, 816, 823
Gould, Jay, 481–82, 511, 523
Grady, Henry W., 521
Graham, Otis, 651
Graham, Sylvester, 333
Grain farmers, 571–72
Grain Stabilization Corporation, 734
Gramm-Rudman-Hollings Act (1986), 917
Grand Army of the Republic (GAR), 487, 499, 580
Grand Canyon, 8
Grand Coulee Dam, 756
Granger Laws, 574–75
Grant, Ulysses S.: Civil War and, 419, 432–34, 436–37; election of, 480–81; Mexican War and, 286; presidency of, 483–86, 502
Grapes of Wrath, The (John Steinbeck), 758
Grasse, Admiral de, 122
Grasshoppers, 572
Gray, Asa, 338
Gray, Robert, 276–77
Great Awakening, 64–66. See also Second Great Awakening
Great Britain, 3; American destroyers transferred to, 783; American lend-lease to, 785–89; American Revolutionary War and, 103–4, 115–25; Caroline affair and, 273, 274; Civil War and, 419, 432–34, 436–37, 441–43; civil wars in, 16; claims to Oregon Country by, 276–78, 280, 283; Clayton-Bulwer Treaty and, 383; colonial exports to, 61–62; colonial wars with France, 78–79; colonial wars with Spain, 79–80; the Confederation and, 135–36; cotton economy and, 290, 350, 423, 426; defeat of the Spanish Armada by, 11; early colonization attempts by, 11; Emancipation Proclamation and, 431; embargo on goods shipped to, 192–94, 197; French and Indian War and, 82–86; Glorious Revolution in, 30; government of colonies by, 90; immigration from (1860–1877), 421; impressment of American seaman by, 191–92; industrial revolution in, 289; law of primogeniture

in, 12–13; literary war with, 273; Maine boundary dispute with, 273–74; mercantilism and, 90–93; Monroe Doctrine and, 228; Napoleonic War and, 190; naval blockade of Atlantic coast by, 205; Navigation Laws of, 29, 30, 91, 92, 94, 99, 130, 135; New World empire of, 12, 13–19; Orders in Council of, 190, 191, 194, 200; Reform Bill of 1867 in, 455; rivalry with Spain of, 11–12; seizure of merchant ships by, 166; Seven Years' War and, 94; Stuart dynasty in, 29; Texas war for independence and, 275; trade with Latin America and, 226–27; Treaty of 1818 with, 224; Tudor dynasty in, 13; Venezuelan crisis and, 597–98; War of 1812 and, 202–6, 207, 208; in World War II, 664–65, 780, 781, 805

Great Depression, 736–39; causes of, 736–37; World War I veterans and, 740–41

Great Lakes, 124, 299–301, 514; canal system and, 301; St. Lawrence waterway project and, 857; War of 1812 and, 202, 209

Great Northern Railroad, 508

Great Society program, 867–70

Great White Fleet, 629

Greece, 825–26, 829; emigration from, 532

Greeley, Horace, 330, 484–85

Greenback Labor party, 486, 575, 631

Green Berets, 862

Greene, Gen. Nathanael, 121

Greenstein, Fred, 858

Greenville, Treaty of (1795), 166

Grenada, 914–15

Grenville, George, 94–95

Griffith, D. W., 711

Grimké, Sarah and Angelina, 337

Gross national product (GNP), 799

Grundy, Felix, 199

Guadalcanal Island, 802

Guadalupe Hidalgo, Treaty of (1848), 285, 369

Guam, 608, 801, 804

Guatemala, CIA-directed coup in, 854

Guerrilla warfare, 615

Guiteau, Charles J., 493

Gulf of Mexico, 78, 135

Gullah (black universal language), 44

Gunboats, 184

Gustavus Adolphus, King, 33

Gutman, Herbert, 367, 527

Gutter journalism, 330

Haiti, 648, 730, 774; Duvalier ouster, 919; treaty with, 662, 742

Hale, Edward Everett, 449

"Half-Way Covenant," 49

Hall, Basil, 353

Halsey, Harlan F., 545

Halsey, William F., 813

Hamilton, Alexander, 131, 165, 168, 290; Constitutional Convention and, 137, 138; the Constitution and, 144; death of, 189; as head of army, 171; Jefferson presidency and, 176; Monroe Doctrine and, 229; political antagonism toward, 158–59; quoted, 149; as secretary of the treasury, 151–56, 167

Hamilton, Andrew, 69

Hamiltonian Federalists, 158, 163

Hammond, Sen. James H., 410

Hancock, John, 92, 103, 138

Hancock, Winfield S., 492

Handy, W. C., 714

Hanna, Marcus Alonzo (Mark), 587–88, 590, 603, 609, 619

Harding, Warren G., 693–94, 720–26; death of, 726; presidency of, 721–26; quoted, 697; scandals in administration of, 726

"Hard-money" policy, 486

Harper's, 544

Harpers Ferry, John Brown's raid on, 404–5

Harrison, Benjamin, 500–501, 578–82

Harrison, William Henry, 261, 264–66, 500; as Indian fighter, 199, 202, 209, 218; presidency of, 270–71, 272

Hart, Gary, 915

Harte, Bret, 547, 563

Hartford Convention (1814), 206–8

Harvard College, 10, 48, 67, 543

Harvey, William Hope, 587

Hatch Act of 1887, 541

Hatch Act of 1939, 766

Havana Conference (1940), 782

Hawaii, 622; annexation of, 599–600, 605, 610; statehood for, 857; sugar production in, 599

"Hawks," 884

Hawley-Smoot Tariff of 1930, 734, 736, 775

Hawthorne, Nathaniel, 345–46

Hay, John, 612, 617–18

Hayes, Lucy Webb, 490

Hayes, Rutherford B., 488, 489–91, 502

Haymarket Square bombing, 525

Hayne, Robert Y., 246–47

Hays, Samuel P., 651

Hays, Will H., 712

Haywood, William D. ("Big Bill"), 677

"H-bomb" (hydrogen bomb), 830

Hearst, William Randolph, 544, 595, 601, 663

Hebrew schools, 533

Heller, Joseph, 944

Helper, Hinton R., 393

Helsinki accords (1975), 895–96

Hemingway, Ernest, 546, 715, 943–44

Henry, Patrick, 114, 138, 144, 146

Henry Street Settlement, 535

Henry VII, King, 13

Henry VIII, King, 13, 22

Hepburn Act of 1906, 639–40

Herter, Christian A., 851

Herzog (Saul Bellow), 945

Hessian soldiers, 103, 110

Hiawatha, 7

Hickok, James B. ("Wild Bill"), 563–64

Hicks, John D., 594, 743

High schools, 540

High-technology industries, 926

Highways, 708; interstate, 847

Hill, James J., 508, 640

Hirohito, Emperor, 815

Hiroshima, Japan, 814

Hispanics, 934

Hiss, Alger, 833

Historians, 346–47

Hitler, Adolf, 694, 726, 735, 773, 775–76, 781; Allied strategy for defeat of, 792; appeasement of, 779; German invasion of Russia and, 787–88; halting of, 804–6, 811–12; suicide of, 812

Ho Chi Minh, 848

Hoe, Richard, 330

Hoffa, James R., 851

Hofstadter, Richard, 594, 651, 770

HOLC, 752

Holidays, in colonial America, 71

Hollywood, 711–12

Holmes, Dr. Oliver Wendell, 340, 345

Holt, Michael, 268, 269

Home Owners' Loan Corporation (HOLC), 752

Homer, Winslow, 552

Homestead Act of 1862, 447, 465, 565–67

Homesteaders, 565; loss of frontier lands, 569, 570; Oklahoma Territory opened to, 568

Homestead plant strike, 581

Honduras, 648

Hone, Philip, 256, 263, 296

Hong Kong, 801

Hooker, "Fighting Joe," 435

Hooker, Rev. Thomas, 27

Hoover, Herbert, 732–43; campaign of 1932 and, 745, 747–48; Great Depression and, 737–39; Latin American policy of, 742–43; Manchurian crisis and, 741–42; presidency of, 734–43; public works spending by, 739–40; quoted, 720; as secretary of commerce, 721, 722, 733; stock-market crash and, 735; in World War I, 680

Hoover Dam, 739–40

Hoover-Stimson Doctrine (1932), 742

Hopkins, Harry L., 751–52, 754

Hopkinson, Francis, 144

Horizontal integration, 514

Horse racing, 325

Horseshoe Bend, Battle of, 203

House Made of Dawn (N. Scott Momaday), 944

House of Burgesses (Virginia), 15, 45, 99

House of Representatives: the Constitution and, 139–41; slavery and, 365; vote on Tariff of 1828 and, 237; vote on Tariff of 1832 and, 251; vote on Tariff of 1833 and, 252; vote on Tariff of 1846 and, 279; War of 1812 and, 199, 200. *See also* Congress

Housing Act of 1949, 835

Housing and Urban Development, Department of (HUD), 869

Housing construction, 760

Houston, Sam, 259, 260

Howard, Oliver O., 461
Howard University, 461
Howe, Elias, 292
Howe, Gen. William, 116, 117
Howells, William Dean, 547, 714
How the Other Half Lives (Jacob A. Riis), 632
Hudson, Henry, 30–31
Hudson River, 36, 299
Hudson River school of painting, 341
Hudson's Bay Company, 276, 280
Hughes, Charles Evans, 637, 669–71, 721, 724
Hughes, Langston, 716
Huguenots, 21, 56, 74
Hull, Cordell, 774
Hull House, 535
Human rights, Carter and, 899–900
Humboldt's Gift (Saul Bellow), 945
Humphrey, Hubert H., 877–79
Hungary, 824; freedom fighters' uprising in, 847–48, 849
Huron Indians, 74
Hutchinson, Anne, 26, 27
Hydrogen bomb ("H-bomb"), 830

IBM, 926
ICC. *See* Interstate Commerce Commission (ICC)
Ickes, Harold L., 755, 756
Idaho, statehood of, 568
Illinois, 121
Illinois State Journal, 397
IMF, 822, 827
Immigrants: British, 56, 421; Chinese, 491; Dutch, 56; federal restrictions on, 536–37; French, 56; frontier farmland and, 570; German, 53, 56, 315, 318, 421; industrial exploitation of, 506, 513; Irish, 56, 315, 316–18, 421; Jewish, 56, 63; 1900–1914, 631; post–Civil War increase of, 532–33; Scotch, 56; social reformers and, 534–35; from southern Europe, 533–34; Swiss, 56; Welsh, 56
Immigration: African immigrants, 56; Alien Laws and, 172; antiforeignism against, 319–20; effect of slavery on, 353; from 1840s and 1850s, 316; from 1861 to 1866, 421–22; during 1970s and 1980s, 933–34; quota system of the 1920s, 699–701
Immigration Act of 1924, 699
Impending Crisis of the South, The (Hinton R. Helper), 393
Imperialism, 595–96; as issue in 1900 presidential campaign, 619–20; McKinley and, 610–11; T. Roosevelt and, 621–23
Imprisonment for debt, 334
Incas, 6
Income tax, 586; establishment of, 445; graduated, 658
Indentured servants, 15–16, 40–41, 58
Independent, The (religious journal), 398
Independent Treasury Bill (1840), 263–64
India, 2

Indian Affairs, Bureau of, 257
Indian Reorganization Act (1934), 562
Indians, American, 6–7; American Revolutionary War and, 121; as barrier to white pioneers in West, 557–58; British colonists and, 166; the Confederation and, 136; effect of Old World diseases on, 7–8; ethnic pride of, 935; federal policies for, 561–62; forcible removal west of the Mississippi River of, 256–58; French colonization and, 75–76; Jamestown and, 14; loss of territories by, 209, 217–18; missionary work among, 66, 77; resistance against settlers by, 198–99; warfare between whites and, 558–59. *See also names of Indian tribes*
Indian Territory, 257
Indochina, French colonial war in, 848
Industrialists, immigrant labor for, 533
Industrialization: after Civil War, 513; economic impact of, 522; labor unions and, 523–27; railroad networks and, 510; in the South, 520–22; women and, 522
Industrial revolution, 289
Industrial Workers of the World (IWWs), 677, 679, 698
Industry: automobile, new businesses created by, 708–9; Harding presidency and, 722; high-technology, 926; F. Roosevelt presidency and, 754–56
Inflation, 130; "double-digit," 900; Ford and, 895; oil crisis and, 924; during seventies, 887, 892–93
Influence of Sea Power upon History, 1660–1783, The (Alfred Thayer Mahan), 596
Ingersoll, Robert G., 540
Inness, George, 552
Insanity, treatment for, 334
Installment-plan buying, 708, 736
Institutes of the Christian Religion (John Calvin), 21
Insull, Samuel, 759
Integration, vertical, 514
Interchangeable parts, principle of, 292
International Bank for Reconstruction and Development (World Bank), 822–23, 827
International Business Machines Corporation (IBM), 926
International Monetary Fund (IMF), 822, 827
Interstate Commerce Act (1887), 501, 512–13, 520
Interstate Commerce Commission (ICC), 512, 639–40, 722
Interstate highways, 847
"Intolerable Acts" (1774), 100–102
Inventions, patents issued for, 513
Invisible Man (Ralph Ellison), 944
Iran, 825; CIA-backed coup in, 849; hostage crisis in, 903–4; Pahlevi, Shah Mohammed Reza and, 849, 901; revolution in (1979), 901
Iraq, 688
Irish immigrants, 315, 316–18; from 1860 to 1866, 421

Iron ore, 513
Iroquois Indians, 7, 75
Irrigation, 567
Irving, Washington, 32, 34, 212, 341
Isabella, Queen, 4
Isolation: of Coolidge presidency, 730–31; Harding presidency and, 723–25
Isolationism: F. Roosevelt and, 776–81; World War II and, 782–83, 786
Israel, 823; invasion of Lebanon, 914; October 1973 war, 892; Six-Day War, 873. *See also* Middle East
Italians, immigration of, 532
Italy, 665; Monroe Doctrine and, 227; in World War II, 775, 807–8
Ivanhoe (Sir Walter Scott), 543
Iwo Jima, 814
IWWs, 677, 679, 698

J. P. Morgan & Company, 666
Jackson, Andrew, 56, 216, 311, 445, 451, 453; appeasement of South Carolina by, 251–52; appraisal of presidency of, 261–62; cabinet of, 245–46; forcible removal of Indian tribes by, 256–58; inauguration of, 243; as Indian fighter, 203, 225, 331; as personification of the new East, 242, 253; plantation economy and, 352; Polk presidential candidacy and, 278; presidency of, 234–35, 241–46, 248, 261–62; quoted, 231, 250; reelection of, 254–55; spoils system and, 243–45; as states' rights champion, 246, 248; Texas war for independence and, 260; two-party system and, 266–67; van Buren election and, 261–62; War of 1812 and, 203–4, 209, 218; war with the Bank of the United States of, 252–56
Jackson, Helen Hunt, 561
Jackson, Jesse, 915
Jackson, Rachel Robards, 240
Jackson, Thomas J. ("Stonewall"), 419, 429, 435
Jacksonian Democrats, 161, 195, 231–32; anti-British feelings of, 273; causes of, 232–34; panic of 1819 and, 217; spoils system and, 244; Tariff of 1828 and, 237–38
Jackson State College, 884
Jamaica, 54
James, Henry, 547, 714
James, William, 535, 543, 547, 610, 612n
James I, King, 13, 15, 22, 29
James II, King, 29, 30, 36
Jamestown, Virginia, 13–14, 22; slavery in, 42
Japan, 665, 773; atomic bombing of, 814–15; attack on Pearl Harbor, 789–90, 793, 794; bombing attacks on, 803–4, 813; bombing of Shanghai by, 742; commercial trade with, 383; embargoes on, 789; immigrants from, 628–29, 700; invasion of China by, 778; invasion of Manchuria by, 741–42; naval buildup by, 776; postwar reconstruction of, 829; Russo-Japa-

nese War, 626–28; Shantung peninsula to, 689, 690n; surrender of, 815; Wilsonian diplomacy and, 661–62; in World War II, 789–90, 794–95, 801–4, 812–15

Japanese-Americans, internment of, 794

Japanese suicide pilots, 814

Jay, John, 123, 124, 136, 144, 153, 158; treaty with Great Britain and, 166–67, 169

Jay Cooke and Company, 445, 485

Jazz music, 714

Jefferson, Thomas, 128, 131, 165, 168, 215; on J. Adams, 168; Alien and Sedition Laws and, 173–74; as amateur inventor, 338; anti-Federalists and, 159; as an architect, 340; Articles of Confederation and, 132, 133; Bank of the United States and, 155, 181; Canning proposal and, 227; as champion of the common people, 159–60; compared with Washington, 195; Constitutional Convention and, 137, 138; the Constitution and, 127, 129; Declaration of Independence and, 112–13; embargo acts and, 192–94; inaugural address of, 179; on Jackson, 243; J. Kennedy on, 181; Louisiana Purchase and, 184–89; Monroe Doctrine and, 229; as a pacifist, 183–84; on political parties, 159; on popular disorders, 137, 139; presidency of, 175–76, 179–95; private citizen versus public official, 180, 186; quoted, 130, 179; reelection of, 189–90; F. Roosevelt compared to, 769–70; as secretary of state, 152; slavery and, 58, 220, 349, 350; spoils system and, 244; state debts and, 154; Supreme Court and, 182–83; on the town meeting, 48; Tripoli pirates and, 183–84; University of Virginia and, 327

Jeffersonian Republicans, 157–61, 163, 166, 179, 180, 215, 216, 232, 240, 261; breaking up of, 236; Democrats and, 266; Supreme Court and, 222; Whigs and, 266

Jenkins, Capt. Robert, 79

Jenkins' Ear, War of (1739), 79–80

Jensen, Richard, 502

Jesuits, as missionaries, 77

Jewish faith, urban growth and, 538

Jewish immigrants, 56, 63

Jews, 533; Hitler's liquidation of, 779, 812

Jiang Jieshi (Chiang Kai-shek), 801, 821, 829–30, 850

Jim Crow laws, 582

Johns Hopkins University, 542

Johnson, Andrew, 355, 459, 461–63, 480; Congress and, 465–67; impeachment charges against, 474–75; presidency of, 457–58, 461–63; Reconstruction and, 463–69

Johnson, Dr. Samuel, 54

Johnson, Hiram W., 637, 689, 691

Johnson, Lyndon B., 855, 938; appraisal of, 879–80; civil rights movement and, 870–72; 879; Great Society program of, 867–70; presidency of, 866–77; Vietnam and, 872–77, 879–80

Johnson, William T., 356

Johnson Debt Default Act (1934), 776

Joint Chiefs of Staff, 828

Jolson, Al, 711

Jones, James, 944

Jones, John Paul, 121

Jones, LeRoi, 944

Jones Act (1916), 661

Joseph, Chief, 559

Josephson, Matthew, 527

Journalism, 543–44; golden age of, 330; yellow, 595–96

Jousting, 351n

Judicial nationalism, 221–24

Judiciary Act of 1789, 153, 182

Judiciary Act of 1801, 181–82

Jungle, The (Upton Sinclair), 641

Juvenile delinquency, 637

Kahn, Louis, 946

Kaiser, Henry J., 795

Kansas, 386; slavery and, 393–95

Kansas City, stockyards in, 563

Kansas-Nebraska Act (1854), 386–88, 397, 400; Lincoln and, 402

Kansas Pacific Railroad, 560

KDKA (Pittsburgh radio station), 710

Kearney, Denis, 491

Kelley, Florence, 535

Kelley, Oliver H., 573–74

Kellogg, Frank B., 724

Kellogg-Briand Pact, 724

Kelly, William, 515

Kennan, George F., 825

Kennedy, Edward, 906–7

Kennedy, John F., 855–57; assassination of, 866–67; Bay of Pigs invasion and, 864; civil rights movement and, 865–66; Cuban missile crisis and, 864; foreign policy of, 862–64; on Jefferson, 181; meeting with Khrushchev, 861; New Frontier policies of, 860–61; presidency of, 859–67; quoted, 859; television debate with Nixon, 854–55; Vietnam and, 862–63

Kennedy, Robert, 859, 875–76; assassination of, 877

Kent State University, 884

Kentucky, 55, 121, 149, 150, 417; importance to the Union of, 448; Jefferson resolutions and, 174, 182

Kerouac, Jack, 941

Key, D. M., 490

Key, Francis Scott, 203

Khomeini, Ayatollah Ruhollah, 903, 904

Khrushchev, Nikita, 849, 868; Camp David meeting with Eisenhower, 853; Cuban missile crisis and, 864; "kitchen debate" with Nixon, 855; meeting with Kennedy, 861; Soviet missile program and, 852–53

Kindergartens, 318, 540

King, Coretta, 857

King, Martin Luther, Jr., 343, 846, 857; assassination of, 871–72; civil rights movement and, 865, 866; voter-registration campaign and, 870

King George's War, 79

King William's War, 78–79

Kipling, Rudyard, 313, 611

Kirkpatrick, Jeane, 916

Kissinger, Henry A., 885, 888, 892

Kitchen Cabinet, 245–46

Kleppner, Paul, 502

Knickerbocker group of writers, 341–42

Knickerbocker's History of New York (Washington Irving), 341

Knights of Labor, 524

Know-Nothing party, 319, 388, 397

Knox, Henry, 152

Kolko, Gabriel, 651

Kooning, Willem de, 946

Korea, 626

Korean War, 835–36, 839; cost of, 839; Eisenhower and, 839; Truman and, 835–36

Kristol, Irving, 943

Ku Klux Klan, 472–74, 699, 729

Labor: benefits provided for laborers (1805), 295–96, 306; child, 635; Clayton Anti-Trust Act and, 660; Eisenhower and, 851–52; factory working conditions, 294–96, 306; Harding presidency and, 722; F. Roosevelt and, 754–56, 761–63; Square Deal for, 639, 646; strikes, 296; Taft-Hartley Act and, 832; women and children in labor force, 292, 295, 937–40; World War I and, 678–79. See also Factory system

Labor Day, 527

Labor unions, *see* Unions

Ladd, William, 334

Lafayette, Marquis de, 104, 113

LaFeber, Walter, 613

La Follette, Robert M., 637, 650, 729

La Follette Seaman's Act of 1915, 660, 722

Lake Erie, 202

"Lame-duck" period, 176n, 409n

Lancaster Pike, 298

Land Act of 1800, 217

Land Act of 1820, 217, 218

Land-grant colleges, 327, 541

Landon, Alfred M., 763–64

Land Ordinance of 1785, 134

Landrum-Griffin Act (1959), 852

Lanier, Sidney, 545–46

Laos, 862

La Salle, Robert de, 78

"Last Leaf, The" (Dr. Oliver Wendell Holmes), 345

Latin America: Alliance for Progress, 836; "Big Sister" policy and, 596; communism in, 872; Eisenhower presidency and, 853; Good Neighbor policy for, 774; Hoover's policy in, 742–43; Marshall Plan for, 854; Monroe Doctrine and, 227–28; newly formed republics in, 225, 226; T. Roosevelt's "preventive intervention" in, 625–26

Laud, Archbishop William, 23, 24

Laughing gas, 340

Lawson, Thomas W., 634

Lawyers, in colonial America, 59
Lazarus, Emma, 537
League of Augsburg, War of, 79
League of Nations, 676, 688–90, 723; Ethiopian crisis and, 776; Manchurian crisis and, 741–42; Wilson and, 688, 690–94, 695
Lease, Mary Elizabeth, 575
Leatherstocking Tales (James Fenimore Cooper), 342
Leaves of Grass (Walt Whitman), 343–44, 545
Lebanon, 852
Lecompton Constitution, 395, 405
Lee, Richard Henry, 112, 144
Lee, Robert E., 286, 419, 421, 429–30
Leisler's Rebellion (1689–1691), 52
Leland Stanford Junior (a university), 542
LeMay, Curtis, 878
Lend-lease, 785–89
Leuchtenberg, William, 770
Levin, N. Gordon, Jr., 695
Levine, Lawrence, 367
Lewis, John L., 761, 762, 796
Lewis, Meriwether, 188
Lewis, Sinclair, 716
Lewis and Clark expedition (1804–1806), 188, 277
Lexington, Massachusetts, 103, 108, 118
"Lexington Massacre" (1775), 103
Leyte Gulf, Battle of, 813
Liberal arts colleges, 327
"Liberal establishment," 882
Liberal Republican party, 484, 485
Liberator, The (antislavery newspaper), 362, 364
Liberia, 361
Liberty party, 278
Libraries, 327–28, 347; public, 543
Library of Congress, 543
Libya, American air raid on (1986), 918
Life-style, urban, 530
Liliuokalani, Queen, 599–600
Lincoln, Abraham, 401–4, 463; abolitionism and, 366; appraisal of presidency of, 452–54; arbitrary powers used by, 447–48; assassination of, 452–54; on black soldiers, 423; Border States and, 417–18; cabinet of, 415–16; Crittenden Compromise and, 410–11; debates with Douglas, 402–4; 1860 election and, 406–8; 1864 election and, 450–52; Emancipation Proclamation of, 429–32; forcible removal of Indians from their homeland and, 257; Fort Sumter and, 416–17; on his education, 326; Mexican War and, 282; on the patent system, 293; political criticism against, 450; presidency of, 414–16, 425, 430–32, 447–48, 450; quoted, 391, 414, 440, 448, 457; Reconstruction plans of, 463–64; Webster-Hayne debate and, 247
Lindbergh, Charles A., 709–10; as champion of isolationism, 783; kidnapping of son of, 703
Lindbergh Law, 703

Lindsay, Vachel, 590, 592
Linotype, 543
Lister, Joseph, 543
Literacy test, 537
Literature, 341–47, 545–48, 943–45; in colonial America, 68; nationalism in, 212–13, 341–42; post–Civil War landmarks in, 546–48; in the 1920s, 714–16; transcendentalism in, 342–43
Livingston, Robert R., 185, 187, 188
Lloyd, Henry Demarest, 632
Lloyd's of London, 205
Locke, John, 342
Lockout, 523
Lockridge, Kenneth, 72
Lodge, Henry Cabot, 596, 687, 689; League of Nations and, 689, 691–93
Lodge, Henry Cabot, Jr., 855
Lodges, 552
Logrolling, 154*n*
London, Jack, 547
London Economic Conference (1933), 772–73
London Morning Chronicle, 274
London Saturday Review, 344
London *Spectator*, 431
London *Times*, 205, 418, 424; appraisal of Lincoln by, 453
Lonely Crowd, The (David Riesman), 943
Long, Huey P., 752
Long Drive, cattle-raising and, 563
Longfellow, Henry Wadsworth, 344
Long Island, Battle of (1776), 116
Looking Backward (Edward Bellamy), 544
Lotteries, 71
Louis XIV, King, 74
Louis XVI, King, 118, 164
Louisiana, 78; Reconstruction in, 470, 471; slavery in, 357
Louisiana Purchase, 172, 184–89; Missouri Compromise and, 220
L'Ouverture, Toussaint, 185
Lovejoy, Rev. Elijah P., 366
Lowell, James Russell, 282, 286, 345, 412
Lowell, Robert, 945
Loyalists (Tories), 113–15, 119, 124, 157; effect of American Revolutionary War on, 127, 129, 130; as Hamiltonians, 158
Luce, Clare Booth, 810
Lumbering, in colonial America, 61
Lusitania, sinking of, 668–69
Luther, Martin, 21
Lutherans, in colonial America, 55, 63
Lyceum lecture associations, 328
Lynchings: lynching bees, 325; of persons in America (by race—1882–1970), 474
Lyon, Mary, 327
Lyon, Matthew, 173

MacArthur, Douglas, 801–2, 813, 815, 816; Korean War and, 836–37; reconstruction of Japan and, 829; Truman and, 837; veterans' Bonus Army and, 741
McAuliffe, A. C., 811
McCarran Internal Security Bill, 833–34
McCarthy, Eugene, 875, 877

McCarthy, Joseph R., 833; Eisenhower and, 843–44
McCarthyism, 844
McClellan, George B., 427–28, 429, 435, 451
McClure's, 633, 634
McCormick, Cyrus, 297
McCoy, Drew, 161
McCulloch v. Maryland (1819), 222, 253
Macdonough, Thomas, 202–3, 208
McGovern, George, 888
McGuffey, William H., 327
McGuffey's Readers, 327
McKay, Claude, 716
McKinley, William, 520, 580, 587; Hanna's campaign for, 587–91; Philippine insurrection and, 616; presidency of, 592–93; second term of, 619, 620; Spanish-American War and, 603, 608, 609
McKinley Tariff Bill, 580
McNamara, Robert S., 859, 862, 875
McNary-Haugen Bill, 728–29
Macon's Bill No. 2, 197
Madison, James, 131, 182, 185, 195, 212, 215, 292; Alien and Sedition Laws and, 173; Canning proposal and, 227; Constitutional Convention and, 138; the Constitution and, 144, 152–53; presidency of, 197–98; War of 1812 and, 201, 203
Magazines, 328, 544
Magellan, Ferdinand, 8
Maggie: A Girl of the Streets (Stephen Crane), 547
Mahan, Alfred Thayer, 596
Mailer, Norman, 944
Maine: boundary dispute in, 273–74; statehood for, 219
Maine (battleship), 601–2
Maine Law of 1851, 335
Maize, *see* Corn (maize)
Malaria, 7, 39
Malcolm X, 871
Manchuria, 626; Japanese invasion of, 741–42; Taft's dollar diplomacy and, 648; U.S.S.R. granted control of, 821
Manifest Destiny, 278–79, 382, 383, 384, 600; Mexican War and, 285–86
Man in the Gray Flannel Suit, The (Sloan Wilson), 943
Mann, Horace, 326
Manufacturing: British competition and, 292; as cause of economic inequality between the North and South, 305–6; in colonial America, 60–61, 290; establishments operating in 1860, 420; in New England, 291–93, 304; principle of interchangeable parts and, 292; tariffs and, 214. *See also* Factory system
"Man without a Country, The" (Edward Everett Hale), 449
Mao Zedong (Mao Tse-tung), 829
"Maple Leaf, The," 209
Marble Faun, The (Nathaniel Hawthorne), 346
Marbury, William, 182
Marbury v. Madison (1803), 182, 221, 247
"March on Washington," 866

Marconi, Guglielmo, 710
Marcos, Ferdinand, 919
Marianas, 804
Marine Corps: establishment of, 171; Mexican War and, 286; Tripoli pirates and, 183–84
Mariner's compass, 3
Marines, in World War II, 803
Marne, Second Battle of, 684
Marriage (1890–1980), 549
"Marseillaise, The," 163
Marshall, George C., 816, 827, 843
Marshall, John, 144, 170, 181–82, 183, 221–22, 246; on interpreting the Constitution, 182; on property rights, 222–24; on states' rights, 222
Marshall, Thurgood, 936
Marshall Field Building, 552
Marshall Plan, 827–28, 854
Mary, Queen (Stuart dynasty), 29, 30
Mary, Queen (Tudor dynasty), 13
Maryland, 55, 417; colonization of, 15–16, 17; established churches in (1775), 64; hardships of colonial life in, 39–40; legislative system of, 69; plantation economy of, 19
Mason-Dixon line, 373, 388
Massachusetts, 55, 207; colonization of, 17, 23–26; established churches in (1775), 64; popular disorders in, 136; ratification of the Constitution by, 142–43; social structure of, 52; state constitution for, 129
Massachusetts Bay Colony, 23–26
Masses, The, 677
Mass production, 292, 513–14
Masterson, "Bat," 565n
Maury, Matthew F., 338
Maximilian, Archduke, 440, 443
Maximum-hour laws, 638
Mayaguez crisis, 897
Mayans, 6
Mayer, Arno, 695
Mayflower, 22, 23
Mayflower Compact, 23
Meade, George G., 436
Meat industry, 518
Meat Inspection Act of 1906, 641–42
Meat-packing business, 563–65
Mechanical reapers, 446–47
Medical schools, 543
Medical science, 543
Medicare, 869
Medicine, 338–40. See also Physicians, in colonial America
Medicines, patent, 635
Megalopolis, 530
Mein Kampf (Adolf Hitler), 781
Mellon, Andrew W., 705, 718, 721, 727
Melville, Herman, 346
Mencken, Henry L., 715, 752–54
Mercantilism, 90–93
Merchant marine, 168, 191, 308, 660
Merchant Marine Act of 1920, 722
Meredith, James, 865–66, 871
Merrimack (wooden warship), 426
Mesabi iron ore range, 274, 513, 514

Mestizos, 10
Methodists, 19, 319, 321, 322; in colonial America, 63
Metropolitan Opera house, 552
Metternich, Prince, 228
Meuse-Argonne offensive, 684–85
Mexican War (1846), 281–87, 369, 382; as background for Civil War, 286–87
Mexico: agricultural workers from, 797; Good Neighbor policy and, 774; Napoleon III's attempt at empire in, 440, 443; oil resources in, 730; purchase of California from, 281, 282; revolution in, 662–64; Texas independence and, 258–60, 275–76, 281; Wilson's policy on, 662–64
Mexico City, 284
Middle Ages, 3
Middle East: oil-drilling concessions in, 723; Reagan's foreign policy in, 913–15, 918; Suez crisis, 849–50
Midway Island, 802
Miles, Nelson A., 608
Military: budget, 922–25; unification of armed forces, 828
Military academies, in the South, 351
Military Academy (West Point), 286
"Military-industrial" complex, 848, 857
Military pensions, 499
Military Reconstruction Act (1867), 468–70
Mill, John Stuart, 312
Miller, Arthur, 945
Miller, Perry, 37
Miller, William, 322
Millerites, 322
Millionaires, 305, 513, 518; private philanthropies for higher education given by, 542; in railroad industry, 511; in steel industry, 515–16
Mills, C. Wright, 943
Mines, Bureau of, 648
Minimum wages, 638, 847
Mining, 562–63
Minnesota, 274
Minow, Newton, 942
Minstrel shows, 341
Minute Men, 103, 108
Miranda case, 886
MIRVs (Multiple Independently Targeted Reentry Vehicles), 886
"Missile gap," 852
Missile program, Eisenhower presidency and, 852
Mississippi: murder of civil rights workers in, 870; Reconstruction in, 470, 471; slavery in, 357
Mississippi, University of, 865–66
Mississippi River, 78, 167; canal system and, 301; Civil war and, 425–26; cotton economy and, 304; importance to frontier farmers of, 184–85; railroads and, 303; steamboats and, 299
Missouri, 417; slavery in, 219–21
Missouri Compromise (1820), 219–21, 386; as cause for rise of Jacksonian democracy, 233

Missouri (ship), 815
Moby Dick (Herman Melville), 346
Molasses Act (1733), 62
Momaday, N. Scott, 944
Mondale, Walter, 915
Money: elastic currency, 658, 659; emergency currency, 645
Monitor (ironclad warship), 426
Monk, Maria, 320
"Monkey Trial" (1925), 704–5
Monopolies, see Trusts
Monroe, James, 185, 187, 208, 215–16, 221; foreign policy of, 224–29; presidency of, 215–16, 224–29
Monroe Doctrine (1823), 227–28, 443; appraisal of, 228–29; T. Roosevelt's perversion of, 624–26; Venezuelan crisis and, 597, 598
Montana, 563; statehood of, 568
Montcalm, Marquis de, 84
Montgomery, Bernard L., 805
Montgomery, David, 527
Montgomery, Gen. Richard, 110
Monticello, 159, 340
Moody, Dwight Lyman, 538
Moody Bible Institute, 538
Moon landing, 860–61
Moral Majority, 907
Morgan, Edmund S., 52, 367
Morgan, J. Pierpont, 514, 515–16, 538, 583, 640, 641
Morill Tariff, 465
Mormons, 322–24, 556
Morrill Act (1862), 541
Morrill Tariff Act (1861), 445, 465
Morris, Roger, 129
Morrison, Tony, 944
Morse, Samuel F. B., 293
Morse code, 293
Moscow, Nixon in, 884–86
Moscow-Washington "hot line," 864
Mott, Lucretia, 336
Mound Builders, 6
Mountain whites, 355
Mount Holyoke Seminary, 327
Mount Vernon, 150
Movies, 711–12
Mower-reaper, 296
"Muckrakers," 633–35
Mugwumps, 496, 497
Mulattoes, 356, 357
"Mulligan letters," 496
Multiple Independently Targeted Reentry Vehicles (MIRVs), 886
Muscle Shoals Bill, 740
Music, 341, 552; jazz, 714
Mussolini, Benito, 775–77, 779, 807
My Lai massacre, 883
Myra Breckinridge (Gore Vidal), 944

NAACP, 740, 798
Nagasaki, 815
Naismith, James, 554
Naked and the Dead, The (Norman Mailer), 944

Nantes, Edict of (1598), 74
Napoleon I, 171, 172; defeat and exile of, 202, 210; embargo on goods shipped to France and, 194, 197–98; invasion of Russia by, 208; Louisiana Purchase and, 184–86, 187
Napoleonic Wars, 79, 190
Napoleon III, 440, 441, 443
Nash, Gary, 37
Nash, Guy, 72
Nasser, Gamal Abdel, 849
Nast, Thomas, 482
Nation, 544
Nation, Carrie A., 551
National American Women's Suffrage Association, 549
National Association for the Advancement of Colored People (NAACP), 540, 798
National Banking Act (1863), 445, 658
National Banking System, authorization by Congress of, 445
National banks, issuing of emergency currency by, 645
National Consumers League, 535
National debt, *see* Debt, national
National Defense, Council of (1915), 677
National Defense and Education Act (NDEA) (1958), 852
National Grange (Patrons of Husbandry), 573–75
Nationalism, 212–14; judicial, 221–24
National Labor Relations Act (Wagner Act), 761, 766
National Labor Relations Board, 761
National Labor Union, 524
National literature, 212–13, 341–42
National Progressive Republican League, 650
National Prohibition party, 550
National Recovery Administration (NRA), 754–55
National Republican party, 240, 255
National Security Act (1947), 828
National Security Council (NSC), 828
National university, 236
National War Labor Board, 678–79
National Women's party, 712
Native Son (Richard Wright), 944
Nativism (antiforeignism), 535–37
NATO, 829, 849, 873
Naturalization Law of 1802, 181
Natural resources, conservation of, 642–45
Naval Academy (Annapolis), establishment of, 347
Navigation Laws (British), 29, 30, 91, 92, 94, 99, 130, 135
Navy, American: American Revolutionary War and, 121–22; the Great White Fleet, 629; imperialism and, 596; Mexican War and, 286; Spanish-American War and, 604–5; two-ocean, 781; War of 1812 and, 204; Washington "Disarmament" Conference, 724; in World War II, 802, 804, 813–14
Navy Department, 171
Nazism, 776, 823. *See also* Hitler, Adolf; World World II

Nebraska, 385; slavery and, 394
Nelson, Lord Horatio, 190
"Neoconservatives," 943
Netherlands, the, 3, 157; American Revolutionary War and, 119; immigrants from, 56; rebellion against Spain, 30
Neutrality: legislation on, under F. Roosevelt, 777–81; Wilson's proclamation of, 665–66, 669; in World War I, 665–66
Neutrality Acts of 1935, 1936, and 1937, 777
Neutrality Proclamation (1793), 165–66
Nevada, mining in, 563
New Amsterdam (New York City), 32
Newark, New Jersey, race riots in, 871
New Deal, 646, 748–63, 764, 766–69; congressional termination of programs, 794; criticism of, 767–68; objectives of, 748–50, 767
New Democracy, *see* Jacksonian Democrats
New England: abolitionism in, 361–62, 366; anti-Jefferson campaign in, 175; cotton economy and, 366; family life in 46–47; Hartford Convention and, 206–8; immigrants in, 56; industry and commerce of, 50–51; manufacturing in (1860), 420; pioneer heritage of, 51; Salem witch trials in, 49; social structure of, 47–48, 57–58; soil and climate of, 49–50; town meetings in, 49; transcendentalist movement in, 342–43; War of 1812 and, 200–201; the West as rival of, 246–47
New England Confederation (1643–1684), 28–29, 140; New Netherlands and, 32
New England Emigrant Aid Company, 393
Newfoundland, 11, 124, 224
New France, *see* Canada
New Freedom platform, 654, 655
New Frontier policies, 860–61
New Guinea, 802, 803, 813
New Hampshire, 207; colonization of, 17, 27–28; established churches in (1775), 64; ratification of the Constitution by, 144
New Harmony, Indiana, 337
New Immigrants, 532–35; antiforeignism against, 535–37
New Jersey, 136; colonization of, 17, 36; the Constitution and, 139; established churches in (1775), 64
Newlands Act of 1902, 643
New Mexico, 188, 373, 378, 385
New Nationalism doctrine, 650, 654
New Netherlands, 31–34
New Orleans, Louisiana, 315; Battle of (1815), 203–4, 208, 209
New Panama Canal Company, 622
Newport, Rhode Island, 325
Newspapers, 330; in colonial America, 69; sensationalism in, 543–44
New Sweden, 32–33
New World: Columbus's discovery of, 3–4; indirect discoverers of, 2–3; native plants introduced to Europe from, 7
New York, 136; American Revolutionary War and, 115–16; colonization of, 17; effect of Erie Canal on economy of, 299–300; established churches in

(1775), 64; General Incorporation Law and, 293; ratification of the Constitution by, 144–45
New York Central Railroad, 509
New York City, 33–34, 55, 314–16; American Revolutionary War and, 120; Civil War draft riots in, 443–44; Irish immigrants in, 317–18; as nation's seaport, 303–4; New Immigrants to, 532–33; population in 1790, 149; population in 1900, 529; slavery revolt in, 45
New York *Evening Post,* 285, 342, 575
New York *Herald,* 330
New York *Sun,* 330
New York Times, The, 884
New York *Tribune,* 330, 484; on secession, 409
Nez Percé Indians, 559
Ngo Dinh Diem, 848
Nicaragua, 383, 648, 730, 743, 914, 919
Nimitz, Chester W., 802, 803, 816
Nine-Power Treaty of 1922, 724
Nineteenth Amendment (1920), 678
Ninth Amendment, 152
Nixon, Richard M., 924; Arab oil embargo and, 892–93; in Beijing (Peking), 884–86; "Checkers" speech of, 838; Communist witch-hunt and, 833; domestic policy of, 887; energy crisis and, 892–93; Ford's pardon of, 895; foreign policy of, 882–86; "kitchen debate" with Khrushchev, 855; in Moscow, 884–86; presidency of, 877–79; reelection of, 887–88; resignation of, 893–95; secret bombing of Cambodia and, 891–92; South American tour of, 854; Supreme Court and, 886–87; television debates with J. Kennedy, 854–55; as vice-president, 838, 850; Vietnam War and, 882–84; War Powers Act and, 891–92; Watergate scandal and, 889–91
Nixon Doctrine, 882
Nobel Peace Prize, 627–28
"No-growth" economy, 947
Non-Intercourse Act (1809), 193, 197
Norfolk, Virginia, 111
Norris, Frank, 547–48
Norris, George W., 759
Norris–La Guardia Anti-Injunction Act of 1932, 740
North, Lord, 98, 99, 103, 104, 122, 123
North, the: abolitionism and, 356, 361–62, 366; Compromise of 1850 and, 377, 379–80; cotton economy and, 349–50, 353; decline of, 930–31; freed blacks in, 356; Fugitive Slave Law and, 381; Missouri Compromise and, 220–21; panic of 1857 and, 401. *See also* Union, the
North Africa, Allied forces in, 805
North African pirates, 136
North American Review, 213, 328
North Atlantic Pact, 828
North Atlantic Treaty Organization (NATO), *see* NATO
North Carolina, 55, 121, 136; colonization of, 17, 18; plantation economy of, 19; ratifi-

cation of the Constitution by, 145; Reconstruction in, 470; secession of, 417
North Dakota, statehood of, 568
Northern Pacific Railroad, 508, 567
Northern Securities Company, 640
North Korea, *Pueblo* incident and, 873
North Vietnam: bombing of, 872; Paris peace talks, 877. *See also* Vietnam War
Northwest Ordinance of 1787, 132, 134
Northwest Territory, 134–35
Norway, 781
Nova Scotia, 79
Novels: dime, 545; writing, 546–48
NRA (National Recovery Administration), 754–55
Nuclear arms race, 830; SALT treaty and, 899
Nuclear test–ban treaty, 864
Nuremberg trials, 823

Oakley, Annie, 553
Oates, Joyce Carol, 944
Oberlin College, 321–22, 327
O'Connor, Flannery, 944
O'Connor, Sandra Day, 915–16
Octopus, The (Frank Norris), 547
Office of Price Administration, 795
Of Plymouth Plantation (William Bradford), 23, 39
Oglethorpe, James, 18
Ohio, 149, 150
"Ohio fever," 217
Ohio River, 312
Ohio Valley, 218; importance to colonists of, 81–82
Oil embargo, Arab, 892–93; inflation and, 924
Oil industry, 516–18; automobile industry and, 708
Okinawa, 814
Oklahoma, statehood of, 568
Oldenburg, Claes, 946
Old Man and the Sea, The (Ernest Hemingway), 943
Old Northwest, 134–35
Olds, Ransom E., 706
O'Leary, J. A., 671
Olney, Richard, 512, 597
O'Neal, Peggy, 245–46
Oneida Colony (New York), 338
O'Neill, Eugene, 716
On the Origin of Species (Charles Darwin), 539
OPEC (Organization of Petroleum Exporting Countries), 900–901, 924
Open Door note, 617
Open Housing Bill, 870
Operation Rolling Thunder, 872
Oregon, 188, 224, 225, 371, 383, 384
Oregon Country, 276–80, 283
Oregon Trail, 278
Organization Man, The (William H. Whyte, Jr.), 943
Organization of Petroleum Exporting Countries (OPEC), 900–901, 924

Organized crime, annual income from (by 1930), 703
Organized philanthropy, 551
Orlando, Vittorio, 688
Osceola (Seminole chieftain), 258
Ostend Manifesto, 383–84
O'Sullivan, John L., 270
Oswald, Lee Harvey, 866
Other People's Money and How the Bankers Use It (Louis D. Brandeis), 658
Our Country: Its Possible Future and Its Present Crisis (Josiah Strong), 595
Overland stages, 308
Owen, Robert, 337

Pabst, Frederick, 318n
Pacific, war in, 801–4, 812–16
Pacific Railroad Act, 465
Pahlevi, Mohammed Reza, 849, 901
Paine, Robert Treat, 163
Paine, Thomas, 108, 111–12, 320, 341; opposition to Washington of, 167
Painters, 551–52
Painting, 340–41; in colonial America, 67–68
Palmer, A. Mitchell, 698
Panama, 8, 774; revolution (1903), 622
Panama Canal, 622–23, 899
Panama Canal Tolls Act of 1912, 661
Pan-American Conference (1889), 596
Panay (gunboat), 778
Panic of 1819, 217, 221
Panic of 1837, 263, 273
Panic of 1857, 401
Panic of 1873, 485–86, 490
Panic of 1907, 645
Paris, liberation of, 809
Paris, Treaty of (1783), 123–25
Paris Peace Conference, 687–90
Parkman, Francis, 347
Parks, Rosa, 846
Parochial schools, 533, 540
Parrington, Vernon Louis, 502
Passell, Peter, 947
Pasteur, Louis, 543
Patent medicines, 340, 635
Patent Office, 293
Patent system, 293
Patriots, *see* Whigs
Patronage system, 487, 490, 494, 495
Patton, George S., 809
Paxton Boys, 56
Payne-Aldrich Bill (1909), 648, 649
Peace Corps, 859
Peace movements, 334–35
Peale, Charles Wilson, 67, 341
Pearl Harbor: Japanese attack on, 789–90, 793, 794; naval base at, 599
Peking, *see* Beijing (Peking)
Pendleton Act of 1883, 494–95
Penicillin, 815
Penn, William, 34–35
Pennsylvania, 55; colonization of, 17, 34–36; established churches in (1775), 64; legislative system of, 69; ratification of the

Constitution by, 142; Whiskey Rebellion in, 156–57
Pennsylvania, University of, 67
Pennsylvania Dutch, 55
Pennsylvania Gazette, 82
Penn Warren, Robert, 944
Pension Act of 1980, 579
Pensions, military, 499
Pentagon Papers, 884
People's party, *see* Populists (People's party)
Percy, Walker, 944
Perry, Matthew C., 383
Perry, Oliver Hazard, 202, 208
Pershing, John J., 664, 684
Personal journalism, 330
Peru, 9
Petigru, James L., 417
Petroleum, discovery of, 447
Petroleum business, *see* Oil industry
Philadelphia, 35, 36, 55, 314, 529; American Revolutionary War and, 117, 120; national government in, 133, 179; population of (1790), 149; religious persecution in, 320
Philanthropy, organized, 551
Philip, King (Indian chieftain), 28
Philip II, King, 11
Philippines, 621–22; annexation of, 609–10, 612–13; independence agreement for, 773–74; insurrection in, 615–17; Marcos ouster, 919; Spanish-American War in, 604–5; territorial status given to, 661; in World War II, 801, 802, 813
Phillips, David G., 634
Phillips, Ulrich Bonnell, 367
Phillips, Wendell, 362, 430
Phips, Williams, 47
Phonograph, 552
Photography, 341
Physicians, in colonial America, 58–59
Pickett, Gen. George, 436
Pierce, Franklin, 381, 395; Cuba and, 383–84; presidency of, 382–83, 386–87, 397
Pike, Zebulon, 188
Pike's Peak gold rush, 562, 567
Pilgrims, 23. *See also* Puritans (Puritanism)
Pillsbury, John S., 567
Pilots, Japanese, 814
Pinchot, Gifford, 642, 649
Pinckney Treaty of 1795, 167
Piracy, 136, 183–84
Pit, The (Frank Norris), 548
Pitt, William, 82, 83–84, 86, 104
Pittsburgh, 514
Pizarro, Francisco, 9
Plagues, 59
Plains Indians, 557
Plantation system: aristocracy of, 350–51; in colonial America, 19; financial instability of, 352; importance of slavery to, 350–53, 356–57
Plath, Sylvia, 945
Platt Amendment, 612
Play It as It Lays (Joan Didion), 944
Plessy v. *Ferguson* (1896), 844

Plunkitt, George Washington, 483
Plutocracy, 518
Plymouth Bay, Massachusetts, 23
Plymouth Colony, 23
Pocahontas, 14
Podheretz, Norman, 943
Poe, Edgar Allan, 345
Poetry, 545–46, 716, 945
Poker games, 314
Poland, 820, 821, 824; immigration from, 532; invasion of, 780; Solidarity movement in, 912–13
Political abolitionists, 364
Political essays, 341
Political parties, 157–60, 254–55; 261; evolution of, 161; two-party system, 158, 266–68. *See also* Democratic party; Republican party; Third parties
Political progressivism, 635–37
Politics, impact of television on, 942. *See also* Democratic party; Republican party
Polk, James K., 228, 275, 278, 369, 371; Mexican War and, 282, 283, 285, 287; Oregon Country and, 280; presidency of, 279–80; purchase of California and, 281
Pollock, Jackson, 946
Polo, Marco, 3
Polygamy, 322, 324
Ponce de León, Juan, 8
Pontiac (Indian chieftain), 86
Pony Express, 308
Poor Richard's Almanack (Benjamin Franklin), 58, 68
Pope, Alexander, 68
Pope, Gen. John, 429
Popular sovereignty, 369–70, 393, 395, 400, 402, 405
Population: in colonial America (1700–1775), 54; in 1870, 481; elderly, increase in, 932–33; ethnic diversity in (1790–est.), 56; growth in Sunbelt, 929–31; in major cities (1790), 149; in mid–nineteenth century, 314–16; new immigration and, 933–34; in 1900, 529; postwar baby boom, 931–32; World War II and, 798
Populists (People's party), 575–76, 581–82, 631; silver issue and, 587, 589
Portman, John, 946
Portnoy's Complaint (Philip Roth), 945
Portrait of a Lady, The (Henry James), 547
Portugal, New World empire of, 3–4, 8
Postal system: intercolonial, 62; Pony Express, 308
Potatoes, 7; famine in Ireland, 316–17
Potsdam Conference (1945), 814
Potter, David M., 331, 389
Pound, Ezra, 716, 945
Powderly, Terence V., 525
Power Elite, The (C. Wright Mills), 943
Pragmatism, 543
Prayer in school, 886, 917–18
Predestination, 21
Presbyterians (Presbyterianism), 65, 319, 322; in colonial America, 63; Scotch, 21
Prescott, William H., 347

"Preventive intervention" policy (of T. Roosevelt), 625–26
Pride, ethnic, 934–35
Prime rate, 901
Primogeniture, law of, 12–13, 128
Princeton, New Jersey, 116
Princeton College, 66, 67, 653
Printing presses, 3, 330; in colonial America, 69
Privateering, 122; War of 1812 and, 205
Privy Council (British), 90, 91
Proclamation of 1763, 87
Productivity, 923–24
Professional schools, 542
Progress and Poverty (Henry George), 544
Progressive education, 704
Progressive party, 729, 834
Progressivism, 631–33, 669; in cities and states, 637–39; muckrakers and, 633–35; political progressivism, 635–37; presidential election of 1912 and, 654–55, 656; T. Roosevelt and, 839–50; Wilson and, 656, 660–61
Prohibition, 551, 701–2; gangsterism and, 702–3; repeal of, 756
Prohibitionists, 336
Promised Land, The (Mary Antin), 533
Promise of American Life, The (Herbert Croly), 654
Propaganda for World War I, 676–77
Property rights, Supreme Court and, 222–24
Prophet, The (Shawnee Indian), 198
Proposition 13, 929
Prosperity in the 1920s, 705–6, 717–18. *See also* Economy
Prostitution, 634, 637
Protective tariff, 272
Protestant churches, urban growth and, 538
"Protestant ethic," 25
Protestant Reformation, 11, 21–22
Protestants (Protestantism), *see names of Protestant denominations*
Providence, Rhode Island, 26, 27
Public education, 325–27, 540
Public libraries, 543
Public utility: holding companies, 759; TVA, 759–60
Public Utility Holding Company Act of 1935, 759
Public welfare, government expenditures for, 925
Public works, Hoover presidency and, 739. *See also* New Deal
Public Works Administration (PWA), 755–56
Pueblo incident, 873
Pueblo Indians, 6
Puerto Rico, 608, 611, 621, 623
Pugilism, 553–54
Pujo, Arsene, 658
Pulitzer, Joseph, 595, 601
Pullman Palace Car Company, 303, 509, 584
Pullman strike (1894), 584–85
Pure Food and Drug Act of 1906, 642
Puritans (Puritanism), 12, 22, 23; in colonial America, 64; Massachusetts Bay Com-

pany and, 23–24, 25; New England Confederation and, 28, 29; slavery and, 47–48; social structure of New England and, 47
PWA, 755–56

Quakers, 25, 26, 34; abolitionism and, 361; in colonial America, 63; Emerson on, 36; in Pennsylvania, 35, 36; slavery and, 35
"Quarantine" speech of F. Roosevelt, 772, 778
Quartering Act of 1765, 94, 97
Quebec, Canada, 110; Battle of, 84
Quebec Act of 1774, 100–101, 110
Queen Anne's War, 78–79
Quemoy, 850
Quincy, Josiah, 100

Rabbit Run (John Updike), 944
Race riots, 317, 722, 798; in Newark and Detroit, 871; in Watts, 870–71
Radar, 805
Radical abolitionism, 362–64
Radicalism, 697–98
Radio, 710–11; influence on presidential campaigns of, 732
Ragtime (E. L. Doctorow), 945
Railroad Act, 465
Railroads, 301–3; automobile industry and, 708; congressional subsidies for, 504, 505; construction of, 504, 506–7; corruption caused by, 510–11; government regulation of, 511–13; massacre of buffalo herds and, 560; meat-packing business and, 563; private management of, 722; taming of the Indians and, 559; transcontinental, 385, 504–13
Railway Labor Board, 722
Raleigh, Sir Walter, 1, 11, 13
Ramona (Helen Hunt Jackson), 561
Randolph, A. Philip, 798
Randolph, John, 167, 192, 198, 235, 238, 292
Rankin, Jeannette, 675
Rauschenberg, Robert, 946
Rauschenbusch, Walter, 534
"Raven, The" (Edgar Allan Poe), 345
Reagan, Ronald, 906–19, 929; budget and, 910–12, 917; election of (1980), 906–9; foreign policy under, 912–15, 918–19; Reagan revolution, 909–10, 919; reelection of (1984), 915–17
"Reaganomics," 911, 917
Reaper-thresher (the "combine"), 571
Rearmament, the Cold War and, 828–30
Rebel without a Cause (film), 941
Reciprocal Trade Agreements Act of 1934, 775
Reconstruction, 457–59; Black Codes and, 464–65, 467; Congress and, 463, 465–70; congressional, 465; heritage of, 477; Ku Klux Klan and, 472–74; Lincoln's plans for, 463–64; military, 468–70; official end of, 490, 491; presidential, 463–64; principal proposals and plans

for, 466; realities of, 470–72; Republican party and, 463, 465–66, 468, 477

Reconstruction Finance Corporation (RFC), 740

Red Badge of Courage, The (Stephen Crane), 547

"Red scare" of 1919–1920, 698

Reed, Thomas B., 579, 580

Reed, Walter, 612

Reform, social, 631–33. *See also* Progressivism

Reformatories, 334

Reform Bill of 1867 (British), 455

Reform campaigns, 333–36

Religion: in colonial America, 58–59, 62–66; effect of Darwinism on, 539–40; Great Awakening, 64–66; liberalism in, 320–21; missionary work, 66, 77; 1928 presidential campaign and, 733; post–1960s resurgence of, 942; as practiced by slaves, 360; religious intolerance, 319–20; revivalism, 333–34; Second Great Awakening, 320–22, 333; separation of church and state, 128; slavery and, 322. *See also specific religions and sects*

Remington, Frederic, 601

Renaissance, the, 3

Reorganization Act (1939), 766

Republican Committee for the Re-election of the President (CREEP), 889

Republican party: abolitionism and, 364; Dred Scott decision and, 400; 1856 presidential election and, 397, 398–99; 1860 presidential election and, 406; 1864 presidential election and, 450–51; ethnic and cultural difference between Democrats and, 486–88; evolution of, 161; "hard-money" policy of, 486; Kansas-Nebraska Act and, 388; 1912 presidential election and, 654, 656; 1932 presidential election and, 745, 747–48; Reconstruction and, 463, 465–68, 476–77; the silver issue (1896) and, 588, 590; Taft causes split in, 648–50

Republic Steel Company, 762

Resumption Act of 1875, 486

Revels, Hiram, 471

"Revenue-sharing" bill, 887

Revere, Paul, 98

"Reverse discrimination," 936

Revivalists, urban, 538

Rhineland, 689

Rhode Island, 207; colonization of, 17, 18, 26–27; Constitutional Convention and, 137; established churches in (1775), 64; legislative system of, 69; ratification of the Constitution by, 141, 145; state constitution for, 129

Rice, 17, 19, 349

Richardson, Henry H., 552

Richmond, Virginia, 458; as Confederacy capital, 417; destruction of, 458

Rickover, H. G., 602

Riesman, David, 943

Rights, human, 899

Riis, Jacob A., 632

Riots, race, 722, 798, 870–71

Rise of Silas Lapham, The (William Dean Howells), 547

Roads, federal funding for, 215, 236, 246

Roanoke Island, 11

Robin Moor, torpedoing of, 787

Robinson, Edgar E., 770

Robinson, Jackie, 832

Rochambeau, Comte de, 120, 122

Rockefeller, John D., 443, 514, 517, 518, 523, 538, 542

Rockefeller Foundation, 704

Rocketry, 926

Roethke, Theodore, 945

Roe v. *Wade,* 939

Rogers, Will, 767

Rolfe, John, 14

Roman Catholics (Catholicism): catholicism as presidential election issue, 855–56; in colonial America, 15–16; 63, 64; intolerance against, 319–20; urban growth and, 538

Romania, 820

Rome-Berlin Axis, 776

Rommel, Field Marshal Erwin, 805

Roosevelt, Eleanor, 746

Roosevelt, Franklin D., 167n, 646, 698; at Casablanca, 807; Churchill and, 788, 807, 816; compared to Jefferson, 769–70; death of, 812; election of 1932 and, 745, 746–48; election of 1940 and, 783–85; election of 1944 and, 809–10; foreign policy of, 772–74; neutrality legislation of, 777–81; New Deal program of, 748–63, 764, 766–69; political appeal of, 746; presidency of, 748–57, 792–816; "Quarantine" speech of, 772, 778; quoted, 745, 772, 792; reciprocal trade policy of, 775; Supreme Court and, 764–66; at Teheran, 808; war message of, 789; wartime preparedness and, 781–82; at Yalta Conference, 820–22

Roosevelt, Theodore, 93, 578, 596; attack on Wilson's neutrality by, 669, 670–71; attempt at third-term presidency, 650–51, 654–55; background of, 620–21; conservation of natural resources and, 642–45, 650; construction of Panama canal and, 622–23; consumer reform by, 641–42; corporate trust-busting of, 639–41; lasting contributions of, 646; on muckraking, 634; Nobel Peace Prize to, 627–28; on patronage system, 494; progressivism and, 639–50; quoted, 615, 631; rift between Taft and, 648, 650–51, 654; Russo-Japanese War and, 626–28; Spanish-American War and, 603, 604, 606–7, 608; Square Deal for labor of, 631, 639, 646; Taft as presidential choice of, 646; as vice-president, 619, 620; on woman suffrage, 637

Roosevelt, Theodore, Jr., 723

Roosevelt Dam, 643

Root, Elihu, 613

Root-Takahira agreement of 1908, 629

Rosenberg, Julius and Ethel, 834

Ross, E. S., 535

Ross, Leonard, 947

Roszak, Theodore, 940

Roth, Philip, 944–45

Roughing It (Mark Twain), 546

"Rough Riders," 606–7

Rousseau, Jean Jacques, 118

Royal African Company, 42

Royster, Charles, 125

Ruby, Jack, 866

Rush-Bagot Agreement (1817), 209

Russia, 120, 533; Allied invasion of during World War I, 683; invasion by Napoleon of, 208; Monroe Doctrine and, 227; North American trading posts of, 226, 228; Oregon Country and, 276; purchase of Alaska from, 475–77; revolution in, 674, 682, 697; World War I and, 664

Russo-American Treaty of 1824, 228

Russo-Japanese War, 626–28

Rutgers College, 66, 67

Ruth, George H. ("Babe"), 706

Saarinen, Eero, 946

Saar Valley, 689

Sacco, Nicola, 698

Sackville-West, Sir Lionel, 501

Sadat, Anwar, 899, 913

"Sagebrush Rebellion," 909

St. Bartholomew's Day massacre (1672), 74

Saint-Gaudens, Augustus, 552

St. Lawrence River, 273–74

St. Lawrence waterway project, 857

St. Leger, Col. Barry, 116, 118

Salem witch trials, 49

Salinger, J. D., 944

Salk, Jonas, 932

SALT (Strategic Arms Limitation Talks), 885, 899, 902

Salvation Army, 538

Samoan Islands, 596

Sandinistas, 914

Sanger, Margaret, 712

Santa Anna (Mexican dictator), 259–61, 385; Mexican War and, 283–85, 287

Santo Domingo, 185

Saratoga, New York, 118

Saratoga Springs, New York, 325

Sargent, John Singer, 551–52

"Saturday Night Massacre," 890–91

Savannah, Georgia, 18

Savannah (steamer), 305

"Scalawags," 471

Scandinavia, discovery of the New World and, 2

Scarlet Letter, The (Nathaniel Hawthorne), 345–46

Schechter decision (1935), 755

Schlesinger, Arthur M., Jr., 248, 770

Schlitz, Joseph, 318n

School prayer and Bible reading, 886, 917–18

Schools: Hebrew, 533; high schools, 540; medical, 543; parochial, 533, 540; post–Civil War, 540–43; professional and technical, 542

Schurz, Carl, 318, 422, 459

Science: achievements in, 338–40; in colonial America, 68

Scopes, John T., 704–5

Scotch Highlander. 56

Scotch-Irish immigrants, 56

Scotch Presbyterians, 21

Scott, Dred, 399

Scott, Michael, 207

Scott, Sir Walter, 351

Scott, Winfield, 284, 285, 381, 416

Scribner's Monthly, 544

Sculptors, 552

SDI, 917

SEATO, 848

Secession, 408–12, 417

Second Agricultural Adjustment Act of 1938, 756

Second Continental Congress (1776), 108–9, 129, 138, 140

Second Greaat Awakening, 320–22, 333

Second party system, 592*n*

Sectional balance, 372–75

Securities and Exchange Commission (SEC), 758

Sedition Act, 172–73, 677

Segregation, education and, 936. *See also* Blacks; Civil rights

"Self-Reliance" (Ralph Waldo Emerson), 313

Seminole Indians, 257–58

Senate: Compromise of 1850 and, 375–78; the Constitution and, 139, 141. *See also* Congress

Seneca, New York, Woman's Rights Convention in, 337

Senior citizens, 932–33

Separatist Pilgrims, 23. *See also* Puritans (Puritanism)

Serbia, 664

Servants, indentured, 15–16, 40, 41, 58

Settlement houses, 535

Seventeenth Amendment (1913), 636

Seventh Pan-American Conference (1933), 774

Seven Years' War, 79, 82, 94, 118

Seward, William H., 377, 406, 415, 416, 441, 443, 476–77; purchase of Alaska and, 476–77

Sewing machines, 292–93, 446

Sexual frontiers, 1920s life-styles and, 714

Sexual revolution, 942

Seymour, Horatio, 481

Shafter, William R., 606–7

Shakers, 338

Shakespeare, William, 12

Shanghai, 742

Shantung peninsula, 689, 690*n*

Sharecroppers, 520–21

Shawnee Indians, 198

Shays, Capt. Daniel, 136, 139, 140

Shays's Rebellion (1786), 136

Sheepherders, 565

Sheffield, Lord, 135

Shepard, Sam, 945

Sheridan, Philip H., 558

Sherman, William Tecumseh, 434–35, 451–52, 558

Sherman Anti-Trust Act of 1890, 519–20, 580

Sherman Silver Purchase Act of 1890, 580, 583

Sherman tanks, 805

Sherwin, Martin J., 817

Shipyards, 308

Showboats, 325

Shy, John, 125

Sicily, 807

Sigel, Franz, 422

Silent majority, 883

Silliman, Benjamin, 338

Silver, 563; dollars, 486; free-silver issue, 580, 588–91, 593, 611

Silverites, 580, 587; presidential election of 1896 and, 588, 589

Silver senators, 563

Simms, William Gilmore, 345

Sinclair, Harry F., 726

Sinclair, Upton, 641

Singer, Isaac, 292

Singer, Isaac Bashevis, 945

Sioux Indians, 7, 557, 558

Sioux War of 1876–1877, 558–59

Sister Carrie (Theodore Dreiser), 548

Sit-down strike, 762

"Sit-ins," 865

Sitting Bull, 558, 559

Six-Day War, 873

Sixteenth Amendment (1913), 586*n*, 658

Skyscrapers, 529–30, 531

Slater, Samuel, 290, 295

Slave auctions, 357–58

Slavery: African roots of, 360; American Revolutionary War and, 128; in colonial America, 14–15, 16, 19, 42–45, 57, 58; Compromise of 1850 and, 377–81; the Constitution and, 140; cotton economy and, 349–50, 357; Crittenden Compromise and, 410–11; crusades against, 333, 337; Declaration of Independence and, 128; Emancipation Proclamation and, 430–32; family life among slaves, 360; Freedmen's Bureau and, 460–61, 465, 467; fugitive-slave laws, 375, 379–81; Harpers Ferry raid and, 404–5; inhuman treatment of slaves, 356–61; Jacksonian democracy and, 233; Kansas and, 393–95; Kansas-Nebraska Act and, 387–88; Lincoln-Douglas debates on, 402–4; missionary work among slaves, 66; Missouri Compromise and, 219–21; nonslaveholding whites and, 354–55; in Old Northwest, 134; percentage of slaves in South, 56; plantation system and, 350–53, 356–57; popular sovereignty and, 369–70; Quakers and, 35; response to emancipation among slaves, 459–60; sectional balance and, 372–74; slave culture, 44–45, 360; slave insurrections, 237, 360–61; slaveowners and, 353–55; Tallmadge amendment and, 219; in Texas, 260–61, 379; Underground Railroad and, 374–75, 379–80, 414–15; Wilmot Proviso and, 287, 369–70, 376. *See also* Abolitionism; Blacks; Civil rights

Slidell, John, 281

Slovaks, immigration of, 532

Slums, 315, 531–32

Smallpox, 7, 59, 339

Smith, Adam, 90

Smith, Alfred E., 732, 733, 747, 764, 855

Smith, Capt. John, 14

Smith, Joseph, 322

Smith, Sydney, 246

Smith Act of 1940, 833

Smith-Connally Anti-Strike Act (1943), 796

Smuggling, 92

SNCC, 871

Social democracy, 314

Socialism, Fabian, 544

Socialists, 632–33, 646, 656

Social mobility, 305–6

Social reform, 631–33; New Deal and, 750

Social Security, 760, 847

Social Security Act of 1935, 760, 766

Social Security Act of 1950, 835

Social structure: in colonial America, 45–48, 52, 57–58; first families of Virginia, 45–46; Jacksonian democracy and, 232; in the South, 45–46, 58, 350–51

Social workers, women, 534–35

Society of the Cincinnati, 127

Soil Conservation and Domestic Allotment Act of 1936, 756–57

Solidarity union, 912–13

Sons of Liberty, 96

Soup kitchens, 583

South, the: American Revolutionary War and, 121, 123; civil rights movement and, 865–66, 870; colonization of, 13–19; Compromise of 1850 and, 376–81; cotton economy of, 290, 291, 349–50, 352, 353; Crittenden Compromise and, 410–11; Cuba and, 383–84; economic collapse of, 447, 457–59; effect of slavery on European immigration to, 353; 1860 presidential election and, 405, 406–8; ethnic diversity of, 56; expansion of the West and, 246; freed blacks in, 356; Freedmen's Bureau and, 460–61; Fugitive Slave Law and, 380–81; industrialization and, 520–22; Ku Klux Klan in, 472–74; manufacturing in (1860), 420; Military Reconstruction Act and, 468–70; Missouri Compromise and, 220–21; panic of 1857 and, 401; plantation system of, 350–53, 356–57; proslavery arguments of, 365; public education in, 540–41; public-health program in, 704; reaction to abolitionism in, 364–65; Reconstruction in, 470–72, 477; Republican party and, 388, 412; resistance to desegregation in, 844–45; response to emancipation in, 459–60; runaway slave problem in, 374–75; secession and, 408–12, 417; social structure of, 45–46, 58, 350–51; suffrage in, 232; tariffs as yoke for, 237–39; treatment of plantation slaves in, 356–61; voter-registration campaign in, 870, 871–72; white majority of, 353–55; World War II economic development of, 797

South Africa, racial violence in, 918–19

South America, 120, 225

South Carolina: colonization of, 16–18; established churches in (1775), 64; Fort Sumter and, 416; plantation economy of, 19; Reconstruction in, 470, 471; secession of, 408; slavery in, 42, 43, 45, 58, 140, 357; Tariff of 1828 and, 237, 239, 250–52

"South Carolina Exposition, The" (John C. Calhoun), 239, 246

South Dakota, statehood of, 568

Southeast Asia Treaty Organization (SEATO), 848

Southern Pacific Railroad, 508, 519

"Southern strategy," 887

South Vietnam: Americanized fighting in, 872–73; U.S. troops sent to (1961), 863. See also Vietnam War

Soviet Union, see U.S.S.R.

Space race, Eisenhower and, 852

Spain: American Revolutionary War and, 119, 123; "black legend" of, 10; colonial wars with Britain of, 79–80; the Confederation and, 135–36; conquistadores of, 8–11; Cuba and, 383–84; defeat of the armada of, 12; Florida Treaty of 1819 and, 84; loss of empire, 608–10; loss of Florida by, 225; mercantilism in, 93; Netherlands' rebellion against, 30; New World empire of, 3, 4, 8–11; Pinckney Treaty with, 167

Spanish-American Treaty (1795), 225

Spanish-American War, 603–13; battle of Manila, 603–4; explosion of the *Maine*, 601–2; peace negotiations and treaty, 608–10, 611

Spanish Civil War (1936–1939), 777–78

Spanish Succession, War of, 79

Spargo, John, 635

SPARS (Coast Guard), 796

Spas, 325

Speakeasies, 702

Special Forces (Green Berets), 862

Specie Circular, 256, 263

Spice Islands (Indonesia), 2

Spinning, 61

Spirit of St. Louis, 709

Spock, Benjamin, 940

Spoils system, 243–45

Sports, 325; as big business, 706; blacks in, 832

Spruance, Raymond A., 802

Sputnik I, 852

Sputnik II, 852

Square Deal, 631, 639, 646

Squatters, 18

Stagecoaches, 298, 299, 308

Stalin, Joseph, 775, 808; the Cold War and, 825, 828; pact with Hitler, 779–80, 787; shaping the postwar world, 822; U.S.S.R. denunciation of, 849; at Yalta Conference, 820–22

Stalingrad, siege of, 805

Stamp Act (1765), 94–96

Stamp Act Congress, 95–96, 140

Stampp, Kenneth, 367, 478

Standard Oil Company, 514, 517, 634, 648

Standish, Capt. Myles, 222–23

Stanton, Edwin M., 415, 474

Stanton, Elizabeth Cady, 336, 549

"Star-Spangled Banner, The" (Francis Scott Key), 203

"Star Wars," 917

State banks, 213

States' rights, 246, 248; Supreme Court and, 222

States' Rights party, 834

State-supported universities, 327

Statue of Liberty, 537

Statute for Religious Freedom, 128

Steamboats, 218, 299, 303, 308

Stedman, E. C., 405

Steel, 513, 515–16; industry, pricing system of, 521–22; rail, 509, 515

Steel plow, 296

Steffens, Lincoln, 634

Stein, Gertrude, 311

Steinbeck, John, 754, 758, 943–44

Stenographers, 522

Stephens, Alexander H., 405, 465

Steuben, Baron von, 106, 118

Stevens, Thaddeus, 468, 475, 477

Stevens, Wallace, 945

Stevenson, Adlai E., 583, 837–39, 850

Stimson, Henry Lewis, 742, 799

Stock market: crash of 1929, 735, 736; 1920s bull market, 717–18; speculation in, 717–18. See also Economy

Stock watering, 511

Stockyards, 563

Stone, Lucy, 337

Stoughton, William, 21

Stowe, Harriet Beecher, 329, 358, 361, 391–93

Strategic Arms Limitation Talks (SALT), 885, 899, 902

Strategic Defense Initiative (SDI), 917

Streetcar Named Desire, A (Tennessee Williams), 945

Strikes, 296, 523–27, 581, 584–85, 639, 722, 762, 796, 832

Strong, Josiah, 596

Stuart, Gilbert, 341

Stuart dynasty in Great Britain, 29

Student Non-Violent Coordinating Committee (SNCC), 871

Stuyvesant, Peter, 33

Styron, William, 944

Submarine warfare: during World War I, 680–81; during World War II, 787, 788–89, 804–5, 812–13

Suburbs, 532, 708, 930

Sudentenland, 779

Suez crisis, 849–50

Suffrage, 232, 678; for blacks, 466, 469, 470–72

Sugar, 94, 349

Sugar Act of 1764, 94

Sugar production: in Cuba, 600; in Hawaii, 599

Sullivan, John L., 554

Sullivan, Louis, 529–30, 552

Summit conferences: in Paris (1960), 853–54; in Vienna (1961), 861

Sumner, Charles, 395–96, 468

Sumner, William Graham, 518, 543

Sunbelt, population growth in, 929–31

Sunday, W. A. ("Billy"), 540, 697, 705

"Supply-side" economics, 911, 917

Supreme Court, 153; civil rights rulings by, 844–45; dissolution of Standard Oil Company by, 648; Dred Scott decision and, 399; Harding presidency and, 721; nationalism and, 221–22; New Deal programs and, 755, 757, 758, 761, 764–66; Nixon and, 886–87; property rights and, 222–24; on the question of constitutionality, 181–82, 247*n*; F. Roosevelt and, 764–66; "rule of reason" doctrine of, 648; states' rights and, 222. See also names of Supreme Court cases

Susquehanna River, 36

Sussex (ship), 669

Swartwout, Samuel, 245

Sweatshops, 638

Swedish immigrants, 56

Swift, Gustavus F., 518

Swiss immigrants, 56

Switchboard operators, 522

Syria, 688

Taft, Robert A., 783, 832, 837, 843

Taft, William Howard, 616, 640–41, 645–51, 656

Taft-Hartley Act (1947), 832

Taiwan, *see* Formosa (Taiwan)

"Talkie," 711

Talleyrand, 169, 171

Tallmadge amendment, 219

Tammany, Chief (Indian), 35

Tammany Hall (New York City), 318

Taney, Roger B., 399

Tanks, Sherman, 805

Tappan, Arthur, 361

Tappan, Lewis, 361, 366

Tarbell, Ida M., 634

Tariff of 1816, 214

Tariff of 1824, 250

Tariff of 1828, 237–38, 250–52

Tariff of 1832, 250–51

Tariff of 1833, 251–52

Tariff of 1842, 279

Tariff of 1846, 445

Tariff of 1857, 401, 412

Tariff of 1890, 585–86, 599

Tariffs, 214–15, 238, 239, 251–52, 272, 445, 522; first laws imposing, 154–55; Harding presidency and, 725–26; Wilson's assault on, 658–60

Taverns, 52

Taxes, 70*n*, 133; excess-profits, 718; excise tax, 155, 156, 181; graduated income, 658; income tax, 445, 586; Reagan and, 917; resistance to, 928–29; windfall profits, 901

Taylor, Frederick W., 707

Taylor, Zachary, 281, 284, 370–71; Compromise of 1850 and, 377; presidency of, 327, 377, 378

Teamsters Union, 851

Teapot Dome scandal, 726, 727

Technical schools, 542

Tecumseh (Shawnee Indian), 198, 202

Teheran Conference, 808

Telegraphy, 293, 330; wireless, 710

Telephone, 513, 530

Television, impact of, 942

Teller Amendment of 1898, 603, 612

Temperance movement, 318, 335–36

Tenant farmers, 572

Ten-hour working day, establishment of (1840), 296

Tennessee, 55, 149, 150; Reconstruction in, 470; secession of, 417

Tennessee Coal and Iron Company, 641

Tennessee River, 759

Tennessee Valley Authority (TVA), 740, 759–60

Ten Nights in a Barroom (T. S. Arthur), 325, 335

Tennyson, Alfred Lord, 598

Tenth Amendment, 152

Tenure of Office Act (1867), 474

Terrorism, American air raid on Libya and, 918

Texas, 369, 385; Reconstruction in, 470; slavery and, 260–61, 379; statehood for, 275–76, 278, 279, 280; war for independence, 258–60, 275–76, 281

Textbooks, 327

Thames, Battle of (1813), 202, 209, 264

"Thanatopsis" (William Cullen Bryant), 342

Thanksgiving Day, celebration of, 23, 71

Theater, 324–25, 553

Theory of the Leisure Class, The (Thorstein Veblen), 632

Third parties: Anti-Masonic party, 234, 254–55, 261; Constitutional Union party, 406; Free-Soil party, 364, 370, 371; Know-Nothing party, 319, 388, 397; Liberty party, 278; system of, 592*n*

Third-term presidency, 167

Thirteenth Amendment (1865), 431, 464

Thirty Years' War, 33

Thoreau, Henry David, 343

Thurmond, J. Strom, 834

Tilden, Samuel J., 482, 488

Tippecanoe, Battle of (1811), 199, 264

Tobacco, 7, 13, 19, 59, 92, 93, 349; in colonial America, 40–41; foreign markets for, 62; importance to colonial economy of, 14–15; slavery and, 44

Tobacco, mass-produced cigarettes and, 521

Tocqueville, Alexis de, 314, 320, 331, 336

Tokyo, firebombing raid on, 813

Tomatoes, 7

Tonkin Gulf episode, 868–69

Tonkin Gulf Resolution, 869

Tordesillas, Treaty of (1494), 8

Tories, *see* Loyalists (Tories)

Totalitarianism, post–World War I growth in Europe of, 775–76

Town meetings, 48

Townsend, Francis E., 754

Townshend, "Champagne Charley," 96

Townshend Acts, 96–98

Townshend taxes (1767), 70*n*

Trade: foreign, 522; reciprocal policy of, 775

Trade Expansion Act (1962), 862

Trafalgar, Battle of (1805), 190

Tramp steamers, 308

Transcendentalism, 342–43

Transcontinental airmail route, 709

Transcontinental railroad, 385

Transportation: canals, 299–301; 303; in colonial America, 62; Cumberland Road, 218, 298–99; growth of automobile industry and, 708; Pony Express, 308; railroads, 301–3, 385; stagecoaches, 298, 299, 308; steamboats, 218, 299, 303, 308; turnpikes, 298–99

Transportation, Department of, 869

Travis, Col. W. B., 259

Treasury, 151, 153; gold reserve of, 583–84. *See also* Bank of the United States

Treaty of 1818, 224, 277

Treaty of Versailles, collapse of, 694

Trent affair (1861), 441

Triangle Shirtwaist Company, 638

Triangular trade, 60

Tripoli, Pasha of, piracy and, 183–84

Trolleys, electric, 530

Troy Female Seminary, 327

Truman, Harry S., 810, 812; civil rights for blacks and, 832, 834; the Cold War and, 825–27; development of the H-bomb and, 830; election of 1948 and, 834–35; Fair Deal program of, 835; Korean War and, 835–36; loyalty program of, 832–34; MacArthur and, 837; Marshall Plan and, 827–28; at Potsdam Conference, 814; presidency of, 819–37; quoted, 787, 819, 833

Truman Doctrine, 826

Trumbull, John, 67, 341

Trusts, 514, 518–20; government regulations against, 520; T. Roosevelt's actions against, 640–41; Taft's actions against, 648; Wilson's attack on, 658–60

Truth, Sojourner, 363

Tubman, Harriet, 374

Tudor dynasty in Great Britain, 13

Turgot, Anne Robert, 150

Turkey, 664, 825–26, 829

Turner, Frederick Jackson, 248, 556, 576

Turner, Nat, 360, 364

TVA, 740, 759–60

Twain, Mark, 308, 314, 486, 502, 540, 546–47, 563, 610; on causes of Civil War, 351

Tweed, William Marcy ("Boss"), 482, 483, 534

Tweed Ring, 482

Twelfth Amendment (1804), 176*n*, 235

Twentieth Amendment (1933), 409*n*, 488, 764

Twenty-first Amendment (1933), 756

Twenty-second Amendment (1951), 167*n*, 195, 857

Twenty-fourth Amendment (1964), 870

Twine binders, 571

Tyler, John, 264; presidency of, 271–72; Texas statehood and, 275

Typhoid, 39, 608

Typhoid fever, 608

U.S.S. *Oregon*, 607, 621

U.S.S.R.: American lend-lease to, 787–88; détente policy and, 864; German invasion of, 805–6; grain deal with, 885; Hitler's invasion of, 787–88; invasion of Afghanistan by, 903; missile program, 852–53; Nixon's visit to Moscow, 884–86; nuclear weapons developed by, 830; recognition of, 773; shaping the postwar world, 822; space satellites of, 852; totalitarianism in, 775; Warsaw Pact with Eastern Europe, 849; World War II casualties in, 815

U-2 spy plane incident, 853–54

UFWOC, 934

Uncle Tom's Cabin (Harriet Beecher Stowe), 358, 362, 391–93, 418

Uncle Tom's Cabin (play), 325

Underground Railroad, 374–75, 380, 414–15

Underwood Tariff Bill, 658

Unemployment: Great Depression and, 736, 745; in 1939, 768; F. Roosevelt presidency and, 751–54

UNESCO, 823

Union, the: assets of, 420–22; blacks in armies of, 422; blockade of the Confederacy by, 425–26; casualties of, 454; cotton economy and, 365; Emancipation Proclamation and, 431–32; European immigrants and, 421–22; federal financial aid for, 445; Fort Sumter and, 416–17; idealism of, 423, 427–28; mountain whites and, 355; number of men in uniform from (1861–1865), 444; wartime prosperity of, 446–47; Webster-Hayne debate and, 247–48. *See also* North, the

Union Pacific Railroad, 483, 505–8

Union party, 451

Unions, 294, 295, 523–27; automobile industry and, 762; Harding presidency and, 722; World War II production and, 796

Unitarianism, 320, 322

United Farmworkers Organizing Committee (UFWOC), 934

United Mine Workers, 761, 796

United Nations: founding of, 820; Korean War and, 836

United Nations Relief and Rehabilitation Administration (UNRRA), 827

United States Housing Authority (USHA), 760

United States Steel Corporation, 516, 641, 648, 762, 926
Universities, 541–42; in Spain's New World empire, 10; state-supported, 327. *See also names of universities*
UNRRA, 827
Updike, John, 944
Urban centers, 522; growth of, challenge to the Church of, 538–39; life-style of, 530. *See also* Cities
Urban growth, *see* Cities
Urban revivalists, 538
USHA, 760
Utah, 373, 378; Mormons in, 323–24; statehood of, 568
Utopian communes, 337–38
Utrecht, Treaty of (1713), 79

Vallandigham, Clement L., 449
Valley Forge, 105, 106, 115
Van Buren, Martin, 245, 260, 261, 371, 501; presidency of, 262–64; ten-hour working day established by, 296
Vance, Cyrus, 900
Vanderbilt, Cornelius, 509
Vanderbilt, William H., 504, 511
Vanderbilt University, 509
Vanzetti, Bartolomeo, 698
Vassar College, 540
Vaudeville, 553
Veblen, Thorstein, 632
V-E Day, 812
Venezuela, 624
Venezuelan crisis (1895–1896), 596–98
Vermont, 149, 207, 232
Versailles, Treaty of, 687–90
Vertical integration, 514
Vesey, Denmark, 37, 360
Veterans, bonuses for, 723
Vicksburg, Battle of (1862), 434, 436
Victoria, Queen, 306
Vidal, Gore, 944
Viet Cong, 872, 875
Vietnam: division of, 848; Eisenhower's policy on, 848
Vietnam War: Cambodianizing of, 884; casualties of, 875; cease-fire of January 23, 1973, 888–89; Johnson presidency and, 872–77, 879–80; J. Kennedy presidency and, 862–63; Nixon's visit to Beijing (Peking) and Moscow and, 884–86; North Vietnamese across DMZ, 887–88; North Vietnamese victory in, 896–97; resistance to, 873–75; "Vietnamization" of, 882–84
Villa, Francisco ("Pancho"), 663–64
Vinland, 2
Virginia, 11, 13, 35; colonization of, 14–15, 17; Constitutional Convention and, 137; the Constitution and, 139, 144; established churches in (1775), 64; first families of, 45–46; freemen in, 41–42; hardships of colonial life in, 39–40; House of Burgesses in, 14, 45, 99; importance of tobacco to economy of, 92,

93; Madison resolutions and, 174; plantation economy of, 19; Reconstruction in, 470; secession of, 417; separation of church and state in, 128; slavery in, 15, 42, 357, 364; social structure of, 52; state debt of, 154
Virginia, University of, 327, 340
Virginia Company of London, 13, 14, 22, 23
Virginia Military Institute, 351
Virgin Islands, purchase of, 662
V-J Day, 815
"Voice of America," 828
Volstead Act, 701
Voltaire, 74
Vonnegut, Kurt, Jr., 944
Voter-registration campaign for southern blacks, 870, 871–72
Voting Rights Act of 1965, 870

WAACS (army), 796
Wabash Railroad decision (1886), 512, 575
Wade, "Bluff Ben," 474, 475
Wade-Davis Bill (1864), 463
Wage, minimum, 638, 847
Wage-and-price freeze (1971), 887, 924
Wagner Act, 761, 766
Wake Island, 801
Wald, Lillian, 535
Walden; or, Life in the Woods (Henry David Thoreau), 343
Walker, Alice, 944
Walker, David, 362–63
Walker, Robert J., 279
Walker Tariff of 1846, 445
Walkouts, 526
Wallace, George, 866, 878
Wallace, Henry A., 834
Wallace, Lewis, 545
Wall Street, dollar diplomacy and, 647–48
Wapshot Chronicle, The (John Cheever), 944
Wapshot Scandel, The (John Cheever), 944
War College, 613
Ward, Aaron Montgomery, 570
War Democrats, 450
Warehouse Act of 1916, 660
Warhol, Andy, 946
War Industries Board, 678, 722
War Labor Board (WLB), 796
Warner, Charles Dudley, 502, 546
War of 1812, 79, 184, 194, 200–206, 207, 208; as second war for independence, 208–10
"War on Poverty," 927
War Powers Act (1973), 891–92
War Production Board, 795
Warren, Earl, 844, 886–87
Warsaw Pact, 849
Washington, Booker T., 361, 540
Washington, D.C.: burning of, 203, 209; as nation's capital, 179; rebuilding of, 213; slavery in, 374, 379
Washington, George, 59, 131, 136, 142, 311, 349; American Revolutionary War and, 104, 106, 108–9, 115–16, 118, 120, 122–23; compared with Jefferson, 195;

Constitutional Convention and, 138, 139; the Constitution and, 144; contributions as president of, 168; Farewell Address of, 167; foreign policy of, 164–67; French and Indian War and, 81–82, 83, 85; French Revolution and, 164–66; Monroe Doctrine and, 229; portrait of, 67; presidency of, 150–52, 155, 156–57; quoted, 103; reelection of, 167; as a secessionist, 412; as a sportsman, 71
Washington, Martha, 231
Washington, statehood of, 568
Washington "Disarmament" Conference (1921–1922), 723–25
Washington *Federalist*, 191
Washington *National Intelligencer*, 217
Washington Naval Treaty, 776
Watergate scandals, 889–91, 893–94
Waterloo, Battle of (1815), 210
Watson, James, 784
Watt, James, 909–10
Watts race riots, 870–71
WAVES (navy), 796
Wayne, Gen. "Mad Anthony," 166
WCTU, 551, 638
Wealth against Commonwealth (Henry Demarest Lloyd), 632
Weaver, James B., 575, 581
Weaver, Robert, C., 870
Weaver, Walter R., 508
Weaving, 61, 291
Webster, Daniel, 214, 223, 231, 237, 270, 272, 274, 369, 382; abolitionism and, 366; Bank of the United States and, 254; Compromise of 1850 and, 376, 378; debate with Hayne, 246–47; on Hamilton, 153; Union ideal as expressed by, 247–48
Webster, Noah, 327
Weld, Theodore Dwight, 361, 362
Welfare state, 925
Welsh immigrants, 56
Welty, Eudora, 944
Wesley, John, 19
West, Benjamin, 67
West, the: agricultural development in, 567–68; cattle-raising in, 563–65; colonization of, 556–58; expansion of, 217–18; frontier spirit of, 311–12; Gadsden Purchase and, 385; homesteaders in, 565–67; importance of the frontier as symbol, 569–70; Louisiana Purchase and, 188–89; mining and, 562–63; panic of 1819 and, 217; population growth in (1870s–1890s), 568–69; surrender of Indian tribes, 557–59, 561–62
West Germany, 824–25
West Indies, 23, 62
Westinghouse air brake, 509
West Virginia, 417
Weyler, "Butcher," 600, 601
Wharton, Edith, 714
Wheat, 567; farms, increasing size of, 571
Wheatley, Phillis, 68
Whigs, 113–15, 157, 161, 261, 266; Clay and, 261, 270, 271, 275, 278, 370; 1840

Whigs (*continued*)
  presidential election and, 264–65, 266;
    1844 presidential election and, 278; 1848
    presidential election and, 370, 371; 1852
    presidential election and, 381, 382; phi-
    losophy and policy of, 267–68
Whip Inflation Now campaign, 895
Whiskey, excise tax on, 155, 156; temper-
    ance movement and, 318, 335–36
Whiskey Rebellion (1794), 156–57
Whiskey Ring, 483–84
Whistler, James, 551
White, William Allen, 654, 656
Whitefield, George, 65
"White flight" from cities, 932
Whiteman, Paul, 714
White supremacy, 354–55, 472–74
Whitman, Walt, 343–44, 545
Whitney, Eli, 290, 291, 513
Whittier, John Greenleaf, 344–45, 376, 399
Who's Afraid of Virginia Woolf? (Edward
    Albee), 945
WHO (World Health Organization), 823
Whyte, William H., Jr., 943
Wiebe, Robert H., 651
Wigglesworth, Michael, 25
"Wildcat" currency, 256
"Wild West" shows, 553
Wilentz, Sean, 309
Wiley, Harvey W., 635
Wilhelm II, Kaiser, 597, 665–66
Willard, Emma, 327
Willard, Frances E., 551, 638
William and Mary College, 48, 63, 67
William III, King, 29, 30, 79
Williams, Roger, 26
Williams, Tennessee, 945
Williams, William Appleman, 613
Williams, William Carlos, 945
Williamsburg, Virginia, 68
Williams College, 187
Willkie, Wendell L., 783–85
Wilmot, David, 287
Wilmot Proviso (1846), 287, 369–70, 376
Wilson, Sloan, 943
Wilson, Woodrow, 542, 653–71; attack on
    tariff, the banks, and trusts, 658–60; col-
    lapse and stroke of, 691–92; death of,
    694; foreign policy of, 661–65; "Fourteen
    Points" address of, 675–76, 685–86;
    League of Nations and, 688, 690–94;
    Mexican policy of, 662–64; neutral-
    ity proclamation of, 665–66, 669; New
    Freedom platform of, 654, 655; at Paris
    Peace Conference, 687–90; political ide-

alism of, 656–58, 675; progressivism
    and, 656, 660–61; quoted, 653; reelec-
    tion of, 669–71; Treaty of Versailles and,
    687–90; war message of, 673–75
Wilson-Gorman Bill of 1894, 585–86, 592
Windfall profits tax, 901
Wings of the Dove, The (Henry James), 547
Winthrop, John, 24–26
Wireless telegraphy, 710
Wisconsin, 318
WLB, 796
Wolfe, James, 84, 85
Woman's Christian Temperance Union
    (WCTU), 551, 638
Woman's Rights Convention (Seneca Falls,
    New York—1848), 337
Women: American Revolutionary War and,
    128; in colonial America, 39–40, 46–47,
    51, 61; economic opportunities for,
    328–30; education for, 327, 541; effect
    of urban life on, 548–50; employment
    for, 712, 937–40; factory system and,
    295; increasing self-consciousness of,
    328–30; industrialization and, 522; labor
    unions and, 525, 526; minimum-wage
    law for, 721; new morality and, 548;
    1920s independence of, 714; pioneer life
    for, 312; reform campaigns and, 333–36;
    social reform and, 633; social workers,
    534–35; suffrage battle, 549–50, 637;
    World War I work of, 678; in World War
    II, 796–98
Women and Economics (Charlotte Perkins
    Gilman), 548
Women's movement, 938–40
Wood, Gordon S., 147
Wood, Leonard, 606, 612
Woodhull, Victoria, 548
Woodhull and Claflin's Weekly, 548
Wool, 237
Workmen's compensation laws, 638
Work force, changing composition of,
    925–26. *See also* Labor
Workingmen's Compensation Act of 1916,
    660
Works Progress Administration (WPA), 754
World According to Garp, The (John Irving),
    944
World Bank, 822–23, 827
World Court, 730
World's Fair (E. L. Doctorow), 945
World War I, 79; aftermath of, 694–96; air-
    planes in, 709; American business aid to
    Allies, 666–69; American casualties,
    684–85; conscription, 681–82; Fourteen

Points and, 675–76, 685–86; mobiliza-
    tion for a war economy, 679–82; pre-
    paredness for, 677–79; propaganda for,
    676–77; roots of, 664–65; shipbuilding
    program, 680–81; submarine warfare,
    667–69, 674; Treaty of Versailles,
    687–90; troops in France, 682–86; U.S.
    entry into, 673–75; U.S. neutrality in,
    665–66; verterans' Bonus Army, 740–41
World War II, 79; American casualties in,
    815; American lend-lease for Allies,
    785–89; armed services manpower (and
    womanpower), 796–99; atomic bombing
    of Japan, 814–15; blacks in, 797–98;
    cost of, 801; D-Day invasion, 808–9; dec-
    laration of war, 790; demographic
    changes due to, 798; economic prosper-
    ity due to, 799–801; events leading to,
    775–80; events leading to American en-
    try in, 789–90; halting of Hitler, 804–6,
    811–12; invasion of Italy, 807; isolation-
    ists and, 782–83, 786; national unity
    during, 793–95; North African cam-
    paign, 806–7; submarine warfare, 787,
    788–89, 804–5, 812–13; war in the
    Pacific, 801–4, 812–16; war production,
    781–82, 795–96
World wars, 79
Wounded Knee, 935; Battle of (1890), 562
WPA, 754
Wright, Frank Lloyd, 716, 946
Wright, Orville and Wilbur, 709
Wright, Richard, 944
Wyoming, statehood of, 568
Wyoming Stock-Growers' Association, 565
Wyoming Territory, woman suffrage in, 550

Yale University, 67, 175, 543, 656
Yalta, Big Three conference at (1945),
    820–23
Yellow fever, 7, 339, 608, 612, 624
Yellow journalism, 544, 595–96
York, Alvin C., 685
York, Duke of, 33
Yorktown, Virginia, 131; Battle of (1781),
    122
Young, Andrew, 899
Young, Brigham, 323, 324
Young, James S., 195

Zenger, John Peter, 69
Zimmerman note, 674